THE OXFORD DICTIONARY FOR WRITERS AND EDITORS

The
Oxford Dictionary
for
Writers and Editors

SECOND EDITION
Edited and compiled by
R. M. RITTER

OXFORD
UNIVERSITY PRESS

OXFORD
UNIVERSITY PRESS

Great Clarendon Street, Oxford OX2 6DP

Oxford University Press is a department of the University of Oxford.
It furthers the University's objective of excellence in research, scholarship,
and education by publishing worldwide in

Oxford New York

Athens Auckland Bangkok Bogotá Buenos Aires Calcutta
Cape Town Chennai Dar es Salaam Delhi Florence Hong Kong Istanbul
Karachi Kuala Lumpur Madrid Melbourne Mexico City Mumbai
Nairobi Paris São Paulo Singapore Taipei Tokyo Toronto Warsaw
with associated companies in Berlin Ibadan

Published in the United States
by Oxford University Press Inc., New York

© Oxford University Press 2000

Database right Oxford University Press (maker)

First edition 1981
Second edition 2000

British Library Cataloguing in Publication Data
Data available

Library of Congress Cataloging in Publication Data
Data available
ISBN 0-19-866239-4

1 3 5 7 9 10 8 6 4 2

Designed by Andrew Boag, Typographic problem solving, London
Typeset in Swift and Arial by
Latimer Trend and Company Ltd, Plymouth
Printed by
T. J. International, Padstow

Contents

Ταράσσει τοὺς ἀνθρώπους οὐ τὰ πράγματα, ἀλλὰ τὰ περὶ τῶν πραγμάτων δόγματα.

Epictetus, *Manual*

('Not things, but opinions about things, trouble folk.')

Editor's note

This dictionary is a completely expanded, revised, and updated edition of the original *Oxford Dictionary for Writers and Editors*, first published in 1981. That work was itself successor to eleven editions of the *Authors and Printers Dictionary*, originally published under the editorship of F. Howard Collins in 1905—at which time it was considered to be the first style-book of its kind to have been produced in any country. This edition is designed to be used in conjunction with *Hart's Rules for Compositors and Readers* (thirty-ninth edition, 1983; to be revised and enlarged as *The Oxford Guide to Style*, available in spring 2001), as well as with *The New Fowler's Modern English Usage* (revised third edition, 1998), and the *New Oxford Dictionary of English* (1998) or *Concise Oxford Dictionary* (tenth edition, 1999).

The text is derived from the archives, experience, and practical knowledge of Oxford University Press, especially the Oxford English Dictionary Department and the former Arts & Reference Desk-Editing Department. It also represents the accumulated experience and wisdom of countless people throughout the many editions of this work's precursors. As such my first debt of gratitude is to the generations of compositors, editors, academics, proofreaders, and authors whose labour established and moulded the material included in this book, and whose influence endures on every page. I should like also to thank the many people associated with the Press and University who have generously shared their considerable talents in many areas, in particular Bonnie Blackburn, Edwin and Jackie Pritchard, J. S. G. Simmons, Della Thompson, George Tulloch, Hilary Walford, and John Waś. I am grateful to Barbara Horn for her editorial assistance in the unenviable task of thoroughly revising and streamlining the text at galley stage.

In creating this new edition I have been fortunate in being able to draw upon the extraordinary range and depth of knowledge of my colleagues at the Press, many of whom have taken considerable time and trouble to help me over the years. In particular I thank Elizabeth Stratford, Milica Djuradjević, Enid Barker, Cyril Cox, and Mick Belson, all of whom represent an irreplaceable source of editorial expertise. Here I must single out Leofranc Holford-Strevens, whom it has been my great good fortune to count as both colleague and friend, and who has remained a patient and tireless fount of knowledge for this book in particular and OUP in general: in doing so he amply fulfils the role of a Laudian 'Architypographus'.

Finally—and most importantly—I thank my wife Elizabeth who, while this book was in preparation, endured (with varying degrees of good humour) passive exposure to eight years of editorial ephemera; and my children Olivia, James, and Theodore.

RMR

Michaelmas Term 1999
Oxford

How to use this dictionary

Arrangement of the text and cross-references

1. ARRANGEMENT. Entries are ordered alphabetically, letter by letter.

2. CROSS-REFERENCES. Cross-references are set in normal boldface type **thus.** Semicolons are always used to separate references, so as to distinguish those with internal commas. So the cross reference

    See also **Mac-, Mc-, Mᶜ**

    refers to only one entry, and the cross-references

    See also **Smith; Smythe**

    are to two entries. In addition to these cross-references, the direction 'cf.' (meaning 'compare') may be used in text to cite another entry or entries.

    cf. **assurance; assure; ensure**

    cf. **de La; du; van, van den, van der**

Conventions used in the text

1. BOLD. Boldface type is used for headwords, cross-references, and for all approved forms and spellings; a rejected form or spelling is printed in light face except when it stands as a headword cross-referring to the preferred form. Italic boldface is used for words to be printed in italics.

2. SOLIDUS. A solidus (/) is used to mark the end of that part of the headword to which boldface elements introduced with a dash (*see* **3**) or a hyphen (*see* **4**) later in the same entry should be attached. Thus the entry

    collegi*/*um . . . pl. ***-a***

    shows that the plural form should be *collegia*, and the inflections given as

    gallop/ . . . **-ed, -er, -ing**

    are to be understood as *galloped*, *galloper*, and *galloping*. Only boldface elements follow this rule; note for example in the entry

    metal/, -led, -ling, -lize . . . *not* -ise

    that **-led, -ling,** and **-ling** join the headword, forming *metalled*, *metalling*, and *metallize*, but the rejected termination *-ise* is independently given.

3. DASH. An em-rule dash is used to stand for the repetition of a single headword already given, and the solidus again marks the end of a common element. Thus in the entry

    paddle/ boat, — steamer, — wheel (two words)

    the three combinations are *paddle boat*, *paddle steamer*, and *paddle wheel*. In the entry

    Einstein,/ Albert (1879-1955) German physicist, naturalized US citizen 1940; **— Alfred** (1880–1952) German musicologist, naturalized US citizen 1945

    the names are *Albert Einstein* and *Alfred Einstein*.

    Use of more than one dash indicates the repetition of a corresponding number of words.

4. HYPHEN. In headwords the hyphen serves two purposes: to indicate that a compound is normally hyphenated whenever used, and to introduce a further second element to form a compound with a first element marked off earlier in the entry by means of a solidus. In the second case the intended form of that compound will be clear from scrutiny of the first compound given, and by recourse to the comment given in parentheses at the end of the sequence, e.g. '(hyphen)', '(hyphens)', '(one word)'. The entry

    bird/cage, -seed (one word)

therefore indicates that *birdcage* and *birdseed* are both to be written as one word, and the entry

    multi/-role, -stage, -storey, -user (hyphens,
      one word in US)

indicates that *multi-role*, *multi-stage*, *multi-storey*, and *multi-user* are all to be written with hyphens in British English (but as one word in US English—*see* 8).

5. PARENTHESES. These are used to supply information directly after the headword, portraying the discipline, context, or language the headword may be found in, or describing some special aspect of its spelling, formation, or use. Where a foreign word is not assimilated into the English language, its gender and case are given, as required. This information has been dispensed with as irrelevant where a foreign word has been assimilated into English and is no longer given in italic, unless the original and assimilated forms differ:

    gateau/ cake, pl. **-s**; (Fr. m.) **gâteau/**, pl. **-x**

In addition to their normal function, parentheses are used to formulate a concise definition that will serve two or more parts of speech, the part in parentheses being included or omitted as appropriate. Thus the definition

    oxytone (Gr. gram.) (a word) with an acute
      accent on the last syllable

covers both the noun ('a word with an acute accent on the last syllable') and the adjective ('with an acute accent in the last syllable'). Similarly, the definition

    Cherokee (of or relating to) (a member of) a
      Native American tribe, or the language of this
      people

encompasses the adjectival and noun forms, as well as the singular and collective forms, of the headword.

6. FULL POINT. The full point or period is used in the normal way to mark an abbreviated form, where appropriate, or the end of a sentence. Entries are normally not in complete sentences, and do not end in full points: this enables the user to determine at a glance whether an abbreviation that occurs as the last word in an entry—as is frequently the case—ends in a full point:

    cosine (math., no hyphen) abbr. **cos**
    cosmogony, cosmography abbr. **cosmog.**

7. RESTRICTED USAGES. If the use of a word is restricted in any way, such as limited to a specific geographical area (e.g. Austral., Can., NZ), register (e.g. colloq., derog., sl.), or field of activity (e.g. gram., her., math.),

this is indicated by any of various labels set within parentheses (*see* the List of abbreviations, p. xi). These refer only to the definition immediately following, so that in

> **FA** (statistics) factor analysis, (Fr.) Fédération Aéronautique, Fine Art, Football Association

the label '(statistics)' refers only to factor analysis, and '(Fr.)' refers only to Fédération Aéronautique, not to Fine Art or Football Association.

8. BRITISH AND US ENGLISH VARIANTS. 'US' indicates that the use is found chiefly in US English (though often including e.g. Canadian, Australian, and New Zealand English) but not in British English except as a conscious Americanism. Other geographical designations restrict uses to the areas named.

> **whole note** (US) = **semibreve**

Where an exact British equivalent exists this is set (following an equals sign) in boldface whether it forms a headword or not; where no exact British equivalent exists, a short definition follows instead:

> **muffin**/ a light flat round spongy cake, eaten toasted and buttered; (US) a round cake made from batter or dough; a British — = US **English** — (savoury), a US — = British **American** — (sweet)

Where the word and meaning are the same, but the spelling or treatment differs, this is indicated parenthetically:

> **color** *use* **colour** (except in US)
>
> **colourant** *not* color- (US)
>
> **empanel**/ enrol, *not* im-; **-led, -ling** (one *l* in US)
>
> **tender-hearted**/, **-ness** (hyphen, one word in US)

9. DATES. All dates given in the dictionary are AD unless otherwise specified.

List of abbreviations

Abbreviations used regularly are listed below; others are given in the itself. Abbreviations of subjects (anthropology, botany, etc.) are also valid for their corresponding adjectival forms (anthropological, botanical, etc.).

abbr.	abbreviation	Du.	Dutch
adj.	adjective	dyn.	dynamics
adv.	adverb	eccl.	ecclesiastical
Afr.	Africa(n)	econ.	economics
Afrik.	Afrikaans	elec.	electrical
alt.	alternative	Eng.	English
Amer.	American	esp.	especially
anat.	anatomy	Est.	Estonian
anthrop.	anthropology	f.	feminine
Apocr.	Apocrypha	fig.	figurative(ly)
apos.	apostrophe	Fin.	Finnish
approx.	approximately	Fl.	Flemish
Arab.	Arabic	*fl.*	*floruit* (flourished)
arch.	archaic	Fr.	French
archaeol.	archaeology	Gael.	Gaelic
archit.	architecture	gen.	general
astr.	astronomy	geog.	geography
attrib.	attributive	geol.	geology
Austral.	Australian	geom.	geometry
AV	Authorize Version	Ger.	German
b.	born	Gr.	Greek; Greater
bibliog.	bibliography	gram.	grammar
bind.	binding	Heb.	Hebrew
biol.	biology	her.	heraldry
bot.	botany	Hind.	Hindi
Brazil.	Brazilian	hist.	historical
Brit.	British	hort.	horticulture
c.	century	Hung.	Hungarian
c.	*circa*	Icel.	Icelandic
Can.	Canadian	Ind.	India(n)
cap.	capital	indep.	independent
cc.	centuries	intr.	intransitive
Cent.	Central	Ir.	Irish
cf.	compare	It.	Italian
chem.	chemistry	ital.	italic
Chin.	China, Chinese	Jap.	Japan(ese)
Co.	County	joc.	jocular
colloq.	colloquial	Lat.	Latin
comput.	computing	lit.	literally; literary
contr.	contraction	m.	masculine
cook.	cookery	math.	mathematics
d.	died	ME	Middle English
Dan.	Danish	mech.	mechanics
dép.	*département*	med.	medicine
derog.	derogatory	meteor.	meteorology

mil.	military	print.	printing
mod.	modern	pron.	pronounced
MS	manuscript	propr.	proprietary
mus.	music	pseud.	pseudonym
myth.	mythology	psychol.	psychology
n.	neuter	pt.	point
naut.	nautical	q.v.	*quod vide* (which see)
NEB	New English Bible	RC	Roman Catholic
NODE	*New Oxford Dictionary*	relig.	religion
	of English	rep.	republic
Norw.	Norwegian	rhet.	rhetoric
NT	New Testament	Rom.	Roman
NZ	New Zealand	rom.	roman
obs.	obsolete	Russ.	Russian
OE	Old English	Sc.	Scottish
OED	*Oxford English Dictionary*	sci.	science
off.	official	SI	Système International
offens.	offensive		d'Unités
opp.	opposite, opposed	sing.	singular
orig.	original(ly)	Skt.	Sanskrit
ornith.	ornithology	sl.	slang
OT	Old Testament	Sp.	Spanish
Pak.	Pakistan	spec.	specifically
parl.	parliamentary	Swed.	Swedish
part.	participle	theat.	theatre
Pers.	Persian	theol.	theology
philol.	philology	tr.	transitive
philos.	philosophy	trad.	traditional(ly)
photog.	photography	trans.	translated
phys.	physics, physical	TS	typescript
physiol.	physiology	Turk.	Turkish
pl.	plural	typ.	typography
poet.	poetical	US	United States (style)
Pol.	Polish	var.	variant
Port.	Portuguese	Vulg.	Vulgate
prep.	preposition	zool.	zoology

Note on trade marks and proprietary status

This guide includes some words that have, or are asserted to have, proprietary status as trade marks or otherwise. Their inclusion does not imply that they have acquired for legal purposes a non-proprietary or general significance, nor any other judgement concerning their legal status. In cases where some evidence exists that a word has proprietary status this is indicated by the word 'propr.', but no such judgement concerning the legal status of such words is made or implied thereby.

A Advanced (level examination), ampere, *avancer* (on timepiece regulator); the first in a series

Ⱥ austral (currency of Argentina)

A. Academician, Academy, Acting (rank), alto, amateur, answer, artillery, Associate

a are (unit of area), atto-, year (no point)

a. accepted (Fr. *accepté*, Ger. *acceptiert*) (on bills of exchange), acre, active (in grammar), adjective, anna, area, arrive, (Lat.) *ante* (before)

Ä, ä in German, Swedish, etc. should *not* be replaced by *Ae*, *ae* (except in some proper names), or *A*, *a*, or *Æ*, *æ*. Only the first of two vowels takes the umlaut, as *äu*

Å angstrom

Å, å the 'Swedish *a*', used in Danish, Norwegian, and Swedish

@ at, the 'commercial *a*' used in calculating from prices; used in the domain name in email addresses

A0 ('A nought' or 'A zero') a paper size; *see* **DIN**

A1 first class (originally of ships)

AA Advertising Association, Alcoholics Anonymous, anti-aircraft, Architectural Association, Associate in Arts, Automobile Association; a film-censorship classification

AAA (US) Agricultural Adjustment Acts *or* Administration; Amateur Athletic Association, American Automobile Association

AAC *anno ante Christum* (in the year before Christ) (small caps.)

Aachen Germany; cf. **Aix-la-Chapelle**

AAF (US) Army Air Force; Auxiliary Air Force (till 1957)

AAG Assistant Adjutant General

AAIA Associate of the Association of International Accountants

Aalborg Denmark, in Dan. **Ålborg**

Aalto, (Hugo) Alvar (Henrik) (1896–1976). Finnish architect and designer

A. & M. agricultural and mechanical; (Hymns) Ancient and Modern

A. & N. Army and Navy (Stores, Club)

A. & R. artists and recording, artists and repertoire *or* repertory

a. a. O. (Ger.) *am angeführten Orte* (at the place quoted) (spaces in Ger.)

AAR against all risks (insurance)

aard/vark, -wolf different animals (one word)

Aarhus Denmark

AAS *Academiae Americanae Socius* (Fellow of the American Academy of Arts and Sciences), *Acta Apostolicae Sedis* (Acts of the Apostolic See), Agnostics' Adoption Society

A'asia Australasia

aasvogel a vulture

AAU (US) Amateur Athletic Union

AB able-bodied (seaman), Alberta, *Artium Baccalaureus* (US Bachelor of Arts), a blood type

ab (Lat.) from

ABA Amateur Boxing Association, American Bankers' Association, American Bar Association, Antiquarian Booksellers' Association, Association of British Archaeologists

aba a sleeveless outer garment worn by Arabs; *not* abaya, abba

ABAA Associate of British Association of Accountants and Auditors

abac/us a counting frame, (archit.) a plate at the top of a column; pl. **-uses**

Abaddon hell or the Devil; *see also* **Apollyon**

Abailard, Peter *see* **Abelard, Peter**

abalone a shellfish

à bas (Fr.) down with

abattoir a slaughterhouse (not ital.)

Abb. (Ger.) *Abbildung*

abb. abbess, abbey, abbot

Abbasid (of) a member of a dynasty of Baghdad caliphs ruling 750–1258, *not* Abassid

abbé (Fr. m.) an ecclesiastical title (not ital.)

Abbevillian (of) the culture of the earliest palaeolithic period in Europe

Abbildung/ (Ger. typ. f.) an illustration (cap.), pl. **-en**; abbr. **Abb.**

Abbotsinch Airport Glasgow

abbr. abbreviat/ed, -ion

abbreviat/e, -or *not* -er

abbreviation in general do not use points in abbreviations with several full or small caps.: BBC, MA, QC; with numbers: 1st, 4to; of units of measurement: lb, yd (*but* in.), cc, mm, °C, °F. Use full points with initials of personal names (H. G. Wells) and in abbrs. with mixed upper- and lower-case letters: Sun., Jan.; and with lower-case initials: l. 5, p. 7 (*but* p for pence); abbr. **abbr.**; *see also* individual entries; **acronym**; **contraction**

ABC the alphabet; Argentina, Brazil, and Chile; Associated British Cinemas, Audit Bureau of Circulations, Australian Broadcasting Corporation (*formerly* Commission)

ABCA Army Bureau of Current Affairs, *now* **BCA**

ABC Guide (no points)

abdicat/e, -ion, -or

abecedarian (adj.) arranged alphabetically, (noun) a person learning the alphabet

à Becket, Thomas *use* **Thomas Becket**

Abelard, Peter (1079–1142) French dialectician and theologian, in Fr. **Pierre Abé-**

lard; learned spellings include **Abailard** and **Abaelard** (more authentically **Abaëlard**); editors may accept this spelling but should not impose it

Abendlied (Ger.) an evening song (cap., ital.)

Aberdeen/ Angus (two caps.), — **terrier** (one cap.)

Aberdonian (adj. and noun) (a native or citizen) of Aberdeen

Abergavenny Gwent

Abernethy biscuit (one cap.)

Aberystwyth Dyfed, *not* -ith

abest (Lat.) he, she, *or* it, is absent; pl. ***absunt***

abett/er, in law **-or**

ab extra (Lat.) from outside

abgekürzt (Ger.) abbreviated; abbr. **abgk., abk.**

Abhandlungen (Ger. f. pl.) Transactions (of a society), abbr. **Abh.**

abide past tense **abided** *not* abode (except in arch. usage)

Abidjan Ivory Coast

abigail a lady's maid

Abilene Kans., Tex.

abîme (Fr. m.) abyss, in literary or heraldic sense *use* **abyme**; *see also* **mise en abyme**

ab incunabulis (Lat.) from the cradle

Abingdon Oxon. and Va.

Abington Cambs., Northants., Strathclyde, Co. Limerick; Mass.

ab/ initio (Lat.) from the beginning, abbr. ***ab init.***; — ***intra*** from within

abjure renounce on oath; cf. **adjure**

Abl. (Sp.) *abril* (April)

abl. ablative

ablaut variation in the root vowel of a word (e.g. *sing, sang, sung*)

able-bodied (hyphen)

ABM anti-ballistic missile

ABMM anti-ballistic-missile missile

Åbo Swed. for **Turku**

A-bomb atomic bomb (hyphen, no point)

aboriginal (adj.) indigenous (with initial cap., in technical sense in Australia); **aborigin/es** (pl. noun, for sing. *use* **-al**) also with initial cap. in Australia

ab origine (Lat.) from the beginning

ABO Area Beat Officer, — **system** a system of four types (A, AB, B, and O) used to classify human blood

aboul/ia loss of will power, *not* abulia; **-ic**

about-face noun and verb (hyphen)

above/-board, -mentioned, -named (hyphens)

ab ovo/ (Lat., from the egg) from the beginning, — — ***usque ad mala*** (Lat., from egg to apples) from (the) beginning to (the) end

Abp. Archbishop

abr. abridged, abridgement

abracadabra a supposedly magic word, a spell or charm

abrégé (Fr. m.) abridgement

abréviation (Fr. f.) abbreviation

abridgement abbr. **abr.**

ABS *Antiblockier-System* (Ger. n.), an antilocking brake system

abs. absolute(ly), abstract

abscess a swollen area accumulating pus within body tissue

Abschnitt/ (Ger. typ. m.) section, part, chapter, or division (cap.); pl. **-e**

absciss/a (math.) pl. **-ae**

abseil (noun and verb) (US) = **rappel**

absenter *not* -or

absente reo (Lat.) the defendant being absent, abbr. ***abs. re.***

absent-minded/ (hyphen); **-ly, -ness**

absinth/ the plant, **-e** the liqueur

absit/ (Lat.) let him, her, *or* it, be absent; — **omen** (Lat.) let there be no (ill) omen, may what is threatened not become fact

absolute(ly) abbr. **abs.**

absorb/ soak up, incorporate, consume; **-able, -ability, -ent** but **absorption, absorptive** (*not* -btion, -btive); cf. **adsorb**

abs. re. *absente reo*

abstract abbr. **abs.**

absunt *see* **abest**

abt. about

ABTA Association of British Travel Agents

Abteilung (Ger. f.) division, abbr. **Abt.**

Abu Dhabi United Arab Emirates

abulia *use* **abou-**

ab/ uno disce omnes (Lat.) from one (sample) judge the rest; — ***urbe condita,*** abbr. ᴀᴜᴄ (but ᴀ.ᴜ.ᴄ. in printing classical Latin texts), from the foundation of the city (Rome), 753 ʙᴄ (small caps.)

Abu Simbel the site of Egyptian rock temples built by Rameses II

abusus non tollit usum (Lat.) abuse does not take away use, i.e. is no argument against proper use

abut/, -ment, -ted, -ter (law), **-ting**

ABV alcohol by volume

abyme (Fr. m., lit., her.) *not abîme*; *see also* **mise en abyme**

abys/s a deep cavity, **-mal**

abyssal at or of the ocean depths or floor, (geol.) plutonic; cf. **abysmal**

Abyssinia *now* **Ethiopia**

AC (hist.) Aircraftman, Alpine Club, Assistant Commissioner, Athletic Club, Companion of the Order of Australia

A/C account current, in printing *use* **acct.**; air conditioning (also **a/c**)

AC *anno Christi*, in the year of Christ, occasionally useful to distinguish chronologies based on non-standard Nativity dates from normal AD reckoning, but otherwise inadvisable because also used in the past for *ante Christum* (before Christ) (small caps.)

Ac actinium (no point)

a.c. (elec.) alternating current, author's correction

ACA Associate of the Institute of Chartered Accountants in England and Wales (*or* Ireland)

Academe originally a garden near Athens sacred to the hero Academus (*or* Hecademus), the site of Plato's Academy; now refers to the academic community, world of university scholarship (cap.)

Academician abbr. **A.**

Académie française (one cap.)

Academy a learned body, abbr. **A.**, **Acad.** (cap.)

Academy, the the Platonic school of philosophy; *see also* **Academe**

Acadian of Nova Scotia (Fr. **Acadie**), *not* Ar-

a capite ad calcem (Lat.) completely

a cappella (It.) (mus.) unaccompanied, *not* alla cappella

Acapulco/ Mexico, *in full* **— de Juárez**

ACAS Advisory, Conciliation, and Arbitration Service

ACC Army Catering Corps

acc. acceptance (bill), according (to), accusative

Acca Israel, *use* **Acre**

Accademia (It.) Academy

Accademia della Crusca an Italian literary academy

Accadian *use* **Akk-**

acced/e, -er *not* -or

accedence a giving consent

accelerando/ (mus.) accelerating; as noun, pl. **-s**; abbr. **accel.**

accelerat/e, -or *not* -er

accep^{on} acceptance (bill)

acceptance abbr. **acc.**

accept/er in law and science **-or**

accessible *not* -able

access/it (Lat.) he, she, *or* it, came near; pl. *-erunt*

accessory (noun and adj.) *not* -ary

access time (comput.)

acciaccatura (mus.) a grace note

accidence inflections of words

accidental (mus.)

accidentally *not* -tly

accidie listlessness

acclimat/e, -ize *not* -ise

ACCM Advisory Council for the Church's Ministry (*formerly* **CACTM**)

Acco Israel, *use* **Acre**

accommodat/e, -ion (two *c*s, two *m*s)

accompanist *not* -yist

accouche/ment, -ur, -use (ital.)

account abbr. **A/C**, in printing *use* **acct.**

Accountant-General abbr. **A.-G.**

accoutre/, -ment; *not* accouter (US)

Accra Ghana, *not* Akk-

acct. account, *or* account current

accumulat/e, -or (two *c*s)

accusative abbr. **acc.**, **accus.**

ACE after Common Era (in place of AD) (small caps.); *see also* BCE; CE

acedia *use* **accidie**

ACF Army Cadet Force

ACGB Arts Council of Great Britain

ACGBI Automobile Club of Great Britain and Ireland

ACGI Associate of the City and Guilds of London Institute

Achaean of or relating to Achaea in ancient Greece, (lit., esp. in Homeric contexts) Greek

Achaemenid (*also* **Achaemenian**) of or relating to the dynasty ruling in Persia from Cyrus I to Darius III (553–330 BC); a member of this dynasty; *not* Achai-

acharnement (Fr. m.) bloodthirsty fury, ferocity; gusto

Acheson, Dean (**Gooderham**) (1893–1971) US diplomat

Acheulian (of or concerning) the culture of the palaeolithic period following the Abbevillian and preceding the Mousterian; *not* -ean

à cheval (Fr.) on horseback

Achilles/ heel, — tendon (no apos.)

Achin Sumatra, Indonesia; *not* Atch-

Achnashellach Highland, *not* **Auch-**

achy *not* -ey

ACI Army Council Instruction

ACIA Associate of the Corporation of Insurance Agents

ACIB Associate of the Corporation of Insurance Brokers

acid rain (two words)

ACII Associate of the Chartered Insurance Institute

ACIS Associate of the Institute of Chartered Secretaries and Administrators

ack-ack anti-aircraft gun, fire, etc. (hyphen)

ackee a tropical tree, fruit, *not* ak-

acknowledgement *not* -ledgment (US)

Acland, Sir Antony Arthur (b. 1930) British diplomat

ACLU American Civil Liberties Union

ACMA Associate of the Institute of Cost and Management Accountants

acolyte *not* -ite

Açores (Port.) **Azores**

acoustics (noun sing.) the science of sound, (noun pl.) acoustic properties

ACP Associate of the College of Preceptors; Association of Clinical Pathologists; Association of Correctors of the Press, part of **NGA**

acquit/, -tal (verdict), **-tance** (settlement of debt)

Acre Israel; *not* Acca, Acco

acre abbr. **a.**

acriflavine an antiseptic, *not* -vin

Acrilan (propr.)

acronym a word formed from initials, as *Anzac, laser, scuba,* pron. as words; *see also* **abbreviation; contraction**

acrylic (chem.)

ACS American Chemical Society, Association of Commonwealth Students

ACSA Associate of the Institute of Chartered Secretaries and Administrators

ACT Australian Capital Territory

act. active

Actaeon (Gr. myth.) a hunter

ACTH adrenocorticotrophic hormone

actini/a (zool.) pl. **-ae**

actinium symbol **Ac**

actinomy/ces (bot.) pl. **-cetes**

actionnaire (Fr. m.) shareholder

active abbr. **a., act.**

actor (person) *but* **one-acter** (play)

acts of a play titles, when cited, to be in italic; in text use cap. *A* for Act only when a number follows: *Hamlet*, Act I, Scene ii, *but* 'in the second act'

Acts of Parliament (two caps.)

Acts of Sederunt (Sc. law)

Acts of the Apostles (NT) abbr. **Acts**

ACTT Association of Cinematograph, Television and Allied Technicians

actualité (Fr. f.) present state

actuel/ (Fr.) f. *-le* present

acushla (Ir.) darling

ACW (hist.) Aircraftwoman

AD (*anno Domini*) precedes numerals, *but* follows numbers written as words: 'AD 250', '16 July AD 622', 'the first century AD'; use only when using BC dates as well, or where there is some other reason to fear misunderstanding (small caps.); *see also* **BC, CE**

ad advertisement (no point)

ad. adapted, adapter (point)

a.d. after date

a.d. *ante diem* (before the day)

Ada (propr. comput.) a real-time programming language

adagio/ (mus.) slow; as noun, pl. **-s**

Adams,/ Ansel (**Easton**) (1902–84) US photographer; — **John** (1735–1826) US statesman, President 1797–1801; — **John Quincy** (1767–1848) his son, President 1825–9

Adam's Peak Sri Lanka

adapt/able, -er (person), **-or** (device)

adaptation *not* adaption (US)

a dato (Lat.) from date

ADC aide-de-camp, analogue–digital converter

ad captandum vulgus (Lat., to catch the rabble) claptrap, applied to unsound arguments

ADD *American Dialect Dictionary*

Addams,/ Charles (**Samuel**) (1912–88) US cartoonist; — **Jane** (1860–1935) US social worker and writer, Nobel Peace Prize 1931

Addenbrooke's Hospital Cambridge

addend/um something to be added, pl. **-a** (not ital.)

addio (It.) goodbye

Addis Ababa Ethiopia

additive (something) in the nature of an addition

addorsed (her.) *not* ador-, -ossed

adducible *not* -eable

Adélie/ Land Antarctica (two caps.), — **penguin** (one cap.)

Adenauer, Konrad (1876–1967) German statesman, Chancellor of W. Germany 1949–63

ad eundem (*gradum*) (Lat.) to the same degree at another university

à deux/ (Fr.) of (or between) two, — *temps* *see* **valse**

ad/ extra (Lat.) in an outward direction; — *extremum* to the last; — *finem* near the end, abbr. *ad fin.*; — *hanc vocem* at this word

ad hoc for this (purpose) (roman)

ad/ hominem to the (interests of the) person, personal; — *hunc locum* on this passage, abbr. *a.h.l.*; — *idem* to the same (point)

adieu/ pl. **-s** (not ital.); in Fr. *adieu*, pl. *adieux*

ad infinitum (Lat.) to infinity (not ital.)

ad interim (Lat.) meanwhile, abbr. *ad int.*

adios (Sp.) goodbye (not ital., no accent)

Adirondack Mountains a mountain range in New York State, part of the Appalachians, *not* -dac

Adj. Adjutant

Adj. Gen. Adjutant General

adjectiv/e abbr. **a., adj.**; **-al, -ally**

adjudicator not -er

adjure charge or request (a person) solemnly or earnestly; cf. **abjure**

adjutage a nozzle, *not* aj-

Adjutant/ abbr. **Adj.** (cap. as rank); — **General** (two words) abbr. **AG, Adj. Gen.**

adjuvant (adj.) helpful, auxiliary; (noun) an adjuvant person or thing

Adler, Alfred (1870–1937) Austrian psychologist

ad lib (adv., noun, and verb)

ad/ libitum (Lat.) at pleasure, — *litem* appointed for a lawsuit

ad locum (Lat.) to or at the place, abbr. **ad loc.**, pl. **ad locos**, abbr. **ad locc.** (abbr. not ital.)

Adm. Admiral, Admiralty

admin short for administration (no point)

adminicle a thing that helps, (Sc. law) collateral evidence of the contents of a missing document

administrable *not* -atable

administrat/or abbr. **admor.**, **-rix** abbr. **admix.**

Admiral abbr. **Adm.**, in Fr. *amir/al* pl. *-aux*

Admiralty, the abbr. **Adm.**; *see* **MOD**

ad misericordiam (Lat.) appealing to pity

admissible *not* -able, *but* **admittable**

admix. administratrix

ad modum (Lat.) after the manner of

admonitor/ *not* -er, **-y**

admor. administrator

ad nauseam (Lat.) to a sickening degree (not ital.), *not* -um

ado work, trouble (one word)

adobe a form of sun-dried brick (not ital.)

Adonai (Heb.) the Lord; *see also* **Yahweh**

advocatus diaboli Keats, in P. B. Shelley's elegy, 1821

Adonis (Rom. myth.) a youth beloved of Venus

adopter *not* -or

adorable *not* -eable

Adorno, Theodor (**Wiesengrund**) (1903–69) German philosopher, sociologist, and musicologist; b. **Theodor Wiesengrund**

adorsed, adossed (her.) *use* **addorsed**

ADP adenosine diphosphate, automatic data processing

ad patres (Lat.) deceased (not ital.)

ad personam (Lat.) personal

ADR American Depository Receipt

ad/ referendum (Lat.) for further consideration, — *rem* to the point

adrenalin *not* -ine; in US, **adrenaline** is the hormone, **Adrenalin** (propr.) the synthetic drug

adresse (Fr. f.) address

Adrianople *use* **Edirne**

à droite (Fr.) to the right

A.d.S. Académie des Sciences

adscriptus glebae (Lat.) bound to the soil (of serfs)

adsor/b hold as condensation a gas, liquid, or solute on the surface of a solid; **-bable, -pent, -ption**; cf. **absorb**

adsum (Lat.) I am present

adulator *not* -er

ad/ unguem (Lat.) perfectly; — *unum omnes* all, to a man; — *usum* according to custom, abbr. *ad us.*

adv. adverb, -ially; advocate

adv. (Lat.) adversus (against)

ad valorem (Lat.) according to value, abbr. *ad val.*

adverb/, -ially abbr. **adv.**

ad verbum (Lat.) to a word, verbatim

adverse (often followed by *to*) contrary or hurtful: 'adverse reaction to the drug'; cf. **averse, aversion**

adversus (Lat.) against, abbr. *adv.*

advertise *not* -ize

advertisement abbr. **ad, advt.**; pl. **ads, advts.**

advis/e *not* -ize; **-able** *not* -eable

advis/er *not* -or; **-ory**

ad/ vitam aut culpam (Lat.) for lifetime or until fault, — *vivum* lifelike

ad voc. *use* **s.v.**

advocaat a liqueur

advocate abbr. **adv.**

Advocate General abbr. **AG**

Advocates, Faculty of (law) the Bar of Scotland

advocatus diaboli (Lat.) devil's advocate (ital.)

advt/., -s. advertisement, -s

adyt/um the innermost part of an ancient temple, pl. **-a**

adze *not* adz (US)

AE Air Efficiency Award

A.E. or **AE** (originally and properly **Æ**) pseud. of George (William) Russell (1867–1935) Irish poet, playwright, and journalist

Æ (numismatics) = copper (Lat. *aes*)

AEA Atomic Energy Authority

Aeaea (Gr. myth.) an island inhabited by Circe

AEC Army Educational Corps (*now* **RAEC**), (US) Atomic Energy Commission (*since* 1975 **ERDA**)

aedile *not* e-

AEF Allied (*or* American *or* Australian) Expeditionary Force, Amalgamated Union of Engineering and Foundry Workers

Aegean Sea the Mediterranean between Greece and Turkey

aegis a shield, protection; *not* e-

aegrot/at he *or* she is ill (a certificate that an examination candidate is ill, or the degree thus awarded), pl. *-ant*

AEI Associated Electrical Industries

Ælfred *prefer* **Alfred**

Ælfric (*c*.955–*c*.1010) English writer, also called **Grammaticus** in the 17th–18th cc.

Ælfthryth (*c*.945–*c*.1000) wife of King Edgar and mother of Ethelred the Unready

Aelia Laelia an insoluble riddle

Ælla a tragic interlude by Chatterton, 1768–9

Aemilius a character in Shakespeare's *Titus Andronicus*

Aeneas, *Aeneid*

Aeolian, Aeolic (caps.) *not* E-

aeon *not* eon (except in scientific use)

aepyornis (zool.) *not* epi-, epy-

aequales (Lat.) equal (pl. adj.), (pl. noun) equals (in age or performance); abbr. *aeq.*

AERA Associate Engraver, Royal Academy

aerate etc. *not* aë-

AERE Atomic Energy Research Establishment (Harwell), *now* **UKAEA**

AERI Agricultural Economics Research Institute (Oxford)

aerial *not* aë-

aerie *use* **eyrie**

aer/ify, -obic *not* aë-

aerodrome *use* **airfield**

aero/dynamics, -elasticity, -foil, -gramme, -logy (one word)

aeronaut/, -ical, -ics *not* aë-

aero/nomy, -phagy, -phone (one word)

aeroplane (US **airplane**) superseded by **aircraft** in some contexts

aerosol *not* air-

aerospace (one word)

aeruginous of the nature or colour of verdigris

Aeschylus (525–456 BC) Greek playwright

Aesculapi/us Latin form of the Greek god Asclepius, **-an** of or relating to medicine or physicians; *not* E-

Aesir the collective names of the gods in Scandinavian mythology

Aesop (6th c. BC) Greek fable-writer

aesthete, etc. *not* e-

aestiv/al, -ation *not* e- (US)

aet. or *aetat.* *anno aetatis suae* (of age, aged)

aetheling *use* **atheling**

aether in all meanings *use* **e-**

aetiology *not* e- (US)

Aetna *use* **Etna**

AEU Amalgamated Engineering Union

AEU (TASS) Technical, Administrative, and Supervisory Section of the AEU

AF audio frequency

AFA Associate of the Faculty of Actuaries

Afars and Issas, French territory of the *formerly* French Somaliland, *now* **Djibuti**

AFAS Associate of the Faculty of Architects and Surveyors

AFC Air Force Cross, Association Football Club

AFDCS (UK) Association of First Division Civil Servants (cf. **FDA**)

aff. affirmative, affirming

affairé (Fr.) busy (accent)

affaire d'amour (Fr. f.) love affair

affaire (**de cœur**) affair of the heart

affaire d'honneur duel

affenpinscher a small breed of dog (not ital.)

afferent (physiol.) conducting inwards or towards

affettuoso (mus.) with feeling

affidavit abbr. **afft.**

affranchise *not* -ize

Afghan a breed of hound (cap.), a blanket or shawl (not cap.)

Afghanistan abbr. **Afghan.**

aficionado/ an enthusiast for a sport or hobby, pl. **-s** (not ital.)

afield (one word)

AFL-CIO American Federation of Labor and Congress of Industrial Organizations (hyphen)

AFM Air Force Medal

à fond/ (Fr.) in depth, in detail, thoroughly (cf. *au fond*); — *de train* at full speed

aforethought (one word)

a fortiori with stronger reason, *not* à (not ital.)

Afr. Africa, -n

A.F.R.Ae.S. Associate Fellow of the Royal Aeronautical Society

afreet a demon in Muslim mythology; *not* afrit, efreet

African-American (adj. and noun) term preferred in most contexts to e.g. **black** (q.v.) or Afro-American

Africander a S. African breed of cattle or sheep; *not* Afrikander, Afrikaner

Afridi a people of Cent. Asia

Afrikaans a S. African Dutch language, abbr. **Afrik.**

Afrikaner an Afrikaans-speaking white S. African, *formerly* -cander; *not* -caner

after/birth, -care (one word)

after/-effect, -image (hyphens, one word in US)

afternoon abbr. **aft., p.m.**

after/shave, -taste, -thought (one word)

after-wit *see* *esprit de l'escalier*

AFV armoured fighting vehicle

AG Adjutant General, Air Gunner, (Ger.) *Aktiengesellschaft* (public limited company), Attorney General

A-G Accountant-General, Agent-General (of Colonies)

Ag argentum (silver) (no point)

Agadah *use* **Hagga-**

Aga Khan the leader of Ismaili Muslims

Aganippides (**the**) (Gr. myth.) alternative name for the Muses

agape gaping, open-mouthed; a love-feast, divine love (one word)

à gauche (Fr.) to the left

age group (two words)

ageing *not* agi- (US)

age/ism, -ist *not* agism, agist

agenda/ list of items for discussion, pl. **-s**; formally, **agend/um** (things to be done) is preferred, pl. **-a**

agent abbr. **agt.**

Agent General abbr. **A-G**

agent/ **provocateur** (not ital.) pl. **-s pro-vocateurs**

ages *use* numerals for specific ages: 'a girl of 3', or 'a 3-year-old girl', *not* 'a girl of 3 years old'; *but* write 'in his fortieth year', 'in his forties'; in more literary contexts, 'a man of forty', 'a three-year-old'

aggiornamento (It.) bringing up to date

aggrandize *not* -ise

aging *use* **ageing** (except in US)

agitato (mus.) hurried

agitator *not* -er

AGM Advisory Group Meeting, Annual General Meeting

agma the symbol ŋ, or the sound represented by it

agnail *use* **hangnail**

agnostic/, -ism (not cap.)

à gogo in abundance, e.g. 'whisky à gogo' (two words, not ital.) (in US, a-go-go, no accent)

agonize *not* -ise

agouti a S. American rodent; *not* -y, agu-

agreeable in Fr. *agréable*

agric. agricultur/e, -al, -ist

agriculturist *not* -alist

agrimony (bot.)

agronomy rural economy

AGSM Associate of the Guildhall School of Music

agt. agent

Agᵗᵒ (Sp.) *agosto* (August)

Aguascalientes a city and state, Mexico

Agulhas, Cape S. Africa, *not* L'A-

aguti *use* **agou-**

AH *anno Hegirae*, the Muslim era; precedes the year number (small caps.); *see also* **hegira**

ah when it stands alone, takes an exclamation mark (!); as part of a sentence usually followed by a comma, the ! being placed at the end of the sentence: 'Ah, no, it cannot be!'

AHA American Heart Association, American Historical Association

aha an exclamation of surprise; *see also* **ha ha**

ahem an interjection used to attract attention, gain time, or express disapproval

ahimsa (Skt.) in the Hindu, Buddhist, and Jainist tradition, respect for all living things and avoidance of violence towards others

a.h.l. (Lat.) *ad hunc locum* (on this passage)

Ahmad/abad, -nagar India; *not* Ahmed-, Amed-

Ahmadu Bello University Nigeria

AHMI Association of Headmistresses, Incorporated; *see also* **IAHM**

à huis clos (Fr.) in private

Ahura Mazda (Old Pers.) the Zoroastrian spirit of good; *not* the many variants, although **Ormuzd** (Middle Pers.) is a common later and lit. form

a.h.v. (Lat.) *ad hanc vocem* (at this word)

Ahvenanmaa (Fin.) **Åland Islands**

AI American Institute, Anthropological Institute, artificial insemination, artificial intelligence

AIA American Institute of Aeronautics, American Institute of Architects, Associate of the Institute of Actuaries, automated image analysis

AIAA Architect Member of the Incorporated Association of Architects and Surveyors

AIAC Associate of the Institute of Company Accountants, Association internationale d'archéologie classique

AIAS Surveyor Member of the Incorporated Association of Architects and Surveyors

AIB Associate of the Institute of Bankers

AICC All India Congress Committee

AICS Associate of the Institute of Chartered Shipbrokers

AID Army Intelligence Department, artificial insemination by donor

Aida an opera by Verdi, 1871 (no diaeresis)

aide-de-camp abbr. **ADC**, pl. **aides-de-camp** (not ital.)

aide-memoire aid to memory, pl. **aides-memoires** *or* (properly) **aide-memoires** (not ital.); in Fr. m. *aide-mémoire*, pl. same

Aids acquired immune deficiency syndrome (one cap.); **AIDS** (four caps.) in technical use

aigrette a spray; *not* ei-, -et; *see also* **egret**

aiguillette (Fr. f.) a thin slice of meat, *not* an-

AIH artificial insemination by husband

ail/ (Fr. m.) garlic; **-e** (Fr. f.) bird's wing

Ailesbury, Marquess of; *see also* **Ayl-**

A.I.Loco.E. Associate of the Institute of Locomotive Engineers

aimable (Fr.) amiable

A.I.Mech.E. Associate of the Institution of Mechanical Engineers

A.I.Min.E. Associate of the Institution of Mining Engineers

AIMM Associate of the Institution of Mining and Metallurgy

AIMTA Associate of the Institute of Municipal Treasurers and Accountants

Ain a dép. of France

ʿ**ain** (Arab.) *prefer* ʿ**ayn**

aîn/**é** (Fr.) f. **-ée** elder, senior; opp. to *puîné*, f. *puînée* or *cadet*/, **-te** younger

A.Inst.P. Associate of the Institute of Physics

AIQS Associate of the Institute of Quantity Surveyors

Air, Point of Clwyd; *see also* **Ayre**

air/ bag, — bed, — bladder (two words)

air/borne, -brick (one word)

Airbus (cap., propr., one word)

Air Commodore abbr. **Air Cdre**; *see also* **Commodore**

air condition/, **-ed, -er, -ing** (two words)

aircraft/ sing. and pl. (one word), **— carrier** (two words)

aircraft/man, -woman *not* aircrafts- (one word)

Airedale/ W. Yorks.; a terrier; **Baron —**

air/field, -flow (one word)

Air Force, Royal *see* **Navy, Army, and Air Force**

airgun (one word)

Air Gunner abbr. **AG**

air/lift, -line, -mail (one word)

Air Ministry *now* in **MOD**

airplane (US) *use* **aircraft** or **aeroplane**

airport (one word)

air raid (two words)

air/ship, -sick, -space, -tight (one word)

air-to-air (adj., hyphens)

airworthy of aircraft (one word)

AISA Associate of the Incorporated Secretaries Association

Aisne a dép. of France

ait an islet, *not* eyot (cap. when part of name)

aitchbone (one word) *not* H-, edge-

Aix-la-Chapelle (hyphens) the Fr. name for **Aachen**

Aix-les-Bains (hyphens)

Ajaccio Corsica

Ajax pl. **Ajaxes**

ajutage *use* **adj-**

AK Alaska (postal abbr.), Knight of the Order of Australia

aka also known as (used before an alias)

AKC Associate of King's College (London)

akee *use* **ack-**

akimbo (one word)

Akkadian of Akkad in ancient Babylonia, or its Semitic language; *not* Acc-

Akkra Ghana, *use* **Acc-**

Akmola cap. of Kazakhstan, *formerly* **Almaty**

Aktiengesellschaft (Ger. f.) public limited company, abbr. **AG**

akvavit *use* **aquavit** except when describing a specific (e.g. Scandinavian) variety

AL Alabama (postal abbr.), autograph letter

Al aluminium (no point)

al- an Arabic article, used in proper names (hyphen)

ALA Associate of the Library Association

Ala. Alabama (off. abbr.)

à la short for *à la mode* (Fr., in the manner of); the *la* does not need to agree with the gender of the person or thing to which it refers: *à la reine, à la maître d'hôtel*

Alabama off. abbr. **Ala.**, postal **AL**

à la carte (a meal) that may be ordered from a wide range of available dishes (not ital.); *see also* **table d'hôte**

Aladdin *not* Alladin

Alanbrooke, Viscount (one word)

Åland Islands Baltic Sea, in Fin. **Ahvenanmaa**

à la page (Fr.) up to date

alarm/ *not* alarum except in 'alarums and excursions', **— clock** (two words)

à la russe (Fr.) in the Russian style (not cap.)

alas when it stands alone, takes an exclamation mark (!); as part of a sentence, usually followed by a comma, the ! being placed at the end of the sentence: 'Alas, it is true!'

Alaska/ postal abbr. **AK**; **baked —** (one cap.)

Alb. Albania, -n

Alba. Alberta, *use* **Alta.**

alba Provençal for **aubade** (not ital.)

Alban. *formerly* the signature of the Bishop of St Albans (point), *now* **St Albans:** (colon)

Albania/ republic, abbr. **Alb.**; **-n** (of or related to) (the people or language) of Albania

albedo/ a fraction of radiation reflected, pl. **-s**

Albee, Edward (**Franklin**) (b. 1928) US playwright

albeit though (one word, not ital.)

Albigens/es a S. French Manichaean sect, 12th–13th c.; **-ian**

albin/o pl. **-os**, f. **-ess**; **-ism** *not* -oism; **-otic**

Ålborg Dan. for **Aalborg**

Albrighton Shropshire

album/en the natural white of an egg, **-in** its chief constituent; adj. **-inous**

Albuquerque N. Mex.

Albury Herts., Oxon., Surrey

Alcaeus of Mytilene (b. *c.*620 BC) Greek lyric poet

alcahest *use* **alka-**

alcaic a form of verse metre in four-line stanzas

alcaide (Sp. m.) governor, jailer

alcalde (in Spain) a magistrate, mayor

Alcatraz a former US prison, San Francisco Bay, Calif.

alcázar (Sp.) palace, fortress, bazaar

Alceste an opera by Gluck, 1767

Alcestis *not* Alk-

alcheringa (Aboriginal myth.) the 'dreamtime' or golden age when the first ancestors were created

Alcibiades *not* Alk-

ALCM Associate of the London College of Music

Alcoran *use* **Koran**

Alcyone (Gr. myth.) daughter of Aeolus and wife of Ceyx, *not* Hal-; *see also* **halcyon**

Aldborough Norfolk, N. Yorks.

Aldbrough Humberside

Aldbury Herts.

Aldeburgh Suffolk

al dente cooked but not soft (not ital.)

Alderbury Wilts.

Alderman abbr. **Ald.**

Aldermaston Berks.

Alderney Channel Islands, in Fr. **Aurigny**

Aldiborontiphoscophornia character in *Chrononhotonthologos*

Aldine (adj.) printed by the Manutius family, who introduced italic type

Aldis lamp a hand lamp for signalling

Aldsworth Glos., W. Sussex

Aldus Manutius printer, *see* **Manutius**

Aldworth Berks.

aleatoric depending on the throw of a die or on chance; *not* -ory except in music and the arts, where it describes stochasticism

Alecto (Gr. myth.) one of the three Furies

alef (Heb.) a smooth-breathing mark ('), typographically largely equivalent to the Arab. *hamza* or Gr. lenis (ital.); *not* -eph

alehouse (one word)

Alençon lace (cedilla)

Aleutian Islands Bering Sea

A level 'advanced level' examination (no hyphen)

alexandrine a metrical line of verse having six iambic feet

ALF Animal Liberation Front, Arab Liberation Front (Iraq)

Alf Automatic Letter Facer (Post Office sorting machine)

Alfa-Romeo an Italian make of car (hyphen)

Alford Grampian, Lincs., Som.

Alfred 'the Great' (849–99) King of Wessex; abbr. **A.**, **Alf.**

alfresco (adj. and adv.) (one word, not ital.)

Alfreton Derby.

Alg. Algernon, Algiers

alg/a (bot.) pl. **-ae** (not ital.)

Algarve, (the) Portugal

algebra abbr. **alg.**

ALGOL (comput.) Algorithmic Language

algology (bot.)

Algonkian (geol.) US term for the **Proterozoic** era

Algonqui/an of a large group of Native American Indian tribes or their languages; **-n** (of or concerning) one people in this group or their language, a dialect of Ojibwa; *not* -nki-

Algonquin Round Table the name given to the informal meetings of a group of literary wits at the Algonquin Hotel (New York City), mainly 1920–40

alguacil a mounted official at a bullfight in Spain, a constable or officer of justice in Sp.-speaking countries; *not* -zil (not ital.)

Alhambr/a a Moorish palace at Granada; **-esque**

alia (Lat. pl.) other things

alias/ (adv. and noun) pl. **-es**

alibi/ (noun) pl. **-s**

alienator *not* -er

Aligarh Uttar Pradesh, India

Alighieri the family name of **Dante**

align/, -ment *not* aline

alii (Lat. pl.) other people

alimentative/, -ness *not* alimentive, -ness

A-line (of a garment) having a narrow waist or shoulders and flared skirt (cap., hyphen)

aline *use* **-ign**

alinéa (Fr. m.) paragraph

Alipore India

Alipur India, Pakistan

Alitalia the Italian national airline

ali/us (Lat. m.) another person, pl. **-i**

Aliwal E. Punjab, India; S. Africa

alkahest *not* alca-

alkali/ pl. **-s**

alkalize *not* -ise

Alkestis, Alkibiades *use* **Alc-**

Alkoran *use* **Koran**

alla breve (mus.) two or four minims in bar

alla cappella (mus.) *use* **a cappella**

Alladin *use* **Aladdin**

Allahabad Uttar Pradesh, India

Allah il Allah corruption of Arab. *lā ilāha illa'llāh*, There is no god but God (Muslim prayer and war cry)

Allan-a-Dale a companion of Robin Hood and minstrel hero

allargando (mus.) broad, spread out

allée (Fr. f.) alley, avenue

Allegany Pittsburgh, Pa.

Allegheny US mountains, river, and airline

allegretto/ (mus.) fairly brisk; as noun, pl. **-s**

allegro/ (mus.) brisk, merry; as noun, pl. **-s**

allele one of the alternative forms of a gene; *not* -l, -lomorph

alleluia Lat. form (also liturgical) for Heb. and biblical **hallelujah**

allemande the name of several German dances

Allen, (William) Hervey (1889–1949) US novelist, *not* Harvey

Allendale Northumb.

allerg/y a sensitivity to certain foods, pollens, etc.; **-ic**

alleviator *not* -er

Alleynian a member of Dulwich College

All Fools' Day (caps., no hyphen)

allgemein (Ger.) general (adj.); abbr. **allg.**, **allgm.**

All-Hallows All Saints' Day, 1 Nov. (caps., hyphen)

Allhallows Kent (one word)

allineation alignment, *not* alin-

Allingham, Margery (1904–66) English novelist

allodium an estate held in absolute ownership, *not* alo-

allons! (Fr.) let us go!, come!

allot/, -ment, -table, -ted, -ting

all' ottava (mus.) an octave higher than written, abbr. **all' ott.**

all ready completely or entirely prepared; cf. **already**

all right *not* alright, all-right

all round (prep., two words) ('all round the Wrekin')

all-round/ (adj., hyphen) ('an all-round man') **-er** noun

All Saints' Day 1 Nov.

all/seed, -spice (one word)

All Souls College Oxford (no apos.), **— Souls' Day** 2 Nov., **— Souls' Eve** 1 Nov. (caps., no hyphens)

all together (in a body) *but* **altogether** (entirely)

alluvi/um pl. **-a**

Alma-Ata former Russian name of **Almaty**

almacantar *use* **almu-**

Alma Mater fostering mother, one's school or university

almanac *but* **Oxford Almanack**, ***Whitaker's Almanack***

Almanach de Gotha an annual publication (in Fr.) giving information about European royalty, nobility, and diplomats, published in Gotha 1763–1944; a smaller-scale version was revived in Paris in 1968 (ital.)

Alma-Tadema, Sir Lawrence (1836–1912) Dutch-born English painter

Almaty former cap. of Kazakhstan

Almighty, the cap. except when used attributively, e.g. 'an almighty bang'

Almondbury W. Yorks.

Almondsbury Avon

almucantar *not* alma-

Alnmouth Northumb.

Alnwick Northumb.

alodium *use* **allod-**

A.L.O.E. A Lady of England, pseud. of **Charlotte M. Tucker** (1821–93)

à l'outrance *use* **à outrance**

ALP Australian Labor Party

Alpes-de-Haute-Provence a dép. of France (hyphens)

Alpes-Maritimes a dép. of France

Alphaeus the father of Apostle James 'the Less'

alphanumeric (comput.) of instructions containing alphabetic, numerical, and other characters (one word)

alpha/ the first letter of the Gr. alphabet (A, α); **— particle, — ray** (two words)

Alpinist (cap.)

already (adv.) before the time in question (I knew that already), as early or as soon as this (already at the age of 6); cf. **all ready**

alright *use* **all right**

ALS Associate of the Linnean Society, autograph letter signed

Alsace-Lorraine (hyphen)

Alsirat (Arab.) the bridge to paradise

Alsop en le Dale Derby. (four words)

alt. alternative, altitude (point)

Alta. Alberta, Canada; *not* Alba

alter/ ego (Lat.) one's second self, pl. **— egos** (not ital.)

alter idem another self

Altesse (Fr. f.), **Altezza** (It.) Highness

Althing the Icelandic Parliament, in Icel. **Alþingi**

Althorpe Humberside

Althorp/ House, — Library, — Park
Northants.

Althusser, Louis (1918–90) French philosopher

altitude abbr. **alt.**

alto/ (mus.) pl. **-s**, abbr. **A.**

altogether *see* **all together**

alto-relievo/ high relief, pl. **-s**; Anglicized version of It. *alto rilievo*

aluminium symbol **Al** (no point) *not* -num (US)

alumn/us pl. **-i**; f. **-a**, pl. **-ae**; abbr. **alum.**

AM Academy of Management, air mail, Air Ministry, Albert Medal, amplitude modulation,
Artium Magister (US Master of Arts), *Ave Maria*
(Hail, Mary!), Member of the Order of Australia
(caps.)

A.-M. Alpes-Maritimes

ᴀᴍ *anno mundi* (in the year of the world) (small
caps.)

Am americium (no point)

Am. America, -n

a.m. (Lat.) *ante meridiem* (before noon) (lower
case, points)

AMA American Management/Marketing/Med-
ical/Missionary Association; Assistant Masters' Association, *now* **AMMA**

amadavat *use* **ava-**

amah a child's nurse, esp. in the Far East and
India (not ital.)

Amalek *not* -ech, -eck

amanuens/is pl. **-es**

amateur abbr. **A.**

Ambala India, *not* Umbal(l)a

ambassad/or f. **-ress**

ambergris a waxy secretion from the intestine
of the sperm whale, used in perfumery

ambiance Fr. spelling of **ambience**, used in
English esp. of accessory details in a work
of art (ital.)

ambidextrous *not* -erous

ambience the surroundings (*not* -cy); *see also*
ambiance

ambivalen/t, -ce

amblyop/ia impaired vision, **-ic**

Amboina Indonesia, *properly* **Ambon**; *not* -oyna
(except in hist. contexts)

amboyna a type of decorative wood

ambry *use* **aum-**

AMDG *ad majorem Dei gloriam* (for the greater
glory of God)

ameba *use* **amoeba**

Amedabad, Amednagar India; *use* **Ahmad-**

âme damnée (Fr.) a 'cat's-paw', a devoted
adherent (lit. 'damned soul')

Ameer *use* only with reference to British India;
use **Amir** for Arabic titles, **Emir** for Turkish
and Indian titles

amend correct an error, make minor improve-
ments; cf. **emend**

amende/ honorable (Fr. f.) honourable repar-
ation, pl. **-s honorables**

a mensa et toro (Lat.) 'from board and bed',
legal separation, *not* thoro; cf. **a vinculo matrimonii**

Amer. American

amerc/e (law) punish by fine *or* punish arbi-
trarily; **-ement, -iable**

American Indian (of or relating to) a member
of the aboriginal peoples of America or their
descendants or languages; *prefer* Native American

Americanize *not* -ise

American plan (US) = **full board** (of hotels)

American Revolution (US) = **War of American Independence**

America's Cup, the a yachting race and
trophy

americium symbol **Am**

Amerind/ (also **Amerindian**) American Indian;
-ic

à merveille (Fr.) perfectly, wonderfully

AMG(OT) Allied Military Government (of Occu-
pied Territory) (Second World War)

Amharic the official language of Ethiopia

amiable friendly and pleasant in temperament, likeable; in Fr. *aimable*

amicable showing or done in a friendly spirit,
peaceable; in Fr. *amiable*

amic/us curiae a friend of the court, a disinterested adviser; pl. **-i curiae** (not ital.)

amidships *not* -ship (one word)

amigo (Sp.) friend (not ital.)

amino acid (chem., two words)

Amir (in Arab. *'amīr*) Arabic title, cap. when
forming part of the name; *see also* **Emir**; **Ameer**

Amis,/ (**Sir**) **Kingsley** (1922–97) English novelist and poet; **— Martin** (b. 1949) his son,
English novelist

Amish (of or relating to) a strict US Mennonite
sect

AMMA Assistant Masters' and Mistresses'
Association, *formerly* AMA

Ammal (Ind.) a suffix used to indicate that a
name belongs to a woman, e.g. Dr E. K. Janaki
Ammal

Amman Jordan

Ammergau Bavaria

ammeter for measuring electric current

amoeb/a pl. **-as** (not ital.), *not* ame-

à moitié (Fr.) half

amok *not* amuck, amock

Amoor *use* **Amur**

amorett/o (It. m.) a cupid, pl. **-i**

amortize *not* -ise

Amos (OT) do not abbreviate

amour-propre (Fr.) self-respect, proper pride

amp amperage, ampere, amplifier

Ampère, André Marie (1775–1836) French physicist (accent)

ampere an electric unit of current (no accent); abbr. **A** (sing. and pl.) *or* **amp** (no point)

ampersand = **&**, used in some formulae, references, and lexicographic work, in Acts of Parliament, and in business names. Since it may imply a closer relationship than *and*, the ampersand can be useful in grouping items: 'cinnamon & raisin and onion' are two, not three, types of bagels. However, in general *prefer* **and**. For **&c.** *use* **etc.**, except when reproducing antique typography

amphetamine (med.) a synthetic drug used esp. as a stimulant

amphibian (zool.) a member of the Amphibia; a vehicle adapted for land and water

amphor/a a jar, pl. **-ae**

ampoule a glass container for hypodermic dose; *not* -pule (US), -pul

Amritsar India, *not* Umritsur

amt. amount

amuck *use* **amok**

Amundsen, Roald (1872–1928) Norwegian explorer, S. Pole 1911

Amur Siberia, *not* -oor

amygdalin *not* -e

AN Anglo-Norman, autograph note

ana/ anecdotes or sayings, collective pl.; or sing. with pl. **-s**

-ana a suffix denoting anecdotes or other publications concerning, as Shakespeariana, Victoriana

anacoluth/on (gram.) a sentence or construction that lacks grammatical sequence (e.g. 'while in the garden the door banged shut'), pl. **-a**; **-ic**; *not* -outhon, -kolouthon, -koluthon

Anacreon (6th c. BC) Greek poet, abbr. **Anacr.**

anacreontic (noun and adj.) (a poem written) after the manner of Anacreon, convivial and amatory in tone; a classical verse form

anaemi/a, -c *not* anemi/a, -c (US)

anaerob/e, -ic

anaesthetist a doctor specializing in administering anaesthetics = (US) **anesthesiologist**; in the USA an anesthetist may be either a nurse or a doctor with a subordinate role

anaesthetize *not* ane- (US), -ise

anal. analog/y, -ous; analys/e, -er, -is; analytic, -al

analects (also **analecta**) a collection of short literary extracts

analog (comput.) the use of physical variables to represent numbers; cf. **digital**

analog/ous, -y abbr. **anal.**

analogue an analogous or parallel thing, *not* -log (US); *see also* **analog**

analys/e, -er, -is pl. **-es**, abbr. **anal.**; *not* -lyze (US)

analyst

analytic/, -al abbr. **anal.**

Anam *use* **Annam**

anamorphos/is pl. **-es**

anapaest (prosody) a foot of three syllables, *not* -pest (US)

anastase *use* **anat-**

anastomos/is communication by cross-connections, pl. **-es**; **-ist**

anastrophe (rhet.) the inversion of the usual order of words or clauses

anat. anatom/y, -ical

anatase a mineral, *not* anast-

anathema/ a curse (not used with an article), pl. **-s**; **-tize**

anatomize dissect, *not* -ise

anatom/y, -ical, -ist abbr. **anat.**

anatta (bot.) *use* **annatto**

ANB *American National Biography*

ANC African National Congress, Army Nurse Corps, Australian Newspapers Council

anc. ancient, *not* anct.

ancest/or if a feminine form is required, *use* **-ress**, *not* -rix

anchor/ite hermit, *not* -et; **-etic**

anchylosis *use* **ank-**

ancien régime (Fr. m.) the old order of things (not caps.); of France before 1789 (caps.)

ancient abbr. **anc.**, *not* anct.

Ancient Mariner, Rime of the a poem by Coleridge, 1798

Ancient Order of/ Druids abbr. **AOD**, — — — **Foresters** abbr. **AOF**, — — — **Hibernians** abbr. **AOH**

Ancrene/ Wisse *also called* — **Riwle**, *not* Ancren

Andalusia a region of Spain, in Sp. **Andalucía**

andante (mus.) moving easily, steadily

andantino/ (mus.) rather quicker (*formerly* but erroneously slower) than andante; as noun, pl. **-s**

Andersen, Hans Christian (1805–75) Danish writer

Andhra Pradesh an Indian state

Andoni Basque for **Anthony**

and/or signifying either or both of the stated alternatives; useful in legal, official, and business contexts—'soldiers and/or sailors'—as it compresses a lengthier clarification; avoid elsewhere

Andrea del Sarto (1486–1531) Italian painter

Androcles *not* -kles (except in specialist use)

androgen/ic, -ous (adj.) capable of developing and maintaining male characteristics

androgynous (adj.) of ambiguous gender

Andropov, Yuri (**Vladimirovich**) (1914–84) President of the USSR 1983–4

anent (prep.; arch., Sc.) concerning; a legal term used in Scottish law courts

aneurysm *not* -ism

Angeles, Victoria de los (b. 1923) Spanish soprano

Angelico, Fra (*c*.1400–55) Florentine painter and Dominican friar, *born* **Guido di Pietro**

Angelman syndrome *not* Angelman's

Angers, Marie-Louise-Félicité (1845–1924) French-Canadian novelist, pseud. **Laure Conan**

Angevin a native or inhabitant of Anjou; a Plantagenet, esp. any of the English kings from Henry II to John; certain kings and queens of Naples and Hungary

anglais/ (Fr.) f. *-e* English (not cap.); *but Anglais/, -e* English/man, -woman

angle the sign ∠, angle between the two lines ∧, right angle ∟, two right angles ⊥

angle brackets <> (wide), 〈 〉 (narrow)

Anglesey/ Gwynedd, *not* -ea; in Welsh **Ynys Môn**; Marquess of —

Angleterre (Fr. f.) England

anglice in English (not ital., no accent); abbr. **angl.**

Anglicize *not* -ise (cap.)

Anglo- prefix meaning 'English', although commonly used to encompass 'British'; can sometimes be replaced by 'British' to avoid offending non-English Britons

Anglo/-American; **-French** abbr. **AF**; **-Norman** abbr. **AN** (hyphens)

Anglophile *not* -phil

anglophone (not cap.)

Anglo-Saxon abbr. **AS**; as a language, **Old English** is now usually preferred; avoid as a term for 'English-speaking', except in disciplines where its use has become entrenched

Angora Turkey, *now* **Ankara**

Angostura *now* **Ciudad Bolívar**, Venezuela; — **Bitters** (propr., caps.) a kind of tonic

angostura/ (in full — **bark**) an aromatic bitter bark used as a flavouring

angst fear, anxiety; from (Ger. f.) *Angst*; ultimately from (Dan.) *Angest*, *now* **angst**

angstrom a unit of length equal to 10^{-10} metre (no accents), abbr. **Å**; now largely replaced by the **nanometre**

Ångström/, Anders Jonas (1814–74) Swedish physicist, created the — **pyrheliometer**

anguillette (Fr. f.) eel, *not* ai-

aniline a source of dyes (also adj.)

animalcule/ pl. **-s**, *not* -ae

animalcul/um *pl.* **-a**

animé a W. Indian resin, (Fr. mus.) animated (not ital.)

anion (elec.) an ion carrying a negative charge

Ankara Turkey, *formerly* Angora

ankylos/is the fusion of bones, pl. **-es**; *not* anch-

Anmerkung/ (Ger. f.) a note (cap.), pl. *-en*; abbr. **Anm.**

ann. annals, *anni* (years), *anno*, annual

anna/ (Ind., Pak.) *formerly* one-sixteenth of a rupee, *now* replaced by decimal coinage; pl. **-s**; abbr. **a.**

annales (Fr. pl. f.) annals, abbr. *ann.*

annals abbr. **ann.**

Annam/ *not* Anam; *formerly* a kingdom within French Indo-China, *now* merged in Vietnam; **-ite** the formal name for the Vietnamese language

Annan Dumfries & Galloway

Ann Arbor Mich.

annatto (bot.) an orange-red dye; *not* an-, -a

Anne,/ Queen (1702–14) (b. 1665); — **Saint**

Anne of Cleves (1515–57) fourth wife of Henry VIII of England

Anne of Geierstein a novel by Scott, 1829

annex verb, **annexe** noun (except in US, where 'annex' is both noun and verb)

anno/ (Lat.) in the year, abbr. *ann.*; — *aetatis suae* aged, abbr. *aet.*, *aetat.*; — *Domini* (cap. A, D) abbr. **AD** (small caps); — *Hegirae* (Muslim era) abbr. **AH** (small caps); — *mundi* in the year of the world, abbr. **AM** (small caps); all three abbrs. to be placed *before* the numerals

annonce (Fr. f.) advertisement

annotat/ed, -or *not* -er; abbr. **annot.**

annual abbr. **ann.**

annul/ar ringlike; **-ate, -ated, -et, -oid**

ann/us (Lat.) year, pl. *-i*; *-us horribilis* terrible year; *-us mirabilis* remarkable year

anonymous abbr. **anon.**

anorexic *not* -ectic

Anouilh, Jean (1910–88) French playwright

anschluss unification, esp. *Anschluss* (Ger. m.), the annexation of Austria in 1938 by Germany

ANSI American National Standards Institute

answer abbr. **A., ans.**

answerphone (not cap.)

Ant. Anthony, Antigua

ant. antonym

Antaeus (Gr. myth.) a giant with whom Hercules wrestled

antagonize *not* -ise

Antananarivo Madagascar

Antarctic/ -a

ante a stake in card game (not ital.)

ante/ (Lat.) before, — *bellum* before the war

ante-bellum (adj., hyphen, not ital.) occurring or existing before a particular war, esp. the US Civil War (one word in US)

antechamber *not* anti-

ante diem (Lat.) before the day, abbr. *a.d.*

antediluvian (one word)

ante medium (Lat.) before the middle, abbr. *ante med.*

antemeridian (one word)

ante meridiem (Lat.) before noon, abbr. **a.m.**

ante-mortem (adj., hyphen)

antenatal (one word)

antenn/a (zool.) pl. **-ae**; (US) radio or television aerial, pl. **-s**

ante-post in racing (hyphen)

ante-room (hyphen; one word in US)

anthelmintic a drug or agent used to destroy parasitic worms, *not* -thic

Anthony abbr. **Ant.** Anglicized from Lat. **Antonius**, from which came the variant **Antony** (NB *Antony and Cleopatra*); also **Antaine** (Ir. Gael.), **Antal** (Hungarian), **Antoine** (Fr.), **Andoni** (Basque), **Anton** (Ger., Russ.), **Antoni** (Catalan, Polish), **Antonio** (Castilian Sp., Galician, It.), **António** (European Port.), **Antônio** (Brazil. Port.), **Antonín** (Czech)

anthropolog/y -ical abbr. **anthrop.**

anthropomorphize *not* -ise

anthropophag/us a cannibal, pl. **-i**; adj. **-ous**

antichamber *use* ante-

Antichrist (cap.) *but* **antichristian**

anticline (geol.)

anticlockwise (one word)

antifreeze (one word)

Antigua abbr. **Ant.**

anti-hero a principal character noticeably lacking traditional heroic qualities (hyphen, one word in US)

antilogarithm (one word) abbr. **antilog**

antimacassar a covering put over furniture for protection (not cap.)

antimatter (one word)

antimony symbol **Sb**

antinomy conflict of authority

antinovel a novel in which formal conventions are studiously avoided (one word)

anti-nuclear (hyphen)

antiparticle (one word)

antipathize *not* -ise

antiq. antiquar/y, -ian

antiqs. antiquities

Antiqua (Ger. typ. f.) roman type (cap.)

antique paper a moderately bulky, opaque book paper with roughish surface

antisabbatarian (one word)

anti-Semit/e, -ic, -ism (hyphen, one cap.)

antistrophe a stanza corresponding to the strophe in a Greek dramatic chorus

antistrophon (rhet.) a retort

antitetanus (adj., one word)

antithes/is pl. **-es**

antithesize *not* -ise

antitoxin (one word)

antitype that which is represented by a type or symbol, *or* a person or thing of the opposite type; *not* ante-

António (European Port.), **Antônio** (Brazil. Port.)

antonym a word of opposite meaning, abbr. **ant.**

Anvers Fr. for **Antwerp**, in Fl. **Antwerpen**

Anwick Lincs.

any- pronouns and adverbs beginning with *any-*, *every-*, and *some-* are single words ('anyone you ask', 'everything I own', 'somebody to talk to'), *but* where each word retains its own meaning, the words are printed separately ('any one item', 'every thing in its place', 'some body in motion').

any/body, -how (one word)

any more (two words, one in US)

any/one, -place, -thing (one word)

anyway one word in conventional sense, *but* 'you can do it any way you like' (two words)

anywhere (one word)

Anzac Australian and New Zealand Army Corps (First World War)

Anzeige/ (Ger. f.) notice, advertisement; pl. *-n*

Anzus Australia, New Zealand, and the USA, as an alliance for the Pacific area (one cap.)

AO Accountant Officer, Army Order, Officer of the Order of Australia

AOB any other business

A.O.C.-in-C. Air Officer Commanding in Chief

AOD Ancient Order of Druids, Army Ordinance Department

AOF Ancient Order of Foresters

AOH Ancient Order of Hibernians

A-OK (caps., hyphen)

AOR adult-oriented rock, advance of rights, album-oriented radio

aorist abbr. **aor.**

aort/a (anat.) pl. **-ae**

Aotearoa (Maori) a poetic name for New Zealand, meaning 'land of the long white cloud', originally referring solely to the North Island

août (Fr. m.) August (not cap.)

à outrance (Fr.) to the bitter end, *not à l'outrance*

AP anti-personnel, *à protester* (Fr., on bills of exchange), armour-piercing, Associated Press

Ap. Apostle

ap. (Lat.) *apud* (quoted in)

a.p. above proof, author's proof

Apache a Native American people (cap.), a Parisian ruffian (not cap.)

apanage *not* app-

à part (Fr.) apart

apartheid (Afrik.) segregation (not ital.)

apatosaurus a huge herbivorous dinosaur of the Jurassic period, *formerly* called brontosaurus

ap/e, -ed, -ing, -ish

Apelles (4th c. BC) Greek painter

Apennines Italy (one *p*, three *ns*), in It. **Appennini**

aperçu an outline (not ital.)

aperitif/ an alcoholic drink taken as an appetizer, pl. **-s** (not ital., no accent)

APEX Association of Professional, Executive, Clerical, and Computer Staff

Apex (often attrib.) a system of reduced fares, abbr. of Advance Purchase Excursion (one cap.)

apex/ pl. **-es**, adj. **apical**

apfelstrudel a dish of baked apples in pastry (not cap., not ital.)

aphaere/sis the omission of a sound from the beginning of a word as a morphological development, pl. **-ses**; **-tic**

apheli/on (astr.) pl. **-a**, symbol **Q**

aphid/ pl. **-s**

aphi/s pl. **-des**

APL (comput.) A Programming Language

à plaisir (Fr.) at pleasure

apnoea the temporary cessation of breathing, *not* -nea (US)

Apocalypse (NT) abbr. **Apoc.**

apocalypse a grand or violent event; a revelation, esp. of the end of the world (not cap.)

Apocrypha (cap.) abbr. **Apoc.** (for abbr. of books *see* under names), adj. **apocryphal**

apodictic clearly established, *not* -deictic

apodos/is (gram.) pl. **-es**

apog/ee (astr.) abbr. **apog.**; **-ean**

Apollinaire, Guillaume born **Wilhelm Apollinaris de Kostrowitzky** (1880–1918) French poet and critic

Apollinaris (**water**) a mineral water from Ahr Valley, Germany

Apollin/arius (*sometimes* **-aris**) (*c.*310–*c.*390) Christian heretic, **-arianism**

Apollo/ a Greek god, **-nian**; — **Belvedere** a statue in the Vatican

Apollonius Rhodius (*c.*250 BC) Greek poet

Apollos a follower of St Paul (Acts 18: 24)

Apollyon the Devil

apologize *not* -ise

apophthegm a pithy maxim, *not* apothegm (US)

a-port (hyphen)

apostasy *not* -cy

apostatize *not* -ise

a posteriori (reasoning) from effects to causes (not ital., hyphen in attrib.); cf. **a priori**

Apostle abbr. **Ap.**, pl. **App.**

Apostles' Creed (caps.)

Apostroph/ (Ger. m.) apostrophe, pl. **-e** (cap.)

apostrophize *not* -ise

apothecaries' weight, signs ℳ minim; ℈ scruple; ʒ drachm; ℥ ounce; print quantities in lower-case letters close up behind symbol: final *i* becomes *j*, as vij = 7, j = 1

apothegm *use* **apophthegm** (except in US)

apotheos/is pl. **-es**

apotropaic averting ill luck

App. Apostles

app. appendix

appal/, -led, -ling

Appalachia/, -n Mountains, -n Trail E. North America; this mountain system includes the Adirondacks, Alleghenies, Catskills, and Great Smoky Mountains

appanage *use* **apan-**

apparatchik/ a member of a (usually Communist) party administration, esp. one who executes policy; pl. **-s**, **-i** (not ital.)

apparatus/ pl. **-es**, *not* -ati (*but* use an alternative, e.g. appliances, when possible)

apparatus criticus a collection of variants accompanying a printed text, abbr. **app. crit.**

apparel/, -led, -ling

apparitor an officer of ecclesiastical court, *not* -er

app. crit. apparatus criticus

appeal/, -ed, -ing

appeasement *not* -sment

appell/ant, -ate, -ation, -ative

append/ix pl. **-ices** for the supplement, **-ixes** for the anatomical organ, abbr. **app.**, pl. **apps.** (in all senses)

appetiz/e *not* -ise; **-er, -ing**

applesauce (one word)

appliqué/ (noun, adj., and verb) **-d**

appoggiatura (mus.) a type of grace note, leaning note

appraise estimate value

appreciat/or *not* -er; **-ive, -ory**

apprentice abbr. **appr.**

apprise inform

apprize (arch.) esteem highly

appro (on) approval (no point)

appro. approbation

approver one who turns Queen's evidence; the term is virtually obsolete in British law, but still used elsewhere (e.g. Pakistan)

approximat/e, -ely, -ion abbr. **approx.**

appurts. appurtenances

APR annual percentage rate (of interest), annual progress report

Apr. April

APRC *anno post Romam conditam* (in the year after the building of Rome in 753 BC) (small caps.), *but use* AUC

apr. J.-C. (Fr.) *après Jésus-Christ* (= AD)

après/ (Fr.) after, — *coup* after the event, — *-midi* afternoon (hyphen), — *moi* (or *nous*) *le déluge* after me (*or* us) the deluge

après-ski (of) the time after a day's skiing

April abbr. **Apr.**

April Fool's Day (one fool) *not* Fools' (US)

a/ primo (Lat.) from the first, — *principio* from the beginning

a priori (reasoning) from causes to effects (not ital., hyphen in attrib.); cf. **a posteriori**

apriorism the doctrine of a-priori ideas (one word, not ital.)

apropos (adj. and adv.) (one word, no accent)

à propos de bottes (Fr.) beside the mark

APS Aborigines' Protection Society, American Philosophical Society, American Physics Society, Associate of the Philosophical Society

apse/ a semicircular recess, esp. in a church; pl. **-s**

apsi/s in an orbit, point of greatest or least distance from central body; pl. **-des**

APT advanced passenger train, advanced process technology, Association of Polytechnic Teachers, Association of Printing Technologists, automatic picture transmission (from satellites)

apud (Lat.) according to, in the work, *or* works, of; abbr. **ap.**

Apuleius, Lucius (2nd c. AD) Roman satirist

Apulia a region of Italy, in It. **Puglia**

aqua/ fortis, — regia (chem.) (two words, not ital.)

aquarium/ pl. **-s**

à quatre mains (Fr. mus.) for two performers (lit. 'for four hands')

aquavit an alcoholic drink; *see also* **akvavit**

aqua vitae (two words, not ital.)

Aquinas, St Thomas (*c.*1225–74) Italian theologian

AR Arkansas (postal abbr.)

AR *anno regni* (in the year of the reign) (small caps.)

Ar argon (no point)

a/r all risks

ARA Associate of the Royal Academy, London

Arabi/a, -an, -c abbr. **Arab.**

Arabian Nights' Entertainments, The

Arabic the Semitic language of the Arabs, now spoken in much of N. Africa and the Middle East

arabic numerals the numerals used in ordinary computation, as 1, 2, 3 (not cap.)

arach. arachnology

arachnid (zool.) a member of the Arachnidae

arachnoid (bot.) having long hairs, (anat.) one of meninges

ARAD Associate of the Royal Academy of Dancing

Aragon a region of Spain, *not* Arr-; in Sp. **Aragón**

Araldite (propr.)

ARAM Associate of the Royal Academy of Music

Aramaic abbr. **Aram.** a Semitic language, esp. that of Syria; written in Hebrew characters

Aran, Island of Co. Donegal; *see also* **Arran**

Aran Islands Galway Bay, Ireland; *see also* **Arran**

ARAS Associate of the Royal Astronomical Society

ARB Air Registration Board, Air Research Bureau

ARBA Associate of the Royal Society of British Artists

arbalest a crossbow, *not* arblast

arbit/er, -rary, -ration abbr. **arb.**

arbiter elegantiae (Lat.) a judge of taste

arbitrageur *not* -ger

arbitrament *not* -ement

arbitrator a legal or official word for arbiter

arbor a spindle, axis

arboret/um (bot.) a tree garden, pl. **-a**

arboriculture abbr. **arbor.**

arbor vitae a conifer

arbour a bower, *not* -or (US)

ARBS Associate of the Royal Society of British Sculptors

ARC Aeronautical Research Council, Agricultural Research Council, Architects' Registration Council

Arc, Jeanne d' (Fr.) **Joan of Arc** (1412–31)

ARCA Associate of the Royal College of Art

Arcades ambo (Lat.) two with like tastes

arcan/um pl. **-a**

Arc de Triomphe Paris

arced (elec.) *not* arck-

arc-en-ciel (Fr. m.) rainbow, pl. **arcs-en-ciel**

arch. archa/ic, -ism; archery, archipelago; architect, -ural, -ure

Archaean of or relating to the earlier part of the Precambrian era, *not* -hean (US)

archaeolog/y, -ical, -ist abbr. **archaeol.**, *not* arche- (US)

Archangel Russia, in Russ. **Arkhangelsk**

archangel (one word, cap. when part of name)

Archbishop abbr. **Abp.**

Archd. Archdeacon, Archduke

archetype *not* archi-

archidiaconal of or relating to an archdeacon, *not* archide-

archiepiscopal of or relating to an archbishop

Archimedean *not* -ian

archipelago/ pl. **-s**, abbr. **arch.**

Archipiélago de Colón off. Sp. name for **Galá-pagos Islands**

architect/, -ural, -ure abbr. **arch., archit., archt.; orders of classical architecture** Doric, Ionic, Corinthian, Tuscan, and Composite

architype *use* **arche-**

arcing (elec.) *not* arck-

ARCM Associate of the Royal College of Music

ARCO Associate of the Royal College of Organists

ARCS Associate of the Royal College of Science

arctic (not cap.) cold

Arctic Circle (two caps.)

Arctic regions (one cap.)

Arctogaea (zool.) the land mass including Europe, Asia, Africa, and N. America; cf. **Neogaea**; **Notogaea**

Ardleigh Essex

Ardley Oxon.

ARE Arab Republic of Egypt, Associate of the Royal Society of Painter-Etchers and Engravers

are a unit of square measure, 100 sq. m.

areol/a a small area, pl. **-ae** (not ital.); *not* au-

Arequipa Peru

arête a sharp mountain ridge (not ital.)

argent (her.) silver, abbr. **arg.**

Argentina the country, *or* **Argentine Republic** (in very formal discourse), *not* 'the Argentine'

Argentin/e (adj.) *also* (noun) the inhabitant; *also* **-ian** *not* -ean

argentum silver, symbol (chem.) **Ag**, (numismatics) **Ꞃ**

argon symbol **Ar**

argot slang (not ital.)

arguable *not* -eable

argumentum ad/ crumenam (Lat.) argument to the purse; **— — hoc** argument for this (purpose); **— — hominem** argument to the person's interests; **— —ignorantiam** argument based on the adversary's ignorance; **— — invidiam** argument to hatred or prejudice; **— — rem** argument to the purpose; **— — verecundiam** appeal to modesty; **argumentum baculinum** or **— — baculum** argument of the stick, club-law; **argumentum e silentio** argument from silence

argy-bargy a dispute, wrangle; *not* argle-bargle (hyphen)

Argyle Minn.

Argyll/ and Bute District, — and Sutherland Highlanders, — and the Isles (Bishop of), **Duke of —**

Argyllshire a former county of Scotland

Århus (Dan.) **Aarhus**

Arian (theol.) a follower of Arius, (one) born under Aries

ARIBA Associate of the Royal Institute of British Architects

ARICS Professional Associate of the Royal Institution of Chartered Surveyors

Ariège a dép. of France

Aristotelian *not* -ean

Arius (*c*.250–*c*.336) Christian heretic

Ariz. Arizona (off. abbr.)

Arizona off. abbr. **Ariz.**, postal **AZ**

Ark. Arkansas (off. abbr.)

Arkansas off. abbr. **Ark.**, postal **AR**

Arlay dép. Jura, France

Arle Glos.; *not* -s

Arles dép. Bouches-du-Rhône, France

ARM adjustable-rate mortgage

ArM Master of Architecture (from Lat. *Architecturae Magister*)

Arm. Armenian, Armoric

armadillo/ pl. **-s**

armchair (one word)

Armenia/ an ancient country, a former Soviet Socialist Republic, now an independent republic; **-n** (of or related to) (the people or language) of Armenia

armes blanches (Fr.) side arms (bayonet, sabre, sword)

armful/ pl. **-s**

armhole (one word)

Arminians followers of Arminius

Arminius, Jacobus Latinized form of **Jacob Harmen** (1560–1609) Dutch theologian

armory heraldry, (US) = **armoury**

armoury a collection of arms

armpit (one word)

ARMS Associate of the Royal Society of Miniature Painters

arm's length (two words)

Army/ Dental Corps *now* **RADC**; — **Nursing Service** abbr. **ANS**; — **Order** abbr. **AO**; — **Ordnance Corps** *now* **RAOC**; — **Service Corps** *later* **RASC**, *now* **RCT**; — **Veterinary Department** abbr. **AVD**, *now* **RAVC**

arnotto *use* **annatto**

Arola Piedmont, Italy

Arolla Switzerland

Arolo Lombardy, Italy

Aroostook War settled the border of Maine and New Brunswick, 1842

ARP air-raid precautions

arpeggio/ (mus.) the striking of notes of chord in (usually upward) succession, pl. **-s**

ARPS Associate of the Royal Photographic Society, Association of Railway Preservation Societies

arquebus *use* **harq-**

ARR *anno regni Regis* or *Reginae* (in the year of the King's, *or* Queen's, reign) (small caps.)

arr. arranged; arriv/e, -ed, -es, -als

Arragon *use* **Aragon**

Arran, Earl of

Arran, Isle of Scotland; *see also* **Aran**

arrant utter, notorious; cf. **errant**

arrester a device for slowing an aircraft during landing, *not* -or

arrêt (Fr. m.) decree

Arrhenius, Svante August (1859–1927) Swedish scientist

arrière/-garde (Fr. f.) rearguard; **— -pensée** ulterior motive or mental reservation, pl. **-pensées** (hyphens)

arrivis/me (Fr. m.) ambitious behaviour, **-te** one who behaves thus

arrondissement (Fr. m.) a subdivision of a *département* (not ital. in Eng.)

arrowhead (one word)

Arrows of the Chace by Ruskin (1880), *not* Chase

arroyo/ a brook, stream, or gully; pl. **-s**

ARSA Associate of the Royal Scottish Academy, Associate of the Royal Society of Arts

ARSCM Associate of the Royal School of Church Music

arsenic symbol **As**

ars est celare artem (Lat.) the art is to conceal art

ARSL Associate of the Royal Society of Literature

ARSM Associate of the Royal School of Mines

ARSW Associate of the Royal Scottish Society of Painting in Water Colours

art. article, artillery, artist

art deco a decorative art style of 1920s (not cap.)

artefact *not* arti- (US)

artel an association of craftsmen, peasants, etc. in the former USSR

arteriosclerosis hardening of the arteries (one word)

arthropod/ a member of Arthropoda, animals with jointed body and limbs; pl. **-s**

article abbr. **art.**

articles of roup (Sc. law) conditions of sale (by auction)

articles, titles of (typ.) when cited, to be roman, quoted

artifact (US) *use* **arte-**

artillery abbr. **A.**, **art.**

artisan *not* -zan

artiste a professional singer, dancer, or other performer of either sex; *different from* **artist**

artizan *see* **artis-**

art nouveau a late 19th- to early 20th-c. ornamental art style (not cap.)

art paper a high-quality coated paper used for illustrations

art. pf. artist's proof

Arts and Crafts movement (two caps.)

artwork (one word) abbr. **a/w**

Arundel W. Sussex

Arundell of Wardour, Baron title now extinct

ARV (Bible) American (Standard) Revised Version

Arva Co. Cavan, *not* Arvagh

ARWS Associate of the Royal Society of Painters in Water Colours

Aryan Indo-European, *not* -ian

AS Academy of Science, Admiral Superintendent, Advanced Supplementary (level, in education), Angelman syndrome, Anglo-Saxon

AS (Lat. *anno Seleuci*) in the year of Seleucus (era beginning 312/11 BC); formerly also used for *anno salutis*, in the year of salvation, or *anno Salvatoris*, in the year of the Saviour, both equivalent to AD (small caps.)

As arsenic (no point)

As. Asia, -n, -tic

ASA Advertising Standards Authority, Amateur Swimming Association, Associate Member of the Society of Actuaries, Associate of the Society of Actuaries (USA)

asafoetida (med.) an ill-smelling gum resin; *not* ass-, -fetida (US)

Asahi Shimbun a Japanese newspaper

Asante the modern form of **Ashanti**

asap as soon as possible (no points)

Asbjörnsen, Peter Christian (1812–85) Norwegian writer

ascendan/ce *not* -ence; **-cy, -t**; cap. when referring to a specific period of Irish history

ascender (typ.) the top part of letters such as b, d, f, h, k, l

Ascension/ Day (caps., two words), **— Island** S. Atlantic

ascetic austere

Ascham, Roger (1515–68) English writer

ASCII (comput.) American Standard Code for Information Interchange (caps. or small caps.)

ascites (sing. and pl.) abdominal dropsy

Asclepiad a verse metre, *not* Ask-

Asclepius the Greek hero and god of healing, *not* Asklepios (except in specialist contexts); *see also* **Aesculapius**

a/s de (Fr.) *aux soins de*, = **c/o**

ASDIC Anti-Submarine Detection Investigation Committee, used for a form of hydrophone; *later* **Asdic**, *now* officially **sonar**

ASE American Stock Exchange, Associate of the Society of Engineers

ASEAN Association of South East Asian Nations

as follows: (use colon only, *not* :—)

Asgard the heaven of Norse mythology

ASH Action on Smoking and Health

ash Old English letter æ also used in phonetic script, Danish, and Norwegian

Ashanti Ghana, *not* -ee; *now also* **Asante**

Ashby de la Zouch Leics. (no hyphens)

Ashgabat the capital of Turkmenistan, *formerly* Poltoratsk in Russ. **Ashkhabad**

Ashkenazi/ a Jew of N. or E. European descent, pl. **-m** (cap.); cf. **Sephardi**

ashlar (archit.) *not* -er

Ashmolean Museum Oxford

Ashtar/oth, -eth in biblical and Semitic use, otherwise *use* **Astarte**

Ashton/-in-Makerfield, -under-Lyne Gr. Manchester (hyphens), *not* -Lyme; **— upon Mersey** Gr. Manchester (no hyphens)

ashtray (one word)

Ash Wednesday first day of Lent (two words)

ASI air-speed indicator, Association soroptimiste internationale

Asian (adj. and noun) of Asia; *not* Asiatic except for e.g. 'Asiatic cholera'

A-side the main side of a gramophone record

asinin/e like an ass, *not* ass-; **-ity**

Asir ('the inaccessible') former name for Saudi Arabia

askance *not* askant

Asklepi/ad *use* **Asclepiad**; **-os** *see* **Asclepius**

a.s.l. above sea level (points)

Aslef Associated Society of Locomotive Engineers and Firemen (one cap.)

Aslib Association of Special Libraries and Information Bureaux (one cap.)

ASM air-to-surface missile

Asnières a Paris suburb

Asola Lombardy, Italy

Asolo Venetia, Italy

asper (Gr.) a rough-breathing mark ('), typographically largely equivalent to the Arab. ʿayn or Heb. ʿayin (not ital.)

asperg/e (Fr. f.) asparagus, **-é** (Fr.) sprinkled with (something)

asperges (noun sing.) a sprinkling with blessed water

asphalt *not* ash-, -e

asphodel an immortal flower in Elysium

asphyxia an interruption of breathing

aspic a savoury jelly

aspic (Fr. m.) an asp, a serpent

ASPR Anglo-Saxon Poetic Records

ASR (comput.) answer send and receive

ass a donkey, a stupid person; (US) = arse

ass. assistant

assafoetida *use* **asa-**

assai (mus.) very

assailant a person who attacks another physically or verbally, *not* -ent

Assam/ NE India, **-ese** (of or related to) a native or the language of Assam

assassin the killer of a political or religious leader (not cap.); (hist.) any of a group of Muslim fanatics sent on murder missions in the time of the Crusades (sometimes cap.), *properly* **Nizari Ismaili**

assegai a spear, *not* assa-

Assembly (Church of Scotland) (cap.) *properly* **General Assembly** (also in other Presbyterian Churches); *see also* **Church Assembly**

assent/er one who assents, **-or** one who subscribes to a nomination paper

Asserbaijan, -i *use* **Azer-**

assert/er one who asserts, **-or** an advocate

assess/able *not* -ible, **-or** *not* -er

ASSET Association of Supervisory Staffs, Executives, and Technicians

assign/ee one to whom a right or property is assigned, **-or** one who assigns

Assiniboine Canada, *not* Assinn-

Assisi Italy

assistant abbr. **ass., asst.**

assize (hist.) a court sitting at intervals in each county of England and Wales to administer civil and criminal law

assizer an officer with oversight of weights and measures; *not* -ser, -sor, -zor

assoc. associat/e, -ion

ASSR (hist.) Autonomous Soviet Socialist Republic

asst. assistant

Assuan *use* **Aswan**

assurance the insurance of life (the technical term); *see also* **life insurance**

assure convince or make certain of; *see also* **ensure; insure**

assymmetry *use* **asy-**

Assyr. Assyrian

AST Atlantic Standard Time

a-starboard (hyphen)

Astarte a Syro-Phoenician goddess; *not* Ashtaroth, -eth

astatine symbol **At**

Asterabad Iran

asterisk a symbol (*); in specialist linguistic use a 'star', so a word is 'starred' *not* 'asterisked'; consequently, 'a *' *not* 'an *'

Asti/ an Italian white wine; — **spumante** a sparkling form of this, from Asti in Piedmont (one cap., not ital.)

ASTMS Association of Scientific, Technical, and Managerial Staffs; *now* part of the **MSF**

astr. astronom/y, -er, -ical

astrakhan lambskin from Astrakhan (not cap.)

astrol. astrolog/y, -er

Astronomer Royal (caps., no hyphen)

astronomical unit a unit of length reckoned as 1.496×10^{11} m; *not* an SI unit (though it may be used with SI units); has no internationally agreed symbol; abbr. **AU**

astrophysic/s (pl. noun, treated as sing.) **-al, -ist** (one word)

AstroTurf (propr.) (one word, two caps.)

Asturias Spain, *not* The —

Asunción Paraguay

ASVA Associate of the Incorporated Society of Valuers and Auctioneers

Aswan Egypt, *not* the many variants

asymmetry *not* ass-

asymptote a line approaching but not meeting a curve

asyndet/on the omission of a connecting word (usually a conjunction), **-ic**

Asyut Egypt

AT (Ger.) *Altes Testament* (the Old Testament)

At astatine (no point)

at. atomic

Atahualpa the last Inca

Atalanta (Gr. myth.) a great huntress

atar *use* **attar**

Atatürk, (Mustapha) Kemal (1881–1938) Turkish statesman, President 1923–38

ATC Air Traffic Control, Air Training Corps

Atchin Sumatra, Indonesia; *use* **Ach-**

ATCL Associate of Trinity College of Music, London

atelier a studio (not ital.)

a tempo (mus.) in time; it indicates that, after a change in time, the previous time must be resumed

Athabasca Sask., Canada; *not* -ka

Athanasi/us, St (d. 373) Greek patriarch, **-an**

atheling a prince, lord, or member of a noble family in Anglo-Saxon England; *not* aeth-, although **æth-** is acceptable

Athenaeum a London club; (ital.) a British literary review, 1828–1921

Athene (Gr. myth.) goddess of wisdom, war, and handicrafts, patron of Athens, in which contexts *use* **Athena**

Atheneum publishers, *not* -ae-

Athol New Zealand; Mass.

Atholl/, Duke of; — *also* forest, Sc.

Atholville New Brunswick, Can.

Atl. Atlantic

Atlanta Ga.

ATM automated (*or* automatic) teller machine

atm. atmosphere, atmospheric

atmosphere the gaseous envelope around the Earth and other planets, the pressure exerted by it; abbr. **atm.**

at. no. atomic number

atoll a ring-shaped coral reef surrounding a lagoon

atomize *not* -ise

atonable *not* -eable

ATP adenosine triphosphate

atri/um the hall of a Roman house or a central court in a modern building, pl. **-a**; a cavity in the body, esp. one of two in the heart, pl. **-ums**

Atropos (Gr. myth.) the Fate that cuts the thread of life

ATS Auxiliary Territorial Service (*superseded by* **WRAC**), (Austral.) Amalgamated Television Services

attaché/ pl. **-s** (not ital.)

attar (as of roses) *not* atar, ott-, otto

Attawapiskat a Canadian river

Att. Gen. Attorney General

Attic salt delicate wit (one cap.)

Attila (*c*.406–43) king of the Huns

attitudinize *not* -ise

Attlee, Clement (Richard) (1883–1967) British politician, Prime Minister 1945–51; created earl 1955

attn. for the attention of

atto- (as prefix) 10^{18}, abbr. **a**

attorn (law) to transfer

attorney-at-law (hyphens)

Attorney General (two words) abbr. **AG, Att. Gen.**

attractor *not* -er

ATV all-terrain vehicle, Associated Television (*now* **ITV**)

Atwood, Margaret (b. 1939) Canadian writer

Atwood's machine (phys.) *not* Att-

at. wt. atomic weight

AU (US) Actors' Union, angstrom unit, astronomical unit

Au aurum (gold) (no point)

aubade a dawn-piece

AUBC Association of Universities of the British Commonwealth

auberg/e (Fr. f.) inn, *-iste* (m. *or* f.) innkeeper

aubergine the fruit of the eggplant; in the USA the fruit is called eggplant as well

Aubigné dép. Deux-Sèvres, France

Aubigny dép. Nord, France

aubrietia a dwarf perennial, *not* -retia

AUC (**AVC** in classical transcriptions) *anno urbis conditae* (in the year from the building of the city of Rome in 753 BC), also *ab urbe condita* (from the foundation of the city) (small caps.; no points except in Latin composition)

Auchinleck, Field-Marshal Sir Claude (**John Eyre**) (1884–1981) British soldier

Auchnashellach Highland, *use* **Ach-**

au/ contraire (Fr.) on the contrary, *— courant de* fully acquainted with

Audenarde *see* **Oudenarde**

Audi a German make of car

audio/ frequency, — typist (two words)

audio-visual (hyphen, one word in US)

Auditor-General abbr. **Aud.-Gen.**

auditori/um pl. **-ums**, **-a**

Audubon, John (**James**) (1785–1851) US ornithologist and artist

AUEW/ Amalgamated Union of Engineering Workers, **— (TASS)** Amalgamated Union of Engineering Workers (Technical and Supervisory Section)

au fait (Fr.) thoroughly conversant (not ital.)

Aufklärung (Ger. f.) enlightenment, esp. the 18th-c. intellectual movement

Auflage/ (Ger. f.) edition, impression; pl. *-n* (cap.); abbr. **Aufl.**; note the 'fl' is set as a ligature in Ger.; *unveränderte —* reprint, *verbesserte und vermehrte —* revised and enlarged edition; *see also* **Ausgabe**

au fond (Fr.) at the bottom; used in Eng. to mean basically, in reality, in fact; cf. *à fond*; *dans le fond*

Aufsteiger (Ger. m.) social climber

auf Wiedersehen (Ger.) till we meet again, goodbye

Aug. August

aug. augmentative

Augean (Gr. myth.) (stables) filthy (cap.)

auger a tool for boring; cf. **augur**

aught anything (cf. **naught**)

au grand sérieux (Fr.) in all seriousness

au gratin browned with cheese etc. (not ital.)

augur (noun) a Roman soothsayer, (verb) foresee, portend; cf. **auger**

August abbr. **Aug.**

Augustan of the Roman Emperor Augustus (63 BC–AD 14); or an era compared to this, most usually the early to mid-18th c. in England

Augustine an Augustinian monk, **St —** (354–430) Bishop of Hippo, **St —** (d. 604) first Archbishop of Canterbury

Augustinian a monk of an order following St Augustine of Hippo

au jus (Fr.) in gravy

auk a diving bird, *not* awk

auld lang syne (caps., quotation marks for song title)

Auld Reekie literally 'Old Smoky', i.e. Edinburgh

aumbry a closed recess in the wall of a church, *not* ambry

Aumerle, Duke of a character in Shakespeare's *Richard II*

au mieux (Fr.) on excellent terms

au naturel in its natural state, plainly cooked

Aung San/ (1914–47) Burmese nationalist leader, **— — Suu Kyi** Burmese political leader, daughter of Aung San

auntie *not* -y; a nickname for the BBC (cap.)

au pair (Fr.) at par, on mutual terms

au pair a person helping with childcare, housework (not ital.)

au pied de la lettre (Fr.) literally

Aurangzeb (1618–1707) Mogul Emperor, *not* the many variants

aurar pl. of **eyrir**

aurea mediocritas (Lat.) the golden mean

aureole a saint's halo, a circle of light; *also* **aureola**; *not* ar-

au reste (Fr.) besides

au revoir till we meet again, goodbye

Aurignacian a flint culture of the palaeolithic period in Europe, following the Mousterian and preceding the Solutrean

Aurigny Fr. for **Alderney**

aurochs an extinct wild ox, ancestor of domestic cattle; *not* urus; cf. **wisent**

auror/a australis (astr.) pl. **-ae australes**, **-a borealis** pl. **-ae boreales**

aurum gold, symbol (chem.) **Au** (no point)

Aus. Austria, **-n**

Auschwitz a town and a German concentration camp in Poland in Second World War, in Pol. **Oświęcim**; Poles use the Ger. for the camp and the Pol. for the town

au/ secours (Fr.) a cry for help, — *sérieux* seriously

Ausgabe (Ger. f.) edition (refers to the form, not to a revision), abbr. **Ausg.** (cap.); *see also* **Auflage**, and the compounds **Buch-**; **Pracht-**; **Volks-**

auspicious of good omen, favourable, prosperous; *not* a synonym for notable, significant, important

Aussie Australian; *not* -y, Ossie, Ozzie, or other variants

Austen, Jane (1775–1817) English writer

Austin/ an English form of the name Augustine; **—, Alfred** (1835–1913) Poet Laureate 1896–1913; **—, John Langshaw** (1911–60) English philosopher; — Tex.

austral/ southern (not cap.); of Australia or Australasia (e.g. 'Austral English') (cap.); a basic unit of currency in Argentina; pl. **-es** (not cap.)

Australasia abbr. **A'asia**, a collective term, referring either to (*a*) Australia, New Zealand, and the islands of Melanesia, *or* to (*b*) Australia, New Zealand, Fiji, and Western Samoa; **Oceania** includes Micronesia and Polynesia as well

Austral/ia, -ian abbr. **Austral.**

Australian Capital Territory abbr. **ACT**

Australian Labor Party *not* Labour

Austrasia a Frankish kingdom of 6th–8th cc.

Austria abbr. **Aus.**

Austria-Hungary (*but* **Austro-Hungarian**), hyphen *not* en rule, 1867–1918, in Ger. **Österreich-Ungarn**

Austro- combining form of Austrian (e.g. *Austro-Hungarian*) *or* Australian (e.g. *Austro-Asiatic*)

Austronesian a family of *c.*600 languages spoken in the S. Pacific, also called **Malayo-Polynesian**

AUT Association of University Teachers

autarchy absolute sovereignty

autarky self-sufficiency

Auteuil a Paris suburb

auteur/ (Fr. m.) author, also (esp. in cinema) used of a person who controls all aspects of the creative process, hence *-iste*

auth. authentic; author, -ess, -ity, -ized

author refer to oneself in writing as 'I', *not* 'The author'; avoid using *author* or *co-author* as a verb where *write* or *co-write* will serve

author–date system a form of referencing, often called the Harvard system (en rule)

authorize *not* -ise

Authorized Version (of the Bible) (caps.) abbr. **AV**

autis/m a mental condition obstructing response to environment, **-tic**

autobahn/ a German motorway, pl. **-s**, in Ger. *Autobahn/*, pl. **-en** (not ital.)

autochthon/ an original inhabitant, pl. **-s**; **-ous**

autocracy absolute monarchy

autocue (propr.)

auto/-da-fé (Port.) pl. **autos-da-fé**, 'act of the faith', burning of heretic by Inquisition (not ital.); (Sp.) *auto de fe* (ital.)

autogiro an early form of helicopter, *not* -gyro

autolithography (typ.) printing by lithography from stones or plates prepared by the artist personally

automat/on a piece of mechanism with concealed motive power, a person who acts like such a piece; pl. **-a, -ons**

autonomy self-government

autonym a book published under an author's real name

autopista a Spanish motorway (not ital.)

autore (It.) author, abbr. *aut.*

autoroute a French motorway (not ital.)

autostrad/a an Italian motorway, pl. **-e** (not ital.)

autres temps, autres mœurs (Fr.) other times, other manners

AUT(S) Association of University Teachers (Scotland)

autumn (not cap.)

Auvergne (Fr.) *not* The —

Auvers dép. Seine-et-Oise, France

Auverse dép. Maine-et-Loire, France

auxiliary abbr. **aux., auxil.**

Auxiliary Forces (caps.)

A/ (numismatics) = gold (Lat. *aurum*) (no point)

AV audio-visual, Authorized Version (of the Bible)

a/v ad valorem

av. average

avadavat *not* ama-

avant/-courier in Fr. m. *-courrier* or *-coureur*, f. *-coureuse* forerunner

avant-gard/e the advanced guard, the innovators; **-ism, -ist**

avant-propos (Fr. m.) preface, pl. same (hyphen)

avaunt (arch.) begone

av. C. (It.) *avanti Cristo* (BC)

avdp. avoirdupois

ave. avenue, average

ave atque vale (Lat.) hail and farewell

Ave Maria (Hail, Mary!) abbr. **AM**

Avenue abbr. **Ave.**

Avenue of the Americas off. name of Sixth Avenue, New York City

average abbr. **av.**

Averroes (1126–98) Spanish-Muslim physician, astronomer, philosopher; *also* **-ës** (though less correct); *also called* **ibn-Rushd** *or* **the Commentator**

averse, aversion opposed or disinclined: 'he is not averse to grumbling', 'Mary-Jane's aversion to rice pudding'; cf. **adverse**

avertible *not* -able

avertissement (Fr. m.) notice, warning

aviculture the rearing of birds

Avignon dép. Vaucluse, France

a vinculo matrimonii (Lat.) 'from the bond of marriage', full divorce (cf. *a mensa et toro*)

avis au lecteur (Fr.) notice to the reader

avizandum (Sc. law) a judge's consideration of case in private

av. J.-C. (Fr.) *avant Jésus-Christ* (BC)

AVM Air Vice-Marshal

avocad/o pl. **-os**

avocet a bird, *not* -set

Avogadro/, Amedeo (1776–1856) Italian scientist, *not* Avro-; — **constant** (symb. *L*, N_A) 6.022 1367 × 10^{23} mol^{-1}, *not* Avogadro number (no apos.); *but* **Avogadro's hypothesis**

avoirdupois/ (*in full* — **weight**) a system of weights based on a pound of 16 ounces or 7,000 grains, abbr. **avdp.**

à volonté (Fr.) at pleasure, at will

Avon/ a county of England, and name of several English rivers; **Earl of —**

à votre santé! (Fr.) (here's) to your health!

avril (Fr. m., not cap.) April

a/w (typ.) artwork

AWACS Airborne Warning And Control System (a long-range radar system for detecting enemy aircraft)

Awdry, Revd W(ilbert Vere) (1911–97) children's author, creator of the 'Railway Series' (Thomas the Tank Engine)

awesome *not* aws-

awhile (adv.) *but* for a while; *see also* **while**

awing (part. of **awe**) *not* aweing

awk *use* auk

awk. awkward

AWOL absent without (official) leave

AWRE Atomic Weapons Research Establishment

ax. axiom

axe *not* ax (US)

axel a jumping movement in skating

ax/is pl. **-es**; (cap., hist.) the German alliance formed in 1939

ay/ yes: 'Ay, ay, sir'; pl. **-es**: 'The ayes have it'

ayah an Indian nursemaid

ayatollah a Shi'ite religious leader in Iran (cap. when used as title)

Aycliffe Dur., 'new town', 1947

aye ever: 'For ever and for aye'

Ayer's Cliff Quebec, Canada (apos.)

Ayers Rock Australian Western Desert (no apos.), in Pitjantjatjara **Uluru**

AYH American Youth Hostels

ʿ**ayin** (Heb.) a rough-breathing mark (' *properly* ʿ), typographically largely equivalent to the Arab. ʿayn or Gr. asper (ital.); also expressed as **ayin** (no accent)

Aylesbury Bucks. *See also* **Ail-**

ʿ**ayn** (Arab.) a rough-breathing mark (' *properly* ʿ), typographically largely equivalent to the Heb. ʿayin or Gr. asper (ital.); *not* ain

Ayr Strathclyde

Ayr. Ayrshire

Ayre, Point of IoM

Ayub Khan, Muhammad (1907–74) Pakistani soldier and politician, President 1958–69

AZ Arizona (postal abbr.)

az. azure

Azerbaijan/ a province of NW Iran and former Soviet Socialist Republic, **-i** (adj); **-ian** *or* **Azeri** the language, formerly written in the Arabic or (later) Cyrillic alphabet, now in the roman alphabet; *not* Asser-

Azikiwe, (Benjamin) Nnamdi (1904–96) Nigerian leader, President 1963–6

Azilian a transitional period between the palaeolithic and neolithic ages in Europe

Azores in Port. **Açores**, 'Islands' no longer forms part of the name

Azov, Sea of *not* -off, -of

Azrael the Muslim angel of death

AZT azidothymidine, a drug intended for use against the Aids virus

Aztec (a member) of, *or* concerning, a people dominant in Mexico before the Spanish conquest; adj. same, *not* -ian; *see also* **Nahuatl**

B b

B bel, (mus.) B flat in German system, (chess) bishop, (pencils) black (*see also* **BB, BBB**), boron, the second in a series

B. Bachelor, Baron, bass, basso, Bay, Blessed (*Beat/us, -a*), British

b (phys.) barn, (compass) by

b. base, (Heb.) ben, billion, (meteor.) blue sky, book, born; (cricket) bowled, bye; (Arab.) ibn

BA Bachelor of Arts, Booksellers Association, British Academy, British Airways, British America, British Association

Ba barium (no point)

BAA British Airports Authority, British Astronomical Association

Baader–Meinhof Group (en rule, hyphen in Ger.)

Baalbek Syria

baas (Afrik.) master, boss

baaskap (Afrik.) domination, esp. of non-whites by whites

Ba'ath an Iraqi and Syrian political party, in Arab. *Ba'ṯ*; a loose transliteration for non-technical contexts is **Baath**

Babbitt/ by Sinclair Lewis, 1922 (roman in allusive use, as character's name); **-ry**

babel not cap., except in **Tower of Babel**

babiroussa a wild hog; *not* baby-, -russa

babu an Indian title of respect, *not* -boo except in hist. use

Babygro (propr.) an all-in-one garment for babies

babysitter (one word)

BAC British Aerospace Corporation

baccalaureate the university degree of bachelor (not ital., no accent); *baccalauréat* (Fr. m.) the Fr. equivalent of A levels (ital., accent)

baccarat a card game; in Fr. m. *baccara*

Bacchanalia/ the festival of Bacchus, strictly pl. but used in Eng. as sing.; **-n** (not cap.) riotous or drunken (revelry)

bacchant/ a male or female follower of Bacchus, **-e** female only

Bach,/ German musical family, more than fifty in number in seven generations, of whom the greatest was — **Johann Sebastian** (1685–1750) (of the fifth generation) composer of orchestral, instrumental, and choral music; also important were his father's cousin, — **Johann Christoph** (1642–1703) composer; and of J.S.B.'s twenty children, — **Wilhelm Friedemann** (1710–84); — **Carl Philipp Emanuel**, usually referred to as **C. P. E.** (1714–88), developer of sonata and symphony form; — **Johann Christoph Friedrich** (1732–95); — **Johann Christian** (1735–82) 'the English Bach'

Bacharach/ a small (wine-producing) Rhineland town, —, **Burt** (b. 1929) US composer

Bachelier ès/ lettres (Fr.) Bachelor of Letters, abbr. **B. ès L.**; — — *sciences* Bachelor of Science, abbr. **B. ès S.** (no hyphens)

Bachelor/ abbr. **B. — of Agriculture**, abbr. (US) **B.Agr.**; — — **Architecture**, abbr. **B.Arch.**; — — **Arts**, abbr. **BA**; — — **Art of Obstetrics**, abbr. **BAO**; — — **Canon and Civil Law**, abbr. **BUJ**; — — **Civil Engineering**, abbr. **BCE**; — — **Civil Law**, abbr. **BCL**; — — **Commerce**, abbr. **B.Com.**; — — **Dental Surgery**, abbr. **BDS**, **B.Ch.D.**; — — **Divinity**, abbr. **BD**; — — **Education**, abbr. **B.Ed.**; — — **Engineering**, abbr. **BE, B.Eng.**, (Dublin) **B.A.I. Dub.**; — — **Law**, abbr. **BL**; — — **Laws**, abbr. **B LL** (no point, thin space); — — **Letters**, abbr. **B.Litt., Litt.B.**; in Fr. **B. ès L.**; — — **Medicine**, abbr. **BM, MB**; — — **Metallurgy**, abbr. **B.Met.**; — — **Mining Engineering**, abbr. **BME**; — — **Music**, abbr. **B.Mus., Mus.B.**; — — **Obstetrics**, abbr. **BAO**; — — **Philosophy**, abbr. **B.Phil.**; — — **Science**, abbr. **B.Sc.**, (US) **BS**, in Fr. **B. ès S.**; — — **Surgery**, abbr. **BC, B.Ch., BS, Ch.B.**; — — **Technical Science**, abbr. **B.Sc. Tech.**; — — **Theology**, abbr. **B.Th.**

bacill/us pl. **-i** (not ital.)

back (typ.) the margin of a book nearest the binding; *see also* **margins**

backbench(er) (Parliament) (one word)

Backhuysen, Ludolf (1631–1708) Dutch painter, *not* Bakhuisen

backing up (typ.) printing on the second side

backstreet (one word)

back-up (noun, hyphen, one word in US)

backwoodsman (one word)

baclava *use* **baklava**

Bacon,/ Sir Francis (*often incorrectly* Lord) (1561–1626) Baron Verulam and Viscount St Albans; — **Francis** (1909–92) Irish painter; — **Roger** (*c*.1214–94) English philosopher, scientist, and Franciscan friar

Baconian pertaining to Roger Bacon, *or* to Sir Francis Bacon, *or* to the theory that Sir Francis Bacon wrote Shakespeare's plays

bacshish *use* **baksheesh**

bacteri/um a microscopic organism, pl. **-a**; **-cide**

bade see **bid**

Baden-Baden Germany (hyphen)

Baden-Powell,/ Robert (Stephenson Smyth), Baron (1857–1941) founder of Boy Scouts, 1908, and, with his sister — **Agnes** (1858–1945), Girl Guides, 1910 (hyphen)

Baden-Württemberg a German *Land* (hyphen) (two *t*s); *see also* **Württemberg**

badinage humorous ridicule (not ital.)

BAe British Aerospace

Baedeker, Karl (1801–59) guidebook publisher

Baffin/ Bay, — Island, NE America: *not* -ns, -n's

BAFU Bakers', Food, and Allied Workers' Union

bagarre (Fr. m.) scuffle, brawl

Bagehot, Walter (1826–77) English economist and writer

bagel *not* beigel

Baghdad Iraq, *not* Bagd-

Bagnères/ de Bigorre dép. Hautes-Pyrénées, France; **— de Luchon** dép. Haute-Garonne, France

bagnio/ a bathing-house, oriental prison, brothel; pl. **-s**

Bagnoles dép. Orne, France

Bagnols dép. Gard, France

bagpip/e(s), -er (one word)

B.Agr. (US) Bachelor of Agriculture

Baha'/i a religion initiated by Bahá'u'lláh (1817–92), **-ism**

Baham/as W. Indies, indep. 1973; **-ian**

Bahasa Indonesia the official language of Indonesia

Bahrain islands, Persian Gulf; *not* -ein

Baiae Naples

B.A.I. Dub. Bachelor of Engineering, University of Dublin

baignoire (Fr. f.) a theatre box at stalls level

Baikal, Lake Russia

bail (noun) a security for the appearance of prisoner, a cross-piece over stumps in cricket, (hist.) the outer line of fortifications; (verb) deliver goods in trust, secure release on bail, (naut.) scoop water out of; cf. **bale**

bailee (law) one to whom goods are entrusted for a purpose

bailer (naut.) one who bails water out, a scoop used for bailing; cf. **bailor; bale**

bailey the outer wall of a castle; **Old Bailey** London's Central Criminal Court

bailie/ (Sc.) an alderman; **-ry** the jurisdiction of a bailie, *not* -iary

bailiwick the office or jurisdiction of a bailiff

Baillie, Joanna (1762–1851) Scottish poet

Baillière Tindall Ltd publishers (accent)

bailor (law) one who entrusts goods to a bailee; cf. **bailer**

Baily's/ Magazine, — Directory (apos.)

bain-marie a double boiler, pl. **bains-**

Bairam/ either of two annual Muslim festivals; **Greater —** falls at the end of the Islamic year, **Lesser —** falls at the end of Ramadan

Baireuth Bavaria, *use* **Bay-**

Bairut Lebanon, *use* **Beirut**

Bakelite (propr.)

Bakewell/ tart *properly* **— pudding**

baklava a Turkish pastry, *not* bac-

baksheesh (Arab., Turk.) a gratuity or alms, *not* the many variants (not ital.)

bal. balance

balaclava (in full **— helmet**) *not* -klava (not cap.)

balalaika a Russian stringed instrument

balanceable *not* -cable

Balboa, Vasco Núñez de (1475–1519) Spanish explorer and discoverer of the Pacific Ocean

Balbriggan Co. Dublin, also knitted cotton goods

baldachin *not* -quin

bale/ (noun) a package, abbr. **bl.**, pl. **bls.**; (arch.) destruction, woe; (verb) make into a package; **— out** escape from an aircraft by parachute; cf. **bail**

Bâle Fr. for **Basle**

Balearic Islands a group of Spanish islands in the Mediterranean

Balfour,/ Baron, of Burleigh; **— Baron, of Inchrye**; **— Earl of** three distinct titles

Bali/ Indonesia, **-nese**

Baliol an Anglo-Norman family; *see also* **Balliol**

balk *use* **baulk** (except in US)

Balkan Mountains Bulgaria

Balkhan Mountains Transcaspia

Ball/aarat Victoria, Australia; *use* **-arat**

ballade a medieval French poem, also its imitation (esp. in the 19th c.)

Ballantine,/ James (1808–77) Scottish artist and poet; **— William** (1812–86) English serjeant-at-law

Ballantyne/, James (1772–1833) and **—, John** (1774–1821), Sir W. Scott's printers and publishers; **— Press** founded by them in 1796; **—, R(obert) M(ichael)** (1825–94) Scottish writer for boys

Ballarat Victoria, Australia; *not* -aarat

ballet dancer (two words)

ball game (two words)

Balliol College Oxford; *see also* **Baliol**

ballistic/ (adj.), **-s** (pl., usually treated as sing.) the science (two ls)

ballon/ d'essai (Fr. m.) an experiment to see how a new policy etc. will be received, pl. **-s d'essai**

ballot/, -ed, -ing (one *t*)

ballpark/ (one word), **— figure** an approximately correct number

ballroom (one word)

Ballsbridge Co. Dublin (one word)

ballyhoo commotion, sensational publicity

Balnibarbi the country of the 'projectors' in Swift's *Gulliver's Travels*

baloney humbug, blather, drivel, *not* boloney; a type of sausage, *use* **bologna**

BALPA British Air Line Pilots' Association

Baluchi a native of Baluchistan; *not* Be-, Bi-

baluster an upright supporting a rail, commonly of stone and outdoors, the whole structure being a **balustrade**; cf. **banister**

Balzac/, Honoré (self-styled) **de** (1799–1850) French writer, **-ian**; **—, Jean Louis Guez de** (1596–1654) French writer

Bamberg Germany, *not* -burg

bambin/o (It. m.) baby, pl. **-i**; f. **-a** pl. **-e**

Bamburgh Northumb.

banal commonplace

Banaras Hind. for **Benares**

Band (Ger. m.) a volume, pl. **Bände**; abbr. **Bd.**, pl. **Bde.**

bandanna a handkerchief, *not* -ana

Banda Oriental (hist.) Uruguay

Bandaranaike, Sirimavo Ratwatte Dias (b. 1916) Sinhalese stateswoman, Prime Minister of Sri Lanka 1960–5, 1970–7, and since 1994

b. & b. bed and breakfast

bande/ dessinée (Fr. f.) a comic strip, pl. **-s dessinées**, abbr. **BD**

banderole *not* banderol

bandolero a Spanish brigand

bandolier a belt for cartridges; *not* -oleer, -alier

Bandung Indonesia, *not* Bandoeng

bang an Indian hemp, *use* **bh-**

Bangalore Mysore, India

Bangkok Thailand, *not* Bank-

Bangladesh 'Land of the Bengalis', formerly E. Pakistan (one word)

banian *use* **banyan**

banister an upright supporting a rail, commonly of wood, used indoors on a staircase, the whole structure being **banisters** (pl.); *not* bannister; cf. **baluster**

banjo/ pl. **-s**

bank abbr. **bk.**

banking abbr. **bkg.**

banknote (one word)

Bankok *use* **Bang-**

bank paper a thin, strong paper

banlieue (Fr. f.) precinct, suburb

banneret/ (law) a knight commanding his own troops in battle, *or* a knight made on the field of battle; **-te** a small banner

bannister *use* **bani-**

banns *not* bans

banquet/, -ed, -ing (one *t*)

banquette a raised way behind a firing-rampart, a seat; (S. US) a pavement

banshee a wailing female spirit, in Ir. **bean sídhe**

Bantu designating a large group of Cent., E., and S. African native peoples and languages

banyan an Indian fig tree, *not* -ian

Banyoles Catalonia, Spain

banzai a Japanese battle cry; a greeting used to the Japanese emperor (not ital.)

BAO Bachelor of Art of Obstetrics

BAOR British Army of the Rhine

baptism the religious rite symbolizing admission to the Christian Church; cf. **christening**

Baptist abbr. **Bapt.**

baptistery *not* -try

baptize *not* -ise, abbr. **bap.**

Bar (law) called to the (cap.); a unit of pressure, 10^5 newtons per sq. m., approx. one atmosphere (not cap.)

bar. barleycorn; baromet/er, -ric; barrel

Barbad/os *not* -oes; abbr. **Barb.**, adj. **-ian**

barbarize *not* -ise

Barbary N. Africa

barbecu/e *not* -que; **-es, -ed, -ing**

barbed wire (two words), *not* barbwire (US)

barberry a shrub of genus *Berberis*, *not* ber-, -ery

barbet a tropical bird

barbette a gun platform

Barbirolli, Sir John (1899–1970) English conductor

barbitone a sedative drug, *not* barbital (US)

barbiturate any derivate of barbituric acid

Barbour (propr.)

barcarole a Venetian gondolier's song, in Fr. **barcarolle**

B.Arch. Bachelor of Architecture

Barclays Bank plc. (no apos.)

Barclays de Zoete Wedd a British financial company, abbr. **BZW**

bard (hist.) a Celtic minstrel; the winner of a prize for Welsh verse at an Eisteddfod; a poet (not cap.); **the Bard** (**of Avon**) Shakespeare (cap.)

Bareilly Uttar Pradesh, India; *not* -eli

Barenboim, Daniel (b. 1942) Argentinian-born Israeli musician

Barents Sea N. of Norway and Russia; *not* -'s, -'z

bargain/er a haggler; **-or** (law) the seller

bargepole (one word)

Bar Harbor Me.

Baring-Gould, Revd Sabine (1834–1924) English author (hyphen)

barite (US) = **barytes**

baritone (mus.) *not* bary- (except for Gr. accent)

barium symbol **Ba**

bark a vessel (arch., poet.), in the technical sense *use* **barque**

barkentine *use* **barquen-** (except in US)

Barkston Lincs., N. Yorks.

barleycorn (one word) abbr. **bar.**

bar/maid, -man (one word)

Barmecide (one who offers) illusory benefits, *not* -acide

bar mitzvah the Jewish initiation rite for boys; *see also* **bat mitzvah**

Barmston Humberside

barn (phys.) a unit of area, abbr. **b**

Barnaby Bright St Barnabas' Day, 11 June; the longest day in the Old Style calendar

Barnard, Dr Christiaan (b. 1922) S. African surgeon

Barnardo, Dr Thomas John (1845–1905) British philanthropist

Barnstable Mass.

Barnstaple Devon

baro/graph a recording barometer; **-gram** the record; **-logy** science of weight; **-meter, -metric,** abbr. **bar.**

baron member of the lowest order of British nobility; cap. with name (*but* **Lord** more common); lower case with a foreign name (*but* cap. in Ger.); abbr. **B.**

baron/ (Fr.) Baron, f. **-ne** (not cap.)

baron and feme (law) husband and wife regarded as one

baronet/ a member of the lowest hereditary titled British order; cap. with name; abbr. **Bt.; -age** baronets collectively, or a book about them; **-cy** the patent or rank of baronet

Barons Court London (no apos.)

baroque (not cap., not ital.) highly ornate style, esp. of architecture, music, and other arts, of the 17th and 18th cc.; cap. when followed by 'age', 'era', or when this is to be understood

barouche a four-wheeled carriage, *not* baru-

barque a vessel, *not* bark (except in poet. senses)

barquentine a three-masted vessel with foremast only square-rigged and remaining masts fore-and-aft rigged; *not* -antine, barke- (US)

barr. barrels, barrister

barrac/uda a large and voracious tropical marine fish of the family *Sphyraenidae,* **-outa** only with reference to *Thyrsites atun* (Austral. and NZ)

barrator (law) a malicious litigant; *not* -ater, -etor

barratry (marine law) a master's or crew's fraud or negligence, (law) vexatious litigation, (hist.) trade in the sale of Church or State appointments

Barrault, Jean-Louis (1910–94) French actor, director, producer

barré a method of using a finger to raise the pitch of a (guitar) chord (not ital., in rock and pop music no accent)

barrel/, -s abbr. **bar., barr., bl., bls.**

barrel/led, -ling (one *l* in US)

barrico/ a small cask, pl. **-es**

Barrie, Sir James Matthew (1860–1937) Scottish novelist and playwright

barrister abbr. **barr.**

Barrow-in-Furness Cumbria (hyphens)

Bart. Baronet, *use* **Bt.**

bartender (one word)

Barth,/ Heinrich (1821–65) German explorer; **— John** (b. 1930) US writer; **— Karl** (1886–1968) Swiss theologian

Barthes, Roland (1915–80) French writer and critic

Bartholomew Day 24 Aug. (caps., two words for London local terminology *but* **St Bartholomew's Day** for the massacre, 1572)

Bartók, Béla (1881–1945) Hungarian composer; in Hung. **Bartók Béla** (surname and given name transposed)

Bartolommeo, Fra (1475–1517) Italian painter

Bartolozzi, Francesco (1727–1813) Italian engraver

Bart's St Bartholomew's Hospital, London

Baruch (Apocr.) not to be abbreviated except in narrow measure or marginal notation

baruche *use* **barou-**

barytes a mineral form of barium sulphate, *not* barite (US)

barytone *use* **bari-** except for the Greek accent

bas bleu (Fr. m.) a bluestocking

base abbr. **b.**

baseball US national game, played by two teams of nine; the ball used in it

baseboard (US) = **skirting board**

Basel Ger. for **Basle**

bashaw *use* **pasha**

Bashi-Bazouk (hist.) a Turkish mercenary of the 19th c. (hyphen)

Bashkirtseff, Marie K. *properly* **Mariya Konstantinovna Bashkirtseva** (1860–84) Russian diarist

BASIC (comput.) Beginners' All-Purpose Symbolic Instruction Code

Basic English (two caps.) a simplified form of English proposed by C. K. Ogden, 1929

Basildon Essex, 'new town', 1949

basinet a light steel headpiece, *not* bass-

bas/is pl. **-es**

Baskerville, John (1706–75) typefounder and printer, designer of Baskerville type

Basle Switzerland; in Fr. **Bâle,** Ger. **Basel;** the trad. Eng. form was **Basil** until the 19th c., when **Basle** replaced it; now being replaced by **Basel**

Basque (of or relating to) one or more members of a people of the Western Pyrenees, or their language (cap.); a close-fitting bodice (not cap.)

Basra Iraq, *not* -ah

bas-relief *not* bass-

Bas-Rhin a dép. of France (hyphen)

bass the lowest part in music, the common perch, *not* -e

bassinet a (wicker) cradle, perambulator; *not* basi-, -ette, berceaunette (except in Fr.)

basso/ (mus.) abbr. **B.**, — **profundo** (It. mus.) the lowest male voice

basso-rilievo (It.) bas-relief, pl. **bassi-rilievi** (hyphen)

bastaard (S. Afr.) a person of mixed white and black parentage, whether legitimate or not (not ital.)

bastardize *not* -ise

bastard/ size (typ.) a non-standard size, — **title** *see* **half-title**

Bastille (Fr. f.) a Paris prison

bastille a fortified tower, *not* -ile

bastinado/ *not* basto-, pl. **-s**

Basuto/, -land S. Africa, *now* **Lesotho**

Batak an Austronesian language of Sumatra, Indonesia, also called **Toba Batak**

bateau/ (Fr. m.) a boat, *not* batt-; pl. **-x**

Bath: et Well: the signature of the Bishop of Bath and Wells (two colons)

Bath/ brick, — bun, — chair, — chap (not chop), — **Oliver, — stone** (one cap., two words)

bath/os an anticlimax through an unintentional shift from sublime to ridiculous mood, adj. **-etic**; cf. **pathos**

bat mitzvah the Jewish initiation rite for girls; *see also* **bar mitzvah**

baton a music conductor's stick, a twirler's rod

Batswana (sing. and pl.) inhabitant(s) of Botswana

battalion abbr. **battn., bn.**

battels an account for provisions etc. in Oxford colleges

batter (typ.) a damaged letter

batterie de cuisine (Fr. f.) a set of cooking utensils

battery abbr. **batt., bty.**

battle/axe, -cruiser (one word)

battle cry (two words)

battle/dress, -field, -ground, -ship (one word)

Batumi Georgia; *not* -oum, -um

baud (comput.) abbr. **Bd**, pl. same

Baudelaire, Charles (1821–67) French poet, *not* Beau-

Bauhaus a German school of architectural design 1919–33, founded by Walter Gropius

baulk *not* balk (US)

Bavaria/, -n abbr. **Bav.**, in Ger. **Bayern**

bawbee (Sc.) a halfpenny, *not* bau-

bayadère a Hindu dancing girl

Bayard, Pierre de Terrail, Chevalier de (1475–1524) 'The knight without fear and without reproach'

Bayern Ger. for **Bavaria**

Bayeux Tapestry a linen embroidery depicting the invasion of England, 1066

bayonet/, -ed, -ing; — fitting, — plug (elec.) two words

Bayreuth Bavaria, *not* Bai-; *see also* **Beirut**

Bayrūt Arab. for **Beirut**

bazaar (one *z*, two *a*s)

BB (pencils) double black, *also* **2B**

BBB (pencils) treble black, *also* **3B**

BBC British Broadcasting Corporation

bbl. barrels (esp. of oil)

BC Bachelor of Surgery, Board of Control, British Columbia (Canada)

BC before Christ, to be placed *after* the numerals: 250 BC, the second century BC (small caps.); *see also* **BCE**

b.c. (meteor.) partly cloudy sky

BCA Bureau of Current Affairs

B.C.B.G. (Fr. abbr.) **bon chic bon genre** (points in Fr.)

BCC British Copyright Council, British Council of Churches, British Crown Colony

BCD (comput.) binary coded decimal

BCE Bachelor of Civil Engineering

BCE before Common Era (small caps.); *see also* ACE; BC; CE

BCG bacillus of Calmette and Guérin (anti-TB inoculation)

B.Ch., B.Chir. Bachelor of Surgery

B.Ch.D., BDS Bachelor of Dental Surgery

BCL Bachelor of Civil Law

B.Com., B.Comm. Bachelor of Commerce

B.Com.Sc. Batchelor of Commercial Science

BCP Book of Common Prayer

BD Bachelor of Divinity, *bande dessinée*

Bd. baud; (Ger.) *Band* (a volume)

bd. board, bond, bound

BDA British Dental Association

Bde. (Ger.) *Bände* (volumes)

Bde. Maj. Brigade Major

bdg. binding

bdl. bundle, pl. **bdls.**

Bdr. Bombardier

BDS Bachelor of Dental Surgery (*also* **B.Ch.D.**), Bomb Disposal Squad

bds. (bound in) boards

BE Bachelor of Engineering

Be beryllium (no point)

b.e. bill of exchange

BEA British Epilepsy Association, British Esperanto Association, (hist.) British European Airways

Beach-la-mar (one cap.) *use* **Bislama**

beard (typ.) the space between the bottom of the **x-height** and the upper edge of the shank

beargarden (one word)

Béarnaise a rich white sauce (cap.)

bearskin a military cap (one word)

beastings *use* **bee-**

beasts of the/ chase (law) buck, doe, fox, marten, roe; — — — **forest** (law) boar, hare, hart, hind, wolf; — — — **warren** (law) cony and hare; **beasts of venery** (law) = **beasts of the forest**

beatae memoriae (Lat.) of blessed memory, abbr. **BM**

Beata/ Maria, or — *Virgo* (Lat.) the Blessed Virgin, abbr. **BM**, **BV** (no points); *see also* **BMV**; **BVM**

beat generation (not cap.)

Beatles, the a pop group, 1960–70

beat music (not cap.)

beatnik a member or follower of the beat generation

beau/ pl. **-x** (not ital.)

Beauclerc the sobriquet of Henry I

Beauclerk family name of the Duke of St Albans

Beaudelaire *use* **Baud-**

beau-fils (Fr. m.) son-in-law, stepson; (two words) beautiful son

Beaufort scale of wind force (one cap.)

beau/ idéal the highest type of excellence or beauty, *not* beautiful ideal (not ital.); pl. **-x idéals**

beauidealize *not* -ise (one word)

Beaujolais a red or white burgundy

Beaulieu Hants.

beau monde the fashionable world

Beaune a burgundy

beau-père (Fr. m.) father-in-law, stepfather; (two words) beautiful father

Beauvoir, Simone de (1908–86) French author

beaux arts (Fr. pl. m.) (noun) fine arts, (attrib.) relating to the rules and conventions of the École des Beaux-Arts in Paris (later, Académie des Beaux-Arts); therefore *beaux-arts* is historically acceptable

beaux/ esprits (Fr. pl. m.) brilliant wits; sing. *bel esprit*; — *yeux* good looks

bebop (mus.) (one word)

beccafico/ a small edible Italian bird, *not* beca-; pl. **-s**

béchamel (Fr. cook.) a white sauce named after Béchamel, steward of Louis XIV (not cap.)

bêche-de-mer the sea slug, a Chinese delicacy

Bechstein,/ Friedrich Wilhelm Carl (1826–1900) German pianoforte maker, — **Johann Matthäus** (1757–1822) German naturalist

Bechuana/, -land *see* **Botswana**

Becket, Thomas (?1118–70) Archbishop (one *t*); *not* à Becket

Beckett, Samuel (1906–89) Irish writer

Becquerel/, a French family of physicists: —, **Antoine César** (1788–1878) father of —, **Alexandre Edmond** (1820–91) father of —, **Antoine Henri** (1852–1908) discoverer of radioactive — **rays** *now* **gamma rays**

becquerel a unit of radioactivity, abbr. **Bq**

bed (typ.) the part of the press on which the forme lies

B.Ed. Bachelor of Education

Bedaw/een, -i, -in *use* **Bedouin**

bed/bug, -chamber, -clothes (one word)

Beddgelert Gwynedd, *not* Beth-

bedel in Oxford the official form of beadle, at Cambridge and London **bedell**

Bedfordshire abbr. **Beds.**

Bedouin a desert Arab, *not* the many variants; pl. same; in specialist usage, *prefer* sing. **Bedu** and pl. **Beduin**

Bed/owy *use* **Bedouin**

bed/pan, -post, -ridden, -room (one word)

Beds. Bedfordshire

bed/sitter (one word), *but* **-sittingroom** (one hyphen)

bed/sore, -time (one word)

Beduin *see* **Bedouin**

Beeb (preceded by **the** *or* **Auntie**) (Brit. colloq.) the BBC

beefsteak (one word)

beehive (one word)

beer glass (two words)

beerhouse (law) where beer is sold to be drunk on or off the premises

beer mat (two words)

beershop (law) where beer is sold to be drunk off the premises

beestings the first milk from a mammal (pl. also treated as sing.); *not* bea-, bie-

beeswax (noun and verb)

Beethoven, Ludwig van *not* von (1770–1827) German composer; divide **Beet-hoven**

beeves pl. of beef, *not* beefs (US)

BEF British Expeditionary Force

be/fall *not* -fal, past **-fell**

Beggar's Opera by John Gay, 1728; *not* -s'

Begin, Menachem (1913–92) Israeli politician, Prime Minister 1977–84

begum a Muslim lady of high rank, in the Indian subcontinent; (cap.) the title of a married Muslim woman, equivalent to **Mrs**

behemoth a biblical animal (Book of Job), thought to be the hippopotamus

Behmenism concerning the doctrines of the German mystic Jakob Boehme

Behn, Aphra (1640–89) English novelist and dramatist

behoof (noun) benefit

behove (verb) be incumbent on, *not* behoove (US)

Behring, Emil von (1854–1917) German bacteriologist

Behring/ Isle, — Sea, — Strait *use* **Ber-**

beigel *use* **bag-**

beignet (Fr. m.) a fritter

Beijing (Pinyin) **Peking**

Beinn Bhuidhe near Inveraray, Strathclyde; cf. **Ben Buie**

Beirut Lebanon, *not* Ba-, Bai-, Beyrout(h); in Arab. **Bayrūt**; *see also* **Bayreuth**

bel a unit of sound pressure levels equivalent to ten decibels (**decibel** is more often used), abbr. **B**

Belalp Switzerland (one word)

Bel and the Dragon (Apocr.) abbr. **Bel & Dr.**

Belarus formerly **Belorussia**, *properly* **Belarus´**

bel canto (not ital.)

beldam (arch.) a hag, *not* -e

Belém Brazil, *formerly* Pará

bel/ esprit (Fr. m.) a brilliant wit, pl. *beaux esprits*; — *étage* the first floor, *not* belle

belge (Fr.) Belgian (not cap., unless used as a noun)

Belgic of the ancient Belgae of N. Gaul *or* of the Low Countries

Belgique (Fr. f.) Belgium

Belg/ium, -ian, -ic abbr. **Belg.**

Belgrade Serbia, capital of the former Yugoslavia; in Serbo-Croat **Beograd**

believable *not* -eable

bélinogramme (Fr. Canadian m.) a cablegram or fax, abbr. *bélino*

Belisha beacon (one cap.)

Belitung Indonesia, *not* Billiton

Belize/ Cent. America, *formerly* British Honduras; **-an**

Bell,/ Acton, — Currer, — Ellis *see* **Brontë**

belladonna (bot.) deadly nightshade (one word)

belle (not ital.)

belle/ amie (Fr. f.) female friend; *-de-jour* (bot.) convolvulus; *-de-nuit* (bot.) marvel of Peru

Belleek Co. Armagh, Co. Fermanagh, N. Ireland; also name of a type of china

belle/ époque (Fr. f.) before 1914; *-fille* (hyphen) daughter-in-law, stepdaughter; (two words) beautiful girl

Belle-Île-en-Mer dép. Morbihan, France (hyphens)

Belle Isle, Straits of between Newfoundland and Labrador

Belleisle Co. Fermanagh

belle/ laide (Fr. f.) fascinatingly ugly woman; *-mère* (hyphen) mother-in-law, stepmother; (two words) beautiful mother

belles-lettres literature, pl. but treated as sing. (hyphen)

belletris/t one devoted to belles-lettres, **-m, -tic** *not* -ettr-

Bell Island off NE coast of Newfoundland

Bell Rock North Sea; *also* **Inchcape Rock**

bell-wether *not* -weather (hyphen)

Bel/oochee, -uchi *use* **Baluchi**

Belorussia/ (White Russia) a former Soviet Socialist Republic, *not* Bye-; *now* **Belarus´, -n** of or relating to the country, language, or inhabitants of Belarus´

Beltane an ancient Celtic festival celebrated on May Day

Belvedere Kent; Calif.

belvedere (It.) a raised building, *not* belvi- (not ital.)

Belvidere Ill.

Belvoir Castle Leics.

BEM British Empire Medal

Benares India, officially **Vārānasī**; in Hind. **Banaras**

Benavente y Martínez, Jacinto (1866–1954) Spanish playwright and critic

Ben Buie Mull, Strathclyde; cf. **Beinn Bhuidhe**

benchmark (one word)

Ben Day (typ.) a mechanical method for producing shading and stippling effects

Benedic a canticle from Psalm 103

Benedicite the 'Song of the Three Children' (Apocr.), as canticle

benedick a confirmed bachelor newly married, *not* -ict (from a character in Shakespeare's *Much Ado about Nothing*)

Benedictus the Canticle of Zacharias (Luke 1: 68 ff.), or a choral passage in the mass, beginning *Benedictus qui venit* (Matt. 21: 9)

benefactor *not* -er

beneficent *not* -ficient

benefit/, -ed, -ing (one *t*)

Benelux Belgium, the Netherlands, Luxembourg

Beneš, Edvard (1884–1948) Prime Minister of Czechoslovakia 1921–2; President 1935–8, 1939–45 (in exile), 1946–8

Benet an English form of the name Benedict; used of St Benedict and institutions bearing his name, e.g. St Benet's Church, St Benet's Hall

Benét,/ Stephen Vincent (1898–1943) and — **William Rose** (1886–1950) his brother, US poets

Bene't Street Cambridge

ben for (Dan.) = **lbw**, abbr. **bf** (no points)

B.Eng. Bachelor of Engineering

Bengali/ (of) person born in, language of, Bengal; *not* -ee; pl. **-s**; abbr. **Beng.**

Benghazi Libya, *not* -gasi

Ben-Gurion, David (1886–1973) Israeli statesman, Prime Minister 1948–53, 1955–63

Ben-Hur historical novel by Lew (Lewis) Wallace, 1880; Hollywood films, 1925, 1959 (hyphen)

Ben/ Lawers Tayside, — **Macdhui** Grampian

Bennet/ the family name of the Earl of Tankerville; a family in Austen's *Pride and Prejudice*; —, **John** (*c.*1600) English madrigalist

Bennett,/ (Enoch) Arnold (1867–1931) English writer; — **Richard Rodney** (b. 1936) and — **William Sterndale** (1816–75) English composers

benth/al of ocean depths exceeding 6,000 feet; **-os** the flora and fauna of the sea bottom; cf. **plankton**; adj. **-ic** *not* -onic

Bentham,/ George (1800–84) botanist; — **Jeremy** (1748–1832) English political philosopher

ben trovato (It.) well invented, characteristic if not true

Ben Venue Central (two words)

ben venuto (It.) welcome

Ben/ Vorlich, — Vrackie Tayside

Benzedrine (med.) propr. term for an inhalant or nerve stimulant, *not* -in (cap.)

benzene a liquid obtained from coal tar, petroleum, etc.

benzine a mixture of liquid hydrocarbons obtained from petroleum

benzoin an aromatic resin from various E. Asian trees

benzol crude benzene, *not* -ole

benzoline benzine

benzoyl, benzyl two different chemical radicals

Beowulf an Anglo-Saxon epic

bequeather a testator

Béranger, Pierre Jean de (1780–1857) French poet

Berber (of or relating to) (a member of) the indigenous mainly Muslim Caucasian peoples of N. Africa, or their languages; in Arab. *barbar*

berberry *use* **bar-**

berceau (Fr. m.) a cradle

berceaunette *use* **bassinet** (except in Fr.)

berceuse (Fr. f.) a lullaby

Beretta an Italian arms manufacturer, *not* Bir-

Berg/ (Ger. m.) a mountain, pl. **-e** (cap.)

berg (Afrik.) a mountain

Bergamask a native of Bergamo, Lombardy; **bergamasque** a rustic dance attributed to the Bergamasks

bergamot a tree of citrus family, a type of pear or herb; *not* burg-

Bergerac/ dép. Dordogne, France; wine made there; —, **Savinien Cyrano de** (1619–55) French writer

Bergman,/ Ingmar (b. 1918) Swedish film and theatre director; — **Ingrid** (1917–82) Swedish actress

bergschrund a crevasse or gap at the head of a glacier or névé (not cap.)

Bergson, Henri (1859–1941) French philosopher

beriberi a tropical disease, *not* -ria (one word)

Bering, Vitus Jonassen (1680–1741) Danish navigator

Bering/ Isle, — Sea, — Strait *not* Beh-, -ings

berk a fool, *not* burk

Berkeleian of the philosopher Berkeley

Berkeley/ Calif.; —, **George, Bishop** (1685–1753) Irish philosopher; —, **Sir Lennox** (1903–89) English composer

berkelium symbol **Bk**

Berkhamsted Herts.

Berks. Berkshire

Bermudian a person from Bermuda, *not* -dan

Bernard, Claude (1813–78) French physiologist

Bernardine Cistercian, from St Bernard of Clairvaux (1091–1153)

Berne/ a Swiss canton and town, in Ger. **Bern**; — **Convention** 1886, with later revisions; deals with copyright; each of the more than 110 member states extends benefit of its own copyright law to works by citizens of other member states; *see also* **Universal Copyright Convention**

Berners,/ Gerald Hugh Tyrwhitt-Wilson, Baron (1883–1950) English composer; — **John Bourchier, Baron** (1467–1533) English translator; — **Dame Juliana** wrote *Boke of St Albans*, first edn. 1486

Bernhardt, Sarah, b. **Henriette Rosine Bernhard** (1845–1923) French actress

ber/noose, -nouse *use* **burnous** in general use

Bernoulli a family of Swiss mathematicians, *not* -illi

bersaglier/e (It.) a rifleman, pl. **-i**

Berthelot, Pierre Eugène Marcelin (1827–1907) French chemist and statesman

Berthollet, comte Claude Louis (1748–1822) French chemist

Berwickshire a former county in Scotland

Berwick-upon-Tweed Northumb. (hyphens)

beryllium symbol **Be**

Berzelius, Jöns Jakob, baron (1779–1848) Swedish chemist

B. ès A. *now* **B. ès L.**

Besançon dép. Doubs, France

beseech (past and past part.) **besought**

B. ès L. (Fr.) *Bachelier ès lettres* (Bachelor of Letters)

beso/ las manos (Sp.) 'I kiss the hands' (frequently said or written), **— los pies** 'I kiss the feet'

B. ès S. (Fr.) *Bachelier ès sciences* (Bachelor of Science)

Bessarabia (hist.) a district in Moldavia and Ukraine, ceded by Romania to USSR 1940

Bessbrook Co. Armagh

Bessemer process in steel manufacturing (one cap.)

Besses o' th' Barn Gr. Manchester

bestialize *not* -ise

beta/ the second letter of the Gr. alphabet (*B*, *β*); **— blocker**, **— coefficient**, **— decay**, **— particle**, **— ray** (two words)

betatron an apparatus for accelerating electrons

betel the leaf of a betel pepper, chewed in the East and Far East

Betelgeuse (astr.) a red star in Orion, *not* -x

betel nut a misnomer for the areca nut, chewed with betel

bête/ noire (Fr. f.) one's pet aversion, *not noir*; pl. **-s noires**

bethel a Nonconformist chapel (not cap.)

bêtise (Fr. f.) a foolish or ill-timed remark or action, stupidity

Betjeman, Sir John (1906–84) English poet and writer on architecture, appointed Poet Laureate 1972

betony (bot.) *not* bett-

better one who bets, *not* -or

Betws-y-coed Gwynedd (hyphens)

BeV (abbr.) billion (10⁹) electron volts, *also called* **GeV**

Bevan, Aneurin (1897–1960) Welsh politician who introduced the National Health Service 1948; *see also* **Bevin**

bevel/, -led, -ling (one *l* in US)

Beveridge, William Henry, Baron (1879–1963) English economist

Beverley Humberside

Beverly Miss.

Beverly Hills Calif.

Bevin, Ernest (1881–1951) English politician; *see also* **Bevan**

bevy the proper word for a company of ladies, larks, maidens, quails, or roe deer; also in general use

Bewick, Thomas (1753–1828) English engraver

Bexleyheath London (one word)

bey (hist.) the title of a provincial governor in the Ottoman Empire; **Bey of Tunis** (hist.) the ruler of Tunisia (cap.)

beylik the jurisdiction of a bey, *not* -ic

Beyrout/, -h Lebanon, *use* **Beirut**

bezahlt (Ger.) paid, abbr. **bez.**

bezant a gold coin first struck at Byzantium; a gold roundel in heraldry; *not* by-

beziehungsweise (Ger.) respectively, abbr. **bzw.**

bezüglich (Ger.) with reference to, abbr. **bez.**

BF Bachelor of Forestry, Banque de France, Belgian franc

bf (Dan.) *ben for* = **lbw**

b.f. bankruptcy fee, beer firkin, bloody fool, (typ.) boldface, brought forward

BFA Bachelor of Fine Arts

BFBS British and Foreign Bible Society

BFI British Film Institute

BFPO British Forces' Post Office

BGC bank giro credit

Bhagavadgītā a philosophical dialogue in the Hindu epic **Mahābhārata**

B'ham Birmingham

bhang Indian hemp, *not* ba-

bharal a Himalayan wild sheep, *not* burhel

BHC British High Commissioner

b.h.p. brake horsepower (points)

BHS British Home Stores

Bhutan/ a protectorate of the Republic of India since 1949, **-ese**; **-i** the official language of Bhutan, *properly* **Dzonghka**

Bhutto,/ Benazir (b. 1953) Pakistani politician, Prime Minister 1988–90, 1993–6; daughter of **— Zulfikar Ali** (1928–79) Pakistani politician, President 1971–3, Prime Minister 1973–7

Bi bismuth (no point)

Biafra the name taken by the provinces seceding from eastern Nigeria 1967–70

biannual twice every year, every six months, cf. **biennial**

bias/, -ed, -ing

Bib. Bible

bib. biblical

bibl. *bibliotheca* (library)

Bible abbr. **Bib.**

Biblia Pauperum a medieval 'Bible of the poor', in pictures (caps.)

biblical (not cap.) abbr. **bib.**

bibliograph/er, -ic, -ical, -y abbr. **bibliog.**

bibliomancy foretelling the future by the analysis of a randomly chosen passage from a book, esp. the Bible

bibliopeg/y bookbinding as a fine art, **-ist**

bibliophile not -phil

bibliopole a seller of (esp. rare) books

biblio/theca (Lat.) a library, *-thécaire* (Fr. m., f.) a librarian, *-thèque* (Fr. f.) a library

Bibliothek/ (Ger. f.) a library, *-ar* (Ger. m.) a librarian (caps.)

Bibliothèque nationale/ Paris, now — — **de France**

bicenten/ary a 200th anniversary; **-nial** of or relating to a bicentenary, (esp. US) = **bicentenary**

Bickleigh Devon

Bickley Ches., London, N. Yorks.

bid past **bid** or **bade**, past part. **bid** or **bidden**; *use* bid for the past and past part. in context of auctions and card-playing; and *bade, bidden* for archaic meanings 'command', 'invite', 'utter', or 'proclaim'

Biedermeier a German bourgeois artistic and literary style 1815–48

biennial every two years; cf. **biannual**

bienni/um a two-year period, pl. **-ums**

bienséance (Fr. f.) propriety

bienvenu/ (Fr.) f. **-e** (a) welcome

Bierce, Ambrose (**Gwinnett**) (1842–?1914) US journalist and author

BIF British Industries Fair

biff/é (Fr.) f. **-ée** cancelled

Big Dipper, the (US astron.) = **the Great Bear**

Bigelow,/ Erastus Brigham (1814–79) US inventor and industrialist, — **John** (1817–1911) US journalist and diplomat

Biglow Papers, The anti-slavery poems 1848 and 1857–61, by James Russell Lowell

bigot/, -ed (one *t*)

bijou/ (Fr. m.) a jewel, trinket; in the general sense of something small and elegant, not ital.; pl. **-x**

bijouterie (Fr. f.) jewellery, a jeweller's shop

Bilbao Spain

bilberry (*Vaccinium myrtillus*), not bill-

bilbo/ a Spanish sword or rapier, pl. **-s**

bilboes pl. fetters

Bildungsroman (Ger. m.) a novel of early life and development

bill (parl.) (cap. when part of title)

Billericay Essex

billet/, -ed, -ing

billet-doux a love letter, pl. **billets-doux** (hyphens, not ital.)

billiard/ ball, — cue, — table, etc., *not* billiards- (two words)

billion in the USA and now largely in Britain, a thousand million (10^9), or what formerly was a **milliard**; in France and Germany, a million million (10^{12}). Be careful to avoid ambiguity, particularly when writing for a transatlantic audience; pl. *billions* used only for general sense of a very large number ('billions of years'); abbr. **bn.**; *see also* **trillion**

Billiton Indonesia, *use* **Belitung**

bill of/ exchange abbr. **b.e.**; — — **lading** abbr. **b.l.**; — — **sale** abbr. **b.s.**

Biloxi Miss.

biltong (Afrik.) sun-dried meat

Biluchi *use* **Bal-**

BIM British Institute of Management

bimanal *not* bimanous

bimbo/ pl. **-s**, *not* -es

bimetall/ic, -ism, -ist

bimillenary (designating) a period of 2,000 years; a 2,000th anniversary

bi-monthly avoid as ambiguous; *prefer* (adj. or adv.) fortnightly, semi-monthly or (adv.) twice a month, every two months, as appropriate

bindery a bookbinder's establishment

binnacle (naut.) a compass stand

binocle a field glass

binocular/ (adj.) for two eyes, **-s** (pl. noun) field or opera glasses

Binstead IoW

Binsted Hants., W. Sussex

Binyon, Laurence (1869–1943) English poet

biochemist/, -ry (one word)

biocoenos/is an association of or relationship between different organisms forming a community, pl. **-es**; *not* -cenosis (US)

biodegradable (one word)

biograph/er, -ic, -ical, -y abbr. **biog.**

biolog/y, -ical abbr. **biol.**

bio/mathematics, -physics (one word)

Bipont/, -ine books printed at **Bipontium** (Zweibrücken), Germany

bird bath (two words)

bird/cage, -seed (one word)

bird's-eye view (one hyphen)

birdsong (one word)

bird table (two words)

biretta a square cap worn by (RC) clergymen, *not* bar-, ber-

Birmingham/ abbr. **Birm., B'ham**; — **Small Arms** abbr. **BSA**

Birnam Tayside, immortalized in Shakespeare's *Macbeth*

Biro (Brit. propr.) a kind of ballpoint pen (cap.)

Birstall Leics., W. Yorks.

birth/ certificate, — control (two words)

birthmark (one word)

birthplace abbr. **bpl.**

birth rate (two words)

birthright (one word)

BIS Bank for International Settlements

bis (Fr., It., Lat.) twice, encore; in references, space from preceding figure: '12 *bis*'

bis. bissextile

Biscayan pertaining to Biscay, Spain; Basque; abbr. **Bisc.**

bis dat qui cito dat (Lat.) he gives twice who gives quickly

bise (Fr. f.) dry, cold N. wind in Switzerland, S. France, etc.

BISF British Iron and Steel Federation

Bishop abbr. **Bp.**, (chess) **B**

Bishopbriggs Strathclyde

Bishop *in partibus infidelium* a RC bishop taking title from an ancient see situated 'in territory of unbelievers', *now* termed **Titular Bishop**

Bishop Rock a lighthouse, Scilly Isles

Bishop's/ Castle Shropshire, — **Cleeve** Glos., — **Frome** Hereford, — **Lydeard** Som. (apos.)

bishop's signature usually consists of Christian name and diocese (John Birmingham); for special spellings and punctuation, *see* individual entries

Bishop's Stortford Herts. (apos.)

Bishopsteignton Devon (one word)

Bishopston Avon, W. Glam.

Bishopstone Bucks., Hereford, Kent, E. Sussex, Wilts.

Bishop's Waltham Hants. (apos.)

Bishopthorpe the residence of the Archbishop of York (one word)

Bishopton Dur., N. Yorks., Strathclyde

bisk *use* **bisque**

Bislama the pidgin English of W. Pacific, also called **Beach-la-mar**

Bismarck, Karl Otto Eduard Leopold, Fürst von (1815–98) German statesman, *not* -ark

bismillah (Arab.) 'in the name of God', *not* biz-

bismuth symbol **Bi**

bison either of two wild oxen of the genus *Bison*, native to Europe (*B. bonasus*) or to N. America (*B. bison*) (pl. same). Where the latter inhabits the plains rather than forests, it is usually called **buffalo** (pl. same)

bisque in tennis, croquet, golf; unglazed white porcelain; rich soup (not ital.)

bissextile (noun and adj.) leap year, abbr. **bis.**

bistoury a surgeon's scalpel

bistro a small restaurant (not ital.)

bit (US) 12½ cents (used only in multiples of two); (comput.) binary digit; *see also* **byte**

bitts (naut., pl.) a pair of posts on deck for fastening cables etc.

bitumin/ize, -ous

bivouac/, -ked, -king

biweekly avoid as ambiguous; prefer (adj. or adv.) 'semi-weekly' *or* 'fortnightly', (adv.) 'twice a week' *or* 'every two weeks', as appropriate

bizarre, bizarrerie (not ital.)

Bizet, Georges (1838–75) French composer

Bjørnson, Bjørnstjerne (1832–1910) Norwegian writer

Bk berkelium (no point)

bk. bank, book

bkg. banking

bkt. basket, pl. **bkts.**

BL Bachelor of Law, Bachelor of Letters, Bachelor of Literature, (hist.) British Leyland, British Library

bl. bale, barrel; pl. **bls.**

b.l. bill of lading

black (not cap.) preferred term for people having dark-coloured skin, except for those from the Indian subcontinent, who are usually referred to generally as *Asian*; avoid *coloured*, *Negress*, and *Negro* (cap.) except as a specific ethnologic term; *African-American* is commonly used to describe a black person in the USA

black (typ.) a space inked in

Blackburn: signature of the Bishop of Blackburn (colon)

blackcock *see* **black game**

Black/foot (of or relating to) (a member of) a Native American tribe, or the language of this people; pl. **-feet**

Blackfriars London

black game (two words) black grouse; m. **blackcock** (one word), f. **greyhen**

black letter (typ.) a general term for Gothic or Old English (q.v.) type; *see also* **Fraktur**

blacklist (noun and verb, one word)

Black Maria a prison van (two words, caps.)

Blackmoor Hants.

Blackmore/ Essex, Shropshire; **—, Richard Doddridge** (1825–1900) English writer

blackout (adj., noun, one word)

black out (verb, two words)

Blackrock Co. Cork, Corn., Co. Dublin, Gwent, Co. Louth

Blackrod Gr. Manchester

Black Rod abbr. for 'Gentleman Usher of the Black Rod'

blackshirt/ a Fascist, **-ed** (one word)

blad (print.) a booklet of sample pages from a forthcoming book, used for promotion purposes

blaeberry Sc. and N. Eng. for **bilberry**

Blaenau Ffestiniog Gwynedd (no hyphen), *but* the **Festiniog Railway**

blague/ (Fr. f.) humbug; *-ur* (m.) hoaxer, pretentious talker

Blairadam Fife (one word)

Blair Atholl Tayside (caps., no hyphen)

Blairgowrie Tayside (one word)

Blairs College Aberdeen (no apos.)

blameable *not* blamable (US)

blancmange (cook.) (one word, not ital.)

Bland, Edith *see* **Nesbit**

Blandford, Viscount title of eldest son of the Duke of Marlborough

blanket/, **-ed, -ing** (one *t*)

blanquette (Fr. cook. f.) white meat in white sauce

Blantyre Strathclyde, Malawi

blas/**é** bored through overfamiliarity or a surfeit of pleasure (not ital.); f. **-ée** (not usually used in English)

blastula/ pl. **-e** (US pl. -s)

blather/, **-skite** *not* blether, -skate

Blatherwycke Northants.; *not* -wyck, -wick

bldg. building, pl. **bldgs.**

bleed (typ.) an illustration going to the trimmed edge

bleed (bind.) overcut the margins and mutilate the printing

Blenheim Orange a type of golden-coloured apple (two caps.)

Blériot, Louis (1872–1936) French aviator, first to cross the English Channel in an aeroplane, 1909

blesbok (Afrik.) an antelope, *not* -buck

blessed *not* blest, blessèd (except in poet.)

bletherskate *use* **blatherskite**

Blighty England *or* home

blind (noun, US) = **hide**

blind/ (typ.) a paragraph mark with solid loop, a pilcrow; symbol ¶; **— blocking** *or* **— tooling** (bind.); *see also* **blocking**

Blindheim Ger. for **Blenheim**

B.Lit. Bachelor of Literature

B.Litt. *Baccalaureus Literarum* (Bachelor of Letters)

blitzkrieg (not ital.) a swift, intense military campaign; **blitz** (colloq. Eng.) any violent attack; **the Blitz** the German air raids on London in 1940 (cap.)

Blixen, Karen (**Christentze**), Baroness Blixen-Finecke (1885–1962) Danish novelist and short-story writer; born Karen Dinesen; pseud. **Isak Dinesen**

blk. (typ.) block, -s

BLL Bachelor of Laws (no point, thin space following 'B')

bloc (Fr.) a combination of nations or parties

Bloch, Ernest (1880–1959) Swiss-American composer

block (typ.) a letterpress printing plate for an illustration, (brass) a stamp to impress book-cover; (US) the area between streets in a town or suburb, often used as a measure of distance

Block, Maurice (1816–1901) French economist

blocking/ (bind.) impressing lettering or a design into the case of a book; **blind** — without foil or colour, **gold** — with gold foil

Bloemfontein Orange Free State, S. Africa

Blok, Aleksandr (**Aleksandrovich**) (1880–1921) Russian poet

blond/ fair-complexioned, light-coloured (of hair); f. **-e** (not ital.)

blood/ **bank, — cell, — count** (two words)

blood group (two words) antigens are designated by capital letters, sometimes combined with lower-case letter(s), such as A, B, AB, O, Rh; while defined as groups, blood is described as types, e.g. type A, *not* group A; genes encoding these antigens are represented by the same letters printed in italic; antibodies corresponding to antigens are prefixed by 'anti-', e.g. anti-A

blood pressure (two words)

blood sport (two words)

bloodstain/, **-ed** (one word)

bloodstream (one word)

blood supply (two words)

bloody hand (her.) the armorial device of a baronet

Bloody Mary (two caps.)

Bloomsbury Group (two caps.)

Blot on the 'Scutcheon, A a tragedy in blank verse by R. Browning, 1843

blottesque painting with blotted touches (not ital.)

blow past part. **blown**, *but* **blowed** in the sense of 'cursed' ('Well I'm blowed')

blow-up (noun) an enlarged picture (hyphen, one word in US)

blow up (verb) enlarge (two words)

blowzy coarse-looking, *not* blou-, -sy

Blubberhouses N. Yorks. (one word)

Blücher, Gebhard Leberecht von (1742–1819) German field marshal

Blue a person who has represented a university in a sport, esp. Oxford or Cambridge, *also* **Full Blue, Half Blue** (caps.)

bluebell (one word)

Blue Book a parliamentary or Privy Council report (two words, two caps.); cf. **Green Paper**; **White Paper**

blueing *use* **bluing**

blueish *use* **bluish**

bluejacket a RN sailor (one word)

Bluemantle one of four pursuivants of the English College of Arms

blueprint/ a photographic print, **-ing** this process (one word)

blues, the (mus.) (a piece of) melancholic music, usually in 12-bar sequence (pl. same); depression

bluestocking *but* **Blue Stocking/ Circle, — — Ladies, — — Society**

bluey bluelike

blu/ing, -ish *not* blue-

Blundellsands Merseyside (one word)

blurb a résumé of a book, printed on the jacket

Blu-Tack (propr.)

Blut und Eisen (Ger.) blood and iron

Blyth Northumb.

Blyth Bridge Borders

Blythebridge Staffs.

BM Bachelor of Medicine, Bachelor of Music, *Beata Maria* (the Blessed Virgin), *beatae memoriae* (of blessed memory), benchmark, British Museum

BMA British Medical Association

BME Bachelor of Mining Engineering

B.Met. Bachelor of Metallurgy

BMJ British Medical Journal

BMR (med.) basal metabolic rate

B.Mus. Bachelor of Music

BMV *Beata Maria Virgo* (Blessed Virgin Mary)

BMW Bayerische Motorenwerke

BMX organized bicycle racing on a dirt track, esp. for youngsters; abbr. of bicycle motocross

bn. battalion, billion

B'nai B'rith sons of covenant, a Jewish fraternity (two apos.)

BNB British National Bibliography

BNC Brasenose College, Oxford

BO body odour

b.o. box office, branch office, broker's order, brought over, buyer's option

BOA British Optical Association, British Olympic Association

Boabdil the last Moorish king of Granada 1482–92 (d. *c.*1533)

Boadicea a fierce woman; *use* **Boudicca** for the historical figure

Boanerges sing. or pl., loud preacher(s)

boarding/ house, — school (two words)

Board of Trade (hist.) abbr. **B.o.T., B. of T.,** absorbed in **Department of Trade and Industry** 1970

boat although usually small, a *boat* can be of any size; a *ship* is a sea-going vessel capable of carrying smaller craft. The Royal Navy classes submarines as *boats*

boatswain contr. and pron. **bo's'n** *or* **bosun**

boatyard (one word)

Bobadil a braggart, from Bobadill in Jonson's *Every Man in his Humour*

bobby pin (US) = **hairpin**, *but* **hairpin turn** in both countries

bobby socks (cotton) ankle socks *but* **bobby-soxer** (hist.) for a teenage girl

bobolink a N. American songbird

bobsleigh (one word), *not* bobsled (except in US)

bobwhite the American quail

bocage the representation of silvan scenery in ceramics (not ital.)

Boccaccio, Giovanni (1313–75) Italian writer (four *c*s)

Boccherini, Luigi (1743–1850) Italian composer

Boche a German, esp. a soldier of the First World War (cap.)

BOD biochemical oxygen demand

Bod Tibetan for **Tibet**

bodega a cellar or shop selling wine and food, esp. in a Sp.-speaking area (not ital.)

Bodensee Ger. for **Lake Constance**

Bodhisattva in Mahayana Buddhism and Hinduism, a person able to reach nirvana

bodhrán a shallow one-sided Irish drum (not ital.)

bodh tree *use* **bo tree**

Bodicote Oxon.

Bodleian Library abbr. **Bod. Lib., Bodl., Bodley**

Bodoni, Giambattista (1740–1813) Italian printer and punch-cutter, designer of Bodoni type

body (typ.) the measurement from front to back of the shank of a piece of type; in the Anglo-American system 12 pt. = 0.166 in.; *see also* **Didot**

body blow (two words)

body/builder, -guard (one word)

Boehme, Jakob (1575–1624) German mystic philosopher

Boeotia/ a district of central Greece, **-n** stupid

Boerhaave, Herman (1668–1738) Dutch naturalist

Boethius, Anicius (470–525) Roman statesman and philosopher

bœuf (Fr. m.) beef, bull

B. of T. Board of Trade

bogey/ in golf, ghost; pl. **-s**; *not* bogy

bogie a wheeled undercarriage

Bogota NJ

Bogotá Colombia, S. America

bogy *use* **-ey**

Bohême (Fr. f.) Bohemia (the territory)

bohème (Fr. m., f.) bohemian person, (f.) collective noun for non-traditional artists

Bohemian/ (a native) of Bohemia (cap.); socially unconventional person, **-ism** (not cap.)

bohémien/ (Fr.) f. *-ne* Bohemian, Gypsy

Bohr,/ Niels (**Hendrik David**) (1885–1962) and his son — **Aage** (b. 1922) Danish physicists

Boïeldieu, François Adrien (1775–1834) French composer

boilermaker (one word)

boiler/ room, — suit (two words)

boiling point (two words) abbr. **BP**, **b.p.**

Bokhara river, NSW, Australia; *see also* **Bu-**

bokmål the literary language of Norway, *formerly* **riksmål**, which is now sometimes used to denote a more conservative form of it (not cap.)

boldface type heavy, **as this**, abbr. **b.f.**

Boldizsár, Iván (b. 1912) Hungarian writer

bolero/ a Spanish dance, a woman's short jacket; pl. **-s**

Boleyn, Anne (1507–36) second wife of Henry VIII of England

bolivar a Venezuelan monetary unit

Bolívar, Simón (1783–1830) S. American patriot

Bolivia/, -n abbr. **Bol.**

Böll, Heinrich (**Theodor**) (1917–85) German writer

Bologna Italy, in Lat. **Bononia**; adj. **Bolognese**, *but* **spaghetti bolognese**

bolometer a radiation measurer

boloney humbug, *use* **bal-**; a type of sausage, *use* **bologna**

Bolshevik an advocate of proletarian dictatorship by soviets; a member of the majority group of the Russian Social Democratic Party, later the Communist Party, opp. to **Menshevik**

bolshie uncooperative

bolts (bind.) the three outer edges of a folded sheet before trimming

Boltzmann constant (phys.) symbol *k*

bolus/ a large pill, soft ball of chewed food, pl. **-es**

bomb (colloq. noun) a large sum of money or a resounding success in British slang, but a disastrous failure in US slang

Bombardier cap. as title, abbr. **Bdr.**

Bombay India, in Maratha and properly **Mumbai**

bombazine a fabric; *not* -basine, -bazeen, -bycine

bombe (Fr. cook. f.) a conical confection, often frozen

bona/ fide (Lat.) genuine(ly), — **fides** good faith (no accent, not ital.)

Bonaparte a Corsican family, *not* Buonaparte

bona/ peritura (Lat.) perishable goods, — *vacantia* (law) unclaimed goods

bon-bon/ a kind of sweet (one word in US), **-nière** a box for sweets (not ital.)

bon chic bon genre (Fr.) (of a person) well dressed, well bred; abbr. **B.C.B.G.**

bon/-chrétien a pear, pl. **-s-chrétiens**

bond abbr. **bd.**

bondholder (one word)

bond paper a hard, strong paper

Bonduca *use* **Boudicca**

Bo'ness (originally **Borrowstounness**) Central Scotland (apos.); *see also* **Bowness**

Boney a sobriquet of Napoleon; cf. **bony**

bon/ goût (Fr. m.) good taste; — *gré*, *mal gré*, whether one likes or not

Bonheur, Rosa (1822–99) French painter

bonhomie geniality, good nature

bonhomme (Fr. m.) pleasant fellow, friar

Bonhomme, Jacques a personification of the French peasant

bonhomous full of bonhomie (not ital.)

bonjour (Fr. m.) good day (one word)

bon marché (Fr.) a cheap shop, cheap (two words)

bon/ mot a witticism, pl. **-s mots** (two words, not ital.)

bonne (Fr. f.) a maid

bonne/ bouche (Fr.) a dainty morsel, pl. *-s bouches*; — *foi* good faith; — *fortune* success, pl. *-s fortunes*; — *grâce* gracefulness, pl. *-s grâces*

bonnet/, -ed, -ing (one *t*)

bonnet rouge (Fr. m.) a Republican's cap

Bononia (Lat.) Bologna, Italy

bonsai (Jap.) a dwarfed tree or shrub

bonsoir (Fr. m.) good evening, goodnight (one word)

bontebok (Afrik.) a pied antelope, *not* -buck

bon ton (Fr. m.) good style

bon vivant/ one fond of luxurious food (no hyphen, not ital.), pl. **-s**; the feminine, **bonne vivante**, is not in French usage

bon viveur a pseudo-Fr. substitute for **bon vivant** (not in French usage)

bon voyage! pleasant journey!

bony of or like bone, *not* -ey; cf. **Boney**

boob tube (sl.) a woman's close-fitting, strapless top; (US sl., usually preceded by **the**) television (two words)

Booerhave *see* **Boerhaave**

boogie/, -d, -ing, -s; **-woogie** (hyphen)

book abbr. **bk.**, pl. **bks.**

bookbind/er, -ing (one word)

bookcase a cabinet with shelves for books (one word)

book case (print.) an outer covering for a book (two words)

bookend (one word)

bookkeep/er, -ing (one word)

bookmak/er, -ing (one word)

bookmark/, -er (one word)

bookmobile (US) = **mobile library**

Book-of-the-Month Club (US) (hyphens)

bookplate (one word)

book-rest (hyphen)

books, titles of when cited, to be in italic; *but* series titles roman, no quote marks

book/seller, -shop, -stall (one word)

Booksellers Association, abbr. **BA**

books of Scripture (typ.) not to be italic, nor quoted; for abbrs. *see* separate entries

book trim (bind.) standard trim is approx. 3 mm off head, foredge, and tail margins

bookwork (one word)

Boole/, George (1815–64) English logician and mathematician, **-an**

Boone, Daniel (1735–1820) American explorer and colonizer

bootee a small (e.g. baby's) boot, *not* -ie

Boötes (astr.) a northern constellation containing Arcturus

booze (to) drink; *not* -se, cf. **bouse**

Bophuthatswana a former black homeland, S. Africa

bor. borough

Borak, Al the winged horse on which Muhammad, in a vision, ascended to heaven

Bordeaux/ dép. Gironde, France; a claret or any wine of Bordeaux; **— mixture** of lime and copper sulphate, to kill fungus and insect parasites on plants

border (typ.) an ornament

bordereau (Fr. m.) a memorandum, docket

borderland (one word)

Borders a region of Scotland

bordure (her.) a border round the edge of a shield

Boreas (Gr. myth.) the god of the north wind

Borehamwood Herts.

Borges, Jorge Luis (1899–1986) Argentinian writer

Borghese an Italian family

Borgia,/ Cesare (1476–1507), **— Lucrezia** (1480–1519), **— Rodrigo** (1431–1503)

born/ of child, with reference to birth, abbr. **b.**; **-e** carried, also of birth when 'by' (with name of mother) follows

born/é (Fr.) f. **-ée** narrow-minded

Borodin, Aleksandr (**Porfirevich**) (1834–87) Russian composer and chemist

boron symbol **B**

borough abbr. **bor.**

borscht a Russian soup, *not* bortsch; in Russ. *borshch*

Borstal (hist.) an institution for reformative training (cap.); *now* called detention centre, young offender institution, or youth custody centre, although **borstal** (not cap.) remains as a slang term to describe any of these

borzoi/ a Russian wolfhound, pl. **-s**

bosbok Afrik. for **bushbuck**

Boscán de Almogáver, Juan (*c*.1487–1542) Italian-born Spanish poet

Bosch, Hieronymus (?1450–1516) Dutch painter

bo's'n, bosun contr. of **boatswain**

Bosnia-Hercegovina a republic of the former Yugoslavia, in Serbo-Croat **Bosna i Hercegovina**

Bosporus strait separating European and Asian Turkey, *not* Bosph-

Bossuet, Jacques Bénigne (1627–1704) French bishop and writer

Boswellize write a laudatory biography (cap.)

B.o.T. Board of Trade

botanize *not* -ise

Botany merino wool, esp. from Australia (cap.)

botan/y, -ical, -ist abbr. **bot.**; genera, species, and varieties to be ital., all other divisions roman: order, family, cultivar

botfly (one word), *not* -tt-

bothy (Sc.) a hut, *not* -ie

bo tree the sacred tree of India, *not* bodh —

Botswana S. African rep. *formerly* Bechuanaland

Botticelli, Sandro (1445–1510) Florentine painter

bottle bank (two words)

bottle/-brush, -feed, -fed, -green (hyphens)

bottle/neck, -nose dolphin (one word)

Boucher de Perthes, Jacques (1788–1868) French archaeologist

Boucicault, Dion (1822–90) Irish playwright

Boudicca (d. AD 61) queen of the Iceni; the name is reconstructed as **Boudikā** in British, **Boudicca** in Tacitus' Latin, and miscopied as **Bonduca**; *see also* **Boadicea**

boudoir (not ital.)

bouffant puffed out, as a dress (not ital.)

bougainvillea a tropical plant

Bouguereau, William Adolphe (1825–1905) French painter

bouillabaisse a thick fish soup (not ital.)

bouilli (Fr. m.) stewed meat (ital.)

bouillon broth (not ital.)

boul. boulevard

Boule a legislative council in an ancient Greek city state

boule a French game akin to bowls (not ital.)

boule, boulle (inlay) *use* **buhl**

boulevard/ abbr. **boul.**; **-ier** a 'man about town'

***boulevers*/é** (Fr.) f. **-ée** overturned, **-ement** (m.) a violent inversion

Boulez, Pierre (b. 1925) French composer

Boulogne déps. Haute-Garonne, Pas-de-Calais, France

bounceable *not* -cable

bouncy *not* bouncey

bound abbr. **bd.**

bouquetin the ibex

bouquinist a second-hand bookseller, (Fr. m.) *bouquiniste*

bourgeois/ (Fr.) f. **-e** one of the middle class, **-ie** the middle class (not ital.)

Bourn Cambs.

bourn a stream, (arch.) a limit; *not* -ne

Bourne Lincs.

Bournemouth Dorset

Bournville Birmingham

bourrée an old lively dance, the music for this (not ital.)

bourse a foreign money-market, esp. in Paris

bouse (naut.) haul, *not* -wse; cf. **booze**; **bowser**

boustrophedon written from left to right and right to left on alternate lines, esp. in Gr. or Etruscan inscriptions

boutonnière a spray of flowers worn in a buttonhole (accent, not ital.)

Boutros-Ghali, Boutros (b. 1922) Egyptian diplomat and politician

bouts-rimés rhymed endings

Bouvet Island (Norw.) Antarctic Ocean

bowdlerize expurgate, from **Dr Thomas Bowdler** (1754–1825) (not cap.)

bowled (cricket) abbr. **b.**

Bowness Cumbria; *see also* **Bo'ness**

bowser a tanker used for fuelling aircraft etc.; cf. **booze**; **bouse**

Boxing Day the first weekday after Christmas Day (caps.)

box/ **number**; **— office** abbr. **b.o.** (two words)

box/**room, -wood** (one word)

boyar (hist.) a member of the old aristocracy in Russia

boycott exclude from society or business (not cap.), from **Capt. Charles C. Boycott** (1832–97)

boyfriend (one word)

Boy Scout *now* **Scout**

BP boiling point, British Petroleum, British Pharmacopoeia

BP before present (calibrated) (small caps.), to be placed *after* the numerals; *but note* **bp** before present (uncalibrated) (lower case)

Bp. Bishop

b.p. below proof, bills payable, blood pressure, boiling point

BPC British Pharmaceutical Codex

B.Phil. Bachelor of Philosophy

b.p.i. (comput.) bits (*see* **bit**) per inch

BPIF British Printing Industries Federation

bpl. birthplace

Bq becquerel

BR (hist.) British Rail, *formerly* — Railways

Br bromine (no point)

Br. British, Brother (monastic title)

bra formerly common colloquialism and now the usual term for **brassiere** (no point)

'Brabançonne, La' the Belgian national anthem

bracket/, **-ed, -ing**

Bradford: the signature of the Bishop of Bradford (colon)

Braggadochio a character in Spenser's *Faerie Queene*

braggadocio empty boasting (not ital.)

Brahe, Tycho (1546–1601) Danish astronomer

Brahma the supreme Hindu god (not ital.)

brahma/, **-putra** an Asian domestic fowl (not cap.)

Brahman/ a member of the highest Hindu caste, whose members are traditionally eligible for the priesthood; pl. **-s**; adj. **-ical** (cap.); *not* Brahmin

Brahmaputra a river flowing through Tibet, India, and Bangladesh

Brahmi one of the two oldest alphabets in the Indian subcontinent; cf. **Kharoshthi**

Brahmin/ (US) a socially or intellectually superior person; pl. **-s**; *not* Brahman

Brahmoism a reformed theistic Hinduism

brail haul up

Braille signs composed of raised dots replacing letters, for the blind (cap.)

Braine, John (1922–86) English novelist

braise (cook.) *not* -ze; cf. **braze**

brake/ (for wheel, a large vehicle, etc.) *not* break, **— horsepower** (two words)

Br. Am. British America(n)

Bramah/, **Ernest** (1867–1942) English writer, **—, Joseph** (1749–1814) English inventor of **— lock** etc.

brand new *not* bran

Brandt, Willy (1913–92) German statesman, Chancellor of W. Germany 1969–74

Brandywine a battle of the American War of Independence, 1777

brant goose *use* **brent-** (except in US)

Brantôme, Pierre de Bourdeille, Seigneur de (1540–1614) French writer

Brasenose College Oxford

Brasília new capital of Brazil, 1960

brass/, (**binder's**) (typ.) a die for blocking book cases, pl. **-es**; — **rule** (typ.) for printing simple borders or lines between columns of type

brassard a badge worn on the arm

brasserie a beer garden, licensed restaurant; *brasserie* (Fr. f.) *also* a brewery

brassie a golf club with a brass sole, *not* -y

brassiere a woman's undergarment supporting the breasts, a **bra** (no accent)

brassière/ (Fr. f.) (baby's) vest or undershirt, (Fr. Can. f.) bra; — *de sauvetage* life jacket; cf. *soutien-gorge*

bratticing (archit.) open carved work, (coal-mining) wooden shaft-lining or screen

Brauneberger a white wine

Braunschweig Ger. for **Brunswick**

brav/a! (It.) 'well done!' (to a woman); *-o!* (to a man)

bravo/ a desperado, pl. **-es**; a cry of 'well done!', pl. **-s**

braze to solder; *not* -ise, -ize; cf. **braise**

brazier a worker in brass, a pan for holding lighted coal; *not* -sier

Brazil/, -ian abbr. **Braz.**

Brazzaville capital of Republic of Congo, Cent. Africa

BRCS British Red Cross Society

BRD (Ger.) *Bundesrepublik Deutschland,* Federal Republic of Germany

bread/board, -crumb, -fruit, -line (one word)

break/ (typ.) the division into a fresh paragraph, **-line** the last one of a paragraph (hyphen); *see also* **brake**

breakdown (noun) a collapse, analysis of statistics (one word)

Breakspear, Nicholas Pope Adrian IV 1154–9, *not* -eare

breakthrough (noun, one word)

breakup (noun, one word)

Breathalyser (noun) a device for testing amount of alcohol in the breath; *not* -iser, -izer, -yzer (US) (cap.); **breathalyse** (verb) carry out test, *not* -yze (US) (not cap.)

breathing/ (typ.) either of two signs in Greek, Arabic, Hebrew, and other languages indicating the presence (**rough** ') or the absence (**smooth** ') of an aspirate

breccia a rock composed of angular fragments, *not* -cchia

Brechin Tayside

Brecht/, Bertolt (1898–1956) German playwright; *not* -th-, -d; adj. **-ian**

Brecon Powys

breech birth (two words)

Breeches Bible the 1560 Geneva Bible, with *breeches* for *aprons* in Gen. 3: 7

breeches buoy a life-saving apparatus (two words)

Bren gun a light machine-gun (two words)

brent goose *not* bra- (US)

Brescia Lombardy, Italy

Breslau Ger. for **Wrocław** (Poland)

Bretagne/ Fr. for **Brittany, Grande** — Great Britain

Breton (an inhabitant) of Brittany, abbr. **Bret.**

Bretton Woods NH (UN Monetary Conference, 1944)

bretzel *use* **pretzel**

Breughel *use* **Brueghel** *or* **Bruegel**

brev. brevet, -ed

breve a curved mark (˘) to indicate a short vowel or syllable

brevet d'invention (Fr. m.) a patent

breveté s.g.d.g. (Fr.) patented without government guarantee (*sans garantie du gouvernement*)

breviary a book containing RC daily service

Brezhnev, Leonid (Ilich) (1906–82) General Secretary, USSR Communist Party 1964–82; President of the Supreme Soviet 1977–82

bri/ar *use* **-er** in all senses, *but* (US) briar pipe, **Sweet Briar College**, Sweet Briar, Va.

Briarean many-handed, like **Briareus**, of Greek myth.; *not* -ian

bribable *not* -eable

bric-a-brac (hyphens, no accent)

brick/bat, -work (one word)

Bridge End Cumbria, Devon, Lincs., Shetland

Bridgend Corn., Cumbria (near Patterdale), Co. Donegal, Glos., Lothian, Mid Glam., Strathclyde, Tayside

Bridge of Allan Central

Bridge of San Luis Rey, The novel by Thornton Wilder, 1927

Bridgeport Ala., Calif., Conn., Nebr., Pa., Tex.

Bridges, Robert (Seymour) (1844–1930) English poet, Poet Laureate 1913–30

Bridges Creek Va., birthplace of George Washington

Bridgeton Glasgow; NJ

Bridgetown Corn., Som., Staffs., Co. Wexford, Barbados; NS, Canada; W. Australia

Bridgewater/ NS, Canada; **Duke of** — (1736–1803), projector of the — **Canal; Earl of** — (1756–1829), founder of the — **Treatises**

Bridgnorth Shropshire

Bridgwater Som., *not* Bridge-

bridle path (two words)

bridle-road (hyphen)

bridleway (one word)

brier/, -root (hyphen); *not* briar, brere

brier rose (two words) *not* briar, brere

Brig. brigad/e, -ier

Brillat-Savarin, Anthelme (1755–1826) French gastronome

brimfull (one word)

bring up (typ.) to underlay or interlay a block to bring it to printing height

brio (mus.) fire, life, vigour

briquette a block of compressed coal dust, *not* -et

brisling a Norwegian sprat, *not* brist-

Bristol: the signature of the Bishop of Bristol (colon)

Bristol-board a cardboard used by artists (hyphen; two words, not cap. in US)

Brit. Britain; Britann/ia, -icus, -ica; British

Britain *more correctly* Great Britain, the land mass of England, Scotland, and Wales, with some of its immediately surrounding islands. The United Kingdom adds Northern Ireland to these, though not the Isle of Man and Channel Islands; British Isles is a geographical, not a political, term, and includes the Republic of Ireland, the Isle of Man, and the Channel Islands

Briticism idiom current in Britain, *not* Britishism

British/ abbr. **Brit.**; **— Academy, — Association** abbr. **BA**; **— America** abbr. **Br. Am.**; **— Columbia** abbr. **BC**; **— Guyana** *now* **Guyana**; **— Honduras** *now* **Belize**; **— Library** abbr. **BL**; **— Museum** abbr. **BM**; **— Rail** abbr. **BR**; **— Standard** abbr. **BS** (*see* **BSI**)

Britisher *use* **Briton**

British Indian Ocean Territory a group of 2,300 islands in the Indian Ocean, governed as a British colony from Diego Garcia

britschka *use* **britzka**

Britt. (on coins) Britanniarum, 'of the Britains' (Roman *Britannia Inferior* and *Britannia Superior*)

Brittany in Fr. **Bretagne**

Britten, (Edward) Benjamin, Baron (1913–76) British composer

britzka a Polish open carriage, in Pol. **bryczka**

Bro. Brother (monastic title)

bro. brother, pl. **bros.**

Broad-Churchman (caps., hyphen)

Broad Haven Dyfed, Co. Mayo

Broadmoor a psychiatric hospital, Crowthorne, Berks.

Broad Oak Cumbria, Dorset, Hereford, E. Sussex

Broadoak Corn., Dorset, Glos., Kent, Shropshire

broadside (US typ.) (adj.) = **landscape**

Brobdingnag the land of giants in Swift's *Gulliver's Travels*, 1726; *not* -dig-

broccoli a hardy cauliflower; It. pl., but Eng. sing. *or* pl.

brochet/ (Fr. m.) freshwater pike; **-te** (Fr. f.) (food cooked on) a skewer

Broderers a livery company

broderie anglaise open embroidery on white linen or cambric (not ital.)

broil (US) = **grill**

Bromberg Ger. for **Bydgoszcz**

bromine symbol **Br**

bronch/i pl. the main forks of the windpipe (sing. **-us**), **-ia**, pl. ramifications of the above; **-ioles** their minute branches

bronco/ a type of Mexican horse, *not* -cho; pl. **-s**

Brontë,/ Anne (1820–49) pseud. **Acton Bell**, **— Charlotte** (1816–55) pseud. **Currer Bell**, **— Emily** (1818–48) pseud. **Ellis Bell**, English writers

brontosaurus former term for **apatosaurus**

Bronx, the a borough of New York City

bronzing (typ.) printing in yellow and then dusting with bronze powder to imitate gold

brooch *not* -ach

Brooke/ Leics., Norfolk; **Baron —**; **—, Rupert** (1887–1915), English poet

Brookings Institution Washington, DC; *not* Institute

Brookline Mass.

Brooklyn a borough of New York City

Brooks's Club London, *not* -es's

broomstick (one word)

Brother (monastic title) abbr. **Bro.**

brother/ abbr. **b., bro.**; pl. **-s, brethren**, abbr. **bros.**; **— german** having same parents; **-in-law**, pl. **brothers-in-law**, **— uterine** having same mother only

brougham (hist.) a horse-drawn closed carriage or motor car with an open driver's seat (not cap.), pron. 'broom'

brouhaha a commotion, uproar (not ital.)

Brown/, Ford Madox (1821–93) English painter, **—, John** (1800–59) US abolitionist, **—, Lancelot** (called **Capability —**) (1716–83) English landscape gardener; **—, Robert** (1773–1858) Scottish botanist

Brown University RI, abbr. **BU**

Browne,/ Charles Farrar *see* **Ward**; **— Hablot Knight** (1815–82) English artist, pseud. **Phiz**, illustrated Dickens; **— Sir Thomas** (1605–82) English physician and author

Brownian motion of particles (observed by Robert Brown)

Brownie a junior Guide (cap.); a Scottish house-spirit (not cap.)

browse to read desultorily, eat; *not* -ze

BRS British Road Services

Bruckner, Anton (1824–96) Austrian composer

Bruegel, Pieter (*c*.1520–69) Flemish painter; **Brueghel, Pieter** (1564–1638) and **Jan** (1568–1625) his sons, also painters; *not* Breu-

Bruges Belgium, in Fl. **Brugge**

Brummagem derogatory form of Birmingham, abbr. **Brum**; (adj.) tawdry

Brummell, George Bryan, 'Beau' (1778–1840)

Brummie from or relating to Birmingham

brummy (Austral. and NZ) counterfeit, showy, or cheaply made

Brunei NW Borneo

Brunel/, Sir Marc Isambard (1769–1849) and —, **Isambard Kingdom** (1806–59) his son, British engineers; — **University** Uxbridge

Brunelleschi, Filippo (1377–1446) Italian architect and sculptor

brunette a woman with dark brown hair *or* this colour of hair; the masculine form is **brown**, **brunet** being seldom used

Brünhild (Ger. (orig. Burgundian) myth.) the queen won by Siegfried for Gunther; (Norse myth.) spelt **Brynhild**, won by Sigurðr for Gunnar; variations include (Middle High Ger.) **Brünhilt** (in Bavarian **Prünhilt**); the Anglicized form most familiar from Wagner is **Brunhilda**, *properly* **Brünnhilde**

Brunonian (noun) an alumnus of **Brown University**; (adj.) of the system of medicine of Dr John Brown of Edinburgh (1736–88)

Brunswick Eng. for **Braunschweig**, Germany

Brussels capital of Belgium; in Fl. **Brussel**, Fr. **Bruxelles**

Brussels sprouts (one cap., no apos.)

brut (Fr.) unsweetened

brutalize *not* -ise

Bruxelles Fr. for **Brussels**

bryczka (Pol.) **britzka**

Brynhild a Norse heroine, *see* **Brünhild**

Brynmawr Gwent

Bryn Mawr College Philadelphia

bryology the study of mosses, abbr. **bryol.**

bryozoan (of or relating to) any aquatic invertebrate animal of the phylum Bryozoa, properly *not* polyzoan

Brython Welsh for Briton, a S. British Celt

Brythonic (the language) of the Celts in Britain or Brittany

Brzezinski, Zbigniew (b. 1928) Polish-born US academic and statesman

BS Bachelor of Surgery *or* (US) Science, Blessed Sacrament, British Standard (*see also* **BSI**)

b.s. balance sheet, bill of sale

BSA Birmingham Small Arms, British School at Athens

BSC British Steel Corporation

B.Sc. Bachelor of Science; **B.Sc.(Econ.)** Bachelor of Science in faculty of Economics; **B.Sc.(Eng.)** Bachelor of Science Engineering, Glas.; **B.Sc.Tech.** Bachelor of Technical Science

BSE bovine spongiform encephalopathy, a usually fatal disease of cattle; commonly called 'mad cow disease'

b.s.g.d.g. *see* **breveté s.g.d.g.**

BSI British Standards Institution; a complete list of British Standards is in the BS Yearbook

B-side the secondary side of a gramophone record

BSJA British Show Jumping Association

BSR British School at Rome

BST British Summer Time (before 1968 and from 1972), British Standard Time (1968–71) (both 1 hr. ahead of GMT)

Bt. Baronet, *not* Bart.

BTA British Tourist Authority

B.Th. Bachelor of Theology

B.th.u. *or* **B.t.u.** *or* **BTU** British Thermal Unit(s)

bty. battery

BU Baptist Union; Boston University, Mass.; Brown University, RI; Bucknell University

bu. bushel, -s

buccaneer *not* -ier

Buccleuch, Duke of *not* -gh

Bucellas a white wine from Bucellas, near Lisbon

Buch (Ger. n.) book, pl. *Bücher*

Bucharest Romania, in Romanian **Bucureşti**; *not* Buka-

Buchausgabe (Ger. f.) edition of a book

Buckinghamshire abbr. **Bucks.**

Bucknall Lincs., Staffs.

Bucknell Oxon., Shropshire; also a university at Lewisburg, Pa.

buckram a coarse fabric, (bind.) a good quality cloth

Budapest Hungary, *not* -pesth (one word). Collective name for two towns, Buda and Pest, fused in the 19th c.

Buddha (Skt.) a title (meaning 'The Awakened One') denoting the founder of Buddhism, **Siddhārtha Gautama** (*c*.490 BC–*c*.410 BC); as this is a title rather than a personal name, it should be preceded by **the**

Buddh/ism, -ist if necessary divide as shown, abbr. **Budd.**

budgerigar a parakeet

budget/, -ed, -ing

buen/as noches (Sp.) goodnight; *-as tardes* good afternoon; *-os días* good day, good morning

Buenos/ Aires cap. of Argentina; also in Panama, *use* — **Ayres** in titles of Argentinian railway companies

buffalo/ pl. **-es**

buffer state (two words)

buffet/, -ed, -ing (one *t*)

buffo (noun) a comic actor, esp. in Italian opera (ital.); (adj.) comic, burlesque (not ital.)

Buffon, Georges Louis Leclerc, comte de (1707–88) French naturalist

Bugatti a sports car manufacturer

buhl (inlaid with) brass, tortoiseshell, etc.; Ger. form of *boule*, from **André Charles Boule** (1642–1732) cabinetmaker to Louis XIV

Bühnenaussprache (Ger. f.) a standard pronunciation of German, free of dialectal variations

building abbr. **bldg.**, pl. **bldgs.**

BUJ (*Baccalaureus utriusque juris*) Bachelor of Canon and Civil Law

Bukarest *use* **Buch-**

Bukhara Uzbekistan; *see also* **Bo-**

buksheesh *use* **bak-**

bulbul (Pers.) the Asian song-thrush, the literary counterpart of a nightingale; a singer or poet

Bulfinch's Mythology *not* Bull-

Bulgaria/, -n abbr. **Bulg.**

bulgur a wholewheat cereal food; *not* -gar, -ghur

bulletin (not ital.) abbr. **bull.**

bullfight/, -er, -ing (one word)

bullring (one word)

bull's-eye the centre of a target, a lantern, a peppermint sweet (apos. and hyphen)

bull terrier (two words)

bulrush *not* bull-

bulwark a defence; *not* bull-, -work

Bulwer-Lytton,/ Edward George Earle Lytton, first **Lord Lytton** (1803–73) English novelist; **— Edward Robert** first **Earl of Lytton** (1831–91) his son, English poet and diplomat, pseud. **Owen Meredith**

bumbag (one word)

bumblebee (one word), *not* humble-

bumf papers, *not* bumph

bumkin (naut.) a projection from bows or stern of ship

bumpkin a yokel

bump out (typ.) increase word or letterspacing to fill a line, or line spacing to fill a page

Bumppo, Natty the hero of James Fenimore Cooper's 'Leather-Stocking Tales'

bun/combe *use* **-kum**

Bundesanstalt a German official institution since 1945; *see also* **Reichsanstalt**

Bundesrat, Bundestag (Ger.) the upper and lower houses of the German Parliament

bundle abbr. **bdl.**, pl. **bdls.**

Bunker Hill Mass., a battle of the American War of Independence, 1775, actually fought at neighbouring Breed's Hill; *not* -er's

bunkum *not* -combe

Bunsen burner (one cap.)

Buñuel, Luis (1900–83) Spanish-born film director

Buonaparte *use* **Bona-**

buona sera (It.) good evening, **buon giorno** good day

buoyan/t, -cy

BUPA British United Provident Association

bur a clinging seed vessel or catkin; cf. **burr**

Burckhardt, Jacob Christoph (1818–97) Swiss historian

Burdett-Coutts, Angela Georgina, Baroness (1814–1906) English philanthropist

bureau/ a writing-desk with drawers, (US) a chest of drawers; pl. **-x** (not ital.); **-cracy, -crat**, adj. **-cratic**

Bureau Veritas a maritime underwriters' association at Brussels (two caps.)

burette a graduated glass tube used in chemical analysis, *not* buret

burg. burgess, burgomaster

burgamot *use* **ber-**

Burgerbibliothek Berne, *not* Bü-

burgess abbr. **burg.**

burgh (hist.) Scottish borough or chartered town; status abolished in 1975

burgomaster (one word) abbr. **burg.**

burgrave a governor, *not* burgg-; in Ger. *Burggraf*

burgundy a wine (not cap.)

burhel *use* **bharal**

burial/ ground, place, — service (two words)

burk *use* **be-**

Burkina Faso W. Africa, *formerly* Upper Volta

burl a lump in cloth

burl. burlesque

Burleigh, William Cecil, Lord (1520–98) English statesman, chief minister to Elizabeth I; also spelt **Burghley**

Burlington House London, headquarters of the Royal Academy, British Association, and other artistic and learned bodies

Burm/a *not* -ah (in Burmese and strict official use **Myanmar**); **-ese** a native, national, or the language of Burma; pl. same; *not* -an, -ans

Burmah Oil Co. *not* Burma

Burne-Jones, Sir Edward Coley (1833–98) English painter (hyphen)

Burnett, Frances Eliza Hodgson (1849–1924) US writer

burnous an Arab or Moorish hooded cloak; *not* -e, bernouse, -noose; in Arab. *burnus*

Burntisland Fife (one word)

burnt sienna an orange-red pigment, *not* siena

burr a rough edge, a rough sounding of the letter *r*; a kind of limestone; cf. **bur**

burrito a flour tortilla rolled round a savoury filling

burro a donkey

burro (It.) butter

Burroughs,/ Edgar Rice (1875–1950) US novelist, — **John** (1837–1921) US naturalist and poet, — **William** (1914–97) US novelist

bursar the treasurer of a college, *not* -er

Burton upon Trent (no hyphens)

Burundi Cent. Africa

Bury St Edmunds Suffolk (no apos., no hyphen)

bus/ *not* 'bus; pl. **-es**; as verb **-ed, -ing**

bushbuck (S. Afr.) an antelope, in Afrik. **bosbok**

bushel abbr. **bu.** (sing. and pl.)

Bushey Herts., *not* -hy

bushido the code of the samurai or Japanese military caste

Bushire Iran

Bushy Park London

businesslike (one word)

business/man, -people, -person, -woman (one word)

buss/ (arch. or US colloq.) a kiss, pl. **-es**; as verb, **-ed, -ing**

busybody *not* busi-

busyness the state of being busy, distinct from business

Buthelezi, Chief Mangosuthu (Gatsha) (b. 1928) S. African politician

Butler, Samuel/ (1612–80) English poet (*Hudibras*), — — (1835–1902) English writer (*Erewhon*)

Butte Mont.

butter/fingers, -milk (one word)

buttonhole (one word)

buyer's option abbr. **b.o.**

buyout the purchase of a controlling share in a company etc. (one word; two words as verb)

Buys Ballot, Christoph Hendrik Didericus (1817–90) Dutch meteorologist (no hyphen)

BV *Beata Virgo* (the Blessed Virgin)

B.V. pseud. of **James Thomson**

BVM *Beata Virgo Maria*, the Blessed Virgin Mary

BWI British West Indies *now* **WI**

BWV *Bach-Werke-Verzeichnis*, a prefix to enumeration of J. S. Bach's compositions

by- (as prefix) tends to form one word with the following noun, but hyphen still sometimes found in the cases below

by and by, by and large (no hyphens)

by-blow a side blow, bastard (hyphen)

Bydgoszcz Poland, in Ger. **Bromberg**

bye/, -s (cricket) abbr. **b.**

bye-bye a familiar form of goodbye (hyphens)

by-election (hyphen)

Byelorussia *now* **Belarus** (since 1991)

by-form (hyphen)

bygone (one word)

by-lane (hyphen)

by-law (hyphen, one word in US), *not* bye-

byline in journalism and football (one word)

byname a sobriquet (one word)

by/pass, -path, -play (one word)

by/-plot, -product *not* bye- (hyphens)

by/road, -stander (one word)

by-street (hyphen) *but* Masefield's *The Widow in the Bye Street*

byte (comput.) a group of eight bits (*see* **bit**)

by the by (three words)

by/way, -word (one word)

byzant *use* **be-**

Byzantine cap. when referring to Byzantium, the Eastern Roman Empire, *or* its architecture, painting, or people; not cap. when referring to something extremely complicated, inflexible, or underhand

BZW Barclays de Zoete Wedd

bzw. (Ger.) *beziehungsweise* (respectively)

Cc

C carbon, Celcius *or* centigrade, centum (a hundred), (elec.) coulomb, (comput.) a programming language, the third in a series, (mus.) common time

¢ cedi (currency of Ghana), colón (currency of El Salvador)

C. Cape, Catholic, century, chairman, chief, Church, Command Paper (q.v.) (1870–99) with number following, congressional, Conservative, consul, contralto, Council, counter-tenor, Court, Gaius

c (as prefix) centi-

c. (cricket) caught, cent, -s; centime, century, chapter (esp. in legal works or where indicating *caput*, otherwise prefer **ch.**), city, (meteor.) cloudy, colt, conductor, constable, copeck, cubic

C (ital. cap.) symbol for capacitance

c. *circa* (about), set close up to figures, spaced from words and letters

Ɔ (inverted 'C') 500

CA California (postal abbr.), Central Africa, Central America, Member of the Institute of Chartered Accountants of Scotland, Chief Accountant, chronological age, Civil Aviation, College of Arms, commercial agent, Consumers' Association, Controller of Accounts, Court of Appeal

C/A capital account, commercial account, credit account, current account

Ca calcium (no point)

ca. (law) cases

ca. *circa* use **c.**

CAA Civil Aviation Authority

Caaba *use* **K-**

caaing-whale *use* **ca'ing-**

CAB Citizens' Advice Bureau, (US) Civil Aeronautics Board

cabal a secret faction

caballero/ a Spanish gentleman, pl. **-s** (not ital.)

cabana (US) a hut or shelter at a beach or swimming pool, from (Sp.) *cabaña*

cabbala Hebrew tradition; *not* k-, cabala, -alla

Cabell, James Branch (1879–1958) US novelist

cabinet a piece of furniture or a small room (not cap.); the committee of senior ministers responsible for controlling government policy (usually cap.)

Cable, George Washington (1844–1925) US writer

cable (naut.) one-tenth of a sea mile

cabochon a gem polished but not faceted, *en cabochon* (of a gem) treated in this way

Cabot Lodge *see* **Lodge**

cabotin/ (Fr.) fem. **-e** a second-rate actor, a strolling player

Cabul *use* **K-**

CAC Central Advisory Committee

ca'canny (Sc.) go carefully!; the practice of 'going slow' at work to limit output

cacao/ a tropical tree from whose seeds cocoa and chocolate are made, **-tree** (hyphen); *see also* **cocco, cocoa**

cache/mere, -mire *use* **cashmere**

cachet a distinctive mark, a capsule containing medicine

cachinnate (lit.) laugh loudly

cachou a lozenge to sweeten breath, *not* cashew

cachucha a Spanish dance

caciqu/e a W. Indian and S. American chief, political boss; **-ism**; *not* caz-

caco/demon, -daemon an evil spirit or malignant person (not ital.)

cacoethes/ (Lat. from Gr.) an urge to do something inadvisable (not ital.); **— loquendi** an itch for speaking, **— scribendi** an itch for writing (ital.)

caco/graphy bad handwriting or spelling, **-logy** bad choice of words or pronunciation, **-phony** dissonance, discord

CACTM Central Advisory Council for the Ministry, *now* **ACCM**

cact/us (bot.) pl. **-i**

CAD computer-aided design

c.-à-d. (Fr.) *c'est-à-dire* (that is to say)

cadastral of or showing the extent, value, and ownership of land for taxation

caddie a golf attendant

caddis/-fly, -worm *not* -ice (hyphens)

caddy a box for keeping tea etc.

cadi a Muslim judge, *not* k-

Cadiz city and port, SW Spain; in Sp. **Cádiz**

Cadmean/ of Cadmus of Thebes, *not* -ian; **— victory** a ruinous one

cadmium symbol **Cd**

cadre a nucleus of personnel (not ital.)

caduce/us the wand of Hermes or Mercury, pl. **-i**

caducous (bot.) tending to fall

Cædmon (d. 670) English poet, *not* Ce-

Caenozoic (geol.) *use* **Cen-**

Caermarthen *use* **Car-**

Caernarfon Gwynedd; *not* Car-, -von

Caerns. Carnarvonshire, former county in Wales

Caerphilly Mid Glam., also the cheese; in Welsh **Caerffili**

caerulean *use* ce-

Caesar/, -ean *not* Cesarian (US)

Caesarea name of several ancient cities

caesium symbol **Cs**, *not* ce- (US)

caesura a division of a metrical line, *not* ce-

CAF (US) cost and freight

café a coffee house etc. (not ital.)

café/ au lait (Fr. m.) coffee with milk, — *noir* strong coffee without milk

Caffre *use* **Kaffir** *or* **Kafir**

caftan *use* k-

cag/ey shrewd, *not* -gy; adv. **-ily**, noun **-eyness**

cagoule a waterproof outer garment, *not* ka-

cahier/ (Fr. m.) a paper book, sheets of a MS, an exercise book; — *de doléances* a register of grievances presented to the States-General in 1789 (cap.)

CAI computer-assisted (or -aided) instruction

Caiaphas a Jewish high priest, Luke 3: 2

caiman *use* **cay-**

Cainan a grandson of Seth; *see also* **Canaan**

Caine, Sir Thomas Henry Hall (1853–1931) Manx novelist

ca'ing-whale the round-headed porpoise, *not* caa-

Cainozoic (geol.) *use* **Ceno-**

caique a Bosporan skiff or Levantine sailing ship, *not* caïque

'Ça ira' ('It will be!') a French revolutionary song; lit. 'It will go!', i.e. the revolutionary process

Caius/ a Roman praenomen, *use* **Gaius** *but* abbr. **C.**; — (*properly* **Gonville and Caius**) **College**, Cambridge, pron. 'keys'; abbr. **Cai.**, **CC**

Cajan *use* **-un**

cajole/ persuade by flattery, noun **-ry** (one *l*)

Cajun a Lousianian descended from French-speaking Acadian immigrants *or* their language; *see also* **Creole**

caky *not* -ey

CAL computer-assisted learning

Cal. (California) *use* **Calif.**

cal calorie (no point)

cal. (mus.) calando; calendar

calamanco/ a woollen stuff, pl. **-es**

calamar/o (It.) a squid, pl. **-i**; the pl. form is found on most English menus for sing. or pl., often rom.; the older form, **calamary**, is still sometimes used

calando (mus.) volume and rate diminished, abbr. **cal.**

calcareous chalky, *not* -ious

calcedony *use* **chal-**

calceolaria a slipper-like flower, *not* calci-

calcium symbol **Ca**

calcspar *use* **calcite**

calculator *not* -er

calcul/us a stony concretion in the body, pl. **-i**, adj. **-ous**; a system of computation, pl. **-uses**, adj. **-ar**

Calderón de la Barca, Pedro (1600–81) Spanish playwright and poet

caldron *use* **caul-**

calecannon *use* **colc-**

calendae calends, *use* **k-**

calendar an almanac, abbr. **cal.**; *not* -er; *not* k-except in some church contexts

calend/er make smooth (cloth, paper, etc.), a machine that does this; **-erer** one who does this, *not* -ar, k-

calender (Pers., Turk.) a dervish, *not* k-

calends/ the first day of a Roman month, **the Greek** — a time that never comes; *not* k-

calf/ abbr. **cf.**; — **leather**, — **love** (two words)

calfskin (one word)

Caliban/ a character in Shakespeare's *The Tempest*; **'— upon Setebos'** a poem by R. Browning, 1864

calibre *not* -er (US)

Caliburn King Arthur's sword; *not* Cala-, Cale-; *also* **Excalibur**

calico/ pl. **-es** *not* -s

California off. abbr. **Calif.**, postal **CA**

californium symbol **Cf**

caligraphy *use* **calli-**

caliper *use* **calli-** (except in US)

caliph/ a Muslim chief civil and religious ruler (common spelling), in Arab. **ḳalīfa**; **-ate**; **kali/ f, -ph** are more learned forms

calisthenics *use* **callis-** (except in US)

cal/ix (physiol., biol.), a cuplike cavity or organ, pl. **-ices**

calk (US) = **caulk**

Callaghan, Leonard James (b. 1912) British statesman, Prime Minister 1976–9

Callander Central

called abbr. **cld.**

calligraphy *not* cali-

Calliope (Gr. myth.) the muse of eloquence and epic poetry (cap.); a steam organ at a fairground (not cap.)

calliper a metal leg-support, (pl.) compasses for measuring diameters of objects; *not* cali- (US)

Callirrhoe (Gr. myth.) the wife of Alcmaeon

callisthenics gymnastic exercises, *not* cali- (US)

callous unfeeling, insensitive; (of skin) hardened or hard

call/us thick skin, pl. **-uses**, adj. **-ous**

Calmann-Lévy publishers

calmia, Calmuck *use* **k-, Kalmyk**

Calor gas (propr.) (cap., two words)

calori/e a unit of heat or energy (not now in scientific use), abbr. **cal**; **-meter** a measurer of heat; **-motor** a voltaic battery (one word)

calotte an RC skullcap

Caltech California Institute of Technology

caltrop (mil.) a horse-maiming iron ball with spikes; *not* -throp, -trap

calumet a Native American peace pipe

calumniator *not* -er

Calvé, Emma (1866–1942) French operatic soprano

Calverleigh Devon

Calverley/ Kent, W. Yorks.; **—, Charles Stuart** (1831–84) English writer

calves-foot jelly *not* -f's, -ves', -feet

cal/x the residue from burning, pl. **-ces**

Calypso (Gr. myth.) a sea nymph in the *Odyssey*, **calypso/** a W. Indian song, usually about current affairs, pl. **-s**

caly/x (bot.) pl. **-ces**, *not* -xes

camaraderie good-fellowship

Camargue, the S. France

Camb. Cambridge

Cambodia Indo-China, *not* Kam-, -oja; in Fr. **Cambodge**

Cambrensis, Giraldus *see* **Giraldus Cambrensis**

cambric a fine white linen or cotton fabric

Cambridge/ abbr. **Camb., Cantab.**; **— University** abbr. **CU**; **— — Press** abbr. **CUP**

Cambridgeshire abbr. **Cambs.**

Cambridge University Press abbr. **CUP**

camel the two-humped Bactrian camel, *Camelus bactrianus*; cf. **dromedary**

camellia a flowering shrub, *not* -elia

camelopard (arch.) the giraffe, *not* -leo-

Camelopardalis (astr.) a northern constellation between Ursa Major and Cassiopeia

Camembert a French cheese (cap.)

cameo/ pl. **-s**

camera/ pl. **-s**; **— obscura** *not* — oscura

camera-ready copy (typ.) material ready for photographing for reproduction; (US) = **mechanical**; abbr. **crc, CRC**

Camera Stellata the Star Chamber

Cameroon/, United Republic of Cent. Africa; *not* the Cameroons; **-ian**; in Fr. **République du Cameroun**

Cammaerts, Émile (1878–1953) Belgian poet

Camões, Luís Vaz de (1524–80) Portuguese poet, *not* Camoëns; the older Eng. form is **Luiz Vas de Camoens**

camomile a medicinal plant, *not* cha- (US)

Camorra a Neapolitan secret society, practising violence and extortion; *see also* **Mafia**

Campagna di Roma the plain around Rome

campanile/ a bell tower, pl. **-s**

campbed (one word)

Campbell-Bannerman, Sir Henry (1836–1908) British statesman, Prime Minister 1905–8 (hyphen)

Campbeltown Strathclyde

Campeche/ Bay, — City, — State Mexico, *not* -peachy

campfire (one word)

camp/o (It.) open ground, pl. *-i*; *campo santo* (It., Sp.) a cemetery

campsite (one word)

Campus Martius the field of Mars in ancient Rome

CAMRA Campaign for Real Ale

Can. Canada, Canadian, Cantoris

can. canon, canto

Canaan a son of Ham; the biblical promised land; *see also* **Cainan**

Canad/a, -ian abbr. **Can.**

Canadian River Okla.

canaille (Fr. f.) the rabble, populace

canaker *use* **kanaka**

Canaletto,/ Giovanni Antonio real surname **Canal** (1697–1768) Italian painter; name also used by his nephew **— Bernardo Bellotto** (1720–80) Italian painter

canalize *not* -ise

canapé/ pl. **-s**

Canar/a, -ese *use* **K-**

canard an absurd story (not ital.)

canasta a card game

canaster a tobacco, *not* k-; cf. **canister**

cancan a high-kicking Parisian dance (one word)

cancel (typ.) incorrect matter, a new-printed leaf correcting this (its signature is preceded by *)

cancel/, -lation, -led, -ler, -ling (one l in US)

cancellate (biol.) porous, marked with cross-lines

cancelled abbr. **cld.**

Candahar *use* **K-**

candela a standard unit of light intensity, abbr. **cd**

candelabr/um pl. **-a**; also sing. **-a**, pl. **-as**

Candide, or Optimism by Voltaire, 1759

candlelight (one word)

Candlemas Day 2 Feb.

candle/power, -stick, -wick (one word)

candour *not* -or (US)

C. & W. country and western

canephor/us (archit.) a sculptured youth or maiden with a basket on the head, pl. **-i**

caneton (Fr. m.) a duckling

canister a small metal box; cf. **canaster**

cannabis Indian hemp, *not* cana- (not cap. except for the bot. genus)

cannelloni (two *n*s, two *l*s)

Cannes dép. Alpes-Maritimes, France

cannibalize *not* -ise

Canning,/ George (1770–1827) and his son — **Charles John, Earl** (1812–62) English statesmen

cannon ball (two words, one word in US)

cannon-bone (hyphen, two words in US)

cannon fodder (two words)

canoe/, -d, -ing, -ist

cañón (Sp.) a gorge, canyon

canonize *not* -ise

'Canon's Yeoman's Tale' by Chaucer

Canopic (cap. except in US)

Canosa Apulia, Italy

Canossa/ Emilia, Italy, the scene of penance of Emperor Henry IV before Pope Gregory VII, 1077; hence **to go to** — 'to eat humble pie'

Canova, Antonio (1757–1822) Italian sculptor

canst (no apos.)

Cant. Canterbury, Canticles

cantabile (mus.) in a singing, graceful style

Cantabrigian of Cambridge, *not* -dgian

Cantabrigiensis (Lat.) of Cambridge (University), abbr. **Cantab.**

cantaloupe a musk melon, *not* cante-, -loup

Cantate Psalm 98 (97 in Vulg.) as a canticle

cantatrice (Fr. and It.) a professional woman singer

cante hondo (Sp.) a mournful song

Canterbury/ abbr. **Cant.**, **— bell** a flower (one cap.)

canticle a hymn, abbr. **cant.**

Canticum Canticorum 'The Song of Songs', *also* **Canticles**; abbr. **Cant.**; same as the Song of Solomon

cantilever *not* canta-, -liver

Cantire Strathclyde, *use* **Kintyre**

canto/ a division of a long poem, a song; pl. **-s**, abbr. **can.**

Canton the capital of Guangdong Province, China; in Pinyin **Guangzhou**, in Wade–Giles **Kuang-chou**

Cantonese of Canton or the Cantonese dialect of Chinese (also called **Yue**); (of) a native of Canton (pl. same)

cantonment military quarters

cantoris of the precentor, i.e. on the north side of the choir; abbr. **Can.**

Cantor Lectures Royal College of Physicians, and Society of Arts

Cantuar. Cantuarius, Cantuariensis (of Canterbury)

Cantuar: the signature of the Archbishop of Canterbury (colon)

Cantuarian of Canterbury

cantus firmus (mus.) the basic melody in counterpoint, pl. **cantus firmi**; in It. *canto fermo*, pl. *canti fermi*

Canute Eng. variant of **Cnut**, not to be used in serious hist. work; *see also* **Knut**

canvas/ a coarse linen; **-ed, -es**

canvass/ solicit votes; **-ed, -er, -es**

canyon a gorge, in Sp. *cañón*

Can You Forgive Her? a novel by Anthony Trollope, 1864–5

caoutchouc unvulcanized rubber

CAP Common Agricultural Policy (EC)

Cap (Fr. geog. m.) Cape

cap. capital letter, chapter, foolscap

cap-à-pie from head to foot (accent, hyphens, not ital.)

Cap d'Ail dép. Alpes-Maritimes, France

Cape/ cap. when with name, abbr. **C.**; **— Breton** NS, Canada, *not* Briton, Britton, Britun, abbr. **CB**; **— Canaveral** Fl. (called **Cape Kennedy** 1963–73); **— Coloured** (S. Afr.) *see* **coloured**; **— of Good Hope** abbr. **CGH**; **— Province** (of S. Africa) abbr. **CP**

'apek,/ Josef (1887–1945) and his brother — **Karel** (1890–1938) Czech writers

capercaillie *not* -lzie

Cape Town S. Africa (two words)

Cape Verde/ Islands off W. Africa; *not* — Verd, — de Verd; **-an**

Cap Haitien Haiti

capias (law) a writ of arrest

Capital Gains Tax abbr. **CGT**

capitalize *not* -ise

capital letter abbr. **cap.**

capitals,/ large indicated in copy by three lines underneath the letter, abbr. **cap.**; **— small** abbr. (typ.) **s.c.**; **small cap.**, pl. **small caps.**; **s. cap.**, pl. **s. caps.**; *see also* **even small caps.**

Capitol the hill in ancient Rome, in Lat. **Capitolium**; the temple of Jupiter was the temple of **Capitoline Jove**; Congress building, Capitol Hill, Washington, DC

capitulary a collection of ordinances, esp. of the Frankish kings

capitulum (bot., anat.) a small head, knob

Cap'n slang abbr. of **Captain**

cappuccino coffee made frothy with milk (not ital.)

capriccio/ (mus.) a short fanciful work, pl. **-s**; adj. **-so**

caps. and smalls (typ.) set in small capitals with the initial letters in large capitals, abbr. **caps.** (or **c.**) **and s.c.**

Capsian (of) a palaeolithic culture of N. Africa and S. Europe

capsiz/e *not* -ise, noun **-al**

Captain abbr. **Capt.**

caption (typ.) descriptive matter printed above or below an illustration; (also US) heading of a chapter, page, or section

Captivity, the of the Jews (cap.)

Capuchin a Franciscan friar of the new rule of 1529, *or* a cloak and hood formerly worn by women (cap.); a S. American monkey (not cap.)

caput/ (Lat.) head, **— mortuum** the worthless residue after distillation

Car. Carolus (Charles)

car. carat

carabineer (hist.) a soldier with a carbine; *not* carb-, -ier; *but* **Carabiniers & Greys**

Carabineers, the Royal Scots Dragoon Guards

carabinier/e an Italian gendarme, pl. **-i**

Caracci a family of painters, 1550–1619; *not* Carr-

Caractacus (*fl.* AD 50) King of Silures, ancient Britain; in hist. writing *use* **Carat-**

caracul *use* **karakul**

carafe a glass container for water or wine; *not* -ff, -ffe

¡caramba! (Sp.) wonderful!, how strange! (turned exclamation mark before, unturned after)

carat a unit of weight for precious stones, 200 mg; *not* caract, caret, carrat, karat; abbr. **K.**, **car.**; cf. **caret**; **karat**

caratch *use* **kharaj**

Caravaggio, Michelangelo Merisi da (1569–1609) Italian painter

caravanserai an Eastern inn with courtyard used as halting-place for caravans; *not* -sary, -sery, -sera; *see also* **khan**

caravel a type of Spanish ship, *not* carvel

caraway *not* carra-

carbineer *use* carab-

carbon symbol **C**

carbon copy abbr. **c.c.**

carbon dating (two words)

carboniferous producing coal (not cap.); the fifth period in the Palaeozoic era (cap.)

carbonize *not* -ise

carburet/ted, **-ting, -tor** *not* -ed, -ing, -or (US), *not* -er

carcass/ *not* -ase; pl. **-es**

Carcassonne dép. Aude, France

carcinom/a a cancer, pl. **-ata**

card. cardinal

cardamom *not* -mon, -mum

Cardigan Dyfed; *see also* **Ceredigion**

card index (two words as noun, hyphen as verb)

cardphone (one word)

card-sharp (hyphen)

card table (two words)

Carducci, Giosuè (1835–1907) Italian poet

CARE Christian Action for Research and Education, computer-aided risk evaluation, Cooperative for American Relief Everywhere (*originally* Cooperative for American Remittances Europe)

careen (US) = **career** (swerve about)

carefree (one word)

carême (Fr. m.) Lent

care of abbr. **c/o**

caret an insertion mark (∧, ⋀), the mark over a letter (e.g. ê) in musical (Schenkerian) analysis; cf. **carat**; **karat**

caretaker (one word)

Carew,/ **Richard** (1555–1620) English poet, **— Thomas** (1595–?1639) English poet and courtier

car/ex a sedge, pl. **-ices**

Carey/, **Henry** (?1690–1743) English poet and composer; **—, Henry Charles** (1793–1879) US economist, son of **—, Mathew** (one *t*) (1760–1839) US publicist; **— Street** London, synonymous with the Bankruptcy Court; *see also* **Cary**

cargo/ pl. **-es**

Carib an aboriginal inhabitant of the southern W. Indies or the adjacent coasts, the language of this people

Caribbean Sea W. Indies, *not* Carr-

Cariboo Mountains BC, Canada

caribou a N. American reindeer, pl. same; *not* -boo

Caribou Highway BC, Canada

Caribou Mountain Ida.

carillon (a chime of) bells

Carington *see* **Carrington**

Carinthia Austria and Slovenia; in Ger. **Kärnten**, in Slovenian **Koroško**

carioca a Brazilian dance, the music for this; a native of Rio de Janeiro (not cap.)

cariole *use* carr-

Carisbrooke IoW

carità (It. art) a representation of maternal love

Carleton, William (1794–1869) Irish novelist

Carlile,/ **Richard** (1790–1843) English reformer and politician; **— Revd Preb. William** (1847–1942) founder of Church Army; *see also* **Carlisle**; **Carlyle**

Carliol: the signature of the Bishop of Carlisle (colon)

Carlisle/ Cumbria, **Earl of —**; *see also* **Carlile**; **Carlyle**

Carlist a supporter of the Spanish pretender Don Carlos (1788–1855)

Carlovingian *use* **Carolin-**

Carlsbad *use* Czech **Karlovy Vary**

Carlsbad Caverns National Park N. Mex.

Carlskrona Sweden, *use* **K-**

Carlsruhe Germany, *use* **K-**

Carlton Club London

Carlyle, Thomas (1795–1881) Scottish writer; *see also* **Carlile**; **Carlisle**

Carlylean *not* -eian, -ian

Carmagnola Piedmont, Italy

'Carmagnole, La' a French revolutionary song and dance

Carmarthen Dyfed, *not* Caer-; in Welsh **Caer-fyrddin**

Carnarvon/ Gwynedd, *use* **Caernarfon**; *but* **Earl of —**

Carnatic Madras, India, *not* K-

Carnaval/ a suite of piano pieces by Schumann, 1834–5; *— des animaux, le* a suite for small orchestra by Saint-Saëns, 1886; *— romain, le* overture by Berlioz, 1844; *see also* *Carnival*

'Carnaval de Venise, le' (mus.) a popular type of air and variations, early 19th c.

Carnegie/, Andrew (1835–1919) Scottish-born US millionaire and philanthropist; **— Institute** Pittsburgh, Pa.; **— Institution** Washington, DC

carnelian *use* **cor-**

carnival in Fr. m. *carnaval*, in Ger. n. *Carneval*

Carnival an overture by Dvořák, 1891; *see also* *Carnaval*

Carnoustie Tayside

carol/, -led, -ler, -ling

Carol/ine of the time of Charles I or II, *also* **-ean**

Carolingian of the Frankish dynasty of Charlemagne; *not* Carlovingian, Karl-

Carolus Lat. for Charles, abbr. **Car.**

carom (US) = **cannon** in billiards

Carothers, Wallace Hume (1896–1937) US scientist

carous/e drink heavily, **-al**

carousel (US) merry-go-round, tournament, rotating conveyor system; *not* carr-; *see also* **Carrousel, place du**

car park (two words)

Carpathian Mountains E. Europe, not K-

carpe diem (Lat.) seize the day

carpet/, -ed, -ing

carport (one word)

carp/us the wrist, pl. **-i**

Carracci *use* **Cara-**

carrageen Irish moss; *not* — moss, -gheen; from Carragheen, near Waterford

Carrantuohill Co. Kerry, the highest mountain in Ireland

Carrara N. Italy, a source of marble

carrat *use* **carat**

carraway *use* **cara-**

carriageway (one word)

Carribbean *use* **Cari-**

Carrigtohill Co. Cork (one word)

Carrington, Baron family name **Carington** (one *r*)

carriole a carriage, *not* cariole

Carroll, Lewis pseud. of **Charles Lutwidge Dodgson** (1832–98) English author

carrousel use **caro-**

Carrousel, place du Paris, from Fr. *carrousel* (m.) a tilting-match

Carrutherstown Dumfries & Galloway (one word)

carry/all, -cot (one word)

carry-on excitement, fuss (hyphen)

carry-out (US) = **take-away**

carsick (one word)

carte (fencing) *use* **quarte**

Carte, Richard D'Oyly *see* **D'Oyly Carte**

carte blanche full discretion (not ital.)

carte-de-visite (not ital.)

Cartesian *see* **Descartes**

carthorse (one word)

cartouche (archit.) a scroll ornament, (archaeol.) a ring enclosing hieroglyphic royal name; *not* -ch

cartridge paper a firm, strong paper

cart/wheel, -wright (one word)

carvel-built (naut.) with smooth planking

Carver (US) a chair with arms, a rush seat, and a back having horizontal and vertical spindles; named after **John Carver,** first Governor of Plymouth Colony in America (cap.)

carver the principal chair, with arms, in a set of dining chairs, intended for the person who carves (not cap.)

Cary,/ Alice (1820–71) and **— Phoebe** (1824–71) US sisters, poets; **— Henry Francis** (1772–1844) English translator of Dante; **— (Arthur) Joyce (Lunel)** (1888–1957) English novelist; **— Lucius** Lord Falkland (1610–43); *see also* **Carey**

caryatid/ a female figure as a column, pl. **-s**

CAS Chief of the Air Staff

Casabianca, Louis de (?1755–98) French seaman

Casablanca Morocco

Casa Grande a prehistoric ruin in Arizona; *see also* **Casas Grandes**

'Casa Guidi Windows' by Elizabeth Barrett Browning, 1851

Casals, Pau (1876–1973) Catalan cellist, in Sp. **Pablo**

Casanova de Seingalt, Giovanni Jacopo (1725–98) Italian adventurer

Casas Grandes a Mexican village with famous ruins; *see also* **Casa Grande**

Casaubon/, Isaac (1559–1614) French scholar and theologian; **—, Méric** (1599–1671) his son, clergyman; **Mr —** a character in G. Eliot's *Middlemarch*

casava *use* **cass-**

casbah *use* **k-**

case/ (bind.) bookbinding consisting of two boards joined by a flexible spine, and usually covered with cloth etc.; **upper —** (typ.) capitals; **lower —** small letters (hyphens when attrib.)

case-bound (bind.) bound in a hard cover

case history (two words)

casein milk protein, *not* -ine

case law (two words)

cases (law) abbr. **ca.**

case study (two words)

casework (one word)

cash card (two words)

Cashmer/, -e *use* **Kashmir**

cashmere a soft wool fabric; *not* -meer, cachemere, -ire; cf. **kerseymere**

cash register (US) = **till** (two words)

Casimir-Perier, Jean Pierre Paul (1847–1907) French President 1894–5 (no accent)

casine *use* **casein**

casino/ pl. **-s** (not ital.)

Caslon, William (1693–1766) typefounder, cutter of Caslon type

Cassandra a prophet of disaster, esp. one who is disregarded (from **Kassandra** (Gr. myth.))

cassata an Italian ice cream (not ital.)

Cassation, Cour de highest court of appeal in France

cassava the manioc; *not* cas-, -ave

Cassel Germany, *use* **K-**

Cassell publishers

cassimere *use* **kerseymere**; *see also* **cashmere**

Cassiopeia (astr.) a constellation

Cassivellaunus (*fl.* 50 BC) British prince

cast the actors in a play

caste a hereditary class

Castellammare Campagna and Sicily, Italy

Castelnuovo-Tedesco, Mario (1895–1968) Italian composer

caster one who casts (cf. **castor**), (typ.) a casting machine

Castil/e Spain, *not* -ille; **-ian** (of or related to) a native or the language of Castile

cast iron (noun), **cast-iron** (adj.)

Castle Cary Som.

Castlecary Central, Co. Donegal

Castlerea Co. Roscommon

Castlereagh, Robert Stewart, Viscount (1769–1822) British statesman

Castleton Borders, Derby., Gr. Manchester, Gwent, N. Yorks.

Castletown Cumbria, Dorset, Highland, IoM, Staffs., Tyne & Wear

cast off (typ.) to estimate amount of printed matter copy would make, **cast-off** the result of this estimate

castor a beaver (hence **castor oil**) or its fur, a small wheel for furniture, a small pot with perforated lid (hence **castor sugar**); cf. **caster**

Castor and Pollux stars, twins in classical myth., also patrons of sailors

castrat/o (mus.) a castrated male soprano, pl. **-i**

casual incidental, not regular; *see also* **causal**

casus/ belli (Lat.) the cause of war, **— foederis** a case stipulated by treaty, **— omissus** a case unprovided for by statute

CAT College of Advanced Technology, (typ.) computer-assisted typesetting, (med.) computerized axial (*or* computer-assisted) tomography

Cat. Catalan, Catullus

cat. catalogue, catechism

cataboli/c, -sm *not* k-

cataclasm a violent disruption

cataclysm/ a deluge, a violent event; **-al, -ic, -ist** *not* -atist

Catalan (of or relating to) (a person from) Catalonia or the language of Catalonia, abbr. **Cat.**

Catalina Sp. for **Catherine**

Cataline *use* **Catiline**

catalogu/e abbr. **cat.**; **-ed, -er, -ing**; *not* -log (US); 'Cataloging in Publication Data' is the correct spelling for Library of Congress data on the title verso of a work

catalogue raisonné an explanatory catalogue (not ital.)

Catalonia in Catalan **Catalunya**, Sp. **Cataluña**

catal/yst, -yse *not* -yze (US); **-ysis, -ytic**

catamaran a raft, a two-hulled boat

catarrh an inflammation of the mucous membrane

catarrhine narrow-nosed (of monkeys), *not* -arhine

Catawba a Native American tribe, a US variety of grape *or* wine made from it

Catch, Jack *use* **Ke-**

catch/-all, -as-catch-can (hyphens)

catchline (typ.) a short line of type containing catchword(s), signature letter, running headline, etc.

catchphrase (one word)

catchpole a sheriff's officer, *not* -poll

catch-22 an inescapable dilemma, after a novel by Joseph Heller, 1961 (not cap. except in title)

catchup *use* **ketchup**

catchword (typ.) the first word of next page printed at bottom of preceding page, word(s) printed at head of dictionary page as guide to its contents

Câteau Cambrésis, Peace of 1559

catechism teaching by question and answer, abbr. **cat.**

catechiz/e, -er, -ing *not* -is-

catechumen a convert under instruction before baptism

categorize classify, *not* -ise

caten/a a connected series of patristic comments on Scripture, a series *or* chain, pl. **-ae**

cater-cousin a good friend, *not* qua-

caters (campanology, pl.) changes on nine bells

Cath. Catherine, Catholic

cath. cathedral

Cathar/ a member of a medieval sect seeking great spiritual purity, pl. **-s** *or* **-i**

Catharine Kan., NY, Pa.; *see also* **Catherine**; **St Catharine**; **St Catherine**

cathars/is purging, pl. **-es**

Cathay poetical for China, *not* K-

cathedral cap. when with name, as Ely Cathedral; abbr. **cath.**

cathemeral (biol. adj.) applied to an organism equally active by day and by night

Catherine/ abbr. **Cath.**; **St** — hence — **pear** and — **wheel**; — **I** and **II** empresses of Russia; — **of Aragon**, — **Howard**, — **Parr** first, fifth, and sixth wives of Henry VIII of England; — **de' Medici** (1519–89) Queen of France, in Fr. — de Médicis; *see also* **Katherine**

cathisma *use* **ka-**

cathod/e a negative electrode; **-e ray tube** abbr. **CRT**; **-ic, -ograph**; *not* k-

Catholic abbr. **C.**, **Cath.**; cap. only when referring to the RC religion (the Catholic Church)

catholic/ism, -ize *not* -ise

Catiline the Eng. form of (**Lucius Sergius**) **Catilina** (108–62 BC) Roman conspirator, *not* Cata-

cation (elec.) an ion carrying positive charge of electricity, *not* k-

cat-o'-nine-tails (hyphens)

cat's/ cradle a children's game; **-eye** a precious stone (hyphen), reflective stud in road (cap., propr., hyphen)

Catskill Mountains NY

cat's-paw a person used as a tool, (naut.) a light breeze; *not* catspaw, cats-paw

catsuit (one word)

catsup *use* **ketchup**

Cattegat *use* (Dan.) **Kattegat**, (Swed.) **Kattegatt**

Cattleya an orchid genus

Catullus, Gaius Valerius (?84–?54 BC) Roman poet, abbr. **Cat.**

Cauchy, Augustin Louis (1789–1857) French mathematician

caucus a political clique, (US) a political meeting

Caudillo Sp. for 'leader', the title assumed by Gen. Franco after the Spanish Civil War

caught (cricket) abbr. **c.**

cauldron *not* cal-

caulk make watertight, *not* calk (US)

caus. causa/tion, -tive

causal having to do with a cause; cf. **casual**

causa/tion, -tive abbr. **caus.**

cause/ célèbre a famous law case, pl. **-s célèbres** (not ital.)

causerie (Fr. f.) informal article or talk, esp. on a literary subject

cauterize *not* -ise

Cavafy, Constantine (1863–1933) Greek poet, *not* K-, -is; **Konstandinos Kavafis** in a Modern Gr. transcription

Cavalleria rusticana ('rustic gallantry') an opera by Mascagni, 1890

cavass *use* **k-**

caveat a formal warning (not ital.)

caveat/ actor (Lat.) let the doer beware

caveat emptor let the buyer beware (not ital.)

caveat/ venditor (Lat.) let the seller beware, — **viator** let the traveller beware

caviar *not* -iare, -ier

cavil/ make trifling objections; **-led, -ler, -ling** (one l in US)

Cavour, Count Camillo (1810–61) Italian statesman

Cawnpore Eng. hist. form, *now* **Kanpur**

Caxton, William (c.1422–91) the first English printer

Cayenne the capital of and district in French Guiana (cap.), a type of hot pepper (not cap.)

cayman/ a type of American alligator; *not* cai-, kai-; pl. **-s**

Cayman Islands W. Indies

cazique *use* **cacique**

CB Cape Breton, Cavalry Brigade, Chief Baron, citizens' band (radio), Coal Board, Common Bench, Companion (of the Order) of the Bath, (naval) Confidential Book, confined to barracks, cost–benefit, County Borough, (mus.) *contrabasso* (double bass)

CBA cost benefit analysis, Council for British Archaeology

CBC Canadian Broadcasting Corporation

CBE Commander (of the Order) of the British Empire

CBEL *Cambridge Bibliography of English Literature* (also rom. as abbr.)

CBI Confederation of British Industry, (US) Cumulative Book Index

CC 200, Caius College, Central Committee, Chamber of Commerce, Chess Club, Circuit Court; City Council, -lor; Civil Court, Common Councilman, Companion of the Order of Canada, Consular Corps, Countryside Commission, County Clerk, County Commissioner; County Council, -lor; County Court, Cricket Club, Cycling Club

cc cubic centimetre (no points)

cc. *capita* (chapters)

c.c. carbon copy

CCC 300, Corpus Christi College, Oxford and Cambridge

CCCC 400

CCCCCC Corpus Christi College, Cambridge, Cricket Club

CCF Combined Cadet Force

C.Chem. chartered chemist

CCP Code of Civil Procedure, Court of Common Pleas, credit card purchase

C.Cr.P. Code of Criminal Procedure

CD 400, Civil Defence, compact disc

Cd cadmium (no point)

cd candela (no point)

Cd. Command Paper (1900–18) with number following

c.d. cum dividend (with dividend)

CDC Commonwealth Development Corporation (till 1963 Colonial Development Corporation)

Cdr. Commander

Cdre. Commodore (naval)

CD-ROM (comput.) compact disc read-only memory

CE Chief Engineer, Church of England, Civil Engineer

CE Common (*or* Christian) Era, used instead of AD in non-Christian contexts; follows the numerals: '250 CE', 'second century CE' (small caps.)

Ce cerium (no point)

ceasefire (noun, one word)

Ceauşescu, Nicolae (1918–89) President of Romania 1967–89

cedar a tree

ceder one who cedes; cf. **Seder**

cedilla a mark under a letter, as ç

Cedron *see* **Kidron**

Ceefax (propr.) the BBC teletext service

CEGB Central Electricity Generating Board

ceilidh (Ir. and Sc.) gathering for music, dancing, etc. and stories

Celanese (propr.) an artificial silk

cela/ va sans dire (Fr.) needless to say, — **viendra** that will come

Celebes *now* **Sulawesi**

Celebrated Jumping Frog of Calaveras County, The sketch by Mark Twain 1865

celebrator *not* -er

celestial hierarchy based on the two enumerations of St Paul, St Gregory the Great arranged the nine orders of angelic beings as seraphim, cherubim, thrones, dominations, principalities, powers, virtues, archangels, and angels; Dionysius the Pseudo-Areopagite transposed virtues and principalities

celiac (US) = **coeliac**

cellar *not* -er

Cellini, Benvenuto (1500–71) Italian goldsmith and sculptor

cell/o a violoncello, pl. **-os**; **-ist** the player

cellophane (propr.) a transparent wrapping material

Celsius a temperature scale (cap.) (*prefer to* centigrade), abbr. **C**

Celt/, -ic, -icism *not* K-, abbr. **Celt.**

celt (archaeol.) stone or metal prehistoric implement with a chisel edge (not cap.)

cembal/o a harpsichord, pl. **-os**; **-ist** the player

CEMS Church of England Men's Society

C.Eng. chartered engineer

cenobite *use* **coe-** (except in US)

Cenozoic (geol.) the most recent era of geological time; *not* Caeno-, Caino-, Kaino- (cap.)

censer an incense vessel

censor (noun) an official with power to suppress (parts of) books etc.; (verb) act as a censor

censure criticize harshly, reprove

cent/, -s a US etc. coin (no point); abbr. **c.**, **ct.**, **cts.**; symbol ¢ (the solidus may be vertical or slanted) close up to the figure, e.g. 49¢, and used only with amounts less than a dollar

cent. central, century; *see also* **per cent**

cental/ a corn measure of 100 lb, pl. **-s**; abbr. **ctl.**

centauromachy (a representation of) centaurs fighting

centaury a plant

centenarian one who is 100 years old

centen/ary a 100th anniversary; **-nial** of or relating to a centenary, (esp. US) = **centenary**

centennial (adj.) lasting for 100 years, (noun) = **centenary**

center *use* **-re** (except in US)

centering a framing for an arch, *not* -reing; *see also* **centre**

Centers for Disease Control a US national medical research facility, Atlanta, Ga.; *not* Center

centesimal reckoning or reckoned by hundredths

centi a prefix meaning one-hundredth, abbr. **c**

centigrade (not cap.) abbr. **C**, *use* **Celsius**

centigram *not* -gramme, abbr. **cg** (no point)

centilitre abbr. **cl** (no point)

centime/ one-hundredth of French franc, pl. **-s**; abbr. **c.**, **cts.**

centimetre 0.394 inch, *not* -er (US); abbr. (sing. and pl.) **cm** (no point)

Cento (hist.) Central Treaty Organization

cent/o writing composed of scraps from various authors, pl. **-os**

Central region of Scotland

central abbr. **cent.**

centralize *not* -ise

Central Provinces (India) *now* Madhya Pradesh

centr/e, -ed, -ing (typ.) set matter in middle of line, measure, etc.; *not* center- (US); *see also* **centering**

centre/board, -fold (one word)

centre-notes (typ.) those between columns

centrepiece (one word)

cents abbr. **c.**, **cts.**

centum 100, abbr. **C** (no point); *see also* **per cent**

centumvir/ a Roman commissioner, pl. **-i**

centurion the commander of a company in the Roman army, *not* -ian

century abbr. **c.** *or* **cent.**

ceorl (hist.) a freeman of the lowest rank in Anglo-Saxon England

cephalic of the head, *not* k-

Cephalonia a Greek island, ancient name **Cephallenia**; in Modern Gr. **Kefallinia**

ceramic etc., *not* k-; abbr. **ceram.**

Cerberus (Gr. myth.) the three-headed dog at the gate of Hades

cerebell/um the hind brain, pl. **-a**; adj. **-ar**

cerebro/spinal, -vascular (one word)

cerebr/um the brain proper, pl. **-a**; adj. **-al**

cere/cloths, -ments grave clothes, originally dipped in wax; *not* sere-

Ceredigion a district of Wales, *formerly* Cardiganshire

Cerenkov/, Pavel (**Alekseevich**) (1904–90) Russian physicist, discoverer of — **radiation**, created — **counter**; *not* Che-

cerge *use* **cie-**

ceriph (typ.) *use* **serif**

cerise (Fr. f.) cherry

cerise a colour

cerium symbol **Ce**

CERN (*formerly* Conseil Européen [*later* Organisation Européenne] pour la Recherche Nucléaire); *now* the European Laboratory for Particle Physics

cert (colloq.) abbr. of certainty (no point)

cert. certificate, certify

Cert. Ed. Certificate in Education

certiorari (law) a writ removing a case to a higher court (not ital. except in legal works)

cerulean blue; *not* cae-, coe-

Cervantes (**Saavedra**), **Miguel de** (1547–1616) author of *Don Quixote*

cervelas (Fr. m.) saveloy sausage

cervelle (Fr. f.) brains

Cervin/ (Fr. m.) the Matterhorn, in It. **-o**

cervi/x (anat.) pl. **-ces**, adj. **-cal**

Cesarean *use* **Cae-** (except in US)

cesare/vitch, -witch *use* **tsarevich**

Cesarewitch an annual Newmarket horse race

cesium *use* **cae-** (except in US)

cesser (law) the coming to an end

c'est/-à-dire (Fr.) that is to say, — **la guerre** it is according to the customs of war, — **le premier pas qui coûte** it is the first step that is difficult

Cestr: the signature of the Bishop of Chester (colon)

Cestrian of Chester

cestui/ que trust (law) a beneficiary, pl. **cestuis que trust** (*not* trustent); — **que vie** he on whose life land is held, pl. **cestuis que trust**

cesura *use* **cae-**

CET Central European Time

cetera/ desiderantur *or* — **desunt** (Lat.) the rest are missing

ceteris paribus (Lat.) other things being equal, abbr. **cet. par.**

Cetinje former capital of Montenegro; *not* Cett-, Zet-, -inge; *see also* **Podgorica**

Ceylon *now* **Sri Lanka**; adj. **Sri Lankan**; *see also* **Sinhalese**

Cézanne, Paul (1839–1906) French painter

CF Chaplain to the Forces

Cf californium (no point)

cf. calf, *confer* ('compare' *not* 'see') (not ital.)

c.f. carried forward

CFA Communauté Financière d'Afrique (African Financial Community)

CFC/ chlorofluorocarbon, pl. **-s** (no apos.)

CFE college of further education

CG Captain of the Guard, coastguard, Coldstream Guards

C.G. Captain General, Commissary General, Consul General

cg centigram, -s (no point)

c.g. centre of gravity

CGM Conspicuous Gallantry Medal

CGPM Conférence Générale des Poids et des Mesures (General Conference of Weights and Measures)

CGS Chief of General Staff

cgs centimetre-gram-second

CGT Capital Gains Tax, Confédération Générale du Travail (General Federation of Labour)

CH clearing house, Companion of Honour, courthouse, custom house

Ch. chaplain; Chin/a, -ese; (Lat.) *Chirurgiae* (of surgery), (mus.) choir organ, Church

ch not to be divided in most languages; a separate letter in Spanish and Welsh (following *c* in the alphabet) and Czech, Slovak, and Serbian (following *b* in the alphabet)

ch. chapter, chief; child, -ren; chorus

Chablis a white burgundy

cha-cha a ballroom dance, originally cha-cha-cha (hyphens)

chaconne a dance

chacun/ *à son goût* (Fr.) everyone to his taste (properly — *son goût*), — *pour soi* everyone for himself

Chad/ Cent. Africa; **-ian**; **Lake —** in Sudan, in Fr. **Tchad**; English saint (also spelt **Ceadda**)

chador (Ind.) a Muslim overgarment worn by women; *not* chadar, chuddar

Chagall, Marc (1889–1985) Russian painter

chaîné (ballet) a quick step *or* turn from one foot to another, or a series of these, performed in a line

chain/ gang, — mail (two words, hyphen when attrib.), — **reaction** (two words)

chain-smok/er, -ing (hyphens)

chair/, -man, -person, -woman (one word), abbr. **C.**

chaise/ longue a couch, daybed; pl. **-s longues** (not ital.)

chal (Romany) a Gypsy, f. *chai*

chalaz/a (biol.) a string attached to the yolk of an egg, pl. **-ae**

chalcedony *not* calce-, chalci-

Chald/aea Babylonia (*but* -ea in AV); **-aic, -aism** (*not* -ism), **-ean, -ee**; abbr. **Chald.**

Chaldee the language of the Chaldaeans *or* a native of ancient Chaldaea; the Aramaic language as used in OT books

chalet *not* châ- (not ital.)

Chaliapine (*strictly* **Shalyapin**), **Fyodor** (**Ivanovich**) (1873–1938) Russian bass singer

chalkboard (US) = **blackboard**

Châlons-sur-Marne dép. Marne, France; battle, 451

Chalon-sur-Saône dép. Saône-et-Loire, France

chamb. chamberlain (cap. as a title of office)

chambermaid (one word)

chamber/ music, — pot (two words)

Chambers's/ (***Edinburgh***) ***Journal*, — *Encyclopaedia***

Chambertin a dry red burgundy

chambray a gingham cloth

chambré (of red wine) brought to room temperature

chameleon a lizard of changeable colour, *not* chamae-

chamois-leather *not* shammy-

chamomile *use* cam- (except in US)

Chamonix dép. Haute-Savoie, France; *not* -ouni, -ounix, -oisny

champagne a sparkling wine from the Champagne region of France

champaign flat open country

champerty (law) an illegal agreement, *not* -arty

champignon (Fr. m.) a mushroom or toadstool, *not* -pinion

Champigny-sur-Marne a Paris suburb (hyphens)

Champlain, Lake between NY and Vt.

Champlain, Samuel de (*c.*1570–1635) French founder of Quebec, Can.

champlevé a kind of enamel

Champollion, Jean François (1790–1832) French Egyptologist

Champs-Elysées Paris

chancellery *not* -ory

chancellor (cap. as title) abbr. **chanc.**

chance-medley (law) a form of homicide (hyphen)

Chancery abbr. **Chanc.**

chancre an ulcer, esp. venereal

Chandler's Ford Hants.

Chanel, Gabrielle 'Coco' (1883–1971) French couturier

change/able, -ability

changeover (one word)

Chang Jiang Pinyin for the **Yangtze River**

channel/, -led, -ling

Channel Islands *not* Isles, abbr. **CI**

chanson/ (Fr. f.) a song, *-nette* (f.) a little song, *-nier* (m.) singer or songwriter in cabaret; — *de geste* a medieval French epic poem, pl. *-s de geste*

chant/ singing; *-er* of a bagpipe, *not* chau-

chanteuse a female singer of popular songs (not ital.)

Chantilly dép. Oise, France

Chantrey/, Sir Francis Legatt (1781–1841) sculptor; — **Fund** Royal Academy of Arts, London

chantry an endowed chapel

chanty *use* **shanty**

Chanukkah a scholarly and US var. of **Hanukkah**

chap. chapel, chaplain, chapter

chaparajos (pl.) a cowboy's leather protection for the front of the legs, *not* -ejos; abbr. **chaps**

chapatti *not* chupatty

chapbook (one word)

chapeau/ (Fr. m.) a hat, pl. *-x*; *-x bas!* hats off!; *-bras* a three-cornered hat carried under arm (hyphen)

chapel/ abbr. **chap.**; (typ.) smallest organized union group in printing and publishing offices; **father/mother of** — elected head of a chapel, abbr. **FOC, MOC**

Chapel-en-le-Frith Derby. (hyphens)

chapelle ardente (Fr. f.) a chapel lighted for a lying-in-state (no hyphen)

Chapel/ Royal pl. *-s Royal*

chaperone *not* -on, -onne

Chap.-Gen. Chaplain-General

chaplain abbr. **chap.**

Chapman, Geoffrey publisher

Chapman & Hall publishers

Chappell, William (1809–88) music publisher

chaps *see* **chaparajos**

chapter/, *-s* abbr. **c., cap., ch., chap.**

char/, *-red, -ring*

char a small trout, *not* -rr

charabanc/ a motor coach, pl. *-s*; *not* char-à-banc

characteriz/e *not* -ise; *-able, -ation, -er*

chargé *more fully* **chargé d'affaires**, pl. **chargés** (not ital.)

charisma/, adj. *-tic*, pl. *-ta*

charivari a mock serenade, *not* shivaree (US); *The London Charivari*, former subtitle of *Punch*

Charlemagne (742–814) king of the Franks from 768, Holy Roman Emperor from 800, adj. **Carolingian**

Charles abbr. **C., Chas.**

Charles's Wain (astr.) the seven stars of Ursa Major = US the Big Dipper

Charleston Ill., SC (source of the dance), W. Va.

Charlestown Mass.; Nevis Island, St Kitts-Nevis

Charlottenburg a Berlin suburb

charlotte russe (cook.) a custard or cream enclosed in sponge cake (not ital.)

Charollais a breed of cattle, *not* -olais

Charon (Gr. myth.) the ferryman of the Styx

charpoy an Indian bedstead

charr *use* **char**

chartbuster (one word)

charter/ **flight,** — **member,** — **party** (two words)

Charters Towers Queensland, Australia (no apos.)

chartreuse a liqueur first made at Carthusian monastery near Grenoble (cap. only as propr.)

Chartreux a Carthusian monk

Charybdis (Gr. myth.) a personified whirlpool supposedly in the Straits of Messina; *see also* **Scylla and Charybdis**

Chas. Charles

Chasid/, -ic *use* **Has-**

Chasles,/ Michel (1793–1880) French mathematician; — **Philarète** (1798–1873) French literary critic

chasse (Fr. f.) a liqueur taken after coffee

châsse (Fr. f.) a reliquary, a rim or frame

chassé/ (Fr. m.) a gliding dance step (not ital.), — *croisé* double chassé (ital.)

chassis a framework as of a motor car; a window sash; pl. same (not ital.)

chastis/e *not* -ize; *-ement, -ing*

chateau/ a castle, pl. *-x* (not ital., no accent)

Chateaubriand, François-René, vicomte de (1768–1848) French writer and statesman (no accent on surname)

chateaubriand (Fr. cook.) a fillet of beef, cut thick and grilled (no accent, no cap.)

Châteaubriant dép. Loire-Inférieure, France

Châteaudun dép. Eure-et-Loir, France

Châteauguay Que., Canada

Château/ Lafite, — **Latour,** — **Margaux** clarets (two words)

châteaux en Espagne (Fr.) = 'castles in the air'

chatelain/ a lord of the manor, f. *-e*

Chattanooga Tenn.; site of a battle in the US Civil War

Chatto & Windus publishers

Chaucer/, **Geoffrey** (?1345–1400) English poet, *-ian*

chaud-froid a dish of cold cooked meat or fish in jelly or sauce (not ital.)

chauffeu/r f. *-se*

chaunt/, *-er* *use* **chant** (except when copying older spelling)

chaussée (Fr. f.) a causeway, the ground level

chaussures (Fr. f. pl.) boots, shoes, etc.

Chautauqua a celebrated resort in New York State; (not cap.) (hist.) a school or similar educational course

chauvin/ism, -ist (not cap.)

Ch.B. *Chirurgiae Baccalaureus* (Bachelor of Surgery)

Ch.Ch. Christ Church, Oxford; *also* **Ch:Ch:** (after a former style of abbreviation)

Chebyshev, Pafnuti (**Lvovich**) (1821–94) Russian mathematician, *not* Tch-

Chech/nya *formerly* the Chechen-Ingushetian Autonomous Republic; **-en** a native or inhabitant of Chechnya, pl. **-ens**

check *see* **cheque**

checkers (US) = **draughts**

check/-in (noun, hyphen)

checking account (US) = **current account**

check/list, -out (one word)

check-up (noun, hyphen)

Cheddar cheese *not* -er

Cheeryble Brothers characters in Dickens's *Nicholas Nickleby*

cheese/board, -cake, -cloth (one word)

cheesy *not* -ey

cheetah *not* chet-

chef (Fr. m.) a cook; *chef/ de cuisine* head cook; — *d'orchestre* leader of the orchestra; — *d'œuvre* a masterpiece, pl. *chefs-d'œuvre*

cheir- *use* **chir-**

Cheka (hist.) Soviet 'Extraordinary Commission (against counter-revolution)', 1917–22; *see also* **KGB**

Chekhov, Anton (**Pavlovich**) (1861–1904) Russian playwright and story-writer, *not* the many variants

CHEL Cambridge History of English Literature (also rom. as abbr.)

Chelonia an order of reptiles comprising tortoises and turtles, *not* Testudinata

Chellean *use* **Abbevillian**

Chelmsford: the signature of the Bishop of Chelmsford (colon)

Chelyabinsk Siberia

chem/ical, -ist *not* chy-; abbr. **chem.**

chemical elements no point after symbols; *see also* individual entries

chemico-physical (hyphen)

chemin de fer (Fr. m.) railway, a form of baccarat

chemistry abbr. **chem.**

Chemnitz Germany, called **Karl-Marx-Stadt** under the GDR

cheque a written money order, *not* check (US)

chequer (noun) a pattern of squares; (verb) variegate, interrupt (*not* -ck-)

Chequers the Prime Minister's official country house in Bucks.

Cherbourg dép. Manche, France

chercheu/r (*associée*) (Fr. m.) (associate) researcher, f. *-se*

cherchez la femme (Fr.) lit. 'look for the woman', i.e. find the woman indirectly responsible for otherwise inexplicable acts or occurrences

chère amie (Fr. f.) a sweetheart

Cherenkov *use* **Cerenkov**

chér/i (Fr.) f. *-ie* darling

Chernenko, Konstantin (**Ustinovich**) (1911–85) General Secretary of Communist Party of the Soviet Union, President of the USSR 1984–5

Chernobyl Ukraine, the site of a nuclear accident 1986

chernozem a Russian black soil

Cherokee (of or relating to) (a member of) a Native American tribe, the language of this people

chersonese a name applied to various peninsulas, cap. when used as name (esp. of Thracian peninsula west of Hellespont)

cherub/ an angelic being, pl. **-s**, Heb. pl. **-im**; the practice in the AV of *-im* as sing. and *-s* as pl. should not be imitated

Cherubini, (**Maria**) **Luigi** (1760–1842) Italian composer

Cherwell a river, Oxon.; pron. 'char-well'

Chesapeake Bay between Md. and Va.

che sarà sarà (It.) what will be, will be

Cheshire abbr. **Ches.**

Chesil Beach Dorset

chess/board, -man (one word)

chess/ piece, — player, — problem (two words)

Chester the formal name for Cheshire, now only in hist. use, esp. in 'County palatine of Chester'

Chester-le-Street Co. Durham (hyphens)

chestnut *not* chesnut

chetah *use* **chee-**

chetniks Serbian guerrilla forces during Second World War, now used of Serbian irregulars or pejoratively of Serbian troops in general; in Serbo-Croat *četnici*

cheval/ (Fr. m.) a horse, pl. *chevaux*; — *de frise* (mil.) an obstacle to cavalry advance, usually in the pl. *chevaux de frise*

cheval glass a tall mirror on a frame

Chevalier,/ Albert (1861–1923) English music-hall artiste; — **Maurice** (1888–1972) French entertainer

chevalier/ (Fr. m.) knight, — *d'industrie* a swindler

Chevallier, Gabriel (1895–1969) French novelist

cheville a violin peg; a stopgap word in a sentence or verse

chèvre goat's-milk cheese (not ital.)

chevreau/ (Fr. m.) kid goat, pl. *-x*

chevreuil (Fr. m.) roe deer, (cook.) venison

chevrotain a deerlike animal, *not* -tin

Chevy abbr. of Chevrolet, US make of car

chevy *use* **chivvy**

Chevy Chase Md.

Chevy Chase, The Ballad of 15th-c. Eng. ballad

Cheyenne Wyo.; also a Native American tribe, the language of this people

Cheyne–Stokes respiration (en rule)

Cheyne Walk Chelsea

chez (Fr.) at the house of

chi/ the twenty-second letter of the Gr. alphabet (*X*, *χ*); **-square** a method of comparing statistical experiment with theory (hyphen)

Chi. Chicago

Chiang/ **Ching-kuo, General** (1910–88) President of Taiwan 1978–87, son of — **Kai-shek** (1887–1975) Nationalist Chinese statesman and first President of Taiwan 1950–75

Chianti an Italian wine (cap.)

chiaroscuro/ light and shade, pl. **-s**

chias/**mus** inversion in the second of two parallel phrases of the order followed in the first (e.g. 'He saved others; himself he cannot save'), **-tic**

chibouk a Turkish pipe, *not* -bouque

chic stylish(ness) (not ital.)

Chicago Ill.; abbr. **Chi.**

chiccory *use* **chicory**

Chichele Oxford professorships, *not* -ley

Chichén Itzá Mexico, site of antiquities

Chickahominy Va.

Chickamauga Ga.; battle, 1863

Chickasaw a Native American people

chickenpox (one word)

Chico Calif., often erroneously altered to Chicago in references

chicory *Chichorium intybus*, cultivated for its flowers and root; *not* chicc-; (US) = **endive**

chief abbr. **C.**, **ch.**; **Chief**/ **Accountant** abbr. **CA**; — **Baron** abbr. **CB**; — **Justice** (caps., no hyphen) abbr. **CJ**; — **of General Staff** abbr. **CGS**

chield (Sc.) a young man, *not* chiel

chiffonier a sideboard, *not* -nnier (not ital.)

chiffre (Fr. m.) figure, numeral, monogram

chignon a coil of hair

chigoe a W. Indian parasite; *not* jigger, chigger (except in dialect)

child/**bed, -birth, -care** (one word)

Childe Harold's Pilgrimage a poem by Byron, 1811–17

Childermas 28 Dec.

child/**like, -minder, -proof** (one word)

Chile/ S. America, *not* Chili; **-an**

chile *use* **chilli** (except in US)

Chilianwala Pakistan; *not* -wallah, Killian-

chilli/ a red, *or* Guinea, pepper; *not* chile, chili (US), chilly; pl. **-es**

Chiltern Hundreds (noun pl.) a Crown manor, whose administration is a nominal office for which an MP applies as a way of resigning from the House of Commons

chimaera *use* **chimera**

Chimborazo Ecuador

chimera a creation of the imagination, (biol.) an organism with two cells of two or more genetically distinct types; *not* -aera

chimere a bishop's upper robe, *not* -er

chincapin dwarf chestnut; *not* -kapin, -quapin

chin-chin a drinking toast

Chindits the British troops behind Japanese lines in Burma 1943–5

Chinese abbr. **Ch.** *or* **Chin.**

Chinese Classics the sacred books of Confucianism

chinoiserie imitation Chinese decorative objects

chin-up (US) = **pull-up**

chipmunk a N. American ground squirrel, *not* -uck

Chipping Campden Glos.

chi-rho the monogram of *XP* (☧), first letters of Gr. *Khristos*

chiromancy palmistry, *not* cheir-

Chiron (Gr. myth.) a centaur, *not* Cheir-

chiropodist one who treats hands and feet; *not* cheir-, -pedist

chiropract/**ic** removal of nerve interference by manipulation of spinal column, **-or** one who does this

Chiroptera the bat order

chirosophy palmistry, *not* cheir-

chirrup/, **-ed, -ing**

chirurgiae (Lat.) of surgery, abbr. **Ch.**

chisel/, **-led, -ling**

Chişinău cap. of Moldavia, *not* Kishinev; in Russ. **Kishinyov**

chit, chitty (Anglo-Ind.) a letter

Chittagong Bangladesh

chivvy harass; *not* che-, chivy

chlorine symbol **Cl**

chlorodyne a medicine containing chloroform, *not* -ine

chlorophyll (bot.) the green colouring matter of plants; *not* -il, -yl

Ch.M. *Chirurgiae Magister* (Master of Surgery)

chm. chairman (m. and f.)

choc. chocolate

chock/-a-block, -full (hyphens)

Choctaw (of or relating to) a Native American people, their language

choir a part of a church, singers; *not* quire

cholera morbus acute gastroenteritis

cholesterol a fatty substance found in parts of the body, *not* -in

choliamb (prosody) a Greek or Latin metre of limping character, esp. a trimeter of two iambuses and a spondee or trochee; also called **scazon**

Chomsk/y, (Avram) Noam (b. 1928) US linguist and writer, **-yan** *also* **-ian**

choosy *not* -ey

Chopin, Frédéric François (1810–49) Polish composer

'Chops of the Channel' the west entrance to the English Channel

chop suey (two words)

choreograph/y ballet design, **-er** the arranger

chorography description of districts (intermediate between geography and topography)

chorus/ pl. **-es, -ed**

chose (law) a thing

Chose, Monsieur (Fr.) Mr So-and-so

chose jugée (Fr. f.) a matter already decided

chota hazri (Anglo-Ind.) a light early breakfast

Chota Nagpur Bihar, India

chota peg a small measure of spirits (usually whisky)

chou/ (Fr. m.) cabbage, puff (pastry), a dress rosette; pl. **-x**; *-fleur* cauliflower (hyphen), pl. *choux-fleurs*; *choux de Bruxelles* Brussels sprouts; *chou marin* sea-kale

Chou En-lai in Pinyin **Zhou Enlai**

choux a rich light pastry

chow mein (two words)

Chr. Christ, Christian, Chronicles

Chr. Coll. Cam. Christ's College, Cambridge

Chrétien de Troyes (12th c.) French poet

Christ Church Oxford, *not* — — College; abbr. **Ch.Ch., Ch:Ch:** (older)

Christchurch Dorset, and NZ

Christe eleison (eccl.) 'Christ, have mercy'

christening the act of giving a Christian name during the rite of **baptism**

Christian/ -ity (cap.)

Christiania former name of Oslo, Norway (sometimes **K**-); a type of turn in skiing, abbr. **Christie**, *not* -y

Christianize *not* -ise (cap.)

Christie, Manson, & Woods auctioneers ('**Christie's**')

Christmas Day/ (caps.), **Old** — — 5 Jan. (1753–1800), 6 Jan. (1801–1900), 7 Jan. (1901–2100)

Christoff, Boris (1919–93) Bulgarian bass singer

Christ's College, Cambridge abbr. **Chr. Coll. Cam.**

chromatography (chem.) technique for separation of a mixture

chrome yellow a pigment

chromium symbol **Cr**

chromo/ (typ.) (no point) abbr. of **chromolithograph** a picture printed in colours from stone or plates, pl. **-s**

chromolithography (one word)

chromo paper one with a special heavy coating for lithographic printing

chromosome (biol.) a structure carrying genes in cell

chromosphere the gaseous envelope of the sun

chron. chronolog/y, -ical, -ically; chronometry

Chronicles, First, Second Book of (OT) abbr. **1 Chr., 2 Chr.**

chronological age abbr. **CA**

Chrononhotonthologos a burlesque drama by Henry Carey, 1734

chrysal/is pl. **-ides**

Chrysaor (Gr. myth.) the son of Neptune

Chryseis (Gr. myth.) the daughter of Chryses, a Trojan priest

chryselephantine (Gr. sculpture) overlaid with gold and ivory

Chrysler/ a US make of car, — **Building** New York City

chrysoprase green chalcedony, *not* -phrase

Chrysostom, St John (347–407) Greek patriarch

chthon/ian, -ic (Gr. myth.) dwelling in the underworld, *not* -ean

chuddar *use* **chador**

chukka a period of play in polo, *not* -er

Chunnel a portmanteau slang word for the *Channel tunnel* (cap., not in official use)

chupatty *use* **chapatti**

Chur Graubünden, Switzerland; in Fr. **Coire**

Church institutions or organizations of Christianity, e.g. the Church of England, the Methodist Church (cap.); a building for (usually Christian) worship (not cap.); in the NT 'church' (*ekklesia*, othewise trans. 'congregation' or 'assembly') is lower case, as not yet a formal title or entity; abbr. **C., Ch., ch.**

Church Assembly (*properly* National Assembly of the Church of England) set up 1920, absorbed into the General Synod 1970

Church Commissioners *formerly* Ecclesiastical Commissioners and Queen Anne's Bounty

church/goer, -going (one word)

Churchill,/ Winston (1871–1947) US writer; — **Sir Winston Leonard Spencer** (1874–1965) British statesman, Prime Minister, grandfather of — **Winston Leonard** (b. 1940) British politician

church mouse (two words)

church/warden, -yard (one word)

churinga a sacred object, esp. an amulet, among the Australian Aboriginals

Churrigueresque a lavishly ornate Spanish baroque style

chute a slide

chutney *not* -nee, -ny

chutzpah (Yiddish) shameless audacity, cheek (not ital.)

Chypre Fr. for Cyprus

chypre (Fr. f.) a heavy perfume made from sandalwood (not ital.)

CI Channel Islands, Chief Inspector, Chief Instructor, Commonwealth Institute, Communist International

Ci curie (no point)

CIA (US) Central Intelligence Agency

ciao (It.) hello, goodbye (not ital. in Eng.)

Cibber, Colley (1671–1757) Poet Laureate 1730–57

Cic. Cicero

cicad/a tree cricket; *not* cig-, -ala; pl. **-ae** (biol.), **-as** (general)

cicatri/ce a scar, pl. **-ces**; (med.) **-x**, pl. **-ces**

cicatrize *not* -ise

Cicero, Marcus Tullius, 'Tully' (106–43 BC) Roman orator, abbr. **Cic.**

cicero (typ.) Continental type-measure of 12 **Didot** points

ciceron/e a guide, pl. **-i**

Cicestr: the signature of the Bishop of Chichester (colon)

cicisbe/o (It.) a married woman's gallant, pl. **-i**

CID Criminal Investigation Department

Cid (**Campeador**), **El** (*c*.1040–99) Spanish warrior

ci-devant (Fr.) formerly

CIE Companion of the Order of the Indian Empire

Cie (Fr. abbr.) *compagnie* (company) (no point)

cierge a large candle; *not* cer-, ser-

c.i.f. cost, insurance, and freight

cigala *use* **cicada**

ci-gît (Fr.) here lies

CIGS Chief of Imperial General Staff

CII Chartered Insurance Institute

cili/um a hairlike appendage, pl. **-a**; **-ary, -ate, -ation**

cill *use* **sill**

Cimabue, Giovanni (*c*.1240–1302) Italian painter

cimbalom a dulcimer

cim/ex a bedbug, pl. **-ices**

Cimmerian intensely dark; (pl.) a nomadic people, 7th c. BC (cap.)

C.-in-C. Commander-in-Chief (no hyphens in US)

Cincinnati Ohio

Cincinnatus, Lucius Quinctius (5th c. BC) Roman hero

cine-camera (hyphen)

CinemaScope (propr., one word, two caps.)

cinematheque a film library or archive *or* a small cinema

cinéma-vérité art or process of making realistic films

cinerari/a a plant with ash-coloured foliage, pl. **-as**

cinerari/um a niche for urn with ashes of the deceased, pl. **-a**

Cingalese *use* **Sinhal-**

cingul/um a girdle *or* zone, pl. **-a**

Cinquecento 1500–99, and the Renaissance art of that century (usually cap. in It. and often in Eng.)

Cinque Ports Hastings, New Romney, Hythe, Dover, and Sandwich, plus Winchelsea and Rye

cinques (campanology pl.) changes on eleven bells

cion *use* **scion**

cipher *not* cy-

cipolin (one l) veined white and green marble; in It. **cipollino**

Cipriani, Giambattista (1727–85) Italian painter and engraver

circ. *circiter* (about), *prefer* abbr. **c.**

circa (Lat. prep.) about, in Eng. used mainly with dates and quantities; abbr. **c.** (set close up to figures)

circa mediem (Lat.) about the middle (as of a work), abbr. **circa med.**

Circean of Circe, *not* -aean *but* **Circaeus** in Lat.

circiter (Lat. adv.) about, approximately; abbr. **c.**

circle sign ○; **arc of a circle** sign ∩

Circuit Court abbr. **CC**

circuit edges (bind.) limp covers turned over to protect the leaves

circulariz/e issue circulars, *not* -ise; **-ing**

circum (Lat.) about; in Eng. used as a (roman) prefix meaning around, surrounding (no hyphen)

circumcise *not* -ize

circumflex (typ.) the accent ^

circumflexion *not* -flect-

Cirencester Glos.

cire perdue (Fr. f.) the lost-wax process of bronze-casting

cirque a (natural) amphitheatre or arena, a ring; (geol.) a hollow or gully at the head of a valley or on a mountainside (not ital.)

cirrhos/is a liver disease, pl. **-es**; 'cirrhosis of the liver' is a tautology

cirriped a marine crustacean, *not* -de

cirr/us (bot.) a tendril, (zool.) a slender append-age, (meteor.) a tuftlike cloud formation; pl. **-i**

CIS Confederation of Independent States

cis- prefix meaning 'on this side of'

cis- (chem.) a prefix denoting a type of isomer, e.g. *cis*-decalin (ital., always hyphenated); *not* syn-

cisalpine on the Roman side of the Alps (not cap. except in **Cisalpine Gaul**)

cisatlantic on this side of the Atlantic

cislunar on the side of the moon facing Earth

cispontine on the north side of the Thames; *see also* **transpontine**

cist (archaeol.) a tomb or coffin, *not* k-; cf. **cyst**

cit. citation, cited, citizen

citizens' band (radio) abbr. **CB**

Citlaltépetl a dormant Mexican volcano

citoyen/ (Fr.) f. **-ne** citizen

citrine lemon-colour(ed)

Citroën a French make of car

cittadin/o (It.) a citizen, pl. **-i**; f. **-a**, pl. **-e**

city abbr. **c.**, **the City** London's financial centre

City Company a corporation descended from an ancient trade guild (caps.)

City editor the supervisor of financial reports, *but* (US) **city editor** the editor of local news

ciudad (Sp.) city, *not* cui-

Ciudad Bolívar Venezuela, *formerly* Angostura

Ciudad Trujillo *now* **Santo Domingo**, capital of Dominican Republic

civ. civil, -ian

civics (pl. used as sing.) the study of citizenship

Civil/ Court abbr. **CC**, **— Engineer** abbr. **CE**

civiliz/e *not* -ise; **-able**, **-er**

Civil/ Servants, — Service (caps.) abbr. **CS**

Civitavecchia Italy (one word)

CJ Chief Justice

Cl chlorine (no point)

cl. class, clause, cloth; centilitre, -s (no point)

Clackmannan a district and former county of Scotland (three *n*s)

Clairaut, Alexis Claude (1713–65) French mathematician, *not* -ault

claire-cole *use* **clearcole**

clairvoyant/ f. **-e** (not ital.)

clam/ to clog, smear; **-miness, -my**

clamjamphrie (Sc.) rubbish, a mob; *not* the many variants

clam/our *not* -or (US), *but* **-orous**

clampdown (noun, one word)

clang/our *not* -or (US), *but* **-orous**

Claparède, Jean Louis (**René Antoine Édouard**) (1832–70) Swiss naturalist

claptrap empty words (one word)

claque/ hired applauders, **-ur** a member of a claque (not ital.)

clar. (mus.) clarinet, (typ.) clarendon

clarabella (mus.) an organ stop, *not* clari-

Clarenceux (her.) the second King of Arms (q.v.), *not* -cieux

Clarendon/ Press named after **— Building** a former printing house of the University Press at Oxford; hence an imprint on certain learned books published by OUP

claret red wine of Bordeaux

clarinet/, -tist *not* -ionet, -ist; abbr. **clar.**

Clarissa Harlowe the heroine of the novel *Clarissa* by S. Richardson, 1748

class abbr. **cl.**

class. classic, -al; classification

classes (bot., zool.) (typ.) to be in roman with capital initials

classic of acknowledged excellence, remark-ably typical, outstandingly important, *or* simple and harmonious, as in art, music, etc.

classical of ancient Greek or Latin literature or art, or having the linguistic form used by ancient standard authors; serious or con-ventional *or* following traditional principles; within disciplines *classical* may have a sense that is more temporal and less qualitative: in music studies 'classical music' refers to the period after Baroque and before Romantic; in Greek studies 'classical Greek' is Hellenic (rather than modern or Byzantine)

clause (typ.) lower case as part of a name, e.g. 'clause 3.2'; abbr. **cl.**, pl. **cll.**

Clausewitz, Karl von (1780–1831) Prussian military writer

clayey of the substance of clay

cld. called, cancelled, cleared (goods or ship-ping), coloured

clean (typ.) said of proofs or revises with few errors, or pulled after matter has been cor-rected

clearcole (noun and verb) (to paint with) a coating of size, *not* claire-

clear-cut (adj., hyphen)

clear days time to be reckoned exclusive of the first and last

cleared (goods or shipping) abbr. **cld.**

clear/-eyed, -headed (hyphens)

clearing bank (two words)

clearing house (two words, one word in US) abbr. **CH**

clear-sighted (hyphen)

clearstory *use* **clere-**

clearway (one word)

clef (mus.) three are in use: the C clef 𝄡 (movable), the treble clef 𝄞, and the bass clef 𝄢

cleistogam/ic, -ous (bot.) permanently closed and self-fertilizing, *not* k-

Clemenceau, Georges Eugène Benjamin (1841–1929) French politician, *not* Clé-

Clemens, Samuel Langhorne (1835–1910) US writer, pseud. **Mark Twain**

clench secure (a nail or rivet), grasp firmly; the action or result of these; cf. **clinch**

clepsydra/ an ancient water clock, *not* k-; pl. **-s**

cleptomania *use* k-

clerestory (archit.) the upper part of wall with row of windows, *not* clear-

clerihew a short comic verse on a famous person

clerk abbr. **clk.**

Clerke, Agnes Mary (1842–1907) English astronomer

Clerk-Maxwell, James *see* **Maxwell, James Clerk**

Clerk/ of the Closet, — of Parliaments, — of the Peace abbr. **CP, — of the Privy Council** abbr. **CPC** (caps.)

Clermont-Ferrand dép. Puy-de-Dôme, France (hyphen)

Cleveland a county of England

clevis/ a U-shaped iron at end of beam for attaching tackle, pl. **-es**

clew a ball of thread, (naut., verb *or* noun) (draw up) the lower corner of a sail; cf. **clue**

cl. gt. (bind.) cloth gilt

cliché (typ.) a block or stereotype, hackneyed phrase or opinion

clicker (typ.) the former title of foreman of a companionship

Clicquot, Veuve a brand of champagne

clientele clients collectively (no accent, not ital.)

cliffhang/er, -ing (one word)

climacteric/ (pertaining to) a critical period, **grand —** the age of 63

climactic pertaining to a climax

climatic pertaining to climate

clinch make fast a rope in a special way, embrace, settle conclusively; the action or result of these; cf. **clench**

clincher-built *use* **clinker-**

***Clinker, Humphrey** *not* -ey, a novel by Smollett 1771

clinometer an instrument for measuring slopes, *not* k-

Clio (Gr. myth.) the muse of history

cliometrics (pl. used as sing.) a statistical method of historical research

clippings (US) = **cuttings** (from a newspaper etc.)

cliqu/e, -ish, -ism, -y *not* -eish, -eism, -ey (not ital.)

clish-ma-claver (Sc.) gossip (hyphens)

C.Lit. Companion of Literature

Clitheroe Lancs.

clitor/is (anat.) a part of the female genitalia, **-al**

clk. clerk

cll. clauses

Cllr. Councillor

Cloaca Maxima the major sewer of ancient Rome (caps.)

cloche (hort.) a translucent cover for plants, a woman's close-fitting hat (not ital.)

clock/ face, — radio, — tower (two words)

clock/wise, -work (one word)

cloff an allowance on commodities, *not* clough

***cloisonné** (Fr.) a kind of enamel finish

close (typ.) the second of any pair of punctuation marks, as ']); pron. 'kloze'

close/ up (typ.) push together, remove spacing; **— matter** unleaded *or* thinly spaced

close-up (noun)

closure a stopping, esp. of debate in Parliament; in Fr. f. *clôture*

Clos Vougeot a burgundy

clotbur (bot.) burdock; *not* clote-, cloth-

clote (bot.) burdock and similar burry plants, *not* clote bur

cloth/ abbr. **cl.; — of Bruges** gold brocade

Clotho (Gr. myth.) the Fate that draws the thread of life

***clôture** (Fr. f.) closure

***clou** (Fr. m.) point of chief interest

cloud-cuckoo-land in general senses, hyphens, no cap.; in direct reference to Aristophanes' *Birds*, one word, one cap.

cloudy (meteor.) abbr. **c.**

clough a ravine

clove hitch a knot (two words)

cloze text a comprehension exercise

clubbable sociable

club foot a congenital malformation (two words, one word in US)

club/house, -land (one word)

club line (typ.) *see* **orphan**

clue information to be followed up; cf. **clew**

Cluniac (a monk or nun) of a branch of the Benedictine order stemming from Cluny, France

Clwyd a river and county, N. Wales

Clydebank Strathclyde

Clytaemestra (Gr. myth.) the wife of Agamemnon, *also* **Klytaimestra** (in Gr. contexts); do not impose the trad. Eng. spelling **Clytemnestra** (with an *n*), but do not alter in hist. contexts

CM Certified Master *or* Mistress, *Chirurgiae Magister* (Master of Surgery), (mus.) common metre, Corresponding Member, Member of the Order of Canada

Cm curium (no point)

Cm. Command Paper (1986–) with number following

c.m. *causa mortis* (by reason of death)

cm centimetre(s) (no point)

Cmd. Command Paper (1919–56) with number following

cmdg. commanding

Cmdr. Commander

Cmdre. Commodore

CMG Companion of (the Order of) St Michael and St George

Cmnd. Command Paper (1956–86) with number following

CMP Commissioner of the Metropolitan Police

CMS Church Missionary Society

CNAA Council for National Academic Awards

CND Campaign for Nuclear Disarmament

Cnossus *use* **Knossos**

cnr. corner

Cnut (995–1035) king of Norway, Denmark, and England; this more correct (OE) form of **Canute** is favoured by historians; *see also* **Knut**

CO Colorado (postal abbr.), Commanding Officer, conscientious objector, criminal offence, Crown Office

Co cobalt (no point)

Co. Colón, Company, County

c/o care of

coad. coadjutor

coaetaneous *use* **coe-**

coagul/um a clot, pl. **-a**

Coalbrookdale Shropshire

coal dust (two words)

coal/face, -field, -man (one word)

coal mine/, -r (two words)

coalmouse (ornith.) the coal titmouse, *not* cole-

coal pit (two words)

Coalville Leics.

Coast, the (US) the Pacific coast of the USA, usually California

coastguard an individual *or* the organization (one word), abbr. **CG**

coat of arms (three words), *properly* **achievement of arms**

co-author acceptable as a noun, to be avoided as a verb (hyphen)

coaxial (one word)

cobalt symbol **Co**

Cobbe, Frances Power (1822–1904) British social writer

coble boat, *not* cobble

Coblen/ce, -z Germany, *use* **Koblenz**

COBOL (comput.) common business oriented language; caps. *or* even small caps.

cobra de capello an Indian snake; *not* da, di

Coburg/ Ia.; Saxe- — Germany; *not* -ourg, -urgh

coca a S. American shrub, the source of cocaine; cf. **cocoa**

Coca-Cola (propr.) abbr. **Coke** (cap.)

Cocagne *use* **Cockaigne**

cocaine *not* -ain, popular abbr. **coke** (not cap.)

cocco (bot.) a Jamaican plant tuber; *not* coco; cf. **cocoa**; **coca**

coccy/x (anat.) the end of the spinal column, pl. **-ges**

cochle/a the ear cavity, pl. **-ae**

cochon de lait (Fr. m.) sucking pig

Cockaigne an imaginary land of luxury and idleness, the 'land of cakes'; in the 19th c. applied humorously to London as the country of the cockneys; *not* Cocagne, Cockayne

cock-a-leekie (Sc.) a soup; *not* cockie-leekie, cocky-leeky

cockatiel a small crested Australian parrot, *not* -teel

cockatoo/ a large crested Australian parrot, pl. **-s**

cockatrice a fabulous serpent

Cockcroft, Sir John Douglas (1897–1967) British nuclear scientist

Cocker, Edward (1631–75) reputed author of *Arithmetic*, thus **'according to Cocker'**, accurate

cockney a native of E. London, esp. one born within the sound of Bow Bells (not cap.)

cockscomb a plant; *see also* **coxcomb**

cockswain *use* **cox-**

Cocles, Horatius (Rom. hist.) kept the Sublician Bridge

cocoa a tropical palm tree bearing coconut; cf. **cacao**; **cocco**

COCOM Coordinating Committee for Multinational Export Controls

COCOMO (comput.) constructive cost model, *also* **CoCoMo**

coconut *not* coker-

Cocos Islands (**Keeling Islands**) Bay of Bengal, an external territory of Australia

cocotte a small dish, (arch.) a prostitute

Cocytus a river in Hades

COD cash on delivery

COD *Concise Oxford Dictionary*

cod. codex

CODASYL Conference on Data Systems Languages

Code Napoléon (Fr. m.) a civil code promulgated 1804–11

cod/ex an ancient MS, abbr. **cod.**; pl. **-ices**, abbr. **codd.**

codfish (one word)

codling a small cod, an elongated apple

cod liver oil (three words)

Cody, William Frederick, 'Buffalo Bill' (1846–1917), US frontiersman and showman

co-ed (a girl at a) co-educational (institution), (no point; hyphen, one word in US)

co-education/, -al (hyphen, one word in US)

coefficient (one word)

coelacanth a large bony marine fish, formerly thought to be extinct

Coelebs in Search of a Wife a novel by Hannah More, 1809, *but* **caelebs** Lat. for bachelor

Coelenterata a zool. phylum (not ital.)

coeliac abdominal, *not* ce-

coenobite a member of a monastic community, *not* cen- (US)

co-equal (hyphen, one word in US)

coerulean *use* ce-

coetaneous of the same age, *not* coae-

coeternal (one word)

Cœur de Lion Richard I of England ('the Lionheart'), *or* Louis VIII of France (no hyphens)

coeval of the same age (one word)

coexist/, -ence (one word)

coextensive (one word)

C. of E. Church of England

coffee/ bar, — bean, — cup, — house, — pot, — table (two words)

cofferdam a watertight enclosure

cogito, ergo sum (Lat.) I think, and therefore I exist (the motto of Descartes)

cognac a high-quality brandy (not cap.)

cognate abbr. **cog.**

cogniz/e become conscious of, *not* -ise; **-able, -ance, -ant**

cognoscent/e (It.) a connoisseur, pl. **-i**; *not* con-

cognovit (**actionem**) (law) an acknowledgement that the action is just

coheir/, -ess (one word)

COHSE Confederation of Health Service Employees

COI Central Office of Information

COID Council of Industrial Design, *now* Design Council

coiff/eur, f. **-euse** hairdresser; **-ure** (f.) headdress, hairstyle (not ital.)

coign of vantage a favourable position

Cointreau (propr.) an orange-flavoured liqueur (cap.)

Coire Graubünden, Switzerland; *use* **Chur**

coits *use* **quoits**

Coke abbr. for **Coca-Cola** (cap.)

coke popular abbr. for **cocaine** (not cap.)

Coke, Sir Edward (1552–1634) Lord Chief Justice of England, pron. 'cook'

cokernut *use* coco-

Col. Colonel, Colossians

col. colonial, column

cola a W. African tree and its seed, *not* k-

colander a strainer; *not* colla-, culle-

colcannon an Irish dish; *not* cale-, cole-

cold composition *see* **hand-setting**

Cold Harbor Va.; scene of three Civil War battles

Cold Harbour Lincs., Oxon.

Coldharbour Dorset, Glos., Surrey

cold/ metal, — type (typ.) sorts cast up for hand composition or correction; (compositing) *see* **strike-on**

Coldstream/ a town, Borders; **— Guards** *not* The Coldstreams, abbr. **CG**

cold war, the (not caps.)

colemouse *use* coal-

Coleoptera (zool.) the beetles

cole-pixy *use* **colt-pixie**

Colerain NC

Coleraine Co. Londonderry

Coleridge,/ Hartley (1796–1849) English minor poet and critic, son of next; **— Samuel Taylor** (1772–1834) English poet and critic; **— Sara** *not* -ah (1802–52) English writer

Coleridge-Taylor, Samuel (1875–1912) English composer

coleslaw (one word)

Colette pseud. of **Sidonie Gabrielle Claudine Colette** (1873–1954) French writer

colic/, -ky

Coligny, Gaspard de (1519–72) French Huguenot leader

Coliseum London theatre; *see also* **Coloss-**

coliseum a large stadium

coll. colleague; collect/ed, -ion, -or; college

collage art composition with components pasted onto a surface

collander *use* **colan-**

colla/ parte *or* **— voce** (mus.) adapt to the principal part or voice; abbr. **col. p.**, **col. vo.**

collapsar (astron.) an old star that has collapsed to form a white dwarf, neutron star, or black hole; *not* -er

collapsible *not* -able

coll'arco (mus.) with the bow

collar of SS *see* **SS, collar of**

collat. collateral, -ly

collat/e, -or *not* -er

colla voce *see* **colla parte**

colleague abbr. **coll.**

collect. collectively

collectable *not* -ible

collectanea (Lat. pl.) collected notes

collect/ion, -or abbr. **coll.**

collections/ an examination at some universities

college abbr. **coll.** (cap. when used as part of name)

Collège de France (m.)

College of Arms abbr. **CA**

College of Justice (Sc.) supreme civil courts

collegi/an a member of a college, **-ate** belonging to a college

collegi/um an ecclesiastical body uncontrolled by the State, pl. *-a* (not cap., ital.); the name for the orchestra at some US universities (cap., not ital.)

col legno (mus.) with the wood of the bow

Colles fracture (med., of the wrist)

collie a dog, *not* -y

Collins a letter of thanks for hospitality (from the character in Austen's *Pride and Prejudice*)

collogue talk confidentially

collop a piece of meat

colloq. colloquial, -ly, -ism

colloqui/um a conference, pl. **-a**

colloqu/y talk, pl. **-ies**; **-ize** *not* -ise

collotype (typ.) a printing process

Colo. Colorado (off. abbr.)

Cologne Germany, in Ger. **Köln**

Colombia, Republic of S. America; *see also* **Colu-**

Colombo capital of Sri Lanka, *not* Colu-

Colón Cent. America, abbr. **Co.**; *see also* **Columbus**

Colonel/ abbr. **Col.**; **— Blimp** a pompous, jingoistic person; **— Bogey** (golf) the imaginary good player, eponymous subject of a marching song (ital.)

colonial abbr. **col.**

coloniz/e *not* -ise; **-able, -ation**

colonnade a row of columns

colophon (typ.) publisher's device or imprint

colophony rosin

color *use* **colour** (except in US)

Colorado off. abbr. **Colo.**, postal **CO**

coloration *not* colour-

Colosseum Rome, *properly* the **Flavian Amphitheatre**; *see also* **Colis-**

Colossians (NT) abbr. **Col.**

coloss/us pl. **-i**

Colossus of Rhodes (cap.)

Colour, Trooping the *not* Colours

colourant *not* color- (US)

coloured/ (S. Afr.) of Asian or mixed ancestry, speaking Afrikaans or English as the mother tongue (adj.); **-s** Cape Coloured people (cap.); *see also* **black**

colourist *not* colorist (US)

Colour-Sergeant *not* -jeant; abbr. **Col.-Sgt.**, **Col.-Sergt.**

col. p. (mus.) **colla parte**

colporteur a hawker of books, esp. bibles (not ital.)

Colquhoun pron. 'ko-hoon' (stress on second syllable)

colt abbr. **c.**

colter *use* **cou-** (except in US)

colt-pixie a mischievous fairy, *not* cole-pixy

colubrine snakelike

columbari/um a dovecote; a place for cremation urns; pl. **-a**

Columbia, British Canada, abbr. **BC**

Columbia, District of USA, abbr. **DC** (no points); comma precedes: 'Washington, DC'; *see also* **Colo-**; **Washington**

columbium *now* **niobium**

Columbo *use* **Colombo**

Columbus, Christopher (1451–1506) Genoese navigator, in Sp. **Cristóbal Colón**

column abbr. **col.**

colure (astr.) each of two great circles of the celestial sphere

Colville of Culross, Viscount

col. vo. (mus.) **colla voce**

COM computer output on microfilm *or* microfiche

Com. Commander, Communist

com. comedy, comic, commercial; commission, -er; committee; common, -er, -ly; commun/e, -ity; communicat/e, -ed, -ion

coma/ (med.) stupor, pl. **-s**; (astr.) the nebulous envelope round head of comet, (bot.) a tuft of hair; pl. **-e**

comb. combin/e, -ed, -ing

combat/, -ed, -ing, -ive

Combermere, Viscount

combin/e, -ed, -ing abbr. **comb.**

Comdr. Commander

Comdt. Commandant

come-at-able accessible (hyphens)

come back (verb, two words; noun, one word)

Comecon Council for Mutual Economic Assistance, a former economic association of Communist countries

Comédie-Française, La official name of **Le Théâtre français** (caps.)

Comédie Humaine, La a series of novels by Balzac, 1842–8

comédien/ (Fr.) actor, f. **-ne**

comedy abbr. **com.**

comedy of manners (no caps.)

come/ prima (mus.) as at first; **— sopra** as above, abbr. **co. sa.**

comfit (arch.) a sweet consisting of a nut, seed, etc., coated in sugar; cf. **confit**

comfrey (bot.) any of various plants of the genus *Symphytum*; *not* cum-

comic abbr. **com.**

comillas (Sp. f.) quotation marks « », equivalent to guillemets

Comintern the Communist (Third) International 1919–43; *not* Kom-

comitadji a band of irregulars in the Balkans; *not* k-, -aji

comitatus (Lat.) a retinue, a county or shire; pl. same

comitia (Lat. pl.) a Roman assembly

Comitia/ (pl.) a meeting of the Senate of Dublin University; **— Aestivalia** the same in summer; **— Hiemalia** the same in winter; **— Vernalia** the same in spring

comity of nations international courtesy

Comm. (naval) Commodore

comm. commentary, commerce, commonwealth

commandant abbr. **comdt.**

commandeer seize for military or other service

Commander/ abbr. **Cdr.** (Admiralty), **Com.**, **Comdr.**; **-in-Chief** (hyphens) abbr. **C.-in-C.**; **— of the Faithful** a title of a caliph

commanding abbr. **cmdg.**, **Commanding Officer** abbr. **CO**

commando/ (a member of) a body of troops, esp. shock troops; pl. **-s**

Command Paper a paper laid before Parliament by command of the Crown; abbr. **C.** (1870–99), **Cd.** (1900–18), **Cmd.** (1919–56), **Cmnd.** (1956–86), **Cm.** (1986–), with number following

comme ci, comme ça (Fr.) indifferently, so-so

commedia dell'arte Italian Renaissance comedy

comme il faut (Fr.) as it should be, properly

Commemoration at Oxford, an annual ceremony in memory of founders and benefactors

commencement the ceremonial conferring of university degrees, as at Cambridge and US universities (often cap. as the name of the ceremony)

commendam an ecclesiastical benefice held *in commendam*, i.e. without duties

commentary abbr. **comm.**

commentator *not* -er

commerce abbr. **comm.**

commère a female compère (not ital.)

commingle *not* comingle

Commissary-General (hyphen) abbr. **CG**

commission/, **-er** abbr. **com.**

commissionaire a uniformed door-attendant (not ital.); the Fr. m. **commissionnaire** is less specific in meaning

commit/, **-ment, -table** (*not* -ible), **-tal, -ted, -ting**

committee (collective sing., with sing. verb), abbr. **com.**

committ/er one who commits, **-or** (law) a judge who commits someone to the care of a **-ee** (stress on final syllable)

Commodore (naval) abbr. **Cdre, Cmdre, Comm.**

common/, **-er, -ly** abbr. **com.**

Common Bench abbr. **CB**

common law (two words, hyphen when attrib.)

Common Market *now* **European Community**

common metre (mus.) abbr. **CM**

commonplace/ (adj.) (one word), **— book** (two words)

Common Pleas abbr. **CP**

common sense noun, hyphen when attrib.

commonsensical (adj.) (one word)

Common Serjeant *not* -geant; abbr. **CS, Com.-Serj.**

common stock (US) = **ordinary shares**

common time (mus.) abbr. **C**

Common Version (of the Bible) abbr. **CV, Com. Ver.**

commonwealth (cap. when part of name) abbr. **comm.**

Commonwealth (Austral.) abbr. **Cwlth**

Commonwealth, the *not* the British Commonwealth

Communard (hist.) a supporter of the Paris Commune (cap.)

communard a member of a commune

Commune, the (hist.) communalistic government in Paris in 1871 (cap.)

commune a communal group (esp. sharing accommodation), a small territorial division (France and elsewhere); abbr. **com.**

communicat/e, -ed, -ion abbr. **com.**

communications satellite *not* -ation (two words)

communiqué an official report

Communis/m the specific communistic form of society established in the former USSR and elsewhere, *or* any movement or political doctrine advocating communism; **-t** a member of a Communist Party (cap.)

communis/m the political theory derived from Marx, **-t** a person advocating or practising the general theories of communism (not cap.)

Communist/ abbr. **Com.**, **— Party** abbr. **CP**

communize make common, *not* -ise

commutator an apparatus for reversing electric current

commuter one who travels regularly to work in a town

Comor/o Islands Indian Ocean, indep. 1975; adj. **-an**

comp. comparative, comparison; compil/e, -ed, -er, -ation; compos/er, -ite, -ition, -itor; compounded

compagnie (Fr. f.) company, abbr. *Cie*

compagnon de voyage (Fr. m.) travelling companion

Companies Act (no apos.)

companionship (typ.) the former name of a group of compositors working together under a clicker (q.v.), abbr. **'ship**

company abbr. **Co.**, (mil.) **Coy.** (point); *see also* *compagnie*

comparative abbr. **comp.**

compare abbr. **cf.** (*confer*) or **cp.**

comparison abbr. **comp.**

compass points (typ.) not caps. unless part of an accepted geographical designation: *the mysterious East, the West End, Northern Ireland, the South Bronx* (*but* e.g. *the south of the Bronx*); the compound points, when printed in full, to be hyphenated: *south-south-east* (*but* in US *south-southeast*); no points for abbreviation of compound points: *SSE*

compendi/ous comprehensive but fairly brief; **-um** pl. **-a**

compère a master of ceremonies

competit/or f. **-ress**

Compiègne dép. Oise, France

compil/e, -ed, -er, -ation abbr. **comp.**

complacen/t self-satisfied, **-cy**

complaisan/t obliging, **-ce**

Compleat Angler, The by Izaak Walton, 1653

complement (verb and noun) make complete, that which makes complete

completor/ium (Lat.) compline, pl. **-a**

complexion *not* -ction

compliment (to) praise, flatter(y)

compline the last service of the day (RC), *not* -plin

compos/er, -ite, -ition, -itor abbr. **comp.**

compos mentis (Lat.) in one's right mind

compote stewed fruit

compound/, -ed abbr. **comp.**

compound ranks *or* **titles** each main word to be cap., as Assistant Adjutant-General, Vice-President

comprehensible that can be understood, intelligible; *not* -able

comprehensive complete; including all or nearly all elements, aspects, etc.

compromise *not* -ize

compte/ (Fr. m.) an account; **— rendu** official report, pl. **-s rendus**

Comptes Rendus reports of the French Academy (caps.)

Compton-Burnett, Dame Ivy (1884–1969) English novelist (hyphen)

comptroller retain when citing official title that has it, otherwise *use* **controller**

Comptroller-General of the National Debt Office, Comptroller-General of the Patent Office (caps., hyphen)

computer *not* -or

computerize *not* -ise

Com. Serj. Common Serjeant

Comsomol *use* **K-**

Comt/e, Auguste (1798–1857) French philosopher; **-ian, -ism, -ist**

comte (Fr.) a count, f. **comtesse** (not cap.)

Con. Consul

con/ to direct a ship's course, *not* -nn (US); examine, swindle; *not* -un; **-ning**

con. conclusion, conics, conversation

con. contra (against, in opposition to)

Conakry Guinea

con amore (It.) with affection (not ital. in mus.)

Conan, Laure pseud. of **Marie-Louise-Félicité Angers**

con brio (mus.) with vigour

conc. concentrat/ed, -ion

Conceição the name of many places in Portugal and Brazil

concensus *use* **conse-**

concentre *not* -er (US)

Concepción the name of many Cent. and S. American places (*but* **Conceição** in Brazil)

Concertgebouw Orchestra Amsterdam

concert-go/er, -ing (hyphen, one word in US)

concert hall (two words)

concertina/, -s, -ed *not* 'd, **-ing**

concertino/ (mus.) a group of soloists, a short concerto; pl. **-s**

concert master (two words)

Concert/*meister, -stück* (Ger. mus.) *now* **Konzert-** (cap.)

concerto/ (mus.) pl. **-s** (but **concerti grossi**), abbr. **cto.**

concessionaire a holder of a concession or grant (not ital.), in Fr. m. *concessionnaire*

conch/ a shell, pl. **-s**

conch. conchology

conchie *not* -y; *see* **conscientious objector**

concierg/**e** a caretaker, **-erie** (no accent) a caretaker's flat

Conciergerie, La a former Paris prison

concinnity elegance or neatness of literary style

concision conciseness (esp. of literary style)

conclusion abbr. **con.**

Concord Calif., Mass., NC, NH

concordance an index of words or phrases used in a book or by an author

concordat an agreement (not ital.)

Concorde a make of aircraft

concours/ (Fr. m.) a competition, — *d'élégance* parade of vehicles

concur/, **-red, -ring**

conde (Sp., Port.) a count, *not* -dee

Condé, Louis II de Bourbon, Prince de, 'The Great' (1621–86) French general

condensed type a narrow typeface

condominium (law) the joint control of a State's affairs by other States, (US) a building complex containing individually owned flats or houses

condottier/*e* (It.) a captain of mercenaries, pl. *-i*

conductor *not* -er, abbr. **c.**

conduct/*us* (medieval mus.) pl. *-uses* or *-ûs*, *not* -i

con espressione (mus.) with expression, *not* ex-; abbr. **con esp.**

coney *use* **cony**

Coney Island NY

conf. conference

confection/**ery** (noun), **-ary** (adj.)

Confederacy (US hist.) the league of seceding states in the Civil War

Confederation of Independent States abbr. **CIS**

confer/, **-red, -ring, -rable, -rer** *but* **-ee, -ence, -ment**

confer (Lat.) compare, abbr. **cf.** (not ital.)

conference abbr. **conf.**

conférence (Fr. f.) lecture

Confessio Amantis a poem by Gower, 1393

confetti bits of coloured paper etc.

confidant/ a trusted friend, f. **-e**

confit/ (Fr. m.) a preserve or conserve, either sweet or savoury; **-ure** (Fr. f.) jam, or preserves; cf. **comfit**

confrère a colleague (not ital.)

Confucius (551–479 BC) Chinese sage; latinized as **Kongfuze** (Pinyin), **K'ung Fu-tzŭ** (Wade–Giles)

con fuoco (mus.) with passion

cong. congregation, -al, -alist, -ist; congress, -ional

congé/ (Fr. m.) leave, dismissal; — *d'élire* leave to elect, *not* — *de lire*

Congo, Democratic Republic of Cent. Africa, *was* **Zaire** 1971–97

Congo/, **Republic of the** Cent. Africa, *formerly* French Middle Congo, People's Republic of the Congo; **-lese**

congou a black tea; *not* -o, kongo

congregation/, **-al, -alist** (cap. as religious denomination) abbr. **cong.**

Congresbury Avon

Congress India, the political party; US, the legislative body (cap.); spell out the number, as 'fifty-fourth Congress', not '54th'

congress/, **-ional** abbr. **C., cong.**

conics the geometry of the cone and its sections, abbr. **con.**

conjugation the inflections of a verb, abbr. **conj.**

conjunction connection, abbr. **conj.**; (astr.) apparent proximity of two heavenly bodies, symbol ☌

conjunctiv/**a** the mucous membrane between eyelid and eyeball, pl. **-ae** (not ital.); **-itis** an inflammation of this

conjuror a magician, *not* -er

con moto (mus.) with movement

Conn. Connecticut (off. abbr.)

Conna Co. Cork

Connacht a province of Ireland containing the counties of Galway, Leitrim, Mayo, Roscommon, and Sligo

Connah's Quay Clwyd

connect/**er** one who connects, **-or** that which connects

Connecticut off. abbr. **Conn.**, postal **CT**

connection *not* -xion except in use by Wesleyans and other related Methodist associations to describe the concept of 'religious society' or 'denomination'; also for Lady Huntingdon's Connexion

connivance tacit assent, *not* -ence

connoisseur a well-informed judge in matters of taste (not ital.)

connotation that which is implied by a word, phrase, etc. in addition to its literal or primary denotation

conoscente *use* **cogno-**

conquistador/ a conqueror, esp. of Mexico and Peru; pl. **-es** (not ital.)

Conrad, Joseph pseud. of **Teodor Józef Konrad Korzeniowski** (1857–1924) Polish-born English novelist, *not* K-

Cons. Conservative

cons. consecrate(d), conservation, consonant, constable; constitution, -al

Conscience, Hendrik (1812–83) Belgian novelist

conscience' sake *not* -e's

conscientious objector abbr. **CO**, (First World War colloq.) **conchie**

consenescence general decay

consensus/ *not* -census, -pl. **-es**

Conservative cap. when referring to specific groups so called, e.g. the British political party, or to Conservative Judaism; lower case for other meanings: conservative in dress; a conservative estimate; abbr. **Cons.**

conservatoire a school of music or other arts, *not* -tory (US)

conservat/oire (Fr. m.), **-orio** (It., Port., Sp.), **Konservatorium** (Ger. n., cap.)

consol. consolidated

console (archit.) a bracket; the key-desk of an organ, a cabinet for radio etc.

Consolidated Annuities abbr. **Consols**

consommé a clear soup (not ital.)

consonant abbr. **cons.**

consonantize make consonantal, *not* -ise

con sordino (mus.) with a mute

conspectus (Lat.) a general view (not ital.)

con spirito (mus.) spiritedly

constable abbr. **c., cons.**

Constance a lake (in Ger. **Bodensee**) and town (in Ger. **Konstanz**), Switzerland

Constans/ Roman Emperor (337–50); — mythical king of Britain

Constant,/ Benjamin (in full **Henri Benjamin Constant de Rebecque**) (1767–1830) French-Swiss political novelist, — **Benjamin Jean Joseph** (1845–1902) French painter

Constantino/ple *now* **Istanbul**; -politan

Constitution of a country (cap.)

constitution/, -al abbr. **cons.**

construction abbr. **constr.**

Consuelo a novel by George Sand, 1842

consuetude (law) a custom, esp. one having legal force in Scotland

Consul diplomat, abbr. **C., Con.**; Lat. **consul/**, as Roman magistrate, abbr. **cos.**; pl. **-es**, abbr. **coss.**

Consul-General abbr. **C.-G.**

Consumers' Association abbr. **CA**

consummat/e (verb) to perfect or complete; (adj.) perfect, complete; noun **-ion**

consummatum est (Lat.) it is finished

cont. containing, contents, continent; continue, -d; *not* con't (US)

contadin/o an Italian peasant, pl. **-i**; f. **-a**, pl. **-e**

contagi/um contagious matter; pl. **-a**

containing abbr. **cont.**

contakion *use* **k-**

contang/o (Stock Exchange) a charge for carrying over, pl. **-os**

conte (Fr. m.) a short story, a medieval narrative tale; (It. m.) a count

contemptible deserving contempt, despicable; *not* -able

contemptuous showing contempt, scornful

contents abbr. **cont.**

conterminous coextensive; having a common boundary or border; cf. **coterminous**

Contes drolatiques by Balzac, 1832–7

contessa (It.) a countess

Continent/, -al cap. when referring to mainland Europe as distinct from Britain, lower case when referring to countries that are also continents, such as Australia; *continental USA* is the USA excluding Hawaii but including Alaska; abbr. **cont.**

continual constantly or frequently recurring; cf. **continuous**

continuance (US law) = **adjournment**

continu/e, -ed abbr. **cont.**

continuo/ (mus.) an improvised keyboard accompaniment, pl. **-s**

continuous unbroken, uninterrupted, connected throughout in space or time; cf. **continual**

continu/um (philos., phys.) a continuous quantity, pl. **-a**

cont-line (naut.) a spiral space between rope strands, a space between stowed casks

contr. contract, -ed, -ion, -s; contrary

contra against, in opposition to; abbr. **con.**

contrabasso (It. mus.) the double bass, abbr. **CB**; in Eng. **contrabass**

contract/, -ed, -ion, -s abbr. **contr.**

contracting-out (noun, hyphen)

contraction a word shortened by elision; verbal forms use an apostrophe to mark omission (e.g. *cannot* = *can't*); nouns usually are not punctuated (e.g. *Mister* = *Mr*); *see also* **abbreviation**; **acronym**

contractor *not* -er

contrafagotto (It. mus.) the double bassoon (one word)

contra jus gentium (Lat.) against the law of nations

contralto/ (mus.) the lowest female voice, pl. **-s**; abbr. **C.**

contra/ mundum (Lat.) against the world, — **pacem** (law) against the peace

contrariwise *not* -ry-

contrary abbr. **contr.**

contratenor (mus.) a singing part, abbr. **Ct** (no point)

Contrat social, Le by Rousseau, 1762

contretemps a mishap (not ital.)

control/, -led, -ling

controller *see* **comptroller**

Controller-General *but* **Comptroller-General**, National Debt Office, Patent Office

Controller of Accounts abbr. **CA**

conundrum/ a riddle, pl. **-s**

convector an apparatus for heating by convection

convenances, les (Fr. f. pl.) the conventional proprieties

convener a caller of a meeting

convention/, -al abbr. **conv.**

conventionalize *not* -ise

conversation abbr. **con.**

conversazione/ a meeting for learned conversation, pl. **-s**

converter *not* -or

convertible *not* -able

convey/er (person), **-or** (thing) esp. in **conveyor belt**

Convocation a provincial assembly of the Church of England, a legislative assembly of certain universities

convolvulus/ a flower, bindweed; pl. **-es**

Conwy a river and town, Gwynedd

cony/ a rabbit, *not* coney, pl. **conies**

Conyngham, Marquess

Cooch Behar India, *not* Kuch

cooee (a) call (one word); *not* -ey, -hee, -ie

Cook,/ Captain James (1728–79) British explorer, — **Thomas** (1808–92) English travel agent

cookie (Sc.) a bun, (US) a sweet biscuit; *not* -ey, -y

coolabah an Australian gum tree, *not* -ibah

coolie (Ind., Chin.) a native hired labourer, *not* -y

Coomassie Ghana, *use* **Kumasi**

Cooper, James Fenimore (1789–1851) US novelist, (one *n*)

cooperat/e, -ion, -ive (one word); *but* **co-operative society** (hyphen), abbr. **co-op**

Coopers & Lybrand Deloitte British accountancy firm

co-opt (hyphen)

coordinat/e, -ely, -ion, -ive, -or (one word)

Cop. Copernican

cop. copper, copulative

copaiba (med.) a balsam from a S. American tree, *not* -va

coparcen/ary (law) joint heirship to an undivided property, *not* -ery; **-er** a joint heir

COPEC Conference on Christian Politics, Economics, and Citizenship

copeck a hundredth of a rouble; *not* -ec, -ek, ko-; abbr. **c.**

Copenhagen capital of Denmark, in Dan. **København**

Copernican abbr. **Cop.**

copier *not* copyer

Copland, Aaron (1900–90) US composer, *not* Cope-

copper abbr. **cop.**, symbol **Cu** (cuprum)

copperas ferrous sulphate, green vitriol

copperize to impregnate with copper, *not* -ise

copro- (in compounds) dung-, *not* k-

Copt a native Egyptian in the Hellenistic and Roman periods, a native Christian of the independent Egyptian Church

Coptic the language of the Copts, now used as the liturgical language of Egyptian Christians; abbr. **Copt.**

copul/a (gram., logic, anat., mus.) that which connects; pl. **-as, -ae**

copulative abbr. **cop.**

copy (typ.) matter to be reproduced in type

copy/book, -cat (one word)

copy editor a person who edits copy for printing (two words, one word in US), *but* **copy-edit/, -ing** (verb, one word in US)

cop/yer *use* **-ier**

copyholder (typ.) a stand or clasp holding sheets of copy, *formerly* a proofreader's assistant; (hist.) a type of feudal tenant (one word)

copyreader (one word)

copyright notice the symbol ©, date of publication, and name of copyright owner must appear (usually on title-page verso) in every copy of a publication claiming protection under the Universal Copyright Convention; *see also* **Berne Convention**

copy typist (two words)

copywriter (one word)

coq/ (Fr. m.) cock, — **au vin** chicken cooked in wine (not ital.), — **de bruyère** black game

coquet/ f. **-te** a flirt; **-ry, -ting, -tish**

coquille (Fr. typ. f.) a misprint

Cor. Corinthians

cor. corpus; (mus.) cornet, corno (horn); coroner

coram/ (Lat.) in presence of, — **judice** (law) before a judge, — **nobis** before us, — **paribus** before one's equals, — **populo** before the people

Coran *use* **K-**

cor anglais (mus.) an instrument of the oboe family

coranto *use* **courante**

Corbière, (Édouard Joachim) Tristan (1845–75) French poet

Corbusier, Le *see* **Le Corbusier**

Corcoran Gallery of Art Washington, DC

Corcyra the ancient name of **Corfu**

Corday, Charlotte (1768–93) French revolutionist

cordillera/ a mountain chain, pl. **-s**

Córdoba in Eng. **Cordova** (as in *cordovan*) (cf. **Cordova** in Alabama, Arkansas, and Maryland); in Sp., **Córdoba** (Spain, Argentina, Colombia, Mexico) or **Córdova** (Peru); in Lat. **Corduba**; in Arab. **Qurtuba**

córdoba monetary unit of Nicaragua

cordon bleu (cook.) pl. **cordons bleus** (not ital., two words)

cordon-bleu (ornith.) an African waxbill, pl. **cordon-bleus** (hyphen)

cordon sanitaire pl. **cordons sanitaires** (not ital., two words)

CORE (US) Congress of Racial Equality

Corea/, -n *use* **K-**

co-respondent in divorce case (hyphen, one word in US)

cor/f a lobster cage, pl. **-ves**

Corfe Castle Dorset, castle and village

Corflambo the giant in Spenser's *Faerie Queene*

Corfu a Greek island, ancient name **Corcyra**; in Modern Gr. **Kerkyra**

Corinthians, First, Second Epistle to the (NT) abbr. **1 Cor., 2 Cor.**

Corn. Cornish, Cornwall

corncrake a bird (one word)

Corneille, Pierre (1606–84) French playwright

cornelian *not* car-, -ion

cornemuse French bagpipe

cornerstone (one word)

cornet (mus.) abbr. **cor.**

cornett/o (mus.) an old form of woodwind instrument, pl. **-i**

corn/ field -flour, -flower (one word)

Corniche, La the coast road from Nice to Genoa, in It. **La Cornice**

Cornish/ abbr. **Corn.**, **— gillyflower** a variety of apple

Corn Laws (caps.)

corn/o (mus.) a horn, pl. **-i**; **-o inglese** (It.) cor anglais (ital.)

cornstarch (US) = **cornflour**

cornu/ (anat.) a hornlike process, pl. **-a**

Cornubia (Lat.) Cornwall

cornucopia/ horn of plenty, pl. **-s**, adj. **-n**

Cornwall abbr. **Corn.**, in Cornish **Kernow**, in Fr. f. **Cornouailles**

corolla/ (bot.) pl. **-s**

coron/a (archit., bot., anat., astr.) pl. **-ae**

coroner (cap. as title) abbr. **cor.**

coronis a mark of contraction (crasis) in Gr.

Corot, Jean Baptiste Camille (1796–1875) French painter

Corp. (US) corporation

Corporal abbr. **Cpl.**

corpor/al of the human body; **-eal** physical, as opposed to spiritual

corporealize materialize, *not* -ise

corposant St Elmo's fire

corps sing. and pl.

corps/ d'armée (Fr. m.) army corps

corps de ballet company of ballet dancers (not ital.)

corps de bataille the central part of an army, **— d'élite** a picked body, **— des lettres** (Fr. typ.) the body of the type, **— diplomatique** diplomatic body

corp/us body, pl. **-ora**, abbr. **cor.**

Corpus Christi the festival of institution of the Eucharist, on the Thursday after Trinity Sunday

Corpus Christi College Oxford and Cambridge, abbr. **CCC**

corpus delicti (law) the facts constituting an alleged offence

corp/us luteum (physiol.) an ovarian body, pl. **-ora lutea**

corp/us vile worthless substance, pl. **-ora vilia**

corr. correct/ion, -ive, -or; correspond, -ence, -ent, -ing; corrupt, -ed

correcteur (Fr. typ. m.) corrector of the press

correct/ion, -ive, -or abbr. **corr.**

Correggio, Antonio Allegri da (1494–1534) Italian painter

corregidor (Sp.) a magistrate

correlative abbr. **correl.**

correspond/, -ence, -ent, -ing abbr. **corr.**

Corresponding Member abbr. **CM, Corr. Mem.**

Corrèze dép. France

corrida a bullfight (not ital.), **corrida de toros** (Sp.) a bullfight (ital.)

corrigend/um a thing to be corrected; pl. **-a**; *see also* **erratum**

Corr./ Mem. Corresponding Member, **— Sec.** Corresponding Secretary

corroboree an Australian aboriginal dance; *not* -bery, -borie, -bory

corrupt/, -ed, -ion abbr. **corr.**

corrupter *not* -or

Corsica abbr. **Cors.**, in Fr. f. **Corse**

corslet (armour) a cuirass, *not* -elet

corso (It.) (horse) race, a street for it

Corstorphine Edinburgh

cort. cortex

cortège a (funeral) procession

Cortes the legislative assembly of Spain

Cortés, Hernando (*or* **Cortez, Hernán**) (1485–1547) Spanish conqueror of Mexico

cort/ex bark, pl. **-ices**; abbr. **cort.**

Corunna in Sp. **La Coruña**

corvée feudal forced labour, drudgery (not ital.)

corvette a small naval escort vessel

Coryate, Thomas (?1577–1617) English traveller

corybant/ a Phrygian priest, pl. **-es** (not ital.); adj. **-ic** frenzied

Corycian nymphs the Muses

coryphae/us a chorus leader, *not* -eus; pl. **-i**

coryphée a leading dancer in a corps de ballet (not ital.)

COS Chief of Staff

Cos Greek island, *use* **K-**; *but* **cos lettuce**

cos (math.) cosine (no point)

co. sa. (mus.) come sopra, as above

Cosa Nostra (US) a criminal organization resembling and related to the Mafia

cosec (math.) cosecant (no point)

cosh (math.) hyperbolic cosine (no point)

cosh/ar, -er (Heb.) *use* **kosher**

Così fan tutte ('All women are like that') an opera by Mozart 1790

co-signatory (hyphen, one word in US)

cosine (math., no hyphen) abbr. **cos**

cosmogony, cosmography abbr. **cosmog.**

COSPAR Committee on Space Research

coss. consules (consuls)

cosseted pampered, *not* -etted

co-star (hyphen, one word in US)

cost–benefit (**analysis**) (en rule)

costumier a person who makes or deals in costumes, *not* -mer

cosy *not* -zy (US)

cot a small bed with high sides, esp. for a baby or small child; (US) a small folding bed

cotangent (math., no hyphen) abbr. **cot**

cote a shelter, esp. for animals or birds; a shed or stall

cote (Fr. f.) market quotation, figure, mark, share

côte (Fr. f.) hillside, shore

côté (Fr. m.) side

Côte d'Azure the eastern Mediterranean coast of France

Côte-d'Or dép. France

côtelette (Fr. f.) a cutlet

coterie an exclusive 'set' of persons (not ital.)

coterminous coextensive; having the same or coincident boundaries; cf. **conterminous**

Côte-rôtie (Fr. f.) a red wine

côtes de bœuf (Fr. f.) ribs of beef

Côtes-du-Nord dép. France

cotillion a dance, in Fr. m. *cotillon*

cotoneaster a rosaceous shrub with berries

cottar a peasant, *not* -er

cotter a pin, wedge, etc.

Cotter's Saturday Night, The a poem by Burns, 1786

Cottian Alps France and Italy

cottier a cottager

cotton candy (US) = **candyfloss**

Cottonian Library in British Library, Reference Division

cotton/tail American rabbit (one word); **— wool** raw cotton (two words)

cottonize to make cotton-like, *not* -ise

couch a kind of grass; *see also* **cutch**

coudé (astr.) a telescope with its light path bent at an angle

Couéism psychotherapy by auto-suggestion, named after **Émile Coué** (1857–1926)

cougar (US) a puma

couldst (no apos.)

coulé (mus.) a slur

coulée a stream of molten or solidified lava; (US) a deep ravine or gulch (not ital., no accent in US), *not* cooley

couleur/ (Fr. f.) colour, **— de rose** roseate (fig.)

coulis a fruit purée thin enough to pour (not ital.)

coulisse/ a place of informal discussion or negotiation; **-s** (pl.) the wings in a theatre, 'behind the scenes'

couloir a gully

Coulomb, Charles Augustin de (1736–1806) French physicist; **coulomb** (elec.) a unit of charge, abbr. **C**

coulter a plough blade, *not* col- (US)

council/ assembly; **-lor** member of a council (one *l* in US), abbr. **Cllr.**

council/ estate, — flat, — house (two words) properties owned by council *or* a place in which a council meets

Council of Europe an association of European states, independent of the European Union, founded in 1948 to safeguard the political and cultural heritage of Europe and promote economic and social cooperation

counsel/ advice, a barrister; **-led, -ling; -lor** one who counsels (one *l* in US)

count/, -ess (cap. as title) abbr. **Ct.**

countdown (noun, one word)

counter (typ.) space wholly or mainly enclosed within a letter, e.g. the centre of 'O'

counter/act, -balance, -charge, -claim (one word)

counterclockwise (US) = **anticlockwise**

counter/-culture, -espionage, -intelligence, -intuitive (hyphens, one word in US)

counter-quarte (fencing) (hyphen) *not* -carte

counter/-reformation (caps. with hist. reference); **-revolution** (hyphens)

counter-tenor (mus.) a singing-voice, abbr. **C.**; cf. **contratenor**

Countesthorpe Leics.

Counties palatine Ches. and Lancs. (one cap. only)

countrif/y, -ied *not* country-

country/ dance, — house (two words)

country/side, -wide (one word)

county abbr. **Co.** (as part of name)

County Council/, -lor abbr. **CC**

County court (one cap.) abbr. **CC**

coup a stroke, esp. a political revolution

Coupar Angus Tayside (no hyphen) *not* Cu-

coup/ de foudre (Fr. m.) stroke of lightning; **— de fouet** (fencing) a 'beat', lit. a lash of the whip; **— de grâce** a finishing stroke; **— de main** sudden attack to gain a position; **— de maître** a master stroke; **— de pied** a kick; **— de poing** blow with the fist; **— de soleil** sunstroke; **— d'essai** first attempt; **— d'état** sudden or violent change in government (often not ital. in Eng.); **— de théâtre** sudden sensational act; **— d'œil** a glance, wink

coupe a shallow dish

coupé a covered motor car, usually for two (not ital.)

coupee in dancing, a salute to the partner

couper (Sc.) a dealer

Couperin the name of a French musical family, esp. **François** (1688–1733) composer

coup manqué (Fr. m.) a failure

courante (music for) a dance with a gliding step, *not* coranto

Cour de Cassation *see* **Cassation**

courier in Fr. m. *courrier*

Court abbr. **C.**, **Ct.**

Courtauld Institute of Art London

court bouillon (Fr. cook. m.) a fish stock

Courtenay the family name of the Earl of Devon

courthouse (one word), abbr. **CH**

Courtmantle *use* Cu-

court/ martial (noun, two words) pl. **-s martial**; **court-martial** (verb, hyphen)

Court of/ Appeal abbr. **CA**, **— — Common Pleas** abbr. **CCP**, **— — Probate** abbr. **CP**, **— — St James's** (apos.), **— — Session** abbr. **CS**

Courtrai Belgium, *not* -ay; in Fl. **Kortrijk**

Courts of Justice (caps.)

courtyard (one word)

couscous a NW African dish of granulated flour steamed over broth; *see also* **cuscus**

cousin/ german *not* -aine, -ane; pl. **-s german**

coûte que coûte (Fr.) at any cost, *not* qui

Coutts & Co. bankers, pron. 'coots'

coutur/ier, -ière a dressmaker

Covenanter (Sc. hist.)

covenantor (law)

Coventry: the signature of the Bishop of Coventry (colon)

cover girl (two words)

covering letter *not* **cover letter** (US)

Coverley, Sir Roger de a character described in the *Spectator* by Addison and Steele; a dance

cover-up (noun, hyphen)

covin (law) conspiracy to commit a crime etc. against a third party; (arch.) fraud, deception

Coward, Sir Noel (**Pierce**) (1899–1973) English actor, dramatist, and composer; *also* sometimes **Noël**

Cowling Lancs., N. Yorks.

Cowlinge Suffolk

Cowper, William (1731–1800) English poet

cowrie a shell, used as money in Africa and S. Asia; *not* -ry; cf. **kauri**

Cox a variety of eating apple, in full **Cox's orange pippin**

coxcomb a fop; *see also* **cocks-**

coxswain (naut.) *not* cocks-, colloq. **cox**

Coy. (mil.) company

coyote a N. American prairie wolf

coypu a S. American aquatic rodent, source of nutria fur; *not* -ou

cozen cheat, defraud, beguile

cozy *use* **cosy** (except in US)

CP Cape Province (of S. Africa); Central Provinces, *now* Madhya Pradesh (India); Chief Patriarch, Civil Power, Civil Procedure, Clarendon Press, Clerk of the Peace, Code of Procedure, College of Preceptors, Common Pleas, Common Prayer, Communist Party, *Congregatio Passionis* (Passionist Fathers), Court of Probate

cp. compare, *prefer* **cf.**

c.p. candlepower, carriage paid

CPC Clerk of the Privy Council

c.p.i. characters per inch

Cpl. Corporal

c.p.l. characters per line

c.p.m. characters per minute

CPO Chief Petty Officer, Compulsory Purchase Order

CPR Canadian Pacific Railway

CPRE Council for the Protection of Rural England

CPS *Custos Privati Sigilli* (Keeper of the Privy Seal)

c.p.s. characters per second, cycles per second

CPSA Civil and Public Services Association

CPU (comput.) central processing unit

CR *Carolina Regina* (Queen Caroline), *Carolus Rex* (King Charles), *Civis Romanus* (Roman citizen), Community of the Resurrection, credit rating, current rate, *Custos Rotulorum* (Keeper of the Rolls)

Cr chromium (no point)

Cr. credit, -or; Crown

cr. created

Crabb, George (1778–1854) English philologist

Crabbe, George (1754–1832) English poet

Cracow Anglicized spelling of **Kraków**, Poland

Craigton Glasgow

crampon *not* -oon (US)

Crane,/ (Harold) Hart (1899–1932) US poet, — **Stephen** (1871–1900) US novelist and poet

cranesbill plant of the genus *Geranium* (one word)

crani/um the skull, pl. **-a**

crank an eccentric person, esp. one obsessed by a particular theory; (US) a bad-tempered person; adj. **-y**

crap/e a (usually black) gauzelike fabric, for mourning; adj. **-y**; *see also* **crêpe**

craquelure a network of fine cracks in a painting or its varnish

crash/ helmet, — pad (two words)

crassa negligentia (law) criminal negligence

crawfish a large marine spiny lobster, pl. same

crayfish a freshwater crustacean, pl. same

crc, CRC camera-ready copy

cream/-laid a writing paper with wire marks, **-wove** a writing paper without wire marks (hyphen)

created abbr. **cr.**

Creation, the (cap.)

crèche a day nursery, (US) a representation of a Nativity scene

Crécy, battle of 1346, *not* Cressy, Créci

credible believable, convincing

creditable bringing credit or honour

credit/, -or abbr. **Cr.**

credit card (two words)

crédit/ foncier (Fr. m.) a society for loans on real estate, *— mobilier* a society for loans on personal estate

credo/ creed; capitalize as part of title, e.g. Apostles' *or* Nicene Credo; pl. **-s**

creese *use* **kris**

Crefeld Germany, *use* **K-**

Creighton, Mandell (1843–1901) bishop and historian

crematori/um pl. **-a**

crème/ anglaise, — brulée, — caramel, — de cassis, — de la crème the very best, **— de menthe, — fraîche** (not ital.); *not* crê-

Cremona Italy, also a violin made there (cap.)

crenate (bot.) notched (of leaves)

crenellate(d) (mil.) furnish(ed) with battlements

crenulate (bot.) finely notched

Creole in strict use, a pure-blooded descendant of French, Spanish, Portuguese settlers in W. Indies, Louisiana, Mauritius, Africa, and E. Indies, in loose use (cap.) a Creole–Negro speaking a Spanish or French dialect, a black person born in the USA, or a pidgin grown more sophisticated through use (not cap.); *see also* **Cajun**; **pidgin**

creosote *not* k-

crêpe/ (Fr. m.) crape fabric other than black, (f.) pancake; **— de Chine** raw silk crêpe; **— lisse** smooth crêpe; **— Suzette** small pancake; *see also* **crape**

crescendo/ (mus.) growing in force; abbr. *cres.*, *cresc.*; (non-technical) gradually increasing noise; pl. **-s**

Cressy *use* **Crécy**

crest (her.) a device above the shield and helmet of a coat of arms

cretaceous chalky, *not* -ious; (cap.) of or relating to the last period of the Mesozoic era

Cretan of Crete

cretin (a person affected by) a type of physical and mental handicap; in Fr. m. *crétin*, f. *crétine*

cretonne a cotton cloth

Creusot, Le dép. Saône-et-Loire, France; *not* -zot

Creutzfeldt–Jakob disease (en rule)

crevasse a large fissure, esp. in the ice of a glacier

Crèvecœur, Michel Guillaume Jean de (1735–1813) French-born US writer (ligature)

crève-cœur (Fr. m.) heartbreak, pl. same

crevette (Fr. f.) prawn

crevice a small fissure

crib (US) a small bed with high sides, esp. for a baby or small child (UK = **cot**)

Criccieth Gwynedd

Crichton/, James, 'the Admirable' (1560–?1585) Scottish scholar and soldier

cricket/, -er, -ing

cri de cœur (Fr. m.) a passionate appeal

crim. con. (law) criminal conversation, adultery

crime passionnel (Fr. m.) a crime caused by sexual passion (two *n*s)

crimplene (propr.) bulked Terylene

cring/e, -ing

crinkum-crankum intricate, crooked; *not* -cum -cum

cris/is pl. **-es**

crispbread a thin biscuit (one word)

crit. critic/al, -ized

criteri/on standard of judgement, pl. **-a**

criticaster a petty critic

criticize *not* -ise

critique a review (not ital.)

Critique of Pure Reason by Kant, 1781, in Ger. *Kritik der reinen Vernunft*

CRMP Corps of Royal Military Police

Crna Gora Serbo-Croat for **Montenegro**

Croat/ a native of Croatia, in Serbo-Croat **Hrvat**; *not* Croatian (US); **-ia** a republic of the former Yugoslavia, in Serbo-Croat **Hrvatska**

crochet/ hooked-needle work; **-ed, -ing**

Crockford in full *Crockford's Clerical Directory*, the 'Who's Who' of the clergy

Crockford's a London club

crocus/ pl. **-es**

Croesus (6th c. BC) a rich king (and the last) of Lydia

croissant *not* croisant

Croix de Guerre a French military decoration

Cro-Magnon/ (anthrop.) of a prehistoric race, from remains found at –, dép. Dordogne, France

Cromartie, Earl of

cromesquis (Fr. cook. m.) *see* **kromesky**

Crome Yellow by Aldous Huxley, 1921

Cronos *use* **K-**

Crookback sobriquet of Richard III, *not* Crouchback

Crookes, Sir William (1832–1919) English physicist

Croonian Lecture of the Royal Society

croquet/ a game (not ital.), as verb **-ed, -ing**

croquette rissole (not ital.)

crore (Ind.) ten million, point thus: 1,00,00,000; *see also* **lakh**

crosette *use* **crossette**

crosier a bishop's or archbishop's staff, *not* -zier

croslet *use* **crosslet**

cross/ (typ.) a proof-correction sign for a battered sort; **Greek +**; **Latin †**; **Maltese ✠**; **tau —** of St Anthony ⊤; *see also* **crux**

crossbar (one word)

cross-bench(er) (parl.) (hyphen)

crossbill a passerine bird (one word)

cross-bill (law) a promissory note given in exchange, a bill brought by defendant against plaintiff in a Chancery suit (hyphen)

crossette (archit.) a ledge, *not* crose-

Crossgates Cumbria, Fife, Powys, N. Yorks.

Cross Gates W. Yorks.

cross-heading (typ.) a heading to a paragraph printed across a column in the body of an article in a newspaper, journal, etc.

Crosshill Fife, Strathclyde

Cross Hill Derby., Shropshire

Crosskeys Co. Antrim, Co. Cavan, Gwent

Cross Keys Kent, Wilts.

crosslet (her.) a small cross, *not* cros-

cross-link (hyphen)

crossmatch (one word)

cross-reference abbr. **x-ref.**

crossroad(s) (one word)

cross section (noun, two words)

crosswalk (US) = **pedestrian crossing**

crossways *not* -way, -wise (US)

crosswind (one word)

crossword (puzzle)

crotchet/ a musical note, a whim; **-ed, -ing, -y**

Crouchback *use* **Crook-**

croupier a gaming table attendant

crouton a bit of crust or toast, in Fr. m. *croûton*

Crowland Lincs., Suffolk, *not* Croy-

Crown, the (cap. C) abbr. **Cr.**

crown a former British coin equal to five shillings (25p); a former size of paper, 15 × 20 in.; **crown 4to** 10 × 7.5 in.; **crown 8vo** 7.5 × 5 in. (untrimmed); the basis for size of **metric crown** is 768 × 1008 mm

Crowner's quest dialectal for Coroner's inquest (one cap. only)

Crown Office abbr. **CO**

Crowther-Hunt, Baron (hyphen)

crozier *use* **cros-**

CRP *Calendarium Rotulorum Patentium* (Calendar of the Patent Rolls)

CRR Curia Regis Roll

CRT cathode-ray tube

cru (Fr. m.) a French vineyard or wine-producing region, the wine produced from it, a specific growth (no accent)

Crucifixion, the (cap.)

crudités an hors d'oeuvre of mixed raw vegetables, in pl. (not ital.)

Cruft's Dog Show *not* -s'

Cruikshank, George (1792–1878) English caricaturist and illustrator

crumhorn Eng. spelling of **krummhorn**

cruse a jar, *not* cruise

crush/ bar, — barrier (two words)

Cruso NC

Crusoe, Robinson by Defoe, 1719

cru/x (of an argument) the decisive point at issue, pl. **-xes** *or* **-ces** (not ital.)

crux/ ansata cross with a handle, †; — ***commissa*** tau cross, ⊤; — ***decussata*** cross of St Andrew or St Patrick, ×

cruzeiro former monetary unit of Brazil, from 1986 one-thousandth of a **cruzado**

Crying of Lot 49, The novel by Thomas Pynchon, 1966

cryogenics the study of low-temperature refrigeration

cryptogam/ (bot.) any member of the Cryptogamia, flowerless plants; **-ous**

crypto/gram anything written in code; **-grapher, -graphic, -graphy**

crypton (chem.) *use* **k-**

cryptonym a private name

crystal. crystallography

crystalliz/ation, -e *not* -is-; **-ed, -ing**

CS Chemical Society (now part of Royal Society of Chemistry), Civil Service, Clerk to the Signet, College of Science, Common Serjeant, Court of Session, *Custos Sigilli* (Keeper of the Seal)

Cs caesium (no point)

c/s cycles per second

Csar etc., *use* **Ts-**

csárdás a Hungarian dance, pl. same; *not* cz-

CSC Civil Service Commission, Conspicuous Service Cross (*now* DSC)

CSE Certificate of Secondary Education, replaced in 1988 by GCSE

CS gas a gas used to control riots etc. (two caps.)

CSI Companion of the Order of the Star of India

CSM Company Sergeant Major

CSU Civil Service Union

CT Connecticut (postal abbr.)

Ct. Count, Court

ct. cent

CTC Cyclists' Touring Club

Ctesiphon city of ancient Mesopotamia

ctl. central, -s

cto. (mus.) concerto

cts. centimes, cents

CU Cambridge University

Cu cuprum (copper) (no point)

cu. cubic

cube root (two words)

cubic abbr. **c., cu., cub.**

cubicul/um (archaeol.) burial chamber, pl. **-a**

Cúchulainn (Ir. myth.) warrior hero

cuddl/y tempting to cuddle, given to cuddling; **-lier, -liest**

cudgel/, -led, -ling (one *l* in US)

CUDS Cambridge University Dramatic Society

cue/, -ing; cf. **queue**

cuffs (US) = (**trouser**) **turn-ups**

Cufic *use* **K-**

cui bono? (Lat.) who gains by it?

cuidado (Sp. m.) danger, care, worry; *not* ciu-

Cuillins mountains in Skye

cuirass/ body armour, **-ier** a soldier wearing it

cuisine cookery (not ital.)

culch oyster spawn, *not* cultch

cul-de-sac pl. **culs-de-sac**

cul/ex a gnat, pl. ***-ices***

cullender *use* **colan-**

Cullinan a famous diamond

Culpeper/, Nicholas (1616–54) English herbalist; — Va. from **Thomas, Lord** — (1578–1662) former Governor

cultivar (bot.) a variety made by cultivation, abbr. **cv.**

Culzean Castle Strathclyde

CUM Cambridge University Mission

cum (Lat.) with (not ital.)

Cumaean of Cumae, near Naples

Cumbernauld Strathclyde

Cumbria a county of England

cum dividend with dividend, abbr. **c.d.**

cumfrey *use* **com-**

cum grano salis (Lat.) with a grain of salt

cumin a plant with aromatic seeds (one *m*)

cum laude/ (Lat.) with distinction, ***magna*** — — with high distinction, ***summa*** — — with highest distinction

cummerbund a waistbelt; *not* cumber-, ku-, -band

Cummings, E(dward) E(stlin) (1894–1962) US writer and poet who renounced use of capital letters; thus properly **e. e. cummings**

cum multis aliis (Lat.) with many others

cum. pref. cumulative preference

cumquat *use* **k-**

cumul/us (meteor.) a cloud form, pl. **-i**; abbr. **k.**

cuneiform wedge-shaped; *not* cunif-, cunef-

Cunninghame Graham, Robert Bontine (1852–1936) British writer (no hyphen)

CUP Cambridge University Press

Cupar/ Fife; — **Angus** Tayside, *use* **Coupar Angus**

cupbearer (one word)

Cup Final *but* **cup-tie**

cupful/ the amount held by a cup, esp. (US) a half-pint or 8-ounce measure in cookery (one word); pl. **-s**; *but* 'cups full' (two words)

cupronickel an alloy of copper and nickel (one word)

cuprum copper, symbol **Cu**

cur. currency, current

curable not -eable

curaçao a liqueur named after the Caribbean island, *not* -oa (not cap.)

curare a drug; *not* -a, -i, urari

curb for verb, and part of a bridle (used for all senses in US); cf. **kerb**

curbstone *use* **kerb-**

curé/ French priest (not ital.), *petit* — French curate (ital.)

cure-all a universal remedy (hyphen)

curfuffle *use* **ker-**

Curia/ the papal court (cap.); — *advisare vult* the court desires to consider, abbr. *c.a.v.*

Curie,/ **Marie Sklodowska** (1867–1934) and her husband — **Pierre** (1859–1906) French scientists

curie a unit of radioactivity, abbr. **Ci** (cap.); *now* replaced by **becquerel**

curio/ an object of art, pl. **-s** (not ital.)

curium symbol **Cm**

curlicue a decorative curl; *not* -eque, -ycue

curly brackets (typ.) braces { }

currach a coracle, *not* -agh

Curragh, The Co. Kildare

curren/cy, -t abbr. **cur.**

current (elec.) abbr. **cur.**; symbol *I*, *i* (ital.)

currente calamo (Lat.) easily, fluently

curricul/um pl. **-a**; **-um vitae** pl. **-a vitae**, abbr. **CV, c.v.** (not ital.)

Currie Lothian

Curry Co. Sligo

cursor (comput.) a movable indicator on a VDU screen, identifying the active position

curtain-raiser (theat.) in Fr. *lever de rideau*

Curtiss, Glenn Hammond (1878–1930) US pioneer aviator

Curtmantle sobriquet of Henry II, *not* Cou-

curts/y *not* -sey, **-ied, -ies, -ying**

curvilinear (one word)

Curwen, John (1816–80) pioneer of tonic sol-fa

cuscus/ a marsupial, — **grass** of India; *see also* **couscous**

Cushitic (of or pertaining to) a group of E. African languages of the Hamitic type

custodia legis (Lat.) in the custody of the law

custom house (two words) abbr. **CH**

cust/os (Lat. m.) a custodian, pl. **-odes**

Custos/ *Privati Sigilli* Keeper of the Privy Seal, abbr. **CPS**; — *Rotulorum* Keeper of the Rolls, abbr. **CR**; — *Sigilli* Keeper of the Seal, abbr. **CS**

cut and dried (adj., no hyphens)

cutback (noun, one word)

Cutch India, *use* **K-**

cutch catechu, an extract of Indian plants, the tough paper sheets used by gold-beaters; *not* k-; *see also* **couch**

cut/-off, -out (nouns), **-price** (adj.) (hyphens)

cuts (typ.) illustrations

cut-throat (hyphen)

Cutty Sark a famous clipper, now in dry dock at Greenwich

cutty-stool a stool of repentance

cuvée a vatful, jugful, or sort of wine

Cuyp Dutch artists, *not* K-

CV curriculum vitae

cv. (bot.) cultivar

CVO Commander of the Royal Victorian Order

Cwlth (no point) Commonwealth (Australian)

Cwmbran Gwent

Cwmcarn Gwent

c.w.o. cash with order

CWS Co-operative Wholesale Society

cwt. hundredweight (no point in scientific and technical work)

cybernetics the study of communication processes in animals and machines (sing. treated as pl.)

cyc. cycloped/ia, -ic

Cycle of the Saros (astr.) $6{,}585\frac{1}{2}$ days

cyclo-cross cross-country bicycle racing

cycloped/ia, -ic *but use* -paed- in quoting titles using that form; abbr. **cyc.**

Cyclop/s a giant with one eye, pl. **-es**; adj. **-ean**

cygnet a young swan, *not* cig-

Cym. Cymric

cyma (archit.) a moulding of the cornice

cymbalist a cymbal-player; cf. **cembalo**

cymbal/o a dulcimer, pl. **-os**

cymbiform boat-shaped, *not* cymbae-

Cymmrodorion, Honourable Society of (two *m*s)

Cymrae/g (Welsh) the Welsh language, **-s** a Welsh woman

Cymreig/ (Welsh, adj.) Welsh, **-esau** Welsh women

Cymric Welsh

Cymr/o (Welsh) a Welshman; **-u** Wales; **-y** Welshmen, the Welsh nation; *not* K-

CYMS Catholic Young Men's Society

Cynewulf (8th c.) Anglo-Saxon poet

cynghanedd a form of Welsh poetic alliteration, pl. **cynganeddion**

cynocephalus (classical myth.) a dog-headed creature

Cynthia the moon

Cynthius an epithet of Apollo

cypher *use* **ci-**

cy près (law) as near as possible to a testator's intentions

Cyprian/ of Cyprus and Cypriot; — **Aphrodite** Venus, — in Lat. **Thascius Caecilius Cyprianus** (*c.*200–58) Christian writer and martyr

Cypriot an inhabitant or the language of Cyprus

Cyprus indep. rep. 1960

Cyrenaic pertaining to Cyrene *or* its school of philosophy

Cyrillic (pertaining to) the alphabet used by Slavonic peoples of the Eastern Church (two ls)

cyst/ (biol.) a sac, **-ic**; *not* ci-

Cytherean pertaining to Aphrodite, *not* -ian

CZ Canal Zone (Panama)

Czar etc., *use* **Ts-** (except in US)

czárdás *use* **cs-**

Czech (of or relating to) (a native) of the Czech Republic, or Bohemia, *or* the language of this people

Czechoslovak (hist.) (a person) belonging to the former **Czechoslovakia**; *not* -ian, *now* **Czech** *or* **Slovak**

Czech Republic formed 1993

Czerny, Karl (1791–1857) Austrian composer

D 500, deuterium (= heavy hydrogen), the fourth in series

D. (US) Democrat, Deputy, *Deus* (God), *Dominus* (Lord), Duke, prefix to enumeration of Schubert's works (*see* **Deutsch**)

đ a lower-case letter found in Old Saxon and (with quite different value) modern Serbo-Croat

d (prefix) deci-

d. date, daughter, day, dead, degree, departs; desert/ed, -er; died, dime, dioptre, dose; (Fr.) *douane* (customs), *droite* (the right hand); (It.) *destra* (right), (Lat.) *decretum* (a decree), *denarii* (pence), *denarius* (penny); (meteor.) drizzling

d' as prefix to an un-Anglicized proper name should, in accordance with Fr. practice, be lower case and *not* cap., as 'd'Arsonval', except at beginning of sentence; it is always cap. in It., as 'D'Annunzio'. Signatures to be copied

Ð ð Icelandic, Norse, OE (lower case ð), and phonetic letter, pron. like the soft *th* in '*that*'; *see also* **eth**

∂ (math.) sign of partial derivative

δ (typ.) delete

DA deposit account, (US) District Attorney

Da. Danish

da (prefix) deca-

DAB *Dictionary of American Biography*

da/ ballo (mus.) a dance style; **— capo** *or* **— capo al fine** repeat from the beginning to the word *fine*, abbr. **DC**; **— capo al segno** repeat from the beginning to the sign ❦, abbr. **DS**; **— capella** *or* **— chiesa** in church style

DAC digital–analogue converter

Dacca *use* **Dhaka**

d'accord (Fr.) I agree

dacha a country house or cottage in Russia (not ital.)

Dachau a Nazi concentration camp, 1933–45

dacoit an Indian robber; *not* dak-, dec-

dactyl/ (prosody) a foot of three syllables (- ⌣ ⌣), **-ic**

Dada/ unconventional art, literature, music, and film *c.*1920; **-ism, -ist, -istic**

daddy-long-legs the crane-fly (of the family *Tipulidae*) or the harvestman (of the family *Opilionidae*), *not* daddy longlegs (US)

dado/ pl. **-s**

Daedalus (Gr. myth.) the builder of the Cretan labyrinth and father of Icarus; cf. **De-**

daemon *use* **demon** except for the sense in Greek mythology of a supernatural being or indwelling spirit, *not* dai- (except when using Hellenic transcription)

daffadowndilly a daffodil; *not* daffi-, daffo-, daffy (one word)

Dafydd Wales, Welsh for **David** (the saint is **Dewi**); *not* Daff-

Dagapur Ethiopia

dagger/ (†), **double —** (‡) (typ.) in Eng. before (in Ger. after) a person's name signifies 'dead' or 'died'; this should be used only of Christians. When in Ger. ✕ follows the name it signifies 'killed in battle'; the normal double dagger should not be used for this symbol

daggle-tail *use* **draggle-**

Dagonet, Sir King Arthur's fool

Daguerre, Louis Jacques Mandé (1789–1851) French pioneer of photography

daguerreotype (not cap.)

dahabeeyah a Nile sailing boat

Dahomey W. Africa, *now* **Benin**

Dáil Éireann the Lower House of the Irish Parliament

d'ailleurs (Fr.) besides, however

daimio/ a Japanese noble, pl. **-s**

Daimler a make of motor car

daimon Hellenistic transcription of **daemon**; *see also* **demon**

daiquiri a rum-based cocktail (not cap.)

dais a small platform, *not* daïs

dakoit *use* **dac-**

Dakota (**North, South**) off. abbrs. **N. Dak., S. Dak.**, postal **ND, SD**

Dalai Lama the Grand Lama of Tibet, spiritual head of Tibetan Buddhism

Dalarö Sweden, *not* — Island, as the suffix *-ö* indicates 'island'

Dalí, Salvador (1904–89) Catalan painter

Dalila *see* **Delilah**

Dallapiccola, Luigi (1904–75) Italian composer

Dalmatian a breed of spotted dog, of Dalmatia; *not* -ion

dal segno (It. mus.) repeat from the sign ❦, abbr. **DS**

damageable *not* -gable

Damara/, -land SW Africa, *now* **Namibia**

damascen/e (noun, verb, adj.) (of or relating to) ornament in metal; *not* -keen, -kin; **-er**

Dame the title given to a woman with the rank of Knight Commander or holder of the Grand Cross in the Orders of Chivalry

Dame aux camélias, La a play by Dumas *fils*, 1848

Damien de Veuster, Joseph, 'Father Damien' (1840–89) Belgian priest to a leper colony in the Hawaiian Islands

damnosa hereditas (Lat.) an inheritance involving loss

damnum absque injuria (Lat.) damage without wrong

Damon and Pythias (Gr. myth.) model friends; the correct spelling is **Phintias**

Dan. (Book of) Daniel

Dan/aë (Gr. myth.) the mother of Perseus, also an asteroid; *Danaea* a fern genus; **-aïd** a daughter of Danaus; **-aus** the son of Belus

d. and c. dilatation (of the cervix) and curettage (of the uterus)

Dandie Dinmont a breed of Scottish terrier, from **Andrew Dinmont** a farmer in Scott's *Guy Mannering*

dandruff scurf, *not* -riff

Dane/geld *not* -lt; **-law** (one word)

Daniel, Book of (OT) abbr. **Dan.**

Daniell's battery (elec.) usually called a **Daniell cell**

Danish abbr. **Da.**

danke schön (Ger.) many thanks

Dannebrog the Danish national standard, *also* an order of knighthood; *not* Dane-

D'Annunzio, Gabriele (1864–1938) Italian writer (cap. *D*)

danse macabre (Fr. f.) dance of death

dans/eur a male dancer, **-euse** a female dancer (not ital.)

dans le fond (Fr.) basically, in fact; cf. *au fond*

Dant/e Alighieri (1265–1321) Italian poet; **-ean, -esque, -ist** (caps.)

Danzig Ger. for **Gdańsk**

daou *use* **dhow**

DAR Daughters of the American Revolution

d'Arblay, Mme (1752–1840) the English novelist **Fanny Burney**

Darby and Joan a devoted old married couple, *not* Derby

d'Arc, Jeanne (Fr.) **Joan of Arc**, alphabetized **Arc, Jeanne d'**

Darcy de Knayth, Baroness

Dardanelles the strait linking the Sea of Marmara to the Aegean, in antiquity called **Hellespont**

daredevil (one word)

dare say (two words)

Dar es Salaam the former capital of Tanzania (no hyphens)

Dar the modern Persian language of Afghanistan

Darjeeling *not* Darji-

Dark Ages, the the period of European history preceding the Middle Ages, especially the 5th–10th cc. Beware of using the term too liberally, since not all European cultures underwent the same degree of unenlightenment during this period, or feel the same about it: the traditional French right wing holds the age in high esteem

darkroom (one word)

darshan (Hind.) seeing a revered person

Darwen Lancs., *not* Over —

Darwin/, Charles Robert (1809–82) author of *Origin of Species*; **—, Erasmus** (1731–1802) English physician and poet, grandfather of Charles; **-ian, -ism, -ist**

das (Ger.) the (n. sing. nominative and accusative), *also* that (demonstrative); *see also das heißt*; *dass*

dashboard (one word)

das/ heißt (Ger.) that is to say, abbr. **d. h.**; **— ist** that is, abbr. **d. i.** (spaces in Ger. abbrs.)

dass (Ger.) that (conjunction)

DAT digital audio tape

dat. dative

data (pl.) in computing and related fields, treated as collective noun taking singular verb; *see also* **datum**

data bank (two words)

database (one word)

datable capable of being dated, *not* -eable

data processing (hyphen when attrib.)

data-set (hyphen)

date/ abbr. **d.**, **-line** (hyphen)

dative the indirect object, abbr. **dat.**

Datta, Michael Madhusudan (1824–73) Bengali poet and dramatist

Datta, Sudhindranath (1901–60) Indian poet

datum a thing known or granted, pl. **data**

daube a braised meat stew

Daudet,/ Alphonse (1840–97) French novelist, **— Léon** (1867–1942) French writer and politician

daughter/ abbr. **d.**, **dau.**; **-in-law**, pl. **daughters-in-law** (hyphens)

Daumier, Honoré (1808–79) French painter

Dauntsey's School Devizes

dauphin the eldest son of the King of France 1349–1830; **Dauphiné** his traditional lands in SE France; **dauphiness** his wife, in Fr. *dauphine*

Dav. David

D'Avenant, Sir William (1606–68) English playwright and poet, Poet Laureate 1660–8; also spelt **Davenant**

Davies,/ Sir Henry Walford (1869–1941) musician, **— William Henry** (1871–1940) poet

da Vinci, Leonardo *see* **Leonardo da Vinci**

Davis, Jefferson (1808–89) US senator and President of the Confederate States 1862–5

Davis/ apparatus for escape from a submarine, **— Cup** a tennis trophy

Davy/, Sir Humphry *not* -ey (1778–1829) English chemist, inventor of the **— lamp**

Davy Jones's locker the seabed

Dawley Shropshire

Day, John (1522–84) English printer, also spelt **Daye**, **Daie**

day abbr. **d.** (typ.) initial caps for days of the week, and of fasts, feasts, festivals, holidays; abbr., when necessary, to **Sun.**, **Mon.**, **Tue.**, **Wed.**, **Thur.**, **Fri.**, **Sat.** In Fr., no caps., as *lundi*

Dayak *use* **Dyak**

daybed (one word)

daybook (one word), abbr. **d.b.**

day-boy (hyphen)

day/break, -dream (one word)

day-girl (hyphen)

Day-Glo (propr.) (of) a make of fluorescent paint or other colouring

Day-Lewis, Cecil (1904–72) Poet Laureate 1968–72 (hyphen), wrote under the name **C. Day Lewis** (no hyphen)

daylight (one word)

Daylight Saving Time (US) one hour in advance of local US time, largely equivalent to British Summer Time (three words); abbr. **DST**

day/-long (hyphen)

day/ nursery, — room (two words)

dayside (one word)

day's journey (Heb.) about 17 miles

daytime (one word)

Dayton Ohio

Daytona Beach Fla.

DB Domesday Book

dB decibel (no point)

d.b. daybook, double bed, double-breasted

DBE Dame Commander of the Order of the British Empire

dbk. drawback

dbl. double

DBS direct-broadcast satellite, direct broadcasting by satellite

DC 600, (mus.) da capo (from the beginning), deputy-consul, direct current (*not* d.c.), District of Columbia (USA)

DCB Dame Commander of the Order of the Bath

DCC digital compact cassette

D.Ch. Doctor of Surgery

DCL Doctor of Civil Law

DCM Distinguished Conduct Medal

DCMG Dame Commander of the Order of St Michael and St George

DCVO Dame Commander of the Royal Victorian Order

DD direct debit, *Divinitatis Doctor* (Doctor of Divinity)

D.d. *Deo dedit* (gave to God)

dd in Welsh a separate letter, not to be divided

dd. delivered

d.d. *dono dedit* (gave as a gift)

DDA Dangerous Drugs Act

D-Day 6 June 1944 (hyphen)

DDD *dat, dicat, dedicat* (gives, devotes, and dedicates); *dono dedit dedicavit* (gave and consecrated as a gift)

DDR (Ger.) *Deutsche Demokratische Republik* (German Democratic Republic) East Germany, 1949–90

DDS Doctor of Dental Surgery

DDT dichlorodiphenyltrichloroethane (an insecticide)

DE Delaware (postal abbr.)

de (as prefix to proper name) not cap. ('de Candolle', 'de Talleyrand-Périgord'), except when Anglicized ('De Quincey', 'De Vinne') or starting a sentence; where lower-case, alphabetize by surname ('Mairan, Jean-Jacques de', 'Chazelles, Jean-François, comte de'), though Anglicized names may be treated differently by their bearers. In Sp. and Port. not cap. ('Figueiredo, Adelpha Silva Rodrigues de') and omitted in bare surname references, as for It. ('Medici, Lorenzo de'') unless of Lat. form ('De Sanctis'). In Du. generally not cap. and not used in alphabetizing ('Groot, Huijg de'); in Flemish the reverse is true ('De Bruyne, Jan'); Afrikaans varies; follow established convention or the bearer's preference; cf. **de La**; **du**; **van, van den, van der**

deacon/al, -ate *use* **diac-**

dead abbr. **d.**

dead/beat, -bolt, -eye, -fall (one word)

dead-head (hyphen)

dead heat (noun), **dead-heat** (verb)

dead/line, -lock, -pan (one word)

dead reckoning (naut.) calculating a ship's position from the log, compass, etc. when observations are impossible; often inexact, and the term should not be used in contexts where precision is meant; abbr. **DR**

deadweight (one word, two in US), abbr. **dw**

deaf-and-dumb alphabet *use* **sign language** unless this specific system is meant

dean *not* a synonym for **doyen**; *see also* **dene**

Dean of Faculty (Sc.) (*not* of the) president of the Faculty of Advocates, abbr. **DF**

Dear/ Madam, — Sir in printed letter full left

deasil (Sc.) clockwise, opp. to **widdershins**

deathbed (one word)

death/ blow, — knell, — mask, — penalty, — rate, — rattle, — roll, — row, — squad, — tax, — threat, — toll, — trap, — warrant (two words)

death-watch beetle (hyphen, two words in US)

death wish (two words)

deb (colloq.) debutante (no point, no accent)

deb. debenture

debacle a downfall (no accents)

débat (Fr. m.) discussion, debate; (poet.) a poem in the form of a debate between two characters representing opposed principles (ital.)

debatable *not* -eable

debauchee a libertine

debenture/ abbr. **deb.**, **-holder** (hyphen, two words in US)

debonair gaily elegant, *not* -aire; in Fr. *débonnaire*

Debrett (Peerage)

debris ruins (no accent), in Fr. m. *débris*

debut/, **-ant** f. **-ante** (not ital., no accent); *see also* **deb**

Dec. Decani, December, (archit.) Decorated

dec. deceased, declaration, declared, declension, declination, decorative

dec. (mus.) decrescendo

déc. (Fr.) *décéd/é*, f. *-ée* (deceased); *décembre* (not cap.) (December)

deca- prefix meaning ten, abbr. **da**

décade (Fr. f.) a period of ten days, substituted for a week in the French Republican calendar 1793–1805

decalitre 10 litres, abbr. **dl** (no point)

Decalogue the Ten Commandments

Decameron, The by Boccaccio, 1352

decametre 10 metres, abbr. **dm** (no point)

Decan India, *use* **Decc-**

decani dean's or south side of a choir (north side in Durham Cathedral), abbr. **Dec.**; opp. to **cantoris**

decanter a bottle to hold decanted liquor

Deccan India, *not* Decan

deceased abbr. **dec.**

décéd/é (Fr.) f. **-ée** deceased, abbr. *déc.*

December abbr. **Dec.**; in Fr. m. *décembre*, abbr. *déc.* (not cap.), *also* **X**^bre

decenni/um a decade, pl. **-a**

decentralize *not* -ise

decern (Sc. law) to judge; *see also* **discern**

deci- a prefix meaning one-tenth, abbr. **d**

decibar one-tenth of a bar

decibel a unit for comparing intensity of noises, power, etc.; abbr. **dB**; *see also* **bel**

Decies, Baron

decigram one-tenth of a gram, *not* -mme; abbr. **dg** (no point)

decilitre one-tenth of a litre, abbr. **dl** (no point)

decimalize *not* -ise

decimal point (two words)

decimate kill or remove one in ten, kill a large proportion of; do not use to mean 'exterminate totally', or when any other proportion is specified

decimator one who decimates, takes every tenth part or person; *not* -er

decimetre one-tenth of a metre, 3.937 in.; *not* -er; abbr. **dm** (no point)

decimo-octavo (typ.) 18mo (not ital.); *see* **eighteenmo**

deckle edge the ragged edge of handmade paper, *not* -el

declar/ation, -ed abbr. **dec.**

Declaration of/ Independence USA, 4 July 1776 (caps.); — — **Indulgence** a royal proclamation of religious liberties, esp. under Charles II in 1672 and James II in 1687 (caps.)

déclass/é f. **-ée** who (or that) has fallen to an inferior status (not ital.)

declension (gram.) a system of case-endings, abbr. **dec.**

declinable *not* -eable

declination (astr.) the angular distance from the celestial equator, abbr. **dec.**; (US) a formal refusal

Deco, deco *use* **art deco**

decoit *use* **dac-**

decollate behead; **Decollation** of St John the Baptist, 29 Aug.

décollet/age a low neckline on a woman's dress etc.; **-é** having a low neckline (not ital.)

decolorize *not* -colour-, -ise

decolour render colourless, *not* -or (US)

deconstruct/-ion, -ionist, -ing, -ive (philos. and lit. theory) (one word, not cap.)

decor stage or room furnishings and fittings (no accent)

decorat/e, -or

Decoration Day (US) *see* **Memorial Day**

decorative abbr. **dec.**

decorum propriety of conduct

découpage (not ital.)

decree nisi (law) the first stage in the dissolution of a marriage (not ital.)

decrepit decayed, *not* -id

decrescendo/ (mus.) decreasing in loudness; abbr. *dec.*, **decres.**; as noun, pl. **-s**

decret/um (Lat.) a (papal) decree, pl. **-a**; abbr. *d.*

Dedalus, Stephen a character in Joyce's *A Portrait of the Artist as a Young Man*, 1914–15, and *Ulysses*, 1922; cf. **Dae-**

Dedlock, Sir Leicester *and* **Lady** characters in Dickens's *Bleak House*, *not* Dead-

deducible able to be inferred, *not* -eable

deductible able to be subtracted, *not* -able

de-emphasize (hyphen)

deemster a judge in the Isle of Man, *not* demp-

de-escalat/e, -tion (hyphens)

def. defective, defendant, deferred (shares), defined, definite, definition, defunct

de facto (Lat.) in actual fact (not ital.)

defecat/e, -or *not* defae-

defector *not* -er

defence *not* -se (US), *but* **defensive, defensible**

Defence of Poetry, A an essay by P. Sidney, 1579–80; original title *The Defence of Poesie*

Defence of Poetry an essay by P. B. Shelley, 1821

defendant abbr. **def.**

défense/ d'afficher (Fr.) stick no bills, — *de fumer* no smoking, — *d'entrer* no admittance

defens/ive *not* -cive; **-ible** *not* -ceable, -sable

defensor fidei (Lat.) Defender of the Faith, abbr. **DF**

defer/, -ence, -rable, -red, -rer, -ring

deferred (shares) abbr. **def.**

de fide (Lat.) authentic, to be believed as part of the (Christian) faith

definable *not* -eable

defin/ed, -ite, -ition; abbr. **def.**

deflate remove air, reverse economic inflation

defle/ct bend away, **-ction** this act or process

Defoe, Daniel (1661–1731) English writer, *not* de Foe

defunct abbr. **def.**

deg. degree(s)

dégag/é f. **-ée** easy, unconstrained (not ital.)

Degas, Hilaire (Germain Edgar) (1834–1917) French painter (no accent)

de Gaulle, Charles *see* **Gaulle, de**

degauss/, -ing a device or method for neutralizing magnetism

degradable *not* -eable

degree/ abbr. **deg.**, symbol °, set close up to the scale (10 °C) or, where none, figure (35°)

dégringolade (Fr. f.) rapid deterioration

de/ haut en bas (Fr.) contemptuously, — *haute lutte* with a high hand

de Havilland, Sir Geoffrey (1882–1965) English aircraft designer and manufacturer

Deïaneira (Gr. myth.) the wife of Hercules; *also* an asteroid

de-ic/e, -er (hyphens)

deictic (philol., gram.) (a word that is) pointing, demonstrative

Dei/ gratia (Lat.) by the grace of God, abbr. **DG**; —*judicium* the judgement of God; *see also* **Deo**

Deity, the the one God (cap.)

déjà vu seen before (not ital.)

déjeuner/ (Fr. m.) breakfast or lunch; *petit* — coffee and rolls on rising; — *à la fourchette* meat breakfast, early lunch

de jure (Lat.) by right (often not ital. in legal contexts)

Dekker, Thomas (*c*.1570–1640) English playwright

de Klerk, F(rederik) W(illem) (b. 1936) President of S. Africa 1989–94

de Kooning, Willem (b. 1904) Dutch-born US painter

del (math.) the symbol ∇

Del. Delaware (off. abbr.)

del. delegate, delete

del. delineavit (drew this)

de La (as prefix to proper name) one cap. ('de La Condamine'), two if starting a sentence; *de* is dropped in the absence of a forename; alphabetized under *La* ('La Fontaine, Jean de'). When Anglicized, the prefix may deviate from this practice ('de la Mare', 'De La Warr'); follow established convention or the bearer's preference; cf. **de**; **du**

Delacroix, Ferdinand Victor Eugène (1799–1863) French painter

de La Fontaine *see* **La Fontaine**

de la Mare, Walter (1873–1956) English poet, novelist, and critic

de la Ramée, Marie Louise (1839–1908) English novelist, pseud. **Ouida**

De la Roche, Mazo (1885–1961) Canadian novelist

Delaroche, Paul (1797–1856) French painter

de La Tour *see* **La Tour**

Delaware off. abbr. **Del.**, postal **DE**

De La Warr, Earl (three caps.)

dele (typ.) delete

deleatur (Lat.) let it be deleted

delegate abbr. **del.**

delenda (Lat.) things to be deleted

delft/, -ware glazed earthenware made at Delft (*formerly* Delf) in Holland

Delibes, Léo (1836–91) French composer

delicatesse delicacy (not ital.), in Fr. f. *délicatesse*

delicatessen a shop or department selling prepared foods

Delilah (OT) *but* Dalila in Milton's *Samson Agonistes*

delineable that can be delineated

delineavit (Lat.) drew this; abbr. *del.*

delirium/ a disordered state of mind, with hallucinations, pl. **-s**; — **tremens** delirium with trembling induced by heavy drinking, abbr. **d.t., d.t.s**

De L'Isle, Viscount

deliverer *not* -or

Della Cruscan (noun and adj.) (a member) of the Florentine Accademia della Crusca, concerned with the purity of the Italian language, 16th c.; or of an English poetical group in Florence, late 18th c.

Della Robbia an enamelled terracotta invented by Luca della Robbia; *see also* **Robbia**

Delph/i Greece, the site of an ancient oracle, in Gr. **Delphoi**; **-ic**, *not* -ian

delta/ the fourth letter of the Gr. alphabet (Δ, δ); **— rays, — rhythm, — wing** (two words)

deltiology the collecting and study of post-cards

de luxe luxurious (not ital., two words, one word in US)

dem (Ger.) to the, for the (m. and n. sing., dative)

Dem. (US) Democrat

dem. (typ.) demy

demagog/ue *not* -gog (US); **-y, -uery, -ic**

dem/ain *use* **-esne**

de mal en pis (Fr.) from bad to worse

demarcate mark the limits of, *not* -kate

demarch the chief officer of an ancient Attic deme, a modern Greek mayor

démarche political step or initiative (not ital.)

demean to lower in dignity

demeanour bearing towards another

démenti (Fr. m.) official denial of a rumour etc.

dementia mental enfeeblement (not ital.)

demesne *not* -ain

demi/god, -goddess, -john (one word)

demilitarize *not* -ise

demi/-mondaine (Fr. f.) a woman of the *demi-monde*; *-monde* a class of women considered to be of doubtful social standing and morality, esp. those in 19th-c. France; *-pension* accommodation with one main meal per day; *-saison* spring or autumn fabric (ital., hyphens)

demise death, bequeath; *not* -ize

demi-sec (of champagne or other wines) moderately sweetened (hyphen)

demisemiquaver also called (esp. US) **thirty-second note**

demitasse a small coffee cup, in Fr. f. *demi-tasse*

demiurg/e, -ic (one word)

demo/ (colloq.) demonstration, pl. **-s** (no point)

demobilize discharge from the army, *not* -ise; colloq. **demob**

Democrat/ cap. for US political party; abbr. **D.**; lower case for a believer in a government of social equality, adj. **-ic**

democratize *not* -ise

Democrit/us (5th c. BC) Greek philosopher, adj. **-ean**

démod/é (Fr.) f. **-ée** out of fashion

demoiselle a young lady (not ital.)

Demoivre, Abraham (1667–1754) French mathematician (one word)

demon an evil spirit or devil, *or* a cruel or destructive person; *see also* **daemon**; **daimon**

demon. demonstrative

demonetize divest of value as currency, *not* -ise

demon/ic, -ize *not* dae-

demonstrable *not* -atable

demonstrator *not* -er

demoralize *not* -ise

De Morgan,/ Augustus (1806–71) English mathematician; **— William Frend** (1839–1917) his son, English novelist

de mortuis nil nisi bonum or **bene** (Lat.) speak nothing but good of the dead

demos the people (not ital.)

demotic the popular colloquial form of a language (not cap.); the later form of Ancient Egyptian cursive writing, or the form of the language used in such texts (cf. **hieratic**); the normal spoken form of modern Greek (cf. **katharevousa**)

dempster *use* **deem-**

demurr/able (law) **-age, -er**

dem/y a scholar at Magdalen College, Oxford; pl. **-ies**

demy/ (pron. 'dĕ-meye', with stress on second syllable) (typ.) former size of paper, $17\frac{1}{2}$ × $22\frac{1}{2}$ in.; **— 4to** $11\frac{1}{4}$ × $8\frac{3}{4}$ in.; **— 8vo** $8\frac{3}{4}$ × $5\frac{5}{8}$ in. (untrimmed); basis for size of **metric —** 564 × 444 mm

den (Ger.) the (m. sing., accusative), to the (pl., dative)

Den. Denmark

denar *use* **din-**

denar/ius (Lat.) an ancient Roman silver coin, often translated as a penny; pl. **-ii**; abbr. **d.** (ital.)

denationalize *not* -ise

dene a wooded valley, *not* dean

D.Eng. Doctor of Engineering

dengue not — fever, denga, -gey

Deng Xiaoping (1904–97) Chinese Communist statesman, Vice-Premier 1973–6 and 1977–80, Vice-Chairman of the Central Committee of the Chinese Communist Party 1977–80; even after retirement in 1989 was effective leader of China until death; in Wade–Giles **Teng Hsiao-P'ing**

Denholm Borders

Denholme W. Yorks.

deniable *see* **deny**

denier a unit of silk, rayon, or nylon yarn weight; (hist.) one-twelfth of a French sou

denim a twilled cotton fabric

Denmark abbr. **Den.**

de nos jours (Fr.) of our time (placed after the noun)

denouement a final unravelling, as of a plot or complicated situation *not* the climax of a story etc. (no accent, not ital.)

denounce give notice to terminate (treaty)

de nouveau (Fr.) afresh

de novo (Lat.) afresh

dent. dent/al, -ist, -istry

dentelle (Fr. f.) lacework

dentil one of the toothlike blocks under the bed-moulding of a cornice; *not* -el, -ile

dentine a hard, dense, bony tissue in teeth; *not* -tin (US)

den/y, -iable, -ial, -ier

deoch an doris (Sc.) a drink taken at parting, a stirrup cup; *not* the many variants (no hyphens, not ital.); in Gaelic *deoch an doruis*, in Ir. *deoch an dorais*

deodand (law, hist.) a personal chattel that has caused death, forfeited to the Crown for religious or charitable use

deodar an E. Indian cedar

deodoriz/e *not* -ise, **-er**

Deo/ favente (Lat.) with God's favour; — *gratias* (we give) thanks to God; — *volente* God willing, abbr. **DV**; *see also Dei*

dep. departs, deposed, deputy

dép. (Fr.) *département*, *député* (deputy)

département (Fr. m.) shire, county; abbr. **dép.**

department abbr. **dept.**, *not* dep't

departmentalize *not* -ise

Department for Education and Employment abbr. **DFEE** (no points)

Department of/ — Health abbr. **DoH** (no points); — **the Environment** abbr. **DoE** (no points); — — **Social Security** abbr. **DSS**; — — **Trade and Industry** abbr. **DTI**

dépays/é (Fr.) f. **-ée** out of one's habitual surroundings

dependant (noun) a person who relies on another, esp. for financial support; *not* -ent (US)

dependen/t, -ce, -cy depending, conditional, or subordinate; *or* unable to do without (esp. a drug)

de pis en pis (Fr.) from bad to worse

de plano (law) clearly

depolarize *not* -ise

deposed abbr. **dep.**

depositary a person to whom something is entrusted

deposition the act or an instance of deposing *or* (law) testimony under oath; cap. for the taking down of the body of Christ from the Cross, or its representation

depositor *not* -er

depository a storehouse

depot in Fr. m. *dépôt*

depressible *not* -able

Depression, the Great the depression of 1929–34 (caps.)

De profundis (Lat.) out of the depths; the first words of Psalm 130, used as the title of the mass for the dead (one cap.); *De Profundis* a prose apologia by Wilde, 1905 (two caps.)

de proprio motu (Lat.) of his, *or* her, own accord

dept. department

député a member of the lower French Chamber

deputize *not* -ise

deputy abbr. **dep.**

Deputy Lieutenant abbr. **DL**

De Quincey/, Thomas (1785–1859) English essayist, **-an**

der (Ger.) the (m. sing., nominative) of *or* to *or* for the (f. sing., genitive and dative, or m., f, and neut. pl., genitive)

der. deriv/ation, -ative, -ed

derby (US) = **bowler** (hat)

Derbyshire abbr. **Derby.**

de règle (Fr.) in order, proper

de rigueur according to etiquette or custom (not ital.)

derisible laughable, *not* -able

derisory derisive, scoffing

deriv/ation, -ative, -ed abbr. **der.**

derm the true skin, *also* **derm/a, -is**

dernier/ (Fr.) last, — *cri* the very latest, — *ressort* a last resource

Derrid/a, Jacques (b. 1930) French philosopher, **-ean**

derrière the buttocks (not ital.)

derrière (Fr. m.) the buttocks, behind (prep.)

derring-do daring action, *not* -doe

derringer a small large-bore pistol (three *r*s), invented by **Henry Deringer** [*sic*] (1786–1868) (not cap.)

Derry postally acceptable abbr. of **Londonderry** (city or county)

der Tag (Ger.) the (great) day

derv a fuel oil for diesel-engined road-vehicles (not cap.)

des (Fr.) of the (pl.); as prefix to a proper name, treat as **de**

dès (Fr.) since

des (Ger.) of the (m. and neut. sing., genitive)

Descartes/, René (1596–1650) French mathematician and philosopher, adj. **Cartesian**, possessive **—'s**

descend/ant (noun) a person or thing descended, **-ent** (adj.) descending

descender (typ.) the lower part of letters such as g, j, p, q, y, which extends below the line

descendible that may descend or be descended, *not* -able

desert a wilderness, to abandon; *see also* **dessert**

desert/ed, -er abbr. **d.**

déshabillé (Fr. m.) a state of being only partly or carelessly clothed, undressed; *not déshabille*; *see also* **dishabille**

desiccate to dry, *not* dessicate

desiderat/um something desired, pl. **-a** (not ital.)

desirable *not* -eable

desktop (one word)

D. ès L. (Fr.) Docteur ès Lettres

desman/ pl. **-s**, *not* -men

Des Moines Ia.

desorb, desorption release from adsorbed state

despatch *use* **dis-**

desperado/ a desperate man, pl. **-es** (not ital.)

despicab/le vile, (morally) contemptible; **-ly**

despise *not* dis-, -ize

Des Plaines a city and river, Ill.

despot in Byzantine times used for territorial rulers subject to an overlord, e.g. 'Despot of Morea'; cap. in such hist. contexts only

despotize act like a despot, *not* -ise

des Prez *see* **Josquin des Prez**

des res a desirable residence (no points)

D. ès S. (Fr.) Docteur ès Sciences, *also* **D. ès Sc.**

D. ès Sc. Pol. (Fr.) Docteur ès Sciences Politiques

dessert a dinner course; *see also* **desert**

dessertspoonful/ pl. **-s** (one word)

dessicate *use* **desicc-**

destra/ (It.) right-hand side, abbr. **d.**; — **mano** (mus.) the right hand, abbr. **DM**

destructible *not* -able

destructor a refuse-burning furnace, *not* -er

desuetude a state of disuse

desunt/ cetera (Lat.) the rest are missing, — **multa** many things are wanting

Detaille, Jean Baptiste Édouard (1848–1912) French painter (no accent)

detector (person or thing) *not* -er

de te fabula narratur (Lat.) of thee is the story told

detent a catch (mechanical)

détente easing of strained relations between states (not ital.)

détenu/ (Fr.) f. **-e** one detained in custody

deterrent *not* -ant

detestable *not* -ible

detonat/e, -or

detour a circuitous way, in Fr. m. **détour**

detract/or f. **-ress**

detritus debris (not ital.)

de trop not wanted, superfluous (not ital.)

Deus/ (Lat.) God, abbr. **D.**; — **avertat!** God forbid; — **det** God grant

deus ex machina an unexpected power or event that saves a seemingly hopeless situation, esp. in a play or novel (not ital.)

Deus misereatur God be merciful

deuteragonist the person second in importance to the protagonist in a drama

deuterium/ symbol **D** (no point), — **oxide** heavy water

Deutero-Isaiah the supposed later author of Isaiah 40–55

Deuteronomy (OT) abbr. **Deut.**

Deutsch,/ André, Ltd publishers; — **Otto Erich** (1883–1967) compiler of a thematic catalogue of Schubert's works, *see* **D.**

Deutsche Mark chief monetary unit of Germany; usually written and spoken in Eng. **Deutschmark** *or* **D-Mark**; abbr. **DM** (no point), set close up to following (also preceding) figure; *see also* **mark**; **Ostmark**

Deutsches Reich (Ger.) the official name of Germany 1871–1945 (including the Weimar period)

Deutschland (Ger.) Germany as a geopolitical entity, and the shorthand term for the political entity (*formally* **Bundesrepublik Deutschland**)

de Valéra, Éamon (1882–1975) US-born Prime Minister of Ireland 1932–48, 1951–4, 1957–9; President 1959–73

Devanagari the alphabet used for Indian languages; more properly transcribed as **Devanāgarī**, also called **Nāgarī**.

develop/, -abie, -ment *not* -pe

devest *see* **divest**

deviat/e, -or *not* -er

devil not cap. unless referring to Satan

deviling a young devil

devilled *not* -viled (US)

devilling working as a hack, *not* -iling (US)

devilry *not* -try

devil's advocate an official at papal court appointed to challenge proposed canonization (officially the *Promotor Fidei*); a person who opposes a proposition to test it

Devil's Island a penal settlement, French Guiana; in Fr. **Île du Diable**

Devils/ Playground, — Postpile Calif. (no apos.)

Devils Tower Wyo. (no apos.)

devis/e *not* -ize, **-er** one who devises (non-legal)

devis/ee one who is bequeathed real estate, **-or** one who bequeaths it

devitalize render lifeless, *not* -ise

devoir an act of civility (not ital.)

Devon/ the official name of the county; **Earl of —** *but* **Duke of Devonshire**

Devonian of or relating to Devon; (of or relating to) the fourth period of the Palaeozoic era

Devonshire abbr. **Devon.**

De Vries, Hugo (1848–1935) Dutch botanist

DEW Distant Early Warning

Dewalee use **Diwali**

dewan the prime minister or finance minister of an Indian state

dewar a vacuum flask (not cap.)

De Wet, Christian Rudolph (1854–1922) Boer general and statesman

Dewey/, George (1837–1917) US admiral; —, **John** (1859–1952) US philosopher; —, **Melvil** (1851–1931) US librarian, inventor of the — **decimal system**, a library classification using three-figure numbers to cover the major branches of knowledge; —, **Thomas Edmund** (1902–71) US politician

De Witt, Jan (1625–72) Dutch statesman

dexter/ (her.) the shield-bearer's right, the observer's left, opp. of **sinister**

dextrous/ not -erous; **-ly**

DF *Defensor Fidei* (Defender of the Faith), Dean of Faculty; direction-find/er, -ing

DFC Distinguished Flying Cross

DFEE Department for Education and Employment

DFM Distinguished Flying Medal

dft. draft

DG *Dei gratia* (by the grace of God), *Deo gratias* (thanks to God), Director General, Dragoon Guards

dg decigram(s) (no point)

d. h. (Ger.) *das heißt* (that is to say) (space in Ger. abbr.)

Dhaka Bangladesh

dhal (a dish made with) a kind of split pulse, a common foodstuff in India; not dal

dharma (Ind.) social custom, the right behaviour; the Buddhist truth; Hindu social or moral law

dhobi an Indian washerman

dhooly use **doolie**

dhoti a loincloth worn by male Hindus; not -ee, -ootie

dhow a lateen-rigged ship used on the Arabian sea (accepted misspelling of **dow**), not daou, daw

DHSS (hist.) Department of Health and Social Security

Dhuleep use **Du-**

dhurra use **durra**

dhurrie an Indian cotton fabric, not durrie

DI Defence Intelligence

d. i. (Ger.) *das ist* (that is) (space in Ger. abbr.)

dia. diameter

diablerie devilry, *not* -ry (not ital.)

diachylon a plaster; *not* -um, -culum

diaconate the office of deacon, *not* de-

diacritic a sign (e.g. accent, diaeresis, cedilla) used to indicate different sounds or values of a letter

diaeresis (typ.) a sign (¨) over the second of two vowels, showing that it is to be pronounced separately, as in 'naïve'; *not* die-

Diaghilev, Sergei (**Pavlovich**) (1872–1929) Russian ballet impresario

diagnos/is pl. **-es**

dial/, -led, -ling

dialect/, -al, -ic, -ical abbr. **dial.**

dialectic/ pl. **-s** (usually treated as sing.); **-al, -ian**

diallage (rhet.) a figure of speech in which various arguments are brought to bear on one point; (mineralogy) a brown, grey, or green mineral similar to augite

dialling/ code, — tone *not* dial tone (US) (two words)

dialogue conversation in drama, novels, etc., not necessarily between two persons only; *not* -log (US)

dialyse (chem.) separate by filtration through a membrane; *not* -ize, -yze (US)

dialys/is pl. **-es**

diamanté (not ital.)

diameter abbr. **dia., diam.**

diarchy rule by two authorities (esp. in India 1921–37), *not* dy-

diarrhoea *not* -hea (US)

diaspora a dispersal, (cap.) that of the Jews among the Gentiles mainly in the 8th–6th cc. BC

diatessaron (mus.) Greek and medieval name for the perfect fourth, hence metaphorically a harmony of the four Gospels (not cap.)

diathes/is (med.) a constitutional predisposition to a certain (esp. diseased) state, pl. **-es**

DIC Diploma of Membership of Imperial College, London

dic/ey risky, *not* -cy; **-ier, -iest**

dichotom/y a division into two classes, parts, etc., a sharp or paradoxical contrast; does not mean *dilemma* or *ambivalence*; **-ize** divide into two parts, *not* -ise

Dichter/ (Ger. m.) an author, esp. one of superior merit (suggesting, but not confined to, a writer of verse), f. **-in**; cf. **Schriftsteller**; **Verfasser**

Dickens/, Charles (1812–70) English novelist, **-ian**

Dickens House London, headquarters of the Dickens Fellowship (no apos.)

dickey use **-ky**

Dicksee, Sir Frank (1853–1928), English painter, FPRA 1924–8

dicky a rear seat (usually a folding type), a false shirt-front, a small bird; *not* -ey

dict. dictator, dictionary

Dictaphone (propr.)

dictionnaire (Fr. m., two *n*s) dictionary

dict/um a saying, pl. **-a**

dicy *use* **-cey**

didactyl two-fingered, *not* -le

didgeridoo an Australian Aboriginal musical wind instrument of long tubular shape, *not* -jeridoo

didicoi (sl.) a gypsy, an itinerant tinker; *not* didakai, diddicoy

Didot (typ.) a European system for type measurement; 12 pt. Didot = 4.512 mm; *see also* **body**; **cicero**

didrachm a coin worth two drachmas

didst (no apos.)

die (Ger.) the (f. sing., and m., f., and neut. pl., nominative and accusative)

diecious *use* **dioe-**

died abbr. **d.**; *see also* **dagger**

diehard (one word)

dieresis *use* **diae-**

dies (Lat.) day(s)

diesel a compression-ignition engine

dies/ fausti (Lat.) auspicious days, — *infausti* inauspicious days, — *irae* day of wrath (cap. *D* as Latin hymn sung in a mass for the dead)

dies/is (mus.) variously used for 'quartertone' and sharp sign, (typ.) a rare name for the double dagger (‡); pl. **-es**

dies/ juridicus (Lat.) a day on which courts sit; — *nefasti* blank days (*properly* days on which the Roman praetor did not hear lawsuits, popularly (in Rome) unlucky days); — *non* (law) a day on which no business is done, or that does not count for legal purposes

die-stamping (typ.) an intaglio process leaving a raised impression

dietitian *not* -cian

'Dieu et mon droit' God and my right (English royal motto)

'Die Wacht am Rhein' (Ger.) the Watch on the Rhine, a famous German patriotic song

differ/, -ence abbr. **diff.**

différance (Fr. m.) a term coined by philosopher Jacques Derrida to combine two senses of the French verb *différer* (to differ, and to defer or postpone) in a noun, to indicate simultaneously two senses in which language denies us the full presence or identity of any meaning

differenti/a a distinguishing mark, esp. between species within a genus; pl. **-ae**

diffuser *not* -or

digamma the sixth letter (Ϝ, ϝ) of the early Greek alphabet; original name *wau*

Digest, the the compendium of Roman law compiled in the reign of Justinian (6th c. AD)

digester a person or instrument, *not* -or

digestible *not* -able

digital/ something giving a reading by means of displayed digits; (comput.) operating on data represented as a series of binary digits or in similar discrete form, *see also* **analog**; — **audio tape** a magnetic tape on which sound is recorded digitally, abbr. **DAT**

digitiz/ation (comput.) electronic reduction of characters, by scanning, to a series of digital signals; **-ed font** font so prepared stored electronically in photosetter (also called **ECM**)

diglot (a book containing text) using two languages, *not* -lott

digniora sint priora (Lat.) let things worthier precede

dignitary *not* -atory

Dijck, Christoffel Van (1601–?1669) type founder; his work (now largely lost) served as the model for Caslon and for the Monotype 'Van Dijck' (1935)

dike *use* **dy-** in all senses (except in US for the sense of a long wall, embankment, etc.)

diktat a categorical statement (not ital.); *but* **Diktat** (Ger. n.) the German view of the Treaty of Versailles, 1919 (cap., ital.)

dil. dilute

dilapidat/e, -ed, -ion *not* de-

dilatable *not* -eable

dilat/ation widening or expansion, *not* dilation; **-or, -ator**

dilemma/ a position involving a choice between two unsatisfactory lines of argument or action, *not* simply a synonym for 'problem'; pl. **-s**

dilettant/e (It.) a lover of the fine arts, an amateur dabbler in the fine arts; pl. **-es** *or* **-i** (not ital.)

Dilhorne, Viscount family name Manningham-Buller

diligence (hist.) a public stagecoach, esp. in France (not ital.)

Dillon, Viscount

diluvi/um (geol.) an aqueous deposit, pl. **-a**; **-al** of a flood, esp. of the Flood in Genesis or the Glacial Drift formation in geology (not ital.)

dim. *dimidium* (one half), diminutive

dim. diminuendo

DiMaggio, Joe (1914–99) US baseball player

dime (US) ten cents, abbr. **d.**

diminuendo (It. mus.) getting softer, abbr. *dim.*

dim sum a meal or course of savoury Chinese-style snacks, *not* dim sim

DIN (Deutsche Industrie-Norm) (hist.) a series of technical standards used internationally, esp. to designate electrical connections, film speeds, and paper sizes; *now* **ISO** (International Standards Organization)

Dinan dép. Côtes-du-Nord, France

Dinant Belgium

dinar a Byzantine gold coin (*denarius*, in Arab. *dīnār*); a unit of currency in Bosnia-Hercegovina, Macedonia, and various Middle East and N. African countries; *not* de-

Dinard dép. Côtes-du-Nord, France

d'Indy, Paul Marie Théodore Vincent (1851–1931) French composer

Dinesen, Isak pseud. of **Baroness Karen Blixen** (1885–1962) Danish writer

Ding an sich (Ger. philos. n.) thing in itself

ding-dong (hyphen)

dinghy a small boat; *not* -gey, -gy

dingo/ an Australian native dog, pl. **-es**

dingy grimy; *see also* **dinghy**

dining/ car, — room, — table (two words)

dinner jacket abbr. **DJ**

dioces/e, -an abbr. **dioc.**

dioecious (bot.) *not* die-

Diogenes (412–323 BC) Cynic philosopher

Diogenes Laertius (*c.* AD 200) biographer of philosophers

dionym a binomial, as *Homo sapiens*

Dionysia (pl. noun) the orgiastic and dramatic festival(s) of Dionysus

Dionysi/ac of Dionysus, **-an** of Dionysius

Dionysius (430–367 BC) and his son (*fl.* 350 BC) tyrants of Syracuse

Dionysus the Greek god of living growth, wine, and ecstasy

dioptre a unit of a lens's refractive power, abbr. **d.**; *not* -ter (US)

Dioscuri, the (Gr. myth.) Castor and Pollux

DIP/ (comput.) a form of integrated circuit, **— switch** an arrangement of switches on an electronic device for selecting an operating mode (abbr. of *dual in-line package*)

Dip. Diploma

Dip. A.D. Diploma in Art and Design

Dip. Ed. Diploma in Education

Dip. H.E. Diploma of Higher Education

diphtheria *not* dipth-

diplomaed *not* -a'd, *but prefer* 'with a diploma'

diplomat *not now* -matist, abbr. **dipl.**

diplomate (esp. US) one holding a diploma, esp. in medicine; in Fr. **diplôm/é** f. **-ée**

Diplomatic Lectureship in, *not* Diplomatics

dipsomania/, -c *not* dyp-

diptych *not* -tich

Dirac constant (math.) Planck constant divided by 2π, pron. 'h bar'; symbol **$\hbar$**

Directoire the French Directory of 1795–9; (adj.) of the dress or furniture of the period (cap.)

directress female director; *not* -ice, *but prefer* **director**

directr/ix (geom.) a fixed line used in describing a curve or surface, pl. **-ices**

dirham the principal monetary unit of Morocco and the United Arab Emirates

Dirichlet series (math.)

dirigible capable of being guided; a dirigible balloon or airship

dirig/isme economic control by the State, **-iste** (not ital.)

dirndl an Alpine peasant bodice and full skirt

dirt track (two words, hyphen when attrib.)

dis. discipline; discontinu/e, -ed; discount, (typ.) distribute

disaffirm (law) reverse (a previous decision); repudiate (a settlement)

dis aliter visum (Lat.) the gods (have) thought otherwise

disappoint (one *s*, two *p*s)

disassemble take (a machine) apart; cf. **dissemble**

disassociate *use* **disso-**

disbound (of a pamphlet etc.) removed from a bound volume

disburden *not* -then

disbursement *not* -sment

disc/ a flat thin circular object, a mark of this shape, a layer of cartilage between vertebrae, a gramophone record; **compact —** and **optical —, — brakes**; *see also* **disk**

disc. discover/ed, -er; discount

discern/ to see; **-ible**; *see also* **decern**

discerpt/ible able to be plucked apart, divisible; **-ibility**

discerption (arch.) (an instance of) a pulling apart, severance; a severed piece

disciplinary *not* -ery

discipline abbr. **dis.**

discipular disciple-like

disc jockey abbr. **DJ**

disco/ pl. **-s**

discobol/us a discus thrower, *not* -ulus; pl. **-i** (not cap.); the 'Discobolus' (cap.) is the lost statue by Myron, of which **discoboli** are copies

discoloration *not* discolour-

discolour/, -ed, -ment *not* discolor (US)

discombobulate (US) disturb, disconcert

discomfit/, -ed, -ing disconcert, thwart; **-ure**

discomfort lack of ease, to make uneasy

disconnection not -xion

discontinu/e, -ed abbr. **dis.**

discothèque (not ital., no accent in US)

discount/ abbr. **dis.,** — **rate** (US) the minimum lending rate, — **store** a shop that sells goods at less than the normal retail price

discover/ed, -er abbr. **disc.**

Discovery Day (US) = **Columbus Day**

discreet tactful, judicious

discrete distinct, separate

discus/ pl. **-uses**

disect use **diss-**

disenfranchise or **disfranchise** not -ize

disenthral/ not -enthrall (US), -inthral(l); **-led, -ment**

disenthrone use **dethrone**

disentrain (mil.) get off a train

diseu/r (Fr. m.) f. **-se** artist entertaining with monologues

disguis/e, -er

dishabille Eng. form of **déshabillé**

dishevel/led with hair or dress in disorder, not -eled (US); **-ling** not -eling (US)

dishonour/, -able not -or, -orable (US)

disinterested impartial; cf. **uninterested**

disjecta membra (Lat.) scattered remains, but 'disiecti membra poetae' (Horace)

disk/ (US) = **disc**; (comput.) — **drive, floppy** —, **hard** —, **magnetic** —; **-ette**; see also **disc**

diskette (comput.) a floppy disk

dismissible not -able

Disneyland Anaheim, Calif.

Disney World Orlando, Fla.

disorganiz/e, -er not -ise

disorient/ed, -ing prefer to **disorientat/ed, -ing**; see also **orientate**

dispatch/, -er, -ing not des-

dispensable not -ible

dispensary abbr. **disp.**

Dispersion, the the Diaspora

display/ (typ.) the setting and leading of titles, advertisements, etc., or a direction to set in this style; — **type** of a size or cut suited to this

Disraeli,/ Benjamin (1804–81) Earl of Beaconsfield; — **Isaac** (1766–1848) writer, father of the foregoing, originally spelt his surname **d'Israeli**

dissect/, -ion, -or not dise-

disseis/e dispossess wrongfully, not -ze; **-ee, -in, -or, -oress**

dissemble conceal (one's thoughts or intentions); cf. **disassemble**

disseminat/e scatter abroad, **-or**

dissension disagreement giving rise to discord, not -tion

Dissenter from Church of England (cap.)

dissertation abbr. **diss.**

dissociate to separate, not disasso-

dissoluble able to be disintegrated, loosened, or disconnected; not -uable

dissolvable not -ible

dissyllable use disy-

dissymmetry not disy-

dist. distance, distilled; distinguish, -ed; district

distension not -tion

distich/ a pair of verse lines, a couplet; pl. **-s**

distil/ not distill (US) but **-lation, -led, -ling**; abbr. **dist.**

distingu/é (Fr.) f. **-ée**, having a distinguished air

distinguish/, -ed abbr. **dist.**

distrait/ f. **-e** absent-minded (not ital.)

distraught extremely agitated or distracted

distributary one of the streams of a river delta

distributor one who or that which distributes

district abbr. **dist.**

District/ Attorney (US) abbr. **DA**; — **Court** abbr. **DC**; — **of Columbia** the seat of the US federal government, covering the same area as the city of Washington, abbr. **DC**; — **Registry** abbr. **DR**

disulphide not -sulfide (US)

disyllab/le, -ic, -ize of two syllables, not diss-; in Fr. m. **dissyllabe**

disymmetry use **diss-**

dit/ (Fr. m) ditty; (verb) called, used after a name to indicate a better-known pseudonym etc., f. **-e**

ditheism belief in two gods, not dy-

dithyramb a wild hymn of Bacchic revellers, not dythi-

ditto/ abbr. **do.**, often represented by ,, under the word or sum to be repeated; **-graphy** (an example of) a copyist's mistaken repetition of a letter, word, or phrase

div. divide, -d; dividend, divine, division, divisor, divorce, (Fr.) divers (diverse)

dive-bomber (hyphen)

divers sundry

diverse different

diverticul/um a byway, esp. of the intestines; pl. **-a**

divertiment/o (mus.) a light and entertaining composition, often in the form of a suite for chamber orchestra; pl. **-i**, not -os

divertissement a diversion, an entertainment; a short ballet

Dives a rich man, from the Vulgate translation of Luke 16

divest *not* de- (except in law, as *devest out of*)

divi *use* **divvy**

divid/e, -ed, -end abbr. **div.**; sign for divide ÷

divided highway (US) = **dual carriageway**

divide et impera (Lat.) divide and rule

Divina Commedia, la by Dante, 1300–18; *not* a Come-

diving/ bell, — board, — suit (two words)

Divis (Ger. typ. n.) the hyphen

divisi (mus.) in several parts

divisible *not* -able

divisim (Lat.) separately

division mark ÷

divisor (math.) a factor, *not* -er; abbr. **div.**

divorc/é (Fr.) f. **-ée** a divorced person; Eng. **divorcee** is common gender

divvy *not* divi

Diwali a Hindu festival with illuminations, held between September and November; *not* Dewalee

dixi (Lat.) I have spoken (marking the end of a speech)

Dixie/ *or* **-land** (one word) the US Southern states

DIY do it yourself

DJ dinner jacket, disc jockey

Djakarta Indonesia, *use* **Jak-**

djellaba a hooded woollen Arab cloak; *also* **jel-laba**

djib/ba, -bah *use* **jibba**

Djibouti *not* Jibuti

djinn *use* **jinnee**

DL Deputy-Lieutenant

dl decilitre(s) (no point)

D.Lit. Doctor of Literature, **D.Litt.** Doctor of Letters; *see also* **Lit.D.**; **Litt.D.**

DLM (mus.) double long metre

DM Deputy Master, (It. mus.) *destra mano* (the right hand), Deutsche Mark (Ger. currency), Doctor of Medicine (Oxford), (Fr.) *Docteur en Médecine* (Doctor of Medicine)

dm decimetre(s) (no point)

D-Mark *see* **Deutsche Mark**

D.Mus. Doctor of Music

DMZ (US) Demilitarized Zone

DN *Dominus noster* (our Lord)

DNA deoxyribonucleic acid

DNB *Dictionary of National Biography*

Dnieper River Belarus–Ukraine, in Russ. **Dnepr**

Dniester River Ukraine, in Russ. **Dnestr**

D-notice a government notice to news editors not to publish items on specified subjects, for reasons of security

DNS (typ.) do not set

do (noun) pl. **dos**, *not* do's

do (mus.) *use* **doh** in the tonic sol-fa system

do. ditto, the same

DOA dead on arrival

doat *use* **dote**

Dobbs Ferry NY (no apos.)

Dobermann pinscher a German breed of hound, *not* -man (US)

doc. document(s)

Docent (Ger. m.) a university teacher, now *Doz-*

doch-an-doris *use* **deoch an doris**

docket/, -ed, -ing

docklands (not cap.) *but* **Docklands** E. London

dockyard (one word)

Docteur ès/ Lettres (Fr. m.) Doctor of Letters, abbr. **DèsL**; — — **Sciences** Doctor of Science, abbr. **DèsS** *or* **DèsSc**; — — **Sciences Politiques** Doctor of Political Science, abbr. **DèsScPol**

Doctor abbr. **D.** *but* 'Dr' before name (although not in combination with any of the following after the name); **Doctor of/ Canon Law** *or* **Civil Law DCL**; — — **Dental Surgery DDS**; — — **Divinity DD**; — — **Laws LLD**; — — **Letters D.Litt., Lit(t).D.**; — — **Literature Lit.D.**; — — **Medicine MD, DM**; — — **Music D.Mus., Mus.D.**; — — **Philosophy Ph.D., D.Phil.**; — — **Science D.Sc., Sc.D.**; — — **Veterinary Science** *or* **Surgery DVS**

Doctors' Commons London, where marriage licences were formerly issued by the Bishop of London's Registry (apos.)

doctrinaire an unpractical theorist or political extremist; theoretical and unpractical (not ital.)

docudrama a dramatized television film based on real events (one word)

document/, -ation abbr. **doc.**

documentary (noun) a factual report or film

DOD (US) Department of Defense

dodecaphonic (mus.) of the twelve-note scale

dodgem a funfair car

dodo/ an extinct flightless bird, pl. **-s**

DoE Department of the Environment

doek (S. Afr.) a cloth, esp. a head-cloth

dogana (It. f.) custom house

dogaressa the wife of a doge (not ital.)

dogate the office of doge, *not* -eate (not ital.)

dog/ cart, — days hottest period of the year (two words)

doge the chief magistrate of Venice (not ital.)

dog/fight, -fish (one word)

doggerel unpoetic verse, *not* -grel

Doggett's Coat and Badge trophies of Thames Watermen's championship

dogg/ie a pet name for a (little) dog, **-y** of or like a dog; *see also* **dogie**

doghouse (one word)

dogie (US) a motherless or neglected calf

dog Latin barbarous Latin (two words)

dogma/ authoritative doctrine, pl. **-s**

dogmatize *not* -ise

dogsbody (naut. sl.) a junior officer, a general drudge

dog-star (hyphen)

DoH Department of Health

doh (mus.) *not* do

Dohnányi/, Ernő (1877–1960) Hungarian composer (double acute on first name, *not* umlaut), *formerly* known as **Ernst von —**

doily a napkin; *not* -ey, doyley, -ly, d'oyley, -ie

Dolby (propr.) an electronic noise-reduction system used to reduce tape hiss in recording

dolce (mus.) sweetly

dolce/ far niente (It.) delightful idleness, — *vita* sweet life

doleful *not* -ll

Dolgellau Gwynedd, *not* -ey

Dolittle, Dr John the hero of a series of children's books by Hugh Lofting (1886–1947)

dollar mark $ *or* $, to be before, and close up to, the figures, as $50. Various dollars should be differentiated as $A (Australian), $CAN (Canada), $HK (Hong Kong), $US

Dollfuss, Engelbert (1892–1934) Austrian politician, Chancellor 1932–4

doll's house *not* -s' house, dollhouse (US)

Dolly Varden a character in Dickens's *Barnaby Rudge*, 1841; a type of woman's large hat; a brightly spotted char of western N. America

dolman a Turkish robe, a hussar's jacket, a woman's mantle

dolmen a prehistoric megalithic tomb

dolorous doleful, *but* **dolour** *not* -or (US)

DOM *Deo optimo maximo* (To God the best and greatest), *Dominus omnium magister* (God the Master, or Lord, of all)

Dom (Ger. m.) cathedral; (Russ.) house (not cap.)

dom (Port.) a title of nobility, (Brazilian) a title of respect, as for priests (= **don**); f. **dona**, *not* doña (cap. as part of name), abbr. **D.** (m. and f.); also a title prefixed to the names of some Roman Catholic dignitaries and Benedictine and Carthusian monks, e.g. Dom Gasquet, Dom Pérignon; *see also* **don**

dom. domestic, dominion

domaine a vineyard

Domenichino real name **Domenico Zampieri** (1581–1641) Italian painter

Domesday Book *not* Dooms-; abbr. **DB**

domestic abbr. **dom.**

domicile *not* -cil

Domine dirige nos (Lat.) O Lord, direct us (motto of the City of London)

Dominica one of the Windward Islands, W. Indies

Dominican Republic W. Indies, the eastern portion of the island of Hispaniola

dominie (Sc.) headmaster

dominion abbr. **dom.**

Dominion Day Canada, 1 July

domino/ pl. **-es**

Dominus/ (Lat.) Lord, abbr. **D.**; — *noster* our Lord, **DN**

Domus Procerum (law) the House of Lords; abbr. **DP**, **Dom. Proc.**

don/ a Sp. and S. American title prefixed to a forename, and in It. used with a priest's Christian name and with certain noble families (cap. as part of name, except in Peru); (Port. f.) **dona**, (Sp. f.) **doña**, (It. f.) **donna**; abbr. **D.** (m. and f.); *see also* **dom**; — a university teacher, by convention reserved for a senior member of a college, esp. at Oxford or Cambridge

Donegal Ireland

Donegall/, Marquess of; — **Square, — Street** Belfast

dong the chief monetary unit of Vietnam

dongle (comput.) a security attachment required by a computer to enable protected software to be used

Donizetti, Gaetano (1797–1848) Italian composer

donjon the great tower or innermost keep of a castle; cf. **dungeon**

donna (It.) a lady (ital.), the title of such a lady (cap., not ital.)

Donne, John (1573–1631) English poet

donnée (Fr. f.) a basic fact, the subject or theme of story etc.

Don/ Quixote a novel in two parts (1605, 1615) by Cervantes; in Sp. — *Quijote* (in full *El ingenioso hidalgo don Quijote de la Mancha*, and alphabetized under 'Q')

donut *use* **dough-**

doohickey (US) a small (esp. mechanical) object

doolie (Ind.) a litter, palanquin; *not* dhooley, -lie, -ly, dooly

Doolittle,/ Eliza the heroine of Shaw's *Pygmalion*, — **Hilda** (1886–1961) US poet

Doomsday Book *use* **Domes-** *not* the — —

doorkeeper (one word)

doormouse *use* **dor-**

Doornik Fl. for **Tournai**

dop (Afrik.) cheap brandy, a tot

Doppelgänger/ (Ger. m.) an apparition or double of a living person, pl. same; f. **-in**, pl. **-innen**; in Eng. not cap., not ital., and takes an *s* for the plural

Doppelpunkt (Ger. typ. m.) the colon

Dopper (S. Afr.) a member of the Ge-reformeerde Kerk

doppio (*movimento*) (It.) double (speed)

Doppler effect (phys.) apparent change of frequency when source of vibrations is approaching or receding, from **Christian Johann Doppler** (1803–53) Austrian physicist; *not* -ö-

dopy *use* -**pey**

Dor. Doric

DORA Defence of the Realm Act, 1914

Doré, Paul Gustave (1833–83) French painter and engraver

Dori/an of or relating to the Dorians in ancient Greece, or to Doris in Cent. Greece; -**c** (of) the dialect of the Dorians, (of) a rustic accent, (archit.) (of) the oldest Greek order

dormeuse (Fr. f.) a settee, nightcap, travelling sleeping carriage

dor/mouse *not* door-, pl. -**mice**

dormy (golf) as many up as there are holes to play, *not* -ie

Dorneywood Bucks., a country house used as the official residence by any minister designated by the Prime Minister

doronicum (bot.) leopard's bane

dorp (Afrik.) village, country town

d'Orsay, Alfred Guillaume Gabriel, Count (1801–52) 'the last dandy'

Dorset *not* -shire

dory a fish, (US) a flat-bottomed boat; *not* -ey

DOS (comput.) disk operating system

dos-à-dos (Fr.) back to back, a sofa made for sitting so; also a kind of bookbinding

dosage the size or the giving of a dose, *not* -eage

dos and don'ts *not* do's and don't's

dose an amount of medicine taken at one time, abbr. **d.**

do-se-do/ pl. -**s**; *not* do-si-do

dosimeter *not* dose-

Dos Passos, John (**Roderigo**) (1896–1970) US novelist

dossier papers referring to some matter (*not* ital.)

Dostoevsky, Fyodor (**Mikhailovich**) (1821–81) Russian novelist

dot (Fr. f.) a woman's dowry

dot/e show great fondness, *not* doat; -**age**, -**ard**

dots (**...**) *see* **ellipsis**

Douai/ dép. Nord, France; *not* -y; — **School** *but* **Douay Bible** the RC translations

douane a foreign custom house, abbr. **d.**

double (typ.) a word etc. erroneously repeated

double agent (two words)

double-barrelled (hyphen) *not* -eled (US)

double bass (mus.) (two words)

double/ bill, — bluff, — boiler, — bond (two words)

double/-book, -breasted, -check (hyphens)

double/ concerto, — cream (two words)

double-cross, (hyphen)

double dagger (typ.) the reference mark ‡, formerly called a diesis (two words)

double/-dealer, -decker (hyphens)

double entendre a word or phrase of two meanings, one of them usually indecent (obs. Fr., now Anglicized (hyphen in US); the modern Fr. is *double entente, un mot à*)

double obelus (typ.) a double dagger (‡)

double/-stopping, -talk (hyphens)

doublethink (one word)

double-tonguing (mus.) (hyphen)

doubloon (hist.) a Spanish gold coin

doublure (Fr. typ. f.) ornamental inner lining (usually of leather) to a book cover

doubting Thomas an incredulous or sceptical person (after John 20: 24–9) (one cap.)

doucement (Fr. mus.) sweetly

douceur (Fr. f.) a gratuity

douche a jet of water directed at the body (not ital.)

doughboy (US) a dumpling; a US infantryman, esp. in the First World War (one word)

doughnut (one word) *not* donut

Douglas/ fir, — pine, — spruce (one cap.)

Doukhobors *use* **Dukh-**

Dounreay Highland, atomic research station

douse drench with water, extinguish; cf. **dowse**

douzaine (Fr. f.) dozen, abbr. *dzne.*

dove (US past and past part.) = **dived**

dovecote *not* -cot

dow *use* **dhow**

dowager a widow with a dower or retaining her title, abbr. **dow.**

dowel/ (fasten with) a headless pin, usually of wood; -**led, -ling** (one *l* in US)

dower a widow's life-interest in her husband's property

Dow-Jones New York Stock Exchange index (hyphen)

Down a county of N. Ireland

down/beat, -cast (one word)

Downe, Viscount

down/fall, -grade, -hearted, -hill, -land, -load, -market, -pour, -right, -scale, -side, -stairs, -state, -stream (one word)

down-stroke (hyphen)

Down syndrome *not* 's — (*see* **syndrome**); *not* mongol, -oid

down time (two words)

downtown (US) the more central or business part of a town or city, = **city centre** (one word); cf. **uptown**

down/trodden, -turn (one word)

down wind (noun), **downwind** (adj. and adv.)

dowry money or property brought by a bride to her husband

dowse use a divining rod; cf. **douse**

doyen/ the senior member of a society (not ital.), f. **-ne**

d'oyl/ey, -ie *use* **doily**

D'Oyly Carte, Richard (1844–1901) English theatrical impresario

dozen/, -s abbr. **doz.**

Dozent (Ger. m.) a university teacher, *not now* Doc- (cap.)

DP data processing, displaced person (refugee), (law) *Domus Procerum* (the House of Lords)

DPAS Discharged Prisoners' Aid Society

DPH Diploma in Public Health

D.Phil. Doctor of Philosophy; Ph.D. is the more usual title

DPP Director of Public Prosecutions

DR (naut.) dead reckoning, dispatch rider, District Railway, District Registry, (Ger.) *Deutsches Reich* (German Empire)

Dr doctor (before name)

dr. drachm, -s; drachma (dram *or* coin), -s; dram, -s; drawer, drive, debtor

drachm a weight or measure formerly used by apothecaries, sign ℥, abbr. **dr.**; for other senses *use* **dram**

drachma/ the chief monetary unit of Greece; pl. **-s**, abbr. **dr.**

draconian very harsh or severe, esp. of laws and their application (not cap.); of or relating to Drako, 7th-c. BC Athenian legislator (cap.)

draft a deduction in weighing, a military party, a money order, a rough sketch; *or* to draw off, sketch (US) = **draught**; abbr. **dft.**; cf. **draught**

draftsman one who drafts documents; cf. **draughtsman**

drafty (US) = **draughty**

dragée a sweetmeat enclosing a drug or nut or fruit

draggle-tail a slut, *not* daggle-

drag/line, -net (one word)

dragoman/ an Arabic, Turkish, or Persian interpreter; pl. **-s**, *not* -men

dragonfly (one word)

dragonnade the French persecution of Protestants from 1681; *not* -onade, -oonade

Dragoon Guards abbr. **DG**; these are not 'Guardsmen'

drag/ queen, — race (two words)

drainboard (US) = **draining board**

dram 60 grains, one teaspoonful, 60 minims, small drink; *see* **drachm**; pl. **-s**, abbr. **dr.**

dramat/ic, -ist abbr. **dram.**

dramatis personae (a list of) characters in a play, abbr. **dram. pers.** (not ital.)

dramatize *not* -ise

Drambuie (propr.) a Scotch whisky liqueur

Drang nach Osten (Ger.) desire for expansion eastwards

Drapier's Letters by Swift, 1724

draught the act of drawing or drinking, a take of fish, 20 lb of eels, a dose, a vessel's depth in water, a current of air, liquor 'on draught'; cf. **draft**

draughtsman one who makes drawings, plans, etc.; a piece in the game of draughts; cf. **draftsman**

Dravidian (of or relating to) (a member of) a dark-skinned aboriginal people of S. India and Sri Lanka, including the Tamils and Kanarese; any of the languages spoken by this people

drawback in technical meaning of excise duty remitted, abbr. **dbk.**

drawbridge (one word)

drawer abbr. **dr.**

drawing/ board, — paper, — pin, — room (two words)

draw-on cover (bind.) a limp cover glued to the back of a book

Drdla, Franz (1868–1944) Czech composer

dreadnought (hist.) a type of battleship (from the name of the first, launched in 1906) (cap.); *not* -naught

Dred Scott (19th c.) black slave, subject of US law case, 1857

Dreiser, Theodore (1871–1945) US novelist

Dresden china (one cap.)

dressing/ case, — down, — gown, — room, — station, — table (two words)

drey a squirrel's nest, *not* dray

driblet a trickle, *not* dribb-

dri/er (adj.), **-est, -ly**; *but* **dry/ish, -ness**; cf. **dryer**

drift/-ice, -net (hyphens)

driftwood (one word)

drily *not* dryly (US)

drip/-dry, -proof (hyphens)

drivable *not* -eable

drivell/ed, -er, -ing (one *l* in US)

drive out (typ.) to set matter with wide word spacing, such setting

driving licence (two words), *not* driver's — (US)

drizzling (meteor.) abbr. **d.**

droit/ moral and legal right; **— de seigneur** (not ital.)

droite (Fr. f.) the right hand, abbr. **d.**

dromedary the one-humped Arabian camel, *Camelus dromedarius*; cf. **camel**

Drontheim *use* **Trond-**

drop initial (typ.) the first letter of a chapter opening etc., descending one or more lines below the first line

drop kick (two words)

drop-leaf, -out (hyphens)

dropped head (typ.) an opening title of chapter etc. set lower than first line of text on other pages

droshky (Russ. pl. *drozhki*) a low four-wheeled open carriage, *not* -sky

drought/, -y arid(ity), *not* drouth

DRP *Deutsches Reichspatent*, a German patent

drug/gist (US) a pharmacist, **-store** (US) a chemist's shop (one word)

Druid/ f. **-ess** (cap.)

drum/beat, -fire, -head (one word)

drum major/ an NCO commanding regimental drummers, a baton-twirling leader of a marching band, f. **-ette**

drum set (US) = **drum kit**

drumstick (one word)

drunkenness (three *n*s)

Druze a member of a political or religious sect linked with Islam and living near Mount Lebanon, *not* Drus, -e

Dryasdust a dull pedant (character in prefaces of Scott's novels) (one word, cap.)

dry/er (noun) one who or that which dries, *not* drier; **-est** *use* **dri-** (except in US); *see also* **drier**

dry/ish, -ness *not* dri-

dryly *use* **drily** (except in US)

dry point an etching needle, the work produced by it (two words)

DS (mus.) dal segno (from the sign), disseminated sclerosis

Ds. *dominus*, at Cambridge, a Bachelor of Arts

DSC Distinguished Service Cross

D.Sc. Doctor of Science

DSIR Department of Scientific and Industrial Research

DSM Distinguished Service Medal, (mus.) double short metre

DSO (Companion of the) Distinguished Service Order

d.s.p. *decessit sine prole* (died without issue)

DSS Department of Social Security

DST (US) Daylight Saving Time

d.t., dt's delirium tremens

Du. Dutch

du (as prefix to proper name) where cap. ('Du Deffand, Marie, marquise', 'Duchamp, Marcel'), used in alphabetizing; where not cap. (except when starting a sentence), alphabetized by surname, even if formed from a title ('Maine, Louise de Bourbon, duchesse du'); follow established convention or the bearer's preference; cf. **de**; **de La**

Dual Monarchy (caps.)

Duarte, José Napoleón (1925–90) President of El Salvador 1972, 1980–2, 1984–9

dub. *dubitans* (doubting), *dubius* (dubious)

Du Barry, Marie Jeanne Bécu, comtesse (1746–93) favourite of Louis XV of France

dubbin a grease for leather, *not* -ing

Dubček, Alexander (1921–92) Czechoslovak politician

Dublin/ abbr. **Dubl.**, — **Bay prawn** (two caps.)

Dubois-Raymond, Emil (1818–96) German physiologist, *not* du Bois

Dubonnet (propr.) a sweet French aperitif

duc (Fr.) Duke, f. *duchesse* (not cap., not ital. as part of name)

duces tecum (Lat.) a subpoena (lit. 'you will bring with you')

du Chaillu, Paul Belloni (1837–1904) French-American explorer in Africa

duchess a duke's wife or widow, *or* a woman holding the rank of duke in her own right (cap. as title); in Fr. *duchesse* (not cap.)

duchesse/ a soft heavy kind of satin, a dressing table with a pivoting mirror; — **lace,** — **potatoes,** — **set** (two words)

duchy a dukedom, **the Duchy** the royal dukedom of Cornwall or Lancaster (cap.)

duckbill (one word), *but* **duck-billed platypus** (one hyphen)

duckboard (one word)

duck-rabbit (philos.) *see* **hare-duck**

duckweed (one word)

ductus (Lat. med.) a duct, pl. same (*not* -i)

Dudevant *see* **Sand, George**

dudgeon a feeling of offence, resentment; *not* dun-

duel/ler, -ling, -list (one *l* in US)

duello the rules or practice of duelling

duende an evil spirit, personal magnetism, inspiration (not ital.)

duenna a chaperon (not ital.), in Sp. *dueña*

Dufay, Guillaume (*c*.1400–75) Franco-Flemish composer, *also* **Du Fay**

duffel/ a coarse woollen cloth, *not* -le; — **bag,** — **coat** (two words)

Dufy, Raoul (1877–1953) French painter

dugout (one word)

Duguesclin, Bertrand *see* **Guesclin, du**

duiker (Afrik.) a small antelope, *not* duy-

duke cap. as title, abbr. **D.**; in Fr. *duc* (not cap.)

Dukhobors a Russian sect, *not* Doukh-

Duleep Singh *not* Dhuleep, Dulip

dulia (RC) the reverence accorded to saints and angels (not ital.)

dullness *not* dul-

Dulong and Petit, law of (phys.)

Duma a Russian council of State

Dumas/, Davy de la Pailleterie, Alexandre (1762–1806) French general, father of — **Alexandre** (1802–70) French writer; — *fils,* **Alexandre** (1824–95) his son, French writer; —, **Jean Baptiste André** (1800–84) French chemist

du Maurier,/ George (**Louis Palmella Busson**) (1834–96) English artist and author; — **Sir Gerald** (1873–1934) his son, actor-manager; — **Dame Daphne** (1907–89) his daughter, author

Dumbarton Strathclyde

Dumbarton Oaks/ an estate in Washington, DC, at which — — **Conference** was held, 1944

dumb-bell (hyphen)

dumbfound/, -ed, -er, -ing *not* dumf-

dumdum bullet (no hyphen)

Dumfries & Galloway a region of Scotland

dummy (print.) a prototype

dump truck (US) = **tipper lorry, dumper truck**

dum sola (*et casta*) (law) while unmarried (and chaste)

Dunbarton a former Scottish county; *see also* **Dumbarton**

Dunblane Central, *not* Dum-

Duncan-Sandys, Baron (hyphen)

Dunelm: the signature of the Bishop of Durham (colon); of Durham University (no point, no colon)

dungaree/ a coarse calico material, **-s** overalls made of this; *not* -eree(s)

dungeon an underground cell for prisoners, *not* dud-; cf. **donjon**

dunghill (one word)

duniwassal (Sc.) a Highland gentleman, *not* dunni-

Dunkirk dép. Nord, France; in Fr. (and often now in Eng.) **Dunkerque**

Dún Laoghaire port and suburb of Dublin

Dunnottar Castle Grampian

Duns Scotus, Johannes (*c.*1266–1308) metaphysician

duodecimo/ *or* **twelvemo/** (typ.) a book based on twelve leaves, twenty-four pages, to the sheet; pl. **-s**; abbr. **12mo**

duologue a (stage) conversation between two

duotone (print.) a half-tone illustration in two colours from the same original with different screen angles

Du Pont a family of American industrialists

duppy (W. Ind.) a malevolent spirit or ghost

du Pré, Jacqueline (1945–87) English cellist

Duquesne/, Abraham, marquis (1610–88) French admiral; **Fort** — French fort, 1754, renamed Fort Pitt (Pittsburgh, Pa.) on its capture by the English in 1758

dur (Ger. mus.) major

dura *use* **durra**

durab/le, -ility

durchkomponiert (mus.) having different music for each stanza in a song

Dürer/, Albrecht (1471–1528) German painter; **-esque**

duress constraint, *not* -e

Durex (propr.) a condom

D'Urfey, Thomas (1653–1723) English playwright

Durham abbr. **Dur.**

Durkheim, Émile (1858–1917) French sociologist

durra a kind of sorghum, = **jowar**, *not* dhurra, dura

Dürrenmatt, Friedrich (1921–90) Swiss playwright, novelist, and critic

durrie *use* **dhurrie**

Dushanbe capital of Tajikistan

Dussek, Jan Ladislav (1760–1812) Bohemian composer

Düsseldorf Germany

dustbin (one word)

dust bowl an area denuded of vegetation by drought or erosion (two words, not cap.); the region along the western edge of the Great Plains, USA (caps.)

dustcart (one word)

dust jacket (two words); the parts of a dust-jacket are usually divided into front, front flap, back, back flap, and spine

dust/man, -pan (one word)

dust sheet (two words)

dust-shot (hyphen, two words in US)

dust storm (two words)

dust-trap (hyphen, two words in US)

Dutch of, relating to, or associated with the Netherlands; (US arch.) German; abbr. **Du.**

Dutchess County New York State

Dutch Guiana *now* **Suriname**

dutiable subject to duty

duumvir/ one of a pair of Roman officials, Eng. pl. **-s**

dux a top pupil at certain schools (not ital.)

dux/ (Lat.) a leader, pl. *duces*; — *gregis* leader of the flock

duyker *use* **dui-**

DV *Deo volente* (God willing)

Dvořák, Antonín (1841–1904) Bohemian composer

Dvr. Driver

DVS Doctor of Veterinary Science (*or* Surgery)

dw deadweight, delivered weight

dwale *use* **belladonna**

dwarf/ pl. **-s**, *not* -ves (except in Tolkien and other fantasy writing)

dwt deadweight tonnage, pennyweight, -s; 24 troy grains; *not* pwt.

Dy dysprosium (no point)

dyad a pair, a group of two, (math.) an operator that is a combination of two vectors

Dyak (an indigenous inhabitant) of Borneo or Sarawak, *not* Day-

dyarchy *use* **di-**

dybbuk/ a malevolent spirit in Jewish folklore, pl. **-im**

Dyce Airport Aberdeen

dyeing colouring cloth etc.; cf. **dying**

dye-line (print.) a diazo print (hyphen)

dyestuff (one word)

Dyfed a Welsh county

dying ceasing to live; cf. **dyeing**

Dyirbal (of or relating to) (a member of) an Aboriginal people of northern Queensland, Australia, or their language

dyke *not* di- (US, for a long wall, embankment, etc.)

dynamics the science of matter and motion (sing.), abbr. **dyn.**

dynamo/ pl. **-s**

dyne a unit of force, abbr. **dyn** (no point); in SI units 10 μN

dyotheism *use* **dith-**

dys- a prefix meaning difficult or defective; distinguish it from **dis-**, meaning apart

dysentery a severe infection of the intestines

dyslex/ia a disorder marked by difficulty in reading and spelling, adj. **-ic**

dyspep/sia chronic indigestion, *not* dis-; **-tic**

dysphasia (med.) a lack of coordination in speech, owing to brain damage

dysphoria a state of unease or mental discomfort

dysplasia (med.) the abnormal growth of tissues etc.

dyspno/ea (med.) difficult or laboured breathing, *not* -nea (US); **-eic**

dysprosium symbol **Dy**

dyss/ a megalithic chambered tomb of a kind found in Denmark, pl. **-er**; in Dan. *dysse*

dytheism *use* **di-**

dythiramb *use* **dithy-**

dziggetai a Mongolian wild ass, *not* the many variants

dzne. (Fr.) *douzaine* (dozen)

dzo a cow–yak hybrid, pl. same; *not* the many variants; in Tibetan *mdso*

Dzonghka *also* **-gka** a Tibetan dialect, also called **Bhutani**, the official language of Bhutan

D-Zug (Ger. m.) *Durchgangszug* (an express train)

Ee

E Egyptian (as in £E), (prefix) exa-, the fifth in a series

E. Earl; east, -ern; English

e a symbol used on packaging (in conjunction with specification of weight, size, etc.) to indicate compliance with EC regulations

€ symbol for the euro

e (It., Port.) and

e. (meteor.) wet air but no rain

e eccentricity of ellipse, (dyn.) coefficient of elasticity, (elec.) electromotive force of a cell

e, e, *or* **ε** (math.) the base of natural or Napierian logarithms

é (Port.) is

è (It.) is

è (**e grave accent**) to be used in Eng. for the last syllable of past tenses and participles when that otherwise mute syllable is to be separately pronounced, as 'Hence, loathèd Melancholy!'

each abbr. **ea.**

eadem (Lat.) the same (female) author, abbr. **ead.**, pl. **eaedem**, abbr. **eaed.** (not ital., not cap. except to begin a sentence or note); *see also* **eidem**; **idem**

EAEC European Atomic Energy Community (*now* **Euratom**)

eagre a tidal wave, *not* -er

E. & O. E. errors and omissions excepted

ear/ache, -bash (one word)

ear drops (two words)

ear/drum, -ful (one word)

Earhart, Amelia (1898–1937) US aviator

earl (cap. as title) abbr. **E.**

Earl Grey a type of tea flavoured with bergamot

Earl Marshal the officer presiding over the College of Heralds

ear lobe (two words, except in US)

Earl Palatinate (hist.) an earl having royal authority within his country or domain (caps.)

Earls Court London (no apos.)

ear/mark, -muff, -phone, -piece, -plug, -ring, -shot (one word)

earth, the cap. only in astronomical, poetical, mythological, and anthropomorphic contexts; not cap. and not preceded by 'the' in electrical contexts; symbol ⊕

earthwork (one word)

east abbr. **E.**; *see also* **compass points**

eastbound (one word)

East Bridgford Notts.

East Chester, Eastchester two different towns in NY

East End London (caps.)

East Ender (two words) *but* the television programme is *EastEnders* (one word)

Easter Day the first Sunday after the ecclesiastical full moon on, or next after, 21 Mar.

eastern abbr. **E.**; *see also* **compass points**

easternmost (one word)

East Indiaman (hist.) a large ship engaged in trade with the East Indies

East Kilbride Strathclyde

easy chair (two words)

easygoing (one word)

eau/ de Cologne (three words); **-de-Nil, -de-vie** (hyphens); **— forte** nitric acid, *also* an etching; **— fortiste** an etcher; **— sucrée** sugar and water (not ital.)

Eaudyke Lincs.

EB Encyclopaedia Britannica

Ebbets Field a baseball stadium, New York (no apos.)

Ebbw Vale Gwent, in Welsh **Glynebwy**

ebd. (Ger.) *ebenda*, ibid.

Eblis the chief of the fallen angels in Muslim mythology, *also* **I-** (following Persian pron.)

ebonize *not* -ise

Ebor. *Eboracum* (York)

Ebor: the signature of the Archbishop of York (colon)

EBU European Broadcasting Union

eburnean like ivory, *not* -ian

EC East-Central (postal district of London), Education(al) Committee, Electricity Council, Engineer Captain, Episcopal Church, Established Church, European Community, Executive Committee

écarté a two-person game of cards *or* a position in classical ballet (not ital.)

ECB English Cricket Board

Ecce Homo 'Behold the Man' (John 19: 5)

eccentric/, -ally, -ity; for mathematical sense *see* **excentric**

Ecclefechan Dumfries & Galloway, birthplace of Carlyle

Ecclesiastes (OT) abbr. **Eccles.**

ecclesiastical/ abbr. **eccles.**; **— signs**; Greek Cross ☧ used in service books to notify 'make the sign of the cross', also before signatures of certain Church dignitaries; in service books use ℞ response, ℣ versicle, * words to be intoned; *see also* **cross**; **crux**

Ecclesiasticus (Apocr.) abbr. **Ecclus.**; *also called* **Sirach**, **Sirah**, **Ben Sirach**

ECG electrocardiogram

ECGD Export Credits Guarantee Department

Echegaray, José (1833–1916) Spanish poet, playwright, economist, mathematician, and statesman

echelon (not ital., no accent)

echo/ pl. **-es**, *not* -os

echt (Ger.) genuine

éclair a small pastry filled with cream

éclaircissement (Fr. m.) explanation

éclat a brilliant display, dazzling effect, *or* social distinction, universal renown (not ital.)

eclectic borrowing freely from various sources

eclogue a short pastoral poem

ECM electronic character master; *see also* **digitization**

Eco, Umberto (b. 1932) Italian academic and writer

ecology the study of organisms in their environment, *not* oe-; abbr. **ecol.**

econometrics (pl. noun, usually treated as sing.)

Economist, The (cap. *T*) the definite article is traditionally included in references

economize *not* -ise

econom/y, -ical, -ics, -ist abbr. **econ.**

écossais/ (Fr.) f. **-e** Scottish (not cap.)

écossaise an energetic dance (not ital.)

ecphras/is (lit.), **-tic** a description used as a device to halt a narrative so as to include ancillary information; in Gr. **ekph-**

ecraseur a surgical instrument (no accent)

écrevisse (Fr. f.) crayfish

ecru an unbleached linen colour (no accent, not ital.)

ECSC European Coal and Steel Community

ecstas/y rapture, *not* ex-, -cy; (cap., sl.) a powerful stimulant and hallucinatory drug, MDMA; **-ize** *not* -ise

ECT electroconvulsive therapy

ecu (hist.) European currency unit (*also* **ECU**)

écu (Fr. m.) a French coin; (Fr. her.) a shield or escutcheon (ital.)

Ecuador/ *not* Eq-; abbr. **Ecua.**

ecumenic/, -al belonging to the entire Christian Church, *not* oec- except in specialist uses, e.g. Oecumenical Council

eczema a skin inflammation

ed. edited, editor

EDD *English Dialect Dictionary*

Edda/ a collection of Icelandic legends, pl. **-s**; **The Elder** (*or* **Poetic**) — a collection of poems, 11th c. and earlier; **The Younger** (*or* **Prose**) — 13th-c. stories, prosody, and commentary

Eddy, Mary Morse Baker (1821–1910) founder of Christian Science

Eddystone/ Lighthouse, — Rocks off SW coast of Britain

edelweiss an Alpine plant

edema/, -tous *use* oed-

Edgbaston Birmingham, *not* Edge-

edge tool *not* edged

edgeways *not* -way, -wise (except in dialect)

Edgeworth,/ Maria (1767–1849) Irish novelist; **— Richard Lovell** (1744–1817) her father, Irish educationist

Edgware/ London, **— Road**

edh alternative (esp. US) spelling for **eth**

edidit (Lat.) edited this

edile *use* aed-

Edinburgh abbr. **Edin.**, **E'boro**

Edipus *use* Oe-

Edirne *formerly* Adrianople, Turkey

Edison, Thomas Alva (1847–1931) US inventor

édit/é f. **-ée**; **édité(e) par** (Fr.) published by

éditeur (Fr. m.) publisher, *not* editor; *édité par* is now used in Fr. also to describe the role of a volume editor, as distinct from e.g. a publisher's editor; cf. *rédacteur*

edition (print.) abbr. **edn.** (*not* ed.), pl. **edns.** (*not* eds.) the state of a book (also the copies, or any one copy, so printed) at its first publication, and after each revision, enlargement, abridgement, or change of format (2nd, 3rd, etc.); *not* a reprint containing no substantial alteration; *see also* **impression**; **reprint**

édition de luxe (Fr.) sumptuous edition (ital.)

editio/ princeps first printed edition, pl. **-nes principes**

editor abbr. **ed.**; pl. **eds.** (preferred) *or* **edd.**

edn. edition, pl. **edns.**

edn. cit. the edition cited

Edo a former name for Tokyo; *see also* **Yeddo**

EDP electronic data processing

EDS English Dialect Society

EDT (US) Eastern Daylight Time

educ/ate, -able

educationist *not* -alist

educ/e, -ible

Eduskunta the Parliament of Finland

EE Early English

ee (Sc.) eye, pl. **een**

E.E. & M.P. Envoy Extraordinary and Minister Plenipotentiary

EEC European Economic Community (the Common Market); *see also* **European Community**; **European Union**

EEG electroencephalogram

eerie weird, *not* -y; **eerily**

Eestimaa (Est.) Estonia, *also* **Meiemaa**

EETPU Electrical, Electronic, Tele-communications, and Plumbing Union

EETS Early English Text Society

effect/er one who effects, **-ive** having a definite or desired result, **-or** (biol.) an organ that effects a response to a stimulus, **-uate** cause to happen (*prefer* **effect**)

effendi/ a man of education or standing in eastern Mediterranean or Arab countries, (cap.) a former title of respect or courtesy in Turkey; *not* -dee; pl. **-s**

Efficients a 19th-c. economic school (cap.)

effluvi/um the vapour from decaying matter, pl. **-a**

effluxion that which flows out, *not* -ction

EFL English as a Foreign Language

Efrog (Welsh) York, *also* **Caer —**; **— Newydd** New York

Efta (*also* **EFTA**) European Free Trade Association

e.g. (Lat.) *exampli gratia* (for example) (not ital., comma before)

egg/cup, -head (one word)

eggplant (US) = **aubergine** (one word)

eggshell (one word)

ego/ (psychol.) the self that is conscious and thinks, pl. **-s**

egotize act egotistically, *not* -ise

egret the lesser white heron; *see also* **aigrette**

Egypt/, -ian *see* **United Arab Republic**

Egyptolog/ist, -y abbr. **Egyptol.** (cap.)

eh to be followed by exclamation mark when used as an exclamation, by question mark when used as a question

Ehrenburg, (Ilya Grigorevich) (1891–1967) Russian writer and poet

ehrenhalber (Ger.) honorary, abbr. **eh.**

Eid/ (*correctly* **Id**) either of two Muslim festivals; (in full) **— ul-Fitr**, marking the end of the fast of Ramadan, or (in full) **— ul-Adha**, marking the culmination of the annual pilgrimage to Mecca

eidem (Lat.) the same authors (at least one of whom is male), abbr. **eid.** (not ital., not cap. except to begin a sentence or note); *see also* **eadem**; **idem**

eidol/on a phantom, pl. **-a**

Eifel Mountains Germany

Eiffel/, Alexandre Gustave (1832–1923) French engineer; **— Tower** Paris, in Fr. **Tour Eiffel**

eigen/frequency, -function, -value (math., phys.; one word)

Eigg Inner Hebrides, Scotland

eighteenmo/ (typ.) a book based on eighteen leaves, thirty-six pages, to the sheet; also called **octodecimo, decimo-octavo**; pl. **-s**, abbr. **18mo**

Eighteenth Amendment to the Constitution of the USA, 1920, introducing prohibition of intoxicating liquor; repealed by Twenty-First Amendment, 1933

8vo octavo

eigret/, -te *use* **aigrette**; *see also* **egret**

eikon *use* **icon**

Eikon Basilike a pamphlet (1648/9) reputedly by Charles I, more probably by John Gauden (1605–62), bishop and writer; another, written by Titus Oates, dedicated to William III and attacking James II

Eileithyia the Greek goddess of birth

ein (Ger.) a, an *or* one, a person, they; to differentiate between indefinite article and pronoun in Ger., the latter is sometimes styled with an acute (*éin*); the use of cap. (*Ein*) or letterspacing (*e i n*) is now considered old-fashioned

einschließlich (Ger.) including, inclusive; abbr. **einschl.**

Einstein,/ Albert (1879–1955) German physicist, naturalized US citizen 1940; **— Alfred** (1880–1952) German musicologist, naturalized US citizen 1945

einsteinium symbol **Es**

Éire in Gaelic means 'Ireland'; former off. name of the Republic of Ireland (or 'the Irish Republic'); note the accent, as *eire* in Gaelic means 'burden'

eirenicon a peace proposal, *not* ir-

Eisenhower, Dwight David (1890–1969) US general, Supreme Commander of Allied Expeditionary Force in the Second World War; US President 1953–61

Eisenstein, Sergei (Mikhailovich) (1898–1948) Russian film director

eisteddfod/ a congress of Welsh bards, a national or local festival for musical competitions; pl. **-s, -au** (in Welsh); not cap. except as part of title

eiusdem/ (Lat.) of the same, abbr. **eiusd.**; **— generis** of the same kind; *also* (esp. in law) ***ejusdem***

ejector *not* -er

ejemplo (Sp.) example, abbr. **ej.**

EKG (US var., Ger.) electrocardio/gram, -graph

ekphrasis *use* **ecph-**

El (Heb.) God

el (Sp. m.) the

él (Sp.) he (*but* **el que** (no accent) for 'he who', as *el* is the article)

Elagabalus (204–22) Emperor of Rome 218–22; *not* Elio-, though Helio- is found in late Roman sources

El Al Israel Airlines, Ltd

El Alamein Egypt; battle, 1942

élan dash, spirit (accent, not ital.)

élan vital life force (ital.)

elasticated *not* -cized (US)

E-layer a layer of the ionosphere able to reflect medium-frequency radio waves, *not* E-region

Elbrus, Mount Caucasus; *not* -ruz, -urz

Elburz mountains, Iran, *not* -bruz

elchee Anglicized version of *elçi*, a Turkish ambassador

Elder Brethren of Trinity House (caps.)

eldorado/ any imaginary country or city abounding in gold, a place of great abundance; in specialist use (hist.) **El Dorado** (two words, not ital.); pl. **-s**

elec. electricity, electrical, electuary

elector (hist.) a German prince electing an emperor (cap. as title); a member of a US electoral college, a voter, *not* -er

Electra complex the f. analogue of **Oedipus complex**

electress *not* -toress

electro/ electrotype (no point), pl. **-s**

electrocute *not* -icute

electroencephalograph an instrument recording the electrical activity of the brain (one word), abbr. **EEG**

electrolyse break up by electric means, *not* -yze (US)

electrolyte a solution able to conduct electric current

electromagnet/**ic, -ism** (pertaining to) electricity and magnetism (one word)

electro/**meter** an electricity measurer, **-motive** producing electricity, **-motor** an electric motor (one word)

electron spin resonance (no hyphen) abbr. **ESR**

electronvolt a unit of energy (one word), abbr. **eV** (one cap.)

electrotype a duplicate printing plate made by copper electrolysis (one word), abbr. **electro**

electuary a sweetened medicine, abbr. **elec.**

eleemosynary of or dependent on alms; charitable, gratuitous

eleg/**y** a funeral song, a pensive poem; **-iac**; **-ist** the writer of an elegy, *not* -iast; **-ize** write elegy, *not* -ise; *see also* **elogy**; **eulogy**

elementary abbr. **elem.**

elements (chem.) no point after symbols

elench/**us** (logic) a refutation, pl. **-i**; **elenctic** *not* -chtic

Elephantine Egypt, famed for archaeological yields

elevator *not* -er

Elgin Marbles transported to British Museum from Athens, 1805–12, by the Earl of Elgin

El Giza Egypt, site of the pyramids; *use* **Giza**

Elia pseud. of **Charles Lamb**

Elias Gr. form of Elijah used in NT (AV)

Elien: the signature of the Bishop of Ely (colon)

eligible *not* -able

Eliogabalus *use* **Ela-**

Eliot/ family name of the Earl of St Germans; **—, George** (1819–90) pseud. of **Mary Ann** (*later* **Marian**) **Evans**, English novelist; **—, T**(homas) **S**(tearns) (1888–1965) US (naturalized British) poet; *see also* **Elliot**; **Elyot**

elision (typ.) the suppression of letters or syllables in contractions

elite (not ital., no accent)

Elizabeth abbr. **Eliz.**, in Fr. and Ger. **Elisabeth**, in It. **Elisabetta**, in Sp. **Isabel**, in Scandinavian languages **Elisabet**

Ellice a river in NW Canada

Ellice Islands the former name of **Tuvalu**, W. Pacific

Elliot in the family name of the Earl of Minto; the family in Jane Austen's *Persuasion*; *see also* **Eliot**; **Elyot**

ellips/**is** the omission of words, pl. **-es**; symbol …

Ellis Island the former immigration centre in New York Bay

éloge (Fr. m.) an oration of praise, Anglicized as **eloge** (no accent)

elogi/**um** pl. **-a, elogy** a (funeral) oration of praise, also **eloge**; *see also* **elegy**; **eulogy**

Elohim (Heb.) the Deity

eloin (law) abscond, *not* -gn

Elois/**a, -e** *see* **Héloïse**

E. long. east longitude

El Paso Tex.; *not* -ss-

El Salvador Cent. America, capital San Salvador

Elsass-Lothringen *use* **Alsace-Lorraine**

Elsevier *see* **Elze-**

Elsinore trad. Eng. (as in *Hamlet*) for Dan. **Helsingør**

ELT English language teaching

elucidator one who makes clear, *not* -er

elusive difficult to grasp, mentally or physically; cf. **illusory**

elver a young eel

Elyot, Sir Thomas (?1499–1546) English writer; *see also* **Eliot**; **Elliot**

Élysée palace, Paris

Elysium (Gr. myth.) the abode of dead heroes (cap., not ital.), also **Elysian Fields**

elytr/**on** the hard wing-case of a beetle, pl. **-a** (not ital.)

Elzevier a Dutch family of booksellers and printers, in business ?1583–1712, *not* -vir, although the form is found in some bibliographical sources; the name of the modern publisher is **Elsevier**

EM Earl Marshal, Edward Medal, *Equitum Magister* (Master of the Horse)

Em. Emmanuel, Emily, Emma

em (typ.) a horizontal unit of space, the square of the body of any size of type, originally figured as the width of a capital M; *also* the standard unit of typographic measurement, equal to 12 pt., the 'pica' em; *see also* **em rule**, **en**

'em them

EMA European Monetary Agreement

email electronic mail, *also* **e-mail** (hyphen), *not* E-mail

ém/ail (Fr. m.) enamel, pl. *-aux*, adj. *-aillé*

email/ ink a type of ink used on glass, porcelain, etc.; **— ombrant** a process in which the impressions of the design appear as shadows (two words, not ital.)

Emanuel School Wandsworth

embalmment the preservation of a dead body (three *m*s); **embalming** is the more usual noun

embargo/ a temporary ban on trade, pl. **-es**

embarkation *not* -cation

embarras/ (Fr. m.); **— de richesse(s)** a superfluity of good things; **— de voitures** traffic jam; **— du choix** difficulty of choosing, *not* de

embarrass/, -ment

embassy *not* am- (not cap.)

embathe *not* im-

embed/, -ded, -ding *not* im-

embezzlement *not* -lment

emblaz/e, -onry *not* im-

embod/y, -ied, -ier, -iment *not* im-

embolden *not* im-

embonpoint plumpness (not ital.)

embosom receive into one's affections, *not* im-

emboss raise in relief, *not* im-

embouchement a river mouth (not ital.)

embouchure (mus.) the shaping of the mouth, a mouthpiece (not ital.)

embower shelter with trees, *not* im-

embrangle entangle, confuse; *not* im-

embrasure a door or window recess, widening inwards; *not* -zure

embrocation a liquid used for rubbing on the body to relieve muscular pain etc.; cf. **imbrication**

embroglio *use* im-

embroil confuse, involve in hostility; *not* im-

embrue *use* im-

embryo/ pl. **-s**

embryology abbr. **embryol.**

embue *use* im-

emcee (*also* **MC**) a master of ceremonies, compère

em dash (typ.) = **em rule**

emend alter or remove errors in a text etc.; *see also* **amend**

emerit/us retired and retaining one's title as an honour, pl **-i**, f. **-a**

emerods *use* **haemorrhoids**

Emerson, Ralph Waldo (1803–82) US poet, essayist, and philosopher

emeu (bird) *use* **emu**

émeute (Fr. f.) insurrection

emf electromotive force

EMI Electrical and Musical Industries (Ltd.)

-emia (suffix) *use* **-aemia** (except in US)

emigra/te leave one's own country to settle in another, **-nt** one who does this; cf. **immigrate**

émigr/é f. **-ée** an emigrant, esp. a political exile (not ital.)

éminence grise (Fr. f.) power behind the throne, confidential agent

eminent distinguished, notable, remarkable; cf. **immanent**; **imminent**

Emir a Turkish title (cap.), not cap. in nonspecific Eng. contexts; *see also* **Ameer**, **Amir**

Emmanuel/ College Cambridge; **— (I–III)** Kings of Italy, *properly* **Emanuele**

Emmental a Swiss cheese, *not* -thal

emmesh *use* enm-

Emmet, Robert (1778–1803) Irish patriot

emollient softening or soothing the skin

emolument a salary, fee, or profit from employment or office

Emp. Emperor, Empress

empaestic connected with embossing, *not* -estic

empanel/ enrol, *not* im-; **-led, -ling** (one *l* in US)

empassion *use* im-

Emperor abbr. **Emp.**

emphas/is pl. **-es**

emphasize *not* -ise

emplane *not* en-

empolder *use* im-

empori/um a centre of commerce, a large shop; pl. **-a**

emprise (arch.) a chivalrous enterprise, *not* -ize

emptor a purchaser

empyre/an the highest heaven, **-al**

empyreum/a the 'burnt' smell of organic matter, *not* -ruma; pl. **-ata**

em rule (typ.) a rule (—) the width of an em, set with no space either side in OUP style; *see also* **em**; **en rule**

EMS European Monetary System

EMU European Monetary Union

emu an Australian running bird, *not* emeu

e.m.u. electromagnetic unit(s)

emulator rival, *not* -er

en (typ.) a horizontal unit of space equal to half an em, originally the width of a capital N; *see also* **em**; **en rule**

enactor *not* -er

enamel/led, -ler, -ling

enamorato *use* **in-**

enamoured inspired with love

en/ arrière (Fr.) behind, — ***attendant*** meanwhile, — ***avant*** forward

en bloc in the mass (not ital.)

en brosse bristly cut

enc. enclos/ed, -ure

Encaenia Commemoration at Oxford University, *also* the Graeco-Latin name for Hanukkah; *not* -cenia (not ital.)

encage, encapsulate, encase *not* **in-**

encephalin *use* **enk-**

enchase put in a setting, engrave; *not* **in-**

enchilada (Mexican cook.) a tortilla with chilli sauce and a filling

enchiridi/on a handbook or manual; pl. **-ons**, **-a** (not ital.)

en clair (Fr.) in ordinary language (i.e. not in cipher)

enclos/e, -ure *not* **in-** (*but* **Inclosure Acts**)

encomi/um a eulogy; pl. **-ums**, **-a** (not ital.)

encore again (not ital.)

encroach intrude usurpingly, *not* **in-**

encrust *not* **in-**, *but* **incrustation**

encrypt (comput.) convert (data) into code, esp. to prevent unauthorized access; conceal by this means

encumber to hamper, burden; *not* **in-**

Encyclopaedia Britannica abbr. ***EB***, **Ency. Brit.**

encycloped/ia, -ic, -ical, -ism -ist, -ize abbr. **ency.**, *but use* **-paed-** in quoting titles where that spelling was followed

Encyclopédie the French encyclopedia edited by Diderot, 1751–72; ***encyclopédiste*** a writer for it (not cap.)

en dash (typ.) = **en rule**

endemic regularly found in a specified place; cf. **epidemic**

endemn/ify, -ity *use* **in-**

endent/, -ure *use* **in-**

en/ dernier ressort (Fr.) as a last resource, — ***déshabille*** in undress

endive a curly-leaved plant, *Cichorium endivia*, used in salads; (US) = **chicory**

end leaves *see* **endpapers**

endnote a note printed at the end of (a section of) a book

endors/e write on the back of, *not* **in-**; **-able** *not* -eable, -ible

endpapers (bind.) the sheets at the beginning and end of a book, half of each pasted to the inside of the cover, half forming a flyleaf

endue to invest, *not* **in-**

endur/e, -able, -ed, -er, -ing *not* **in-**

endways *not* -wise

Endymion (Gr. myth.) lover of Selene; ***Endymion***, a poem by Keats; *also* Disraeli's last novel

ENE east-north-east

ENEA European Nuclear Energy Agency

enema/ pl. **-s** (not ital.)

Enemy, the cap. to denote Satan only, *not* the other side in a conflict

energize *not* -ise

enervate deprive of vigour or vitality, *not* **in-**; cf. **inn-**

en/ face (Fr.) facing, — ***famille*** with one's family

enfant/ gâté (Fr. m.) spoilt child, — ***prodigue***, **l'** the prodigal son, —***terrible*** indiscreet person

enfeoff (hist.) transfer land to possession of a subordinate tenant; *see also* **fee**; **feoffee**

en fête (Fr.) in festivity

enfin (Fr.) finally (one word)

enfold *not* **in-**

enforce/, -able *not* **in-**

enfranchis/e, -able, -ement, -ing *not* -ize

ENG electronic news-gathering

Eng. England, English

eng. engineer, -ing; engrav/ed, -er, -ing

Engadine Switzerland, in Ger. **Engadin**

engag/é (Fr.) f. **-ée** morally committed

en garçon (Fr.) as a bachelor

Engels, Friedrich (1820–95) German socialist, associate of Karl Marx

engineer/, -ing abbr. **eng.**

engine room (no hyphen)

Engl/and, -ish abbr. **Eng.**, *not* a synonym for **Britain, British**

English horn *use* **cor anglais**

engraft *not* **in-**

engrain to dye in the raw state, *not* in; cf. **ingrain**

en grande/ tenue *or* — — toilette (Fr.) in full dress

en grand seigneur magnificently

engross *not* **in-**

engulf *not* **in-**, -gulph

enigma/ a riddle, pl. **-s**

enjambment (prosody) the continuation of a sentence without a pause beyond the end of a line, couplet, or stanza (not ital.); in Fr. (m.) ***enjambement***

enkephalin either of two morphine-like peptides occurring naturally in the brain, *not* ence-

en masse in a body (not ital.)

enmesh entangle; *not* emm-, imm-

Enniskillen/ Co. Fermanagh, **Earl of —**, *see also* **Inniskilling**

ennui boredom (not ital.)

ennuy/é f. **-ée** bored (not ital.)

ENO English National Opera

enoculate *use* **in-**

enology *use* **oen-** (except in US)

enormity extreme wickedness *or* error; *not* immensity, of great size, for which *use* **enormousness**

en pantoufle (Fr.) relaxed

en/ passant by the way, in passing; a kind of pawn capture in chess, abbr. **ep** (no points); **— pension** as a boarder or resident (ital.)

enplane *use* **em-**

en/ poste (Fr.) in official position, **— prince** in princely style, **— prise** (chess) in a position to be taken

enquir/e (Brit.) ask, **-y** a question; cf. **inquire**

en/ rapport (Fr.) in sympathy; **— règle** as it should be, in order; **— revanche** in revenge

enrol/, -ment *not* enroll (US), *but* **-led, -ler, -ling**

en route on the way (not ital.)

en rule (typ.) a rule (–) half the width of an em, in OUP style set with no space either side; it is longer than a hyphen (-) and distinct from it in purpose; *see also* **em rule**; **en**

en/s (Lat.) an entity, pl. **-tia**

En Saga ('A Saga'), a tone poem by Sibelius, 1892

Enschede the Netherlands, *but* **Enschedé en Zonen** a printing house at Haarlem

ensconce *not* ins-, es-

en secondes noces (Fr.) by second marriage

ensemble (not ital.)

ensheath *not* -the

ensilage the storage of green fodder in pits or silos

ensnare/, -ment *not* in-

en somme (Fr.) in short

ensuing *not* -eing

en suite to match, forming a unit (not ital.)

ensuite (Fr.) after, following (one word)

ensure make safe or certain; *see also* **assurance**; **assure**; **insure**; **insurance**

enswathe wrap, *not* in-

ENT (med.) ear, nose, and throat

entablature the upper part of a classical building supported by columns or a colonnade

entablement a platform supporting a statue, above the dado and base

entail *not* in-

entente a group of States having an *entente cordiale* (not ital.)

entente/ meaning; **— cordiale** cordial understanding, (caps., not ital.) that between Britain and France, 1904 onwards; *un mot à double* — a word or phrase with two meanings, pl. *mots à double —*; *see also* **double entendre**

enterprise *not* -ize

enthral/ *not* -ll (US), **-led, -ler, -ling, -ment**

enthron/e, -ization *not* in-

entitle *not* in-; *see also* **intitule**

entomology the study of insects, abbr. **entom.**

entourage (not ital.)

en-tout-cas (Fr.) an umbrella-cum-parasol, *En-Tout-Cas* (propr.) a type of hard tennis court

entozo/on an internal parasite, pl. **-a** (not ital.)

entr'acte/ (a performance in) the interval between two acts, pl. **-s**

en train (Fr.) in progress

entrain go or put aboard a train, carry or drag along

entrain (Fr. m.) heartiness

entrammel/ entangle; **-led, -ling** (one *l* in US)

entrap/, -ped, -ping *not* in-

entreat beseech, *not* in-

entrechat (not ital.)

entrecôte (cook.) a boned steak cut off the sirloin (not ital.)

entrée a dish served between the fish and meat courses, (US) the main dish of the meal; the right of admission (not ital.)

entremets side dishes (ital.)

entrench *not* in-

entre nous (Fr.) confidentially

entrepôt a market (not ital.)

entrepreneur/ a person in control of a business enterprise, a contractor (not ital.); **-ial**

entresol a low storey between the ground floor and first floor, mezzanine (not ital.)

entrust *not* in-

entryism infiltration into a political organization to change or subvert its policies or objectives, *not* entrism; (noun) **entrist**

entryphone (propr.) an intercom device at an entrance to a building

en/twine, -twist *not* in-

E-number the letter *E* followed by a code number, designating food additives according to EU directives

enunciat/e, -or

enure *use* **in-**

envelop/ (verb), **-ed, -ment**

envelope (noun)

Enver Pasha (1881–1922) Turkish political and military leader

Env. Extr. Envoy Extraordinary

enweave *use* **in-**

enwrap/, -ped, -ping *not* in-

enwreath *not* in-

enzootic endemic in animals

enzyme (chem.) a protein with catalytic properties

EO Education Officer, Entertainments Officer, Equal Opportunities, (US) Executive Officer, Executive Order

EOC Equal Opportunities Commission

Eocene (geol.) (of or relating to) the second epoch of the Tertiary period (cap., not ital.)

e.o.d. entry on duty, every other day

e.o.h.p. except otherwise herein provided

eo ipso (Lat.) by the fact itself

EOJ (comput.) end of job

EOL (comput.) end of line

eolian *use* **aeo-** (except in US)

eon *use* **aeon** (except in US and scientific use)

Eōthen ('From the East') an account of travels by Kinglake, 1844

EP electroplate, extended play (gramophone record)

Ep. Epistle

ep (chess) *en passant*

EPA (US) Environmental Protection Agency

épat/ant (Fr.) shocking, **-er les bourgeois** shake up the hidebound

epaulette a shoulder-piece, *not* -et (except in US)

EPCOT Experimental Prototype Community of Tomorrow, Fla.

EPDA Emergency Powers Defence Act

épée a sharp-pointed duelling-sword, used (with blunted end) in fencing

epeirogenesis (geol.) the regional uplift of extensive areas of the Earth's crust, *not* -geny

epenthes/is the insertion of a letter or sound within a word (e.g. *b* in *thimble*), pl. **-es**

epergne a table ornament to hold flowers or fruit (not ital., no accent)

Épernay a French white wine

epexeges/is the addition of words to clarify meaning (e.g. *to do* in 'difficult to do'), the words added; pl. **-es**

Eph. Ephesians, Ephraim

ephah a Hebrew measure, *not* epha

ephedrine *not* -in

ephemer/a *same as* **-on**, pl. **-as** (not ital.)

ephemer/is an astronomical almanac, pl. **-ides**

ephemer/on an insect that lives for a day, pl. **-ons** (not ital.); (bibliog.) a printed item intended for transient use (e.g. theatre programme, bottle label), pl. **-a**; **-ist** a collector of ephemera

Ephesians (NT) abbr. **Eph.**

ephod a Jewish priestly vestment

ephor/ a Spartan magistrate, pl. **-s**

ephphatha (Aramaic) 'Be opened'

epicedi/um a funeral ode, pl. **-a**

epicentre the point over centre of earthquake, *not* -er (US)

Epicoene, or the Silent Woman a play by Ben Jonson, 1609

epicure/ a person with refined tastes, esp. in food and drink; **-an** (noun and adj.) (one) devoted to (esp. sensual) enjoyment

Epicurean a philosopher who identifies pleasure with virtue, following the Greek **Epicurus** (342–270 BC)

epideictic adapted for display, *not* -ktic

epidemic (a disease) breaking out locally and lasting only for a time; cf. **endemic**

epidermis the outer skin or cuticle

epigon/e one of a later (and less distinguished) generation; pl. **-es, -i**

epigram a short, witty poem, *or* a pointed remark

epigraph an inscription on a statue or coin, or at the head of a chapter, section, etc.

epilogue the concluding part of a literary work

epiornis *use* **aepy-** (except in US)

epiphany the manifestation of a god; (cap.) 6 Jan., the manifestation of Christ to the Magi; *properly* the Baptism of Christ with the revelation in the heavens, the connection with the Magi being confined to the Western churches

epiphyte a plant that lives on the surface of another

'Epipsychidion' a poem by P. B. Shelley, 1821

Epirot an inhabitant of Epirus, *not* -te

episcopal/ belonging to bishops, abbr. **episc.**; (cap.) the title of Anglican Churches in Scotland and USA; **-ian**

epistem/e the accepted mode in a hist. period of acquiring and arranging knowledge, **-ic, -ology**; in Michel Foucault's work it is spelt (Fr. f.) **épistème**; the original Gr. is **epistēmē**, with different technical uses in both Plato and Aristotle

'Epithalamion' a hymn by Spenser, 1595

epithalami/um a nuptial song, pl. **-a**

epitheli/um surface tissue, pl. **-a**

epitomize *not* -ise

epizo/on (zool.) an animal that lives on the surface of another, pl. **-a**; **-otic** epidemic in animals

e pluribus unum (Lat.) out of many, one (motto of the USA)

EPNS electroplated nickel silver

EPOS electronic point-of-sale (of retail outlets recording information electronically)

eppur si muove (It.) and yet it does move (ascribed to Galileo, after his recantation)

épreuve (Fr. typ. f.) proof

épris/ (Fr.) f. **-e** enamoured

epsilon the fifth letter of the Gr. alphabet (*E*, ε)

Epstein, Sir Jacob (1880–1959) English sculptor

épuis/**é** (Fr.) f. **-ée** exhausted, out of print

epylli/**on** a miniature epic poem, pl. **-a**

epyornis *use* **ae-** (except in US)

eq. equal

equable uniform, not easily disturbed; *see also* **equatable**

Equador *use* **Ecu-**

equal/ *to* (not *with*), **-led, -ling** (one *l* in US)

equaliz/**e, -ation** *not* -ise

equal sign (typ.) = (normal interword space before and after, *not* set close up)

equanimity evenness of mind or temper

equatable able to be regarded as equal; *see also* **equable**

Equator/**, -ial** abbr. **Eq.**

Equatorial Guinea W. Africa

equerry *not* -ery

equestri/**an** a horseman, f. **-enne**

equilibri/**um** balance, pl. **-a**

equinoctial *not* -xial

equinox/ pl. **-es**

equivalent abbr. **equiv.**

equivocator a user of misleading words, *not* -er

equivoque a quibble (not ital.)

ER Eastern Region, *Edwardus Rex* (King Edward), *Elizabetha Regina* (Queen Elizabeth)

Er erbium (no point)

eraser one who, *or* that which, rubs out; *not* -or

Erasmus, Desiderius (1466–1536) Dutch scholar

Erato (Gr.) the lyric muse

erbium symbol **Er**

Erckmann–Chatrian joint pseud. of two French writers collaborating from 1848 to 1870 (en rule)

Erdgeist (Ger. myth.) an earth spirit

Erechtheum a temple at Athens

erector one who, *or* that which, erects; *not* -er

E-region *use* **E-layer**

erethism (med.) excitement, *not* ery-

Erevan Armenia, *use* **Yere-**

Erewhon a novel by Butler, 1872

erf (Afrik.) a plot of ground, pl. **erven**

erg/ a unit of energy and work, now largely replaced by the joule (in SI units $10^{-1}\mu$J), pl.

-s; an area of shifting sand dunes in the Sahara; pl. **-s**, **areg**; in Arab. ʿ**irj**

ergo therefore

Erie one of the Great Lakes (USA and Canada)

Erin (arch., poet.) Ireland, in Ir. Gael. **Éireann**

Érin go brágh (Ir.) Ireland for ever

Eriny/**s** (Gr. myth.) any of the three Furies, Eumenides, or avenging deities; pl. **-es**

Eris/ the Greek goddess of discord; **-tic** of or characterized by disputation, aiming at winning rather than at reaching the truth (not cap.)

erl-king (Ger. myth.) a bearded giant who lures small children to the land of death, in Ger. **Erlkönig** (roman quoted as title of poem by Goethe and of songs by Loewe, Schubert, and others)

ERM exchange-rate mechanism

erne (poet.) a sea eagle, *not* ern (US)

Ernie a device for selecting weekly and monthly winners in Premium Savings Bonds

'Eroica' Symphony by Beethoven, 1804

Eros the Greek god of love

erpetolog/**y, -ist** *use* **h-**

errant erring, deviating from an accepted standard; (lit., arch.) travelling in search of adventure, 'a knight errant'; cf. **arrant**

errat/**um** an error in writing or printing, pl. **-a** (not ital.)

erroneous wrong, *not* -ious

errors (**on proof**) alterations to proofs are marked in different colours of ink, depending on who makes them and why. Normal convention is for printing errors marked by the printer to be in *green*, printing errors marked by the proofreader to be in *red*, and all other errors (or alterations or inclusions) to be in *blue* or *black*

ersatz (Ger.) substitute (not ital.)

Erse of the Highland or Irish Gaelic language

erstens (Ger.) in the first place, **erstgeboren** first-born

Erté (1892–1990) Russian-born French fashion designer and illustrator, born **Romain de Tirtoff**

Ertebølle (archaeol.) a late Mesolithic culture in the Westen Baltic

erup/**t** break out suddenly or dramatically; **-tion** cf. **irrupt**

erven *see* **erf**

erysipelas a skin disease, St Anthony's fire, *not* -us

erythism *use* **ere-**

Erzurum Turkish Armenia; *not* -oum, -om

ES (paper) engine-sized

Es einsteinium (no point)

ESA European Space Agency

escalade mount and enter by a ladder

escalat/e rise, steadily and inevitably, like an escalator; **-ion**

escallop a shellfish, *use* **scallop** (except in heraldry)

escalope a thin slice of boneless meat (not ital.) (US) = **scallop**

escargot an edible snail

escarp/, -ment a steep slope, *not* -pe

Escaut Fr. for **Schelde**

eschalot *use* **shallot**

eschatology (theol.) the doctrine of last things

escheator an official who watches over forfeited property, *not* -er

eschscholtzia a yellow-flowered plant

esconce *use* **ens-**

Escorial, El Spain, *not* Escu-

escritoire *not* -oir (not ital.)

escudo/ the principal monetary unit of Portugal and Cape Verde; pl. **-s**

Esculap/ius, -ian *use* **Ae-**

escutcheon a heraldic shield, a plate for keyhole, etc.; *not* scut- except for *A Blot on the 'Scutcheon* by Browning

Esdras, First, Second Book of (Apocr.) abbr. **1, 2 Esd.**

ESE east-south-east

esker a long ridge of post-glacial gravel in river valleys, *not* -ar

Eskimo/ a native inhabitant of N. Canada, Alaska, Greenland, and E. Siberia; pl. same *or* **-s**; in Fr. **Esquimau/**, pl. **-x**; *prefer* **Inuit**; *see also* **Inuk; Yupik**

ESN educationally subnormal

esophag/us, -eal *use* **oes-** (except in US)

esp. especially

ESP extrasensory perception

espagnol/ (Fr.) f. **-e** Spanish

espagnolette the fastening for a french window

espalier a latticework, a trained fruit tree (not ital.)

especially abbr. **esp.**

Esperanto an artificial universal language invented by L. L. Zamenhof, 1887

espièglerie roguishness (not ital.)

espionage spying, in Fr. **espionnage**

espressivo (mus.) with expression, *not* ex-

espresso an apparatus for making coffee under pressure, the coffee thus produced; *not* exp- (not ital.)

esprit/ (Fr. m.) genius, wit; **— de corps** members' respect for a group; **— de l'escalier** tardy inspiration for an apt retort or clever remark; **— fort** a strong-minded or free-thinking person, pl. **-s forts** (ital.)

Esquimalt Vancouver Island, Canada; *not* -ault

Esquimau Fr. for **Eskimo**

Esquire abbr. **Esq.** a title appended to a man's surname only in the absence of any other form of address preceding or following a name, esp. in (usually Brit.) correspondence. Except in the case of e.g. 'Jr.' or 'III' (which it follows), it is placed immediately after the name; in the USA it is often used in writing to denote a lawyer of either sex

ESR electron spin resonance

ess the name of the letter *s*, pl. **esses**

ess. essences

essays (typ.) cited titles to be roman quoted unless published as a separate work

Essene a member of an ancient Jewish ascetic sect

Essouan *use* **Aswan**

EST (US) Eastern Standard Time

established abbr. **est.**

Established Church the Church recognized by the State as the national Church (caps.), abbr. **EC**

Establishment, the (the values held by) the established sector of society (cap.)

estamin a woollen fabric, *not* ét-

estaminet (Fr. m.) a small café selling alcoholic drinks

estanci/a (Sp.-Amer.) a cattle farm, **-ero** its keeper

Estate/s of the Realm the Parliament of Scotland before union with England in 1707; **the Three Estates** Lords Spiritual (i.e. bishops, the Church of England), Lords Temporal (the House of Lords), Commons (the House of Commons); **the Third —** French bourgeoisie before the Revolution (cap.); **the fourth —** the press (not cap.)

Esther (OT) not to be abbr., *but* **Rest of Esth.** (Apocr.)

esthet/e, -ic *use* **aes-**

estimator *not* -er

estiv/al, -ate, -ation *use* **aes-** (except in US)

Estonia a Baltic republic and former Soviet Socialist Republic, *not* Esth-; in Est. **Eestimaa**, *or* **Meiemaa; Eesti**, in Ger. **Estland** (*formerly* Ehstland, *earlier* Esthland), in Latvian **Igaunija**

estoppel *not* -ple, -pal

estr/ogen, -us *use* **oe-** (except in US)

ESU English-Speaking Union

e.s.u. electrostatic unit(s)

Eszett (Ger.) the character ß, representing a double *s*

ET English translation

ETA estimated time of arrival, Basque separatist movement (Euzkadi ta Azkatasuna, 'Basque homeland and liberty')

eta the seventh letter of the Gr. alphabet (*H*, *η*)

et *alibi* (Lat.) and elsewhere, abbr. ***et al.***

et *alii* (Lat.) and others; abbr. **et al.**, *not* et als.

etalon (phys.) an interference device (no accent, not ital.)

étamin *use* **est-**

état-major (Fr. m.) a staff of military officers

et cetera and other things (not ital.), abbr. **etc.**; comma before if more than one term precedes

etceteras extras, sundries (one word)

Eternal City, the Rome

Etesian winds NW winds blowing each summer in the E. Mediterranean (cap.)

eth *or* (esp. US) **edh** OE, Icel., and Norse letter (Ð, ð), also used in phonetic script; lowercase OE form *properly* ð; distinguish from **thorn** and **wyn**

ether a medium filling all space, *not* ae-

ethereal/, -ity, -ly *not* -ial

Etherege, Sir George (?1635–91) English playwright

ethics the science of morals (treated as sing.)

Ethiopi/a the modern name of Abyssinia; **-c** the liturgical language of the Ethiopian Coptic Church

ethn/ic concerning races, or national or cultural traditions; **-ology, -ological** abbr. **ethnol.**

et hoc genus omne (Lat.) and all this kind of thing

ethology the study of character formation or human or animal behaviour

etiology *use* **ae-** (except in US)

etiquette (not ital.)

Etna Sicily, *not* Ae-

étrier a short rope ladder (not ital.)

et sequen/s and the following; abbr. **et seq.**, **et sq.** (not ital.); pl. **-tes**, n. **-tia** abbr. **et sqq.** (not ital.)

étude a study (not ital.)

étude de concert (mus.) concert study (ital.)

étui a case for small articles such as needles, *not* etwee (not ital.)

etymolog/y the study of derivations; **-ical, -ically, -ist, -ize**; abbr. **etym.**

etym/on a root-word, pl. **-a**

EU European Union

Eu europium (no point)

eucalypt/us (bot.) pl. **-uses**

euchre a card game; *not* eucher, eucre

Euclid/ (*c.*300 BC) Athenian geometer, his treatise (cap.); **-ean** (cap.)

eudemon/ a good angel; **-ic** conducive to happiness, **-ism** a system of ethics that bases moral obligation on the likelihood of actions producing happiness; *not* -dae-

Euer (Ger. m.) your, abbr. **Ew.**

Eugène/ a French given name (*è*); **Prince — of Savoy** (1663–1736) Austrian general

Eugénie, Empress (1826–1920) wife of Napoleon III (*é*)

eulogium/ a eulogy, pl. **-s**

eulogize *not* -ise

eulogy (a *not* an) spoken or written praise; *see also* **elegy**; **elogium**

Eumenides (Gr. myth.) the avenging Furies: Alecto, Tisiphone, and Megaera; (ital.) a play by Aeschylus

euonymus (a *not* an) a plant of genus *Euonymus*, e.g. spindle tree

euphem/ism (a *not* an) a mild term for something unpleasant, **-istic(ally)**; abbr. **euphem.**

euphemize *not* -ise

euphonize *not* -ise

euphony (a *not* an) an agreeable sound

euphorbia (bot.) any plant of the genus *Euphorbia*, including spurges

euphor/ia a feeling of well-being, **-ic**

Euphues a prose romance in affected style, 1579, by John Lyly; hence **euphuism** an affected or high-flown style of writing or speaking

Euratom European Atomic Energy Community

Eure-et-Loir Fr. dép., *not* Loire; not to be confused with Fr. dép. **Eure**

eureka I have found (it), *not* heu- (not ital.); *see also* **heuristic**

eurhythmic *not* eury- (US)

euro the single European currency, symbol €; the common wallaroo (not cap.)

Euro- prefix denoting Europe(an); usually capitalized and occasionally hyphenated (**Eurocentric, Euro-sceptic, Eurotrash**); terms in specialist financial or economic usage (*eurobond, eurocredit, eurocurrency, eurodeposit, euroequity, euronote*) are usually not cap.

Europe abbr. **Eur.** geographically ends at the Urals, and includes Scandinavia and the British Isles

European (a *not* an) abbr. **Eur.**

European Atomic Energy Community abbr. **Euratom**

European Bank for Reconstruction and Development to assist formerly state-controlled economies in eastern Europe and the Soviet Union to make the transition to free-market economies

European Coal and Steel Community established 1952 to regulate pricing, transport, etc. for the coal and steel industries of the member countries; abbr. **ECSC**

European Commission the initiator of European Community action and the guardian of its treaties; appointed by agreement among the governments of the European Community

European Commission for Human Rights part of the Council of Europe, created under the European Convention on Human Rights to examine complaints of alleged breaches of the Convention

European Community abbr. **EC**, formed from the ECSC, EEC, and Euratom; since 1993 called the **European Union**

European Conventions any of the international agreements established by the **Council of Europe**

European Court of Human Rights part of the Council of Europe, separate from the UN and EU, but working in conjunction with the European Commission for Human Rights

European Court of Justice an EU body dealing with disputes between member states

European currency unit ecu

European Economic Community *formerly* the Common Market, *now* part of the EC; abbr. **EEC**

European Free Trade Association a trade association of countries not members of the EC, abbr. **EFTA**

Europeanize *not* -ise (cap.)

European Monetary/ System an EC programme designed to harmonize and stabilize member states' currencies, as a prelude to monetary union, abbr. **EMS**; — — **Union** an EU programme intended to work towards full economic unity in Europe, abbr. **EMU**

European Organization for Nuclear Research *see* **CERN**

European Parliament the Parliament of the European Community

European Recovery Program the Marshall Plan

European Space Agency devoted to advancing space research and technology; formed from the European Space Research Organization and the European Launcher Development Organization; abbr. **ESA**

European Union an organization of Western European countries, *formerly* the **European Community**

europium symbol **Eu**

Europoort a major European port facility near Rotterdam

eurythmic *use* **eurhy-** (except in US)

Euskar/a the Basque language, **-ian**

Euterpe (Gr. myth.) the muse of music

eV electronvolt

evangelize inform about the gospel, *not* -ise

Evans-Pritchard, Sir Edward (**Evan**) (1902–73) English anthropologist

evaporimeter an instrument to measure evaporation, *not* -ometer

evening abbr. **evng.**

even pages (typ.) the left-hand, or verso, pages

even small caps. (typ.) word(s) set entirely in small capitals

everglades (US) tracts of low swampy ground; (cap.) a large area like this in Fla.

evermore for ever, always (one word)

Everyman the eponymous character in a 15th-c. morality play, later applied generally to an ordinary or typical human being (cap., one word); ital. for title of the play, *but* Jonson's plays are *Every Man in his Humour* (1598) and *Every Man out of his Humour* (1599)

evildoer (one word)

Ew. (Ger.) *Euer* etc. (your)

ewe (**a** *not* an) a female sheep

ewer (**a** not an) a jug

Ewigkeit (Ger. f.) eternity

ex (Lat.) out of, excluding (not ital.)

ex. example, executed, executive

exa- prefix meaning 10^{18}, abbr. **E**

exactor one who exacts, *not* -er

exaggeration (two *g*s)

exalt/ raise in rank, power, etc.; praise highly; **-er** *not* -or; cf. **exult**

examination/ colloq. **exam**, — **paper** the questions, — **script** the answers

examplar *use* **exem-**

example abbr. **ex.**, pl. **exx.**; in Fr. m. *exemple*

exanimate lifeless, depressed

ex animo (Lat.) from the mind, earnestly

ex ante (Lat.) as a result of something done before

exasperate irritate, *not* -irate

Exc. Excellency

exc. excellent; except, -ed, -ion

exc. *excudit* (engraved this)

Excalibur King Arthur's sword; *not* -bar, -boor (not ital.); *also* **Caliburn**

ex cathedra (Lat.) with full authority

excavator *not* -er

excellence/ superiority; pl. **-s**, *not* -cies

Excellenc/y pl. **-ies** (persons), abbr. **Exc.**

excellent abbr. **exc.**

excentric (math.) used instead of *eccentric* to avoid the sense of 'odd'

except/, -ed, -ion abbr. **exc.**

exceptionable open to objection

exceptional out of the ordinary

exceptis excipiendis (Lat.) with the necessary exceptions

excerpt an extract

exch. exchange, exchequer

exchange/ abbr. **exch.**, **Stock** — (caps.) abbr. **St. Ex.**

exchangeable *not* -gable

exchequer abbr. **exch.**

excisable liable to excise duty, removable by excision; *not* -eable

excise (verb) *not* -ize

Excise Office *now* Board of Customs and Excise

excit/able *not* -eable, **-ability** *not* -ibility

exciter one who, or that which, excites; (elec.) an auxiliary machine supplying current for another; *not* -or

excitor (anat.) a nerve stimulating part of the body, *not* -er

exclamat/ion, -ory abbrs. **excl., exclam.**

exclamation mark *not* − point (US)

excreta (pl.) excreted matter (not ital.)

excudit (Lat.) engraved this, abbr. *exc.*

ex curia (Lat.) out of court, not -*â*

excursus/ a detailed discussion of a special point in a book (usually in an appendix) *or* a digression in a narrative, pl. **-es** (not ital.)

excusable *not* -eable

ex-directory (hyphen)

ex dividend without next dividend; abbr. **ex div., x.d.**

exeat/ 'let him depart', a formal leave of temporary absence; pl. **-s** (not ital.); *see also* **exit**; *exit*

execut/ed, -ive abbr. **ex.**

execut/or one who carries out a plan etc.; (law) a person appointed to execute a will, *not* -er; abbr. **exor.**; f. **-rix**, abbr. **exrx.**, pl. **-rices**

exege/sis an explanation, pl. **-ses** (not ital.); **-tic**

exemplaire (Fr. m.) a specimen, a copy; (Ger. n.) *Exemplar*

exemplar a pattern, *not* exa-

exemple (Fr. m.) example

exempli gratia (Lat.) for example, abbr. **e.g.**

exempl/um an example or model, esp. a moralizing or illustrative story; pl. **-a**

exequatur/ an official recognition by a foreign government of a consul or other agent, pl. **-s** (not ital.)

exequies (pl.) a funeral ceremony (not ital.)

exercise *not* -ize

Exeter in Lat. *Exonia*, abbr. **Exon.**; *see also* **Exon:**

exeunt/ *see* **exit**, **− omnes** (Lat. stage direction) they all leave

ex gratia voluntary (not ital.)

exhibitor *not* -er

exhilarat/e enliven; **-ing, -ion**

ex hypothesi (Lat.) according to the hypothesis proposed

exigen/cy urgency, **-t** urgent

exiguous small, scanty

ex interest without next interest; abbr. **ex int., x.i.**

existence *not* -ance

existentialism the philosophy that individuals are free and responsible agents determining their own development (not cap.)

exit/ a way out, pl. **-s**

exit (Lat. stage direction) he, *or* she, goes out, pl. *exeunt* they go out (ital.); *see also* **exeat**

ex/ lege (Lat.) arising from law, **− lex** beyond or outside the law

ex-libris (sing. and pl.) 'from the library of', a bookplate (not ital.); abbr. **ex-lib.**

ex new without the right to new shares; abbr. **ex n., x.n.**

ex nihilo nihil fit (Lat.) out of nothing, nothing comes

Exocet missile (propr., one cap.)

exodi/um the conclusion of a drama, a farce following it; pl. **-a**; Anglicized as **exode**; cf. **exordium**

exodus a departure, esp. of a body of people; (cap., OT) the departure of Israelites from Egypt, a biblical book, abbr. **Exod.**

ex officiis (Lat.) by virtue of official positions

ex officio by virtue of one's official position (not ital.)

exon an officer of the Yeomen of the Guard

Exon: the signature of the Bishop of Exeter (colon)

exor. executor

exorcize expel an evil spirit from, *not* -ise

exordium/ the introductory part of a discourse, pl. **-s**; cf. **exodium**

exp. export, -ation, -ed; express

expanded type (typ.) a type with unusually wide face

ex parte (law) in the interests of one side only or of an interested outside party

ex pede Herculem (Lat.) judge from the sample

expedient advantageous, advisable on practical rather than moral grounds; suitable

expeditious acting or done with speed and efficiency, suited for swift performance

expendable able to be sacrificed

expense *not* -ce

experimenter *not* -or

expertise (noun) expert skill, knowledge, or judgement

expertize (verb) give an expert opinion, *not* -ise

experto crede (Lat.) believe one who has tried it

expi/ate, -able

explanation abbr. **expl.**

explicit (Lat.) (here) ends; as noun, the conclusion (of a book)

export/, **-ation, -ed** abbr. **exp.**

exposé an explanation, exposure (not ital.)

expositor one who expounds, *not* -er

ex post facto (Lat.) after the fact

expostulator one who remonstrates, *not* -er

ex-president (caps. as title)

express abbr. **exp.**

expressible *not* -able

expressivo (mus.) *use* **es-**

expresso *use* **es-**

exrx. executrix

ex silentio (Lat.) by the absence of contrary evidence

ext. extension, exterior; external, -ly; extinct, extra, extract

extasy, extatic *use* **ecs-**

extempore (adj., adv.) unprepared, without preparation (not ital.)

extemporize *not* -ise

extender *not* -or

extendible *not* -able, *but in general use* **extensible** *not* -able

extension abbr. **ext.**

extensor a muscle, *not* -er

extent (typ.) the amount of printed space, expressed in ens (*see* **en**) or pages, filled by a given batch of copy

exterior abbr. **ext.**

external/, **-ly** abbr. **ext.**

externalize *not* -ise

externe a non-resident hospital physician, a day-pupil

exterritorial *use* **extra-**

extinct abbr. **ext.**

extirpator one who destroys completely, *not* -er

extol/, **-led, -ler, -ling**

extra, extract abbr. **ext.**

extractable *not* -ible

extractor *not* -er

extra/**marital** outside marriage, **-mural** outside the scope of ordinary teaching (one word); *but* **Extra-Mural Studies** (of Brit. universities)

extraneous brought in from outside, *not* -ious

extrasensory perception abbr. **ESP**

extraterritorial not under local jurisdiction, *not* exter-

extraversion *see* **extroversion**

extremum/ (math.) the maximum or minimum value of a function, pl. **-s**

extrover/**sion, -sive, -t, -ted** *not* extra- (except in Jungian psychology)

exult be greatly joyful, feel triumphant; cf. **exalt**

ex ungue leonem (Lat.) judge from the sample

exuviae cast coverings of animals

ex-voto/ an offering made in pursuance of a vow, pl. **-s**

exx. examples

Exxon Corporation *formerly* Esso, originally Standard Oil of New Jersey

Exzellenz (Ger. f.) Excellency, abbr. *Exz.*; *not* Exc-

Eyck *see* **Van Eyck**

eye/**ball, -bath, -bright, -brow, -ful, -glass** (one word)

eyeing *not* eying

eye/**lash** (one word)

eye/ **lens, — level** (two words, hyphen when attrib.)

eye/**lid, -liner** (one word)

eye muscles (two words)

eye/**patch, -piece** (optics), **-shadow, -sight** (one word)

eye socket (two words)

eye/**sore, -wash, -witness** (one word)

eyot an islet, *use* **ait**

eyrie *not* aerie, eyry

eyrir a coin of Iceland, one-hundredth of a króna; pl. **aurar**

Ezekiel (OT) abbr. **Ezek.**

Ezra (OT) not to be abbr.

Ff

F Fahrenheit, fail, farad, (on timepiece regulator) fast, (pencils) fine, fluorine, (photog.) focal length, (math.) function, the sixth of a series

F. fair, Fellow, felon; formul/a, -ae; Friday, all proper names with this initial except those beginning ff

f femto-, (math.) function

f. farthing, fathom, female, feminine, filly, (photog.) focal length (cf. **f-number**), (meteor.) fog, following, franc, free, from, furlong

ƒ (mus.) forte (loud); (Du.) guilder(s) (no point, space between abbr. and amount), *see also* **fl.**

f. (Lat.) *fortasse* (perhaps), (Ger.) *für* (for)

FA (statistics) factor analysis, (Fr.) Fédération Aéronautique, Fine Art, Football Association

Fa. Florida, *use* **Fla.**

fa (mus.) *use* **fah**

FAA (US) Federal Aviation Administration, Fleet Air Arm

Faber & Faber publishers

Fabian/ism, -ist (cap.)

fabliau/ a metrical tale in French poetry, pl. **-x**

fabula in Lat. lit. the name for several types of play, e.g. *fabula Atellana* and *fabula palliata*; in Russ. Formalism, the 'raw material' of a story's events; cf. *sjužet*;

fac. facsimile, *use* **facs.**; *see also* **fax**

façade (not ital.)

face (typ.) the printing surface of type, the design of a particular font

facet/ one side or aspect; **-ed, -ing** *not* -tt-

facetiae pleasantries, witticisms; (in book-selling) pornography (not ital.)

facia/ the instrument panel of a motor vehicle, *or* any similar panel or plate for operating machinery; the upper part of a shopfront with the proprietor's name etc.; pl. **-s**; cf. **fascia**

facies (med., geol.) general aspect, features

facile princeps (Lat.) easily best (ital.)

facilis descensus Averni (*not* Averno) (Lat.) easy is the descent to Avernus

façon de parler (Fr.) mere form of words

facsimile/ an exact copy, pl. **-s**; abbr. **facs.**; *see also* **fax**

facta, non verba (Lat.) deeds, not words

factional of or characterized by faction, belonging to a faction

factious characterized by, or inclined to, faction

factitious specially contrived, artificial

factorial (math.) (of) the product of a number and all the whole numbers below it (factorial four = 4 × 3 × 2 × 1); symbol **!** (as in 4!)

factorize *not* -ise

factotum/ a servant or employee who attends to everything, pl. **-s** (not ital.)

factum/ (law) an act or deed, a statement of the facts; pl. **-s**

factum est (Lat.) it is done

facul/a a bright solar spot or streak, pl. **-ae**; *not* fae-

fado/ a Portuguese folk song, pl. **-s**

faec/es (pl.) excrement, **-al**; *not* feces (US)

faerie (arch., and poet.) fairyland, the (realm of) fairies, esp. as represented by Spenser in *The Faerie Queene*, 1590–6; *not* faery, faërie, fairy

Faeroe/ Isles Danish, in N. Atlantic; *use* **the Faeroes**, adj. **Faeroese**; in Dan. **Færøerne**, in Faeroese **Føroyar**, in Fr. **les îles Féroé**, in Ger. **Färöer, -se** the language of the Faeroes

fag end (two words)

faggot/ a bundle of sticks etc., a seasoned meatball; (Brit.) derog. name for a woman, (US) derog. name for a male homosexual; *not* fagot (US); **-ted, -ting** (one *t* in US), **-y**

fah (mus.) in the tonic sol-fa system, *not* fa

Fahrenheit abbr. **F**

FAIA Fellow of the Association of International Accountants

faience glazed pottery; *not* faï-, fay-

fainéant idle, idler (not ital.)

faint ruled (paper) *use* **feint**

fair abbr. **F.**

fair and square (no hyphens except when attrib.)

fair copy a transcript free from corrections, abbr. **f. co.**

fair game (two words)

fairground (one word)

Fair Isle Shetland, and knitting design

fair/ name, — play, — rent, — sex (two words)

fair-spoken (hyphen)

fairway *not* fare- (one word)

fairyland (one word)

fairy/ story, — tale (two words, hyphen when attrib.)

fait accompli an accomplished fact, pl. **faits accomplis** (not ital.)

faith heal/er, -ing (two words)

Faizabad Uttar Pradesh, India; *not* Fyz-

fakir a Muslim or (rarely) Hindu religious mendicant or ascetic, *not* the many variants (Arab. *faḳīr*)

falafel *use* **fela-** (except in US)

Falang/e, -ism, -ist (a member of) the Fascist movement in Spain; cf. **Phalange**

faldstool *not* fold- (one word)

Falernian wine of ancient Campania

Falkland/ Islands S. Atlantic, in Sp. **Islas Malvinas**; **Viscount —**

Falk Laws 1874–5, German anti-Catholic laws introduced by Adalbert Falk

fall (US) = **autumn** (although both terms are used in US)

Falla, Manuel de (1876–1946) Spanish composer

fal-lal a piece of finery, *not* fallol; collective noun **fallallery**

fallible liable to err, *not* -able

Fallodon, Edward, Viscount Grey of (1862–1933) English statesman, *not* -en

fallout (noun) (one word)

falsa lectio (Lat.) a false reading, abbr. **f.l.**

falsetto/ pl. **-s**

falucca *use* **fel-**

falutin *see* **high-falutin**

FAM Free and Accepted Masons

fam. familiar, family

familiarize *not* -ise

famille/ a Chinese enamelled porcelain with a predominant colour, e.g. **— jaune, — noire, — rose, — verte**

family abbr. **fam.**; *see also* **botany**; **zoology**

famul/us (hist.) an attendant on a magician or scholar, pl. **-i**

fan/ belt, — club, — dance (two words)

fandango/ a Spanish dance or its music, pl. **-es** (not ital.)

Faneuil Hall a historic building, Boston, Mass.

fanfaronade arrogant talk, *not* -nnade; in Fr. f. **fanfaronnade**

fanlight (one word)

fanny/ (Brit. coarse sl.) the female genitals, (US sl.) the buttocks; usually considered a taboo word in Britain, but mild slang in the USA **— pack** (US) = **bumbag** (two words)

fantasia/ (mus.) a free composition (not ital.), pl. **-s**

fantasize *not* -ise

fantasmagoria *use* **phantas-**

fantas/t, -y *not* ph-

Fanti (of or relating to) (a member of) a tribe native to Ghana, the language of this people; *not* -te, -tee

Fantin-Latour, Henri (1836–1904) French painter

fantoccini (It.) marionettes

fantom *use* **ph-**

FAO Food and Agriculture Organization (of UN), for the attention of

FAP First Aid Post

faqu/eer, -ir *use* **fakir**

far. farriery, farthing

farad/ (elec.) a unit of capacitance, abbr. **F** (no point); **-ic current** inductive, induced; *not* -aic

Faraday/, Michael (1791–1867) English chemist; **— cage, — constant, — effect**

farandole a lively Provençal dance or its music

farceur a joker, wag, writer of farces (not ital.)

fareway *use* **fair-**

farewell (one word)

far/-fetched, -flung (hyphens)

Far from the Madding Crowd a novel by Hardy, 1874; *not Maddening* (orig. a line from Gray's *Elegy*)

farinaceous starchy, *not* -ious

Faringdon Oxon., *not* Farr-

farm/hand, -house, -stead, -yard (one word)

Farne Islands N. Sea; *not* Farn, Fearne, Ferne

far niente (It.) doing nothing; *see also* **dolce**

Faro Brazil, Canada, Chad, Portugal

Fårö Sweden

Faroe Denmark, *use* **Faeroe**

farouche sullen from shyness (not ital.)

Farquhar, George (1678–1707) Irish dramatist

farrago/ a hotchpotch, *not* fara-; pl. **-s**

Farrar, Frederick William, Dean (1831–1903) English divine and writer

Farrar, Straus & Giroux publishers (one comma)

farriery horse-shoeing, abbr. **far.**

Farringdon/ Within, — Without wards of the City of London

Farsi the modern Persian language of Iran

far-sighted having foresight, prudent; (esp. US, one word) = **long-sighted**

farthing abbr. **f.**, **far.**

FAS Fellow of the Anthropological Society, Fellow of the Antiquarian Society

Fas Arab. for **Fez**

fasces (pl.) a bundle of rods, the symbol of power

fasci/a (archit.) a long flat surface between mouldings on the architrave in classical architecture, *or* a flat surface covering the ends of rafters; pl. **-ae**; cf. **facia**

fascicle an instalment of a book, usually not complete in itself; a bunch or bundle; *not* -icule

fascicul/us (anat.) a bundle of fibres, pl. **-i**

Fasc/ism, -ist (noun, adj.), **-istic** (adj.) cap. when referring to the principles and organization of the extreme nationalist movement in Italy (1922–43); lower case when referring generally to any similar movement

Fassbinder, (Rainer) Werner (1946–82) German film actor, director, and writer

Fastens/-een, -eve, -even (Sc.) Shrove Tuesday, *not* Feastings-

Fastnacht (Ger. f.) Shrove Tuesday

fata Morgana a mirage seen in the Straits of Messina (ital.)

Fates, the Three (Gr. myth.) Atropos, Clotho, and Lachesis

Father/ (relig.) abbr. **Fr.**; **the —** as Deity (cap.)

father-in-law pl. **fathers-in-law** (hyphens)

fatherland (one word)

father of (**the**) **chapel** *see* **chapel**

fathom abbr. **f., fm.**

fatigu/able, -e, -ed, -ing

Fatiha the short first sura of the Koran, used by Muslims as a prayer; *not* -hah

Fatimid a descendant of Fatima, the daughter of Muhammad; a member of a dynasty ruling in N. Africa in the 10th–12th cc.; *not* -mite

fatstock livestock fattened for slaughter (one word)

fatwa (in Islamic countries) an authoritative ruling on a religious matter (not ital.)

faubourg (Fr.) a generic (Parisian) suburb, cap. when with the full name

Faulkland a character in Sheridan's *The Rivals*

Faulkner/, William (1897–1962) US novelist, **-ian**

fault-find/er, -ing (hyphen)

faun/ (Rom. myth.) a rural deity, pl. **-s**

fauna/ (collective sing.) the animals of a region or epoch, pl. **-s** (not ital.)

Faure, François Félix (1841–99) French statesman

Fauré, Gabriel (1845–1924) French composer

faute de mieux (Fr.) for want of a better alternative

fauteuil/ (Fr.) armchair, membership of the French Academy; pl. **-s**

Fauves, Les a group of painters led by Matisse; **fauv/ism, -ist** (concerning) the style of painting associated with them (not cap.)

faux pas a blunder, tactless mistake; pl. same (two words, not ital.)

favela (Port.) a Brazilian shack, slum, or shanty town

favour/, -able, -ite, -itism *not* favor- (US)

Fawkes, Guy (1570–1606) Catholic rebel and conspirator

fawn a young deer, its colour; (verb) grovel

fax (dispatch) (a copy produced by) facsimile transmission via electronic scanning (not cap.); *see also* **facs.**

fayence *use* **fai-**

FBA Fellow of the British Academy, *not* FRBA

FBAA Fellow of the British Association of Accountants and Auditors

FBCS Fellow of the British Computer Society

FBI (US) Federal Bureau of Investigation

FBIM Fellow of the British Institute of Management

FBOA Fellow of the British Optical Association

FC Football Club, Free Church (of Scotland)

FCA Fellow of the Institute of Chartered Accountants in England and Wales (*or* Ireland) (off.)

FCC (US) Federal Communications Commission

FCGI Fellow of the City and Guilds of London Institute

FCIA Fellow of the Corporation of Insurance Agents

FCIB Fellow of the Corporation of Insurance Brokers

FCII Fellow of the Chartered Insurance Institute

FCMA Fellow of the Institute of Cost and Management Accountants

FCO Foreign and Commonwealth Office

f. co. fair copy

FCP Fellow of the College of Preceptors

fcp. foolscap

FCS *see* **FRSC**

FCSA Fellow of the Institute of Chartered Secretaries and Administrators

FCSP Fellow of the Chartered Society of Physiotherapy

FCST Fellow of the College of Speech Therapists

FD *fidei defensor* (Defender of the Faith)

FDA (UK) First Division (Civil Servants) Association (cf. **AFDCS**); (US) Food and Drugs Administration

FDIC (US) Federal Deposit Insurance Corporation

Fe *ferrum* (iron) (no point)

Fearne Islands *use* **Farne**

feasible practicable, *not* -able

Feastings- *use* **Fastens-**

feather bed (noun, two words; verb, hyphen)

feather-brain (hyphen)

feather edge (two words)

featherfew *use* **fever-**

featherweight paper a light but bulky book paper

February abbr. **Feb.**

fecal, feces *use* **fae-** (except in US)

fecerunt (Lat. pl.) made this, abbr. **ff.**

fecial *use* **fet-**

fecit (Lat.) made this, abbr. **fec.**

fedayeen Arab guerrillas (pl.), in colloq. Arab. *fidā'iyīn*

Federalist abbr. **Fed.**

federalize *not* -ise

fee/ (law) an inherited estate of land, — **simple** estate unlimited as to class of heir, — **tail** estate so limited (two words); *see also* **fief**

feed/back, -stock (one word)

feeoff/ *use* **fief, -ee** *use* **feoffee**

feff/ *use* **fief, -ment** *use* **feoffment**

Fehmgericht/ a medieval German secret tribunal, Anglicized as **Vehmgericht**; (Ger. pl.) **-e**

Feilding the family name of the Earl of Denbigh; *see also* **Fie-**

feint (noun) a sham attack, (verb) pretend

feint ruled (paper) *not* faint

felafel *not* fala- (US), in Arab. *falāfil*

feld/spar a rock-forming mineral, *not* felspar; **-spathic**

Félibre a member of **Félibrige**, a school of Provençal writers

Felixstowe Suffolk

Fell a general term used to describe the type-faces and ornaments secured by **John Fell** (1624–86) Dean of Christ Church and Bishop of Oxford

fellah/ an Egyptian peasant; pl. **-in**, *not* -s, -een; *see also* **Fulahs**

Fellini, Federico (*not* Fr-) (1920–93) Italian film director

fellmonger a hide dealer

felloe a wheel rim, *not* felly

Fellow abbr. **F.**; in Lat. *socius*, in the Royal Society *sodalis*

fellow/ **citizen, — feeling, — men** (two words)

fellow-traveller (hyphen)

felly *use* **felloe**

felo de se (Anglo-Lat.) suicide, pl. **felos de se**

felon abbr. **F.**

felspar *use* **felds-**

felucca a small Mediterranean sailing vessel; *not* fal-, fil-

fem. feminine

female (bot., zool., sociology) abbr. **f.**, sign ♀

feme/ (law) wife, *not* -mme; — **covert** a married woman; — **sole** a woman without a husband, e.g. spinster, widow, or (esp.) divorcee (two words); *see also* **femme**

Femgericht (Ger.) *use* **Fehm-**

feminine abbr. **f., fem.**

feminize make feminine, *not* -ise

femme/ **de chambre** (Fr. f.) chambermaid, lady's maid; pl. **-s de chambre**; *see also* **feme**

femme fatale a dangerously attractive woman (not ital.); *see also* **feme**

femme/ **galante** (Fr. f.) a prostitute, — **incomprise** an unappreciated woman, — **savante** a learned woman; *see also* **feme**

femto- a prefix meaning 10^{-15}, abbr. **f**

fem/ur pl. **-ora** (not ital.); **-oral**

fencible able to be fenced, (hist., noun) a soldier liable only for home service; *not* -able

Fénelon, François de Salignac de La Mothe (1651–1715) French ecclesiastic and writer, *not* Féné-

fenestr/a (anat.) a small hole in a bone etc., pl. **-ae** (not ital.)

feng shui in Chinese thought, a system of influences in natural surroundings (not ital.)

fenugreek a leguminous plant, *not* foenu-

feoff *use* **fief**

feoff/ee (hist.) one enfeoffed, *not* feeo-; **-ment** act of enfeoffing; *see also* **enfeoff; fee; fief**

ferae naturae (law, adj.) wild (of animals), literally 'of a wild nature'

Ferd. Ferdinand

Ferdausi *use* **Fir-**

fer de lance a venomous snake (Cent. and S. Amer.)

Ferghana Cent. Asia, *not* -gana

Feringhee in the Orient, a European, esp. a Portuguese; *not* the many variants

Fermanagh a county of N. Ireland, abbr. **Ferm.**

fermata (mus.) an unspecified prolongation of a note or rest, a sign indicating this

Fermi, Enrico (1901–54) Italian-American physicist

Fermi–Dirac–Sommerfeld law (en rules)

fermium symbol **Fm**

Ferne Islands *use* **Farne**

Ferrara/ Italy; **—, Andrea** (16th c.) Italian swordsmith

Ferrari, Paolo (1822–89) Italian dramatist

Ferrero, Guglielmo (1871–1942) Italian historian

ferret/, **-ed, -er, -ing**

Ferris wheel (one cap.)

ferrule a metal cap or band on the end of a stick or tube (two *r*s); *not* ferrel, ferule

ferrum iron, symbol **Fe**

ferryman (one word)

fertilize *not* -ise

ferule a cane or rod for punishment (one *r*); *see also* **ferrule**

fess/ (her.) a horizontal stripe across the middle of a shield, *not* fesse; — **point** (two words)

festa (It.) festival

Festiniog Railway Wales, *not* **Ffest-**

Festschrift/ (Ger. f.) a collection of writings published in honour of a scholar, pl. **-en** (cap., not ital.)

feta cheese *not* -tta

fêt/e entertainment, **-ed** (not ital.)

fête champêtre an outdoor entertainment, a rural festival (not cap.); **Fête-Dieu** feast of Corpus Christi, pl. **Fêtes-Dieu** (ital., caps., hyphen)

fetial ambassadorial, *not* fec-

fetid ill-smelling, *not* foe-

fetish/ *not* -ich, -iche; **-eer, -ism, -ist** (not ital.)

fetor a bad smell, *not* foe-

fet/us pl. **-uses; -al, -ation, -icide**, *not* foe-

feu/ (Sc.) a perpetual lease at a fixed rent, the land so held; pl. **-s**

feu/ (Fr.) f. **-e**, late, deceased; note *la feue reine* but *feu la reine*

Feuchtwanger, Lion (1884–1958) German novelist

feud. feudal

feudalize make feudal, *not* -ise

feu/ d'artifice (Fr. m.) firework, pl. **-x d'artifice**; **— de joie** a salute by firing rifles etc., pl. **-x de joie**

feu-duty (hyphen)

feuille (Fr. typ. f.) sheet

Feuillet, Octave (1821–90) French novelist and playwright

feuillet/ (Fr. typ. m.) leaf, **— blanc** blank leaf

feuilletage (Fr. cook. m.) puff pastry

feuilleton fiction, criticism, light literature, etc. (not ital.); in Fr. m. the part of newspaper etc. devoted to this

Feulhs *use* **Fulahs**

feverfew (bot.) a herb, *Chrysanthemum parthenium*; *not* feather-, fetter-, -foe

février (Fr. m.) February, abbr. **fév.** (not cap.)

Fez Morocco; in Arab. **Fas**, in Fr. **Fès**

fez/ a cap, pl. **-zes** (not ital.); **-zed**

FF *Felicissimi Fratres* (Most Fortunate Brothers), Fianna Fáil, French Franc

ff, cap. **Ff** in Welsh, a separate letter, not to be divided, alphabetized after 'f'

ff (typ.) as initial letters for a proper name, follow the bearer's preference in capitalization: ffolkes, Fforde, Ffowcs, ffrench

ff. folios; following pages etc. (pl.) preferred to *et seqq.*

ff (mus.) fortissimo (very loud), to be set as a special music sort in scores

ff. *fecerunt*

FFA Fellow of the Faculty of Actuaries (Scotland)

FFAS Fellow of the Faculty of Architects and Surveyors

Ffestiniog Wales, *not* **Fest-**

fff (mus.) fortississimo (as loud as possible), to be set as a special music sort in scores

F.F.Hom. Fellow of the Faculty of Homoeopathy

FFPS Fellow of the Faculty of Physicians and Surgeons

FFR Fellow of the Faculty of Radiologists

Ffrangcon-Davies, David (**Thomas**) (1855–1918) Welsh baritone, *not* ff-, -çon

FG Fine Gael

FGS Fellow of the Geological Society

FH fire hydrant

FHA (US) Federal Housing Administration, (UK) Fellow of the Institute of Health Service Administrators

FHS Fellow of the Heraldry Society

FIA Fellow of the Institute of Actuaries

FIAC Fellow of the Institute of Company Accountants

fiacre a four-wheeled cab

FIAI Fellow of the Institute of Industrial and Commercial Accountants

fianc/é f. **-ée** one betrothed (not ital.)

fianchetto/ (chess) placing the bishop on long diagonal, pl. **-es** (not ital.)

fianna the militia of Finn and other legendary Irish kings; **Fianna**/ (pl.) the Fenians, **— Éireann** the Fenians of Ireland, **— Fáil** an Irish political party

F.I.Arb. Fellow of the Institute of Arbitrators

FIAS Fellow Surveyor Member of the Incorporated Association of Architects and Surveyors

fiasco/ a failure, pl. **-s**

Fiat Fabbrica Italiana Automobile Torino (Italian motor car, company, and factory)

fiat a formal authorization (not ital.)

fiat/ justitia (Lat.) let justice be done, **— lux** let there be light

FIB Fellow of the Institute of Bankers

F.I.Biol. Fellow of the Institute of Biology

fibre/board, -glass (one word) *not* -er (US)

fibrin blood protein appearing as network of fibres, *not* -ine

fibul/a a leg bone, a brooch; pl. **-ae**

FICE Fellow of the Institute of Civil Engineers

fiche a microfiche, pl. same

fichu a woman's small triangular neckerchief (not ital.)

FICS Fellow of the Institute of Chartered Shipbrokers, Fellow of the International College of Surgeons

fictile of pottery

fic/tion, -titious abbr. **fict.**

fictionalize *not* -ise

fictive/ly, -ness

FID Fellow of the Institute of Directors

fidalgo (Port.) a noble

fiddle-de-dee nonsense (hyphens)

Fidei Defensor (Lat.) Defender of the Faith; abbr. **FD**, **Fid. Def.**

fides Punica (Lat.) Punic faith, bad faith

fidget/, -ed, -ily, -ing, -y (one *t*)

Fido Fog Intensive Dispersal Operation, to enable aeroplanes to land

fidus Achates (Lat.) a trusty friend, devoted follower

FIEE Fellow of the Institution of Electrical Engineers

fief (hist.) land held by tenant of a superior, *not* feoff; *see also* **enfeoff**; **fee**; **feoffee**

field/-book, -cornet (hyphens)

field/ day, — glasses (two words)

field hockey (US) = **hockey**

Fielding, Henry (1707–54) English novelist; *see also* **Fei-**

field marshal (two words, caps. as title) abbr. **FM**

field officer (two words, caps. as title) abbr. **FO**

fieldwork/, -er (one word)

Fiennes, Sir Ranulph (Twisleton-Wykeham) (b. 1944) English explorer (one hyphen); *see also* **Twisleton-Wykeham-Fiennes**

fieri facias (Lat.) 'see that it is done', a writ; abbr. **fi. fa.**

FIFA International Football Federation (Fr. Fédération internationale de football association)

FIFST Fellow of the Institute of Food Science and Technology

fifth/ column, columnist (two words, not cap.)

Fifth/ Monarchy the last of the five great kingdoms predicted in Dan. 2: 44 (two caps.); **— -monarchy-man** (hist.) a 17th-c. zealot expecting the immediate second coming of Christ (one cap., hyphens)

fift/y, -ieth symbol **L**

fifty-year rule (hist.) *now* **thirty-year rule**

fig. figure; figurative, -ly

figura a person or thing representing or symbolizing a fact etc.

figural figurative, relating to figures or shapes, (mus.) florid in style

figurant/ (Fr. m.) ballet dancer appearing only in a group, pl. **-s**; f. **-e**, pl. **-es**; in It. (m. or f.) **-e**, pl. **-i**

figure/ (typ.) a numeral, esp. arabic; an illustration, abbr. **fig.**, pl. **figs.**

figurehead (one word)

figure skat/er, -ing (two words)

FIHE Fellow of the Institute of Health Education

F.I.Inst. Fellow of the Imperial Institute

FIJ *use* **FJI**

Fiji/ W. Pacific; adj. **-an** only of Polynesians, otherwise **Fiji**

fllagree *use* **fili-**

Fildes, Sir Luke (1844–1927) English painter

filemot a yellowish-brown, 'dead leaf' colour; *not* filamort, filmot, phil-

filet (cook.) a fillet of meat or fish

filfot *use* **fy-**

filibeg (Sc.) a kilt, *not* the many variants; in Gaelic ***feileadh-beag***

filibuster *not* fill-

filigree/ ornamental metallic lacework, **-d**; *not* fila-, file-; **— letter** (typ.) an initial with filigree background

filing cabinet (two words)

Filipin/as Sp. for Philippine Islands; (m.) **-o**(s), (f.) **-a**(s) native(s) of the islands; *see also* **Pilipino**

fille de/ chambre (Fr. f.) chambermaid, lady's maid, pl. ***filles de chambre***; **— — joie** a prostitute

fillet/ in Fr. m. *filet*; **-ed, -ing**

fillibeg *use* **fili-**

filling station (two words)

fillip/ a stimulus; **-ed, -ing**

fillipeen *use* **philippina**

fillister a kind of plane tool (two **l**s)

filmot *use* **file-**

filmsetting (typ.) typesetting on photographic film (one word)

filo a thin pastry, *not* phyllo (US)

Filofax (propr.)

filoselle floss silk (not ital.)

fils (Fr. m.) son, junior, added to a surname to distinguish a son from a father, as 'Dumas *fils*'; *see also* **père**

filter/ a device for separating solid matter from liquid, **-able** *not* filtrable; **-bed, -paper** (hyphens); cf. **philtre**

filucca *use* **fel-**

FIMBRA (UK) Financial Intermediaries, Managers, and Brokers Association

F.I.Mech.E. Fellow of the Institution of Mechanical Engineers

Fin. Finland, Finnish

finable liable to a fine

finale a conclusion (not ital.)

finalize *not* -ise

fin de/ siècle (Fr. f.) (characteristic of) the end of the (19th) century, decadent; **— — millénaire** (characteristic of) the end of the millennium

fine (mus.) end of the piece

fine champagne old liqueur brandy

Fine Gael an Irish political party

fine-paper edition abbr. **FP**

fines herbes mixed herbs used in cooking

finesse subtlety (not ital.)

fine-tooth comb (one hyphen)

fingerboard (one word)

finger bowl (two words)

finger/mark, -nail (one word)

finger/-paint, -painting, -plate (hyphens, two words in US)

finger/print, -tip (one word)

finick/ing, -y over-particular, fastidious

finis the end (not ital.)

finis (Lat.) the end (as of a work), abbr. *fin.*

Finistère a dép. of France

Finisterre/ a weather-forecast sea area, **Cape — Spain**

Finland in Fin. **Suomi**

Finn a native or national of Finland, or a person of Finnish descent

finnan haddock smoked haddock (two words), *not* the many variants

Finnegans Wake a novel by Joyce, 1939 (no apos.)

Finnish/ abbr. **Fin.**

Finno/-Karelia *formerly* the Karelian Soviet Socialist Republic; **-Ugric** (or **-Ugrian**) (belonging to) the group of Ural-Altaic languages including Finnish, Estonian, Sami, and Magyar

fino a light-coloured dry sherry

Fin. Sec. Financial Secretary

F.Inst.P. Fellow of the Institute of Physics

FIOB Fellow of the Institute of Building

FIOP Fellow of the Institute of Printing

fiord *use* **fj-**

fioritura (mus.) decoration of melody

FIPA Fellow of the Institute of Practitioners in Advertising

FIQS Fellow of the Institute of Quantity Surveyors

fir. firkin, -s

Fırat (Turk.) the Euphrates (undotted *i*); *not* Frat, Furāt

Firbank, Ronald (1886–1926) English novelist

Firdausi (?930–1020) Persian poet; *not* Fer-, -dousi, -dusi

fire alarm (two words)

fire/arm(s), -back, -ball, -box, -brand (one word)

fire brigade (two words)

fire/cracker (US) an explosive firework, **-dog** (one word)

fire-drake a fire-breathing dragon in Teutonic myth. (hyphen)

fire/ drill, — engine, — escape (two words)

fire/fighter, -fighting, -fly, -guard (one word)

fire hose (two words)

fire hydrant abbr. **FH** (two words)

fire insurance (two words)

fire/light, -man (one word)

Firenze (It.) Florence

fire-opal a girasol (hyphen, two words in US)

fireplace (one word)

fire-plug (hyphen, one word in US) abbr. **FP**

fire/proof, -side (one word)

fire station (two words)

firestorm (one word)

fire trap (two words, one word in US)

fire/water, -wood (one word)

firkin/ a small cask for liquids, pl. **-s**; abbr. **fir.**

firman/ an edict, pl. **-s**

firn névé, granular snow not yet compressed into ice at the head of a glacier (not ital.)

first aid (two words)

first/-born, -class (adj. and adv.) (hyphens)

first floor (two words, hyphen as adj.)

first-fruit(s) (hyphen)

first-hand (adj., hyphen) *but* **at first hand** (two words)

first proof (typ.) the first impression taken

first-rate (hyphen)

First World War 1914–18 (caps.) is common British style; **World War I** is common US style

firth an estuary, *not* fri-

fir tree (two words)

FIS Fellow of the Institute of Statisticians

FISA Fellow of the Incorporated Secretaries Association

Fischer, Bobby (**Robert James**) (b. 1943) US chess grand master

Fischer-Dieskau, Dietrich (b. 1925) German baritone

fisgig *use* **fiz-**

fish/ pl. same, unless describing differing types or species, in which case *use* **-es**

fish cake (two words)

Fisher,/ Andrew (1862–1928) Australian statesman, Prime Minister 1908–9, 1910–13, 1914–15; **— Sir Ronald Aylmer** (1890–1962) British statistician and geneticist

fish finger (two words)

fishing/ line, — rod (two words)

fish/monger, -net, -pot, -tail, -wife (one word)

fissile able to undergo fission, *not* fissionable

FIST Fellow of the Institute of Science Technology

fist (typ.) the ☞ or ☞, used to draw attention to a note

fisticuffs *not* fisty-

fistul/a the opening of an internal organ to the exterior or to another organ; pl. **-as, -ae** (not ital.)

fit past **fitted** (except in US)

fit (arch.) a section of a poem, *not* fytte

FitzGerald/ the family name of the Duke of Leinster; —, **Edward** (1809–83) English poet and translator (one word); —, **George Francis** (1851–1901) Irish physicist, devised the theory of — **contraction**, in full **Lorenz–FitzGerald contraction** (en rule); cap. *G*

Fitzgerald,/ Ella (1918–96) US singer and composer; — **F**(**rancis**) **Scott** (**Key**) (1896–1940) US novelist, surname *not* Scott Fitzgerald; lower-case g

Fitzwilliam/ College, — Museum Cambridge

fivefold (one word)

Five Towns, the in the novels of Arnold Bennett: Tunstall ('Turnhill'), Burslem ('Bursley'), Hanley ('Hanbridge'), Stoke-on-Trent ('Knype'), and Longton ('Longshaw'); *see also* **the Potteries**

fix (US verb) mend, prepare (food or drink)

fixed star (astron.) sign ✭ or ✶

fizgig a flirtatious girl, a small firework, (Austral. sl.) a police informer; *not* fis-, fizz-

fizz a sound, *not* fiz

FJI Fellow of the Institute of Journalists, *not* FIJ

fjord (Norw.) a deep arm of the sea (not ital.), *not* **fi**-

FL (naval) Flag Lieutenant, Florida (postal abbr.)

Fl. Flanders, Flemish

fl. florin, fluid, (Du. etc.) gulden (space between abbr. and amount); *see also* **f**

fl. *flores* (flowers), *floruit* (flourished)

f.l. *falsa lectio* (a false reading)

FLA Fellow of the Library Association

Fla. Florida (off. abbr.)

flabbergast/, -ed dumbfound(ed), *not* flaba-, flaber-

flabell/um (eccl., bot.) a fan, pl. **-a**

flack *use* **flak**

flag-boat (hyphen)

flag day a day on which money is raised for a charity by the sale of small paper flags (two words); (US, caps.) 14 June, the anniversary of the Stars and Stripes in 1777

flageolet (mus.) a small flute, (bot.) a French kidney bean; *not* -elet (not ital.)

flagitious deeply criminal

flag-officer (hyphen)

flagpole (one word)

flag-rank (hyphen)

flag/ship, -staff, -stone (one word)

flair instinct for selecting or performing what is excellent, useful, etc.; a talent or ability; *cf.* **flare**

flak anti-aircraft fire, *not* -ck

flambé (cook.) served in flames (not ital.)

flambeau/ a torch, pl. **-s** (not ital.)

flamboyant showy, (archit.) with flame-like lines (not ital.)

flame/less, -like (one word)

flamenco/ a type of song or dance performed by Spanish gypsies, pl. **-s** (not ital.)

flameproof (one word)

flame-thrower (hyphen, two words in US)

flame tree (bot.) any of various trees with brilliant red flowers (two words)

flamingo/ a tropical bird, pl. **-s**

flammab/le inflammable, **-ility**; negative form = **non-flammable**

Flamsteed, John (1646–1719) first English Astronomer Royal, 1675–1719; *not* -stead

flanch slope inwards, *not* -aunch

Flanders abbr. **Fl.**; in Fl. **Vlaanderen**, in Fr. **Flandre**, in Ger. **Flandern**

flân/erie (Fr. f.) idling, idleness; **-eur** f. **-euse** an idler, a lounger

flannelette a cotton imitation of flannel, *not* -llette

flannel/led, -ling (one *l* in US), **-board** (one word)

flapjack a biscuit-like cake made from oats, golden syrup, etc.; (esp. US) a pancake

flare a sudden outburst of flame, a bright light or signal, or a gradual widening; *cf.* **flair**

flash/back, -bulb (one word)

flash/ burn, — flood (two words)

flash/gun, -light, -point (one word)

flat (mus.) sign ♭

flatback (bind.) *see* **square back**

flat/fish, -ware, -worm (one word)

Flaubert, Gustave (1821–80) French novelist

flaunch *use* **flanch**

flautist *not* flut- (US)

flavour/, -ed, -ing, -less *not* -or (US) *but* **flavorous**

F-layer the highest and most strongly ionized region of the ionosphere (one cap.)

flèche (Fr. f.) an arrow, (archit.) a slender spire

flection *use* **flexion** (except in US)

fledgling *not* -geling

Fleming a native of medieval Flanders, or a member of a Flemish-speaking people inhabiting N. and W. Belgium; *cf.* **Walloon**

Fleming,/ Sir Alexander (1881–1955) Scottish bacteriologist, discovered penicillin; — **Ian** (**Lancaster**) (1908–64) thriller writer and journalist

flense cut up, flay (a whale or seal); *not* -ch, flinch

fleur-de-lis a heraldic lily, *not* fleur-de-lys, flower-de-luce; pl. **fleurs-de-lis** (not ital.); no hyphens in Fr.

fleuret an ornament like a small flower

fleuron a flower-shaped ornament in a type-face, or on a building, coin, etc.

fleury (her.) decorated with fleurs-de-lis, *not* -ory

flexible *not* -able

flexion *not* -ction (US)

flexitime the system of working variable hours, *not* flext-

flexography (print.) a rotary letterpress technique using rubber or plastic plates and synthetic inks or dyes for printing on fabrics, plastics, etc., as well as on paper

flibbertigibbet a gossiping or frivolous person

fliegende Holländer, Der (*The Flying Dutchman*) an opera by Wagner, 1843; but e.g. 'Wagner's *Fliegender Holländer*' when the article is omitted

flier *use* **flyer** in all senses

flintlock (one word)

floatage *but* **flotation**

floccul/us (Lat.) a small tuft, (astr.) a small solar cloud, (anat.) a small lobe in the cerebellum; pl. **-i**

Flood, the in Genesis (cap.)

flood/gate, -light, -plain (one word)

flood tide (two words)

floor in Brit. usage, the *ground floor* is the floor of a building at ground level, the floor above it being the *first floor*. In US usage, the ground floor is called the *first floor*, the floor above it being the *second floor*. Most Continental languages agree with British usage, Russian with US

floor/board, -cloth (one word)

floorlamp (US) = **standard lamp** (one word)

floor/ manager, — plan, — sample, — show (two words)

floozie *not* -sie, -zy

flophouse (US) = **dosshouse**

flor. *floruit* (flourished), *prefer **fl.***

flora/ (collective sing.) the plants of a region or epoch, pl. **-s** (not ital.)

floreat may he, she, *or* it, flourish (not ital.)

Floren/ce in It. **Firenze**; **-tine**

flores (Lat.) flowers, abbr. ***fl.***

florescen/ce, -t

floriat/e, -ed florally decorated, *not* -eate

Florida off. abbr. **Fla.**, postal **FL**

florilegi/um an anthology, pl. **-a**

florin abbr. **fl.**, (Du.) **f**

floruit (Lat.) flourished; abbr. ***fl.*** (preferable), ***flor.*** (not ital. when used as noun); use only to precede approx. date of activity for a person whose birth or death date is unknown: 'William of Coventry (*fl.* 1360)', 'Edward Fisher (*fl.* 1627–56)', 'Ralph Acton (*fl.* 14th c.)'; *see also **circa***

flotation *not* float-.

flotsam and jetsam (naut.) floating wreckage and goods thrown overboard; rubbish

flourished abbr. ***fl.*** (*floruit*)

flow chart (two words, one word in US)

flower-de-luce *use* **fleur-de-lis**

FLS Fellow of the Linnean Society (off. spelling), *not* Linnae-

Flt. Lt. Flight Lieutenant

Flt. Sgt. Flight Sergeant

flu influenza (no apos., no point)

fluffing (typ.) a release of paper fluff or dust during printing

Flügel, Johann Gottfried (1788–1855) German lexicographer

flugelhorn (mus.) a kind of cornet

flugelman *use* **fugle-**

fluid abbr. **fl.**

fluidize *not* -ise

fluky *not* -ey

flummox confound; *not* -ix, -ux

flunkey/ pl. **-s**, *not* -ky

fluoresce/, -nce, -nt be made luminous

fluoridate add fluoride to

fluorinate introduce fluorine into

fluorine *not* -in, symbol **F**

fluoroscope an instrument for X-ray examination, with fluorescent screen

fluorspar (chem.) calcium fluoride as mineral

flush/ (typ.) set to the margin of columns or page; **— left, — right** text is aligned to left or right margin

Flushing the Netherlands, in Du. and Ger. **Vlissingen**, in Fr. **Flessingue**; Queens, New York City

flustr/a a seaweed, pl. **-ae** (not ital.)

flutist *use* **flautist** (except in US)

fluty flutelike, *not* -ey

fluxions (math.) *not* -ctions

flyer *not* -ier

flyleaf (print.) a blank leaf at beginning or end of a book; the blank leaf of a circular (one word)

flyover a bridge carrying one road or railway over another (one word)

flysheet (print.) a two- or four-page tract (one word)

fly/weight, -wheel (one word)

FM field magnet, Field Marshal, Foreign Mission, frequency modulation

Fm fermium (no point)

fm. fathom

FMS Fellow of the Medical Society

fn. footnote, *but prefer* **n.** (except in contexts requiring a distinction between footnotes and other notes)

f-number (photog.) the ratio of the focal length to the effective diameter of a lens (e.g. f5)

FO Field Officer, (naval) Flag Officer, (RAF) Flying Officer, (hist., in UK) Foreign Office

fo. folio

f.o.b. free on board

FOC father of the chapel; *see* **chapel**

focalize *not* -ise

Foch, Ferdinand (1851–1929) French general

fo'c'sle *use* **forecastle**

focus/ pl. **-es**, (sci.) **foci**

focus/ed, -es, -ing *not* -uss-

foehn *use* **föhn**

foenugreek *use* **fe-**

Foerster, Friedrich Wilhelm (1869–1966) German philosopher and political writer

foet/id, -or *use* **fe-**

foetus *use* **fe-**

fog (meteor.) abbr. **f.**

Fogg, Phileas the hero of J. Verne's *Around the World in Eighty Days*

foggy obscured by fog

fog/y one with antiquated notions; *not* -ey, -ie; pl. **-ies**

föhn a warm Alpine south wind, *not* foehn

FOIA (US) Freedom of Information Act

foie (Fr. m.) liver

Fokine, Michel (1880–1942) Russian-born US ballet dancer and choreographer

fol. folio (*use* **fo.**), following

-fold as a suffix forms one word (e.g. threefold), except after numerals (10-fold)

fold-out an oversize page in book, unfolded by the reader (hyphen)

foldstool *use* **fald-**

foliaceous leaflike, *not* -ious

Folies Bergère (not ital.)

folio/ (typ.) a sheet of MS or TS copy; a page number; a book based on two leaves, four pages, to the sheet; pl. **-s**; as verb, **-ed** *not* -'d; abbr. **fo.**, *not* fol.

foli/um (Lat.) a leaf, pl. **-a**

folk/ art, — dance (two words)

Folketing the Danish Parliament, *not* -thing

folk-like (hyphen, one word in US)

folklor/e, -ism, -ist, -istic (one word)

folk singer (two words, one word in US)

folk song (two words)

folk tale (two words, one word in US)

folkways (one word)

follic/le (bot., med.) a small sac, *not* -cule; *but* **-ular, -ulated**

following abbr. **f., fol.**

fonda (Sp.) an inn

fondant a soft sweet of flavoured sugar

fondue a dish of melted cheese, eggs, chocolate, etc.; *not* -du

fons et origo (Lat.) source and origin

font a receptacle in a church for baptismal water; (typ.) a set of type of one face or size; cf. **fount**

Fontainebleau dép. Seine-et-Marne, France

fontanelle *not* -el (US)

Fontarabia *use* **Fuenterr-**

Fonteyn, Dame Margot (1919–91) English prima ballerina, born **Margaret Hookham**

foodstuff (one word)

foolproof (one word)

foolscap a former size of paper, $17 \times 13\frac{1}{2}$ in.

foot 30.48 cm; abbr. (sing. and pl.) **ft**, sign ′; not now in scientific use

foot-and-mouth disease (hyphens)

foot/ball, -board, -brake, -bridge, -hills, -hold, -lights (one word)

footline, running (typ.) a running headline set at the foot of a page

foot/loose, -man (one word)

footnote (typ.) a note printed at the foot of a page; *see also* **reference marks**

foot/pad, -path, -plate, -print, -rest (one word)

Foots Cray London

Footscray Victoria, Australia

foot/sore, -step, -stool, -way, -wear, -work (one word)

for. foreign, forestry

f.o.r. free on rail

fora pl. of **forum**

foram/en (anat., bot.) an orifice, pl. **-ina**

forasmuch (arch., one word)

foray a raid, *not* forr-

forbade *see* **forbid**

for/bear abstain, past **-bore**, past part. **-borne**; cf. **forebear**

Forbes-Robertson, Sir Johnston (1853–1937) Scottish actor

for/bid past **-bade**, past part. **-bidden,** present part. **-bidding**

force majeure (Fr. f.) irresistible compulsion or coercion, an unforeseeable course of events excusing a person from the fulfilment of a contract

forcemeat meat or vegetables finely chopped and seasoned, *not* forced- (one word)

forceps surgical pincers, pl. same

forcible *not* -eable

Ford, Ford Madox, b. **Ford Hermann Hueffer** (1873–1939) English writer

forearm (noun and verb, one word)

forebear an ancestor; cf. **forbear**

forebod/e, -ing *not* forb-

forecast predict, *not* forc-

forecastle *not* fo'c'sle

foreclose *not* forc-

foredge (typ.) the margin of a book opposite the binding, *not* fore-edge; *see also* **margins**

fore-edge (hyphen in non-technical uses)

fore-end *not* forend

forefend *use* forf-

fore/finger, -front (one word)

foregather *not* forg-

fore/go to go before, past **-went**, past part. **-gone**, present part. **-going**; cf. **forgo**

fore/head, -hock (one word)

foreign abbr. **for.**

Foreign and Commonwealth Office formed 1968 from the two separate Offices, abbr. **FCO**

Foreign/ Mission abbr. **FM**; — **Office** (caps.) abbr. **FO**, *now* **FCO**

forel an early vellum-like covering for books, *not* forr-

fore/leg, -lock, -mast, -play (one word)

fore/run past **-ran**, past part. **-run**; -runner (one word)

fore/said, -see, -shadow, -shore -shorten, -sight, -skin, -stall *not* for- (one word)

Forester, C(ecil) S(cott) (1899–1966) English novelist

foretell *not* fort-, fortel

for ever for always (two words, one word in US); **forever** continually (one word)

forewarn *not* for- (one word)

foreword (of book) *not* forw-, -ward; an introduction to a book by someone other than the author or editor

forfeit/, -able, -ure

forfend (US) protect by precautions, (arch.) avert; *not* fore-

forgather *use* fore-

forget/, -ting, past **forgot**, past part. **forgotten** *or* (esp. US) **forgot**; **-table**

forget-me-not (bot.)

forgivable *not* -eable

for/go abstain from, past **-went**, past part. **-gone**, present part. **-going**; cf. **forego**

forint the chief monetary unit of Hungary

formalin a germicide or preservative, *not* -ine

formalize *not* -ise

format/ (typ.) the size (octavo, quarto, etc.) of a book, periodical, etc.; (loosely) its general typographic style and appearance; (comput.) a defined structure for holding data etc.; as verb, past **-ted**, past part. **-ted**, present part. **-ting** (one *t* in US)

forme (typ.) a body of type secured in the frame called a chase; *not* form (US)

former the first of two; *see also* **latter**

Formica (propr.) (cap.)

formul/a pl. **-ae** (in math., sci., and scholarly uses), **-as** (in common usage, esp. in US) (not ital.); abbr. **F.**

forray *use* **foray**

forrel *use* **forel**

forsaid *use* fore-

Fors Clavigera a series of letters by Ruskin, 1871–84

Forster,/ John (1812–76) English biographer (*see also* **Foster**), — **E(dward) M(organ)** (1879–1970) English novelist

forsw/ear, past **-ore**, past part. **-orn**

forsythia an ornamental shrub

Fort cap. when part of a name; abbr. **Ft.**

fort. fortification, fortified

forte/ person's strong point (not ital.); (mus.) strong and loud, abbr. *f*, **-piano** loud, then immediately soft (hyphen), abbr. *fp*; **-piano** an early form of pianoforte (one word)

fortell *use* fore-

FORTH (comput.) a programming language (caps. or even small caps.)

fortissimo/ (mus.) very loud; as noun, pl. **-s**; abbr. *ff*

fortississimo/ (mus.) as loud as possible; as noun, pl. **-s**; abbr. *fff*

fortiter in re (Lat.) bravely in action; cf. *suaviter in modo*

Fort-Lamy *now* **N'Djamena**, Chad

Fortran (comput.) Formula Translation, a programming language; *also* **FORTRAN** or even small caps

fortuitous due to or characterized by chance; *not* fortunate or well-timed

forty-eightmo (typ.) a book based on forty-eight leaves, ninety-six pages, to the sheet; abbr. **48mo**

for/um a place of or meeting for public discussion; pl. **-ums**, (in Rom. or legal contexts) **-a**

forward/ (adj., noun, adv., and verb), **-s** common alt. adv. meaning towards the front, in the direction one is facing, or in the direction of motion

forwarn *use* fore-

forzando (mus.) forced, abbr. **fz** (no point); *see also* **sforzando**

fos. (abbr.) pl. of **fo.** (folio)

foss/a (anat.) a cavity, pl. **-ae**

fosse a ditch, *not* foss

fossilize *not* -ise

Foster,/ Birket (1825–99) English painter, — **John** (1770–1843) English essayist (*see also* **Forster**), — **Stephen Collins** (1826–64) US songwriter, — **Sir Harry Hylton-** *see* **Hylton-Foster**

Fotheringhay Castle Northants., 1066–1604

Foucault,/ Jean Bernard Léon (1819–68) French physicist, — **Michel** (**Paul**) (1926–84) French philosopher and historian of ideas; **Foucaldian**

Foucquet *use* **Foug-**

fouetté (ballet) a quick whipping movement of the raised leg (not ital.)

foul/, -ly; **-up** (hyphen as noun)

Foulahs *use* **Ful-**

foulard a thin, soft material (not ital.)

foul proof (typ.) a proofreader's marked proof as opposed to the corrected proof that succeeds it

foundry/ *not* -ery, — **proof** a final proof from a forme that has been prepared for plating

fount a source of a desirable quality or commodity; cf. **font**

Fouqué, Friedrich, Baron de la Motte (1777–1843) German poet and dramatist

Fouquet,/ Jean (1416–80) French painter, — **Nicolas** (1615–80) French statesman; *not* Foucq-

four-colour process (typ.) printing in yellow, magenta, cyan, and black to give a complete colour reproduction

fourfold (one word)

4GL (comput.) Fourth-Generation Language

Four Horsemen of the Apocalypse Conquest, Slaughter, Famine, and Death, riding white, red, black, and pale horses respectively (Rev. 6: 1–8)

Fourier/, François Marie Charles (1772–1837) French socialist, hence **-ism, -ist, -ite**; **—, Jean Baptiste Joseph** (1768–1830) French mathematician and physicist, hence **— series**

four/score, -some (one word)

four-stroke (hyphen)

fourth estate (joc.) the press, journalism; *see also* **Estates**

Fourth of July US Independence Day (caps.)

Fourth of June George III's birthday, a day of celebration at Eton

4to quarto

Fowler,/ F(**rancis**) **G**(**eorge**) (1870–1918) English lexicographer; — **H**(**enry**) **W**(**atson**) (1858–1933) English lexicographer, author of *Modern English Usage* and joint author, with brother F. G., of *The King's English*

Fox,/ Charles James (1749–1806) English politician; — **George** (1624–91) English preacher, founder of Society of Friends (Quakers)

Foxe, John (1516–87) English clergyman and martyrologist

foxed paper stained with brown spots

fox/glove, -hole, -hound (one word)

fox/-hunt (hyphen)

fox terrier (two words)

foxtrot (one word)

foxy of or like a fox, sly or cunning, reddish-brown; (of paper) damaged, esp. by mildew; (US sl.) (of a woman) attractive

foyer an entrance hall (not ital.)

FP Fine Paper (the best edition of a work), fire-plug, (Sc.) former pupil(s)

f.p. freezing point

fp (mus.) forte-piano

FPA Family Planning Association, Foreign Press Association

F.Ph.S. Fellow of the Philosophical Society of England

FPS Fellow of the Pharmaceutical Society of Great Britain

Fr francium (no point)

Fr. Father, France, French, Friar, Friday, (Ger.) Frau (Mrs, wife), (It.) *Fratelli* (Brothers)

fr. fragment, franc, from, (Ger.) *frei* (free)

Fra (It.) brother, friar (no point)

fracas a noisy quarrel, pl. same (not ital.)

fractal (math.) a curve having the property that any small part of it, enlarged, has the same statistical character as the whole

fractile fragile, of or relating to breakage; (statistics) *use* **quantile**

fractionalize *not* -ise

fractious irritable, peevish, unruly; cf. **factious, factitious**

FRAD Fellow of the Royal Academy of Dancing

fraenu/lum, -m *not* fre-

F.R.Ae.S. Fellow of the Royal Aeronautical Society

F.R.Ag.Ss. Fellow of the Royal Agricultural Societies

FRAI Fellow of the Royal Anthropological Institute

fraise/ (Fr. f.) strawberry; **— des bois** wild strawberry, **— de veau** (Fr. cook.) calf's mesentery or caul

Fraktur (typ.) a German style of black-letter type, as 𝔉𝔯𝔞𝔨𝔱𝔲𝔯

FRAM Fellow of the Royal Academy of Music

framable *not* -eable

framboesia (med.) yaws, *not* -besia (US)

framework (one word)

franc (Fr. m.) abbr. **F, f., fr.**; pl. same; the chief monetary unit of France, Belgium, Switzerland, Luxembourg, and several other countries (not ital.); in general contexts to be put *after* numerals, as 10 f. 50 c., or 10.50 fr. In financial contexts, *use* **Fr** (pl. same) close up *before* numerals; may be clarified further by country, e.g. 'BFr15' (Belgian franc), 'FFr15' (French franc), 'SwFr15' (Swiss franc)

française, à la (Fr.) in the French style (not cap.)

France abbr. **Fr.**

France, Anatole pseud. of **Jacques-Anatole-François Thibault** (1844–1924) French novelist and critic

Franche-Comté a region of France

franchise *not* -ize

Francic of or pertaining to the ancient Francs or their language

francisc a kind of battleaxe used by the ancient Francs

francium symbol **Fr**

Franck, César Auguste (1822–90) Belgian-born French organist and composer

Franco (y Bahamonde), Gen. Francisco (1892–1975) Spanish head of state 1939–75, titled *el Caudillo*

Franco- of France, French (hyphen) cap. in e.g. 'Franco-Prussian', 'Francophile', *but* 'francophone'

François Premier designating the styles of architecture, furniture, etc. or the characteristics of the reign of Francis I of France (1515–47)

franc-tireur (Fr. m.) guerrilla, partisan; (fig.) freelance; pl. *francs-tireurs*

franglais (Fr. m.) French regarded as including too many borrowings from English

Frankenstein (in Mary Shelley's novel, 1818) the maker of the monster, not the monster itself

Frankfort Ind., Ky.

Frankfurt/ am Main, — an der Oder Germany (no hyphens); *not* -fort, -on-Main, -on-Oder; in Fr. **Francfort**

Frankfurter Allgemeine Zeitung a German newspaper, *not* Frankfor-, -für-; familiarly **FAZ**

Franz Josef Land an archipelago, Arctic Ocean (Russia)

frappant (Fr.) striking, affecting

frappé (Fr.) iced, an iced drink (ital.); (US) a thick milk shake (not ital.)

FRAS Fellow of the Royal Asiatic Society, Fellow of the Royal Astronomical Society

Fraser the family name of Barons Lovat, Saltoun, and Strathalmond; *see also* **Frazer**

Fraser River BC, Canada

frat/e (It.) a friar, pl. *-i*; *-ello* brother, pl. *-elli*; in N. It. dialect these meanings are reversed

fraternize *not* -ise

Frau/ (Ger. f.) Mrs, wife, woman; *not* Fräu; abbr. **Fr.**; pl. *-en*; in Ger. used of any adult woman

Fräulein (Ger. n.) Miss, unmarried girl; pl. same; abbr. **Frl.**

Fraunhofer/, Joseph von (1787–1826) German optician and physicist, discoverer of — **diffraction, — lines** (no umlaut)

Frazer, Sir James George (1854–1941) English anthropologist; *see also* **Fraser**

FRBS Fellow of the Royal Botanic Society, Fellow of the Royal Society of British Sculptors

FRCGP Fellow of the Royal College of General Practitioners

FRCM Fellow of the Royal College of Music

FRCO Fellow of the Royal College of Organists

FRCOG Fellow of the Royal College of Obstetricians and Gynaecologists

FRCP Fellow of the Royal College of Physicians, London

F.R.C.Path. Fellow of the Royal College of Pathologists

FRCS Fellow of the Royal College of Surgeons, England

FRCVS Fellow of the Royal College of Veterinary Surgeons, London

F.R.Econ.S. Fellow of the Royal Economic Society

Fred. Frederic, Frederick; no point when it is a full name, or a diminutive

Fredericton NB, Canada; *not* -ck-

free and easy (three words)

free/base, -board, -booter, -born (one word)

freedman an emancipated slave; cf. **freeman**

Free/fone (US propr.) *also* -phone

free-for-all (adj.) (hyphens)

free/hand, -hold, -holder (one word)

free house an inn or public house not controlled by a brewery (two words)

freelance/ (verb, adj., adv.), *-r* (noun) one word except in hist. sense of a medieval mercenary

freeman one to whom the freedom of a city has been given; cf. **freedman**

Freemantle *use* Frem-

Freemason/, -ry (cap., one word)

Freepost (cap.)

free-range (adj., hyphen)

freest the superlative of **free** (no hyphen)

freethink/er, -ing (one word)

free verse *vers libre*

freeway (US) an express highway, esp. toll-free or with controlled access

free will the power of self-determination (two words), **free-will** (adj., hyphen)

freeze convert to ice; cf. **frieze**

freezing point abbr. **f.p.**

Frege/, Gottlob (1848–1925) German mathematician, logician, and philosopher; *-an*

frei (Ger.) free, abbr. **fr.**

Freiberg Saxony, Germany

Freiburg/ im Breisgau Baden, Germany; Ger. abbr. **— i. B.**

Freiburg Ger. for **Fribourg**

Freightliner (propr.) (one word)

Freiherr Ger. title, abbr. **Frhr.**

Freischütz, Der an opera by Weber, 1819

freize *use* **frieze**

Fremantle W. Australia, *not* Free-

French abbr. **Fr.**

French/ chalk, — cricket (cap.)

french fries (US) = (**potato**) **chips** (not cap.)

French groove (bind.) an extra space between the board and spine

French horn (cap.)

Frenchified (cap.)

French/ kiss, — knickers, — leave, — letter (two words, cap.)

Frenchlike (one word, cap.)

French/ mustard, — polish (noun, hyphen as verb), **— polisher, — seam, — toast, — vermouth, — windows** (two words, cap.)

frenetic delirious, frantic; *not* ph-

frenu/lum, -m *use* **frae-** (except in US)

freon (propr.) any of a group of halogenated hydrocarbons (not cap.)

freq. frequent, -ly, -ative

frère (Fr. m.) brother, friar

FRES Fellow of the Royal Entomological Society

fresco/ a watercolour done on damp plaster, pl. **-s** (not ital.)

freshman a first-year student of either sex at university, college, polytechnic, or (N. Amer.) high school (one word)

fresh water (noun, two words; adj. one word)

Fresnel/, Augustin Jean (1788–1827) French optical physicist; **— biprism, — diffraction, — rhomb** (one cap.), **— lens** (not cap.)

Freud/, Sigmund (1856–1939) Austrian neurologist and founder of psychoanalysis, **-ian**

Freytag, Gustav (1816–95) German writer

FRG Federal Republic of Germany, 1949–90, W. Germany

FRGS Fellow of the Royal Geographical Society

F.R.Hist.S. Fellow of the Royal Historical Society

Frhr. (Ger. title) *Freiherr*

FRHS Fellow of the Royal Horticultural Society

Fri. Friday

friable easily crumbled; cf. **fryable**

friar's balsam tincture of benzoin, *not* -s'

FRIBA Fellow of the Royal Institute of British Architects, pl. **FFRIBA**

Fribourg Switzerland, in Ger. **Freiburg**

FRIC Fellow of the Royal Institute of Chemistry, now **FRSC**

fricandeau/ a braised and larded fillet of veal, pl. **-x** (not ital.)

fricassee/ a white stew, pl. **-s** (not ital., no accent)

FRICS Fellow of the Royal Institution of Chartered Surveyors

Friday abbr. **F., Fr., Fri.**

fridge (colloq.) a refrigerator, *not* frig

Friedman, Milton (b. 1912) US economist

frier one who fries, *use* **-yer**

Friesian a breed of cattle, *not* Fris-; (in US) = **Holstein**

frieze a cloth, (archit.) the part below the cornice; *not* frei-

Friml, Rudolf (1879–1972) Czech-born US pianist and composer

FRIPHH Fellow of the Royal Institute of Public Health and Hygiene

frippery tawdry finery

Fris. Frisia (Friesland, an area comprising the NW Netherlands and adjacent islands), Frisian; *see also* **Friesian**

frisbee (propr.) (not cap.)

frisson an emotional thrill, a shudder (not ital.)

frit/ (Fr. cook.) fried, pl. **-s**; f. **-e**, pl. **-es**

frith an estuary, *use* **firth**

fritto misto (It.) mixed grill

Friuli-Venezia Giulia a region of Italy

frivol/led, -ling (one *l* in US)

frizz curl, roughen; *not* friz

Frl. (Ger.) Fräulein (Miss)

F.R.Med.Soc. Fellow of the Royal Medical Society

F.R.Met.S. Fellow of the Royal Meteorological Society

FRMS Fellow of the Royal Microscopical Society

FRNS Fellow of the Royal Numismatic Society

fro as in 'to and fro' (no point)

froe (US) a cleaving tool, *not* -ow

Froebel/ a kindergarten system developed by **Friedrich Fröbel** (1782–1852) German teacher and educationist, **-ian**

frolic/, -ked, -king

fromage/ (Fr. m.) cheese; **— de tête** pig's head, **— de porc** brawn

Fronde a French rebel party during minority of Louis XIV

frondeur a member of Fronde, political rebel

Frontignan a muscat grape or wine (not ital.)

frontispiece (print.) an illustration facing the title page of a book or of one of its divisions (one word)

frontmatter (print.) pages preceding the text proper (one word)

frost/bite, -bitten (one word)

frosting (US) = **icing** (on food)

Froude, James Anthony (1818–94) English historian

Froufrou a comedy by Meilhac and Halévy, 1869

frou-frou a rustling of a dress; frills or frippery (not ital.)

frow *use* **-oe**

frowsty musty, stuffy

frowzy unkempt, slatternly

FRPS Fellow of the Royal Photographic Society

FRS Fellow of the Royal Society, in Lat. **SRS** (*Societatis Regiae Sodalis*)

frs. francs

FRSA Fellow of the Royal Society of Arts

FRSC Fellow of the Royal Society of Chemistry

FRSE Fellow of the Royal Society of Edinburgh

FRSH Fellow of the Royal Society of Health

FRSL Fellow of the Royal Society of Literature

FRSM Fellow of the Royal Society of Medicine

FRST Fellow of the Royal Society of Teachers

frumenty hulled boiled wheat with milk, sugar, etc.; *not* the many variants

frust/um (geom.) the lower portion of intersected cone or pyramid, pl. **-a**; *not* -rum

FRVA Fellow of the Rating and Valuation Association

fry/able able to be fried (cf. **friable**), **-er**; *not* fri-

FSA Fellow of the Society of Antiquaries

FSAA Fellow of the Society of Incorporated Accountants and Auditors

FSB 'Federal Service of Security' (Federal´naya Sluzhba Bezopasnosti); successor to the KGB in Russia, 1992–; *see also* **KGB**

FSE Fellow of the Society of Engineers

FSIAD Fellow of the Society of Industrial Artists and Designers

FSS Fellow of the Royal Statistical Society

FSVA Fellow of the Incorporated Society of Valuers and Auctioneers

ft foot *or* feet (no point except in US)

Ft. fort

ft. feint (paper), flat, fortified

FTCD Fellow of Trinity College, Dublin

FTCL Fellow of Trinity College (of Music), London

FTI Fellow of the Textile Institute

FTP (comput.) File Transfer Protocol

Fuad/ I (1868–1936) King of Egypt 1923–36; — **II** (b. 1952) King of Egypt 1952–3

fuchsia (bot.) *not* fuschia (not ital.)

fuc/us a seaweed, pl. **-i** (not ital.)

Fuehrer (Ger.) *use* **Füh-**

fuelled *not* -eled

Fuenterrabia Spain, *not* Fontarabia

fugleman a leader in military exercises; *not* flugel-, flugle-, fugal-, fugel-; in Ger. m. *Flügelmann*

fug/ue (mus., psychol.) (not ital.), **-al**

Führer leader, the title assumed by Hitler in Nazi Germany, 1934; *not* Fue-

Fujiyama extinct Japanese volcano, *not* Mount Fujiyama; *properly* **Fujisan** *or* **Fuki-no-Yama**; *not* Fuzi-

-ful a suffix denoting amounts, pl. **-fuls**

Fula a W. African language; *not* Ful, Fulfulde

Fulahs Sudanese; *not* Felláh, Fellani, Feulhs, Foulahs, Fulbe; *see also* **fellah**

Fulbright/, (**James**) **William** (1905–95) US senator, responsible for the — **Act** 1946, which provided the foundation for the — **scholarship**

fulcr/um the point of leverage, pl. **-a** (not ital.)

fulfil/, -led, -ling, -ment *not* fulfill/, -ment (US)

fulgor splendour, *not* -gour

full-bound (bind.) completely cased in the same material (hyphen)

full capitals (typ.) large capital letters

fuller's earth (not cap.)

full/ left, — right (typ.) set text to align with respective margin of a page, same as **range**; cf. **ragged/ left, — right**; *see also* **full out**

full/-length not shortened, **-scale** not reduced (hyphens)

fullness *not* ful-

full out (typ.) set to the margin of a column or page, not indented

fulmar a petrel

fulness *use* **full-**

fulsome excessive and cloying; *not* full-

fumatory a place for smoking or fumigation; cf. **fumitory**

fumigator *not* -er

fumitory (bot.) any plant of the genus *Fumaria*, esp. *F. officinalis*; cf. **fumatory**

function (math.) abbr. **F**, **f**; symbol *f*

funfair (one word)

fung/us pl. **-i**, adj. **-ous** (not ital.)

funnel/led, -ling (one l in US), **-like** (hyphen)

funny bone (two words)

funny-face (hyphen)

fur. furlong

für (Ger.) for, abbr. *f.*

Furat *use* **Fırat**

furbelow a flounce, *not* -llow

furfuraceous scaly

furlong one-eighth of mile; abbr. **f.**, **fur.**

furmenty *use* **fru-**

Furness,/ Christopher, Baron (1852–1912) English shipping magnate, — **Horace Howard** (1833–1912) or his son (1865–1930) US Shakespearian scholars

Furniss, Harry (1854–1925) English caricaturist and illustrator

Furnivall, Frederick James (1825–1910) English philologist

furor (Lat.) rage (ital.)

furore uproar (not ital.); *not* -or (US)

Fürst/ (Ger. m.) ruling or reigning prince (not necessarily of the blood royal), pl. *-en*; f. *-in* pl. *-innen* (cap.; not ital. as part of title, no comma preceding); cf. *Prinz*

furth/er (adv., adj., and verb), **-est** (adv. and adj.)

Furtwängler,/ Adolf (1853–1907) German archaeologist; — **Wilhelm** (1886–1954) his son, German conductor

fusable *use* **fusi-**

fus/e, -ee, -elage *not* fuz-

fusible *not* -able

fusil a musket, *not* -zil

fusilier *not* -leer

fusillade *not* -ilade

fut. future

futhorc the Scandinavian runic alphabet; *see also* **rune**

futur/e, -ism (often cap. as a specific hist. movement), **-ist, -istic, -ity**

fuz/e, -ee, -elage, -il *use* **fus-**

Fuzhou (Pinyin) Foochow, China

Fuziyama *use* **Fuji-**

f.v. *folio verso* (on the back of the page)

FWA Family Welfare Association

fwd forward

f.w.d. four-wheel drive, front-wheel drive

fylfot (typ.) the swastika, esp. when used as a decorative page-filler rather than a political or religious emblem; *not* fil-

fyrd the English local militia before 1066

fytte *use* **fit**

Fyzabad *use* **Faiz-**

fz (mus.) forzando

FZS Fellow of the Zoological Society

G g

G gauss, the seventh in a series, (as prefix) giga-, Group

₲ guarani (currency of Paraguay)

G. Graduate, Grand, Gulf, (naval) gunnery

g (dyn.) local gravitational acceleration; gram(s)

g. (meteor.) gale; (Fr.) *gauche* (left), *gras*, *-se* (big); guinea, *-s*

GA General Assembly (Sc. Church); Georgia, USA (postal abbr.)

Ga gallium (no point); a language spoken in Ghana

Ga. Gallic; Georgia, USA (off. abbr.)

gabardine a durable cotton cloth; cf. **gaber-**

gabbey *use* **gaby**

gabbro/ (geol.) an igneous rock, pl. **-s**

gaberdine (hist.) a loose, long cloak worn esp. by Jews and almsmen; cf. **gabar-**

Gabon/ W. Africa; **-ese**

Gaborone Botswana

gaby a simpleton; *not* -ey, gabbey, gawby

Gadarene (adj.) involving or engaged in headlong or suicidal rush or flight as in Matt. 8: 28–32

Gaddafi *see* **Qaddafi**

Gaddi a family of Florentine painters, 1259–1396

Gadhel *use* **Goidel**

Gaditanian of Cadiz, SW Spain

gadolinium symbol **Gd**

Gadshill Kent, site of **Gad's Hill Place**, Charles Dickens's residence 1860–70; character in Shakespeare's *1 Henry IV* (one word)

Gaekwar the title of the prince of Baroda, India; *not* Gaik-

Gaelic (of or relating to) any of the Celtic languages spoken in Ireland, Scotland, and the Isle of Man; abbr. **Gael.**

Gaeltacht any region of Ireland where the vernacular language is Irish

gaff a hooked or barbed fishing spear

gaffe a blunder, an indiscreet act or remark

gaga senile, incapable (one word)

Gagarin, Yuri (**Alekseevich**) (1934–68) Russian cosmonaut, first to orbit earth, 1961

gage a, *or* to, pledge; cf. **gauge**

Gaia/, Gaea, Ge (Gr. myth.) personification of the Earth; later, the Earth-goddess, daughter of Chaos; **Ge** is the classical Attic and commonest prose form; **Gaia** (Latinized as **Gaea**) the epic and poetic form normally preferred in general discussion of myth. or in (sci.) viewing the Earth as a vast living organism; **— hypothesis, -n**

gai/ety, -ly; *not* gay-

Gaikwar *use* **Gaek-**

gaillardia (bot.) a plant

gairfish *use* **gar-**

gairfowl *use* **gare-fowl**

gairish *use* **gar-**

Gair Loch Strathclyde, *use* **Gare Loch**

Gairloch Highland, *not* **Gare-**

Gaitskell, Hugh Todd Naylor (1906–63) British statesman

Gaius a Roman praenomen, *not* Caius; abbr. **C.**

gal a unit of acceleration, with numbers **Gal** (no point)

Gal. Galatians

gal. gallon, *-s*

gala/ a festive occasion, pl. **-s** (not ital.)

galaena *use* **-lena**

galangale *use* **gali-**

galantine white meat served cold in aspic, *not* gall-

Galantuomo, Il Re King Victor Emmanuel I of Italy

galanty show a shadow pantomime; *not* -tee, gallantee, -ty

Galápagos Islands in the Pacific Ocean, official Sp. name **Archipiélago de Colón**

Galatea, Acis *or* **Pygmalion and** (Gr. myth.)

Galaţi Romania; *not* -acz, -atch, -atz

Galatia Asia Minor

Galatians (NT) abbr. **Gal.**

galaxy (astr.) any of the many independent systems of stars, gas, dust, etc. held together by gravitational attraction (not cap.); the galaxy of which the solar system is part, the Milky Way (cap.)

galena lead ore, *not* -aena

galera (Sp. typ.) a galley

galère/ (Fr. f.) galley (ship), *qu'allait-il faire dans cette —?* how did he get into this scrape? (with the implication 'by his own stupid fault')

Galician (of or relating to) (a person from) Galicia, or the language of Galicia

Galilean of Galilee, of Galileo

Galileo Galilei (1564–1642) Italian astronomer and mathematician; **Galileo** is the given name, **Galilei** the surname; in Fr. **Galilée**, It. and Ger. **Galilei**

galingale *not* gala-

galiot a vessel, *use* **gall-**

galipot a resin; cf. **gall-**

galivant *use* **galli-**

gall. gallon, *-s*

gallantine *use* **gal-**

gallanty show *use* **gala-**

gallaway *use* **gallo-**

gall bladder (two words)

Galle Sri Lanka, *formerly* Point de Galle

Galles, le pays de Wales; adj. **gallois**/ f. **-e**

galley/ (typ.) oblong tray for set type, **— proofs** those supplied unpaginated

Gallic of Gaul, French; abbr. **Ga.**

gallice in French

Gallic/ism a French idiom; **-ize** make Gallic or French, *not* -ise

Galli-Curci, Amelita (1889–1963) Italian soprano

galliot a Dutch cargo-boat

Gallipoli S. Italy, Turkey; in Turk. **Gelibolu**, which should be used for modern references, but **Gallipoli** for the First World War campaign

gallipot a small jar; cf. **gali-**

gallium symbol **Ga**

gallivant gad about; *not* gala-, gali-

gallon/, **-s** abbr. **gal.**, **gall.**

galloon a dress trimming

galloot *use* **gal-**

gallop/ a horse's movement; **-ed, -er, -ing**; cf. **gal-**

gallopade a Hungarian dance; *not* galop-, gallopp-

Gallovidian of Galloway

Galloway SW Scotland

galloway a breed of cattle; *not* galla-

gallows treated as sing.

gallstone (one word)

Gallup/, **Dr George Horace** (1901–84) founded the American Institute of Public Opinion, 1936; **— poll** a measure of public opinion (two words, one cap.)

galoot an awkward fellow; not gall-, geel-

galop a dance; cf. **gall-**

galosh/ an overshoe; *not* gol-, -oshe; **-ed**

galumph move noisily or clumsily

galv. galvan/ic, -ism

Galvani, Luigi (1737–98) discoverer of galvanism

galvanize not -ise

Galway W. Ireland

Galwegian of Galloway

Gama, Vasco da (1467–1524) Portuguese navigator, first round Africa to India

gambade/ a horse's leap or bound, a fantastic movement, an escapade; *not* -do; pl. **-s**

Gambia, The W. Africa; no definite article in US

Gambier Ohio

gambier a gum; *not* -beer, -bir

gamboge yellow pigment, *not* -booze

gambol/ to frisk; **-led, -ling** (one *l* in US)

Game at Chesse, A an allegorical comic play by Middleton, 1624

game bird (two words)

game/book, -keeper (one word)

game/ **machine, — plan, — point, — show, — theory, — warden** (two words)

gamin/ f. **-e** a street urchin (not ital.)

gamma/ the third letter of the Gr. alphabet (Γ, γ); unit of magnetic flux density, in SI units 1 nT; **— globulin** a protein; **— ray** (two words)

gammon a cured ham, *not* gam-

gamy having the flavour or scent of game left till high, *not* -ey

Gand Fr. for Ghent, Belgium

Gandhi,/ **Mohandas Karamchand** (**'Mahatma Gandhi'**) (1869–1948) Indian nationalist leader; **— Mrs Indira** (1917–84) Prime Minister of India 1966–77, 1980–4, daughter of Pandit Nehru, not related to preceding; **— Rajiv** (1944–91) Prime Minister of India 1984–9, her son

gangli/on a knot on a nerve, pl. **-a**

gangue rock or earth in which ore is found

gangway (one word)

ganister a hard stone, *not* gann-

ganja marijuana

gantlet (US) a stretch of railway track where two lines of track overlap; *see also* **gauntlet**

gantry platform to carry travelling crane etc.; *not* gau-

Ganymede (Gr. myth.) cup-bearer to the gods, fourth moon of Jupiter

gaol/, **-bird, -break, -er** *use* **jail**/ except in hist. contexts

Garamond a typeface

Garamont, Claude (*c*.1500–61) French type-designer, -cutter, and -founder

garbage can (US) = **dustbin**

García Lorca, Federico (1898–1936) Spanish poet and playwright, often alphabetized under **Lorca**

García Márquez, Gabriel (b. 1928) Colombian novelist

Garcilaso de la Vega/ (1503–36) Spanish poet, **— — —** (**'the Inca'**) (1540–1616) Spanish historian

garçon (Fr. m.) waiter, boy, bachelor (ital.)

Garda Síochána (Ir.) the police force of Ireland; **garda**/ a member of that force, pl. **-í** (not cap.)

Garde nationale (Fr.) national guard (one cap.)

gardenia (bot.) (not ital.)

Gardens abbr. **Gdns.**

gare (Fr. f.) railway station

garefish *use* **gar-**

gare-fowl the great auk; *not* gair-, gar- (hyphen)

Gare Loch Strathclyde, *not* Gair

Gareloch Highland, *use* **Gair-**

garfish similar to pike; *not* gair-, gare-

gargantuan enormous (not cap.)

gargoyle (archit.) *not* -ile, -oil

Garhwal Uttar Pradesh, India

gari *use* **gharry**

garish gaudy, *not* gair-

garlic *but* **-licky**

Garmisch-Partenkirchen Germany

garni/ (Fr.) f. **-e** furnished

garrott/e to throttle, or the apparatus used; *not* -ote (US), garo-; **-er**

garryowen a type of high kick in Rugby Union, in League Rugby called an **up-and-under** (not cap., one word)

garter belt (US) = **suspender belt**

Garter King of Arms a chief herald (at the College of Arms), *not* -at-

Gascogne Fr. for Gascony

Gascon a native of Gascony

gascon a braggart, *gasconnade* (Fr. f.) boasting

gaseous *not* -ious

Gaskell, Mrs Elizabeth (**Cleghorn**) (1810–65) English novelist

gasoline a volatile liquid from petroleum, esp. (chiefly US and technical) petrol; *not* -ene

Gaspé a peninsula, cape, and town, Que., Canada

gas poisoning (two words)

gas station (US) = **filling station**

Gast/haus (Ger. n.) an inn, pl. **-häuser** (cap.)

Gast/hof (Ger. m.) a hotel, pl. **-höfe** (cap.)

gastroenteri/c, -tis (one word)

gastropod any member of the Gastropoda, mollusc class (not ital.); *not* -ster-

gât/é (Fr.) f. **-ée** spoiled

gateau/ cake, pl. **-s**; (Fr. m.) *gâteau/*, pl. **-x**

gatecrash/, -er (one word)

gate/fold a folded oversize page (one word)

gate/house, -keeper, -leg, -post, -way (one word)

gather (bind.) assemble the printed and folded sections in sequence

Gatling gun a machine gun with clustered barrels (cap.)

GATT General Agreement on Tariffs and Trade

gauch/e awkward, **-erie** awkwardness (not ital.)

gauche (Fr.) left, abbr. **g.**

gaucho/ a cowboy from the S. Amer. pampas, *not* gua-; pl. **-s**

Gaudí (**y Cornet**)**, Antonio** (1853–1926) Catalan architect

Gaudier-Brzeska, Henri (1891–1915) French sculptor

gauge a measure; *not* gua-; cf. **gage**

Gauguin, (**Eugène Henri**) **Paul** (1848–1903) French painter

Gaul ancient France; adj. **Gallic,** (Fr.) *gaulois/*, f. **-e**

gauleiter a regional party official governing a district under Nazi rule, a local or petty tyrant (not ital.)

Gaull/e, General Charles (**André Joseph Marie**) **de** (1890–1970) French President 1944–5, 1959–69; **-ist**

Gauloise (propr.) a French cigarette

gauntlet/ a long glove, *not* gant-; **-ed**

gauntr/ee, -y *use* **gantry**

gaur an Indian ox, *not* gour

Gauss, Karl Friedrich (1777–1855) German mathematician and physicist

gauss a unit of magnetic induction, abbr. **G**; pl. same

Gautama Buddha *see* **Buddha**

Gauthier-Villars publishers

Gautier, Théophile (1811–72) French writer

gauzy *not* -ey

gavel/ a president's or auctioneer's hammer; **-led, -ling** (one l in US)

gavial *use* **gharial**

gavotte a dance, music for it

gawby *use* **gaby**

gay/ety, -ly *use* **gai-**

Gay-Lussac, Joseph Louis (1778–1850) French chemist and physicist

gaz. gazett/e, -ed, -eer

gazebo/ a summer-house, belvedere; pl. **-s**

gazett/e, -ed, -eer abbr. **gaz.**

gazpacho a cold vegetable soup

gazump raise the price to a would-be buyer after agreement but before completion

GB Great Britain

GBE Knight, *or* Dame, Grand Cross (of the Order) of the British Empire

GBH grievous bodily harm (caps.)

G.B.S. George Bernard Shaw (1856–1950) Irish-born British dramatist and critic

GC George Cross, Golf Club

GCA Ground Controlled Approach (radar)

GCB Knight, *or* Dame, Grand Cross (of the Order) of the Bath

GCE General Certificate of Education

GCF *or* **g.c.f.** (math.) greatest common factor

GCHQ Government Communications Headquarters

GCI Ground Controlled Interception (radar)

GCIE Knight, *or* Dame, Grand Commander (of the Order) of the Indian Empire

GCLH Grand Cross of the Legion of Honour

GCM general court martial, (math.) greatest common measure

g.c.m. (math.) greatest common measure

GCMG Knight, *or* Dame, Grand Cross (of the Order) of St Michael and St George

GCSE General Certificate of Secondary Education

GCSI Knight, *or* Dame, Grand Commander (of the Order) of the Star of India

GCVO Knight, *or* Dame, Grand Cross of the Royal Victorian Order

GD Grand Duchess, Grand Duchy, Grand Duke

Gd gadolinium (no point)

Gdańsk Poland, *formerly* Danzig

Gdns. Gardens

GDP gross domestic product

GDR (hist.) German Democratic Republic; *see* **DDR**

Gdsm. Guardsman

Ge germanium (no point)

g.e. (bind.) gilt edges

gearbox (one word)

gear lever (two words)

gearwheel (one word)

geboren/ (Ger.) born, **-e** = née (e.g. 'Jenny Marx, geb. von Westfalen'); abbr. **geb.**

gebunden (Ger.) bound, when used of a stringed instrument the term is retained in Eng.; abbr. **geb.**

GEC General Electric Company

gecko/ any of various house lizards, pl. **-s**

gee-ho a call to horses, *not* jee-

geeloot *use* **gal-**

gee-string *use* **G-string**

gee-up a call to horses, *not* jee-

Ge'ez the classical literary language of Ethiopia, surviving as **Ethiopic**

geezer (sl.) an old man, *not* geyser

gefallen (Ger.) killed in battle, abbr. **gef.**; symbol ✕ (follows the name); cf. **gestorben**

gefuffle *use* **ker-**

Geg one of two main dialects of Albanian, *not* Gheg; *see also* **Tosk**

Gehenna (NT) hell

Geiger counter (*in full* **Geiger–Müller counter**) an instrument for detecting radioactivity

Geisenheimer a white Rhine wine

geisha a trained Japanese hostess, pl. same

Geissler/, **Heinrich** (1814–79) German physicist, inventor of — **tube**

gel (phys.) (form) a semi-solid colloidal suspension or jelly

gelatin/, **-ize**, **-ous** *not* -e, -ise

Geld (Ger. n.) money (cap.)

Gelderland E. Netherlands, *not* Guel-

gelder rose *use* **gue-**

gelée (Fr. f.) frost, jelly

Gelée, Claude *see* **Lorrain**

Gelert a faithful dog of Welsh legend

Gellert, Christian Fürchtegott (1715–69) German poet

Gelsemium (bot.) *not* -inum

Gemara second part of the Talmud

gemm/**a** a bud, pl. **-ae**

gemütlich (Ger.) leisurely; agreeab/le, -ly; comfortab/le, -ly

Gemütlichkeit (Ger. f.) geniality, friendliness

Gen. General, Genesis

gen. gender, genera; general, -ly; genitive, genus

gendarme/ pl. **-s**; **-rie** a body of soldiers used as police (not ital.)

gender abbr. **gen.**

gên/**e** (Fr. f.) constraint; **-é**, f. **-ée** constrained

gene/ the unit of heredity, pl. **-s**

genealog/**y** a family's pedigree, *not* -olog-; **-ical**

genera *see* **genus**

General abbr. **Gen.**

General Assembly (Sc. Church) abbr. **GA**

general election (not caps.)

generalia (Lat. pl.) general principles

generalissimo/ supreme commander, pl. **-s**

generalize *not* -ise

generator *not* -er

Genesis (OT) abbr. **Gen.**

genes/**is** the origin of a thing, pl. **-es** (not cap.)

genet a catlike mammal of genus *Genetta*, *not* -tte; cf. **jennet**

Geneva/ Switzerland, in Fr. **Genève**, Ger. **Genf**, It. **Ginevra**; adj. **Genevan**; **Genevese** (sing. and pl.) native(s) of —, in Fr. **genevois**/, f. **-e**(**s**)

genev/**a** (lit.), **-er** Dutch (Hollands) gin

Geneva Convention an international agreement governing the status and treatment of captured and wounded military personnel in wartime, 1864, revised 1950, 1978

Geneviève, Saint (*c.*422–*c.*512) patron saint of Paris

Genghis Khan (1162–1227) Mongol conqueror of N. China and Iran, *not* Jenghiz; in Mongolian **Chingiz Khan** *or* **Čiṇgiz Khan**

genie/ (Muslim myth.) a spirit, pl. **-s** *see also* **jinnee**

genit *use* **jennet**

genitive abbr. **gen.**, **genit.**

geni/us since the Romantic era, (a person of) consummate intellectual power, pl. **-uses**; *previously* innate disposition *or* (Roman myth.) personal spirit, pl. **-i**; *see also* **genie**

geni/us loci (Lat.) the pervading spirit of a place, pl. *-i loci*

Gennesaret, Sea of *not* -eth

gennet *use* j-

Geno/a Italy; in Fr. **Gênes**, It. **Genova**; **-ese** *not* -ovese (except in It.)

genre (not ital.)

gen/s a clan, pl. **-tes**

Gens de Lettres, Société des French society of authors

Gensfleisch *see* **Gutenberg**

Gent Fl. and Ger. for **Ghent**, Belgium

gent a gentleman

genteel/ affectedly refined, **-ly**

Gentele's green a colour

gentil/ (Fr.) f. *-le* gentle, kind

Gentile (a person who is) not Jewish (*see also* **goy**), not Mormon; *or* of or relating to a nation or tribe (cap.); (gram.) a word indicating nationality (not cap.)

gentilhomme (Fr. m.) nobleman (by ancestry rather than creation), gentleman; pl. **gentilshommes**

gentleman-at-arms (hyphens)

Gentleman's Magazine UK periodical 1731–1914; *not* -men's

Gentlemen's Quarterly US periodical, *now called* **GQ**; *not* -man's

Gents, the men's lavatory (cap., no apos.)

genuflection a bending of the knee, *not* -xion

genus pl. **genera**, abbr. **gen.**

Geo. George

geod. geode/sy (large-scale earth measurement), -tic

Geoffrey-Lloyd, Baron

Geoffroy Saint-Hilaire, Étienne (1772–1844) French zoologist, *not* -frey (one hyphen)

geog. geograph/er, -ical, -y

geographical qualifiers forming everyday terms often have lower-case initials, as chinese white, roman type, venetian blinds; *but* Brussels sprouts, India ink, London pride

geol. geolog/ical, -ist, -y

geological *not* geologic (US)

geologize *not* -ise

geology the names of formations to have caps., as Old Red Sandstone

geom. geome/ter, -trical, -try

Geordie a native of Tyneside

Georg Ger. for George

George abbr. **Geo.**

George/ Cross (also — **Medal**) decorations for bravery awarded esp. to civilians, instituted by King George VI

George Town Bahamas, Cayman Islands, Malaysia, and many places in Australia, Canada, and USA

Georgetown Guyana, and many places in Australia, Canada, and USA (one word)

Georgia USA, off. abbr. **Ga.**, postal **GA**; a Caucasian state, *formerly* a Soviet Socialist Republic

Georgian of or characteristic of the time of Kings George I–IV (1714–1830), esp. architecture; *or* of the time of Kings George V and VI (1910–52), esp. of the literature of 1910–20; of or relating to (the language of) Georgia in the Caucasus, *or* a native thereof; of or relating to Georgia in the USA, *or* a native thereof

Georgium sidus (astr.) an old name for Uranus

Ger. German, Germany

ger. gerund, -ial

geranium/ (bot.) pl. **-s** (not ital.)

Gerard, John (1545–1612) English botanist, *not* -arde

gerbil a mouselike desert rodent of the subfamily *Gerbillinae*, distinct from the **jerboa**; *not* jer-

gerfalcon *use* gyr-

Géricault, Jean Louis André Théodore (1791–1824) French painter

gerkin *use* ghe-

German abbr. **Ger.**

german (placed after *brother* or *sister*) having both parents the same; (placed after *cousin*) having both grandparents the same on one side

germane relevant

germanium symbol **Ge**

Germanize *not* -ise

German/ measles, — shepherd (esp. US) = **alsatian, — silver** (two words, one cap.)

Germany abbr. **Ger.**

germon *use* **albacore**

Gernika (Basque) **Guernica**

Gérôme, Jean Léon (1824–1904) French painter

gerrymander manipulate an electoral district unfairly, *not* je-

gerund/, -ial abbr. **ger.**

Ges. (Ger.) *Gesellschaft* (cap.)

gesammelte Werke (Ger. pl.) collected works (one cap.)

Gesellschaft (Ger. f.) a company or society (cap.), abbr. **Ges.**; *see also* **GmbH**

gesso/ gypsum used in art, pl. **-es**

gest. (Ger.) **gestorben**

gestalt (psychol.) an organized whole that is perceived as more than the sum of its parts (not cap., not ital.)

Gestapo the German secret police under Hitler

Gesta Romanorum (Lat. pl.) a medieval collection of anecdotes

gesticulator one who moves his hands and arms in talking, *not* -er

gestorben (Ger.) deceased, abbr. ***gest.***; symbol † (follows the name); cf. ***gefallen***

Gesundheit (Ger.) expressing a wish of good health (said before drinking or to one who sneezes)

get-at-able accessible (hyphens)

getaway an escape (one word)

gettable (two *t*s)

Getty, Jean (*not* John) **Paul** (1892–1976) US oil businessman

Gettysburg Pa.; scene of battle and of Lincoln's address, 1863

Geulinex, Arnold (1625–69) Dutch philosopher

GeV giga-electronvolt

Gewandhaus (Ger. n.) Clothworkers' Hall, a concert hall in Leipzig (not ital. for its orchestra)

gewgaw a gaudy plaything (one word)

geyser a hot spring, water heater (not ital.); *not* geezer

G5 Group of Five

GFS Girls' Friendly Society

GG Girl Guides, Governor-General, Grenadier Guards

Gg gigagram

g.gr. a great gross, or 144 dozen

GGSM Graduate of the Guildhall School of Music

Ghadames Libya

Ghana/ W. Africa; adj. and noun **-ian**

Ghandi *use* **Gandhi**

gharial a large Indian crocodile, *not* gavi-

gharry a vehicle used in India, *not* gari

ghat (Anglo-Ind.) a mountain pass, steps to a river; *not* ghât, ghát, ghaut

Ghazi a Muslim fighter against non-Muslims

ghee Indian clarified butter, *not* ghi

Gheel a Belgian commune long celebrated for its treatment of mentally ill people, in Fl. **Geel**

Gheg *use* **Geg**

Ghent Belgium; in Fr. **Gand**, Fl. and Ger. **Gent**

gherao (Ind., Pak.) a lock-in of employers

gherkin a small cucumber; *not* ge-, gi-, gu-

ghetto/ pl. **-s** (not ital.)

ghi *use* **ghee**

ghiaour *use* **gi-**

Ghibelline one of the Emperor's faction in medieval Italian states, opposed to Guelf; *not* -in, Gib-, Guib-

Ghiberti, Lorenzo (1378–1455) Italian sculptor, painter, goldsmith

ghillie *use* **gill-**

Ghirlandaio, Domenico (1449–94) Italian painter

Ghizeh *use* **Giza**

Ghom Pers. pronunciation of **Qom**

Ghonds *use* **Gonds**

Ghoorkas *use* **Gurkhas**

ghost/-write (hyphen, one word in US), — **writer** (two words, one word in US)

ghoul an evil spirit; *not* -ool, -oule, -owl

GHQ General Headquarters

Ghurkas *use* **Gurkhas**

GI (US) Government Issue, (colloq.) serviceman

Giacometti, Alberto (1901–66) Swiss sculptor, painter, poet

giallo antico (It.) a rich yellow marble

Giant's Causeway Co. Antrim, *not* -ts'

giaour (derog.) Turk. name for a non-Muslim; *not* ghiaour, giaur; in Turk. now ***gâvur***

Giaour, The a poem by Byron, 1813

Gib Gibraltar

gibber to chatter, *not* j-

gibbet/, -ed, -ing

Gibbon, Edward (1737–94) English historian

Gibbons,/ Grinling (1648–1720) English carver, — **Orlando** (1583–1625) English composer

gibbo/us humpbacked, convex; **-sity**

gib/e to sneer; **-er, -ing**; cf. **gybe**

Gibeline *use* **Ghibell-**

Gibraltar/ abbr. **Gib**; **-ian**

Gibran, Khalil (1883–1931) Lebanese-born US writer and artist, *not* Jubran

gibus an opera hat (not ital.)

Gide, André Paul Guillaume (1869–1951) French writer

Gideon a biblical character, a member of a body distributing bibles

Gielgud, Sir (Arthur) John (b. 1904) English actor, director, and producer

giga- a prefix meaning one thousand million (10^9), abbr. **G**

GIGO (comput.) garbage in, garbage out

gigolo/ pl. **-s** (not ital.)

gigot/ (cook.) leg of mutton or lamb, — **sleeve** (two words); *not* j-

gigue a lively dance

Gilbert, Sir William Schwenck (1836–1911) English librettist

Gil Blas a picaresque satire by Le Sage, 1715

gild an association, *use* **gui-**

Gilead/ a mountainous district east of River Jordan, 'balm in —' (Jer. 8: 22)

gill a quarter of a pint; a deep ravine, narrow mountain torrent, *not* ghy-

Gill, (Arthur) Eric (Rowton) (1882–1940) artist, sculptor, and type designer

Gillette/, King Camp (1855–1932) US inventor of safety razor, **— William** (1857–1937) US actor and writer

gillie (Sc.) a man or boy attending a person hunting or fishing, (hist.) a Highland chief's attendant; *not* ghi-

Gillray, James (1757–1815) English caricaturist

gillyflower a clove-scented flower, *not* jilli-

gilt abbr. **gt.**

gimcrack trumpery, *not* jim-

gimlet a tool, *not* gimb-

gimmick a contrivance, device

gimp a trimming, a fishing line; *not* gui-, gy-

Ginevra It. for Geneva

ginger/ ale, — beer (two words)

gingerbread (one word)

ginger/ nut, — snap (two words, one word in US), **— wine** (two words)

ginglym/us (anat.) a hingelike joint such as the elbow, pl. **-i**; **-oid**

ginkgo an oriental tree, *not* gingko

ginn *see* **jinnee**

Gioconda, La *see* **Mona Lisa**; an opera by Ponchielli, 1876; a play by D'Annunzio, 1898

Giorgione, Giorgio Barbarelli da Castelfranco (1475–1510) Italian painter

Giott/o di Bondone (1266–1337) Italian painter and architect, **-esque**

gipsy *use* **gyp-**

Giraldus Cambrensis (de Barri) (*c*.1146–*c*.1220) Welsh churchman and historian

girandole a firework (not ital.)

girasol a fire opal, *not* -ole

Giraudoux, Jean (1882–1944) French novelist and playwright

girkin *use* **ghe-**

girlfriend (one word)

Girl Guide *now* **Guide**

giro a system of money transfer, *not* gy-

Girobank (cap., one word)

Girond/e a dép. of France, **-ist** a French moderate republican 1791–3

Giscard d'Estaing, Valéry (b. 1926) President of France 1974–81

gismo *use* **giz-**

gitan/ (Fr.) f. **-e** Spanish gypsy

gitan/o (Sp.) f. **-a** gypsy

gîte (Fr. m.) a rural holiday house in France

Guilia an Italian name, *not* Gui-

Giulini, Carlo Maria (b. 1914) Italian conductor

Giulio an Italian name, *not* Gui-

Giulio Romano (*c*.1499–1546) Italian architect

giuoco piano (It.) quiet play (a chess opening, 'the Italian game'); *giuoco* is in modern It. *gioco*, but the older spelling is retained in Eng. refs.

Giuseppe an Italian name, *not* Gui-

giveable *not* givable

given name a name given in addition to a surname; *prefer to* 'Christian name', which implies that Christian baptism is the norm; and to 'forename', since it includes names that follow the surname (e.g. Hungarian, Chinese, and Japanese)

Giza Egypt; *not* El-Ghiz-, -eh

gizmo *not* gis-

Gk. Greek

glace (Fr. cook. f.) ice

glacé glazed (not ital.)

gladiol/us (bot.) pl. **-i** (not ital.)

Gladstone/ bag, — cap (two words)

Gladstonian *not* -ean

Glagolitic of or relating to the alphabet ascribed to St Cyril, formerly used in writing some Slavonic languages

glair the white of an egg, *not* glaire

Glam. Glamorgan

glamorize *not* -ise

glamorous/, -ly *not* -our-

glamour *not* -or (even in US)

glandular fever = **(infectious) mono-nucleosis** (the usual US term)

glan/s the rounded part forming the end of the penis or clitoris, pl. **-des**

Glas. Glasgow

glaserian fissure (anat.) *not* glass-

glasnost (not ital.)

Glasse, Mrs Hannah wrote *The Art of Cookery* in 1747

glassful pl. **glassfuls**

glasshouse greenhouse, (sl.) military prison

Glaswegian of Glasgow

Glauber/, Johann Rudolf (1604–68) German chemist; **—'s salt** a cathartic (apos.), *not* salts

glaucoma an eye condition

glaucous greyish green or blue; (bot.) covered with a bloom

Glazunov, Aleksandr (Konstantinovich) (1865–1936) Russian composer

GLC (hist.) Greater London Council

Glen written separately when referring not to a settlement but to the glen itself, as Glen Almond, Glen Coe

Glenalmond Tayside

Glencoe Highland, *but* **Glen Coe** (pass)

Glendower, Owen (*c*.1354–*c*.1416) Welsh chieftain; in Welsh **Owain Glyn Dŵr**, *also called* **Owain ap Gruffydd**

Glenealy Co. Wicklow

Gleneely Co. Donegal

Glenfarclas, Glenfiddich, Glenforres whiskies

glengarry a Scottish cap

Glenlivet/ a Speyside village; *not* -at, -it (one word); **The —, Braes of —** whiskies

Glenmorangie a whisky

Glenrothes Fife

glissade a slide down a steep slope (not ital.)

glissand/o (mus.) slurred, in a gliding manner; pl. **-os** *not* -i

glissé a sliding step in dance (not ital.)

glockenspiel/ an orchestral percussion instrument, pl. **-s**

Gloria/ (liturgy) pl. **-s**

Gloria/ in Excelsis, — Patri hymns

Gloria Tibi glory to Thee (two caps.)

Glorious Twelfth, the (UK) 12 Aug., the start of grouse-shooting season

Glos. Gloucestershire

gloss a superficial lustre, a marginal note

gloss. glossary, a collection of glosses

glosseme (not ital.)

Gloucestershire abbr. **Glos.**

Gloucestr: the signature of the Bishop of Gloucester (colon)

glovebox (one word)

glove/ compartment, — puppet (two words)

glower gaze angrily, *not* -our

glow-worm (hyphen)

gloxinia/ (bot.) pl. **-s** (not ital.)

Gluck, Christoph Willibald Ritter von (1714–87) German composer, *not* Glü-

glu/e, -ed, -ey, -ing

glue/-pot, -sniffer (hyphen)

glut/en *not* -in; *but* **-inize, -inous**

glutton one excessively greedy (esp. for food); a voracious animal, *Gulo gulo*, called **wolverine** in N. Amer.

glycerine *not* -in (US)

Glyn Dŵr *see* **Glendower**

GM genetically modified, George Medal, Grand Master

gm. gram, *use* **g** (no point)

gm² *properly* **g/m²** grams per square metre, *use* **gsm**

G-man (US colloq.) a special agent of the FBI

GmbH (Ger.) *Gesellschaft mit beschränkter Haftung* (limited liability company)

GMC General Medical Council

Gmelin, Leopold (1788–1853) German chemist

GMT Greenwich Mean Time

GMWU General and Municipal Workers' Union

gn. guinea

gnamma (Austral.) a waterhole; *not* n-

GNC General Nursing Council

gneiss (geol.) a laminated rock (not ital.)

gnocchi small dumplings (not ital.)

gnos/is the knowledge of spiritual mysteries, pl. **-es**; **-tic** having spiritual knowledge

Gnosticism an eclectic philosophy of the redemption of the spirit from matter through knowledge; cap. when referring to the ancient world, but lower case for more modern systems

GNP gross national product

Gnr. (mil.) gunner

gns. guineas

gnu/ antelope, pl. **-s**

GO general order, great (*or* grand) organ

goalkeeper (one word)

goal/ kick, — line (two words)

goal/mouth, -post, -tender (one word)

goatee a chin-tuft like a goat's beard

goat/herd (one word)

goat's-beard a plant or fungus (hyphen)

goat/skin, -sucker (bird) (one word)

goaty goatlike

gobbledegook pompous jargon, *not* -dyg- (US)

Gobbo/, Launcelot a character in Shakespeare's *The Merchant of Venice*; **Old —** his father

Gobelin tapestry *not* -ins

gobemouche/ a credulous person, pl. **-s**; (Fr. m. sing. and pl.) *gobe-mouches*

Gobi a desert in Mongolia and E. Turkistan

gobsmack/, -ed, -ing (one word)

goby a fish (not ital.)

GOC General Officer Commanding

go-cart *use* -kart

God cap. when referring to the monotheistic deity, but lower case for pronouns referring to him; lower case for the gods of polytheistic religions and for the idiom 'make a god of something'

God-awful (hyphen, cap.)

god/child, -dam (one word)

god-daughter (hyphen, one word in US)

goddess (not cap.)

godfather (one word)

godhead divine nature, *but* **the Godhead** (cap.)

godless (one word)

Godley, Arthur *see* **Kilbracken**

godlike (one word)

god/mother, -parent (one word)

God's acre a burial ground (apos., one cap.)

god/send, -sent -son (one word)

Godspeed (one word, cap.)

Godthåb *use* **Nuuk**

Goebbels, Joseph (**Paul**) (1897–1945) German minister of propaganda 1933–45, *not* Gö-

Goehr,/ Alexander (b. 1932) German-born composer; **— Walter** (1903–60) his father, German conductor

Goering, Hermann (1893–1946) German field marshal, *not* Gö- (except in Ger.)

Goeth/e, Johann Wolfgang von (1749–1832) German poet and playwright; *not* Gö-, Got-; **-ean**

Goetheaner (Ger. m.) a follower of Goethe

gofer (US sl.) a person who runs errands, a dogsbody; cf. **goffer**, **gopher**

goffer to crimp, emboss; *not* gau-; animal, wood, *use* **goph-**

Goffs Oak Herts. (no apos.)

Gogh, Vincent (**Willem**) **Van** (1853–90) Dutch painter; in Eng. sometimes alphabetized under 'Van'

Gogmagog (Br. myth.) a giant, named **Göemot** by Spenser in the *Faerie Queene*

goi *use* **goy**

Goidel a member of Goidelic peoples (Irish, Highland Scottish, Manx), a Gael; *not* Gadhel; *Gaidheal* in Sc. Gaelic

goitre *not* -er (US)

go-kart a miniature racing car, *not* -cart (hyphen)

Golconda a rich source of wealth (from a ruined city near Hyderabad)

gold symbol **Au**

gold-digger (hyphen, two words in US)

gold dust (two words)

Golders Green NW London (no apos.)

goldfield (one word)

gold leaf (two words, hyphen when attrib.)

gold mine (two words)

Goldsmiths College University of London (no apos.)

golf/ bag, — ball, — cart (two words)

golf/ club the implement, the premises, or the association, **— course, — links, — match, — player** (two words)

Goliath a Philistine giant, a type of crane; *not* -iah

Gollancz,/ Sir Israel (1864–1930) English writer, **— Sir Victor** (1893–1967) British publisher and writer

golliwog *not* golly-

golosh *use* **gal-**

GOM Grand Old Man (esp. W. E. Gladstone)

Gomorr/ah (OT); **-ha** (AV NT) *but* **-ah** in NEB

Goncharov, Ivan (**Aleksandrovich**) (1812–91) Russian novelist

Goncourt/, Edmond Louis Antoine (1822–96) and his brother **—, Jules Alfred Huot** (1830–70) French novelists; **Prix —** (named after Edmond)

gondola/ pl. **-s** (not ital.)

Gonds a people of Cent. India, *not* Gh-

Gongo a tributary of the Zaïre

Góngora y Argote, Luis de (1561–1627) Spanish poet

gongorism a Spanish form of euphuism

gonorrhoea *not* -hea (US)

Gonville and Caius College Cambridge, *see also* **Caius**

good afternoon (salutation) (two words)

goodbye (one word), *not* -by

good/ day, — evening (salutations) (two words)

Good Friday (caps., two words)

good humour (two words), **good-humoured** (hyphen)

good morning (salutation) (two words)

Good-Natur'd Man, The a comedy by Goldsmith, 1768

good nature (two words), **good-natured** (hyphen)

goodnight (salutation) (one word)

good-quality (adj.)

Good/ Samaritan, — Templar (caps.)

goodwill of a business etc. (one word)

Goorkhas *use* **Gur-**

gooroo *use* **guru**

goose pl. **geese**, (in tailoring) **gooses**

gooseberry (one word)

goose/ bumps (US) = **gooseflesh, — egg** (US) a zero score in a game

gooseflesh (one word)

goose pimples (two words)

goose/-skin, -step (hyphens)

goosey a diminutive of goose; *not* -sie, -sy

Goossens a 19th–20th-c. Anglo-Belgian family of musicians

GOP Grand Old Party (Republican Party in USA)

gopher a burrowing animal, a kind of wood; cf. **gofer**; **goffer**

Gorbachev, Mikhail (**Sergeevich**) (b. 1931) General Secretary of Communist Party of the USSR 1985–91, President of the Supreme Soviet of the USSR 1988–91, President of the USSR 1990–1

Gordian knot tied by Gordius, cut by Alexander the Great

Gordonstoun School Elgin, Grampian

Gordonstown Grampian

Gorgio/ the Gypsy name for a non-Gypsy, pl. **-s**

Gorgonzola a cheese (cap.)

Gorky Russia, *formerly*, and once again, **Nizhni Novgorod**

Gorky, Maxim pseud. of **Aleksei Maksimovich Peshkov** (1868–1936) Russian writer and playwright

gormand *use* **gour-**

gormandize eat greedily; *not* gour-, -ise

gors/e furze, **-y**

Gorsedd/ a meeting of Welsh bards and druids, pl. **-au**

Goschen, Viscount

Göschen, Georg Joachim (1752–1828) German publisher (accent), grandfather of the first **Viscount Goschen** (1831–1907) (no accent)

Goshen a land of plenty, name of several towns in the USA and Canada

go-slow (noun, hyphen)

gospel cap. only when referring to the record of Christ's life and teaching in the first four books of the NT, *or* the north side of the altar (*Gospel side*)

gospodin (Russ.) Lord, Mr; f. **gospozha**; Russian practice now is to use initials instead of the title; *see also* **grazhdanin**

Goss, Sir John (1800–80) English organist and composer

Gosse,/ Sir Edmund William (1849–1928) English writer; — **Philip Henry** (1810–88) his father, English naturalist

gossip/, -ed, -er, -ing, -y (one *p*)

Göteborg Sweden, in Ger. **Gothenburg**

Gotham/ a village proverbial for the folly of its inhabitants, sometimes applied to Newcastle; **wise men of** — i.e. fools; — **City** (US colloq.) New York City, **-ite** a New Yorker

Gothic architecture, writing, etc. (cap.); abbr. **Goth.**

Gothic (typ.) a loose name for (esp. bold) sans serif faces, *formerly* OE black-letter faces

gotten past part. of **get**; *use* **got** except in the common expression 'ill-gotten gain', and in US

Götterdämmerung (Twilight of the Gods) the last part of Wagner's *Ring des Nibelungen*, 1876

Göttingen University Germany

Gouda a Dutch cheese

gouge a concave chisel

goujons deep-fried strips of chicken or fish (not ital.)

gouk *use* **-wk**

gour an Indian ox, *use* **ga-**

gourmand/ a glutton; **-ise** indulgence in gluttony; *see also* **gormandize**

gourmet a connoisseur of good food

goût (Fr. m.) taste

Goutte d'or a white burgundy wine

gov. govern/or, -ment

Government meaning the State (cap.), abbr. **Govt.**

Governor General abbr. **Gov. Gen.**, **GG**

Gowers, Sir Ernest (1880–1966) English civil servant, author of *Plain Words*, reviser of Fowler's *Modern English Usage*

gowk a cuckoo, a fool; *not* -uk

goy/ (derog.) Jewish name for a Gentile, pl. **-im**

Goya (**y Lucientes**), **Francisco José de** (1746–1828) Spanish painter

GP general practitioner, Graduate in Pharmacy, Grand Prix, Gloria Patri (glory be to the Father)

Gp. Group

g.p. great primer

Gp/Capt (RAF) Group Captain (no points)

GPO (hist.) General Post Office, (US) Government Printing Office

GPS Global Positioning System

GPU the Soviet 'State political administration for struggle against espionage and counter-revolution' (1922–3); *see also* **KGB**

GR *Georgius*, or *Gulielmus, Rex* (King George, *or* William)

Gr. Grand, Greater, Grecian, Greece, Greek

gr. grain, -s; *for* gram *use* **g**; gross, grey

Graaff, Robert Jemison van de *see* **van de Graaff**

Graafian follicle in ovary

Graal *use* **-ail**

Grabar the classical Armenian language

graben (Geol.) a depression of the Earth's surface between faults, pl. same

Gracchus,/ Gaius Sempronius (153–121 BC) and his brother — **Tiberius Sempronius** (163–133 BC), the **Gracchi,** Roman reformers

grace note (mus.) (two words)

Gracián, Baltasar (1601–58) Spanish moralist

gradatim (Lat.) step by step

gradine a tier of low steps or seats, a ledge at the back of an altar; *not* -in

gradus ad Parnassum (Lat.) step(s) to Parnassus, Lat. or Gr. poetical dictionary, any series of graded exercises; in short **gradus** (not ital.)

Graeae (Gr. myth.) three sisters who guarded the abode of the Gorgons

Graec/ism a Greek characteristic, *not* Grec- (US); **-ize, -o** (combining form), **-ophile**

Graf/ (Ger.) a count (equivalent to an earl), pl. **-en**, f. **Gräfin/**, pl. **-nen** (cap.; not ital. as part of title, no comma preceding)

graffit/o scribbling, usually on a wall; pl. **-i**; cf. **sgraffito**

Grahame, Kenneth (1859–1932) English author

Graian Alps France and Italy

Grail, the Holy *not* Graal, Graile

grain apothecaries', avoirdupois, or troy weight, all 0.0648 gram; abbr. **gr.**

Grainger, Percy (**Aldridge**) (1882–1961) Australian-born US composer

gram a unit of mass, abbr. **g**; in SI units 0.001 kg

gram. gramm/ar, -arian, -atical

gramaphone *use* **gramo-**

graminivorous feeding on grass, *not* gramen-

gramm/ar, -arian, -atical abbr. **gram.**

grammar school (two words)

gramme *use* **gram**

Grammont E. Flanders, Belgium

Gramont, Philibert, comte de (1621–1707) French courtier, adventurer, and soldier; *not* Gramm-

gramophone *not* grama-, grammo-

Gram's stain (bacteriology) (cap.)

Granada Spain, a British television network

granadilla *use* **gren-**

Gran Chaco, El a region in Bolivia, Paraguay, and Argentina

Grand abbr. **G., Gr.**

grandad *use* **-ddad**

grandam grandmother, old woman; *not* -dame

grand aunt (two words) *prefer* **great-aunt**

Grand Canyon Ariz.

grandchild (one word)

Grand Coulee Dam Wash.

granddad *not* grandad, grand-dad

granddaughter (one word)

Grand/ Duchess, — Duchy, — Duke (two words, both caps. if used as title) abbr. **GD**

grande dame (Fr.) a dignified lady

grande/ passion violent love affair, **— tenue** or **— toilette** full dress

grandeur (not ital.)

grandeur naturelle (Fr. f.) life-size

grandfather (one word)

Grand Guignol a sensational or horrific drama (not ital.)

grandiloquence pompous or inflated language, *not* -elo-

grand jury (not caps.)

grand mal a serious form of epilepsy (not ital.)

grand master a chess player of highest class

Grand Master (caps.) abbr. **GM**

grand-messe (Fr. f.) high mass (hyphen), before 1932 **grand' messe** (apos.)

Grand Monarque, le Louis XIV

grand monde, le (Fr.) the court and nobility

grandmother (one word)

grand/-nephew, -niece (hyphen)

Grand Old Party (US) the Republican Party, abbr. **GOP**

grandparent (one word)

Grand/ Prix an international motor-racing event, pl. **-s Prix** (not ital.); abbr. **GP**

Grand Rapids Mich.

grand siècle a classical or golden age, esp. the 17th c. in France

grand signior one of high rank (not cap.), the Sultan of Turkey (caps.); in Fr. **grand seigneur**, It. **gran signore**, Sp. **gran señor**

grandson (one word) abbr. **g.s.**

grand uncle (two words)

Grant Duff, Sir Mountstuart Elphinstone (1829–1906) Scottish politician (no hyphen)

granter one who grants

Granth the Sikh scriptures, *not* Grunth

grantor (law) one who makes a grant

gran turismo (It.) touring car

Granville-Barker, Harley (1877–1946) English playwright, producer, and actor

grapefruit pl. same

grapey *not* -py

graphology the study of character from handwriting, *not* graphio-

gras/ (Fr.) f. **-se**, fat; **— double** tripe; cf. **gros**

Grasmere Cumbria

Grass, Günter (**Wilhelm**) (b. 1927) German writer

Grasse dép. Alpes-Maritimes, France

grass/hopper, -land (one word)

gratia Dei (Lat.) by the grace of God

gratin *see* **au gratin**

gratis for nothing, free (not ital.)

Grattan, Henry (1746–1820) Irish statesman and orator

Gratz Pa.

Gratz Austria, *use* **Graz**

Grätz Czech Republic, *use* **Hradec Králové**

Grätz Poland, *use* **Grodzisk**

Graubünden a Swiss canton; in Fr. **Grisons**, in Romansh **Grisun**, in It. **Grigioni**

grauwacke *use* **grey-**

gravam/en the essence or most serious part of an argument, or a grievance; pl. **-ens**, *properly* **-ina**

grave (mus.) slow, solemn

grave accent (`)

gravel/, -led, -ling (one *l* in US)

Graves a Bordeaux wine

Graves' disease exophthalmic goitre (apos.)

grave/stone, -yard (one word)

gravitas (Lat.) solemn demeanour

gravure (typ.) the intaglio printing process (from photogravure)

gravy/ boat, — train (two words)

gray a colour, *use* **grey** (except in US)

gray a unit of absorbed radiation dose, abbr. **Gy** (no point); in SI units 1 J/kg

Gray,/ Asa (1810–88) US botanist, **— Louis Harold** (1905–65) English radiobiologist, **— Thomas** (1716–71) English poet; *see also* **Grey**

grayling a fish, *not* grey-

Gray's Inn London

graywacke *use* **grey-** (except in US)

Graz the capital of Styria, Austria, *not* Gratz

grazhdan/in (Russ.) citizen, f. *-ka*, pl. *-e*; formal term, often replaced by *tovarishch*

grazier one who pastures cattle, *not* -zer

GRCM Graduate of the Royal College of Music

greasy not -ey

great-aunt (hyphen)

Great Britain abbr. **GB**; *see also* **Britain**

Greater Manchester a metropolitan county

great gross 144 dozen, abbr. **g.gr.**

Great Lakes between USA and Canada: Superior, Huron, Michigan, Erie, Ontario

great/-nephew, -niece (hyphen)

Great Power (caps. only with hist. reference)

Greats the Oxford BA final examination for honours in Lit. Hum.

great-uncle (hyphen)

Grecian/ *use* **Greek** except as an adj. referring to architecture and facial outline, and as a noun for a boy in the top form at Christ's Hospital, or a Greek-speaking Jew of the Dispersion; also **— bend, — knot, — slippers**; abbr. **Gr.**

Grec/ism, -ize, -ophile *use* **Grae-** (except in US)

Greco, El (1541–1614) Spanish painter, born in Crete, real name **Domenico Theotocopuli** *or* **Kyriakos Theotokopoulos**

Greece abbr. **Gr.**

greegree *use* **gris-gris**

Greek abbr. **Gr., Gk.** (to avoid confusion with abbr. for 'German')

Greek calends, at the never, in Lat. *ad kalendas Graecas*

Greeley, Horace (1811–72) US journalist and politician

Greely, Adolphus Washington (1844–1935) US general and Arctic explorer

Green, John Richard (1837–83) English historian

Greenaway, Kate (1846–1901) English artist and illustrator of children's books

green/back (US) a note of legal tender, **-bottle** (one word)

Green Cloth (in full **Board of Green Cloth**) the Lord Steward's department of the Royal Household

Greene,/ Sir Conyngham (1854–1934) British diplomat, **— Graham** (1904–91) English novelist, **— Harry Plunket** (1865–1936) English singer, **— Nathanael** (1742–86) American Revolutionary War general, **— Robert** (1560–92) English dramatist and pamphleteer

green fee (golf) *not* **greens fee** (US)

green/gage, -grocer, -house (one word)

Greenland/ in Dan. **Grønland**, in Inuit **Kalaallit Nûnaat**; **-er, -ic**

Green Paper (UK) a consultative preliminary report of government proposals, for discussion (two caps.); cf. **Blue Book**; **White Paper**

green room a room off stage for actors

greensand/ a sandstone (not cap.), **Lower —** and **Upper —** two strata of the Cretaceous system (caps.)

green thumb (US) = **green fingers**

Greenwich Mean Time (caps.) abbr. **GMT**

greetings card *not* greeting (US)

gregale the Mediterranean NE wind; *not* -cale, grigale (not cap.)

grège a colour between beige and grey, *not* grei-

Gregorian/ calendar, — chant, — telescope (one cap.)

Greifswald university town, Germany

Grenada W. Indies

grenadilla a passion fruit, *not* gran- (not ital.)

grenadine a syrup made from pomegranates or currants; a loosely woven silk fabric; (cook.) a dish of veal or poultry fillets, (Fr. m.) *grenadin*

Grenadines, The chain of islands between Grenada and St Vincent, W. Indies

Gresham/'s Law 'bad money drives out good', from **Sir Thomas —** (1519–79) English financier

Grétry, André Ernest Modeste (1741–1813) French composer

Greuze, Jean Baptiste (1725–1805) French painter

Grévy, François Paul Jules (1807–91) French President 1879–87

grey colour, *not* gray (US)

Grey, Lady Jane (1537–54) proclaimed Queen of England 1553, deposed, beheaded; *see also* **Fallodon**; **Gray**

greybeard an old man, large jug, clematis (one word)

Greyfriars College Oxford

greyhen a female black grouse

greyhound/ (one word), **— racing** (two words)

greyling *use* gray-

grey matter (two words)

greywacke (geol.) a sedimentary rock; *not* grau-, gray- (US) (not ital.)

Grieg, Edvard (*not* Edward) **Hagerup** (1843–1907) Norwegian composer

Grieve *see* **MacDiarmid**

grievous *not* -ious

griffin a fabulous creature; *not* -on, gryphon

griffon a vulture, a breed of dog

grigale *use* gre-

Grigioni It. for **Graubünden**

grill cook under or on a grill etc.

grille a grating, a latticed screen, *not* -ill (except in US) (not ital.)

grill/é f. **-ée** (Fr. cook.) broiled, grilled

Grimm,/ Jakob (1785–1863) and his brother — **Wilhelm** (1786–1859) German philologists, collectors of fairy tales

Grimm's Law deals with consonantal changes in Germanic languages

Grimsetter Airport Orkney

grimy begrimed, *not* -ey

Grindelwald Switzerland, *not* Grindle-

grindstone (one word)

gringo/ a foreigner, esp. a Brit. or N. Amer. in a Sp.-speaking country (derog.); pl. **-s** (not ital.)

Griqua/ a child of Cape Dutch and Khoikhoi parents, **-land**, S. Africa (one word)

grisaille a method of decorative painting (not ital.)

Griselda a patient wife (after Boccaccio and Chaucer), in Sc. **Grizel**

grisette a working-class French girl

gris-gris/ an African *or* voodoo charm or fetish, **— bag, — maker, — man** (hyphen, two words); *not* greegree, gri-gri

grisly terrible, *not* grizz-

Gris-Nez, Cap dép. Pas-de-Calais, France (hyphen)

Grisons Fr. for **Graubünden**, in Romansh **Grisun**

grissini (pl.) long sticks of crispbread

gristly having or like gristle, *not* -ey

Grizel Sc. form of **Griselda**

grizzly/ grey-haired, **— bear** (two words)

gro. gross

groat (hist.) a silver coin worth four old pence, a small sum ('don't care a groat')

groats hulled or crushed grain, esp. oats

Grodzisk Poland, *not* Grätz

groin the fold between belly and thigh, (archit.) line of intersection of two vaults; cf. **groyne**

grommet not gru-

Gromyko, Andrei (**Andreevich**) (1909–89) Soviet Foreign Minister 1957–85, President of the Supreme Soviet 1985–8

Gropius, Walter (1883–1969) German architect

gros/ (Fr.) f. **-se** big; cf. **gras**

grosbeak (ornith.) the hawfinch

Groschen (Ger. m.) an Austrian and old German small coin, pl. same

grosgrain a corded silk fabric

gros point (Fr. m.) cross-stitch embroidery on canvas

gross (144) is sing. and pl., abbr. **gro.**

Grosse Point Mich.

Grosseteste, Robert (1175–1253) Bishop of Lincoln

grosso modo (It.) approximately

Grote, George (1794–1871) English historian of Greece

grotesque (typ.) a 19th-c. sans-serif typeface, abbr. **grot.**

grotesquerie *not* -ery (not ital.)

Grotius, Hugo (1583–1645) Dutch jurist and statesman (Latinized form of De Groot)

grotto/ pl. **-es**

ground/ floor, — level (two words, hyphen as adj.)

ground/ plan, — rent (two words)

ground/sheet, -sman, -water, -work (one word)

Group of/ (econ.) various combinations of industrial nations that meet to consider economic and trade concerns; **— — Three** (abbr. **G3**); **— — Five** (abbr. **G5**); **— — Seven** (abbr. **G7**); **— — Ten** (abbr. **G10**)

grovel/, -led, -ler, -ling (one *l* in US)

grove of Academe (one cap., not pl.) from Milton's *Paradise Regained*, refers specifically to Plato's Academy; *see also* **Academe**

Grove's Dictionary of Music and Musicians the current edn. is *The New Grove Dictionary of Music and Musicians*, usually abbr. *New Grove*

grown-up (adj. and noun) (hyphen)

groyn/e a breakwater, *not* -in (US); **-ing**; cf. **groin**

GRSM Graduate of the Royal Schools of Music (the Royal Academy and the Royal College)

GRT gross registered tonnage

Grub Street haunt of literary hacks and impoverished authors, later Milton Street, now demolished

gruelling (one *l* in US)

Gruffydd *see* **Glendower**

grummet *use* gro-

Grundy, Mrs in Thomas Morton's *Speed the Plough*, 1798, an embodiment of conventional propriety

Grunth the Sikh scriptures, *use* **Gra-**

Gruyère a cheese (cap., not ital.)

Gruyères Switzerland

Gryphius, Sébastien (1491–1556) German-born French printer, *not* Gryptinus

gryphon *use* **griffin**

grysbok (Afrik.) an antelope, *not* -buck

GS General Secretary, General Service, (mil.) General Staff, Grammar School

gs (hist.) guineas

g.s. grandson

G7 Group of Seven

GSM Guildhall School of Music

gsm grams per square metre, metric method for measuring weight of paper and card (no points)

GSO General Staff Officer

GSP (naval) Good Service Pension

G/-string the garment, a string for a violin etc.; **-suit** (hyphens)

GT Good Templar, *gran turismo*

gt. gilt, great, gutta

g.t. (bind.) gilt top

G10 Group of Ten

gtt. guttae

gu. gules

guacho *use* **gau-**

Guadalajara Mexico, Spain

Guadalupe/ Spain; — **Hidalgo** Mexico, *formerly* **Gustavo A. Madero**; — **Mountains** Texas and New Mexico

Guadeloupe W. Indies

guage *use* **gau-**

guaiacum (bot.) a tropical American tree, the resin obtained from it; *not* guaiac

Guaira, La Venezuela, *not* Guay-

Guam Marianas Islands; *not* Guaham, Guajam

guana a lizard, shortened from **iguana**

Guangdong (Pinyin) a Chinese province, *also* **Kwantung**

Guangzhou (Pinyin) a Chinese province, *not* Canton

guano fertilizer from seabirds' excrement

Guarani a member of a S. American Indian people, their language (cap.)

guarani the monetary unit of Paraguay (not cap.), symbol **G** *or* **₲**

guardhouse (one word)

Guardia Civil (Sp.) national guard (two caps.)

guard rail (two words)

guardroom (one word)

guards are *mounted*, **sentries** are *posted*

guard-ship (hyphen)

guardsman (one word)

Guareschi, Giovanni (1908–68) Italian novelist

Guarneri violin makers; *not* -nieri, -nerius

Guatemala Cent. America

Guayaquil Ecuador

Guayra *use* **La Guaira**

guazzo (It.) = gouache

Guedalla, Philip (1889–1944) British writer

Guelderland *use* **Geld-**

guelder rose *not* ge-

Guelf one of the Pope's faction in medieval Italian states, opposed to Ghibelline; *also* **Guelph**

Guenevere, Defence of by W. Morris, 1858; *see also* **Guinevere**

Guernica Spain, in Basque **Gernika**; subject of painting by Picasso, 1937

Guernsey a Channel Island, in Fr. **Guernesey**

guernsey a heavy knitted woollen pullover; the jersey worn by Australian footballers

guerre (Fr. f.) war

guerrilla/ a person or body engaged in — **warfare** irregular fighting by small bodies; *not* -eri-, gor-

Guesclin, Bertrand du (1314–80) Constable of France

guesstimate (colloq.) an estimate based on a mixture of guesswork and calculation, *not* guest-

guesswork (one word)

guest house (two words)

Gueux a league of Dutch rebels 1565–6

Guevara (de la Serna), Ernesto 'Che' (1928–67) leader of the Cuban revolution, *not* 'Ché'

Guggenheim/ Fellowship; — **Museum** (*formerly* **Solomon R. — Museum**) NYC

Guglielmo (It.) **William**

Gui, Vittorio (1885–1975) Italian conductor and composer

Guiana/, British *now* **Guyana**, — **Dutch** *now* **Suriname**

Guibelline *use* **Ghi-**

guide/book, -line, -post (one word)

Guides a girls' organization (cap.) (US) = **Girl Scouts**

Guido (It.) **Guy**

Guilbert, Yvette (1869–1944) French *diseuse*

guild an association, *not* gild

guilder a silver florin, the chief monetary unit of the Netherlands, abbr. **f**; in Du. **gulden**

Guildford Surrey, *not* Guilf-

Guildford: the signature of the Bishop of Guildford (colon)

guildhall *not* gi-; *but* **Guildhall**, London (*not* the —), York, and elsewhere (cap.)

Guilford, Earl of

Guili/a, -o It. names, *use* **Giu-**

Guillaume (Fr.) **William**

guillemets (typ.) quotation marks (« ») used in Fr., Ger., Russ., Sp., etc. (not ital.)

guillemot a seabird

Guillermo (Sp.) **William**

guilloche an architectural ornament (not ital.)

guillotine a beheading apparatus, a paper-cutting machine, a device for terminating parliamentary debates

guimp *use* **gi-**

Guinea/ W. Africa, adj. **-n**; — **Bissau** W. Africa; **New** — E. Indies; **Equatorial** — W. Cent. Africa

guinea/ (Brit. hist.) 21 shillings (21/–, £1.05), used esp. in determining professional fees; pl. **-s**; abbrs. **g., gn., gns., gs.**

guinea fowl (two words)

guinea pig a small S. American rodent; the subject of an experiment (two words)

Guinevere the wife of King Arthur; *see also* **Guenevere**

Guiranwala Pakistan

Guisborough Cleveland

Guiscard, Robert (11th c.) Norman leader

Guiseppe an Italian name, *use* **Giu-**

Gujarat/ an area in W. India, *not* Guze-; **-i** (of or relating to) (a native or the language) of Gujarat

Gujrat Pakistan

Gulag (Russ. acronym) Chief Administration for Corrective Labour Camps, the Soviet network of these camps, or a camp or prison within it (cap., not ital.); originally transliterated as **GULag**

gulden *see* **guilder**

gules (her.) red (usually placed after the noun), abbr. **gu.**

Gulf/ cap. when with name, as Gulf of Corinth, Persian Gulf; abbr. **G.**; — **Stream** (no hyphen)

Gulielmus (Lat.) William

gullible easily cheated, *not* -able

Gulliver's Travels a novel by Swift, 1726

gully a channel, *not* -ey

GUM a Moscow department store (caps.)

gum arabic (two words)

Gumbo a patois of blacks and Creoles spoken esp. in Louisiana (cap.)

gumbo/ okra, a kind of soup thickened with these; pl. **-s** (not cap.)

gum/boil, -boot, -shield (one word)

gum tree (two words)

gun. gunnery

gun/ **barrel, — battle** (two words)

gunboat (one word)

gun/ **bore, — carriage, — dog** (two words)

gun/fight, -fire (one word)

gung-ho enthusiastic, eager (hyphen)

Gungl, Josef (1810–89) Hungarian composer

gun/lock, -man, -metal (one word)

gunnel *use* **gunwale**

gunnery (naval) abbr. **G., gun.**

gunny sacking

gun platform (two words)

gun/point, -powder, -room (one word)

gun-runner (hyphen)

gun/ship, -shot (one word)

gun-shy (hyphen)

gun/slinger, -smith, -stock (one word)

Gunter's chain a surveyor's chain, 66 ft long

Gunther a character in the *Nibelungenlied* (no umlaut)

gunwale *not* gunnel

gurdwara a Sikh temple

Gurkhas Nepali soldiers in Ind. or Brit. service; *not* Ghoor-, Ghur-, Goor-

gurkin *use* **gher-**

Gurmukhi the alphabet in which Punjabi is written

gurnard a fish, *not* -net

guru a religious teacher; *not* gooroo

Gutenberg (*or* **Gensfleisch**), **Johann** (*c.*1399–1468) German inventor (so generally assumed) of movable metal types

gutt/a a drop, abbr. **gt.**; pl. **-ae**, abbr. **gtt.**

gutta-percha a hard rubber-like substance (hyphen, not ital.)

gutter (typ.) the space between imposed pages of type allowing for two foredge margins; in a book, the inner space between two columns or pages

guttural connected with the throat

Guyan/a S. America, **-ese**; *not* Gui-

Guyot, Yves (1843–1928) French economist

Guy's Hospital London (apos.)

Guzerat India, *use* **Gujarat**

Gwalior India

Gwent a Welsh county

GWR Great Western Railway

Gwyn, Nell (1650–87) (born **Eleanor Gwynne**) English actress, mistress of Charles II; *not* -nne

Gwynedd a Welsh county

Gwynn, Stephen (1864–1950) English writer

Gy gray (no point)

gybe (naut.) change course, *not* ji- (US); cf. **gibe**

gym (colloq.) gymnasium (no point)

gymkhana an athletic display, a pony-club competition; *not* -kana (not ital.)

gymnasium/ pl. **-s** (not ital.), colloq. **gym**

gymnot/us the electric eel, pl. **-i** (not ital.)

gymp *use* **gi-**

gymslip (one word)

gynaeceum (Gr., Rom.) the women's apartments in a house

gynaecology the study of women's diseases, *not* gyne- (US); abbr. **gyn.**

gynoeci/um (bot.) the female organ of a flower, pl. **-a**

gypsum hydrated calcium sulphate

Gypsy a member of a nomadic people of Europe and N. America speaking Romany (cap.); *not* Gip-; a person resembling or living like this people (not cap.)

gyrfalcon a large falcon; *not* ger-, jer-

gyro money transfer, *use* **gi-**

gyro/ short for gyroscope, -compass, pl. **-s**

gyr/us a fold or convolution, esp. of the brain; pl. **-i**

gyttja (geol.) a lake deposit of a usually black organic sediment

H h

H henry (unit of inductance), hydrogen, (pencils) hard (*see also* **HH**, **HHH**), (mus.) B natural in German system, the eighth in a series

H. harbour, hydrant

h hour, -s (in scientific and technical work), (as prefix) hecto-

h. hardness, height, husband, (meteor.) hail

H. (Ger.) *Heft* (number, part)

h Planck constant

h Planck constant divided by 2π, also called the Dirac constant, pronounced 'h bar'

HA Historical Association, Horse Artillery

Ha hahnium (no point)

ha. hectare(s) (no point)

h.a. *hoc anno* (in this year), *hujus anni* (this year's)

Haag, Den informal Du. for **The Hague**; cf. **'s-Gravenhage**

Haakon the name of seven Norwegian kings; in Old Norse **Hákon**, in Modern Norw. **Håkon**

haar a raw sea-mist (E. coast of England and Scotland)

Haarlem Netherlands; cf. **Harlem**

hab. habitat

Habakkuk (OT) abbr. **Hab.**

Habana, la Sp. for **Havana**

habeas corpus a writ to produce a person before court, abbr. **hab. corp.** (not ital.)

Habeas Corpus Act 1640 (amended 1679), 1816, 1862

habendum (law) part of deed defining estate or interest granted

Haberdashers' Aske's School Elstree

habet (Lat.) he is hit (lit. he has); *see also* **hoc habet**

habile skilful, able; *not* -ille (not ital.)

habitat the normal abode of an animal or plant (not ital.), abbr. **hab.**

habitu/é f. **-ée**, a frequenter (not ital.)

Habsburg, House of the Austrian Imperial family, *not* Hap-

HAC Honourable Artillery Company

háček a diacritic mark (˘) placed over letters to modify the sound in some Slavonic and Baltic languages

Hachette publishers

hachis (Fr. cook. m.) minced meat, hash

hachisch *use* **hashish**

hachure a line used in map hill-shading (usually in pl.)

hacienda (not ital.)

hackberry the bird cherry, *not* hag-

Hackluyt *use* Hak-

hackney/ (verb) make trite, **-ed**; (noun) a horse pl. **-s**; — **carriage** off. term for 'taxi'

hacksaw (one word)

hac lege (Lat.) on these terms

Hades (Gr. myth.) the abode or god of the dead (cap.)

Hadith a body of traditions relating to Muhammad, in Arab. *ḥadīt*

hadj/, -i *use* **haj**

Hadramaut S. Arabia, *not* Hadhra-

haecceity (philos.) the individual quality of a thing that makes it unique

Haeckel, Ernst Heinrich (1834–1919) German philosopher, *not* Hä-

haem/, -al, -atin, -atite *not* heme, hem/al, -atin, -atite (US)

haema-, haemo- prefix meaning blood, *not* hema-, hemo- (US)

haemorrh/age, -oids *not* hem- (US)

haere mai (Maori) welcome (not ital.)

Haffner a serenade and symphony by Mozart

hafiz a Muslim who knows the Koran by heart

Hāfiz (d. 1388) Persian poet, real name **Shams ud-din Muhammad**

hafnium symbol **Hf**

Hag. Haggai

hagberry *use* **hack-**

Haggad/ah a legend etc. used to illustrate a point of the Law in the Talmud; a book recited at the Seder; *not* Agadah, Hagada, -ah; **-ic**

Haggai (OT) abbr. **Hag.**

haggard wild-looking; an untamed hawk

haggis a Scottish dish; *not* -ess, -ies

Hagiographa last part of the Hebrew Scriptures (cap.)

hagio/grapher, -graphy, -latry, -logy (not cap.)

Hague, Cap de La NW France

Hague, The in Du. **'s-Gravenhage** *or* **Den Haag**, in Fr. **La Haye** (caps.) Amsterdam is the capital of the Netherlands; The Hague is its seat of government. The definite article in 'The Hague' is cap. in running text, unlike that in 'the Netherlands'

ha ha laughter (two words)

ha-ha a trench dug as a garden boundary; *not* aha, haw-haw (hyphen)

hahnium symbol **Ha**

Haidarabad *use* **Hyder-**

haik an outer covering for head and body worn by Arabs, *not* haick, -ek

haiku a Jap. verse form, pl. same; *not* hokku

Haile/ Selassie I (1892–1975) Emperor of Ethiopia 1930–74; *also* — **Sellassie**

Haileybury College Herts.

hail-fellow-well-met (adj.) friendly, often excessively (three hyphens)

hail/stone, -storm (one word)

Hainault London

Hainaut a province, Belgium

hair/bell, -brain *use* **hare-**

hairbreadth (adj. one word), *but* **hair's breadth** (noun, two words)

hair/brush, -cloth, -cut (one word)

hairdo/ a coiffure (one word), pl. **-s**

hairdress/er, -ing (one word)

hairdryer *not* -drier

hair/grip, -like, -line (one word)

hairlip *use* **hare-**

hair/net, -piece, -pin (one word)

hair's breadth *see* **hairbreadth**

hair shirt (two words, hyphen when attrib.)

hairslide (one word)

hair space (typ.) a very thin space, thinner than a thin space (hyphen); (US) = **thin space** (two words)

hair/-splitter, -splitting (hyphens, one word in US)

hair/spray, -spring, -style, -stylist (one word)

hair-trigger (hyphen, one word in US)

Haiti W. Indies, *not* Hay-; *formerly* the island of Hispaniola, *now* its western part

haj/ the Islamic pilgrimage to Mecca, **-i** a Muslim who has been to Mecca as a pilgrim (cap. used as a title); *not* hadj, -i, hajj, -i

Hakenkreuz (Ger. n.) the swastika

hakim (in Ind. and Muslim countries) a physician, in Arab. **ḥakīm**; also a judge, ruler, or governor, in Arab. **ḥākim**; *not* -keem

Hakluyt/, Richard (*c.*1552–1616) English historian and geographer, — **Society**; *not* Hack-

Hákon, Håkon *see* **Haakon**

Halach/a Jewish law and jurisprudence, based on the Talmud; **-ic**; *not* -kah

halal/ (verb) kill (an animal) as prescribed by Muslim law, (noun) the meat thus prepared; **-led, -ling**; in Arab. **ḥalāl**; *not* -llal

halberd/ (hist.) combined spear and battleaxe, *not* -ert; **-ier**

Halcyone (Gr. myth.) *use* **Al-**

Halevi, Judah (*c.*1085–1140) Spanish-Jewish philosopher and poet

Halévy,/ Élie (1870–1937) French historian; — **Jacques François Fromental Élie** (1799–1862) his great-uncle, French composer; — **Joseph** (1827–1917) French traveller; — **Ludovic** (1834–1908) father of Élie, French playwright and novelist

half a dozen etc. (no hyphens) *but* **half-dozen** (hyphen)

half-and-half (hyphens)

half an hour (no hyphens) *but* **half-hour** (hyphen)

half/-binding (bind.) when the spine and corners are bound in a different material from the sides (hyphen), **-bound** (hyphen)

half-breed (hyphen)

half-brother (hyphen, two words in US)

half/-caste, -cut, -deck, -hardy, -hearted (hyphens)

half/ hitch, — holiday (two words)

half/-hour, -hourly, -life, -light (hyphens)

half/ mast, — measures (two words)

half-moon (hyphen)

half nelson (two words, no caps.)

half note (esp. US mus.) = **minim**

half past, — pay (two words)

halfpenny (one word)

halfpennyworth (one word) colloq. **ha'p'orth**

half-price (hyphen)

half-sister (hyphen, two words in US)

half/-term, -timber, -timbered, -time (hyphens)

half-title (typ.) the short title printed on the leaf before the full title (hyphen, two words in US); *also called* **bastard title**

half-tone (typ.) reproduction in which tones are produced by varying sizes of dots, a black-and-white photograph; (esp. US mus.) = **semitone** (hyphen)

half/-track, -truth (hyphens)

halfway (one word)

half/wit (one word), **-witted** (hyphen)

half-year(ly) (occurring at) an interval of six months, biannual

Haliburton, Thomas Chandler (1796–1865) Canadian-born British writer, pseud. **Sam Slick**

haliotis a type of edible gastropod mollusc

halitosis bad breath

hallabaloo *use* **hulla-**

hallal *use* **halal**

Hallé/, Sir Charles (1819–95) German-born Mancunian pianist and conductor (born **Karl Halle**), founded — **Orchestra** 1857, — **Concerts**

Halle an der Saale Germany, abbr. **Halle a/S.**

hallelujah *see also* **alleluia**; 'Hallelujah Chorus' in Handel's *Messiah*

Halles, Les Paris, former central market

Halley, Edmond (1656–1742) English astronomer, *not* -und

halliard *use* **haly-**

Halliwell-Phillipps, James (**Orchard**) (1820–89) English Shakespearian scholar

hallo *use* **he-**

halloo/ (a cry) inciting dogs to the chase; **-ed, -s**

Hallow/e'en 31 Oct. (no apos. in US); **-mas** (one word) 1 Nov., All Saints' Day

Hallstatt (of or relating to) the early Iron Age in Europe, *not* -stadt

hall/ux the great toe, pl. **-uces**

halm a stalk or stem, *use* **haulm**

halo/ a ring of light round moon, head, etc.; **-ed, -es**

Hals, Frans (1582/3–1666) Dutch painter

halva a sweet confection of sesame flour and honey, *not* -ah

halves pl. of **half**

halyard (naut.) a rope for raising sail; *not* halli-, hauly-

hamadryad/ a wood nymph, a king cobra; pl. **-s**

hamadryas a large Arabian baboon, pl. same

hamba (S. Afr.) go away, be off (not ital.)

Hambleden/ Bucks., **Viscount —**

Hambledon Hants., Surrey

Hambleton Lancs., Leics., N. Yorks.

Hambros Bank, Ltd (no apos.)

Hamburg/ Germany; a fowl, a grape (not cap.), **-er** (not cap.)

'Hamelin, The Pied Piper of' a poem by R. Browning, 1842

ham/-fisted, -handed (hyphens)

Hamit/es a group of peoples in Egypt and N. Africa, by tradition descended from Noah's son Ham; **-ic** (of or relating to) a group of African languages

hammam a Turkish bath; *not* hummum, -aum

Hammarskjöld, Dag (**Hjalmar Agne Carl**) (1905–61) Swedish statesman, Secretary-General of the UN 1953–61

hammer/beam, -head (one word)

Hammergafferstein, Hans pseud. of **Henry W. Longfellow**

Hammerklavier (Ger.) former name of the pianoforte, as opposed to harpsichord; Beethoven labelled Op. 101 and Op. 106 'für das Hammerklavier'; Op. 106 is popularly known as the *Hammerklavier* Sonata

Hammerstein II, Oscar (1895–1960) US lyricist and playwright

Hammett, (**Samuel**) **Dashiell** (1894–1961) US writer of detective novels

Hampden, John (1594–1643) English patriot and statesman

Hampshire abbr. **Hants.**

Hampton Court London

hamsin *use* **kham-**

ham/string past and past part. are correctly **-stringed**, but **-strung** is favoured by usage

Hamtramck Mich.

hamza (Arab.) a glottal-stop mark ('), typographically largely equivalent to the Gr. lenis or Heb. *alef* (ital.)

hand/bag, -bell, -bill, -book, -brake (one word)

Hand/buch (Ger. n.) a handbook (cap.), pl. *-bücher*

hand/clap, -cuffs (one word)

Handel, George Frederick (1685–1759) German composer resident in England, in Ger. **Georg Friedrich Händel**; *see also* **Handl**

Handels/blatt (Ger. n.) trade journal (cap.), pl. *-blätter*

handful/ *not* -ll, pl. **-s**

hand grenade (two words)

hand/grip, -gun, -hold (one word)

handicap/, -per, -ping

handiwork *not* handy-

handkerchief/ pl. **-s**, abbr. **hdkf.**

Handl, Jacob (1550–91) Slovenian composer, *not* Hä-; also known as **Gallus**; *see also* **Handel**

hand/list, -made, -maid(**en**) (one word)

handout (noun, one word)

hand-pick/ (verb, hyphen), **-ed** (adj., one word in US)

handrail (one word)

Handschrift/ (Ger. f.) MS, abbr. **Hs.**; pl. *-en*, abbr. **Hss.** (caps.); printer's copy is usually *Manuskript* (Ger. n.)

handsel/, -led, -ling (one *l* in US); *not* hans-

handset a combined mouthpiece and earpiece (one word)

hand-setting (typ.) manual composition (hyphen)

hand/shake, -spike, -spring, -stand, -writing (one word)

handyman (one word)

handywork *use* **handi-**

hangar/ a large shed (cf. **hanger**), **-age**

hangdog shamefaced (one word)

hanged past tense or past part., used of capital punishment; other senses *use* **hung**

hanger one who, *or* that which, hangs; a sword, a wood; cf. **hangar**

hang-glid/e, -er, -ing (hyphen, two words in US)

hanging/ paragraph *or* **— indent** (typ.) set with second and following lines indented under first line

hangnail *not* agnail

Hang Seng/ Bank, — — index Hong Kong

hang-up (noun, hyphen)

hanky-panky (hyphen)

Hanover/ in Ger. **Hannover, -ian** of or relating to the British sovereigns from George I to Victoria (1714–1901)

Hans/ (Du., Ger.) Jack, **— Niemand** 'Mr Nobody'

Hansa a medieval guild of merchants, the entrance fee to a guild; *not* -se

Hansard the verbatim record of debates in Parliament (not ital.)

Hanseatic League a medieval political and commercial league of Germanic towns

hansel *use* **hand-**

hansom a two-wheeled horse-drawn cab

Hants. Hampshire, *not* Hants

Hanukkah the Jewish festival of lights; *see also* **Chanukkah**

hanuman/ an Indian langur; (cap.) (Hindu myth.) the monkey-god; pl. **-s** *not* -men

hapax legomen/on a word found once only (not ital.) pl. **-a**

haphazard (one word)

ha'p'orth (colloq.) a halfpennyworth

happi a loose Japanese coat

happy-go-lucky (hyphens)

happy hunting ground (no hyphen)

Hapsburg *use* **Hab-**

hara-kiri (Jap.) ritual suicide by disembowelment with a sword; *not* hari-, -kari, hurry-curry; the more refined term is **seppuku**

haram a Muslim sacred place, forbidden to non-Muslims; *not* -em

harangu/e address like an orator, **-ed**

Harare the capital of Zimbabwe

harass *not* harr-

harbour/, -age abbr. **H., har.**; *not* -or, -orage (US)

Harcourt Brace Jovanovich publishers (no commas)

hard (pencils) abbr. **H**

hard/-a-lee, -a-port, -a-starboard, -a-weather (two hyphens each)

hardback (of) a book bound in stiff covers

hard/ball, -bitten, -board (one word)

hard-boiled (hyphen)

hard copy (comput.) printed material produced by computer (two words); cf. **soft copy**

Hardecanute accepted var. of **Harthacnut** (1019–42) King of Denmark and England

hard hat (two words)

hard hit severely affected (hyphen when attrib.)

Hardie, James Keir (1856–1915) British socialist

hardi/hood, -ness *not* hardy-

Harding, Baron, of Petherton

Hardinge/, Viscount; Baron — of Penshurst

hard/line unyielding, **-liner** a person who adheres rigidly to policy (one word)

hardness (mineralogy) abbr. **h.**

hard rock (two words)

hards coarse flax, *not* hur-

hardshell (attrib. one word)

hard shoulder on motorway (two words)

hard sign (typ.) a double prime ("), used in e.g. transliterated Russ.; cf. **soft sign**

Hardt Mountains Bavarian Palatinate; cf. **Harz**

Hardwicke, Earl of

hard-wired (hyphen)

hardwood (one word) *but* **hard-wooded**

hard-working (hyphen)

harebell (bot.) *not* hair- (one word)

hare-brain/, -ed *not* hair- (hyphens)

hare-duck (philos.) in Wittgenstein's illustration of ambivalent diagrams; *not* rabbit-duck, duck-rabbit (hyphen)

Harefoot the sobriquet of Harold I

Hare/ Krishna (a member of) a sect devoted to the worship of the Hindu deity Krishna, pl. **— Krishnas**

harelip *not* hair- (one word)

harem the women of a Muslim household living in a separate part of the house; their quarters; *not* -am, -eem, -im (not ital.)

harem-scarem *use* **harum-scarum**

Hargreaves, James (1720–78) English weaver, inventor of the spinning jenny

haricot a variety of French bean

haricot/ de mouton Irish stew, **-s blancs** haricot beans, **-s d'Espagne** scarlet runners, **-s rouges** kidney beans, **-s verts** French beans

haridan *use* **harr-**

harier *use* **harr-**

Harijan a member of the caste of untouchables in India (cap.)

hari-kari *use* **hara-kiri**

harim *use* **-em**

Haringey Greater London borough, 1965; *not* -ay; *see also* **Harringay**

Harington, Sir John (1561–1612) English poet and pamphleteer; *see also* **Harri-**

hark/ (arch.) listen attentively, **-en** *use* **hearken**

harl a fibre, *not* -le

Harlech Gwynedd, *not* -ck

Harleian of Harley or his manuscript collection

Harlem New York; cf. **Haarlem**

Harlequin/ a character in pantomime and in It. *commedia dell'arte* (cap.); **-ade** (not cap.); **— duck** an Icelandic duck (not cap.)

Harlesden London

Harleston Devon, Norfolk, Suffolk

Harlestone Northants.

Harley,/ Robert (1661–1724) first Earl of Oxford, statesman and bibliophile; **— Edward** (1689–1741), his son, the second Earl

Harlow (1911–37) US film actress

harmattan a parching dusty land-wind of the W. African coast; in Fanti or Twi *haramata*

Harmen *see* **Arminius**

harmonize *not* -ise

HarperCollins publishers (one word)

Harper's Bazaar a US fashion magazine, founded 1867; Brit. version, founded 1929, *now Harpers & Queen* (*H&Q*)

Harpers Ferry W. Va. (no apos.)

Harper's Magazine a US magazine, founded 1850

harquebus/ (hist.) an early type of portable gun; *not* -ss, arque-; **-ier**

Harraden, Beatrice (1864–1936) English writer

harrass *use* **har-**

harridan a haggard old woman, *not* hari-

harrier a hound for hunting hares, a hawk; (cap. as pl.) group of cross-country runners; *not* har-

Harringay N. London; *see also* **Haringey**

Harrington, Earl of, *see also* **Hari-**

Harris Manchester College Oxford, *formerly* Manchester College

Harris tweed a kind of tweed woven by hand in Harris in the Outer Hebrides

Harrogate N. Yorks., *not* Harrow-

Harrovian a member of Harrow School

harrumph clear the throat or make a similar sound, esp. ostentatiously

Hart, Horace (1840–1916) Printer to the University of Oxford 1883–1916

hartal the closing of Indian shops or offices as a mark of protest or sorrow

Harte, (Francis) Bret (1836–1902) US novelist and story-writer

hartebeest a large African antelope, *not* hartb-; in Afrik. *hartebees*

Hartford Conn.

Harthacnut a more correct form of the commonly spelt **Hardecanute**; **Hǫrðaknútr** the technically correct Old Norse form

Hartlepool Cleveland

hartshorn (one word)

Hart's Rules for Compositors and Readers at the University Press, Oxford 1st (pub.) edn. 1904, 39th edn. 1983

Hartz Mountains *use* **Harz**; cf. **Hardt**

harum-scarum reckless (hyphen), *not* harem-scarem

Harun-al-Rashid (763–809) Caliph of Baghdad, hero of the *Arabian Nights*; (two hyphens) *not* -oun, -ar-, -sch-

harusp/ex a Roman religious official who interpreted omens from the inspection of animals' entrails, pl. **-ices**

Harvard references an author–date system of referencing sources

Harvard University at Cambridge, Mass.; abbr. **Harv.** or **HU**

harvestman *see* **daddy-long-legs**

Harv/ey, William (1578–1657) English physician, discovered blood circulation; **-eian** *not* -eyan

Harz Mountains Cent. Germany, *not* Hartz; cf. **Hardt**

has-been/ a person or thing that is no longer of importance or use, pl. **-s** (hyphen)

Hašek, Jaroslav (1883–1923) Czech novelist and satirist

Hashemites an Arab princely family

hashish hemp smoked or chewed as a drug; *not* hach-, hasch-, -eesh, -isch

Hasid/ a member of any of several mystical Jewish sects; adj. **-ic**, pl. **-im**; *not* Hass-, Ch-

Haslemere Surrey; *see also* **Haz-**

Hasse, Johann Adolph (1699–1783) German composer

Hassler, Hans Leo (1564–1612) German composer

hatable *not* -eable

hat/band, -box (one word)

hatch/back, -way (one word)

hatha yoga a system of exercises in yoga

hatpin (one word)

Hatshepsut (*c*.1500 BC) Queen of Egypt

hatt short form of *hattı humayun* or *hattı şerif* a Turkish edict made irrevocable by a Sultan's mark

hat-trick (hyphen)

hauberk (hist.) a coat of mail

hauler one who or that which hauls

haulier (Brit.) a firm or person engaged in road transport, a miner who moves coal

haulm (bot.) a stalk or stem, *not* halm

haulyard *use* **hal-**

Hauptmann,/ Gerhart (1862–1946) German poet and dramatist, — **Moritz** (1792–1868) German composer

Hausa (of or relating to) (a member of) a people of W. Africa and the Sudan, or the language of this people, widely used in W. Africa as a lingua franca; pl. same; *not* -ssa, Housa

hausfrau/ housewife (not cap.); in Ger. f. *Hausfrau*/ pl. **-en**

Haussmann, Georges Eugène, baron (1809–91) Paris architect

haussmannize open out and rebuild

haut/bois, -boy (hist. mus.) *use* **oboe** in an orchestral or chamber context

haute bourgeoisie (Fr. f.) upper middle class

haute/ couture high fashion; — **cuisine** cooking of a high standard (not ital.)

haute école advanced horsemanship

Haute/-Garonne a dép. of SW France, **-Loire** a dép. of Cent. France, **-Marne** a dép. of E. France (hyphens)

Hautes-Alpes a dép. of SE France (hyphen)

Haute/-Saône a dép. of E. France (hyphen)

Haute-Savoie a dép. of SE France (hyphen)

Hautes-Pyrénées a dép. of SW France (hyphen)

hauteur haughty demeanour (not ital.)

Haute-Vienne a dép. of Cent. France (hyphen); cf. **Vienne**

haute volée (Fr. f.) the upper ten

haut-goût (Fr. m.) high flavour

haut monde (Fr. m.) fashionable society

Haut-Rhin a dép. of E. France (hyphen)

Hauts-de-Seine a dép. of N. France (two hyphens)

Haüy, René Just (1743–1822) French mineralogist and crystallographer

Havana Cuba; *not* -ah, -annah; in Sp. **la Habana**

Havas a French news agency

Havel, Václav (b. 1936) Czech playwright and politician, President of Czechoslovakia 1990–3, President of Czech Republic 1993-

haver (Sc.) talk nonsense (*not* vacillate)

Haverfordwest Dyfed

Havergal, Frances Ridley (1836–79) English hymn-writer

Havering-atte-Bower Essex

haversack a bag for carrying food, *not* -sac

havoc/ (noun); as verb, **-ked, -king**

Havre France, *use* **Le Havre** (always cap. *L* in Eng., lower case in Fr.)

Hawaii/ one or all of the Hawaiian Islands, or the US state comprising most of them, *properly* **Hawai'i**; off. and postal abbr. **HI**; adj. **-an**

haw-haw *use* **ha-ha**

Haw-Haw, Lord nickname of William Joyce, American-born German propagandist in the Second World War, executed 1946

hawk-eyed (hyphen)

hawksbill a small turtle, *not* hawk's-bill

hawse/ (naut.) part of ship's bows; **-hole, -pipe** (hyphens)

Hawthorne,/ Julian (1846–1934) US writer; — **Nathaniel** (1804–64) his father, US novelist

hay/ a country dance, *not* hey (*but Shepherd's Hey*, by P. A. Grainger); **-box, -cock** (one word)

Haydn,/ Franz Joseph (1732–1809) and his brother — **Johann Michael** (1737–1806) Austrian composers; — **Joseph** (d. 1856) compiled *Dictionary of Dates*

Haydon, Benjamin Robert (1786–1846) English painter

hay fever (two words)

hay/field, -maker, -rick, -seed, -stack -wire (one word)

hazel-hen (hyphen)

hazelnut (one word)

Hazlemere Bucks.; *see also* **Has-**

Hazlitt,/ William (1778–1830) English essayist, — **William Carew** (1834–1913) English bibliographer

hazy indistinct, *not* -ey

HB (pencils) hard black

Hb haemoglobin (no point)

HBM Her, *or* His, Britannic Majesty('s)

H-bomb hydrogen bomb (no point, hyphen)

HC habitual criminal, Heralds' College, High Church, Holy Communion, Home Counties, (Fr.) *hors concours* (not competing), House of Commons, House of Correction

h.c. *honoris causa*

HCF *or* **h.c.f.** (math.) highest common factor; **HCF** (Brit.) Honorary Chaplain to the Forces

hd. head

hdkf. handkerchief

H. Doc. (US) House of Representatives Document

hdqrs. headquarters

Hdt. Herodotus

HE His Eminence; His, *or* Her, Excellency; high explosive

He helium (no point)

head (typ.) the blank space at the top of a page; *see also* **margins**

headach/e (one word); **-y** *not* -ey

headband a band worn round head, (bind.) strengthening band of multicoloured silk etc. sewn or stuck to head (and sometimes tail) of back of book

headbang/er, -ing (one word)

head-butt (hyphen)

head/board, -count, -dress, -gear (one word)

headhunt/, -er, -ing

head/lamp, -land (one word)

Headlesscross N. Lanarkshire (one word)

headlight (one word)

headline *see* **running heads**

head/lock, -long, -man a chief (one word)

head/master, -mistress as general term (one word, no caps.); off. title at certain schools (two words, caps.), abbr. **HM**

headnote a summary at the head of a chapter or page, (mus.) a tone produced in the head register (one word)

head-on (hyphen)

head/phone(s), -piece (one word)

headquarters used as sing. of the place, pl. of the occupants (one word); abbr. **HQ, hdqrs.**

head/rest, -room, -sail, -scarf (one word)

head sea waves from forward direction (two words)

headship the position of chief (one word)

headsman an executioner (one word)

headstock the bearings in a machine (one word)

head/stone, -strong (one word)

head teacher (two words)

head voice the high register of the voice in speaking or singing (two words)

head/water, -way, -wind (one word)

headword (typ.) an emphasized word opening a paragraph or entry etc. (one word)

headwork (one word)

heal *see* **hele**

health/ centre, — certificate, — farm, — food (two words)

healthful *not* -ull

health/ officer, — service, — visitor (two words)

Heap *see* **Heep**

hear, hear! an exclamation of agreement; *not* here, here!

hearken *not* hark-

Hearn, Lafcadio (1850–1904) US author

heart/ache, -beat (one word)

heartbreak/, -er, -ing (one word)

heartbroken (one word)

heartburn pyrosis (one word)

heart-burn jealousy (hyphen)

heart/ disease, — failure (two words)

heartfelt (one word)

hearth/rug, -stone (one word)

heartland (one word)

heart/-rending, -searching (hyphens)

heartsease *or* **heart's-ease** a pansy

heart/sick, -sore, -strings (one word)

heart/-throb, -warming (hyphen)

heartwood (one word)

Heath Robinson (a contraption) having absurdly ingenious and impracticable machinery (no hyphen); (US) = **Rube Goldberg**

heatproof (one word)

heat-resistant (hyphen)

heat/stroke, -wave (one word)

heave ho! (two words)

Heaven cap. when equivalent to the Deity; lower case when a place

heaven/-born, -sent (hyphens)

Heaviside/, Oliver (1850–1925) British electrical engineer; **— layer** (in full **Heaviside–Kennelly layer** (en rule)) the E-layer, a stratum of the atmosphere that reflects radio waves; *not* Heavy-

heavy/-duty, -footed, -handed, -hearted (hyphens)

heavy/ metal, — water, — weather (two words)

heavyweight (one word)

Heb. Hebrew, -s; Epistle to the Hebrews (NT)

hebdomad/ a group of seven, a week; *not* -ade; **-al**

Hebraize make Hebrew; *not* -ise, -aicize

Hebrew abbr. **Heb.**

Hebrews (NT) abbr. **Heb.**

Hebridean *not* -ian

Hecat/e the Greek goddess of dark places, **-aean**

hecatomb a great public sacrifice, originally of 100 oxen

heckelphone (mus.) a bass oboe

Heckmondwike W. Yorks.

Hecla a mountain, Western Isles; *not* Hek-; cf. **Hekla**

hectare 10,000 sq. m.; abbr. **ha** (no point)

hecto- prefix meaning 100; abbr. **h**; **hectogram** (**hg**) *not* -gramme; **hectolitre** (**hl**) *not* -liter (US); **hectometre** (**hm**) *not* -meter (US)

Hedda Gabler a play by Ibsen, 1890

hedgehog/ adj. **-gy**

hedgerow (one word)

hedgrah *use* **hegira**

hee-haw (noun, verb) bray, *not* he-

heel *see* **hele**

Heep, Uriah a character in Dickens's *David Copperfield, not* Heap

Heer (Ger. n.) army (cap.)

Heft (Ger. n.) number, part; abbr. **H.**

Hegel/, Georg (*not* -e) **Wilhelm Friedrich** (1770–1831) German philosopher, **-ian**

hegemon/y leadership, esp. political; **-ic**

hegira a general exodus or departure; (cap.) denotes the flight of Muhammad from Mecca to Medina, 16 July AD 622, from which the Muslim era is reckoned; *not* hedgrah, heijira (not ital.), in Arab. *hijra*

Heidegger, Martin (1889–1976) German philosopher

Heidelberg a university town, Germany

Heidsieck a champagne

Heifetz, Jascha (1901–87) Russian-born US violinist

heighday *use* **hey-**

heigh-ho an audible sigh, *not* hey-

heijira *use* **heg-**

heil (Ger.) hail!

Heiland, der (Ger.) the Saviour (cap.)

heilig (Ger.) holy, abbr. **hl.**

Heilige Schrift (Ger. f.) Holy Scripture (caps.), abbr. *Hl. S.*

Heimskringla 'the round world', a history of Norse kings by Snorri Sturluson

Heimweh (Ger. n.) homesickness

Heine/, Heinrich (*but* signed **Henri** when in France) (1797–1856) German poet, **-sque**

Heinemann, William publishers

Heinrich Ger. for Henry

Heinz Ger. for Harry

heir apparent a legal heir, whoever may subsequently be born (two words); abbr. **heir app.**

heir presumptive the legal heir if no nearer relative should be born (two words), abbr. **heir pres**.

Heisenberg/, Werner Karl (1901–76) German physicist, discoverer of — **uncertainty principle**

Hejaz 'the boundary', *not* Hi-; *see also* **Saudi Arabia**

hejira *use* **heg-**

Hekla a volcano, Iceland, *not* Hec-; cf. **Hecla**

Hel (Norse myth.) originally, the abode of the dead; later, the abode of the damned, as opposed to Valhalla; later still, the goddess of the dead (in Ger. and Lat. **Hela**)

Hela a Polish holiday resort, in Polish **Hel**

HeLa a strain of human cells (one word, two caps.)

Heldentenor (Ger. m.) 'hero-tenor', with robust operatic voice

hele to set (plants) in the ground; *not* heal, heel

Helensburgh Strathclyde, *not* -borough

Helicon (Gr. myth.) a mountain range in Boeotia, home of the Muses, site of fountains Aganippe and Hippocrene

Heliogabalus *use* **Elag-**

heliport a landing pad for helicopters (one word)

helium symbol **He**

hel/ix a spiral curve like the thread of a screw, pl. **-ices**

hell (not cap.)

hell (Ger.) clear, bright

Helladic of or belonging to the Bronze Age culture of mainland Greece

hell-bent (hyphen)

hellcat (one word)

Helle (Gr. myth.) the sister of Phrixus, fell from the golden ram into the strait afterwards named **Hellespont** (the Dardanelles)

Hellen (Gr. myth.) the son of Deucalion and Pyrrha, progenitor of the Greek people

Hellen/e a (modern or ancient) Greek, pl. **-es**; **-ic** (cap.)

Hellenist one skilled in Greek; one who has adopted Greek ways, esp. a Jew of the Dispersion

Hellenistic denoting the Greek language and culture of the period after Alexander the Great

Hellenize make Greek, *not* -ise

Hellespont *now* **the Dardanelles**

hell/fire, -hole, -hound (one word)

hell-like (hyphen)

hello *not* ha-, hu-

helmet/, -ed (one *t*)

Helmholtz, Hermann Ludwig Ferdinand von (1821–94) German scientist

helmsman one who steers (one word)

Héloïse (1101–64) beloved of Peter Abelard; *not* El-, -sa, *but* Pope's poem is 'Eloisa to Abelard', 1717

helpline (one word)

helpmate *not* -meet (one word)

Helsingør (Dan.) **Elsinore**

Helsinki Finland, in Swed. **Helsingfors**

helter-skelter (hyphen)

Helvellyn a mountain, Cumbria

Helvetia/ (Lat.) Switzerland (used as a linguistically neutral term), **-n** a native of Switzerland

Hely-Hutchinson/ an Irish name, the family name of the Earl of Donoughmore (hyphen); **—, Victor** (1901–47) British composer

hema- prefix, *use* **haema-** (except in US)

Hemel Hempstead Herts. (two words)

hemidemisemiquaver (mus.) a sixty-fourth note; *not* semidemi-

Hemingway, Ernest (**Miller**) (1899–1961) US novelist and journalist

hemistich (prosody) half a line, *not* -itch

hemo- prefix, *use* **haemo-** (except in US)

hemstitch (one word)

hence/forth, -forward (one word)

hendiadys the expression of one idea by two words connected with *and*, instead of one modifying the other, e.g. 'nice and warm' for 'nicely warm'

henge a prehistoric monument consisting of a circle of massive stone or wood uprights

henna/ an oriental shrub, its leaves used for dyeing hair; **-ed**

henpeck/, -ed (one word)

Henri Fr. for Henry

Henry abbr. **Hy**

Henry, O. pseud. of **William Sydney Porter** (1862–1910) US short-story writer

henr/y the SI unit of inductance, pl. **-ies**; abbr. **H**

Henschel, Sir George (1850–1934), German-born English musician

Henslow, John Stevens (1796–1861) English botanist and geologist

Henslowe, Philip (d. *c.*1616) English theatrical manager

heortology the study of (Church) festivals

Hephaestus (myth.) *not* -aistos, except in Greek contexts

Hepplewhite/ an 18th-c. style of furniture, from **George —** (d. 1786); *not* Heppel-

Heptateuch the first seven books of the OT

her. heraldry

her. heres (heir)

Herakles *use* **Hercules**

heraldry abbr. **her.**

Heralds' College the College of Arms, abbr. **HC** (apos.)

Hérault a dép. of France

Herausgeber (Ger. m.) editor (of a text)

herbaceous *not* -ious

herbari/um a collection of dried plants, a book, room, or building for these; pl. **-a** (not ital.)

Herbart, Johann Friedrich (1776–1841) German philosopher and educationist

Hercegovina/ a region in the former Yugoslavia; **Bosnia- —** (hyphen); *not* Herz-

Herculaneum a Roman town overwhelmed by Vesuvius, AD 79; *not* -ium

Herculean strong, difficult

Hercules *not* -akles, except in Greek contexts

Hercynian (geol.) of a late Palaeozoic mountain-forming time in the E. hemisphere

herd book (two words)

here/about(s), -after, -by, (one word)

Hereford: the signature of the Bishop of Hereford (colon)

Hereford and Worcester a former county of England (1974–98)

here, here! *use* **hear, hear!**

herein/, -after, -before (one word)

here/of, -on, -out (one word)

here/s (Lat.) heir, pl. *-des*; abbr. *her.*

here/to, -tofore, -under, -unto, -upon (one word) formal and antiquated terms meaning 'to this matter', 'before this time', 'below', 'to this', and 'after (*or* 'in consequence of') this'; *prefer* the more familiar modern words

herewith (one word)

Hergesheimer, Joseph (1880–1954) US novelist

Heriot-Watt University Edinburgh

heritor (Sc. law) a person who inherits

heritrix an heiress; *not* -tress, here-

Her Majesty('s) (caps.) abbr. **HM**

hermeneutic/ concerning interpretation, esp. of Scripture or literary texts; **-s** the science of interpretation (treated as sing.)

hermetic *not* -ical

hernia/ a rupture, pl. **-s**

hero/ (a *not* an) pl. **-es; -ic**

Herodotus (*c.*484–*c.*420 BC) Greek historian; abbr. **Hdt., Herod.**

heroi-comic combining the heroic with the comic, in Fr. *héroï-comique*; *not* heroic-comic, -al

heroin a drug, *not* -ine

heroine a heroic woman, chief female character in story etc.

heroize make a hero of, *not* -ise

hero-worship/, -ped, -per, -ping (one *p* in US)

herpes a skin disease; *herpes zoster* shingles

herpetolog/y the study of reptiles, **-ist**; *not* er-

Herr/ (Ger. m.) Mr, Sir; pl. **-en**

Herr, der (Ger.) the Lord (cap.)

herr (Norw., Swed.) Mr, abbr. **hr.**

herre (Dan.) Mr, abbr. **hr.**

Herrenvolk (Ger. n.) master race, (in Nazi ideology) the German people

Herrgott (Ger.) Lord God

herringbone a stitch or pattern (one word)

Herrnhuter a member of a Christian Moravian sect (not ital., not -ü- even in Ger.)

Her Royal Highness (caps.) abbr. **HRH**

hers (no apos.)

Herschel,/ Caroline Lucretia (1750–1848) German-born English astronomer; **— Sir John Frederick William** (1792–1871) English astronomer, son of **— Sir William**, b. **Friedrich Wilhelm** (1738–1822) German-born English astronomer

Herschell, Baron

Herstmonceux E. Sussex, former site of the Royal Observatory; *not* Hurst-

hersute *use* **hir-**

Hertfordshire abbr. **Herts.**

Herts. Hertfordshire

Hertz/, Heinrich Rudolf (1857–94) German physicist, discoverer of **-ian waves**, used in radiocommunication

hertz an SI unit of frequency, pl. same; abbr. **Hz**

Hertzog, James Barry Munnik (1866–1942) S. African statesman, Prime Minister 1924–39; *not* Herzog

Herz (Ger. n.) heart (cap.)

Herzegovina *use* **Herce-**

Herzog/ (Ger. m.) duke, pl. *Herzöge*; *-in* (f.) duchess, pl. *-innen*; *-tum* (n.) duchy, *not* -thum (caps.)

Herzog, Werner (b. 1942) German film director, b. **Werner Stipetic**

Hesperian (poet.) western, (Gr. myth.) of or concerning the Hesperides

Hesperis a genus of plants

Hesperus the evening star, Venus

Hesse a German state, in Ger. **Hessen**; **Hessian** an inhabitant of Hesse, in Ger. **Hess/e**, f. **-in**

Hesse, Herman (1877–1962) German-born Swiss writer

hessian a strong coarse sacking

het (Du. n.) the; abbr. **'t**, as van 't Hoff

hetaer/a a courtesan or mistress of ancient Greece, pl. **-ae**; **-ism**; *not* -tair-, -tar-

heterogeneous dissimilar, *not* -nous

heteroousian (theol.) (a person) believing the Father and Son to be of unlike substance, *not* heterou-; cf. **homoiousian**; **homoousian**

het/man a Polish or Cossack military commander, pl. **-men**

Hetton-le-Hole Tyne & Wear (hyphens)

heu (Lat.) alas!

heureka *use* **eu-**

heuristic/ allowing or assisting to discover (an educational method), **-s** the science of heuristic procedure (treated as sing.); *see also* **eureka**

HEW US Department of Health, Education, and Welfare

hex (verb) practise witchcraft, bewitch; (noun) a magic spell, a witch

hex- Gr. prefix for six, in Lat. **sex-**

Hexateuch the first six books of the OT

hey *see* **hay**

heyday the flush or full bloom of youth, prosperity, etc. (one word); *not* heigh-

heyduck a Hungarian of an ennobled military class; in Hung. **hajdú**, pl. **hajdúk**

Heyerdahl, Thor (b. 1914) Norwegian ethnologist (*Kon-Tiki* expedition, 1947)

hey-ho *use* **heigh-**

hey presto a conjuror's exclamation (two words)

HF (pencils) hard firm, high frequency, Home Fleet, Home Forces

Hf hafnium (no point)

hf. half

h.f. high frequency

HFRA Honorary Fellow of the Royal Academy

HG His, *or* Her, Grace; High German, Home Guard, Horse Guards

Hg *hydrargyrum* (mercury) (no point)

hg hectogram, -s (no point)

HGV (Brit.) heavy goods vehicle

HH His, *or* Her, Highness; His Holiness (the Pope); (pencils) double-hard, *also* **2H**

hh. hands (measure of horse's height)

hhd. hogshead, -s

HHH (pencils) treble hard, *also* **3H**

HI Hawaii (official and postal abbr.), Hawaiian Islands, *hic iacet* (here lies)

hiatus/ pl. **-es** (not ital.)

Hiawatha the Native American hero of Longfellow's poem

hibernate (of some animals) spend the winter in a dormant state; *not* hy-

hic (Lat.) this, here

hiccup/ *not* -cough, -kup; **-ed, -ing** (one *p*)

hic et ubique (Lat.) here and everywhere

Hichens, Robert Smythe (1864–1950) English novelist

hic iacet/ (*or* *jacet*) (Lat.) here lies; — — *sepult/us*, f. — — -a here lies buried; abbr. **HIS, HJS**

hidalgo/ a Spanish gentleman by birth, pl. **-s**

hide-and-seek a game (hyphens)

hideaway (noun)

hidebound narrow-minded (one word)

hieing *not* hy-

hier (Ger.) here, *hier spricht man deutsch* German spoken here

hieratic priestly; of the ancient Egyptian writing used by priests (cf. **demotic**); of Egyptian or Greek traditional styles of art

hieroglyph/ a stylized figure representing a word; **-ic(s), -ist, -ize**, *not* -ise

hierogram a sacred inscription or symbol, *not* -graph

hierology sacred literature or lore

hierophant an interpreter of sacred mysteries or esoteric principles

hifalutin *use* **high-**

hi-fi high fidelity (no points), pl. **hi-fis**

higgledy-piggledy haphazard, in confusion

highball (one word)

highboy (US) a type of tallboy; cf. **lowboy**

highbrow (one word)

high chair (two words)

High Church abbr. **HC**; **High Churchman** (caps., two words)

high-class (adj., hyphen)

High Commission an embassy from one Commonwealth country to another

high dudgeon *see* **dudgeon**

highfalutin bombast(ic); *not* -en, -n', -ng, hifa-

high fidelity reproducing sound with little distortion; colloq. **hi-fi/** pl. **-s**

high/-flown, -flyer, -flying (hyphens)

high frequency (hyphen when attrib.)

high hat a top hat, (mus.) a pair of foot-operated cymbals (*also* **high-hat**)

highjacker *use* **hi-**

high jump (two words)

Highland a region of Scotland

highlight/, -er (one word)

high-minded (hyphen)

high pressure (hyphen when attrib.); abbr. **HP**, **h.p.**

high priest abbr. **HP** (two words)

high-rise (a building) having many storeys (hyphen)

high/-risk (adj., hyphen), — **road** (two words)

high school (Eng.) a grammar school, (US, Sc.) a secondary school

high seas, the outside territorial waters (two words)

high/ table, — tea, — tech (hyphen when attrib.), — **tide, — treason** (two words)

high water mark (three words) abbr. **HWM**

highway/, -man (one word)

HIH His, or Her, Imperial Highness

hijack/ seize control of aircraft etc., steal goods in transit; **-er, -ing**

Hijaz use **Hej-**

hijira/, -h use **heg-**

Hil. Hilary

Hilary a session of the High Court of Justice, the university term beginning in January, esp. at Oxford and Dublin universities; from St Hilary of Poitiers (d. c.367), festival 13 Jan.

hill cap. with name, as Boars Hill, Box Hill, Bunker Hill

Hillary, Sir Edmund (Percival) (b. 1919) NZ explorer and mountaineer, climbed Everest 1953

hillbilly (one word)

hill fort (two words)

Hillingdon W. London

Hillington Norfolk, Strathclyde

hillside (one word)

hill station (two words)

hill/top, -walker, -walking (one word)

HIM His, or Her, Imperial Majesty

Himachal Pradesh an Indian state

Himalaya/ or **the -s** India and Tibet; **-n**

Hinayana Skt. for **Theravada**

hinc/ (Lat.) hence, — **illae lacrimae** hence those tears

Hinckley Leics., not Hink-

Hind. Hindu, -stan, -stani

Hindi not -dee (not ital.)

hind leg (two words)

hindmost (one word)

Hindoo use **Hindu**

hindquarters (one word)

hindrance not -erance

hindsight (one word)

Hindu/ not -doo, abbr. **Hind.** (not ital.); **-ism, -ize**

Hindu Kush mountains, Afghanistan

Hindustani abbr. **Hind.**, not Indo-

hing/e, -ed, -ing

Hinkley Point Som., the site of a nuclear power station

Hinshelwood, Sir Cyril Norman (1897–1967) British chemist

hinterland the (often deserted or uncharted) areas beyond a coastal district or a river's banks, a remote or fringe area (one word)

hip/ bath, — bone, — flask, — joint (two words)

hip-length (hyphen)

hippie use **-y** in all senses

hippo/ hippopotamus, pl. **-s**

hip pocket (two words)

Hippocrat/es (fl. 400 BC) Greek 'Father of Medicine', **-ic**

Hippocrene a fountain on Mt. Helicon sacred to the Muses, a term for poetic or literary inspiration

hippogriff a fabulous monster, not -gryph (not ital.)

hippopotamus/ pl. **-es**

hipp/y a person of unconventional appearance, associated with a rejection of conventional values; also a person with broad hips; pl. **-ies**

hiragana the cursive form of Japanese syllabic writing or kana; cf. **katakana**

hirdy-girdy (Sc.) in disorder; cf. **hurdy-gurdy**

hireable obtainable for hire, not -rable

hire car (two words)

hire purchase (two words) abbr. **HP, h.p.**

hirly-birly use **hurly-burly**

Hiroshima Japan

Hirschhorn Museum Washington, DC

hirsute hairy, not her-

HIS hic iacet sepult/us, -a (here lies buried)

His/ Eminence abbr. **HE, — Excellency** abbr. **HE, — Majesty('s)** abbr. **HM** (caps., not ital.)

Hispanic of or relating to Iberia or Spain and other Spanish-speaking countries; a Spanish-speaking person, esp. one of Latin-American descent, living in the USA

Hispanicize render Spanish, not -ise

Hispanist an expert in or student of the language, literature, and civilization of Spain; not -icist

His Royal Highness (caps.) abbr. HRH

hist. histor/ian, -ic, -ical

Hitchens, Sydney Ivon (1893–1979) English painter

hitch-hik/e, -er, -ing (hyphen, one word in US)

Hitchin Herts., not -en

hi-tech use **high tech** (hyphen when attrib.)

HIV human immunodeficiency virus, a retrovirus that causes Aids; 'HIV virus' is tautologous

HJ *hic jacet* (here lies)

HJS *hic jacet sepult/us, -a* (here lies buried)

HK Hong Kong; House of Keys, Isle of Man

HL House of Lords

hl hectolitre(s) (no point)

hl. (Ger.) *heilig* (holy)

Hl. S. (Ger.) *Heilige Schrift* (Holy Scripture)

HM Head Master, Head Mistress; Her, *or* His, Majesty('s); Home Mission

hm hectometre(s) (no point)

h.m. *hoc mense* (in this month), *huius mensis* (this month's)

HMC Headmasters' Conference; Her, *or* His, Majesty's Customs; Royal Commission on Historical Manuscripts

HMG Her, *or* His, Majesty's Government

HMI Her, *or* His, Majesty's Inspector

HMP *hoc monumentum posuit* (erected this monument)

HMS Her, *or* His, Majesty's Service, *or* Ship

HMSO Her, *or* His, Majesty's Stationery Office; *not* the —

HMV His Master's Voice

HNC, HND Higher National Certificate, Higher National Diploma

HO Home Office, (Ger.) *Handelsorganisation* (state shop in GDR, taken over in 1990)

Ho holmium (no point)

ho. house

Hoangho *use* **Hwang-Ho**

hoard a store of money or possessions, to save these; cf. **horde**

hoar frost (two words, one word in US)

hoarhound *use* **hore-**

hoarstone (Brit.) an ancient boundary stone, *not* hore-

Hobbema, Meindert (1638–1709) Dutch painter

Hobbes,/ John Oliver pseud. of **Pearle Mary Teresa Craigie** (1867–1906) English writer, — **Thomas** (1588–1679) English philosopher

hobbledehoy a raw youth, *not* the many variants

hobby horse (two words)

hobnob (one word)

hobo/ (US) a migrant worker or tramp, pl. **-es**

Hoboken NJ

hoboy (mus.) *use* **oboe**

Hobson-Jobson/ism (hyphen) the assimilation of adopted foreign words to the sound-pattern of the adopting language, e.g. *Sir Roger Dowler* for the 18th-c. Indian prince Siraj-ud-Dawlah

Hobson's choice a choice between taking the thing offered or nothing, *not* between two equally unacceptable or unpleasant alternatives

hoc/ age (Lat.) attend!; — **anno** in this year, abbr. **h.a.**

Hoccleve, Thomas (?1370–?1450) English poet, *not* O-

hoc/ genus omne all of this kind, — **habet** he has a hit (of gladiators)

hochepot (Fr. cook. m.) hotchpotch, stew, ragout

Ho Chi Minh/ adopted Chinese name of **Nguyen That Thanh** (1890–1969) Vietnamese politician, President of Vietnam 1945–54 and North Vietnam 1954–69; ——— **City** Vietnam, *formerly* Saigon

hock/ a joint of a quadruped's hind leg; a Rhineland white wine (properly from Hochheim); (esp. US) (verb) pawn, pledge, **in** — in pawn or in debt

hockey/ in Britain this general term suggests **field** —, in the USA it suggests **ice** —

Hocking,/ Joseph (1855–1937) and his brother — **Silas Kitto** (1850–1935) British novelists

hoc/ loco (Lat.) in this place; — **mense** in this month, abbr. **h.m.**; — **monumentum posuit** erected this monument, abbr. **HMP**; — **sensu** in this sense, abbr. **h.s.**; — **tempore** at this time, abbr. **h.t.**; — **titulo** in, or under, this title, abbr. **h.t.**

hocus/ to hoax, drug; **-sed, -sing**

hocus-pocus deception, trickery (hyphen)

Hodder & Stoughton publishers

hodgepodge *use* **hotchpotch** (except in US)

Hodgkin's disease a malignant disease of lymphatic tissues, named after **Thomas Hodgkin** (1798–1866) English physician

hodmandod a snail

hodograph (math.) a curve

hodometer *use* **od-**

Hoe Plymouth

Hoe,/ Robert (1784–1833), — **Richard March** (1812–86) his son, — **Robert** (1839–1909) his grandson, all US printers

hoeing *not* hoing

Hofer, Andreas (1767–1810) Tyrolese patriot

Hoff, Jacobus Hendricus van 't (1852–1911) Dutch physicist and chemist

Hoffmann,/ August Heinrich (1798–1874) German writer ('Hoffmann von Fallersleben'; *Deutschland über Alles*, 1841); — **Daniel** (1576–1601) German theologian; — **Ernst Theodor Amadeus** (originally **Wilhelm**) (1776–1822) German writer and composer, source of Offenbach's *Tales of Hoffmann*; — **Friedrich** (1660–1742) German chemist; *see also* **Hofmann**

Hoffnung (Ger. f.) hope (cap.)

Hoffnung, Gerard (1925–59) English humorous artist and musician

Hofmann,/ August Wilhelm von (1818–92) German chemist, — **Johann Christian Conrad von** (1810–77) German theologian, — **Josef Casimir** (1876–1957) Polish pianist and composer; *see also* **Hoffmann**

Hofmannsthal, Hugo von (1874–1929) Austrian poet, librettist of some operas by Richard Strauss

hog a castrated pig

hogan a Navajo Indian hut of logs etc.

hoggin a gravel mixture

Hogmanay (Sc.) the last day of the year

hogshead/ a large cask; pl. **-s**, abbr. **hhd.**

Hogue, La dép. Manche, France

Hohenzollern, House of the Prussian Imperial family

Ho Ho Kus NJ (three words)

hoiden *use* **hoy-**

hoing *use* **hoe-**

hoi polloi (Gr.) the masses; *not* oi, *not* the – –, as *hoi* = the (not ital.)

hokey (US sl.) sentimental, melodramatic, artificial; *not* -ky

hokey-cokey a communal dance performed in a circle with synchronized shaking of the limbs in turn

hokey-pokey (hist.) ice cream, *not* hoky-poky (hyphen)

hokku *use* **haiku**

hokum stage business used for cheap effect

Holbein, Hans 'the Elder' (1465–1524), 'the Younger' (1497–1543) both German painters

Hölderlin, Johann Christian Friedrich (1770–1843) German poet

hold-up (noun) a delay, a robbery (hyphen)

holey having holes

Holi a Hindu religious festival

Holiday, Billie born **Eleanora Fagan** (1915–59) US jazz singer

holidaymaker (one word)

holily in holy manner

Holinshed, Raphael (d. *c*.1580) English chronicler; *not* -ings-, -head

Holland/ *use* **the Netherlands**; **North —, South —** (provinces), **Parts of —** (former division of Lincs.)

holland a linen (not cap.)

hollandais/ (Fr.) f. **-e** Dutch (not cap.)

hollandaise a creamy sauce (not ital.)

Hollands Dutch gin (cap.)

hollow (bind.) a paper reinforcement of the back, and sometimes the spine, of a book

hollowware hollow articles of metal, china, etc. such as pots, kettles, jugs, etc. (one word)

hollyhock a plant

Hollywood Los Angeles, Calif.

Holman-Hunt, William (1827–1910) English painter (hyphen)

Holmes, Oliver Wendell (1809–94) US professor, author, and essayist; and his son (1841–1935) US jurist, Associate Justice of the US Supreme Court 1902–32

holmium symbol **Ho**

Holm Patrick, Baron

holocaust a whole burnt offering, wholesale sacrifice or destruction (cap. with hist. reference to the mass murder of the Jews by the Nazis, 1939–45)

Holocene (of or relating to) the most recent epoch of the Quaternary period; also called **Recent**

Holofernes an Assyrian general (-ph- in NEB); a pedantic and pretentious teacher in Rabelais's *Gargantua*, 1534, and Shakespeare's *Love's Labour's Lost*, 1598

hologram (a photograph of) a three-dimensional image formed by the interference of light beams from a coherent light source

holograph (a document) wholly written by hand by the person named as the author

Holstein (US) = **Friesian**

holus-bolus all at once (hyphen)

Holy Communion (caps.), abbr. **HC**

Holy Cross Day (three words, caps.), Holy Rood Day, feast of the Exaltation of the Cross, 14 Sept.

Holy/ Family, — Ghost, — Land (two words, caps.)

Holyoake,/ George Jacob (1817–1906) English writer and agitator, — **Rt. Hon. Sir Keith Jacka** (1904–83) Prime Minister of New Zealand 1960–72

holy of holies the inner chamber of the Jewish tabernacle (not caps.)

Holy Roman Empire (caps.) abbr. **HRE**

Holy Rood Day *see* **Holy Cross Day**

Holyroodhouse, Palace of Edinburgh

Holy Saturday the day before Easter Sunday (caps.)

Holy Spirit as Deity (caps.)

holystone (naut.) (scour decks with) soft sandstone (one word)

Holy Thursday Ascension Day in English Church; but Thursday in Holy Week, or Maundy Thursday, in Roman Church

Holy Week the week before Easter (two words, caps.)

Holywood Co. Down

Hom. Homer

homage public acknowledgement of allegiance, in Fr. *hommage* (m.)

homard (Fr. m.) lobster

hombre (Sp. and US sl.) man (not ital.)

Homburg a soft felt hat

Home/ a surname, pron. 'Hume'; **— of the Hirsel, Baron**

homebody (one word)

home/ boy, -girl someone from the same hometown, community, or neighbourhood

home/-brew, -brewed, -brewing (hyphen, two words in US)

homecoming (one word)

Home Counties, the the counties closest to London, i.e. Essex, Herts., Kent, Surrey; sometimes includes Berks., Bucks., Sussex; abbr. **HC**

home/-grown (hyphen, one word in US)

Home Guard (two words, caps.) (a member of) the British citizen army, 1940–57; abbr. **HG** (no points); *see also* **LDV**

home/land, -like (one word)

homely suggesting home, cosy; (US) unattractively plain, ugly

home-made (hyphen, one word in US)

home/maker (one word), **-making** (hyphen, one word in US)

Home Office the British government department

home of lost causes Oxford University (from Arnold's *Essays in Criticism*) (not cap.)

homeopath/, -y use **homoeo-** (except in US)

Homer (*c*.9th c. BC) Greek poet, abbr. **Hom.**

homeroom (US) (one word)

Home Rule (two words, caps.), abbr. **HR**

homesick/, -ness (one word)

homespun (one word)

home town (two words, one word in US)

homework (one word)

homey homelike

homing *not* -eing

homin/id a member of the family *Hominidae*, **-oid** a humanlike animal

Hommage/ d'auteur, — de l'auteur (Fr.) with the author's compliments; **— *d'éditeur*, — *de l'éditeur*** with the publisher's compliments, *not* editor's (*but see* **éditeur**)

homme/ d'affaires (Fr.) businessman, *not des*; **— *de bien*** a respectable man; **— *de cour*** a courtier; **— *de lettres*** author; **— *de paille*** man of straw; **— *d'épée*** a military man; **— *de robe*** lawyer; **— *d'esprit*** man of wit; **— *d'État*** statesman; **— *de tête*** man of resource; **— *du monde*** man of fashion

Homo (zool.) genus of humans

hom/o (Lat.) human being, pl. **-ines**

homoeopath/y the treatment of diseases by minute doses of drugs that excite similar symptoms; **-ic, -ist**; *not* homeo- (US)

homogene/ous of the same kind, consistent, uniform; (math.) containing terms all of the same degree; **-ity**

homogenize to make (milk) homogeneous, *not* -ise

homogen/ous, -etic (biol.) having a common descent or origin

homogeny (biol.) similarity due to common descent

homograph a word spelt like another but of different meaning or origin

homoiothermic warm-blooded

homoiousian (theol.) (a person) believing the Father and Son to be of like substance (not ital.); cf. **heteroousian**; **homoousian**

homolog/ue a homologous thing, *not* -log (US); **-ize** be or make homologous, *not* -ise

homonym a homograph or homophone; *not* -me

homoousian (theol.) (a person) believing the Father and Son to be of the same substance, *not* homou- (not ital.); cf. **heteroousian**; **homoiousian**

homophone a word having the same sound as another but of different meaning or origin (e.g. *pair, pear*)

Homo sapiens (zool.) the species modern humans

homosexual (a person of either sex) feeling (or involving) sexual attraction only to persons of the same sex

Homs Syria

homy use **homey**

Hon. Honorary, Honourable (son or daughter of a peer, MP)

Honble. Honourable (former Indian title)

honch/o (US sl.) the person in charge, an admirable man; pl. **-os**; in Jap. **han'chō**

Hondura/s Cent. America, **-n**

Honegger, Arthur (1892–1955) French-born Swiss composer

honey/ badger, — bee, — buzzard (two words)

honey/comb, -dew (one word)

honeyed sweet, *not* -ied

honey/moon, -suckle (one word)

Hong Kong S. China (no hyphen), abbr. **HK**

HongKongBank Hongkong and Shanghai Banking Corporation (one word)

Honi soit qui mal y pense shamed be he who thinks evil of it (motto of the Order of the Garter)

honnête homme (Fr. m.) a decent, cultivated man

honor/, -able use **honour-** (except in US)

Honorable (US) abbr. title for a congressman or judge, abbr. **Hon.**

honorand one to be honoured

honorarium/ a voluntary fee for professional services, pl. **-s** (not ital.)

honorary/ (of office etc.) bestowed as an honour, unpaid; **— secretary** abbr. **Hon. Sec.**

honorific (utterance) expressing honour or respect

honoris/ causa or **— gratia** (Lat.) for the sake of honour

Honourable title for the son or daughter of a peer (used with name) or for an MP (used with constituency, e.g. 'the Hon. Member for —'), abbr. **Hon.**; for Indian title abbr. **Honble.**; *see also* **Honorable**

Hons. Honours

Hon. Sec. honorary secretary

hoodwink (one word)

hoof/ usual pl. **-s**, *not* -ves

Hooghly India, *not* Hugli

Hook, Theodore Edward (1788–1841) English humorist; *see also* **Hooke**

hookah an oriental pipe, *not* the many variants

hook and eye (no hyphens)

Hooke/, Robert (1635–1703) English physicist, **—'s law**; *see also* **Hook**

Hooker,/ Sir William Jackson (1785–1865) and **— Sir Joseph Dalton** (1817–1911) his son, English botanists

hooping cough *use* wh-

hoopoe S. European bird

hoor/ah, -ay *use* hurr/ah, -ay

Hooray/ Henry a rich but ineffectual young man, esp. one who is fashionable, extroverted, and conventional; f. **— Henrietta**

Hoover/ (propr.) a vacuum cleaner (cap.); (not cap.) to vacuum-clean, **-ed, -ing**

hooves *use* **hoofs**

hophead (US sl.) a drug addict, (Austral. and NZ sl.) a drunkard

Hopi/ (of or relating to) (a member of) a Native American tribe, or the language of this people; pl. **-s**; *not* -ki, -qui

Hopkins/, Gerard Manley (1844–89) English poet; **—, Johns** (*not* John) (1795–1873) US financier; **Johns — University Medical Center** Baltimore, Md. (no apos.)

hop-o'-my-thumb a dwarf (hyphens)

hop-picker (hyphen)

Hoppner, John (1758–1810) English painter

hopscotch a children's game (one word)

hor. horizon, -tal

hor/a (Lat.) hour, pl. **-ae**

Horace (in Lat. **Quintus Horatius Flaccus**) (65–8 BC) Roman poet, abbr. **Hor.**

horae/ canonicae hours for prayer, **— sub-secivae** leisure hours

Horatius Cocles (Rom. hist.) who kept the Sublician Bridge

horde a troop of nomads, a crowd of people; cf. **hoard**

horehound a plant; *not* hoar-

horizon/, -tal abbr. **hor.**

horn,/ English a woodwind instrument, *use* **cor anglais**; **— French** a brass instrument

hornblende a mineral, *not* -d

hornpipe a dance, music for it (one word)

horology abbr. **horol.**

horresco referens (Lat.) I shudder to mention it

hors/ (Fr.) beyond, out of; **— concours** not for competition (*not* de); **— de combat** out of the fight, disabled; *-de-la-loi* outlaw (hyphens); **— de pair** without an equal

hors d'oeuvre an appetizer, pl. **-s**; in Fr. m. *hors d'œuvre*, pl. same

Horse Artillery (caps.) abbr. **HA**

horse/back, -box (one word)

horse brass (two words)

horse chestnut *not* chesnut (two words)

horse/flesh (one word), **-fly** (hyphen)

Horse Guards abbr. **HG** (two words, caps.)

horse/hair, -play (one word)

horsepower a unit of power (746 watts), abbr. **hp**

horse rac/e, -ing (two words), *but* **Horserace** (one word) **Betting Levy Board** and **Horserace Totalisator Board**

horse/radish, -shoe (one word) *but* **horse-shoeing** (hyphen)

Horseshoe Falls Niagara river, Ont.; **Horse Shoe Falls** Guyana

horse/tail, -whip, -woman (one word)

horsey horselike, *not* -sy (US)

horst (geol.) a raised elongated block of land bounded by faults on both sides

'Horst Wessel Song' the song of the German Nazi *Sturm-Abteilung*, after the writer of the words

hort. horticulture

hortus siccus an arranged collection of dried plants

Hos. Hosea

hosanna a shout of praise, 'save, we pray'; *not* -ah (not ital.); **Hosanna Sunday** Palm Sunday

Hosea (OT) abbr. **Hos.**

hospital/ abbr. **hosp.**, **-ize** *not* -ise

hospitaller one of a charitable brotherhood (one l in US)

hostell/er, -ing (one l in US)

hostler a stableman at an inn, *use* **ostler** (except in US); (US) a person who services machines, esp. railway engines

hotbed (one word)

hotchpot (law) the reunion and blending of properties for the purpose of securing equal division (one word); *not* hodgepodge (US)

hotchpotch a confused mixture, a jumble; a dish of many mixed ingredients; *not* hodge-podge (US)

hotdog perform ostentatious stunts, e.g. while skiing or surfing; a person who does this (one word); a frankfurter sandwiched in a soft roll (two words)

hôte (Fr. m.) innkeeper, host; *also* guest

hotel preceded by *a*, not *an*; name is roman, quoted *only* where necessary to avoid ambiguity: 'The Farmhouse'

Hôtel des Invalides Paris, founded 1670 as a hospital for disabled soldiers; contains Napoleon's tomb (caps.)

hôtel/ de ville (Fr. m.) town hall; ***-Dieu, l'*** chief hospital of a town (one cap.); — ***garni***, — ***meublé*** furnished lodgings

hotelier a hotel-keeper (not ital., no accent)

hot/foot, -head, -house (one word)

hot metal (typ.) type made from molten metal

hot/plate, -pot (cook.), **-shot** (one word)

Hottentot *use* **Khoikhoi**

houdah *use* **how-**

Houdan a breed of fowls

Houdin, Jean Eugène Robert (1805–71) French conjuror

Houdini, Harry b. **Erik Weisz** (1874–1926) US escapologist

Houdon, Jean Antoine (1741–1828) French sculptor

Houghton-le-Spring Tyne & Wear (hyphens)

hoummous *see* **hummus**

hour/, -s abbr. **hr., hrs.**, *but* **h** (no point, same in pl.) in scientific and technical work; **-glass** (one word)

houri/ a beautiful young woman, esp. in the Muslim Paradise; pl. **-s**

Housa *use* **Hau-**

house the number of, in a street, has no comma after, as '6 Fleet Street'; abbr. **ho.**

House, the Christ Church (Oxford), the House of Commons, the Stock Exchange

house/ agent, — arrest (two words)

houseboat (one word)

housebote (law) a tenant's right to wood to repair house (one word)

housebreak/er, -ing (one word)

housecarl (hist.) a member of the bodyguard of a Danish or English king or noble, *not* -e

housecoat (one word)

house flag the distinguishing flag of a shipping company (two words)

house/fly, -holder, -keeper, -keeping, -maid (one word)

house martin (two words)

house-mother (hyphen, one word in US)

House of Keys in the Isle of Man, the elected chamber of Tynwald

House of Representatives (US) the lower house of the US Congress and other legislatures (cf. **Senate**), abbr. **HR**

house party (two words)

house physician abbr. **HP** (two words)

house style (typ.) a printer's or publisher's preferred way of presenting text

house surgeon abbr. **HS** (two words)

house-to-house performed at or carried to each house in turn (hyphens)

house/wife, -work (one word)

Housman,/ A(lfred) E(dward) (1859–1936) English scholar and poet; — **Laurence** (1865–1959) his brother, English writer and artist

Houssaye,/ Arsène (1815–96) French novelist and poet; — **Henri** (1848–1911) his son, French historian

Houyhnhnm in Swift's *Gulliver's Travels*, one of a race of horses with noble human characteristics, pron. 'hwinnim'; contrasted with **Yahoo**

hovercraft (not cap.) pl. same

Hövsgöl lake, Mongolia

Howards End a novel by E. M. Forster, 1910 (no apos.)

howdah an elephant-seat; *not* -a, houda, -ar

how-do-you-do *or* **how-d'ye-do** awkward situation (hyphens)

howitzer a short cannon for high-angle firing of shells at low velocities

howsoever *not* howsoe'er (except in poet. contexts)

Hoxha, Enver (1908–85) Prime Minister of Albania 1944–54, First Secretary of the Labour Party in Albania 1954–85

Hoxnian (geol.) (designating or pertaining to) an interglacial state of the Pleistocene in Britain, identified with the Holsteinian of northern Europe

hoyden tomboy, *not* hoi-

Hoyle/, Edmond (1672–1769) English writer on card games; **according to** — correctly, exactly

HP high pressure (*also* **h.p.**), high priest, hire purchase (*also* **h.p.**), house physician, Houses of Parliament

h.p. horsepower (*also* **HP, hp**)

HQ Headquarters

HR Home Rule, (US) House of Representatives

hr. (Norw., Swed.) herr (Mr); (Dan.) herre (Mr); hour, pl. **hrs.** (non-technical use)

Hradec Králové Czech Republic, *not* Königgrätz

Hrdlička, Aleš (1869–1943) Bohemian-born US anthropologist

HRE Holy Roman Empire

H. Rep. (US) House of Representatives Report (space)

H. Res. (US) House of Representatives Resolution (space)

HRH Her, *or* His, Royal Highness

HRIP (Lat.) *hic requiescit in pace* (here rests in peace)

hrsg. (Ger.) *herausgegeben* (edited)

Hrvatska (Croat) **Croatia**

HS *hic sepult/us, -a* (here buried), house surgeon; symbol for sesterce, a Roman coin equivalent to a quarter of a denarius

Hs. (Ger.) *Handschrift* (manuscript)

h.s. (Lat.) *hoc sensu* (in this sense)

HSE *hic sepult/us, -a est* (here lies buried)

HSH His, *or* Her, Serene Highness

HT high tension

ht. height

h.t. *hoc tempore* (at this time), *hoc titulo* (in, *or* under, this title), (elec.) high tension

HTML (comput.) Hypertext Mark-up Language

HTTP (comput.) Hypertext Transport (*or* Transfer) Protocol

ht. wkt. (cricket) hit wicket

HU Harvard University

Huanghe *see* **Hwang-Ho**

huarache a leather-thonged sandal, *not* gua-

Hubble/, Edwin Powell (1889–1953) US astronomer, **— classification, — constant, — Space Telescope**, *but* **—'s law**

hubble-bubble a rudimentary hookah; confused talk (hyphen)

Huberman, Bronisław (1882–1947) Polish violinist

hübnerite a form of manganese tungstate, *not* hue-

hubris/ (Gr. drama) presumptuous pride that invites disaster, *not* hy- (not ital.); **-tic**

huckaback a rough-surfaced linen fabric, *not* hugga-

Hucknall Notts., where Byron is buried

Hudibras a satiric poem by S. Butler, 1663–80

hudibrastic in the style of *Hudibras*, in octosyllabic couplets with comic rhymes, mock-heroic (not cap.)

Hudson Bay N. America, *but* **Hudson's Bay Company**

Hueffer *see* **Ford Madox Ford**

huggaback *use* **huck-**

hugger-mugger secret(ly) (hyphen)

Hughenden Bucks., *not* -don

Hugli *use* **Hooghly**

Hugo, Victor (**Marie**) (1802–85) French poet, novelist, and playwright

Huguenot (hist.) a 16th–17th-c. French Protestant, *not* -onot

huissier (Fr. m.) bailiff, doorkeeper

huîtres (Fr. f. pl.) oysters

huius/ anni (Lat.) of this year, abbr. **h.a.**; — **mensis** of this month, abbr. **h.m.**

hullabaloo uproar, *not* the many variants

Hullah, John Pyke (1812–84) English musician

hullo *use* he-

Hulsean Lectures Cambridge

Humanae vitae (Lat.) of human life, name of an encyclical on contraception, by Pope Paul VI, 1968

Humaniora (Lat.) the humanities, abbr. **Hum.**; *see also* **Lit. Hum.**

humanize *not* -ise

humankind (one word)

Humberside a county of England

humble-bee *use* **bumblebee**

humble pie (to eat), *not* umble (two words)

Humboldt,/ Friedrich Heinrich Alexander, Baron von (1769–1859) German naturalist; **— Karl Wilhelm, Baron von** (1767–1835) his brother, German philologist, statesman, and poet

humdrum commonplace (one word)

Humean of **David Hume** (1711–76) Scottish historian and philosopher, *not* -ian

humer/us the upper-arm bone, pl. **-i** (not ital.)

hummingbird (one word)

hummum a Turkish bath, *use* **hammam**

hummus a purée of chickpeas and sesame oil, *often* **houmous**; *not* hoummos; in Turk. *humus*

humor *use* **-our** (except in US)

humoral (med.) relating to body fluids, esp. (hist.) of the four bodily humours

humoresque a musical caprice, *not* humour-

humor/ist, -ize *not* -ise

humorous/, -ly, -ness

humoursome capricious

humous *see* **humus**

humpback(ed) (one word)

Humperdinck, Engelbert/ (1854–1921) German composer; **— —** adopted name of **Arnold** (**Gerry**) **Dorsey** (b. 1935) British popular singer

Humphrey, Duke of Gloucester (1391–1447) son of Henry IV of England, Protector during minority of Henry VI; *but* **Duke Humfrey's Library** in the Bodleian

Humphrey's Clock, Master by Dickens, 1840

Humphry (not -ey) **Clinker** by Smollett, 1771

Humpty-Dumpty (hyphen)

hum/us the organic constituent of soil, adj. **-ous**

hunchback(ed) (one word)

hundert (Ger.) hundred

hundred symbol **C**

hundred-and-first etc. (hyphens)

hundred-per-cent (adj.) entire

hundredweight (one word), pl. same, abbr. **cwt.**

Hundred Years War between England and France, 1337–1453 (caps., no apos.)

hung *see* **hanged**

Hung. Hungar/y, -ian

Hungary abbr. **Hung.**; in Hung. (Magyar) **Magyarország**; in Fr. **Hongrie**, in Ger. **Ungarn**

Hunstanton Norfolk

Hunter's Quay Strathclyde (apos.)

Huntingdon Cambs.

Huntington/ Cheshire, Hereford, E. Lothian, Staffs., N. Yorks., W. Virginia; — **Library** San Marino, Calif.

Huntley Glos., Staffs.

Huntly/ Grampian; **Marquess of —**; *not* -ey

Hunyadi János a Hungarian mineral water

Hunyadi, János (1387–1456) Hungarian general of Romanian descent, *not* -ady; in Hung. the order is **Hunyadi János**

hurds *use* **ha-**

hurdy-gurdy (mus.) *not* hi-, gi-

hurly-burly a commotion; *not* hi-, bi-

hurrah *or* **hurray** *not* hoo-, except in **Hooray Henry**

hurry-curry *use* **hara-kiri**

hurry-scurry pell-mell, *not* -sk-

Hurstmonceux E. Sussex, *use* **Herst-**

Hurstpierpoint W. Sussex (one word)

Husák, Gustáv (1913–91) Czechoslovak politician, leader of the Communist Party of Czechoslovakia 1969–87, President 1975–89

husband abbr. **h.**

Husbands Bosworth Leics. (no apos.)

Huss/, **John** (1369–1455) Bohemian religious and nationalist reformer, in Czech **Jan Hus**, in Ger. **Johann Hus**; **-ite**

hussar a soldier of a light cavalry regiment; a Hungarian light horseman of the 15th c., in Magyar *huszár*

hussy impudent or immoral woman, *not* -zzy

Huxley,/ **Aldous** (**Leonard**) (1894–1963) English novelist; — **Sir Julian Sorell** (1887–1975) his brother, biologist and scientific administrator; — **Thomas Henry** (1825–95) their grandfather, biologist and essayist

Huygens, Christiaan (1629–95) Dutch mathematician and astronomer, *not* -ghens

Huysmans, Joris Karl (1848–1907) French novelist

huzzy *use* **-ssy**

h.w. (cricket) hit wicket

h/w herewith

Hwang-Ho the Yellow River, China, *not* Hoangho; in Pinyin **Huanghe**; either

'Hwang-Ho' *or* 'the River Hwang', *but not* 'the Hwang-Ho River'

HWM high water mark

Hy Henry (man's name) (no point)

Hyacinthe, Père born **Charles Jean Marie Loyson** (1827–1912), French priest

Hyades a group of stars in Taurus

hyaena *use* **hye-**

hybernate *use* **hi-**

hybrid (bot.) symbol ×

hybridize etc., *not* -ise

hybris *use* **hu-**

hyd. hydrostatics

Hyderabad Deccan, India; Sind, Pakistan; *not* Haidar-, Hydar-

hydrangea a shrub, *not* -ia

hydro/ (colloq.) hydropathic establishment, hydroelectric plant (no point); pl. **-s**

hydro/**carbon, -dynamics, -electric** (one word)

hydrogen symbol **H**

hydro/**lysis** decomposition by water, **-lyse** *not* -lyze (US)

hydrophobia rabies, aversion to water

hydroplane a kind of motor boat (one word)

hydrostatics abbr. **hyd.**

hydrotherapy (one word)

hyena *not* hyae-

Hyères dép. Var, France

Hy/**gieia** (Gr.) goddess of health, **-geia** *or* **-gīa** the later Rom. spelling; *not* -gea, -giea

hygien/**e** the science of health, **-ic**

hying *use* **hie-**

Hyksos rulers of Egypt, 17th–16th cc. BC

Hylton-Foster, Sir Harry (1905–65) Speaker of the House of Commons 1959–65

Hymen (Gr. and Rom. myth.) the god of marriage, **hymeneal**

hymen/ (anat.) virginal membrane (not ital.), **-al**

hymn book (two words, one word in US)

hyp. hypothesis, hypothetical

hypaesthesia diminished capacity for sensation, *not* hypes- (US)

hypaethral open to the sky, roofless; *not* hype- (US)

hypallage (rhet.) the transposition of the natural relations of two elements in a proposition (e.g. 'Theo shook his angry curls')

hyperaem/**ia** an excess of blood, **-ic**; *not* -rhaemia, -remia (US)

hyperaesthesia excessive physical sensibility, *not* hyperes- (US)

hyperbaton (rhet.) the separation or rearrangement of the normal order of words, esp. for the sake of emphasis (e.g. 'This I must see')

hyperbol/a a curve, **-ic**

hyperbol/e exaggeration, **-ical**

hypercritical excessively critical

hypermarket (Brit.) a very large supermarket, usually outside a town (one word)

hyphen (typ.) sign (-) used to join words, indicate word breaks at the end of a line, or indicate a missing implied element (e.g. hard- and paperback)

hypnotize *not* -ise

hypochondria a morbid anxiety about health, *not* -condria

hypocri/sy, -te, -tical

hypota/xis (gram.) the explicit subordination of one clause to another, **-ctic**; cf. **parataxis**

hypotenuse (geom.) *not* hypoth-

hypothecate to mortgage

hypothermia abnormally low body temperature

hypothes/is a provisional explanation, pl. **-es**; abbr. **hyp.**

hypothesize form a hypothesis; *not* -ise, -tize

hysterectomy (med.) the removal of the womb

hysteresis (phys.) a lagging of variation in effect behind variation in cause

hysteron proteron (rhet.) a figure of speech in which what should come last is put first (e.g. 'I die! I faint! I fail!') (not ital.)

hysterotomy (med.) cutting into the womb

Hz hertz, an SI unit of frequency (no point)

I iodine, (roman numeral) one (no point), the ninth in a series, Elizabethan spelling of *ay* (meaning 'yes'), (Dan.) familiar or solemn nom. pl. of 'you'

I. Island, -s; Isle, -s; *imperator* (emperor), *imperatrix* (empress)

i (med. prescriptions) one, (math.) square root of minus one

i. *id* (that)

I or *i* (ital.) symbol for electric current

I, the (metaphysics) the ego

ı (typ.) undotted *i*, a sort used in Turk.

ι (Gr.) iota (no dot)

IA Indian Army, infected area, Iowa (postal abbr.)

Ia. Iowa (off. abbr.)

IAA indoleacetic acid

IAAF International Amateur Athletic Federation

IAEA International Atomic Energy Agency

IAHM Incorporated Association of Headmasters; *see also* **AHMI**

IAM Institute of Advanced Motorists

iamb/us a foot of two syllables (˘ -), *not* iamb (US); pl. **-uses** *not* -bi (except in context of classical Greek poetry); adj. **-ic**; **-ics** iambic verse

Iaşi Romania, in Ger. **Jassy**

IATA International Air Transport Association

IBA Independent Broadcasting Authority

Ibáñez, Vicente Blasco (1867–1928) Spanish novelist

Ibárruri Gómez, Dolores (1895–1989) Spanish communist politician and Republican leader, known as **La Pasionaria**

I-beam a girder with an I-shaped section (use a serif typeface to approximate actual shape)

Iberian pertaining to the Spanish peninsula (including Portugal)

ibex/ a wild mountain-goat, pl. **-es**

ibidem (Lat.) in the same place, abbr. **ibid.** (*preferred*), **ib.** (not ital., not cap. except to begin sentence or note); *see also* **idem**

ibis/ a wading bird, pl. **-es**

Ibiza Balearic Islands, *not* Iv-; in Catalan **Eivissa**

Iblis *use* **E-**

IBM International Business Machines

ibn *also* **bin** (Arab.) son of (used in personal names), abbr. **b.**

ibn Abdul Aziz,/ Saud (1902–69) son of Abdul Aziz ibn Saud, King of Saudi Arabia 1953–64, succeeded by his three brothers: — — — **Feisal** (1904–75) King of Saudi Arabia 1964–75; — — — **Khalid** (1913–82) King of Saudi Arabia 1975–

82; — — — **Fahd** (b. 1923) King of Saudi Arabia 1982–

ibn Saud, Abdul Aziz (1880–1953) King of Saudi Arabia 1932–53

Ibo (of or relating to) (a member of) a people of SE Nigeria, or their Kwa language; *not* Ig-

IBRD International Bank for Reconstruction and Development (UN), also known as the **World Bank**

Ibsen, Henrik (1828–1906) Norwegian writer and playwright

IC (comput.) integrated circuit

i/c in charge, in command

ICA Institute of Contemporary Arts

ICAN International Commission for Air Navigation

ICAO International Civil Aviation Organization (UN)

Icarian of Icarus, *not* -ean

ICBM intercontinental ballistic missile

ICE Institution of Civil Engineers, internal-combustion engine

Ice. Iceland, -ic

ice age a glacial period (not cap.)

ice axe (two words)

ice/berg, -block, -box (one word)

ice/ bucket, — cap (two words)

ice-cold (hyphen)

ice/ cream, — cube, — hockey (two words)

ice house (two words, one word in US)

Icelandic/ (typ.) roman alphabet now used, **Old —** called **Old Norse** in its lit. form

ice lolly (two words)

Iceni an ancient people of E. England

ice/ pack, — pick, — rink (two words)

ice-skate(r) (hyphen, two words in US)

ice station (two words)

ICFTU International Confederation of Free Trade Unions

ich (Ger.) I (cap. only at the beginning of a sentence)

Ich dien (Ger.) I serve (motto of the Princes of Wales)

I.Chem.E. Institution of Chemical Engineers

I Ching an ancient Chinese manual of divinations (caps.)

ichneumon a wasp, a N. African mongoose

ichor (Gr. myth.) a fluid flowing like blood in the veins of the gods

ichthyology the study of fishes, abbr. **ichth.**

ichthyosaur/us an extinct marine animal, pl. **-i**

Ichthys (Gr. 'fish', early Christian symbol) initial letters of *Iesous Christos Theou Uios Soter* (Jesus Christ, Son of God, Saviour)

ICI Imperial Chemical Industries

ici (Fr.) here, **— on parle français** French spoken here (no caps.)

Icknield/ Street, — Way, etc.

icky *not* ikky

ICN *in Christi nomine* (in Christ's name)

icon/ pl. **-s**; **-ic**; *not* ik-, eik- (not ital.)

icon. iconograph/y, -ic

ICS Indian Civil Service

ictus (prosody) rhythmical or metrical stress, (med.) a stroke or seizure; pl. same

ICU Intensive Care Unit

ICV International Code Use (signals)

ID (US) identification, identity, (mil.) Intelligence Department, (postal abbr.) Idaho

id (psychol.) not cap.

id. *idem*

i.d. inner diameter

id (Lat.) that, abbr. **i.**

IDA International Development Association (UN)

Idaho off. abbr. **Ida.**, postal **ID**

IDB (S. Afr.) illicit diamond buy/er, -ing

idea'd having ideas, *not* -aed

idealize *not* -ise

idealogical etc., *use* ideo-

idée/ fixe (Fr. f.) fixed idea, **— reçue** accepted opinion

idem/ (Lat.) the same (man), as mentioned before; abbr. **id.** (not ital., not cap. except to begin sentence or note); **id.** generally used to avoid repetition of male author's name in bibliographic matter when citing more than one work in uninterrupted succession; *use* **ead.** (for *eadem*) for a female author, pl. **eaed.** (for *eaedem*), and **eid.** (for *eidem*) for two or more authors of whom at least one is male and one female; *see also* **ibidem**; **— quod** the same as, abbr. **i.q.**

identikit (propr.) a system for producing a composite drawing of a face; cf. **photofit**

ideo/gram, -graph a character symbolizing the idea of a thing without expressing its name

ideologue a visionary

ideolog/y the study of ideas, a way of thinking; **-ical, -ist**; *not* ideal-

ides (pl.) in Roman calendar the fifteenth day of March, May, July, October, the thirteenth of other months

id est (Lat.) that is, abbr. **i.e.** (not ital., lower case, comma before)

id genus omne (Lat.) all of that kind

idiolect the linguistic system of one person, *not* ideo-

idiosyncra/sy a peculiarity of temperament, *not* -cy; **-tic**

idl/ing, -y *not* -eing, -ey

IDN *in Dei nomine* (in God's name)

Ido an artificial universal language based on Esperanto

idolater *not* -or

idolize *not* -ise

idol/um a false mental image, pl. **-a**

Idumaea *not* -mea

idyll a work of art depicting innocence or rusticity; a blissful period, *not* -yl

IE (Order of the) Indian Empire, Indo-European

i.e. *id est* (that is)

IEA International Energy Agency

IEE Institution of Electrical Engineers

IEEE (US) Institute of Electrical and Electronics Engineers

Ieper (Fl.) **Ypres**

IERE Institution of Electronic and Radio Engineers

Iesu (Lat.) Jesus (vocative)

IF intermediate frequency

IFC International Finance Corporation (UN)

iff (conjunction, logic and math.) if and only if (no points)

IG Indo-Germanic, (mil.) Inspector-General

I. Gas E. Institution of Gas Engineers

Igaunija Latvian for **Estonia**

Igbo *use* **Ibo**

igloo/ an Inuit snow hut, pl. **-s**

ign. *ignotus* (unknown)

igneous of, *or* like, *or* produced by, fire; *not* -ious

ignis fatuus a will-o'-the-wisp, pl. **ignes fatui** (not ital.)

ignitable *not* -ible

ignoramus/ an ignorant person, pl. **-es**

ignoratio elenchi (Lat.) refuting a proposition differing from that one professes to be refuting

ignotum per ignotius (Lat.) the unknown by means of the more unknown, *not* ignotus

ignotus (Lat.) unknown, abbr. **ign.**

IGO intergovernmental organization

IGY International Geophysical Year

i.h. *iacet hic* (here lies)

IHC same as **IHS**, *C* being a form of the Gr. cap. S

ihm (Ger.) to him

Ihnen (Ger.) to you (cap.); (not cap.) to them

i.h.p. indicated horsepower

Ihr (Ger.) your (cap.); to her, her, their, (familiar) you (not cap.)

IHS abbr. of Gr. *Iesous* (*H* being Gr. cap. long *E*); later interpreted as Lat. *Iesus Hominum Salvator* (Jesus Men's Saviour); *In Hoc Signo* (*vinces*) in this sign (thou shalt conquer); *In Hac* (*Cruce*) *Salus*, in this (cross) is salvation

IHVE Institution of Heating and Ventilation Engineers

II (roman numeral) two (no point)

III (roman numeral) three (no point)

IIII (roman numeral) *use* **IV** (except in classical or medieval texts)

IJ a water area (in the Netherlands); (typ.) a (one-piece) capital letter; *not* Ij, Y

ij (typ.) a (one-piece) lower-case letter in Du. used instead of **y** *but* alphabetized as *y*

ij (med.) two

i. J. (Ger.) *im Jahre* (in the year) (spaces in Ger.)

i. J. d. W. (Ger.) *im Jahre der Welt* (in the year of the world) (spaces in Ger.)

IJ/muiden town, **-ssel** river, **-sselmeer** *formerly* Zuider Zee, **-stein** a town, the Netherlands; *not* Ij-, Y-

Ijo (of or relating to) (a member of) a people of SE Nigeria, or their Kwa language; *not* -aw

ikky *use* **icky**

ikon *use* **ic-**

IL Illinois (postal abbr.)

il (Fr.) he, it; (It., m. sing.) the

ilang-ilang *use* **ylang-ylang**

île (Fr. f.) island

Île-de-France a French region, province, Paris square

Île-de-Montréal a county in Quebec

Île-Jésus a county in Quebec

Île-St-Louis a Paris square

ile/um (anat.) a part of the intestine, pl. **-a**

ilex/ the holm oak, pl. **-es**

Iliad of Homer (ital.)

Ilium (Lat.) Troy

ili/um (anat.) a part of the pelvis, pl. **-a**

ilk, of that (Sc.) of the same place, name, or estate; (colloq.) of family, class, or set, often considered derogatory

Ill. Illinois (off. abbr.)

ill. *illustrissimus* (most distinguished)

ill/-advised, -advisedly, -affected, -assorted (hyphens)

ill at ease (hyphens when attrib.)

ill/-behaved, -bred (hyphens)

ill breeding (two words)

ill/-considered, -defined, -disposed (hyphens)

Ille-et-Vilaine a dép. of France

illegalize *not* -ise

illegible (of handwriting, print, etc.) not clear enough to read; cf. **unreadable**

illegitimize *not* -atize, -ise

ill-equipped (hyphen)

ill fame (two words)

ill/-fated, -favoured *not* -favored (US) (hyphens)

ill feeling (hyphen when attrib.)

ill/-founded, -gotten (hyphens)

ill/ health, — humour (two words)

ill-humoured *not* -humored (US) (hyphen)

illimitable limitless

Illinois off. abbr. **Ill.**, postal **IL**

ill/-judged, -mannered (hyphens)

ill nature (two words)

ill/-natured, -omened, -starred (hyphens)

ill temper (two words)

ill/-tempered, -timed, -treat, -treatment (hyphens)

illuminati (pl.) enlightened people, cap. with reference to particular historical movements (not ital.)

ill use (two words)

ill-used (hyphen)

illusory of more apparent than real value, *not* -ive; cf. **elusive**

illustrat/ed, -ion abbr. **illus.**

illustrator *not* -er

ill will (two words)

il n'y a pas de quoi (Fr.) don't mention it

ILO International Labour Organization

ILP Independent Labour Party

'Il Penseroso' a poem by Milton, 1632

ILR Independent Local Radio

ILS instrument landing system

ILTF International Lawn Tennis Federation; *see also* **tennis**

IM intramuscular

imag/o a winged insect, pl. **-ines**; idealized mental picture, pl. **-s**

imam a leader of prayers in a mosque; a title of various Muslim leaders; *not* -âm, -aum

I.Mar.E. Institute of Marine Engineers

imbed *use* **em-**

imbrication an overlapping of tiles, scales, feathers, etc.; cf. **embrocation**

imbroglio/ a tangle, pl. **-s**; *not* em- (not ital.)

imbrue to stain, dye; *not* em-

imbue to saturate, inspire; *not* em-

IMCO Inter-Governmental Maritime Consultative Organization (UN), *now* **IMO**

I.Mech.E. Institution of Mechanical Engineers

IMF International Monetary Fund (UN)

imfe *use* **-phee**

I.Min.E. Institution of Mining Engineers

im Jahre (Ger.) in the year, abbr. **i. J.**

IMM Institution of Mining and Metallurgy

immanent indwelling, inherent, the antonym of transcendent; cf. **imminent**; **eminent**

Immelmann a kind of looping aircraft turn (cap.)

immesh *use* **en-**

immigra/te come as a permanent resident to a country other than one's native land, **-nt** one who does this; cf. **emigrate**

imminent impending; cf. **eminent**; **immanent**

immobiliz/e *not* -ise; **-ation**

immortalize *not* -ise

immortelle an everlasting flower (not ital.)

Immortels, Les the members of the French Academy

immov/able, -ability, -ableness, -ably *not* -eab- (except for feasts and (law) property); *see also* **movable**

immunize render immune, *not* -ise

immutable unchangeable

IMO International Maritime Organization

imp. imperative, imperfect, imperial, impersonal; import/ed, -er; impression, imprimatur

imp. (Fr.) *imprimeur* (printer); (Lat.) *imperator* (emperor), *imperatrix* (empress)

impanel *use* **em-**

impassable that cannot be traversed

impasse a deadlock (not ital.)

impassible that cannot feel, passive

impassion/ stir emotionally, **-ed**; *not* em-

impasto/ the thick laying-on of colour, pl. **-s**

impayable (Fr.) invaluable, priceless

impeccable *not* -ible

impedance (elec.) hindrance to alternating current

impedimenta (pl.) encumbrances, baggage

impel/, -led, -ler *not* -lor, **-ling**

imperative (gram.) mood expressing command, abbr. **imp.**

imperat/or (Lat.) f. **-rix** absolute ruler, emperor; abbr. **I.,** *imp.*

imperf. imperfect, (stamps) imperforate

imperfect abbr. **imp.**, **imperf.**

imperial abbr. **imp.**

imperil/, -led, -ling (one l in US)

imperium absolute power (not ital.)

imperium in imperio (Lat.) an empire within an empire

impermeable that cannot be passed through

impersonal abbr. **imp.**

impetus/ momentum, incentive; pl. **-es**

imphee a sugar cane; *not* -fe, -phie

impi (S. Afr.) an armed band, (hist.) a Zulu regiment

imping/e make an impact, encroach, **-ing**

implacable *not* -ible

impolder reclaim from the sea; *not* em-

import/ed, -er abbr. **imp.**

impose (typ.) arrange pages so that they will read consecutively when the printed sheet is folded

impost/or *not* -er, **-orous** *not* -rous

impracticable that cannot be effected or accomplished; *see also* **practical**

Impractical not practical, **unpractical**; *see also* **practical**

impregn/able that cannot be taken by force, **-atable** that can be impregnated

impresa (It.) an undertaking

impresario/ a manager of operatic or other cultural undertakings (one s, not ital.); pl. **-s**

impressa (It.) an imprint (obs.)

impression (print.) the product from one cycle of a printing machine; all the copies of a book etc. printed at one press-run from the same type, plates, etc.; abbr. **imp.**; *see also* **edition**; **imprint**; **reprint**

impressionable *not* -ible

Impressionis/m, -t, -tic a specific artistic movement or style of music or writing (cap.); a general tendency or style (not cap.)

imprimatur an official licence to print, sanction; abbr. **imp.** (not ital. except in a RC context)

imprimatura (It.) coloured transparent glaze

imprim/er (Fr.) to print, **-erie** (f.) printing office, **-eur** (m.) printer

imprimi potest (Lat.) a formula giving imprimatur (ital.)

imprimis (Lat.) in the first place, not *in primis* (ital.)

imprint/ the name and address of the printer; **publisher's —** the name of the publisher or publishing division, place of publication, and date

impromptu pl. **-s** (not ital.)

improvable *not* -eable, -ible

improvis/e *not* -ize; **-ator** one who speaks or plays music extempore; **-er** in general, one who improvises

improvvisat/a (It.) improvisation; **-ore** improvisator, pl. **-ori**; f. **-rice**, pl. **-rici**

I.Mun.E. Institution of Municipal Engineers

IN Indiana (postal abbr.)

In indium (no point)

in. inch, -es

in (Ger.) in, into

in- (Fr.) prefix in stating book sizes, as *in-8°*, octavo

in/ *absentia* (Lat.) in (one's) absence, —
abstracto in the abstract

inadmissible *not* -able

inadverten/t (of people) negligent, (of actions)
unintentional; **-ce**

inadvisable (of thing or course of action) not
recommended; cf. **unadvisable**

in aeternum for ever

inamorat/o f. **-a** a lover, pl. **-i** (not ital.); in It.
innamorat/o, -a; *not* en-

in articulo mortis (Lat.) at the moment of
death

inartistic not following the principles of art,
lacking artistic skill or talent; cf. **unartistic**

inasmuch (one word)

Inauguration Day (of the US President) 20 Jan.;
before 1937, 4 Mar.

in banco (Lat.) as a full court of judges

Inbegriff (Ger. m.) epitome, embodiment (cap.)

in/board, -born, -bred, -built (one word)

INC *in nomine Christi* (in Christ's name)

Inc. (US) Incorporated

Inca/ (one of) the pre-Columbian people of
Peru, **-n**

incage *use* en-

in camera not in open court

in/capsulate, -case *use* en-

in/ *cathedra* (Lat.) in the chair of office, —
cautelam for a warning

inch/ in metric system 25.4 mm (not now in
scientific use), pl. **-es**; abbr. **in.** (sing. and
pl.); sign "

inchase *use* en-

Inchcape Rock *or* **Bell Rock**, North Sea (two
words)

incidentally *not* -tly

incipient beginning, in an initial stage; *not*
insi-

incipit the first words (of book etc.)

incise cut into, engrave; *not* -ize

incl. including, inclusive

inclose *use* en-

includible *not* -able

inclu/ding, -sive abbr. **incl.**

'In Coena Domini' a former annual papal bull
against heretics

Incogniti a cricket club

incognito/ with one's name or identity concealed or disguised, the pretended identity;
pl. **-s**; abbr. **incog.** (not ital.)

income/ group, — tax (two words)

in/ *commendam* (Lat.) temporarily holding a
vacant benefice

incommunicado without means of communication (not ital.), in Sp. *incomunicado*

in concreto in material form, definite

incondensable *not* -ible

inconnu/ (Fr.) f. **-e** unknown

incontrovertible *not* -able

incorrigible *not* -eable

increas/ed, -ing abbr. **incr.**

incredible *not* -able

incroach *use* en-

incrust *use* en-, *but* **incrustation**

incubous (bot.) having the upper leaf-margin
overlapping the leaf above

incub/us a person or thing that oppresses like
a nightmare, esp. a male demon believed to
have sexual intercourse with sleeping women;
pl. **-uses** (in extended meaning), **-i** (of
demons); cf. **succubus**

incumber etc., *use* en-

incunable (Fr.) = **incunabulum**

incunabul/a (sing. **-um**) the earliest examples
of any art, (bibliog.) books printed before
1501

incur/, -red, -ring, -rable

incurable that cannot be cured

in curia (Lat.) in open court

incu/s (anat.) a bone in the ear, pl. **-des**

IND *in nomine Dei* (in God's name)

Ind poetical for India (no point)

Ind. India, -n; Indiana (off. abbr.)

ind. independen/ce, -t; index, indication, industrial

Ind Coope an English brewer

indebted *not* en-

indeclinable (gram.) having no inflections,
abbr. **indecl.**

indefatigabl/e tireless, **-y**

indefeasible that cannot be forfeited, *not* -able

indefensible that cannot be defended, *not*
-cible, -able

indefinite abbr. **indef.**

indelible that cannot be rubbed out; *not* -able,
-eble

indemni/fy protect against harm or loss; **-ty**;
not en-

indent (typ.) begin a line, or lines, with a blank
space; *not* en-; *see also* **hanging**

indenture a sealed agreement, esp. one binding apprentice to master; *not* en-

independen/ce, -t abbr. **ind., indep.**

Independence, Declaration of USA, 4 July
1776 (caps.)

Independence Day a day celebrating national
independence, esp. (US) 4 July

independency a country that has attained
independence

Independent a person who is politically independent, (hist.) Congregational (cap.)

Independent Order of Odd Fellows *not* Oddfellows, abbr. **IOOF**

in deposito (Lat.) in deposit

indescribable *not* -eable, -ible

ind/ex pl. **-exes**, abbr. **ind.**; (sci., math.) pl. **-ices**; (print.) *see* **fist**

'Index/ Expurgatorius' (Lat.) an index of the passages to be expunged; **'— Librorum Expurgandorum'** (RC) a list of books that might be read only in expurgated editions; **'— Librorum Prohibitorum'** (RC) a list of books that the Church forbade to be read

index/ nominum (Lat.) index of names; **— locorum** index of places, **— rerum** subject index, **— verborum** index of words; pl. **indices —** (not ital.)

India/, -n abbr. **Ind.**

India/man a large ship in the Indian trade, pl. **-men**

Indiana off. abbr. **Ind.**, postal **IN**

Indianapolis Ind.

Indian/ clubs, — corn, — file, — ink (two words, one cap.), *not* India ink (US)

Indian summer a period of warm weather in late autumn, a tranquil late period of life

India paper/ a thin book paper, *not* -ian (no hyphen); **Oxford — —** very thin, strong bible paper made only for OUP

India rubber (two words, no cap. in US)

Indic (of) the group of Indo-European languages comprising Sanskrit and its modern descendants

indication abbr. **ind.**

indicative (gram.) abbr. **indic.**

indicia (pl.) signs, identifying marks (not ital.)

indict/ accuse formally by legal process, cf. **indite**; **-er** *not* -or

indiction (later Rom. Empire and Middle Ages) a cycle of fifteen years, used for administrative and dating purposes; 'first [etc.] indiction' = the first (etc.) year of the cycle, *not* the first cycle

indie (colloq.) an independent record or film company, *not* -dy

indigestible *not* -able

indiscreet injudicious

indiscrete not divided into distinct parts

indispensable *not* -ible

indite put into written words; cf. **indict**

indium symbol **In**

individualize *not* -ise

individu/um (Lat.) the indivisible, pl. **-a**

Indo-Aryan (of or relating to) a member of any of the Aryan peoples of India, the Indic group of languages

Indo-Chin/a an unofficial collective name for the countries of the SE peninsula of Asia (hyphen; one word, one cap. in US), **-ese**

Indo-European (of or relating to) the family of languages spoken over the greater part of Europe and Asia as far as N. India, the hypothetical parent language of this family; abbr. **IE, Indo-Eur.**

Indo-Germanic *use* **Indo-European**

Indo-Iranian (of or relating to) the subfamily of Indo-European languages spoken chiefly in N. India and Iran

Indonesia indep. 1950; *formerly* Dutch East Indies, with W. New Guinea added 1962 and E. Timor annexed 1974; abbr. **Indon.**; *see also* **Bahasa Indonesia**

indoor/, -s (one word)

indorse etc., *use* **en-**

Indostan *use* **Hindu-**

indraught a drawing in, *not* -aft (US)

indubitabl/e *not* -ible; **-y**

inducement (often followed by *to*) an attraction that leads one on, a thing that induces

induction *not* -xion

indu/e, -re *use* **en-**

Indulgence, Declaration of proclamation of religious liberties, esp. under Charles II in 1672 and James II in 1687 (caps.)

industrial abbr. **ind.**

Industrial Revolution (two caps.)

inédit/ f. **-e** (Fr.) unpublished, *not* unedited

inedita (Lat.) unpublished compositions

inedited not published, *or* published without editorial alterations or additions

ineducable incapable of being educated; *not* -atable, -ible

ineffaceable that cannot be effaced

inefficacious ineffective

ineligible *not* -able

inequable not fairly distributed, not uniform

inequitable unfair, unjust

inertia (not ital.) *but* **vis inertiae**

in esse (Lat.) actually existing

inessential (something) not necessary, dispensable

in/ excelsis in the highest (degree); **— extenso** in full, at length; **— extremis** at the point of death, in great difficulties

in f. in fine (finally)

inf. infantry, inferior, infinitive

inf. (Lat.) infra (below)

infallib/le *not* -able; **-ilist** a believer in the Pope's infallibility, *not* -blist

infant/a daughter of the King and Queen of Spain; **-e** a younger son of the same (not ital., cap. as title); cf. **príncipe**

infantry abbr. **inf.**

infantryman (one word)

infected area abbr. **IA**

infer/, **-red**, **-ring**

infer/able *not* -rr-; **-ence**

inferior abbr. **inf.**

inferior (typ.) a small character set below the baseline, usually to the side of ordinary characters, e.g. ₁₂ₐᵦ; *also called* **subscript**; cf. **superior**

inferno/ a raging fire, a scene of horror, pl. **-s**; (cap. and ital.) the first part of Dante's *Divina Commedia*

in fieri (Lat.) in course of completion

infighting boxing at close quarters, internal conflict (one word)

infill/ fill in, **-ing**

infin. infinitive

in fine finally, abbr. **in f.** (not ital.)

infinitive abbr. **inf.**, **infin.**

infinity symbol ∞

in flagrante delicto in the very act of committing an offence (not ital.)

inflamma/ble easily set on fire, flammable; *not* non-flammable; **-tory** *not* flammatory; *see* **flammable**

inflatable *not* -eable

inflater one who, *or* that which, inflates, *not* -or

inflection modulation of voice, grammatical termination; *not* -xion

inflexible *not* -able

inflexion *use* **-ction**

infold etc., *use* **en-**

inforce etc., *use* **en-**

in forma pauperis (Lat.) as a pauper

infra/ (Lat.) below, abbr. **inf.**; **— dignitatem** undignified, abbr. **infra dig.**, (colloq.) **infra dig**

infra/red, **-sonic**, **-sound**, **-structure** (one word)

inful/a each of the ribbons of a bishop's mitre, pl. **-ae**

infuser one who, *or* that which, steeps something in a liquid; *not* -or

infusible that cannot be melted

in futuro (Lat.) in, *or* for, the future

Inge, William Ralph, Dean (1860–1954) English divine

Ingelow, Jean (1820–97) English poet

in genere (Lat.) in kind

ingenious inventive

ingénue an artless girl (not ital.)

ingenuity inventiveness

ingenuous/ free from guile, **-ness**

inglenook a chimney corner (one word)

Ingoldsby Legends by R. H. Barham, 1840

ingraft, ingrain (verb) *use* **en-**

ingrain/ (adj.) dyed in the yarn; **-ed** (adj., less specific) deeply rooted, inveterate; cf. **engrain**

Ingres/, Jean Auguste Dominique (1780–1867) French painter (no accent), **violon d'—** an additional skill

ingross *use* **en-**

in-group a small exclusive group of people (hyphen)

ingulf *use* **en-**

inhabitant abbr. **inhab.**

in hac parte (Lat.) on this part

in hoc/ (Lat.) in this respect, **— — salus** safety in this

in-house (adj. and adv., hyphen)

INI *in nomine Iesu* (in the name of Jesus)

in infinitum for ever

Inishfail poetical for Ireland, *not* Inn-

init. (Lat.) initio (in the beginning), *initium* (beginning)

initial/, **-led**, **-ling** (one *l* in US)

initial letter (typ.) a large letter used at beginning of chapter

Initial Teaching Alphabet (caps.) abbr. **i t a** (spaced lower case, no points)

initium (Lat.) beginning (as of a work), abbr. **init.**

injuri/a (law) a wrong, pl. **-ae**

ink-blot test (one hyphen; inkblot one word in US)

Inkerman Crimea, *not* -ann

ink-jet printer (hyphen)

inkling a slight knowledge or suspicion

Inklings, the an Oxford group, 1930s–1960s, composed of C. S. Lewis, J. R. R. Tolkien, C. Williams, and others

ink/pot, **-stand**, **-well** (one word)

in-laws relatives by marriage (hyphen)

in/ limine (Lat.) at the outset, abbr. **in lim.**; **— loco** in place of; **— loco citato** in the place cited, abbr. **loc. cit.**; **— loco parentis** in the position of parent; **— medias res** into the midst of affairs; **— medio** in the middle; **— medio tutissimus ibis** the middle course is safest; **— memoriam** to the memory (of)

inn, name of *see* **hotel**

innamorat/o f. **-a** *see* **inam-**

inner (typ.) the side of a sheet containing the second page

innervate supply (an organ etc.) with nerves; cf. **ener-**

Innes,/ Cosmo (1798–1874) Scottish historian, **— James Dickson** (1887–1914) British painter, **— Michael** pseud. of **John Innes Mackintosh Stewart** (1906–94) British novelist, **— Thomas** (1662–1744) Scottish historian

Inness, George (1825–94) US painter

innings a portion of a game played by one side, pl. same; *not* inning (except in US)

Innisfail *use* **Inishfail**

Inniskilling/ Dragoon Guards, — Fusiliers; *see also* **Enniskillen**

innkeeper (one word)

Innocents' Day 28 Dec. (caps.)

innoculate *use* **ino-**

in nomine (Lat.) in the name (of a person)

Innsbruck Austria

Inns of Court, the Inner Temple, Middle Temple, Lincoln's Inn, Gray's Inn

in/- nubibus (Lat.) in the clouds, *— nuce* in a nutshell

innuendo/ an oblique, disparaging, or suggestive remark; pl. **-es**; *not* inu- (not ital.)

Innuit *use* **Inuit**

inoculate inject an immunizing serum into; *not* en-, inn-

in/ pace (Lat.) in peace; *— pari materia* in an analogous case; *— partibus infidelium* in the regions of unbelievers, abbr. **i.p.i.**, *in partibus*; cf. **Bishop**

in-patient (hyphen, one word in US)

in petto (It.) secretly

in/ pontificalibus in pontifical vestments; *— posse* potentially; *— potentia* potentially; *— primis use* **imprimis**; *— principio* in the beginning, abbr. *in pr.*; *— propria persona* in his, *or* her, own person; *— puris naturalibus* naked

input/ (verb) **-ting,** past and past part. **-ted** or **input**

inquir/e undertake a formal or intellectual investigation; **-y** such an investigation; cf. **enquire**

inquorate lacking a quorum

in/ re (Lat.) in the matter of, *— rem* (law) relating to a matter, *— rerum natura* in the nature of things

INRI *Iesus Nazarenus Rex Iudaeorum* (Jesus of Nazareth, King of the Jews) (John 19: 19)

in/road, -rush (one word)

INS Immigration and Naturalization Service

ins. insurance

in saecula saeculorum (Lat.) for ever and ever

insconce *use* **en-**

in se (Lat.) in itself, in themselves

Insecta (zool.) (Lat. pl.) insects, *not* -ae

inselberg an isolated hill or mountain rising abruptly from its surroundings (not cap.)

insert (bind.) a bookmark, advertisement, etc., slipped loose inside bound pages; a folded section of book printed separately but bound in with the book, *formerly* inset

inset (typ.) a small map etc. printed within the borders of a larger one

inshallah (Arab.) if Allah wills

insign/ia (pl. and sing.); badges of office (not ital.); **-e** (rare) sing. form

insipient unwise, foolish; *not* inci-

insisten/ce, -t *not* -ance, -ant

in situ (Lat.) in position

insnare *use* **en-**

in so far (three words, one word in US)

insomuch to such an extent; inasmuch (one word)

insoucian/ce lack of concern, **-t** unconcerned (not ital.)

Inspector abbr. **Insp.**

Inspector-General abbr. **IG, Insp.-Gen.**

INST *in nomine Sanctae Trinitatis* (in the name of the Holy Trinity)

inst. instant; institut/e, -es, -ion

Inst. Act. Institute of Actuaries

install/, -lation (two *l*s), **-ment** (one *l* except in US)

instant of this month, abbr. **inst.**

instantaneous occurring or done instantly

instanter at once (joc.) (not ital.)

in statu/ pupillari (Lat.) in a condition of pupillage, *— — quo* (*ante, prius; nunc*) in the same state (as formerly; as now)

instauration (formal) restoration, renewal

Inst./D. Institute of Directors, **—F.** Institute of Fuel

instil/ inculcate gradually (one *l* except in US); **-led, -ling**

Institut de France the association of five French academies: Académie des beaux-arts, Académie française, Académie des inscriptions et belles-lettres, Académie des sciences, Académie des sciences morales et politiques

Institute *see* separate entries beginning **I.** or **Inst.** (Institute of), **FI** (Fellow of the Institute of), **RI** (Royal Institute of)

Institut français du Royaume-Uni the French Institute, London

Institution *see* separate entries beginning **I.** (Institution of), **FI** (Fellow of the Institution of), **RI** (Royal Institution of)

institutionalize *not* -ise, -ionize

institutor *not* -er

Inst./P. Institute of Physics, **—R.** Institute of Refrigeration

instruct/or *not* -er; f. **-ress**

instrument/, -al abbr. **instr.**

insurance when effected against a risk, *but* **assurance** of life

insur/e provide for a possible contingency, **-er** (spelling in all insurance senses); abbr. **ins.**; cf. **assurance; assure; ensure**

inswathe *use* en-

int. interest, interior, interjection, internal, international, interpreter

intaglio/ an incised design, pl. **-s** (not ital.); (typ.) a printing process based on an etched or incised plate

intailed *use* en-

intangible *not* -able

intarsia mosaic woodwork

integration, sign of (math.) ∫

intelligentsia (collective noun) the intellectual part of a population, *not* -zia

Intelpost International Electronic Post

Intelsat International Telecommunications Satellite Consortium

in tenebris (Lat.) in darkness, in doubt

inter/ bury; **-red, -ring**

inter (Lat.) between

inter intermediate

inter/ alia among other things, — *alios* among other persons

intercity (*but* 'InterCity' (propr.), a type of train) (one word)

inter-class (hyphen, one word in US)

inter/collegiate, -colonial, -com (no point), **-continental** (one word)

interdict/, -ion, -ory

interest abbr. **int.**, in Fr. m. *intérêt*

interface (comput.) a boundary or link between two computer units (one word)

interim (not ital.)

interior abbr. **int.**

interjection abbr. **int., interj.**

interlea/f an extra leaf inserted between the regular leaves of a book; pl. **-ves**; **-ve** insert such a leaf

interlinear matter (typ.) small type between lines of larger type

intermarr/iage, -y (one word)

intermedi/ate abbr. **inter.**

intermezz/o a short piece of entertainment, pl. **-i**; (cap., ital.) an opera by Richard Strauss, 1924

intermission a pause or cessation; interval between parts of a play, film, etc.

intermit/ stop for a time; **-ted, -tent, -ting**

internal/ abbr. **int.**; **-combustion engine** (one hyphen)

Internal Revenue Service (US) = **Inland Revenue Service**

international abbr. **int., internat.**, (US) **internat'l, int'l**

International,/ the first an association of working classes of all countries (Marxist 1862–73); **— the second** ('Socialist' 1889–); **— the third** (Russian Communist 1919–43)

also called the Comintern; **— the fourth** (Trotskyist 1938–)

'Internationale, The' French poem adopted internationally as a socialist hymn, until 1944 the Soviet anthem

internationalize *not* -ise

Internet (comput.) (cap., one word)

internist (med.) a specialist in internal diseases, (US) a general practitioner

inter nos (Lat.) between ourselves

internuncio/ a papal ambassador, pl. **-s** (not ital.)

interoceanic (one word)

interpellate (parl.) interrupt to demand explanation

interplanetary (one word)

Interpol International Criminal Police Commission

interpolate make insertions

interpret/, -ed, -er abbr. **int.**, **-ing**; **-ative** (adj.) *not* -pretive; **-atively** (adv.)

interregnum/ a period between one ruler and another, pl. **-s** *or* (esp. in classical contexts) **-a** (not cap.); **the —** in Germany (1254–73), in England (1649–60) (cap.)

interrelat/ed, -ionship (one word)

interrog. interrog/ation, -ative, -atively

in terrorem (Lat.) as a warning

interrupter *not* -or

inter se (Lat.) among, *or* between, themselves

inter vivos from one living person to another

inter-war in the period between two wars, esp. the two world wars (hyphen, one word in US)

in testimonium (Lat.) in witness

inthral *use* en-

inthrone *use* en-

intitule etc., *not* en-; *but* **entitle**

intonaco (It.) a plaster surface for fresco painting, *not* -ico

in toto (Lat.) entirely

intra/ (Lat.) within, — *muros* privately

intramuscular within a muscle (one word), abbr. **IM**

intrans. intransitive

intransigent (adj.) uncompromising, in Fr. *intransigeant* (m. and adj.) (no accent)

intrap *use* en-

intrauterine within the womb (one word)

intravenous within a vein (one word), abbr. **IV**

intra vires (Lat.) within one's powers

in-tray (hyphen)

intreat *use* en-

intrench *use* en-

intrigant/ f. **-e** an intriguer (not ital.)

introduction abbr. **introd.**

introvert *not* intra-

intrust *use* **en-**

intubate *not* en-

intussusception (physiol.) the taking in of foreign matter by living organism, withdrawal of one portion of a tube into another (double *s*)

intwine, intwist *use* **en-**

Inuit (of or relating to) (a member of) a Canadian Native American people, or the language of this people (*properly* **Inupiaq**); *not* Inn-; *see also* **Eskimo**; **Inuk**; **Yupik**

Inuk/ (of or relating to) (a member of) a Canadian or Greenland Native American people, or the language of this people (*properly* **-titut**); *not* Inn-

Iñupiat (of or relating to) (a member of) an Alaskan Native American people, or the language of this people; *not* Inn-

inure accustom, (law) take effect; *not* en-

in/ usu (Lat.) in use, — **utero** in the womb, — **utroque iure** under both laws (canon and civil)

inv. invent/ed, -or; invoice

inv. invenit (designed this)

in vacuo (Lat.) in empty space

Invalides, Hôtel des Paris, *see* **Hôtel**

invenit (Lat.) designed this, abbr. *inv.*

invent/ed, -or *not* -er, abbr. **inv.**

Inveraray Strathclyde, *not* -ry

inverness a sleeveless coat with removable cape (not cap.)

Inverness-shire a former county of Scotland (hyphen)

Invertebrata (collective noun) all animals other than vertebrates

inverted commas *see* **quotation marks**

inverter *not* -or

Inverurie Grampian

investor *not* -er

in vino veritas (Lat.) a drunken person speaks the truth

invita Minerva (Lat.) uninspiredly

in/ vitro (Lat.) in the test tube, — **vitro fertilization** abbr. **IVF** (caps.), — **vivo** (Lat.) in the living organism

invoice abbr. **inv.**

involucre (anat., bot.) a covering, envelope (not ital.)

inwards *use* **inward**

inweave *not* en-

inwrap, inwreathe *use* **en-**

inyala a large S. African antelope, *not* ny-

I/O (comput.) input/output

io (Gr., Lat.) an exclamation of triumph or strong emotion (ital.)

IOC International Olympic Committee

iodine symbol **I**

IOF Independent Order of Foresters

IOGT International Order of Good Templars

IoM Isle of Man (*also* **IOM, IM**)

Ion. Ionic

Ion/ian (hist.) of Ionia, (mus.) the mode; **-ic** (of) the dialect and architectural order (cap.)

ioni/c of, relating to, *or* using, ions; **-ze** to convert into ions, *not* -ise

IOOF Independent Order of Odd Fellows

IOP Institute of Painters in Oil Colours

IOR Independent Order of Rechabites

iota/ the ninth letter of the Gr. alphabet (*I*, ι); — **adscript** printed after lower-case alpha, eta, and omega: αι, ηι, ωι; — **subscript** printed beneath alpha, eta, and omega: ᾳ, ῃ, ῳ

IOU I owe you

IoW Isle of Wight (*also* **IOW, IW**)

Iowa off. abbr. **Ia.**, postal **IA**

IP input primary

IPA India Pale Ale, International Phonetic Alphabet, International Phonetic Association

IPCS Institution of Professional Civil Servants

IPD (Sc. law) *in praesentia Dominorum* (in the presence of the Lords [of Session])

ipecacuanha (bot., med.) a purgative root

IPI International Press Institute

i.p.i. *in partibus infidelium* (in the regions of unbelievers)

IPM Institute of Personnel Management

I.Prod.E. Institution of Production Engineers

i.p.s. inches per second

ipse dixit (Lat., 'he himself has said it') a dogmatic statement resting merely on the speaker's authority

ipsissima verba (Lat.) the precise words

ipso facto (Lat.) by that very fact or act, thereby; *prefer* **eo ipso**

IPTS International Practical Temperature Scale

IQ intelligence quotient

i.q. idem quod (the same as)

Iqbal, Sir Muhammad (1875–1938) Punjabi poet and philosopher, 'father of Pakistan'

Iquique Chile

IR infrared, Inland Revenue

Ir iridium (no point)

Ir. Irish

IRA Irish Republican Army

irade (Turk.) a written decree signed by the Sultan himself

Iran/, -ian, -ic; abbr. **Iran.**

Iraq/ *not* Irak; adj. **-i**

Irawadi *use* **Irrawaddy**

IRBM intermediate-range ballistic missile

IRC International Red Cross

Ireland abbr. **Ire.**, in Gaelic **Éire**

Irena Ireland personified

irenic (lit.) aiming or aimed at peace; *not* -ical, ei-

irenicon *use* **ei-**

Irian Jaya Indonesian for **W. New Guinea**

iridescen/ce the play of rainbow colours, **-t**; *not* irr-

iridium symbol **Ir**

iris/ (anat., bot.) pl. **-es**

Irish abbr. **Ir.**

Irishism *not* Iricism, *but prefer* **Hibernicism**

Irkutsk E. Siberia; *not* Irkoo-, Irkou-

IRO Inland Revenue Office, International Refugee Organization

iron symbol **Fe** (ferrum)

ironclad (one word)

Iron Curtain (two words, caps.)

ironic *not* -ical

iron mould (two words) *not* -mold (US)

iron ration (two words)

Ironside/ the sobriquet of Edmund II, **—, William Edmund, Baron** (1880–1959) British soldier; **-s** Cromwell's troops in the Civil War

Ironsides, Old nickname of the USS *Constitution*, a forty-four-gun frigate

iron/ware, -work (one word)

Iroquoian (of or relating to) a language family of eastern N. America

Iroquois a Native American Indian confederacy of peoples formerly inhabiting New York State; (of or relating to) a member of any of these peoples or their languages (pl. same)

Irrawaddy a river in Burma, *not* Irawadi

irreconcilable *not* -eable, -iable

irredentist one who (re)claims regions for his country, esp. (cap.) Italian

irrefragable unanswerable, *not* -ible

irreg. irregular, -ly

irregardless *use* **regardless**

irreparable *not* -pairable

irreplaceable *not* -cable

irresistibl/e, -y *not* -able, -ably

irridescen/ce, -t *use* **iri-**

irrupt/ enter forcibly or suddenly; cf. **erupt**; **-tion**

IRS Inland Revenue Service, (US) Internal Revenue Service

Irtysh a river in Cent. Asia

Irún Spain

Irvine Strathclyde

IS input secondary, Irish Society

is. island, -s; isle, -s

Isa. Isaiah

Isaiah (OT) abbr. **Isa.**

Isaian of the prophet Isaiah, *not* Isaiahian

ISBN International Standard Book Number

Isère a river and dép. SE France

Iseult Tristram's lady-love; the many variants reflect different retellings (e.g. **Isode** in Malory, **Isolde** in Wagner's opera)

Isfahan Iran, *not* Isp-

Isherwood, Christopher (**William Bradshaw**) (1904–86) English novelist

ISI International Statistical Institute, Iron and Steel Institute

Isidore of Seville (570–636) Archbishop of Seville and encyclopedia writer

isl. island, -s (*prefer* **I.** *or* **is.**); isle, -s

Islam literally 'surrender (to God)', the Muslim religion; *see also* **Muslim**

island/, -s abbr. **I., is.**; when with name to have cap., as Cape Verde Islands; in Fr. f. *île*

Island (Ger., Dan. n.) Iceland, *Isländer* (Ger. m.) an Icelander

Ísland Icelandic for **Iceland**

Islay Strathclyde, *not* Isla

isle/, -s abbr. **I., isl.**

Isle of/ Man abbr. **IoM, IOM, IM**; **— Wight** abbr. **IoW, IOW, IW**

Isleworth London

ISM Imperial Service Medal, Incorporated Society of Musicians

ism the suffix used as generic noun (no hyphen)

Ismaili (a member) of a Muslim sect

ISO (Companion of the) Imperial Service Order, International Organization for Standardization

isobar (meteor.) *not* -are (not ital.)

Isocrates (436–338 BC) Athenian orator

isola (It.) island

Iso/ld, -lde, -lt, -lte, -ulde *see* **Iseult**

isosceles (geom.) of a triangle, having two sides equal

isotop/e a form of an element differing from other forms in the mass of its atoms, **-ic**

isotron a device for separating isotopes by accelerating ions

isotrop/ic (phys.) having same properties in all directions, **-y**

ISP (comput.) Internet service provider

Ispahan *use* **Isfa-**

Israel/i (noun and adj.) (a citizen) of the modern state of Israel, est. 1948; **-ite** (noun) one of the ancient Jewish people, adj. **-itic, -itish** (in Bible only)

ISSN International Standard Serial Number

issue, second (bibliog.) state resulting from sheets of same edition being bound up with new title page and additional matter, or in a different order; the original state of that edition is then called the first issue; *see also* **impression**

Istanbul Turkey

isth. isthmus

isthmian of or relating to an isthmus, esp. (cap.) to the Isthmus of Corinth in S. Greece

Isthmian games one of the four principal Panhellenic festivals

I.Struct.E. Institution of Structural Engineers

It. Italian, Italy

i t a (spaced lower case, no points) Initial Teaching Alphabet

ital. italic

Italian abbr. **It.**

italic (typ.) abbr. **ital.**

italice (Lat.) in Italian

italicize to print in italic type, *not* -ise

italienne, à l' (Fr.) in Italian style (lower-case i)

Italiote of the ancient Greek colonies in S. Italy, *not* -ot

Italy abbr. **It.**; in Fr. f. *Italie*, Ger. n. *Italien*, It. *Italia*

ITAR-TASS the official news agency of Russia, renamed from **TASS** 1992; *see also* **TASS**

item a separate thing (as in a list)

item (Lat.) also, likewise

itemize give item by item, *not* -ise

itin. itinerary

ITN Independent Television News

ITO International Trade Organization

its possessive pronoun (no apos.)

it's it is, it has

itsy-bitsy *or* **itty-bitty**

ITU International Telecommunication Union (UN), Intensive Therapy Unit

ITV Independent Television

IU international unit

IUD intrauterine (contraceptive) device, intrauterine death (of the fetus before birth)

Iun. Lat. abbr. for **Iunius**

IUPAC International Union of Pure and Applied Chemistry

IV intravenous, (roman numeral) four (no point); *see also* **IIII**

Ivanovich, Ivan a nickname for a Russian, as in English 'John Bull'

Iveagh, Earl of

IVF *in vitro* fertilization

ivied clothed with ivy, *not* ivyed

Iviza *use* **Ib-**

Ivory Coast W. Africa

ivy pl. **ivies**

Ivybridge Devon (one word)

Ivy League a group of universities in the E. USA, usually considered to consist of Brown, Columbia, Cornell, Dartmouth, Harvard, Princeton, University of Pennsylvania, and Yale

IW Isle of Wight

IWES Institution of Water Engineers and Scientists

Iwo Jima an island in N. Pacific, taken by the US Marines 1945

IWW Industrial Workers of the World (US)

IX (roman numeral) nine (no point)

I Zingari a cricket club

İzmir Turkey, *formerly* Smyrna

Jj

J (at cards) jack, (phys.) joule, Joule's mechanical equivalent of heat, (after judge's name) justice; traditionally (and often still) not used in the numeration of series

J. Journal (in abbr. title), judge, *judex* (judge), (Ger.) *Jahr* (year)

j (med. prescriptions) one, (math.) square root of minus one

JA Judge Advocate

Jabalpur Madhya Pradesh, India; *formerly* Jubbulpore

Jac. *Jacobus* (James)

jacana a small tropical wading bird; *not* jaç-, jass-

jacaranda any tropical American tree of the genus *Jacaranda* or *Dalbergia*

jacconet *use* jaco-

jack (naut.) a small ship's flag, esp. one showing nationality; *see also* **Union Jack**

jack, every man each and every person (three words, not cap.)

jackanapes (sing.) a pert or insolent fellow (one word)

Jack and Jill *not* Gill

jackaroo (Austral. sl.) originally a newcomer (usually from England), now a novice on a sheep- or cattle-station; *not* -eroo

jackass a male ass, a stupid person

jack/boot, -daw (one word)

jacket/, -ed, -ing

Jack Frost frost personified (two caps.)

jack/fruit, -hammer (one word)

jack-in-the-box (hyphens)

Jack Ketch the hangman; *not* Ca-, Ki-

jackknife (one word)

jack of all trades (four words)

jack-o'-lantern (hyphens) *not* -a-

jack/pot, -rabbit (one word)

Jack Russell a breed of terrier (caps.)

Jackson/, Andrew, 'Old Hickory' (1767–1845) US President 1829–37, **-ian**; **—, Thomas Jonathan, 'Stonewall'** (1824–63) Confederate general at the first battle of Bull Run, 1861

jack/staff, -stone, -straw (one word)

Jack tar a sailor (one cap.)

Jacob/ean of or relating to the reign of James I of England; of St James the Less, of the apostle St James or the Epistle of St James; *see also* **Jacobi**

Jacobethan (design) displaying a combination of Elizabethan and Jacobean styles

Jacobi, Karl Gustav Jakob (1804–51) German mathematician, hence (in math.) **Jacobian, Jacobi polynomial**; *see also* **Jacobean**

Jacobin/ (hist.) a French Dominican friar, a member of a radical democratic club established in Paris in 1789, any extreme radical; **-ic, -ism**; *see also* **Jacobean**

jacobin a pigeon with reversed feathers on the back of its neck like a cowl, *not* -ine

Jacobit/e an adherent of James II of England/James VII of Scotland after his departure, or of the Stuarts; **-ical, -ism**

Jacob's/ ladder a plant, *Polemonium caeruleum*; **— staff** a surveyor's iron-shod rod

Jacobus Lat. for James, abbr. **Jac.**

jacobus a gold coin of James I

jaconet a medium cotton cloth, *not* jacc-

Jacquard/, Joseph Marie (1752–1834) French weaver, hence **— loom** (not cap.)

jacquerie any brutal peasant revolt; (cap.) that in France, 1358

Jacques/ Fr. for **James**; **— Bonhomme** James Goodfellow, a popular name for a French peasant; cf. **Robin Goodfellow**

jacta est alea (Lat.) the die is cast

jactation boasting

jactitation (med.) restless tossing of the body, (law) the offence of falsely claiming to be someone's husband or wife

jacuzzi/ (propr.) a large bath with underwater jets of water to massage the body, pl. **-s** (*properly*, and in US, cap., often used lower case)

j'adoube (Fr.) 'I adjust', said by a chess player touching, but not moving, a man

Jaeger (propr.) a woollen clothing material from which vegetable fibres are excluded (cap.)

jaeger a hunter; a seabird of the skua family; *not* ya-; *see also* **Jäger**

JAG Judge Advocate General

Jäger (Ger. m.) huntsman, rifleman

Jag/gernaut, -anath *use* **Juggernaut**

jaghire Indian land tenure; *not* -gheer, geer, -gir

Jago Cornish for **James**

Jahr/ (Ger. n.) year, pl. **-e** (*not* Jä-) abbr. **J.**; **-buch** (n.) yearbook, abbr. **Jb.**, pl. **-bücher**, abbr. **Jbb.**; **-esbericht** (m.) annual report; **-gang** (m.) year's issue, number, etc., abbr. **Jg.** (caps., one word)

jährlich (Ger. adj.) annual

Jahveh *use* **Yahweh**

jai alai (Sp.) a game like pelota

jail/, -bird, -break, -er (one word) *not now* gaol (except in hist. contexts)

Jaime Sp. for **James**

Jain (of or relating to) (an adherent of) a non-Brahmanical Indian religion

Jaipur Rajasthan, India; *see also* **Jeypore**

Jakarta Indonesia, *not* Da-, Dj-

Jakob Ger. for **Jacob**, **James**

Jakutsk Siberia, *use* **Yak-**

Jalalabad Afghanistan; Uttar Pradesh, India; *not* Jela-

Jalandhar *use* **Jullundur**

jalapeño/ a hot green chilli pepper, pl. **-s**

jalopy a dilapidated motor car, *not* -ppy

jalousie an external window shutter

Jam (hist.) (a hereditary title of) any of certain princes and noblemen in the Indian subcontinent (ital.)

jam/ pack tightly; **-med, -ming**; cf. **jamb**

Jamaica a Caribbean island, abbr. **Jam.**

jamb a side post, as of a door; cf. **jam**

jambon/ (Fr. cook. m.) ham, **-neau** a small ham

jamboree a celebration or merrymaking, a large rally of Scouts

James abbr. **Jas.**

Jamesone, George (1588–1644) Scottish painter

Jameson/ **Raid** S. Africa, 1895–6; from **Sir Leander Starr** — (1853–1917) S. African statesman

James's Day, St 25 July (caps., apos.)

Jamieson, John (1759–1838) Scottish lexicographer; *see also* **James-**

jam satis (Lat.) enough by this time

Jan. January

Janáček, Leoš (1854–1928) Czech composer

Jane Doe (US) a hypothetical average woman; *see also* **John Doe**

Jane Eyre a novel by C. Brontë, 1847

Janeite an admirer of Jane Austen's writings

Jane's yearbooks on aircraft, ships, etc. (apos.); italicize as part of title

Janglish *use* **Japl-**

janizary *not* -issary; in Turk. **yeniçeri**

Jan Mayen an Arctic island (Norw.)

Jansen/, **Cornelius** (1585–1638) RC Bishop of Ypres; **-ist** (cap.)

janséniste (Fr. m., f.) (of or relating to) a Jansenist (not cap.)

Janssen/ **Cornelius** (**Otto**) (1590–1665) Dutch painter, — **Johannes** (1829–91) German historian, — **Pierre Jules César** (1824–1907) French astronomer

Janssens, Abraham (1569–1631) Dutch painter

January abbr. **Jan.**

Janus the Roman god of doors and beginnings, depicted as having two faces

janvier (Fr. m.) January, abbr. **janv.** (not cap.)

Jap/ (colloq., usually derog.) (a) Japanese, pl. **-s** (no point)

Jap. Japan/, -ese

Japan abbr. **Jap.**, in Jap. **Nippon**

japan/ to lacquer with a hard varnish; **-ned, -ner, -ning**

Japanese/ abbr. **Jap.**; — **paper** handmade (usually in Japan), used for proofs of etchings and engravings

Japheth the third son of Noah, *not* -et

Japlish a blend of Japanese and (pseudo-)English, used in Japan, *not* Jang-

Jaques a character in Shakespeare's *As You Like It*; *not* -cq-

jar/, **-red, -ring**

Jardin/ **d'Acclimatation**, — **des Plantes** Paris, botanical and zoological gardens

jardinière an ornamental flowerpot, a dish of mixed vegetables (not ital.)

jargon words or expressions used by a particular group or profession; a translucent, colourless, or smoky variety of zircon; *not* -oon

jargonelle a pear, *not* -el (not ital.)

jarl (hist.) a Norse or Danish chieftain, *not* y-

Järnefelt, (**Edvard**) **Armas** (1869–1958) Finnish composer

Jaroslav (Russ.) *use* **Yaroslavl'** (place), **Yaroslav** (person); in Pol. **Jarosław**

jarrah an Australian mahogany gum tree

Järvefelt, Göran (1947–89) Swedish opera director

Jarvie, Bailie Nicol a character in Scott's *Rob Roy*

Jas. James

jasmine (bot.) *not* -in, jessamine, -in

jaspé mottled, veined, of materials and floor coverings (not ital.)

jassana *use* **jac-**

Jassy Ger. for **Iaşi**

Jaume Catalan for **James**

Jaunpur Uttar Pradesh, India

Jaurès, Jean Léon (1859–1914) French socialist

Javanese of or relating to Java in Indonesia, its people, or its language; *not* Javan; abbr. **Jav.**

Javelle water a bleach or disinfectant; *not* -el, -elle's

jawbone (one word)

jawohl (Ger.) yes, certainly (one word); *not* -woll

Jaycees (US) a national and international civic organization

jaywalk/, **-er, -ing** (one word)

Jb. (Ger.) *Jahrbuch* (yearbook)

JC Jesus Christ, Julius Caesar, Justice Clerk

J.-C. (Fr.) *Jésus-Christ* (hyphen)

JCB (propr.) a type of mechanical excavator

JCL (comput.) job-control language

JCR Junior Common Room, (Cambridge University) Junior Combination Room

JD Junior Deacon, Junior Dean, *Jurum Doctor* (Doctor of Laws)

je (Fr.) I (cap. only at beginning of sentence)

Jeaffreson, John Cordy (1831–1901) English historical writer

Jean (Fr.) **John**

Jeanne d'Arc (Fr.) Joan of Arc

Jean Paul pseud. of **J. P. F. Richter**

Jedda *use* **Jiddah**

jee-ho *use* **gee-**

Jeejeebhoy, Sir Jamsetjee (1783–1859) Indian philanthropist

jeep a small sturdy esp. military motor vehicle with four-wheel drive; (propr.) a similar civilian vehicle (cap.)

jee-up *use* **gee-**

Jefferies, Richard (1848–87) English naturalist

Jefferson, Thomas (1743–1826) third US President

Jefferys, Thomas (*fl.* 1732–71) English cartographer

Jeffrey, Francis, Lord (1773–1850) Scottish jurist and literary critic

Jeffreys, George, Baron (1648–89) the infamous judge

jehad *use* **ji-**

Jehlam *use* **Jhelum**

Jehovah traditional form of **Yahweh**

jejune meagre, insipid (not ital.)

Jekyll and Hyde the eponymous character in *The Strange Case of Dr Jekyll and Mr Hyde*, by R. L. Stevenson, 1886

Jelalabad, Jellalabad *use* **Jala-**

jellaba accepted spelling var. of **djellaba**

jellify convert into jelly, *not* -yfy

Jell-o (US propr.) a fruit-flavoured gelatin dessert, = **jelly**

jelly/ baby, — bean (two words)

jellyfish (one word)

Jemappes, battle of Belgium, French victory over Austrians, 1792; *not* Jemm-

jemmy a short crowbar, *not* ji- (US)

je ne sais/ quoi (Fr.) an indescribable something, — — — *trop* I don't exactly know

Jenghis Khan *use* **G-**

Jenis/esi *use* **Yeniseisk**, **-sei** *use* **Yenisei**

Jenkins's Ear an incident that precipitated war with Spain, 1739

jennet a small Spanish horse; *not* genit, gennet, -tt; cf. **genet**

Jenůfa opera by Janáček, 1904; originally *Její pastorkyňa*

jeopardize endanger, *not* -ise

Jephthah a judge of Israel; *Jephtha* an oratorio about him by Handel, 1752

jequirity an Indian shrub with ornamental and medicinal seeds, *not* -erity

Jer. Jeremiah

jerbil *use* **ger-**

jerboa any small desert rodent of the family Dipodidae, distinct from the **gerbil**

jeremiad a doleful complaint or lamentation, a list of woes; *not* -de

Jeremiah (OT) abbr. **Jer.**

Jerez Spain, Mexico (no accent); *not* Xerez, in Fr. **Xérès**

jerfalcon *use* **gyr-**

jeroboam a wine bottle of four times the ordinary size (not cap.); a king of Israel (cap.) (1 Kgs. 12–14)

Jérôme Bonaparte (1784–1860) brother of Napoleon I

jerry/-builder a builder of unsubstantial houses (hyphen); **-building, -built**

jerrycan *not* jerri-

jerrymander *use* **ge-**

Jersey/ a light brown dairy cow from Jersey; (US colloq.) New Jersey (cap.); a knitted (usually woollen) pullover or similar garment, a plain-knitted (originally woollen) fabric (not cap.); pl. **-s**

Jerusalem artichoke (one cap.)

Jervaulx Abbey N. Yorks.

Jes. Jesus

Jespersen, Jens Otto Harry (1860–1943) Danish philologist, *not* -son

jessamin/, -e *use* **jasmine**

Jesse the father of David (OT)

Jesuits, Order of *Societas Jesu* (Society of Jesus), abbr. **SJ**

Jesus abbr. **Jes.**, in vocative (arch.) **Jesu**

jet black (two words, hyphen when attrib.)

jeté (ballet) a spring or leap with one leg forward and the other stretched backwards (not ital.)

jet/ engine, — lag (two words)

jet-propelled (hyphen)

jet propulsion (two words)

jetsam (naut.) goods thrown overboard; *not* -som, -some, -son; *see also* **flotsam and jetsam**

jet/ set (two words), **-setter** (hyphen)

jet stream (two words)

jeu/ (Fr. m.) game, pl. **-x**; — *de mots* a play on words; — *de paume* real tennis (court); **Musée du Jeu de Paume** (caps.) Paris; — *d'esprit* a witty (usually literary) trifle

jeune fille (Fr. f.) a girl

jeune/ premier (Fr.) a stage lover, f. — *première*

jeunesse dorée (Fr. f.) gilded youth

Jewel, John (1522–71) English bishop

jewel/, -led, -ler, -lery (one *l* in US)

jew's harp a small lyre-shaped instrument played against the teeth (initial cap. in US)

Jeypore Orissa, India; *see also* **Jaipur**

Jezebel a shameless or immoral woman (cap.)

Jg. (Ger.) *Jahrgang* (year's issues etc.)

Jhelum Pakistan, *not* Jehlam

Jhind *use* **Jind**

JHS *use* **IHS**

-ji in India, an honorific suffix attached to names, e.g. *guruji*

jiao a monetary unit of China, pl. same

jib of horse, also a sail; *not* -bb

jibba a Muslim man's long coat; *not* dj-, -bah

jibber *use* **g-**

jibe (US) agree, be in accord (usually followed by *with*); cf. **gibe**; **gybe**

Jibuti *use* **Djibouti**

JIC Joint Industrial Council

Jiddah Saudi Arabia, *not* Jedda

jiffy a short time, *not* -ey

jigger *use* **chigoe**

jigot *use* **gi-**

jigsaw/ (one word), **— puzzle** (two words)

jihad a holy war undertaken by Muslims against unbelievers, *not* je-; in Arab. **jihād**

Jilin Chinese province (Pinyin), in Wade–Giles **Kirin**

jillaroo (Austral. sl.) female station hand, *not* -eroo

jilliflower *use* **gilly-**

jimcrack *use* **g-**

Jim Crow/ (US) the practice of segregating blacks, **-ism**; (offens.) a black person; an implement for straightening iron bars or bending rails by screw pressure

Jiménez, Juan Ramón (1881–1958) Spanish poet

jimmy (US) = **jemmy** (crowbar)

Jind a town and former state, India; *not* Jh-

Jingis Khan *use* **Ge-**

jingo/ in declaration '**by —!**'; a fanatical patriot, pl. **-es**; **-ism**, **-istic**

jinnee (Muslim myth.) *not* djinn, ginn; pl. **jinn**; in Arab. **jinnī**, pl. **jinn**; *see also* **genie**

jinricksha *use* **rickshaw**

JIT, JiT *see* **Just in Time**

jiu-jitsu *use* **ju-**

JJ Justices

Jno. John, but use only in exact reprints of documents etc.

jnr. junior

JO *Journal Officiel*

Joan Catalan for **John**

joannes *use* **johan-**

Joan of Arc (1412–31) French national heroine, in Fr. **Jeanne d'Arc**

João Port. for **John**

jobcentre (Brit.) government offices displaying information about available jobs (one word)

job lot (two words)

job/sheet, -work (one word)

'Jock o' Hazeldean' a ballad mainly by Scott

jockstrap (one word)

jodel *use* **y-**

Jodhpur Rajasthan, India

jodhpurs riding breeches, *not* jhod-

Joe Blow (US colloq.) a hypothetical average man, = **Joe Bloggs**; *see also* **John Doe**

Joel (OT) not to be abbr.

johannes a gold coin of John V of Portugal, *not* joa-

Johannesburg S. Africa

Johannine of the apostle John, *not* -ean

Johannisberg Hesse, Germany

Johannisberger a Rhine wine, *not* -berg (not ital.)

John abbr. **J.**; *see also* **Jno.**; (NT) not to be abbr.

John Doe (US) a hypothetical average man, = **Joe Bloggs**; an anonymous man; *see also* **Jane Doe**

John Dory a fish, *not* -ey; also **dory**

Johnian (a member) of St John's College, Cambridge

johnny a fellow, man (not cap.)

John o' Groat's (**House**) a Highland site; the possessive apostrophe is often omitted

Johns Hopkins/ University, — — Medical Center Baltimore, Md.; *not* John (no apos.)

Johnson/, Lyndon Baines (1908–73) President of USA 1963–9, abbr. **LBJ** (no points); **—, Samuel** (1709–84) English prose-writer and lexicographer, **-ian**; *see also* **Jonson**

Johnsonese a florid style, *not* Jon-

John the Baptist (caps.)

Johore *see* **Malaya, Federation of**

joie de vivre (Fr.) joy of living (no hyphens)

joint/ capital, — stock etc. (hyphen when attrib.)

Jökulsárgljúfur (lit. 'Glacier River Gulch') **National Park** Iceland

jolie/ laide (Fr. f.) a fascinatingly ugly woman, pl. **-s laides**

Jon. Jonathan

Jonah, Book of (OT) not to be abbr.

Joneses/ as in 'keeping up with the —'; *not* Jones', -s's

jongleur (hist.) an itinerant minstrel (ital.)

jonquil a narcissus (not ital.)

Jonson, Benjamin ('**Ben**') (1572–1637) English playwright; *see also* **Johnson**

Joppa ancient name of **Jaffa**, Israel

Jordaens, Jakob (1593–1678) Dutch painter

Jordan/ adj. **-ian**

Jorrocks' Jaunts by R. S. Surtees, 1831–4

Jos. Joseph

Josephine, the Empress b. **Marie Josèphe-Rose Tascher de la Pagerie**, (1763–1814) widow of Viscount Beauharnais, married Napoleon I 1796, divorced 1809

Josh. Joshua (OT)

Josquin/ **des Prez**, b. — **Lebloitte** (d. 1521) Franco-Flemish composer and musician; the shortened form is 'Josquin', *not* 'des Prez'; *not* Prés

jostl/e push; **-er, -ing**

jot/, **-ted, -ting**

joule (phys.) an SI unit of energy, abbr. **J**

jour. journal, journey

jour/ (Fr. m.) day, abbr. **jr.**; — *de fête* a festival; — *de l'an* New Year's Day; — *des morts* All Souls' Day, 2 Nov.; — *gras* flesh day; — *maigre* fish day

journal abbr. **jour.**, **J.** (in abbr. title)

journ/*al* (Fr. m.) newspaper, pl. **-aux**; — *intime* a private diary

Journal officiel the French and EU daily publications of legislation, abbr. **JO**

Journals, the a record of daily proceedings in Parliament (cap.)

journey abbr. **jour.**

joust a knightly combat, *not* just

Jovian of or like the god or planet Jupiter

jowar a kind of sorghum = **durra**, in Hindi **jawār**

Joycean of or characteristic of **James** (**Augustine Aloysius**) **Joyce** (1882–1941) Irish novelist and poet, or his writings; a specialist in or admirer of Joyce's works

joy/ful, -ride, -stick (one word)

JP Justice of the Peace

JR *Jacobus Rex* (King James)

Jr. junior

jr. (Fr.) *jour* (day)

jt. joint

Juan Sp. for John

Juárez, Benito Pablo (1806–72) Mexican President 1861–5, 1867–72

Jubbulpore *use* **Jabalpur**

Jubilate Deo Ps. 100 as canticle (99 in Vulg.)

jud. judicial

Judaean of Judaea, *not* -ean

Judaeo- Jew(ish), *not* Judeo- (US)

Judaize follow Jewish customs or rites, make Jewish; *not* -ise

Judg. Judges (OT)

Judge/ abbr. **J.**; — **Advocate** (no hyphen), abbr. **JA**; — **Advocate General** (no hyphen), abbr. **JAG** (caps.)

judgement/, **-al** a moral, practical, or informal deduction *but* **judgment**/, **-al** (law) a judge's or court's formal ruling; and in US in all contexts

Judgement Day, Last Judgement (caps.)

Judges (OT) abbr. **Judg.**

judicial abbr. **jud.**

Judith (Apocr.) not to be abbr.

judo/ a form of ju-jitsu, **-ist**

jug/, **-ged, -ging, -ful**

juge/ *d'instance* (Fr. m.) a legally trained justice of the peace, *formerly* — *de paix*; — *d'instruction* examining magistrate

Jugendstil (Ger.) art nouveau (ital., cap.)

Juggernaut an institution or notion to which persons blindly sacrifice themselves or others (cap.); *not* Ja-; in Hindi **Jagannath**; (Brit.) a large heavy motorized vehicle (not cap.)

Jugoslav/, **-ia** *use* Y-

juillet (Fr. m.) July (not cap.)

Juilliard/ **Quartet**, — **School of Music** New York City

juin (Fr. m.) June (not cap.)

ju-jitsu a Japanese system of unarmed combat and physical training; *not* jiu-, -jutsu; in Japanese *jūjutsu*; *see also* **judo**

ju-ju a charm or fetish of some W. African peoples, or its supernatural power (hyphen)

jukebox (one word)

julep a medicated drink; (US) a drink of spirits, sugar, ice, and mint; *not* -ap, -eb

Julian/ (331–63) Emperor of Rome, 'the Apostate'; — **Alps** Italy–Slovenia; — **calendar**

Julien, Saint- a claret (hyphen)

julienne (not ital.)

Juliet cap (two words, one cap.)

Jullundur India, *not* Jalandhar

July not to be abbr.

jumble sale (two words)

jumbo/ pl. **-s**; — **jet** (two words)

jumelles (Fr. f. pl.) opera glasses

jump rope (US) = **skipping rope**

jumpsuit (one word)

Jun. Junius, as Latin month *use* **Iun.**

jun. junior

junction abbr. **junc.**

June not to be abbr.

Juneau Alaska

Jung/, **Carl Gustav** (1875–1961) Swiss psychologist, **-ian**

junior abbr. **Jr.**, **jun.**; *not* jnr., jr., junr. Use **Jr.** when it forms part of the bearer's name: 'J.

Doe, Jr.'; the comma preceding it is sometimes left out: follow the bearer's preference, if known. Use **jun.** where it is an ad hoc designation (like *fils*); here a comma always precedes it: 'J. Doe, jun.'

Junker (Ger. m.) a young squire or noble, a member of an exclusive (Prussian) aristocratic party (cap.)

junket/, -ed, -ing

junk food (two words)

junkie a drug addict

junk/ mail, — shop (two words)

junky of or like junk

junkyard (US) = **scrapyard**

Juno (Rom. myth.) wife of Jupiter, = **Hera**

junr. junior; *see* **junior**

junta a political or military clique; a council in Spain, Portugal, or S. America (not ital.)

Junto the Whig chiefs in reigns of William and Anne

jupe (Fr. f.), **jupon** (m.) a skirt or petticoat

jural of law, of rights and obligations

Jurassic (of or relating to) the second period of the Mesozoic era (cap., not ital.)

jure/ divino (Lat.) by divine right, — **humano** by human law

jurisp. jurisprudence

Juris utriusque Doctor (Lat.) Doctor of both civil and canon law, abbr. **JUD**

jury box (two words)

jury/man, -woman (one word)

jury-rigged (hyphen)

jus (Fr. cook. m.) natural juices from cooking

jus/ (Lat.) law, — **canonicum** canon law, — **civile** civil law, — **divinum** divine law, — **gentium** law of nations, — **gladii** the right of the sword

jusjurandum (Lat.) an oath, pl. **jurajuranda**

jus/ mariti (Lat.) right of husband to wife's property, — **naturae** law of nature, — **primae**

noctis droit de seigneur, — **relictae** right of the widow

Jussieu,/ Adrien de (1797–1853) and his father — **Antoine Laurent de** (1748–1836) French botanists

Just. Justinian

just a knightly combat, *use* **jou-**

juste milieu (Fr. m.) the golden mean

Justice a judge; abbr. **J**, pl. **JJ**; outside court the form of address or reference to a Supreme Court judge is **Mr**, *or* **Mrs**, **Justice**, followed by the surname

Justice Clerk, Lord the second highest Scottish judge (caps.), abbr. **JC**

Justice General, Lord the highest Scottish judge (caps.)

Justice of the Peace abbr. **JP**

justiciar/, -y a judge; *not* -er, -itiar (not ital.)

Justiciary, High Court of the supreme Scottish criminal court

justify (print.) put equal spaces between the words in a line of type so that they range on the measure; *see also* **full/ left, — right, — out**; **ragged left/, — right**

Justinian (483–565) Roman Emperor of the East, codified Roman law; abbr. **Just.**

Just in Time a Japanese manufacturing strategy designed to minimize stockpiling raw materials or finished product, in Jap. **kanban**; abbr. **JIT, JiT**

justitiar *use* **-ciar**

jut/, -ted, -ting

Juvenal (in Lat., **Decimus Junius Juvenalis**) (*c.*60–140) Roman poet, abbr. **Juv.**

juvenescen/ce, -t (the process of) passing from infancy to youth

juvenilia (pl.) works produced in one's youth (not ital.)

Jylland (Dan.) Jutland

j'y suis, j'y reste (Fr.) here I am, here I stay

K *kalium* (potassium), Kelvin (temperature scale), kelvin (unit of temperature), (chess) king (no point), the tenth in a series, thousand (*prefer* **k**)

K. (assaying) carat, king(s), King('s), Köchel (Mozart thematic catalogue number); *see also* **Kp.**

k (as prefix) kilo-, thousand; *see also* **kilo-**

k. (meteor.) cumulus

k (phys.) Boltzmann constant

K2 the second highest mountain in the world, in Karakoram Mountains

Kaaba the most sacred shrine at Mecca, in Arab. *al-Ka'bah*; *not* Caaba

kaan *use* **khan**

kabbala *use* **c-**

kabuki a popular traditional Japanese drama with highly stylized song

Kabul Afghanistan, *not* C-

kabushiki kaisha (Jap.) = public limited company, abbr. **KK**

Kádár, János (1912–89) Hungarian politician, Prime Minister 1956–8, 1961–5

kadi *use* **c-**

Kaffeeklatsch (Ger. m.) an informal gathering for coffee and conversation (not cap. or ital. in US)

Kaffir *use* **Xhosa**; (S. Afric. offens.) any black African; *not* Caffre, Kafir

kaffiyeh *use* **ke-**

Kaffraria S. Africa

Kafir a native of the Hindu Kush mountains of NE Afghanistan; *not* Caffre, Kaffir

kāfir (Arab.) infidel

Kafka/, Franz (1883–1924) Czech-born Austrian novelist and poet, **-esque**

kaftan long, belted garment worn in the Near East; *not* **c-**

kagoule *use* **c-**

Kahn-Freud, Sir Otto (1900–79) German-born English lawyer and scholar

kail Scots for **kale**

kaiman *use* **cay-**

Kainozoic *use* **Ceno-**

Kaisar-i-Hind/ (Anglo-Ind.) (the Caesar of India) former Indian title of the English monarch; *not* Q-, -er-; **— medal**, abbr. **K.i.H., KIH**

Kaiser (Ger. m.) emperor (cap., not ital.)

kal. *kalendae*

kala-azar a tropical disease (hyphen)

Kalamazoo Mich.

kalarippayat an Indian martial art (ital.)

Kalashnikov any of various Russian automatic rifles, esp. the AK-47

kale the cabbage genus; *see also* **kail**; **kaleyard**

kalendae (Lat.) the calends (first day of the month), not *c-*; abbr. *kal.*

kalend/ar, -er, -s *use* **c-**

Kalevala the national epic of Finland, *not* -wala

kaleyard/ (Sc.) a kitchen garden, **kail-** in strict Scots; **— school** a group of 19th-c. fiction writers including J. M. Barrie, who described local town life in Scotland; *not* kailyard school

kali/f, -ph more learned forms of **caliph**, in Arab. *ḳalīfa*

Kalimantan Indonesian name for part of Borneo

Kaliningrad Russia, *formerly* Königsberg

kalium (Lat.) potassium, symbol **K**

kalmia (bot.) American evergreen shrub, *not* c-

Kalmyck a member of a Buddhist Mongolian people, their Ural-Altaic language; of this people; *not* -muck, -muk, C-

Kama the Hindu god of love (cap.)

kamarband *use* **cummerbund**

Kamboja *use* **Cambodia**

Kamchatka E. Siberia; *not* Kams-, -mtchatka, -mtschatka

Kamerun *use* **Cameroon**

kamikaze (the pilot of) a Japanese suicide aircraft (not ital.)

Kampuchea off. name of **Cambodia** 1975–89

kamsin *use* **kh-**

Kan. Kansas (off. abbr.)

kana any of various Japanese syllabaries

kanaka a South Sea Islander, esp. an indentured labourer; *not* canaker

Kanar/a a district of W. India, *not* C-; **-ese** a member of a Dravidian people in this area, their language; *see also* **Kannada**

kanaster *use* **c-**

Kanchenjunga a mountain in Himalayas, *not* Kinchin-

Kandahar Afghanistan, *not* C-

Kandy Sri Lanka

Kannada the Kanarese language written in the Kannada alphabet

Kanpur Uttar Pradesh, India; *not* Cawnpore

Kans/as off. abbr. **Kan.**, postal **KS**; **-an**

Kansas City Mo., Kan.

Kant, Immanuel (1724–1804) German philosopher

KANU Kenya African National Union

kaolin a fine white clay

kaon (phys.) a meson having a mass several times that of a pion, *not* K-meson

Kap. (Ger.) *Kapitel* (chapter)

kapellmeister a director of orchestra or choir (not cap., not ital.)

kappa the tenth letter of the Gr. alphabet (*K*, κ)

Kapurthala E. Punjab, India

kaput (sl.) broken, ruined (not ital.); from Ger. *kaputt*

karabiner a mountaineer's coupling link with a safety closure, *not* ca- (US)

Karachi Pakistan, *not* Kurrachee

Karafuto *use* **Sakhalin**

Karaite a member of Jewish sect that interprets scriptures literally

Karajan, Herbert von (1908–89) Austrian conductor

Karakoram Mountains Kashmir, *not* -um

karakul (fur of) Asian sheep; *not* c-, -cul

karaoke a form of entertainment in which people sing popular songs against a pre-recorded backing, *not* kari- (not ital.)

karat *use* **c-** (except in US as a measure of gold purity)

karate/ the Japanese art of unarmed combat, **-ka** an expert in this (one word)

kari *use* **karri**

Karl-Marx-Stadt the former name of **Chemnitz** during E. German sovereignty (hyphens)

Karlovingian *use* **Carolin-**

Karlovy Vary Czech Republic (no accent); *not* Carlsbad (except in historical contexts), Karlsbad

Karlsbad *use* **Karlovy Vary**

Karls/krona (Sweden) **-ruhe** (Germany) etc., *not* C-

karma (Buddhism) destiny (not ital.)

Kármán, Theodor von (1881–1963) Hungarian-born US physicist

Karnatic *use* **C-**

Kärnten (Ger.) **Carinthia**, Austria and Slovenia

Karoo a high pastoral plateau in S. Africa, *not* Karr- (cap.)

karoshi in Japan, death through overwork; in Jap. *karōshi*

Karpathian Mountains *use* **C-**

karri an Australian blue gum tree, *not* kari; *see also* **kauri**

Kartoum *use* **Kh-**

kasbah the citadel of a N. African city, or an Arab quarter near this; *not* c-

Kashmir/ NW India, *not* Cashmer(e); **-i** (of or relating to) (a native or the Dardic language of) Kashmir

Kassel Germany, *not* C-

kataboli/sm, -c *use* **c-**

katakana an angular form of Japanese kana

katana a long samurai sword

katharevousa *also* **katharévusa** (not cap.) a form of Greek favoured for official, learned, and technical writing (but not literature) before 1976, then combined with demotic to form Modern Greek

Katharina a character in Shakespeare's *The Taming of the Shrew*

Katharine/ characters in Shakespeare's *Love's Labour's Lost, Henry V*, and (**— of Aragon**) in *Henry VIII*; *see also* **Catherine**

Kathāsaritsāgara a Sanskrit epic

Kathay *use* **C-**

Katherine *see* **C-**; **Katharine**

kathism/a a section of the Greek Psalter, pl. **-ata**; *not* ca-

Kathmandu capital of Nepal, *not* Katm-

kathode *use* **c-**

kation *use* **c-**

Kattegat (Dan.), **Kattegatt** (Swed.) the strait between Denmark and Sweden, *not* C-

Kauffmann, Angelica (1741–1807) Swiss-born English painter

Kaufman, George Simon (1889–1961) US playwright

Kaunas Lithuania, *not* Kovno

kauri New Zealand coniferous tree etc., *not* the many variants (not ital.); cf. **cowrie**; **karri**

Kavafis *use* **Cavafy** in Eng. use

kavass a Turkish armed attendant, *not* the many variants

Kawabata, Yasunari (1899–1972) Japanese novelist

kayak/ an Eskimo canoe, *not* the many variants; **-er, -ing**

Kaye-Smith, Sheila (1889–1955) English novelist (hyphen)

Kazakhstan a former Soviet Socialist Republic; adj. **Kazakh**

Kazan' Russia (prime accent), *not* Kas-

Kazantzakis, Nikos (1885–1957) Greek writer

KB (chess) king's bishop (no points), King's Bench, Knight Bachelor, Knight of the Order of the Bath

KBD King's Bench Division

KBE Knight Commander of the Order of the British Empire

kbit kilobit

KBP (chess) king's bishop's pawn (no points)

kbyte kilobyte

KC King's College, King's Counsel

kc kilocycle; *see also* **kc/s**

KCB Knight Commander of the Order of the Bath

KCIE Knight Commander of the Order of the Indian Empire

KCL King's College London

KCMG Knight Commander of the Order of St Michael and St George

kc/s *prefer* **kHz**

kčs koruna (Czechoslovakia), since 1993 commonly abbr. **kč** (Czech Republic) and **ks** (Slovakia)

KCSI Knight Commander of the Order of the Star of India

KCVO Knight Commander of the Royal Victorian Order

KD knocked down

KE kinetic energy

Keats House Hampstead (no apos.)

Keäwe a character in R. L. Stevenson's *The Bottle Imp*

kebab *not* the many variants, *not* **kabob** (US)

keblah *use* **ki-**

Kedah *see* **Malaya, Federation of**

kedgeree *not* the many variants (not ital.)

Kedron *see* **Kidron**

Keele Staffs.

keelhaul a naval punishment (one word)

keelson (naut.) a line of timber fastening a ship's floor-timbers to its keel, *not* kelson

keepsake (one word)

keep standing (typ.) keep type or film stored in page from after first printing for possible reprint, abbr. **KS**

Kees, Weldon (1914–55) US poet and author

keeshond/ a Dutch breed of dog, pl. **-en**

kef a drowsy state induced by marijuana etc., the substance smoked to produce this state; the enjoyment of idleness; *not* kif (not ital.)

keffiyeh a Bedouin Arab headdress; in Arab. *keffiyya*, *kūfiyya*

kefir (Russ.) a drink of fermented cow's milk

Kelantan *see* **Malaya, Federation of**

kell/eck, -ick (naut.) *use* **killick**

Kellner/ (Ger.) f. **-in** waiter (cap.)

Kellogg College Oxford, *formerly* Rewley House

Kellogg Pact Paris 1928, fifteen leading nations renounced war

Kelly's Directories (apos.)

Kelmscott Press 1891–8, founded by W. Morris

kelpie a water spirit, *not* -y

kelson *use* **keel-**

Kelt/, -ic, -icism *use* **C-**

kelter *use* **ki-**

kelvin (sci.) symbol **K** (no point); *see also* **Thomson**

Kemal, Mustafa *see* **Atatürk**

Kempis, Thomas à (1379–1471) German monk, reputed author of *Imitatio Christi*

kendo the Japanese art of fencing with bamboo swords

Kenmare Co. Kerry

Kenmore Highland, Tayside

kennel/, -led, -ling (one *l* in US)

Kenney, James (1780–1849) Irish playwright

kentle *use* **quintal**

Kents Bank Cumbria (no apos.)

Kentucky off. abbr. **Ky.**, postal **KY**

Kenwigs a family in Dickens's *Nicholas Nickleby*

Kenya/ E. Africa; **-n**

Kenyatta, Jomo (1893–1978) Kenyan statesman

kephalic *use* **c-**

kepi (no accent, not ital.) Anglicized form of Fr. m. *képi* military cap

Kepler/, Johann (1571–1630) German astronomer, *not* Kepp-; **-ian**

keramic etc., *use* **c-**

kerb/, -side, -stone (one word); cf. **curb**

Kerch Crimea, *not* Kertch

kerfuffle disorder, fuss; *not* cur-, ge-, kur-

Kerguelen Island Indian Ocean

keris *see* **kris**

Kerkyra Modern Gr. name of **Corfu**

kermis *not* -ess, kirmess

kern/ (typ.) modify spacing between characters to allow for each letter's shape, **-ed**; (hist.) a light-armed Irish foot-soldier; *not* kerne

kernel/ a seed within a hard shell; **-led, -ly**

Kernow Cornish for Cornwall

keros/ene paraffin oil; *also* **-ine** (except in US)

Kerouac, Jack (1922–69) US novelist

kerseymere twilled woollen cloth, *not* cassi-; cf. **cashmere**

Kertch *use* **Kerch**

keskidee *use* **kiska-**

ketch (naut.) a two-masted vessel

Ketch, Jack the hangman; not Ca-, Ki-

ketchup *not* cat-, catsup

kettledrum (one word)

Keuper (geol.) the upper division of the Trias

keV kilo-electronvolt

key a wharf, *use* **quay**

keyboard/ (comput., mus., etc.) (one word); **-er** one who uses a computer keyboard, **-ist** one who plays a keyboard musical instrument

key-bugle (hyphen)

keyhole (one word)

Keynes/, John Maynard, Baron (1883–1946) British economist; **-ian** (adj.) of Keynes's economic theories; (noun) an adherent of these theories; **-ianism**

key/note, -pad, -punch, -ring (one word)

Keys, House of IoM (caps.), abbr. **HK**

key signature (mus.) (two words)

key/stone, -stroke, -way (one word)

Key West Fla. (two words)

keyword (one word)

KG Knight of the Order of the Garter, (Ger.) *Kommanditgesellschaft* (limited partnership)

kg kilogram(s) (no point)

KGB USSR state secret police, 'Committee of State Security' 1953–92; earlier post-revolution manifestations: **Cheka** 1917–22, **GPU** 1922–3, **OGPU** 1923–34, **NKVD** 1934–43, **NKGB** 1943–6, **MGB** 1946–53, **MVD** 1953–60; *see also* **FSB**

Kgotla an assembly of Bantu elders, the place for this; *not* kotla

Kgs., 1, 2 First, Second Book of Kings

Khachaturyan, Aram (**Ilich**) (1903–78) Armenian composer

khaddar an Indian homespun cloth

Khaibar Oasis Saudi Arabia

Khaiber Pass *use* **Khyber**

khaki (not ital.)

khal/eefate, -ifat *use* **caliphate**

khalif/, -a *use* **caliph**

khamsin an Egyptian hot wind in March, April, and May; *not* ha-, ka-, -seen

khan/ a title given to rulers and officials in Cent. Asia, Afghanistan, etc.; (hist.) the supreme ruler of the Turkish, Tartar, and Mongol tribes, *or* the emperor of China in the Middle Ages; **-ate**; **-um** a lady of high rank; a polite form of address affixed to a Muslim woman's name

khan an inn in an Eastern town or village, *not* kaan; *see also* **caravanserai**

Khan, Muhammad Ayub *see* **Ayub Khan, Muhammad**

Khanty (of or relating to) (a member of) a people living in the Ob River basin in W. Siberia, or (of) the Ob-Ugrian language of this people; *formerly* Ostyak

kharaj (Turk.) a tax on Christians; not *-ach, -age, caratch*

Kharoshthi one of the two oldest alphabets in the Indian subcontinent; cf. **Brahmi**

Khartoum capital of Sudan; *not* Ka-, -tum

Khaskura the Nepali language

Khayyám, Omar *see* **Omar Khayyám**

Khediv/e a viceroy of Egypt under Turkish rule 1867–1914; **-a** his wife; **-ate** his office; **-al** *not* -ial

khidmutgar (Ind.) a male waiter (*not* the many variants)

Khmer/ (of) a native of the ancient Khmer kingdom or of modern Cambodia, *or* (of) their language; **— Republic** name of Cambodia 1970–5; **— Rouge** Cambodian communists

Khoikhoi a S. African people (pl. same), *formerly* called Hottentot; their language is **Nama**

Khomeini, Ayatollah Ruhollah (1908–89) Iranian religious and political leader, head of state 1979–89

Khrushchev, Nikita (**Sergeevich**) (1894–1971) Soviet politician, Secretary-General of the Communist Party 1953–64, Prime Minister 1958–64

Khyber Pass NW Frontier Province, Pakistan; *not* Khai-

kHz kilohertz, 1,000 hertz (no point, cap. H); *not* kc/s

kiak *use* **kayak**

kiang a wild Tibetan ass

kibbutz/ an Israeli communal agricultural (etc.) settlement, pl. **-im**; **-nik** a member of it

kibitz/ look on at cards, be meddlesome; **-er** one who does this; *not* -bb-

kiblah the direction of the Kaaba, to which Muslims turn in prayer; a niche or slab in a mosque showing this direction (= **mihrab**); *not* ke-; in Arab. **ḳibla, qibla**

kibosh/ nonsense, *not* ky-; **put the — on** put an end to, finish

kickback a recoil, a payment for collaboration (one word)

kick-off (noun, football) (hyphen, one word in US)

kick/shaw, -sorter, -stand (one word)

kick-start (noun and verb) (hyphen)

kiddie (colloq.) a young child, *not* -y

kidmutgar *use* **khid-**

kidnap/, -ped, -per, -ping

kidney bean (two words)

Kidron (*or* **Ce-**) Palestine, **Ke-** in NEB; in Arab. **Wadi en Nar**

Kierkegaard, Søren (**Aabye**) (1813–55) Danish philosopher

Kiev capital of Ukraine, *not* -eff; **Kyiv, Kyjiw** are alt. Ukrainian forms

kif *use* **kef**

K.i.H. (*or* **KIH**) Kaisar-i-Hind medal

Kikuyu (of) the largest Bantu-speaking group in Kenya, or their language; pl. same

kil. kilderkin(s)

Kilauea a volcano in Hawaii, *not* -aua

Kilbracken, Baron (1847–1932) Sir Arthur Godley, of the India Office

kilderkin/ a cask for liquids etc., holding 16 or 18 gallons; pl. **-s**; abbr. **kil.**

Kilimanjaro extinct volcano, E. Africa (one word, divide Kilima-njaro)

Killala Co. Mayo, also Bishop of

Killaloe Co. Clare, also Bishop of

Killaloo Co. Londonderry

Killea Co. Donegal

Killeagh Co. Cork

Killen Highland

Killianwala *use* **Chili-**

killick a stone used as anchor; *not* -ock, kelleck, -ick

Killiecrankie Tayside

Killin Central

Killylea Co. Armagh

Killyleagh Co. Down

'Kilmansegg, Miss' a poem by T. Hood, 1828; *not* -eg

kilo/ shortened form of kilogram or kilometre (no point), pl. **-s**

kilo- usually indicates 1,000 (10^3) times a unit of measurement, e.g. *kilometre, kilowatt*, but in computing it indicates a multiple of 1,024 (2^{10}), e.g. *kilobit, kilobyte*; abbr. **k**, *not* K

kilobit (comput.) 1,024 (2^{10}) bits, abbr. **kbit**

kilobyte (comput.) 1,024 (2^{10}) bytes, as a measure of memory size; abbr. **kbyte**

kilocycle a former measure of frequency = 1 kilohertz, abbr. **kc**; *but use* **kHz** for **kc/s**

kilogram an SI unit of mass, *not* -me; abbr. **kg** (no point)

kilojoule 1,000 joules, esp. as a measure of the energy value of foods; abbr. **kJ**

kilolitre 1,000 litres, abbr. **kl** (no point); *not* -er (except in US)

kilometre/ 1,000 metres, *not* -er (except in US); **-age** *not* -rage; abbr. **km** (no point)

kiloton a unit of explosive power equivalent to 1,000 tons of TNT, *not* -tonne; abbr. **kT**

kilowatt/ 1,000 watts, abbr. **kW**; **-hour** (hyphen) abbr. **kWh**

kilter/ good condition, alignment (usually used in the phrase **out of —**); *not* ke-

Kimeridgian (geol.) (*not* -mm-) an Upper Jurassic clay found at Kimmeridge, Dorset (cap.)

Kim/ Il Sung (1912–94) Prime Minister and President of N. Korea 1948–94, father of — **Jong Il** (b. 1942) President of N. Korea 1994–

kimono/ a kind of gown, pl. **-s**

Kimric Welsh, *use* **Cym-**

kinaesthesia the sense of muscular effort, *not* kine (US)

Kincardine(shire) a former county of Scotland

Kincardine O'Neil Grampian (three caps.)

Kinchinjunga *use* **Kanchen-**

kindergarten/ a school for young children (not ital., not cap.), **-er** a student (*formerly* the teacher)

kinesthesia *use* **kinae-** (except in US)

kinfolk *use* **kins-** (except in US)

King/ abbr. **K.** (in chess, no point); (typ.) print as e.g. Edward VII, *or* the Seventh, *not* the VII,

VIIth; — **Charles's head** an obsession; — **Charles spaniel** (two caps.), *not* -s's

kingd. kingdom

kingmaker (one word)

King of Arms (her.) a chief herald, at the College of Arms: **Garter, Clarenceux**, and **Norroy and Ulster**; in Scotland: **Lyon** (three words); *not* King at Arms

kingpin (one word)

King's abbr. **K.**

Kings, First, Second Book of (OT) abbr. **1 Kgs., 2 Kgs.**

Kingsale, Baron *see also* **Kinsale**

King's Bench (apos.) abbr. **KB**

Kingsbridge Devon, Som. (one word)

King's/ College London (no comma) abbr. **KCL**; — **Counsel** abbr. **KC**; — **Cross** London and Sydney (apos.)

king-size(d) (hyphen)

King's/ Langley Herts., — **Lynn** Norfolk (apos.)

Kings Norton/ Leics., **Baron —** (no apos.)

King's Printer *see* **printer**

Kings Sutton Oxon.

Kingsteignton Devon (one word)

Kingston Australia, Canada, Jamaica, USA

Kingstone Hereford, Som., Staffs., S. Yorks.

Kingston/ upon Hull Humberside, — **upon Thames** London (no hyphens)

Kingstown Dublin, off. **Dun Laoghaire**

Kingswinford W. Midlands (one word)

Kington Glos., Worcs.

Kinloss, Baroness

Kinnoull, Earl of

Kinross/, Baron, -shire a former county in Scotland (hyphen)

Kinsale Co. Cork; *see also* **Kingsale**

kinsfolk *not* kinfolk (US)

Kinshasa the capital of the Democratic Republic of Congo (Zaire)

kintle *use* **quintal**

Kintyre Strathclyde, *not* Cantire

Kioto Japan, *use* **Kyoto**

kip the basic monetary unit of Laos, *properly* **New —**

Kirchhoff, Gustav Robert (1824–87) German physicist

Kirghiz/ *use* **Kyrgyz**; **-ia** a former Soviet Socialist Republic, *now* **Kyrgyzstan**

Kiribati W. Pacific; adj. same

kirk/ a church (not cap.), **the — of Scotland** the Church of Scotland (cap.)

Kirkby in Ashfield Notts. (three words)

Kirkbymoorside N. Yorks. (one word)

Kirkcaldy Fife

Kirkcudbright Dumfries & Galloway

Kirkpatrick, Ralph (1911–84) US harpsichordist, compiler of catalogue of Domenico Scarlatti's keyboard works; catalogue abbr. usually **K.**

kirmess *use* **kermis**

kirschwasser a cherry liqueur, *not* kirschen-

Kishinev *use* **Chişinău**

kiskadee a tyrant flycatcher, *not* keski-

kissogram (not cap.) *but* **Kissagram** (propr.)

kist *use* c-

Kiswahili one of the six languages preferred for use in Africa by the Organization for African Unity

kitbag (one word)

kit-cat a portrait 36 × 28 in., like those painted of members of the Kit-Cat Club in the reign of James II

Kitch, Jack *use* Ke-

kitchen garden/, -er, -ing (two words)

kitchen-sink (in art forms) depicting extreme realism (e.g. '— school of painting', '— drama') (hyphen)

Kitemark the official kite-shaped mark on goods approved by the British Standards Institution (cap.)

kitmutgar **use** *khid-*

kitsch *not* -itch

Kit's Coty House Aylesford, Kent, a dolmen; *not* Coity, Cotty

Kitzbühel Austria

KK (Jap.) *kabushiki kaisha* (public limited company)

KKK Ku Klux Klan

KKt (chess) king's knight (no points)

KKtP (chess) king's knight's pawn (no points)

Klang (Ger. m.) quality of musical sound

klaxon a horn or warning hooter (not cap.)

Kleenex (cap., propr.)

kleistogam/ic, -ous *use* c-

Klemperer, Otto (1885–1973) German conductor

klepht a member of the original body of Greeks who refused to submit to the Turks in the 15th c., their descendants (not cap.)

klepsydra *use* c-

kleptomania an irresistible tendency to theft, *not* c-

klieg light an arc light used in making motion pictures (not cap.)

klinometer *use* c-

Klischograph (typ., propr.) an electronic photoengraving machine

KLM Koninklijke Luchtvaart Maatschappij NV (Royal Dutch Air Lines)

Klondike Yukon, Canada; *not* -yke

Klopstock, Friedrich Gottlieb (1724–1803) German poet

kludge (originally US sl.) an ill-assorted collection of poorly matching parts; (comput.) put a machine, system, or program together badly, the result of this

Klytaimestra wife of Agamemnon, in non-Gr. contexts usually **Clytaemestra**

km kilometre(s) (no point)

K Mart US retail chain (no hyphen)

K-meson *use* **kaon**

K.Mess. King's Messenger

KN (chess) king's knight (no points)

kn. knot, -s

kneecap the patella (one word)

kneel/, knelt *or* (esp. US) **kneeled, -ing**

Knesset the Israeli Parliament

knickerbocker (in pl.) loose-fitting breeches gathered at the knee or calf (not cap.); a New Yorker (cap.)

knickers a woman's or girl's underpants; (esp. US) knickerbockers, *or* a boy's short trousers

knick-knack (hyphen) *not* nick-nack

knight abbr. **K., Knt., Kt.**, (chess) **Kt** *or* **N** (no point); *see also* **KB**; **KBE**; **KCB**; **KCIE**; **KCMG**; **KCSI**; **KCVO**; **KG**; **KP**; **KT**

Knightbridge a Cambridge professorship, *not* Knights-

knight errant pl. **knights errant** (two words), *but* **knight-errantry** (hyphen)

Knightsbridge London

Knights/ Hospitallers a charitable military brotherhood (otherwise **— of St John, — of Rhodes, — of Malta**)

knit/, -ted, -ting

knitting/ machine, needle (two words)

knobby knob-shaped

knobkerrie (S. Afr.) a short stick with knobbed head; *not* -kerry, -kiri, -stick; in Afrik. **knopkierie**

knockabout (noun and adj., one word)

knock-down (adj.) (hyphen)

knocking shop (two words)

knock/ knees (two words) *but* **-kneed** (hyphen)

knock on wood (US) = **touch wood**

knockout (noun) (one word) abbr. **KO**

Knole Kent, Som.

knopkierie *use* **knobkerrie** (except in Afrik.)

Knossos Crete, *not* Cnossus

knot/, -ted, -ting

knot (naut.) abbrs. **kn., kt.**

know-how (noun, hyphen)

Knowl W. Yorks.

Knowle Avon, Devon, Shropshire, Som., W. Midlands

knowledgeable *not* -dgable

KNP (chess) king's knight's pawn (no points)

Knt. Knight, *use* **Kt.**

knur/ a knot, **— and spell** a game; *not* -rr

knurl a small projection, *not* nurl

Knut (Ger.) **Cnut**, in Dan. **Knud**, in Old Norse **Knútr**; *see also* **Canute**

Knutsford Ches.

KO *or* **k.o.** kick-off (football), knockout (boxing); **KO'd**

koala/ *not* **— bear**

København Dan. for **Copenhagen**

Koblenz Germany; *not* C-, -ce

Koch,/ **Ludwig** (1881–1974) German-born, English-domiciled musician and recorder of birdsong; **— Robert** (1843–1910) German bacteriologist

Köchel, Ludwig von (1800–77) Austrian scientist and music bibliographer, cataloguer of Mozart's works; abbr. **K.**

Kock, Charles Paul de (1794–1871) French novelist

Kodaikanal Observatory Madras, India

Kodály, Zoltán (1882–1967) Hungarian composer

koedoe *use* **kudu**

Koestler, Arthur (1905–83) Hungarian-born British novelist

Koh-i-noor diamond *not* -núr, -nûr (hyphens, one cap.)

kohlrabi a turnip-rooted vegetable of the cabbage family

koine (not cap.) a lingua franca, (cap.) that of the Greeks *c.*300 BC–AD 500

Kokoschka, Oskar (1886–1980) Austrian-born painter

kola *use* **cola**

kolkhoz a collective farm in the former USSR (not ital.)

Kołłątaj, Hugo (1750–1812) Polish politician, writer, and reformer, 'the Polish Machiavelli'

Köln Ger. for **Cologne**

Komi (of or relating to) (a member of) an Autonomous Republic, NW Russia; *also* the Finnic language of this people, *formerly* called Zyryan

Komintern *use* **C-**

komitadji, komitaji *use* **comitadji**

Komsomol a Soviet youth organization, *not* C-

Kongfuze *see* **Confucius**

kongo *use* **congou**

Königgrätz Czech Republic, *use* **Hradec Krá-lové**

Königsberg *now* **Kaliningrad**

Konrad *see* **Conrad**

Konstanz Ger. for **Constance**

kontaki/**on** a liturgical hymn in the Eastern Church, pl. **-a**; not c-

Konzert/**meister** (Ger. m.) orchestra leader, **-stück** (n.) concert piece (one word)

koodoo *use* **kudu**

kookaburra an Australian bird

Koord *use* **Kurd**

koori an indigenous generic term for an Australian aborigine (from the Awabakal)

Kootenai Ida., Mont.

Kootenay BC, Canada

kopeck, kopek *use* **copeck**

koppa the Gr. letter ϙ, ϙ

koppie (S. Afr.) a small hill, *not* kopje

kopro- *use* **copro-**

Koran the Islamic sacred book; *not* Coran, Q'ran; *see also* **Qur'ān**

Korea/ since 1948 divided into South Korea (off. the **Republic of Korea**) and North Korea (off. the **People's Democratic Republic of Korea**); adj. **-n**, *not* C-

Kortrijk Fl. for **Courtrai**

koruna major unit of currency in the former Czechoslovakia (abbr. **kčs**), in the Czech Republic (abbr. **kč**), and in Slovakia (abbr. **ks**); pl. same in English, in Czech the form varies with the amount; *see also* **krona**; **króna**; **krone**

Kos Greek island, *but* **cos** lettuce

KOSB King's Own Scottish Borderers

Kosciusko, Thaddeus (1746–1817) Polish patriot, in Pol. **Tadeusz Andrzej Bonawentura Kościuszko**

kosher (of food) prepared according to the Jewish law; *not* coshar, -er, koscher

Kosygin, Aleksei (**Nikolaevich**) (1904–80) Soviet Prime Minister 1964–80

kotow *use* **kow-**

Kotzebue, August Friedrich Ferdinand von (1761–1819) German playwright

koumiss a preparation from mare's milk; *not* ku-, -mis

kourbash a whip used for punishment in Turkey and Egypt, *not* kur-; in Arabic **kurbāj**

kourie *use* **kauri**

Koussevitsky, Serge Alexandrovich (1874–1951) Russian conductor

Kovno Lithuania, *use* **Kaunas**

kowrie *use* **kauri**

kowtow/ a Chinese form of submissive bow, act obsequiously; *not* kot-; in Pinyin **ketou**; **-ed, -ing**

KP (chess) king's pawn (no points), (US mil.) kitchen duty, Knight of the Order of St Patrick

k.p.h. kilometres per hour

KR (chess) king's rook (no points), King's Regiment, King's Regulations

Kr krypton (no point)

kr. kreuzer, krona, króna, krone

kraal (Afrik.) an enclosure, a native village

Krafft-Ebing, Richard von, Baron (1840–1902) German physician and psychiatrist

kraft paper a strong brown wrapping paper, *not* c-

Krakat/au volcano, Sunda Strait; common Western spelling **-oa**; *not* -ao

Kraków Pol. for **Cracow**

krans (Afrik.) a cliff, *not* krantz

Krapotkine, Prince *use* **Kropotkin**

K ration an emergency field ration (one cap., two words)

kreese *use* **kris**

Krefeld Germany, *not* C-

Kreisler, Fritz (1875–1962) Austrian-born US violinist

kremlin/ a citadel within a Russian town (not cap.); **the —** the citadel in Moscow, (hist.) the USSR Government housed within it (cap.)

kreosote *use* **c-**

Kreutzer, Rodolphe (1766–1831) German-French violinist; **'Kreutzer' Sonata** by Beethoven, 1803; *The Kreutzer Sonata* a novella by Tolstoy, 1889, also nickname of Janáček's String Quartet No. 1 (1923–4), inspired by Tolstoy's work

kreuzer an Austrian and old German copper coin, abbr. **kr.**

kriegspiel a war game, a form of chess with an umpire; in Ger. n. *Kriegsspiel*

Krio/ an English creole spoken in Sierra Leone, **-s** those who originally developed it

Kriol an English creole spoken in N. Australia

kris a Malay or Indonesian dagger, *also* **keris**; *not* creese, kreese

Krishnaism (Hinduism) the worship of Krishna as an incarnation of Vishnu (cap.)

kromesky a Russian dish of minced meat or fish, fried in bacon; in Fr. m. *cromesquis*

kron/a a Swedish silver coin, pl. **-or**; abbr. **kr.**; *see also* **koruna**

krón/a an Icelandic silver coin, pl. **-ur**; abbr. **kr.**; *see also* **koruna**

kron/e a silver coin, Austrian (pl. **-en**), Danish (pl. **-er**), Norwegian (pl. **-er**); all abbr. **kr.**; *see also* **koruna**

Kronos (Gr. myth.) *not* C-, -us

Kroo *use* **Kru** (not ital.)

Kropotkin/, Pyotr (Alekseevich), Prince (1842–1921) Russian geographer, revolutionist, and author; *not* Kra-, -ine

KRP (chess) king's rook's pawn (no points)

Kru (of or relating to) (a member of) a black seafaring people on the coast of Liberia; *not* -oo, -ou, (not ital.)

Kruger, Stephanus Johannes Paulus (1825–1904) S. African statesman

krugerrand a S. African gold coin (one word, not cap.)

krummhorn a medieval wind instrument, often spelt **crumhorn** in Eng.

krypton symbol **Kr** (no point); *not* c-

KS Kansas (postal abbr.), King's Scholar

Kshatriya the warrior caste of the Hindus (cap., not ital.)

K. St. J. Knight of the Order of St John of Jerusalem

KT Knight of the Order of the Thistle, Knight Templar

Kt (chess) knight (no point)

kT kiloton (no point)

Kt. Knight (Bachelor)

kt. knot

Kt. Bach. Knight Bachelor

κτλ (Gr.) *kai ta loipa* (and the rest *or* etc.)

Ku kurchatovium (no point)

Kuala Lumpur capital of Malaysia

Kublai Khan (1214–94) first Mongol Emperor of China

'Kubla Khan' a poem by Coleridge, 1816

Kuch Behar *use* **Cooch**

kudos (Gr.) renown (sing., not ital.)

kudu a S. African antelope, *not* koodoo; in Afrik. **koedoe**

Kufic (of) an early angular form of Arabic writing, *not* C-

Ku Klux Klan a US secret society (no hyphens, not ital.), abbr. **KKK**

kukri (Ind.) a curved knife, *not* the many variants (not ital.)

kulak (hist.) a Russian peasant proprietor

Kultur/ (Ger. f.) culture; (derog.) German civilization and culture, seen as racist, authoritarian, and militaristic; **-kampf** (Ger. m.) the war of culture (between Bismarck's Government and the Catholic Church, *c.*1872–7)

Kumasi Ghana; *not* Coo-, -assie

kumis(s) *use* **koumiss**

kümmel a sweet liqueur

kummerbund *use* **c-**

kumquat an orange-like fruit; *not* c-

Kung (of or related to) (the language of) a San people of the Kalahari Desert, *properly* **!Kung** (exclamation mark, close up)

kung fu a Chinese unarmed martial art

K'ung Fu-tzŭ *see* **Confucius**

Kunstlied (Ger. n.) art-song

Kuomintang the Chinese nationalist people's party, founded 1912; abbr. **KMT**; in Pinyin **Gwomindang**

kupfernickel (mineralogy) (one *f*, not cap.)

kupfferite (mineralogy) (two *f*s)

kurbash *use* **kour-**

kurchatovium symbol **Ku**

Kurd/ (an inhabitant) of Kurdistan, pl. **-s**; *not* Koo-; **-ish**

kurdaitcha (Austral.) the tribal use of a bone in spells intended to cause sickness or death, a man empowered to point the bone at a victim (not ital.)

kurfuffle *use* **ker-**

Kurile Islands NW Pacific

kursaal a hall for visitors at a spa or resort

Kursiv, Kursivschrift (Ger. typ. m., f.) italic type

kurta a loose shirt or tunic worn by esp. Hindu men and women, *not* -tha

Kutch India, *not* C-

kutch *use* **c-**

Kutchuk-Kainardja (**Treaty**) 1774, *properly* **Küçük-Kaynarca**

Kuwait/ Persian Gulf, adj. **-i**

Kuyp *use* **C-**

kV kilovolt (no point)

kVA kilovolt-ampere (no point)

kvass rye beer, *not* quass; in Russ. *kvas*

kW kilowatt (no point)

Kwa a branch of the Niger–Congo language family

KWAC (comput., indexing, etc.) keyword and context

kwacha chief monetary unit of Zambia

KwaNdebele a former black homeland in Transvaal, S. Africa (one word, two caps.)

KwaThema (S. Afric.) a township (one word, two caps.)

KwaZulu/Natal a S. African province, *formerly* Natal, incorporating the former homeland of KwaZulu

Kweyol the preferred name in Dominica and St Lucia for their French-based patois

kWh kilowatt-hour

KWIC (comput., indexing, etc.) keyword in context

KWOC (comput., indexing, etc.) keyword out of context

KY Kentucky (postal abbr.)

Ky. Kentucky (off. abbr.)

kybosh *use* **ki-**

Kyd, Thomas (1558–94) English playwright

kylie (W. Austral.) a boomerang

Kymric Welsh, *use* C-

Kyoto Japan, *not* Ki- in Jap. **Kyōto**

Kyrgyz a Mongol people living in Cent. Asia, *not* Kirghiz

Kyrgyzstan *formerly* Soviet Republic of Kirghizia

Kyrie eleison (eccl.) 'Lord, have mercy', abbr. **Kyrie**; *not* elee-

Kyrle, John (1637–1724) English philanthropist, 'the Man of Ross'

Kyzylkum a desert, Kazakhstan and Uzbekistan

Kyzyl-Orda Kazakhstan

L l

L fifty, Lake; learner (motor vehicle), Liberal; (biol.) Linnaeus; lir/a, -e; the eleventh in a series

L. Lady, Latin, (theat.) left (from actor's point of view), (Lat.) *liber* (book), licentiate; (Fr.) *livre* (book, pound); Loch, (Lat.) *locus* (place), London, Lough, prefix to enumeration of D. Scarlatti's works (*see* **Longo**)

l left, (mech.) symbol for length; litre, -s (spell out word when there is danger of confusion)

l. leaf, league, (Ger.) *lies* (read), (meteor.) lightning, line, link

l. (hist.) pound, to be placed *after* figures, as 50*l.* (ital.); *see also* **£**

L (elec.) symbol for inductance

£ pound, to be placed *before* figures, as £50; **£E** Egyptian pound (100 piastres); **£m.** (one) million pounds, with figure inserted after symbol, as £3m.

Ł, ł Polish letter 'the Polish l'

LA law agent, Legislative Assembly, Library Association, Local Authority, Los Angeles, Louisiana (postal abbr.)

La lanthanum (no point)

La. Lane, Louisiana (off. abbr.)

la (mus.) *use* **lah**

laager an encampment, esp. in a circle of wagons; in Afrik. *laer*

Lab. Labour (party), Labrador

lab (no point) laboratory

label/, -led, -ling

labi/um (anat.) a lip or liplike structure, pl. **-a**

Labor Day (US, Canada) the first Monday in September, *not* Labour

Labor Party (Austral.) *not* Labour

lab/our, -orious

Labour Day (UK and other countries) 1 May

Labourers Act (caps., no apos.)

labourite a supporter of the Labour Party (not cap.)

labour market (two words, hyphen when attrib.)

Labrador/ abbr. **Lab.,** — **retriever** a breed of retriever (one cap.)

labr/um (Lat.) the lip of a jug etc., pl. **-a**

La Bruyère, Jean de (1645–96) French writer and moralist

labyrinth/, -ian, -ic, -ine

LAC Leading Aircraftman, Licentiate of the Apothecaries' Company, London Athletic Club

lac a resin; cf. **lakh**

Laccadive/ Sea off the Malabar Coast, India; — **Islands** *use* **Lakshadweep Islands**

lace-up (adj. and noun) (shoe) having laces (hyphen)

lace/wing, -wood, -work (one word)

Lachaise, Père a Paris cemetery (two words, caps.)

lâche (Fr.) lax, cowardly (ital.)

laches (law) negligence or unreasonable delay (not ital.)

Lachesis (Gr. myth.) the Fate that spins the thread of life

lachryma Christi any of various wines from the slopes of Mount Vesuvius

lachrym/al of tears; **-ation, -atory, -ose**; *not* lacry-; *but* **lacri-** usual in scientific use

lackadaisical listless

lacker *use* **-cquer**

lackey a servile person; *not* -kay, -quey

Lackland sobriquet of King John

lacklustre *not* -er (US)

Laconian Spartan

laconic concise (not cap.)

lacquer a varnish, *not* -ker

lacquey *use* **-key**

lacrimal etc., *use* **lachry-**

La Crosse Wis.

lacrosse a ball game

lacrymal etc., *use* **lachry-**

lacuna/ a missing portion, esp. in an ancient MS; pl. **-e**, (esp. in US) **-s** (not ital.)

LACW Leading Aircraftwoman

lacy lacelike, *not* -ey

ladanum a plant resin used in perfumery etc.; *not* labd-; cf. **laud-**

laddie a young fellow, *not* -y

la-di-da (someone) pretentious or snobbish

Ladies, the a women's lavatory (cap., no apos.)

ladies' fingers okra; cf. **ladyfinger, lady's finger**

Ladies' Gallery House of Commons

ladies' man (apos., two words)

Ladies' Mile Hyde Park, London

ladies' night (apos., two words)

Ladikia *use* **Latakia**

Ladin the Rhaeto-Romanic dialect of the Engadine in Switzerland

Ladino/ the Spanish dialect of the Sephardic Jews, also called **Judaeo-Spanish**; a mestizo or Spanish-speaking non-Indian in Cent. America; pl. **-s**

Ladismith Cape Province; *see also* **Ladysmith**

Lady abbr. **L.**

Lady, Our (caps.)

ladybird (one word), *not* -bug (US)

Lady Bountiful a patronizingly generous lady of the manor etc., after a character in Farquhar's *The Beaux' Stratagem*, 1707

Lady Day/ 25 Mar. (two words, caps.), — — **in Harvest** 15 Aug.

lady-fern (hyphen)

ladyfinger (US) a finger-shaped sponge cake; cf. **ladies' fingers**, **lady's finger**

ladyf/y make a lady of, **-ied**; *not* ladi-

lady-in-waiting (hyphens)

lady/killer, -like (one word)

lady-love a man's sweetheart (hyphen, one word in US)

Lady Margaret Hall Oxford, abbr. **LMH**

lady's finger kidney vetch; cf. **ladies' fingers**, **ladyfinger**

lady's maid pl. **ladies' maids** (no hyphen)

Ladysmith Natal; *see also* **Ladismith**

lady's slipper (apos.)

lady's smock cuckoo flower (two words)

laemergeier *use* **lammergeyer**

laer (Afrik.) *use* **laager**

laesa majestas (Lat.) *lèse-majesté*

Laetare Sunday fourth in Lent

laevo- prefix meaning left, *not* levo- (except in US)

Lafayette/, Marie Joseph, marquis de (1757–1834) French general, aided Americans in Revolution (one word); — **College** Easton, Pa.

Laffitte, Jacques (1767–1844) French statesman

Lafite, Chateau a claret (two words)

Lafitte, Jean (1780–c.1826) buccaneer of unknown origin

La Follette, Robert Marion (1855–1925) US politician

La Fontaine, Jean de (1621–95) French writer

LAFTA Latin-American Free Trade Association

lagan goods or wreckage lying on the bed of the sea; *not* li-

lager a light, effervescent beer

Lagerkvist, Pär (1891–1974) Swedish novelist

Lagerlöf, Selma Ottilia Lovisa (1858–1940) Swedish novelist

lager lout (two words)

Lagrange, Joseph Louis, comte (1736–1813) French mathematician

Lagting the Upper House of the Norwegian Parliament

La Guaira Venezuela, *not* -yra

LaGuardia/, Fiorello (Henry) (1882–1947) mayor of New York (one word, two caps.); — **Airport** New York

LAH Licentiate of Apothecaries' Hall, Dublin

lah (mus.) *not* la

La Hague, Cape NW France

La Haye (Fr.) The Hague

La Hogue a roadstead, NW France; in Fr. **La Hougue**

Lahore Pakistan, *not* -or

Laibach Slovenia, Ger. for **Ljubljana**

laic/ (someone) non-clerical, lay, secular; **-ity, -ize**

laid paper that which when held to the light shows close-set parallel lines; cf. **wove paper**

Laïs (4th c. BC) Greek courtesan and beauty

laissez/-aller (Fr.) absence of restraint; **-faire** letting people do as they think best, let well alone!; **-passer** (m.) pass, permit (for persons and things) (hyphens, not ital.); *not* laisser-

Lake cap. as part of the name, as Bala Lake, Lake Superior; abbr. **L**

Lakeland the Lake District in Cumbria (one word)

Lake Poets, the Coleridge, Southey, and Wordsworth

Lake Windermere *use* **Windermere**, as 'Lake Windermere' is a tautology

Lake Wobegon a fictional US town in the stories of Garrison Keillor, *not* Woe-

lakh/ (Ind.) one hundred thousand, 100,000; *not* -ck, -c (not ital.); in quantities of rupees, pointing above one lakh is with a comma after the number of lakhs: thus 25,87,000 is 25 lakhs 87 thousand rupees; *see also* **crore**

Lakshadweep Islands in the Laccadive Sea, SW coast of India

Lalitpur Uttar Pradesh, India; *not* Lalat-

Lallan/ of or concerning the Lowlands of Scotland; the Lowland Scots dialect, now usually **-s**

Lalla Rookh a novel by Moore, 1817

'L'Allegro' a poem by Milton, 1632

Lam. Lamentations (OT)

lama a Tibetan or Mongolian Buddhist monk (cap. when part of title); *not* lla-

Lamarck/, Jean Baptiste Pierre Antoine de Monet, chevalier de (1744–1829) French naturalist; **-ian, -ism**

Lamarque, comte Maximilien (1770–1832) French general

Lamartine, Alphonse Marie Louis de (1790–1869) French poet and statesman

lamasery a monastery of lamas

lambada a fast Brazilian dance

lambaste thrash, criticize; *not* -bast

lambda the eleventh letter of the Gr. alphabet (Λ, λ), (phys.) the symbol for wavelength

Lamborghini an Italian make of sports car

lamb's fry (cook.) (apos., two words)

lambskin (one word)

lamb's lettuce (apos., two words)

lambswool *not* lamb's-wool

LAMDA London Academy of Music and Dramatic Art

lamé (adj. and noun) (a material) with inwoven gold or silver thread (not ital.)

lamell/a a thin plate, pl. **-ae**

Lamentations, Book of (OT) abbr. **Lam.**

lamin/a a thin plate, pl. **-ae**

Lammas/ (in full — **Day**) 1 Aug., formerly observed as a harvest festival

lammergeyer the bearded vulture; *not* lae-, le-, -geier

lampblack (one word)

lamp holder (two words)

lamplight/, -er (one word)

lamp-post (hyphen)

lampshade (one word)

Lancashire abbr. **Lancs.**

Lancaster, County *or* **County palatine, of** the formal name of Lancashire

Lance Bombardier abbr. **L.Bdr.** *or* **L/Bdr.**

Lance Corporal abbr. **L/Cpl.**

lancelet a small fish-like chordate

lancet small surgical knife

lancewood a tough W. Indian wood (one word)

Lancing College W. Sussex

Lancs. Lancashire

Land (Ger. n.) a province of Germany or Austria, pl. *Länder* (ital., cap.)

landau/ pl. **-s**; **-let** a small landau (not ital.)

landdrost (S. Afr.) a district magistrate (not ital.)

landfall (one word)

landgrav/e (hist.) a count having jurisdiction over a territory, the title of certain German princes; f. **-ine**; **-iate** a landgrave's territory, *not* -vate

landholder (one word)

ländler an Austrian dance

land/locked, -lord, -lubber, -mark, -mine (one word)

Landor, Walter Savage (1775–1864) English poet and prose writer

landowner (one word)

Land-Rover (hyphen) *but* **Range Rover** (two words)

landscape (typ.) book, page, or illustration of which the width is greater than the depth, in US **broadside**; cf. **portrait**

Land's End Cornwall

landslide (one word)

landsmål *formerly* Landsmaal; *see* **nynorsk**

lands/man pl. **-men**

land tax (two words)

Lane abbr. **La.**

Lang,/ Andrew (1844–1912) Scottish man of letters, — **Cosmo Gordon** (1864–1945) Archbishop of Canterbury

lang. language

Langeberg Mountains S. Africa, in Afrik. **Langeberge**

langouste the spiny lobster, rock lobster, or crawfish; in Fr. f. *langouste*

langoustine the Norway lobster, in Fr. m. *langoustine*

langsam (Ger. mus.) slowly

lang syne long ago (two words)

Langtonian (an inhabitant) of Kirkcaldy, Fife

language abbr. **lang.**

langue de chat (Fr. f.) a finger-shaped biscuit or chocolate

Languedoc/ a former French province, between the Loire and the Pyrenees; **-ian** dialect of *langue d'oc* spoken in Languedoc

langue/ d'oc (Fr. f.) any of the dialects of medieval France spoken south of the Loire (*see also* **Occitan**; **Provençal**); — *d'oïl* any of the dialects of medieval France spoken north of the Loire, largely equivalent to Old French and forming the basis of modern French

languor/ lassitude, **-ous**

langur an Asian long-tailed monkey

laniard *use* **lany-**

Lankester, Sir Edwin Ray (1847–1929) English zoologist

lanolin the fat in sheep's wool, *not* -ine

Lansdown Avon, Glos.; battle, 1643

Lansdowne, Marquess of

Lansing Mich.

lansquenet a card game of German origin, a German mercenary soldier in the 16th–17th cc. (not ital.)

lantern slide (two words)

lanthanum symbol **La**

lanyard a short rope attached to something, *not* lani-

Lao a SE Asian people, the Tai language spoken in Laos and Thailand, *not* Laotian

Laocoön a Trojan priest, subject of a famous sculpture

Laodicean lukewarm (of feelings)

Laois a county of Ireland

Lao/s adj. **-tian**

Lao-tzu (*fl.* 6th c. BC) founder of Taoism (hyphen), in Pinyin **Laoze**; *not* the many variants

Lap. Lapland; *see also* **Lapp**

La Paz Bolivia

lapdog (one word)

lapel/ *not* -elle, lappelle; **-led**

Laphroaig an Islay village and Scotch whisky

lapis lazuli a rich blue stone or its colour (two words, not ital.)

Laplace, Pierre Simon, marquis de (1749–1827) French astronomer

Lapland in Norw. the same, in Fr. **Laponie**, in Ger. and Swed. **Lappland**; abbr. **Lap.**

Lapp/ a native of Lapland, (adj. and noun) **-ish**

lappelle *use* **lapel**

lapsus/ (Lat.) a slip; — *calami* a slip of the pen; — *linguae* a slip of the tongue; — *memoriae* a slip of memory, pl. same; a person who falls from a high standard, pl. *lapsi*

laptop a portable microcomputer suitable for use while travelling (one word)

Laputa/ a flying island in Swift's *Gulliver's Travels*; **-n** visionary, absurd

lar/ a Roman household god, pl. **-es**; **lares and penates** one's home

la Ramée, Marie Louise de (1839–1908) French writer of English novels (l.c. *la*), pseud. **Ouida**

lardon bacon for larding, *not* -oon

lardycake, lardy-cake a cake made with lard, currants, etc.

lares *see* **lar**

La Reyne/ le veult, — — s'avisera forms of *Le Roy* etc. when a queen is reigning

largesse a free gift, generosity; *not* -ess (not ital.)

larghetto (mus.) fairly slow

largo (mus.) slow, broad

lariat a rope for tethering animals; *not* -iette, -rriet (not ital.)

Larissa Greece, in Gr. **Lárisa**

larkspur (bot.) (one word)

La Rochefoucauld, François, duc de (1613–80) French writer

La Rochelle dép. Charente-Maritime, France

Larousse/, Pierre Athanase (1818–75) French lexicographer, — French publishers

larrikin (Austral.) a hooligan, *not* lari-

larv/a pl. **-ae** (not ital.)

laryn/x (anat.) pl. **-ges**; **-geal**, **-gitis**

lasagne (It. pl.) pasta in wide sheets or ribbons, *not* -na (It. sing.) (US)

Lasalle, Antoine Chevalier Charles Louis, comte de (1775–1809) French general; *see also* **Lassalle**

La Salle,/ Antoine de (c.1400–60) French soldier and poet, — **René Robert Caveller** (1643–87) French explorer, — **St Jean Baptiste de** (1651–1719) French founder of the order of Christian Brothers

Lascar an E. Indian sailor (not ital.)

Las Casas, Bartolomé de (1474–1566) Spanish missionary

Las Cases, Emmanuel Augustin Dieudonné, comte de (1766–1842) friend of Napoleon I on St Helena

Lascaux SW France, site of palaeolithic cave art

laser a device using light *a*mplification by *s*timulated *e*mission of *r*adiation (acronym); *see also* **maser**

laser/disc an optical disc for reproducing sound and pictures (one word), **-Vision** a system for the reproduction of video signals recorded on a disc with a laser (one word, two caps.)

lashkar a body of Indian irregular troops (not ital.)

Las Meninas by Velázquez and Picasso (after Velázquez), *not* -iñas

La Spezia NW Italy, *not* -zzia

Lassa/ Nigeria, source of — **fever**; *see also* **Lhasa**

Lassalle, Ferdinand (1825–64) German Socialist (one word); *see also* **Lasalle**; **La Salle**

Lassell, William (1799–1880) English astronomer

lassie (Sc. and N. Eng.) a young girl, *not* -y

lasso/ pl. **-s**; as verb **-ed**, **-es**, **-ing**

Lassus, Orlandus (1532–94) Belgian-born composer

'Last Post' (caps.) it is sounded, not played

Last Supper, the (caps.)

Lat. Latin

lat. latitude

Latakia Syria; *not* Ladi-, -ieh, -yah

latchkey (one word)

latecomer (one word)

lateish *use* **latish**

La Tène of or relating to the second Iron Age culture of Cent. and W. Europe

Lateran/, St John a church in Rome, — **Council** one of five held there

latex/ a fluid derived esp. from rubber trees, a synthetic material resembling this; pl. **-es**

lath a thin strip of wood

lathe a machine for turning wood, metal, etc.

lathi a heavy stick carried by the Indian police

Latin abbr. **L.**, **Lat.**

Latin America/ the parts of Cent. and S. America where Spanish or Portuguese is the main language, **-n** (two words, no hyphen even when attrib.)

Latin Cross +

latine (Lat.) in Latin

Latinity the quality of one's Latin

Latinize make Latin, *not* -ise

latish fairly late, *not* late-

latitude abbr. **lat.** (no point in scientific work)

Latour, Chateau a claret (two words)

La Tour, Maurice Quentin de (1704–88) celebrated French painter of pastel portraits

La Trobe University, Melbourne

Latrobe Pa.; Tasmania, Australia

latten a metal like brass (not ital.)

latter the second of two, *not* the last of a series (for which *use* **last**); *see also* **former**

Latter-Day Saints the Mormons' name for themselves

lattice-work (hyphen)

Latvia a Baltic republic; in Latvian **Latvija**, in Fr. **Lettonie**; adj. **Latvian, Lettish**

Latymer Upper School Hammersmith, London

laudanum a solution formerly used as a narcotic painkiller; cf. **lad-**

laudator temporis acti (Lat.) a praiser of past times

laughing/ gas, — stock (two words)

launderette *not* -drette

laura/ (hist.) a group of hermits' cells, pl. **-s**

laurel/, -led, -ling (one *l* in US)

Laurence, Friar a character in Shakespeare's *Romeo and Juliet; see also* **Law-**

Laurentian mountains and (geol.) rocks, near the St Lawrence River, Canada

laurustinus an evergreen; *not* laures-, lauris-

Laus Deo (Lat.) Praise (be) to God, abbr. **LD**

lav (colloq.) lavatory (no point)

Lavoisier, Antoine Laurent (1743–94) French chemist (one word)

law agent abbr. **LA**

law/ binding *or* **— calf, — sheep** a binding in smooth pale brown calfskin or sheepskin, formerly much used for law books

law court (two words)

Law Courts, the (caps., no hyphen)

lawgiver (one word)

lawnmower (one word)

Lawrence/, D(avid) H(erbert) (1885–1930) English novelist; **—, Sir Thomas** (1769–1830) English painter; **—, T(homas) E(dward), 'Lawrence of Arabia'** (1888–1935) English archaeologist and soldier, (from 1927) Aircraftman Shaw; adj. **Lawrentian** *or* **Lawrencian; St —** Canadian river; *see also* **Lau-**

lawrencium symbol **Lw**

Laws abbr. **LL**

law sheep *see* **law binding**

law-stationer (hyphen)

lawsuit (one word)

Laxness, Haldór Kiljan (b. 1902) Icelandic writer

lay untilled land, *use* **lea**

layabout (one word)

Layamon (*fl.* late 1200) English priest and author of the *Brut*, properly **Laʒamon**

layaway (US) a system of paying a deposit to secure an article for later purchase, in Austral. and NZ **lay-by**

lay brother etc. (two words)

lay-by/ pl. **-s** (hyphen)

layette a complete outfit for a baby (not ital.)

lay/man, -out (noun), **-person** (one word)

lay/ reader, — sister (two words)

laywoman (one word)

lazaretto/ a place for quarantine (not ital.), pl. **-s**

lazybones (one word)

lazy-tongs (hyphen, two words in US)

lazzaron/e one of a low class at Naples, *not* lazar-; pl. *-i*

lb pound, -s (weight) (not in scientific use)

l.b. (cricket) leg-bye

L.Bdr., L/Bdr. Lance Bombardier

lbs (US) pounds

lbw (cricket) leg before wicket (no points)

LC (theat.) left centre, Legislative Council, (US) Library of Congress, Lord Chamberlain, Lord Chancellor, letter of credit

l.c. *loco citato* (in the place cited); (typ.) lower case, that is *not* caps.

LCB Lord Chief Baron

LCD liquid crystal display

L.Ch. Licentiate in Surgery

LCJ Lord Chief Justice

LCM (math.) least common multiple, London College of Music

l.c.m. (math.) least common multiple

LCP Licentiate of the College of Preceptors

L/Cpl. Lance Corporal

LD Lady Day, *Laus Deo* (praise be to God), Low Dutch

Ld. Lord

LDC (econ.) less developed country

Ldg. (naval) Leading

L.d'H. Légion d'honneur

Ldp. Lordship

LDS Licentiate in Dental Surgery

£E Egyptian pound(s)

lea untilled land; *not* lay, lee; *see also* **ley**

lead (typ.) a strip of metal used to separate lines of type

lead (chem.) symbol **Pb**

leaded/ matter, — type (typ.) having the lines separated by leading

leader *see* **leading article**

leaders (typ.) dots used singly or in groups to guide the eye across the page

leading (typ.) extra spacing between lines of type

leading article newspaper article expressing editorial opinion; *also called* **leader**

leaf (typ.) single piece of paper, two pages back to back; abbr. **l.**, pl. **ll.**

leaflet (typ.) a minor piece of printing, usually two, four, or six pages

leaf mould (two words), *not* mold (US)

league abbr. **l.**

Leakey,/ Louis (**Seymour Bazett**) (1903–72) English palaeontologist and anthropologist, — **Mary Douglas** (1913–96) his wife, — **Richard** (**Erskine Frere**) (b. 1944) his son

Leamington Spa War.; *see also* **Lem-**; **Lym-**

lean/, -ed *or* **-t**

lean-to (hyphen)

leap/, -ed *or* **-t**

leapfrog/, -ged, -ging

leap year (two words)

learn/, -ed *or* **-t**

leasehold/, -er (one word)

leatherette imitation leather

leatherneck a member of the US Marine Corps. (not cap., one word)

'Leatherstocking Tales' the collective name for five novels by J. F. Cooper

leaves abbr. **ll.**

Leban/on no longer The Lebanon; **-ese**

Lebensraum (Ger. m.) territory for natural expansion

Lebesgue/, Henri Léon (1875–1941) French mathematician, — **theory of integration** (math.)

Lebewohl! (Ger. n.) farewell!

Lecocq, Alexandre Charles (1832–1918) French composer

Leconte de Lisle, Charles Marie René (1818–94) French poet

Le Corbusier pseud. of **Charles Édouard Jeanneret-Gris** (1887–1965), Swiss architect and town planner

Lecouvreur, Adrienne (1692–1730) French actress; (ital.) play (1849) by E. Scribe and E. Legouvé; *Adriana Lecouvreur* an opera by Cilea, 1902

lect. lecture

lectern a church reading desk, *not* -urn

lecture/ship the post of lecturer (as at Cambridge), *but* **-rship** at Oxford University (cap. as title)

LED light-emitting diode

lederhosen leather shorts (not ital.)

ledger/ a book of accounts, — **tackle** in fishing; *see also* **leger line**

lee untilled land, *use* **lea**

Lee, Laurie (1914–97) English writer and poet

Leeuwenhoek, Anton van (1632–1723) Dutch microscopist

leeward (the region) on or towards the side sheltered from the wind; cf. **windward**

leeway (one word)

Le Fanu, Joseph Sheridan (1814–73) Irish writer and newspaper proprietor

left/ (theat., from actor's point of view) abbr. **L**; — **centre** abbr. **LC**

left/-hand, -handed adjs. (hyphens)

left wing (hyphen as adj.), **left-winger** (hyphen)

Leg. legislat/ive, -ure

leg. legal; (Lat.) *legit* (he, *or* she, reads), *legunt* (they read, present tense)

legalize *not* -ise

Le Gallienne,/ Richard (1866–1947) English author and journalist; — — **Eva** (1899–1991) his daughter, US actress

legato (mus.) smooth

leg-bye (cricket) abbr. **l.b.**

legenda (Lat.) things to be read

Léger, Alexis St-Léger (1887–1975) French poet, pseud. **St John Perse**

legerdemain sleight of hand (not ital.)

leger line (mus.) *not* led-

leges (Lat.) laws, abbr. **ll.**

leggiero (mus.) light, swift, delicate

Legh the family name of Baron Newton; *see also* **Leigh**

Leghorn the former English name for the Italian port **Livorno**; a straw plait, a breed of domestic fowl (not cap.)

Légion d'honneur, la a French order of merit

legionnaire/ a member of a legion, a legionary (not ital.); **-s' disease** a form of bacterial pneumonia (not cap.)

legislat/ive, -ure abbr. **Leg.**

Legislative Assembly abbr. **LA** (no points)

legit (Lat.) he, *or* she, reads; abbr. **leg.**

legitim/ate (verb) (law) render (a child) legitimate, **-ation**; elsewhere use **-ize, -ization**; *not* -atize, -ise

leg/-pull, -rest (hyphens)

legroom (one word)

legume the seed pod of a leguminous plant, esp. as used for food

legunt (Lat.) they read (present tense), abbr. **leg.**

Le Havre dép. Seine-Maritime, France

Lehigh University Bethlehem, Pa.

lei a Polynesian garland; *see also* **leu**

Leibniz, Gottfried Wilhelm, Baron von (1646–1716) German mathematician and philosopher, *not* -itz

Leicester: the signature of the Bishop of Leicester (colon)

Leicestershire abbr. **Leics.**

Leiden the Netherlands, in Fr. **Leyde**; *see also* **Leyden**

Leigh, Baron *see also* **Legh**

Leighton Buzzard Beds. (two words)

Leipzig Germany; abbr. **Lpz.**, **Leip.**

leishmaniasis a disease caused by a parasite

leitmoti/v *or* **-f** (mus.) a theme associated with person, situation, or sentiment; *not* -ive; pl. **-vs**, **-fs** (one word, not ital.)

Leix a county of Ireland, formerly Queen's County; *now* **Laois**

le juste milieu (Fr.) the golden mean; *see also* **milieu**

L.E.L. pseud. of **Letitia Elizabeth Landon** (1802–38)

Lely, Sir Peter (1618–80) Dutch-English painter

Lemberg Ger. for **Lvov**

Lemington Glos., Tyne & Wear; *see also* **Lea-**; **Ly-**

lemm/a a title or theme, proposition taken for granted, pl. **-as**; heading of an annotation, pl. **-ata** (not ital.)

lemmergeyer *use* **la-**

Lemprière, John (1765–1824) English lexicographer

Le Nain,/ Antoine (1588–1648), — — **Louis** (1593–1648), and — — **Mathieu** (1607–67) brothers, French painters

Lenclos, Ninon de (1616–1706) a French beauty

lending library (two words)

length abbr. **l.**, (mech.) symbol **l**

Lenin assumed name of **Vladimir Ilich Ulyanov** (1870–1924) Russian political leader

Leningrad *see* **St Petersburg**

len/is (Gr.) a smooth-breathing mark ('), typographically largely equivalent to the Arab. *hamza* or Heb. *alef*; pl. **-es** (not ital.)

Lennoxtown Strathclyde (one word)

Lenox Library New York

lens/ *not* lense; pl. **-es**

Lent from Ash Wednesday to Easter (cap.)

lento (mus.) slow

Leonardo da Vinci (1452–1519) Italian painter, sculptor, engineer; a work by him is 'a Leonardo' *not* 'a da Vinci'

Leoncavallo, Ruggiero (1857–1919) Italian composer

Leonid/ a meteor, pl. **-s** (not ital.)

Lepcha the language of Sikkim

Lepidoptera (zool.) butterflies and moths

LEPRA British Leprosy Relief Association

leprechaun an Irish sprite; *not* lepra-, -awn

Le Queux, William Tufnell (1864–1927) English novelist and traveller

Lermontov, Mikhail (**Yurevich**) (1814–41) Russian poet

Le Roy/ le veult the royal assent to bills in Parliament, — — *s'avisera* the royal dissent to bills in Parliament; cf. *La Reyne*

lès or *lez* (Fr. topographical) near (with names of towns)

Le Sage, Alain René (1668–1747) French novelist and dramatist

Lesbian (an inhabitant) of Lesbos

lesbian a homosexual woman (not cap.)

lèse-majesté (Fr. f.) treason (ital.), Anglicized as **lese-majesty** (not ital.)

L. ès L. *Licencié ès lettres* (Licentiate in, *or* of, Letters)

Lesotho S. Africa

L. ès S. *Licencié ès sciences* (Licentiate in, *or* of, Science)

Lethe/ a river in Hades, **-an**

let-in notes (typ.) those set inside the text area (usually in a smaller-size type), as distinct from side notes

Letraset (propr.) a system of lettering using transfers

letter/, **-ed**, **-ing**

letterhead (typ.) printed (heading on) stationery (one word)

letter/press, **-set** (typ.) one word

letters of distinction as FRS, LLD, etc., are usually put in large caps., although even small caps. can improve the general effect in contexts laden with them

letterspacing (typ.) shown in copy by short vertical dashes between letters (one word)

letters patent a formal writing conferring patent or privilege (two words)

Lettish *see* **Latvia**

lettre/ de cachet (Fr. f.) warrant for imprisonment, bearing the royal seal, pl. **-s de cachet**; — *de créance*, — *de crédit* letter of credit, pl. **-s de créance**, **-s de crédit**; — *de marque* letter of marque, pl. **-s de marque**

Letzeburgesch Ger. dialect of Luxembourg

leu a unit of currency in Romania, pl. **lei**

leucotomy a brain operation, *not* -k-

leukaemia an excess of white corpuscles in blood; *not* -c-, -ch-, -kemia

Leuven in Fl. the same, Fr. **Louvain**, Ger. **Löwen**; the Katholieke Universiteit Leuven is separated into two distinct bodies, one Flemish (Katholieke Universiteit Leuven, at Leuven) and one French (Université Catholique de Louvain, at Louvain-la-Neuve)

Leuwenhoek *use* **Leeu-**

Lev. Leviticus

lev/ a Bulgarian monetary unit, pl. **-a**

Levant/, the (arch.) the eastern part of the Mediterranean with its islands and neighbouring countries (cap.), *not* -ante; **-er** a strong easterly Mediterranean wind (not cap.), a native or inhabitant of the Levant (cap.); **-ine** of or trading in the Levant, a native or inhabitant of the Levant; — **morocco** (bind.) a superior quality leather with prominent grain (one cap.)

Levante the collective name for four Mediterranean provinces of Spain, forming two autonomous regions, Comunidad Valenciana and Murcia

levee an assembly (no accent, not ital.), (US) a river embankment

level/, -led, -ler, -ling (one medial *l* in US), **-ly**

lever de/ rideau (Fr. m.) opening piece at the theatre; — — **séance** closing of a meeting

leviable that may be levied

Leviathan a book by Hobbes, 1651

leviathan a sea monster

Levi's (cap., propr.) jeans manufactured by Levi Strauss

Lévi-Strauss, Claude (b. 1908) French anthropologist and ethnographer

Leviticus (OT) abbr. **Lev.**

Levittown NY, Pa.

Levkosia Gr. for **Nicosia**

levo- a prefix, *use* **laevo-** (except in US)

Lewes E. Sussex

Lewes,/ Charles Lee (1740–1803) English actor, — **George Henry** (1817–78) English philosopher and critic; *see also* **Lewis**

Lewis Western Isles

Lewis/, Cecil Day (1904–72) Poet Laureate 1968–72, *see* **Day-Lewis**; —, **Clive Staples** (1898–1963) English writer; —, **Sir George Cornewall** *not* Cornw- (1806–63) English statesman and man of letters; —, **Harry Sinclair** (1885–1951) US novelist; —, **Isaac Newton** (1858–1931) US soldier, inventor of — **gun**; —, **Matthew Gregory, 'Monk'** (**1775–1818**) English writer of romances; —, **Meriwether** (1774–1809) US explorer; *see also* **Lewes**; **Wyndham Lewis**

lex (Lat.) law, pl. *leges*

lexicog. lexicograph/er, -y, -ical

lexicon/ a dictionary, esp. of Greek, Hebrew, Arabic; pl. **-s**; abbr. **lex.** (not ital.)

lex/ loci (Lat.) local custom, — *non scripta* unwritten law, — *scripta* statute law, — *talionis* 'an eye for an eye', — *terrae* the law of the land

ley/ untilled land, *use* **lea**; *but* — **farming** alternate growing of grass and crops; — **line** the supposed straight path connecting prehistoric sites

Leyden/ the Netherlands, *use* Lei-; *but* — **jar** (elec.)

leylandii Leyland cypress (not cap., pl. same)

Leys School Cambridge

lez see **lès**

LF *or* **l.f.** low frequency

Lfg. (Ger.) *Lieferung*

LG (gunpowder, leather, wheat) large grain, Life Guards, Low German

L.Ger. Low German

L.Gr. Late Greek, Low Greek

LGSM Licentiate of the Guildhall School of Music

LGU Ladies' Golf Union

l.h. left hand

LHA Lord High Admiral

Lhasa Tibet, *not* -ssa; *see also* **Lassa**

Lhasa apso a breed of dog (one cap.)

LHC Lord High Chancellor

LHD *Literarum Humaniorum Doctor* (*literally* doctor of the more humane letters)

LHT Lord High Treasurer

LI Light Infantry, Long Island (NY)

Li lithium (no point)

Liadov, Anatoli (**Konstantinovich**) (1855–1914) Russian composer; *not* Lya-

liais/e, -on *not* -as-

Líakoura Greece, modern name of **Mount Parnassus**

liana a tropical climbing plant, *not* -ne

Liapunov, Sergei (**Mikhailovich**) (1859–1924) Russian composer; *not* Lya-

Lib colloq. abbr. of (Men's, Women's, etc.) Liberation (cap., no point)

lib./ librarian, library; — **cat.** library catalogue

lib. (Lat.) *liber* (a book)

libel/ (law) a published false statement damaging to a person's reputation (cf. **slander**); the act of publishing such a statement; **-led, -ler, -ling, -lous** (one medial *l* in US)

liber (Lat.) a book, abbr. **L.**, *lib.*

Liberal/ abbr. **L.**, — **Unionist** (caps., no hyphen)

liberalize *not* -ise

Liberia W. Africa

libertarian an advocate of liberty, a believer in free will; cf. **necessitarian**

libertine (one who is) dissolute, licentious

libid/o sex drive, pl. **-os**; **-inal**

libr/a (Lat.) pound, pl. **-ae**; abbr. **£, l., lb**

librair/e (Fr. m.) bookseller, **-ie** (f.) bookshop

librar/ian, -y abbr. **lib.**

library sigla abbreviated references to libraries and other archives, for use in MS citations on music etc.

librett/o (It.) the text of an opera etc.; pl. **-os, -i** (not ital.); **-ist** writer of this

libris, ex- *see* **ex-libris**

libr/o (It.) a book, pl. *-i*

Libya/ N. Africa; **-n** of ancient N. Africa or modern Libya

licence (noun) a permit, *not* -se (US)

licens/e (verb) authorize; **-ee, -er, -ing**

licensed victualler

licentiate abbr. **L.**

licet (Lat.) legal, it is allowed

lichee *use* **lychee**

lichen epiphytic vegetable growth

Lichfield Staffs.; *see also* **Litch-**

Lichfield: the signature of the Bishop of Lichfield (colon)

lich-gate a roofed gateway at the entrance to a churchyard, *not* lych- (US)

lichi *use* **lychee**

lickerish desirous, greedy; cf. **liquorice**

Lick Observatory Calif.

licorice *use* **liquor-** (except in US)

Liddell, Henry George (1818–98) English lexicographer, father of the original of *Alice in Wonderland*

Lido a famous bathing beach near Venice

lido/ an open-air swimming pool or bathing beach, pl. **-s**

Lie,/ **Jonas Lauritz Edemil** (1833–1908) Norwegian novelist, — **Trygve Halvdan** (1896–1968) Secretary-General of UN 1946–53

Liebfraumilch a hock, in Ger. f. *Liebfrauenmilch*

Liebig/, **Justus, Baron von** (1803–73) German chemist, — a beef extract first prepared by him; — **condenser** (cap.)

Liechtenstein a principality on the Upper Rhine

lied/ a song, pl. **-er** (not ital.)

Lieder ohne Worte songs without words

Lieferung (Ger. f.) a part of a work published in instalments, abbr. *Lfg.*

Liège Belgium, *formerly* Lié- (in Belgian Fr. till 1946); in Fl. **Luik,** Ger. **Lüttich,** Lat. **Leodium; Liégeois/** f. **-e** an inhabitant of Liège

lieu, in in place (of) (not ital.)

Lieutenant/ abbr. **Lt., Lieut.;** — **Colonel** abbr. **Lt. Col., Lieut. Col.;** — **Commander** abbr. **Lt. Com., Lieut. Com.;** — **General** abbr. **Lt. Gen., Lieut. Gen.; Governor** abbr. **Lt. Gov., Lieut. Gov.** (two words)

life/belt, -blood, -boat, -buoy (one word)

life/ **cycle,** — **force,** — **form** (two words)

life-giving (hyphen)

lifeguard (one word)

Life Guards a regiment of the Household Cavalry (two words), **Life-guardsman** (hyphen)

life insurance is the general (though technically incorrect) term; *see also* **assurance**

life jacket (two words)

life/like, -line (one word)

lifelong lasting for life (one word); cf. **live-**

life/-preserver, -raft (hyphens, two words in US)

life-saver (Austral., NZ, and alt. US) = **life-guard**

life-size(d) (adj., hyphen)

life/span, -style, -time (one word)

ligature (typ.) two or more letters joined together and forming one character or type as Æ, fl, ffi

liger the hybrid offspring of a lion and tigress; cf. **tigon**

light bulb (two words)

lightening making less heavy, esp. (med.) a drop in the level of the womb during the last weeks of pregnancy

light/-headed, -hearted (hyphens)

lighthouse (one word)

Light Infantry abbr. **LI, Lt. Inf.**

lighting-up time (one hyphen)

light meter (two words)

lightning/ (meteor.) abbr. **l.,** — **bug** (US) = **firefly**

light-o'-love a fickle woman (hyphens, apos.)

light/proof, -ship (one word)

light show (two words)

light/weight, -wood (one word)

light year (astron.) the distance light travels in one year, nearly 6 million million miles (two words)

ligneous of wood, woody

-like use a hyphen in formations intended as nonce-words, or not generally current, and with nouns ending in 'l'; omit the hyphen when the first element is of one syllable

likeable *not* lika- (US)

likeli/hood *not* -lyhood, *but* **-ly**

Lilienthal, Otto (1849–96) German aviator

Liliput, liliputian *use* **Lilli-, lilli-**

lillibullero a 17th-c. song refrain, *not* the many variants (not ital.)

Lilliput the country of the pygmies in Swift's *Gulliver's Travels*, **lilliputian** diminutive (not cap.)

Lilo (propr.) type of inflatable mattress

lily of the valley (no hyphens)

lima bean a tropical American plant, *Phaseolus limensis*; its flat, pale-green seeds are different from, but sometimes confused with, those of the broad bean, *Vicia faba*

limbo/ the borderland of Hell, a place of oblivion; a W. Indian dance; pl. **-s** (not ital.)

Limburg province of Belgium, province of the Netherlands; in Fl. and Du. the same, in Fr. **Limbourg**

limbus/ fatuorum (Lat.) a fool's paradise, — *infantum* limbo of unbaptized children, — *patrum* limbo of pre-Christian good men

lime-green (hyphen)

lime juice (two words)

lime/kiln, -light, -pit (one word)

limerick a humorous or comic form of five-line stanza with a rhyme scheme *aabba* (not cap.)

limes (Lat.) Roman frontier (ital.)

limestone (one word)

Limey (derog., US sl.) a British sailor, an Englishman; cf. **limy**

limn/ (arch.) paint (esp. a miniature portrait), (hist.) illuminate (MSS); **-er**

limy limelike, sticky; cf. **Limey**

lin. line/al, -ar

linable able to be covered on the inside, *not* linea-

linage number of lines, payment by the line; cf. **lineage**

linament *use* **linea-** *or* **lini-**

linchpin *not* ly- (one word)

Linch's law *use* **lynch law**

Lincoln: the signature of the Bishop of Lincoln (colon)

Lincoln Center New York, a nexus of theatres, opera house, concert hall, etc.

Lincoln green (one cap.)

Lincolnshire abbr. **Lincs.**

Lindbergh, Charles (**Augustus**) (1902–74) US aviator

linden a lime tree of the genus *Tilia*

Lindley, John (1799–1865) English botanist

Lindsay,/ Earl of family name Lindesay-Bethune, — **Sir Coutts** (1824–1913) English artist, — **Sir David** (1490–1555) Scottish poet, — (**Nicholas**) **Vachel** (1879–1931) US poet; *see also* **Lindsey**

Lindsey, Earl of family name Bertie

line abbr. **l.**, pl. **ll.**

lineage ancestry; cf. **linage**

line/al, -ar abbr. **lin.**

lineament a distinctive feature or characteristic, *not* lina-; cf. **liniment**

Linear/ A the earlier of two forms of ancient Cretan writing; — **B** the later form, found also on the Greek mainland (no hyphens)

line block (typ.) a letterpress block for lines and solids

line drawing (two words)

linen-draper (hyphen)

linenfold a type of carved scroll (one word)

line printer (two words)

linga/, -m a phallus, esp. as the Hindu symbol of Śiva; in Skt. (nominative sing.) *liṅgam*, (noun) *liṅga*, a distinguishing feature

lingerie women's underwear collectively (not ital.)

lingo/ a (foreign) language, pl. **-s**

lingua/ franca an international language (not ital.); pl. — **francas**

liniment an embrocation, *not* lina-; cf. **lineament**

lining numerals (typ.) those that align (or range) at top and bottom, as 1234567890

lining paper (bind.) a paper glued inside the cover

link 7.92 in., one-hundredth of a chain; abbr. l.

Linn/aean abbr. **Linn.**; *but* **-ean Society** London (off. spelling), abbr. **LS**

Linnaeus, Carolus (1707–78) Swedish naturalist; in Swed. **Carl von Linné**; abbr. **L.**, **Linn.**

Linnhe, Loch Highland

linocut (a print from) a design or form carved in relief on a block of linoleum (one word)

Linotype (propr.) abbr. **Lino**

linsey-woolsey a thin coarse fabric of linen and wool, gibberish; *not* linsy-, -wolsey

Linson (propr.) (bind.) a strong paper used in place of bookcloth

lintel/, -led

liny full of lines, *not* -ey

Lion, Gulf of the *or* **Lion Gulf** off the Mediterranean French coast; in Fr. **golfe du Lion**; *not* Lions, Lyon, Lyons

Lionardo da Vinci *use* **Le-**

lionize *not* -ise

lipography the omission of letters or words in writing

Lippi,/ Fra Filippo *or* **Lippo** (*c.*1406–69) and — **Filippino** (*c.*1457–1504) his son, Italian painters

Lippizaner a horse of a fine white breed used esp. in displays of dressage, *not* Lipizzaner

lipsalve (one word)

lip-service (hyphen)

lipstick (one word)

liq. liquid, liquor

lique/faction, -factive, -fiable, -fy *not* liqui-

liqueur a strong alcoholic liquor, sweetened and flavoured (not ital.)

liquid abbr. **liq.**

liquidambar a genus of balsam-bearing trees, *not* -er (one word, not ital.)

liquid crystal display a form of visual display in electronic devices (no hyphen), abbr. **LCD**

liquidize *not* -ise

liquor/ (esp. US) = **spirits** (in common usage), abbr. **liq.**; — **on draught** *not* draft (US)

liquorice *not* licor- (US)

liquorish desirous, greedy; *use* **licker-**

lir/a a unit of Italian (pl. **-e**) or Turkish (pl. same) currency; abbr. **L.**

Lisbon Portugal; in Port. **Lisboa**, in Fr. **Lisbonne**, Ger. **Lissabon**, It. **Lisbona**

LISP (comput.) a list-processing programming language (caps. or even small caps.)

lissom lithe, supple; *not* -e

Liszt, (Abbé) Franz (1811–86) Hungarian pianist and composer

lit. literal, -ly; literary, literature, litre, little

Litchfield/ Hants.; Conn.; **Earl of —.**; *see also* **Lich-**

litchi *use* **lychee**

Lit.D. *Literarum Doctor* (Doctor of Letters); *see also* **D.Lit.**; **D.Litt.**; **Litt.D.**

lite pendente (Lat.) during the trial

liter *use* **-re** (except in US)

liter/al, -ally, -ary, -ature abbr. **lit.**

literal (typ.) printing of wrong sort, of turn, or of sort in battered state or wrong font

literalize etc., render literal; *not* -ise

litera (or *littera*) *scripta manet* (Lat.) the written word remains

literat/i the learned as a class, sing. **-us**; *not* litt-

literatim (Lat.) letter for letter, textually, literally

Lith. Lithuanian

lithium symbol **Li**

lithography (typ.) a planographic printing process from a smooth plate, originally a stone; abbr. **litho** (no point)

Lithuania/ a Baltic country; in Lithuanian **Lietuva**, Fr. **Lituanie**, Ger. **Litauen**, **-n** (of or relating to) (the people or language) of Lithuania

Lit. Hum. *Literae Humaniores* Faculty (Classics and Philosophy) at Oxford

litmus/ paper, — test (two words)

Litolff, Henri Charles (1818–91) French pianist, composer, music-publisher

litotes (rhet.) a form of meiosis, esp. one using ironical negative, e.g. 'no mean feat', 'I shan't be sorry'

litre/ abbr. **l** (no point), **lit.**; one-thousandth of a cubic metre, 1.76 pints; **-age** a number of litres

Litt.B. *Literarum Baccalaureus* (Bachelor of Letters)

Litt.D. *Literarum Doctor* (Doctor of Letters, Camb. and TCD); *see also* **D.Lit.**; **D.Litt.**; **Lit.D.**

littera see *litera*

littérateur a literary man (not ital.)

litterati *use* **lite-**

Little England/, -er (two words, caps.)

Littlehampton W. Sussex (one word)

Little Russian (hist.) (a) Ukrainian

Littleton/ the family name of Baron Hatherton; **—, Sir Thomas** (?1407–81) English jurist; *see also* **Lyttelton**

littoral (of or on) the shore region of the sea, a lake, etc.

Littré, Maximilien Paul Émile (1801–81) French lexicographer

liturg. liturg/ies, -ical, -y

liv. (Fr.) *livre* (m. book, f. pound)

liveable *not* liva-

livelong intensive and emotional form of long; cf. **life-**

Liverpool: the signature of the Bishop of Liverpool (colon)

Liverpudlian (an inhabitant) of Liverpool, *also* **Liverpolitan**

livestock (one word)

Livingston Lothian

Livingstone, David (1813–73) Scottish explorer and missionary

Livorno an Italian seaport

livraison (Fr. f.) a part of a work published in instalments

livre (Fr. m.) book, (f.) pound; abbr. **L.**, *liv.*

Livy (in Lat., **Titus Livius**) (59 BC–AD 17) Roman historian

LJ Lord Justice, pl. **L JJ** Lords Justices (thin space, no points)

Ljubljana Slovenia, in Ger. **Laibach**

LL late, law, *or* Low, Latin; Lord Lieutenant, -s

ll a separate letter in Sp. and Welsh, not to be divided; in Catalan not alphabetized separately, but also not to be divided

l·l a letter group in Catalan, which is divided l-|l over a line; distinguish from **ll**

ll. leaves, lines, (Lat.) *leges* (laws)

-ll (words ending in) followed by -ful *or* -ly, usually omit one *l*

llama a S. American ruminant; *not* la-

Llandeilo/ Dyfed, **— Group** (geol.) (caps.)

Llandrindod Wells Powys

Llanelli Dyfed (*not now* -y)

Llanfairpwllgwyngyllgogerychwyrndrobwllllantysiliogogogoch Gwynedd, usually shortened to **Llanfairpwllgwyngyll** (the original name, the rest being 19th-c. whim) or **Llanfair P. G.**

llano/ a treeless grassy S. American plain or steppe, pl. **-s**

Llantwit Major S. Glam., in Welsh **Llanilltud Fawr**

LL B *Legum Baccalaureus* (Bachelor of Laws) (no points, thin space)

LL D *Legum Doctor* (Doctor of Laws) (no points, thin space)

LL M *Legum Magister* (Master of Laws) (no points, thin space)

Llosa, Mario Vargas *see* **Vargas Llosa**

Lloyd, Norddeutscher the North German Lloyd Steamship Co. (two words), abbr. **NDL**

Lloyd George, David (1863–1945) British Prime Minister 1916–22; created Earl Lloyd-George of Dwyfor; *properly* 'George' is the surname, *but* double-barrelled through usage

Lloyd's/ an incorporated society of underwriters, *not* -s; **Lloyd's List** a daily publication devoted to shipping news (ital.); **Lloyd's Register of Shipping** an institution, ital. for published annual of the same name; *see also* **Loyd**

Lloyds Bank, plc (no apos.)

Llull, Ramon (*c.*1233–*c.*1315) Catalan lay missionary and philosopher; in Sp. **Ramón Lull**, older Eng. **Raymond Lull**(**y**); adj. **Lullian** (Eng. from the Lat.)

LM Licentiate in Midwifery, (mus.) long metre

£m. (one) million pounds; figure follows symbol, e.g. £3m.

l. M. (Ger.) *laufenden Monats* (of the current month)

lm lumen(s) (no point)

LMBC Lady Margaret Boat Club (St John's College), Cambridge

LMD long metre double

LMH Lady Margaret Hall (Oxford)

LMSSA Licentiate in Medicine and Surgery, Society of Apothecaries

LMT Local Mean Time

ln natural logarithm (no point)

LO Liaison Officer

loadline (one word) *see* **Plimsoll line**

load/star, -stone *use* **lode-**

Loanda Angola, *not* St Paul de —; *but use now* **Luanda**

loath averse, disinclined, reluctant; *not* loth

loath/e regard with disgust, detest; **-some** *not* loth-

LOB Location of Offices Bureau

Lobachevsky, Nikolai (**Ivanovich**) (1793–1856) Russian mathematician

'Lobgesang' Mendelssohn's 'Hymn of Praise', 1840

lobscouse a sailor's stew; *see also* **Scouse**

lobworm (one word)

locale a scene or locality

localize *not* -ise

loc. cit. *loco citato* (in the place cited), pl. **locc. citt.** *or* **ll. cc.** (not ital.)

loch a Scottish lake, *not* -ck; cap. when with name, abbr. **L.**

Lochalsh Highland

lochan a small Scottish lake, *not* lock-

Loch Awe Strathclyde

Lochearnhead Central (one word)

Lochgilphead Strathclyde

Loch Leven Highland, Tayside

Lochnagar a mountain in Grampian (one word)

loci pl. of **locus**

lock (naut.) a confined section of a canal or river where the water level can be raised or lowered by the use of gates and sluices, *not* loch

Lock/e, John (1632–1704) English philosopher; **-ian, -ean**

lockjaw (one word)

lock-keeper (hyphen)

lockout/ an employers' refusal of work, pl. **-s** (one word)

locksmith (one word)

lock-up/ (noun or adj.; hyphen, one word in US)

loco/ locomotive, pl. **-s** (no point)

loco/ (Lat.) in the place; — **citato** in the place cited, abbr. **l.c., loc. cit.**, pl. **locc. citt.** *or* **ll. cc.** (not ital.); — **laudato** in the place cited with approval, abbr. **loc. laud.**; — **sigilli** in the place of the seal, abbr. **LS**; — **supra citato** in the place cited above, abbr. **l.s.c.** (not ital.)

Lok Sabha the lower house of the Indian parliament; cf. **Rajya Sabha**

locum/-tenency (hyphen); — **tenens** a substitute, pl. — **tenentes** (not ital.)

locus/ (Lat.) a written passage, a curve, pl. **loci**; — **citatus** the passage quoted; — **classicus** an authoritative passage from a standard book, pl. **loci classici**; — **communis** a commonplace; — **delicti** the place of a crime; — **in quo** the place in which; — **poenitentiae** a place of repentance; — **sigilli** the place of the seal, abbr. **LS**; — **standi** a recognized position, (law) right to appear

LOD *Little Oxford Dictionary*

lode/star a star steered by, **-stone** (a piece of) magnetite (one word); *not* load-

lodg/e, -eable, -ement, -ing

Lodge, Henry Cabot (1850–1924) US senator, author, and scholar; also his grandson (1902–85) diplomat

lodging house (two words)

Łódź Poland

Loeb/, James (1867–1933) US banker, founder of the — **Library** of classical authors

loess (geol.) a deposit of fine yellowish loam in certain valleys; *not* loëss, löss

L. of C. line of communication

Lofoten Islands Norway; *not* -den, -ffoden

log logarithm (no point)

log. logic

logan-stone a rocking stone; *not* loggan-, logging-

logarithm/ abbr. **log**; **natural —** to base *e*, abbr. **ln** *or* **log**ₑ

logbook (one word)

log cabin (two words)

loge (Fr. f.) theatre stall (not ital.)

loggia/ (It.) a gallery, pl. **-s**

logi/on a saying of Christ not in the Gospels, pl. **-a** (not ital.)

logo/ a device used as a printed identifier of an organization, pl. **-s** (no point)

logogram a sign or character representing a word, esp. in shorthand

logomachy a dispute about words, controversy turning on merely verbal points

logorrhoea an excessive flow of words, esp. in mental illness; *not* -hea (US)

logroll/, -er, -ing (give, one who gives) mutual aid among politicians or reviewers (one word)

logwood (one word)

Lohengrin a German hero; (ital.) an opera by Wagner, 1850

Loir, Loire, Loiret different forms used for various French rivers and déps.

Lollard any of the followers of the 14th-c. religious reformer John Wyclif

lollipop/ a large boiled sweet on a small stick, *not* lolly-; **— lady, — man** (Brit. colloq.) a traffic controller for schoolchildren

Lombard/ (of or relating to) (a member of) a Germanic people who conquered Italy in the 6th c., a native or the dialect of Lombardy in N. Italy; **-ic**; **-y** in It. **Lombardia**, in Fr. **Lombardie**, in Ger. **Lombardei**

Lombroso, Cesare (1836–1909) Italian criminologist

Lomé Togo

Londin: the signature of the Bishop of London (colon)

Londinii (Lat.) at London

Londini Scanorum (Lat.) at Lund

London/ abbr. **L., Lond.;** in Du. **Londen**, Fr. **Londres**, It. **Londra**; **— Apprentice** a hamlet in Cornwall

long. longitude

long/board, -boat -bow (one word)

long-distance (adj., hyphen)

longe *use* **lu-**

long/eval long-lived, *not* -aeval; **-evity**

Longfellow, Henry Wadsworth (*not* Words-) (1807–82) US poet

long/hair, -hand, -horn, -house (one word)

Long Island NY, abbr. **LI**

longitude abbr. **long.** (no point in scientific work), symbol λ

long jump (two words)

Longleat House Wilts.

long/ letter (typ.) *ā, ē*, etc.; **— mark** that placed over the long letter; the macron

Long Mynd, The Shropshire, **Longmynd Group** (geol.) (caps.)

Longo, Alessandro (1864–1945) compiler of edition of Domenico Scarlatti's keyboard works, abbr. **L.**

longo intervallo (Lat.) at a long interval

long page (typ.) one having a line or lines more than its companion pages

Longridge Lancs.

long s (typ.) former letter ſ, italic ſ, *not* set in final position

Longshanks sobriquet of Edward I

Longships islands and lighthouse off Cornwall

longshore/ (adj.) *not* 'long-, **-man** (US noun, one word) = **docker**

long-sighted having long sight; cf. **far-sighted**

long/-sleeved, -standing (hyphens, one word in US)

Longton Lancs., Staffs.

long ton 2,240 lb, abbr. **l.t.**

Longtown Cumbria, Hereford

longueur a tedious passage in book, play, film, usually pl. (ital.)

long vowel (typ.) *ā, ē*, etc.

long/ways, -wise = **lengthways** (one word)

loof *use* **luff**

loofah *not* luffa

lookalike (as noun, one word)

Look Homeward, Angel autobiographical novel by Thomas Wolfe, 1929 (comma)

looking glass (two words)

lookout/ pl. **-s** (one word)

loophole (one word)

Loos,/ Adolf (1870–1933) Austrian architect, **— Anita** (1893–1981) US author

loosestrife (bot.) (one word)

lop-eared (hyphen)

Lope de Vega *see* **Vega Carpio**

loping with long strides, *not* lope-

lopsided (one word)

loquitur (Lat.) he, *or* she, speaks, with the speaker's name following, used as a stage direction or to remind the reader; abbr. **loq.**

Lorca, Federico García *see* **García Lorca**

Lord (with name) may be substituted for Marquess, Earl, or Viscount, and is more often used than Baron; also prefixed to the given name of the younger son of a duke or marquess; abbr. **Ld.**

Lord/ Chamberlain, — Chancellor abbr. **LC**; **— Chief Baron** abbr. **LCB**; **— Chief Justice** abbr. **LCJ**; **— Justice** abbr. **LJ**, pl. **LJJ** (thin space); **Lieutenant** pl. **Lord Lieutenants**, abbr. **LL**; — **Mayor** (two words, caps.); — **of hosts**, — **of lords** as Deity (one cap.); — **President of the Council** abbr. **LPC**; — **Privy Seal** abbr. **LPS**; — **Provost** abbr. **LP**

Lord's Cricket Ground London (apos.)

Lord's Day (caps.)

Lordship abbr. **Ldp.**

Lord's/ Prayer, — **Supper**, — **Table** (caps.)

Lorelei the siren of the Rhine; *not* Lurlei/, -berg; *Die Lore Lay*, poem by Brentano, 1802; *Die Loreley*, poem by Heine, 1823

Lorentz/, Hendrik Antoon (1853–1928) Dutch theoretical physist, — **force**, — **transformation**; Lorentz–FitzGerald contraction (en rule) *preferred* to FitzGerald–Lorentz contraction

Lorenz, Konrad Zacharias (1903–89) Austrian zoologist and ethnologist

Lorenzo *see* **Lourenço**

Loreto Colombia, Italy, Mexico, Peru

Loretto Anglicized version of the It. **Loreto**; also a Scottish school

lorgnette opera glass, or pair of eyeglasses with a long handle

loris a small tailless lemur; *not* lori, lory

Lorrain, Claude born **Gelée** (1600–82) French painter, *not* -aine

Lorraine in Ger. **Lothringren**; *see also* **Alsace-Lorraine**

lory one of the parrots; cf. **loris**

losable *not* -eable

Los Angeles Calif.

löss (geol.) *use* **loess**

lost generation a generation with many of its men killed in war, esp. that of 1914–18; an emotionally and culturally unstable generation coming to maturity, cap. esp. with reference to 1915–25

Lot-et-Garonne a dép. of France

loth/ averse, *use* **loath**; **-some** *use* **loathsome**

Lothario/ a rake in Nicholas Rowe's *The Fair Penitent*, 1703; pl. **-s**

Lothian a region of Scotland

Loti, Pierre pseud. of **Julien Viaud** (1850–1923) French writer

lotus/ Egyptian and Asian water lily, pl. **-es**

lotus-eater *not* lotos-, *but* 'The Lotos-Eaters' by Tennyson

louche disreputable, shifty (not ital.)

loudspeaker (one word)

lough an Irish lake, cap. with name, abbr. **L.**

louis d'or (hist.) a former French gold coin worth about 20 francs, pl. same

Louisiana off. abbr. **La.**, postal **LA**; *not* Lou.

Louis-Philippe (1773–1850) French king

Louis/-Quatorze reign 1643-1715; **-Quinze** 1715–74; **-Seize** 1774–93; **-Treize** 1610–43 (Louis XIV, XV, XVI, XIII), art styles (hyphens)

loung/e, -er, -ing

lounge/ bar, — **lizard**, — **suit** (two words)

loupe a small magnifying glass used by jewellers etc., *not* loop

loup-garou (Fr. m.) a werewolf, a surly man or recluse; pl. *loups-garous*

lour/ to frown, **-y**; *not* lower/, -y (US)

Lourenço Marques Mozambique, *now* **Maputo**; *not* Lorenzo Marques, -ez

Louvain Belgium, in Fl. **Leuven**

louvre a shutter, ventilator; *not* -er (US)

lovable *not* -eable

love affair (two words)

love/bird, -bite (one word)

love child (two words)

love–hate relationship (en rule)

love letter (two words)

love/lock, -lorn, -making (one word)

love/ match, — **nest**, — **seat** (two words)

lovesick (one word)

Love's Labour's Lost a play by Shakespeare, 1598 (two apos.)

love song, — **story** (two words)

loving/ cup, — **kindness** (two words)

lowboy (US) a low chest or table with drawers and short legs; cf. **highboy**

Low/ Church (two words, no hyphen even when attrib.) — **Churchman** (two words, caps.)

low/-cut, -down (adj., hyphens)

low-down, the (noun, colloq.) the relevant information (hyphen, one word in US)

lower to frown, *use* **lour**

Lower California (caps.)

lower case (typ.) the small letters 'a–z' (hyphen when attrib.), abbr. **l.c.**

Lowland a region of Scotland

Low Sunday the first after Easter (caps.)

low water/ (two words), — — **mark** (three words) abbr. **LWM**

lox liquid oxygen, (US) smoked salmon

Loyd, Sam (1841–1911) US puzzle composer; *see also* **Lloyd**; **Lloyd's**; **Lloyds**

LP large paper, long-playing record, Lord Provost, low pressure, (paper) large post

l.p. low pressure

LPC Lord President of the Council

LPG liquefied petroleum gas

L-plate a learner driver's sign (hyphen)

LPO London Philharmonic Orchestra

L'pool Liverpool

LPS Lord Privy Seal

Lpz. (Ger.) Leipzig

lr. lower

LRAD Licentiate of the Royal Academy of Dancing

LRAM Licentiate of the Royal Academy of Music

LRCP Licentiate of the Royal College of Physicians

LRCS Licentiate of the Royal College of Surgeons

LRCVS Licentiate of the Royal College of Veterinary Surgeons

LRSC Licentiate of the Royal Society of Chemistry

LS Leading Seaman, Linnean Society; *loco* or *locus sigilli*, (in) the place of the seal

l.s. left side

LSA Licentiate of the Society of Apothecaries

l.s.c. *loco supra citato* (in the place cited above)

LSD least significant digit; Lightermen, Stevedores, and Dockers; lysergic acid diethylamide

l.s.d. (hist.) *librae, solidi, denarii* (pounds, shillings, and pence, also **£.s.d.**)

LSE London School of Economics and Political Science

L-shape (cap., hyphen); *see also* **sans serif**

LSI (comput.) large-scale integration

LSO London Symphony Orchestra

Lt. Lieutenant

l.t. long toll, low tension

LTA Lawn Tennis Association, London Teachers' Association

LTCL Licentiate of Trinity College of Music, London

Lt. Col. Lieutenant Colonel

Lt. Com. Lieutenant Commander

Ltd Limited

LTE London Transport Executive

Lt. Gen. Lieutenant General

Lt. Gov. Lieutenant Governor

L.Th. Licentiate in Theology (Durham)

Lt. Inf. Light Infantry

LTM Licentiate in Tropical Medicine

Lu lutetium (no point)

Luanda Angola, *not* Lo-

Luang Prabang Laos

Lübeck Germany, *not* Lue-

lubricious *not* -cous

Lubumbashi Zaire (Democratic Republic of Congo)

Lucan of St Luke, *not* Luk-; (in Lat., **Marcus Annaeus Lucanus**) (39–65) Roman poet

lucarne a dormer window

Lucayo (of or relating to) (a member of) an extinct aboriginal Arawakan tribe of the Bahamas, or their language

Lucerne Switzerland; in Fr. same, in Ger. **Luzern**

lucerne alfalfa, *not* -ern

Lucian (2nd c.) Greek writer

Lucknow Uttar Pradesh, India

Lucullan profusely luxurious (cap.), from **Licinius Lucullus** (1st c. BC) Roman general famous for his lavish banquets

lucus a non lucendo (Lat.) *approx.* inconsequent or illogical

Ludd/ite, -ism (cap.)

ludo a board game, a simplified form of parcheesi (not cap.); *see also* **pachisi**

LUE (theat.) left upper entrance

Luebeck *use* **Lü-**

luff *not* loof

Luftwaffe (hist.) the German air force 1935–45 (not ital. in contemporary use)

Luger a type of German automatic pistol (cap.), named after **George Luger** (1849–1923) German engineer and firearms expert

Luggnagg an island in Swift's *Gulliver's Travels*

lug/hole, -sail, -worm (one word)

Luik Fl. for **Liège**

Lukács, György (1885–1971) Hungarian philosopher, literary critic, and politician

Luke (NT) not to be abbr., **Lucan** *not* Luk-

lukewarm/, -ness tepid(ity) (one word)

Lull/, -ian *see* **Llull, Ramon**

Lulsgate Airport Bristol

lumbar (anat.) of the loins, esp. the lower back

lumber move clumsily; unused furniture etc.; (US) = **timber**

lum/en (anat.) a cavity, pl. **-ina**; (phys.) the unit of luminous flux, pl. **-ens**, abbr. **lm**

lumpenproletariat the lowest elements of the proletariat (beggars, drifters, etc.), a term originally used by Karl Marx (one word, not cap., not ital.)

lunate/ crescent-shaped, a crescent-shaped prehistoric implement etc. **— sigma** a form of sigma (Ϲ, ϲ)

lunation the time from one new moon to next, about $29\frac{1}{2}$ days

lunge a long rope for exercising horses, *not* lo-

lunging *not* longeing

lunula/ a crescent-shaped mark, esp. the white area at the base of the fingernail; a crescent-shaped Bronze Age ornament; pl. **-e**

lupin a garden plant, *not* -e

lupine of or like a wolf or wolves

lur a bronze S-shaped trumpet; *not* -e

Lurlei/, -berg *use* **Lorelei**

Lusatian *use* **Sorbian**

Lusiads, The a poem by Camões, 1572; original title *Os Lusíadas* ('The Sons of Luso')

Lusitania Portugal

Luso- of Portugal, Portuguese; cap. in e.g. 'Luso-Brazilian' (hyphen), 'Lusophile'; *but* 'lusophone'

lustre *not* -er (US)

lustr/um a five-year period, pl. **-a**

lusus naturae (Lat.) a freak of nature, pl. same

lutenist a lute-player, *not* -anist

lutetium *not* -tec-, symbol **Lu**

Luth. Lutheran

Luthuli (*also* **Lutuli**), **Albert John** (*c*.1898–1967) S. African political leader

Lutine bell a bell rung at Lloyd's, once to announce the loss, twice for the arrival, of a vessel overdue

Lutosławski, Witold (1913–94) Polish composer

lux (phys.) unit of illuminance, abbr. **lx**

Luxembourg/ city, district, province, airport of Belgium; *also* **Grand Duchy of —** (sometimes spelt *-burg* to avoid French influence); *also* Gardens and Palace, Paris; in Fr. the same, in Letzeburgesch **Letzebuerg**, in Ger. **Luxemburg**; **-er**

Luxemburg Wis.

Luxemburg, Rosa (1870–1919) German socialist

luxuriant lush, profuse in growth; (of literary or artistic style) florid, richly ornate

luxurious supplied with luxuries, self-indulgent, voluptuous

Luzern Ger. for **Lucerne**

LV luncheon voucher

L'viv Ukraine, in Eng. **Lvov** (after 1945), in Ger. and Yiddish **Lemberg**, in Pol. **Lwów**, in Russ. **L'vov**

Lw lawrencium (no point)

LWL load-water-line

LWM low water mark

lx lux (no point)

LXX the Septuagint, seventy

Lya/dov, -punov *use* **Lia-**

lycée (Fr. m.) higher secondary school

Lyceum/, the (cap.) the Aristotelian school of philosophy; (not cap.) a college of literary studies, pl. **-s**

lychee a sweet fleshy fruit and tree; *not* the many variants (not ital.)

lych-gate *use* **lich-** (except in US)

Lycra (propr.) an elastic fibre or fabric used for close-fitting clothing (cap.)

lyddite an explosive (two *d*s)

lyke wake a night watch over a dead body (hyphen); **'Lyke Wake Dirge'** medieval English song (three words)

Lyly, John (*c*.1554–1606) English author; *see also Euphues*

Lymington Hants.; *see also* **Lea-**; **Le-**

lymphoma/ any malignant tumour of the lymph nodes, excluding leukaemia; pl. **-ta**

lynch law *not* -'s, Linch's (two words)

lynchpin *use* **li-**

lynx/ a medium-sized wild cat, pl. **-es**; **-eyed** keen-sighted (hyphen), **-like** (one word)

Lyon King of Arms the chief Scottish herald

Lyonnais, Crédit French banking corporation

Lyons in Fr. **Lyon**; *see also* **Lion**

lyricist a person who writes the words to a song

lyrist a person who plays the lyre, a lyric poet

lysin (chem.) a lysing substance

lysine (chem.) an amino acid

Lyte, Henry Francis (1793–1847) English hymn writer

Lytham St Annes Lancs. (no apos.)

Lyttelton/ family name of Viscounts Chandos and Cobham (*see also* **Littleton**); **—, Humphrey** (**Richard Adeane**) (b. 1921) English jazz musician

Lytton *see* **Bulwer-Lytton**

M m

M 1,000, (typ.) em, (as prefix) mega-, (chem.) molar, motorway, sea mile, the twelfth in a series

M. Majesty, Marquess, Marquis, Member, metronome, middle, militia, (in Peerage) minor, Monday; (Fr.) *main* (hand), *mille* (a thousand), monsieur; (It.) *mano* (hand), *mezzo, -a* (half); (Lat.) *magister* (master), *medicinae* (of medicine)

M' *see* **Mac-, Mc-**

m metre, -s; (as prefix) milli-; minute, -s

m. male, married, masculine, meridian, meridional; mile, -s; mill, million; (meteor.) mist; month, -s; moon, (Lat.) *meridies* (noon), *metrum* (verse metre)

m (mech.) mass, (Fr.) *mois* (month)

m- (chem. prefix) meta- (ital., hyphen)

ɱ minim (drop)

MA *Magister Artium* (Master of Arts), Massachusetts (postal abbr.), Military Academy

mA (elec.) milliampere (no point)

m/a (bookkeeping) my account

Ma, Yo Yo (b. 1955) French-born Chinese cellist

ma (It.) but

ma'am *see* **madam**

Maartens, Maarten pseud. of **Joost Marius van der Poorten-Schwartz** (1858–1915) Dutch novelist, wrote in English

Maas *see* **Meuse**

Maasai *see* **Masai**

Maastricht the Netherlands, *not* Maes-

Mabinogion a collection of ancient Welsh romances

Mac-, Mc-, M'- the spelling depends on the custom of the name's bearer, and this must be followed, as: MacDonald, Macdonald, McDonald, McDonald, M'Donald (*properly* turned comma, *not* apos.); however spelt, alphabetize as *Mac*

mac (colloq.) mackintosh, *not* mack (no point)

macadam/ a material for road-making; from **John Loudon McAdam** (1756–1836) Scottish engineer; **-ize** *not* -ise; *see also* **tarmac**

Macao E. Asia, *not* -au

macao a parrot, *use* **-aw**

macaron/i (*not* macc-) long tubes of pasta; an 18th-c. dandy, pl. **-ies**; **-ics** (in pl.) burlesque verses containing Latin (or other foreign) words and vernacular words with Latin etc. terminations

MacArthur, Douglas (1880–1964) US general

Macassar/ (in full **— oil**) oil formerly used on hair (cap.), *but* **antimacassar** (not cap.)

Macaulay,/ Dame Rose (1881–1958) British novelist, **— Thomas Babington, Baron** (1800–59) British writer

macaw a parrot, W. Indian palm; *not* -ao, -cc-

Macc., 1, 2 First, Second Book of Maccabees (Third and Fourth are in the Greek Bible)

Maccabean of the Maccabees, *not* -baean

Maccabees/ (in full **Books of the —**) four books of Jewish history and theology, abbr. **Macc.**

McCarthy,/ Eugene Joseph (b. 1916) US politician; **— Joseph Raymond** (1909–57) US politician, responsible for **McCarthyism**; **— Mary** (1912–89) US writer

MacCarthy, Sir Desmond (1878–1952) British writer

McCormack, John (1884–1945) Irish-born US singer

McCoy, the real the genuine article

McCullers, Carson (1917–67) US novelist and playwright

MacCunn, Hamish (1868–1916) Scottish composer

MacDiarmid, Hugh pseud. of **Christopher Murray Grieve** (1892–1978) Scottish poet

MacDonald,/ George (1824–1905) Scottish novelist and poet; **— Rt. Hon. James Ramsay** (1866–1937) British Prime Minister 1924, 1929–35

Macdonald,/ Alexandre (1765–1840) Duke of Taranto, French marshal; **— Flora** (1722–90) Jacobite heroine

McDonald's (one of) a fast-food restaurant chain; *not* Mac-, despite e.g. its product named 'Big Mac'

McDonnell Douglas US aircraft manufacturer (no hyphen)

Macdonnell Ranges Northern Territory, Australia

MacDowell, Edward Alexander (1861–1908) US composer

macédoine mixed fruit or vegetables, esp. cut up small or in jelly (not ital.)

Macedonia/ a republic of the former Yugoslavia, in Serbo-Croat **Makedonija**; *properly*, the 'Former Yugoslav Republic of Macedonia' to distinguish it from the Greek province of that name; **-n** (of or related to) (the people or language) of Macedonia; abbr. **Maced.**

M'Fingal (*also* **M'**) a mock epic by John Trumbull, the first two cantos of which were published separately 1775–6, complete work published 1782

McGill University Montreal, Canada

Macgillicuddy's Reeks mountains in Co. Kerry

McGonagall, William (1830–1902) Scottish poet noted for his bad verse

McGraw-Hill publishers (hyphen)

MacGregor family name of Rob Roy

ma chère (Fr. f.) my dear; *see also* **mon cher**

machete a broad, heavy large knife, *not* matchet

Machiavell/i, Niccolò dei (1469–1527) Florentine statesman, playwright, writer on political opportunism, *not* Macch-; **-ian** (cap. only in literal or hist. usage); noun, **-ianism**, *not* -ism

machicolation (archit.) openings between supporting corbels

machina (Lat.) a machine; *see also* **deus ex machina**

machinab/le, -ility *not* machine-

machine abbr. **M/C**

machine gun (noun two words, verb and adj. hyphen), abbr. **MG**; *see also* **sub-machine gun**

machine-readable in a form that a computer can process

machine tool *but* **machine-tooled**

machismo (a show of) exaggeratedly assertive manliness (not ital.)

Mach/ number ratio of speed of a body to speed of sound in surrounding atmosphere (one cap.), expressed as e.g. Mach 1, Mach 2; **-meter** instrument indicating air speed in the form of a Mach number (one word); from **Ernst Mach** (1838–1916) Austrian physicist

macho (a person) showily manly or virile (not ital.)

M'Choakumchild, Mr and Mrs (*also* **M'-**) schoolmaster and -mistress in Dickens's *Hard Times*, 1854

Machpelah the burial place of Abraham, *not* Macp-

Machtpolitik power politics (cap.)

Machu Picchu Peru, site of ancient Incan city

Macià, Francesc (1859–1933) Catalan leader and founder of Estat Català

McIntosh a variety of apple

Macintosh/ (propr.) a make of computer; **—, Charles Rennie** (1868–1928) Scottish architect and designer

Mackenzie, Sir Edward Montague Compton (1883–1972) British novelist

Mackinac an island, fort, and straits, Great Lakes, USA

Mackinaw city, Mich., and river, Ill.

mackinaw a heavy woollen blanket, a short thick coat (not cap.)

McKinley, William (1843–1901) US President 1896–1901

mackintosh a waterproof, (colloq.) **mac** (no point), patented by **Charles Macintosh** (1766–1843) Scottish chemist; *not* maci-

mackle (print.) a blurred impression

Mackmurdo, Arthur H(eygate) (1851–1942) Scottish architect and designer, worked in England

macle a twin crystal, spot in a mineral

MacLeish, Archibald (1892–1982) US poet

Macleod, Fiona pseud. of **William Sharp** (1856–1905) Scottish poet and novelist

McLuhan, (Herbert) Marshall (1911–81) Canadian sociologist

MacMahon, Marie Edmé Patrice Maurice de (1808–93) Duke of Magenta, French marshal, President 1873–9

McMaster University Hamilton, Ont., Canada

Macmillan, Maurice Harold (Earl of Stockton) (1894–1986) British statesman

Macmillan/ Publishers Ltd London, **— Publishing USA** New York

McNaghten rules on insanity as defence in criminal trial (one cap.); *not* named after the English judge **Edward Macnaghten** (1830–1913), but after **Daniel McNaghten** (also spelt **M'Naghten** *or* **Macnaughton**), the murderer of Sir Robert Peel's private secretary, 1843

MacNeice, Frederick Louis (1907–63) Anglo-Irish poet, critic, traveller

Macon Ga.

Mâcon dép. Saône-et-Loire, France; *also* a burgundy; *not* -çon

Macpelah *use* **Mach-**

Macquarie University Sydney

macramé lace a trimming of knotted thread, *not* -mi

Macready, William Charles (1793–1873) English actor

macroeconomics the study of large-scale or general economic factors (one word); cf. **microeconomics**

macron a mark (ˉ) to indicate a long or stressed vowel or syllable

macroscopic visible to the naked eye

macrurous (zool.) long-tailed, *not* -rour-

McTaggart, John McTaggart Ellis (1866–1925) British philosopher

macul/a a spot, pl. **-ae**

Madagascar off SE coast of Africa

madam/ pl. **-s**; colloq. abbr. **'m, ma'am** (cap. for the correct form of address to the Queen)

Madame (Fr.) abbr. **Mme**, *not* Mdme; pl. **Mesdames**, abbr. **Mmes** (no point after abbrs.)

Mädchen (Ger. n.) young girl, pl. same (cap.)

mad cow disease (colloq.) BSE

Madeira an island, fortified wine, cake

madeleine a small sponge cake

Mademoiselle (Fr.) abbr. **Mlle**, *not* Mdlle; pl. **Mesdemoiselles** abbr. **Mlles**, *not* Mdlles (no point after abbrs.)

Madhya Pradesh an Indian state; abbr. **MP**

madonna (a representation of) the Virgin Mary (cap. as name)

madonna (It.) my lady, madam (not cap.)

madrasah (Ind.) a school or college, in Arab. *madrasa*

Maecenas/ a generous patron of literature or the arts, *not* Me-; pl. **-es**, Lat. pl. **Maecenates**; from **Gaius Maecenas** (*c.*74–8 BC) Roman statesman and patron of Horace and Virgil

maelstrom a great whirlpool; *not* mahl-, mal-; *but Descent into the Maelström* by E. A. Poe, 1841

Maelzel, Johann Nepomuk (1772–1838) German musician; *see also* **metronome**

maenad/ a female follower of Bacchus, *not* me-; pl. **-s**

maestoso (mus.) majestic, stately

Maestricht the Netherlands, *use* **Maas-**

maestr/**o** (mus.) master, composer, conductor; pl. **-i** (not ital.)

Maeterlinck, Count Maurice (1862–1949) Belgian poet, playwright, essayist, philosopher

Mae West an inflatable life jacket named after the film actress (two words, caps.)

MAFF Ministry of Agriculture, Fisheries, and Food

Mafia a Sicilian secret society, extending to the USA and elsewhere (*see also* **Camorra**); (not cap.) a group regarded as exerting a hidden, sinister influence

Mafikeng S. Africa; **Mafeking** is the hist. spelling, e.g. for the Boer War siege, retained for the town in Manitoba, Canada

mafios/**o** a member of the Mafia, pl. **-i** (not cap.)

ma foi! (Fr.) upon my word!

Mag. Magyar (Hungarian)

mag. magazine, magnetism

Maga (colloq.) *Blackwood's Magazine*

magazine abbr. **mag.**

magazines, titles of (typ.) when cited, to be in italic

magdalen a repentant prostitute, a home for such; *but* **Mary Magdalene**

Magdalen College Oxford

Magdalene College Cambridge

Magdalenian (archaeol.) (of or relating to) the latest palaeolithic culture or period in Europe

Magellan, Ferdinand (1480–1521) Portuguese explorer, in Port. **Fernão de Magalhães**

maggot a grub; cf. **magot**

Maghrib/ countries of N. Africa joined in economic cooperation 1964–5: Algeria, Libya, Morocco, Tunisia, and Western Sahara; Mauritania became involved in 1970, Chad and Mali are sometimes associated; *not* -eb; **-i** inhabitants of this region or the form of Arabic spoken by them

magi pl. of **magus**

magic/ (verb) **-ked, -king**

magilp *use* **meg-**

magister (Lat. m.) master, abbr. **M.**; — *artium* Master of Arts, abbr. **MA**; — *chirurgiae* Master of Surgery, abbr. **M.Ch.**

magistrand an arts student ready for graduation, esp. now at Aberdeen University; at St Andrews a fourth-year student

Maglemosian (archaeol.) (of or relating to) a N. European mesolithic culture

magma/ a mass; pl. **-ta**, or **-s** in general use

Magna Carta (1215) *not* Cha-, *not* preceded by 'the'

magnalium an alloy of magnesium and aluminium

magnesium symbol **Mg**

magnetism abbr. **mag.**

magnetize *not* -ise

magneto/ a type of electric generator, pl. **-s**

magnificat a song of praise, (cap.) the hymn of the Virgin Mary (Luke 1: 46–55) used as a canticle

magnification sign × (followed by a numeral)

magnifico/ a Venetian grandee, pl. **-es** (not ital.)

magnif/**y, -ied, -ying**

magnifying glass (two words)

magnum a wine bottle about twice the standard size

magnum bonum a large, good variety, esp. of plums or potatoes; pl. **magnum bonums** (two words, not ital.)

magn/**um opus** (Lat.) an author's chief work, pl. **-a opera**; cf. *opus magnum*

magot an ape; a Chinese or Japanese figure; cf. **magg-**

Magritte, René (1898–1967) Belgian painter

mag/**us** a member of a priestly Zoroastrian caste of ancient Persia, a sorcerer, pl. **-i**; **the** (**three**) **Magi** the wise men from the East who brought gifts to the infant Christ (Matt. 2: 1) (one cap.)

Magyar (of or relating to) a member of a Ural-Altaic people now predominant in Hungary, the language of this people; a Hungarian; abbr. **Mag.**

magyar a type of blouse or the style of its sleeves

Mahabharata an Indian epic (accent on third syllable), *Mahābhārata* in specialist contexts

Mahame/**dan, -tan** *see* **Muhammad**

mahara/**ja** (hist.) an Indian prince, *not* -jah (cap. as title); **-ni** (hist.) the wife of a maharaja, *not* -nee (not ital.)

maharishi a Hindu sage

mahatma in esoteric Buddhism one possessing supernatural powers; (with cap.) title prefixed to exalted persons, esp. **Gandhi**

mahaut *use* **-out**

Mahayana a school of Buddhism practised in China, Japan, and Tibet

Mahdi a spiritual and temporal leader expected by Muslims, (esp. hist.) a leader claiming to be this person

Mahican (a member of) a Native American people between the Hudson River and Narragansett Bay; *see also* **Mohegan**; **Mohican**

mah-jong a Chinese game played with tiles, *not* -ngg (hyphen)

Mahler, Gustav (1860–1911) Austrian composer

mahlstick *use* **maul-**

mahlstrom *use* **mael-**

Mahomet *not* -ed; *use* **Muhammad** for the Prophet except when reproducing hist. spelling

mahout an elephant-driver, *not* -aut

Mahratta *use* **Maratha**

Mahratti *use* **Marathi**

mahseer a large Indian freshwater fish, *not* the many variants

mahwa an Indian tree

mai (Fr. m.) May (not cap.)

Maia (Gr. myth.) the mother of Hermes

maidan (Ind., Pers.) a plain, an esplanade; *not* -aun

maiden/hair, -head (one word)

maiden name (two words)

maieutic of Socratic method of educing latent ideas

maigre day (RC) one when no flesh is eaten

mail carrier postman or -woman (two words)

Maillol, Aristide (1861–1944) French sculptor

maillot a dancer's tights *or* a woman's one-piece bathing suit (not ital.)

main/ (Fr. f.) a hand, a quire, abbr. **M.**; — *droite* right hand, abbr. **MD**; — *gauche* left hand, abbr. **MG**

Maine off. abbr. **Me.**, postal **ME**

Maine-et-Loire dép. of France (hyphens)

mainframe the central processing unit and primary memory of a computer, (often attrib.) a large computer system (one word)

mainland a large continuous extent of land, excluding neighbouring islands etc.; (cap.) the largest island in Orkney and in Shetland, *or* the continental USA, as from Hawaii

main line (hyphen when attrib.)

mainline (verb) inject drugs intravenously

main/sail, -spring, -stay (one word)

mainstream the principal current of a river; (attrib.) the prevailing trend in opinion, fashion, etc., esp. a type of jazz

Mainz am Rhein Germany (no hyphens); *not* Mayence, Mentz (local form)

mai/olica a white tin-glazed earthenware decorated with metallic colours; *use* **maj-** for the 19th-c. trade name for such earthenware

maisonette a small house, a flat; Anglicized form of Fr. f. *maisonnette*

maison garnie (Fr. f.) furnished house

Maisur *see* **Mysore**

maître title of French advocate

maître d'hôtel/ head steward (not ital.), *à la* — — plainly prepared with parsley (ital.) (no hyphen)

maîtresse (Fr. f.) mistress

maiuscol/a (It. typ.) capital letter, *-etto* small capital letter

maize a cereal plant, *Zea mays*, commonly called **corn** in N. America and Australia

Maj. Major

maj. majority

Majesté, Sa (Fr. f.) His, *or* Her, Majesty; *not* Son —

Majesty abbr. **M.**

Majlis the parliament of various N. African and Middle Eastern countries, esp. Iran

majolica *see* **maiolica**

Major/ abbr **Maj.**; **-General** (caps. as title, hyphen except in US) abbr. **Maj.-Gen.**

Major, John (1470–1550) Scottish humanist; — — (b. 1943) British politician, Prime Minister 1990–7

Majorca Balearic Islands, in Sp. and Catalan **Mallorca**

major-domo/ a house steward, pl. **-s** (hyphen)

majority abbr. **maj.**

majuscule a cap. or uncial letter

make-believe (hyphen as noun)

Makedonija Serbo-Croat for **Macedonia**

makeready (typ.) the preparation of forme or plate, fitting of new offset blankets, on printing machine (one word)

makeshift (one word)

make-up cosmetics, (typ.) arrangement of matter into pages (hyphen)

makeweight (one word)

Mal. Malachi, Malayan

Malabo Equatorial Guinea, *formerly* Santa Isabel

Malacca *see* **Malaya, Federation of**

Malachi (OT) abbr. **Mal.**

malacology study of molluscs, abbr. **malac.**

maladroit clumsy (not ital.)

mala/ fide (Lat.) treacherously, — *fides* bad faith

Málaga Spain (accent); a sweet, fortified wine from there (no accent)

Malagasy a native or the language of Madagascar

Malagasy Republic *now* **Madagascar**

malagueña a fandango-like dance from Málaga

mala in se (Lat.) acts that are intrinsically wrong

malaise discomfort, uneasiness

malamute an Inuit dog, *not* male-

malanders *use* **mallen-**

malapropism the mistaken use of a word in place of one that sounds similar, to comic effect, from **Mrs Malaprop**, a character in *The Rivals* by Sheridan, 1775

malapropos inopportunely, in Fr. *mal à propos*

Malawi/ Cent. Africa, in Chichewa **Malaŵi**; **-an**; **Lake —** *formerly* Lake Nyasa

Malay the language and people predominating in Malaysia and Indonesia

Malaya, Federation of till 1957 consisted of nine states (Johore, Kedah, Kelantan, Negri Sembilan, Pahang, Perak, Perlis, Selangor, Trengganu) and the two British settlements of Penang and Malacca; adj. **Malayan**; abbr. **Mal.**; *see also* **Malaysia**

Malayalam a Dravidian language of the State of Kerala, Malabar coast, SW India

Malayo-/ a combination form of Malayan, e.g. *Malayo-Chinese* (hyphen); **-Polynesian** Austronesian

Malaysia/ since 1957 an independent state within the Commonwealth, consisting of Malaya, Sabah, and Sarawak; **-n**; *formerly* (Federation of) Malaya

Malcolm X assumed name of **Malcolm Little** (1925-65) US black nationalist leader

malcontent *not* male-

mal de mer (Fr. m.) seasickness

Malden Surrey

mal de tête (Fr. m.) headache

Maldiv/es, The SW of Sri Lanka, **-ian**

Maldon Essex

mal du pays (Fr. m.) homesickness

male (bot., zool., sociology) abbr. **m.**, sign ♂

maleable *use* **mall-**

malecontent *use* **malc-**

malee *use* **mall-**

maleficence (lit.) evildoing, harmfulness

malemute *use* **mala-**

malentendu (Fr. m.) misunderstanding (one word)

Malesherbes, Chrétien Guillaume de Lamoignon de (1721-94) French statesman; *see also* **Malherbe**

malfeasance (law) evildoing; cf. **misfeasance**

malgré (Fr.) in spite of

Malherbe, François de (1555-1628) French writer; *see also* **Malesherbes**

Mali/ NW Africa; **-an**

mali a member of the Indian gardener caste, a gardener; cf. **mallee**

Malines Belgium, in Flemish **Mechelen**; *see also* **Mechlin**

Mallarmé, Stéphane (1842-98) French poet

malleable *not* male-

mallee the Australian eucalyptus; cf. **mali**

mallemuck *use* **mollymawk**

mallenders an eruption behind a horse's knee, *not* malan-

Mallorca Sp. and Catalan for **Majorca**; the local language (a dialect of Catalan) is *Mallorqúi*

Mallow Co. Cork

Malmaison near Paris (one word)

Malmesbury Wilts.

malmsey a sweet wine; *not* malv-, -sie, -esie, -asye

Malone, Edmond (*not* -und) (1741-1812) British literary critic

Malplaquet, battle of 1709

malpractice misbehaviour, *not* -se

malstrom *use* **mael-**

Maltese/ (of or related to) (a native or the language) of Malta, **— cross** ✠; *see also* **cross**; **crux**

Malthus/, Thomas Robert (1766-1834) English writer on population, **-ian**

Malton N. Yorks.

maltster a person who makes malt, *not* -ser

Maluku Indonesian islands, *not* Moluccas

malvoisie *use* malmsey

mama var. of **mamma**

mamba any venomous African snake of the genus *Dendroaspis*

mambo a Lat. American dance like the rumba, the music for this

mameluco in Brazil, the offspring of a white and an Indian

Mameluke (hist.) a member of the military caste that ruled Egypt 1254-1811; *not* the many variants; in Arab. *mamlūk*

mamill/a a nipple, pl. **-ae**; **-ary**; *not* mamm- (US)

mamma a child's name for mother, *also* **mama**

mamm/a a breast, pl. **-ae**; **-ary**

mammee a tropical American tree, *not* the many variants

Mammon wealth personified (cap.)

Man. Manila, Manitoba

man. manual

Man, Isle of *see* **Isle of Man**

mana (Maori) might, authority, prestige; supernatural or magical power; cf. **manna**

man about town (three words)

manacle a fetter, *not* -icle
Manacles rocks off Cornish coast
manage/able, -ment
manakin a tropical American bird; cf. **manikin**; **mannequin**; **mannikin**; **minikin**
Manama the capital and free-trade port of Bahrain, in Arabic **Al Manamah**
mañana (Sp.) tomorrow *or* an indefinite future time
Manassas Va.; scene of two American Civil War battles, 1861, 1862; named **Bull Run** by the North
Manasseh, tribe of
Manasses, Prayer of (Apocr.) abbr. **Pr. Man.**
man-at-arms pl. **men-at-arms** (hyphens)
manatee the sea cow
Manaus Brazil, *formerly* Manáos
Manche a dép. of France
Manche, La (Fr.) the English Channel
manche (Fr. m.) handle, (f.) sleeve
Manchester abbr. **Manch., M/c**
Manchester: the signature of the Bishop of Manchester (colon)
man-child pl. **men-children** (hyphens)
Manchu a member of a Mongolian people in China, who formed the last imperial dynasty (1644–1912); the language of the Manchus, now spoken in part of NE China (Manchuria); of or relating to the Manchu people or their language; *not* -choo, -chow
Manchukuo Japanese puppet state 1932–45, formed out of Manchuria, Chinese Jehol, and part of Inner Mongolia
Manchuria a region in NE China, named (1643) after an invading Mongolian people (*see* **Manchu**)
Mancunian (an inhabitant) of Manchester
Mandaean (of or concerning) (a member of) a Gnostic sect surviving in Iraq and claiming descent from John the Baptist; the language of this sect
mandala a symbolic circular figure representing the universe in various religions; (psychol.) such a symbol in a dream, representing the dreamer's search for completeness and self-unity
Mandalay Burma, *not* Mande-
mandamus a writ issued from a higher court to a lower, *not* -emus (not ital.)
mandarin a person of importance, esp. reactionary or secretive bureaucrat; a small orange; official language of China (cap.); *not* -ine
mandatary (law, hist.) one to whom a mandate is given
mandatory (adj.) compulsory
Mandelay, mandemus *use* -da-
mandioc *use* mani-

mandolin a stringed instrument, *not* -ine
mandorla *use* **vesica**
mandrel a spindle, *not* -il
mandrill a baboon
maneater (one word)
manège horsemanship, riding school; cf. **menage**
Manes the classical form of **Mani**; *see also* **Manichee**
Manet, Édouard (1832–83) French painter; cf. **Monet**
man/et (Lat., theat.) he, *or* she, remains; pl. *-ent*
maneuver *use* **manoeuvre**
manganese symbol **Mn**
mangel-wurzel a large beet; *not* mangle-, mangold-
mango/ a tropical fruit, *not* -oe; pl. **-es**
mangold-wurzel *use* **mangel-**
mangosteen a tropical fruit; *not* -an, -ine
mangy having mange, *not* -gey
manhaden *use* **men-**
manhandle (one word)
manhattan a cocktail (not cap.)
Manhattan Island borough, New York City
Manhattan Project the production of the first atomic bombs in USA
Manheim Germany, *use* **Mann-**
man/hole, -hood (one word)
man-hour/ the work of one person per hour, pl. **-s** (hyphen)
manhunt (one word)
Manich/ee originally a religious follower of the Persian **Mani** (also **Manes**) (c.216–76); **-aeism, -aean** *not* -chean (US); used generally to describe an adherent of any dualist religious system; (philos.) (often **Manichaean**) any dualist or dualistic system of conflict
manicle a fetter, *use* **-acle**
manifesto/ a declaration of policy, pl. **-s**
manikin a dwarf, an anatomical model; *not* mana-, manni-; cf. **manakin**; **mannequin**; **mannikin**; **minikin**
Manila/ Philippine Islands, abbr. **Man.**; — **cigar, — hemp** (cap.); *not* -illa
man/illa a type of sturdy paper (*also* **-ila**), an African metal bracelet used as a medium of exchange (not cap.)
manille the second best trump or honour in ombre or quadrille
manioc the cassava plant, flour made from it; *not* the many variants
maniple a subdivision of a Roman legion, a Eucharistic vestment
manipulator *not* -er
Manipur NE India, *not* Munnepoor

Manitoba a Canadian province, abbr. **Man.**

manitou (Amer. Ind.) a good or evil spirit as an object of reverence; something regarded as having supernatural power

man-made (hyphen)

manna unexpected benefit; cf. **mana**

mannequin a dressmaker's (live) model, a window dummy; *not* mani-; cf. **manakin**; **manikin**; **mannikin**; **minikin**

manner born, to the *not* manor (*Hamlet* I. iv. 17)

Mannheim Germany, *not* Manh-

mannikin any small finchlike bird of the genus *Lonchura*; cf. **manakin**; **manikin**; **mannequin**; **minikin**

Mannlicher rifle invented by **Ferdinand Ritter von Mannlicher** (1848–1904) (no umlaut)

mano (anthrop.) a primitive stone implement (not ital.)

mano/ (It. f.) a hand, abbr. **M.**, pl. *mani*; — *destra* right hand, abbr. **MD**; — *sinistra* left hand, abbr. **MS**

manoeuvrab/le, -ility (no ligature) *not* maneuverable, -ility (US)

manoeuvr/e, -ed, -ing (no ligature) *not* maneuver, -ed, -ing (US)

man-of-war an armed ship, pl. **men-of-war** (hyphens)

man-of-war's-man (apos., hyphens)

ma non troppo (mus.) but not too much so (qualifying a tempo indication)

manpower the power generated by a man working (one word); for the number of people available for work etc., *prefer* **workers**, **staff**, **personnel**, **people**, **human resources**

manqu/é (Fr.) f. *-ée* unsuccessful, unfulfilled (placed after the noun)

Man Ray pseud. of **Emmanuel Radinski** (some sources **Rudnitsky**) (1890–1977) US artist, photographer, and film-maker; usually alphabetized thus

Mansard/, François (1598–1666) French architect, — **roof** lower part steeper than upper (not cap.)

Mansfield, Katherine pseud. of **Kathleen Beauchamp**, later **Murry** (1888–1923) New Zealand-born British writer of short stories; *see also* **Murry**

Mansion House, the off. residence of the Lord Mayor of London (caps.); the house of a lord mayor or a landed proprietor (no caps.)

mansuetae naturae (law, adj.) tame (of animals), literally, of a tame nature

mantel a shelf above a fireplace

mantelet a short cloak, a movable screen to protect gunners; *not* mantlet

mantelpiece *not* mantle-

mantilla (Sp.) a veil covering head and shoulders

mantis an orthopterous insect, pl. same

mantissa the part of a logarithm after the decimal point

mantle a cloak

mantlet *use* **-telet**

mantling (her.) (a representation of) ornamental drapery etc. behind and around a shield

mantrap (one word)

Mantua Italy, in It. **Mantova**

mantua (hist.) a woman's loose gown of the 17th–18th cc.

manual an organ keyboard, abbr. **man.**

manual alphabet *use* **sign language** except when differentiating finger spelling

manufactur/e, -er abbr. **mfr.**; **-ed** abbr. **mfd.**; **-ers, -es** abbr. **mfrs.**; **-ing** abbr. **mfg.**

Manufacturers Hanover Corp. a US bank (no apos.)

manum/it set (a slave) free; **-itted, -itting**; **-ission**

manu propria (Lat.) with one's own hand

manus (Lat. f.) a hand, pl. same

manuscript abbr. **MS** (**a** *not* an, as it is pronounced 'manuscript' *not* 'em-ess'), pl. **MSS** (*but* spell out except in bibliog. enumeration)

manuscrit (Fr. m.) manuscript; abbr. **ms.**, pl. **mss.**

Manuskript (Ger. n.) printer's copy; MS is usually *Handschrift*

Manutius,/ Aldus (1450–1515) in It. **Aldo Manuzio**, — **Aldus** 'the younger' (1547–97), — **Paulus** (1512–72) Italian printers

Manx/ of the Isle of Man, of the Celtic language formerly spoken there; — **cat** (two words), **-man, -men, -woman, -women** (one word)

many-sided (hyphen)

manzanilla a dry sherry, a type of dive (not cap.)

manzanilla (Sp. f.) camomile tea

Mao/ism the doctrine of Mao Zedong, **-ist**

Maori/ *properly* **Māori** (of or relating to) (a member of) the Polynesian aboriginal people of New Zealand, or their language; pl. same

Mao/ Zedong (Pinyin), — **Tse-tung** (traditional) (1893–1976) Chairman of Chinese Communist Party 1954–76, **-ism**

Mapplethorpe, Robert (1947–89) US photographer

Maputo Mozambique, *formerly* Lourenço Marques

maquillage (the application of) make-up

Maquis the resistance movement in France 1940–5

Mar, Earl of family name: of Mar (no other family name); *see also* **Mar and Kellie**

Mar. March

mar/, **-red**, **-ring**

mar. maritime

marabou/ **feather,** — **stork** *not* -bout, -bu

marabout a Muslim monk or hermit, esp. in N. Africa, *or* a shrine marking a marabout's burial place; *not* -but

Maracaibo Venezuela, *not* -ybo

maranatha (Syriac) 'our Lord cometh'

Mar and Kellie, Earl of family name Erskine; *see also* **Mar**

maraschino/ a strong sweet liqueur made from Dalmatian cherries; — **cherry** cherry preserved in maraschino (not cap.)

Marat, Jean-Paul (1743–93) French revolutionary

Maratha a member of a warrior people native to the modern Indian State of Maharashtra, *not* Mahratta

Marathi the Indo-European language spoken in Maharashtra, NW India; *not* Mahratti

Marazion Cornwall

marbling (bind.) staining endpapers or book edges to resemble marble

marbly marble-like, *not* -ley

marbré (Fr.) marbled, the marbled edges of books

Marcan of St Mark or the Gospel according to him, *not* Mark-

marcato (mus.) emphasized

March (month of) abbr. **Mar.**

Märchen (Ger. n.) a fairy tale, pl. same

marches/**e** (It.) marquis, f. **-a** marchioness

marchioness the wife or widow of a marquess, *or* a woman holding the rank of marquess in her own right; abbr. **march.** (cap. as title)

Marcobrunner a hock

Marconi, Guglielmo, Marchese (1874–1937) inventor of radio telegraphy; **marconigram** a message sent by his system (not cap.)

Marcuse, Herbert (1898–1979) German-born US philosopher

Mardi Gras Shrove Tuesday

mare (Lat.) sea, (astr.) lunar plain, pl. *maria*

maréchal/ (Fr. m.) field marshal, **-e** his wife

Maréchal Niel a rose

mare/ *clausum* (Lat.) a sea under one country's jurisdiction; — *liberum* a sea open to all countries

mare's/**-nest, -tail** (apos., hyphen)

marg. margin, -al

margarine a butter substitute, colloq. **marge**

margarita a tequila-based cocktail

margarite a mineral or rock-formation

Margaux, Chateau a claret (two words)

marge colloq. for margarine, *not* marg

marge (Fr. f.) margin

margin/, **-al** abbr. **marg.**

marginalia (pl.) marginal notes (not ital.)

margins (typ.) the four are called back or gutter (at binding) head (top), foredge (opposite binding), and tail (foot); an acceptable ratio for the size of margins, in order as above, is $1 : 1\frac{1}{2} : 2 : 2\frac{1}{2}$

Margoliouth, David Samuel (1858–1940) British orientalist

Margrethe (b. 1940) Queen of Denmark 1972–

marguerite the ox-eye daisy

mariage de convenance (Fr. m.) marriage in order to keep up appearances, *not* marr-

Mariamne the name of two wives of Herod the Great

Marian (RC) of or relating to the Virgin Mary

Marianne a woman symbolizing France

Mariánské Lázně Czech Republic, in Ger. **Marienbad**

Marie/ **de' Medici** (1573–1642) wife of Henry IV of France (*not* de), in Fr. — **de Médicis**

Marienberg Germany

Marienbourg Belgium

Mariënburg Suriname

marijuana *not* -huana

marin/**ade** (cook.) a liquid in which food is cooked, **-ate** steep in it

Mariolatry (derog.) worship of the Virgin Mary, *not* Mary-

marionette a puppet worked by strings, in Fr. f. *marionnette*

maritime abbr. **mar.**

Maritimes, the the Canadian provinces of New Brunswick, Nova Scotia, Prince Edward Island, and sometimes Newfoundland; in full **Maritime Provinces**

marivaudage (Fr. m.) daintily affected style, from **Pierre Carlet de Chamblain de Marivaux** (1688–1763) French playwright and novelist

marjoram either of two herbs, *Origanum majorana* (or *hortensis*) *or O. onites*, used for seasoning; *see also* **oregano**

Mark (NT) not to be abbr.; **Marcan** *not* Mark-

mark/ German coin, pl. in English contexts **-s**; *see also* **Deutsche Mark**; **Ostmark**

markdown (noun) a reduction in price (one word)

Market, the (hist.) the European Economic Community (cap.)

market/ abbr. **mkt.**; **-ed, -ing**

market day (two words)

Market Drayton Shropshire

market garden/, **-er** (two words)

Market Harborough Leics.

Marketors, Worshipful Company of

market overt (law) open market

marketplace (one word)

market/ research, — town, — value (two words)

Market Weighton Humberside

markka the basic monetary unit of Finland

marks of reference (typ.) *, †, ‡, §, ‖, ¶

mark-up (noun) an increase in price, (typ.) final copy preparation (hyphen, one word in US)

Marlburian (a member) of Marlborough College

marlin any marine fish of the family *Istiophoridae*

marline (naut.) a thin line of two strands

marlinspike for separating strands of rope in splicing; *not* -ine-, -ing- (one word)

Marlow Bucks.

Marlowe, Christopher (1564–93) English playwright

Marmara, Sea of *not* -ora

Marmite (Brit. propr.) a preparation made from yeast extract and vegetable extract (cap.); an earthenware cooking vessel (not cap.)

marmoset a monkey

Marocco *use* **Mor-**

Maronite a member of a sect of Syrian Christians dwelling chiefly in Lebanon

Marprelate Controversy, the a war of pamphlets 1588–9, between Puritan 'Martin Marprelate' and defenders of the Established Church

marq. marquis

marque/ the make (not type or model) of a car; **letters of —** a licence to fit out an armed vessel and employ it in the capture of an enemy's merchant shipping at sea, as a form of reprisal

marque de fabrique (Fr. f.) trade mark

marquee a large tent, (US) a canopy of the entrance to a building

Marquesas Islands S. Pacific

marquess a British nobleman ranking between a duke and an earl (cap. as title); abbr. **M.**, **marq.** Some British peers of this rank prefer **marquis**; *see also* **marchioness**

marquetry inlaid work, *not* -terie

Márquez, Gabriel García *see* **García Márquez, Gabriel**

marquis/ a (usually Continental) nobleman ranking between a duke and a count, abbr. **M.**, **marq.**; **-e** the wife or widow of a marquis, *or* a woman holding the rank of marquis in her own right, *not now* marchioness; during 16th and 17th cc. a marquis could be a woman (cap. as title only in Eng.); in Fr. ***marquis/*** abbr. **Mⁱˢ**; f. **-e**, abbr. **Mⁱˢᵉ**

Marrakesh Morocco; *not* Mara-, -kech

marriageable *not* -gable

Marriage-à-la-Mode a tragicomic play by Dryden, 1672

married abbr. **m.**

marron (Fr. m.) chestnut, **marron glacé** a sugared chestnut (not ital.)

Marsala a dark sweet fortified dessert wine (cap.)

'Marseillaise, La' French national anthem

Marseilles Bouches-du-Rhône, France; in Fr. (and increasingly in Eng.) **Marseille**, *but* **Marseilles** Ill.

marshal/ (noun and verb) *not* -ll (US); **-led, -ler, -ling** (one *l* in US)

Marshall/, General George (**Catlett**) (1880–1959) US soldier and statesman, initiator of **— Plan** for W. European recovery, 1947

Marshall Islands W. Pacific

Marsham, Viscount eldest son of the Earl of Romney; *see also* **Masham**

martellato (mus.) played with heavy strokes

Martello/ a small circular fort, pl. **-s** (cap.)

marten a weasel; cf. **martin**

Martens, Dr *or* **'Doc'** (propr.) a brand of footwear, before 1960 spelt **Maertens** (no apos.)

Martha's Vineyard an island, Mass.

Martial (in Lat. **Marcus Valerius Martialis**) (*c*.40–*c*.102) Roman poet, abbr. **Mart.**

martin a bird; *see also* **marten**

Martineau, Harriet (1802–76) English writer

martingale the strap from a horse's noseband to girth, *not* -gal

Martini (propr.) a vermouth

martini a cocktail made from gin and dry vermouth

Martinique W. Indies

Martinmas 11 Nov.

martlet (her.) an imaginary footless bird borne as a charge, (arch.) a swift or house-martin

martyrize etc., *not* -ise

marvel/, -led, -ling, -lous (one *l* in US)

Marvell, Andrew (1621–78) English poet and satirist

Marx/, Karl (1818–83) German socialist, author of *Das Kapital*; **-ism** *not* -ianism; **-ian** a student of Marx or Marxism; **-ist** an ideological follower of Marx's doctrines

Marxism-Leninism Marxism as developed by Lenin (hyphen)

Mary Turkmenistan, *formerly* Merv

Maryland off. abbr. **Md.**, postal **MD**

Marylebone/ London, **St —** parliamentary constituency

Marymass 25 Mar.

Maryolatry *use* **Mari-**

mas (Lat.) a male, pl. ***mares***

Masai (of or relating to) (a member of) a pastoral people living in Kenya and Tanzania, their language; pl. same; *properly* **Maasai**

Masaryk,/ Tomáš (Thomas) Garrigue (1850–1937) first President of Czechoslovakia; **— Jan Garrigue** (1886–1948) his son, Czechoslovak politician

masc. masculine

Mascagni, Pietro (1863–1945) Italian composer

masculine abbr. **m., masc.**

Masefield, John (1878–1967) Poet Laureate 1930–67

maser microwave amplification by stimulated emission of radiation (acronym); cf. **laser**

mashallah! (Arab., Pers., Turk.) an exclamation of wonder (lit. 'what God wills!')

Masham/, Baron family name Lister, **— of Ilton, Baroness** family name Cunliffe-Lister; *see also* **Marsham**

mashie a golf club, *not* -y

Mashona/, -land Zimbabwe

Mashraq Arab countries of the E. Mediterranean: Egypt, Jordan, Lebanon, Sudan, and Syria; cf. **Maghrib**

masjid (Arab.) a mosque; not *mes-, mus-*

maskinonge a large N. American pike; *not* muskellunge

masochism perversion in which a person delights in being cruelly treated; from **Leopold von Sacher-Masoch** (1835–95) Austrian novelist

Mason/, -ic, -ry (Freemasonry) (cap.)

Mason–Dixon line USA, separated slave-owning South from free North; surveyed 1763–7 by English astronomers Charles Mason and Jeremiah Dixon (en rule)

Masor/ah a body of trad. information and comment on the text of the Hebrew Bible, *not* the many variants; **-ete** a Jewish scholar contributing to the Masorah; **-etic Text** abbr. **MT**, 𝔐

masque a dramatic and musical entertainment esp. of the 16th and 17th cc.

mass/ (mech.) symbol **m** (not cap.); (esp. RC mus.) the Eucharist, **high —, low —** (often initial caps. in liturgical contexts)

Massachusetts off. abbr. **Mass.**, postal **MA**

massé a stroke at billiards

Masséna, André (1758–1817) French marshal

Massenet, Jules Émile Frédéric (1842–1912) French composer

Massereene, Viscount

masseu/r f. **-se** (not ital.)

massif (geol.) a mountain mass (not ital.)

Massora *use* **Masorah**

mastaba/ (archaeol.) an ancient Egyptian tomb, a stone bench attached to a house in Islamic countries; pl. **-s**

Master/ abbr. **M. — of Arts** abbr. **MA; — — Commerce** abbr. **M.Com.; — — Dental Surgery** abbr. **MDS; — — Education** abbr. **M.Ed.; — — Laws** abbr. **LL M; — — Letters** abbr. **M.Litt.; — — Music** abbr. **M.Mus.**, (Camb.) **Mus.M.; — — Philosophy** abbr. **M.Phil.; — — Science** abbr. **M.Sc.**, (US) **MS; — — Surgery** abbr. **M.Ch., M.Chir., MS, Ch.M.; — — Theology** abbr. **M.Th.**

master-at-arms (naut.) first-class petty officer (hyphens)

master mariner the captain of a merchant vessel (two words)

mastermind (noun, adj., and verb, one word)

Master of courtesy title of the eldest son of a Scottish viscount or baron, e.g. The Master of Lovat

Master of Ceremonies abbr. **MC**

Master of the Rolls abbr. **MR**

masterpiece (one word)

master printer head of a printing firm

Master Printers Association abbr. **MPA**

master/ stroke, — switch (two words)

masterwork (one word)

masthead (one word)

mastic a gum resin; *not* -ich, -ick

mat dull, *use* **matt**

Matabele/ pl. same, *now* officially **Ndebele; -land** Zimbabwe (one word)

matador a bullfighter, *not* -ore

match/board, -box (one word)

matchet *use* **machete**

match/lock, -maker (one word)

match point (two words)

match/stick, -wood (one word)

maté an infusion; in Sp. m. *mate*, in Quechua *mati*

matelot (sl.) a sailor, a shade of blue (not ital.); *not* matlo, matlow

matelot (Fr. m.) a sailor

matelote (Fr. cook. f.) a rich fish stew

mat/er (Lat.) mother, pl. **-res**

materialize *not* -ise

materia medica the science of drugs, the drugs themselves (not ital.)

matériel (mil.) everything except personnel (ital.)

matey sociable, *not* -ty

math. mathemat/ics, -ical, -ician

mathematics abbr. **math.**

Mather,/ Cotton (1663–1728), son of **— Increase** (1639–1723), American Puritan theologians and writers

Mathew, Lord Justice (1830–1909)

Mathews,/ Charles (1776–1835) English actor; **— Charles James** (1803–78) his son, English actor and playwright; **— Shailer** (1863–1941)

US educator and theologian; *see also* **Matthews**

matin (Fr. m.) morning

matinée an afternoon entertainment (no accent in US); **matinée musicale** an afternoon entertainment with music (ital.)

matins sometimes in Prayer Book **mattins**

matlo/, -w *use* **matelot**

matriculator *not* -er

matr/ix pl. **-ices**

matronymic a name taken from a female ancestor, as *Margisson*, *Dvorin*; *not* me-

matt/ (of colour, surface) dull, without lustre; a mount for a picture; *not* mat; **-e** an impure product of smelting, a mask used in film-making

Matt. St Matthew's Gospel

Mattei, Tito (1841–1914) Italian composer

matter (typ.) MS or TS copy to be printed, type that has been set

Matterhorn an Alpine peak; in Fr. **Mont Cervin**, It. **Monte Cervino**

Matthew (NT) abbr. **Matt.**

Matthew Paris *see* **Paris, Matthew**

Matthews the usual spelling, *but see* **Mathews**

mattins *see* **matins**

maty *use* **-tey**

matzo/ unleavened bread; pl. **-s**, (more correctly) **-th**

Mau Uttar Pradesh, India; *see also* **Mhow**

Maugham, (William) Somerset (1874–1965) English novelist and playwright

Maugrabin, Hayraddin a character in Scott's *Quentin Durward*

Maulmain Burma, *but* **Moulmein** in Kipling

maulstick a painter's hand rest, *not* mahl-

Mau Mau a Kikuyu secret society in Kenya, rebelled 1952 (two words)

Maundy Thursday the day before Good Friday, *not* Maunday (two words)

Maupassant, Guy de (1850–93) French writer

Mauresque *use* **Mor-**

Mauretania an ancient region of NW Africa; cf. **Mauri-**

Mauretania name of two successive Cunard liners

Maurist a member of the reformed Benedictine congregation of St Maur (Fr.)

Mauritania NW Africa; cf. **Maure-**

Mauriti/us in Indian Ocean, **-an**

mausoleum/ a magnificent tomb, pl. **-s**

mauvaise honte (Fr. f.) shyness

mauvais/ goût (Fr. m.) bad taste; — *pas* a difficulty; — *quart d'heure* a bad quarter of an hour, a short unpleasant time; — *sujet* a ne'er-do-well; — *ton* bad style

maverick an unbranded animal, masterless person, rover (not cap.)

Má Vlast (My Country) a cycle of six symphonic poems by Smetana, 1874–9

Max. Maximilian I or II, Holy Roman Emperors

max. maxim, maximum

maxill/a the jaw, pl. **-ae**

maximize *not* -ise

maxim/um the greatest, pl. **-a**; abbr. **max.** (not ital.)

maxwell a unit of magnetic flux, abbr. **Mx**

Maxwell, James Clerk (1831–79) Scottish physicist, *not* Clerk-Maxwell

Maxwell-Lyte, Sir Henry Churchill (1848–1940) English historical writer

May (month of) not to be abbr.

may (tree) (not cap.)

Maya/ one of an Indian people of Cent. America and S. Mexico, pl. same; **-n**

maya (Hindu philos.) illusion

maybe perhaps (one word)

May-bug (hyphen)

May Day 1 May (caps., two words)

mayday international radio distress signal (one word, not cap.)

Mayence on the Rhine *use* **Mainz am Rhein**

Mayfair London (one word), *but* **May Fair Intercontinental Hotel** London

may/flower, -fly (one word)

mayor cap. only as title or in the City of London

maypole (one word)

May queen (two words, one cap.)

mayst (no apos.)

mazagran (Fr. m.) black coffee served in a glass

Mazarin Bible 42-line, first book printed from movable type, by Gutenberg and Fust, *c.*1450; **Cardinal Mazarin** (1602–61) had twenty-five copies

mazarine deep blue

Mazatlán Mexico

mazel tov (Yiddish) congratulations! (lit. 'good luck!')

Mazepa, Ivan (1644–1709) Cossack chief, hero of Byron's poem *Mazeppa*, 1819

mazurka a Polish dance, not mazou-

Mazzini, Giuseppe (1805–72) Italian patriot

MB *Medicinae Baccalaureus* (Bachelor of Medicine)

mb millibar

MBA Master of Business Administration

Mbabane Swaziland

mbar millibar

MBCS Member of the British Computer Society

MBE Member of the Order of the British Empire

MBIM Member of the British Institute of Management

MC Master of Ceremonies, Master of Surgery, (US) Member of Congress, Member of Council, Military Cross

Mc *see* **Mac-, Mc-, Mᶜ-**

M/c Manchester, machine

MCC Marylebone Cricket Club

M.Ch., M.Chir. *Magister Chirurgiae* (Master of Surgery)

mCi millicurie, -s

M.Com. Master of Commerce

MCP male chauvinist pig, Member of the College of Preceptors

MCR Middle Common Room

MCS Military College of Science

Mc/s *use* **MHz**

MCSP Member of the Chartered Society of Physiotherapy

MD managing director, Maryland (postal abbr.), (Lat.) *Medicinae Doctor* (Doctor of Medicine), mentally deficient, Middle Dutch, (It. mus.) *mano destra* (right hand), (Fr. mus.) *main droite* (right hand)

Md mendelevium (no point)

Md. Maryland (off. abbr.)

Mdlle *use* **Mlle** (Mademoiselle)

MDMA methylenedioxymethamphetamine; *see also* **ecstasy**

Mdme *use* **Mme** (Madame)

MDS Master of Dental Surgery

MDT (US) Mountain Daylight Time

MDu. Middle Dutch

ME Maine (postal abbr.), Marine Engineer, Mechanical Engineer, Middle English, Military Engineer, Mining Engineer, Most Excellent, myalgic encephalomyelitis

Me. Maine (off. abbr.)

Mᵉ (Fr.) *maître* (title of a French advocate)

me (mus.) *not* mi

me, it is, it is I both are used in speech, but the former should not be printed, except as a colloquialism

mea culpa (Lat.) by my fault

meagre *not* -er (US)

mealie/ (S. Afr.) an ear or grain of maize, pl. **-s**

meal ticket (two words)

mealtime (one word)

mealy-mouthed hypocritical (hyphen)

mean time that based on mean sun (two words)

meantime (adv.) *but* 'in the mean time'

meanwhile (adv.) *but* 'in the mean while'

measur/e, -able, -ing abbr. **meas.**; (typ.) the width to which type is set, usually stated in 12-pt. (pica) ems; (US mus.) = a bar or its time-content

measuring/ cup, — device, — glass, — jug, — line, — tape (two words)

meatball (one word)

Mebyon Kernow (Corn.) 'sons of Cornwall', movement for Cornish independence

MEC Member of Executive Council

Mecca the capital of Hejaz, and one of the federal capitals of Saudi Arabia; *not* Mekka, -ah, -eh; *see also* **Riyadh**

Mecenas *use* **Mae-**

mech. mechan/ics, -ical

mechanics is sing. as name of the science

Mechelen Belgium, in Fr. **Malines**

Mechlin lace etc., *but see* **Mechelen**; **Malines**

Mecklenburgh Square London, WC

Mecklenburg/-Schwerin, -Strelitz Germany

Mec Vannin (Manx) 'sons of Man', movement for Manx independence

M.Ed. Master of Education

med. medical, medicine, medieval, medium

medal/, -led, -lion, -list *not* -ist (US)

Mede a member of an Indo-European people that established an empire in Media in Persia in the 7th c. BC

Médecin malgré lui, Le a play by Molière, 1666

media pl. of **medium**, remains plural in all senses.

mediaeval *use* **medie-**

medic (sl.) a doctor or medical student (no point)

Medicaid (US) a government programme of health insurance for those requiring financial assistance

medical/ abbr. **med.**; **— signs** ʒ drachm, ♏ minim, M *misce* (mix), ʒ ounce, ○ pint, ℞ *recipe*, ℈ scruple

Medicare (US) government programme of medical care, esp. for the aged

Medic/i Florentine ruling family, 15th–18th cc.; **-ean**; individual names are *de' Medici*, *see also* **Catherine de' Medici**

medicinae (Lat.) of medicine, abbr. **M.**

medicine abbr. **med.**

medico/ (colloq.) a doctor or medical student, pl. **-s**

medieval/ abbr. **med.**; **-ism, -ist, -ize**, etc., *not* mediae-

Medina a river, IoW; Arabia, in Arab. **al-Madinah**

Medit. Mediterranean

meditatio fugae (Lat., Sc. law) contemplation of flight

medi/um pl. **-a**, in spiritualism **-ums** (not ital.); abbr. **med.**; *see also* **media**

med. jur. medical jurisprudence

Médoc SW France, a claret from this region

meerschaum (not cap.)

Meerut Uttar Pradesh, India; *not* Merath, Mirat

mega- a prefix meaning a million or very large; abbr. **M**

Megaera (Gr. myth.) one of the Furies

megahertz a million hertz, esp. as a measure of frequency of radio transmissions, abbr. **MHz**

Megara a city and port, ancient Greece

megaton a unit of explosive power equal to one million tons of TNT, *not* -tonne; abbr. **MT**

megavolt (elec.) a million volts, abbr. **MV**

megawatt (elec.) a million watts, abbr. **MW**

megilp an artist's medium, a vehicle for oil colours; *not* mag-, -ilph

megohm (elec.) a million ohms, abbr. **MΩ**

megrim/, -s headache, 'the blues'

Mehmetçik (Turk.) a general name (lit. 'Little Mehmet'), equivalent to 'Tommy Atkins' or 'GI Joe'

mehrab *use* **mi-**

Meiji Tenno born **Mutsuhito** (1852–1912) emperor of Japan, **Meiji** the period of his rule

Meilhac, Henri (1831–97) French playwright

mein Herr (Ger.) a form of address, as 'sir'; pl. *meine Herren*; f. *meine Dame*, pl. *meine Damen*

meios/is (rhet.) diminution, understatement (*see also* **litotes**); (biol.) cell division before fertilization, pl. **-es**

Meiringen Switzerland, *not* Mey-

Meirionnydd a district of Gwynedd

Meissen a porcelain, from German town

Meissonier, Jean Louis Ernest (1815–91) French painter

Meissonnier, Juste Aurèle (1693–1750) French goldsmith, architect, furniture designer

Meistersinger a member of one of the 14th- to 16th-c. German guilds for lyric poets and musicians, pl. same

Meistersinger von Nürnberg, Die an opera by Wagner, 1867

Méjico Sp. for **Mexico**, in Amer. Sp. **México**

me judice (Lat.) in my opinion

Mekk/a, -ah, -eh *use* **Mecca**

Melanchthon, Philip Graecized form of **Philipp Schwarzerd** (1497–1560) Luther's associate

Melanesia/ the islands between the Equator and the Tropic of Capricorn, and between New Guinea and Fiji (a region and archbishopric, *not* a political unit); **-n** (of or relating to) (a member of) the dominant Negroid people of Melanesia or their group of

Oceanic languages (the pidgin is officially **Neo-Melanesian**)

mélange (Fr. m.) a mixture, medley

Melchior, Lauritz (1890–1973) Danish tenor

Melchi/zedek (OT) King of Salem; **-sedec** in NT, *but* **-zedek** in NEB

mêlée a fray (not ital., no accents in US)

Meliboean (poet.) alternating; *not* -aean, -bean

Melos a Greek island; *see also* **Milo**

Melpomene (Gr. myth.) the muse of tragedy

melt spleen, *use* **milt**

meltdown (noun, one word)

melting/ point, — pot (two words)

Melton Mowbray Leics. (two words)

mem. memento, memorial

Member abbr. **M.**

Member of Parliament (caps.) abbr. **MP**, pl. **MPs**

memento/ a souvenir, pl. **-es**; abbr. **mem.** (not ital.)

memento mori (Lat.) an object reminding one of death, 'remember that you must die', pl. same (not ital.)

Meml/ook, -uk *use* **Mameluke**

memo/ memorandum, pl. **-s** (no point)

mémoire (Fr. m.) bill, report, treatise; (f.) memory

memorabilia (pl.) noteworthy things

memorand/um a written note, pl. **-ums**; pl. **-a** things to be noted; *see also* **memo**

memorial abbr. **mem.**

Memorial Day (US) the last Monday in May

memorialize to commemorate by a memorial, *not* -ise

memoria technica a system or contrivance used to assist the memory, mnemonics (not ital.)

memorize *not* - ise

memsahib *see* **sahib**

menad *use* **mae-**

ménage a household (not ital.), cf. **manège**; *ménage à trois* an arrangement in which three people live together, typically a married couple and the lover of one of them

menagerie (a place for) a collection of wild animals, *not* -ery

menarche the onset of menstruation

Mencken, H(enry) L(ouis) (1880–1956) US author, critic, and editor

mendacity falsehood

Mendel/, Gregor Johann (1822–84) Austrian botanist; **-ian, -ism**

Mendeleev, Dmitri (Ivanovich) (1834–1907) Russian chemist

mendelevium symbol **Md**

Mendelssohn(**-Bartholdy**), **Jacob Ludwig Felix** (1809–47) German composer

mendicity begging

meneer (Afrik.) Mr, sir

menhaden N. American fish of herring family, *not* man-

menhir (archaeol.) a tall, upright, usually pre-historic monumental stone

meningitis an inflammation of the meninges

Mennonite a member of a Protestant sect

meno (It. mus.) less

Menorca Sp. for Minorca

mensa (Lat.) a table; *a mensa et toro* from bed and board (a kind of divorce), not *thoro*

Mensa a constellation, an organization for those with a high IQ (one cap.)

Menshevik a member of the non-Leninist wing of the Russian Social Democratic Party before 1917; *see also* **Bolshevik**

Men's Lib (caps., no point)

mens/ rea (Lat.) criminal intent, the knowledge of wrongdoing; *— sana in corpore sano* a sound mind in a sound body

menstru/um a solvent, pl. **-a**

mensur. mensuration

menswear (one word, no apos.)

menthe (Fr. cook. f.) mint, not *mi-*

Menton French Riviera, in It. **Mentone**

mentor an experienced and trusted adviser (not cap.)

menu/ pl. **-s**

Menuhin, Sir Yehudi (1916–99) US-born British violinist

meow *use* **miaow**

MEP Member of the European Parliament

m.e.p. mean effective pressure

Mephistophele/s; **-an** a fiendish person like Mephistopheles (cap.); malicious, cynical (not cap.); *not* -ian

mer. meridian, meridional

Merano Italian Tyrol

Merath *use* **Meerut**

Mercator projection a method of map making (one cap.); *not* -'s

Mercedes(**-Benz**) a German make of car (hyphen); **Mercédès** (Fr.), **Mercedes** (Sp.) a woman's name

mercerize *not* -ise

merchandise (noun and verb) *not* -ize

Merchant/ Company Schools Edinburgh, **— Taylors Company**, *but* **— Taylors' School** (apos.)

merci (Fr. m.) thanks; no, thank you; (f.) mercy

mercur/y symbol **Hg**; **-ial** swift, volatile, (cap.) of the planet Mercury

Meredith/, George (1828–1909) English novelist and poet, adj. **-ian**; **—, Owen** *see* **Bulwer-Lytton, Edward Robert**

meretricious befitting a prostitute, showy

meridian abbr. **m.**, **mer.**

meridies (Lat.) noon, abbr. **m.**

meridional of a meridian; abbr. **m.**, **mer.**; (noun) an inhabitant of S. Europe, esp of S. France

Mérimée, Prosper (1803–70) French novelist and historian

merino/ a sheep, pl. **-s**

merissa a Sudanese drink made from fermented maize

meritocracy government by the best people

meritorious deserving reward or praise

merle the common blackbird, *not* merl

merlin a small falcon

merlon the solid part of an embattled parapet

Merovingian (a king) of a Frankish dynasty in Gaul and Germany, *c*.500–700

Merrimack town and river in NH; (ital.) the name of the Confederate ironclad warship that fought the *Monitor* during the US Civil War

merry andrew a buffoon (two words, not cap.)

merry-go-round (hyphens)

merrythought the wishbone (one word)

Merseyside a metropolitan county

Merthyr Tydfil Mid Glam. (two words), *not* -vil

Merv Turkmenistan, *now* **Mary**

mesa a flat-topped mountain

mésalliance (Fr. f.) marriage with a social inferior, in Eng. *use* **misalliance**

mescal/ a maguey, or the liquor obtained from this (cf. **tequila**); **— buttons**; **-ine**, *not* -in

Mesdames (Fr.) pl. of **Madame**, abbr. **Mmes**

Mesdemoiselles (Fr.) pl. of **Mademoiselle**; abbr. **Mlles**, *not* Mdlles

mesjid *use* **mas-**

mesmerize hypnotize, fascinate; *not* -ise

Mesolongi *use* **Missolonghi**

Mesozoic (geol.) (of or relating to) an era of geological time marked by the development of dinosaurs, and with evidence of the first mammals, birds, and flowering plants (cap.)

mesquite/ a N. American tree, *not* -it; **— bean** (two words)

Messeigneurs pl. of **Monseigneur**

Messerschmitt, Willy (**Wilhelm Emil**) (1898–1978) German aircraft designer, *not* -dt

Messiaen, Olivier (**Eugène Prosper Charles**) (1908–92) French organist and composer

Messia/h, -nic a (would-be) liberator of an oppressed people, the promised deliverer of the Jews (caps.); *Messiah* oratorio by Handel, 1742, *not The —*

Messieurs (Fr.) pl. of **Monsieur**; abbr. **MM.**

mess/jacket, — kit (two words)

Messrs pl. of **Mr** (no point)

mess tin (two words)

messuage (law) a dwelling house with out-buildings and land assigned to its use

mestiz/o a person of Spanish and American Indian blood, *not* -ino; pl. **-os**; f. **-a,** pl. **-as**

Met, the (UK) the Meteorological Office, the Metropolitan Police in London, (US) the Metropolitan Opera House in New York

met. metallurg/y, -ical, -ist; metronome

meta- combination form (usually **met-** before a vowel or *h*)

metal/, -led, -ling, -lize (one *l* in US), *not* -ise

metallurg/y, -ical, -ist abbr. **met., metall.**

metamorphos/e transform; *not* -ise, -ize; noun **-is,** pl. **-es**

metaph. metaphys/ics, -ical, -ically, -ician; metaphor, -ical, -ically

metaphras/e (noun) a literal translation, (verb tr.) put into other words; (adj.) **-tic**

metathes/is pl. **-es**

meteor/, -ite, -oid

meteor. meteorology

meter measuring device, (US) = **metre**

Meth. Methodist

methodize *not* -ise

Methuselah a very old person or thing, from the name of an OT patriarch said to have lived 969 years (Gen. 5: 27); a wine bottle of about eight times the standard size (not cap.)

métier (Fr. m.) one's trade, profession, or forte

Metis a person of mixed race, esp. the offspring of a white person and a Native American in Canada; pl. same; f. **Metisse/,** pl. **-s;** in Fr. *métis,* f. *métisse*

metonymy abbr. **meton.**

metre/ SI unit of length, 39.37 in.; *not* -er (US); abbr. **m** (no point); **-age** number of metres, *not* -rage

Métro, Le (no point) abbr. of *Le Métropolitain,* the Paris underground railway

metrology the science of weights and measures, abbr. **metrol.**

metronome/ (mus.) an instrument for fixing tempos; abbr. **M., met.; Maelzel's —** abbr. **MM**

metronymic *use* ma-

metropol/is pl. **-ises; -itan;** abbr. **metrop.**

metr/um (Lat. verse) metre, abbr. **m.;** pl. **-a,** abbr. **mm.**

meubl/é (Fr.) f. **-ée** furnished

meum/ (Lat.) mine; **— and** *tuum* mine and thine, *not et tuum*

meunière (esp. of fish) floured and cooked or served in lightly browned butter with lemon juice and parsley (not ital.)

Meuse a river of France, Belgium, and the Netherlands; in Du. **Maas**

MeV mega-electronvolt

meV milli-electronvolt

mews a street of stables converted into garages or houses, pl. same

Mex. Mexic/o, -an

Mexican (noun) a native or national of Mexico, a person of Mexican descent; a language spoken in Mexico, esp. Nahuatl; (adj.) of or relating to Mexico or its people, *or* of Mexican descent

Mexico/ in Amer. Sp. **México,** in Sp. **Méjico; — City** in Amer. Sp. **Ciudad México,** often shortened to **México; Mexican**

Meynell,/ Alice (1847–1922) English poet, **— Sir Francis** (1891–1975) English typographer, **— Wilfrid** (1852–1948) English writer

Meyringen *use* **Mei-**

MEZ (Ger.) *Mitteleuropäische Zeit* = **Central European Time,** one hour in advance of GMT

mezereon (bot.) a spring-flowering shrub, *not* -eum

mezuz/ah a parchment inscribed with religious texts and attached in a case to the doorpost of a Jewish house as a sign of faith, pl. **-oth**

mezzanine a low storey between two others; (UK) a floor or space beneath the stage, (US) a dress circle

mezza voce (It. mus.) not with full strength of sound, abbr. *m.v.*

mezzo/ short for mezzo-soprano, pl. **-s**

mezz/o (It. mus.) f. **-a** half, medium; abbr. **M.**

mezzo-relievo half-relief

mezzo-soprano (mus., hyphen)

mezzotint (typ.) an intaglio illustration process from a roughened plate

MF (paper) machine finish, medium frequency, (typ.) modern face

mf (mus.) mezzo forte (fairly loud)

mfd. manufactured

mfg. manufacturing

MFH Master of Foxhounds

MFHom. Member of the Faculty of Homoeopathy

MFN most favoured nation

MFr. Middle French

mfr. manufactur/e, -er

mfrs. manufactur/ers, -es

m.ft. *mixtura* (or, in early modern texts, *mistura*) *fiat* (let a mixture be made)

MG (paper) machine glazed, machine gun, (Fr. mus.) *main gauche* (left hand), Morris Garages (as a make of car)

Mg magnesium (no point)

mg milligram (no point)

MGB USSR 'Ministry of State Security', 1946–53; *see also* **KGB**

M.Glam. Mid Glamorgan

MGM Metro-Goldwyn-Mayer, US film studio

Mgr Monseigneur, Monsignor (no point)

MGr. Middle Greek

Mgr. Manager, pl. **Mgrs.**

MH Master of Hounds (usually beagles or harriers)

MHG Middle High German

MHK Member of the House of Keys (IoM)

mho (elec.) a former unit of conductance, the reciprocal of an **ohm**

M.Hon. Most Honourable

Mhow Madhya Pradesh, India; *see also* **Mau**

MHR Member of the House of Representatives

MHz megahertz (no point, two caps.)

MI Michigan (postal abbr.), Middle Irish, Military Intelligence, Mounted Infantry

MI5 Military Intelligence department concerned with state security, **MI6** Military Intelligence department concerned with espionage (neither is in official use) (no points)

MIAE Member of the Institute of Automobile Engineers

M.I.Ae.E. Member of the Institute of Aeronautical Engineers (also without points)

mi. mile(s)

miaow the cry of a cat; *not* meow (US), miaou (Fr.), miau (Sp.), miaul

miasm/a (Gr.) a noxious emanation, pl. **-ata** (not ital.)

M.I.Biol. Member of the Institute of Biology

Mic. Micah (OT)

micaceous pertaining to mica, *not* -ious

Micawber/, Wilkins a character in Dickens's *David Copperfield*, **-ish** unpractical but hopeful; **-ism**

MICE Member of the Institution of Civil Engineers

Mich. Michaelmas, 29 Sept.; Michigan (off. abbr.)

Michelangelo Buonarroti (1475–1564) Italian sculptor, painter, architect, poet (two words, not three)

Michelson/, Albert Abraham (1852–1931) German-American physicist; **–Morley** experiment (en rule)

M.I.Chem.E. Member of the Institution of Chemical Engineers

Michener, James (**Albert**) (1907–97) US novelist

Michigan off. abbr. **Mich.**, postal **MI**

mickey/ (to take the — out of) to make fun of, *not* micky

Mickey Finn (US) a drugged drink

Mickiewicz, Adam (1798–1855) Polish poet

Micmac (of or relating to) (a member of) a Native American tribe (one word)

micro- a prefix meaning very small, or one-millionth; symbol μ, e.g. **microhm**, μΩ; **micrometre** (*preferred* to **micron**), μm; **microvolt**, μV

microchip (one word)

microeconomics the branch of economics dealing with individual commodities, producers, etc. (one word); cf. **macroeconomics**

microelectronics (one word)

microfiche a sheet of film, suitable for filing, containing microphotographs of pages of book, periodical, manuscript, etc.; pl. same

microfilm film bearing microphotographs

microgram one-millionth of a gram, abbr. **μg**

micrography the description or delineation of microscopic objects

micrometer an instrument for measuring minute distances or angles; cf. **micrometre**, *see also under* **micro-**

micromillimetre *or* **millimicron** abbr. **mμ**, *but* use **nanometre** abbr. **nm**

micron symbol **μ**, *but* use **micrometre** (*see under* **micro-**)

Micronesia islands north of Melanesia

micro-organism (hyphen)

microphotograph a photograph reduced to microscopic size; cf. **photomicrograph**

microprocessor (one word)

micros. microscop/y, -ist

microsecond one-millionth of a second, abbr. **μs**

Microsoft (propr.) (the manufacturer of) an operating system for microcomputers, abbr. **MS**

microwave oven (two words)

mid. middle

midbrain (one word)

Mid Calder Lothian (caps., no hyphens)

midday (one word)

middle abbr. **M.**, **mid.**

middle age (two words) *but* **middle-aged** (hyphen)

Middle Ages, the roughly from the fall of the Western Roman Empire to the Renaissance and the Reformation (two words, caps.)

middle class (two words, hyphen when attrib.)

middle common room a common room for the use of graduate members of a college who are not Fellows, abbr. **MCR**

Middle East *not* Mideast (US)

Middle English the English language in use *c.*1150–1500, abbr. **ME**

Middle French the French language in use 12th–15th cc. (the French do not make this distinction), abbr. **MFr.**

Middle Greek the Greek language in use 7th–15th cc., abbr. **MGr.**

Middle High German the High German language in use *c.*1100–1500, abbr. **MHG**

Middle Irish the Irish language in use 11th–15th cc., abbr. **MI**

Middle Low German the Low German language in use *c.*1100–1500, abbr. **MLG**

middleman (one word)

middle-of-the-road (adj.) moderate, avoiding extremes (no hyphens as a noun)

Middlesbrough Cleveland, *not* -borough

Middle Scots the Scots language in use late 15th–early 17th cc., abbr. **MS**

Middlesex a former county of England, abbr. **Middx.**

Middleton,/ Baron family name Willoughby; **— Thomas** (*c.*1570–1627) English playwright; *see also* **Midleton; Mydd-**

Middle Welsh the Welsh language in use *c.*1150–1500, abbr. **MW**

Middle West (US) N. Cent. states as geographical area; *see also* **Midwest**

Middx. Middlesex

Mideast (US) = **Middle East**

midfield/ (noun and adj., one word), **-er**

Midgard (Norse myth.) abode of human beings

Mid Glamorgan a county of Wales, abbr. **Mid Glam., M.Glam.**

MIDI musical instrument digital interface

midi a thing of medium length or size

Midianite member of an ancient N. Arabian people

midinette a Parisian shop girl (not ital.)

Midland Bank plc

Midlands, the inland counties of central England, the region south of the Humber and Mersey and north of the Thames, excepting Norfolk, Suffolk, Essex, Middlesex, Hertfordshire, Gloucestershire, and the counties bordering on Wales; in hunting, the champaign country including parts of Leicestershire, Northamptonshire, Warwickshire, Nottinghamshire, and Derbyshire

Mid Lent the fourth Sunday in Lent (two caps., two words)

Midleton, Viscount family name Brodrick; *see also* **Midd-; Mydd-**

mid-life (hyphen, one word in US)

Midlothian former county of Scotland (one word)

mid/night, -rib, -ship (one word)

Midsomer Norton Avon

midsummer (one word)

Midsummer Day 24 June (two words, caps.)

midway (one word)

Midwest/, the (US) N. Cent. states considered as a single political or social region (one word); *see also* **Middle West; -erner**

midwi/fe pl. **-ves; -fery**

midwinter (one word)

MIEE Member of the Institution of Electrical Engineers

mielie *use* **meal-**

Miers, Sir Henry Alexander (1858–1942) English mineralogist; *see also* **Myers; Myres**

Mies van der Rohe, Ludwig (1886–1969) German-born US architect

MiG any of several aircraft designed by Mikoyan and Gurevich; individual models are cited with a hyphen, e.g. MiG-15, MiG-21 (two caps.)

mightest *not* mightst

mignonette a fragrant plant, in Fr. f. *mignonnette*

Mihailović, Draža (b. **Dragoljub**) (1893–1946) Yugoslav soldier, sometimes Anglicized as **Drazha Mihailovich**

mihrab a niche or slab in a mosque, indicating the direction of Mecca; *not* me-, mirh-; in Arab. *miḥrāb*; *see also* **kiblah**

MIJ *use* **MJI**

mijnheer (Du.) Sir, Mr; cf. **mynheer**

mil one-thousandth of an inch (no point)

mil. military, militia

Milan Italy, in It. **Milano**

milch cow a source of easy profit, *not* milk (two words)

mile/ abbr. **m.**, pl. **mls.; nautical —** = 6,076 feet; **statute —** = 5,280 feet; in Fr. m. *mille*, pl. *milles*

mileage a number of miles, *not* -lage

Milesian (an inhabitant) of ancient Miletus in Asia Minor, (joc.) an Irishman

milestone (one word)

milieu/ environment (not ital.), pl. **-x**; *see also* *juste milieu*

military abbr. **mil.**

Military Academy abbr. **MA**

militate have effect; cf. **mitigate**

militia abbr. **M., mil.**

milk/ bar, — chocolate, — float (two words)

milkman (one word)

milk/ pudding, — round, — run, — shake (two words)

milksop (one word)

Milky Way (astr.) (caps.)

mill abbr. **m.**

Mill,/ James (1773–1836) Scottish historian and economist; **— John Stuart** (1806–73) his son, English economist and political philosopher

Millais, Sir John Everett (1829–96) English painter; *see also* **Millet**

Millay, Edna St Vincent (1892–1950) US poet, 'St.' (point) in US use

millboard a stout pasteboard for bookbinding etc. (one word)

mille/ (Fr. m.) a thousand, pl. same, abbr. **M.**; also a mile, pl. *-s*; *-feuille* (m.) a confection, (f.) a plant (one word)

millenar/y of a thousand, (celebration of) the thousandth anniversary; **-ian**

millenni/um a thousand years; pl. **-a** in literal senses, **-ums** in general contexts (two *l*s, two *n*s), **-al**

mille passus (Lat.) 1,000 paces of 5 feet, or the Roman mile; abbr. **MP**, **m.p.**; pl. *milia passuum*

millepede *see* **millipede**

Milles-Lade family name of Earl Sondes; *see also* **Mills**

Millet,/ Aimé (1819–91) French sculptor, — **Jean-François** (1814–75) French painter; *see also* **Millais**

milli- prefix meaning one-thousandth; abbr. **m**, e.g. **milliampere** abbr. **mA**

milliard one thousand million; *see* **billion**

millibar a unit of pressure, one-thousandth of a bar; abbr. **mbar**, (meteor.) **mb** (no point)

milligram one-thousandth of a gram; abbr. **mg** (no point); *not* -gramme

millilitre one-thousandth of a litre, abbr. **ml** (no point)

millimetre one-thousandth of a metre, 0.039 in.; abbr. **mm** (no point)

millimicron *use* **nanometre**

million abbr. **m.**; for millions of pounds use e.g. £150m.

millionaire not -onnaire

millipede (zool.) *not* mille- (though most correct)

Mills the family name of Baron Hillingdon; *see also* **Milles-Lade**

Milngavie Strathclyde

Milo Fr. and It. for **Melos**, a Greek island, esp. in Venus de Milo

M.I.Loco.E. Member of the Institute of Locomotive Engineers

Milošović, Slobodan (b. 1941) president of Serbia 1992–7, president of the Federal Republic of Yugoslavia 1997–

milt the spleen, *not* melt

Milton Keynes Bucks.

Milwaukee Wis.

M.I.Mech.E. Member of the Institution of Mechanical Engineers

mimeograph (noun) (often attrib.) a duplicating machine that produces copies from a stencil, a copy produced in this way; (verb) produce copies by this process; abbr. **mimeo**

mimic/, -ked, -king, -ry

M.I.Min.E. Member of the Institution of Mining Engineers

MIMM Member of the Institution of Mining and Metallurgy

Min any of the Chinese languages or dialects spoken in Fukien province, SE China

min. minim, minimum, mining, minister, ministry, minor; minute, -s (no point in scientific and technical work)

min/a an ancient Greek unit of weight and currency, pl. **-ae**; for the bird, *use* **mynah**

minac/ious threatening, **-ity**

minatory threatening

minauderie affected, simpering behaviour (not ital.)

mincemeat (one word)

mince pie (two words)

Mindanao one of the Philippine Islands, *not* -oa

Mindererus/ Latinized name of **R. M. Minderer** (*c.*1570–1621) German physician, — **spirit** a diaphoretic

mine-detector (hyphen, two words in US)

mine/field, -hunter, -layer (one word)

mineralog/y, -ical abbr. **mineral.**; *not* minerological, -ology

minever *use* **mini-**

mingy mean, *not* -ey

Mini (propr.) a make of car (cap.); a short skirt or dress (not cap.)

mini/bus, -cab, -car, -computer (one word)

Minié, Claude Étienne (1814–79) inventor of a type of bullet and rifle

minikin a diminutive person or thing; cf. **manakin**; **manikin**; **mannequin**; **mannikin**

minim a drop, one-sixtieth of fluid drachm; abbr. **min.**; sign ℥; (mus.) a halfnote

minimize *not* -ise

minim/um pl. **-a** (not ital.), abbr. **min.**

mining abbr. **min.**

miniscule *use* **minu-**

miniseries a short series of television programmes on a single theme (one word)

miniskirt (one word)

minister abbr. **min.**

Minister without Portfolio (two caps.)

minium a red oxide of lead

miniver a plain white fur, *not* -ever

minke a small baleen whale

Minn. Minnesota (off. abbr.)

Minneapolis Minn.

Minnehaha wife of Hiawatha in Longfellow's poem

minnesinger one of a school of medieval German lyric poets (not cap. or ital.)

Minnesota off. abbr. **Minn.**, postal **MN**

Minoan pertaining to the Bronze Age civilization, language, or scripts of ancient Crete, *c*.3000–1100 BC (from King Minos)

minor abbr. **min.**, (in Peerage) **M.**

Minorca Balearic Islands, in Sp. **Menorca**

Minories a street in London

Minotaur (Gr. myth.) the monstrous offspring of a bull and Pasiphaë, wife of King Minos

Min./ Plen. *or* **Plenip.** Minister Plenipotentiary, **— Res.** Minister Residentiary

M.Inst.P. Member of the Institute of Physics

Mint, the (cap.)

minthe use **menthe**

minuet a dance, its music; *not* -ette

minus/ sign −; pl. **-es**

minuscule (palaeography) a kind of cursive script developed in the 7th c.; a small or lower-case letter; (adj.) tiny; *not* mini-

minute/, -s abbr. **m.**, **min.** (no point in scientific and technical work); sign ′; **— mark** (′) symbol for feet, minutes, also placed after a stressed syllable

minuti/ae small details, sing. **-a** (not ital.)

MIOB Member of the Institute of Building

Miocene (geol.) (of or relating to) the fourth epoch of the Tertiary period (cap., not ital.)

mi/osis the contraction of the pupil of the eye, *not* my-; **-otic**

MIPA Member of the Institute of Practitioners in Advertising

mirabile/ dictu (Lat.) wonderful to relate, **— *visu*** wonderful to see

MIRAS mortgage interest relief at source

Mirat *use* **Meerut**

mirepoix (Fr. cook. m.) sautéd chopped vegetables

mirhab *use* **mihr-**

mirky dark, *use* **mur-**

Miró, Joan (1893–1983) Catalan painter

MIRV multiple independently targeted re-entry vehicle (a type of ballistic missile)

miry mirelike, *not* -ey

Mirzapur Uttar Pradesh, India; *not* -pore

mis/advice bad counsel, **-advise** give it (one word)

misalliance marriage with a social inferior, in Fr. f. *mésalliance*

misan/dry the hatred of men, **-thropy** the hatred of humankind

misc. miscellaneous, miscellany

miscellanea miscellaneous matter, is plural

miscellany a mixture, medley, collection

mischievous *not* -ious

miscible capable of being mixed, esp. in scientific and technical contexts; *see also* **mixable**

misdemeanour *not* -or (US)

Mise (Fr.) *marquise* (marchioness) *not Mise*

mise en abyme (Fr. lit. f.) an internal duplication of (part of) a literary work; *not abîme*, no hyphens

mise-en-scène (Fr. f.) scenery, stage effect (no hyphens as Eng. lit. term)

misère a declaration to win no tricks in cards

Miserere (a musical setting of) the 50th Psalm of the Vulgate

miserere (*properly* **misericord**) a bracket on a turn-up seat used as support for a person standing

misfeasance a wrongful act; (law) a transgression, esp. the wrongful exercise of lawful authority; cf. **malfeasance**

mishmash a mixture (one word)

Mishna/h a collection of Jewish precepts forming the basis of the Talmud, and embodying Jewish oral law; **-ic**

misle *use* **mizz-**

misletoe *use* **mistle-**

misogam/y the hatred of marriage, **-ist**

misogyn/y the hatred of women, **-ist**

misprint (typ.) a typographical error

Miss (cap. as title, no point)

Miss. Mission, -ary; Mississippi (off. abbr.)

missal (RC) a book containing the texts used in the service of the mass throughout the year; a book of prayers

missel thrush *use* **mistle**

misseltoe *use* **mistle-**

mis/send, -sent (one word)

misshape/, -n (one word)

Mission/, -ary abbr. **Miss.**

missis (sl.) Mrs, *not* -us (US sl.)

Mississippi a river and state, USA; off. abbr. **Miss.**, postal **MS**

Missolonghi Greece

Missouri a river and state, USA; off. abbr. **Mo.**, postal **MO**

mis/spell, -spend, -spent, -state, -step (one word)

missus (US sl.) = **missis**

mist (meteor.) abbr. **m.**

mistakable *not* -eable

Mister abbr. **Mr**

Mistinguett pseud. of **Jeanne Marie Bourgeois** (1875–1956) French entertainer, *not* -e

mistle *use* **mizzle**

mistle thrush *not* missel

mistletoe *not* missel-, misle-

Mistral,/ Frédéric (1830–1914) Provençal poet, **— Gabriela** pseud. of **Lucila Godoy de Alcayaga** (1889–1957) Chilean poet

mistral (not ital.)

Mistress abbr. **Mrs**

M.I.Struct.E. Member of the Institution of Structural Engineers

MIT Massachusetts Institute of Technology

miter *use* **mitre** (except in US)

Mithra/s the Persian sun-god; **-ic, -ism**

Mithridat/es (VI, 136–63 BC) King of Pontus, *not* Mithra-; **-ize, -ic, -ism** (not cap.)

mitigate (verb) moderate; cf. **militate**

Mitilini *see* **Mytilene**

mitre/ *not* miter (US); **-block, -board, -box** (hyphens)

mitre wheels (two words)

mitring *not* mitreing

Mitterrand, François (1916–96) President of France 1981–95

mixable in gen. use, *not* -ible; *see also* **miscible**

Mizen Head Co. Cork

mizzen/ the aftermost of the fore-and-aft sails; **-mast** the aftermost mast of a three-masted ship (one word); *not* miz-

mizzle a fine rain; *not* misle, mistle

MJI Member of the Institute of Journalists, *not* MIJ

Mk. identifying a particular design, as Mk. V; mark (Ger. coin), *use* **DM**

mks metre-kilogram-second (no points)

mkt. market

ML Licentiate in Midwifery, Medieval Latin, Middle Latin, motor launch

Ml. mail

ml millilitre, -s (no point)

MLA Member of the Legislative Assembly, Modern Languages Association

MLC Member of the Legislative Council

MLD minimum lethal dose

MLF Multilateral Nuclear Force

MLG Middle Low German

M.Litt. Master of Letters

Mlle/ Mademoiselle, pl. **-s** (no point)

MLR minimum lending rate

MLS Member of the Linnean Society

mls. miles

MM 2,000, (mus.) Maelzel's metronome, (Their) Majesties, (Fr.) Messieurs, Military Medal

mm millimetre, -s (no point)

mm. (Lat.) *metra* (verse metres)

m.m. *mutatis mutandis* (with the necessary changes)

Mme/ (Fr.) Madame, pl. **-s** (no point)

m.m.f. magnetomotive force

M.Mus. Master of Music

MN Merchant Navy, Minnesota (postal abbr.)

Mn manganese (no point)

Mn. Modern (with names of languages)

M'Naghten rules *use* **McNaghten rules**

mnemonics (pl. noun treated as sing.)

MO mass observation, Medical Officer, Missouri (postal abbr.), money order

Mo molybdenum (no point)

Mo. Missouri (off. abbr.)

mo. (US) month

mob/, -bed, -bing

Mobilian Jargon a Native American pidgin used as a lingua franca among different tribes in south-eastern USA, and as a contact language between tribes and European settlers (caps.)

mobilize *not* -ise

Möbius/, August Ferdinand (1790–1868) German mathematician, discoverer of the — **strip**

Mobutu Sese Seko (full name **Mobutu Sese Seko Kuku Ngbendu Wa Za Banga**, b. **Joseph-Désiré Mobutu**) (1930–97) president of Zaire 1965–97

Moby-Dick a novel by H. Melville, 1851 (hyphen)

MOC mother of the chapel; *see* **chapel**

moccasin a Native American shoe, a N. American venomous snake; *not* the many variants

Mocha an Arabian port on the Red Sea

mocha a coffee, a sheepskin (not cap.)

mock turtle soup (three words)

MOD Ministry of Defence, *formerly* M.o.D.

mod. moderate, modern

mod. moderato (mus.)

mode (Fr. m.) method, (gram.) mood; (f.) fashion

model/, -led, -ler, -ling (one *l* in US)

modem (comput.) (not cap.)

moderate abbr. **mod.**

Moderations the first public examination in some faculties for the Oxford BA degree

moderato (mus.) in moderate time, abbr. **mod.**

modern abbr. **mod.**, (with names of languages) **Mn.**

modern English the English language from about 1500 onwards

modern face (typ.) a type design with contrasting thick and thin strokes and serifs at right angles; abbr. **MF**

modernism (not cap.)

modernismo a school of 19th-c. Spanish-American poetry

modernize *not* -ise

modicum/ a small quantity, pl. **-s** (not ital.)

modif/y, -iable, -ied, -ier, -ying

Modigliani, Amedeo (1884–1920) Italian painter and sculptor

modiste a milliner, dressmaker (not ital.)

modo praescripto (Lat.) as directed

Mods. Moderations

modus/ operandi (Lat.) the particular way a person performs a task or action, a plan of working; **— vivendi** a way of living or coping, a temporary compromise

Moët et Chandon champagne manufacturers

mœurs (Fr. f. pl.) manners, customs

Mogadishu Somalia

mogul (colloq.) an important or influential person; (cap., hist.) any of the emperors of Delhi in the 16th–19th cc. (often **the Great Mogul**); cf. **Mughal**

MOH Master of Otter Hounds, Medical Officer of Health

Mohammed the Prophet, *use* **Muhammad**

Mohammedan *use* **Muslim**

Mohave Desert *use* **Moj-**

Mohawk (of or relating to) (a member of) a Native American tribe, their language; also a skating step; *not* -hock

Mohegan (of or relating to) (a member of) the eastern branch of the Native American Mahican tribe, *or* their language

Mohican (of or relating to) (a member of) the western branch of the Native American Mahican tribe, *or* their language

Mohocks 18th-c. London ruffians, *not* -hawks

Moholy-Nagy, László (1895–1946) Hungarian-born US painter, sculptor, and photographer

Mohorovičić discontinuity *or* **moho** (geol.); named after **Andrija Mohorovičić** (1857–1936) Yugoslav geophysicist

moidore (hist.) a Portuguese gold coin

moire (noun) a watered fabric, usually silk (not ital.)

moiré (adj.) (of silk etc.) watered, (noun) a patterned appearance like watered silk (not ital.)

mois (Fr. m.) month, abbr. **m** (no point)

Mojave Desert Calif.; *not* Moh-

mol (chem.) abbr. of **mole**

molar (chem.) abbr. **M**

molasses an uncrystallized syrup from raw sugar, (US) = **treacle**, *not* moll-

Mold Clwyd

mold/, -er, -ing, -y (US) = **mould/, -er, -ing, -y**

Moldau the Ger. name for two rivers, the Moldova and the Vltava

Moldavia a province of Romania (in Rom. **Moldova**)

Moldova an independent state, *formerly* the **Moldavian Soviet Socialist Republic**

mole (chem.) an SI unit of amount of substance, abbr. **mol**

Molière pseud. of **Jean Baptiste Poquelin** (1622–73) French playwright

moll (hist. sl.) a gangster's female companion, a prostitute

moll (Ger. mus.) minor

mollah *use* **mu-**

mollasses *use* **mola-**

mollusc *not* -sk (US)

mollymawk any of various small kinds of albatross or similar birds, *not* mallemuck

Molnár, Ferenc (1878–1952) Hungarian playwright

Mol/och a Canaanite idol to whom children were sacrificed (often fig.); sometimes **-ech** in the OT; *not* -eck (cap.); a spiny Australian reptile (not cap.)

Molotov/, Vyacheslav (Mikhailovich) assumed name of **V. M. Skriabin** (1890–1986) Soviet statesman; **— cocktail**

molt *use* **moult** (except in US)

Moltke,/ Count Helmuth Karl Bernard von (1800–91) Prussian field marshal; **— Helmuth Johannes Ludwig von** (1848–1916) his nephew, German general in the First World War

molto (mus.) much, very

Moluccas Indonesian islands, *use* **Maluku**

mol. wt. molecular weight

molybdenum symbol **Mo**

MoMA Museum of Modern Art, New York City (three caps.)

Mombasa Kenya, *not* -assa

momentarily lasting only a moment; *also* (US) at any moment, instantly

moment/um impetus, mass × velocity; pl. **-a** (not ital.)

Mommsen, Theodor (1817–1903) German historian

Mon. Monday

Monaci (Lat.) Munich

Monaco a principality adjoining Mediterranean France, adj. **Monégasque**

Monaco di Baviera (It.) Munich

Mona Lisa a portrait by Leonardo da Vinci, also called **La Gioconda**

mon/ ami (Fr.) f. **— amie** my friend

monandry marriage with one husband at a time

monarch, the (not cap.) *but* **the Sovereign, the Crown** for the British monarch

monaural of reproduction of sound by one channel, *also* **monophonic**

Mönchen-Gladbach Germany

mon cher (Fr. m.) my dear; *see also* **ma chère**

Monck,/ Viscount; — George, Duke of Albemarle (1608–70) English general; *see also* **Monk**

Monckton,/ Lionel (1861–1924) English composer, **— Walter Turner, Viscount** (1891–1963) British lawyer and politician

Moncreiff, Baron different from **Moncreiffe of that Ilk**

Moncrieff the more usual spelling

Moncton NB, Canada

mondaine (Fr. f.) (a woman who is) of the fashionable world, worldly

Monday abbr. **M.**, **Mon.**

Mondrian, Piet(er **Cornelis**) (1872–1944) Dutch painter

Monégasque from or of Monaco

Monel metal (propr.)

Monet, Claude Oscar (1840–1926) French painter; cf. **Manet**

monetar/y, -ist

money/, -ed *not* monied; pl. **-s**, *but* **monies** in legal contexts and in Acts of Parliament

money/bags, -lender, -maker (one word)

money/ market, — order abbr. **MO** (no point), **— spider** (two words)

money/-spinner, —'s-worth (hyphens)

moneywort a trailing evergreen plant (one word)

Monghyr Bihar, India

Mongol/ a member of an Asian people; **-ian**; **-oid** (cap.); *see also* **Down syndrome**

mongoos/e an Indian animal, pl. **-es**; *not* mun-

moniker (sl.) a name; *not* -icker

Monk Bretton, Baron; *see also* **Monck**

monkey business (two words), *not* — shine/, -s (US)

monkshood a poisonous garden plant (one word, no apos.)

Mono *see* **Monotype**

mono/ short for monaural; as noun, pl. **-s**

monochrom/e in one colour (one word), **-atic**

monocle a single eyeglass

monocoque/ an aircraft or vehicle with body of single rigid structure, pl. **-s**

monocycle *use* **uni-**

Monoecus Lat. for **Monaco**

monogam/y marriage with one person at a time, **-ist**

monogyny marriage with one wife at a time

monologue *not* -log (US)

monomark a combination of letters, with or without figures, registered as an identification mark for goods, articles, etc.

mononucleosis (med.) (US) = **glandular fever**

monophonic *see* **monaural**

Monophoto (typ.) (propr.) a filmsetting system (cap.)

Monophysite a person who holds that there is only one nature in the person of Christ (cap.)

monopol/ism, -ist, -istic, -ize, -y

Monotype (typ.) (propr.) a hot-metal composition system; abbr. **Mono**

Monroe Doctrine that European powers should not interfere in American affairs, from **James Monroe** (1758–1831) US President

Mons Belgium, in Fl. **Bergen**

Mons. incorrect abbr. for **Monsieur**

Monseigneur a title of an eminent French person, esp. a prince, cardinal, archbishop, or bishop; abbr. **Mgr**; pl. *Messeigneurs*, abbr. **Mgrs**; *see also* **Monsignor**

Monserrat Leeward Islands, *use* **Mont-**

Monsieur/ (Fr.) Mr, Sir; abbr. (to be used in third person only) **M.**; pl. **Messieurs** abbr. **MM.**; **— Chose** Mr So-and-so; *see also* **Mons.**

Monsignor/ (RC title) abbr. **Mgr**; pl. **-s**, abbr. **Mgrs**; It. **-e**, pl. **-i** (ital.); *see also* *Monseigneur*

mons/ pubis (not cap.), **— Veneris** (one cap.)

Mont. Montana (off. abbr.)

montage (not ital.)

Montagu, Lady Mary Wortley (1689–1762) English writer

Montague Romeo's family in Shakespeare's *Romeo and Juliet*

Montagu of Beaulieu, Baron

Montaigne, Michel Eyquem de (1533–92) French essayist

Montana Switzerland; USA, off. abbr. **Mont.**, postal **MT**

Montaña/ a forest, **La —** a region, Peru

Mont Blanc (caps.)

mont-de-piété (Fr. m.) a government pawnshop, pl. *monts-de-piété* (hyphens)

Monte Albán Mexico

Monte Cristo *not* Christo

Montefiascone an Italian wine, *not* -sco (one word)

Montenegr/o a republic *formerly* in Yugoslavia, **-in**; in Serbo-Croat **Crnagora**

Monterey Calif.

Monte Rosa Switzerland (caps., two words)

Monterrey Mexico

Montesquieu, Charles Louis de Secondat, baron de (1689–1755) French jurist and political philosopher

Montesquiou, Pierre de, comte d'Artagnan (1645–1725) marshal of France

Montesquiou(-Fezensac), comte Robert de (1855–1921) aesthete and dandy

Monteverdi, Claudio Giovanni Antonio (1567–1643) Italian composer

Montevideo capital of Uruguay (one word)

Montgomerie/ family name of the Earl of Eglinton, **—, Alexander** (1556–1610) Scottish poet

Montgomery second title of the Earl of Pembroke, a town and former county in Wales, also towns in Ala. and W. Va., and in Pakistan

Montgomery of Alamein, Bernard Law, Viscount (1887–1976) British field marshal in the Second World War

month/, -s abbr. **m.**; **day of the —** to be thus: 25 Jan., *not* Jan. 25 (US). When necessary, months to be abbreviated thus: Jan., Feb., Mar., Apr., Aug., Sept., Oct., Nov., Dec.; spell out May, June, and July. In Fr. and many other languages the names of months do not take caps., as *janvier*

Montpelier Vt.

Montpellier dép. Hérault, France

Mont-Saint-Michel dép. Manche, France (caps., hyphens); in Cornwall, **Mount Saint Michael,** *use* **St Michael's Mount**

Montserrat Leeward Islands, Spain; *not* Mons-

Montyon prizes of French Academy, *not* Month-

mooch (colloq.) loiter or saunter desultorily, (esp. US) beg or steal

Moodkee *use* **Mudki**

Moog/, Robert (b. 1934) US inventor, creator of **— synthesizer** electronic musical instrument (one cap.)

Mooltan *use* **Mu-**

moolvi/ a Muslim doctor of the law, pl. **-s**; *not* -vee, -vie

moon cap. only in astr. or anthrop. contexts, and in list of planets; abbr. **m.**; sign for new ●; first quarter ☽; full ○; last quarter ☾

moon/beam, -calf (one word), **-fish** *use* **opah**

Moonie (sl.) a member of the Unification Church

moon/light, -lit, -quake, -rise, -scape, -set (one word)

moonshee an Indian writer or teacher, *not* munshi (not ital.)

moon/shine, -shot, -stone, -struck (one word)

Moor/ (of or relating to) a member of a Muslim people of mixed Berber and Arab descent, inhabiting NW Africa; **-ish**

Moore,/ George (1852–1933) Irish novelist; **— Sir John** (1761–1809) British general, killed at Corunna; **— Thomas** (1779–1852) 'the bard of Erin'; *see also* **More**

Moosonee, Archbishop of Ont., Canada

mop/e, -ed, -ing, -ish

mopoke the boobook, a brown spotted owl native to Australia and New Zealand; *not* morepork

Mor. Morocco

moral (adj.) concerned with principles of right and wrong, virtuous; (noun) a moral lesson or principle, in Fr. f. *morale*

morale state of mind, esp. in respect of confidence and courage, in Fr. m. *moral*

moralize *not* -ise

Moral Re-Armament *see* **Oxford Group**

moratorium/ pl. **-s**

Moravia/ part of the Czech Republic; **-n Brethren** (members of) a Protestant sect

Moray/ a former Scottish county, *not* Morayshire; **Earl of —**

morbidezza (It. art) extreme delicacy

morbilli (med.) measles, *not* -bilia

morbus, cholera (not ital.)

morceau/ (Fr. m.) a morsel, a short music piece; pl. **-x**

mordant biting, pungent, corrosive; (a substance) fixing dye

mordent (mus.) a type of ornament, a pralltriller

more (Lat.) in the manner of

More,/ Hannah (1745–1833) English religious writer; **— Sir Thomas** (1478–1535) English writer and statesman, canonized 1935; *see also* **Moore**

Morea medieval name for ancient and modern **Peloponnese**

'more honoured in the breach than the observance' (*Hamlet*, I. iv. 14) 'more honourable to breach it than observe it', *not* 'more often breached than observed'

moreish so pleasant one wants more, *not* -rish

morel an edible fungus, *not* -lle

morello/ a bitter dark cherry, pl. **-s**

more majorum (Lat.) in the style of one's ancestors

morendo (mus.) dying away

morepork *use* **mopoke**

mores (Lat. pl.) social customs (not ital.)

Moresco an Italian dance (cap.); cf. **Morisco**

Moresque Moorish, *not* Mau-

more suo (Lat.) in his, *or* her, own peculiar way

Moretonhampstead Devon (one word)

Moreton-in-Marsh Glos. (hyphens), *not* -in-the-Marsh

morganatic marriage between royalty and commoner, the children being legitimate but not heirs to the higher rank (not cap.)

morgue a mortuary

morgue (Fr. f.) haughtiness

MORI Market & Opinion Research Institute, *not* Mori

Morisco/ Moorish, a Moor; pl. **-s**; cf. **Moresco**

morish *use* **moreish**

Morison,/ James (1816–93) Scottish founder of the Evangelical Union 1843, **— James Augustus Cotter** (1832–88) English historical writer, **— Stanley** (1889–1967) typographer

Morisot, Berthe (1841–95) French Impressionist painter

Morland, George (1763–1804) English painter

Mormon a member of Church of Jesus Christ of Latter-Day Saints; *not* -an

morn. morning

mornay (cook.) a sauce flavoured with cheese

Morny, Charles, duc de (1811–65) French statesman

Moro a Muslim living in the Philippines

Morocc/o abbr. **Mor.**; **-an**; *not* Ma-; in Fr. **Maroc**

morocco leather/ (bind.) (not cap.), **french —** — a low grade with small grain; **levant — —** a high grade with large grain; **persian — —** the best, usually finished on the grain side

morphemics (linguistics) study of word structure (noun pl., usually treated as sing.)

morphology the study of forms (bot., linguistics), abbr. **morph.**

Morpheus Roman god of sleep, *not* -aeus

morphia a drug (pop. for **morphine**)

Morrell, Lady Ottoline (1873–1938) English hostess

Morrells (hist.) an Oxford brewer (no apos.)

Morris,/ Gouverneur (1752–1816) US statesman, and his great-grandson (1876–1953) US writer; **— William** (1834–96) English craftsman, poet, and socialist; **— William Richard, Lord Nuffield** (1877–1963) English industrialist and philanthropist

Morris chair an adjustable-backed easy chair (cap.)

morris dance (two words, not cap.)

Morrison, Toni (b. **Chloe Anthony Wofford**) (b. 1931) US novelist

mortgag/ee the creditor in a mortgage; **-er** the debtor; in law, **-or**

mortice *use* **-ise**

mortician (US) = undertaker, funeral manager

mortis causa (Lat., Sc. law) in contemplation of death

mortise/ hole for receiving tenon in joint, **— lock** one recessed in frame etc. (two words); *not* -ice

Morton/, John (*c*.1420–1500) English statesman, deviser of **—'s Fork**

Morvan, Le a French district

Morven Grampian

Morvern Highland

MOS (comput.) metal oxide semiconductor

Mosaic of Moses

mosaic/ a representation using inlaid pieces of glass, stone, etc.; as verb **-ked, -king**; **-ist** a maker of mosaics

Moscow Russia, in Russian **Moskva**

Moseley a Birmingham suburb; *see also* **Mossl-**

Moseley, Henry Gwyn Jeffreys (1887–1915) English physicist; *see also* **Mosl-**

Moselle a river, France–Germany; a white wine; in Ger. **Mosel**

moshav/ a cooperative association of Israeli smallholders, pl. **-im**

Moslem *use* **Muslim**

Mosley, Sir Oswald Ernald, Bt. (1896–1980) English politician; *see also* **Mose-**

mosquito/ pl. **-es**, *not* mu-

Mossley Ches., Gr. Manchester, Staffs.

mosso (mus.) 'moved' (e.g. più mosso, more moved = quicker)

Most/ High as Deity (caps.), **— Honourable** a title given to marquises and to members of the Privy Council and the Order of the Bath, **— Reverend** a title given to archbishops and to RC bishops

Moszkowski, Moritz (1854–1925) Polish composer

MOT Ministry of Transport, *now* Department of Transport, but still used colloq. in **MOT test** for motor vehicles

mot/ (Fr. m.) a word; **— à —** word for word, abbr. *m. à m.*; *le — juste* the most appropriate expression, pl. *les mots justes*

Mother Carey's chicken the storm petrel

Mother Hubbard a character in a nursery rhyme, a gown such as she wore

Mother Hubberds Tale by Spenser, 1591

Mothering Sunday the fourth Sunday in Lent

mother-in-law pl. **mothers-in-law** (hyphens)

motherland (one word)

mother-of-pearl (hyphens)

Mother's Day (US) second Sunday in May (for commercial purposes), = Mothering Sunday (for traditional purposes)

motif/ (not ital.); pl. **-s** (*not* motives)

motley a mixture, *not* -ly

moto/ (It. mus.) motion, **— continuo** constant repetition, **— contrario** contrary motion, **— obbliquo** oblique motion, **— perpetuo** a piece of music speeding without pause from start to finish, **— precedente** at the preceding pace, **— primo** at the first pace

motorbike (one word)

motor boat (two words, hyphens when attrib., one word in US)

motorcade (one word)

motor/ car, — coach (two words, hyphens when attrib.)

motorcycle (one word)

moto retto (It. mus.) direct or similar motion

motorized *not* -ised

motorway (one word)

Motown music with rhythm-and-blues elements, associated with Detroit

mottl/ed, -ing

motto/ pl. **-es**

motu proprio (Lat.) of his, *or* her, own accord (usually of the Pope)

moue pout (not ital.)

mouezzin *use* **mue-**

moufflet/ (Fr. m.) small child, scamp; f. *-te*

mouflon a wild sheep; *not* mouffl-, muf-

mouillé (Fr.) softened, wet, (phonetics) palatalized (of consonant)

moujik *use* **muzhik**

mould/, **-er**, **-ing**, **-y** *not* mol- (US)

moulin (Fr. m.) mill, a nearly vertical shaft in a glacier

Moulmein *see* **Maulmain**

moult a shedding, *not* molt (US)

Mount/, **-ain** abbr. **Mt.**, pl. **Mts.**

Mountain Ash Mid Glam.

Mount Auburn Mass., a noted cemetery

Mount Edgcumbe, Earl of *not* Edge-

Mountevans, Baron (one word)

Mountgarret, Viscount (one word)

Mountie (colloq.) a member of the Royal Canadian Mounted Police

Mount Saint Michael Corn., *use* **St Michael's Mount**; *see also* **Mont-Saint-Michel**

Mourne Mountains Ireland

Mourning Becomes Electra a play by E. O'Neill, 1931

mourning cloak (US) a butterfly, *Nymphalis antiopa*; = **Camberwell beauty**

mousetrap (one word)

Mousquetaire a French musketeer, esp. one of the 17th- to 18th-c. royal musketeers

moussaka a Greek dish, *not* -s-

mousseline/ a muslin-like fabric; **-de-laine** a wool and cotton muslin; **-de-soie** a muslin-like silk (hyphens)

mousseu/x (Fr.) f. *-se* foaming or sparkling, as wine

moustache *not* mu- (US)

Mousterian (archaeol.) of or relating to the flint workings of the middle palaeolithic epoch; in Fr. *moustérien*

mousy mouselike, *not* -ey

mouth organ (two words)

mouth/piece -wash (one word)

mouton (Fr. m.) sheep, mutton

movable (something) that can be moved

moveable a form of *movable* used in legal work (for property) and the Prayer Book (for feasts); E. Hemingway's memoir is *A Moveable Feast*, 1964

moyen/ (Fr. m.) medium, **— âge, le** the Middle Ages

moyenne (Fr. f.) average

Mozambi/que SE Africa; in Port. **Moçambique**; **-can**

Mozart/, **Wolfgang Amadeus** (1756–91) Austrian composer, **-ian**

mozzarella an Italian curd cheese

MP Madhya Pradesh, Member of Parliament (pl. **MPs**), Metropolitan Police, Military Police

m.p. melting point, *mille passus*

mp (mus.) mezzo piano (fairly soft)

MPA Master Printers Association

mpg miles per gallon

mph miles per hour

M.Phil. Master of Philosophy

MPO Metropolitan Police Office ('Scotland Yard')

MPS Member of the Pharmaceutical Society

MR Master of the Rolls, Municipal Reform

Mr Mister, pl. **Messrs**

MRA Moral Re-Armament

MRAC Member of the Royal Agricultural College

M.R.Ae.S. Member of the Royal Aeronautical Society

MRAS Member of the Royal Asiatic Society

MRBM medium-range ballistic missile

MRC Medical Research Council

MRCA multi-role combat aircraft

MRCO Member of the Royal College of Organists

MRCOG Member of the Royal College of Obstetricians and Gynaecologists

MRCP Member of the Royal College of Physicians, London

MRCS Member of the Royal College of Surgeons, England

MRCVS Member of the Royal College of Veterinary Surgeons, London

MRE Microbiological Research Establishment

MRGS Member of the Royal Geographical Society

MRH Member of the Royal Household

MRI Member of the Royal Institution

MRIA Member of the Royal Irish Academy

MRICS Member of the Royal Institution of Chartered Surveyors

MRINA Member of the Royal Institution of Naval Architects

mRNA messenger RNA

Mrs Missis, Missus (corruptions of Mistress)

MRSC Member of the Royal Society of Chemistry

MRSH Member of the Royal Society of Health

MRSL Member of the Royal Society of Literature

MRSM Member of the Royal Society of Medicine, Member of the Royal Society of Musicians of Great Britain

MRST Member of the Royal Society of Teachers

MS *manuscriptum, manu scriptus* (manuscript, codex, narrative, etc.); pl. **MSS** (no point); *see also* **typescript**

MS Master of Science (esp. US), Master of Surgery, multiple sclerosis, (Lat.) *memoriae sacrum* (sacred to the memory of), Middle Scots, Mississippi (postal abbr.), (It. mus.) *mano sinistra* (the left hand)

Ms the title of a woman whether or not married (no point)

m/s metres per second, SI unit of speed

ms. (Fr.) *manuscrit* (= **MS**)

MSA Member of the Society of Apothecaries (of London), Mutual Security Agency

M.Sc. Master of Science

MS-DOS (comput.) Microsoft disk operating system (caps. or even small caps.)

MSF Manufacturing, Science, and Finance (union)

MSH Master of Staghounds

MSI (comput.) medium-scale integration

MSIAD Member of the Society of Industrial Artists and Designers

m.s.l. mean sea level (points)

MSM Meritorious Service Medal

MSP Member of the Scottish Parliament

MSS *manuscripta* (manuscripts)

mss. (Fr.) *manuscrits* (= **MSS**)

MT Masoretic Text (of OT), Mechanical (Motor) Transport, megaton, Montana (postal abbr.)

Mt. Mount, Mountain

MTB motor torpedo-boat

M.Tech. Master of Technology

M.Th. Master of Theology

Mts. Mounts, Mountains

mu the twelfth letter of the Gr. alphabet (M, μ), (math.) modulus, (phys.) symbol for magnetic permeability, micron, (as prefix) micro-; **μm** micrometre; **mμ** millimicron, *use* **nm**

muc/us a slimy substance, adj. **-ous**

Muddiford Devon

mud/dy (verb), **-died, -dying**

Mudeford Dorset

Mudford Som.

Mudki E. Punjab, India; *not* Moodkee

muesli a breakfast food (not ital.)

muezzin a Muslim crier, *not* mou-

muffetee a worsted cuff worn on the wrist

muffin/ a light, flat, round spongy cake, eaten toasted and buttered; (US) a round cake made from batter or dough; a British — = US **English** — (savoury), a US — = British **American** — (sweet)

muflon *use* **mou-**

mufti/ (Arab.) a magistrate, not -tee (not ital.); **in** — in civilian dress (not ital.)

Mughal a Mongolian; (attrib.) denoting the Muslim dynasty in India in the 16th–19th cc.; *not* Mog/hal, -hul, -ul; cf. **Mogul**

Muhammad the preferred form, but a compromise between the literary 'Mohammed' and the learned 'Muḥammad' (with subscript dot); adj. ending '-an' is both incorrect and often regarded as offensive; replace by the more correct **Muslim** or **Islamic**. Older forms such a 'Mahometan' and 'Mohammedan' are acceptable only in reproducing older texts

Mühlhausen Thuringia, Germany; cf. **Mulhouse**

mujahid/ a guerrilla fighter in Islamic countries, esp. one supporting Muslim fundamentalism; pl. **-in**; *not* -edin, -deen; in Arab. and Pers. *mujāhidīn*

mujik a Russian peasant, *use* **muzh-**

Mukden China

mulatto/ the offspring of one white and one black parent, pl. **-s**

mulch (treat soil with) a mixture of wet straw, leaves, etc.; *not* -sh

Mulhouse Alsace, France; in Ger. **Mülhausen**

mull (bind.) coarse muslin glued to the backs of books

mullah (Muslim) a learned man (not cap.); *not* moll-, mool-, -a

mullein a tall yellow-flowered plant, *not* -en

Müller, Friedrich Max (1823–1900) German-born English philologist; *also* later **Max-Müller** (hyphen)

mulligatawny a soup; *not* muli-, mulla-

mullion a vertical bar dividing the lights in a window, *not* munn-

mulsh *use* **-ch**

Multan Pakistan, *not* Moo-

multangular having many angles, *not* multi-

Multatuli pseud. of **Edward Dowes Dekker** (1820–87) Dutch writer

multiaccess (comput.) the simultaneous connection to a computer of a number of terminals (one word)

multiaxial of or involving several axes (one word)

multimillionaire (one word)

multinational (one word)

multipartite divided into many parts (one word)

multiple mark (typ.) the sign of multiplication ($\times$); if a medial full point is to be used instead, ensure that sufficient instruction is given

multiplepoinding (Sc. law) a process which safeguards a person from whom the same funds are claimed by more than one creditor (one word)

multiplication point to be set medially, as m·s (metre-second)

multiprocess/er, -ing (one word)

multiprogramm/er, -ing (one word)

multi-purpose (hyphen, one word in US)

multiracial (one word)

multi/-role, -stage, -storey, -user (hyphens, one word in US)

multi/valent, -valve, -vocal (one word)

multi-way (hyphen, one word in US)

multum in parvo (Lat.) much in small compass

Mumbai Maratha for **Bombay**

mumbo-jumbo/ a meaningless ritual or language; pl. **-s** (hyphen)

Munch, Edvard (1863–1944) Norwegian artist

Munchausen, Baron (1720–97) Hanoverian nobleman whose extravagant adventures are the theme of *Adventures of Baron Munchausen*, collected by Rudolph Eric Raspe *c*.1785; in Ger. **Münchhausen**

München (Ger.) Munich

Mundt, Theodor (1808–61) German journalist and writer

municipalize etc., *not* -ise

muniment (usually in pl.) a document kept as evidence of rights or privileges etc.

Munnepoor *use* **Manipur**

munnion *use* **mull-**

Munro,/ General character in J. F. Cooper's *Last of the Mohicans* based on Lieutenant Colonel Monro; **— H**(ector) **H**(ugh) *see* **Saki**

munshi (Ind.) *use* **moonshee**

Munster Ireland

Münster Germany, Switzerland

muntjac a S. Asian deer; *not* -jack, -jak

Muntz (**metal**) an alloy of copper and zinc for sheathing ships etc., *not* Muntz's

Murdoch,/ (**Jean**) **Iris** (1919–1999) British writer, **— John** (1747–1824) friend of Burns

Murdock, William (1754–1839) inventor of coal-gas lighting, *not* -och

Murfreesboro, Battle of US Civil War, 1863

murky dark, *not* mi-

Murphy's Law any of various maxims about the perverseness of things (caps.)

Murray,/ (**George**) **Gilbert** (**Aimé**) (1866–1957) Australian-born British classical scholar, **— Sir James** (**Augustus Henry**) (1837–1915) Scottish lexicographer and chief editor of the *OED*; *see also* **Murry**

Mürren Oberland, Switzerland

murrey the colour of a mulberry, a deep red or purple

murrhine fluorspar ware; *not* murrine, myrrh-

Murrumbidgee a river in New South Wales, Australia

Murry,/ John Middleton (1889–1957) English writer, *not* -ay; **— Kathleen** wife of above, *see* **Mansfield**; *see also* **Murray**

Murshidabad W. Bengal, India

mus. museum; music, -al

musaeo/graphy, -logy *use* **museo-**

Musalman *see* **Mussul-**

Mus.B., Mus. Bac. *Musicae Baccalaureus* (Bachelor of Music)

musc/a (Lat.) a fly, pl. *-ae*

Muscadet a dry white wine from Brittany, made from muscadine grapes; cf. **muscatel**

Muscat the capital of Oman, S. Arabia

muscatel a raisin from a muscadine grape, the general name for a sweet wine made from the muscadine grape; *not* -del; *also* **muscat**; cf. **Muscadet**

Muschelkalk (geol.) shell limestone (cap.)

Musc/i the true mosses, sing. *-us*

muscovado/ unrefined sugar, pl. **-s**

Muscovite a native or citizen of Moscow, of or relating to Moscow; (arch.) a Russian, of or relating to Russia

muscovite a silver-grey form of mica

Muscovy (arch.) Russia

Mus.D., Mus. Doc. *Musicae Doctor* (Doctor of Music)

museo/graphy museum cataloguing, **-logy** the science of arranging museums; *not* musae-

Muses, the nine Calliope, Clio, Erato, Euterpe, Melpomene, Polyhymnia, Terpsichore, Thalia, Urania

musette a kind of small bagpipe; a small oboe-like instrument; a dance; (US) a small knapsack

museum abbr. **mus.**

Music/, Bachelor of abbr. **Mus.B., B.Mus.; —, Doctor of** abbr. **Mus.D., D.Mus.; —, Master of** abbr. **M.Mus.,** (Camb.) **Mus.M.**

music/, -al abbr. **mus.**

music/ drama, — hall, — paper, — stand, — stool (two words)

Musigny a red burgundy

musique concrète (Fr. f.) music constructed from recorded sounds

musjid *use* **mas-**

muskellunge *use* **maskinonge**

Muslim (a member) of the faith of Islam; *not* Moslem, Muhammadan

muslin-de-lain *use* **mousseline-de-laine**

Mus.M. Master of Music (Camb.)

musquito *use* **mos-**

muss (US) (throw into) a state of disorder

Mussadeq, Muhammad (1881–1967) Iranian Prime Minister 1951–3

Mussalman *see* **Mussul-**

Musselburgh Lothian, *not* -borough

Mussolini, Benito (**Amilcaro Andrea**) (1883–1945) Italian Fascist politician, Prime

Minister 1922–43; known as **Il Duce** ('the leader')

Mussorgsky (common Eng. form, more exact form **Musorgski**) **Modest** (**Petrovich**) (1839–81) Russian composer

Mussul/man (arch.) a Muslim, from Pers. *musulmān*; *not* the many variants; pl. **-mans**, *not* -men

mustache *use* **mous-** (except in US)

Mustafa Algeria

Mustafabad Uttar Pradesh, India

Musulman *see* **Mussul-**

mutable likely to change

mutand/um (Lat.) anything to be altered, pl. *-a*

mutatis mutandis (Lat.) with the necessary changes, abbr. **m.m.**

mutato nomine (Lat.) with the name changed

mutual fund (US) = **unit trust**

mutuel (US) a totalizer, a pari-mutuel

muu-muu a (Hawaiian) woman's loose-fitting dress

Muybridge, Eadweard (1830–1904) English photographer

Muzaffarabad Kashmir

Muzaffarpur Bihar, India

Muzak (propr.) a system of piped music (cap.); any (recorded) light background music (not cap.)

muzhik a Russian peasant; *not* moujik, mujik

MV megavolt, -s; motor vessel, muzzle velocity

mV (elec.) millivolt, -s (no point)

m.v. (It. mus.) *mezza voce*, muzzle velocity

MVD USSR 'Ministry of Internal Affairs' 1953–60; *see also* **KGB**

MVO Member (of fourth or fifth class) of the Royal Victorian Order

M.V.Sc. Master of Veterinary Science

MW medium wave; megawatt, -s; Middle Welsh, Most Worshipful, Most Worthy

mW milliwatt, -s (no point)

Mx maxwell, -s; Middlesex (no point)

MY motor yacht

myalism a W. Indian witchcraft, adj. **myal**

myall an Australian acacia, an Australian Aboriginal living in the traditional way

myceli/um (bot.) the thallus of a fungus, pl. **-a**

Mycenaean of or relating to the late Bronze Age civilization in Greece; its inhabitants (*c.*1500–1100 BC)

Myddelton Square Clerkenwell, London; *see also* **Mi-**

Myddleton, Sir Hugh (1560–1631) London merchant

Myers,/ Frederic William Henry (1843–1901) English poet, essayist, spiritualist; **— Leopold Hamilton** (1881–1944) English novelist; *see also* **Miers**; **Myres**

mynah/ a starling of SE Asia, pl. **-s**; *not* mina, myna

mynheer (hist.) Eng. term for a Dutchman, from *mijnheer* (Du.) sir, Mr

myop/ia shortness of sight, adj. **-ic**

myosis *use* **mi-**

myosotis the forget-me-not

Myres, Sir John Linton (1869–1954) English archaeologist; *see also* **Miers**; **Myers**

myriad (of) an indefinitely great number, innumerable, *or* 10,000; 'myriad of' is correct

Myriapoda the centipedes and millepedes, *not* Myrio-

myrobalan a plum, *not* -bolan

myrrhine *use* **murrh-**

myrtle *not* -tel

Mysore Deccan, India (common form); *properly* **Maisur**

myst. mysteries

myth. mytholog/y, -ical

mythopoei/a the construction of myths; **-c** myth-making; *not* -pae-, -pei-, -poeit-

myth/us (lit.) a myth, pl. **-i**

Mytilen/e Lesbos, Greece; **-aean**; Mitylene in AV NT; **Mitilíni** the modern city

myxoedema a metabolic disease, *not* myxed- (US)

myxomatosis a contagious and fatal viral disease in rabbits

N n

N (typ.) en; (chess) knight; newton(s); nitrogen; the thirteenth in a series

₦ naira (currency of Nigeria)

N. Norse; north, -ern; (Lat.) *nom/en, -ina* (name, -s); *noster* (our)

(N.) (naval) navigat/ing, -ion

n (math.) an indefinite integer, whence (gen.) **to the nth** (**degree**); (as prefix) nano-

n. name, nephew, neuter, new, nominative, noon, note, noun

n (chem.) symbol for amount of substance

n. (Lat.) *natus* (born), *nocte* (at night)

ñ (Sp.) called '*n* with tilde', or 'Spanish *n*'; pron. as *n* in 'cognac' or 'onion'; follows *n* without tilde in Spanish alphabetical sequence

NA National Academ/y, -ician; Nautical Almanac, Naval Auxiliary; North America, -n

Na *natrium* (sodium) (no point)

n/a (banking) no account, not applicable, not available

NAACP (US) National Association for the Advancement of Colored People

NAAFI Navy, Army, and Air Force Institutes

naamloze vennootschap (Du.) public limited company, abbr. **NV**

Naas Co. Kildare

nabob (hist.) an official or governor under the Mogul empire, a person of conspicuous wealth or high rank; cf. **nawab**

Nabuchodonosor *see* **Nebuchadnezzar**

nach *use* **nautch**

nach/ Christi Geburt, — *Christo* (Ger.) AD, abbr. **n. Chr.**

Nachdruck (Ger. typ. m.) reprint, pirated edition; *nachdrucken* to reprint, or pirate

nacho/ (usually in pl. **-s**) a tortilla chip, usually topped with melted cheese, guacamole, etc.

nach und nach (Ger.) little by little

nacre/ mother-of-pearl (not ital.), **-ous** *not* -rous

nacré (Fr.) like mother-of-pearl (ital.)

Na-Dene (*also* **Na-Déné**) a linguistic group of more than twenty Amerind languages spoken in N. America

nadir the lowest point, as opposed to **zenith**

naev/us a form of birthmark, pl. **-i**; *not* nevus (US)

Naga Hills Assam, India; Burma

Nagaland an Indian state

Nagar W. Bengal, Mysore, E. Punjab, Kashmir, India

-nagar (in Indian place names) a town, as Ahmadnagar; *not* -naggore, -nagore, -nugger, -ur

Nagpur Maharashtra, India; *not* -pore

Nah. Nahum

Nahuatl (*also* **Nahua**) (of or concerning) (a member of) a group of peoples native to S. Mexico and Cent. America, including the Aztecs, and their Uto-Aztecan language

Nahum (OT) abbr. **Nah.**

naiad/ (Gr. myth.) a water nymph, an aquatic plant; *not* naid; pl. **-s, -es**

naïf *use* **naive**; in Fr. *naï/f* f. **-ve**

Naini Tal Uttar Pradesh, India

nainsook an Indian muslin, *not* -zook

Nairne, Baroness b. **Caroline Oliphant** (1776–1845) Scottish poet

Nairnshire a former county of Scotland

naive/ artless; *not* naï-, naïf; **-ty**

naïveté (Fr. f.) artlessness

Najd a province of Saudi Arabia

NALGO National and Local Government Officers' Association

Nama a member of the Khoikhoi people (pl. same) *or* their language; *not* Hottentot

namable *use* **name-**

Namaqualand S. Africa (one word)

namby-pamby weakly sentimental (hyphen)

name abbr. **n.**

nameable *not* namable (US)

namely *preferred to* viz.

N. Amer. North America(n)

namesake (one word)

names of periodicals *see* **periodicals**

names of ships to be italic: the *Cutty Sark*, RMS *Titanic*, USS *New Jersey*, the *Charles W. Morgan*

Namibia *formerly* South West Africa

namma *use* **gn-**

N&Q Notes and Queries

nankeen a fabric, *not* -kin

nano- prefix meaning one-thousand-millionth (10^{-9}), abbr. **n**

nanometre one-thousandth of a micrometre, abbr. **nm**

nanosecond one-thousandth of a microsecond, abbr. **ns**

Nansen/, Fridtjof (1861–1930) Norwegian diplomat and Arctic traveller, — **passport** a document of identification given to stateless persons after the First World War

Nantasket Beach Mass.

Nantucket Island Mass.

Nap. Napoleon

nap/, -ped, -ping

Napa Calif.

napa *use* **-ppa**

naphtha an inflammable oil

naphthal/ene a crystalline substance used in the manufacture of dyes etc.; **-ic**

Napierian logarithms from **John Napier** (1550–1617) Scottish mathematician, *not* -perian

Naples Italy; in It. **Napoli**, Ger. **Neapel**; adj. **Neapolitan**

napoleon/ a gold 20-franc piece of Napoleon I, **double —** a 40-franc piece; in Fr. m. **napoléon**

Napoleonic of, relating to, *or* characteristic of, Napoleon I (1769–1821) or his time

napolitaine, à la (Fr. cook.) in the Neapolitan style (not cap. *n*)

nappa a soft leather made by a special process from the skin of sheep or goats, *not* napa

Narbada an Indian river, *not* Nerbudda

narciss/us a flower, pl. **-i**; **-ism** excessive admiration of oneself

narcos/is a stupor induced by narcotics, pl. **-es**

narghile a hookah, *not* the many variants; in Pers. **nārgīleh**

Narragansett Bay RI; *not* -et

narrow measure (typ.) type composed in narrow widths, as in columns

narrow-minded (hyphen)

narwhal/ the sea unicorn; *not* -e, -wal; **— tusk** *not* horn

NAS National Association of Schoolmasters, Noise Abatement Society

NASA, Nasa (US) National Aeronautics and Space Administration

nasalize *not* -ise

NASD National Amalgamated Stevedores and Dockers

Nash,/ Ogden (1902–71) US poet; **— Richard, 'Beau'** (1674–1762) Bath Master of Ceremonies

Nash *or* **Nashe, Thomas** (1567–1601) English pamphleteer and playwright

Nasirabad Pakistan

Nasmith, James (1740–1808) English theologian and antiquary

Nasmyth/, Alexander (1758–1840) Scottish painter, **—, James** (1808–90) Scottish engineer, **— hammer** *not* -th's

nasturtium/ (bot.) *not* -ian, -ion; pl. **-s**

NAS/UWT National Association of Schoolmasters and Union of Women Teachers

Nat. Natal; Nathanael, -iel; National, -ist

nat. natural, -ist

Natal now **KwaZulu/Natal**

natch (colloq.) naturally; cf. **nautch**

NATFHE National Association of Teachers in Further and Higher Education

nat. hist. natural history

national abbr. **nat.**, (US) **nat'l**

National/ — Academy, — Academician abbr. **NA**; **— Bureau of Standards** (USA) abbr. **NBS**; **— Engineering Laboratory** East Kilbride, abbr. **NEL**

National Enquirer US publication, *not* — *Inquirer*

National Graphical Association abbr. **NGA**

nationalist not cap.; *but* cap. with reference to a particular party or institution, abbr. **Nat.**

nationalize *not* -ise

National/ Physical Laboratory Teddington, abbr. **NPL**; **— Playing Fields Association** abbr. **NPFA**; **— Research Council** abbr. **NRC**; **— Research Development Corporation** abbr. **NRDC**; **— Rifle Association** abbr. **NRA**; **— Rivers Authority** abbr. **NRA**

National Westminster Bank plc abbr. **NatWest** (one word)

nationwide (one word)

NATO, Nato North Atlantic Treaty Organization

nat./ ord. natural order, **— phil.** natural philosophy

natrium sodium, symbol **Na**

NATSOPA National Society of Operative Printers, Graphical and Media Personnel (*originally* Printers and Assistants)

nattier blue a soft blue, from **Jean-Marc Nattier** (1685–1766) French painter

natt/y trim; **-ier, -ily, -iness**

natura (Lat.) nature

natural/ abbr. **nat.**; **-ism -ist**; cf. **naturism**

natural (mus.) sign ♮

naturalize *not* -ise

natura non facit salt/um, -us (Lat.) Nature makes no leap, **-s**

nature the processes of the material world (cap. only when personified)

natur/ism the worship of nature, (advocacy of) (collective) nudism; **-ist**; cf. **naturalism**

natus (Lat.) born, abbr. **n.**

naught nothing, *but* HMS *Dreadnought*; (US) = **nought**

Nauheim, Bad Hesse, Germany

Nauru/ W. Pacific, **-an**

nause/a sickness, esp. with an inclination to vomit; **-ate** affect with nausea; **-ous** causing nausea, offensive in taste or smell

Nausicaa a character in Homer's *Odyssey* (no accent)

nautch/ an Indian dancing entertainment, **— girl**; *not* nach, natch

nautical abbr. **naut.**

Nautical Almanac abbr. **NA**

nautical mile *see* mile

nautil/us a shell; pl. **-uses, -i**

nav. naval, navigation

Nava/jo (of or relating to) (a member of) a Native American people, or their language; *pl.* **-jos**; *also* **-ho, -hos**

navarin a stew of mutton or lamb

Navarrese of Navarre

navigat/ing, -ion abbr. **(N.)**, **nav.**

navv/y (Brit.) (work as) a labourer employed in building or excavating roads, canals, etc.; **-ies, -ied**

Navy, Army, and Air Force in toasts etc. the Navy precedes, being the senior service

navy blue (not cap.)

Navy List (two words)

navy yard (US) a government shipyard with civilian labour (not cap.)

nawab a distinguished Muslim in Pakistan, (hist.) a governor or nobleman in India; cf. **nabob**

Nazarene/ a Christian, a native of Nazareth; *not* -arite, -irite; **-s** a group of early 19th-c. German religious painters

Nazarite (hist.) a Hebrew who had taken vows of abstinence; *not* -arene, -irite

Nazi/ a member of the German National Socialist Party; **-fy, -ism** not -sm

NB New Brunswick, North Britain, (Lat.) *nota bene* (mark well)

Nb niobium (no point)

n.b. (cricket) no ball

NBA (US) National Basketball Association, (hist.) Net Book Agreement

NBC National Book Council, *now* **NBL**; (US) National Broadcasting Company; National Bus Company

NBG no bloody good

NBL National Book League

NBS National Broadcasting Service (of New Zealand)

NC North Carolina (off. and postal abbr.)

NCB (hist.) National Coal Board, since 1987 **British Coal**

NCCL National Council for Civil Liberties

n. Chr. (Ger.) *nach Christo* or *nach Christi Geburt* (AD)

NCL National Carriers, Ltd.

NCO non-commissioned officer

NCR no carbon (paper) required

NCU National Communications Union, National Cyclists' Union

NCW National Council of Women

ND North Dakota (postal abbr.)

N.D. (Fr.) *Notre Dame*

Nd neodymium (no point)

n.d. (bibliog.) no date given

N. Dak. North Dakota (off. abbr.)

N'Djamena Chad

NDL Norddeutscher Lloyd

NE Nebraska (postal abbr.), new edition, New England; north-east, -ern

Ne neon (no point)

né (Fr.) f. **née** born (not ital.)

n/e new edition, (banking) no effects

Neal,/ Daniel (1678–1743) English Puritan writer, — **John** (1793–1876) US writer; *see also* **Neele; Neill**

Neale, John Mason (1818–66) English hymnologist; *see also* **Neele; Neill**

Neanderthal/ common name for a subspecies of palaeolithic hominid; individuals are **-er** *not* — men; *not* -tal-

Neapel (Ger.) **Naples**

Neapolitan/ (an inhabitant) of Naples, — **ice** ice cream layered in different colours, — **violet** sweet-scented double viola

neap tide a tide when there is least difference between high and low water (two words)

near abbr. **nr.**; **near by** (adv., two words), **nearby** (adj., one word)

Nearctic (zool.) of northern N. America, *not* Neoarctic

near letter quality (comput.) abbr. **NLQ**

nearside (Brit.) the left side of a vehicle, animal, etc.; cf. **offside**

nearsighted (US) = **short-sighted**

neat's-foot oil (one hyphen)

NEB National Enterprise Board, New English Bible

Nebraska off. abbr. **Nebr.**, postal **NE**

Nebuchadnezzar King of Babylon, destroyed Jerusalem in 586 BC; a wine bottle of about twenty times the standard size (not cap.); **Nabuchodonosor** in the AV Apocrypha and the Vulgate; **Nebuchadrezzar** is the spelling in Jer. 43: 10 etc.

nebula/ pl. **-ae**

nebuly (her.) wavy in form, cloud-like

necess/ary, -arily

necessitarian (philos.) (of or concerning) a person who holds that all action is predetermined and free will is impossible (cf. **libertarian**); *not* necessarian

necess/itate, -ity

Neckar river in Württemberg, Germany

Necker, Jacques (1732–1804) French statesman

nec pluribus impar (Lat.) a match for many (motto of Louis XIV)

NED *New English Dictionary*, original name for the **OED** (*Oxford English Dictionary*)

NEDO National Economic Development Office

née (Fr. f.) born

needle/cord, -craft, -fish, -point (one word)

needle time an agreed maximum allowance of time for broadcasting commercially recorded music (two words)

needle/woman, -women, -work (one word)

Neele, Henry (1798–1828) English poet; *see also* **Neal; Neale; Neill**

neelghau *use* **nilgai**

ne'er/ never, **-do-well** (hyphens)

ne exeat regno (law) a writ to restrain a person from leaving the kingdom

nefasti (*dies*) (Lat.) black (ill-omened) days

Nefertiti (*fl.* 14th c. BC) Egyptian queen; *also* **Nofretete**

neg. negative, -ly

Negev, the a desert region of S. Israel, *not* -eb; in Fr. **Néguev**

neglig/ee a woman's dressing gown of diaphanous fabric; *not* neglige; in Fr. m. **négligé**

negligible *not* -eable

negotiate *not* -ciate

nègre (Fr. m.) Negro, black; (lit.) ghost writer

Negrillo/ (of or relating to) a member of a dwarf Negroid people in Cent. and S. Africa, pl. **-s** (cap.)

Negri Sembilan *see* **Malaya, Federation of**

Negrito/ (of or relating to) a member of a dwarf Negroid people in the Malayo-Polynesian region, pl. **-s** (cap.)

Negritude the quality of being black, African-ness (cap.)

négritude (Fr. f.) a cultural movement launched by black students in Paris, 1932, to reassert traditional African values (ital.)

Negro/ pl. **-es**, a member of a dark-skinned race originally native to Africa (cap.); outside the field of ethnology *use* **black** (q.v.); *see also* **African-American**

Negroid *not* -rooid

Negus (hist.) the title of the Emperor of Abyssinia (Ethiopia), in Amharic **n'gus**

negus (hist.) a hot drink of port or sherry, sugar, lemon, and spice, invented by **Col. Francis Negus** (d. 1732)

Neh. Nehemiah (OT)

Nehru/, **Jawaharlal, 'Pandit'** (1889–1964) Indian nationalist leader, Prime Minister 1947–64; **-vian**

n.e.i. *non est invent/us, -a, um* (he, she, *or* it, has not been found)

neice *use* **niece**

neige (Fr. f.) snow, (Fr. cook. f.) whisked white of egg

neighbour/, **-hood, -ly** *not* -or (US)

Neilgherry Hills *use* **The Nilgiris**

Neill,/ **A**(lexander) **S**(utherland) (1883–1973) British educationist; — **Patrick** (d. 1705) first printer in Belfast, of Scottish birth; — **Patrick**

(1776–1851) Scottish naturalist, *see also* **Neal; Neale; Neele**

neither (of two) *is*; neither he nor she *is*; but neither he nor they *are*, neither these nor those *are*

Nejd *use* **Na-**

nekton aquatic animals able to swim independently; cf. **plankton**

NEL National Engineering Laboratory

nematode (noun or adj.) (of) a roundworm or threadworm, *not* -oid

nem./ con. nemine contradicente, — *diss. nemine dissentiente*

Nemean/ (adj.) of the vale of Nemea in ancient Argolis, — **games** one of the four principal Panhellenic festivals, — **lion** (Gr. myth.) slain by Hercules

nemes/is (cap. when personified) pl. **-es**

nemine/ contradicente (Lat.) unanimously, abbr. *nem. con.*; — *dissentiente* no one dissenting, abbr. *nem. diss.*

nemo/ (Lat.) nobody, — *me impune lacessit* no one attacks me with impunity (motto of Scotland, and of the Order of the Thistle)

nemophila (bot.) a garden flower, *not* -phyla

N. Eng. New England

ne nimium (Lat.) shun excess

nenuphar the great white water lily; cf. *Nuphar*

neo- freely added (usually with hyphen) to names of philosophies and institutions and to their adjectival forms, to designate their revivals or new forms (retain caps. of words that have them), e.g. neo-Christianity, *but* neo-classical, Neoplatonism

Neoarctic *use* **Near-**

neocolonial/, **-ism, -ist** (one word)

Neocomian (geol.) (cap.)

neodymium symbol **Nd**

Neogaea (zool.) the land mass including S. and Cent. America; cf. **Arctogaea; Notogaea**

neolithic (archaeol.) of or relating to the later Stone Age (not cap.)

neolog/ize use new terms, *not* -ise; **-ism** abbr. **neol.**; **-ist**

neon symbol **Ne**

Neoplaton/ism a philosophical and religious system developed in the 3rd c., combining Platonic thought with oriental mysticism; **-ic** (one word, one cap.)

Nep. Neptune

Nepal/ a kingdom between Tibet and India, *not* -aul; adj. **-i** *not* -ese; the Nepali language is also called **Gurkhali**

neper unit for comparing power levels

nephew abbr. **n.**

ne plus ultra (Lat.) the furthest attainable point, perfection; *not* non

neptunium symbol **Np**

ne quid nimis (Lat.) be wisely moderate, nothing too much

Nerbudda *use* **Narbada**

NERC Natural Environment Research Council

nerd (esp. US sl.) a foolish, feeble, or uninteresting person; *not* nu-

nereid/ (Gr. myth.) a sea nymph; pl. **-s**, (with cap.) **-es**

Neri, Saint Philip (1515–95) Italian founder of the Congregation of the Oratory

nero antico (It.) a type of black marble

Neruda,/ Jan (1834–91) Czech writer; **— Pablo** pseud. of **Neftali Ricardo Reyes** (1904–73) Chilean poet

nerve/ cell, — centre, — gas (two words)

nerve-racking *not* wr-

Nesbit (**Bland**), **E**(**dith**) (1858–1924) English poet, novelist, and writer of children's stories

Nesbitt, Cathleen (1890–1982) English actress

nescien/t (followed by *of*) lacking knowledge, ignorant; **-ce**

Nessler's reagent (chem.) after **Julius Nessler** (1827–1905) German chemist

n'est-ce-pas? (Fr.) is it not so? aren't you?

Nestlé Rowntree part of **Société des Produits Nestlé SA** (accent)

net not subject to deduction; *not* nett

net/, -ted, -ting

net curtain (two words)

Netherlands, the formerly Holland was only part of, not equal to, the Netherlands (*or* Low Countries), which also included Belgium and Luxembourg. Now, however, these three countries are known collectively as Benelux, and the Netherlands is the official name of the province of Holland only. The definite article in 'the Netherlands' is lower case in running text, unlike that of its seat of government, The Hague; abbr. **Neth.**; (Du.) **Nederland**, (Fr.) **les Pays-Bas**

netsuke a carved Japanese button-like ornament, pl. same

nett *use* **net**

nettlerash (one word)

network (one word)

Neuchâtel Switzerland, or a white or red wine from there

Neue Folge (Ger.) new series, abbr. **NF** (small caps.)

Neufchâtel déps. Aisne and Seine-Maritime, France; a kind of cheese

Neuilly dép. Seine, France

neuma (mus.) passages sung to a single vowel, e.g. the final vowel of *alleluia*

neume (mus.) a written note in medieval music, often used specifically of staffless notation; the symbol indicating this (a ligature); *not* neum

neuralgia an intense intermittent pain in a nerve (a symptom, not a disease)

neurasthenia a general term for nervous prostration, chronic fatigue, etc. (not in medical use)

neurine a poisonous ptomaine, *not* -in

neuritis an inflammation of nerve fibres

neuron a nerve cell and its appendages, *not* -one

Neuropter/a an order of insects, sing. **-on**

neuros/is a functional derangement through nervous disorder, pl. **-es**

neurotic/ (adj. and noun), **-ally, -ism**

neurotransmitter (one word)

neuter abbr. **n.**, **neut.**

neutralize *not* -ise

neutrino/ (phys.) an uncharged particle with very small mass, pl. **-s**

neutron/ (phys.) an uncharged particle, pl. **-s**

Nevada off. abbr. **Nev.**, postal **NV**

névé (Swiss Fr. m.) an expanse of granular snow not yet compressed into ice at the head of a glacier (not ital.)

never/-ending, -failing (hyphens)

nevermore (one word)

never-never (colloq.) hire purchase (hyphen)

nevertheless (one word)

Nevill the family name of the Marquess of Abergavenny

Neville the family name of Baron Braybrooke

new abbr. **n.**

Newbery/, John (1713–67) English printer, **— Medal** (USA)

Newbiggin Cumbria, Durham, Northumb., N. Yorks.

Newbigging Strathclyde, Tayside

new-blown (hyphen)

newborn (one word)

Newborough, Baron

New Brunswick Canada, New Jersey; abbr. **NB**

Newburgh/ Fife, Grampian, Lancs.; **Countess of —**

New Castle Ind., Pa.

Newcastle: the signature of the Bishop of Newcastle (colon)

Newcastle/ upon Tyne Tyne & Wear; **— under Lyme** Staffs. (no hyphens)

newcomer (one word)

New Criticism an approach to the analysis of literary texts concentrating on the organization of the text itself (caps.)

New Deal/, the a US programme of social and economic reform in the 1930s (caps.), **-ish**

Newdigate, Sir Roger (1719–1806) founder of the Oxford prize for English verse

new edition abbr. **NE**, **n/e**

New England/ (US) NE states of Maine, New Hampshire, Vermont, Massachusetts, Rhode Island, and Connecticut; **-er**

New English Bible, The first part (the NT) pub. 1961, completed 1970; abbr. **NEB**

New English Dictionary original name for the *Oxford English Dictionary*

newfangled (one word)

New Forest Hants. (two words)

Newfoundland/ (one word) Canada; abbr. **NF**, **Nfld.**; **-er** an inhabitant

New Greek the Greek language in use since the end of the Middle Ages, called **Romaic** in the 19th c.; *prefer* **Modern Greek**

New Guinea *see* **Papua**

New Hall Cambridge

Newham a borough of Gr. London (one word)

New Hampshire off. and postal abbr. **NH**

New Haven Conn. (two words)

Newhaven Lothian, E. Sussex (one word)

New Hebrew the Hebrew language used in modern Israel, *prefer* **Modern Hebrew**

New Hebrides *use* **Vanuatu**

Ne Win (b. 1911) Burmese general and politician, Prime Minister 1958–60, head of state 1962–74, President 1974–81.

New Jersey off. and postal abbr. **NJ**

New Journalism a style of journalism characterized by the use of subjective and fictional elements so as to elicit an emotional response from the reader (caps.)

new-laid egg (one hyphen)

New Latin the Latin in use since the close of the Middle Ages, esp. in the sciences; *also called* **Neo-Latin**

New Mexico off. abbr. **N. Mex.**, postal **NM**

New Mills Ches., Powys

Newmilns Strathclyde

Newnes, Sir George (1851–1910) English publisher

Newnham College Cambridge

New Orleans La., abbr. **NO**

new paragraph (typ.) abbr. **n.p.**

New Quay Dyfed, Essex (two words)

Newquay Corn. (one word)

New Red Sandstone (geol.) (caps.)

newsagent (Brit.) (one word) *but* **news agency** (two words)

news/boy, -break, -brief (one word)

news bulletin (two words)

newscaster (one word)

newsdealer (US) = **newsagent**

new series abbr. **NS** (small caps. in refs.)

newsflash (one word)

news-gather/er, -ing (hyphen, one word in US)

news/girl, -letter, -man, -monger (one word)

New South Wales Australia (three words, caps., no hyphens), abbr. **NSW**

newspaper/boy, -girl, -man (one word)

Newspaper Publishers' Association abbr. **NPA**

newspapers, titles of *see* **periodicals**

Newspeak ambiguous euphemistic language (one cap.)

newsprint a low-quality paper on which newspapers are printed

news/reader, -reel, -room (one word)

news/-sheet, -stand (hyphens, one word in US)

news theatre (two words)

New Style according to the Gregorian calendar, adopted in 1752; abbr. **NS** (full caps., no point); *see also* **Old Style**

new-style numerals (typ.) ranging, lining numerals, with uniform ascenders and no descenders

news/vendor *not* **-er, -woman, worthy** (one word)

New Testament abbr. **NT**, **New Test.**

newton an SI unit of force, abbr. **N**

Newton Abbot Devon

Newton-le-Willows Merseyside, N. Yorks. (hyphens)

Newtonmore Highland (one word)

Newton Poppleford Devon

Newton Stewart Dumfries & Galloway (two words); *see also* **Newtownstewart**

Newtown Powys

Newtownabbey Co. Antrim (one word)

Newtownards Co. Down (one word)

Newtownbutler Co. Fermanagh (one word)

Newtowncunningham Co. Donegal (one word)

Newtownforbes Co. Longford (one word)

Newtownmountkennedy Co. Wicklow (one word)

Newtownsands Co. Limerick (one word)

Newtownstewart Co. Tyrone (one word); *see also* **Newton Stewart**

New Wav/e the *nouvelle vague*, or a form of 1970s–1980s rock music (caps.); **-er, -ish**

New Year's Day (caps.) always 1 Jan. even when the year is reckoned from some other day

New York US state, abbr. **NY**; the city, often abbr. **NYC**, but officially **New York, NY**

New Yorker a person born or living in New York (City)

New Yorker, The a US magazine (ital.)

nexus (Lat.) a tie, a linked group; pl. same, *not* nexi

Ney, Michel (1769–1815) French marshal

Nez Percé (of or pertaining to) a Native American people of Idaho, Oregon, and Washington, or their Penutian language

NF National Front, Newfoundland, New French, Norman French

NF (Ger.) *Neue Folge* (new series) (small caps.)

NFL (US) National Football League

Nfld. Newfoundland

NFU National Farmers' Union

NFWI National Federation of Women's Institutes

NG National Giro, National Guard, New Granada

ng in Welsh usually a separate letter, following g in alphabetical sequence; not to be divided

n.g. no good

ngaio/ a small New Zealand tree, with edible fruit and light white timber; pl. **-s**

Ngbaka (of or related to) a group of related languages spoken in Cent. Africa

Ngbandi (of or related to) a Niger–Congo language

NGO non-governmental organization

Ngoko the form of Javanese used in Indonesia among intimates and when addressing certain people of lower status

ngoma a dance, or a night of dancing, in E. Africa

Ngoni a member of an Nguni people now living chiefly in Malawi

N.Gr. New Greek

Nguni (of or related to) (a member of) a Bantu-speaking people living mainly in southern Africa, or a group of closely related Bantu languages

ngwee a monetary unit of Zambia, pl. same

NH New Hampshire (off. and postal abbr.)

N.Heb. New Hebrew, New Hebrides

NHG New High German

NHI National Health Insurance

n.h.p. nominal horsepower

NHS National Health Service

NI National Insurance, Northern Ireland

Ni nickel (no point)

Niagara/ a river separating Ontario, Canada, from New York State, **— Falls** the waterfalls of the Niagara river, also towns in NY and Ontario

Nibelungenlied a German epic, 12th–13th c.

niblick a golf club

NiCad a nickel-cadmium battery (one word, two caps.), (US propr.) **Nicad** (one cap.)

Nicam a digital stereo system used in British television; also **NICAM**

Nicar. Nicaragua

Nicene Creed issued in 325 by the Council of Nicaea (in Asia Minor); to be distinguished from the longer **Niceno-Constantinopolitan Creed** of the Thirty-Nine Articles, issued in 371

niche a recess, *not* -ch

Nicholas Anglicized spelling of the names of five popes, two Russian emperors, and the patron saint of Russia; in Russ. **Nikolai**, in Fr. **Nicolas**

Nicholson the usual spelling, *but see* **Nicolson**

nicht wahr? (Ger.) is it not so?

nickel/ (US) a 5-cent coin; (chem.) symbol **Ni**; **-plated, -plating** (hyphen); **— silver** (two words)

nick-nack *use* **knick-knack**

nickname (one word)

Nicobar Islands Indian Ocean, *not* Nik-

niçois/ (Fr.) of Nice, f. **-e** (not cap.); a native of Nice, f. **-e** (cap.)

nicol prism from **William Nicol** (1768–1851) Scottish physicist

Nicolson, Hon. Sir Harold George (1886–1968) British politician and man of letters

Nicomachean Ethics by Aristotle, *not* Nicho-

Nicosia Cyprus (Gr. **Levkosia**), Sicily; *not* Nik-

NID Naval Intelligence Division

nid/us (Lat.) a nest, pl. **-i**

Niebelungenlied *use* **Nib-**

Niebuhr,/ Barthold Georg (1776–1831) German historian and philologist, **— Karsten** (1733–1815) German traveller, **— Reinhold** (1892–1971) US theologian

niece *not* nei-

niell/o Italian metalwork, pl. **-i** (not ital.)

nien hao (part of) the reign of a Chinese emperor, used in imperial China as a system of dating; a dating mark on Chinese pottery or porcelain; pl. same; in Chinese **niánhào**

Niepce/, Joseph Nicéphore (1765–1833) French physicist, originator of photography; **— de Saint-Victor, Claude Marie François** (1805–70) his nephew, inventor of heliographic engraving

Niersteiner a Rhine wine

Nietzsche/, Friedrich Wilhelm (1844–1900) German political philosopher; **-an, -anism**

Nièvre a dép. of France

Niger, Republic of W. Cent. Africa; adj. **Nigérien**

Nigeria/, Republic of W. coast of Africa; adj. **-n**, in Fr. **nigérian**

night-blindness (hyphen, two words in US)

night/cap, -clothes, -club, -dress, -fall, -gown (one word)

night-hawk (hyphen, one word in US)

nightlife (one word)

night light (two words)

night-long (adj. and adv., hyphen)

nightmarish *not* -reish

night nurse (two words)

night owl (two words, one word in US)

night/ safe, — school (two words)

nightshade (bot.) (one word)

night shift (two words)

night/shirt, -spot (one word)

nightstick (US) = **truncheon** (one word)

night-time (hyphen, one word in US)

night watch (two words)

nightwatchman (one word)

night-work (hyphen, two words in US)

nihil/ (Lat.) nothing, — **ad rem** nothing to the purpose, — **obstat** no objection is raised (to publication etc.)

Nihon *use* **Nippon**

Nijinsk/y, Vaslav (1890–1950) Russian ballet dancer; **-a, Bronislava** (1891–1972) his sister, Russian choreographer

Nijni Novgorod, Russia, *use* **Nizhni Novgorod**

Nikobar Islands, Nikosia *use* **Nic-**

nil/ (Lat.) nothing; — **admirari** wondering at nothing (*not* admiring nothing); — **conscire sibi** to be conscious of no fault; — **desperandum** despair of nothing, *not* never despair

nilgai a short-horned Indian antelope; *not* neelghau, nylghau

Nilgiris, The hills, S. India; *not* Neilgherry Hills

nil nisi bene (speak) only well (of the dead)

Nilotic of or relating to the Nile, the Nile region, or a group of E. African Negroid peoples or their languages

ni l'un (or **une** f.) **ni l'autre** (Fr.) neither the one nor the other

nimbostrat/us (meteor.) a low grey layer of cloud, pl. **-i**

nimb/us a halo, a rain cloud; pl. **-i, -uses**; adj. **-used**

niminy-piminy affectedly delicate, *not* -i -i

n'importe! (Fr.) never mind!

Nin, Anaïs (1903–77) French-born US writer

nincompoop a simpleton (one word)

ninepins a game (one word)

ninja (Jap.) a person skilled in the Japanese martial art of **ninjutsu**

ninth *not* -eth

niobium symbol **Nb**

nip/, -ped, -per, -ping

Nippon the native name for Japan, *not* Nihon

NIREX Nuclear Industry Radioactive Waste Executive

nirvana (not cap., not ital.)

nisi (Lat.) unless, — **prius** unless before

Nissen/, Peter Norman (1871–1930) British mining engineer, inventor of — **hut**

nisus (Lat.) an effort, pl. same

nitrate a salt of nitric acid

nitre saltpetre (potassium nitrate), *not* -er (US)

nitrite a salt of nitrous acid

nitrogen symbol **N**

nitrogenize *not* -ise

nitrogenous *not* -eous

nitroglycerine an explosive yellow liquid, *not* -in (one word)

nizam a Turkish soldier, (cap.) title of the ruler of Hyderabad; pl. same

Nizhni Novgorod Russia, named Gorky during the Soviet era

NJ New Jersey (off. and postal abbr.)

NKGB (hist.) Soviet 'People's Commissariat of State Security' 1943–6; *see also* **KGB**

Nkrumah, Dr Kwame (1909–72) Ghanaian politician, President 1960–6

NKVD (hist.) Soviet 'People's Commissariat for Internal Affairs' 1934–43; *see also* **KGB**

NL New Latin, Neo-Latin

n.l. (Lat.) *non licet* (it is not allowed), *non liquet* (it is not clear), (typ.) new line

N. lat. north latitude

NLC National Liberal Club

NLQ (comput.) near letter quality

NM New Mexico (postal abbr.)

n. M. (Ger.) *nächsten Monats* (next month)

nm nanometre

N. Mex. New Mexico (off. abbr.)

NMR nuclear magnetic resonance

nn. notes

NNE north-north-east

NNW north-north-west

NO Navigation Officer, New Orleans

No Japanese drama, *use* **Noh** (q.v.)

No nobelium (no point)

No., no. number, from It. *numero*; pl. **Nos., nos.**; in Fr. **n°**, pl. **n°ˢ**; in Ger. **Nr.**

no (the negative) pl. **noes**

n.o. (cricket) not out

Noachian pertaining to Noah

Nobel/, Alfred (Bernard) (1833–96) Swedish inventor of dynamite; — **Prizes** (six) awarded annually for physics, chemistry, physiology or medicine, literature, peace, economics

nobelium symbol **No**

nobiliary/ of the nobility, — **particle** a preposition forming part of a title of nobility, e.g. in Fr. *de*, in Ger. *von*.

noblesse/ (Fr. f.) nobility, — *oblige* nobility imposes obligations

nobody (one word) *but* **no one** (two words)

nocte (Lat.) at night, abbr. **n.**

'Noctes Ambrosianae' articles in *Blackwood's Magazine*, 1822–35

nocturn (RC) a part of matins originally said at night

nocturne (painting) a night scene, (mus.) a night-piece (not ital. except as part of title)

NOD Naval Ordnance Department

NODE *New Oxford Dictionary of English*

nod/, **-ded**, **-ding**

nod/**us** a difficulty, pl. **-i**

Noel Christmas, in Fr. m. **Noël**; the Eng. **Nowel(l)** is obsolete except in carols

Noël the name

Noether, Emmy (1882–1935) German mathematician

noetic of the intellect

Nofretete *see* **Nefertiti**

Noh a traditional Japanese drama with dance and song, *not* No (cap.)

noisette/ a hazelnut; (cook.) in pl. **-s**, small choice pieces of meat; (bot.) a hybrid between China and moss rose

noisome noxious, ill-smelling (no connection with noise)

noisy *not* -ey

nolens volens (Lat.) willy-nilly, pl. *nolentes volentes*

noli me tangere (Lat.) don't touch me (no hyphens)

nolle prosequi (law) relinquishment of a suit by plaintiff or prosecutor, abbr. *nol. pros.*

nolo/ (Lat.) I do not wish to, — *contendere* I will not contest, — *episcopari* I do not wish to be a bishop (formula for avoiding responsible office)

nom. nominal, nominative

no man's land (apos., three words)

nombre (Fr., Catalan m.) number, (Sp. m.) name

nombril (her.) the point halfway between fess point and the base of the shield

nom de guerre (Fr. m.) an assumed name under which one fights, plays, writes, etc.

nom de plume a pseudonym under which one writes (not in Fr. usage) (not ital.), *prefer* **pen name**

nom de théâtre (Fr. m.) a stage-name

nom/**en** a name, pl. **-ina**; abbr. **N.**

nomen/ **genericum** a generic name, — *specificum* a specific name

nomin. nominative

nominative (gram.) the case of the subject; abbr. **n.**, **nom.**, *or* **nomin.**

non/ (Lat.) not, — *assumpsit* a denial of any promise

nonagenarian a person from 90 to 99 years old, *not* nona-

nonce-word one coined only for the occasion (hyphen)

nonchalan/**ce** indifference, **-t** (not ital.)

non-commissioned officer/ abbr. **NCO**; pl. **-s** (one hyphen, two words in US)

non-committal (hyphen)

non compos mentis of unsound mind (not ital.)

non con. non-content, dissentient

Nonconform/**ist** an English Protestant separated from the Church of England (cap. only in this sense), **-ity**

non constat (Lat.) it is not clear

non-cooperation (one hyphen, one word in US)

none can be followed by sing. or pl. verb according to the sense

Nones (pl.) in Roman calendar the ninth day, counting inclusively, before the Ides

non est (Lat.) it is wanting; *non est invent*/*us*, **-a**, **-um** he, she, *or* it, has not been found, abbr. **n.e.i.**

nonesuch *use* **nonsuch** (except in US)

Nonesuch Press founded by Sir Francis Meynell

nonet (mus.) a composition for nine performers

nonetheless = nevertheless (one word); = not any the less (for that) (three words)

non-Euclidean (hyphen, one cap.)

nonfeasance failure to perform an act required by law (one word)

non-hero the opposite of a hero (hyphen, one word in US); cf. **anti-hero**

nonillion originally (esp. Brit.) the ninth power of a million (10^{54}), *but now* usually (originally US) the tenth power of a thousand (10^{30})

non inventus (Lat.) not found

nonjur/**or** a person who refuses to take an oath (one word); **-ing**

non-jury (of a trial) without a jury

non/ **libet** it does not please (me); — *licet* it is not permitted, abbr. **n.l.**

non-lining numerals (typ.) those that have ascenders and descenders, as 1234567890

non/ **liquet** (Lat.) it is not clear, abbr. **n.l.**; — *mi ricordo* (It.) I do not remember

non-net book one that a retailer may sell at less than the published price (hyphen)

non/ **nobis** (Lat.) not unto us, the first words of Ps. 115; — *obstante* notwithstanding, abbr. **non obst.**; — *obstante veredicto* notwithstanding the verdict

nonpareil unequalled

non-person a person regarded as non-existent or insignificant (hyphen, one word in US); cf. **unperson**

non placet (Lat.) it does not please (used as a negative vote in a Church or university assembly)

nonplus/ perplex; **-sed, -sing**

non plus ultra (Lat.) perfection, *use* **ne plus ultra**

non/ possumus (Lat.) we cannot; **— pro-sequitur** he does not prosecute, abbr. *non pros.*

non-resident/ , -ial (hyphen)

non sequitur it does not follow logically, abbr. **non seq.**

non/-skid, -slip, -stick, -stop (hyphen)

nonsuch a person or thing that is unrivalled; *not* nonesuch (US)

nonsuit the stoppage of suit by judge when plaintiff has failed to make a case (one word)

non-toxic (hyphen, one word in US)

non-U not characteristic of the upper class (hyphen, no point)

noon abbr. **n.**

noonday (one word)

no one no person (two words) *but* **nobody**

noontide (one word)

n.o.p. not otherwise provided for

Nor. Norman

Noraid Irish Northern Aid Committee (one cap.)

Norddeutscher Lloyd (two words) abbr. **NDL**

Nordenfelt gun a form of machine gun invented by the Swedish engineer **Thorsten Nordenfelt** (1842–1920)

Nordenskjöld, Nils Adolf Erik, Baron (1832–1901) Swedish Arctic explorer

Nordic of or relating to the tall blond dolichocephalic Germanic people found in N. Europe, esp. in Scandinavia or Finland

Norge Norw. for **Norway**, in New Norse (nynorsk) **Noreg**

norm/a (Lat.) a rule or measure, pl. **-ae**

normalize standardize, *not* -ise

Normanby, Marquess of

normande, à la (Fr. cook.) apple-flavoured (not cap.)

Norn any of three goddesses of destiny in Scandinavian myth.

Norroy and Ulster (her.) third King of Arms

Norse abbr. **N.**

North, Christopher pseud. of **Prof. John Wilson** (1785–1854) Scottish poet

north abbr. **N.**; *see also* **compass points**

Northallerton N. Yorks. (one word)

North Americ/a, -an abbr. **NA, N. Amer.**

Northamptonshire abbr. **Northants.**

northbound (one word)

North Britain a name for Scotland, offensive to Scots; abbr. **Scot.**, *not* NB

North Carolina off. and postal abbr. **NC**

Northd. Northumberland

North Dakota off. abbr. **N. Dak.**, postal **ND**

North Downs Kent etc.

north-east/, -ern (hyphen, one word in US) abbr. **NE**

northeaster a wind (one word)

northern abbr. **N.**; *see also* **compass points**

Northern Ireland abbr. **NI**

Northern Territory (Australia) abbr. **NT**

Northesk, Earl of

North-German Gazette (one hyphen)

North-Holland publisher (hyphen)

Northleach Glos. (one word)

North Pole (caps.)

Northumberland abbr. **Northumb.**, (postal) **Northd.**

North Wales abbr. **NW**

north-west/, -ern (hyphen, one word in US) abbr. **NW**

northwester a wind (one word)

Norvic: the signature of the Bishop of Norwich (colon)

Norw. Norway, Norwegian

Norway in Norw. **Norge**, in New Norse (nynorsk) **Noreg**, in Fr. **Norvège**, in Ger. **Norwegen**, in It. **Norvegia**

nor'wester a northwester, a glass of strong liquor, an oilskin hat (= **sou'wester**)

Nos., nos. numbers

n°s (Fr.) *numéros* (numbers)

nosce teipsum (Lat.) know thyself

nose/bag, -band, -bleed (one word)

nose-cone (hyphen, two words in US)

nosedive (noun and verb, one word)

nosegay (one word)

nose job rhinoplasty (two words)

nose-piece (hyphen, one word in US)

nose wheel (two words, one word in US)

nosey *use* **nosy**

no sooner/ ... than *not* — — ... when

nostalgie/ (Fr. f.) nostalgia; **— de la boue** a desire for depravity, lit. 'mud-nostalgia'

noster (Lat.) our, our own; abbr. **N.**

Nostradamus (1503–66) French astrologer and physician, in Fr. **Michel de Nostredame**

nostrum/ a quack remedy, pl. **-s** (not ital.)

nosy *not* -ey

nosy parker an inquisitive person (not cap.)

nota bene (Lat.) mark well, abbr. **NB**

notabilia (Lat. pl.) notable things

notab/ility, -le *not* note-

notand/um (Lat.) a thing to be noted, pl. *-a*

notarize (US) certify (a document) as a notary

notar/y public a person authorized to perform certain legal formalities, esp. to draw up or certify contracts, deeds, etc. (two words); pl. **-ies public**; abbr. **NP**

notation a method of recording music or movement in written form; (US) a note or annotation, a record

note/, -s abbr. **n.**, pl. **nn.**

note/book, -case, -paper, -worthy (one word)

notic/e, -eable, -ing *not* notica-

noticeboard (one word, two words in US)

notif/y, -iable, -ied, -ying

notiti/a (Lat.) a list, pl. *-ae*

Notogaea (zool.) the land mass of Australasia; cf. **Arctogaea**; **Neogaea**

notorious well known, esp. unfavourably: 'a notorious criminal', 'notorious for its climate'; it does not mean *villainous*

not proven (Sc. law) a verdict pronouncing evidence insufficient to determine guilt or innocence

Notre Dame Ind., university and town

Notre Dame (Fr.) Our Lady, abbr. **N.D.** (no hyphen); (part of) the Fr. name of many churches (hyphen), abbr. **N.-D.**; *not* Nô-

Notre Seigneur (Fr.) Our Lord, abbr. **N.S.**

Nottinghamshire abbr. **Notts.**

Nouakchott Mauritania

n'oubliez pas (Fr.) don't forget

nougat a confection

nought the figure zero (0); *see also* **naught**

noughth immediately preceding what is regarded as 'first' in a series (e.g. 'noughth week'), also **zeroth**

noumen/on an object of intellectual intuition, not perceptible by the senses, opp. to **phenomenon**; pl. **-a**; **-al, -ally**

noun abbr. **n.**

nouns, German all have initial caps. in Ger. usage

nous (Gr.) intellect, shrewdness (not ital.); *Noûs* a journal (accent)

nous avons changé tout cela (Fr.) we have changed all that

nous verrons (Fr.) we shall see

nouveau/ riche a parvenu, pl. **-x riches** (not ital.)

nouvelle cuisine a style of cookery (not ital.)

nouvelles (Fr. f. pl.) news

nouvelle vague (Fr. f.) new wave, esp. describing French film-making of the early 1960s

Nov. November

nov/a (astr.) a new star, pl. **-ae**

Novalis pseud. of **Baron Friedrich von Hardenberg** (1772–1801) German writer

Nova/ Scotia Canada, abbr. **NS**; **— Zembla** Arctic islands, *use* **Novaya Zemlya** (two words, caps.)

Noveboracensian of New York, *not* Nova- (one word); cf. **Novi Eboraci**

novelette a short novel, (Brit. derog.) a light romantic novel, (mus.) a piano piece in free form with several themes

novella/ a short novel or narrative story, pl. **-s**

November abbr. **Nov.**; in Fr. m. *novembre*, abbr. *nov.* (not cap.)

noviciate the state or period of being a novice, *not* -tiate (US)

Nov/i Eboraci (Lat.) at New York (two words), **-um Eboracum** (Lat.) New York; *see also* **Noveboracensian**

Novotný, Antonín (1904–75) Czechoslovak politician, President 1957–68

nov/us homo (Lat.) a self-made man, pl. *-i homines*

NOW (US) National Organization for Women

nowadays (one word)

Nowel(l) *see* **Noel**

nowhere (one word)

noyade (Fr. f.) execution by drowning

noyau/ a liqueur of brandy flavoured with fruit kernels, pl. **-x**

NP New Providence, Notary Public

Np neptunium (no point)

n.p. net personalty, (typ.) new paragraph, (bibliog.) no place of publication given

NPA Newspaper Publishers' Association

NPL National Physical Laboratory

NPO New Philharmonia Orchestra (*earlier and later* **Philharmonia Orchestra**)

NR North Riding

Nr. (Ger.) *Nummer* (number)

nr. near

NRA (US) National Rifle Association, (UK) National Rivers Authority

NRC National Research Council

NRDC National Research Development Corporation

NRSV New Revised Standard Version (of the Bible)

NRT net registered tonnage

NS New Side, Newspaper Society, New Style (after 1752), Nova Scotia

ns New Series (small caps. in refs.)

N.S. (Fr.) *Notre Seigneur* (Our Lord)

n.s. not specified

n/s (banking) not sufficient, (advertisements) non-smoker, -ing

NSB National Savings Bank

NSC National Security Council

NSF (US) National Science Foundation

NSPCC National Society for the Prevention of Cruelty to Children

NSW New South Wales

NT National Theatre, National Trust, New Testament, (Austral.) Northern Territory, (bridge) no trumps

NTP normal temperature and pressure

nu the thirteenth letter of the Gr. alphabet (*N*, *ν*)

n.u. name unknown

nuance a shade of difference (not ital.)

NUBE National Union of Bank Employees

nucle/us pl. **-i**

nuclide (phys.) an atom having a specified type of nucleus, *not* -eide

-nugger in Indian place names, *use* **-nagar**

NUGMW National Union of General and Municipal Workers

NUI National University of Ireland

Nuits-Saint-Georges a red burgundy (two hyphens)

NUJ National Union of Journalists

Nuku'alofa Tonga

nulla bona (law) no goods that can be distrained upon

nullah (Anglo-Ind.) a dry watercourse or ravine (not ital.)

nulla-nulla an Australian club, *not* -ah -ah

nullif/y, -ied, -ying

nulli secundus (Lat.) second to none

NUM National Union of Mineworkers

Num. Numbers (OT), *not* Numb.

num. numeral, -s

number abbr. **No., no.**; pl. **Nos., nos.**

Numbers (OT) abbr. **Num.**

numbskull *use* **num-**

num/en a presiding deity or spirit, pl. **-ina**

numeraire (econ.) the function of money as a measure of value, a standard for currency exchange rates (no accent, not ital.)

numéraire (Fr. m.) cash, legal tender

numér/o (Fr. m.) number, abbr. **n°**, pl. **n°s**; *-oter* to number (e.g. pages), *-oteur* a numbering machine

numis. numismatic, -s; numismatology

Nummer (Ger. f.) number, abbr. **Nr.**

numskull a dunce, *not* numb-

nunatak (Inuit) a hill or mountain protruding through glacial ice, *not* -ck

Nunc Dimittis (Lat.) (the musical setting of) the Song of Simeon as a canticle

nunchaku a Japanese martial arts weapon consisting of two hardwood sticks joined together at one end by a strap or chain (not ital.)

nunci/o a papal ambassador; pl. **-os**; **-ature** the office or tenure of a nuncio

nuncupat/e declare (a will or testament) orally, not in writing; **-ion, -ive**

NUPE National Union of Public Employees

Nuphar (bot.) the yellow water-lily genus; cf. **nenuphar**

NUR National Union of Railwaymen (merged with the NUS to form the RMT, 1990)

nurd *use* **ne-**

Nuremberg *not* -burg, in German **Nürnberg**

Nureyev, Rudolf (**Hametovich**) (1939–93) Russian ballet dancer

nurl *use* **kn-**

Nürnberg Anglicized as **Nuremberg**

nurs/e, -ing, -ling

nursemaid (one word)

nurseryman (one word)

nursery/ rhyme, — school (two words)

NUS National Union of Seamen (merged with the NUR to form the RMT, 1990), National Union of Students

NUT National Union of Teachers

nut/, -ted, -ting, -ty

nutcrackers (one word)

NUTG National Union of Townswomen's Guilds

nut/hatch a bird, **-shell** (one word)

Nuuk Greenland, *not* Godthåb

nux vomica a seed of E. Indian tree, source of strychnine (two words, not ital.); abbr. **nux vom.**

NV *naamloze vennootschap* (public limited company), Nevada (postal abbr.), New Version

NVM Nativity of the Virgin Mary

NW north-west, -ern; North Wales

NWFP North-West Frontier Province, Pakistan

NWT North-West Territories, Canada

NY New York (City *or* State); *see also* **New York**

nyala an antelope, *use* **iny-**

Nyasaland Cent. Africa, *not* Nyassa- (one word); *now* **Malawi**

NYC New York City

nyctalopia night-blindness

nyet (Russ.) no (to avoid confusion the normal transliteration, *net*, is not used)

nylghau an antelope, *use* **nilgai**

nylon (not cap.)

Nymegen the Netherlands; in Du. **Nijmegen**, Fr. **Nimègue**, Ger. **Nimwegen**

nymph/ae (anat.) the *labia minora*, sing. **-a**

Nymphaea (bot.) the white water-lily genus

nymphet a young or little nymph, a sexually attractive young girl; *not* -tte

nympho/ (colloq.) a nymphomaniac, pl. **-s**

nympholep/sy ecstasy or frenzy caused by desire of the unattainable; **-t** a person inspired by violent enthusiasm, esp. for an ideal

nynorsk 'new Norwegian', a Norwegian peasant dialect given literary form *c*.1850; *formerly* landsmål (not cap.)

Nyquist/, Harry (1889–1976) Swedish-born US physicist, responsible for — **criterion**, — **diagram**, — **limit**, — **noise theorem**

Nyx (Gr. myth.) the female personification of Night, daughter of Chaos

NZ New Zealand

O (exclamation)

O oxygen (no point), (Lat.) *octarius* (a pint), the fourteenth in a series; a blood group

O. Odd Fellows, Order (as DSO), owner, (Fr. m.) *ouest* (west), (Ger. m.) *Osten* (east)

O' Irish patronymic prefix ('grandson of') (apos., *not* turned comma); **o** or **ó**, or corresponding caps., followed by thin space, also used

o. old, (meteor.) overcast

o- (chem. prefix) *ortho-* (ital., always hyphenated), *prefer to ortho-*

o' abbr. for *of*, to be set close up in common constructions (o'clock), but according to sense in reproducing archaic or dialectal constructions (cock o' th' walk)

Ö, ö in Ger., Swed., etc., may *not* be replaced by *Oe, oe* (except in some proper names), *O, o,* or *Œ, œ*

ö (Swed.), **ø** (Dan.) island

Ø, ø Danish and Norwegian letter

% per cent

‰ per mille

o/a on account of

oaf/ a stupid or loutish person, pl. **-s**

Oak-apple Day 29 May

Oaks, the annual race at Epsom (treated as sing.)

O. & M. organization and methods

OAP Old Age Pension, **-er**

oarlock (US) = **rowlock**

oarweed seaweed, *not* ore-weed

OAS on active service, Organization of American States, Organisation de l'Armée Secrète

oas/is pl. **-es**

oatcake (one word)

Oates, Titus (1649–1705) the man who fabricated the Popish Plot, 1678

oatmeal (one word)

OAU Organization of African Unity

Oaxaca Mexico

OB Old Boy, outside broadcast

ob. oboe

ob. *obiit* (he, she, *or* it, died)

Obadiah (OT) abbr. **Obad.**

obbligato (mus.) an accompaniment, *not* obl-; abbr. **obb.**

OBE Officer of the Order of the British Empire, overtaken by events

obeah W. Indian sorcery; *not* -ea, -eeyah, -i

obeisance a courtesy bow

obelisk a tapering, usually four-sided, monument or landmark; *not* -isc

obel/us (typ.) dagger-shaped reference mark in printed matter (†); **double obelus** ‡; a mark (— or ÷) used in ancient manuscripts to mark a word or passage, esp. as spurious; pl. **-i**; **-ize** mark with an obelus as spurious etc.

Oberammergau Bavaria, Germany

obi a broad Japanese sash worn with a kimono; for sorcery *use* obeah

obiit/ (Lat.) he, she, *or* it died, abbr. **ob.**; **— sine prole** died without issue, abbr. **ob.s.p.**

obit a date of death, a funeral or commemoration service; (colloq.) obituary (no point, not ital.)

obiter/ dictum (Lat.) a thing said by the way, pl. **— dicta**; **— scriptum** a thing written by the way, pl. **— scripta**

object/, -ion, -ionable, -ive, -ively abbr. **obj.**

object language a language described by means of another language (two words)

object lesson (two words)

object-oriented/ architecture abbr. **OOA, — design** abbr. **OOD, — language** abbr. **OOL, — planning system** abbr. **OOPS** (comput.); *not* -orientated (one hyphen)

objet/ d'art a work of artistic value, pl. **-s d'art** (not ital.)

objet/ trouvé (Fr. m.) thing found, pl. **-s trouvés**

obl. oblique, oblong

obligato *use* obb-

obligee (law) a person to whom another is bound

obliger one who does a favour

obligor (law) one who binds himself to another

oblique abbr. **obl.**

oblong abbr. **obl.**

obloquy the state of being generally ill spoken of; abuse, detraction

o.b.o. or best offer

obo/e (mus.) *not* the many variants, abbr. **ob.**; **-ist** *not* -eist

obol a coin and weight of ancient Greece

obole a small French coin in use 10th–15th cc.

obol/us an apothecaries' weight of 10 grains; various small coins in medieval Europe; pl. **-i**

O'Brien,/ Conor Cruise (b. 1917) Irish politician, **— Edna** (b. 1932) Irish writer, **— Flann** pseud. of **Brian O'Nolan** (1911–66) Irish writer, **— William Smith** (1803–64) and **— William** (1852–1928) Irish patriots

obs. observation, observatory, observed, obsolete

obscurum per obscurius (Lat.) (explaining) the obscure by means of the more obscure, *not obscurus — —*

obsequi/es funeral rites, the sing. -y *not used*; **-al**

obsequious fawning

observanda (Lat. pl.) things to be observed

observat/ion, -ory abbr. **obs.**

obsidian (mineral.)

obsolescen/t becoming obsolete; the state is **-ce**

obsolete/ disused, antiquated, abbr. **obs.**; the state is **-ness**

ob.s.p. *obiit sine prole* (died without issue)

obstetric/s abbr. **obstet.**; **-ian**

obstructor *not* -er

OC Officer Commanding, Officer of the Order of Canada

ocarina a small (usually terracotta) wind instrument, *not* och-

Occam, William (**of**) *see* **Ockham, William** (**of**)

Occidental (cap. as noun, not cap. as adj.)

occip/ut the back of the head (not ital.), **-ital**

Occitan (of or concerning) a Romance language related to Catalan, also called *langue d'oc*

Occleve *use* **Hoccleve**

occulist *use* **ocu-**

occur/, -red, -rence, -rent, -ring

Oceania the islands of the Pacific and adjacent seas

ocell/us (zool.) simple (as opp. to compound) eye (of insect), pl. **-i**

ocharina *use* **oca-**

ochlocracy mob rule

ochone (Sc., Ir.) expressing regret or lament, *not* oh-; in Gaelic and Ir. *ochóin*

ochra *use* **okra**

ochr/e a yellow pigment; *not* ocher (US), oker; **-eous, -y**

Ockeghem, Johannes (d. 1497) Franco-Flemish composer, *also* **Okeghem**

Ockham Surrey; *see also* **Occam**

Ockham/, William (**of**) (*c.*1285–*c.*1347) English Franciscan philosopher, deviser of **—'s razor** the principle of the fewest possible assumptions; **-ism, -ist**; *also* **Occam, Ockam**

o'clock to be printed close up (not to be abbr.)

O'Connell, Daniel (1775–1847) Irish statesman

O'Connor,/ Feargus Edward (1794–1855) Irish-born Chartist leader; **— Rt. Hon. Thomas Power** (1848–1931) Irish-born journalist and British politician

OCR (comput.) optical character recognition (reading of print etc. by electronic eye for computer input)

ocra *use* **okra**

Oct. October

octachord eight-stringed (musical instrument), *not* octo-

octahedr/on a solid figure with eight faces, pl. **-ons**; **-al**; *not* octae-, octoe-, octoh-

octaroon *use* **octo-**

octastyle (archit.) having eight columns, *not* octo-

Octateuch the first eight books of OT, *not* Octo-

octave a fencing position

octavo/ (typ.) a book based on eight leaves, sixteen pages, to the sheet; pl. **-s**, abbr. **8vo** (no point)

octet (mus.) *not* -ett, -ette

October abbr. **Oct.**; in Fr. m. *octobre*, abbr. *oct.* (not cap.)

Octobrist (Russ. hist.) *not* -erist, in Russ. *oktyabrist*

octochord *use* **octa-**

octodecimo *see* **eighteenmo**

octo/edron, -hedron *use* **octa-**

octogenarian a person from 80 to 89 years old

octop/us pl. **-uses**, formal pl. **-odes**; *not* -i

octoroon a person of one-eighth Negro blood, *not* octa-

octostyle *use* **octa-**

Octoteuch *use* **Octa-**

octroi (Fr. m.) municipal customs duties (not ital.)

OCTU *or* **Octu** Officer Cadets Training Unit

ocularist a maker of artificial eyes, *not* occ-

oculist a medical specialist in eyes, *not* occ-

Oculi Sunday third in Lent

ocul/us (Lat.) an eye, pl. *-i*

OD Old Dutch, Ordnance datum, overdose

O/D on demand, overdraft

od a hypothetical force; (arch.) God, *not* 'od

o.d. outer diameter

odal *use* **ud-**

odalisque (Turk.) a female slave or concubine, *not* -isk (not ital.)

O.Dan. Old Danish

Oddfellow a member of fraternity (off. title **Independent Order of Odd Fellows**)

oddments (typ.) parts of a book other than main text, such as contents, index; a section containing oddments

odd pages (typ.) the right-hand, or recto, pages

Odelsting the lower house of Norwegian Parliament

Odendaalsrus (off. spelling) Orange Free State, *not* -st

Odéon a Paris theatre

Oder–Neisse line between Poland and Germany (en rule)

Odets, Clifford (1906–63) US dramatist and playwright

odeum/ a building for musical performances, pl. **-s**

Odeypore *use* **Udaipur**

odi profanum vulgus (Lat.) I loathe the common herd

odium a widespread dislike

odium/ aestheticum (Lat.) the bitterness of aesthetic controversy, — *medicum* the bitterness of medical controversy, — *musicum* the bitterness of musical controversy, — *theologicum* the bitterness of theological controversy

odometer an instrument for measuring distance travelled, *not* ho-

O'Donoghue of the Glens, The (cap. *T*)

O'Donovan, The (cap. *T*)

odontoglossum/ an orchid, pl. **-s**; cap., ital., as genus

odor/iferous, -ize, -izer, -ous

odour/, -less *not* odor- (US)

Odra ancient region corresponding to the modern Indian state of Orissa

Odysseus Greek hero (spelling used in classical contexts); in Lat. **Ulixes**, Eng. **Ulysses** (e.g. Shakespeare, Tennyson, and Joyce)

Odyssey of Homer (ital., not quoted); **Odyssean** (not ital.)

odyssey a long wandering (not cap., not ital.)

OE Old English

Oe (phys.) oersted

OECD Organization for Economic Cooperation and Development

oecist the founder of a Greek colony, *not* oik-

oecology *use* **ec-**

oecumenic/, -al *see* **ecumenic**

Oecumenical Council an assembly of ecclesiastical representatives deciding on Christian matters

Oecumenical Patriarch the Archbishop of Constantinople, head of the Orthodox Church

OED Oxford English Dictionary, originally *NED* (New English Dictionary)

oedema/ a swelling, **-tous**; *not* ed- (US)

Oedipus/ the Theban hero, *not* Edi-; — **complex** (psych.) a boy's subconscious desire for his mother and hostility to his father (two words); **Oedipal**

OEEC Organization for European Economic Co-operation, *now* **OECD**

Oehlenschläger, Adam (1779–1850) Danish writer, *not* Oh-

œil (Fr. m.) eye, pl. *yeux*; *œil-de-bœuf* a small round window, pl. *œils-de-bœuf*; *œil-de-perdrix* a soft corn, pl. *œils-de-perdrix*

œillade (Fr. f.) a glance

oeno/logy the study of wine, **-phile** lover of wines; *not* en- (US), oin-

oersted (phys.) unit of magnetic field strength, from **Hans Christian Oersted** (1777–1851) Danish physicist, *not* œr-; abbr. **Oe**; in SI units $1000/4\pi$ A/m

oesophag/us the gullet, pl. **-i**; **-eal** (not ital.); *not* es- (US)

Oesterreich (Ger.) Austria, *use* **Ös-**

oestrogen, oestrus *not* es- (US)

œuf (Fr. m.) egg, *œufs*; *à la coque* boiled eggs, — *à la neige* whisked eggs, — *à l'indienne* curried eggs, — *de Pâques* Easter eggs, — *sur le plat* fried eggs

œuvre work, esp. a writer's or artist's work taken as a whole (not ital.)

OF Odd Fellows, Old French, (typ.) old-face type

of (US) in time-keeping, used in relation to the following (*not* preceding) hour: 'quarter of three' = 2.45 *not* 3.15

O'Faoláin, Seán (1900–91) Irish writer

off. offic/e, -er, -ial, -inal

Offaly Ireland

Offa's Dike between England and Wales (apos.)

offbeat (one word)

off-centre (hyphens)

off colour not in good health, (esp. US) somewhat indecent (-or)

offcut a remnant of paper, wood, etc.

off day (two words)

Offenbach, Jacques (1819–80) German-born French composer

offence *not* -se (US)

offer/, -ed, -ing, -tory

offg. officiating

off guard (two words, hyphen when attrib.)

offhand/, -ed casual, extempore (one word)

offic/e, -er abbr. **off.**

official abbr. **off., offic.**

Official Report of Parliamentary Debates, The the official name for Hansard since 1892

officiating abbr. **offg.**

officina (Lat.) workshop; *see also* *oficina*

officinal abbr. **off.**

off/-key, -licence (hyphens)

offload (one word)

off/-peak, -piste, -price (hyphens)

offprint (typ.) a separately printed copy, or small edition, of an article that originally appeared as part of a larger publication

off/-putting, -screen, -season (hyphens)

offset/ (print.) **-litho, -lithography** a planographic printing process in which ink is transferred onto an intermediate rubber blanket cylinder and then offset onto the paper (hyphens)

offshoot (one word)

offshore (adj. and adv., one word)

offside (sport); (Brit.) right side of a vehicle, animal, etc. (cf. **nearside**) (one word)

offspring (one word)

offstage (one word)

off-street (hyphen)

off-the/-cuff, -record, -shelf, -wall (adj., hyphens)

off/-time, -white (hyphen)

oficina (Sp.) a S. American factory; *see also* **off-**

Oflag a German prison camp for officers

O'Flaherty, Liam (1896–1984) Irish novelist

OFM Order of Friars Minor

OFS Orange Free State

oft-times (hyphen)

ogam *use* **ogh-**

ogee (archit.) a moulding, adj. **ogeed**

ogham an ancient alphabet, used to write Pictish and Irish; *not* -gam, -gum, -hum

ogiv/e the diagonal rib of a vault, a pointed arch; **-al**

OGPU *or* **Ogpu** the Soviet 'United state political administration for struggle against espionage and counter-revolution' 1923–34; *see also* **KGB**

O'Grady, The (cap. *T*)

ogr/e a man-eating giant, pl. **-es**; f. **-ess**; adj. **-ish** *not* -eish

OH Ohio (postal abbr.)

OHBMS On Her, *or* His, Britannic Majesty's Service

O. Henry *see* **Henry**

OHG Old High German

Ohio postal abbr. **OH**; spell out in other contexts (such as refs.)

ohm SI unit of electrical resistance; symbol Ω; *see also* **mho**; from **Georg Simon Ohm** (1787–1854) German physicist; **ohmic/ contact, — loss** (two words), **ohmmeter** (one word, two *m*s)

OHMS On Her, *or* His, Majesty's Service

oho! an exclamation of surprise; *not* O ho, Oh ho, etc.

ohone *use* **och-**

oidium a fungus, *not* oï-

oikist *use* **oec-**

oilcake (one word)

oil can (two words)

oilcloth (one word)

oil-colour (hyphen)

oilfield (one word)

oil-fired (hyphen)

oil-gauge (hyphen, two words in US)

oil/ paint, — painting (two words)

oil-press (hyphen, two words in US)

oil rig (two words)

oil/skin, -stone (one word)

oil/ tanker, — well (two words)

oino/logy, -phile *use* **oen-**

oi polloi (Gr.) the masses, *use* **hoi polloi**

O.Ir. Old Irish

Oireachtas the legislature of the Irish Republic: the President, Dáil, and Seanad

OIRO offers in the region of, only in receipt of offer; *also* **o.i.r.o.**

Oistrakh,/ David (Fyodorovich) (1908–74) and **— Igor (Davidovich)** (b. 1931) his son, Russian violinists

O.It. Old Italian

Ojibwa Wis.

Ojibway a Native American tribe

OK 'all correct'; *not* Ok, ok, okay; Oklahoma (postal abbr.)

okapi a bright-coloured African ruminant

O'Keeffe, Georgia (1887–1986) US painter

Okeghem *see* **Ockeghem**

Okehampton Devon

O'Kelly, The (cap. *T*)

oker *use* **ochre**

Oklahoma off. abbr. **Okla.**, postal **OK**

okra an African plant, its edible seed pods; *not* oc(h)-, -o

OL Old Latin

Ol. Olympiad

Olaf, St the patron of Norway

old/ abbr. **o.**, **-clothes-man** (hyphens)

Old Bailey *see* **bailey**

Old Believer dissenter from the Orthodox Church, *formerly* **Raskolnik**

Old Church Slavonic the Slavonic language from the 9th c., also called **Old Bulgarian**

Old English the English language up to *c*.1150, abbr. **OE**; (typ.) a name for the English style of black letter: 𝔒𝔩𝔡 𝔈𝔫𝔤𝔩𝔦𝔰𝔥

old face (typ.) a type design based on the original roman type of the 15th c.; abbr. **OF**

old-fashioned (hyphen)

Old French the French language before *c*.1400, abbr. **OF**

'Old Glory' the US stars-and-stripes flag

'Old Hickory' *see* **Jackson, Andrew**

Old High German the High German language up to *c*.1200, abbr. **OHG**

'Old Hundredth' a hymn tune, *not* Hundred

Old Icelandic *see* **Old Norse**

Old Ionic the Greek dialect found in Homeric epics, abbr. **OI**

Old Irish the Irish language used in the 7th–11th cc., abbr. **O.Ir.**

Old Italian the Italian language used in the 4th–10th cc., abbr. **O.It.**

Old Latin pre-classical Latin, abbr. **OL**

old maid an elderly spinster, prissy man, card game (two words); *but* **old-maidish** (hyphen)

Old Man and the Sea, The novelette by Hemingway, 1952

Old Man of the Sea a character in *Arabian Nights* (caps.)

Oldmeldrum Grampian (one word)

Old Norse the Germanic language from which the Scandinavian languages are derived, specifically the language of Norway and its colonies until the 14th c.; abbr. **ON**; its general (non-lit.) form is sometimes called **Old Icelandic**, abbr. **O.Ic.**

Old Pals Act (three words, caps., no apos.)

Old Peculier a beer, *not* -iar

Old Possum's Book of Practical Cats a collection of humorous poems by T. S. Eliot, 1939

Old Pretender, the James Stuart (1688–1766) son of James II

Old Prussian a Baltic (*not* Germanic) language used before the 17th c. in E. Prussia, abbr. **OP**

Old Red Sandstone (geol.) (caps.)

Old Saxon the Saxon language in use until *c.*12th c. in NW Germany, abbr. **OS**

old school tie (three words)

Old Style according to the Julian calendar (before 1752), abbr. **OS** (full caps., no point); cf. **New Style**

old style/ (typ.) a type design, being a regularized old face; abbr. **OS**

old-style numerals (typ.) *see* **non-lining numerals**

Old Testament abbr. **OT**, **Old Test.**

old-time/ (adj., hyphen), **-r**

Old Welsh the Welsh language found in documents up to *c.*1150, abbr. **OW**

old woman a fussy man (two words), *but* **old-womanish** (hyphen)

¡olé! (Sp.) bravo!

olefin (chem.) a hydrocarbon, *not* -ine

oleiferous oil-producing, *not* olif-

oleograph a picture printed in oil colours

O level (hist.) 'ordinary level' examination (no hyphen)

OLG Old Low German

Olifants River S. Africa (no apos.)

Oligocene (geol.) (of or relating to) the third epoch of the Tertiary period (cap., not ital.)

olive/**branch, — drab, — oil** (two words)

Olivetan an order of monks, *not* -tian

Olivier, Laurence (**Kerr**), **Baron** (1907–89) English actor; *see also* **Ollivier**

olla podrida the Spanish national dish; a medley (not ital.)

Ollivier, Olivier Émile (1825–1913) French statesman and writer; *see also* **Olivier**

oloroso/ (a drink of) a medium-sweet sherry, pl. **-s**

Olympiad a celebration of Olympic Games (ancient *and* modern); period of four years between celebrations; abbr. **Ol.**

Olympian of Olympus, the abode of the Greek gods; as a noun, a dweller in Olympus or a superhuman person

Olympic of Olympia in Greece, of the games held there in antiquity, of the modern games

OM (Member of the) Order of Merit

o.m. old measurement

-oma a suffix forming nouns denoting tumours and other abnormal growths

omadhaun an Irish term of contempt (*not* the many variants)

Omagh Co. Tyrone

Omaha Nebr.

Oman/ SE Arabia, adj. **-i**

Omar Khayyám (1050–1123) Persian poet, astronomer, and mathematician

ombre a card game for three, popular in Europe in the 17th–18th cc.

ombré (of a fabric etc.) having gradual shading of colour from light to dark (not ital.)

ombuds/**man** a parliamentary commissioner or official appointed to investigate complaints against government departments; pl. **-men**

Omdurman Sudan

omega the last letter of the Gr. alphabet (Ω, ω); Ω the symbol for **ohm**

omelette *not* -et (US)

omertà a code of silence, esp. as practised by the Mafia

omicron the fifteenth letter of the Gr. alphabet (O, o), *not* omik-

omit/, **-ted, -ting**

omnibus/ pl. **-es**; *see also* **bus**

omnium gatherum a confused medley (not ital.)

ON Old Norse

oncoming (one word)

oncost an overhead expense (one word)

Ondaatje, (**Philip**) **Michael** (b. 1943) Sri-Lankan-born Canadian writer

ondes martenot (mus.) electronic keyboard producing one note of variable pitch (not caps., not ital.)

on dit (Fr. m. sing./pl.) gossip, hearsay ('people say'); pl. **on dits** (not used in Fr.)

one-and-twenty etc. (hyphens)

Oneida a socialist community started at Lake Oneida, NY, 1847

one-idea'd (hyphen)

O'Neill/, Eugene (**Gladstone**) (1888–1953) US playwright, **—, Moira** pseud. of **Agnes Higginson Skrine** (*fl.* 1900) Irish poet; **— of the Maine, Baron** the family name of Baron Rathcavan

oneiro/critic an interpreter of dreams; **-logy, -mancy**; *not* oniro-

oneness (**a** *not* an) (one word)

one/-night stand, -off (hyphens)

oneself is reflexive or intensive, **one's self** one's personal entity

one/-sided, -upmanship (hyphens)

ONF Old Norman French

ongoing continuing (one word)

onion-skin a thin, smooth, translucent paper

onirocritic etc., *use* **oneiro-**

online (one word)

onlook/er, -ing (one word)

on ne passe pas (Fr.) no thoroughfare

o.n.o. or near(est) offer

O'Nolan, Brian *see* **O'Brien, Flann**

onomastic/ relating to names, **-on** a vocabulary of proper names, **-s** the study of the origin and formation of (esp. personal) proper names (treated as sing.)

onomatopoe/ia word-formation by imitation of sound, abbr. **onomat.**; **-ial, -ian, -ic -ical, -ically**

onomatopo/esis, -etically *not* -poë-, -poie-

onrush (one word)

on-screen (hyphen)

onshore (adj., adv., one word)

onside (sport) (one word)

onstage (one word)

on-street (adj., hyphen)

Ontario Canada, abbr. **Ont.**

onto (prep., one word, *but* two words for *on* followed by prep. *to*)

ontolog/y the metaphysical study of the essence of things, **-ize** *not* -ise

onus/ a burden, pl. **-es** (not ital.)

onus probandi (Lat.) burden of proof (ital.)

% per cent symbol; *prefer* the words to the symbol except in scientific or heavily statistical work, in notes and parenthetical matter, and in tables and captions

o-o (ornith.) a Hawaiian honeyeater; cf. **ou**

oo- (biol.) prefix denoting egg, ovum; *not* oö- (US)

Oodeypore India, *use* **Udaipur**

oolong a cured Chinese tea, *not* ou-

oomiak *use* **umiak**

‰ per mille

Oostanaula a river, Ga.

Oostende Fl. for **Ostend** (Eng. spelling)

Ootacamund Madras, India; *not* Utakamand; colloq. abbr. **Ooty**

oozy muddy, *not* -ey

OP observation post, *Ordinis Praedicatorum* (of the Order of Preachers, or Dominicans)

op. operation; optime; *opus* (work), *opera* (works)

o.p. (theat.) opposite the prompter's side, or the actor's right; (bibliog.) out of print; (typ.) overproof

opah a deep-sea fish

op art art in geometrical form giving the optical illusion of movement (no point)

op. cit. *opere citato* (in the work quoted) (not ital.)

OPEC Organization of Petroleum Exporting Countries

op-ed (US) (of or relating to) (articles) opposite the editorial page in a newspaper (hyphen, not cap.)

open-and-shut case (two hyphens)

opencast in mining, with removal of the surface layers (one word)

open-door policy an opportunity for free trade and immigration (one hyphen)

open-heart/ of surgery, **-ed** (hyphens)

open-mouthed (hyphen, one word in US)

open-plan (adj., hyphen)

open sesame (not caps., two words)

openwork/, -ed, -ing (one word)

opera *see* **opus**

operable that can be operated (on)

opera buffa comic opera, in Fr. **opéra bouffe**

Opéra-Comique a Paris theatre (hyphen)

opéra comique (Fr. m.) opera with spoken dialogue

opera/ glasses, — house (two words)

opera seria (It.) 18th-c. opera on heroic theme

operation abbr. **op.**, pl. **ops.**

opercul/um (biol.) a cover, pl. **-a** (not ital.)

opere/ citato (Lat.) in the work quoted, abbr. **op. cit.**; **— in medio** in the midst of the work

operetta/ a light opera, pl. **-s**

ophicleide (mus.) the serpent, a bass or alto key-bugle; *not* -eid

ophiolatry the worship of serpents

ophiology the study of serpents, *not* ophid-

ophthalmic of the eye

Opie,/ Amelia (1769–1853) English novelist, wife of **— John** (1761–1807) English painter; **— Iona** (b. 1923) and **— Peter** (1918–82) her husband, authors and folklorists

opinion poll (two words)

o.p.n. *ora pro nobis* (pray for us)

opodeldoc a liniment

opopanax a perfume

Oporto Portugal, in Port. **Porto**

opp. opposed, opposite

opposite font (typ.) type set in a contrasting typeface, e.g. *italic* in roman text, *or* roman *in italic text*

oppressor *not* -er

ops. operations

opt. optative, optical, optician, optics

optical centring (typ.) positioning of text on the page so that it appears to the reader to be centred, although by measurement it is not

optime at Cambridge University, one next in merit to a **wrangler** (not ital.); abbr. **op.**

optimize make the best of, *not* -ise

optim/um pl. **-a**

optometrist (esp. US) a person who practises optometry, = **ophthalmic optician**

opus (Lat.) a work, pl. **opera** (not ital.); abbr. **op.**

opus/ anglicanum a type of fine pictorial embroidery produced in England during the Middle Ages, **— anglicum** a type of lavish manuscript illumination regarded as characteristically English

opuscul/um (Lat.) a minor work; pl. **-a**; in Eng. **opuscule** pl. **opuscules**

opus Dei (eccl.) the work of God, specifically the Divine Office, or liturgical worship in general (one cap.); a RC organization founded in Spain in 1927 (two caps.)

Opusdeista (RC) a member of the Opus Dei

opus magnum a great work, pl. *opera magna*; cf. *magnum opus*

opus number (mus.) (two words)

opus/ operantis (Lat.) the effect of a sacrament resulting from the spiritual disposition of the recipient (the Donatist view); **— operatum** the effect of a sacrament resulting from the grace flowing from the sacrament itself (the RC view)

OR operating room, operational research, Oregon (postal abbr.), other ranks

or (her.) gold or yellow colour

or. oriental

o.r. owner's risk

ora (Lat. pl.) mouths, *see* **os**

oral of or relating to the mouth, spoken; cf. **verbal**

orangeade *not* -gade

orange blossom (two words)

Orange Free State a province of S. Africa (three words), abbr. **OFS**

Orange/ism *not* -gism; **-man** (one word, cap.)

Orangeman's Day 12 July

orange/ peel, — squash, — stick (two words)

orange-wood (hyphen, one word in US)

orang-utan *not* ourang-, -outang, -utang (hyphen, one word in US; not ital.)

Oranmore and Browne, Baron

ora pro nobis (Lat.) pray for us, abbr. **o.p.n.**

orat. orator, -ical, -ically

oratio/ obliqua (Lat.) indirect speech, **— recta** direct speech

oratorio/ pl. **-s**; **titles of —** when cited, to be in ital.

orca any of various whales, esp. the killer whale; *not* -ka

Orcadian of or pertaining to Orkney

orchid a member of a family of mainly exotic flowering plants; **orchis** an (esp. wild) orchid or one of genus *Orchis*

Orczy, Baroness Emmuska (Emma) (1865–1947) Hungarian-born English novelist

ord. ordained, order, ordinal, ordinance, ordinary

Order abbr. **O.**; when referring to a society, to be cap., as the Order of Jesuits

order abbr. **ord.**; for the orders of classical architecture *see* **architect**; for the orders of angels *see* **celestial hierarchy**

order/ book, — form (two words)

order paper (esp. parl.) a written or printed order of the day, an agenda (two words)

ordin/ance a regulation, **-ary**; abbr. **ord.**

ordnance artillery, military stores

Ordnance/ Survey Department (caps.) abbr. **OSD**; **— datum** (one cap.) the standard sea level of the Ordnance Survey, abbr. **OD**

ordonnance the proper disposition of parts of a building or picture (not ital.)

Ordovician (geol.) (of or relating to) the second period of the Palaeozoic era

ordre du jour (Fr. m.) agenda of a meeting

öre a Swedish coin, equal to one-hundredth of krona; pl. same

øre a Danish or Norwegian coin, equal to one-hundredth of krone; pl. same

Ore. Oregon (off. abbr.)

oregano (*Origanum vulgare*) wild marjoram used for seasoning; *see also* **marjoram**

Oregon off. abbr. **Oreg.**, postal **OR**

O'Rell, Max pseud. of **Paul Blouet** (1848–1903) French author and journalist

oreo/graphy, -logy *use* **oro-**

Oresteia a trilogy by Aeschylus, 458 BC

Øresund (Dan.) the sound between Denmark and Sweden, in Sw. **Öresund**

oreweed *use* **oar-**

orfèvrerie (Fr. f.) goldsmith's work

orfray *use* **-phrey**

org. organ, -ic, -ism, -ization, -ized

organdie a fine translucent cotton muslin; *not* -di, -dy (US); in Fr. m. *organdi*

organize *not* -ise

organon (Gr.) instrument of thought, esp. a means of reasoning or system of logic; title of Aristotle's logical writings (cap., ital.)

organ/um (Lat.) organ, (mus.) polyphony; pl. **-a**

organza a thin, stiff transparent dress fabric

org/y *not* -ie; pl. **-ies**

oriel a small room built out from a wall, its window

Oriel College Oxford

Orient, the the East

orientate *prefer* **orient** in all senses, and with prefixes (e.g. dis-, re-) and suffixes (e.g. -ed, -able); -tate form not used in US

oriental/ (cap. as noun), **-ist**, abbr. **or.**, **orient.**

orientalize *not* -ise (not cap.)

oriflamme *not* -flamb

orig. origin, -al, -ally, -ate, -ated

Origen (185–253) a Father of the Church

original (Sp. typ.) copy

Origin of Species, The by C. Darwin, 1859

orinasal of the mouth and nose, *not* oro-

Orinoco river, S. America; cf. **oro-**

oriole any of two genera of birds: in the Old World genus *Oriolus*, in the New World genus *Icterus*

Orissa state in NE India

Oriya a native of Orissa, or the Indic language of Orissa or Odra, an ancient region corresponding to modern Orissa

orka *use* **-ca**

Orkney a region of Scotland

Orkneys an island group

orle (her.) a narrow band or border of charges near the edge of a shield

Orléans House of; a dép. of France (accent); **Orlean/ism, -ist** (no accent in Eng. or It.)

Orme's Head, Great *and* **Little** Gwynedd (apos.)

ormolu a gilded bronze or gold-coloured alloy (one word, not ital.)

Ormonde, Marquess of

Ormuzd (Middle Pers.) the Zoroastrian spirit of good; *not* the many variants, although **Ahura Mazda** (Old Pers.) is a common early form

orn/é (Fr.) f. **-ée** adorned

ornith. ornitholog/y, -ical

ornithorhynchus duck-billed platypus

orogen/esis (geol.) the process of formation of mountains; **-etic, -ic**

oro/graphy, -logy mountain description and science, *not* oreo-

oronasal *use* **ori-**

oronoco a Virginian tobacco, *not* the many variants; cf. **Ori-**

Oroonoko a novel by Aphra Behn, *c.*1678

orotund magniloquent, imposing

orphan (typ.) first line of a paragraph at the foot of a page or column; also called **club line**; *see also* **widow**

Orphe/us (Gr. myth.) a Thracian lyrist; **-an** like his music, entrancing

Orphic pertaining to **Orphism**, the mystic cult connected with Orpheus

orphrey an ornamental border, *not* -fray

orpine a purple-flowered plant, *not* -pin

orrery a model of the solar system

orris/ lace or embroidery, an iris plant; **-powder** (hyphen), **— root** (two words)

Or San Michele a church at Florence, *not* Saint

Ortega y Gasset, José (1883–1955) Spanish philosopher

ortho- (chem. prefix) *use* **o-**

orthoepy the scientific study of the correct pronunciation of words

ortho/paedic concerned with the cure of bone deformities; **-paedics, -paedist**; *not* -ped- (US)

ortolan a small edible bird (not ital.)

Orvieto an Italian white wine

Orwell/, George pseud. of **Eric Arthur Blair** (1903–50) English novelist and essayist, **-ian**

OS Old Saxon, Old School, Old Series, Old Side, Old Style (before 1752), old style (type), ordinary seaman, Ordnance Survey, (clothing) outsize

os Old Series (small caps.)

Os osmium (no point)

o.s. only son

o/s out of stock, outstanding

os (Lat.) a bone, pl. *ossa*

os (Lat.) a mouth, pl. *ora*

OSA Order of St Augustine

Osaka Japan, *not* Oz-

OSB Order of St Benedict

Osborn, Sherard (1822–75) British rear admiral and Arctic explorer

Osborne IoW

Osborne/ family name of Duke of Leeds; **—, John James** (1929–94) British playwright

Osbourne, (Samuel) Lloyd (1868–1947) US novelist and playwright (stepson of R. L. Stevenson)

Oscan (of or written in) the ancient language of Campania in Italy, related to Latin and surviving only in inscriptions

oscill/ate move between two points (cf. **vacillate**); **-ation, -ator, -atory, -ogram, -ograph, -oscope**

oscul/ate kiss, adhere closely; **-ant, -ation, -atory**

oscul/um (Lat.) a kiss, pl. **-a**; *osculum pacis* the kiss of peace

OSD Ordnance Survey Department, Order of St Dominic

Oset *use* **Ossett**

OSF Order of St Francis

O.Sl. Old Slavonic

Osler, Sir William (1849–1919) Canadian physician

Oslo capital of Norway, *formerly* Christiania

Osmanlı of the family of **Osman** (1259–1326) (*not* Othman) founder of the Ottoman Empire; *not* -lee, -lie, -ly (undotted 'i', not ital.)

osmium symbol **Os**

Osnabrück Germany, the Eng. form Osnaburg(h) is obsolete

o.s.p. *use* **ob.s.p.**

ossa (Lat. pl.) bones, *see* **os**

ossein bone cartilage, *not* -eine

Ossett W. Yorks.; *not* Oset, Osset

ossia (It. mus.) or

Ossie *use* **Aussie**

osso bucco (It. cook.) shin of veal stewed with vegetables (not ital.); in It. *ossobuco*, pl. *ossibuchi*

Ossory, Ferns, and Leighlin, Bishop of

o.s.t. (naut.) ordinary spring tides

Ostend Belgium; in Fr. and Ger. **Ostende**, in Fl. **Oostende**

ostensibl/e outwardly professed, **-y**

ostensive/ indicating by demonstration, **-ly**

osteomyelitis an inflammation of the marrow of the bone (one word)

osteria (It.) an inn

Österreich/ (Ger.) Austria, *not* Oe-; **-Ungarn** Ger. for Austria-Hungary (hyphen)

Ostiak *see* **Osty-**

ostinato/ (mus.) repeated melodic figure, pl. **-s**

ostler (hist.) a stableman at an inn; *see also* **hostler**

Ostmark (hist.) W. German name for the chief monetary unit of the former Democratic Republic of Germany, correctly the **Mark der DDR**, superseded in 1990 by the **Deutsche Mark**; *see also* **mark**

Ostpolitik the foreign policy of many Western European countries with reference to the former Communist bloc (not ital.)

ostrac/on a potsherd, used in ancient Greece for inscribing and voting; pl. **-a** (*not* -k- except in Gr. contexts); **-ize** exclude from favour; *not* -ise; **-ism**

Ostrogoth/ (hist.) a member of the E. branch of the Goths, who conquered Italy in the 5th–6th cc.; **-ic**

Ostrovsky, Aleksandr (**Nikolaevich**) (1823–86) Russian playwright

Ostyak/ former name for **Khanty**, **— Samoyed** former name for **Selkup**

O.Sw. Old Swedish

Oswaldtwistle Lancs., *not* -sle

Oświęcim Pol. for **Auschwitz**

OT occupational therapy, Old Testament

Otaheite *now* **Tahiti**

OTC *now* **STC**

O tempora! O mores! (Lat.) what times, what manners!

O.Teut. Old Teutonic

other-world/ly, -liness (hyphen, one word in US)

Othman *use* **Os-**

otium/ (Lat.) leisure, **— cum dignitate** leisure with dignity, **— sine dignitate** leisure without dignity

otolith any of the small particles of calcium carbonate in the inner ear, *not* -lite (not ital.)

otorhinolaryngology the study of the ears, nose, and larynx

o.t.t. over the top

ottar (of roses) *use* **attar**

ottava rima (It.) a stanza of eight lines of ten or eleven syllables, rhyming *ababbabcc*, as in Byron's *Don Juan*

Ottawa Canada, *not* Otto-

otto (of roses) *use* **attar**

Ottoman/ (adj.) (hist.) of or concerning the dynasty of Osman I, the branch of the Turks to which he belonged, or the empire ruled by his descendants; (noun) an Ottoman person; a Turk; pl. **-s** (cap.); **— Turkish** Old or Middle Turkish, written in the Arabic alphabet

ottoman/ an upholstered sofa, a fabric; pl. **-s** (not cap.)

Otway, Thomas (1652–85) English playwright

OU Open University, Oxford University

ou (ornith.) a Hawaiian honeycreeper; cf. **o-o**

Ouagadougou Burkina Faso, *not* Wagadugu

oubliette a secret dungeon (not ital.)

Oudenarde Belgium; battle, 1708; in Modern Fr. **Audenarde**, in Fl. **Oudenaarde**

Oudh India, *not* Oude

OUDS Oxford University Dramatic Society

Ouessant, l'île d' an island off Brittany; in Eng. **Ushant**, in Breton **Enez Eusa**

Oughtred, William (1575–1660) English mathematician

Ouida *see* **de la Ramée**

ouï-dire (Fr. m. sing./pl.) hearsay

Ouija (propr.) a board used in spiritualistic seances (cap.)

oukaz *use* **ukase**

Ouless, Walter William (1848–1933) British painter

oulong *use* oo-

ounce/, -s (not in scientific use), abbr. **oz**

OUP Oxford University Press

ourang-outang *use* **orang-utan**

Our/ Father, — Lady, — Lord (caps.)

ours (no apos.)

Our Saviour (cap.)

ousel *use* ouz-

out (typ.) an accidental omission of copy in composition

out- prefixed to a verb nearly always forms a single word unless the verb begins with *t*, as *out-talk*, *out-turn*.

out-and-out unreserved(ly) (hyphens)

out/back (noun), **-board, -building** (one word)

outcast (person) cast out (the general word)

outcaste (Anglo-Ind.) (a person) with no caste

out/dated, -door (adj.), **-doors** (noun and adv.) (one word)

Outeniqua Mountains S. Africa

outer (typ.) the side of a sheet containing the signature and first page

Outer House (Sc. law) the hall where judges of the Court of Session sit singly

outfield (sport) (one word)

outfit/, -ted, -ter, -ting

outgeneral/ outdo in generalship; **-led, -ling** (one *l* in US)

outgo/ expenditure, pl. **-es**

outgrowth (one word)

out-Herod Herod (hyphen, two caps.)

outhouse a building, esp. a shed, lean-to, barn, etc. built next to or in the grounds of a house; (US) an outdoor lavatory (one word)

outl/ie, -ier, -ying

outmanoeuvre (one word, no lig.) *not* -neu- (US)

outmoded (one word)

out/ of date, — of doors (hyphens when attrib.); **— of sorts** unwell

outpatient (one word)

output/ (verb), **-ting**, past and past part. **output**

outrance, à (Fr.) to the bitter end, all-out; *not* à l'outrance

outr/é (Fr.) f. **-ée** eccentric

outrider (one word)

outrival/led, -ling (one *l* in US)

out/rush, -size (one word)

outspan (S. Afr.) unyoke, a place for doing this

out/standing, -station (one word)

outstrip/, -ped, -ping

out-swinger (sport) (hyphen)

out/-take, -talk, -think, -thrust, -top, -trade, -tray, -turn (hyphens, one word in US)

outv/ie, -ier, -ying (one word)

outward bound (hyphen when attrib.)

Outward Bound Trust (no hyphen)

outwit/, -ted, -ting

outwork (one word)

ouvert/ (Fr.) f. **-e** open

ouvri/er (Fr.) a workman, f. **-ère**

ouzel/ a type of thrush (**ring —**), a type of diving bird (**water —**); (arch.) a blackbird; *not* ous-

ouzo/ a Greek aniseed-flavoured spirit, pl. **-s**

oven/proof (one word)

oven-ready (hyphen)

ovenware (one word)

over/-abundant (hyphen, one word in US)

over/act, -active (one word)

overage an excess or surplus

over age above an age limit (two words, hyphen when attrib.)

overall (noun, adv., and adj., one word)

overambitious (one word)

over-anxious (hyphen, one word in US)

over/balance, -blown, -board, -book -burden, -burdensome, -careful (one word)

overcast (meteor.) abbr. **o.**

over/confidence, -confident, -critical (one word)

overcrowd/, -ed (one word)

over-curious (hyphen, one word in US)

Over Darwen Lancs., *use* **Darwen**

over-delicate (hyphen, one word in US)

overdevelop/, -ed, -ing (one word)

overemphas/is, -ize *not* -ise (one word)

overexcite (one word)

over-exercise (hyphen, one word in US)

over/exert, -familiar (one word)

overfulfil *not* -fill (US)

over/generalize, -generous (one word)

Overijssel a province of the Netherlands

over/joyed -land (one word)

over-large (hyphen, one word in US)

over/long, -look (one word)

over-many (hyphen)

overnice (one word)

overnight/, -er (one word)

over/-optimistic, -particular (hyphens)

over/pass, -populate, -produce, -rate, -reach, -react, -ride, -ripe, -rule (one word)

overrun (typ.) carry over words from one line or page to the next (one word)

overseas (one word)

oversensitive/, -ness (one word)

overset (typ.) set up (type) in excess of the available space

over/sexed, -sight, -simplify, -slaugh, -solicitous, -subscribe, -subtle, -use, -value, -view, -weight, -winter, -work (one word)

Ovid (in Lat., **Publius Ovidius Naso**) (43 BC–AD 17) Roman poet

ovol/o (archit.) a moulding, pl. **-i**

ov/um an egg, pl. **-a** (not ital.)

Owens College Manchester (no apos.)

owner abbr. **O.**

Ox. Oxford

Oxbridge Oxford and Cambridge Universities regarded collectively

Oxenstjerna, Count Axel (1583–1654) Swedish statesman

ox-eye/, — daisy (hyphen)

Oxf. Oxford

Oxfam Oxford Committee for Famine Relief

Oxford abbr. **Ox.**, **Oxf.**

Oxford Almanack not -ac

Oxford blue a dark blue, sometimes with a purple tinge; cf. **Blue**

Oxford comma a serial comma

Oxford corners (hist.) ruled border lines crossing and extending slightly beyond each other at the corners

Oxford Down a breed of sheep produced by crossing Cotswold and Hampshire Down sheep (two caps.)

Oxford English Dictionary, The abbr. **OED**, *not NED*

Oxford grey (US hist. sl.) a black jazz musician

Oxford Group a religious movement founded at Oxford in 1921 (two caps.), later named Moral Re-Armament

Oxford hollow (bind.) (a binding with) a flattened paper tube attached to the back of the gatherings and to the spine of the binding

Oxford Movement an Anglican High Church movement started in Oxford in 1833 (two caps.)

Oxfordshire abbr. **Oxon.**

Oxford University/ abbr. **OU**; — — **Press** only the full name is never preceded by the definite article: *not* 'the Oxford University Press' *but* 'the University Press', 'the Press', 'the OUP'; abbr. **OUP**

oxhide (one word)

oxide *not* -id, -yd, -yde

oxidation *prefer to* oxidization; *not* oxy-

oxidize etc.; *not* -ise, oxy-

Oxon. Oxfordshire; (Lat.) *Oxonia, Oxonium* (Oxford), *Oxoniensis* (of Oxford)

Oxon: the signature of the Bishop of Oxford (colon)

Oxonium (Lat.) Oxford

ox/tail, -tongue (one word)

oxychloride *not* oxi-

oxyd/e, -ation, -ize *use* oxi-

oxygen/ symbol **O**, **-ize** *not* -ise

Oxyrhynchus Egypt, a source of papyri

oxytone (Gr. gram.) (a word) with an acute accent on the last syllable

oyez! hear ye! *not* oyes

oz ounce, -s (no point, not in scientific use)

Ozaka Japan, *use* **Os-**

Ozalid/ (propr.) (print.) a photographic reproduction process for generating proofs on paper from film; **combined —** a proof made simultaneously from more than one Ozalid; in the USA proofs prepared by a similar process are called **blues**, from their colour

ozone-friendly (hyphen)

ozone/ hole, — layer (two words)

Ozu, Yasujiro (1903–63) Japanese film director

'Ozymandias' a sonnet by Shelley, 1818

Ozzie *use* **Aussie**

Pp

P (car) park, (chess) pawn, (as prefix) peta-, phosphorus, (phys.) poise, the fifteenth in a series

₱ Philippine peso

P. pastor, post, president, prince, (Fr.) *Père* (Father); (Lat.) *Papa* (Pope), *Pater* (Father), pontifex (a bishop), *populus* (people)

p penny, pennies, pence; (as prefix) pico-

p. page, participle, (meteor.) passing showers, passive, past, per; (Fr.) *passé* (past), *pied* (foot), *pouce* (inch), *pour* (for); (Lat.) *partim* (in part), *per* (through), *pius* (holy), *pondere* (by weight), *post* (after), *primus* (first), *pro* (for)

p- (chem. prefix) *para-* (ital., always hyphenated), *prefer to para-*

p (mech.) pressure, (mus.) piano (softly)

¶ (typ.) paragraph symbol, pilcrow

PA Pennsylvania (postal abbr.), personal assistant, Press Association, public address, Publishers Association

Pa (phys.) pascal, (chem.) protactinium (no point)

Pa. Pennsylvania (off. abbr.)

p.a. per annum (yearly)

Paarl Cape Province, S. Africa

pabulum (not ital.)

PABX private automatic branch exchange

pace/ (Lat.) with due respect to (one holding a different view), — *tua* by your leave

pacha *use* **pasha**

pachinko a Japanese form of pinball

pachisi a four-handed Indian board game with six cowries used like dice, in Hind. *pachīsī*; adopted in the West as **parcheesi** *or* **parchesi** (not cap.), in Sp. **parchís**; a simplified form is known in Europe as **ludo**

pachyderm any thick-skinned mammal, esp. an elephant or rhinoceros

pachymeter an instrument for measuring small thicknesses, *not* pacho-; cf. **micrometer**

pacifier (US) a baby's dummy

package/, -s abbr. **pkg.**; — **holiday**, — **tour** (two words)

pack/ animal, — drill (two words)

packet/, -ed, -ing

packhorse (one word)

packing/ box, — case (two words)

packing/-needle, -sheet (hyphens)

pack rat (two words)

pack/saddle, -thread (one word)

pad/, -ded, -ding

paddle/ boat, — steamer, — wheel (two words)

Paderewski, Ignacy Jan (1860–1941) pianist, first Premier of the Polish Republic 1919

Padishah a title applied to the Shah of Iran, the Sultan of Turkey, the Great Mogul, and the (British) Emperor of India; in Pers. *pādshāh*

padlock (one word)

padre (colloq.) a chaplain

padre (It., Port., Sp.) father, applied also to a priest

padron/e (It.) master, employer; pl. *-i*

Padua in It. **Padova**

paduasoy a strong corded silk fabric, *not* the many variants

p.ae. *partes aequales* (equal parts)

paean a song of triumph, *not* pean; cf. **paeon**, **peon**

paedagogy *use* **ped-**

paederast/, -y *use* **ped-**

paediatric/ (med.) relating to children (esp. their diseases); **-s** the science, usually treated as sing.; **-ian**; *not* ped- (US)

paedo/baptism, -phile, -philia (one word), *not* ped- (US)

paella a Spanish dish of rice, saffron, chicken, and seafood

paeon (Gr. and Lat. prosody) a foot of one long and three short syllables; cf. **paean**, **peon**

paeony *use* **pe-**

Paesiello, Giovanni (1740–1816) Italian composer of operas

Paganini, Niccolò (1782–1840) Italian violinist and composer

paganize *not* -ise

page (typ.) one side of a leaf; type, film, etc., made up for printing on this; abbr. **p.**, pl. **pp.**; (comput.) to present text on a VDU in static full-screen units (cf. **scroll**)

pageboy a boy serving as a page, a hairstyle (one word)

paginate to number pages

pagination (typ.) the numbering of the pages of a book, journal, etc.; may be in headline or at foot of page; generally omitted on opening pages of chapters, main sections, etc.

Pagliacci, I an opera by Leoncavallo, 1892

Pahang *see* **Malaya, Federation of**

Pahlanpur *use* **Pal-**

Pahlavi (of) the language and writing system of Persia under the Sassanians; *not* Pehlevi

paid abbr. **pd.**

pai-hua a modern form of written Chinese based on colloquial speech

paillasse (Fr. f.) a straw mattress, in Eng. **palliasse**

pailles/ (Fr. cook. f.) straws, — *de parmesan* cheese straws

Pain, Barry (**Eric Odell**) (1864–1928) English humorous writer; *see also* **Paine**; **Payn**; **Payne**

pain (Fr. m.) bread

Paine, Thomas (1737–1809) English-born political philosopher and American patriot, author of *The Rights of Man; see also* **Pain**; **Payn**; **Payne**

painim *use* **pay-**

painkill/er, -ing (one word)

paint. painting

paint/box, -brush (one word)

paintings, titles of when cited, to be in italic if named by the painter, roman quoted if popularly identified as such by others

paintwork (one word)

pair/, -s abbr. **pr.**

pais/a a coin of India, Pakistan, Nepal, and Bangladesh; pl. **-e**

paisano/ (in Sp.-speaking areas) a fellow-countryman, a peasant (not cap.); (Mex. and SW US) a name of the roadrunner or chaparral cock; (Mex.) a nickname for a Spaniard (cap.); pl. **-s**

Paisley (a soft woollen garment or fabric having) a distinctive detailed pattern of curved feather-shaped figures (cap. except in US)

Paiute (of or relating to) (a member of) a Native American people, originally inhabiting the south-west, or their language

pajamas (US) = **pyjamas**

Pak. Pakistan, -i

pakeha (Maori) a white man

Pakistan/ adj. **-i**; abbr. **Pak.**; *see also* **Bangladesh**

Pakhto *see* **Pashto**

Pal. Palestine

palace cap. only as part of a name (e.g. Blenheim Palace, Pardo Palace), or as an abbreviated reference to Buckingham Palace

Palaearctic (zool.) of the northern Old World, *not* Palaeoarctic

palaeo- a prefix meaning ancient, *not* -eo- (US)

Palaeocene (geol.) (of or relating to) the earliest epoch of the Tertiary period; *not* Paleocene (US)

palaeography the study of ancient writing, abbr. **palaeog.**

palaeolithic (archaeol.) *not* paleo- (US)

palaeology the study of antiquities, *not* paleo- (US)

palaeontology the study of fossils, abbr. **palaeont.**; *not* paleo- (US)

Palaeozoic (geol.) (of or relating to) an era of geological time marked by the appearance of marine and terrestrial plants and animals, esp. invertebrates; *not* Paleo- (US)

palaestra a Greek or Roman wrestling school, *not* pale-

palais (Fr. m.) palace; dance hall (not ital.)

Palanpur Rajasthan, India; *not* Pahl-

palatable *not* -eable

palate the roof of the mouth, sense of taste; cf. **palette**, **pallet**

palatinate the territory under the jurisdiction of a Count Palatine

palatine/ (hist.) (of an official or feudal lord) having local authority that elsewhere belongs only to a sovereign (Count Palatine); (of a territory) subject to this authority (cap., but often lower case in hist. contexts); (med.) of or connected with the palate, **— bone** each of two bones forming the hard palate

palazz/o (It.) palace, a grand house of a great man or family; pl. **-i**

pal/e, -ish

paleo- *use* **palaeo-** (except in US)

Palestin/e abbr. **Pal.**; **-ian**

palestra *use* **palae-**

paletot an overcoat (no accent, not ital.)

palette/ an artist's thin portable board for colour-mixing, **— knife** (two words); cf. **palate**; **pallet**

Palgrave, Francis Turner (1824–97) English anthologist

Pali an Indic language used in the canonical books of Buddhists

palimony (esp. US colloq.) an allowance made by one member of an unmarried couple to the other after separation

palimpsest a piece of writing material or manuscript on which the original writing has been effaced to make room for other writing; a monumental brass turned and re-engraved on the reverse side

palindrom/e a word or phrase that reads the same backwards as forwards, ignoring punctuation and spacing; **-ic**

Palladian characterized by wisdom or learning, after **Pallas**, epithet of the Greek goddess Athene; also a Renaissance modification of the classic Roman style of architecture, from **Andrea Palladio** (1518–80) Italian architect

palladium a safeguard or source of protection; an image of Pallas Athene; a metallic element, symbol **Pd**

pallet a mattress, projection on a machine or clock, valve in an organ, platform for carrying loads; cf. **palate**; **palette**

palliasse a straw mattress, in Fr. f. *paillasse*

palliat/e alleviate, minimize; (adj. and noun) **-ive**

palli/um an ecclesiastical pall; (hist.) a man's large rectangular cloak; (med.) the cerebral cortex; (zool.) the mantle of a mollusc or brachiopod; pl. **-ums, -a**

Pall Mall a London street (two words)

pall-mall (hist.) a game

pallor paleness, *not* -our

Pallottine Fathers a RC society of priests

Palmers Green London (no apos.)

palmetto/ a small palm tree, pl. **-s**

palm/ honey, — oil (two words)

Palm Sunday one before Easter (two words, caps.)

Palomar, Mount (observatory, telescope) Calif.

palp/us an insect's feeler, pl. **-i**

palsgrav/e a Count Palatinate, f. **-ine**

palstave (archaeol.) a type of bronze etc. chisel

paly (her.) divided into equal vertical shapes

pam. pamphlet

Pamir a tableland in Cent. Asia, *not* -irs

pampas grass (two words)

Pan. Panama

panacea a cure-all (not ital.)

pan-African (hyphen)

panakin *use* **panni-**

pan/-American (*but* **Pan American Union**), **-Anglican** (hyphens)

Panama/ Cent. America, abbr. **Pan.**; **-nian**; a hat of strawlike material (not cap.)

panatella a long thin cigar (not ital.)

panchayat a village council in India

Panchen/ a Tibetan Buddhist title of respect (cap.); **— Lama** the lama of the Tashi Lhunpo monastery, ranking next after the Dalai Lama; **— Rinpoche** a religious teacher held in high regard by Tibetan Buddhists

Pandaemonium the abode of all the demons in Milton's *Paradise Lost* (cap.); cf. **pande-**

Pandean pipes *not* -aean (cap.)

pandect a treatise covering the whole of a subject; the digest of Roman law made under the Emperor Justinian in the 6th c. (pl., cap.)

pandemonium (a scene of) uproar, utter confusion (not cap.); cf. **Pandae-**

Pandit, Mrs Vijaya Lakshmi (1900–90) Indian diplomat

pandit *use* **pun-**, *but* **Pandit** (cap.) as Indian title

P&O Peninsular and Oriental Steamship Company (no points)

p. & p. postage and packing

panegyr/ic a formal speech or essay of praise; **-ical, -ist, -ize** *not* -ise

panel/, -led, -ling, -list (one *l* in US)

panem et circenses (Lat.) bread and circus games

paner (Fr. cook.) dress with egg and breadcrumbs

pan-Hellen/ic, -ism (hyphen) *not* Panhellenic (except in US or in an institutional name)

panic/, -ked, -ky

panikin *use* **panni-**

pan-Islam/, -ic (hyphen)

Panizzi, Sir Antonio (1797–1879) Italian-born English librarian

Panjabi the language of Punjab (*pañjābī*)

panjandrum a mock title

pannikin a small metal drinking cup; *not* pana-, pani-, -can

panopl/y pl. **-ies; -ied**

pan pipe *not* Pan's (two words)

pan-Slav/ic, -ism *not* pan-Scl-

pantagraph *use* **panto-**

Pantaloon a character in Italian comedy

panta rhei (Gr.) all things are in a state of flux

pantheon the deities of a people collectively; a temple to all gods, (cap.) circular one in Rome

Panthéon Paris

panther a leopard, esp. with black fur; (US var.) a puma

panto/ (colloq.) pantomime, pl. **-s**

pantograph an instrument for copying to scale; a framework for transmitting overhead current to electric vehicle; *not* panta-, penta-

pants (US) = **trousers**

pantyhose (US) = women's tights (one word)

panzer/ armoured (not ital.), in Ger. m. *Panzer*; **— division** (two words)

Pão de Açúcar (Port.) Sugarloaf Mountain, Rio de Janeiro, Brazil

Papa (Lat.) Pope, abbr. **P.**

papabile (It.) suitable to be pope, more generally, for high office

papain an enzyme obtained from unripe papayas

papal/, -ly

Papal States, the (hist.) (caps.)

Papandreou,/ Andreas Georgios (1919–96) Greek Prime Minister 1981–9, 1993–6; **— Georgios** (1888–1968) his father, Greek statesman

paparazz/o a freelance photographer who pursues celebrities, pl. **-i** (not ital.)

papaw *use* **pawpaw** (except in US); *see also* **papaya**

papaya tropical Amer. evergreen tree and its fruit; also called **pawpaw**

papel (Sp. m.) paper; (as of an actor) role, part

paperback a softcover book (one word)

paper/ boy, — clip, — girl (two words, one word in US)

paper tiger (two words)

paper/weight, -work (one word)

papet/*ier* (Fr.) f. -*ière* a stationer

Papier (Ger. n.) paper (cap.)

papier (Fr. m.) paper (not cap.)

papier mâché moulded paper pulp (two words, not ital.)

papill/**a** a small protuberance on a living surface, pl. -**ae**; -**ary**, -**ate**, -**ose**

papillon (Fr. m.) butterfly; (not ital.) a breed of dog

papoose a Native American infant, *not* papp-

Pap/ **smear, — test** (US) test to detect cancer of the cervix or womb (cap.), from **Dr George Papanicolaou** (1883–1962) US scientist

Papst (Ger. m.) Pope (cap.)

Papua New Guinea/, -**n**; abbr. **PNG**

papyr/**us** an ancient writing material or a MS written on it, pl. -**i**; -**ology** the study of papyri; -**ologist**

par equality (of exchange etc.) (no point); cf. **parr**

par. paragraph, parallel, parish

par (Fr.) by, out of, in, through

Pará Brazil, *now* **Belém**

Para. Paraguay

para. paragraph, pl. **paras.**

para- (chem. prefix) (ital.)

paracetamol a drug used to reduce pain and relieve fever (not cap.)

Paraclete the Holy Spirit as advocate or counsellor (John 14: 16, 26, etc.) (cap.)

paradiddle a fast drum beat with syncopated alternate strokes, *not* tara-

paradisaical *not* -iacal

paraffin/ *not* -fine; an inflammable waxy or oily substance distilled from petroleum or shale; — **oil** its liquid form = (US) **kerosene**; — **wax** = (US) **paraffin**

paragraph/ a distinct section of type-matter on a page; abbr. **par.**, **para.**; pl. **pars.**, **paras.**; symbol ¶ (pilcrow); — **sign** symbol ¶ used in manuscripts to mark the beginning of a new section or part of a narrative or discourse until replaced by indenting; *now* used to flag marginal notes or to introduce an editorial *obiter dictum* or protest

Paraguay/ S. America, -**an**; abbr. **Para.**

parakeet *not* -quet, -oquet, -okeet, parr-

parakŷïsma see **sampi**

paralanguage elements or factors in communication that are ancillary to language proper, e.g. intonation and gesture

paralipomena things omitted from a work and added as a supplement, esp. the OT books of Chronicles; *not* -leip-

paralips/**is** drawing attention to a subject by affecting not to mention it, pl. -**es**; *not* -leipsis (except in specifically Hellenist contexts), -lepsis, -lepsy

parallel/ abbr. **par.**; -**ed**, -**ing**

parallelepiped a solid figure bounded by six parallelograms; *not* -ipiped, -opiped

parallel mark (‖) (typ.)

paralogize reason falsely, *not* -ise

paralyse *not* -ise, -ize, -yze (US)

Paramatta *use* **Parra-**

parameci/**um** (zool.) *not* -aecium, -oecium; pl. -**a**

parameter (math.) a variable factor constant in a particular case; avoid using in general senses

paranoi/**a** a mental disorder esp. characterized by delusions of persecution and self-importance, *not* -noea; -**ac**, -**d**

paraph the flourish at the end of a signature

paraphernalia (pl.) miscellaneous belongings, items of equipment, etc.

paraquat a quick-acting herbicide

paraquet *use* -**keet**

parasitize *not* -ise

parata/**xis** (gram.) the juxtaposition of clauses etc. one after another, without words to indicate coordination or subordination; cf. **hypotaxis**; -**ctic**

paratroops airborne parachute troops

par avion (Fr.) by airmail

parbleu! (Fr. colloq.) an exclamation of surprise

parcel/, -**led**, -**ling** (one l in US)

parcel post (two words)

parcen/**ary** (law) a joint heirship, -**er** joint heir

parcheesi, parchesi *see* **pachisi**

parchment/ an animal skin prepared for writing, -**paper** imitation parchment (hyphen)

parcimony etc., *use* **parsi-**

Pardo Palace a royal palace outside Madrid; cf. **Prado**

parenthes/**is** the upright curves ( ); pl. -**es**, abbr. **parens.**

parenthesize insert as a parenthesis, *not* -ise

parerg/**on** a subsidiary work, pl. -**a** (not ital.)

par excellence pre-eminently (not ital.)

par exemple (Fr.) for example, abbr. **p. ex.**

pargana in India, a parish or subdivision of a district, *not* pergunnah

parget/**ed**, -**er**, -**ing** (*not* -tt-)

par hasard (Fr.) by chance, *not* haz-

parheli/**on** a bright spot on the solar halo, *also called* **mock sun**, **sun dog**; pl. -**a**

pariah (Ind.) one of low or no caste, a social outcast

parietal (anat.) of the wall of the body or any of its cavities, (bot.) of the wall of a hollow structure etc., (US) relating to residence within a college

pari-mutuel a totalizator (not ital.)

pari passu (Lat.) at the same rate

Paris, Matthew (d. 1259) English monk and historian, *not* 'of Paris'

parish/ abbr. **par.**, — **priest** abbr. **PP**

Parisian of Paris (cap.), **Parisienne** (Fr. f.) a woman of Paris (cap.)

park abbr. **P, pk.**

Park, Mungo (1771–1806) Scottish traveller in Africa

parka a waterproof hooded jacket, originally worn by the Inuit

parking lot (US) = car park

parking/ **meter,** — **ticket** (two words)

Parkinson's/ **disease** a chronic nervous palsy, studied by **James Parkinson** (1755–1824); — **law** the law, facetiously expounded by **Cyril Northcote Parkinson** (1909–93), that work expands to fill the time available for it

parkway (US) an open landscaped highway, (UK) a railway station with extensive parking facilities

parlay/ (US) use money won on a bet as a further stake, exploit a position or circumstance successfully, an act of this, pl. **-s**; **-ed, -ing**

parley/ (hold) a conference to settle a dispute, pl. **-s**; **-ed, -ing**

Parliament/ (UK) the highest legislature, consisting of the Sovereign, the House of Lords, and the House of Commons (cap.), abbr. **Parl.** (not cap. as a general term); — **House** the Scottish Law Courts in Edinburgh

parlour *not* -or (US)

Parmesan a hard cheese made at Parma and elsewhere (cap.), in It. **parmigiano**

Parnass/**us, Mount** Greece, sacred to the Muses; now **Líakoura**; **-ian** poetic, (of or relating to) (a member of) a group of French poets in the late 19th c., emphasizing strictness of form, named from the anthology *Le Parnasse contemporain*, 1866

parochialize *not* -ise

parokeet *use* **para-**

parol (law) oral, not written; *not* -le

parol/**e** release a prisoner before the expiry of sentence; as verb, present part. **-ing**; **-ee** one paroled

paronomasia wordplay

paronym a word cognate with another, a word formed from a foreign word

paroquet *use* **parakeet**

paroxysm a fit of pain, passion, laughter

paroxytone (Gr. gram.) (a word) with acute accent on penultimate syllable

parquet/ wooden flooring, (US) the stalls of a theatre; as verb, past and past part. **-ed**; **-ry**; in Fr. f. **parqueterie**

Parr,/ **Catherine** (1512–48) last wife of Henry VIII; — **Thomas, 'Old'** (?1483–1635) English centenarian

parr a young salmon, *not* par

parrakeet *use* **para-**

Parramatta New South Wales, Australia; *not* -mata, Para-

parramatta a light dress fabric (not cap.)

Parratt, Sir Walter (1841–1924) English organist

parricid/**e** a murder(er) of a near relative or of a revered person, **-al**; *see also* **patri-**

parroquet *use* **parakeet**

pars. paragraphs

parse describe (a word in context) grammatically, stating its inflection, relation to the sentence, etc.; resolve (a sentence) into its component parts and describe them grammatically; (comput.) perform a syntax analysis on a string of input symbols

parsec (astr.) a unit of stellar distance, equal to about 3.25 light years (3.08×10^{16} metres); abbr. **pc**; although not an SI unit, it may be used with SI units and prefixes, e.g. *megaparsec*, abbr. **Mpc**

Parsee/ a descendant of the Zoroastrians who fled from Persia to India in the 7th–8th cc., in Pers. *pārsī*; pl. **-s**

Parsifal an opera by Wagner, 1879

parsimon/**y** meanness, **-ious**; *not* parci-

parsnip (bot.) *not* -ep

part abbr. **pt.**

part. participle

partable (law) *use* **-ible**

parterre a flower bed or garden (not ital.); (US) an area in a theatre between the orchestra and audience

partes aequales (Lat.) equal parts, abbr. **p. ae.**

part-exchange (verb, hyphen), **part exchange** (noun, two words)

Parthenon the temple of Athene on the Acropolis at Athens

Parthian shot etc., a glance or remark made when turning away (one cap.)

parti (Fr. m.) party (faction), match (marriage), resolution (good *or* bad); **Parti québécois** Canadian political party (one cap., not ital)

partible (law) that must be divided, *not* -able

participator *not* -er

participle a verbal adjective, abbr. **p., part.**

particoloured variegated, *not* party- (one word)

particularize *not* -ise

partie/ (Fr. f.) part, — **carrée** a party of two men and two women

partim (Lat.) in part, abbr. **p.**

parti pris (Fr. m.) a preconceived view, a bias

partisan an adherent of a party (frequently derog.), (mil.) a member of a resistance movement; *not* -zan

partita/ (mus.) a suite, an air with variations; pl. **-s**

partout (Fr.) everywhere

part-owner (hyphen)

part-song (hyphen)

part time (hyphen when attrib.)

party (Conservative, Labour, Liberal, Communist, etc.) not cap. unless integral to the official title, as in 'Social Democratic and Labour Party'

party-coloured *use* partic-

party/ **line, — wall** (two words)

parvenu/ f. **-e** an upstart; pl. **-s**, **-es** (not ital.)

Pasadena Calif.

pascal (phys.) the SI unit of pressure and stress, equal to one newton per square metre (not cap.); abbr. **Pa**; (comput.) a programming language (cap. or all caps.); both named after **Blaise Pascal** (1623–62) French mathematician, physicist, and religious philosopher

paschal of or relating to the Jewish Passover, or to Easter

Pas-de-Calais a dép. of France (hyphens), **Pas de Calais** (Fr. m.) Strait of Dover (three words)

pas de/ **chat** a special leap in ballet, — — **deux** dance for two, — — **quatre** dance for four, — — **trois** dance for three (not ital.); *see also* **pas seul**

pasha/ (Turk.) a title placed *after* the name, *not* -cha; in Turk. *paşa*, in Fr. m. *pacha*; **-lic** a pasha's province, in Turk. *paşalık*

Pasha, Enver *see* **Enver Pasha**

Pashto the Iranian language of the Pathans, spoken in Pakistan and Afghanistan and sometimes called Afghan *or* **Pakhto** (to reflect northern pronunciation); *not* -u, Push-

Pašić, Nikola (1845–1926) Serbian statesman, Prime Minister of Serbia five times between 1891 and 1918, and of the Kingdom of Serbs, Croats, and Slovenes 1921–4, 1924–6

paso doble a ballroom dance in march style (not ital.)

pasquinade a lampoon or satire, originally one displayed in a public place

pass. passive

passable barely satisfactory, just adequate, or (of a road, pass, etc.) that can be passed; cf. **passible**

passacaglia (mus.) an instrumental piece based on an old dance

passant (her.) (of an animal) walking and looking to the dexter side, with three paws on the ground and the right forepaw raised

pass/**band, -book** (one word)

Passchendaele Belgium; battle, 1917

passé past, faded; abbr. **p.**; in Fr. *pass*/**é**, f. **-ée**

passed master *use* past

passementerie (Fr. f.) embroidery, *not* passi-

passepartout a master key, a picture frame consisting of glass held to a backing by adhesive tape along the edges (not ital.; hyphen in US); the valet in Verne's *Around the World in Eighty Days* (cap.)

passer-by pl. **passers-by** (hyphen, one word in US)

pas seul a dance for one person; *see also* **pas de**

Passfield *see* **Webb**

passible (theol.) capable of feeling or suffering; cf. **passable**

passim (Lat.) here and there throughout

Passion Week follows Passion Sunday (fifth in Lent)

passive abbr. **p.**, **pass.**

pass/ **key, — mark** (two words)

pass/**port, -word** (one word)

past abbr. **p.**

pastel/ an artist's crayon, **-list**; cf. **pastille**

Pasternak, Boris (**Leonidovich**) (1890–1960) Russian novelist and poet

pasteurize sterilize, *not* -ise

pastiche a medley, esp. a work of art, made up from or imitating various sources; in It. *pasticcio*

pastille a confection, odorizer; *not* -il; cf. **pastel**

pastis an aniseed-flavoured aperitif (not cap.)

past master a former master in a guild, an expert; *not* passed

pastorale/ (mus.) a pastoral composition, pl. **-s**

past participle abbr. **past part.**

pat. patent, -ed

Pata. Patagonia

patchouli (a perfume from) a strongly scented E. Indian plant, *not* -ly

patchwork (one word)

pate (arch., colloq.) the head, esp. representing the seat of intellect

pâte the paste of which porcelain is made (not ital.)

pâté/ spread or paste of meat, fish, etc. (not ital.); **— de foie gras** a spiced paste of fatted goose liver

patell/a (anat.) kneecap, pl. **-ae**; adj. **-ar**

paten the dish used at Eucharist, a circular metal plate; *not* -in, -ine

Patent Office abbr. **Pat. Off.**

Pater (Lat.) Father, abbr. **P.**

paterfamilias the father of a family, pl. **patresfamilias**

paternoster the Lord's Prayer (esp. in Lat.), a bead in a rosary, a lift consisting of a series of doorless moving compartments

pater patriae (Lat.) father of his country

Paterson NJ

Paterson, William (1658–1719) British founder of the Bank of England

path. patholog/y, -ical

Pathan a member of a Pashto-speaking people inhabiting NW Pakistan and SE Afghanistan

Pathétique name of a sonata by Beethoven (in full *Grande sonate pathétique*) and symphony by Tchaikovsky (a subtitle authorized by him)

pathos a quality in speech, writing, events, etc. that excites pity or sadness; cf. **bathos**

Patiala E. Punjab, India

patin/, -e *use* **paten**

patio/ an inner court, paved area of garden; pl. **-s**

pâtisserie pastry (not ital.); *pâtiss/ier*, f. *-ière* (Fr.) pastry cook (ital.)

Patna a long-grain rice (cap.)

patois a (regional) dialect of the common people, differing from the literary language; pl. same (not ital.)

Patres/ (Lat.) fathers, abbr. **PP**; **— Conscripti** Conscript Fathers, abbr. **PP C**

patria potestas (Rom. law) a father's power over his family

patricide a murder(er) of one's own father; *see also* **parricide**

patrol/, -led, -ling

patrolman (US) = **police constable**

patronize *not* -ise

patronymic a name derived from the name of a father or ancestor, as *Johnson, O'Brien, Ivanovich*

pattée (of a cross) having almost triangular arms becoming very broad at the ends so as to form a square

Pattenmakers Company *not* Pattern-

Pattison, Mark (1813–84) Rector of Lincoln College, Oxford

Patton, George S(mith) (1885–1945) US general

PAU Pan American Union

pauca verba (Lat.) few words

pauperize *not* -ise

Pausanias (*fl. c.* AD 150) Greek traveller, author of 'Description of Greece'; abbr. **Paus.**

pavane (hist.) a stately dance, *not* -an; in Fr. f. *pavane*

pavé (Fr. m.) pavement, jewellery setting with stones close together

pavilion *not* pavill-

pavior one who lays pavements; *not* -ver, -vier, -viour; **Paviors Company** (no apos.)

Pavlov/, Ivan (Petrovich) (1849–1936) Russian physiologist; **-ian** of or relating to his work, esp. on conditioned reflexes

pavlova a meringue cake with cream and fruit, named after **Anna Pavlova** (1885–1931) Russian ballet dancer

pawaw *use* **powwow**

pawn (chess) abbr. **P**

pawn/broker, -shop (one word)

pawpaw a N. Amer. deciduous tree and its edible fruit; *not* papaw (US); *see also* **papaya**

PAX private automatic (telephone) exchange

pax vobiscum (Lat.) peace be with you

paxwax the neck cartilages, *not* the many variants

payback (noun) (one word)

pay/ bed, — claim (two words)

pay day (two words, one word in US)

pay dirt (US) a financially promising situation, lit. ground worth working for ore

PAYE pay as you earn, a method of tax collection

payload (one word)

paymaster abbr. **paymr.**, **PM** (one word)

Paymaster-General (caps., hyphen) abbr. **PMG**

payment abbr. **pt.**

Payn, James (1830–98) English novelist and editor; *see also* **Pain**; **Paine**; **Payne**

Payne,/ Edward John (1844–1904) English historian; **— John Howard** (1791–1852) US playwright; *see also* **Pain**; **Paine**; **Payn**

paynim a pagan, *not* pai-

pay-off (noun, hyphen, one word in US)

pay packet (two words)

pay/phone, -roll (one word)

paysag/e (Fr. m.) a landscape (painting), *-iste* (Fr. m.) a landscape painter (ital.)

Pays-Bas (Fr. m. pl.) the Netherlands (caps., hyphen)

PB *Pharmacopoeia Britannica*, Plymouth Brethren, Prayer Book

Pb *plumbum* (lead) (no point)

PBI (mil. sl.) (poor bloody) infantry(man)

PBX private branch exchange

PC Panama Canal; Parish Council, -or; personal computer, Police Constable, politically correct, Privy Council, Privy Counsellor

pc (astr.) parsec

p.c. per cent, police constable, postcard

p/c petty cash, prices current

PCB (comput.) printed circuit board, (chem.) polychlorinated biphenyl

PCC Parochial Church Council

PCM pulse code modulation

PCS (Sc.) Principal Clerk of Session

pct. (US) per cent

PD *Pharmacopoeia Dublinensis*, (US) Police Department, Postal District (London), *privat-docent*

Pd palladium (no point)

pd. paid

p.d. per diem, (elec.) potential difference

p.d.q. pretty damn quick

PDSA People's Dispensary for Sick Animals

PDT (US) Pacific Daylight Time

PE *Pharmacopoeia Edinburgensis*, physical education, Port Elizabeth (Cape Province), potential energy, Protestant Episcopal

p.e. personal estate

p/e price/earnings ratio

PEA Physical Education Association of Great Britain and Northern Ireland

peaceable *not* -cable

peace/keeper, -maker (one word)

peace-offering (hyphen)

peace pipe (two words)

peacetime (one word)

pea-chick a young peafowl (hyphen)

peach Melba ice cream and peaches with liqueur, *not* pêche

pea/cock, -fowl (one word)

pea green (two words, hyphen when attrib.)

peahen (one word)

pea jacket a sailor's short overcoat (two words)

pean (her.) fur represented as sable spotted with or; a song of praise or triumph, *use* **paean**

pearl (knitting) *use* **purl**

Pearl Harbor a US naval base, Hawaii; *not* — Harbour

Pears, Sir Peter (1910–86) English tenor

Peary, Robert Edwin (1856–1920) US Arctic explorer, first at N. Pole 1909

pease pudding (two words)

peat/bog, -moss, -reek (one word)

peau-de-soie a smooth silky fabric (hyphens, not ital.)

pebbl/e, -y

peccadillo/ a trifling offence, pl. **-es**

peccary a S. American wild pig, *not* -i

peccavi a confession of guilt (not ital.)

pêche (Fr. f.) fish/ery, -ing; peach; **pêche Melba** in Eng. *use* **peach Melba**

péch/é (Fr. m.) sin, **-eur** (Fr.) sinner, f. **-eresse**

pêcheu/r (Fr.) fisherman, f. **-se**

peckish (colloq.) hungry, (US) irritable

peckoe, peco *use* **pekoe**

pecorino/ an Italian cheese made from ewes' milk, pl. **-s**

peculat/e embezzle, **-or**

Ped. (mus.) pedal

pedagog/ue (derog.) a pedantic teacher; **-y, -ics** the science of teaching; *not* pae-

pedal/, -led, -ling (one *l* in US)

peddler a person who sells drugs illegally; cf. **pedlar**

pederast/, -y *not* paed-

pedestal/, -led, -ling (one *l* in US)

pediatrics *use* **pae-** (except in US)

pedlar a travelling vendor of small wares, *not* peddler (US)

pedo/baptism, -philia *use* **paedo-**

Peeblesshire a former Scottish county, abbr. **Peebles.**

peekaboo (one word)

peel (hist.) a small square tower, *not* pele

Peele, George (?1558–1597) English playwright

peephole (one word)

peeping Tom a voyeur (one cap.)

peep show (two words)

peer/ f. **-ess** a member of one of the degrees of the nobility in Britain (i.e. (in descending order) a duke, marquess, earl, viscount, or baron), or a noble of any country; **— of the realm** (*or* **of the United Kingdom**) any of the class of peers whose adult members may all sit in the House of Lords; **life —** a person ennobled to the peerage, but whose title dies with him or her (unlike a **hereditary —**)

peer group (two words)

Peer Gynt a play by Ibsen, 1867; incidental music by Grieg, opera by Egk

peewit the lapwing, *not* pew-

Peggotty a family in Dickens's *David Copperfield*

Pehlevi *use* **Pahlavi**

PEI Prince Edward Island, Canada

peignoir a woman's loose dressing gown

peine forte et dure (Fr. f.) severe punishment, a medieval judicial torture

Peirce, Charles Sanders (1839–1914) US logician, founder of philosophical pragmatism

p.ej. (Sp.) *por ejemplo*, for example, e.g.

Pekinese a small dog, colloq. **peke**

Peking/ China; *not* Peip- (except during the Nationalist period), -kin; in Pinyin **Beijing**; **-ese** (an inhabitant) of Peking

pekoe a black tea; *not* peckoe, peco (not cap.)

Pelagian/ (of or concerning) (a follower of) the monk **Pelagius** (*c.*4th–5th cc.) or his theory denying the doctrine of original sin, **-ism**

pelagi/an inhabiting, or an inhabitant of, the open sea; **-c**

pele *use* **peel**

pell-mell confusedly, recklessly

Peloponnese S. Greece; *see also* **Morea**

pemmican a dried meat for travellers; *not* pemi-

Pen. Peninsula

penalize *not* -ise

pen-and-ink (adj., hyphens)

Penang *see* **Malaya, Federation of**

penanggalan a female vampire in Malaysian folklore

penates (pl.) Roman household gods, esp. of the storeroom; *see also* **lar**

penbardd (Welsh) a head or chief bard

pence *see* **penny**

penchant bias (not ital.)

pencil/, -led, -ling (one l in US)

PEN Club International Association of Poets, Playwrights, Editors, Essayists, and Novelists

pendant (noun) anything hanging

pendent (adj.) suspended

pendente lite (Lat.) during the trial

pendragon (hist.) an ancient British or Welsh prince (cap. as title)

pendulum/ pl. **-s**

penetrable that may be penetrated

penetralia (pl.) the innermost recesses (not ital.)

pen feather a quill feather; cf. **pin feather**

penfriend (one word)

pengő the chief unit of currency in Hungary 1927–46, replaced by the forint

penguin an Antarctic bird; cf. **pinguin**

pen holder (two words)

penicillin (med.)

Penicillium (bot.) a genus of fungi, mould (ital.)

Penicuik Lothian

penillion improvised stanzas sung to a harp accompaniment at an eisteddfod etc., sing. **pennill**

peninsula/ (noun) pl. **-s**, adj. **-r**

Peninsular/ Campaign SE Virginia, 1862, in the American Civil War; **—— War** Spain and Portugal, 1808–14, in the Napoleonic Wars

penis/ the male organ, pl. **-es**

penknife (one word)

Penmaenmawr Gwynedd

penman/, -ship (one word)

pen name (two words)

pennant (naut.) a piece of rigging, a flag

penni/ a monetary unit of Finland; pl. **-ä**

penniless *not* penny-

pennill sing. of **penillion**

pennon a long narrow flag

penn'orth (colloq.) a pennyworth

Pennsylvania/ off. abbr. **Pa.**, postal **PA**; *not* Penn., Penna.; **—— Dutch** a dialect of High German spoken by descendants of 17th–18th-c. German and Swiss immigrants

to Pennsylvania etc.; (as pl.) these settlers or their descendants

penny pl. **pennies** (a number of coins), **pence** (a sum of money); abbr. **p** (sing. and pl., no point); pre-1971 penny, abbr. **d.** (sing. and pl.)

penny-a-liner (hyphens)

pennyroyal (bot.) a kind of mint (one word)

pennyweight 24 grains, abbr. **dwt.**

penny/wort, -worth (one word)

penology the science of punishment, *not* poe-

pen pal (US) = **penfriend**

Penrhyn/ Gwynedd, *also* **Baron ——**

Penryn Cornwall

pensée (Fr. f.) thought, maxim; pansy

pension/ a regular payment made by a government, employer, or insurance company; based on age, length of employment, or charitable grounds; **-able, -ary, -er**

pension/ a European, esp. French, boarding house or school; *en* —— as a boarder (ital.)

pensionnat (Fr. m.) a boarding school

penstemon (bot.) *not* pents-

Pent. Pentecost

pentagon/ a figure or building with five sides; the US defence headquarters (cap.); **-al**

pentagram a five-pointed star

pentagraph *use* **panto-**

pentameter (prosody) a verse of five units

Pentateuch/ the first five books of the OT, traditionally ascribed to Moses and called the **Torah** by Jews (cap.); **-al** (not cap.)

Pentecost/ Whit Sunday (cap.), abbr. **Pent.**; **-al** (not cap.)

penthouse (one word)

pentobarbital (US) = **pentobarbitone**

pentstemon *use* **pens-**

penumbr/a (astr.) a lighter shadow round dark shadow of an eclipse, pl. **-ae**

peon a Sp.-Am. day labourer or farm worker; cf. **paean**; **paeon**

peony a flower, *not* pae-

PEP Personal Equity Plan, Political and Economic Planning

pepo/ the fleshy fruit of a melon etc., pl. **-s**

pepper/box, -corn (one word)

pepper/ mill (two words)

peppermint (one word)

pepper pot (two words)

pepsin an enzyme in gastric juice, *not* -ine

Pepys, Samuel (1633–1703) English diarist and civil servant

per (Lat.) by, for (rom. when used with assimilated Eng. terms); abbr. **p.**

per. period

PERA Production Engineering Research Association of Great Britain

per accidens (Lat.) contingently, indirectly (opp. of **per se**)

perai *use* **piranha**

Perak *see* **Malaya, Federation of**

per annum yearly; abbr. **p.a.**, **per ann.**

per caput (Lat. 'by head') for each person; the pl. **per capita**, originally in contrast to **per stirpes**, has acquired the sing. form's meaning except in hist. or legal contexts (not ital.)

perceiv/e, -able, -er

per cent in every hundred (two words, one word in US, no point), symbol **%**

percentage (one word)

perceptible *not* -able

Perceval/ one of King Arthur's knights, —, **Spencer** (1762–1812) English statesman

perchance perhaps

percolat/e, -ing, -or

per contra on the other hand (not ital.)

per curiam (Lat.) by the court

perdendosi (mus.) dying away

per diem daily; (noun) daily allowance (not ital.)

perdu/ (Fr.) f. **-e** concealed, lost

Père (Fr. m.) RC father, not ital. as part of name; abbr. **P.**

père (Fr. m.) father, senior, added to a surname to distinguish a father from a son, as 'Dumas père'; *see also* **fils**

Père David's deer a large slender-antlered deer

Père Lachaise a Paris cemetery (two words, caps.)

Perelman, S(idney) J(oseph) (1904–79) US humorist and author

perestroika (in the former Soviet Union) the policy or practice of restructuring or reforming the economic and political system, in Russ. **perestroïka**

perf. perfect, (stamps) perforated

perfect abbr. **perf.**

perfecta (US) a form of betting in which the first two places in a race must be predicted in the correct order

perfect binding a binding method alternative to sewing, in which the gatherings of each volume are clamped together, their back folds sheared off, and the resultant leaf edges glued to a flexible backing

perfecter one who perfects, *not* -or; (typ.) a printing press which prints both sides of the paper at one pass

perfectib/le, -ility *not* -ab-

perfecting (typ.) printing the second side of a sheet

perfecto a large thick cigar pointed at each end

perforated abbr. **perf.**

perforce of necessity (one word)

Pergamon Press publishers

Pergamum a city and kingdom in ancient Asia Minor

pergana *use* **par-**

Pergolesi, Giovanni Battista (1710–36) Italian composer

pergunnah *use* **pargana**

peri/ (Pers. myth.) a fairy, a good (originally evil) genius; a beautiful or graceful being; pl. **-s**

periagua *use* **pira-**

peridot a green semi-precious stone, *not* -te

perig/ee (astr.) abbr. **perig.**; **-ean**

Périgord (Fr. cook.) cooking based on truffles

peril/, -led, -ling (one *l* in US)

perimeter the outline of a closed figure

per incuriam (Lat.) by oversight

perine/um (anat.) pl. **-ums**, adj. **-al**

per interim (Lat.) in the mean time

period (US) = **full point**, abbr. **per.**

periodicals, titles of when cited, to be italic; as a rule the definite article should be in roman lower case, except by tradition for *The Economist* and *The Times*

peripatetic walking about, (cap.) Aristotelian (school of philosophy)

peripeteia a sudden reversal of fortune, *not* -tia (not ital.)

periphras/is circumlocution, pl. **-es**; **-tic**

perispomen/on (Gr. gram.) (a word) with circumflex on last syllable, pl. **-a**

peristyle (archit.) a row of columns round temple

periton/eum (anat.) pl. **-eums**; **-eal**, **-itis**

perityphlitis (med.)

periwig/, -ged *not* perri-

periwinkle a plant and mollusc

perlé a sparkling S. African wine

Perlis *see* **Malaya, Federation of**

perm colloq. for permanent wave, permutation, and corresponding verbs (no point)

permeable that may be permeated

per mensem for each month (not ital.)

Permian (geol.) (of or relating to) the last period of the Palaeozoic era

per mille in every thousand (not ital.), *not* mil; symbol ‰

permis de séjour (Fr. m.) a residence permit

permissible *not* -able

permit/, -ted, -ting

pernickety fastidious, over-precise; *not* persn- (US)

Perón,/ Juan Domingo (1895–1974) President of Argentina 1946–55, 1973–4; husband of — (**María**) **Eva** (**Duarte de**) (1919–52), called **'Evita'**; **Peronism** (no accent)

per pais (Norman Fr.) by jury (lit. 'by the county')

Perpendicular (archit.) of the third stage of English Gothic (15th–16th cc.), with vertical tracery in large windows (cap.)

perpetuum mobile (Lat.) something never at rest, (mus.) = **moto perpetuo**

per procurationem (Lat.) used in signatures to mean through the agency of (*incorrectly* on behalf of); the correct sequence is 'Smith *per pro.* Jones' (Jones signing for Smith); abbr. *per pro.*, **p.p.**

Perrier/ (propr.) (cap.), — **-Jouët** a champagne (hyphen)

perriwig *use* **peri-**

Pers. Persia, -n

pers. person, -al, -ally

per saltum (Lat.) at a leap (ital.)

per se by himself, herself, itself, *or* themselves, by or in itself, intrinsically (opp. of *per accidens*) (not ital.)

Perse *see* **Léger**

Perseids (astr.) a group of meteors that appear to radiate from the constellation Perseus

Persia/, -n abbr. **Pers.**; *but use* **Iran**, **Iranian**, of the modern state

Persian/ carpet, — **cat**, — **rug** (caps.) *but* — **morocco** (bind.) (no caps.)

persiflage banter (not ital.)

persil (Fr. m.) parsley

persimmon (bot.) the date-plum, *not* -simon

persist/ence (in Fr. f. *persistance*), -ency, -ent

persnickety *use* **pernickety** (except in US)

persona/ perceived characteristics of personality, pl. **-e** (not ital.)

persona/ grata (Lat.) an acceptable person, pl. **-e gratae**; — *gratissima* a most acceptable person, pl. **-e gratissimae**; — *ingrata*, — *non grata* an unacceptable person, pl. **-e ingratae, -e non gratae**

personalize *not* -ise

personalty (law) personal estate, *not* -ality

personnel/ staff employed in any service, members of armed forces; — **carrier**, — **manager** (two words)

persp. perspective

perspex (propr.) a tough transparent plastic (not cap.)

perspicaci/ous mentally discerning, astute; **-ty**

perspicu/ous clearly expressed; **-ity**

per stirpes (Lat.) by the number of families; cf. **per caput**

persuadable able to be induced (e.g. to do something in a particular instance)

persuasible open to persuasion or influence

persuasive able to persuade

PERT project *or* programme evaluation and review technique

pertinac/ity persistence, **-ious**

peruke a wig, *not* -que

Peruv. Peruvian

per viam (Lat.) by way of

pes (Lat.) a foot, pl. *pedes*

Pesach the Passover festival, in Heb. *Pesaḥ*

peseta the chief monetary unit in Spain, abbr. **pta.**

Peshawar W. Pakistan, *not* -ur

peso/ the chief monetary unit in some Latin American countries and the Philippines, pl. **-s**

Pest *see* **Budapest**

Pestalozzi, Johann Heinrich (1746–1827) Swiss educationist

Pet., 1, 2 First, Second Epistle of Peter

peta- prefix meaning 10^{15}, abbr. **P**

Pétain, Henri Philippe (1856–1951) French marshal and politician, head of the Vichy government 1940–4

petal/, -led

Peter, First, Second Epistle of (NT) abbr. **1 Pet., 2 Pet.**

peterel *use* **-trel**

Peterlee Dur.

Peterloo massacre St Peter's Field, Manchester, 1819; named in ironical reference to the Battle of Waterloo

Peter Principle the jocular principle that members of a hierarchy are promoted until they reach the level at which they are no longer competent, propounded by **Laurence Johnson Peter** (1919–90) US educationist and author

Peter Schlemihl a well-meaning unlucky fellow; (ital.) novel by Chamisso, 1814

Peter's pence (hist.) an annual tax, *later* a voluntary contribution on St Peter's Day (one cap.)

petit/ (Fr. m.) small; — *bleu* (in France) a telegram, pl. *-s bleus*

petit/ bourgeois a member of the **petite bourgeoisie**, the lower middle class, pl. **-s bourgeois**; f. **-e bourgeoise** pl. **-es bourgeoises**; the Eng. form, **petty bourgeois/, -ie**, carries a more pejorative tone

petit déjeuner (Fr. m.) breakfast

petit/ four a small fancy cake, biscuit, or sweet; pl. **-s fours** (not ital.)

petitio principii (Lat.) begging the question, a logical fallacy in which a conclusion is taken for granted in the premiss

petit-maître (Fr. m.) a dandy or coxcomb

petit/ mal a mild form of epilepsy, **— point** embroidery in small stitches (not ital.)

petits pois small green peas (not ital.)

petits soins (Fr. m. pl.) little attentions

petit verre (Fr. m.) a glass of liqueur

Petrarc/h, Francesco (1304–74) Italian scholar and poet, in It. **-a**; adj. **-han**

Petre, Baron

petrel a seabird, *not* -erel

Petri dish (one cap.)

Petriburg: the signature of the Bishop of Peterborough (colon)

petro/chemical, -chemistry, -dollar, -glyph (one word)

Petrograd *see* **St Petersburg**

petrol refined petroleum used as fuel

petroleum unrefined oil

petrology abbr. **petrol.**

Pettie, John (1839–93) Scottish painter

pettifog/ to cavil in legal matters; **-ger, -gery, -ging**

petty bourgeois/, -ie Eng. forms of **petit bourgeois, petite bourgeoisie** (qq.v.)

petty/ cash abbr. **p/c, — officer** abbr. **PO** (two words)

peu à peu (Fr.) little by little

Peugeot a French make of car

peut-être (Fr.) perhaps

pewit *use* **pee-**

p. ex. (Fr.) *par exemple* (for example)

PF Patriotic Front, Procurator-Fiscal

pF picofarad (no point)

pf (mus.) più forte (a little louder), piano forte (soft, then loud)

Pfc. (US) Private first class

Pfd. (Ger.) *Pfund* (pound)

Pfennig (Ger. m.) a small German coin, abbr. **Pf.**

Pfitzner, Hans (1869–1949) German composer

Pfleiderer,/ Edmund (1842–1902) and his brother **— Otto** (1839–1908) German philosophers

Pfund (Ger. n.) pound (cap.), abbr. *Pfd.*

PG paying guest, postgraduate

pg picogram (no point)

PGA Professional Golfers' Association

PGM (Freemasonry, Odd Fellows) Past Grand Master

pH (chem.) (one cap.)

ph phot

Phaedo (b. *c.*417 BC) a pupil of Socrates

phaenomenon etc., *use* **phe-**

Phaethon (Gr. myth.) son of Helios; *not* Phaë-, -ton

phaeton a light open four-wheeled carriage, (US) a type of touring car

Phalang/e a right-wing activist Maronite party in Lebanon (cf. **Falange**); **-ism, -ist**

phalan/x a line of battle or a compact body of men, pl. **-xes**; (biol.) a bone or stamen bundle, pl. **-ges**

phall/us pl. **-uses**, (bot., med., relig.) **-i**

phanariot (hist.) a member of a class of Greek officials in Constantinople under the Ottoman Empire

phantasize *use* **fan-**

phantasmagor/ia a shifting scene of real or imagined figures, pl. **-ias**; **-ic**; *not* fa-

phantasy *use* **fan-**

phantom *not* f-

Phar. Pharmacopoeia

Pharao/h *not* -oah; **-nic**

Pharis/ee pl. **-ees**; **-aism, -aic, -aical**

pharm. pharmaceutical, pharmacy

pharmacol. pharmacology

pharmacopoeia a book describing drugs, abbr. **P.** (*see* **BP**), **Phar.**; *Pharmacopoeia/ Dublinensis* (of Dublin) abbr. **PD**; **—** *Edinburgensis* (of Edinburgh) abbr. **PE**; **—** *Londiniensis* (of London) abbr. **PL**; *not* -peia (US)

pharos a lighthouse, (cap.) the one at Alexandria *or* the island on which it stood

pharyn/x the cavity behind the larynx, pl. **-ges**; **-gal, -geal, -gitis**

phas/e, -ic, -ing

phatic (of speech etc.) used to convey general sociability rather than to communicate a specific meaning

Ph.B. *Philosophiae Baccalaureus* (Bachelor of Philosophy)

Ph.D. *Philosophiae Doctor* (Doctor of Philosophy)

Phebe *see* **Phoebe**

Phèdre a play by Racine, 1677

Pheidias (5th c. BC) Athenian sculptor; *not now* **Phidias** except to describe an enthusiastic writer on art

Phenician *use* **Phoe-**

phenix *use* **phoe-**

phenomen/on an appearance, pl. **-a**; **-al**; *not* phae-

phial a small (usually cylindrical) glass vessel, esp. for holding liquid medicines; *see also* **vial**

phi twenty-first letter of the Gr. alphabet (Φ, ϕ)

Phi Beta Kappa (US) an intercollegiate honorary society to which distinguished students may be elected

Phidias *use* **Phei-**

Phil. Philadelphia, Philharmonic, Philippine, Philippians

philabeg *use* **fili-**

Philadelphia abbr. **Phil., Phila.**

philatel/y postage-stamp collecting; **-ic, -ically, -ist**

Philem. Philemon (NT)

philemot *use* **fi-**

philharmonic fond of music (cap. as part of the name of an orchestra or society)

philhellen/e (one) friendly to the Greeks; **-ic, -ism, -ist**

philibeg *use* **fi-**

Philip the name of five kings of Macedonia, six kings of France, and five kings of Spain; any of various French, Spanish, or Burgundian gold or silver coins issued by kings and dukes named Philip

Philippe Fr. for **Philip**

Philippians (NT) abbr. **Phil.**

Philippics (pl.) the speeches of Demosthenes against Philip of Macedon, also those of Cicero against Antony; **philippic** a bitter invective

philippina a game of forfeits, *not* the many variants

Philippine Islands abbr. **PI**

Philippines, Republic of the inhabited by Filipinos

Philipps the family name of Viscount St Davids and Baron Milford; *see also* **Phill-**

Philips/ electronics manufacturer, **—, Ambrose** (1675–1749) English writer of pastoral and nursery poems, hence 'namby-pamby'; **—, John** (1676–1709) parodist of Milton; **—, Katherine** (1631–64) English poet; *see also* **Phill-**

Philip Sparrow *see* ***Phyllyp Sparowe***

Philister (Ger.) a townsman, a non-student; pl. same (cap.)

Philistine an inhabitant of ancient Palestine; a person indifferent to culture (not cap.); **philistinism** (not cap.)

phillipina *use* **philipp-**

Phillipps,/ James Orchard *see* **Halliwell-Phillipps**, **— Sir Thomas** (1792–1872) English book collector; *see also* **Philipps**

Phillips,/ Sir Claud (1846–1924) English art critic; **— Edward** (1630–94) lexicographer, and **— John** (1631–1706) Milton's nephews; **John Bertram** (1906–82) English Bible translator; **— Stephen** (1864–1915) English poet; **— Wendell** (1811–84) US abolitionist; *see also* **Philips**

Phillpotts,/ Eden (1862–1960) English novelist and dramatist, **— Henry** (1778–1869) Bishop of Exeter; *see also* **Philpott**

philogynist a person who likes or admires women

philopoena *use* **philippina**

philosopher's stone a substance thought to change base metals to gold, *properly* **-s'**

philosophize *not* **-ise**

philosophy abbr. **philos.**

Philpott, Henry (1807–92) Bishop of Worcester; *see also* **Phillpotts**

Phil. Soc. Philological Society of London, Philosophical Society of America

Phil. Trans. the *Philosophical Transactions of the Royal Society of London*

philtre an aphrodisiac drink, *not* **-er** (US); cf. **filter**

Phiz illustrator of Dickens; *see* **Browne, Hablot Knight**

phiz, phizog (arch., colloq.) the face, *not* phizz

phlebit/is inflammation of the veins, **-ic**

Phnom Penh Cambodia

phobia/ a morbid fear, pl. **-s**

Phoebe *but* **Phebe** in Shakespeare's *As You Like It*

Phoebus 'bright', an epithet of Apollo

Phoenician *not* Phe-

phoenix a mythical bird that rose rejuvenated from its own ashes, *not* phen-

phon a unit of perceived loudness

phon. phonetics

phone/ short for telephone, *not* 'phone; **— book** (esp. US) = **telephone directory**; **-card** (one word)

phone-in a broadcast incorporating listeners' telephoned views (hyphen)

phonetics (usually treated as sing.)

phon/ey false, *not* phony; **-ier, -ily, -iness**

phonol. phonology

phosphor/us symbol P; (adj.) **-ous**

phosphuretted *not* -eted, -oretted

phot a unit of illuminance, abbr. **ph**

photo/ photograph (no point), pl. **-s**

photo/biology, -call, -chemistry (one word)

photo/composition, -setting (one word) (typ.) setting copy onto film etc. instead of in metal type

photocop/y, -ier (one word) *prefer* to **xerox** in general references

photoelectric (one word)

photo finish (two words)

photofit composite picture using photographs of facial features (one word); cf. **identikit**

photog. photograph/y, -ic

Photograph/ (Ger. m.) photographer; **-ie** (f.) photograph, -y

photograph/e (Fr. m. and f.) photographer; **-ie** (f.) photograph, -y

photogravure (typ.) the intaglio printing process; shortened as **gravure**

photojournalism (one word)

photolithography (typ.) the photographic processes for making a plate for printing by offset lithography; colloq. **photolitho**

photom. photometr/y, -ical

photomicrograph a photograph of a minute object taken with a microscope; cf. **micro-photograph**

photomontage a montage of photographs

photo-offset (typ.) offset printing with plates made photographically (hyphen)

photosetting *see* **photocomposition**

photostat (propr.) a type of machine for making photocopies, (to make) such a copy

phr. phrase

phren. phrenology

phrenetic *use* **fren-**

phrenitic affected with phrenitis, inflammation of the brain

phthalic (chem.) derived from naphthalene

phthisis tuberculosis

Phyfe, Duncan (1786–1854) Scottish-born US furniture maker

phylactery a small leather box containing Hebrew texts on vellum, worn by Jewish men at morning prayer as a reminder to keep the law

Phyllyp Sparowe a poem by Skelton, 1529

phylo- (biol.) a prefix denoting a race or tribe

phyl/um a main division of the animal or vegetable kingdom, pl. **-a**

phys. physical, physician, physics

physic/, -ked, -king, -ky

Physic, Regius Professor of Cambridge University, *not* -cs

physico-chemical (hyphen, one word in US)

physiol. physiolog/y, -ical, -ist

physique constitution (not ital.)

physique (Fr. f.) physics (natural philosophy)

PI Philippine Islands

pi (typ.) *use* **pie** (except in US)

pi the sixteenth letter of the Gr. alphabet (Π, π); ∏ (math.) product; ratio of circumference to diameter of a circle, or 3.14159265 ...

pianissimo (mus.) very soft, abbr. ***pp***

pianississimo (mus.) as softly as possible, abbr. ***ppp***

piano/ (mus.) softly, abbr. ***p***, pl. **piani**; instrument formally called **pianoforte** (one word), pl. **-s**; **-player, -stool** (hyphens)

piano-forte (mus.) softly, then loud (two words)

Pianola (propr.) an automatic player-piano (cap.)

piano nobile (archit.) the main floor of a building (ital.)

piassava a stout fibre from palm trees, *not* -aba

piastre a small coin of Middle Eastern countries, *not* -er (US)

piazza/ an open square, pl. **-s**

pibroch an air on the bagpipe, *not* the bagpipe itself

pica (typ.) the size of letters on some typewriters; the standard for typographic measurement, equalling 12 pt. or about one-sixth of an inch; (med.) the eating of substances other than normal food

picaninny *use* **picca-**

Picard, Jean (1620–82) French astronomer

picaresque of a style of fiction describing the life of an (amiable) rogue (not ital.)

Picasso, Pablo (**Ruiz**) (1881–1973) Spanish painter

picayune a small US coin pre-1857, (colloq.) any trifling coin, person, or thing; (adj.) trifling, mean

piccalilli a pickle of vegetables and mustard

piccaninny (offens.) a black or Australian Aboriginal infant; *not* pica-, picka- (US)

Piccard, Auguste (1884–1962) Swiss physicist

piccolo/ the smallest flute, pl. **-s**

pi character (typ.) one of a set of special sorts; *see also* **pi plaque**

pickaback *use* **piggyback**

pickaxe (one word), *not* -ax (US)

pickelhaube (hist.) a German spiked infantry helmet, in Ger. f. ***Pickelhaube***

picket/ (*also* **picq-, piq-**); as verb, **-ed, -ing**; — **line** (two words)

picklock (one word)

pick-me-up/ a tonic (hyphens), pl. **-s**

pickpocket (one word)

Pickwickian of or like Mr Pickwick in Dickens's *Pickwick Papers*, esp. in being jovial, plump, etc.; (of words or their sense) misunderstood or misused, esp. to avoid offence

picnic/, -ked, -ker, -king, -ky

pico- prefix meaning 10^{-12}, abbr. **p**

picquet *use* **-ket**; *see also* **piquet**

picture/ book, — card (two words)

picturegoer (one word)

picture/ hat, — postcard (two words)

pictures, titles of when cited, to be in italic if named by the artist, roman quoted if popularly identified as such by others

picture window (two words)

pidgin/ a simplified language containing vocabulary from two or more languages, used for communication between people not having a common language; — **English** a pidgin in which the chief language is English, used originally between Chinese and Europeans (two words, one cap.); a pidgin grown more sophisticated through use is a **creole**; cf. **pigeon**

pi-dog *use* **pye-**

pie (typ.) composed type that has been jumbled; *not* pi, pye

pie (hist.) former monetary unit of India, equal to one-twelfth of an anna

piebald of two colours in irregular patches, usually of horses, usually black and white; *not* pye-; cf. **skewbald**

pièce/ de résistance the most important or remarkable item, the principal dish at a meal; pl. **-s de résistance** (not ital.)

piecemeal gradually (one word)

piece-rate (hyphen)

piecework (one word)

pied/ (Fr. m.) a foot, abbr. **p.**

pied-à-terre an occasional residence, pl. **pieds-à-terre** (hyphens)

pie-dog *use* pye-

Pierce, Franklin (1804–69) US President 1853–7

Pierce the Ploughman's Crede anon., *c.*1394; *see also* **Piers**

Pierian Spring the fountain of the Muses in Thessaly

Pierides (Gr. myth) the nine Muses

pierr/ot a seaside entertainer derived from French pantomime, f. **-ette**

Piers Plowman, The Vision of William concerning a poem by Langland, 14th c.; *see also* **Pierce**

pietà the representation of the dead Christ in the Virgin Mary's arms

pietas (Lat.) the respect due to an ancestor, forerunner, etc.

Pietermaritzburg S. Africa

pietr/a dura (It.) a stone mosaic, pl. ***-e dure***

piezoelectric/, -ity (one word)

pig (US) = **piglet**; cf. **swine**

pigeon/ common dove; a person easily swindled; (colloq.) **not my —** not my affair; cf. **pidgin**

pigeon-hol/e, -ed (hyphen, one word in US)

piggyback (one word) *not* pick-a-back

pig-headed (hyphen, one word in US)

pig iron (two words)

pigm/y, -aean *use* pygm-

pigpen (US) = **pigsty**

pig/skin, -sty pl. **-sties**; **-swill, -tail, -wash, -weed** (one word)

Pike's Peak Rocky Mountains (apos.)

pikestaff (one word)

Piketberg (off. spelling) Cape Province, *not* Piquet-

pilaf a dish of spiced rice or wheat with meat, fish, vegetables, etc. in the Middle East (not ital.)

pilau a dish of spiced rice or wheat with meat, fish, vegetables, etc. in India (not ital.)

pilcrow (typ. hist.) the paragraph symbol (¶)

Pilipino the national language of the Philippines, a standardized form of Tagalog; *not* Filipino

pillar box (two words)

pillbox (one word)

pill bug a type of woodlouse (two words)

pillowcase (one word)

pillow-fight (hyphen)

pillow/ lace, — lava, — talk (two words)

pillule *use* pilule

pilot/, -ed, -ing

pilot biscuit (US) = **ship's biscuit**

pilot/ fish, — house, — light (two words)

Piloty, Karl von (1826–86) German painter

Pilsen Czech Republic, in Czech **Plzeň**

Pilsener a light beer (cap.)

Piłsudski, Józef (1867–1935) Polish general, first President of Poland 1918

pilule a small pill, *not* pill-

pimiento/ a sweet red pepper, allspice; pl. **-s**; *not* pime- (though sometimes reserved for allspice)

PIN personal identification number

pin/ a small cask for liquids; pl. **-s**

pina colada a drink made from pineapple juice, rum, and coconut; in Sp. ***piña colada***

pinball (one word)

pince-nez eyeglasses with a nose clip instead of earpieces, pl. same (not ital., hyphen)

pincushion (one word)

Pindar (518–438 BC) Greek poet, abbr. **Pind.**

Pindar, Peter pseud. of **Dr John Wolcot** (1738–1819)

pineapple (one word)

pine/ cone, — nut (two words)

Pinero, Sir Arthur Wing (1855–1934) English playwright

pin feather a small feather; cf. **pen feather**

ping-pong (hyphen)

pinguin a W. Indian plant or fruit; cf. **penguin**

pin/head, -hole (one word)

pinkie (esp. US, Sc.) the little finger

Pinkster (US) = **Whitsuntide**

pin money (two words)

pinochle (US) a card game with a double pack of forty-eight cards (nine to ace only)

pin/point, -prick (one word)

pinscher a breed of dog, *not* pinch-; *see also* **Dobermann pinscher**

pinstripe (one word)

pint (UK) 20 fl. oz (0.568 l); (US) 16 fl. oz (0.473 l); abbr. **pt.**, symbol **O**

pinta (Brit. colloq.) a pint of milk, (med.) a chronic skin disease endemic in tropical America

pin-table (hyphen)

pintado/ a petrel, mackerel-like fish; pl. **-s**

pinto (US, of a horse) = **piebald**

Pinturicchio the nickname of **Bernardino di Betto** (1454–1513) Italian painter

pin-up (noun; hyphen, one word in US)

pinxit (Lat.) painted this; abbr. **pnxt.**, **pinx.**

Pinyin a system of romanized spelling for transliterating Chinese (cap.)

piob mhor the Highland pipes (not cap.), in Gael. **piob-mhór**

pion (phys.) a subatomic particle, a pi meson

pipal *use* **bo tree**

pipeclay (one word)

pipe/cleaner, — dream, — organ (two words)

pipe-rack (hyphen)

pipe rolls (hist.) the annual records of the British Exchequer 12th–19th cc.

pipe/-stem, -stone (hyphens)

pi plaque (typ.) a set of special sorts

Pippa Passes a poem by R. Browning, 1841

pipy like, or having, pipes; *not* -ey

piquan/t sharp, **-cy** (not ital.)

piqu/e resentment; a score in piquet; as a verb, irritate, **-ed, -ing**

piqué a thick cotton fabric; (mus.) short, detached (not ital.)

piqué (Fr.) (of wine) slightly sour; (cook.) larded

piquet a card game, *not* picq-; *see also* **picket**

Piquetberg *use* **Piket-**

PIRA *or* **Pira** Research Association for the Paper and Board, Printing and Packaging Industries, publishers

Piraeus the port of Athens

piragua a S. American dugout canoe, *not* the many variants

Pirandello, Luigi (1867–1936) Italian playwright

Piranesi, Giambattista (1720–78) Italian architect and etcher

piranha a ferocious S. American fish; *not* perai, piraya

pis aller (Fr. m.) a second best

piscin/a a fish pond, a swimming pool; (eccl.) a stone basin for disposing of water used in washing the chalice etc. pl. **-ae**

pisé (Fr. m.) rammed earth (ital.)

piskie *use* **pix-** (except in Cornish dialect)

Pissarro,/ Camille (1830–1903) French painter, father of **— Lucien** (1863–1944) French–British painter

pissed/ (Brit.) drunk, (US) annoyed; **— off** (Brit., US) annoyed, fed up

pistachio/ a nut, pl. **-s**; *not* -acho

piste a ski track (not ital.)

pistol/, -led, -ling (one l in US)

pistole (hist.) a foreign (esp. Spanish) gold coin

pit (US) the stone of a fruit

pita *use* **-tta** (except in US)

pitch-and-toss (hyphens)

pitch/blende, -fork, -stone (one word)

piteous deserving pity, wretched

pitiful causing pity, contemptible

Pitman, Sir Isaac (1813–97) English inventor of shorthand

pitta a flat hollow bread that can be split and filled with salad etc., *not* pita (US)

Pitti, Palazzo an art gallery in Florence

Pitt Rivers/, Augustus Henry Lane Fox (1827–1900) English lieutenant general, archaeologist, and anthropologist, founder of the **— — Museum** Oxford (no hyphen)

Pitt-Rivers/, George Henry Lane-Fox (1890–1966) grandson of above, captain, owner/director of the former **— - — Museum** Dorset (hyphen)

Pittsburgh Pa.; *not* -burg

più (It. mus.) more; **— forte** a little louder, abbr. **pf**

pius (Lat.) holy, abbr. **p.**

pivot/, -ed, -ing

pix *use* **py-**

pixel/s (electronics) the minute areas of uniform illumination from which an image on a display screen is composed; **-ate** divide (an image) into pixels

pix/ie a small fairy or elf; *not* pisk- (except in Corn. dialect), -y; **-ilated** bewildered, *not* pixy-led

pixie/ hat, — hood (two words)

Pizarro, Francisco (*c.*1475–1541) Spanish conquistador

pizz/a pl. **-as**; **-eria** the place where pizzas are made or sold

pizzazz *not* pizazz, pzazz

pizzicato (mus.) pinched, plucked; abbr. **pizz.**

PJ presiding judge, Probate Judge

PK psychokinesis

pk. pack, park, peak, peck(s)

pkg. package, -s

PL Paymaster Lieutenant, *Pharmacopoeia Londiniensis*, Poet Laureate, Primrose League

P/L Profit and Loss

Pl. Plate, -s

pl. place, plate, platoon, plural

PLA Port of London Authority

place (UK) any of the first three or four positions in a race, esp. other than first; (US) second in a horse race

place (Fr. f.) square in a town

place aux dames! (Fr.) ladies first!

place-bet (UK) a bet on a horse to come first, second, third, or sometimes fourth in a race; (US) a bet on a horse to come second

placebo/ (med.) a medicine given with no physiological effect, (RC) the opening antiphon of vespers for the dead; pl. **-s**

place card (two words)

place mat (two words, one word in US)

place name (two words)

placent/a an organ nourishing the foetus in the womb, pl. **-ae**

place setting (two words)

placet (Lat.) it pleases, permission granted, an affirmative vote in a church or university assembly

plafond (Fr. m.) a ceiling, esp. decorated (ital.)

plagiarize take and use the thoughts, writings, inventions, etc. of another person as one's own; *not* -ise

plagu/e, -esome, -ily, -y

Plaid Cymru the Welsh nationalist party

plainchant (one word)

plain clothes (hyphen when attrib., one word in US)

plain sailing (fig.) easy work (two words); cf. **plane sailing**

plain/sman, -song (one word)

plaint (Eng. law) an accusation or charge

plaintiff (law) a person who brings a case against another in court, abbr. **plf.**

plaintive expressing sorrow

Plaisterers, Worshipful Company of

planchet a coin-blank

planchette a small board on castors with a pencil-point, used to trace letters spontaneously at spiritualistic seances (not ital.)

Planck/ constant symbol *h* (6.626 × 10⁻³⁴ J s); — **Law of Radiation** in the quantum theory, from **Max Planck** (1858–1947) German physicist; *not* -'s

plane short for aeroplane, *not* 'plane

plane sailing (naut.) the calculation of a ship's position on the assumption that it is moving on a plane surface (two words); cf. **plain sailing**

planetari/um pl. **-ums**

plankton microscopic organic life drifting in water; cf. **benthal; nekton**

planographic (typ.) of a printing process based on a flat surface, on which the image areas are made greasy so as to accept ink and the rest wet to reject it

Plantagenet family name of the English sovereigns from Henry II to Richard II, 1154–1399

Plantin, Christophe (*c.*1520–89) French printer

plasmolyse (bot.) *not* -ize, -yze (US)

plasterboard (one word)

plaster of Paris (one cap.)

plasticine (propr.) a soft modelling substance (not cap.)

plasticky plastic-like

plastic wrap (US) = **cling film**

plastron a breastplate, bodice front, etc.

plat/ (Fr. cook. m.) a dish, — *du jour* special dish of the day

Plate/, -s (typ.) abbr. **Pl.**

plate/ (typ.) planographic or typographic printing surface of complete page or sheet cast or etched in metal or polymerized resin; half-tone etc. illustration; (photog.) **whole** — 8½ × 6½ in., **half** — 6½ × 4¼ in., **quarter** — 4¼ × 3¼ in.

plateau/ area of fairly level high ground, pl. **-x** (not ital.)

plate/ glass, — rack (two words)

platinize coat with platinum, *not* -ise

platinum/ symbol **Pt**; — **black** platinum in powder form; — **blond** (a person with) silvery-blond hair, f. — **blonde**

Platon/ic (cap. in hist. or philos. contexts) *but* **platonic love** (not cap.); **-ism, -ist, -ize** *not* -ise

Plattdeutsch Low German (one word)

platteland/ (S. Afr.) remote country districts, **-er**

platypus/ the Australian duckbill, pl. **-es**

platyrrhine broad-nosed (of monkeys), *not* -yrrhine

plausible *not* -able

Plautus, Titus Maccius (*c.*254–*c.*184 BC) Roman playwright, abbr. **Plaut.**

play-act/or, -ing (hyphens, one word in US)

playback (noun) (one word)

play/bill, -boy, -fellow, -girl, -goer, -ground, -group, -house (one word)

playing/ card, — field (two words)

play/let, -list, -mate (one word)

play/-off (noun; hyphen, one word in US)

playpen (one word)

plays, titles of when cited to be in italic

play/school, -thing, -time, -wright (one word)

plaza/ a public square, pl. **-s** (not ital.)

plc, PLC public limited company (no points); *use* caps. or lower case according to a company's preferred style; *see also* **AG**; **Inc.**; **KK**; **NV**; **Pty**; **SA**; **SpA**

plead past and past part. **pleaded** *or* (esp. US, Sc.) **pled**

pleased as Punch (one cap.)

pleasur/e, -able

plebeian a commoner in ancient Rome, vulgar, common; *not* -bian

plebiscit/e a vote of the people (no accent, not ital.), **-ary**

plebiscit/um (Lat.) a law passed by the *plebs*, pl. *-a*

plebs (Lat.) the general populace, pl. *plebes*

plectr/um pl. **-ums, -a**

pled *see* **plead**

Pleiad (Gr. myth.) one of the **Pleiades**, the seven daughters of Atlas (cap.); any brilliant group of seven (not cap.)

Pleiades a star-group

plein air (Fr. m.) the open air, outside

pleinairist a painter reproducing effects of atmosphere and light (not ital.)

Pleistocene (geol.) (of or relating to) the first epoch of the Quaternary period; also called the **ice age**

Plen. plenipotentiary

pleno jure (Lat.) with full authority

plethora an excess, glut; (med.) an excess of red corpuscles in the blood; *not* a synonym for *many*

pleur/a a membrane lining the thorax or enveloping the lungs, pl. **-ae**; **-isy** inflammation of this; **-itic**

pleuropneumonia (one word)

Plexiglas (US propr.) = **perspex**, *not* -ss

plexus/ a network (of nerves etc.), pl. **-es**

plf. plaintiff

plié/ (ballet) a bending of the knees with the feet on the ground (not ital.); pl. **-s**

Plimsoll line (naut.) *properly* **loadline**, the marking on a ship's side showing the limit of legal submersion under various conditions; *not* -'s; named after **Samuel Plimsoll** (1824–98) English politician and promoter of the Merchant Shipping Act of 1876

plimsolls rubber-soled canvas shoes, *not* -es

Plinlimmon *use* **Plynlimon**

Pliny/ the Elder in Lat. **Gaius Plinius Secundus** (23–79) and his nephew — **the Younger** (**Gaius Plinius Caecilius Secundus**) (*c.*61–*c.*112) Roman writers

Pliocene (geol.) (of or relating to) the last epoch of the Tertiary period

plissé gathering, kilting, or pleating (not ital.)

PLO Palestine Liberation Organization

plod/, -der, -ding

PL/1 a (comput.) programming language (caps. or even small caps.)

plow (esp. US) = **plough**, *but* **Piers Plowman** by Langland

PLP Parliamentary Labour Party

PLR Public Lending Right

plumb vertical, determine depth using a plumb line

plumbum lead, symbol **Pb**

plummy abounding or rich in plums, (colloq.) (of a voice) sounding affectedly rich or deep in tone

plum pudding (hyphen when attrib.)

plumy plumelike, *not* -ey

plung/e, -ing

Plunket family name of Baron Plunket

Plunkett family name of the Earl of Fingall, and of Barons Dunsany and Louth

pluperfect abbr. **plup.**

plural/ abbr. **pl., -ize** *not* -ise

plus/ with the addition of, sign +; an additional amount, an advantage, pl. **-es**

Plutarch (*c.*50–*c.*120) Greek philosopher and biographer, abbr. **Plut.**

Pluto (Rom. myth.) the god of the underworld, (astr.) planet, symbol ♇

plutonium symbol **Pu**

Plutus (Gr. myth.) the personification of riches

pluviometer a rain gauge, *not* pluvia-

Plymouth Brethren a religious sect formed *c.*1830, abbr. **PB**

Plynlimon a Welsh mountain; *not* Plin-, -limmon

Plzeň Czech for **Pilsen**

PM paymaster, postmaster, post-mortem, Prime Minister, Provost Marshal

Pm promethium (no point)

pm picometre (no point)

pm. premium, premolar

p.m. (Lat.) *post meridiem* (after noon) (not cap., points)

PMG Paymaster-General, Postmaster General

p.m.h. production per man-hour

PMRAFNS Princess Mary's Royal Air Force Nursing Service

PMS (US) premenstrual syndrome = **PMT**, (comput.) processor-memory switch

PMT (typ.) photo-mechanical tint, (finance) post-market trading, premenstrual tension

p.n. promissory note

PNdB perceived noise decibel(s)

PNEU Parents' National Educational Union

pneumatic relating to air or gases, abbr. **pneum.**

pneumon/ic pertaining to the lungs, **-ia**

PNG Papua New Guinea

pnxt. *pinxit* (painted this)

PO petty officer (RN), pilot officer (RAF), postal order, post office

Po polonium (no point)

po/ (colloq.) chamber pot, pl. **-s**

pocketbook (one word)

pocket handkerchief (two words, hyphen in US)

pocket knife (two words, one word in US)

pocket money (two words)

pocket-piece (hyphen)

poco/ (It.) a little, — *a poco* little by little

pococurant/e apathetic, careless (one word, not ital.); **-ism** *not* -eism

POD pay on delivery, Post Office Department

POD *Pocket Oxford Dictionary*

podestà (It. m.) municipal magistrate

Podgorica cap. of Montenegro, *formerly* **Titograd**

podiatr/ist, -y (US) = **chiropod/ist, -y**

podi/um a base or pedestal, pl. **-a**

Podsnappery English self-congratulatory philistinism, from Mr Podsnap in Dickens's *Our Mutual Friend*

podzol/ infertile acidic soil with minerals leached from the surface layers, *not* -sol; **-ization, -ize** *not* -isation, -ise

Poe, Edgar Allan (1809–49) US writer; *not* Alan, Allen

poéle (Fr. m.) stove, (f.) frying pan

poème (Fr. m.) a long poem

poems, titles of when cited to be roman quoted unless long enough to form a separate publication, in which case they are to be in italic

poenology *use* **pen-**

poésie (Fr. f.) poetry, a short poem

poet. poetic, -al; poetry

poetaster a paltry or inferior poet

poeticize *not* -ise

Poet/ Laureate (caps., two words); abbr. **PL**, pl. **-s Laureate**; *see also* **Austin**; **Betjeman**; **Bridges**; **Cibber**; **Lewis**; **Masefield**; **Southey**; **Tennyson**

Poets' Corner Westminster Abbey (caps.)

po-faced solemn (hyphen)

pogrom an organized massacre, esp. of Jews in Russia

poignard *use* **poni-**

poikilothermic (zool.) cold-blooded

poilu (Fr. m.) a French soldier, esp. of the First World War

Poincaré, Raymond (1860–1934) French statesman, President 1913–20

poiniard *use* **poni-**

poinsettia (bot.) *not* point-

point a general term for all marks of punctuation, esp. the full stop; *see also* **compass**, **point system**

point-blank (hyphen)

point/ d'appui (Fr. m.) base of operations, — *d'attaque* base of offensive operations

Point de Galle *see* **Galle**

point-device extremely precise (hyphen)

point duty (two words)

point-virgule (Fr. m.) the semicolon

pointsettia *use* **poins-**

points of omission *see* **ellipsis**

point system (typ.) an Anglo-American standard by which the bodies of all types are multiples, or divisions, of the twelfth of a pica; in the UK and USA 1 point = 0.351mm, in Europe 1 point = 0.376 mm; abbr. **pt.**

poire (Fr. f.) pear

poiré (Fr. m.) perry

poireau/ (Fr. m.) leek, pl. **-x**

poirée (Fr. f.) white beet, Swiss chard

poirier (Fr. m.) pear tree, wood from this

pois (Fr. m. sing. and pl.) pea

poise (phys.) a unit of dynamic viscosity, in SI units 10^{-1} Pa s; abbr. **P**

poisson/ (Fr. m.) fish, — *d'avril* April fool

poivre (Fr. m.) pepper

pokey (US sl.) jail

poky small and cramped, (US) annoyingly slow; *not* -ey

Pol. Poland, Polish

Poland abbr. **Pol.**

polarize *not* -ise

pole/axe, -cat (one word)

pol. econ. political economy

pole-jump (hyphen)

poles, the caps. when used as geographical designations, e.g. North Pole

pole vault (noun, two words; verb, hyphen)

Police (Ger.), *police* (Fr.) policy of insurance; *see also* **Polizei**

police constable (two words), abbr. **p.c.** (**PC** when used before a name)

policeman (one word)

police officer (two words)

police sergeant (two words), abbr. **p.s.** (**PS** when used before a name)

police/ state, — station (two words)

policewoman (one word)

polichinelle (Fr. m.) puppet, buffoon

poliomyelitis infantile paralysis; (colloq.) **polio**/, pl. **-s**

Polish abbr. **Pol.**

Polish notation (logic, math.) a system of formula notation without brackets and punctuation

polit. political, politics

politburo the principal policy-making committee of a Communist party, esp. (hist.) in the USSR (cap. as title); in Russ. *politbyuro*

politesse (Fr. f.) formal politeness

Politian (1454–94) Italian humanist, in It. **Angelo degli Ambrogini**, known as **il Poliziano**

politic/, **-ize** *not* -ise; **-ked, -king**; **-s**

political correctness abbr. **PC**

political economy abbr. **pol. econ.**

politico/ one devoted to politics, pl. **-s**

polity an organized society, form of civil government

Polizei (Ger. f.) police (cap.); *see also* **Police**

polka/, **-ed**

polka dot (hyphen when attrib.)

pollack a sea fish, *not* -ock

pollen/ analysis, — count (two words)

poll/ex thumb, pl. **-ices**

polling/ booth, — day (two words)

Pollock, Jackson (1912–56) US abstract expressionist painter

Pollok, Robert (1798–1827) Scottish poet

Pollok/shaws, -shields Glasgow

pollster a sampler of public opinion

poll tax (two words)

Pollyanna an irrepressibly cheerful optimist, from the eponymous heroine of a novel by Eleanor Porter, 1913

polonaise a dance, music, type of woman's dress, or method of cooking in the Polish style

polonium symbol **Po**

Pol Pot (*c.*1925–98) Cambodian communist leader of the Khmer Rouge, Prime Minister 1976–9, born **Saloth Sar**

Poltoratsk Turkmenistan, *now* **Ashgabat**

poly/ (colloq.) polytechnic, pl. **-s**

polyandr/y marriage to more than one husband at the same time, **-ous**

polyanthus/ (bot.) *not* -os, pl. **-es**

Polybius (*c.*200–*c.*118 BC) Greek historian, abbr. **Polyb.**

polyethylene polymerized ethylene

polygam/y marriage to more than one wife or husband at the same time, **-ous**

polygen/y the theory that humankind originated from several independent pairs of ancestors; **-ism, -ist**

polyglot/, **-tal, -tic**

polygyn/y marriage to more than one wife at the same time, **-ous**

polyhedr/on *not* polye-, pl. **-a**

Polyhymnia (Gr. myth.) the muse of rhetoric

Polynesia/ islands in central Pacific (a bishopric, not a political unit); **-n** (a native) of Polynesia; (of or concerning) the Austronesian family of languages including Maori, Hawaiian, and Samoan

polynya a stretch of open water surrounded by ice, esp. in the Arctic seas (not ital.)

Polyolbion a poem by Drayton, 1613–22

polyp/ (zool.) pl. **-s**

polyp/us (med.) pl. **-i**

polysem/y (philol.) the existence of many meanings (of a word etc.); **-ic, -ous**

polytechnic (cap. when part of name) (colloq.) **poly**

polythene the commercial name for a polyethylene

poly/urethane, -vinyl chloride synthetic resins or plastics

polyzoan *use* **bryozoan**

pomade a preparation for the hair, *not* pomm-

pomelo/ a fruit, the shaddock; pl. **-s**; *not* pomm-, pu-

pomfret-cake *see* **Pontefract-cake**

Pommard a burgundy, *not* Pomard

pommel/ a knob, saddle bow; **-led, -ling** (one *l* in US); cf. **pummel**

pommelo *use* **pom-**

pommes/ (Fr. f. pl.) apples, **— de terre** potatoes

Pommy Austral. and NZ term for a Briton (esp. a recent immigrant); *NODE* and *COD* 10th edn. label it 'informal, derogatory'; the *Australian COD* has no cap. and labels it 'colloq.', adding *pommy bastard* as 'a term of affectionate abuse'; abbr. **Pom**

pompano/ a W. Indian and N. American food-fish, pl. **-s**

Pompeian of Pompeii

pom-pom an automatic quick-firing gun, often on a ship

pompon an ornamental tuft or ball, as worn on a hat or brandished by cheerleaders; *not* -pom (US; hyphen in US)

poncho/ a S. American cloak or one of similar design, pl. **-s**

pondere (Lat.) by weight, abbr. **p.**

Pondicherry India, in Fr. **Pondichéry**

pongo/ an ape, (naut. sl.) a soldier, (Austral., NZ sl. offens.) an Englishman; pl. **-s**

poniard a dagger; *not* poign-, poin-

Poniatowski,/ Józef Antoni (1763–1813) Polish soldier, **— Stanisław August** (1732–98) last King of Poland

pons (Lat.) a bridge, pl. **pontes**

pons asinorum any difficult proposition, originally a rule of geometry from Euclid, lit. 'bridge of asses'

Pontacq a white wine

Pontefract-cake a small liquorice sweet originally made at Pontefract (*earlier* Pomfret) in Yorkshire; *not* pomfret-

pontif/ex (eccl.) a bishop, (Rom. hist.) a member of a priestly college; pl. **-ices**; **Pontifex Maximus** a head of college

pont/iff a bishop, esp. the Pope; **-ifical**

Pont-l'Évêque dép. Calvados, France; a cheese

Pontypridd Mid Glam.

Pooh-Bah a holder of many offices at once, from a character in Gilbert and Sullivan's *The Mikado*, 1885

pooh-pooh to scorn, ridicule; *not* poo-poo

pooja *use* pu-

pooka a hobgoblin, in Ir. *púca*

Pool Corn., W. Yorks.

Poole Dorset

Poole, William Frederick (1821–94) US librarian, compiler of *Poole's Index*

Poona India, *not* -ah; *also now* **Pune**

poor box (two words)

poorhouse (one word)

Poor Law (caps. when hist.)

poor rate (hist.) assessment for relief of poor (two words, no caps.)

Poorten-Schwartz *see* **Maartens**

POP (comput.) point of presence, Post Office Preferred (size of envelopes etc.)

Pop a social club and debating society at Eton College

pop/ (colloq.) popular, **— art, — music** that based on popular culture (two words)

pop. population

popadam, -dom *use* **poppadam**

Pope cap. as title for a specific man: 'the Pope', 'Pope John Paul II'; not cap. for general concept and in ref. to more than one person

Pope/, Alexander (1688–1744) English poet, satirist, and translator; **-an**

Pope Joan a card game (two words)

Popocatepetl a volcano, Mexico

poppadom a thin, crisp, spiced bread eaten with curry etc.; *not* popa-, -dum

Popsicle (US and Canadian propr.) a rectangular ice lolly with two flat handles (cap.)

popularize *not* -ise

population abbr. **pop.**

populus (Lat.) people, abbr. **P.**

porc (Fr. m.) pork, pig

Porch, the the Stoic school of philosophy

Porchester/, Lord; **— Terrace** London; *see also* **Port-**

Porsche a German make of car

Porson/ a sloping Greek typeface, supposedly derived from the Greek hand of **Richard —** (1759–1808) English Greek scholar

Port. Portug/al, -uese

Portakabin (propr.) a portable room or building designed for quick assembly

portament/o (mus.) a continuous glide (not break) from one note to another of different pitch, pl. **-i**

Portarlington, Earl of

Port au Prince Haiti

Port aux Basques Newfoundland

Portchester Hants.; *see also* **Porch-**

Portcullis (her.) one of the four pursuivants of the English College of Arms

Porte/ (hist.) the Turkish court and government, more fully **the Sublime —**

porte cochère (no accent in US)

Port Elizabeth Cape Province, abbr. **PE**

portent/, -ous *not* -ious

Porter, William Sydney *see* **Henry, O.**

portfolio/ pl. **-s**

Port Glasgow Strathclyde

Porthmadog Gwynedd, *formerly* Portmadoc

portico/ pl. **-es**; **-ed**

portière a door curtain (no accent in US)

Portland/ cement, — stone

portmanteau/ pl. **-s**; **— word** one blending the sounds and combining the meanings of two others, e.g. *motel, Oxbridge, smog* (not ital.)

Porto Port. for **Oporto** (o being the definite article), in hist. Port. and Brazilian Port. **Pôrto**

Porto Bello Panama, *use* **Puerto Bello**

Portobello/ Lothian, **— Road** London (one word)

Port of Spain Trinidad

Porto Rico *use* **Puerto Rico**

Portpatrick Dumfries & Galloway (one word)

portrait (typ.) a book, page, or illustration of which the depth is greater than the width; cf. **landscape**

Port-Royal monastery, Versailles and Paris (hyphen)

Port Royal Jamaica; SC (two words)

Port Salut a cheese (two words)

Portsmouth: the signature of the Bishop of Portsmouth (colon)

Portugal abbr. **Port.**

Portuguese abbr. **Port.**

pos. positive

pos/e, -ed, -ing

Posen *use* **Poznań**

pos/er a problem; **-eur** f. **-euse** one who behaves affectedly, pl. **-eurs, -euses**

posey *use* **posy**

posit/, -ed, -ing

posology (med.) the study of dosages

poss. possess/ion, -ive

posse/ a body of men, pl. **-s**; **— comitatus** (hist.) a county force of men over 15

Post, Van der *see* **Van der Post**

post (Lat.) after, abbr. **p.**

postage/ meter (US) = **franking machine**; **— stamp** (two words)

postal code *use* **postcode**

postal order abbr. **PO**

post/bag, -box, -card (one word)

post-classical (hyphen)

postcode (one word)

post-date (verb and noun, hyphen, one word in US)

postdoctoral (one word)

poste restante a post office department where letters remain till called for (not ital.)

post-exilic subsequent to the exile of the Jews in Babylon (hyphen)

postgraduate (one word)

post-haste (hyphen, one word in US)

post hoc/ (Lat.) after this; **— — ergo propter hoc** after this, therefore because of this, the fallacy of consequence for sequence

post horn (mus.) (two words)

posthumous occurring after death, *not* postu-

Posthumus a character in Shakespeare's *Cymbeline*

postilion one who guides post- or carriage-horses, riding the near one; *not* -llion

post-Impressionis/m (hyphen, one word in US; one cap.: I in UK, P in US); **-t**

post-industrial (hyphen)

post initium (Lat.) after the beginning (as of a work), abbr. **post init.**

Post-it (propr.) (one cap., hyphen)

post litem motam (Lat.) after litigation began

post/man, -mark (one word)

postmaster abbr. **PM**; *also* a scholar at Merton College, Oxford (one word)

postmaster general the head of a country's postal service, abolished as an office in the UK; pl. **postmasters general**

post mediem (Lat.) after the middle (as of a work), abbr. **post med.**

post meridiem (Lat.) after noon, abbr. **p.m.**

post-millennial/, -ism, -ist (hyphen, one word in US)

postmistress (one word)

postmodern/ (one word, not cap.), **-ism, -ist**

post mortem (Lat.) after death

post-mortem (adj. and noun) abbr. **PM** (hyphen, one word in US; not ital.)

post/-natal, -nuptial (hyphens, one word in US)

post-obit taking effect, or a bond payable, after death (hyphen, not ital.)

Post Office, The (caps., two words) public corporation, replaced the government department in 1969

post office (not caps., two words) a local office of the above, abbr. **PO**; (US) a children's game = **postman's knock**

post-paid (hyphen, one word in US) abbr. **p.p.**

postpositi/on a word or particle placed after another; **-ve** designating this (one word)

postprandial after dinner (one word)

postscript (one word) abbr. **PS**, pl. **PSS**

post-structural/ (hyphen), **-ism, -ist**

post terminum (Lat.) after the conclusion

postumous *use* posth-

post-war use only as adj., not adv. (hyphen, one word in US)

posy a nosegay, *not* -ey

Pot, Pol *see* **Pol Pot**

pot. potential

potage a thick soup

potassium symbol **K**

potato/ pl. **-es**; **— chips** (US) = **— crisps**

pot-au-feu (Fr. cook. m.) a large cooking pot, a meat broth

poteen alcohol made illicitly, usually from potatoes; *not* pott-, poth-; in Ir. **poitín**

potential abbr. **pot.**

pothole/, -r (one word)

pot-pourri a mixture or medley (hyphen, one word in US)

potsherd a piece of broken earthenware, *not* -ard

potteen *use* **poteen**

Potteries, the general name for a group of six towns in Staffordshire associated with production of pottery and china: Burslem, Fenton, Hanley, Longton, Stoke-on-Trent, and Tunstall; also called 'the Six Towns'; *see also* **the Five Towns**

potter's field a burial place for paupers, strangers, etc. (after Matt. 27: 7); *not* -s'

potting shed (two words)

potto/ a W. African lemur-like animal, a kinkajou; pl. **-s**

pouce (Fr. m.) an inch, a thumb; abbr. **p.**

pouding (Fr. cook. m.) pudding

poudr/é (Fr.) f. **-ée** powdered

Poughkeepsie NY

Pouilly/ dép. Saône-et-Loire, France, source of **-Fuissé** white wine; **-sur-Loire** dép. Nièvre, France, source of **-Fumé** white wine (hyphens)

poulard a fattened domestic hen, in Fr. f. **poularde**

poule (Fr. f.) hen

poulet (Fr. m.) young chicken

poulette (Fr. f.) young hen

POUNC Post Office Users' National Council

pound avoirdupois, approx. 453 g; abbr. **lb**, pl. same (not in scientific use)

pound sign (money) **£** (sing. and pl.); *see also* at **l**.

pour/ (Fr.) for, abbr. **p.**; **— ainsi dire** so to speak

pourboire (Fr. m.) gratuity, tip

pourparler (Fr. m.) preliminary discussion (one word)

pousse-café (Fr. m.) liqueur (after coffee)

poussette a dance with hands joined, to do this (not ital.)

Poussin, Nicolas (1594–1665) French painter

poussin a very young chicken (not ital.)

pou sto (Gr.) standing-place

POW Prince of Wales, prisoner of war

powder/ flask, — keg, — magazine, — monkey, — puff, — room (two words)

power/ boat, — cut, — dive, — factor (two words)

powerhouse (one word)

power/ plant, — station (two words)

Powis, Earl of family name Herbert

powwow a Native American conference, or any meeting compared to this; *not* pawaw (one word)

Powys family name of Baron Lilford; a Welsh county

Poznań Poland, *not* Posen

PP parish priest, Past President, (Lat.) *Patres* (Fathers)

pp. pages

p.p. past participle, post paid, (Lat.) *per procurationem* (q.v.)

pp (mus.) pianissimo (very soft), più piano (softer)

p.p.b. parts per billion (10⁹)

PP C (Lat.) *Patres Conscripti* (Conscript Fathers) (thin space)

PPC (Fr.) *pour prendre congé*

PPE Philosophy, Politics, and Economics (Oxford degree subject)

p.p.m. parts per million

PPP Psychology, Philosophy, and Physiology (Oxford degree subject)

ppp (mus.) pianississimo (as softly as possible)

PPS Parliamentary *or* principal private secretary, *post-postscriptum* (further postscript)

PQ Parliamentary Question, previous (or preceding) question; Province of Quebec, Canada; (Fr.) Parti québécois (Quebec Party)

PR (Lat.) *Populus Romanus* (the Roman people), prize ring, Proportional Representation, Public Relations, Puerto Rico

Pr praseodymium (no point)

Pr. priest

pr. pair, -s; price

PRA President of the Royal Academy

praam a boat, *use* **pram**

Prachtausgabe (Ger. typ. f.) de luxe edition

practicable that can be done or used, possible in practice; *see also* **impracticable**

practical of, concerned with, or suited to practice or use rather than theory; *see also* **impractical, unpractical**

practice (noun, in US also verb)

practise (verb)

Practising Law Institute US legal publishers, *not* -cing

Prado a Madrid art gallery; cf. **Pardo Palace**

praecipe (law) a writ demanding action or an explanation of non-action, an order requesting a writ (ital., roman in US)

praemunire (hist.) a sheriff's writ concerned with papal jurisdiction (not ital.)

praenomen a Roman first name, *not* pren-

praepostor a school prefect; *not* prep-, -itor

praeses *use* **pre-**

praesidium *use* **pres-**

Praeterita Ruskin's (unfinished) autobiography, 1889

praetor/ a Roman magistrate, **-ian**; *not* pre-

Praga a suburb of Warsaw; It. for **Prague**

Prague the Czech Republic; Eng. and Fr. for Czech **Praha**; in Ger. **Prag**

prahu *use* **proa**

Prakrit any of the (esp. ancient or medieval) vernacular dialects of N. and Cent. India

pram a perambulator; a flat-bottomed gunboat or Baltic cargo boat, a Scandinavian ship's dinghy; *not* praam

praseodymium symbol **Pr**

Prayer Book (caps., two words) abbr. **PB**

Prayer of Manasses (Apocr.) abbr. **Pr. of Man.**

PRB Pre-Raphaelite Brotherhood (group of artists), 1848

pre-adam/ic, -ite (hyphens, not cap.)

pre-adolescent (hyphen, one word in US)

preamplifier (one word)

Préault, Antoine Auguste (1809–79) French sculptor

preb. prebend, -ary

prec. preceding, precentor

Precambrian (geol.) (of or relating to) the earliest era of geological time

precede *not* -eed

precent/or a controller of cathedral music, f. **-rix**; abbr. **prec.**

precept/or teacher, f. **-ress**

preces (Lat.) prayers

precession (astr.) the successively earlier occurrence (of the equinoxes), (dyn.) the rotation of the axis of a spinning body about another body

pre-Christian (hyphen, cap. C)

Précieuses ridicules, Les a play by Molière, 1659

précieu/x (Fr.) an affected man, f. **-se**

precipitate hasty

precipitous steep

précis/ (to write) a summary, pl. same (not ital.); as verb **-ed, -ing**

precisian one who is rigidly precise, esp. in religious observance, (hist., in hostile sense) a Puritan

precisionist one who makes a practice of precision

preclassical (one word)

pre-Columbian (hyphen, cap. *C*)

preconce/ive, -ption (one word)

precursor forerunner, *not* -er

pred. predicative, -ly

pre-dat/e, -ed, -ing (hyphen, one word in US)

predecease (noun and verb, one word)

predicant a preacher, esp. Dominican

predictor *not* -er

predikant (Afrik.) a preacher of the Dutch Reformed Church, esp. in S. Africa

predilection partiality

predispos/e, -ition (one word)

pre-echo/, -ing (hyphens, one word in US)

pre-elect/, -ion (hyphens, one word in US)

pre-eminen/t, -ce (hyphens, one word in US)

pre-empt/, -ion, -ive (hyphens, one word in US)

pre-exilic prior to exile of Jews in Babylon (hyphen, one word in US)

pre-exist/, -ence (hyphens, one word in US)

pref. preface, preference, preferred; prefix, -ed

prefab (colloq.) a prefabricated building (no point)

prefabricate (one word)

preface an introductory address to the reader in which the author explains the purpose, prospective readership, and scope of the book and may include a brief acknowledgement to colleagues or advisers in the absence of an acknowledgements section; abbr. **pref.**

préfecture/ (Fr. f.) the county hall in a French town, **— de police** office of the commissioner of police

prefer/, -able, -ably, -ence, -red -ring; abbr. **pref.**

préfet (Fr. m.) prefect

prefix/, -ed abbr. **pref.**

pre/form, -frontal, -heat, -historic (one word)

Preignac a white wine

prejudge/, -ment (one word), *not* prejudgment (US)

prelim. preliminary

preliminary matter (typ.) all matter preceding the main text; (colloq.) **prelims**

pre-makeready (typ.) careful preparation of the forme before it goes to the machine

pre/marital, -menstrual (one word)

premier/ (short for **— minister**) the first or chief minister (of a country or institution), esp. the first minister of the Crown (= **Prime Minister**); (Austral. and Canadian) the chief minister of a state or province, or (US obs.) the Secretary of State

premi/er (Fr.) f. **-ère** first; abbrs. **1er, 1ère**

premiere/ (give) the first performance of a film or play; as verb, **-d** (not ital., no accent)

première danseuse (Fr. f.) the principal female dancer in a ballet

premise (verb) say or write by way of introduction, or (logic) create or apply a premiss

premises (noun, pl.) a house or building with its grounds and appurtenances; (law) the houses, lands, or tenements previously specified in a document or the like

premiss/ a previous statement from which another is inferred or follows as a conclusion, a proposition; pl. **-es**; *also* **premise**

premium/ abbr. **pm.**, pl. **-s**

premolar a tooth, abbr. **pm.**

Premonstratensian (hist.) (of or relating to) (a member of) an order of regular canons founded at Prémontré in France in 1120, or the corresponding order of nuns

prenomen *use* **prae-**

preoccup/y, -ation (one word)

preordain (one word)

prep/ (colloq. Brit.) the preparation of school work by a pupil, the period when this is done; (colloq. US) (as or like) a student in a preparatory school, *see also* **preppy**

prep. preparat/ion, -ory; preposition

pre/paid, -pay (one word)

preparatory school a usually private school preparing pupils for a higher school, or (US) for college or university (= **public school**)

prepositor *use* **praepost-**

prepossess (one word)

preppy (US colloq.) (of or concerning) a person attending a private school, with conservative clothes and outlook; *not* -ie

pre-prandial (hyphen)

pre-preference ranking before preference shares (hyphen, one word in US)

Pre-Raphaelite/ (caps., hyphen), **— Brotherhood** abbr. **PRB**

prerequisite (one word)

Pres. president

Pres, Josquin des *see* **Josquin des Prez**

présalé (Fr. m.) salt-marsh sheep or mutton (one word), pl. **prés-salés** (hyphen)

Presb. Presbyterian

presbyop/ia a failing of near sight in the elderly, **-ic**

Presbyterian (cap.) abbr. **Presb.**

prescribable *not* -eable

prescribe advise the use of, recommend, lay down or impose authoritatively; cf. **proscribe**

pre-select/, -ive, -or *not* -er (hyphens)

Preseli a district of Dyfed

present author, the *prefer* **I** *or* **me**

presentiment a vague expectation or foreboding

presently soon, after a short time; *also* (esp. US and Sc.) immediately, at the present time

presentment the act of presenting information

preses (Sc.) a president or chairman, pl. same; *not* prae-

preset (one word)

pre-shrunk (hyphen)

president abbr. **P., Pres.**

presidium a standing executive committee in a Communist country, esp. in the former USSR; *not* prae-

Presocratic (philos.) prior to Socrates, *not* pre-Socratic (US)

press, the newspapers, journalists, etc., generally or collectively (not cap.); a specific printing establishment or publishing company, with or without the organization's full name: 'Athlone Press', 'the (Oxford University) Press' (cap.)

press agent (two words)

Press Association abbr. **PA**

press box a shelter for reporters at outdoor functions (two words)

press-button (hyphen)

press conference (two words)

Pressensé, Edmond Dehaut de (1824–91) French theologian and statesman

press gallery esp. in House of Commons (two words)

press-gang (hyphen)

pressman (one word)

pressmark that which shows the place of a book in a library (one word), *now usually* **shelf mark**

press-proof (typ.) the last one examined before platemaking or going to press (hyphen)

press stud (two words), colloq. known as *popper* in Britain and *snap* in the USA

press-up (hyphen)

pressure (mech.) symbol *p*

pressurize produce or maintain pressure (in something); in abstract senses *use* **pressure**

presswork (typ.) the preparation for and control of the printing-off of composed material; the work thus produced

Presteigne Powys

Prester John a mythical medieval priest-king of Cent. Asia or Abyssinia; a novel by John Buchan, 1910 (ital.)

prestissimo (mus.) very quickly

presto (mus.) quickly

Prestonpans Lothian (one word)

prestressed (hyphen)

Prestwich Gr. Manchester

Prestwick Northumb., Strathclyde

presum/e, -able, -ably, -ing

presumptive giving grounds for an inference from known facts; *see also* **heir presumptive**

presumptuous unduly or overbearingly confident and presuming

presuppos/e, -ition (one word)

pret. preterite

prêt-à-porter (Fr. m.) ready-to-wear (clothes)

pre/-tax, -teen (hyphen, one word in US)

pretence *not* -se (US)

preten/sion, -tious

preterite the past tense, *not* -it; abbr. **pret.**

preternatural etc. (one word)

pretor *use* prae-

pretzel a crisp knot- or stick-shaped salted biscuit or bread, *not* br-

Preussen Ger. for Prussia

preux chevalier (Fr. m.) a brave knight

prevail/, -ed, -ing

prevaricate speak or act evasively or misleadingly, quibble or equivocate; cf. **procrastinate**

preventive *not* -tative, -titive

previous abbr. **prev.**

Prévost, Marcel (1862–1941) French novelist

Prévost d'Exiles, Antoine François (1679–1765) French novelist, known as **Abbé Prévost**

prévôt (Fr. m.) provost

prevue *use* **preview**

pre-war use only as adj., not adv. (hyphen, one word in US)

Prez, Josquin des *see* **Josquin des Prez**

PRI *Partido Revolucionario Institucional* (Mexican governing party), President of the Royal Institute of Painters in Water Colours

PRIBA President of the Royal Institute of British Architects

Pribilof Island Bering Sea

price abbr. **pr.**

price-fixing (hyphen)

price/ list, ring (two words)

prices current abbr. **p/c**

price tag (two words)

pricey *not* -cy

prie-dieu a kneeling stool (hyphen, not ital.)

priest abbr. **Pr.**

prig/, -gery, -gish, -gism

prim. primary, primate, primitive

prima (typ.) the page of copy on which a new batch of proof begins; also a mark on copy where this begins or where reading is to be resumed after interruption; pron. 'prī-ma'

prima/ ballerina pl. — **ballerinas**, — **donna** pl. — **donnas** (not ital.)

primaeval *use* **prime-**

prima facie (adv., adj., no hyphen, not ital.)

Primate of/ All England the Archbishop of Canterbury, — — **England** the Archbishop of York

prime/ (math.) symbol ', **double** — symbol ''; a fencing position

Prime Minister (two words, caps.) abbr. **PM**

primeval of the first age of the world, *not* -aeval

primigravid/a a woman in her first pregnancy, pl. **-ae**

primipar/a a woman bearing her first child, pl. **-ae**

primitive abbr. **prim.**

primo/ (mus.) the upper part in a duet, pl. **-s**

primo (Lat.) in the first place, abbr. **1°**

primum mobile (Lat.) the central or most important source of motion or action

Primus (propr.) a portable stove (cap.)

primus the presiding bishop of the Scottish Episcopal Church

primus/ (Lat.) first, abbr. **p.**; — *inter pares* first among equals

prin. principal

prince abbr. **P.**; **Prince of/ Glory**, — — **Life**, *or* — — **Peace** as Deity (caps.)

Prince of Wales/ abbr. **POW**, — — — **Island** off Penang

princeps (Lat.) the first, pl. *principes*; *see also* *editio princeps*

Princes Town Trinidad

Princeton town and university, NJ

Princetown Devon, Mid Glam.

principal (adj.) chief; (noun) the chief person (cap. as title of an office); abbr. **prin.**

principe (Fr. m.) principle

principe (Sp. m.) a Spanish crown prince (not ital., cap. as title); cf. **infante**

Principe, Il (It.) Machiavelli's *The Prince*

principessa (It. f.) an Italian princess (cap., not ital., as title)

principle a fundamental truth, moral basis

print. printing

print/, in still on sale; **out of** — new copies no longer obtainable, abbr. **o.p., o/p**

printani/er (Fr. cook.) f. **-ère** with early spring vegetables

printer abbr. **pr.**; **the King's**, *or* **Queen's, Printer/ of Bibles and Prayer Books** may print bibles (AV) and prayer books (1662) to the exclusion of all other English presses, except those of the universities of Oxford and Cambridge; — — — **of the Acts of Parliament** has the duty of providing an authoritative printing of all Acts of Parliament etc., and controls their copyright

printer's error pl. **print/er's**, *or* **-ers', errors** (use hyphen to avoid ambiguity: *bad printers'-errors*)

printing abbr. **ptg.**, **print.**

print/maker, -out, -works (one word)

Prinz/ (Ger. m.) prince (usually of the blood royal), pl. **-en**; f. **-essin** pl. **-essinnen** (cap., not ital., as part of title); cf. *Fürst*

prise force open, *not* -ize (US)

prisonbreak, -er (one word)

Prisoner's Dilemma in game theory, a non-zero-sum game invented by A. W. Tucker (caps.), *not* Prisoners' —

pristine in its original condition, unspoilt, *not* a synonym for spotless

priv. privative

privat-docent (hist.) a German university lecturer paid only by students' fees, abbr. **PD**; in Ger. m. *Privatdozent*

Private (mil.) cap. as title, abbr. **Pte.**

privative denoting the loss or absence of something, esp. in grammar; abbr. **priv.**

privileg/e, -ed

priv/y secret, **-ily, -ity** (law) a recognized relation between two parties, e.g. that of blood, lease, or service

Privy Coun/cil, -sellor (two words, caps.) abbr. **PC**

Privy Seal abbr. **PS**

prix/ (Fr. m.) prize, price; — *fixe* fixed price

prize force open, *use* **-ise** (except in US)

prize/fight, -fighter (one word)

prize-giving (hyphen, two words in US)

prize/ money, — ring (two words)

prize/winner, -winning (one word)

p.r.n. *pro re nata* (as occasion may require)

PRO Public Record Office, Public Relations Officer

pro/ for, abbr. **p.**; (colloq.) professional, pl. **-s** (no point)

proa a Malay outrigged boat, *not* the many variants

proactive creating or controlling a situation by taking the initiative (one word)

pro-am involving professionals and amateurs (no points, hyphen)

pro and con for and against, pl. **pros and cons** (not ital., no points)

prob. probab/le, -ly; problem

probit (statistics) a unit of probability based on deviation from the mean of a standard distribution

probity uprightness, honesty

pro bono publico (Lat.) for the public good

probosci/s a long flexible trunk or snout, pl. **-ses**; *properly* **-des**

Proc. proceedings, proctor

proceed *not* -ede

procès (Fr. m.) lawsuit

process blocks (typ.) those made by photographic and etching processes, for printing illustrations by letterpress

procès-verb/al a written report, minutes; pl. **-aux** (not ital.)

proconsul (one word)

procrastinate defer action, be dilatory; cf. **prevaricate**

Procrustean using force to impose conformity, like Procrustes (Gr. myth.) (cap.)

Procter,/ Adelaide Anne (1825–64) English poet; — **Bryan Waller** *not* Walter (1787–1874) pseud. **Barry Cornwall**, English poet

Proctor, Richard Anthony (1837–88) British astronomer

proctor a university official, an attorney in spiritual courts; abbr. **Proc.**; **King's**, *or* **Queen's**, **Proctor** an official who can intervene in divorce cases

procurator-fiscal a Scottish law officer (not cap., hyphen), abbr. **PF**

prodrome a preliminary treatise or symptom, *not* -dromus

producible *not* -able

product (math.) symbol Π

proem/ a preface or preamble, **-ial**

pro et contra (Lat.) for and against; *see also* **pro and con**

Prof. Professor, pl. **Profs.**, *but* spell out before name (except in narrow measure)

profane secular, irreverent, blasphemous

Professeur (Fr. m.) professor (masculine regardless of the person)

professoriate *not* -orate

proffer/, -ed, -ing

profit/, -ed, -ing

profiterole a confection of choux pastry and sweet filling (not ital.)

Pr. of Man. Prayer of Manasses

pro forma/ (adv. and adj.) (done) as a matter of form, (noun) an invoice sent in advance of goods supplied (in full — — **invoice**); pl. **-s**

progr/amme *but* **-am** (noun and verb) in computing and in US

pro hac vice (Lat.) on this occasion (only), *not* hâc

Prohibition the prevention by law of the manufacture and sale of alcohol, esp. in the USA 1920–33 (cap.)

projector *not* -er

Prokofiev, Sergei (**Sergeevich**) (1891–1953) Russian composer

prolegomen/a preliminary remarks, sing. (rare) **-on**; **-ary, -ous**

proleps/is anticipation, esp. of adjectives in grammar; pl. **-es**

proletari/at the poorest class in a community, *not* -ate; **-an, -anize** *not* -ise

PROLOG (comput.) a programming language (caps. or even small caps.), *also* **Prolog**

prologize deliver a prologue; *not* -ise, -uize

prologue *not* -og

PROM (comput.) programmable read-only memory (caps. or even small caps.)

prom a paved public walk along seafront; (US) a school or university ball or dance, a promenade concert, esp. (Brit.) **The Proms** the Henry Wood Promenade Concerts

prom. promontory

Promethean of or like Prometheus (Gr. myth.)

promethium symbol **Pm**

promissory note abbr. **p.n.**

promoter one who or that which promotes, *not* -or

pron. pronominal, pronoun, pronounced, pronunciation

proneur flatterer, in Fr. *prôneur*

pronoun abbr. **pron.**

pronounc/e, -eable, -ed, -ement, -ing abbr. **pron.**

pronunciamento/ a manifesto, pl. **-s** (not ital.)

pronunciamiento (Sp.) a revolt, insurrection, coup

pronunciation *not* -nounc-

proof errors *see* **errors** (**on proof**)

proofread/, -er, -ing (one word, *but* sometimes hyphenated esp. as verb)

Prop. Propertius

prop (colloq.) (stage) property, propeller (no point)

prop. proposition

propagand/a an activity for the spread of a doctrine or practice, is *singular*; **-ize**, *not* -ise; **-ism, -ist**

proparoxytone (Gr. gram.) (a word) with acute accent on last syllable but two

pro patria (Lat.) for one's country

propel/, -led, -ler, -ling

propell/ant (noun), **-ent** (adj.)

properispomen/on (Gr. gram.) (a word) with circumflex on penultimate syllable, pl. **-a**

Propertius, Sextus (*c.*50–*c.*14 BC) Roman poet, abbr. **Prop.**

prophe/cy (noun), **-sy** (verb)

proportional (math.) symbol ∝

proposition abbr. **prop.**

Proprietary (Austral., NZ, S. Afr.) after name of company, abbr. **Pty.**

proprio motu (Lat.) of his, *or* her, own accord

propter hoc (Lat.) because of this; *see also* ***post hoc***

propylae/um (Lat. from Gr.) the entrance to a temple, pl. **-a**; **Propylaea** the entrance to the Acropolis at Athens (pl., cap.)

propylon/ (Gr.) the entrance to a temple, pl. **-s**

pro rata in proportion (not ital.)

prorate allocate or distribute pro rata (one word, not ital.)

pro re nata as occasion may require (ital.), abbr. **p.r.n.**

pros. prosody

prosceni/um the front part of the stage, pl. **-ums**

proscribe banish; cf. **prescribe**

proselyt/e a religious convert; **-ize** to convert, *not* -ise

prosit! (Lat. and Ger.) your good health!; *see also* ***prost!***

prosod/y the laws of poetic metre, abbr. **pros.**; -ic, -ist

prosopograph/y a description of a person's appearance, personality, social and family connections, career, etc., or the study of such descriptions (esp. in Rom. hist.); **-er, -ical**

prosopopoeia (rhet.) the introduction of pretended speaker

prospector *not* -er

prospectus/ pl. **-es**

prost! (Ger.) your good health! (standard form); *see also* ***prosit!***

prostate a gland surrounding the neck of the bladder in male mammals

prostrate lying face downwards or horizontally

pros/y commonplace, *not* -ey; **-ily**

Prot. Protectorate, Protestant

protactinium symbol **Pa**

protagonist the leading character in a play, novel, or cause (*not* the opp. of antagonist)

pro tanto (Lat.) to that extent

protean assuming different shapes, like Proteus (Gr. myth.); *not* -ian

protector *not* -er

Protectorate abbr. **Prot.**

protég/é one under the protection of a patron, f. **-ée**; pl. **-és**, **-ées** (not ital.)

pro tempore (Lat.) for the time being (not ital. in US), (colloq.) **pro tem** (no point, not ital.); abbr. **p.t.**

Proterozoic (geol.) (of or relating to) the later part of the Precambrian era; in US *also* **Algonkian**

Protestant/ abbr. **Prot.**; **-ism** (cap.)

protester *not* -or

'Prothalamion' a poem by Spenser, 1596

protocol/, **-led**, **-ling**

protonotary a chief clerk, esp. to some law courts; *not* protho-

prototype an original model

protozo/on a single-cell form of life, pl. **-a** (not ital., cap. as grouping of phyla); **-al, -ic**

protractor a drawing instrument, *not* -er

Proudhon, Pierre Joseph (1809–65) French socialist

Prov. Proven/ce, -çal; Proverbs, Province, Provost

prov. proverbially, provincial, provisional

prov/e, -able, -ed, lit., Sc., and US **-en**

proven, not (Sc. law) a verdict pronouncing evidence insufficient to determine guilt or innocence

provenance (place of) origin (not ital.), *not* -venience

Provençal/ (of or relating to) the region of Provence in SE France; a native of Provence, or the language spoken there; **Old —** a medieval form of Provençal

provençale, à la (Fr. cook.) with garlic or onions (not cap.)

Provence SE France (no cedilla), abbr. **Prov.**

provenience *use* **-nance**

Proverbs (OT) abbr. **Prov.**

provinc/e abbr. **Prov.**; **-ial** abbr. **prov.**

Province of Quebec Canada, abbr. **PQ**

Provincetown Mass.

proviso/ a stipulation, pl. **-s** (not ital.)

Provo/ a member of the Provisional IRA; pl. **-s**

Provost/ abbr. **Prov.**, **— Marshal** (caps., two words) abbr. **PM**

proxime/ accessit (Lat.) he, *or* she, came nearest (to winning a prize etc.) abbr. *prox. acc.*; pl. **— accesserunt**

proximo in, *or* of, the next month; do not abbr.

PRS Performing Rights Society, President of the Royal Society

PRSA President of the Royal Scottish Academy

PRSE President of the Royal Society of Edinburgh

Prudhomme/ divide Pru|dhomme; *see also* **Sully —**

prud'homme (Fr. m.) *formerly* good and true man; *now* expert, umpire

Prufrock, J. Alfred in T. S. Eliot's 'The Love Song of J. Alfred Prufrock', 1915

prunella a throat affliction; a strong silk or worsted material; a plant (as genus name, cap. and ital.)

Pruss. Prussia, -n

PS permanent secretary, Police Sergeant (*see also* **police constable**), *postscriptum* (postscript) (pl. **PSS**), private secretary, Privy Seal, (theat.) prompt side

Ps. Psalm

p.s. police sergeant

PSA President of the Society of Antiquaries

Psalm/ abbr. **Ps.**, pl. **-s** abbr. **Pss.**, **Book of Psalms** (OT) abbr. **Ps.**

psalm-book a book containing the Psalms (not cap., hyphen, one word in US)

psalmist the author of a psalm (not cap.); **the — David** or the author of any of the Psalms (cap.)

psalter the Book of Psalms (not cap.); a specific version of this (cap.)

psaltery an ancient and medieval plucked instrument

p's and q's (apos., no points) *or* **ps and qs**

PSBR public sector borrowing requirement

psepholog/y the study of patterns in voting; **-ical, -ist**

pseud (colloq.) (an) intellectually or socially pretentious (person) (no point)

pseud. pseudonym (full point)

pseudepigraph/a (pl.) **-ic, -ical**

pseudo/ pretentious or insincere (person), pl. **-s**

pseudonym an assumed name, abbr. **pseud.**

pseudo/science, -scientific (one word)

pshaw! an exclamation; *not* psha, -h

psi the twenty-third letter of the Gr. alphabet (Ψ, ψ), the lower-case form is used to denote parapsychological factors

p.s.i. pounds per square inch

p.s.i.g. pounds per square inch gauge

psilocybin a hallucinogenic alkaloid found in some mushrooms

psittac/ine of or related to parrots, parrot-like; **-osis** a contagious disease transmissible from birds to humans

PSS *postscripta* (postscripts) (no point)

Pss. *see* **Psalm**

PST (US) Pacific Standard Time

PSV public service vehicle

psych. psychic, -al

psychedelic *not* psycho-

psycho/ (colloq.) psychotic (person), pl. **-s**

psychoanaly/sis, -se, -st, -tic, -tical (one word)

psycho/babble, -drama, -dynamics (one word)

psychokinesis movement by psychic agency, abbr. **PK**

psychol. psycholog/y, -ical

psycho/sis pl. **-ses**, adj. **-tic**

psychotherapy (one word)

PT physical training, post town, pupil teacher

Pt platinum (no point)

Pt. (geog.) Point, Port

pt. part, payment; pint, -s; (math., typ.) point

p.t. (Lat.) *pro tempore* (for the time being)

PTA Parent–Teacher Association, Passenger Transport Authority

pta. peseta

Ptah (Egyptian myth.) the creator of the world

Pte. (mil.) Private

pterodactyl *not* -le

ptg. printing

ptisan a medicated or nourishing drink, esp. of barley water; cf. **tisane**

PTO please turn over, Public Trustee Office

Ptolemaic (hist.) of or relating to **Claudius Ptolemy** (*c.* AD 100–70) Alexandrian astronomer, or his theories; of or relating to the **Ptolemies**, a dynasty of Macedonian rulers of Egypt 323–30 BC

Pty. (Austral., NZ, S. Afr.) Proprietary (company) = **Ltd**

Pu plutonium (no point)

pub/ (colloq.) a public house, (Austral.) a hotel; **— crawl** (two words)

pub./ public, -an; publish, -ed, -er, -ing; **— doc.** public document

public address/, — — system (no hyphen even when attrib.; hyphen in US in all uses), abbr. **PA**

publican the keeper of a public house, (Austral.) the keeper of a hotel

public house (two words)

publicity agent (two words)

publicize *not* -ise

Public Lending Right the right of authors to payment when their work is lent by public libraries, based on an estimate drawn from a pool of libraries; abbr. **PLR**

public limited company abbr. **plc**, **PLC**

public school (Brit.) a private fee-paying secondary school, esp. for boarders; (US, Austral., Sc., etc.) any non-fee-paying school (two words)

publish/, -ed, -er, -ing abbr. **pub.**

Publishers Association/ (no apos.) abbr. **PA**; **Scottish — —** abbr. **SPA**

publisher's/ binding (bibliog.) the standard binding in which an edition is supplied to booksellers, **— imprint** *see* **imprint**

pucka *use* **pukka**

Pudd'nhead Wilson, The Tragedy of a novel by Mark Twain, 1894

pudend/um usually pl. **-a**, genitals (usually female)

Puebla Mexico

Pueblo Col.

pueblo/ a town or village in Spain or Latin America, pl. **-s**

Pueblo Indians any of the Native American tribes of SW USA, esp. the Hopi and Zuni

Puerto/ Bello Panama; — **Rico** W. Indian island, adj. — **Rican**; *not* Porto-

puff adder (two words)

puffball (one word)

puff pastry (two words)

pug/ dog, — nose(**d**) (two words); **-gish, -gy**

puggaree an Indian turban, hat-scarf; *not* the many variants

Pugwash/ NS, Canada; site of the first — **Conference**

puîn/é (Fr.) f. **-ée** younger, opp. to **aîné** senior

puisne (law) subsequent (to)

puja a Hindu rite of worship, a prayer; *not* poo-

pukka *not* puck-, -ah; *see also* **sahib**

pul/e to whine, **-ing**

Pulitzer/, Joseph (1847–1911) US journalist, endowed thirteen — **Prizes** for various genres of literature, journalism, and music

pull (typ.) a proof

Pullman a railway carriage or motor coach (cap.)

pull-out (something) that pulls out (hyphen, one word in US)

pullover a knitted garment (one word)

pull-up (hyphen)

pulque a Mexican fermented drink made from the sap of the maguey

pulsar (astr.) a source of pulsating radio signals

pulse-rate (hyphen)

pulsimeter a pulse measurer

Pulsometer (propr.) a pumping engine

pulverize *not* -ise

pumelo *use* pom-

pumice/, — stone (two words); **-ous**

pummel/ pound with the fists; **-led, -ling** (one *l* in US); cf. **pommel**

pummelo *use* pomelo

pump a light shoe, a plimsoll; (US) = **court shoe**

pumpernickel a black rye bread

Punchinello (cap.) the principal character in an Italian puppet show, hence **Punch** (no point)

punctatim (Lat.) point for point

punctilio/ (scrupulous observance of) a point of behaviour, pl. **-s**; adj. **-us**

punctus/ (Lat.) a point, pl. same; (in MSS) — **elevat/us** : (like an inverted semicolon), pl. — **-i**; — **interrogativ/us** ? (like a question mark), pl. — **-i**; — **vers/us** ; (like a semicolon), pl. — **-i**

pundit a Hindu sage, (gen.) an expert; in Hind. *paṇḍit*; *see also* **pandit**

Pune India, *also* (esp. hist.) **Poona**

Punica fides (Lat.) Punic faith, treachery

Punjab/ India and Pakistan; *not* -aub; **-i** (of or relating to) (a native) of Punjab, *not* -bee; *see also* **Panjabi**

punkah (Anglo-Ind.) a large fan, *not* -a

Punkt (Ger. typ. m.) point, dot, a full stop (cap.); **punktieren** to point, dot, or punctuate; **Punktierung** (f.) punctuation

PUO (med.) pyrexia (fever) of unknown origin

pup/a (zool.) a chrysalis, pl. **-ae** (not ital.)

pupillage (two ls)

puppy love (US) = **calf love**

pur *use* **purr**

-pur (Ind.) a city, as Nagpur, Kanpur

Puran/a any of a class of Sanskrit sacred writings on Hindu mythology, folklore, etc.; **-ic**

Purchas, Samuel (1577–1626) English compiler of voyages

purchas/able *not* -eable, **-er** *not* -or

purdah (Ind.) (a curtain for) seclusion of women of rank, *not* -a

purée pulped vegetables etc. (no accent in US)

purgatory (not cap.)

Purim a Jewish spring festival commemorating the defeat of Haman's plot to massacre the Jews (Esther 9)

puritan/ one strict in religion or morals (cap. in hist. use); **-ical, -ism, -ize** *not* -ise

purl in knitting, *not* pearl

Purleigh Essex

Purley Berks., London

purlieus surroundings, a person's bounds or limits

Purple Heart (US) a decoration for those wounded in action

purpose/, -ful, -less, -ly

purpure (her.) purple

purr (verb, noun), *not* pur

pur sang (Fr. m.) pure blood; (adj.) thoroughbred, total

purslane (bot.) a salad herb, *not* -lain

pursuivant (Brit.) an officer of the College of Arms ranking below a herald, (arch.) a follower or attendant

purveyor one whose business is to supply (food), *not* -er

push-bike (hyphen)

push-button (hyphen; as noun, two words in US)

push/cart, -chair (one word)

pushover (colloq.) something that is easily done; someone who can easily be overcome, persuaded, etc. (one word)

pushrod (one word)

Pushto, Pushtu *use* **Pashto**

pushup (US) = **press-up**

put in golf, *use* **putt**

put over make acceptable or effective, express in an understandable way; also (US) postpone, achieve by deceit

putre/fy go rotten, *not* -ify; **-scent** in the process of rotting; **-scible** liable to rot

putsch a revolutionary attempt (not cap.), in (Swiss) Ger. m. *Putsch*

putt in golf, *not* put

puttees strips of cloth worn round the lower leg for protection, *not* -ies

putt/o (It.) a figure of a child in Renaissance art, pl. **-i**

Puy-de-Dôme a dép. of France (hyphens, two caps.); in phrases, *puy* (Fr. m.) a volcanic plug, to have lower-case *p* and no hyphens, as *le puy de Dôme*

PVC polyvinyl chloride

Pwllheli Gwynedd

PWR pressurized water reactor

pwt pennyweight, *use* **dwt.**

Pwyll (Welsh myth.) a prince of Dyfed and 'Head of Hades'

pyaemia (med.) a type of blood poisoning, *not* pyem- (US)

pycnic (anthrop.) *use* pyk-

pye (typ.) *use* **pie**

pyebald *use* **pie-**

pye-dog a vagrant mongrel, esp. in Asia; *not* pi-, pie-

pygm/y *not* pig-, **-aean** *not* -ean

pyjamas *not* pa- (US)

pyknic (anthrop.) (a person) of short, squat stature; *not* pyc-

Pylon School the nickname for a group of 1930s poets including Auden, Day-Lewis, Mac-Neice, and Spender

Pym,/ Barbara (**Mary Compton**) (1913–1980) English novelist, **— John** (1584–1643) English statesman

Pynchon, Thomas (b. 1937) US novelist

Pyongyang N. Korea

pyorrhoea a periodontal disease, or any discharge of pus; *not* -hea (US)

Pyrenees Mountains France and Spain

Pyrénées/-Atlantiques, Hautes- —, — -Orientales déps. of France

Pyrex (propr.) (cap.)

pyrit/es (in full **iron pyrites**) **-ic**; **-iferous**; **-ize** *not* -ise; **-ous**

pyro/lysis decomposition from heat, pl. **-lyses**; **-lyse** *not* -lyze

pyrotechnics abbr. **pyrotech.**

pyrrhic/ dance an ancient Greek war dance; **— foot** (prosody) a foot of two short syllables; **— victory** one won at too great a cost, like that of **Pyrrhus**, King of Epirus, over the Romans in 279 BC

Pyrrhon/ (*c.*300 BC) Greek sceptic philosopher, **-ism**

Pytchley Hunt, the

Pythagor/as (*c.*580–*c.*500 BC) Greek philosopher and mathematician, formulated **-as' theorem**; **-ean**

Pythian of or relating to Delphi (in Cent. Greece) or its ancient oracle of Apollo

python any of several non-venomous constricting snakes

pythoness the Pythian priestess, a witch

pyx/ (eccl.) the vessel in which the consecrated bread of the Eucharist is kept; a box at the Royal Mint in which specimen gold and silver coins are deposited to be tested annually, the **trial of the —**; *not* pix (not cap.)

Qq

Q quartermaster, Quarto (Shakespeare etc.), Queen('s), (chess) queen (no point), question, the sixteenth in a series

Q. pseud. of Sir Arthur Thomas Quiller-Couch

q. quaere, query, quintal; quire, -s; (meteor.) squalls

QAB Queen Anne's Bounty

Qaddafi, Muammar (Muhammad al-) (b. 1942) Libyan leader 1969– ; *use* Qaddāfī in specialist texts; *not* Gadafi, Gadhdhafi, Qadafy, Gaddafi (though preferred by *The Times*), Gadaffi

Qaisar-i-Hind *use* **K-**

Qantas Queensland and Northern Territory Aerial Service (Australian airline), *not* Qu-

QARANC Queen Alexandra's Royal Army Nursing Corps

QARNNS Queen Alexandra's Royal Naval Nursing Service

Qatar/ Persian Gulf, adj. **-i**

QB Queen's Bench, (chess) queen's bishop

QBD Queen's Bench Division

Q-boat (First World War) a merchant vessel with concealed guns

QBP (chess) queen's bishop's pawn

QC Queen's, *or* Queens', College; Queen's Counsel (title follows name, separated by a comma)

q.e. *quod est* (which is)

QED *quod erat demonstrandum* (which was to be demonstrated)

QEF *quod erat faciendum* (which was to be done)

QEI *quod erat inveniendum* (which was to be found out)

QF quick-firing

qibla *see* **kiblah**

QKt (chess) queen's knight, **QKtP** queen's knight's pawn

q.l. *quantum libet* (as much as you please)

Qld Queensland (no point)

QM Quartermaster

q.m. *quomodo* (by what means)

QMC Queen Mary College, London

Q.Mess. Queen's Messenger

QMG Quartermaster General

QMS Quartermaster Sergeant

QN (chess) queen's knight

QNP queen's knight's pawn

Qom a river, city, and former province, Cent. Iran (common spelling); **Qum** is a more exact transcription, **Ghom** reflects Pers. pronunciation

QP (chess) queen's pawn

q.pl. *quantum placet* (as much as seems good)

QPM Queen's Police Medal

QPR Queen's Park Rangers football club

qq.v. *quae vide* (which see) (refers to pl.) (not ital.)

QR (chess) queen's rook

qr. quarter, quire

QRP (chess) queen's rook's pawn

qrs. quarters

QS quarter sessions, Queen's Scholar

q.s. *quantum sufficit* (as much as suffices)

QSO quasi-stellar object, quasar

qt. quantity; quart(s)

q.t. (colloq.) (on the) quiet

qu. question

qua in the capacity or character of; *not* -à, -â (not ital.)

quad (colloq.) quadrangle; quadraphony; a quadruplet; (typ.) in metal setting, a piece of spacing material; in photosetting, the action of spacing out a line; (paper) a size of printing paper four times (quadruple) the basic size (no point in any sense)

quad. quadrant

Quadragesima the first Sunday in Lent

quadrant a quarter of a circle's circumference, quarter of a sphere, etc.

quadraphon/y sound reproduction using four transmission channels; **-ic, -ically**; *not* quadri-, quadro-; (colloq.) **quad**

quadrat (ecology) a small area marked out for study, *not* -te

quadrate (esp. anat., zool.) (to make) (something) square or rectangular

quadrenni/um a period of four years; pl. **-ums**, **-a**; **-al**; *not* quadrie-

quadrillion a thousand raised to the fifth power, 10^{15}; *formerly* (esp. Brit.) a thousand raised to the eighth power, 10^{24}

quadriplegia *not* tetra-

quadrivium (hist.) a medieval university course of arithmetic, geometry, astronomy, and music; cf. **trivium**

quaere (Lat. imperative) inquire, (as noun) a question; abbr. **q.**

quaestor an ancient Roman magistrate; cf. **que-**

quae vide (Lat.) which see (refers to plural), abbr. **qq.v.**

quag/ a marshy or boggy place, **-gy**

quagga (S. Afr.) an extinct zebra-like animal

quahog any of various edible clams of the Atlantic coast of N. America, *not* -haug

quai (Fr. m.) quay, railway platform

quaich a Scots drinking vessel, *not* -gh; in Gaelic *cuach*

Quaid-e-Azam/ College of Commerce and Business Administration Peshawar, — **Library** Lahore

Quaid-i-Azam University Islamabad

Quai d'Orsay Paris, the French Foreign Office

Quaker a member of the Society of Friends

quand même (Fr.) notwithstanding, all the same

quango/ quasi non-governmental organization, pl. **-s**

quant (propel with) a punting pole with a prong at the bottom to prevent it sinking into the mud

quantile (statistics) *not* fractile

quantity abbr. **qt.**

quantize *not* -ise

quant/um (not ital.) a natural minimum quantity of an entity, pl. **-a**; *see also* **Planck**

quantum/ (Lat.) a concrete quantity, pl. *quanta*; — *libet* as much as you please, abbr. *q.l.*; — *meruit* as much as he, *or* she, deserved; — *placet* as much as seems good, abbr. *q.pl.*; — *sufficit* as much as suffices, abbr. *q.s.*, *quant. suff.*; — *vis* as much as you wish, abbr. *q.v.*

Qu'Appelle/ a river; **Bishop of —** Rupert's Land, Canada

Quarles, Francis (1592–1644) English poet

quarrel/, -led, -ler (*not* -lor), **-ling** (one *l* in US), **-some**

quart two pints (40 fl. oz, (US) 32 fl. oz), abbr. **qt.**; a sequence in piquet

quart. quarterly

Quart (Ger. n.) quarto (cap., not cap. if adj.)

quarte a position in fencing; *also* **quart**; *not* carte

quarter/, -s abbr. **qr., qrs.**

quarterback (one word)

quarter binding the spine in a different material from the rest of the case (two words), *but* **quarter-bound** (hyphen)

quarter day (two words)

quarterdeck (one word)

quarter-final (hyphen, one word in US)

Quarter Horse (caps.)

quarter-hour (hyphen)

quarter-light (hyphen)

quartermaster (one word) abbr. **QM, Q**; **Quartermaster/ General** (two words, caps.) abbr. **QMG**; — **Sergeant** (two words, caps.) abbr. **QMS**

quarter note (esp. US mus.) a crotchet

quarter-plate (hyphen)

quarter sessions (not caps.); abbr. **QS**

quarterstaff (hist.) a stout pole 6–8 feet long, formerly used as a weapon (one word)

quartet *not* -ette

quartier/ (Fr. cook. m.) quarter, — *d'agneau* quarter of lamb, *-général* military headquarters (hyphen), *Quartier Latin* the Latin Quarter of Paris (caps.)

quarto/ (typ.) a book based on four leaves, eight pages, to the sheet; pl. **-s**; abbr. **4to** (no point)

quasar a quasi-stellar object, abbr. **QSO**

quasi- a prefix with the sense 'seeming(ly)', 'almost'

Quasimodo/ the first Sunday after Easter (one word, cap.), a character in Hugo's *Notre-Dame de Paris*; —, **Salvatore** (1901–85) Italian poet

quass *use* **kvass**

quater/centenary (a celebration of) a four-hundredth anniversary, *not* quart-

quater-cousin *use* **cater-**

quaternary having four parts (not cap.); (geol.) (of or relating to) the most recent period in the Cenozoic era (cap.)

quatorzain any fourteen-line poem, an irregular sonnet

quatrain a stanza of four lines usually with alternate rhymes

Quatre-Bras battle, 1815

Quattrocento 1400–99, art and literature of the early Renaissance period (cap.)

quay a wharf, *not* key

QUB Queen's University, Belfast

Quebec/ Canada; abbr. **PQ, Que.**; adj. and noun **-ois**, pl. same; **Québécois** a French-speaking native or inhabitant, in Eng. **Quebecker** (cap.); **Parti québécois** Canadian political party (one cap.)

Quechua a S. American Indian language widely spoken in Peru and neighbouring countries, *not* Qui-

Queen abbr. **Q** (no point)

Queen Anne's Bounty formerly for augmenting Church of England livings (apos.), abbr. **QAB**

Queenborough Sheppey, Kent; *see also* **Queens-**

Queen Mary College London, *not* Mary's; abbr. **QMC**

Queen's abbr. **Q**

Queens a borough of New York City (no apos.)

Queensberry/ Rules the standard rules, esp. of boxing, named after **Sir John Sholto Douglas** (1844–1900) **8th Marquess of —**

Queensboro Bridge New York City, *not* -ough

Queensborough Co. Louth; *see also* **Queenb-**

Queensbury London, W. Yorks.

Queens College Charlotte, NC; Flushing, NY (no apos.)

Queen's College, The Oxford (named after one queen)

Queens' College Cambridge (named after two queens)

Queen's Counsel abbr. **QC**

Queen's County Ireland, *now* **Laois**

Queensland Australia, abbr. **Qld**

Queen's Printer *see* **printer**

Queen's University Belfast; Kingston, Ontario

queensware cream-coloured Wedgwood (one word)

Quelimane Mozambique

Quellen/**angabe** (Ger. f.) reference; **-forschung** (Ger. f.) source research, criticism (one word)

quelque chose (Fr. m.) some thing, a trifle

quenelle (cook.) a forcemeat ball (not ital.)

Quentin Durward a novel by Scott, 1823

¿Qué pasa? (Sp.) What's up? (turned question mark before, unturned after)

query abbr. **q.**, **qy**; sign ?

Quesnay, François (1694–1774) French economist

question/ abbr. **Q.**, **qu.**; **— mark** ?

questionnaire (two *n*s)

questor an official of the RC Church or French Assembly; cf. **quae-**

Quételet, Lambert Adolphe Jacques (1796–1874) Belgian mathematician and astronomer

Quetta Pakistan

quetzal a beautiful bird of Cent. America; the chief monetary unit in Guatemala

Quetzalcoatl the chief hero-god of the Toltecs and Aztecs

queu/e persons in line, to form this; **-ed**, **-ing**; *not* cue

queue/ (Fr. f.) tail, **— de bœuf** oxtail

quiche an open flan (not ital.)

Quichua *use* **Que-**

quick/-fire, -freeze (hyphens)

quicklime (one word)

quick march (two words)

quick/sand, -set, -silver -step, -thorn (one word)

quick time (two words)

quicumque vult (Lat.) whosoever will (be saved) (first words of the Athanasian Creed)

quid (Brit. sl.) one pound sterling, pl. same

quid (Lat.) that which a thing is

quidam (Lat.) an unknown person, pl. same

quiddity (philos.) the essence of a person or thing, what makes a thing what it is

quid pro quo something in return, an equivalent (not ital.)

¿Quién sabe? (Sp.) Who knows? (turned question mark before, unturned after)

quieten (Brit.) (verb tr. and intr., often followed by *down*) = (US) **quiet**

quietus death (not ital.)

Quijote de la Mancha, El ingenioso hidalgo don *see* Don Quixote

Quiller-Couch, Sir Arthur (**Thomas**) (1863–1944) English novelist and essayist (hyphen), pseud. **Q.**

quin (colloq.) for quintuplet (no point), *not* quint (except in US)

quincentenary (a celebration of) a five-hundredth anniversary (one word), *not* -centennial

quincun/x five arranged as on dice, pl. **-xes**; **-cial**

quinine a medicine, *not* -in

Quinquagesima the Sunday before Lent

quinquenni/um a period of five years; pl. **-ums**, **-a**; **-al** lasting for, *or* occurring every, five years; the word's ambiguity makes a more specific wording preferable

quinquereme an ancient Roman galley with five files of oarsmen on each side

quins/y tonsillitis; *not* -cy, -sey, -zy; **-ied**

quint a sequence of five cards in piquet, (US) = **quin**; cf. **quinte**

quint/al *not* kentle, kintle; pl. **-als** (in Fr. **-aux**); abbr. **q.**

quinte a position in fencing; cf. **quint**

quintet (mus.) *not* -ette

quintillion a thousand raised to the sixth power, 10^{18}; *formerly* (esp. Brit.) a thousand raised to the tenth power, 10^{30}

quiproquo (Fr. m.) mistake

quipu the ancient Peruvians' substitute for writing by knotting threads of various colours; *not* -po, -ppo, -ppu

quire/ four sheets of paper etc. folded to form eight leaves; any collection of leaves one within another in a manuscript or book; twenty-five (*formerly* twenty-four) sheets of paper; **in -s** unbound, in sheets; abbr. **q.**, **qr.**, pl. same

Qui s'excuse s'accuse (Fr.) to excuse oneself is to accuse oneself

quisling a traitor, from **Vidkun Quisling** (1887–1945) pro-Nazi leader in Norway

quit/, **-ted**, **-ter** (*not* -tor), **-ting**

Quito Ecuador

Qui va là? (Fr.) Who goes there?

Qui vive? (Fr.) Who goes there?

qui vive, on the on the alert (not ital.)

quixotic extravagantly romantic and visionary, like Don Quixote

quiz/, **-zed**, **-zer**, **-zes**, **-zing**

Qum *see* **Qom**

Qumran Jordan, site associated with Dead Sea Scrolls

quoad/ (Lat.) as far as, — *hoc* to this extent

quod erat demonstrandum etc., *see* **QED** etc.

quod est (Lat.) which is, abbr. **q.e.**

quodlibet/ (hist.) (exercise on) subject of philosophical or theological disputation, (mus.) a medley; **-arian, -ical, -ically**

quod vide (Lat.) which see (refers to sing.), abbr. **q.v.**

quoins (typ.) wedges or expanding devices that secure type, blocks, and furniture in the chase; pron. 'coins'

quoits a game, *not* coits

quo jure? (Lat.) by what right?

quomodo (Lat.) by what means, abbr. **q.m.**

quondam (adj.) former, sometime; from Lat. *quondam* (adv.) formerly

Quonset hut (US) a prefabricated metal building similar to a Nissen hut

quor/um the number of members whose presence is needed to make proceedings valid, pl. **-ums** (not ital.); adj. **-ate**

quot. quot/ation, -ed

quota/ a share, pl. **-s**

quotation marks (typ.) single (' '), double (" "); (colloq.) **quotes** (no point)

quot homines, tot sententiae (Lat.) there are as many opinions as there are people

quo vadis? (Lat.) where are you going?

Qur'ān Arab. and specialist rendering of **Koran**

qursh a monetary unit of Saudi Arabia, pl. same

q.v. *quod vide* (which see) (refers to sing., pl. **qq.v.**)

q.v. *quantum vis* (as much as you wish)

qwerty keyboard of typewriter or computer input (no caps., an acronym from the first letters on top row of this keyboard)

qy query (no point)

R radius, rand, *Regina*, *retarder* (on timepiece regulator), *Rex*, River, roentgen, (chess) rook, the seventeenth in a series, (elec.) symbol for resistance

R. rabbi, Radical, railway, rector, regiment, registered, reply, (US) Republican, Royal, (Fr.) *Rue* (street), (Ger.) *Recht* (law), (naut.) run (deserted), (theat.) right (from actor's point of view), (thermometer) Réaumur

® registered trade mark

℞ *recipe* (take)

℟ response (to a versicle)

r rare, recto, residence, resides, right, rises; rouble, **-s**; (meteor.) rain

RA Rear Admiral, Royal Academy, Royal Academician, Royal Artillery, (astr.) right ascension

Ra radium (no point), Egyptian god of the sun, spelt **Rē^c** by Egyptologists

R/A refer to acceptor, return to author

RAA Royal Academy of Arts

RAAF Royal Australian Air Force, Royal Auxiliary Air Force

Rabat Morocco

Rabb. Rabbinic

rabbet/ a groove in woodwork; **-ed, -ing**; *not* -bit, rebate

rabbi/ a Jewish expounder of the law, pl. **-s**; abbr. **R.** (cap.); **Chief Rabbi** (caps.)

rabbin/ usually in pl. **-s**, Jewish authorities on the law, mainly of 2nd–13th cc.; **-ical, -ism, -ist**

rabbinic/ of or relating to rabbis; **— Hebrew** (noun) late Hebrew (caps.), abbr. **Rabb.**

rabbit/, **-ed, -ing**; **-duck** (philos.) *see* **hare-duck**; cf. **rabbet**

rabbit/ **fever, — punch, — warren** (two words)

rabdomancy *use* **rhab-**

Rabelais/, **François** (?1494–1553) French writer, **-ian** (cap.)

rabscallion *use* **raps-**

RAC Royal Agricultural College, Royal Armoured Corps, Royal Automobile Club

raccoon *not* **rac-**

race use in technical contexts to describe a genus, species, breed, stock, strain, or variety of animal, plant, or micro-organism, *but* use *people, nation, group,* or *community* to describe humans in non-technical contexts as being of a distinct ethnic stock with distinct physical characteristics

race/**card, -course, -goer, -horse, -track, -way** (one word)

racey *use* **-cy**

rach/**is** (bot., zool.) *not* rha-, pl. **-ides** (though incorrectly formed)

rachiti/**s** rickets, **-c**

Rachmaninov, Sergei (Vasilevich) (1873–1943) Russian composer

Rachmanism slum landlordism

rack/ **and ruin, — one's brains**; *see also* **wrack**

racket/, **-eer, -s** (game), **-y**; *not* -quet, *but see* **racquetball**

rackett (mus.) a Renaissance woodwind instrument; *not* -et, rank-

racont/**eur** f. **-euse** (not ital.)

racoon *use* **racc-**

racquet *use* **-ket**

racquetball (US) a court game similar to handball (one word), *not* racket-

RACS Royal Arsenal Co-operative Society

rac/**y** *not* -ey; **-ily**

RAD Royal Academy of Dancing

rad a former unit of absorbed radiation dose, = 0.01 Gy (*now use* **gray**); radian

Rad. Radical

rad. radix (root)

RADA Royal Academy of Dramatic Art

radar radio detection *and* ranging (acronym) (not cap.)

RADC Royal Army Dental Corps

Radcliffe/, **Ann** (1764–1823) English writer; **—, John** (1650–1714) English physician; **— College** Mass.; **— Camera, — Infirmary, — Science Library, — Observatory** Oxford; *see also* **Rat-**

Radhakrishnan, Sir Sarvepalli (1888–1975) Indian philosopher and statesman, President 1962–7

radian the SI unit of plane angle (approx. 57.296°), abbr. **rad**

radiator *not* -er

Radical (politics) abbr. **R., Rad.**

radical/ (chem.) *not* -cle, **— sign** (math.) $\sqrt{}$

radices pl. of radix

radicle (bot.)

radio/ pl. **-s**

radioactiv/**e** (one word), **-ity**

radio-assay (hyphen)

radiobiology (one word)

radio/ **cab, — car** (two words)

radio/**carbon, -cobalt** (one word)

radio-control/, **-led** (hyphen)

radio-element (hyphen, one word in US)

radio frequency (two words, hyphen when attrib.)

radio/**gram, -graph, -immunology, -isotope, -meter, -metric, -paque, -phonic, -scopy** (one word)

radio/-telegraphy, -telephony (hyphens, one word in US)

radio telescope (two words)

radio/telex, -therapy (one word)

radium symbol **Ra**

rad/ius pl. **-ii**, abbr. **R**

rad/ius vector pl. **-ii vectores**

rad/ix a root, pl. **-ices**; abbr. **rad.**

radon symbol **Rn**

RAE Royal Aircraft Establishment(s)

Rae, John (1813–93) Scottish Arctic traveller; *see also* **Ray; Reay**

Rae Bareli Uttar Pradesh, India; *not* Ray Bareilly

Raeburn, Sir Henry (1756–1823) Scottish painter

RAEC Royal Army Education Corps

R.Aero.C. Royal Aero Club of the United Kingdom

R.Ae.S. Royal Aeronautical Society

Raetia *use* **Rh-**

RAF Royal Air Force

RAFA Royal Air Forces Association

Rafferty's rules (Austral., NZ colloq.) no rules at all, esp. in boxing

raffia a palm fibre; *not* -fia, -phia

RAFRO Royal Air Force Reserve of Officers

RAFVR Royal Air Force Volunteer Reserve

rag/, -ged, -ging

raga (Ind. mus.) a pattern of notes used as a basis for improvisation, or a piece using a particular raga; *not* rag

ragamuffin (one word)

rag-and-bone man (two hyphens)

ragbag (one word)

rag doll (two words)

ragee a coarse Indian grain; *not* ragg-, -i; in Hind. *rāgī*

ragged/ left, — right (typ.) set text with even internal spacing to align with, respectively, the right or left margin of a page; *ragged right* is *ranged left*, and vice versa; cf. **full/ left, — right, — out**

raglan (not cap.)

ragout a rich meat stew, in Fr. m. *ragoût*

ragtag (one word) **and bobtail** (one word)

ragtime (mus.) (one word)

raguly (her.) like a row of sawn-off branches

Ragusa (It.) Dubrovnik (Croatia), also a town in Sicily

Rahman, Ziaur *see* **Ziaur Rahman**

RAI Royal Anthropological Institute

Rai (It.) Radiotelevisione Italiana (It. broadcasting corporation), *formerly* Radio Audizioni Italiane (one cap., no point)

raie (Fr. f.) skate (a fish)

Raikes, Robert (1735–1811) English originator of Sunday Schools

rail/car, -card, -head, -man, -road, -way (abbr. **R.**, **rly.**), **-wayman** (one word)

railway yard (two words)

rain/ abbr. **r.**; **-bow, -coat, -drop, -fall, -forest** (one word)

rain gauge (two words)

rain/hat, -proof, -storm, -water (one word)

raise (US noun) an increase in salary, = **pay rise**

raison/ de plus (Fr.) all the more reason, — **d'état** a reason of state, — **d'être** purpose of existence

raisonn/é (Fr.) f. **-ée** reasoned out

Raj, the (hist.) British sovereignty in India (cap.), in Hind. *rāj*

raja/ an Indian title, a Malay or Javanese chief; *not* -h (not cap.); in Hind. *rājā*; *see also* **ranee**

Rajagopalachari, Chakravarti (1878–1972) last Governor-General of India 1948–50

Rajasthan/ an Indian state; **-i** an Indo-Aryan language, spoken in Rajasthan in India and Pakistan

Rajput/ a member of the Hindu soldier caste claiming Kshatriya descent, *not* -poot; **-ana** an Indian region

Rajshahi Bangladesh, *not* -eshaye

Rajya Sabha the upper house of the Indian parliament, *not* Raja —; cf. **Lok Sabha**

raki any of various spirits made in E. Europe and the Middle East

raku a kind of Japanese lead-glazed earthenware

rale/ a noise made in difficult breathing, pl. **-s**; in Fr. m. *râle*

Ralegh, Sir Walter (1552–1618) English courtier, colonizer, soldier, and writer; *formerly* also spelt -eigh

Raleigh NC

Raleigh, Prof. Sir Walter (Alexander) (1861–1922) English writer; *see also* **Rayleigh**

Ralfs, John (1807–90) English botanist

rallentando/ (mus.) (passage performed) with decreasing pace, pl. **-s**; abbr. **rall.**

rallying point (two words)

RAM (comput.) random-access memory, Royal Academy of Music (London)

ram/, -med, -ming

Ramadan the ninth month of the Muslim year, during which strict fasting is observed from sunrise to sunset; in Arab. *ramaḍān*

Raman/, Sir Chandrasekhara Venkata (1888–1970) Indian physicist, — **effect** a change of frequency in scattering of radiation

Ramayana a Hindu epic

Ramblers' Association *not* 's

Rambouillet dép. Seine-et-Oise, France

RAMC Royal Army Medical Corps

ramchuddar an Indian shawl

Ramée, Marie Louise de la *see* **la Ramée, Marie Louise de**

ramekin a small mould, *not* -quin

Rameses the name of kings of ancient Egypt, *not* Ramses (US)

Ramillies battle, 1706

Rampur Uttar Pradesh, India

Ramsay,/ Allan (1686–1758) Scottish poet, — **Allan** (1713–84) Scottish painter, — **Sir William** (1852–1916) Scottish chemist

Ramses *use* **Rameses**

Ramsey Cambs., Essex, IoM

Ramsey,/ Arthur Michael (1904–88) Bishop of Durham 1952–6, Archbishop of York 1956–61, Archbishop of Canterbury 1961–74; — **Ian Thomas** (1915–72) Bishop of Durham 1966–72

ram/us (Lat.) a branch, pl. **-i**

RAN Royal Australian Navy

ranchero/ person who farms or works on a ranch (not ital.); pl. **-s**

ranc/our spite, *not* -or (except in US); *but* **-orous**

Rand (colloq.) the Witwatersrand, S. Africa

rand chief monetary unit of S. Africa and some neighbouring countries, pl. same; abbr. **R**

R & A Royal and Ancient (Golf Club)

R & B rhythm and blues

r. & c.c. riot and civil commotion

R & D research and development

Randolph-Macon College Ashland and Lynchburg, Va. (hyphen)

random-access memory (comput.) abbr. **RAM**

R & R rest and relaxation

ranee (hist.) a Hindu queen, the wife or widow of a raja (q.v.); *also* **rani** (not cap.); *not* rann-; in Hind. *rānī*

rangatira (NZ) a Maori chief or noble

rang/e (typ.) align vertically and/or horizontally (cf. **ragged/ left,** — **right**); **-ing numerals** lining numerals

range a large cooking stove kept continually hot, (US) an electric or gas cooker

rang/é (Fr. m.) f. **-ée** domesticated, orderly

Ranger (UK) a senior Guide (US) a commando (cap.); keeper of a royal park or forest, (not cap.)

Range Rover (two words) *but* **Land-Rover** (hyphen)

Rangoon Burma, *not* -un

rani *see* **ranee**

Ranjit Singh (1780–1839) founder of the Sikh kingdom

Ranjitsinhji, Kumar Shri (1872–1933) Indian cricketer, Maharaja Jam Sahib of Nawanagar 1906–33

Ranke, Leopold von (1795–1886) German historian

ranket(t) *use* **rackett**

rannee *use* **ranee**

Ransom, John Crowe (1888–1974) US poet

Ransome, Arthur (1884–1967) English writer

ranuncul/us a buttercup, pl. **-uses**; (bot.) the genus including buttercups (cap. and ital.)

ranz-des-vaches Swiss alpenhorn melody

RAOB Royal Antediluvian Order of Buffaloes

RAOC Royal Army Ordnance Corps

rap/, -ped, -ping

RAPC Royal Army Pay Corps

rape (hist.) any of the six ancient divisions of Sussex (not ital.)

Raphael/ in It. **Raffaello Sanzio** (1483–1520) Italian painter, **-esque**

raphia *use* **raff-**

raphide (bot., zool.) a needle-like crystal, *not* rha-

rapid eye movement (three words) abbr. **REM**

rapid-fire (hyphen)

Rappahannock a river, Va.

rapparee a 17th-c. Irish freebooter

rappee a coarse snuff

rappel/ (esp. US) abseil; **-led, -ling** (one *l* in US) (not ital.)

rapport fruitful communication or relationship (not ital.)

rapporteur one who prepares account of proceedings (not ital.)

rapprochement the establishment or renewal of friendly relations (not ital.)

rapscallion a rascal, *not* rabs-

rar/a avis (Lat.) a prodigy, literally a rare bird; pl. **-ae aves**

rare abbr. **r.**

rarebit *see* **Welsh rabbit**

rarefaction *not* -efication

rarefy *not* rari-

rarity *not* -ety

RARO Regular Army Reserve of Officers

Rarotonga Cook Islands, NZ

RAS Royal Agricultural, Asiatic, *or* Astronomical, Society

RASC Royal Army Service Corps, *now* **RCT**

rase destroy, *use* **-ze**

Raskolnik/ (Russ.) pl. **-i**; *see* **Old Believer**

Rasoumoffsky *see* **Razumovsky**

Rasselas, Prince of Abyssinia, The History of a novel by S. Johnson, 1759

Rastafarian/ (a member of *or* relating to) a Jamaican religion, **-ism** the religion

Rasumovsky Quartets, the by Beethoven, 1806

rat/, **-ted, -ting**

ratable *use* **rateable**

ratafia a liqueur, a biscuit; *not* -afie, -ifia

ratan *use* **ratt-**

ratany (bot.) *use* **rh-**

ratatouille a vegetable stew

ratbag (one word)

ratchet/, **-ed**

Ratcliffe College Leicester

rateable *not* rata-

ratepayer (one word)

Rathaus (Ger. n.) town hall

rathskeller (US) a beer hall or restaurant in a basement (not cap.), in Ger. m. *Ratskeller* a (restaurant in the) town-hall cellar

ratifia *use* **rata-**

ratiocinat/e go through logical processes, reason, esp. using syllogisms; **-ion, -ive, -or**

rationale a logical cause, reasoned explanation

rationalize *not* -ise

Ratisbon *use* **Regensburg**

ratline (naut.) the ladder-rope on the shrouds; *not* -in, -ing

rat race (two words)

rattan a cane, *not* ratan

rattlesnake (one word)

Raumer,/ **Friedrich Ludwig Georg von** (1781–1873) German historian; **— Rudolf von** (1815–76) German philologist; *see also* **Réaumur**

ravage devastate, plunder

RAVC Royal Army Veterinary Corps

ravel/, **-led, -ling** (one *l* in US)

ravioli (not ital.)

ravish commit rape on (a woman), enrapture

Rawalpindi Pakistan, *not* Rawul-

raw sienna a brownish-yellow pigment, *not* siena

ray (mus.) in tonic sol-fa, *not* re

Ray,/ **John** (1627–1705) English naturalist, spelt Wray till 1670; **— Man** *see* **Man Ray**; *see also* **Rae; Reay**

Ray Bareilly *use* **Rae Bareli**

Rayleigh Essex

Rayleigh, John William Strutt, Baron (1842–1919) English physicist; *see also* **Ralegh; Raleigh**

raze destroy, erase; *not* -se

Razumovsky, Prince Andrei (**Kirillovich**) (1752–1836) Russian statesman, ambassador to Vienna; *not* Rasoumoffsky, Rasumovsky (except in Beethoven's work)

razzmatazz *not* the many variants

Rb rubidium (no point)

RBA Royal Society of British Artists

RBS Royal Society of British Sculptors

RC/ Red Cross, reinforced concrete, (theat.) right centre, Roman Catholic; **— paper** (print.) a resin-coated paper (for photosetting)

RCA Royal College of Art, (US) Radio Corporation of America

RCAF Royal Canadian Air Force

RCC Roman Catholic Church

RCDS Royal College of Defence Studies

RCM Royal College of Music (London)

RCMP Royal Canadian Mounted Police

RCN Royal College of Nursing, Royal Canadian Navy

RCO Royal College of Organists

RCOG Royal College of Obstetricians and Gynaecologists

RCP Royal College of Physicians

RCS Royal College of Science, Royal College of Surgeons, Royal Commonwealth Society, Royal Corps of Signals

RCT Royal Corps of Transport

RCVS Royal College of Veterinary Surgeons

RD Royal Dragoons, Royal Naval Reserve Decoration, Rural Dean, (US) Rural District

R/D refer to drawer (of a cheque)

Rd. road

RDC Royal Defence Corps, (hist.) Rural District Council

RD$ Dominican peso

RDF Radio Direction-Finder, -ing

RDI Royal Designer for Industry (Royal Society of Arts)

RDS Royal Drawing Society

RE Reformed Episcopal, Religious Education, Right Excellent, Royal Engineers, Royal Exchange, Royal Society of Painter-Etchers and Engravers

Re Reynolds number, rhenium, rupee (no point)

re (mus.) *use* **ray**

Re, il (It.) the King (no accent)

re with regard to (as first word in a heading, esp. of a law document); avoid using as substitute for *about, concerning* in general contexts (not an abbr., no point)

re- (prefix) *use* hyphen when followed by *e* and separately sounded (except in US), *re-echo, re-enact*; and when forming a compound to be distinguished from a more familiar one-word form, as with *recover* (= regain) and *re-cover* (= cover again)

react produce response (one word)

re-act act again (hyphen)

Read, Sir Herbert Edward (1893–1968) English critic; *see also* **Reade**; **Rede**; **Reed**; **Reid**

readdress (one word)

Reade, Charles (1814–84) English novelist; *see also* **Read**; **Rede**; **Reed**; **Reid**

Reader a university teacher, in some universities intermediate between Lecturer and Professor (cap. as title)

reader (print.) a proof corrector, one who reports on typescripts to a publisher (not cap.)

Reader's Digest Association Ltd publishers

reading/ desk, — lamp, — light, — room (two words)

readjourn, readjust, readmission (one word)

readmit/, -ted, -ting (one word)

read-only memory (comput.) abbr. **ROM**

read-out (noun, comput., hyphen, one word in US)

ready/-made, -to-wear (adjs., hyphens)

reafforest/ (one word) *not* reforest (US), **-ation**

reagent (one word)

real/ a former Portuguese and current Brazilian coin, pl. *réis*; a former Spanish and Mexican coin, then equivalent to a US 'bit' (12½ cents), pl. *-es*

realiz/e, -able *not* -is-

realpolitik politics based on realities and material needs, rather than on morals or ideals (not cap., not ital.); in Ger. f. *Realpolitik*

real tennis *see* **tennis**

realt/or (US) a real-estate agent, **-y** (law) landed property

ream of paper 500 sheets, abbr. **rm.**

reanimate, reappear, reappoint (one word)

reapprais/e, -al (one word)

Rear Admiral abbr. **RA**, **Rear Adm.** (two words, caps.)

rearguard (one word)

rearm/, -ament (one word)

rearrange, reascend, reassemble (one word)

reassert/, -ed, -ing (one word)

reassur/e, -ance (one word)

Réaumur/, René Antoine Ferchault de (1683–1757) French inventor of the thermometer scale; — the scale itself, abbr. **R.**, **Réaum**; *see also* **Raumer**

reawake etc. (one word)

Reay, Donald James Mackay, Baron (1839–1921) Dutch-born Scottish Governor of Bombay and first president of the British Academy; *see also* **Rae**; **Ray**

Reb a traditional Jewish courtesy title used preceding a man's forename or surname, as 'Mr', 'Rabbi'

rebaptize *not* -ise (one word)

rebate to reduce, a reduction; cf. **rabbet**

rebb/e a rabbi or Jewish religious leader, **-itzin** the wife of a rabbi

rebec (mus.) a medieval stringed instrument, *not* -eck

rebel/, -led, -ling

rebind bind (a book) again, past part. **rebound**

rebound spring back, have an adverse effect on doer of an action (one word)

rebus/ an enigmatic representation of a word (esp. a name), by pictures etc. suggesting its parts; (her.) a device suggesting the name of its bearer; pl. **-es**

rebut/, -tal, -ted, -ting

rec. receipt, recipe; record, -ed, -er

Récamier, Jeanne Françoise Julie Adélaïde, Madame (1777–1849) a leader of French society

recap/ (colloq.) recapitulate (no point); **-ped, -ping**

recast (one word)

recce/ (sl.) a reconnaissance, to reconnoitre; pl. **-s**

recd. received, *not* rec'd (US)

recede withdraw, shrink back (one word)

re-cede cede back to a former owner (hyphen)

receipt abbr. **rec.**

receivable *not* -eable

recension the revision of a text, a particular form or version of a text resulting from such revision

recent not long past or established, (geol., cap.) = **Holocene**

receptor (biol.) *not* -er

Rechabite a total abstainer (cap.)

réchauffé (Fr. m.) a warmed-up dish, (fig.) a rehash

recherché chosen with care, far-fetched (not ital.)

recidiv/ist one who relapses into crime, **-ism**

recipe/ pl. **-s**, abbr. **rec.**

réclame (Fr. f.) notoriety by advertisement, (journalism) an editorial announcement

recogniz/ance a bond given to a court, *not* -sance; **-ant** showing recognition or consciousness, *not* -sant

recognize *not* -ise

recollect remember (one word)

re-collect collect again (hyphen)

recolour (one word) *not* -or (US)

recommit/, -ted, -ting

recompense (noun and verb)

reconcilable *not* -eable

reconciler *not* -or

reconnaissance a preliminary survey, *not* reconnoi- (not ital.)

reconnoitre make a preliminary survey, *not* -er (US); in Fr. *reconnaître*

record/, -ed, -er abbr **rec.**

record player (two words)

recount narrate (one word)

re-count count again, a further count (hyphen)

recoup to recompense, recover, make up for

recover regain possession of, revive (one word)

re-cover cover again (hyphen)

recreate refresh, create again (one word)

recreation an amusement, pastime (one word)

re-creat/ion the act of creating again; **-or** *not* -er (hyphen)

rect. rectified

rectif/y, -iable, -ied, -ier, -ying

recto/ (print.) the right-hand page, opp. of **verso**; abbr. ʳ, **r.** (not ital.); pl. **-s**

rector/ abbr. **R., -ial**

rectri/x a strong tail-feather, pl. **-ces**

rectum/ (anat.) the straight part of the intestine, pl. **-s**

rect/us (anat.) a straight muscle, pl. **-i**

reçu (Fr. m.) a receipt

recueil (Fr. m.) a literary compilation, miscellany

reculer pour mieux sauter (Fr.) withdraw to await a better opportunity

recur/, -red, -ring

redact/ put into literary form, edit for publication; **-or**

rédact/eur (Fr.) (publisher's) editor, f. **-rice**; cf. *éditeur*

rédaction (Fr. f.) editing, editorial department

Redakteur (Ger. m.) editor (cap.)

Redbourn Herts.

Redbourne Humberside

redbreast a robin (one word)

red-brick new (university) (hyphen)

Redbridge Gr. London

redcap (Brit.) a member of the military police, (US) a railway porter

redcoat (hist.) a British soldier (so called from the scarlet uniform of most regiments) (one word, not cap.)

redcurrant (one word)

redd/en, -ish, -y

Reddish Gr. Manchester

Redditch Worc.

Rede Lecture Cambridge University; *see also* **Read; Reade; Reed; Reid**

Redeless, Ethelred the (*c.*968–1016) King of England 978–1016, 'the Unready'

Redemptionists an order of Trinitarian friars devoted to the redemption of Christian captives from slavery

Redemptorists an order of missionaries founded in 1732 by Alfonso Liguori

Redgauntlet a novel by Scott, 1824 (one word)

red-handed (hyphen)

redhead (one word) *but* **red-headed** (hyphen, one word in US)

red-hot (hyphen)

redial/, -led, -ling (one *l* in US)

Red Indian (offens.) *use* Native American

rediviv/us (Lat.) restored to life, pl. **-i**; f. **-a**, pl. **-ae**

red lead (two words)

red/-letter day, -light district (one hyphen)

redneck (one word)

redoubt (mil.) an outwork, *not* -out

redpoll a finch (one word)

red poll a breed of hornless red cattle (two words)

redress to remedy (one word)

re-dress dress again (hyphen)

redskin (one word)

red tape excessive (use of) formalities (two words)

reducible *not* -eable

reductio ad/ absurdum (Lat.) disproof by reaching an obviously absurd conclusion, — **— impossibile** disproof by reaching an impossible conclusion

redwater a cattle disease (one word, two in US)

reebok *use* **rhe-**, *but* **Reebok** (propr.) for the sportswear manufacturer

re-echo (hyphen, one word in US)

Reed,/ Alfred German (1847–95) English actor; **— Edward Tennyson** (1860–1933) English caricaturist; **— Talbot Baines** (1852–93) English writer of boys' books; **— Walter** (1851–1902) US army surgeon; *see also* **Read; Reade; Rede; Reid**

re/-edit, -educate (hyphens, one word in US)

reef knot (two words)

Reekie, Auld Old Smoky (Edinburgh)

re/-elect, -election, -eligible, -embark (*not* reim-), **-emerge, -emergence, -emphasize** (not -ise), **-employ, -enact, -enactment, -enforce** (enforce again), **-enlist, -enslave, -enter, -enthrone** (hyphens, one word in US)

re-entrant (of) an angle pointing inwards, esp. in fortification (cf. **salient**); (geom.) (an angle that is) reflex (hyphen, one word in US)

re/-entry, -equip, -establish, -evaluate (hyphens, one word in US)

reeve (naut.) thread or fasten rope, past **rove**; *see also* **ruff**

re/-examine, -exchange, -exhibit, -export (hyphens, one word in US)

Ref. the Reformation

ref. referee, reference, referred; reform/ed, -er

Ref. Ch. Reformed Church

refer/, -able, -ence, -red, -rer, -ring

refer/ee, -eed abbr. **ref.**

reference/ book, — library (two words)

reference marks (typ.) may be used (esp. in math. setting) as an alternative to superior figures for footnote references in the order * (not used in math. works) † ‡ § ¶ ‖, repeated on the same page in duplicate ** etc. if necessary

reference point (two words)

referendum/ referring to the electorate on a particular issue, pl. **-s**

referrible *use* **-erable**

refit/, -ted, -ting

refl. reflect/ion, -ive; reflexive

reflectible *use* **reflexible**

reflection *not* -exion, abbr. **refl.**; in Fr. f. *réflexion*

reflective (of surfaces) giving back a reflection, abbr. **refl.**; (of people) meditative

reflector *not* -er

reflet lustre or iridescence, esp. on pottery (not ital.)

reflexible able to be reflected, *not* reflect-

reflexion *use* **-ction**

reflexive (gram.) implying that the action is reflected upon the doer, abbr. **refl.**

reforest/, -ation *use* **reafforest-** (except in US)

reform/ improve, correct; **-ation** (one word)

re-form/ form again, **-ation** (hyphen)

Reformation, the (cap.) 16th-c. movement for the reform of abuses in the RC Church; abbr. **Ref.**

Reform Bills 1832, 1867, 1884–5

reform/ed, -er abbr. **ref.**

refractor a type of lens or telescope

refractory stubborn, unmanageable, rebellious, difficult

refrangible that can be refracted

refuel/, -led, -ling (one *l* in US)

refund pay back, reimburse (one word)

re-fund fund again (hyphen)

refuse withhold acceptance or consent (one word)

re-fuse fuse again (hyphen)

refusenik (hist.) a Jew in the Soviet Union who had been refused permission to emigrate to Israel, *also* **refusnik** (not cap., not ital.)

Reg. Regent, *regina* (queen)

reg. regis/ter, -trar, -try; regular, -ly

regalia (pl.) insignia

regardless without regard, consideration, or attention; *not* irre-

regd. registered

regenerator *not* -er

Regensburg Bavaria, *not* Ratisbon, -berg

Regent abbr. **Reg.**

Regent's Park/ London (apos.); — — **College** Oxford

reggae a W. Indian style of music with a strong subsidiary beat

Reg. Gen. Registrar General

régie a government department that controls an industry or service, e.g. in Austria, France, Italy, Spain, and Turkey

regime/ pl. **-s**, **-n** pl. **-ns** (not ital., no accent)

regiment abbr. **regt.**, **R.**

Regina (Lat.) queen; abbr. **R.**, **Reg.**

regisseur a ballet or theatre director (not ital.)

register abbr. **reg.**; (bind.) a bookmarker; (typ.) print so that pages back one another exactly, or the separate colour printings of an illustration superimpose exactly

registered abbr. **regd.**

Registered Nurse (US) = **SRN**, abbr. **RN**

register marks (typ.) the crosses used to help achieve good register

Register Office off. name, *not* Registry

registrable *not* -erable

Registrar an official of Oxford University, *not* Registrary

registr/ar, -y abbr. **reg.**

Registrar General (two words, caps.) abbr. **Reg. Gen.**

Registrary an official of Cambridge University, *not* Registrar

Registry Office *see* **Register Office**

regium donum (Lat.) a royal grant

Regius professor (cap. *P* only when used to refer to a specific chair) abbr. **Reg. prof.**

règle (Fr. f.) a rule

regnal years *not* regal (except in hist. usage)

regret/, -ful, -fully, -table, -tably, -ted, -ting

regt. regiment

regul/a (Lat.) a book of rules, pl. **-ae**

regular/, -ly abbr. **reg.**

regulator *not* -er

re/hash, -heat (noun and verb, one word)

rehoboam a wine bottle of about six times the standard size, named after **Rehoboam**, a king of Israel (1 Kgs. 12)

rei (hist.) erroneous English back-formation for *real*

rei/ (Port. m.) king, pl. **-s** (no accent); **o rei** the king, *but* **El-Rei** His Majesty

Reich/ (hist.) the German State and Commonwealth (cap.); **Deutsches —** the official name of Germany 1871–1945; **First** — the Holy Roman Empire 962–1806; **Second** — the German Empire 1871–1918; **Third** — the Nazi regime 1933–45; of these, only *Third Reich* is normal historical terminology

Reichsanstalt a German official institution 1871–1945

Reichsanzeiger a German gazette

Reichs/kanzler the German Chancellor; **-mark** the former basic monetary unit of Germany, abbr. **RM**; **-tag** (hist.) (the building where met) the legislative body of the North German Confederation 1867–71, of the German Empire 1871–1918, or of post-Imperial Germany until 1945; **-wehr** the German army 1921–35 (one word)

Reid,/ Sir George (1841–1913) Scottish painter, — **Capt. Thomas Mayne** (1818–83) British novelist, — **Thomas** (1710–96) Scottish metaphysician, — **Whitelaw** (1837–1912) US journalist and diplomat; *see also* **Read**; **Reade**; **Rede**; **Reed**

Reikiavik *use* **Reykj-**

Reilly, the life of *use* **Riley**

reimbark etc., *use* **re-embark** etc.

reimburse pay for loss or expense (one word)

réimpression (Fr. f.) a reprint

Reims dép. Marne, France, Fr. adj. **rémois**; *prefer to* Rheims (trad. Eng. spelling) *but* adj. **Rhemish**

reine-claude (Fr. f.) greengage, pl. *reines-claude* (hyphen)

re infecta (Lat.) with the object not attained

reinforce/ strengthen, **-ment**; *see also* **re-enforce**

Reinhardt, Max (1873–1943) German theatrical producer

reinstate (one word)

reis the captain of a boat or ship; a chief or governor; in Arab. *ra'is*

réis pl. of *real*

Reis Effendi (Turk.) the title of the former Secretary of State for Foreign Affairs in the Ottoman Empire (caps.)

rejectamenta (pl.) wasted matter (not ital.)

rel. relative, -ly; religion, religious, (Fr.) *relié* (bound), (Lat.) *reliquiae* (relics)

relabel/, -led, -ling (-ed, -ing in US)

relat/er one who relates something, **-or** (law) one who lays information before the Attorney General

relative/, -ly abbr. **rel.**

relativity the state of being relative, Einstein's theory of space-time

relativize *not* -ise

relator *see* **relater**

relay arrange in relay(s), to pass on, lay again (one word)

releas/er one who releases, **-or** (law) one who grants a release

relent abandon a harsh intention, yield to compassion (one word)

relet/ let again, **-ting** (one word)

relev/é (Fr.) f. **-ée** exalted, noble; (cook.) highly seasoned; *not ré-*

reliable *not* -y-

relié (Fr. bibliog.) bound

relief-printing (typ.) printing from surfaces raised to contact ink and paper, = **letterpress** (hyphen)

relievo (art) = **relief**, in It. **riliev/o**, pl. **-i**

religieuse/ (Fr. f.) a nun, pl. **-s**

religieux (Fr. m.) a monk, pl. same

relig/ion, -ious abbr. **rel.**

religionize *not* -ise

religious denominations as Baptist, Protestant, to have caps.

reliquar/y (esp. eccl.) a receptacle for relics, pl. **-ies**

reliquiae (Lat. pl.) relics, fossils; abbr. **rel.**

rel/y, -ied, -ying

REM rapid eye movement

rem roentgen equivalent man

rem. remarks

remainder (print.) that part of an edition's print-run that is unsaleable at its original price

remanen/t (adj.) remaining, residual, esp. (of magnetism) remaining after the magnetizing field has been removed; **-ce**; cf. **remnant**

Remarque, Erich Maria born **Krämer** (1898–1970) German-born US novelist

remblai/ earth used to form a rampart, pl. **-s**

Rembrandt/ in full — (**Harmenszoon**) **van Rijn** (1606–69) Dutch painter, **-esque**

REME Royal Electrical and Mechanical Engineers

Remembrance Sunday that nearest to 11 Nov.

remerciment (Fr. m.) thanks, *not -îement* (except in 17th-c. spelling)

rem/ex a wing quill feather, pl. **-iges**

Reminiscere Sunday the second in Lent

remise (law) to make over, *not* -ize

remissible capable of being forgiven

remit/, -tal, -tance, -tee, -tent, -ter

remnant a small remaining quantity; cf. **remanent**

remodel/, -led, -ling (one *l* in US)

rémois (Fr.) of Reims, f. **-e** (not cap.); a native of Reims, f. **-e** (cap.)

remonstrator *not* -er

rémoulade or *rémolade* (Fr. f.) a salad dressing, a kind of sauce

remould *not* -mold (US)

removable *not* -eable

Rémusat,/ **Charles François Marie, comte de** (1797–1875) French politician and writer, — **Jean Pierre** (1788–1832) French Chinese scholar

Renaissance, the (the period of) the revival of art and literature under the influence of classical models in the 14th–16th cc. (cap.); (not cap.) any similar revival; *not* -ascence

Renaixença (Catalan f.) the revival of Catalan culture in the 19th c.

Renard the fox, *use* **Rey-** (except in a specifically French context)

renascen/**ce** rebirth, renewal; **-t**

Renault a French make of car

rendezvous/ sing. and pl. (one word, not ital.); as verb **-es, -ed, -ing**; in Fr. m. *rendez-vous* (hyphen)

renege renounce, abandon; *not* -gue

reniform kidney-shaped

Renoir,/ **Auguste** (1841–1919) French painter, — **Jean** (1894–1979) his son, French film director

renounceable *not* -cable

renouncement *use* **renunciation**

renovator *not* -er

renown fame, high distinction; *not* -known

rent-a/**-car, -cop, -crowd** etc. (hyphens)

rentes/ (Fr. f.) independent income, also government stocks; — *sur l'État* interest on government loans

rentier one whose income is derived from investments, in Fr. *rent*/*ier*, f. *-ière*

renuncia/**tion, -nt, -tive, -tory**

reoccup/**y, -ation** (one word)

reometer etc., *use* **rhe-**

re/**open, -order, -organize** *not* -ise (one word)

reorient/**, -ate** (one word); *see also* **orient, orientate**

Rep. (US) Representative, Republican

rep a fabric, *not* repp; (colloq.) representative, (theat.) repertory (no point), (US) reputation

rep. report, -er; republic, -an

rep/**air, -airable** (of material things); **-arable, -aration** (of amends for loss)

repartee (the making of) witty retorts (not ital.), in Fr. f. *repartie*

repêchage a contest between runners-up for a place in the final (not ital.)

repel/**, -led, -lent, -ling, -ler**

repertoire a stock of pieces, techniques, etc. that a company or a performer knows (not ital.)

repertorium (Lat.) a catalogue

repertory the theatrical performance of various plays for short periods by one company, or the company that performs them

repetatur (Lat.) let it be repeated, abbr. *repet.*

répétiteur a private teacher or coach, esp. of opera singers (not ital.), in Fr. *répétit*/*eur*, f. *-rice*

repetitorium (Lat.) a summary

replaceable *not* -cable

réplique (Fr. f.) a reply

repl/**y, -ies, -ier, -ying**

report/**, -er** abbr. **rep., rept.**

report/**age** (not ital.), **-orial** (US) of newspaper reporters

repoussé (ornamental metalwork) hammered from the reverse side (not ital.); cf. **retroussé**

repp *use* **rep**

repr. representing, reprint

reprehensible *not* -able

representable *not* -ible

Representative abbr. **Rep.**

Representatives, House of the lower division of the US Congress (caps.)

repress/**, -ible, -or** *not* -er

reprint (print.) a second or new impression of any printed work, with only minor corrections; a reimpression with no corrections at all; printed matter taken from some other publication for reproduction; or (in imprecise use) printed 'copy'; (one word) abbr. **repr., RP**; *see also* **edition; imprint**

reprisal an act of retaliation, *not* -izal

reprise (law) a yearly charge or deduction, (mus.) repeated passage; *not* -ize

reprize to prize anew

repro./ reproduction, — **pull** (typ., no point) a good proof made for camera use

reproducible *not* -eable

reprogram *not* -mme

reproof (noun) a rebuke, (verb) make waterproof again

reprove to rebuke

rept. report

republic/**, -an** abbr. **rep.**

Republican abbr. **R** (no point)

Republic Day in India 26 Jan.

République française (Fr. f.) French Republic (one cap.), abbr. **RF**

repudiat/**e, -or** *not* -er

reputable respectable

requiem/ the mass for the dead, or its musical setting; pl. **-s**

requies/*cat in pace* (Lat.) may he, *or* she, rest in peace; abbr. **RIP**; pl. *-cant in pace*; *-cit in pace* he, *or* she, rests in peace

reread (one word)

reredos/ an ornamental screen or panelling behind an altar, *not* the many variants; pl. **-es**

re-release (hyphen, one word in US)

re-route/ (hyphen, one word in US), **-ing**

rerun (noun and verb, one word)

res. research, reserve; resid/ence, -es; resigned

res/ (Lat.) a thing or things, — *adjudicata* a matter already decided

re/sale, -sell (one word)

res angusta domi scanty means at home

rescuable *not* -ueable

research abbr. **res.**

reserve that which is kept back, restraint, to keep back (one word); abbr. **res.**

re-serve serve again (hyphen)

Reserve, Army (caps.)

reservist *not* -eist

res gestae (Lat. pl.) things done, matters of fact

resid/ence, -es abbr. **r.**, **res.**

residence permit (two words)

residu/e pl. **-es**, **-um** pl. **-a**

resign/ give up office, employment, etc.; **-ed** abbr. **res.**

re-sign sign again

resin a gum from trees or synthetically produced; cf. **rosin**

resist/ance, -ant *not* -ence, -ent

resist/er person, **-or** thing

res/ judicata (Lat.) a thing already decided, — *nihili* a nonentity

resoluble that can be resolved (one word)

re-soluble that can be dissolved again (hyphen)

resolv/able, -er

resonator an instrument responding to a certain frequency of vibrations

resorb absorb again

resort have recourse to, expedient, a holiday spot (one word)

re-sort sort again (hyphen)

resource in Fr. f. *ressource*

resp. respondent

respecter *not* -or

Respighi, Ottorino (1879–1936) Italian composer

respirator *not* -er

respondent abbr. **resp.**

response mark (print.) R̷

responsible in Fr. *responsable*

restaurateur restaurant-keeper, *not* -rant-

rest/-baulk, -cure (hyphens, two words in US)

rest day (two words)

rest-harrow (hyphen, two words in US)

rest/ home, — house (two words)

resting place (two words)

restor/able, -er

Restoration, the (hist.) the re-establishment of Charles II as king of England in 1660, or the literary period following this; also used for other countries, e.g. the period 1814–30 in France (cap.)

restrain check, hold in (one word)

re-strain strain again (hyphen)

restroom (one word)

resum/e, -able

résumé a summary (not ital., two accents), (US) = **curriculum vitae**

resurgam (Lat.) I shall rise again

resuscitat/e, -or

Reszke,/ Édouard de (1856–1917) Polish bass; **— Jean de** (1850–1925) his brother, Polish tenor

ret. retired, returned

retable a shelf or framed panels above back of altar

retd. retired, returned; *not* ret'd (US)

R. et I. (Lat.) *Rex et Imperator* king and emperor, *Regina et Imperatrix* queen and empress (points); in Eng. **RI**

retin/a the inner membrane of the eyeball; pl. (anat.) **-ae**, (gen.) **-as**

retinol vitamin A

retiral (esp. Sc.) retirement from office etc.

retired abbr. **ret.**, **retd.**

retraceable *not* -cable

retractable *not* -ible

retractor *not* -er

retree slightly defective paper

retrial (one word)

retriever a dog

retrocede cede back again; for the sense 'move back' *prefer* **recede**

retrochoir (archit.) (one word)

retroflex (adj.) turned backwards (one word)

retrorocket (one word)

retroussé turned up (not ital.), in Fr. *retrouss/é*, f. **-ée**; cf. **repoussé**

retry (one word)

returned abbr. **ret.**, **retd.** *not* ret'd (US)

Reuben (OT) a son of Jacob

Reubens, Peter Paul *use* **Ru-**

reunion a social gathering, in Fr. f. *réunion*

Réunion, Île de Indian Ocean

re/unite, -urge, -usable, -use (one word)

Reuters a reporting agency

Rev. Book of Revelation, Review; *see also* **Reverend**

rev. revenue, reverse; revis/e, -ed, -ion; revolution, -s

Reval the former name of (and still Ger. for) **Tallinn**

revalorize establish a new value, *not* -ise

Revd *see* **Reverend**

réveil (Fr. m.) an awaking, a morning call

reveille a morning call to troops (no accents, not ital.)

revel/, -led, -ler, -ling (one *l* in US)

Revelation, Book of (NT) *not* -ions, abbr. **Rev.**

revenons à nos moutons (Fr.) let us return to our subject (lit. '. . . to our sheep')

revenue/ abbr. **rev.**; **— office, — tax** (two words)

reverberator *not* -er

Reverend abbr. (**The**) **Revd**, pl. **Revds** (cap. *T* only in official title of address, not in running text); *not* Rev. (US); **Most Revd** archbishop or Irish RC bishop; **Revd Mother** Mother Superior of a convent; **Right Revd** *or* **Rt. Revd** bishop or moderator; **Very Revd** dean, provost, or former moderator

rever/end deserving reverence, **-ent** showing it

reverie a daydream, *not* -y

revers the front of a garment turned back showing the inner surface, pl. same

reverse abbr. **rev.**

reversed block (typ.) a design in which the illustration or wording appears in white against a background; a block whose contents are transposed left-to-right for offset printing

reversible *not* -able

rêveu/r (Fr.) f. **-se** (day)dreamer

review abbr. **rev.**

revis/e *not* -ize; **-able, -ing**; (print.) a proof including corrections made in an earlier proof; abbr. **rev.**

revis/ed, -ion abbr. **rev.**

Revised Standard Version of the Bible (caps.), abbr. **RSV**

Revised Statutes abbr. **RS, Rev. Stat.**

Revised Version of the Bible (caps.), abbr. **RV**

reviv/er one who revives, **-or** (law) a proceeding to revive a suit

revoir, à (Fr.) to be revised; cf. **au revoir**

revo/ke, -cable, -cation

Revolution, the American 1775–83; Chinese 1911–12; English 1688–9; French 1789–95, 1830, 1848, 1870; Russian 1905, 1917 (cap.); unless otherwise specified, 'the French Revolution' is assumed to be that of 1789–95, and 'the Russian Revolution' that of (esp. October) 1917

revolution/, -s abbr. **rev.**; *see also* **rpm; rps**

revolutionize *not* -ise

Rev. Stat. Revised Statutes

revue a theatrical entertainment (not ital.)

Rewley House Oxford, *now* **Kellogg College** (for matriculated students)

Rex (Lat.) king, abbr. **R.**

Rexine (propr.) imitation leather (cap.)

Reykjavik Iceland, *not* Reiki-

Reynard the fox, *not* Ren- (cap.)

Reynolds/, Osborne (1842–1912) Irish engineer and physicist; **—'s law** (two words, apos.); **— number** (two words, no apos.), abbr. **Re**

Reynolds News (no apos.)

rez-de-chaussée (Fr. m.) ground floor

Rezniček, Baron Emil Nikolaus von (1860–1945) Austrian composer

RF *République française* (French Republic)

Rf rutherfordium (no point)

r.f. radio frequency

rf. see **rinforzando**

RFA Royal Field Artillery, Royal Fleet Auxiliary

RFC Royal Flying Corps, Rugby Football Club

RGS Royal Geographical Society

RH Royal Highness

Rh rhesus, rhodium (no point)

r.h. right hand

RHA Regional Health Authority, Road Haulage Association, Royal Hibernian Academy, Royal Horse Artillery

rhabdomancy divination by rod, *not* ra-

Rhadamanth/ine stern, like **-us** (Gr. myth.) the judge of the dead

Rhaet/ia, -ian, -ic (of) the Austrian Tyrol; *not* Rae-, Rhe-

rhaphis *use* **ra-**

rhapsodize to be enthusiastic, *not* -ise

rhatany (bot.) a S. American shrub with an astringent root, *not* rat-

rhebok an antelope, *not* rhee-, ree-

Rheims *use* **Reims**

Rhein (Ger. m.) the Rhine

Rheingold, Das the first opera in Wagner's *Ring des Nibelungen*, 1869

Rhemish of Reims (trad. Eng. form); *use* **rémois** in specialist texts only

Rhenish (a wine) of the Rhine

rhenium symbol **Re**

rheology (phys.) the science of flow

rheo/meter, -stat, -trope instruments for (respectively) measuring, regulating, reversing electric current; *not* reo-

rhesus/ an Indian monkey; **— factor** (in the blood) abbr. **Rh-factor; Rh-positive, Rh-negative** (hyphens, no point)

rhet. rhetoric

Rhetia *use* **Rhae-**

RHF Royal Highland Fusiliers

RHG Royal Horse Guards (the Blues)

Rhine/ a European river; in Fr. **Rhin**, Ger. **Rhein**; **-land** (one word)

rhinestone an imitation diamond

rhinoceros pl. same; colloq. **rhino/**, pl. **-s** (no point)

R.Hist.S. Royal Historical Society

rho the seventeenth letter of the Gr. alphabet (P, ρ)

Rhode Island off. and postal abbr. **RI**

Rhod/es an island in Aegean Sea, and its capital; **-ian**

Rhodes Scholar/, -ship (at Oxford)

rhodium symbol **Rh**

rhododendron/ pl. **-s**

rhodomontade *use* **rodo-**

rhombus/ (geom.) pl. **-es**

Rhondda a river and town, Mid Glam.

Rhône a French dép. and river, *not* Rhone

RHS Royal Historical, Horticultural, *or* Humane, Society

rhumb any of the thirty-two points of the compass, or the angle between two successive compass points

rhumba *use* **ru-**

rhumb line (naut.) (two words)

rhym/e (noun and verb) *not* rime (except in older use); **-er** (-ester is usually derog.)

rhythm/, -ic

RI (US) Rhode Island, Royal Institute, Royal Institute of Painters in Water Colours, Royal Institution; Eng. form of *R. et I.*

RIA Royal Irish Academy

rial a monetary unit of Iran, Oman, and Yemen

Rialto Venice (cap.)

RIB a rigid inflatable boat (caps.)

rib/, -bed, -bing

RIBA Royal Institute of British Architects

riband *see* **ribbon**

ribband a light spar used in shipbuilding

ribbon *not* riband, except in sport and heraldry

riboflavin *not* -e

Ricard/o, David (1772–1823) English economist, **-ian**

Riccio *use* **Rizz-**

ricercar an elaborate contrapuntal instrumental composition in fugal or canonic style, esp. of the 16th–18th cc.; *not* -e

Richelieu, Armand Jean du Plessis, duc de, Cardinal (1585–1642) French statesman

Richepin, Jean (1849–1926) French writer

Richter/, Charles Francis (1900–85) US seismologist, devised **— scale** for expressing the magnitude of an earthquake; **—, Hans** (1843–1916) German conductor of Wagnerian opera and the Hallé Orchestra; **—, Johann Paul Friedrich** (1763–1825) German writer, pseud.

Jean Paul; **—, Karl** (1926–81) German conductor; **—, Svyatoslav** (**Teofilovich**) (1915–97) Russian pianist

Richthofen, Baron Manfred von (1882–1918) German flying ace

rick to sprain or strain, *not* wrick

rickets a bone disease

rickettsi/a a micro-organism such as typhus, pl. **-ae**; from **Howard Taylor Ricketts** (1871–1910) US pathologist

rickety shaky, *not* -tty

rickrack *use* ricrac

rickshaw a light two-wheeled vehicle, originally a shortening of the Jap. *jinrikisha*; *not* -sha

ricochet/ to skip or rebound (of projectile); **-ed, -ing** (not ital.)

ricrac a zigzag braid trimming, *not* rickrack

RICS Royal Institution of Chartered Surveyors

rid/, -dance, -ded, -ding

rid/e, -eable, -den, -ing

ride to hounds *not* — — the —

ridge piece (two words)

ridge pole (two words, one word in US)

ridge/ tile, — tree (two words)

ridgeway (one word, cap. as a specific name for a geographical feature)

Ridgway Col., Pa.

ridgy *not* -ey

riding each of three former administrative divisions (**East Riding, North Riding, West Riding**) of Yorkshire (caps.), an electoral division of Canada

Riemann/, Georg Friedrich Bernhard (1826–66) German mathematician, **-ian**

Riesling a white wine

Rievaulx Abbey N. Yorks., *not* Riv-

Rif, Er a mountainous region in N. Morocco, *not* Riff

rifaciment/o (It.) a remaking, pl. **-i**

Riff/ a Berber of Er Rif, pl. **-i**

riff (mus.) (play) a short repeated phrase in jazz etc.

riffle turn (pages etc.) quickly, leaf through quickly, shuffle; an instance of this

riff-raff rabble (hyphen, one word in US)

rifl/e, -ing

rifle/ range, — shot (two words)

rigadoon a lively dance, *not* rigaudon

right/ (theat., from actor's point of view) abbr. **R, — centre** abbr. **RC**

right angle symbol ∟

right ascension (astr.) abbr. **RA**

righteous

right/-hand, -handed (adjs.) (hyphens)

right-hand pages (print.) the recto pages

Right Honourable a title given to certain high officials (e.g. Privy Counsellors) and peers below the rank of marquess; abbr. **Rt. Hon.**

Right Reverend (for bishops and moderators in Presbyterian churches and Church of Scotland) abbr. (**The**) **Right Revd, Rt. Revd**

right wing (hyphen as adj.), **right-winger**

Rigi Swiss mountain, *not* -hi

rigor (med.) sudden shivering or rigidity (not ital.)

rigor mortis stiffening of the body after death (not ital.)

rigour severity, *not* -or (US); *but* **rigorous**

Rigsdag the former Danish Parliament

Rig Veda the oldest and principal of the Sanskrit Vedas, in specialist contexts *Rigveda*, *R̩gveda*; *see also* **Veda**

RIIA Royal Institute of International Affairs

Riksdag the Swedish Parliament

riksmål *formerly* **Rigsmaal**; *see* **bokmål**

Riley,/ the life of (sl.) carefree existence, *not* Reilly; — **Bridget Louise** (b. 1931) British painter; — **James Whitcomb** (1849–1916) US poet

riliev/o (It.) raised or embossed work, pl. *-i*; in Eng. **relievo**

Rilke, Rainer Maria (1875–1926) German poet

rill a small stream

rille a narrow valley on the moon

rim/, -med, -ming

rim/a (It.) verse, pl. *-e*

rim/e hoar-frost, **-y**; cf. **rhyme**

Rime of the Ancient Mariner, The a poem by Coleridge, 1798

Rimsky-Korsakov, Nikolai (**Andreevich**) (1844–1908) Russian composer

RINA Royal Institution of Naval Architects

rinderpest pleuropneumonia in ruminants (one word)

rinforz/ando, -ato (It. mus.) with more emphasis; abbr. **rf., rinf.**

Ring des Nibelungen, Der cycle of operas by Wagner, 1869–76

ring/leader, -master (one word)

Ringling Brothers and Barnum & Bailey Circus a US circus organization

rio (Port.) river, (Venetian It.) canal

río (Sp.) river (accent)

Rio de Janeiro Brazil, *not* Rio Janeiro

Rio Grande port, Brazil; — — **do Norte**, — — **do Sul** states, Brazil (no accent)

Río Grande river, Mexico (no accent in US usage)

RIP *requiesc/at* (or *-ant*) *in pace* (may he, she (or they), rest in peace)

RIPA Royal Institute of Public Administration

RIPH & H Royal Institute of Public Health and Hygiene

ripien/o (mus.) a player or instrument additional to a leader or soloist; pl. **-os, -i**

Ripman, Walter (1869–1947) English educationist

rippl/e, -y

Rip Van Winkle by Washington Irving, 1820 (three caps.)

ris de veau (Fr. cook. m.) sweetbread

rises abbr. **r.**

rishi a Hindu sage or saint, in Skr. **r̩ṣi**

risible provoking laughter, *not* -able

Risorgimento (hist.) a 19th-c. movement for the unification and independence of Italy, achieved in 1870 (also used for the ensuing period)

risotto/ rice with stock, onions, etc.; pl. **-s**

risqué slightly indecent (not ital.), in Fr. *risqu/é* f. **-ée**

rissole a fried cake of breaded minced meat (not ital.)

rissolé (Fr. cook.) well-browned

ritardando/ (mus.) holding back, pl. **-s**; abbr. **rit., ritard.**

Ritchie-Calder, Baron (hyphen)

ritenuto (mus.) with immediate reduction of speed, abbr. **riten.**

ritornello/ (mus.) a short repeated instrumental passage in a vocal work, return of full orchestra after a solo passage in a concerto; pl. **-s**

Ritter/ (Ger. m.) (the rank of) knight (cf. *Springer*) (cap.; not ital. as part of title, no comma preceding), pl. same; (f.) *-zeit* the Age of Chivalry (one word)

ritualist/ one devoted to ritual, **-ic** (cap. with hist. reference)

ritualize *not* -ise

Riv. River

rival/, -led, -ling (one *l* in US)

Rivaulx *use* **Rie-**

river abbr. **r., R., Riv.**

river (typ.) a track of white space twisting down a printed page, caused by bad word-spacing

Rivera y Orbaneja, Miguel Primo de (1870–1930) Spanish general, dictator 1923–30

river/ blindness, — capture, — dolphin, — god (two words)

river/scape, -side (one word)

Rivesaltes a French wine

rivet/, -ed, -er, -ing

Riviera the coast of France and Italy from Nice to La Spezia (cap.); a similar region elsewhere (not cap.)

Rivière, Briton (1840–1920) English painter

rivière (Fr. f.) river, (of diamonds) collar

Riyadh capital of Nejd, and one of the federal capitals of Saudi Arabia; *see also* **Mecca**

riz (Fr. m.) rice

Rizzio, David (1540–66) Italian musician, favourite of Mary Queen of Scots, assassinated; *not* Ricc-

RL Rugby League

RLO Returned Letter Office

R.L.S. Robert Louis Stevenson

RLSS Royal Life Saving Society

rly. railway

RM (hist.) Reichsmark, Resident Magistrate, Royal Mail, Royal Marines

rm. ream, room

RMA Royal Military Academy (Sandhurst)

RMCS Royal Military College of Science

R.Met.S. Royal Meteorological Society

r.m.m. relative molecular mass

r months September to April

RMP Royal Military Police

RMS Royal Mail Service, Royal Mail Steamer, Royal Microscopical Society, Royal Society of Miniature Painters

rms root mean square

RMSM Royal Military School of Music

RMT National Union of Rail, Maritime, and Transport Workers

RN Royal Navy, (US) Registered Nurse

Rn radon (no point)

RNA ribonucleic acid

RNC Royal Naval College

RNCM Royal Northern College of Music

RNIB Royal National Institute for the Blind

RNID Royal National Institute for the Deaf

RNLI Royal National Lifeboat Institution

RNR Royal Naval Reserve

RNZAF Royal New Zealand Air Force

RNZN Royal New Zealand Navy

RO Receiving Office, -r; Record Office, Relieving Officer, Returning Officer, Royal Observatory

ro. rood

Road after name to be cap., as Fulham Road; abbr. **Rd.**

road/bed, -block (one word)

road hog (two words)

roadhouse (one word)

road map (two words)

road/runner, -show, -side, -stead (one word)

road/ tax, — test (two words, hyphen when attrib.)

road/way, -works, -worthy (one word)

roan (bind.) a soft and flexible sheepskin, often imitating morocco

Roanoke Va.

Roaring/ Forties the stormy ocean tracts between latitudes 40° and 50° S., **— Twenties** the decade of the 1920s (caps.)

Robarts, Mr a character in Trollope's *Framley Parsonage*

Robbe-Grillet, Alain (b. 1922) French writer

Robben Island S. Africa

Robbia, Luca della (1399–1482) Italian sculptor; *see also* **Della Robbia**

Robespierre, Maximilien François Marie Isidore de (1758–94) French revolutionary

Robin Goodfellow a sprite, the 'Puck' of Shakespeare's *A Midsummer Night's Dream* (caps.); cf. **Jacques Bonhomme**

Robin Hood a hero of medieval legend

robin redbreast (two words)

Robinson Crusoe a novel by Defoe, 1719

Rob Roy Robert ('the Red') MacGregor (1671–1734) Scottish outlaw (caps., two words), a drink named after him

ROC Royal Observer Corps

roc a fabulous bird of eastern legend, *not* the many variants

roccoco *use* roco-

Roch, St

Rochefoucauld *see* **La Rochefoucauld**

roches moutonnées (geol.) a glaciated type of rock surface (not ital.)

rochet a surplice-like linen garment; *not* rotch-, -ette

Rocinante Don Quixote's steed, usually Anglicized as Rosinante

rock (US) a stone of any size

Rock, the Gibraltar

rock and roll/ *also* **rock 'n' roll/, -er** (often no hyphens as adj.)

rock-bottom (adj., hyphen; noun, two words)

rockburst (one word)

rock candy (two words)

Rockefeller/, John D(avison) (1840–1937) head of a family of US capitalists; **—, Nelson** (**Aldrich**) (1908–79) US statesman; **— Center** a nexus of office skyscrapers, NYC; **— Foundation** philanthropic; **— Institute** a university for medical research

rock face (two words)

rockfall (one word)

rock garden (two words)

Rockies, the (N. Amer.) the Rocky Mountains

'Rock of Ages' (caps.)

rock/ plant, — python, — salmon, — salt, — wool (two words)

rococo/ a late baroque ornamental style of decoration in 18th-c. Europe, also in music; pl. **-s**; *not* rocc-

Rod, Édouard (1857–1910) French writer

Rodd, James Rennell, first Baron Rennell (1858–1941) English diplomat and scholar

rodeo/ pl. **-s**

Roderic (d. 711) last king of the Visigoths, *not* -ick

Rodin, Auguste (1840–1917) French sculptor

rodomontade bragging talk, *not* rh-

roebuck (one word)

Roedean School Brighton

roe deer (two words)

roentgen/ former unit of ionizing radiation dose, now expressed in coulombs per kilogram; abbr. **R**; **-ography** photography with X-rays; **-ology** study of X-rays; *see also* **Röntgen**

ROF Royal Ordnance Factory

Roffen: the signature of the Bishop of Rochester (colon)

Rogation Sunday that before Ascension Day

Roget, Peter Mark (1779–1869) English physician and taxonomist, compiled *Roget's Thesaurus of English Words and Phrases*

rognons/ (Fr. m. pl.) kidneys, **— blancs** (Fr. cook) testicles

rogues' gallery *not* rogue's

Rohilkhand Uttar Pradesh, India; *not* Rohilc-, -und

Rohmer,/ Eric (b. 1920) French film director, **— Sax** pseud. of **Arthur Sarsfield Ward** (1883–1959) British mystery-writer

ROI Royal Institute of Oil Painters

roi fainéant (Fr.) do-nothing king, used specifically of any of the late Merovingians

roinek *use* **rooi-**

roisterer a noisy reveller, *not* roy-

rok *use* **roc**

Rokitansky, Karl, Baron von (1804–78) Czech-born Austrian anatomist

role an actor's part, in Fr. m. *rôle*

roll-call (hyphen, two words in US)

roller-coaster (hyphen; noun, two words in US)

roller skate (noun and verb; two words)

rolling pin (two words)

rollmop (one word)

rollock *use* **rowlock**

roll-on (noun and adj., hyphen)

Rolls-Royce (hyphen)

Rölvaag, Ole Edvart (1876–1931) Norwegian-US novelist

roly-poly a pudding, *not* the many variants

ROM (comput.) read-only memory

Rom/ a male Gypsy, pl. **-a** (cap.)

Rom. Roman, Romance, Romans (Epistle to the)

rom. roman type

Romaic the vernacular language of modern Greece, esp. its pure demotic or dialectal form

romaika a national dance of modern Greece

Romain, Jules (*c.*1499–1546) Italian architect, *but use* **Giulio Romano**

romain/ (Fr.) Roman, f. **-e**

romaine lettuce (US) = **cos lettuce**

Romains, Jules (1885–1972) French writer

rōmaji the Roman alphabet used to transliterate Japanese

roman (typ.) the ordinary upright letters as distinct from bold or italic, abbr. **rom.** (not cap.)

roman/ (Fr. m.) novel (*see* e.g. *roman-à-clef*, *roman-fleuve*); (medieval lit.) romance; also used of the language intermediate in time between Latin and Old French; (Fr. adj.) Romanesque (art, architecture), Romance (language, literature); f. **-e**

roman-à-clef (Fr. m.) a novel about real people under disguised identities, pl. *romans-à-clef*

romanais/ (Fr.) of or relating to the city of Romans-sur-Isère; f. **-e**

Roman Catholic/ (caps.) abbr. **RC**; **— — Church** (caps.), abbr. **RCC**

Romance (of or relating to) the languages derived from Latin regarded collectively

romance (Fr. f.) a sentimental song; (Sp. m.) an eight-syllable metre, or a ballad written in it (not ital. in Hispanic studies)

romancear (Sp.) to translate into Spanish; in Chile *also* to waste time chattering, *or* to flirt

Roman de la Rose 13th-c. French allegorical verse romance, the source of *Romaunt of the Rose*, attributed to Chaucer

Romanée-Conti a red burgundy wine

Romanes lectures at Oxford University

Romanesque the style of architecture *c.*900–1200, between classical and Gothic

roman-feuilleton (Fr. m.) a serial, pl. *romans-feuilletons*; *roman-fleuve* (Fr. m.) a long novel or novels about the same characters over a period, pl. *romans-fleuves*

Romania/, -n *not* Roum- or Rum- (except in hist. contexts to distinguish the modern state from the Roman world etc.)

romaniz/e *not* -ise, **-ation**

Romano a strong-tasting hard cheese

Romano- prefix meaning Roman, e.g. 'Romano-British' (hyphen, cap.)

roman/o (It., Sp.) Roman, f. **-a**

Romanov a Russian dynasty 1613–1917; *not* -of, -off

Romans, Epistle to the (NT) abbr. **Rom.**

Romansh (of) Rhaeto-Romanic, (esp.) the dialects of the Swiss canton of Grisons (*also* called **Grishun**); *not* Rou-, Ru-, -ansch, -onsch

Romantic/ of or relating to the 18th–19th-c. movement or style in the European arts (cap.), **-ism, -ist, -s**

Romany (of or concerning) a Gypsy, the Gypsies, or their Indo-European language; *not* -ncy, -mmany (cap.); in Romany *Romani*

romanza (It. f.) romance (medieval lit., music), aria

romanzesco (It.) adventurous, romantic (fiction)

romanz/o (It.) Romance, f. *-a*; (m.) romance, novel, fiction

Romaunt of the Rose *see* ***Roman de la Rose***

Romeo/ a young lover, pl. **-s** (cap.)

Romney, George (1734–1802) English painter

romneya a poppy-like shrub

Romney Marsh Kent

Romsey Hants.

Ronaldsay Orkney

Ronaldshay, Earl of the Marquess of Zetland's heir

Ronaldsway Airport IoM

Ronda Spain

rondavel (S. Afr.) a round tribal hut or any similar building

rondeau/ a poem of ten or thirteen lines with only two rhymes throughout, and with the opening words used twice as a refrain; pl. **-x**

rondel a special form of the rondeau

rondo/ (mus.) a movement with a recurring main theme, pl. **-s**

rone (Sc.) a gutter for carrying off rainwater from a roof

Röntgen,/ Julius (1855–1934) Dutch composer; **— Wilhelm Konrad von** (1845–1923) German physicist, discoverer of Röntgen (or X-) rays; *see also* **roentgen**

roo (Austral. colloq.) a kangaroo, *not* 'roo

rood abbr. **ro.**

roof garden (two words)

roof rack (two words, one word in US)

rooftop/, -s (one word)

rooinek (Afrik. sl. offens.) an Englishman, *not* roi-

rook (chess) abbr. **R**, *also* a bird

Rooke, Sir George (1650–1709) English admiral

room abbr. **rm.**

rooming house (two words)

room-mate (hyphen, one word in US)

room service (two words)

Roosevelt,/ Franklin Delano (1882–1945) US President 1933–45; **— Theodore** (1858–1919) US President 1901–9

root rummage, give support, search out; cf. **rout**

root (math.) sign √

root mean square (hyphens for adj., e.g. 'root-mean-square value') abbr. **rms**

rop/e, -eable, -ing, -y

rope-dancer (hyphen, one word in US)

rope ladder (two words)

rope-walk/, -er (hyphen, one word in US)

Roquefort a French cheese

ro-ro (adj.) roll-on roll-off (of shipping practices)

rorqual a whale

Rorschach test (psychol.) a personality test using ink-blots; *not* -scharch

rosaceous of the rose family

Rosalind a character in Shakespeare's *As You Like It,* and Spenser's *Shepheardes Calendar*

Rosaline a character in Shakespeare's *Love's Labour's Lost* and *Romeo and Juliet*

Rosamond Clifford, 'Fair' (d. *c.*1176) probable mistress of Henry II

rosary (RC) (the beads for) a set of devotions; cf. **rosery**

Roscommon Ireland

rose/ (Fr. m.) pink colour, (f.) a rose; *couleur de —* roseate, attractive

rosé pink wine

Rosebery, Earl of *not* -berry, -bury

rose/bowl, -bud (one word)

rose bush (two words, one word in US)

rose-coloured (hyphen)

rose/ garden, — hip (two words)

rosella an Australian parakeet

Rosencrantz and Guildenstern characters in Shakespeare's *Hamlet*

Rosencrantz and Guildenstern are Dead a comedy by T. Stoppard, 1966

Rosenkranz, Johann Karl Friedrich (1805–79) German metaphysical philosopher

Rosenkreuz *see* **Rosicrucian**

roseola (med.) a rosy rash, German measles

rose/-pink, -red (hyphens)

rosery a rose garden; cf. **rosary**

rose-tinted (hyphen)

rose tree (two words)

Rosetta/ Egypt, **— Stone** (caps.)

rose/ water, — window (two words)

rosewood (one word)

rosey *use* **-sy**

Rosh Hashanah the Jewish New Year's Day (not ital.), *not* -annah

Roshi the spiritual leader of a community of Zen Buddhist monks

Rosicrucian (a member) of a secretive 17th–18th-c. order devoted to metaphysical occult lore, said to be launched by a mythical 15th-c. knight, Christian Rosenkreuz

rosin a solid residue from turpentine distillation, used esp. on the bow of musical instruments; cf. **resin**

Rosinante *see* **Rocinante**

Roskilde/ Denmark; **Treaty of** — 1658, between Denmark and Sweden

Roslin Lothian

Rosny, Joseph Henry joint pseud. of brothers **Joseph Henri Boëx** (1856–1940) and **Séraphin Justin François Boëx** (1859–1948) French novelists

rosolio/ a sweet cordial of S. Europe, pl. **-s**; *not* -oglio, -oli (not cap.)

RoSPA Royal Society for the Prevention of Accidents

Ross,/ **Sir James Clark** (1800–62) English Arctic explorer; — **Sir John** (1777–1856) his uncle, Scottish explorer; — **Sir Ronald** (1857–1932) English physician

Rosse, Earl of

Rossellini, Roberto (1906–77) Italian film director

Rossetti,/ **Christina** (**Georgina**) (1830–94) English poet; — **Dante Gabriel** (1828–82) her brother, English painter and poet; — **Gabriele** (1783–1854) Italian poet and liberal, father of the other three; — **William Michael** (1829–1919) his son, English author and critic

Rosslyn, Earl of *see also* **Roslin**

Ross-shire (hyphen) latterly **Ross and Cromarty**, now part of Highland region

Rostand, Edmond (1868–1918) French playwright

roster a list of persons, showing rotation of duties

Rösti (Ger. f. pl. cook.) thinly sliced fried potatoes

Rostropovich, Mstislav (**Leopoldovich**) (b. 1927) Russian cellist and conductor

rostr/**um** a speaker's platform, pl. **-a** (not ital.)

ros/**y** *not* -ey, **-ily**

rot/, **-ted**, **-ting**

rota/ a roster, pl. **-s**; **the** — the supreme ecclesiastical and secular court of the Roman Catholic Church (cap.)

Rotarian a member of a Rotary Club (cap.)

rotary revolving, *not* rotatory; (print.) a printing machine in which the plate(s) are mounted on a cylinder

Rotary Club a branch of Rotary International, a charitable society (caps.)

rotator a revolving part, (anat.) a muscle that rotates a limb

rotatory *use* **rotary**

Rotavator (propr.) a rotary cultivator, *not* Roto-

rotchet *use* **roch-**

rote mechanical memory or performance

Rothamsted Herts., agricultural station for soil research

Rothe, Richard (1799–1867) German theologian

Rothes/ Grampian, **Earl of** —

Rothschild a European family of bankers

rôti (Fr. m. cook.) roast meat

rotifer/ a minute aquatic animal, pl. **-s**; **Rotifera** the phylum containing them

rotogravure (print.) the printing from photogravure cylinders on a web-fed rotary press

rotor (mech.) a revolving part

rottenstone decomposed siliceous limestone (one word)

Rottingdean E. Sussex (one word)

Rottweiler a tall black-and-tan breed of dog (not cap. in US)

rotunda/ a domed circular building or hall, pl. **-s**

roturl/**er** (Fr.) f. **-ère** a commoner (as opposed to a noble)

Rouault, Georges (1871–1958) French painter

Roubiliac, Louis François (*c*.1705–62) French sculptor, *not* -lliac

rouble a Russian coin and monetary unit, *not* ru- (US); abbr. **r.**; in Russ. *rubl´*

rouche *use* **ru-**

roué a debauchee (not ital.)

Rouge/ **Croix,** — **Dragon** pursuivants

rouge-et-noir a game of chance (hyphens, not ital.)

Rougemont, Louis De assumed name of **Louis Grin** (1847–1921) Swiss-born adventurer and writer

Rouget de Lisle, Claude Joseph (1760–1836) composer of 'La Marseillaise', *not* l'Isle

rough trump, *use* **ruff**

rough-and-/-ready, -tumble (hyphens)

rough breathing (typ.) *see* **breathing**

roughcast (one word)

rough/-dry, -hew (hyphens)

rough house (two words, one word in US)

roughneck (one word)

rough pull (print.) a proof pulled by hand on inferior paper for correction purposes

rough-rider (hyphen, one word in US) *but* Teddy Roosevelt's **Rough Riders** (caps., two words)

roughshod (one word)

Rougon-Macquart a family depicted in a cycle of novels by Émile Zola (hyphen)

roulade (cook.) a dish cooked or served in the shape of a roll, (mus.) a florid passage in solo vocal music on one syllable (not ital.)

rouleau/ a cylindrical roll of coins, pl. **-x** (not ital.)

Roumania/, -n *use* **Rom-**

Roumansh *use* **Rom-**

Roumelia/, -n *use* **Rum-**

round about (adv. and prep., two words) *but*
roundabout (noun and adj., one word)

roundhouse (one word)

rounding (bind.) shaping the back of a book
into a convex curve

round robin (two words)

roundworm (one word)

rouseabout (Austral., NZ) an unskilled
labourer or odd jobber, esp. on a farm; *see
also* **roustabout**

Rousseau,/ Henri (1844–1910) French painter,
called *Le Douanier*; — **Jean Baptiste** (1670–
1741) French poet; — **Jean-Jacques** (1712–72)
Geneva-born French philosopher; — **Pierre
Étienne Théodore** (1812–67) French painter

Roussillon a French province, a red wine from
there

roustabout a labourer on an oil rig, an
unskilled or casual labourer, (US) a dock
labourer or deckhand; *see also* **rouseabout**

rout (verb) to put to flight; (noun) a rabble, a
disorderly retreat; cf. **root**

route/ a way taken from a starting point to a
destination; **-ing**

Routledge publishers

roux (cook.) a mixture of fat and flour

ROW (econ.) rest of the world

rowing boat (two words) *not* rowboat (US)

rowlock (naut.) *not* roll-, rull-

Roxburgh Borders

Roxburghe, Duke of *not* -burg

Roxburghe Club an exclusive club for bibliophiles

royal/ a former size of paper, 20 × 25 in.; —
4to $12\frac{1}{2}$ × 10 in., — **8vo** 10 × $6\frac{1}{4}$ in.
(untrimmed)

Royal/ (cap.) abbr. **R.**; — **Academy, — Academician, — Artillery** abbr. **RA**

Royal Greenwich Observatory Cambridge,
formerly at Herstmonceaux, originally at
Greenwich; abbr. **RGO**

Royal Highness abbr. **RH**

Royal Military Academy Greenwich (no
comma)

Royal Society abbr. **RS**

royal/ standard used solely by the monarch,
other members of the royal family having a
— **banner**

Royal/ Welch Fusiliers, — Welch Regiment
(*but* **Welsh Guards**)

roysterer *use* **roi-**

RP read for press, received pronunciation,
Reformed Presbyterian, reply paid, reprint, (Fr.)
Révérend Père (Reverend Father), Royal Society
of Portrait Painters

RPC Royal Pioneer Corps

RPE Reformed Protestant Episcopal

RPI retail price index

RPM resale price maintenance

rpm revolutions per minute (no points)

RPO Royal Philharmonic Orchestra

rps revolutions per second (no points)

RPS Royal Philharmonic Society, Royal Photographic Society

RQMS Regimental Quartermaster-Sergeant

RR (US) railroad, rural route

RRC (Lady of the) Royal Red Cross

RS (US) Received Standard, Revised Statutes,
Royal Scots, Royal Society

Rs rupees

r.s. right side

RSA Royal Scottish Academ/y, -ician; Royal Society of Arts

RSAA Royal Society for Asian Affairs

RSC Royal Shakespeare Company, Royal Society
of Chemistry

RSD Royal Society of Dublin

RSE Royal Society of Edinburgh

RSFSR Russian Soviet Federative Socialist
Republic, largest republic in the former USSR

RSH Royal Society of Health

R. Signals Royal Corps of Signals

RSL Royal Society of Literature

RSM Regimental Sergeant Major, Royal School
of Mines, Royal Society of Medicine, Royal
Society of Musicians of Great Britain

RSMA Royal Society of Marine Artists

RSO railway sub-office, railway sorting office

RSPB Royal Society for the Protection of Birds

RSPCA Royal Society for the Prevention of
Cruelty to Animals

RSRE Royal Signals and Radar Establishment

RSV Revised Standard Version (of Bible)

RSVP *répondez, s'il vous plaît* (please reply) (do
not use in writings in French, or in the third
person)

RT radio-telegraphy, radio-telephony, received
text

rt. right

RTE Radio Telefis Éireann

Rt. Hon. Right Honourable

RTO Railway Transport Officer

RTR Royal Tank Regiment

Rt. Revd Right Reverend (of a bishop or moderator)

RTS Royal Toxophilite Society

RTYC Royal Thames Yacht Club

RU Rugby Union

Ru ruthenium (no point)

Ruanda *use* **Rw-**

rub-a-dub/ make the sound of a drum, **-bed, -bing** (hyphens)

rubai a quatrain in Persian poetry, pl. *rubaiyat*; in Pers. (and in specialist works) *rubāʿī*, pl. *rubāʿiyāt*; *see also* next entry

Rubáiyát of Omar Khayyám, The a collection of Persian poetry translated by E. FitzGerald, 1859

rubato/ (mus.) (performed at) tempo varied for expressive effect, pl. **-s**

rubber (Brit.) eraser, *or* (colloq.) condom; **-s** (US) galoshes, *or* (colloq.) condoms

rubber stamp (hyphen as verb)

rubef/y to make red, *not* -ify; **-acient, -action**

rubella (med.) German measles; cf. **rubeola**

Rubens, Peter Paul (1577–1640) Flemish painter, *not* Reu-

rubeola (med.) measles; cf. **rubella**

Rubicon, cross the take an irretraceable step (cap.); **rubicon** (noun and verb; in piquet, not cap.)

rubidium symbol **Rb**

Rubinstein,/ Anton (**Grigorevich**) (1829–94) Russian composer and pianist, **— Artur** (1886–1982) Polish-born American pianist

ruble *use* **rou-** (except in US)

RUC (hist.) Royal Ulster Constabulary

ru/c, -ck, -kh *use* **roc**

ruch/e a quilling or frilling, **-ing**; *not* rou-

rudbeckia a composite garden plant of the genus *Rudbeckia*; cf. **rutabaga**

Rüdesheimer a Rhine wine

RUE (theat.) right upper entrance

ru/e a herb, to regret; **-eful, -ing**

rue (Fr. f.) street, (herb) rue; in Fr. not cap. with street names; in Eng. cap., not ital.

ruff a frill worn round the neck, esp. in the 16th c.; a domestic pigeon; a wading bird, f. **reeve**; a perch-like fish (*not* ruffe); (to) trump at cards

rug/a (Lat.) a wrinkle, pl. **-ae**

Rugbeian a member of Rugby School

rugby football (not cap.) colloq. **rugger**

Ruhmkorff/, Heinrich Daniel (1803–77) German-born French electrical inventor, **— coil**

RUKBA Royal United Kingdom Beneficent Association

rule/ (typ.) a line; **dotted** ...; **double** ════; **em** —; **en** –; **French** ──◆──; **milled** ----------; **parallel** ════; **single** ───; **spread** *or* **swelled** ───; **total** ════; **wavy** 〜〜〜

'Rule, Britannia!' (comma, to denote an imperative rather than an invitation)

rullock *use* **row-**

Rumania/, -n *use* **Rom-**

Rumansh *use* **Rom-**

rumba/ a dance; **-ed, -ing, -s**; *not* rhu-

rumb-line *use* **rh-**

Rumelia/ an area of the Balkans, mainly in Bulgaria; **-n**; *not* Rou-

rumen/ a ruminant's first stomach, pl. **-s**

rumin/ant an animal that chews the cud; **-ator** one who ponders, *not* -er

rummage sale (US) = **jumble sale**

Rump, the (hist.) the remnant of the English Long Parliament 1648–53, or after its restoration in 1659

Rumpelstiltskin a dwarf in German folklore, in Ger. **Rumpelstilzchen**

run (naut.) deserted, abbr. **R.**; (US) = **ladder** (in hosiery)

runabout a small light vehicle (one word)

runaway (noun and adj., one word)

rune any of the letters of the earliest Germanic alphabet, used also by Scandinavians and Anglo-Saxons; a Finnish poem or a division of it

Runeberg, John Ludwig (1804–77) Finnish poet

rune-staff a magic wand inscribed with runes, or a runic calendar or almanac (hyphen)

running/ foot(**line**) a line of type set in margin at foot of page; *see also* next entry

running/ head(**line**) *or* **— title** (typ.) a line of type set in the head margin of a page

Runnymede a meadow on the River Thames where King John sealed Magna Carta, 1215

run-off (noun, hyphen, one word in US)

run-of-the-mill (hyphens)

run on (typ.) (matter) to be set without break or paragraph; the continued operation of press subsequent to first (or stated quantity of) copy

run round (typ.) to set text etc. round three or more sides of a block on a page, as with illustrations, tables, etc.

runway (one word)

Runyon/, (Alfred) Damon (1884–1946) US journalist and author, **-esque**

rupee the chief monetary unit of India, Pakistan, Sri Lanka, Nepal, Mauritius, and the Seychelles; in Hind. *rūpiyah*; abbr. **Re**, pl. **Rs**, tens of rupees **Rx**

Rupert's Land, Prince Canada

rupiah the chief monetary unit of Indonesia, abbr. **Rp**

RUR Royal Ulster Regiment, (hist.) Royal Ulster Rifles

RUR *Rossum's Universal Robots* (title of a play by K. Čapek, 1920)

ruralize *not* -ise

Ruritania/ an imaginary setting in SE Europe in the novels of Anthony Hope, **-n** relating to or characteristic of romantic adventure or its setting

RUSI Royal United Services Institute for Defence Studies

rus in urbe (Lat.) the country within a town

Russ. Russia, -n

**Russell/, Bertrand (Arthur William),
Earl** (1872–1970) English philosopher and mathematician; **Baron — of Liverpool**; *also* the family name of Duke of Bedford and Barons Ampthill and De Clifford; **—, George** *see* **A.E.**; **Jack —** a breed of terrier

Russell cord a ribbed fabric (two words)

Russia/, -n abbr. **Russ.**

Russia leather (bind.) a durable bookbinding leather from skins impregnated with birch-bark oil

rut/, -ted, -ting, -ty

rutabaga (US) = **swede**; cf. **rudbeckia**

Ruth (OT) not to be abbr.

ruthenium symbol **Ru**

Rutherford,/ Ernest, Baron (1871–1937) New Zealand scientist; **— Mark** pseud. of **William Hale White** (1831–1913) English writer

rutherfordium symbol **Rf**

Ruthven, Baron

Ruwenzori mountain, Uganda and Congo

Ruy Lopez a chess opening, from **Ruy López** (16th-c.) Spanish chess master; also called 'the Spanish opening'

Ruysbroeck, Jan van (1293–1387) Flemish mystic

Ruysdael,/ Jakob van (1628–82) and **— Salomon van** (1600–70) Dutch painters

RV Revised Version (of the Bible)

RW Right Worshipful, Right Worthy

Rwanda/ Cent. Africa; *not* Ru-; **-n**

RWF Royal Welch Fusiliers

RWS Royal Society of Painters in Water Colours

Rx tens of rupees

Ry. railway

RYA Royal Yachting Association

ryegrass (one word)

Rye House Plot 1682–3 (no hyphens, three caps.)

ryokan a traditional Japanese inn

ryot an Indian peasant, in Urdu *ra'īyat*

RYS Royal Yacht Squadron (a club)

Ryukyu Islands Japan, *not* the many variants

S (Lat.) *semi* (half, e.g. IIS = $2\frac{1}{2}$); siemens; sulphur; (on timepiece regulator) slow; the eighteenth in a series

S. Sabbath, Saint, school, series, *Signor,* Socialist, Society, soprano; south, -ern; sun, Sunday, surplus, (Fr.) *saint* (saint), (Ger.) *Seite* (page), (Lat.) *sepultus* (buried), *socius* or *sodalis* (Fellow)

S/. sucre (currency of Ecuador)

s second, -s (of time or angle)

s. section, see; sets, -s; shilling, -s; sign, -ed; singular, (meteor.) snow, solo, son, spherical, stem, (meteor.) stratus cloud, substantive, succeeded; (Fr.) *siècle* (century), *sud* (south); (Ger.) *siehe* (see), (It.) *sinistra* (left)

s/ (Fr.) *sur* (on) e.g. Boulogne s/M = Boulogne-sur-mer

's abbr. for Du. *des* (of the), as 's-Gravenhage (The Hague); arch. prefix (esp. in oaths) for *God's,* as 'sblood, 'struth

% *see* dal segno

$ *or* $ the dollar sign; to be before, and close up to, numerals

∫ italic form of the **long s**, (math.) sign of integration

SA the Salvation Army, sex appeal, South Africa, South America, South Australia, (Sp.) *Sociedad Anónima* (public limited company), (Port.) *Sociedade Anónima* (public limited company), (Brazilian Port.) *Sociedade Anônima* (public limited company), (Fr.) *Société Anonyme* (public limited company), (Ger.) *Sturm-Abteilung* (the paramilitary force of the Nazi Party)

sa. sable

s.a. *sine anno* (without date)

Saar/ a river and region; **-land** a province of Germany (one word)

Sabaean of ancient Yemen

Sabah a part of Malaysia

Sabaism star worship in ancient Arabia and Mesopotamia (cap.)

Sabaoth, Lord (**God**) **of** (Scripture) Lord of Hosts (cap.), in Heb *ṣᵉbāōṯ*; cf. **sabbath**

Sabatini, Rafael (1875–1950) Anglo-Italian author

Sabbatarian/, -ism (caps.)

sabbath/ (**day**) (not cap.), **— day's journey** (Heb.) about two-thirds of a mile; cf. **Sabaoth**

Sabian (a member) of a sect classed in the Koran with Muslims, Jews, and Christians, as believers in the true God

Sabine (of or relating to) a people of the Cent. Apennines in ancient Italy

sable (her.) black

sabra a Jew born in Israel (not cap.), in Modern Heb. *sābrāh*

sabre/ *not* -er (US)

sabretache *not* -tash, -tasche

sabre-toothed/ cat, — tiger

sabreur a user of the sabre, esp. a cavalryman

SAC Senior Aircraftman, (US) Strategic Air Command

sac (med., biol.) a baglike cavity

saccharimeter an instrument for measuring sugar content by means of polarized light, *not* -ometer

saccharin a non-fattening sugar substitute

saccharine (adj.) sugary, either literally or figuratively

saccharometer an instrument for measuring sugar content by hydrometry, *not* -imeter

sachem the supreme chief of some Native American tribes, (US) a political leader

Sacheverell, Henry (?1674–1724) English ecclesiastic and politician

Sachlichkeit/ (Ger. f.) objectivity, realism; **Neue —** a German art movement

Sachs,/ Hans (1494–1576) German poet; **— Julius** (1832–97) German botanist; *see also* **Sax; Saxe**

Sachsen Ger. for Saxony

sackbut a medieval trombone

sackcloth (one word)

sack race (two words)

Sackville-West, Victoria Mary (**'Vita'**) (1892–1962) English author

sacral (anat.) of or relating to the sacrum, (anthrop.) of or for sacred rites

sacr/é (Fr.) f. **-ée** sacred

Sacred College (RC) the body of cardinals

sacrileg/e, -ious *not* sacre-, -ligious

SACW Senior Aircraftwoman

SAD (med.) seasonal affective disorder

Saddam Hussein (**al-Takriti**) (b. 1937) president of Iraq 1979–

saddlebag (one word)

saddle blanket (two words)

saddle bow (two words, one word in US)

saddlecloth (one word)

saddle/ horse, — shoe, — soap (two words)

saddle-sore (hyphen, two words in US)

saddle stitch (bind.) stitching of thread or wire staple through the centre of a pamphlet or magazine placed open on a saddle-shaped support (two words)

Sadduce/e, -an

sadhu an Indian holy man, sage, or ascetic

Saʿdī (?1184–1291) Persian poet, born **Muslih Addin**

sadism a sexual perversion marked by love of cruelty, from **Donatien Alphonse François, comte ('marquis') de Sade** (1740–1814) French soldier and writer

Sadleir, Michael born **Sadler** (1888–1957) English author, bibliographer, and publisher, son of following

Sadler, Sir Michael Ernest (1861–1943) English educationist

sadomasochism (one word)

sae stamped (self-)addressed envelope

safari/ pl. **-s**

safe/ **conduct, — deposit** (hyphen when attrib.)

safety/ **belt, — catch, — curtain, — film, — glass, — lamp, — match, — net, — pin, — razor, — valve** (two words)

Saffron Walden Essex (no hyphen)

S. Afr. South Africa, **-n**

saga/ pl. **-s** an Old Norse (spec. Icelandic) prose narrative, hence any long or heroic story; in the original, titles of individual sagas have only an initial cap. and no possessive apos., e.g. *Kórmáks saga*, *Njáls saga*; the title may also be compounded with the preceding genitive, e.g. *Sturlungasaga*, but note e.g. *Gunnlaugs saga ormusungu* where the name has a following attribute

sagesse (Fr. f.) wisdom

Saghalien Island *use* **Sakhalin**

sago/ a palm, a starch produced from it, pl. **-s**

Sahara/ desert (in Arab. *ṣaḥrā*) *not* — Desert; **-n**

sahib (Ind.) European master, gentleman; (cap.) an honorific affix, as Smith Sahib; f. **memsahib**; **pukka sahib** perfect gentleman

Saidpur India, *not* Sayyid-

saignant/ (Fr. cook.) f. **-e** underdone, rare

Saigon *now* **Ho Chi Minh City**

sailboat (US) = **sailing boat** (one word)

sailcloth (one word)

sailed abbr. **sld.**

sailer a ship of specified power

sailing/ **boat, — ship** (two words)

sailor a seaman or -woman

Sailors' Home *not* -'s

sailplane (one word)

sainfoin (bot.) a leguminous fodder plant, *not* saint-

Saint abbr. **S., St**; pl. **SS, Sts**

St Abbs *but* **St Abb's Head** Borders

St Albans/ Herts.; **Bishop** *and* **Duke of** — — (no apos.)

St Albans: the signature of the Bishop (colon)

St Alban's Head Dorset (apos.)

St Aldwyn, Earl

St Andrews (**University**) Fife (no apos.)

St Andrew's/ **Cross** ×, — — **Day** 30 Nov.

St Andrews, Dunkeld, and Dunblane, Bishop of

St Anne's/ **College** Oxford; — — **Day** 26 July; — — **on Sea** Lancs. (no hyphens, apos.)

St Anthony's/ **cross** ⊤; — — **fire** erysipelas

St Antony's College Oxford

St Arvans Gwent (no apos.)

St Aubin Jersey, *not* Aubin's

St Barnabas's Day 11 June

St Barthélemy French W. Indies

St Bartholomew's Day 24 Aug.; *see also* **Bartholomew Day**

St Bees (**Head, School**) (St Begha's) Cumbria (no apos.)

St Benet's Hall Oxford

St Bernard (dog or Pass)

St Boswells Borders (no apos.)

St Catharines Ontario (no apos.)

St Catharine's College Cambridge

St Catherine's College Oxford

St Christopher Island W. Indies (no apos.); *see also* **St Kitts-Nevis**

St Clears Dyfed (no apos.)

St Clement's Day 23 Nov.

St Crispin's Day 25 Oct.

St Cross Church *and* **College** Oxford

St Davids/ **Head** Dyfed, *and* **Viscount** — — (no apos.)

St David's Day 1 Mar.

St Denis's Day 9 Oct.

St Dunstan's Day 19 May

St Ebbe's Oxford

Sainte-Beuve, Charles Augustin (1804–69) French literary critic

Sainte-Claire Deville, Henri Étienne (1818–81) French chemist (one hyphen)

St Edm. and Ipswich: the signature of the Bishop of St Edmundsbury and Ipswich

St Edmund Hall Oxford

St Edmund's House Cambridge

St Elmo's fire an electric discharge, a corposant

Saint-Émilion a claret

Saint-Estèphe a claret

Saint-Étienne dép. Loire, France

Saint-Exupéry, Antoine Jean Baptiste (**Marie Roger**) **de** (1900–44) French aviator and writer

St Fillans Tayside (no apos.)

saintfoin *use* **sain-**

St Frideswide/ patron of Oxford (city and university), — —**'s Day** 19 Oct.

Saint-Gall *or* **St Gallen** Switzerland

St George's/ Channel, — — Day 23 Apr. (apos.)

St Germans, Bishop *and* **Earl of**

St Giles' an Oxford street (apos.)

St Gotthard Switzerland, *not* Goth-

St Gregory's Day 12 Mar.

St Helens/ Cumbria, IoW, Merseyside; **Baron** — — (no apos.)

St Helier Jersey

St Ive Corn.

St Ives Cambs., Corn., Dorset (no apos.)

St James's the British court

St James's Day 25 July

St James's/ Palace, — — Park, — — Square, — — Street London

St John as proper name pron. 'sinjun' (stress on first syllable)

Saint John New Brunswick

St John Ambulance/ Association, — — — Brigade *not* John's

St John's/ Antigua; NF, Que., Canada; — — **College** Oxford, Cambridge, Durham; — — **Wood** London; — — **wort** any yellow-flowered plant of the genus *Hypericum* (three words, two hyphens in US)

St John the Baptist's Day 24 June

St John the Evangelist's Day 27 Dec.

Saint-Julien a claret (hyphen)

St Just/ Corn., **Baron** — —

Saint-Just, Louis Antoine Léon de (1767–94) French revolutionary

St Just-in-Roseland Corn. (hyphens)

St Kitts-Nevis St Christopher Island, W. Indies; *properly* **the Federation of St Christopher and Nevis** (no apos.)

St Lambert's Day 17 Sept.

St Lawrence River Canada

St Lawrence's Day 10 Aug.

St Leger a race; as surname pron. 'sillinger' *or* 'sentlejer' (stress on first syllable)

St Leonards/ Bucks., Dorset, Lothian, Strathclyde; **Baron** — — (no apos.)

St Leonards-on-Sea E. Sussex (hyphens, no apos.)

St Lucia W. Indies

St Luke's/ Day 18 Oct.; — — **summer** a warm period in mid-October

St Maarten, St Martin a Caribbean island divided between Dutch and French control respectively

St Margaret's at Cliffe Kent

St Margaret's Day 20 July

St Mark's Day 25 Apr.

St Martin-in-the-Fields a London church, *not* Martin's (hyphens)

St Martin's/ Day 11 Nov.; — — **summer** a warm period in mid-November

St Mary Abbots Kensington (no apos.)

St Mary Church S. Glam. (three words)

St Marychurch Devon (two words)

St Mary Cray London, *not* Mary's

St Matthew's Day 21 Sept.

St Matthias's Day 24 Feb., *not* Matthias'

St Mawes Corn.

St Michael and All Angels' Day 29 Sept.

St Michael's Mount Corn.; *see also* **Mont-Saint-Michel**

St Neot Corn.

St Neots Cambs. (no apos.)

St Nicholas patron of Russia, a town in Belgium

St Nicholas's clerks thieves

St Olaf the patron of Norway

St Patrick's Day 17 Mar.

St Paul Minn.

St Paul de Loanda *use* **Luanda**

saintpaulia any plant of the genus *Saintpaulia*, esp. the African violet

St Paul's/, — — Cray London; — — **Day** 25 Jan.

St Peter Port Guernsey, *not* Peter's

St Peter's/ Rome; — — **College** Oxford; — — **Day** 29 June

St Petersburg capital of Russia 1712–1918; called **Petrograd** Dec. 1914–Feb. 1924, thereafter **Leningrad**, till Oct. 1991, when it regained its original name; in Russ. **Sanktpeterburg** (one *s*), colloq. **Piter**; in Fr. **Saint-Pétersbourg**, in Ger. (**Sankt**) **Petersburg**, in It. (**S.**) **Pietroburgo**

St Philip and St James's Day 1 May

Saint-Pierre a claret

Saint-Pierre, Jacques Henri Bernardin de (1737–1814) French author

Saint-Saëns, Charles Camille (1835–1921) French composer

Saintsbury, George Edward Bateman (1845–1933) English literary critic

St Sepulchre, Church of

Saint-Simon,/ Claude Henri de Rouvroy, comte de (1760–1825) founder of French socialism, whence **-ism** a form of socialism; — **Louis de Rouvroy, duc de** (1675–1755) French diplomat and writer

St Simon and St Jude's Day 28 Oct.

St Stephen Corn.

St Stephen's/ the chapel of the Houses of Parliament; — — **Day** 26 Dec.

St Swithun *see* **Swithun**

St Thomas's Day 21 Dec.

St Valentine's Day 14 Feb.

St Vitus's dance Sydenham chorea, not Vitus'

Sakandarabad Hyderabad, India, *use* **Secunder-**; Uttar Pradesh, India, *use* **Sikandar-**

sake a Japanese fermented liquor; *not* -ké, -ki

Sakhalin an island, E. Asia; *not* Saghalien, Karafuto

Sakharov, Andrei (**Dmitrievich**) (1921–89) Russian physicist and dissident

Saki pseud. of **H**(**ector**) **H**(**ugh**) **Munro** (1870–1916) English writer

saki/ a S. American monkey, pl. **-s**

Sakta a member of a Hindu sect worshipping the Sakti, in Skt. *śākta*

Sakti (in Hinduism) the female principle, esp. when personified as the wife of a god (cap.); in Skt. *śakti*

Śākyamuni the title of Buddha

salaam the oriental salutation 'Peace', *not* -lam (not ital.); in Arab. *salām*

salable *use* **sale-** (except in US)

salad/ days, — dressing, — oil (two words)

salade a helmet, *use* **sallet**

salade (Fr. f.) lettuce, salad

salami/ a highly seasoned sausage, pl. **-s**; in It. *salame*, pl. *salami*; cf. *salume*

Salammbô a novel by Flaubert, 1862

salariat the salaried class, *not* -ate

saleable *not* sala- (US)

Salem Madras; Mass.

Salempur Uttar Pradesh, India

saleroom *not* salesroom (US)

Salesian (a member) of a RC order founded by Don Bosco in honour of St Francis de Sales

sales/man, -woman, -person (one word)

Salian of or relating to the Salii, a 4th-c. Frankish people living near the River Ijssel

Salic law *not* -ique

salicylic acid a chemical used as a fungicide, and in aspirin and dyestuffs

salient jutting out, conspicuous, (of an angle, esp. in fortification) pointing outwards (cf. **re-entrant**); (her.) (of a lion etc.) standing on its hind legs with the forepaws raised

Salinger,/ J(**erome**) **D**(**avid**) (b. 1919) US novelist, **— Pierre** (**Emil George**) (b. 1925) US journalist and writer

salle/ (Fr. f.) hall, **— à manger** dining room, **— d'attente** waiting room

sallenders a dry eruption on a horse's hind leg, *not* sellan-

sallet (hist.) a light helmet with an outward-curving rear part, *not* salade

Sallust in Lat., **Gaius Sallustius Crispus** (86–?34 BC) Roman historian, abbr. **Sall.**

Sally Lunn a teacake (caps., two words)

salmagundi/ a medley, a seasoned dish; pl. **-s**

salmanazar a wine bottle of about twelve times the standard size

salmi a ragout, esp. of game; in Fr. m. *salmis*

salmon trout (two words)

Salomon Brothers, Inc. a US investment bank; *not* So-, -an

salon (Fr.) reception room, hairdresser's etc. establishment (not cap.); an annual exhibition in Paris of living artists' pictures (cap.)

Salonika Greece

saloon/ — bar, — car (two words)

Salop. *now* Shropshire

Salopian (a native *or* inhabitant) of, *or* relating to, Shropshire

Salpêtrière, La a hospital, Paris

salpicon (Sp. m.) cold minced meat, *not* -çon

salsa (not ital.)

salsify (bot.) *not* -afy

SALT Strategic Arms Limitation Talks (*or* Treaty)

saltarello/ an Italian and Spanish dance, pl. **-s**

salt cellar (two words, one word in US)

salt lake (two words)

Salt Lake City Ut. (caps., three words)

salt mine (two words)

Saltoun, Baron

saltpetre *not* -peter (US)

saltus a sudden transition, a breach of continuity; pl. same

salt water (one word when attrib.)

Saltykov(-Shchedrin), M. E., pseud. of **graf Mikhail** (**Yevgrafovich**) **Saltykov** (1826–89) Russian satirical writer and journalist; pen name also **N. Shchedrin**

Saltykov-Shchedrin State Public Library St Petersburg (hyphen *not* en rule); now the **National Library of Russia**

saluki pl. **-s**

salum/e (It. cook.) salt meat (esp. pork), pl. **-*i***; cf. **salami**

salutary beneficial, *not* -ory

salutatory welcoming, *not* -ary

Salvador/, El republic of Cent. America; **-ean** in Sp. *salvadoreño*

salver a tray; cf. **salvor**

salvo/ a simultaneous discharge of guns, bombs, cheers, pl. **-es**; a reservation, excuse, pl. **-s**

salvo jure (Lat.) reserving the right

sal volatile ammonium carbonate, smelling salts

salvor one who salvages; cf. **salver**

Salzkammergut Austria

SAM surface-to-air missile

Sam. Samaritan

Sam., 1, 2 First, Second Book of Samuel

samarium symbol **Sm**

Samarkand Uzbekistan; *not* -cand, -quand

samba/ a Brazilian dance; **-ed, -ing, -s**

sambok (Afrik.) *use* **sjam-**

Sam Browne an army officer's belt with a shoulder strap

sambuca an Italian aniseed-flavoured liqueur, (hist.) a triangular stringed instrument, a kind of siege engine; *not* -cca

S. Amer. South America, -n

Samhain 1 Nov., Celtic festival marking the beginning of winter; in Scots Gaelic *Samhuinn*

Samhita a continuous version of a Vedic text, any of the basic collections of Vedic texts

Sami the preferred native and scholarly term for the Lapps collectively

Samian of or relating to Samon, an Aegean island

samisen a long three-stringed Japanese guitar, played with a plectrum (not ital.)

samizdat the secret publication of banned matter, as in the former USSR (not ital.)

Samnite (of or relating to) a member of a people of ancient Italy often at war with republican Rome, or the language of this people

Samoyed/ a Mongolian of NW Siberia, a breed of dog; *not* -oied, -oide, -oyede; **-ic**

sampan a small flat-bottomed Chinese boat, *not* san-

sampi *or* **sanpi** (Gr.) modern name (derived from 'san' and 'pi') for the character ϡ, used for 900, in Byzantine times called *parakyisma*

Sampson, Dominie a character in Scott's *Guy Mannering*

samsara in Indian philosophy, the endless cycle of death and rebirth to which life in the material world is bound; in Skt. *saṃsāra*

samskara in Indian philosophy, a purificatory ceremony or rite marking an event in one's life; a mental impression, instinct, or memory; in Skt. *saṃskāra*

Samuel, First, Second Book of (OT) abbr. **1 Sam., 2 Sam.**

samurai the Japanese military class (sing. and pl., not cap.), *not* -ourai

Sana'a N. Yemen, *properly* **Ṣanʿāʾ**; *not* Sanaa

sanatorium/ *not* sanitarium (US), pl. **-s**

sanatory healing; cf. **sanitary**

sanbenito/ a penitential garment, pl. **-s**

Sancho Panza Don Quixote's squire

Sancho-Pedro a card game (caps., hyphen)

sanctum/ a retreat, pl. **-s**; **— sanctorum** (Lat.) the holy of holies in a Jewish temple, a special retreat, pl. **sancta sanctorum** (not ital.)

Sand, George (*not* Georges) pseud. of **Madame Amandine Aurore Lucile Dupin, baronne Dudevant** (1804–76) French novelist

sandal/, -led, -wood

sandarac realgar, resin; *not* -ach

Sandars Reader Cambridge University

sand/bag, -bank, -bar (one word)

sandblast (noun and verb, one word)

sandbox (US) = **sandpit**

sandboy, happy as a (one word)

Sandburg, Carl (1878–1967) US poet

sandcastle (one word)

sand dollar a round flat sea urchin of the order *Exocycloida* (two words)

sand/paper, -piper (bird), **-pit, -stone, -storm** (one word)

sandwich/board, — course (two words)

sangar a stone breastwork round a hollow, *not* -ga

sang-de-bœuf (Fr. m.) a deep red colour

sangfroid composure (one word, not ital.)

sangria a Spanish drink made from red wine with fruit etc. (not ital.)

Sanhedrin the supreme council and court of justice in ancient Jerusalem, *not* -im

sanitarium *use* **sanatorium** (except in US)

sanitary healthy, *not* -ory; cf. **sanatory**

sanitize *not* -ise

Sankt (Ger.) saint, abbr. **St.**

sannup (Amer. Ind.) among some Native American peoples, a married man; *not* -op

sannyasi a Hindu religious mendicant, pl. same; *not* sany-; in Hind. and Urdu *sannyāsī*

sanpan *use* **sam-**

sanpi *see* **sampi**

sans (Fr.) without

San Salvador capital of El Salvador

sans/ appel (Fr.) without appeal, **— *cérémonie*** informally, **— *changer*** without changing

Sanscrit *use* **Sansk-**

sans-culott/e in the French Revolution, a lower-class extreme republican or revolutionary, pl. **-es**; **-erie, -ism, -ist** (hyphen); in Fr. m. *sans-culotte* (hyphen), *sans-culottisme*; **-id** (hist.) each of the five (in leap year six) complementary days added at the end of the month Fructidor of the French Republican calendar

sans doute (Fr.) no doubt

sanserif *use* **sans serif**

Sansevieria (bot.) a genus of lily

sans/ façon (Fr.) informally, **— *faute*** without fail, **— *gêne*** free and easy (hyphen if used as a noun)

Sanskrit abbr. **Skt.**

sans/ pareil (Fr.) unequalled, **— *peine*** without difficulty; **— *peur et sans reproche*** fearless and blameless, — **phrase** without circumlocution

sans serif (typ.) a typeface without serifs; use to illustrate shapes only in contexts where it is important to represent actual configuration exactly (e.g. 'K-angled', 'X-joint'), but not where the shape is understood (e.g. *The L-Shaped Room*, 'a T-shirt'); use a serif typeface for *I-beam* when representing the configuration, or the sense may be lost; (two words), *not* sanserif

Sanssouci the palace of Frederick II at Potsdam (one word)

sans/ souci (Fr.) without cares, — **tache** stainless

Santa (It., Sp., Port.) a female saint, abbr. **Sta**

Santa Ana Calif.

Santa Claus *not* Kl-

Santa Fe N. Mex., Argentina (no accent)

Santa Isabel *now* **Malabo**

Santander N. Spain (one word)

Santa Trinita Florence, *not* Trinità

Santayana, George b. **Jorge Agustín Nicolás Ruiz de Santayana y Borrais** (1863–1952) Spanish-born US philosopher and novelist

Santenot a burgundy wine

Santo Domingo a former name of the Dominican Republic, W. Indies; name of its capital

Santos-Dumont, Alberto (1873–1932) Brazilian airman

sanyasi *use* **sannyasi**

São (Port.) saint, e.g. in place names, as **São Miguel** Azores, **São Paulo** Brazil

Saône/ a French river; **Haute-** — a dép. of France (hyphen); **-et-Loire** a dép. of France, abbr. **S.-et-L.** (hyphens)

São Tomé and Príncipe W. Africa

Sapho an opera by Gounod, 1851; a novel by Daudet, 1884

sapienti sat (Lat.) sufficient for a wise man; in full *verbum sapienti sat est*, a word is enough to the wise

Sapper the official term for a private of the Royal Engineers, abbr. **Spr.** (cap.)

sapph/ics verse in sapphic stanzas, **-ism** homosexual relations between women (not cap.)

Sappho (*c*.600 BC) Greek poetess of Lesbos; adj. **Sapphic** *but* **sapphic/ metre**, — **verse** (not cap.)

SAR (US) Sons of the American Revolution

Sar. Sardinia, -n

SARA (comput.) search and replace automatically, pl. **SARAs**

saraband a stately old Spanish dance, the music for this; *not* -bande

Saragossa Spain, in Catalan same, in Sp. **Zaragoza**

sarai *use* **ser-**

Sarajevo Bosnia-Hercegovina

sarape *use* **ser-**

Sarawak a state in Malaysia

sarcenet *use* **sars-**

sarcom/a (med.) a tumour, pl. **-ata**

sarcophag/us a stone coffin, pl. **-i**

Sardinia in It. **Sardegna**, abbr. **Sar.**

Sardou, Victorien (1831–1908) French playwright

saree *use* **-ri**

sargasso/ a seaweed, pl. **-s**

Sargent,/ John Singer (1856–1925) US painter, — **Sir Harold Malcolm Watts** (1895–1967) English conductor

sari/ a garment worn by Indian women, *not* -ee; pl. **-s**; in Hind. **sāṟ(h)ī**

SARL *or* **Sarl** (Fr.) *société à responsabilité limitée* (private limited company)

sarong a Malay or Javanese long garment for man or woman

saros (astr.) a period of about eighteen years between repetitions of eclipses

sarsaparilla a preparation of dried roots used to flavour some drinks and medicines and formerly as a tonic; *not* saspa-, sassper-

sarsen (geol.) a sandstone boulder carried by ice during a glacial period, *not* sara-

sarsenet a fabric, *not* sarc-

Sartor Resartus 'the tailor retailored', by Carlyle, 1833–4

Sartre, Jean Paul (1905–80) French philosopher

Sarum the historical name of Salisbury

Sarum: the signature of the Bishop of Salisbury (colon)

SAS Special Air Service

Sasanian *see* **Sass-**

SASC Small Arms School Corps

s.a.s.e. (US) self-addressed stamped envelope

sashay (esp. US colloq.) walk or move ostentatiously, casually, or diagonally

sash/ cord, — **weight**, — **window** (two words)

sasine (Sc. law) (an act or document granting) the possession of feudal property; cf. **seisin**

Saskatchewan Canada, abbr. **Sask.**

Sasquatch a supposed yeti-like animal of NW America, *also called* **Bigfoot**

sassafras (bot., med.) a N. American tree, an infusion from its bark; *not* sasse-

Sassan/ian, -id (a member) of a Persian dynasty ruling AD 211–651; *properly* **Sasa-**, and thus in specialist contexts

Sassenach (Sc., Ir., usually derog.) (of) an English person or the English generally; in Scots Gaelic **Sasunnoch**, in Ir. **Sasanach**

Sat. Saturday

Satan (cap.)

satanic devilish (not cap. unless directly referring to Satan)

Satan/ism, -ology (caps.)

satay in Indonesian *sate*, in Malayan *satai*

SATB (mus.) (scored for) soprano, alto, tenor, bass

sateen a shiny fabric, *not* satt-

sati *use* **suttee**

satinet a thin satin, *not* -ette

satire a literary work holding up folly or vice to ridicule

satirize *not* -ise

satisfice (esp. econ., social sci.) perform the minimum required

sat sapienti see sapienti sat

satsuma/ a variety of tangerine (not cap.); **— ware** cream-coloured Japanese pottery (cap.)

satteen *use* **sat-**

Saturday abbr. **Sat.**

Saturnalia (Lat. pl.) the ancient Roman orgiastic festival of Saturn (cap.), a time or occasion of wild revelry (in this sense commonly sing., not cap.); adj. **saturnalian** (not cap.)

Saturnian of the god or planet Saturn (cap.)

saturnic (med.) affected with lead poisoning

saturnine of a sluggish, gloomy temperament, or having dark and brooding looks (not cap.)

satyagraha (Ind. hist.) a policy of passive resistance, esp. to British rule, as advocated by Gandhi (not ital.); in Hind. *satyāgraha*

satyr/, -ic; -iasis

Sauchiehall Street Glasgow

saucisse (Fr. f.) fresh pork sausage

saucisson (Fr. m.) a large, highly seasoned sausage

Saudi Arabia *formerly* Hejaz, Nejd, and Asir

sauerkraut (Ger.) chopped pickled cabbage (not ital.)

Saumur a French sparkling white wine

sauna bath (two words)

sausage/ dog (colloq.) a dachshund, **— meat, — roll** (two words)

Saussure/, Ferdinand de (1857–1913) Swiss linguistic scholar, **-an**

saut/é (food) lightly fried, to cook in this way; **-éd** *not* -éed (except in US)

Sauternes dép. Gironde, France; a white Bordeaux wine produced in this district; *not* Sauterne

sauve qui peut (Fr.) let him save himself who can

SAVAK (hist.) the secret intelligence organization of Iran 1957–79; acronym from the Persian Sāzmān-i-Attalāt Va Amnīyat-i-

Keshvar (National Security and Intelligence Organization)

savannah a treeless plain of subtropical regions, *not* -na (US)

Savannah a river and town, Ga.; a town, Tenn.

savant/ a man of learning, pl. **-s**; f. **-e**, pl. **-es** (not ital.)

Savigny a red burgundy

Savile/ the family name of the Earl of Mexborough; **Baron —; — Club, — Row** London; **—, Sir Henry** (1549–1622) founder of the Savilian chairs at Oxford; *not* -ille

savin a kind of juniper; (US) = **red cedar**; *not* -ine

savings/ bank, — certificate (two words)

saviour *not* -ior (US)

savoir-faire skill, tact (not ital.)

savoir-vivre (Fr.) good breeding (hyphens)

Savonarola, Girolamo (1452–98) Italian religious reformer

savory/ the herb (**summer —, winter —**)

savoury appetiz/er, -ing; *not* -ory (US)

Savoyard of Savoy (region or theatre)

saw/dust, -fish, -mill (one word)

sawn-off *not* sawed-off (US)

sawtooth (one word)

saw-wort a composite plant yielding a yellow dye (hyphen)

sax (colloq.) saxophone; a slater's chopper, *not* zax

Sax. Saxon, Saxony

Sax, Adolphe (1814–94) Belgian inventor of saxhorn and saxophone; *see also* **Sachs**; **Saxe**

Saxe Fr. for Saxony, in Ger. **Sachsen**

Saxe,/ Hermann Maurice, comte de (1696–1750) French marshal; **— John Godfrey** (1816–87) US poet and humorous writer; *see also* **Sachs; Sax**

saxe (Fr. m.) Dresden china

Saxe/-Altenburg, -Coburg-Gotha, -Meiningen, -Weimar (hyphens) former duchies in eastern Germany, incorporated in Thuringia (Coburg in Bavaria) 1919; in Ger. **Sachsen-**

saxhorn a brass wind instrument with a long winding tube and bell opening

Saxon/, -y abbr. **Sax.**

saxony a fine kind of wool, cloth made from this (not cap.)

saxophone a brass wind instrument with keys and a reed like that of a clarinet, colloq. **sax**

SAYE save as you earn

Saye and Sele, Baron

say-so (noun, hyphen)

Sayyidpur *use* **Said-**

Sb *stibium* (antimony) (no point)

sb stilb

sb. substantive

s.b. single-breasted

S-bend (cap., hyphen); *see also* **sans serif**

SBN *see* **ISBN**

SC South Carolina, Special Constable, Staff College, Staff Corps, Supreme Court, (Lat.) *senatus consultum* (a decree of the Senate), (law) same case, (paper) super-calendered

Sc scandium (no point)

Sc. Scotch, Scots, Scottish

sc. scene, scruple, (Lat.) *scilicet* (namely)

s.c. (typ.) small capitals

sc. *sculpsit* (carved or engraved this)

Sca Fell an English mountain, Cumbria; *not* Scaw (two words)

Scafell Pike the highest English mountain, Cumbria (two words)

scagliola an imitation marble, *not* scal-

scal/a (anat.) a canal in the cochlea, pl. **-ae**

Scala, La a theatre, Milan; in full **Teatro alla Scala**

scalable *not* -eable

scalar (math., phys.) (of a quantity) having only magnitude, not direction; a scalar quantity

scalawag use **scally-** (except in US)

scald an ancient Scandinavian composer and reciter, *use* **sk-**

scaler one who, *or* that which, scales

Scaliger,/ Joseph Justus (1540–1609) French philologist; **— Julius Caesar** (1484–1558) his father, Italian-born scholar

scaliola *use* **scagl-**

scallop/ a shellfish, a shallow pan or dish, a decorative edging; **-ed, -ing**; *not* sco-, escallop

scallywag a scamp, an ill-fed animal; *not* scalla-, scala- (US)

scampi (pl.) breaded langoustines or large prawns; (sing.) a dish of these; in It. *scamp/o*, pl. *-i*

scan/, **-ned, -ning, -sion**

Scand. Scandinavia, -n

scandalize *not* -ise

scandal/um magnatum (Lat.) defamation of high personages, pl. *-a magnatum*; abbr. *scan. mag.*

Scandinavia/, -n includes Denmark, Norway, Sweden, Iceland, and the Faeroe Islands, but not Finland; abbr. **Scand.**

scandium symbol **Sc**

SCAPA Society for Checking the Abuses of Public Advertising

Scapigliatura, La a 19th-c. Italian literary movement

s. caps. (typ.) small capitals

scar the craggy part of a cliff etc., *not* -aur

scaramouch (arch.) a boastful coward, a braggart, esp. as a stock character in Italian farce; in It. **Scaramuccia**, Fr. **Scaramouche**

Scarborough N. Yorks.

Scarbrough, Earl of

scare/crow, -monger (one word)

scar/f a strip of material worn around the neck, pl. **-ves**; (make) a join in the ends (of timber, metal, leather), pl. **-fs**

scarlatina scarlet fever, *not* scarlet-

Scarlatti,/ Alessandro (1660–1725) and **— Domenico** (1685–1757) his son, Italian composers

Scarlett family name of Baron Abinger

scaur *use* **scar**

Scaw Fell *use* **Sca Fell**

scazon (prosody) *see* **choliamb**

Sc.B. *Scientiae Baccalaureus* (Bachelor of Science)

SCC Sea Cadet Corps

Sc.D. *Scientiae Doctor* (Doctor of Science)

SCE Scottish Certificate of Education

scen/a (It., Lat.) a scene in a play or opera; It. pl. *-e*, Lat. pl. *-ae*

scenario/ an outline of a ballet, play, or film; pl. **-s**

scène/ (Fr. f.) scene, stage; *en* — on the stage

Scenes of Clerical Life by George Eliot, 1858, *not from* or *of a*

scep/sis philosophic doubt, **-tic** one inclined to disbelieve; adj. **-tical**; *not* sk- (US)

sceptre *not* -er (US)

SCGB Ski Club of Great Britain

sch. scholar, school, schooner

schadenfreude malicious glee, delight in others' misfortune; in Ger. f. **Schadenfreude**

Schadow,/ Friedrich (1789–1862) German painter; **— Johann Gottfried** (1764–1850) German sculptor, father of Rudolph and Friedrich; **— Rudolph** (1786–1822) German sculptor

Schäfer, E. A. *see* **Sharpey-Schafer**

schako *use* **sha-**

schallot, schalom *use* **sh-**

Schaumburg-Lippe Germany (hyphen)

Scheele/, Karl Wilhelm (1742–86) German chemist, **—'s green** (apos.)

Scheherazade the relater in *The Arabian Nights*; a more scholarly transliteration from Pers. is 'Shahrazād' *or* 'Šīrazād'; the symphonic suite by Rimsky-Korsakov is *Sheherazade*, 1888; the combined song cycle by Ravel and poems by Tristan Klingsor is *Shéhérazade*, 1903

Schelde a river, Belgium–Holland; *not* -dt; in Fr. **Escaut**

Schelling, Friedrich Wilhelm Joseph von (1775–1854) German philosopher

schem/a (Gr.) an outline, pl. **-ata**

schematize *not* -ise

schemozzle *use* **sh-**

Schenectady NY

scherzando/ (mus.) in a playful or lively manner; as noun, pl. **-s**

scherzo/ (mus.) a playful or vigorous piece or movement, pl. **-s**

Schiedam (cap.) Dutch gin, schnapps

Schiehallion a mountain, Tayside

Schiller, Johann Christoph Friedrich von (1759–1805) German poet

schilling the chief monetary unit of Austria

Schimmelpenninck, Mary Anne (**Mrs**) (1778–1856) English writer

Schimpf/wort (Ger.) an insulting epithet, a term of abuse; pl. **-wörter**

schipperke a breed of small black tailless dog; *not* ski-

schizanthus (bot.) the butterfly flower

schizo/ (colloq.) schizophrenic, pl. **-s**

schlemiel (US colloq.) a foolish or unlucky person (not ital.), in Yiddish **shlemiel**

Schlesinger, Arthur M(eier)**/** (1888–1965) and —— **Jr.** (b. 1917) his son, US professors and historians

Schleswig-Holstein Germany (hyphen)

Schliemann, Heinrich (1822–90) German archaeologist

schmaltz sentimentalism; *not* sh-, -alz (not ital.)

schnapps any of various spirits drunk in N. Europe, *not* -aps

schnauzer German breed of dog (not cap.)

schnitzel/ (Ger.) a veal cutlet, **Wiener —** this fried in breadcrumbs (one cap.)

Schnitzler, Arthur (1862–1931) Austrian playwright

schnorkel *use* **sn-**

Schobert, Johann (*c*.1720–67) German composer

Schoenberg, Arnold (1874–1951) Austrian-born composer, *not* Schö-

Scholar-Gipsy, The a poem by M. Arnold, 1853

scholi/um (Lat.) a marginal note or explanatory comment in a manuscript, pl. **-a**; **-ast** (hist.) an ancient or medieval scholar, esp. a grammarian

Schomberg, Friedrich Hermann, Duke of (1615–90) German-born French marshal and English mercenary officer

Schomburg Center for Research in Black Culture New York City

Schomburgk, Sir Robert Hermann (1804–65) German traveller

Schönbrunn Vienna

school an educational institution for children under 19 years; (US) any level of education, including college or university; abbr. **S.**; — **age**, — **bag**, — **board** (hyphen, one word in US) (US or hist.) a board or authority for local education (two words)

school/book, -boy (one word)

school bus (two words)

schoolchild (one word)

schooldays (one word, two words in US)

school/fellow, -girl (one word)

schoolhouse a building for school (one word); **school house** the headmaster's or housemaster's house at a boarding school (two words)

school leaver (two words)

school-leaving age (hyphen)

school/man, -master, -mate, -mistress, -room, -teacher (one word)

school time (two words, one word in US)

school year (two words)

schooner abbr. **sch.**

Schopenhauer, Arthur (1788–1860) German philosopher

Schreiner, Olive Emilie Albertina (1855–1920) S. African writer

Schrift/ (Ger. f.) (hand)writing, book, publication, paper, review, periodical, work, etc., pl. **-en**

Schriftsteller/ (Ger. m.) writer, author, f. **-in** (cf. **Dichter**, **Verfasser**); **-name** (f.) pen-name

Schrödinger/, Erwin (1887–1961) Austrian physicist, — **equation** *but* —**'s cat**

Schubart, Christian Friedrich Daniel (1739–91) German poet

Schubert, Franz Peter (1797–1828) Austrian composer

Schuman,/ Robert (1886–1963) French statesman, — **William Howard** (1910–92) US composer

Schumann, Robert Alexander (1810–56) German composer

schuss (make) a straight downhill run on skis (not ital.)

Schütz, Heinrich (1585–1672) German composer

Schutzstaffel (Ger. f.) (hist.) the Nazi elite corps, abbr. **SS**

Schuyler,/ Eugene (1840–90) US writer, — **Philip John** (1733–1804) US statesman and soldier

Schuylkill a town and river, Pa.

schwa (phonetics) the indistinct vowel sound, as in 'ago'; symbol ə; *not* sheva, shwa

Schwärmerei (Ger. f.) a sentimental enthusiasm

Schwarzerd *see* **Melanchthon**

Schwarzwald (Ger. m.) the Black Forest

Schweinfurt/ Bavaria; **— blue, — green**, etc.

Schweinfurth, Georg August (1836–1925) German traveller in Africa

Schweitzer, Albert (1875–1965) German philosopher, theologian, organist, and medical missionary

Schweiz, die Ger. for Switzerland

Schwyz a canton and its capital in Switzerland

sci. scien/ce, -tific

scia/graphy the art of the perspective of shadows, X-ray radiography; **-gram, -graph, -graphic; -machy** fighting with shadows; *not* scio-, skia- (US, and in Greek contexts)

science abbr. **sci.**

science fiction (two words), (colloq.) **sci-fi** abbr. **SF**

scienter (law) knowingly, intentionally (not ital.)

scientific/ abbr. **sci.**

Scientology a religious system (cap.)

sci-fi (colloq.) science fiction (hyphen)

scilicet that is to say, namely (introducing a word or an explanation of an ambiguity); abbr. **sc.** (not ital.)

Scill/y, Isles of off Corn., **-onian**

scimitar an oriental curved sword, *not* the many variants

Scind Pakistan, use **Sind**

scintilla/ a spark, a trace; pl. **-s**

sciography etc., *use* **scia-**

sciolist a superficial pretender to knowledge

scion *not* cion

scire facias (law) a writ to enforce or annul a judgment, patent, etc.

scirocco *use* **si-**

Sclavic etc., *use* **Sl-**

sclerom/a pl. **-ata** (med.) hardening

scleros/is pl. **-es** (med.) hardening

SCM State Certified Midwife, Student Christian Movement

Sc.M. *Scientiae Magister* (Master of Science)

Scolar Press publishers, *not* Sch-

scollop *use* **sca-**

Scone Tayside

SCONUL Standing Conference of National and University Libraries

score (bind.) break the surface of a board to help folding

-score (suffix, one word e.g. *threescore*)

score/board, -card (one word)

score sheet (two words)

scori/a slag, pl. **-ae**

Scot a native of Scotland

Scot. Scotch, Scotland, Scottish

Scotch use only in phrases such as **— (whisky), — broth**, etc.; abbr. **Sc., Scot.**

Scotch catch (mus.) a short note on the beat followed by a long one

Scotch/ egg, — gambit, — kale

Scotchman *use* **Scots-**

Scotch mist (two words)

Scotch pine *use* **Scots pine**

Scotch snap (mus.) = **Scotch catch**

Scotch tape (US propr.) transparent adhesive tape; *see also* **Sellotape**

Scotch terrier *use* **Scottish terrier**

Scotchwoman *use* **Scots-**

scot-free (hyphen)

scotice *use* **scott-**

Scotic/ism, -ize *use* **Scott-**

Scotism the doctrine of Duns Scotus

Scots fir = **Scots pine**

Scots Guards (no apos.)

Scotsman *not* Scotchman

Scots pine *not* Scotch pine

Scotswoman *not* Scotchwoman

Scott Fitzgerald, F. *see* **Fitzgerald, F. Scott**

scottice in the Scots dialect (no accent), *not* scotice

Scotticism a Scottish expression, *not* Scoti-

Scotticize make or become like the Scots; *not* -ise, Scoti-

Scottie (colloq.) a Scottish person or terrier

Scottish prefer to Scotch, *not* Scotish; abbr. **Sc., Scot.**

Scottish terrier (one of) a breed of rough-haired short-legged dogs, *not* Scotch terrier

Scouse (colloq.) a native of Liverpool (cap.); the Liverpool dialect, a stew (short for **lobscouse**) (not cap.)

Scout *not* now Boy Scout (cap.)

scow a flat-bottomed boat, *not* sk-

SCPS Society of Civil and Public Servants

SCR Senior Common Room, (Cambridge University) Senior Combination Room

scr. scruple, -s

scrap/book, -yard (one word)

screen (typ.) a fine grating on film or glass that breaks an illustration with various tones into dots of the appropriate size

screenplay the script of a film (one word)

screenwriter a person who writes a screenplay (one word)

screwball (a person who is) crazy or eccentric (one word)

screw cap (two words, hyphen when attrib.)

screwdriver (one word)

screw top (two words, hyphen when attrib.)

screw up bungle, muddle (hyphen when noun, one word in US)

screw valve (two words)

Scriabin(e) *use* **Skriabin**

scribes and Pharisees (cap. *P* only)

scrips/it (Lat.) wrote this; pl. *-erunt*, *-ere*

Script. Scripture

script (typ.) a type resembling handwriting

scriptori/um a writing room, pl. **-a**

scriptural (not cap.)

Scriptures, the (cap.)

scrod (US) a young cod or haddock

scroll (comput.) to move text vertically up or down screen; cf. **page**

Scrooge a miser, from the character in Dickens's *A Christmas Carol* (cap.)

scrot/um (anat.) pl. **-a**

scruple 20 grains; abbr. **sc.**, sign ℈

scrutator a scrutineer

scrutin/ize inspect closely; *not* -ise, **-y**

scry/ divine by crystal-gazing; **-er, -ing**

scuba/ self-contained underwater breathing apparatus (acronym), pl. **-s**; **-diver, -diving** (hyphens, two words in US)

Scud missile (one cap.)

sculduggery *use* **skul-**

sculp. sculpt/or, -ress, -ural, -ure

sculps/it (Lat.) engraved, or carved, this; pl. *-erunt, -ere*; abbr. **sc., sculps.**

sculptures, titles of when cited, to be in italic

scurry (noun and verb) *not* sk-

S-curve (cap., hyphen); use sans serif typeface where it is important to represent the actual configuration exactly

Scutari Albania, *not* Sk-; in Albanian **Shkodër**

scutcheon *use* **escut-**, *but A Blot in the 'Scutcheon* by R. Browning

scuttlebutt (one word)

Scylla and Charybdis (Gr. myth.) a sea monster and whirlpool in the Straits of Messina, two dangers such that avoidance of one increases the risk from the other

scymitar *use* **scim-**

SD South Dakota (postal abbr.)

sd. (books) sewed

s.d. shillings and pence, (Ger.) *siehe dies* (= q.v.), (Lat.) *sine die* (indefinitely)

S. Dak. South Dakota (off. abbr.)

SDI (US) Strategic Defense Initiative, begun 1983; commonly called **Star Wars**

SDLP (N. Ireland) Social Democratic and Labour Party

SDP (UK) Social Democratic Party

SDR special drawing right (from the International Monetary Fund)

SE south-east, -ern; (Fr.) *Son Excellence* (His, *or* Her, Excellency)

S/E Stock Exchange

Se selenium (no point)

Sea cap. with name, as North Sea, Sea of Marmara

sea/bed, -bird, -board, -borne (one word)

sea breeze (two words)

SEAC South-East Asia Command

sea/ change, — cow, — cucumber, — dog (two words)

sea/farer, -faring, -food (one word)

Seaford E. Sussex

Seaforde Co. Down

sea/going, -gull (one word)

sea horse (two words)

Seal Kent

Seale Surrey

sea/ legs, — level (two words)

sealing wax (two words)

sea lion (two words)

Sea Lord a naval member of the Admiralty Board (caps.)

sealskin (one word)

Séamas, Séamus (Anglicized as **Seamus**) Ir. Gael. for **James**; *see also* **Seumas, Seumus**

sea mile *see* **mile**

seamstress a sewing-woman, *not* semp-

Seanad Éireann the Upper House of the Irish Parliament

seance a spiritualist meeting (not ital., no accent), in Fr. f. *séance*

sea/plane, -port (one word)

SEAQ Stock Exchange Automated Quotations (a computerized access to share information)

sear scorch, wither(ed); cf. **sere**

searchlight (one word)

search/ party, — warrant (two words)

seascape (one word)

sea serpent (two words)

sea/shell, -shore, -sick, -sickness, -side (one word)

seasons, names of not cap. except when used poetically or as part of a formal appellation

season ticket (two words)

SEAT a Spanish make of car

SEATO South-East Asia Treaty Organization

sea urchin (two words)

sea/ wall, — water (two words, one word in US)

sea/way, -weed, -worthy (one word)

sebaceous fatty, *not* -ious

Sebastopol (hist.) the spelling generally used in contemporary accounts of the Crimean War; *see also* **Sev-**

SEC (US) Securities and Exchange Commission *but* Securities Exchange Act

sec (math.) secant (no point), (colloq.) second; dry (as of wine) (not ital.), in Fr. *sec*, f. *sèche*

sec. second, -s (of time or angle, no point in scientific and technical work), secondary, secretary

sec. see secundum

secateurs (pl.) a pair of pruning clippers (no accent, not ital.)

secco/ painting on dry plaster, pl. **-s**

Sec.-Gen. Secretary-General

Sechuana the language of the Bechuanas, *use* **Setswana**

Secker and Warburg publishers

second (adj.) abbr. **2nd**

second/, **-s** abbr. **s.**, **sec.** (no point in scientific and technical work); sign ″; — **mark** (″) symbol for inches or seconds; cf. **secund**

seconde a fencing parry

second-hand (adj. and adv., hyphen, one word in US)

second floor (two words, hyphen as adj.)

second lieutenant an army officer next below lieutenant or (in the US) first lieutenant

secondo (mus.) the lower part in a duet

second-rate (hyphen)

Second World War 1939–45 (caps.) is common British style; **World War II** is common US style

secrecy *not* -sy

sec. reg. *secundum regulam* (according to rule)

secretaire an escritoire (not ital.)

secretariat a permanent administrative office or department, esp. a governmental one; *not* -ate

secretary abbr. **sec.**

Secretary/-General pl. —**-Generals**, (US) **Secretaries-General**; (caps.), abbr. **Sec.-Gen.**

Secretary of State, the head of a major government department, (US) chief government official responsible for foreign affairs (caps.)

secret/e to hide, to discharge from a cell (blood, sap, etc.); **-ion, -or, -ory**

section/ abbr. **s.**, **sect.**; symbol §, pl. §§; — **mark** §, the fourth mark for footnotes

secularize *not* -ise

secund (biol.) on one side only; cf. **second**

Secunderabad Hyderabad, India; *not* Sak-, Sek-; *see also* **Sikandar-**

secundo (Lat.) in the second place, abbr. **2°**

secundum/ (Lat.) according to, abbr. **sec.**; — **artem** according to art, abbr. **sec. art.**; — **naturam** naturally, abbr. **sec. nat.**; — **quid** in a particular respect only; — **regulam** according to rule, abbr. **sec. reg.**

SED Scottish Education Department

sedan/ (US) = **saloon car**; — **chair** (two words)

Sedbergh Cumbria

se defendendo (Lat.) in defending himself, *or* herself

Seder Jewish service on the first night or two nights of Passover, *not* ceder; in Heb. *sẹder*

sederunt (Sc.) a sitting of an ecclesiastical assembly or other body (not ital.)

sede vacante (Lat.) when the see is vacant

Sedgemoor Som.; battle, 1685 (one word)

sedil/e a stone seat for a priest in the chancel of a church, usually one of three; pl. **-ia** (not ital.)

seduc/er *not* -or, **-ible** *not* -eable

séduisant/ (Fr.) f. **-e** bewitching

See, the Holy the Papacy

see (verb) often ital. in indexes and reference books to distinguish it from the words being treated, abbr. **s.**

Seefried, Irmgard (1919–88) German soprano

Seeing Eye dog (US propr.) = **guide dog for the blind**

Seeley, Sir John Robert (1834–95) English historian and writer

Seely family name of Baron Mottistone

see-saw (hyphen, one word in US)

seethe boil, bubble over; *not* -th

sego/ a N. American lily, pl. **-s**

segu/e go on without a pause; an uninterrupted transition; **-ed, -es, -ing**

seguidilla/ a Spanish dance, the music for this; pl. **-s**

Sehnsucht (Ger. f.) yearning, wistful longing

Seicent/o the style of Italian art and literature of the 17th c.; in It. = 600, used with reference to the years 1600–99; **-ist, -oist**

seiche a fluctuation in the water level of a lake

seigneur/ a feudal lord or lord of the manor, *not* -ior; **-ial** (not ital.)

seigniorage a superior's prerogative, the Crown's right to revenue from bullion, *not* seignor-

seigniory lordship, sovereign authority, a seigneur's domain; *not* -eury; *see also* **signory**

Seine/-et-Marne abbr. **S.-et-M.**, **-Maritime**, **-St.-Denis** déps. of France (hyphens)

seise (law) put in possession of; cf. **seize**

seisin (law) (taking) possession by freehold, *not* -zin; cf. **sasine**

seismo/gram a record given by a **seismograph**, an instrument used to record the force of earthquakes; **-logy** the study of earthquakes

Seit/e (Ger. f.) a page, pl. **-en**; abbr. **S.** in sing. and pl.

seize grasp; cf. **seise**

seizin *use* **seis-**

sejant (her.) (of an animal) sitting upright on its haunches (placed after noun)

Sejm the Polish parliament

séjour (Fr. m.) sojourn

Sekt a German sparkling white wine (cap., not ital.)

Sekunderabad *use* **Sec-**

sel. selected

Selangor *see* **Malaya, Federation of**

Selassie, Haile *see* **Haile Selassie**

Selborne, Earl of

Selborne, Natural History of by Gilbert White, 1789

selector one who, or that which, selects; *not* -er

selenium symbol **Se**

self- added (with hyphen) as a reflexive prefix to nouns, adjs., and parts., as *self-absorption*, *self-contained*, *self-evident*, *self-made*, etc.; but note *selfsame*

self-conscious (hyphen) *but* **unselfconscious** (one word)

Seljuk (a member) of the Turkish dynasties ruling in 11th–13th cc., *not* -ouk; in Turk. *Selçuk*

Selkup (of or relating to) (a member of) a Samoyedic people of N. Siberia, or (of) the Uralic language of this people; *formerly* Ostyak Samoyed

Sellafield site of a nuclear power station and reprocessing plant, Cumbria; known as Windscale 1947–81

sellanders *use* **sallen-**

sell-by date (hyphen)

selle de mouton (Fr. f.) saddle of mutton

seller's option abbr. **s.o.**

Sellindge Hythe, Kent

Selling Sittingbourne, Kent

Sellotape (propr.) a transparent adhesive tape (cap.); esp. in transatlantic writing *prefer* e.g. *sticking* or *sticky tape*; *see also* **Scotch tape**

Selsey Glos., E. Sussex; *not* -sea

seltzer a German mineral water

selvedge an edging of cloth, *not* -age

Sem. Semitic

semant/ic (adj.) concerning the meaning of words, **-ics** the branch of philology concerned with this (pl. but treated as sing.)

Semei Kazakhstan, *formerly* **Semipalatinsk**; *not* Semey

semeio- *use* **semio-**

semi/ (colloq.) a semi-detached house, (US) a semi-trailer; pl. **-s**

semi (Lat.) half; abbr. *s*, *S*

semi- prefix meaning half, partly, or almost

semi-automatic (hyphen, one word in US)

semi-barbar/ian, -ic, -ism, -ous (hyphens, one word in US)

semi-bold (typ.) a weight between light roman and bold (hyphen, one word in US)

semi/circle, -circular, -colon (;)**, -conductor** (one word)

semi-conscious (hyphen, one word in US)

semidemisemiquaver *use* **hemi-**

semi-final/, -ist (hyphen, one word in US)

semi-monthly twice a month (hyphen, one word in US), *prefer* to bi-monthly

Seminole (of or relating to) (a member of) a Native American people, pl. same

semi-official (hyphen, one word in US)

semi/ology, -otics the branch of linguistics concerned with signs and symbols; (med.) the science of symptoms; *not* semeio-

Semipalatinsk *see* **Semei**

semi/-precious, -skilled, -skimmed, -sweet (hyphens, one word in US)

Semite *not* Sh-

Semitic abbr. **Sem.**

Semitize *not* -ise (cap.)

semi/-transparent, -tropical (hyphens, one word in US)

semi-weekly twice a week (hyphen, one word in US), *prefer* to bi-weekly

semp. (mus.) sempre

semper/ eadem (Lat. f. sing., and n. pl.) always the same; — *fidelis* always faithful, pl. — *fideles*; — *idem* (m. and n. sing.) always the same

semplice (mus.) in simple style

sempre (mus.) always, abbr. *semp.*

sempstress *use* **seams-**

Semtex a highly malleable, odourless plastic explosive (cap.)

SEN State Enrolled Nurse

Sen. Senat/e, -or; Seneca, senior

sen. senior

senari/us (prosody) a verse of six feet, esp. an iambic trimeter; pl. **-i**

Senate abbr. **Sen.**

senator cap. only when used with name

Senatus (Lat.) the Senate

Senatus Academicus the governing body in Scottish universities (not ital.)

senatus consultum a decree of the Senate, abbr. **SC**; in Fr. m. (hist.) *sénatus-consulte*

Seneca, Lucius Annaeus (c.3 BC–AD 65) Roman Stoic philosopher and statesman, abbr. **Sen.**

Senegal/ W. Africa; **-ese**; in Fr. **Sénégal**

seneschal the steward or major-domo of a medieval great house, a judge in Sark

senhor/ (Port.) Mr, abbr. **sr.**; **-a** Mrs, abbr. **sra.**; **-ita** Miss, abbr. **srta.** (cap. when used with name)

senior abbr. **sen.**, **Senr.**; not part of bearer's name, and therefore used only as ad-hoc designation (like *père*); set after surname, with comma preceding, and before degrees or other titles: 'J. Bloggs, sen., Esq.', *not* 'Esq., sen.'

seniores priores (Lat.) elders first

senior nursing officer the official term for a hospital matron

Sennacherib (d. 681 BC) King of Assyria

sennet (hist.) a signal call on a trumpet or cornet; cf. **sennit**; **sinnet**

sennight (arch.) a week

sennit (hist.) plaited straw, palm leaves, etc., used for making hats; cf. **sennet**; **sinnet**

se non è vero è ben trovato (It.) if it is not true, it is well invented

señor/ (Sp.) Mr, abbr. **sr.**; **-es** Messrs; **-a** Mrs, abbr. **sra.**; **-ita** Miss, abbr. **srta.** (cap. when used with name)

senr. senior

sensitize make sensitive, *not* -ise

sensori/um (Lat.) the grey matter of the brain and spinal cord, pl. **-a**

sensory pertaining to the senses or sensation

sensual concerned with the gratification of the senses, carnal

sensualize *not* -ise

sensu/ lato (Lat.) in the wide sense; — **stricto** in the narrow sense, *not strictu*

sens/um (philos.) sense datum, pl. **-a**

sensuous pertaining to or affected by the senses in aesthetic terms

sentimentalize *not* -ise

Senussi a member of a fanatic Muslim sect, pl. same

senza (It. mus.) without

Seoul S. Korea; *not* Seul, Soul; in Korean **Kyongsong**

separate (typ.) a reprint of one of a series of items, abbr. **sep.**

separator *not* -er

Sephardi/ a Jew of Spanish or Portuguese descent, pl. **-m**; adj. **-c** (cap.); *not* Sef-; cf. **Ashkenazi**

sepoy (hist.) an Indian soldier in European (esp. British) service (not cap.); cf. **spahi**

seppuku (Jap.) the formal term for ritual suicide by disembowelment with a sword; **hara-kiri** is colloq.

Sept. September, Septuagint, *not* Sep.

sept a clan, esp. in Ireland

September abbr. **Sept.**; in Fr. m. **septembre**, abbr. **sept.** (not cap.)

septemvir/ (Lat.) one of a committee of seven, pl. **-i**

septenari/us (prosody) a verse of seven feet, esp. a trochaic or iambic tetrameter catalectic; pl. **-i**

septet (mus.) *not* -ett, -ette

septfoil a seven-lobed ornamental figure

septicaemia blood poisoning, *not* -cemia (US)

septillion a thousand raised to the eighth power (10^{24}), *formerly* the fourteenth power (10^{42}); pl. same

septime a fencing parry

septuagenarian a person from 70 to 79 years old

Septuagesima Sunday the third before Lent

Septuagint the Greek version of the OT including the Apocrypha, *c.*270 BC; abbr. **Sept.**, **LXX**

sept/um (biol.) a partition, pl. **-a**

sepulchre/ a burial vault or tomb; **whited —** a hypocrite (Matt. 23: 27); *not* -er (US); **sepulchral**

Sepulchre, Church of St *not* -'s

sepultus (Lat.) buried, abbr. **S.**

seq. (sing.) (Lat.) *sequens* (the following), *sequente* (and in what follows), *sequitur* (it follows)

seqq. (pl.) (Lat.) *sequentes, sequentia* (the following), *sequentibus* (in the following places)

sequel/a (med.) a symptom following a disease, pl. **-ae**

sequen/s, -te *see* **seq.**

sequent/es (Lat. m., f.), **-ia** (n.), **-ibus** *see* **seqq.**

sequitur (Lat.) it follows, abbr. **seq.**

ser. series

sera pl. of **serum**

serac/ a castellated mass of ice in a glacier, pl. **-s** (not ital.)

seraglio/ a harem, (hist.) a Turkish palace; pl. **-s**

serai a caravanserai; *not* sar-, -ay

Serajevo *use* **Sa-**

serang (Anglo-Ind.) a native head of a Lascar crew

serape a Spanish-American shawl or blanket; *not* sar-, zar-

seraph/ a celestial being, pl. **-im** *not* -s

seraskier (hist.) the Turkish Commander-in-Chief and minister of war

Serb. Serbian, (no point) a native of Serbia or a person of Serbian descent

Serb/ia a republic of the former Yugoslavia, in Serbo-Croat **Srbija**

Serbo-Croat/ (of or relating to) the main official language of the former Yugoslavia, combining Serbian and Croatian dialects; also **-ian, Croato-Serbian** (hyphens)

SERC Science and Engineering Research Council

sere a gun-lock's catch, (ecology) a sequence of animal or plant communities; cf. **sear**

sere/cloths, -ments *use* **cere-**

serein (Fr. m.) a fine rain from a cloudless sky in tropical climates

serge a fabric; for candle, *use* **cie-**

sergeant (mil.; but *-j-* in some official contexts) abbr. **Sgt.** (cap. as title)

serial comma a name sometimes given to the comma before *and* in a list of three or more items, e.g. the second comma in 'red, white, and blue'

seriatim serially, point by point

series sing. and pl.; abbr. **S., ser.**

serifs (typ.) the short lines across the ends of arms and stems of letters, *not* ceriphs

Serinagar *use* **Sr-**

Seringapatam Mysore, India

serio-comic (hyphen, one word in US)

Serjeant *see* **sergeant**

sermonize *not* -ise

serra (Port.) a sierra, mountain range

ser/um the fluid that separates from clotted blood, an antitoxin; pl. **-a**

serviceable *not* -cable

service/man, -woman (one word)

serviette a table-napkin (not ital.)

servitor *not* -er

servo/ a mechanism for powered automatic control of a larger system, pl. **-s**; as a combined form denotes a machine with this function, e.g. *servomotor* (one word)

Sesotho a Bantu language, *not* Sesuto

sesquicentenary (the celebration of) a 150th anniversary, *not* -tennial (US)

sesquipedalian (of word) one and a half (metrical) feet long, many-syllabled

sess. session

Session/, Court of the supreme Scottish Court, *not* Sessions; **Parliamentary —** (caps.)

sesterce a Roman coin; in Lat. **sesterti/us** pl. **-i**, symbol **HS** (no point)

sesterti/um 1,000 sesterces, pl. **-a**

sestet the last six lines of a sonnet; cf. **sextet**

Sesuto *use* **Sesotho**

set a shoot for planting; an alignment in weaving; (typ.) amount of spacing controlling the distance between letters, the width of a piece of type or sort; *see also* **sett**

setback (noun, one word)

S.-et-L. Saône-et-Loire

S.-et-M. Seine-et-Marne

set-off (typ.) an unwanted transfer of ink from one sheet to another

set/ piece, — point (two words)

sets abbr. **s.**

Setswana the Bantu language of the Tswana

sett a badger's burrow, a granite paving block, a pattern in a tartan; *not* set

Settecento (It.) the years 1700–99 (esp. in Italy)

Settlement (Stock Exchange) (cap.)

settler one who settles

settlor (law) one who makes a settlement

set-up (adj. and noun, hyphen, one word in US)

Seul Korea, *use* **Seoul**

Seumas, Seumus (Anglicized as **Seamus**) Ir. Gael. for **James**; in Scots Gael. **Seumas** (Anglicized as **Hamish**); *see also* **Séamas, Séamus**

Seuss, Dr pseud. of **Theodor Seuss Geisel** (1904–91) US author-illustrator of children's books

Sevastopol Crimea, Ukraine; in Russ. **Sevastopol´**, in Ukrainian **Sevastopol´** *or* **Sevastopil´**; *see also* **Seb-**

seven deadly sins pride, envy, anger, sloth, covetousness, gluttony, and lust

seven liberal arts *see* **quadrivium**; **trivium**

Sevenoaks Kent (one word)

seven seas the oceans of the world: Arctic, Antarctic, N. Atlantic, S. Atlantic, Indian, N. Pacific, and S. Pacific

Seventh-Day Adventist (three caps., one hyphen)

seven wonders of the world (from antiquity): the Egyptian Pyramids, the Mausoleum at Halicarnassus, the Hanging Gardens of Babylon, the Temple of Artemis at Ephesus, the statue of Zeus by Phidias at Olympia, the Colossus at Rhodes, and the Pharos at Alexandria (*or* alternatively the walls of Babylon)

Seven Years War 1756–63 (caps., no apos.)

Sévigné, Marie de Rabutin-Chantal, Madame de (1626–96) French writer

Sèvres fine porcelain made at Sèvres in the suburbs of Paris (no accent in US)

sewage/ the refuse that passes through sewers; **— farm, — works** (two words)

sewerage a system of sewers

sewin a salmon trout, *not* -en

sewing (bind.) the individual sewing of each book section to its neighbours; *see also* **stitching**

sewing machine (two words)

sexagenarian a person from 60 to 69 years old

Sexagesima Sunday the second before Lent

sex/ appeal, — change, — kitten (two words)

sex-linked (genetics) (hyphen)

sex/ maniac, — object, — symbol (two words)

sextet (mus.) (a work for) a group of six performers; *not* -ett, -ette; cf. **sestet**

sexto (typ.) a book based on six leaves (twelve pages) to the sheet, abbr. **6to**; **sextodecimo** *or* **sixteenmo** a book based on sixteen leaves (thirty-two pages) to the sheet, abbr. **16mo**

sexualize attribute sex to, *not* -ise

Seychell/es, Republic of Indian Ocean; **-ois**

Seymour, Jane (1509–37) third wife of Henry VIII of England

SF San Francisco, science fiction

s.f. sub *finem* (towards the end)

SFA Scottish Football Association

Sforza/ a Milanese ducal family, notably **—, Ludovico** (1451–1508); **—, Carlo, Count** (1873–1952) leader of anti-Fascist opposition in Italy

sforz/ando, -ato (mus.) with sudden emphasis on a chord or note, abbr. **sfz**

sfumato (It.) (the technique of painting) with indistinct outlines

SG (US) senior grade, (law) Solicitor-General, specific gravity

SGA Society of Graphic Artists

Sganarelle the name of several characters in Molière's comedies

sgd. signed

s.g.d.g. (Fr.) *sans garantie du gouvernement* (without government guarantee) (also caps.)

SGML (comput.) Standard Generalized Markup Language

sgraffit/o decorative work in which different colours are got by removing outer layers, pl. **-i**; cf. **graffito**

's-Gravenhage formal Du. for **The Hague**

Sgt. Sergeant

sh. shilling, -s

shadoof an Egyptian water-raising apparatus, in Egyptian Arab. *šādūf*

shagreen the untanned leather from the skin of fish, sharks, etc.

shah (hist.) a title of the former monarch of Iran, cap. when part of a formal title; in Pers. *šāh*

Shahabad Bengal, Hyderabad, Punjab, Uttar Pradesh, India

shaikh *see* **sheikh**

shakedown (noun and attrib. one word)

Shakespear/e, William (1564–1616) English playwright, *not* the many variants (except when approximating hist. usage); abbr. **Shak.**; **-ian, -iana** (OUP preference); *also* **-ean, -eana** (esp. in US)

Shakespeare Society, the *but* **the New Shakespere Society**

shako/ a military headdress, *not* sch-; pl. **-s**

shakuhachi/ a Japanese bamboo flute, pl. **-s**

shaky unsteady, *not* -key

shallop a small boat or dinghy; *not* shalop, -oop

shallot a kind of onion; *not* esch-, sch-, shalott

shalom a Jewish salutation, *not* sch-

Shalott, The Lady of a poem by Tennyson, 1833

sha/man pl. **-mans** *not* -men

shamefaced (one word)

shammy-leather *use* **chamois**

Shandong (Pinyin) Chinese province, also **Shantung** esp. with reference to a type of silk (not cap.)

shandrydan a rickety vehicle, *not* -dery-

Shanghai China; **shanghai/** make drunk and ship as a sailor (not cap.), **-ed**

Shangri-La an imaginary earthly paradise, from J. Hilton's novel *Lost Horizon* (hyphen, two caps.)

shanty/ a hut, a rough dwelling, a sailor's song; *not* ch-; **— town** (two words, one word in US)

shapable *not* shape-

SHAPE Supreme Headquarters, Allied Powers, Europe

Shahrazād *see* **Scheherazade**

sharecropper (one word)

share-farmer (hyphen)

shareholder (one word)

share-list (hyphen)

share-out (noun, hyphen)

shareware (comput.) (one word)

shariah the Muslim code of religious law, in Arab. *šarī'a*

sharif a descendant of Muhammad through his daughter Fatima; a Muslim leader; *not* shereef, -if; in Arab. *šarīf*

sharp/ (mus.) sign ♯, **double —** sign ×

Sharp,/ Becky a character in Thackeray's *Vanity Fair*; **— Cecil James** (1859–1924) English collector of folk songs; **— Granville** (1735–1813) English abolitionist; **— James** (1613–79) Scottish prelate; **— William** (1855–1905) Scottish poet and novelist, pseud. **Fiona Macleod**

Sharpe,/ Charles Kirkpatrick (1781–1851) Scottish antiquary and artist, **— Samuel** (1799–1881) English Egyptologist and biblical scholar

Sharpesburg Ky., Pa.

Sharpesville Pa.

Sharpeville S. Africa

Sharpey-Schafer, Sir Edward Albert b. **Schäfer** (1850–1935) English physiologist

sharpshoot/er, -ing (one word)

sharp/-tongued, -witted (hyphens)

Shasta daisy a European plant, *Chrysanthemum maximum* (one cap.)

Shastra Hindu sacred writings; in Hind. *śāstr*, in Skt. *śāstra*

shaving/-brush, -cream, -soap, -stick (hyphens, two words in US)

Shavu/oth a Jewish holiday commemorating the handing down of the Law on Mt. Sinai, in Heb. *šābu'ōṯ*; also **-ot**

Shaw/, George Bernard (1856–1950) Irish-born English playwright, adj. **Shavian**; **Aircraftman** — *see* **Lawrence, T. E.**

shawm (mus.) a medieval double-reed wind instrument

shaykh *see* **sheikh**

Shchedrin, N. *see* **Saltykov(-Shchedrin)**

shchi a Russian cabbage soup, *not* the many variants

s/he short for 'he or she', used to indicate both sexes; *not* to be used in formal writing

sheaf pl. **sheaves**

shealing *use* **shiel-**

shear/ to cut; past **-ed**, past part. **shorn** *but* **-ed** with reference to mechanical shears (cf. **sheer**); **-hulk, -legs** *use* **sheer-**

shearwater a bird (one word)

sheath/ (noun), **-e** (verb)

shebang (US sl.) a matter or affair, esp. in 'the whole —'

shebeen (Ir.) an unlicensed house selling spirits, in Ir. *síbín*

Shechinah *use* **Shek-**

sheep dip (two words)

sheep/dog, -fold (one word)

sheep run (two words)

sheepshank a type of knot (one word)

sheepskin a rug, a bookbinding leather, a parchment (one word)

sheepwalk a tract of land on which sheep are pastured (one word)

sheer (adj.) mere, very steep, very thin; (adv.) quite, vertically; (verb) deviate, swerve; cf. **shear**

sheer/hulk a dismasted ship, **-legs** a hoisting apparatus for masts (one word)

Sheer Thursday (Maundy Thursday); in Scots also **Shere**, **Skire**

sheet (typ.) a piece of paper of a definite size, a signature of a book

sheet/ metal, — music (two words)

sheets, in (typ.) not folded, or, if folded, not bound

sheet work (typ.) printing the two sides of a sheet from two formes

Sheffield: the signature of the Bishop of Sheffield (colon)

Shéhérazade *see* **Scheherazade**

sheikh (common Eng. spelling) a chief or head of an Arab tribe, family, or village (lit. 'old man'), a Muslim leader; more learned transliterations are **shaikh** (preferred by *The Times*), **shayk**; in Arab. *šayḵ*

sheiling *use* **shie-**

shekel the chief monetary unit of modern Israel, (hist.) a silver coin and unit of weight in ancient Israel and the Middle East; in Heb. *šeḵel*

Shekinah the visible glory of God, *not* Shech-

sheldrake a coastal wild duck, *not* shell-; f. and pl. **shelduck** *not* sheld duck

shelf-ful/ the quantity that fills a shelf, pl. **-s** (hyphen)

shelf-life (hyphen, two words in US)

shelf-like (hyphen, one word in US)

shelf/ mark, — room (two words)

shellac/ a gum; *not* -ack, shelac, shelack; as verb **-ked, -king**

Shelley, Percy Bysshe (1792–1822) English poet

shell/fire, -fish (one word)

shell game (US) = **thimblerig**

shell jacket (two words)

shell pink (two words, hyphen when attrib.)

shellproof (one word)

shell shock/, -ed (two words)

shell suit (two words)

Shelta ancient hybrid secret language used by Irish tinkers, Gypsies, etc.

sheltie a Shetland pony or sheepdog, *not* -y

shelv/e, -ing, -y

Shemite *use* **Sem-**

shemozzle rumpus, *not* sch-

Sheol Hebrew underworld abode of the dead; in Heb. *še'ōl*

Shepheardes Calender, The a poem by Spenser, 1579; several subsequent edns. have variant spellings

Shepheard's Hotel Cairo

Shepherd Market London

Shepherd's Bush London

shepherd's/ crook, — needle, — pie, — plaid, — purse (apos.)

Sheppard, Jack (1702–24) English highwayman

Sheppey, Isle of Kent

Shepton Mallet Som.

Sheraton, Thomas (1751–1806) English furniture designer

sherbet a flavoured sweet effervescent powder or drink; (US) a water ice, sorbet; a cooling drink of sweet diluted fruit juices; (Austral. joc.) beer; *not* -bert

Sherborne Dorset, Glos.; **Baron —**

Sherbourne War.

Sherburn Dur., N. Yorks.

Sherburn in Elmet N. Yorks.

Shere Surrey

shereef, sherif *use* **sharif**

Shere Thursday *use* **Sheer Thursday**

sheriff a county officer

Sheringham Norfolk

Sherpa (a member of) a Himalayan people from borders of Nepal and Tibet, *not* -ah; pl. same

Sherpur Bangladesh

Sherrington, Sir Charles Scott (1857–1952) English physiologist

's-Hertogenbosch the Netherlands, commonly called **Den Bosch**; in Fr. **Bois-le-Duc**

Shetland/ a region of Scotland, **— Islands** *or* **-s** the main group of islands in it

sheva *use* **schwa**

shew *use* **show** except in Scots law, and biblical and Prayer Book citations

shewbread (Scripture) loaves displayed in a Jewish temple, *not* Show-

sheyk *use* **sheikh**

Shia one of the two main branches of Islam, esp. in Iran; *also* **Shiah**; *see also* **Sunni**; in Arab. **šī'a**

shiatsu therapy in which pressure is applied with the thumbs and palms to certain points on the body

shibboleth *not* shibo-

shieling a Highland hut or sheep-shelter; *not* sheal-, she-

shi/est, -ly, -ness *use* **shy-**

Shifnal Shropshire

shih-tzu a breed of dog with long silky hair (hyphen, two words in US)

shiitake an edible mushroom

Shi'ite (a member) of the Shia branch of Islam, *not* Shiite; *also* **Shi'i** in learned contexts

shikaree (Ind.) a hunter, *not* the many variants

Shikarpur Pakistan

shiksa (offens.) a Gentile girl or woman, in Yiddish *shikse*

shillelagh an Irish cudgel, *not* the many variants

shilling/, -s abbr. *s.*, **sh.**; symbol *l-*

shilly-shally/, -ing

Shinto/, -ism the official Japanese religion

shiny *not* -ey

'ship (typ.) *see* **companionship**

ship/board, -builder, -building, -load, -mate, -owner (one word)

shipping agent (two words)

shipping/-bill, -master, -office (hyphens)

ship's biscuit sing. and pl.

shipshape (one word)

ships' names to be italic

Shipston on Stour War. (three words)

Shipton Glos., N. Yorks., Shropshire

Shiptonthorpe Humberside

Shipton under Wychwood Oxon. (three words)

ship/way, -worm, -wreck, -wright, -yard (one word)

Shiraz Iran; *not* Sheraz, Shyraz; in Pers. **Shīrāz**; also the Eng. form of **Syrah**

Shire/brook Derby., **-hampton** Avon, **-newton** Gwent (one word)

Shires, the (cap.) generally, the group of English counties ending in -*shire*, extending NE from Hampshire and Devon

shirtsleeve/, -s (one word)

shirt-tail (hyphen, one word in US)

shirtwaist/ (US) a blouse resembling a shirt, **-er** (US) a dress with a bodice like a shirt (one word)

shish kebab (two words), in Turk. **şiş kebabı**

Shiva *see* **Śiva**

shivaree *use* **charivari** (except in US)

shmaltz *use* **sch-**

shockproof (one word)

shock/ tactics, — therapy, — treatment, — troops, — wave (two words)

shoe/, -ing

shoe/black, -box (one word)

shoe buckle (two words)

shoe/horn, -lace (one word)

shoe leather (two words)

shoe/maker, -shine, -string (one word)

shoe tree (two words)

shogun/ (hist.) any of a succession of Japanese hereditary commanders-in-chief and virtual rulers before 1868, in Jap. **shōgun**; **-ate**

Sholokhov, Mikhail (Aleksandrovich) (1905–84) Russian novelist

Shooters Hill London (no apos.)

shooting box (two words)

shooting brake an estate car, *not* break

shooting/ coat, — gallery, — range, — star (two words)

shooting stick a walking stick with a foldable seat (two words)

shop/ assistant, — boy (two words)

shopfront (one word)

shop girl (two words)

shopkeeper (one word)

shoplift/, -er, -ing (one word)

shopping mall (two words)

shop steward (two words)

shop talk (two words, one word in US)

shopwalker (one word)

shop window (two words, one word in US)

short/bread, -cake (one word)

short-change (verb, hyphen; one word in US)

short circuit (noun, hyphen for verb)

short/coming, -crust, -fall, -hand, -horn (one word)

short mark that placed over a short vowel, a breve; *see also* **short vowel**

short-sighted lacking foresight, the inability to focus except on comparatively near objects (hyphen, one word in US)

short/ ton 2,000 lb, abbr. **s.t.**; — **vowel** ă, ĕ, etc.

shorty (colloq.) a short person or garment, *not* -ie

Shostakovich, Dmitri (**Dmitrievich**) (1906–75) Russian composer

shotgun (one word)

shoulder/ bag, — band, — blade (two words)

shoulder head(**line**) (typ.) a supplementary running head, usually of section, paragraph, or line numbers, or listing the first and last entry on a page

shoulder note (typ.) a marginal note at the top outer corner of the page

shoulder/ pad, — strap (two words)

shovel/, -led, -ler, -ling (one *l* in US), **-ful** pl. **-fuls**

shovelboard (one word)

shoveler a duck, *Anas clypeata*, with a broad shovel-like beak; *not* -ller

shovelhead (one word)

show *see* **shew**

showboat (US) a river steamer on which performances are given

Showbread *use* **shew-**

show business (two words) colloq. **showbiz** (one word)

show/case, -down, -girl (one word)

show house (two words)

showjump/, -er, -ing (one word, two words in US)

showman (one word)

show-off (noun, hyphen)

show/piece, -place, -room (one word)

show-through (typ.) the degree to which printing is visible on the other side of the paper

s.h.p. shaft horsepower

shrieval/ of or relating to a sheriff; **-ty** a sheriff's office, jurisdiction, or tenure

shrill/y, -ness

shrink-wrap (noun and verb, hyphen; one word in US)

shrivel/, -led, -ling (one *l* in US)

Shropshire *formerly* Salop

Shrovetide from the Saturday evening before to Ash Wednesday morning

Shrove Tuesday the day before Ash Wednesday

shufti/ (Brit. colloq.) a look or glimpse, pl. **-s**

shumac *use* su-

'shun! (colloq.) attention!

Shute, Nevil pseud. of **N. S. Norway** (1899–1960) English novelist

shuttlecock (one word)

s.h.v. *sub hac voce* or *sub hoc verbo* (under this word)

shwa *use* **sch-**

shy/er, -est, -ly, -ness *not* shi-

shyster (US) a person, esp. a lawyer, who uses unscrupulous methods

SI Sandwich Islands, (order of the) Star of India, Staten Island (NY), Système International (d'Unités)

Si silicon (no point)

si (mus.) *use* **te**

SIAD Society of Industrial Artists and Designers

sialagogue an agent inducing a flow of saliva, *not* sialo-

Siam *use* **Thailand**

Siamese/ *use* **Thai** except set phrases such as — **cat, — twins**

Sib. Siberia, -n

Sibeli/us, Jean (1865–1957) Finnish composer, **-an**

sibilant (adj.) hissing, (noun) letter(s) sounded with a hiss (e.g. *s, sh*)

sibyl/ a prophetess, **-line**; **the Sibylline books** (one cap.) an ancient Roman collection of oracles; cf. **Sybil**

Sic. Sicil/y, -ian

sic (Lat.) thus, so

sice the six on dice; cf. **syce**

Sichuan (Pinyin) a Chinese province, also **Szechwan**

Sicilian Vespers a massacre of the French in Sicily, 1282; subject of an opera by Verdi, *Les Vêpres siciliennes*, 1855

sick/bay, -bed (one word)

sick benefit (two words)

sick building syndrome (three words)

sick/ call, — flag, — leave (two words)

sick-making (hyphen)

sickroom (one word)

sic transit gloria mundi (Lat.) thus passes the glory of the world

sicut ante (Lat.) as before

sic vos non vobis (Lat.) thus you labour, but not for yourselves

Siddhãrtha Gautama (Skt.) (*c*.490 BC–*c*.410 BC) the Buddha, founder of Buddhism; in Pali **Siddhãttha Gotama**

side arm a weapon worn at the side (two words)

sideband (one word)

side-bet (hyphen)

sideboard (one word)

sideburns = **sideboards**, side whiskers (one word)

sidecar (one word)

side/ chapel, — dish, — door, — drum, — effect (two words)

side head (typ.) a heading or subheading set full left to the margin

side issue (two words)

sidekick a close associate

side/light, -line, -long (one word)

side notes (typ.) those in margin, generally outer (two words)

side/ order, — road (two words)

side saddle (two words, one in US)

side salad (two words)

sideshow (one word)

sidestep (noun and verb) (one word)

side street (two words)

side/stroke, -swipe (one word)

side table (two words)

sidetrack (one word)

side trip (two words)

side valve of an engine (hyphen when attrib.)

side view (two words)

sidewalk (US) = **pavement**

sideways (one word)

side/ whiskers, — wind (two words)

sidewinder a N. American desert rattlesnake, (US) a sideways blow

Sidgwick & Jackson publishers

Sidney, Sir Philip (1554–86) English soldier, courtier, writer; *see also* **Syd-**

SIDS sudden infant death syndrome, cot death

siècle (Fr. m.) century, abbr. **s.**

Siegfried/ a *Nibelungenlied* hero, eponym of the third opera in Wagner's *Ring*, 1876; *not* Sig-; **— Line** the German fortified line on the Franco-German border before 1939

siehe (Ger.) see, abbr. **s.**

siehe/ dies (Ger.) see this (= q.v.), abbr. **s. d.**; **— oben** see above, abbr. **s. o.**; **— unten** see below, abbr. **s. u.** (spaces in Ger.)

Siemens,/ Werner von (1816–92) German founder of the electrical firm; **— Sir William**, born **Karl Wilhelm von** (1823–83) his brother, German-born British engineer; **— Friedrich** (1826–1904) the youngest brother, applied Sir William's open-hearth process to glass making

siemens (elec.) the SI unit of conductance, abbr. **S**

Siena Italy, *not* -nna

Sienkiewicz, Henryk (1846–1916) Polish novelist

sienna/ a pigment in paint; **burnt —, raw —**

sierra/ (Sp.) a mountain chain, pl. **-s**

Sierra/ Leone W. Africa, **— Leonean**; **— Madre** Mexican mountain chains; **— Nevada** a mountain chain in E. Calif. and in Spain

siesta/ (Sp.) afternoon rest, pl. **-s**

Sieyès, Emmanuel Joseph (1748–1836) French statesman

siffleu/r (Fr. m.) f. **-se** a professional whistler

Sig. Signor, -i

sig. signature

Sigfried *use* **Sieg-**

sight-read/, -er, -ing of music (hyphen)

sight screen (two words)

sightsee/r, -ing (one word)

sightworthy (one word)

sigill/um (Lat.) a seal, pl. **-a**

sigla *see* **library sigla**

sigl/um a sign denoting source of text, pl. **-a**

sigma the eighteenth letter of the Gr. alphabet (Σ, σ, final ς), Σ (math.) sum; **lunate —** a form of sigma (C, c)

sign abbr. **s.**

signal/, -ize *not* -ise, **-led, -ler, -ling** (one *l* in US), **-ly**

signal/book, box (two words)

signalman (one word)

signal tower (US) = **signal box**

signatory one who has signed, *not* -ary

signature (mus.) the key or time sign at beginning of the stave, abbr. **sig.**

signature (typ.) a complete part of a book printed on one sheet, usually sixteen or thirty-two pages, abbr. **sig.**

signed abbr. **s., sgd.**

Signor/ (It.) Mr, pl. **-i**, abbr. **Sig.**; **-a** Mrs, pl. **-e**, abbr. **Sig.ra**; **-ina** Miss, pl. **-ine**, abbr. **Sig.na**

signory (hist.) the governing body of a medieval Italian republic; *see also* **seigniory**

signpost (one word)

Sikandarabad Uttar Pradesh, India; *see also* **Secunder-**

Sikes, Bill a character in Dickens's *Oliver Twist*, *not* Sy-

Sikh/ a member of an Indian monotheistic sect founded in the 16th c., **-ism** the religious tenets of the Sikhs

Sikkim/ a former E. Himalayan kingdom, annexed as a state by India 1975; **-ese**

Sikorski, Gen. Władysław (1881–1943) Polish Prime Minister

silent partner (US) = **sleeping partner**

silen/us (Gr. myth.) a bearded old man like a satyr, sometimes with the tail and legs of a horse; pl. **-i** (often cap. in sing. or specific senses, not cap. in pl. or general senses)

siliceous of silica, *not* -ious

silicon a chemical element, symbol **Si**

silicone any of the many polymeric organic compounds containing silicon

siliqu/a a long narrow seed pod, pl. **-ae**

silkworm (one word)

sill (of door, window) *not* c-

sillabub *use* **syll-**

Sillanpää, Frans Eemil (1888–1964) Finnish novelist

Sillery a champagne

silo/ an airtight chamber for storing grain, pl. **-s**

Silurian (geol.) (of or relating to) the third period of the Palaeozoic era

silva/, -n *use* **syl-**

silver/ symbol **Ag** (argentum) (no point); **— age** a period regarded as inferior to a golden age, e.g. that of post-classical Latin literature in the early Imperial period

silverfish pl. same (one word)

silver Latin literary Latin of the early Imperial period (one cap.)

silver/side, -smith, -ware (one word)

silvicultur/e, -ist *not* sylvi-

s'il vous plaît (Fr.) if you please, abbr. **s.v.p.**

similia similibus curantur (Lat.) like cures like

similiter (Lat.) in like manner

simitar *use* **scim-**

Simla Himachal Pradesh, India

simon-pure real, genuine (hyphen, not cap.); from (**the real**) **Simon Pure**, a character in Centlivre's *Bold Stroke for a Wife*

Simonstown Cape Province, S. Africa (one word)

simon/y the buying or selling of ecclesiastical privileges, e.g. pardons or benefices; **-iac, -iacal**

simoom a hot, dry, dust-laden wind blowing at intervals esp. in the Arabian desert; *not* -oon; in Arab. *samūm*

simpatico (It.) congenial, in Sp. *simpático*

simpliciter (Lat.) absolutely, without qualification

simulacr/um an image, a deceptive substitute; pl. **-a**

simultaneous *not* -ious

simurg (Persian myth.) a monstrous bird, in Pers. *sīmorgh*

sin (math.) sine (no point)

Sinaitic of or relating to Mount Sinai or the Sinai peninsula (cap.)

Sind/ Pakistan; *not* -e, -h, Scinde; **-hi** a native of Sind, pl. **-his**; an Indo-Aryan language spoken in Pakistan and NW India

Sindbad a character in the *Arabian Nights*, *not* Sinb-

sine (math.) abbr. **sin**

sine/ (Lat.) without; **— anno** without the date, abbr. **s.a.**; **— cura** without office; **— die** with no appointed day (of business adjourned indefinitely) abbr. **s.d.**; **— dubio** without doubt; **— invidia** without envy; **— legitima prole** without lawful issue, abbr. **s.l.p.**; **— loco, anno, vel nomine** without place, year, or name, abbr. **s.l.a.n.**; **— loco et anno** without place and date (of books without imprints), abbr. **s.l.e.a.**; **— mascula prole** without male issue, abbr. **s.m.p**; **— mora** without delay; **— nomine** without (printer's) name, abbr. **s.n.**; **— odio** without hatred; **— prole** (**superstite**) without (surviving) issue, abbr. **s.p.**(**s.**)

sine qua non an indispensable condition, *not* quâ

sinfon/ia (It. mus.) an overture or symphony, pl. **-ia**; **-ietta** a small-scaled symphony or orchestra, pl. **-iettas**

sing. singular

Singapore/ an island off S. end of the Malay Peninsula, **-an**

sing/e scorch; **-ed, -eing**

Singer Sargent, John *see* **Sargent**, **John Singer**

Singh/ a title adopted by the warrior castes of N. India, a surname adopted by male Sikhs; *not* -ng; **-alese** *use* **Sinhalese**

single-minded (hyphen)

sing-song (adj. and noun, hyphen, one word in US)

singular abbr. **s., sing.**

sinh hyperbolic sine (no point)

Sinha, Baron

Sinhalese (a member of the major population group or Indic language) of Sri Lanka, or (of) the Indic language spoken by this people, *also* **Sinhala**; *not* Sing-, Cing-

sinister (her.) of or on the shield-bearer's left, the observer's right, opp. to **dexter**

sinistra/ (It.) left-hand side, abbr. **s.**; **— mano** (mus.) the left hand, abbr. **SM**

sinnet (naut.) braided cordage made in flat or round or square form from three to nine cords; cf. **sennet**; **sennit**

Sinn Fein/ the movement and political party for Irish independence; in Ir. **Sinn Féin**; **-er, -ism**

Sino- a prefix denoting Chinese

sinus/ (anat.) a cavity in bone or tissue, pl. **-es**

Sion *use* **Zion**

Siou/x (of or relating to) (a member of) a group of Native American peoples, or the language of this group; pl. same; **-an**

siphon *not* sy-

si quis (Lat.) if anyone, first words of a notice of ordination

Sirach *or* **Sirah** (Apocr.) abbr. **Sir.**, *also called* **Ecclesiasticus**

sircar (Ind.) a head, the government; *not* -kar

sirdar (Ind. etc.) a person of high political or military rank, in Urdu *sardār*

siren a sea nymph, temptress, (device that emits) warning sound; *not* sy-

Sirenia an order of aquatic mammals

siringe *use* **sy-**

sirocco/ a Saharan wind reaching Italy and S. Europe, pl. **-s**; *not* sci-

sirup *use* **sy-**

sirvente (Fr. m.) a medieval Provençal narrative poem

SIS Secret Intelligence Service

sissy *not* ci-

sister german having same parents (two words)

sister/-in-law pl. **sisters-in-law, -uterine** having same mother only (hyphens)

Sistine Chapel in the Vatican, *not* Six-

Sisyphean condemned to eternal punishment, like **Sisyphus** (Gr. myth.) (cap.)

Sitapur Uttar Pradesh, India

sitcom (abbr.) a situation comedy (one word)

sitrep a situation report on the current military condition in an area (one word)

sits vac (abbr.) situations vacant (no points)

sitting room (two words)

situs (Lat. sing. and pl.) a site

Sitwell,/ Dame Edith (1887–1964) English poet; **— Sir Osbert** (1892–1969) English poet, novelist, essayist; **— Sir Sacheverell** (1897–1988) English poet and art critic

sitz bath a hip bath (two words)

Śiva/ a Hindu god; **-ism, -ite**; *also* **Shiva** in informal contexts

Siwalik Hills India, *not* Siv-

sixain (prosody) a six-line stanza

Six Day War 1967 (no hyphen)

Six Mile Bottom Cambs. (three words)

Sixmilebridge Co. Clare, Co. Limerick (one word)

Sixmilecross Co. Tyrone (one word)

six/pence, -penny (one word)

Six Road Ends Co. Down (three words)

sixte a fencing parry

sixteenmo *see* **sextodecimo**

Sixth Avenue Manhattan, New York City; former (and still trad.) name for **Avenue of the Americas**

Sixtine *use* **Sistine**

Six Towns the Potteries in Staffordshire; *see also* **Five Towns, The**

sixty-fourmo (typ.) a book based on 64 leaves, 128 pages, to the sheet (hyphen); abbr. **64mo**

sixty-fourth note (US mus.) = **hemidemisemiquaver**

sizable *use* **sizea-** (except in US)

sizeism *not* sizism

sizar an assisted student at Cambridge or Trinity College, Dublin

sizeable *not* -zable (US)

SJ Society of Jesus (Jesuits)

SJAA St John Ambulance Association

SJAB St John Ambulance Brigade

Sjælland an island, Denmark; *not* Zealand; in Ger. **Seeland**

sjambok (Afrik.) (flog with) a hide whip, *not* sam-

SJC (US) Supreme Judicial Court

sjužet (lit.) in Russian Formalism, a narrative work's plot as it is presented to the reader (cf. *fabula*); *also* (in non-specialist contexts) *syuzhet*

Skagerrak the arm of the North Sea between Denmark and Norway (one word), *not* **Skager Rack**

skald in ancient Scandinavia, a composer and reciter of poems honouring heroes and their deeds; *not* scald

Skara Brae Orkney

skateboard/, -er, -ing (one word)

skean/ (hist.) a Gaelic dagger formerly used in Ireland and Scotland, **-dhu** a dirk worn in the stocking as part of Highland costume (hyphen); *not* skene-

skein of silk etc., *not* -ain

Skelmersdale/ Lancs.; **Baron —**

skep a wooden or wicker basket or beehive, *not* skip

skep/sis, -tic, -tical *use* **sc-** (except in US)

skeuomorph *not* skew-

skewbald of two colours in irregular patches, usually of horses, usually white and a colour other than black; cf. **piebald**

ski/ pl. **-s**; as verb **-ed, -ing** (no hyphens)

skiagraphy etc., *use* **scia-** except in US, and in Greek contexts

skier a person using skis; cf. **skyer**

skiey *use* **skyey**

skiing *see* **ski**

ski-joring a sport in which the skier is towed (hyphen), in Norw. *skikjøring*

skilful *not* skill- (US)

skillet a small metal cooking pot with a long handle and (usually) legs; (US) = **frying pan**

skill-less without skill (hyphen, three *l*s)

skin-deep (hyphen)

skin div/e, -er, -ing (two words, one in US)

skinflint a miser (one word)

skin graft (two words)

skinhead (one word)

skinlike (one word)

Skinner, B(**urrhus**) **F**(**rederic**) (1904–90) US psychologist

skin test (two words)

skintight (one word)

skip a large container for builders' refuse etc.; *see also* **skep**

skirting board (two words)

skiver (bind.) a binding leather split from the grain side of sheepskin

Skokie a city and river, Ill.

skol a toast in drinking, *not* **skoal**; in Dan. before 1948 **skaal**, in Swed. and Dan. after 1948 **skål**

Skopje Macedonia

skow *use* **sc-**

Skriabin, Aleksandr (**Nikolaevich**) (1872–1915) Russian composer, *also* **Skryabin**

Skt. Sanskrit

skulduggery trickery; *not* **scul-, skull-**

skullcap (one word)

skull-less (hyphen, three *l*s)

skunk/-bear (US) a wolverine (hyphen), **— cabbage** (US) a herbaceous plant with an offensive-smelling spathe (two words)

skurry *use* **sc-**

Skutari *use* **Sc-**

skydiv/e, -er, -ing (one word)

skyer a high hit at cricket; *cf.* **skier**

Skye terrier (one cap.)

skyey *not* skiey

sky/jack, -lark, -light, -line, -sail, -scraper, -watch (one word)

skywriting (one word)

SL serjeant-at-law, solicitor-at-law

SLADE Society of Lithographic Artists, Designers, Engravers, and Process Workers

slainte a Gaelic toast: good health!; in Gael. **sláinte**

slaked lime *not* slack-

slalom ski race down zigzag course, *not* slallom

Slamannan Central

s.l.a.n. *sine loco, anno, vel nomine* (without place, year, or name)

slander/ (law) false oral defamation; *cf.* **libel**; **-er, -ous, -ously**

slapdash (one word)

slap-happy (hyphen)

slapstick (one word)

S. lat. south latitude

slate (colloq.) criticize severely; (US) schedule, plan; (US) nominate for office etc.

slaty like, or made of, slate; *not* -ey

Slav/ic (esp. in US), **-onian, -onic** (esp. in UK) of the Slavs; *not* Sc-; abbr. **Slav.**

SLBM submarine-launched ballistic missile

SLD (hist.) Social and Liberal Democrats, in 1989 officially replaced by **Liberal Democrats**

sld. sailed

s.l.e.a. *sine loco et anno* (without place or date)

sled (US) = **sledge**

sledgehammer (one word)

sleeping/ bag, — car, — partner, — pill, — sickness (two words)

sleepwalk/, -er, -ing (one word)

sleight of hand, *not* sli-

slenderize *not* -ise

Slesvig (Dan.) a province, Germany and Denmark; in Ger. **Schleswig**

sleuth-hound (hyphen, one word in US)

S level a GCE examination (no hyphen), abbr. of special *or* (hist.) scholarship level

slew *not* slue

slily *use* **slyly**

slip road a road for entering or leaving a motorway etc. (two words)

slip/shod, -stream, -way (one word)

Sloane, Sir Hans (1660–1753) English naturalist

sloe/ (fruit of) blackthorn, **— gin** a liqueur of sloes (two words); **-worm** *use* **slow-**

sloot (Du.) a ditch; *see also* **sluit**

sloping fractions (typ.) those with a solidus or oblique stroke, as ½

sloth laziness, also (zool.) a slow-moving nocturnal S. American mammal

slot machine (two words)

Slough Berks.

slough to shed

Slovak/ a member or the language of a Slavonic people inhabiting Slovakia, **-ian**

Slovene a member or the language of a Slavonic people in Slovenia, of or relating to Slovenia or its people or language; *also* **Slovenian**

Slovenia a republic in the former Yugoslavia, in Serbo-Croat **Slovenija**

slowpoke (US) = **slowcoach** (one word)

slow-worm a small European legless lizard, *not* sloe- (hyphen)

s.l.p. *sine legitima prole* (without lawful issue)

SLR single-lens reflex (camera), self-loading rifle

slue *use* **slew**

slugabed a lazy person (one word)

sluice/, -gate, -valve, -way (hyphens)

sluit (Afrik.) a deep gully formed by heavy rain; *see also* **sloot**

slyly *not* sli-

SM sadomasochism, Sergeant Major, Staff Major, (mus.) short metre, (Fr.) *Sa Majesté*, (Ger.) *Seine Majestat* (His Majesty), (It. mus.) *sinistra mano* (the left hand), (It.) *Sua Maesta*, (Sp.) *Su Majestad* (His, *or* Her, Majesty)

Sm samarium (no point)

sm. small

small arms (two words)

small-bore (of a firearm) (hyphen, two words in US)

small capitals abbr. **s.c.**, **small caps.**, **s. caps.**

smallgoods (Austral.) delicatessen meats

smallhold/er, -ing (one word)

small-minded (hyphen)

smallpox (one word)

Smalls the Oxford 'Responsions' Examination (cap.); small items of laundry (not cap.)

smart alec *not* -eck, -ick (two words)

SMD (mus.) short metre double

SME Sancta Mater Ecclesia (Holy Mother Church)

Smelfungus Sterne's name for Smollett (one l)

smelling/ bottle, — salts (two words)

smell-less (hyphen, three ls)

smelt past of smell, *not* smelled (US); a small sea fish; *see also* **smolt**

smetana sour cream

Smetana, Bedřich (1824–84) Czech composer

SMI (Fr.) *Sa Majesté Impériale* (His, *or* Her, Imperial Majesty)

smidgen *not* -in, -eon

Smith,/ Sydney (1771–1845) English clergyman and wit; **— Sir William Sidney** (1764–1840) English admiral, defender of St Jean d'Acre; *see also* **Smyth**; **Smythe**

Smithsonian Institution Washington, DC, *not* -tute; abbr. **Smith. Inst.**; founded 1846 from funds left by **James Smithson** (1765–1829) English chemist

SMM Sancta Mater Maria (Holy Mother Mary)

smok/e, -able, -y

smoke/screen, -stack (one word)

smoking/ jacket, — room (two words)

smolder *use* **smoulder** (except in US)

Smollett, Tobias (**George**) (1721–71) Scottish novelist and physician

smolt a young salmon; *see also* **smelt**

smooth/ (verb) **-s** *not* -e, -es; **— breathing** (typ.) *see* **breathing**

smorgasbord open sandwiches served with delicacies, as hors d'oeuvres or a buffet (not ital.); in Swed. *smörgåsbord*

smorzando (It. mus.) gradually dying away

smoulder *not* smol- (US)

s.m.p. *sine mascula prole* (without male issue)

smriti Hindu traditional teachings on religion etc., in Skt. *smr̥ti*

Smyrna the former name for **İzmir**, Turkey

Smyrniot (a native) of Smyrna

Smyth,/ Dame Ethel (1858–1944) English composer, **— John** (1586–1612) founder of the English Baptists; *see also* **Smith**; **Smythe**

Smythe, Francis Sydney (1900–49) English mountaineer; *see also* **Smith**; **Smyth**

Sn stannum (tin) (no point)

s.n. (Lat) *sine nomine* (without name), *sub nomine* (under a specified name)

snake charmer (two words)

snake-pit (hyphen, two words in US)

snap (US) (close with) a press stud

snapdragon (bot.) a plant, *Antirrhinum majus*; a Christmas game (one word)

snifter a small drink of alcohol; (US) a balloon glass for bandy etc.

snipe/ a gamebird, pl. **-s** and (collective) same

snivel/, -led, -ler, -ling (one l in US)

snorkel/ a device for underwater swimming etc., **-ler, -ling** (one l in US); *not* schn-

Snorri Sturluson (1178–1241) Icelandic historian and poet; *see also* **Heimskringla**

snow (meteor.) abbr. **s.**

snow/ball, -berry (one word)

snow-blind/, -ed, -ing, -ness (hyphen, one word in US)

snowblower (one word)

snow boot (two words)

snowbound (one word)

snow bunting a mainly white finch (two words)

snow/cap, -drift, -drop, -fall, -field, -flake (one word)

snow/ goose, — leopard (two words)

snow/line, -man, -mobile (one word)

snow/plough *not* -plow (US), **-shoe, -storm** (one word)

snowy owl (two words)

SNP Scottish National Party

Snr. *see* **senior**

snuffbox (one word)

SO Staff Officer, Stationery Office, sub-office

so (mus.) *use* **soh**

s.o. seller's option, (Ger.) *siehe oben* (see above), substance of

so-and-so/ a particular person not specified, pl. **-s** (no apos.); **Mr So-and-so** (one cap.)

Soane's, Sir John (**Museum**) London

soap/bark, -berry, -box (one word)

soap/ flakes, — opera (two words)

soap/stone, -suds, -wort (one word)

SOAS School of Oriental and African Studies

sobriquet nickname, *not* sou- (not ital.)

Soc. Socialist, Society, Socrates

socage a feudal tenure of land, *not* socc-

so-called (adj., hyphen)

Socialist cap. when referring to a political party or its members; not cap. when referring to general principles of socialism or their adherents; abbr. **S., Soc.**

socialize *not* -ise

sociedad/ (Sp. f.) society; — *anónima* public limited company, abbr. **SA**

sociedade/ (Port. f.) society; — *anónima* public limited company, abbr. **SA**; — *anônima* (Brazilian Port.) public limited company, abbr. **SA**

società/ (It. f.) society; — *per azioni* public limited company, abbr. **SpA**

société/ (Fr. f.) society; — *anonyme* public limited company, abbr. **SA**

Société des Bibliophiles françois founded 1820, *not français* (lower-case *f*); abbr. **S**ᵗᵉ

Society abbr. **S., Soc.**

socio/biology, -cultural (one word)

socio-economic (hyphen, one word in US)

sociolinguistic (one word)

sociology abbr. **sociol.**

socius/ (Lat.) Fellow, Associate, abbr. **S.**; — *criminis* associate in crime

Socotra Indian Ocean; *not* -ora, Sok-

Socrat/es (469–399 BC) Greek philosopher, *not* Sok-; **-ic**; abbr. **Soc.**

sodium symbol **Na** (natrium)

sodomize *not* -ise

Sodor and Man, Bishop of; **Sodor & Man:** his signature (one colon)

SOE Special Operations Executive

SOED Shorter Oxford English Dictionary

sœur/ (Fr. f.) sister, nun; — *de charité* Sister of Mercy

Sofar (acronym, one cap.)

soffit (archit.) the under-surface of an arch or eaves

Sofi *use* **Sufi**; *see also* **Sophy**

Sofia Bulgaria, in Bulgarian **Sofiya**

S. of S. Song of Solomon

softa a Muslim student of sacred law and theology (not ital.)

soft copy (comput.) the transient reproduction of keyboard input on VDU (two words); cf. **hard copy**

soft-core (hyphen, one word in US)

soft-headed/, -ness (hyphens, one word in US)

soft-hearted/, -ness (hyphens, one word in US)

S. of III Ch. Song of the Three Children

softie a soft-hearted, silly, or weak person; *not* -y

soft-pedal/, -led, -ling (one *l* in US)

soft sell (noun, two words)

soft-sell (verb, hyphen, two words in US)

soft sign (typ.) a single prime ('), used in e.g. transliterated Russ., cf. **hard sign**

soft-spoken (hyphen)

software programs and other operating information used by a computer (one word)

softwood (one word)

SOGAT *or* **Sogat** Society of Graphical and Allied Trades, from 1982 officially called **SOGAT 82**

sogenannt (Ger.) so-called, abbr. **sog.**

soh (mus.) *not* so

Soho a district of London's West End (one cap.), **SoHo** a district of Manhattan south of Houston Street (two caps.)

soi-disant (Fr.) self-styled (hyphen); do not use for 'so-called' (i.e. by others)

soign/é (Fr.) f. *-ée* carefully finished or arranged, well-groomed

soirée/ an evening party, — *dansante* one with dancing, — *musicale* one with music (not ital.)

Sokotra *use* **Socotra**

Sokrates *use* **Soc-** except in Hellenic contexts, or esp. of a Sokrates other than the philosopher

Sol (Lat.) (the personification of) the sun (cap.)

Sol. Solomon

sol. solicitor, solution

sola *see* **solus**

solan goose the gannet; cf. **solen**

solarize *not* -ise

solati/um (Lat.) compensation, pl. **-a**

sola topi an Indian sun helmet, *not* solar

solecis/m a blunder in speaking, writing, or behaviour; **-tic**

solecize *not* -ise

solemnize *not* -ise

solen a razor-shell mollusc; cf. **solan**

solenoid a cylindrical wire coil acting as a magnet

sol-fa/ (mus.) (hyphen), **-ed**

solfegg/io (mus.) a sol-fa exercise for the voice, pl. **-i**

soli pl. of **solo**

solicitor abbr. **sol., solr.**

Solicitor-General (caps., hyphen, two words in US); abbr. **SG, Sol.-Gen.**

solicitude anxiety, concern; in Fr. f. *sollicitude*

solid (typ.) text matter set without extra spacing between lines or letters

solidarność (Pol.) solidarity, cap. as name of Polish trade-union movement led by Lech Wałęsa

solid/us oblique stroke (/), pl. **-i**, abbr. **s.**

soliloqu/y a speech made alone or regardless of hearers, pl. **-ies**; **-ize** *not* -ise

solipsis/m (philos.) the view that the self is all that exists or can be known; **-t, -tic, -tically**

solmization (mus.) *not* -sation

sol/o abbr. **s.**, pl. **-os**; It. mus. pl. **-i**

Solon (638–?558 BC) Athenian lawgiver

solr. solicitor

solubilize make soluble or more soluble, *not* -ise

soluble that can be dissolved or solved

sol/us (theat.) f. **-a** alone, unaccompanied

solution abbr. **sol.**

Solutrean (the culture of) the palaeolithic period in Europe following the Aurignacian and preceding the Magdalenian, *not* -ian

solvable that can be solved; *not* -eable, -ible

solvent *not* -ant

solvitur ambulando (Lat.) the question settles itself naturally

Solzhenitsyn, Aleksandr (Isaevich) (b. 1918) Russian writer

Som. Somerset

Somali/ (of or relating to) (a member of) a Hamitic Muslim people of Somalia, or the Cushitic language of this people; pl. same

Somalia NE Africa, adj. **Somali**

Somaliland (one word)

sombre *not* -er (except in US)

sombrero/ a broad-brimmed hat, esp. the characteristic hat of Mexico; pl. **-s**; in Sp. *sombrero* a hat of any type

somebody a person (one word); an unspecified group of persons, or thing or collection of thing (two words)

somehow (one word)

someone somebody (one word); a single person or thing (two words)

Somerby Leics., Lincs.

somersault *not* -set, summer-

Somersby Lincs., birthplace of Tennyson

Somerset an English county, abbr. **Som.**

Somers Town London (two words)

Somerstown W. Sussex (one word)

something (one word)

some/what, -when, -where (one word)

sommelier a wine waiter (not ital.)

Somoza (Debayle), Anastasio (1925–80) President of Nicaragua 1967–72, 1974–9

Son, the as the Deity (cap.)

son abbr. **s.**

sonar (acronym, not cap.)

sonata/ (mus.) pl. **-s**

Sondes, Earl *not* of

son et lumière (Fr.) a night entertainment with sound and light effects

song/bird, -book (one word)

song cycle (two words)

Song/ of Solomon (OT) abbr. **S. of S.**, *also called* — **of Songs**; — **of the Three Children** (Apocr.) abbr. **S. of III Ch.**

songs, titles of (typ.) to be roman quoted when cited

song thrush (two words)

songwriter (one word)

son-in-law (hyphens) pl. **sons-in-law**

Son of/ God, — — Man (caps.)

sons/y (Sc.) plump, buxom; of a cheerful disposition; bringing good fortune; **-ier, -iest**; *not* -ie, -zy

soochong *use* **sou-**

Soofee *use* **Sufi**

Sop. soprano, -s

Sophocles (495–406 BC) Greek playwright, abbr. **Soph.**

sophomore a second-year university or (US) high-school student, *not* sophi-

Sophy English name for the Shah, 16th–17th cc.; cf. **Sufi**

sopra (It.) above

sopranino/ (mus.) an instrument higher than a soprano, pl. **-s**

sopran/o (mus.) pl. **-os**, It. pl. **-i**; abbr. **S., Sop.**

sorbefacient (med.) (a drug etc.) causing absorption

Sorbian of or relating to a Slavonic people in southern Brandenburg and eastern Saxony, or to their W. Slavonic language, still spoken around Lusatia, Bautzen, and Cottbus, eastern Germany; *not* Sora-, *not* Lusatian, Wendish (q.v.)

Sorbonne the medieval theological college of Paris, now comprising three of the Paris universities with faculties of science and arts also; formally Académie Universitaire de Paris

sorcer/er f. **-ess** a wizard or magician, **-ous**

sordin/o (mus.) a mute for a bowed or wind instrument, pl. **-i**

sorehead (US) a touchy or disgruntled person (one word)

sorghum a tropical cereal grass, *not* -gum

sortes/ (Lat.) (divination by) lots; — *Biblicae* or *Sacrae*, — *Homericae*, — *Vergilianae* (divination from) random passages of Scripture, Homer, Virgil

sortie/ (make) a sally, esp. from a besieged garrison; (make) an operational flight by a single military aircraft; **-d, -ing, -s**

sortilege divination by sorts

sorts/ (typ.) letters or pieces of type; *see also* **special** —

SOS (a) signal for help, pl. **SOSs**

so-so passable (hyphen)

sostenuto/ (mus.) (a passage played) in sustained manner, pl. **-s**

Sotheby Parke Bernet & Co. auctioneers ('Sotheby's')

sotto/ (It.) under, — **voce** in an undertone

sou (hist.) a French coin of small value (not ital.)

Soubirous, St Bernadette (1844–79) of Lourdes, French nun

soubrette a maid or other pert female character in a (musical) comedy (not ital.)

soubriquet use **sob-**

souchong a fine black China tea, *not* soo-

Soudan/, -ese *use* **Sud-**

souffle (med.) a low murmur heard in the auscultation of various organs etc. (no accent)

soufflé a light spongy dish using egg whites (not ital.)

souffleur (Fr. m.) a theatre prompter

souk a market place in Muslim countries; *not* suk, sukh; in Arab. **sūḳ**

Soul *use* **Seoul**

soul food (two words)

soulless (one word)

soulmate (one word, two words in US)

soul music (two words)

Soult, Nicolas Jean de Dieu (1769–1851) French marshal, Duke of Dalmatia

sound barrier (two words)

sound bite a short extract from a recorded interview, chosen for its pungency or appropriateness; *not* byte

sound effect (two words)

soundhole (one word)

sounding board (mus.) (two words)

sound post (two words)

sound/proof, -track (one word)

sound wave (two words)

soup bowl (two words)

soupçon a very small quantity (not ital.)

souper (Fr. m.) supper, *not* -pé

soup/ kitchen, — plate (two words)

soup spoon (two words, one word in US)

sourcebook (one word)

source criticism (two words)

sour cream *not* -ed —

soutane (RC) a priest's cassock

souteneur (Fr. m.) a pimp

souterrain (esp. archaeol.) an underground chamber or passage

south abbr. **S.**; *see also* **compass points**

South/ Africa, — African abbr. **S. Afr., SA**; — **America, — American** abbr. **S. Amer., SA**; **South Australia, — Australian** abbr. **SA**

southbound (one word)

South/ Carolina off. and postal abbr. **SC**; — **Dakota** off. abbr. **S. Dak.**, postal **SD**

Southdown a breed of sheep (one word)

South Downs Hants. etc.

south-east/, -ern (hyphen, one word in US) abbr. **SE**

southeaster a wind from south-east (one word)

southern abbr. **S.**; *see also* **compass points**

Southern Africa a geographical term, including Zimbabwe and other countries as well as the Republic of South Africa

southernwood a species of wormwood, lad's love

Southern Yemen *see* **Yemen**

Southesk, Earl of

Southey, Robert (1774–1843) Poet Laureate 1813–43

southpaw (a person who is) left-handed (one word)

South Pole (caps.)

South Wales abbr. **SW**

Southwark *or* 'The Borough', formerly in Surrey

Southwark: the signature of the Bishop of Southwark (colon)

Southwell: the signature of the Bishop of Southwell (colon)

south-west/, -ern (hyphen, one word in US) abbr. **SW**

South West Africa (three words)

southwester a wind from south-west (one word)

soutien-gorge (Fr. m.) bra, brassiere; pl. **soutiens-gorge**; cf. **brassière**

souvlaki a Greek dish of pieces of meat grilled on a skewer, *not* -ia

sou'wester a sailor's oilskin hat or coat, a southwester wind

sovereign/, -s abbr. **sov., sovs.**

soviet (Russ.) an elected local, district, or national council, the basis of Russian governmental machinery since 1917; (hist.) a revolutionary council before 1917 (not cap.); (adj.) of or concerning the former Soviet Union (cap.); *see also* **Union of Soviet Socialist Republics**

Sowet/o a group of townships SW of Johannesburg, S. Africa; adj. **-an**

sox *use* **socks** (except in some commercial contexts, or as part of the name of certain US baseball teams)

Soxhlet (chem.) an extraction apparatus

soybean *not* soya-

Sp. Spain, Spanish

sp. species (sing.), specimen, spelling, spirit

s.p. self-propelled, starting price

s.p. *sine prole* (without issue)

SpA (It.) *Società per Azioni* (public limited company)

spacecraft (sing. and pl.) (one word)

space flight (two words)

spaceman (one word)

space rocket (two words)

spaces (typ.) blanks between words or letters

spaceship (one word)

space station (two words)

spacesuit (one word)

space-time (hyphen) *or* **spacetime** (one word)

space travel/, -ler (two words)

space/ vehicle, — walk (two words)

spacewoman (one word)

spacial *use* **spat-**

spae/ (Sc.) foretell, prophesy; **-wife** a female fortune-teller or witch (one word)

spaghetti strings of pasta (not ital.)

spahi a Turkish horse-soldier, Algerian French cavalryman; in Turk. **sipahi**; cf. **sepoy**

Spain abbr. **Sp.**

Spalato It. for **Split**

spandrel (archit.) a space between the curve of an arch and the enclosing mouldings, *not* -il

Spanish (of or relating to) (a person from) Spain or the Castilian language of Spain, abbr. **Sp.**

Spanish n (ñ) 'n with the tilde' or 'curly n'; pron. *ng* in 'cognac' or *ni* in 'onion'

Spanish Town Jamaica

sparagmos (Gr. tragedy) the ritual tearing to pieces of a victim

spare rib/, -s (two words, one word in US)

spark plug (two words)

spatial *not* -acial

spatio-temporal (hyphen, one word in US)

spatterdash (US) = **roughcast**

SPCK Society for Promoting Christian Knowledge

SPE Society for Pure English

speakeas/y pl. **-ies**

spear/head, -man, -mint, -wort (one word)

spec (colloq.) specification, speculation (no point)

spec. special, -ly; specific, -ally, -ation; specimen

spécialité (Fr. f.) a speciality (ital.)

speciality in general senses, *not* specialty (US)

specialize *not* -ise

special sort (typ.) a character or symbol not on the standard keyboard or ASCII character set, one that must be accessed by codes during setting

specialty (law) a contract under seal, (US) = **speciality**

specie coin, as distinct from paper money; pl. same

species abbr. **sp.**; pl. same, abbr. **spp.**

specific gravity relative density, abbr. **sp. gr.**

specimen abbr. **sp.**, **spec.**

specs (colloq.) spectacles

Spectaclemakers Society (no hyphen, no apos.)

spectre *not* -er (US)

spectr/um pl. **-a**

speculat/e, -or

specul/um (surg.) an instrument for dilating body cavities for viewing, a (polished metal) mirror, (ornith.) a bright patch on a bird's wing; pl. **-a**

speech day (two words)

speed/boat, -way (one word)

spele/an (adj.) cave-dwelling; **-ologist, -ology**; *not* spelae-

spel(l)ican *use* **spillikin**

spell past and past part. **spelled** *or* **spelt**

spell/bind, -bound (one word)

speluncar of, pertaining to, or resembling a cave

spelunker (US) a person who explores caves, esp. as a hobby

Spencer,/ Earl (*not* of), **— Herbert** (1820–1903) English philosopher, **— Sir Stanley** (1891–1959) English painter

Spengler, Oswald (1880–1936) German philosopher of history

Spenser/, Edmund (1552–99) English poet; **-ian** of the poet, his style, *or* his stanza (*ababbcbcc*)

Spetsai Greece, *not* Spezzia

spew to vomit, *not* spue

Speyer Germany, *not* Spires

Spezzia *use* **Spetsai** (Greece) *or* **La Spezia** (Italy)

sp. gr. specific gravity

spherical abbr. **s.**

sphinx/ *not* sphy-, pl. **-es** (cap. with reference to Gr. myth. or the huge sphinx near the Pyramids at Giza)

sphygmomanometer an instrument for measuring blood pressure

spianato (mus.) made smooth

spick and span (three words)

spicy not -ey

spiegando (mus.) 'unfolding', becoming louder

spiflicate (joc.) trounce, not spiff-

spiky not -ey

spill past and past part. **spilt** or **spilled** (esp. in US)

spillikin a small rod, or a game using them; not spel(l)ican

spillover (noun) (one word)

spillway a passage for surplus water from a dam (one word)

spina bifida (med.) a congenital defect of the spine (two words, not ital.)

spinach not -age

spin/-dry, -dryer (hyphens) not -drier

spine/ (bind.) that part of the case protecting the back of a book, and bearing **— lettering**

spinney a thicket, not -ny

spinning/ jenny, — machine, — top, — wheel (two words)

spin-off (noun, hyphen)

Spinon/e an Italian gun dog, pl. **-i** (cap.)

Spinoz/a, Baruch (1632–77) Dutch philosopher; **-ism, -ist, -istic**

spiraea (bot.) an ornamental shrub, not -rea (US)

spiral/, -led, -ling (one l in US)

Spires Germany, use **Speyer**

spirit abbr. **sp.**

spirito (mus.) life, spirit

spiritual of the spirit

spiritualize not -ise

spirituel marked by refinement and quickness of mind (not ital); in Fr. **spirituel** f. **-le**

spirochaete any of various flexible spiral-shaped bacteria, not -hete (US)

spirt use **spurt**

spitfire a person of fiery temper (one word)

Spithead the strait between IoW and Portsmouth

Spitsbergen Arctic Ocean, not Spitz-

spiv/ (sl.) a flashy petty black marketeer; **-vish, -very, -vy**

splendour not -or (US)

Split Croatia, formerly **Spalato**

Spode/, Josiah (1754–1827) maker of **— china** at Stoke

Spohr, Louis (1784–1859) German composer

spoil past and past part. **spoilt** or **spoiled** (esp. in US)

spokes/man, -person, -woman (one word)

spolia/ (Lat.) spoils, **— opima** a trophy won by a general who killed the commander of an opposing army in single combat

spoliation not spoil-

spond/ee (prosody) a foot of two long (or stressed) syllables, **-aic**

sponge bag (two words)

sponge bath (US) = **blanket bath**

sponge/ cake, — cloth, — pudding (two words)

spongy like sponge, not -gey

sponsion (law) being a surety for another, a pledge or promise made on behalf of the State by an agent not authorized to do so

sponson a projection from the side of a warship, tank, seaplane, or paddle steamer

spontane/ity, -ous

spoonerism a transposition of the initial letters etc. of two or more words, e.g. 'You have hissed my mystery lectures' (not cap.); from the English scholar **Revd W. A. Spooner** (1844–1930)

spoon-feed (hyphen)

spoonful/ pl. **-s**

sporran a pouch worn over a kilt

spos/a (It.) bride, pl. **-e**; **-o** bridegroom, pl. **-i**

spotlight (one word)

spp. species (pl.)

SPQR Senatus Populusque Romanus (the Senate and Roman people, used as the emblem of the modern City), small profits and quick returns

SPR Society for Psychical Research

Spr. Sapper

Sprachgefühl (Ger. n.) a feeling for (the natural idiom of) a language

Sprechgesang (mus.) a style of dramatic vocalization between speech and song

sprezzatura (It.) ease of manner, studied carelessness, nonchalance, esp. in art or literature

sprightly lively, not spritely

spring (verb); (past) **sprang**, (US past) **sprung**

spring (season of) (not cap.)

spring balance (two words)

springboard (one word)

springbok (Afrik.) an antelope; (cap.) a South African, esp. one who plays or has played for South Africa in international sporting competitions; not -buck

spring/ chicken, — clean, — cleaning (two words)

Springer (Ger. m.) the knight at chess, not Ritter

spring fever (two words)

springtail any wingless insect of the order Collembola

spring/tide, -time the season of spring (one word)

spring tide the tide of greatest range (two words)

spring water (two words, one word in US)

sprinkled edges (bind.) the cut edges of books sprinkled with coloured ink

SPRL (Fr.) *société de personnes à responsabilité limitée* (private limited company)

spry/ active; **-er, -est, -ly, -ness**

s.p.s. *sine prole superstite* (without surviving issue)

spue *use* **spew**

spumante an Italian sparkling white wine (not cap., not ital.)

spumoni (US) a kind of ice-cream dessert (not ital.)

spurrey a slender plant, *not* -y

spurt *not* -irt

sputnik each of a series of Russian artificial satellites launched between 1957 and 1961

sput/um expectorated matter, pl. **-a**

spy/glass, -hole (one word)

sq./ square; **— ft.** square feet; **— in.** square inches; **— m.** square metres, square miles (each sing. and pl.); not used in scientific and technical work

Sqn. Ldr. *or* **Sqn/Ldr** Squadron Leader

squacco/ a small crested heron, pl. **-s**

squaddie (Brit. sl.) a recruit, a private; *not* -dy

squalls (meteor.) abbr. **q.**

square (bind.) that part of the case which overlaps the edges of a book

square back (bind.) a book whose back has not been rounded; *see* **rounding**

square brackets [ ]

square off (US) = **square up**; (Austral.) placate

square root (two words)

squeegee a rubber-edged implement for sweeping wet surfaces, *not* -ie

squirearchy landowners collectively, esp. as a class; *not* -rarchy

squirrel/, -led, -ling (one l in US), **-ly**

squirt gun (US) = **water pistol**

sq. yd. square yards (sing. and pl.)

SR Southern Region

Sr strontium (no point)

Sr. Sister, (Sp.) *Señor*

sr steradian

sr. *use* **sen.**

Sra. (Sp.) *Señora*

Srbija Serbo-Croat for **Serbia**

SRC Science Research Council, Students' Representative Council

Sri Lanka/ 'Resplendent Island'; **-n**

Srinagar Kashmir, *not* Ser-

SRN State Registered Nurse

sRNA soluble (transfer) RNA, *use* **tRNA**

SRO standing room only, statutory rules and orders

Srta. (Sp.) *Señorita*

SS Saints, Secretary of State, steamship, (Fr.) *Sa Sainteté* (His Holiness), (Ger.) *Schutzstaffel* (Nazi elite corps), (It.) *Sua Santità* (His Holiness)

SS, collar of the former badge of the House of Lancaster, *not* esses

ss. subsection, (med.) half

s.s. screw steamer, (mus.) *senza sordini* (without mutes)

SSAFA Soldiers', Sailors', and Airmen's Families Association

Ssangyong a Korean make of car; *also* **SsangYong** (one word)

SSC (Sc.) Solicitor to the Supreme Court

SSE south-south-east

S.Sgt., S/Sgt. Staff Sergeant

SSP statutory sick pay

SSR Soviet Socialist Republic

SSRC Social Science Research Council

SSSI Site of Special Scientific Interest

SST supersonic transport

SSW south-south-west

St Saint, alphabetize under Saint, *not* St-; stokes

St. (in Slavonic languages) *Stari* etc., old; Strait, -s; Street

st. stanza, stem, stone, strophe, (cricket) stumped

s.t. short ton (2,000 lb)

Sta (It., Sp., Port.) Santa (female saint) (no point)

Sta. Station

Staal,/ Georges Frédéric Charles, baron de (1824–1907) Russian diplomat; **— Marguerite Jeanne Cordier De Launay, baronne de** (1684–1750) French writer; *see also* **Staël**; **Stahl**

'Stabat Mater' 'the Mother was standing' (medieval poem, RC hymn)

stabbing (bind.) wire stitching near the back edge of a closed section or pamphlet, the piercing of a book section prior to sewing or stitching

stabilize/ *not* -ise, **-r** (US) the horizontal tailplane of an aircraft

staccato/ in an abrupt or detached manner; as noun, pl. **-s**

stadi/um (Gr. antiquity) a measure of length (about 185 metres), a racecourse, pl. **-a**; (modern use) a sports ground, pl. **-ums**

stadtholder (cap. only as part of title); in Du. *stadthouder*

Staël, Madame de in full **Anne Louise Germaine, baronne de Staël-Holstein**, b.

Necker (1766–1817) French writer; *see also* **Staal**; **Stahl**

staff/ a pole or stick; (mus.) a set of lines on which music is written, pl. **staves**; a body of persons under authority, pl. **-s**; cf. **stave**

Staffs. Staffordshire

Staff Sergeant abbr. **S.Sgt., S/Sgt.**

stag beetle (two words)

stage/coach, -craft (one word)

stage/ direction, — door, — fright (two words)

stagehand (one word)

stage/-manage (hyphen), **— manager** (two words)

stage name (two words)

staghound (one word)

Stagirite, the Aristotle, *not* Stagy-

stag/ night, — party (two words)

stagy excessively theatrical *not* -ey

Stahl,/ Friedrich Julius (1802–61) German lawyer and politician; **— Georg Ernst** (1660–1734) German chemist; *see also* **Staal**; **Staël**

staid solemn; cf. **stayed**

stair/case, -head, -way, -well (one word)

Stakhanovite an exceptionally productive worker (esp. in the former USSR) (cap.)

stalactite a mineral deposit hanging from the roof of a cave

Stalag (hist.) a German POW camp, esp. for non-commissioned officers and privates

stalagmite a mineral deposit rising from the floor of a cave

stalemate (one word)

Stalin, Joseph (1879–1953) b. **Iosif Vissarioniovich Dzhugashvili**, General Secretary of the Communist Party of the USSR 1922–53

Stalingrad *previously* **Tsartisyn**, *now* **Volgograd**

stalking horse (two words)

stamen/ (bot.) pl. **-s**

stamina power of endurance

stamp/ collector, — duty (two words)

stamping ground (two words)

stamp/ mill, — office (two words)

stanch (verb) check a flow; cf. **staunch**

stand-alone (of a computer) operating independently of a network or other system

standardize *not* -ise

standing type (typ.) type not yet distributed after use

stand-off/ a deadlock, **-ish** rather cold and reserved (hyphen)

stand/pipe, -point, -still (noun) (one word)

stannum tin, symbol **Sn**

Stanstead Suffolk

Stansted Essex, Kent

stanza/, -s, -ed; abbr. **st.**

stapes (anat.) a bone in the ear, pl. same

star/, -red, -ring, -ry

Starcross Devon (one word)

star/dust, -fish (one word)

star fruit the carambola (two words)

star/light, -lit (one word)

Stars and Stripes the US flag

'Star-Spangled Banner, The' the US national anthem

START Strategic Arms Reduction Treaty (*or* Talks)

starting/ block, — gate, — pistol, — point, — post, — price, — stall (two words)

Star Wars (US colloq.) **SDI**, from the science-fiction film *Star Wars*, 1977 (caps., not ital.)

stat. statics, statuary, statute

state a nation or territory considered as a political community, often cap. to denote the abstract concept: 'separation of Church and State'

State Department (US) the department of foreign affairs

Staten Island New York, *not* Staa-; abbr. **SI**

state-of-the-art (adj., hyphens; noun, four words)

stater an ancient Greek coin, *not* -or

stateroom (one word)

States, the commonly the United States of America; the legislative body in Jersey, Guernsey, and Alderney

States General (hist.) the legislative body in the Netherlands and in France before 1789

stateside (US colloq.) of, in, or towards the USA (not cap.)

statesman/like, -ship (one word)

statics the science of forces in equilibrium (sing.)

Station abbr. **Sta., Stn.**

stationary not moving

Stationers' Hall the hall of the Stationers' Company in London, at which a book was formerly registered for purposes of copyright (apos. after *s*)

stationery paper etc.

Stationery Office the government's publishing house, which also provides stationery for government offices

stationmaster (one word)

station wagon (US) = **estate car**

statistics the subject is treated as sing., while the numerical facts systematized are treated as pl.

Státní tajná bezpečnost (hist.) Czechoslovak equivalent to the KGB, abbr. **STB**

stator (elec.) a stationary part within which something revolves; *not* -er

statuary abbr. **stat.**

status/ rank, pl. **-es** (not ital.)

status quo/ the same state as now, the existing state of affairs (not ital.)

status quo ante (Lat.) the same state as before (ital.)

statute a written law passed by a legislative body, e.g. an Act of Parliament; abbr. **stat.**

statute/ book, — law (two words)

statute mile *see* **mile**

statutory *not* -ary

staunch firm, loyal; cf. **stanch**

stave/ (mus.) a staff, a stanza or verse (of a song), an alliterative letter in Germanic poetry, a piece of wood in the side of a barrel; pl. **-s**; cf. **staff**

stay-at-home (adj. and noun, hyphens)

stayed stopped, remained; cf. **staid**

STB *Sacrae Theologiae Baccalaureus* (Bachelor of Sacred Theology), Státní tajná bezpečnost (q.v.)

STC Senior (Officers') Training Corps, Short-Title Catalogue

stchi *use* **sh-**

STD *Sacrae Theologiae Doctor* (Doctor of Sacred Theology), sexually transmitted disease, subscriber trunk dialling

Ste (Fr. f.) *sainte* (female saint) (no point)

S^té (Fr.) *Société* (Society)

steadfast *not* sted-

steakhouse (one word, two words in US)

steak knife (two words)

steam/ age, — bath (two words)

steamboat (one word)

steam/ boiler, — engine, — gauge, — hammer, — heat, — iron, — organ, — power (two words)

steam/roller, -ship, abbr. **SS** (one word)

steam shovel (two words)

steam/ train, — turbine (two words)

Steel, Flora Annie (1847–1929) Scottish novelist

Steele, Sir Richard (1672–1729) English essayist and dramatist

Steell,/ Gourlay (1819–94) Scottish painter; — **Sir John** (1804–91) his brother, Scottish sculptor

steel/work, -works, -yard (one word)

steenbok (Afrik.) a small antelope, *not* steinbuck; *see also* **steinbock**

steenkirk (hist.) a neckcloth, *not* stein-

steeplechase/ a cross-country horse race, **-r** the horse or rider taking part

steeplejack (one word)

Steevens,/ George (1736–1800) English Shakespearian commentator; — **George**

Warrington (1869–1900) English journalist; *see also* **Stephen**; **Stephens**; **Stevens**

Stefánsson, Vilhjálmur (1879–1962) Canadian-born US anthropologist, archaeologist, and Arctic explorer

Steinbeck, John (**Ernst**) (1902–68) US novelist

Steinberg a hock (wine)

steinbock an Alpine ibex

steinbuck *use* **steenbok**

steinkirk *use* **steen-**

stel/a (archaeol.) an upright slab or pillar, usually engraved and sculpted, esp. as a gravestone; pl. **-ae**

stem abbr. **s., st.**

stemm/a a family tree or pedigree, pl. **-ata**

stencil/, -led, -ler, -ling (one *l* in US)

Stendhal pseud. of **Marie Henri Beyle** (1783–1842) French novelist

Sten gun a type of lightweight sub-machine gun (one cap.)

Stentor/ a person with a powerful voice, from Homer's herald in the Trojan War; **-ian** (not cap.)

step/brother, -child, -daughter, -father (one word)

Stephen, Sir Leslie (1832–1904) English biographer and critic; *see also* **Steevens**; **Stephens**; **Stevens**

stephengraph *use* **stev-**

Stephens,/ Alexander Hamilton (1812–83) US statesman, — **James** (1882–1950) Irish poet and novelist; *see also* **Steevens**; **Stephen**; **Stevens**

Stephenson,/ George (1781–1848) English locomotive engineer; — **Robert** (1803–59) his son, English engineer; *see also* **Stev-**

step/ladder, -mother (one word)

step-parent (hyphen, one word in US)

steppe a treeless plain, esp. of Russia

stepping stone (two words, hyphen in US)

step/sister, -son (one word)

steradian the SI unit of solid angle, abbr. **sr**

stere a unit of volume, 1 cubic metre

stereophonic of reproduction of sound by two channels, (colloq.) **stereo/**, pl. **-s**

stereotype (typ.) a duplicate plate cast from a matrix moulded from original relief printing material; (colloq.) **stereo**

sterilize *not* -ise

Sterling, John (1806–44) Scottish writer; *see also* **Stir-**

sterling/ (of money) of standard value, abbr. **stg.**; — **silver** silver of $92\frac{1}{4}$ per cent purity

Sterne, Laurence (*not* Law-) (1713–68) English novelist

stet/ (typ.) let the original form stand; **-ted, -ting**

Stetson (US propr.) a wide-brimmed, high-crowned hat (cap.)

Stettin Ger. for Szczecin

Steuart,/ **Sir James Denham** (1712–80) Scottish economist; — **John Alexander** (1861–1932) Scottish journalist and novelist; *see also* **Stewart**; **Stuart**

stevengraph a colourful picture made of silk, *not* steph-

Stevens,/ **Alfred** (1818–75) English sculptor, — **Thaddeus** (1792–1868) US abolitionist, — **Wallace** (1879–1955) US poet; *see also* **Steevens**; **Stephen**; **Stephens**

Stevenson,/ **Adlai** (**Ewing**) (1835–1914) US Vice-President; — **Adlai** (**Ewing**), **III** (1900–65) his grandson, US politician; — **Robert** (1772–1850) English lighthouse engineer; — **Robert Louis** (**Balfour**) (1850–94) his grandson, Scottish novelist, essayist, and poet, abbr. **R.L.S.**; *see also* **Steph-**

Stewart/ family name of the Earl of Galloway, —, **Dugald** (1753–1828) Scottish metaphysician, —, **James** (1831–1905) Scottish African missionary; *see also* **Steuart**; **Stuart**

Stewartry a district of Dumfries & Galloway

stg. sterling

stibium antimony, symbol **Sb**

stichometry the division into, or measurement by, lines of verse; *not* stycho-

stichomythia dialogue in alternate lines of verse

Stieglitz, Alfred (1864–1946) US photographer

stigma/ a mark or sign of disgrace; (Gr.) the name given in modern times to the character ς; pl. **-s**, *but* **-ta** with reference to Christ's wounds (pron. with stress on the first syllable)

stigmatize *not* -ise

stilb an SI unit of luminance, equal to 1 candela per cm²; abbr. **sb**

stilboestrol a powerful synthetic oestrogen, *not* -be- (US)

stile an arrangement of steps over a fence, a vertical piece in framework; cf. **style**

stiletto/ a dagger; (in full — **heel**) a long tapering heel on a woman's shoe; pl. **-s**

still/birth, -born (one word)

still life/ pl. **-s** (hyphen when attrib.)

Stillson wrench (one cap.)

stilly (adv.) in a still, quiet manner

Stilton a kind of strong rich cheese (cap.)

stilus *use* sty-

stimie *use* sty-

stimul/ate, -able

stimul/us pl. **-i**

stimy *use* stymie

stip. stipend, -iary

stir-fry (hyphen)

Stirling a town and district of Central

Stirling,/ **J. Hutchison** (*not* -inson) (1820–1909) Scottish metaphysician; — **Sir William Alexander, Earl of** (?1567–1640) Scottish poet, usually called **William Alexander**; *see also* **Ster-**

stirp/s (biol.) a classification group, (law) a branch of a family or its progenitor; pl. **-es**

stitching (bind.) the sewing together of all the sections of a book in a single operation; *see also* **sewing**

Stn. Station

stoa/ (Gr. archit.) a long building with a colonnade, pl. **-s** (not cap.); a philosophical school of Zeno and the Stoics (*see* **Stoic**) (cap.)

stock/breeder, -broker (one word)

stock company (US) a repertory company performing mainly at a particular theatre

Stock Exchange (caps.) abbr. **S/E**, **St. Ex.**, **Stock Ex.**

Stockhausen, Karlheinz (b. 1928) German composer and theorist

stockholder (one word)

stockinet an elastic fabric; *not* -ette, -inget

stock/jobber, -list, -pile, -pot, -room, -yard (one word)

stodg/e, -y *not* -ey

stoep (Afrik.) a terrace attached to a house; cf. **stoop**; **stoup**

Stoic/ (a member) of a Greek philosophical school founded by Zeno in the 4th c. BC; **-ism**; (gen., not cap.) a person having great self-control in adversity, adj. **-al**

stoichio/logy the doctrine of elements; *not* **stoechio-**, **stoicheio-**; **-metric** (chem.) having elements in fixed proportions; **-metry** (chem.) the proportion in which elements occur in a compound

stoke/hold, -hole (one word)

Stoke-on-Trent Staffs. (hyphens)

stokes a unit of kinematic viscosity, abbr. **St**; in SI units 10⁻⁴ m²/s

STOL short take-off and landing

ston/e a unit of weight, 14 lb (6.35 kg); abbr. **st.**

stone (typ.) the table on which pages of type are imposed

stone/cutter, -fish (one word)

stone/ fly, -ground (one word, hyphen in US)

Stone House Cumbria

Stonehouse Ches., Devon, Glos., Northumb., Strathclyde

stonemason (one word)

stone/wall (verb), **-ware, -washed, -work** (one word)

stony *not* -ey

Stonyhurst College Lancs.

stoop (US) a step or small porch at a house door; cf. **stoep**; **stoup**

stop/cock, -gap (one word)

stop-go alternating progress and lack of it, esp. the alternate restriction and stimulation of economic demand (hyphen)

stop light a red traffic light (two words, one word in US)

stop/off, -over (nouns, one word)

stop press (two words, hyphen when attrib.)

stop valve (two words)

stopwatch (one word)

storable *not* -eable

storage heater (two words)

store/front, -house, -keeper, -room (one word)

storey/ a horizontal division or level of a building, pl. **-s**; *not* story (US), -ies; **-ed**

storied celebrated in story, *not* -yed

storiolog/y the scientific study of folklore, *not* story-; **-ist**

stormbound (one word)

storm petrel (two words) *not* stormy

storm troop/er, -s (two words)

Storting the legislative assembly of Norway

story (of a building) *use* **storey** (except in US)

storyboard (one word)

story book (two words, one word in US)

story/line, -teller (one word)

stoup a holy-water basin, (arch.) a flagon; cf. **stoep**; **stoup**

Stow, John (?1525–1605) English historian

stowaway (one word)

Stowe/ a village and school in Bucks.; **—, Harriet (Elizabeth)** (née) **Beecher** (1811–96) US writer

Stow-on-the-Wold Glos. (hyphens)

STP *Sacrae Theologiae Professor* (Professor of Sacred Theology), standard temperature and pressure

Str. Strait, -s

str. stroke (oar)

Strachey/ the family name of Baron O'Hagan; **—, (Giles) Lytton** (1880–1932) English biographer and essayist

Strad (colloq.) Stradivarius (violin) (cap., no point), italic as journal title

Stradbroke, Earl of

Stradivarius an instrument of the violin family made by **Antonio Stradivari** (in Latin **Antonius Stradivarius**) of Cremona (*c.*1644–1737), (colloq.) **Strad**

Strafford, Earl of

straight away immediately (two words)

straightaway (US) (of a course) straight, straight part of a racecourse (one word)

straightforward (one word)

strait/, -s cap. when with name; abbr. **St., Str.**

straitjacket *not* straight-

strait-laced *not* straight- (hyphen, one word in US)

Straits Settlements now part of Malaysia

Stranraer Dumfries & Galloway

strappado/ a form of torture, pl. **-s**; as verb **-ed, -ing**

Strasburg Eng. form of Fr. **Strasbourg**, Ger. **Strassburg**; if using Fr. spelling, *use* Ger. spelling for the period of German rule, 1871–1919 (but not for the Nazi occupation, 1940–5)

Stratford-upon-Avon War., *but* **Stratford-on-Avon District Council** (hyphens)

strath (Sc.) a broad mountain valley; cap. and separate word when referring to the strath itself, e.g. 'Strath Spey'

Strathclyde/ an ancient kingdom and modern region in Scotland; university; **Baron —**

strathspey a slow Scottish dance

stratigraphy (geol., archaeol.) (the study of) the order and relative position of strata, *not* strato-

stratosphere the upper atmosphere; cf. **tropo-**

strat/um a layer, pl. **-a**

strat/us a low layer of cloud, pl. **-i**; abbr. **s.**

Straus, Oskar (1870–1954) Austrian-born composer

Strauss,/ Johann I (1804–49) Austrian composer of Viennese waltzes; **— Johann II** (1825–99) his son, the best known of the family; **— Joseph** (1827–70) and **— Eduard** (1835–1916) also sons of Johann I; **— Johann III** (1866–1939) son of Johann II; **— Richard Georg** (1864–1949) German composer of operas, songs, and orchestral works

Stravinsky, Igor (Fyodorovich) (1882–1971) Russian-born composer

strawberry/ blonde, — mark, — pear, — roan (two words)

stream of consciousness (hyphens when attrib.)

Streatfeild a family name, *not* -field

street name of, to have initial cap., as in Regent Street; spell out when a number, as Fifth Avenue, *but* follow local conventions, e.g. in New York spell out numbers only for avenues, using arabic numberals for streets: 42nd Street; house number to be in arabic, not followed by any punctuation, as 6 Fleet Street; abbr. **St.**

street/walker, -wise (one word)

stretto/ (mus.) (passage played) in quicker time, pl. **-s**

strew to scatter, *not* -ow; past part. **strewed** *or* **strewn**

strewth (colloq.) God's truth (no apos.), *not* stru-

stri/a (anat., geol.) a stripe, pl. **-ae**

stride past **strode**, past part. **stridden**

strike/-bound, -breaker (hyphens, one word in US)

strike-through (typ.) the penetration of ink into paper (hyphen)

Strine a comic transliteration of Australian speech, e.g. *Emma Chissitt* ('How much is it?') (cap.)

string bass (US) = **double bass**

stringendo (mus.) pressing, accelerating the tempo

strip mine (US) = **opencast mine**

stripping-in (typ.) in filmsetting, making alterations to text by the excision and replacement of the film containing it

strip-search (hyphen; noun, two words in US, verb, hyphen)

striptease (one word)

stripy having stripes, *not* -ey

strive past **strove**, past part. **striven**

Stroganoff (cook.) (designating) a dish of meat cooked in sour cream (cap.)

strong-arm (hyphen)

strong/box, -hold, -man (one word)

strongroom (one word, two words in US)

strontium symbol **Sr**

Strood Kent

Stroud Glos., Hants.

strow *use* **strew**

struth *use* **strew-**

Struwwelpeter a German children's book, a character with straggly unkempt hair and long fingernails

strychnine *not* -in

Sts Saints

Stuart,/ House of (of or relating to) (a member of) the royal family ruling Scotland 1371–1714 and England 1603–49, 1660–1714, **— Leslie** pseud. of **Thomas Barrett** (1866–1928) English composer; *see also* **Steuart; Stewart**

stucco/ (apply) plaster or cement coating to wall surfaces, pl. **-es**; as verb **-es, -ed**

Stück (Ger. n.) a piece

student a graduate recipient of a stipend from the foundation of a college, esp. a Fellow of Christ Church, Oxford

studio/ pl. **-s**

stumbling block (two words)

stupa a round usually domed building erected as a Buddhist shrine, in Skt. *stūpa*

stupefy *not* -ify

stupor *not* -our

Sturla Þórðarson (*c.*1214–84) (sometimes Anglicized as **Thord(h)arson**) Icelandic historian, author of *Sturlungasaga* and nephew of Snorri Sturluson

Sturluson *see* **Snorri Sturluson**

Sturm und Drang (Ger.) a literary and artistic movement in Germany in the late 18th c. (three words)

Sturm-und-Drang-Periode German Romanticism of the late 18th c. (three hyphens)

Stuttgart Germany; *not* Stü-, -ard

Stuyvesant, Peter (1592–1672) Dutch colonial governor

sty an inflamed swelling on eyelid, an enclosure for pigs; *not* stye; pl. **sties**

stycho/metry, -mythia *use* **sticho-**

Stygian (Gr. myth.) of or relating to the River Styx in Hades

style a custom, manner, etc.; *see also* **house style**; cf. **stile**

stylite (eccl. hist.) an ancient or medieval ascetic living on top of a pillar

stylize *not* -ise

styl/us a needle-like device; pl. **-i** *or* (esp. those used in playing gramophone records) **-uses**

stymie thwart, obstruct, an obstruction; *not* sti-, -my

Styx (Gr. myth.) a river in Hades

s.u. (Ger.) *siehe unten* (see below)

Suabia *use* **Swa-**

suable that can be sued, *not* -eable

Suakin Sudan, *not* -im

suaraj *use* **sw-**

suaviter in modo (Lat.) gently in manner; cf. **fortiter in re**

sub/ (colloq.) subaltern, sub-editor, submarine, subscription, substitute; as verb, act as substitute, sub-edit; **-bed, -bing**

sub (Lat.) under

subahdar (Ind.) a native captain

subaltern an officer below the rank of captain, (colloq.) **sub**

subaudi (Lat.) understand, supply

sub/-basement, -branch, -breed (hyphens, one word in US)

sub/category, -class (one word)

sub-clause (hyphen, one word in US)

sub/committee, -conscious, -contract, -deacon, -dean, -divide, -division, -dominant (one word)

sub-edit/, -or, -orial (hyphens, one word in US)

sub finem (Lat.) towards the end (as of a work), abbr. **s.f., sub fin.**

subfusc/, -ous dark, esp. of formal clothing worn at some universities

subgenus (one word)

sub-heading (hyphen, one word in US)

subhuman (one word)

subj. subject, -ive, -ively; subjunctive

subject matter (two words)

sub judice (Lat.) under consideration

subjunctive abbr. **subj.**

subkingdom (one word)

sub/-lease, -let (hyphens, one word in US)

sub lieutenant abbr. **Sub-Lt.** (cap. as title; two words, one word in US)

Sublime Porte, the (hist.) the Turkish court and government

sub-machine gun (one hyphen, no hyphen in US: **submachine gun**)

submarginal (esp. econ.) not reaching minimum requirements, (of land) that cannot be farmed profitably

submarine (one word), in the Royal Navy classed as boats

submerged tenth (econ.) the supposed fraction of the population permanently living in poverty

submicroscopic (one word)

sub/ modo (Lat.) in a qualified sense; — *nomine* under a specified name, abbr. **s.n.**

subnormal (one word)

sub-plot (hyphen, one word in US)

subpoena/ (serve) a writ commanding attendance, pl. **-s**; as verb **-ed**; *not* -pena (one word, not ital.)

sub rosa in secrecy or confidence

subscript (a symbol or letter) written below the line, inferior; cf. **superscript**; *see also* **iota**

subscription (colloq.) **sub**

subsection (one word) abbr. **subsec.**

subsequence a subsequent incident, a consequence; a sequence forming part of a larger one

subsidize pay a subsidy to, *not* -ise

subsidy a grant of public money

sub/ sigillo (Lat.) in the strictest confidence, — *silentio* in silence

sub/sonic, -space (one word)

sub specie aeternitatis (Lat.) under the aspect of eternity, in a universal perspective

subspecies sing. abbr. **subsp.**, pl. abbr. **subspp.**

substance, amount of symbol **n**

sub-standard (hyphen, one word in US)

substantive abbr. **s., sb., subst.**

substitute (noun) colloq. **sub**

substrat/um pl. **-a**

sub/structure, -terranean (one word)

subtil/, -e *use* **subtle** in all senses

subtilize rarefy, *not* -ise

subtitle (one word)

subtl/e fine, rarefied, elusive, cunning; **-er, -est, -ety, -y**; *not* subtil-

subtopia suburban development regarded unfavourably

sub/total, -tropical (one word)

suburbia suburbs and their inhabitants (not cap.)

sub/ voce or — verbo (Lat.) under a specified word, preferred to *ad voc.*; abbr. **s.v.**

subway a tunnel beneath a road etc., (UK) for pedestrians, (US) for an underground railway (one word)

succeeded abbr. **s.**

succès/ de scandale (Fr. m.) success due to being scandalous, — *d'estime* success with more honour than profit, — *fou* extravagant success

Succoth the Jewish Feast of Tabernacles, *not* -ukko- (US); in Heb. *sukkōt*

succour *not* -or (US)

succub/us a female demon believed to have sexual intercourse with sleeping men, pl. **-i**; cf. **incubus**

suchlike (one word)

sucking pig (two words) *also* (esp. in US) **suckling pig**

sucre the basic monetary unit of Ecuador

sud (Fr. m.) south, abbr. **s.**

Süd (Ger. m.) south, abbr. **S.** (cap.)

Sudan/ N. Africa, **-ese**; in Fr. **Soudan**

sudd floating vegetation impeding the navigation of the White Nile

Sudra the Hindu labourer caste, the lowest of the four great castes; in Skt. *śūdra*

Sue, Marie-Joseph *self-styled* **Eugène** (1804–57) French novelist, *not* Suë

su/e, -ed, -ing

Suède Fr. for Sweden, adj. *suédois*

suede dull-dressed kid leather (no accent)

Suetonius, Gaius Tranquillus (*c.*70–*c.*160) Roman biographer and antiquarian, abbr. **Suet.**

suff. suffix

suffic/it (Lat.) it is sufficient, pl. *-iunt*

Sufi a Muslim ascetic and mystic; *not* Sofi, Soofee; in Arab. *ṣūfī*; *see also* **Sophy**

sugar/-bowl (hyphen, two words in US)

sugar/ beet, — cane, — daddy (two words)

sugarloaf (one word)

sugar/ maple, — pea (two words)

sugarplum (one word)

sugar soap (two words)

suggestible capable of being suggested, open to suggestion; *not* -able

suggestio falsi (Lat.) an indirect lie

sui/ generis (Lat.) (the only one or ones) of his, her, its, *or* their, own kind; **— juris** of full age and capacity

suisse (Fr. adj.) of or relating to Switzerland, (m., f., cap.) a Swiss person, (m., not cap.) a beadle of a church; **la Suisse** (Fr.) Switzerland

suite a set of rooms, attendants, *or* musical pieces (not ital.)

suivez (mus.) follow the soloist

suk(h) *use* **souk**

sukiyaki a Japanese dish of sliced meat simmered with vegetables and sauce

Sulawesi Indonesia, formerly **Celebes**

Süleyman/ I (?1495–1566) Sultan of Turkey 1520–66, called 'Kanuni' (the Lawgiver) in Turkey, 'the Magnificent' in Europe; **— II** (1641–91) Sultan of Turkey 1687–91; *not* Sula- though often **Suleiman** in hist. texts

Sully Prudhomme, René François Armand (1839–1907) French poet and critic

sulpha a class of drugs, *not* -fa (US)

sulph/ur symbol **S**, *not* -fur (US); **-ate, -ite, -uretted, -urize** *not* -ise

sultan/ a Muslim ruler, f. **-a**; **Sultan, the** of Turkey, till 1922; abbr. **Sult.**

Sultanpur India

sum (math.) symbol Σ

sumac (bot.) an ornamental tree; *not* sh-, -ach, -ack

Sumburgh Airport Shetland

Sumer/ Babylonia; **-ian** (of or relating to) the early and non-Semitic element in the civilization of ancient Babylonia, a member of this people, or their language

summ/a (Lat.) a summary of what is known of a subject, pl. **-ae** (not cap.)

summa cum laude (esp. US) (of a degree, diploma, etc.) of the highest standard, with the highest distinction (not ital.)

summarize *not* -ise

summer (not cap.)

summersault *use* **somer-**

summertime the summer season (one word); **British Summer Time** in summer only, one hour in advance of GMT 1922–67, and from 1972 (three words); *see also* **BST**; **Daylight Saving Time**

summonsed (law) issued with a summons, *not* -oned

summum bonum (Lat.) the supreme good

Sumter, Fort SC

Sun. Sunday

sun cap. only in astron. and anthropomorphic contexts, and in a list of planets; abbr. **S.**

sun/bathe, -beam, -bed, -belt, -block (one word)

sun bonnet (two words, one in US)

sunburn/, -t *or* **-ed** (one word)

sundae an ice cream dessert

Sunday abbr. **Sun.**

sun/dial, -down, -dress (one word)

sundry various, several

sun-dr/y dry in the sun, **-ied**

sunfast (US) (of dye) not subject to fading by sunlight

sun/flower, -glasses (one word)

sun-god (hyphen, two words in US)

sunhat (one word, two words in US)

sun/light, -like (one word)

Sunna a traditional portion of Muslim law based on Muhammad's words or acts; *not* -ah

Sunni/ (of or relating to) (an adherent of) one of the two main branches of Islam; *see also* **Shia**; pl. same; *not* -ee; also **-te**

sun/rise, -set, -shade, -shine -spot, -stroke, -tan (one word)

suntrap (one word, two words in US)

sunup (US) = **sunrise** (one word)

Sun Yat-sen (Pinyin **Sun Yixian**) (1866–1925) Chinese Kuomintang politician

suo/ jure (Lat.) in one's own right, **— loco** in its own place

Suomi Fin. for **Finland**

sup. superior, supine

sup. (Lat.) *supra* (above)

superannu/ate, -able (one word)

supercalendered paper highly polished but not coated, abbr. **SC**

supercargo/ an officer in a merchant ship managing sales, pl. **-es** (one word)

supercede *use* **-sede**

superego/ (psychol.) the part of mind that exerts conscience, pl. **-s** (one word)

superexcellen/ce, -t (one word)

superficies a surface, pl. same

super/fine, -glue, -highway, -human (one word)

superintendent abbr. **supt.**

superior abbr. **sup.**

superior (typ.) a small character set above the line, usually to the side, of ordinary characters, e.g. $^{1\ 2\ a\ b}$; *also called* **superscript**; cf. **inferior**

superl. superlative

super/man, -market (one word)

supermundane superior to earthly things, *not* exceptionally tedious

super/natural, -power (one word)

superscript (a symbol or letter) written above the line, *also called* **superior**; cf. **subscript**

supersede to set aside, take the place of, *not* -cede

super/sonic, -store, -structure, -tanker (one word)

supervis/e *not* -ize, **-or** *not* -er

supine abbr. **sup.**

suppl/e, -y *not* -ely (US)

supplement abbr. **suppl.**

supposititous hypothetical, assumed

supposititious spurious

suppository *not* -ary

suppressio veri (Lat.) suppression of the truth

suppressor *not* -er

supr. supreme

supra (Lat.) above, formerly; abbr. **sup.**; in text *prefer* 'above' except in legal work

suprême (Fr. f.) a method of cooking, with a rich cream sauce

Supreme Court (two caps.)

supremo/ a leader or ruler, pl. **-s**

supt. superintendent

suq *use* **souk**

sur (Fr. prep.) upon, abbr. **s/** (close up) in addresses

sura a chapter or section of the Koran (cap. when referring to specific chapters), *not* ass-, -ah; in Arab. *sūra*

Surabaya Indonesia

surah a thin silk fabric

Surat Bombay, India

surcingle a belt

Sûreté the French CID, in Paris

surfboard (one word)

surfiction (lit.) postmodernist or metafiction

surf-riding (hyphen)

surg/eon, -ery, -ical abbr. **surg.**

Surgeon General (US) the head of a public health service or of the medical service of an army etc., pl. **Surgeons General**

Surgeons, Royal College of abbr. **RCS**

Suriname S. America

surmise conjecture, *not* -ize

surplus abbr. **S.**

surprise *not* -ize

surrealism (two *r*s) a 20th-c. movement in art and literature, often cap. to distinguish from the looser meaning of a bizarre imaginative effect

surrebutter (law) the plaintiff's reply to the defendant's rebutter

sursum corda (Lat.) lift up your hearts

Surtees, Robert Smith (1805–64) English fox-hunting novelist

surtitle (one word)

surtout an overcoat or greatcoat

surv. survey/ing, -or; surviving

Surv.-Gen. Surveyor-General

survivor *not* -er

Susanna (Apocr.) abbr. **Sus.**

susceptible *not* -able

suspenders a suspender belt, (US) a pair of braces; *not* -ors

sus. per coll. (Lat.) *suspen/sio* (*-sus, -datur*) *per collum*, hanging (hanged, let him be hanged) by the neck

Susquehanna River Pa., *not* -ana

suss/ slang for suspect, suspicion; **— out** to reconnoitre; **-ed, -ing**

susuhunan (hist.) (the title of) the ruler of Surakarta and of Mataram in Java

Sutlej a Punjab river

Sutra an aphorism or set of aphorisms in Hindu literature, a narrative part of Buddhist literature, Jainist scripture

suttee (the custom of) a Hindu widow immolating herself on her husband's pyre, in Hind. and Urdu *sati*

suum cuique (Lat.) let each have his own

SUV sport utility vehicle

Suwannee River Ga., Fla.; *not* Swa- (except as song title)

sužet *use* **sju-**

SV (Lat.) *Sancta Virgo* (Holy Virgin), *Sanctitas Vestra* (Your Holiness)

s.v. sailing vessel; *sub voce* or *sub verbo*

SVA Incorporated Society of Valuers and Auctioneers

Svedberg (**unit**) a unit of time equal to 10^{-13} second used in expressing sedimentation coefficients, symbol **S**; from **Theodor S. Svedberg** (1884–1971) Swedish chemist

svelte slender, lissom, graceful (not ital.)

Svendsen, Johan Severin (1840–1911) Norwegian composer

Svengali a person who exercises a controlling or mesmeric influence on another, esp. for a sinister purpose

Sverige Swed. for Sweden

s.v.p. (Fr.) *s'il vous plaît* (if you please)

SW South Wales; south-west, -ern

Sw. Swed/en, -ish

swab (clean with) a mop or other absorbent device, *not* -ob

Swabia Germany, *not* Su-

Swahili (of or relating to) (a member of) a Bantu-speaking people of Zanzibar and adjacent coasts of Tanzania, properly **Mswahili** (sing.), **Waswahili** (pl.); (of or relating to) their language, used widely as a lingua franca in E. Africa, properly **KiSwahili**

swami/ a Hindu male religious teacher, pl. **-s**; in Hind. *swāmī*

Swammerdam, Jan (1637–80) Dutch naturalist

'Swanee River' song, otherwise known as 'Old Folks at Home', by Stephen Collins Foster, 1851; in all other instances *use* **Suwannee**

swan/sdown, -song (one word)

swan-upping the annual taking up and marking of Thames swans (hyphen)

swap to exchange, *not* -op

Swapo South West Africa People's Organization, in Namibia

Swaraj (hist.) self-government or independence for India, *not* su-

swash (typ.) (of) letters with elaborate tails or flourishes

swat hit sharply; cf. **swot**

swath a line of cut grass or corn

swathe bind or enclose

Swazi/, -land S. Africa

sweat/ past and past part. **-ed** (*sweat* in US)

sweatband (one word)

sweating-sickness an epidemic fever with sweating, prevalent in England in the 15th–16th cc.

sweat/shirt, -shop, -suit (one word)

swede a kind of turnip (not cap.)

Sweden abbr. **Swed., Sw.**; (the latter is acceptable in narrow measure and where no confusion with Switzerland can arise); in Swed. **Sverige**, in Fr. **Suède**

Swedenborg, Emanuel (1688–1772) Swedish philosopher

Swedish/ abbr. **Swed., Sw.**; '**— a'** Å, å

sweepback (of aircraft's wings) noun and adj. (one word)

Sweet, Henry (1845–1912) English philologist; *see also* **Swete**

sweet and sour (cook. adj., no hyphen even when attrib.; no hyphens in US unless attrib.)

sweetbread (one word)

Sweet Briar Va., *not* — Brier

sweetheart (one word)

sweetie a sweet, (esp. US) a term of endearment

sweet/meal, -meat (one word)

sweet potato a tropical climbing plant, *Ipomoea batatas*, or the edible tuberous roots of this; cf. **yam**

sweet-talk (verb, hyphen)

sweet tooth (two words)

sweet william (bot.) (two words, not caps.)

swelled rule (typ.) a rule wider in centre than at ends; *see also* **rule**

Swete, Henry Barclay (1835–1917) English biblical scholar; *see also* **Sweet**

Sweyn the name of three Danish kings, in Dan. **Svend**

SWG standard wire gauge

swimming/ bath, — costume, — pool (two words)

swimsuit (one word)

Swinburne, Algernon Charles (1837–1909) English poet

Swinden N. Yorks.

Swindon Glos., Staffs., Wilts.

swine/ (US and formal Brit.) a mature pig, pl. same; cf. **hog**; **pig**; **— fever** (two words), **-herd** (one word)

swing door (two words)

swingeing hard (blow)

swing-wing (of aircraft) (hyphen)

Swinton Gr. Manchester, N. Yorks., S. Yorks., Borders

swipe card (two words)

switch/back, -board, -blade (one word)

Swithun/, St Bishop of Winchester 852–62, *not* -in; **-'s Day** 15 July

Switzerland abbr. **Switz., Sw.** (the latter is acceptable in narrow measure and where no confusion with Sweden can arise); in Fr. **la Suisse**, Ger. **die Schweiz**, It. **Svizzera**

swivel/, -led, -ling (one *l* in US)

swizz (sl.) a swindle, a disappointment; pl. **-es**; *not* swiz

swop *use* -ap

sword dance (two words)

sword/fish, -play, -sman, -stick (one word)

swot study hard; cf. **swat**

SWP Socialist Workers' Party

swung dash (typ.) ∼

SY steam yacht

Sybil woman's name; cf. **sibyl**

sycamine (NT, AV) the black mulberry tree

sycamore any of three trees: a large maple, *Acer pseudoplatanus*, grown in Europe and Asia; (US) the plane tree, *Platanus*; a fig tree, *Ficus sycomorus* (spelt **sycomore** in the Bible), growing in Egypt, Syria, etc.

syce (Anglo-Ind.) a groom; cf. **sice**

Sydney New South Wales, Australia; *see also* **Sid-**

Sykes *see* **Si-**

syllab/ication *not* -ification, **-ize** *not* -ise

syllabub *not* sill-

syllabus/ pl. **-es**

sylleps/is (gram.) application of a word in differing senses to two others ('he caught his train and a cold'), pl. **-es**; cf. **zeugma**

syllogism a logical argument of two premises and a conclusion

syllogize argue by syllogism, *not* -ise

sylva/, -n *not* si-

Sylvester,/ James Joseph (1814–97) English mathematician, **— Josuah** (1563–1618) English poet sylvicultur/e, -ist *use* si-

symbolize *not* -ise

symmetr/ic, -ical, -ize *not* -ise

sympathique (Fr.) congenial, having the right artistic feeling for

sympathize *not* -ise

symposi/um a conference, a collection of views on a topic (not cap.); one of Plato's Socratic dialogues (cap., ital.); pl. **-a**

syn. synonym, -ous

syn- (chem.) of isomers, *use* **cis-**

synaeres/is (gram.) the contraction of two vowels, pl. **-es**; *not* -neresis (US)

synaesthesia *not* synes- (US)

synagog/ue an assembly of Jews for worship, their place of worship; **-al, -ic**

synchronize (cause to) coincide in time, *not* -ise; colloq. **sync,** *not* synch

syndrome a group of concurrent symptoms; in medical and scientific use, avoid 's in identification of syndromes derived from names of individuals; thus e.g. *Angelman syndrome, Munchausen syndrome*

synecdoche a figure of speech in which a part is made to represent the whole or vice versa

synonym/ a word with the same meaning as another; **-ous** abbr. **syn.**; **-ize** *not* -ise; **-y** *not* -e, -ey

synops/is a summary, pl. **-es**

Synoptic Gospels Matthew, Mark, and Luke, which relate the events from the same point of view

synthes/ist, -ize *not* synthet-, -ise

syphon *use* si-

Syr. Syria, -c, -n

syr. syrup

Syrah a variety of grape, the wine made from this; trad. spelt **Shiraz** in Eng.

syren *use* si-

Syriac (in or relating to) the literary language of ancient Syria, based on W. Aramaic; abbr. **Syr.**

Syringa (bot.) the lilac genus

syringa the mock orange

syringe/ an instrument for squirting or injecting, **-ing**; *not* si-

syrin/x a pan pipe, (anat.) a narrow tube from throat to eardrum, the vocal organ of birds, (archaeol.) a narrow gallery in rock; pl. **-xes, -ges**

syrup *not* sir-, abbr. **syr.**

syst. system

system/atic methodical, **-atize** *not* -ise, **-ic** (physiol.) of the bodily system as a whole

Système International (d'Unités) a coherent system of scientific units based on the metre, kilogram, second, ampere, kelvin, mole, and candela; adopted by the General Conference of Weights and Measures (CGPM) and endorsed by the International Organization for Standardization (ISO); abbr. **SI**

syuzhet see sjužet

syzygy (prosody) a combination of two different feet in one measure, a dipody; (astr.) the moon being in conjunction or opposition; (philos.) a pair of connected or correlative things; a word game invented by Lewis Carroll

Szczecin Poland, in Ger. **Stettin**

Szechwan a Chinese province, in Pinyin **Sichuan**

Szent-Györgyi, Albert von (1893–1986) Hungarian-born US biochemist

Sze Yap (of or relating to) the form of Cantonese spoken in the south of Guangdong Province

Szigeti, Joseph (1892–1973) Hungarian violinist

Szilard, Leo (1898–1964) Hungarian-born US physicist and molecular biochemist

szlach/ta (hist.) the aristocratic or landowning class in Poland before 1945, **-cic** a member of this (ital.)

Szymanowski, Karol (1883–1937) Polish composer

Tt

T (as prefix) tera-, tesla, tritium, the nineteenth in a series

T temperature

T. Tenor, Territory, Testament, (It. mus.) tace (be silent)

t ton, -s; tonne, -s

t. town(-ship); tun, -s; (Fr.) *tome* (volume), *tonneau* (ton); (Lat.) *tempore* (in the time of), (mus.) tempo (time); (It.) *tenor/e, -i* (tenor, -s); (meteor.) thunder

't (Du.) *het* (the, n.) as in 'van 't Hoff'

t time

TA Territorial Army

Ta tantalum (no point)

Taal, the (hist.) an early form of Afrikaans

TA & VRA Territorial Auxiliary and Volunteer Reserve Association

TAB typhoid-paratyphoid A and B vaccine, (Austral.) Totalizator Agency Board

Tabago *use* **To-**

tabasco a pungent pepper, (cap., propr.) a sauce made from this

tabbouleh an Arabic vegetable salad made with cracked wheat, in Arab. *tabbūla*

Tabernacles, Feast of Succoth

tabla (Ind. mus.) a pair of small drums played with the hands

tablature (mus.) a form of notation using letters, figures, or diagrams to indicate placement of fingers on an instrument

table/ alphabétique (Fr. typ. f.) index, — **des matières** table of contents

tableau/ a picturesque presentation, dramatic situation, pl. **-x** (not ital.); — **vivant** a still silent group representing a scene, pl. **-x vivants** (ital.)

tablecloth (one word)

table/ d'hôte a set meal for guests at hotel, pl. **-s d'hôte** (not ital.)

tableland (one word)

table mat (two words)

tablespoonful/ pl. **-s**, abbr. **tbsp**

table/ talk, — tennis (two words)

table top (two words, one word in US)

tableware (one word)

taboo/ (something) forbidden, to prohibit, a prohibition; *not* -pu (NZ), -u; in Tongan *tabu*; **-ed, -s**

tabor a small drum, *not* -our

tabouret a drum-shaped stool, *not* -oret (US)

tabul/a (Lat.) a document, pl. **-ae**; — **rasa** a blank surface, pl. **-ae rasae** (not ital.)

tabulat/e, -or

Tac. Tacitus

tac-au-tac (fencing) parry and riposte (hyphens, not ital.); but *du tac au tac* (Fr. fig.) from defence to attack (no hyphens, ital.)

tace (mus.) be silent, abbr. **T.**

tacet (mus.) is silent

tachism action painting, in Fr. m. *tachisme*

tacho/ (colloq.) tachometer, pl. **-s**

tachograph a device for recording the speed and travel-time of vehicles

tachometer an instrument for measuring the speed of rotation

tachymeter an instrument used in surveying

Tacitus, Gaius Cornelius (*c.*55–120) Roman historian, abbr. **Tac.**

taco/ (Mexican cook.) meat, vegetables, etc. in a folded, fried (maize) tortilla; pl. **-s**

Tadjikistan *use* **Taj-**

taedium vitae (Lat.) weariness of life (often as a pathological state with a tendency to suicide)

taeni/a (archit.) a fillet between a Doric architrave and frieze; (anat.) any flat ribbon-like structure; a large parasitic tapeworm; (Gr. antiquity) a fillet or headband; pl. **-ae**; *not* te- (US)

Tae-ping *use* **Taiping** (one word)

taffeta a fabric, *not* the many variants

Taffy (offens.) colloq. term for a Welshman (cap.)

taff/y (US) a confection like chewy toffee, insincere flattery; *not* tof-; pl. -ies

Tagalog (of or relating to) (a member of) the principal people of the Philippine Islands, or their language; *see also* **Filipino**; **Pilipino**

tag end (US) the last remaining part of something

tagetes (bot.) a type of marigold, *not* -ete; pl. same

tagliatelle (It. cook.) pasta in ribbons, *not* -elli

Tagore, Rabindranath (1861–1941) Indian poet

Tagus a river, Spain and Portugal; Sp. **Tajo**, Port. **Tejo**, Fr. **Tage**, It. **Tago**

Tahiti an island, Pacific Ocean

tahr a goatlike mammal of the Himalayas, *not* thar

tahsil an administrative area in parts of India, in Urdu *taḥsīl*

Tai a language family of SE Asia, including Thai, Lao, and Shan

t'ai chi ch'uan a Chinese martial art and system of callisthenics, often abbr. as **t'ai chi** (not ital.)

taiga a coniferous forest lying between tundra and steppe, esp. in Siberia

tail (typ.) blank space at the bottom of a page; *see also* **margins**

tailback a queue of vehicles in a traffic jam (one word, two words as verb), (US) in American football, one player's position

tail/board, -gate (one word)

tail lamp (two words, one word in US)

taille/ (Fr. f.) engraving, also size etc.; **— douce** copperplate engraving

tailless (one word)

tail light (two words, one word in US)

tailpiece (typ.) the design at the end of a section, chapter, or book

tail/pipe, -plane, -spin, -stock (one word)

Tain Highland

Táin an Old Irish tale

Taine, Hippolyte Adolphe (1828–93) French historian and literary critic

taipan the head of a foreign business in China, a large venomous Australian snake

Taipei the capital of Taiwan

Taiping rebellion 1850–64, *not* Tae-

Tait,/ Archibald Campbell (1811–82) Archbishop of Canterbury; **— Peter Guthrie** (1831–1901) Scottish mathematician and physicist; *see also* **Tate**

Taiwan *formerly* Formosa

taj a tall conical cap worn by a dervish, in Arab. *tāj*

Tajik a member of the Iranian language family, spoken in Tajikistan, Uzbekistan, and Afghanistan

Tajikistan a former Soviet Socialist Republic, *not* Tadj-, Tadzh-

Taj Mahal the mausoleum at Agra, India; *not* Me-

takable able to be taken, *not* -eable

take (typ.) a single batch of copy or of proofs

takeaway (noun and adj., one word)

take back (typ.) transfer (text) to the previous line

take-home pay (one hyphen)

take-off (noun, hyphen, one word in US)

takeout (noun, US) = **takeaway**

take over (typ.) transfer (text) to the next line

takeover the assumption of control over a business, as through a buyout (one word, two words as verb)

Tal (Ger. n.) valley, before 1901 spelt *Th-*

Talbot of Malahide, Baron

talebearer (one word)

tales (law) a suit for summoning jurors to supply a deficiency (ital.); **tales/man** one so summoned, pl. **-men** (not ital.); cf. **talis-**

taletell/er, -ing (one word)

Talfourd, Sir Thomas Noon (1795–1854) English playwright, biographer, and author of the Copyright Act of 1842

Taliesin (6th c.) Welsh bard

talisman/ a charm, amulet, pl. **-s**; cf. **tales-**

talis qualis (Lat.) such as he *or* she is

talking/ blues, — book, — drum, — film, — head, — point, — shop (two words)

talking-to a sharp reprimand (hyphen)

talk show (two words)

talktime the time a mobile phone is in use (one word)

Tallahassee Fla.

Tallahatchie a river in Mississippi

tallboy a tall chest of drawers, sometimes in lower and upper sections or mounted on legs (in US **highboy**)

Talleyrand(-Périgord), Charles Maurice de (1754–1838) French politician

Tallinn capital of Estonia, *formerly* (and still in Ger.) **Reval**

Tallis, Thomas (?1505–85) English composer; *not* Talys, Tallys; **Tallis's canon** a hymn tune

tally-ho/ pl. **-s**, as verb **-ed**, **-es** (hyphen)

Talmud/ (cap.), **-ic** (not cap.) *not* -ical

Tal-y-llyn Gwynedd, Powys (two hyphens)

TAM television audience measurement

Tam. Tamil

tam (colloq.) tam-o'-shanter (no point)

tamable *use* **tameable** (except in US)

tamarin a S. American monkey

tamarind a tropical evergreen tree, or its fruit

tamarisk a shrub of the genus *Tamarix*

tambala a monetary unit of Malawi, pl. same

tambour a drum; a circular frame for holding fabric taut during embroidery; (archit.) the circular part of various structures, esp. those forming the shaft of a column, or a sloping buttress or projection

tamboura (mus.) an Indian stringed instrument used as a drone, in Arab. *ṭanbūra*

tambourin a long narrow drum of Provence, (music for) a dance accompanied by it

tambourine a small drum with jingling metal discs, beaten with the hand

tameable *not* -mable (US)

Tamerlane (1336–1405) Mongol conqueror (*but* Tamburlaine in Marlowe)

Tameside a district, Gr. Manchester

Tamil/ (concerning) (a member of) a Dravidian people inhabiting S. India and Sri Lanka, the language of this people; *not* -ul; adj. **-an**; abbr. **Tam.**

Tammany/ Hall a corrupt political organization or group, or corrupt political activities in general; **-ism**; *not* Tama-

'Tam o' Shanter' a poem by Burns, 1791 (caps., lower-case *o*, apos., no hyphens)

tam-o'-shanter a woollen cap (hyphens, apos.); colloq. **tam**

tampion a plug for the muzzle of a gun or the top of an organ pipe, *not* to-

tampon (med.) an absorbent plug

tam-tam a large metal gong (hyphen)

tan (math.) tangent (no point)

Tánaiste the deputy Prime Minister of Ireland

Tanak/ the Hebrew Scriptures, comprising the three canonical divisions of the Law, the Prophets, and the Hagiographa or Writings; pl. **-im**

Tananarive *use* **Antananarivo**

Tang a dynasty ruling China 618–*c*.906; (attrib.) designating art and artefacts of this period; in Chin. *táng*

tanga a bikini of small panels connected with thin ties

Tanger/ (Fr., Ger.) Tangier, (It.) **-i**

tangerine a citrus fruit, (cap.) a native of Tangier; *not* tangier-

tangible *not* -eable

Tangier Morocco, *not* -iers

tango/ pl. **-s**

tanh (math.) hyperbolic tangent (no point)

tanist/ (hist.) the elected heir apparent to a Celtic chief, **-ry** the system of appointing such as successor while the principal lives; cf. **Tánaiste**

Tanjor/, **-e** *use* **Thanjavur**

tanka a Japanese poem in 5 lines and 31 syllables, giving a complete picture of an event or mood

Tannhäuser an opera by Wagner, 1845

Tannoy (propr.) a type of public address system

tanrec *use* **ten-**

tantalize *not* -ise

tantalum symbol **Ta**

tant/ *bien que mal* (Fr.) with indifferent success, — *mieux* so much the better, — *pis* so much the worse

tantr/**a** any of a class of Hindu or Buddhist mystical and magical writings; **-ic, -ism, -ist**

Tanzania E. Africa

Taoiseach the Prime Minister of the Irish Republic

Taoism a Chinese philosophy based on the writings of Lao-tzu; *not* Tâ-, Taö- (one word)

tap dance (two words)

tape/ **deck,** — **measure** (two words)

tape-record (verb, hyphen)

tape record/**er, -ing** (two words)

tapis a tapestry or covering (not ital.)

tapis, sur le (Fr.) under consideration or discussion

tapisserie (Fr. f.) tapestry

tap pants (US) = **french knickers** (lingerie)

tap/room, -root (one word)

taps (pl., usually treated as sing.) (US) last bugle call of the night in army quarters, or a similar call blown at a military funeral

tap-water (hyphen, two words in US)

Ṭarābulus al-Ġarb (Arab.) **Tripoli**, Libya

Ṭarābulus/ **ash-Shām**, *properly* — **al-Ša'm** (Arab.) **Tripoli**, Lebanon

taradiddle a petty lie, pretentious nonsense; *not* para-, tarra-

tarantella a whirling Italian dance, or the music for it

tarantism (hist.) dancing mania

tarantula a large spider

Tarbert Strathclyde, Western Isles, Co. Kerry; (river) Highland

Tarbet Loch Lomond, Strathclyde, and Loch Nevis, Highland

Tardenoisian (archaeol.) (of or relating to) a mesolithic culture using small flint implements

tariff a duty on particular goods, *not* -if

tarlatan a muslin, *not* -etan

tarmac/ (propr.) tarmacadam, or a surface made of this; (verb) to cover with tarmac, **-ked** (not cap.)

tarot a card game or a trump in this, a similar deck used in fortune-telling; *not* -oc

tarpaulin a waterproof cloth, originally of tarred canvas, *not* -ing; (US and Austral. colloq.) **tarp**

Tarpeian Rock ancient Rome

tarradiddle *use* **tara-**

Tarragona Spain

tarry covered with or like tar, *not* tary; linger, stay, wait

tartan a pattern of coloured stripes crossing at right angles

Tartar/, **-y** *see* **Tatar**

tartar a violent-tempered or intractable person (not cap.), adj. **-ian**; a deposit on the teeth, adj. **-ic**

tartare sauce *not* -r (except in US)

Tartar/**us** (Gr. myth.) the place of punishment in Hades, **-ean**

Tartuff/**e** a religious hypocrite, **-ian**; in Fr. m. *tartufe*

Tartuffe, Le a play by Molière, 1669

tartufo (It.) truffle

Tas. Tasmania

Tashi Lama a title of the **Panchen Lama**

tashinamu (Jap.) dedicate oneself privately to some purpose or design, regardless of whether it will succeed, or one's labour will be recognized

task/master, -mistress (one word)

Tasmania abbr. **Tas.**

TASS the official news agency of the Soviet Union, renamed **ITAR-Tass** 1992; *also* **Tass**

tassel/, -led, -ling (one *l* in US)

taste bud (two words)

ta-ta (colloq.) goodbye (hyphen)

Tatar/ (of or relating to) (a member of) a group of Cent. Asian peoples including Mongols and Turks, or the Turkic language of these peoples; of or relating to Cent. Asia E. of the Caspian Sea; *not* Tartar, -y except in hist. contexts; **-stan** the Tatar Autonomous Republic

Tate/, Nahum (1652–1715) Irish poet and playwright, **—, Sir William Henry** (1842–1921) English industrialist, **— Gallery** London; *see also* **Tait**

tatterdemalion a ragged fellow, *not* -ian

tattersall check a fabric pattern of coloured lines (not cap.)

Tattersalls London (-s' only in the possessive case)

tattoo/ an evening drum or bugle signal, call to quarters, military parade by night; a design on the skin; *not* the many variants; **-ed, -er, -ing, -s**

tau/ the nineteenth letter of the Gr. alphabet (*T*, τ), **— cross** ⊤

Tauchnitz,/ Karl Christoph (1761–1836) founded at Leipzig, 1796, the publishing firm once famous for editions of Latin and Greek authors; **— Christian Bernhard, Baron von** (1816–95) founded at Leipzig, 1837, the Librairie Bernhard Tauchnitz, famous for good-quality reprints of British and US authors, banned in Britain and USA because of copyright infringements

tausend (Ger.) thousand

taut (naut.) tight, in good condition; *not* -ght

tautolog/y, -ize *not* -ise

tavern, name of *see* **hotel**

TAVR (hist.) Territorial and Army Volunteer Reserve (1967–79), *now called* **TA**

tawny tan-colour, *not* -ey

taxa pl. of **taxon**

tax-free (hyphen)

tax haven (two words)

taxi/, -ing

tax/on a taxonomic group, pl. **-a**

taxpayer (one word)

tax return (two words)

Taylor Institution Oxford, strictly *not* Taylorian, Institute

Taylour family name of the Marquess of Headfort

Tayside a region of Scotland (one word)

tazz/a a bowl or cup, pl. **-e**

TB terabyte(s) torpedo boat, tuberculosis (tubercle bacillus)

Tb terbium (no point)

Tbilisi Georgia, *formerly* Tiflis; in Georgian **T'bilisi**

T-bone (hyphen)

tbsp tablespoon(ful)

Tc technetium (no point)

TCD Trinity College, Dublin

Tchad, Lake etc., *use* **Chad**

Tchaikovsky, Pyotr (Ilich) (1840–93) Russian composer, *not* Tschaï-; those with the same surname usually transliterated **Chaïkovskiï**

Tchebyshev, Tchekoff etc. *use* **Che-**

TD (Ir.) *Teachta Dála* (Member of the Dáil), Territorial Decoration, touchdown

Te tellurium (no point)

te tonne, -s

te (mus.) *not* si, ti

tea/ bag, — caddy (two words)

teacake (one word, two words in US)

tea/ chest, — cosy (two words)

teacup (one word)

tea/ dance, — garden, — lady, — leaf (two words)

team/mate, -work (one word)

tea party (two words)

teapot (one word)

teapoy a small three- or four-legged table

tearaway an impetuous or reckless young person, hooligan (one word)

tearoom (one word)

tea rose (two words)

tear sheet (two words)

tease *not* -ze

teasel (bot.) *not* -sle, -zel, -zle

tea shop (two words)

Teasmade (propr., cap.)

teaspoonful/ pl. **-s** (one word), abbr. **tsp**

teatime (one word)

tea/ towel, — tray, — tree (two words)

tech. technical, -ly

technetium symbol **Tc**

Technicolor (propr.) a process of colour cinematography (cap.); (colloq.) a vivid or artificial colour (not cap.); *not* -our

technol. technological, -ly

techy *use* **tetchy**

tectonics/ (pl. treated as sing.) (archit.) the craft of producing practical and aesthetically pleasing buildings; (geol.) the study of large-scale structural features, as in **plate —**

teddy bear (two words, not cap.)

Teddy boy (two words, one cap.)

tedesc/o (It. adj.) f. **-a** German (not cap.)

Te Deum (mus.) a hymn (caps.)

teed (golf)

tee-hee a titter; *not* **tehee**

teenage/, -d, -r (one word)

teepee *use* **te-**

tee shirt *use* **T-shirt**

Teesside Cleveland

teetotal/ advocating or characterized by total abstinence from alcoholic drink; abbr. **TT**; **-ism, -ler** (one *l* in US), **-ly**

teetotum/ a four-sided top spun with the fingers, pl. **-s**

TEFL teaching of English as a foreign language

Tegnér, Esaias (1782–1846) Swedish poet

tehee *use* **tee-**

Tehran Iran, *not* -heran

Teignmouth Devon; *see also* **Tyne-**

Teil/ (Ger. m. *or* n.) a part, pl. **-e**; *not* Th- (cap.)

Teilhard de Chardin, Pierre (1881–1955) French writer

tel *use* **tell**

tel. telegraph, telephone

telaesthesia *not* tele- (US)

telamon/ (archit.) a male figure used as a supporting pillar, pl. **-es**

Tel Aviv Israel

tele/camera, -cine, -communication(s), -conference, -fax (one word)

Telegu *use* **Telu-**

tele/marketing, -message (one word)

telephone/ book, — number (two words)

tele/printer, -prompter (one word)

telesthesia *use* **telae-** (except in US)

teletex/ (propr.) an electronic text transmission system; **-t** a news and information service transmitted to televisions from a computer source

teletype (propr., cap. in US)

televis/e *not* -ize, **-ion**

Telford/ Shropshire, **—, Thomas** (1757–1834) Scottish engineer

tell (archaeol.) an artificial mound in Middle East, *not* tel

Tell-el-Amarna Egypt

telltale (one word)

tellurian (inhabitant) of the earth

tellurion an orrery, *not* -ium

tellurium symbol **Te**

Telstar a communications satellite, launched 1962

Telugu a Dravidian people of SE India, or their language; *not* -oogoo, Tele-

Téméraire, The Fighting a picture by Turner, 1839

temp. temperature, temporary

temp. *tempore* (in the time of)

tempera a method of painting using an emulsion, this paint

temperature symbol *T* (no point)

Templar a member of a religious order, the **Knights Templars**, suppressed in 1312; a student or lawyer living in the Temple, London

template a pattern or gauge, *not* -plet

Temple Bar London

temp/o (mus.) time, pl. **-os**; abbr. **t.**

tempora mutantur (Lat.) times are changing

temporar/y abbr. **temp.**, adv. **-ily**

tempore (Lat.) in the time of; abbr. **t.**, **temp.**

temporize *not* -ise

tempura a Japanese dish of fish, shellfish, or vegetables, fried in batter

tempus edax rerum (Lat.) time consumes everything

ten. tenuto

Tenasserim Burma, *not* Tenn-

Ten Commandments, the (caps.)

tendentious calculated to promote a particular cause or point of view, *not* -cious

tenderfoot a novice (one word)

tender-hearted/, -ness (hyphen, one word in US)

tenderize *not* -ise

tenderloin the middle part of a pork loin; (US) the undercut of a sirloin

Tenerife a peak and island, Canary Islands; *not* -iffe

tenia *use* **taenia** (except in US)

Teniers, David/ (1582–1649) and **— —** (1610–90) his son, Dutch painters

Tenison, Thomas (1636–1715) Archbishop of Canterbury; *see also* **Tennyson**

Tennasserim *use* **Tena-**

Tennessee off. abbr. **Tenn.**, postal **TN**

Tenniel, Sir John (1820–1914) English cartoonist and caricaturist

tennis/ not necessary to use 'lawn tennis', *but see* **ILTF**; **real —** a different game, played on an indoor court

tennis/ ball, — court, — racket (two words)

Tenno, Meiji *see* **Meiji Tenno**

Tennyson/, Alfred, Lord (1809–92) Poet Laureate 1850–92, **-ian**; *see also* **Tenison**

Tenochtitlán former Aztec capital, on the site of Mexico City

tenor a settled course, *not* -our; (mus.) male voice, abbr. **T.**

tenor/e (It. mus. m.) tenor voice, pl. *-i*; abbr. **t.**

tenrec a hedgehog-like mammal native to Madagascar, *not* tan-

tenson a contest between troubadours, *not* tenz-

tenuto (mus.) held on, sustained; abbr. **ten.**

Teotihuacán pre-Columbian city, near Mexico City

tepee a portable conical Native American dwelling, esp. of the Great Plains; cf. **wigwam**

tequila a mescal liquor made in Tequila in Mexico (not cap.)

Ter. Terence, Terrace

ter (Lat.) thrice

tera- prefix meaning 10^{12}, abbr. **T**

teraph/ a small image as a domestic deity or oracle of the ancient Hebrews, pl. **-im**; in Heb. *tᵉrāpim*

terat. teratology (study of malformations

terbium symbol **Tb**

terce (eccl.) the office said at the third daytime hour; cf. **tie-**

tercel a male hawk, *not* tier-

tercenten/ary a 300th anniversary; **-nial** occurring every, or lasting, 300 years, (US) = **tercentenary**

tercet (prosody) a triplet, *not* tier-

Terence in Lat. **Publius Terentius Afer** (190–159 BC) Roman comic playwright, abbr. **Ter.**

Teresa, St of Ávila *not* Th-

tergiversat/e to change one's principles; **-ion, -or**

termagant an overbearing or brawling woman (cap. in hist. use as imaginary deity, as in morality plays)

termination abbr. **term.**

terminator *not* -er

terminology abbr. **term.**

termin/us pl. **-i**

terminus/ ad quem (Lat.) the finish, — *a quo* the starting point

termor (law) a person who holds lands etc. for a term of years, or for life; *not* -er

Terpsichore/ (Gr. myth) the muse of dancing, **-an** of dancing

Terr. Territory

terra alba a white mineral, esp. pipeclay or pulverized gypsum

terrace cap. when with name, abbr. **Ter.**; in Fr. f. *terrasse*

terracotta (an object made of) unglazed kiln-burnt clay and sand; its colour (one word, hyphen in US)

Terra del Fuego *use* **Tierra del Fuego**

terrae/ filius (Lat.) lit. son of the soil, denoting a 'worthless nobody'; pl. — *filii* (ital.); **Terrae filius** (hist.) at Oxford University, a semi-licensed jester in the 'Act' (part of the ancient degree ceremony), permitted to make satirical remarks (but liable for punishment if he went too far) (not ital., one cap.)

terra firma dry land (two words, not ital.)

terr/a incognita (Lat.) an unexplored region, pl. *-ae incognitae* (ital.)

terramare an ammoniacal earthy deposit found in mounds in prehistoric lake-dwellings or settlements, *or* the dwelling or settlement itself (not ital.)

terrarium/ a vivarium for small land animals or growing plants, pl. **-s**

terra sigillata an astringent clay, or Samian ware (ital.)

terrazzo/ a floor of stone chips set in concrete and smoothed, pl. **-s**

terret the ring for a driving rein, *not* -it

terre-verte a soft green earth used as a pigment (hyphen, not ital.)

Territory (cap. in geog. names) abbr. **T.**, **Terr.**

terrorize *not* -ise

Tertiary (geol.) (of or relating to) the first period in the Cenozoic era (cap., not ital.); *see also* **Eocene; Miocene; Oligocene; Palaeocene; Pliocene**

tertio (Lat.) in the third place, abbr. **3°**

tertium quid a third something, an intermediate course (not ital.)

terz/a rima (It.) a particular rhyming scheme, pl. *-e rime*

terzetto/ (mus.) a piece for three voices or instruments, pl. **-s**

TES Times Educational Supplement

TESL teaching of English as a second language

tesla the unit of magnetic induction, from **Nikola Tesla** (1856–1943) Croatian-American physicist

TESOL teaching of English to speakers of other languages

tessellate(d) pave(d) with tiles, *not* -ela-

tesser/a a small square tile, pl. **-ae**; **-act** a cube in four dimensions (not ital.)

tessitura (mus.) the ordinary range of a voice

Tess of the D'Urbervilles a novel by Hardy, 1891

Testament abbr. **T.**, **Test.**

testamur (Lat.) examination certificate

test/ drive (hyphen as verb), — **flight** (two words)

test/is (anat.) pl. **-es**

test/ match, — paper, — pilot (two words)

test tube (two words), **test-tube baby** (one hyphen)

Testudinata *use* **Chelonia**

Tet the Vietnamese New Year, observed for three days following the first new moon after 20 Jan. (cap.); in Vietnamese *tết*

tetchy peevish, *not* techy

tête-à-tête (adv., adj., *and* noun, hyphens, accents, not ital.)

tête-bêche (of a postage stamp) printed upside down or sideways relative to another (ital.)

Tetragrammaton the Hebrew name of God written in four (usually small-cap.) letters (YHVH, YHWH), articulated as Yahweh, Jehovah, etc.

tetralogy a group of four related literary or operatic works, (Gr. antiquity) a trilogy of tragedies with a satyric drama

tetrameter (prosody) a verse of four measures

tetraplegia *use* **quadri-**

Teufelsdröckh, Herr Diogenes a character in Carlyle's *Sartor Resartus*

Teut. Teuton, -ic

Teutonic/ relating to or characteristic of the Germanic peoples or their languages; **-ism**

Tevere It. for the Tiber river

Tex. Texas (off. abbr.), Texan (originally Texian)

textbook (one word)

textus receptus (Lat.) the received text, abbr. **text. rec.**

Teyte, Maggie (1888–1976) English soprano

t.g. type genus

TGV (Fr.) *Train à Grande Vitesse*

TGWU Transport and General Workers' Union

Th thorium (no point)

Th. Thomas, Thursday

th a separate letter in Welsh, not to be divided

thagi *use* **thuggee**

Thai of or relating to Thailand, or (a member of) its people; pl. same

Thailand adj. **Thai**

Thaïs (4th c. BC) Greek courtesan

thaler (hist.) a German silver coin

Thalia (Gr. myth.) the muse of comedy

thallium symbol **Tl**

thalweg (geog.) the deepest point or lowest line along a river bed or valley, (law) a boundary between states along the centre of a river etc.; in Modern Ger. m. *Talweg*

Thames a river; in Du. **Theems**, Fr. **Tamise**, Ger. **Themse**, Sp. **Támesis**

Thanjavur India; *not* Tanjor, -e

Thanksgiving Day (US) the fourth Thursday in November, (Canada) second Monday in October

Thant, U (1909–74) Burmese diplomat; 'U' is a Burmese honorific (equivalent to 'Mr') and not a first name

thar *use* **tahr** (except for despot)

Tharrawaddy Burma, *not* Tharawadi

thé/ (Fr. m.) tea, **— dansant** afternoon tea with dancing

Theaetetus a dialogue by Plato, named after a disciple of Socrates

theat. theatrical

theatre/ *not* -er (US), **— -in-the-round** (hyphens), **— nurse, — sister** (two words); in Fr. m. *théâtre*; *Théâtre français* Paris (one cap.)

thec/a (anat., bot.) a case, sheath, sac; pl. **-ae**

thegn (hist.) an English thane

theirs (no apos.)

them/a (Gr.) a theme, pl. **-ata**

Theo. Theodore

theocracy a priest- or god-governed state (cap. with hist. ref. to Jews), *not* -sy

theocrasy the mingling of several divine attributes in one god, *not* -cy

Theocritus (3rd c. BC) Greek poet, abbr. **Theoc.**

theodicy (an instance of) the vindication of divine providence in view of the existence of evil

theodolite a surveying instrument

theol. theolog/y, -ian, -ical

theologize *not* -ise

Theophrastus (*c.*370–*c.*288 BC) Greek philosopher and botanist, abbr. **Theoph.**

theor. theorem

theoret. theoretic, -al, -ally

theorize *not* -ise

theosoph/y a philosophy professing knowledge of God by inspiration; **-ical, -ist, -ize**

Theoto/copuli, -kopoulos *see* **Greco, El**

therapeutic/ healing, **-s** the study of healing agents; abbr. **therap.**

Theravada a conservative form of Buddhism, in Pali *theravāda*

thereanent (Sc.) about that matter

therefor (arch.) for that object or purpose

therefore for that reason, accordingly, consequently; (math.) sign ∴

therein/ in that place or respect, **-after** later in the same document etc., **-before** earlier in the same document etc. (one word)

theremin an electronic musical instrument with a tone varied by the proximity of the hand etc. to the sounding rod (not cap.)

Theresa, St of Ávila, *use* **Ter-**

Thérèse (Fr.)

thereto/ to that or it, in addition; **-fore** before that time (one word)

thereupon in consequence of that, soon or immediately after that (one word)

therm a unit of heat

thermodynamics (one word, pl. usually treated as sing.)

thermomet/er, -ric abbr. **thermom.**

thermonuclear (one word)

Thermopylae, Pass of Greece; battle, 480 BC

thermos (propr.) a vacuum flask

THES *Times Higher Education Supplement*

thesaur/us pl. **-i**

thes/is pl. **-es**; titles to be printed in roman, quoted

Thess./ Thessaly, **1, 2** — Thessalonians (NT)

theta the eighth letter of the Gr. alphabet (*Θ, θ*)

THI temperature-humidity index

thiamine a vitamin, *not* -in

thias/os (Gr. antiquity) a gathering to worship a deity, *not* -us; pl. **-oi**

thicken/, -ed, -er *not* -or, **-ing**

thickset (one word)

thick space (typ.) a third of an em space

thimblerig/ (play) a swindling trick or game; **-ger, -ging** (one word)

thin/, -ner, -nish

thing/amy, -umabob, -umajig, -ummy, -y are the usual British variants; **-amabob, -amajig** are the usual US versions

think tank an advisory organization (two words)

thin space (typ.) a fifth of an em space, symbol ‡ *or* ⌒

third/ (adj.) abbr. **3rd**, **— country** (econ.) a country that does not participate in a customs union, specifically the EU

Third World (caps., no hyphen when attrib.)

Thirty-Nine Articles, the (hyphen, caps.)

thirty-second note (US mus.) a demi-semiquaver

thirty-twomo (typ.) a book based on thirty-two leaves, sixty-four pages to the sheet; abbr. **32mo** (no point)

thirty-year rule (hyphen)

Thirty Years War 1618–48 (caps., no apos.)

tho' though

thole-pin (naut.) one of two which keep an oar in position; *not* -owl, -owel (hyphen)

thol/os (Gr. archit.) a dome-shaped building, esp. a tomb; pl. **-oi**

Thomas abbr. **Th.**, **Thos.**

Thom/ism the doctrine of St Thomas Aquinas, **-ist**

Thompson,/ Sir Benjamin, Count von Rumford (1753–1814) American-born founder of the Royal Institution, London; **— Sir D'Arcy Wentworth** (1860–1948) Scottish biologist; **— Sir Edward Maunde** (1840–1929) English librarian and palaeographer; **— Francis** (1859–1907) English poet; **— Silvanus** (*not* Sy-) **Phillips** (1851–1916) English physicist

Thomson/, Prof. Arthur (1858–1935) Scottish anatomist; **—, Sir Charles Wyville** (1830–82) Scottish zoologist; **—, James** (1700–48) Scottish poet, 'The Seasons'; **—, James** (1834–82) Scottish poet, pseud. **B.V.**, 'City of Dreadful Night'; **—, Prof. Sir John Arthur** (1861–1933) Scottish zoologist and writer; **—, Joseph** (1858–95) Scottish African traveller; **—, Prof.**

Sir Joseph John (1856–1940) English physicist; **—, Sir William, Baron Kelvin** (1824–1907) British mathematician and physicist (hence **kelvin**); **Barons — of Fleet** *and* **of Monifieth**

thor/ax (anat., zool.) the part of the body between neck and abdomen or tail, pl. **-aces**; adj. **-acic**

Thord(h)arson *properly* Þórðarson *see* **Sturla** Þórðarson

Thoreau, Henry David (1817–62) US author and philosopher

thorium symbol **Th**

thorn a runic letter, = *th*; in OE þ, þ; by the late medieval period similar in form to y; in Icelandic Þ, þ. Distinguish from **eth** and **wyn**

thorough bass (mus.) harmony above bass indicated by system of numerals (two words)

thorough/bred, -fare, -going (one word)

Thos. Thomas

thou (colloq.) thousand, -th (no point or apos.)

though abbr. **tho'**

thousand-and-first etc. (hyphens)

thow(e)l-pin *use* **thole-**

thr. through

thral/l slave, bondage; **-dom** bondage

thrash/ beat soundly, strike the waves, make way in water; **— out** discuss exhaustively; cf. **thresh**

thread/bare, -fin (one word)

thread mark (in banknote paper)

Threadneedle Street/ London (two words), **The Old Lady of — —** the Bank of England

threadworm (one word)

three/fold, -pence, -penny (one word)

three-point turn (one hyphen)

three-quarter(s) (adj., hyphen)

three quarters (noun, two words)

three Rs, the reading, writing, arithmetic (no point, no apos.)

threescore (one word)

threescore and ten seventy (three words)

threesome (one word)

thresh beat and separate grain from corn etc.; cf. **thrash**

threshing/ floor, — machine (two words)

threshold *not* -hhold

thrips a plant pest (sing.)

thrive past **thrived** *or* **throve**, past part. **thrived**

thro' *use* **through**

Throckmorton, Sir Nicholas (1515–71) English diplomat

throes violent pangs

Throgmorton/ Avenue, — Street London

Throndhjem *use* **Trondheim**

throne a chair of State for a sovereign or bishop etc. (not cap.)

through *not* thro'; (US) up to and including, e.g. *Monday through Friday*, abbr. **thr.**

Thucydides (*c.*460–*c.*400 BC) Greek historian, abbr. **Thuc.**

thug/ a brutal ruffian (cap. with hist. ref. to assassins in India); **-gee** (hist.) the practice of the Thugs (*not* thagi except in modern specialist contexts), **-gery**

thuja Eng. form of the botanical *Thuya*, the arbor-vitae genus

Thule/ Greenland; **Southern —** S. Atlantic

thulium symbol **Tm**

thumb index (two words, hyphen as verb)

thumb/nail, -print, -screw, -tack (one word)

thunder (meteor.) abbr. **t.**

thunder/bolt, -box, -clap, -cloud, -head, -storm, -struck (one word)

Thüringen Austria; in (hist.) Eng. **Thuringia**, Fr. **Thuringe**, It. **Turingia**

Thursday abbr. **Th., Thur., Thurs.**

thuya *see* **thuja**

THWM Trinity High-Water Mark

thym/e the herb, adj. **-y** *not* -ey

Thynne family name of the Marquess of Bath

Ti titanium (no point)

ti (mus.) *use* **te**

Tiananmen Square Beijing, China

Tian-Shan a mountain range, Kyrgyzstan and China

tiara/ a turban, diadem, ornamental coronet; **-ed** *not* -'d

Tiber a river, Italy; in It. **Tevere**, Fr. **Tibre**

Tiberias ancient Palestine, *now* **Teverya** Israel

Tiberius (**Claudius Nero Caesar**) (42 BC–AD 37) second Emperor of Rome 14–37

Tibet/ in Tibetan **Bod**, in Pinyin **Xizang**; **-an** of or relating to Tibet, or (a member of) its people or its Tibeto-Burman language

Tibeto-Burman a family of languages distributed throughout Cent. and SE Asia

tibi/a (anat.) the inner bone from knee to ankle, pl. **-ae**

Tibullus, Albius (*c.*50–19 BC) Roman poet, abbr. **Tib.**

tic douloureux facial neuralgia, *not* dol-, not ital. (two words)

ticket/, -ed, -ing

ticket office (two words)

tickety-boo (hyphen)

tick-tack a regular beat, racecourse semaphore; *not* tic-tac

tick-tack-toe *or* **tic-tac-toe** (US) **= noughts and crosses**

Ticonderoga NY; a battleship (ital.)

t.i.d. (med.) *ter in die* (three times a day)

tidbit *use* **tit-** (except in US)

tiddly (sl.) tiny, slightly drunk; *not* -ey

tiddlywink/ a counter, **-s** the game; *not* tiddle(d)y- (US)

tideland (US) land that is submerged at high tide (one word)

tidemark (one word)

tide mill (two words)

tide table (two words)

tide/waiter, -water, -wave, -way (one word)

tie, tying *not* tieing

tie/-back, -break, -dye, -in (hyphen)

tiepin (one word)

tierce/ (arch.) a wine measure, (mus.) an interval of two octaves and a major third, a fencing position, a sequence of three cards; **-d** (her.) divided into three parts of different tinctures; cf. **terce**

tierc/el, -et *use* **terc-**

Tierra del Fuego S. America, *not* Terra

***Tiers/ État** (Fr. m.) third estate, the common people; **— Monde** (Fr. m.) Third World (caps.)*

Tietjens, Therese Cathline Johanna (1830–77) German-born Hungarian soprano, *not* Titiens

Tiffany,/ Charles Lewis (1812–92) US jeweller, founder of the New York jewellery store; his son **— Louis Comfort** (1848–1902) US interior designer

tiffany a gauze muslin (not cap.)

tiffin (Anglo-Ind.) a light lunch, *not* -ing

Tiflis *use* **Tbilisi**

tigerish *not* tigr-

Tighnabruaich Strathclyde

tight back (bind.) the cover glued to the back, so that it does not become hollow when open

tightrope (one word)

tigon the hybrid offspring of a tiger and lioness, *not* -glon (US); cf. **liger**

Tigre, Tigrinya two different Semitic languages of N. Ethiopia

tigrish *use* **tiger-**

TIH Their Imperial Highnesses

tike *use* **ty-**

tiki/ (NZ) a large wooden or small ornamental greenstone image representing a human figure, pl. **-s**

tilde a mark (˜) over a letter, e.g. in Sp. over *n* when pron. *ny* (as in *señor*), in Por. over *a* or *o* when nasalized (as in *São Paulo*); in Sp. may mean 'accent' in general; in Port. **til**

Tilsit/ a cheese (cap.); **Treaty of —** 1807; *not* -tt

Tim., 1, 2 First, Second Epistle to Timothy

timar/ (hist.) a fief held by military service under the feudal system of Turkey, in Pers. *tīmār*; **-iot** one holding a timar (not ital.)

timbal (arch.) the kettledrum

timbale/ (biol.) a drum-shaped membrane in certain insects (e.g. cicada), used to produce a shrill chirping sound; (cook.) a drum-shaped dish of minced meat or fish cooked in pastry or a mould; **-s** (mus.) a pair of single-headed drums played with drumsticks

timber dressed lumber for building etc., (US) rough (undressed) wood, forest

timbre the characteristic quality of sounds of a voice or instrument (not ital.)

Timbuktu Mali, *not* -buctoo; *but* **'Timbuctoo'** in Tennyson's prize-poem, 1829, and usually in a figurative sense; in Fr. **Tombouctou**

time symbol *t*

timeable *not* -mable

time-and-motion (adj., hyphens)

time/ bomb, — capsule, — clock, — exposure (two words)

time/-fuse, -honoured *not* -ored (US) (hyphens)

time immemorial (two words)

timekeeper (one word)

time/ lag, — limit (two words)

time of day (typ.) to be in numerals, with full point (colon in US) where time includes minutes and hours: 9.30 a.m. *or* 09.30; *but* phrases such as 'half past two', 'a quarter to four' to be spelt out

timeout (comput.) (one word)

timepiece (one word)

Times, The established 1788 (caps.), *not The London Times. The* (cap. T, ital.) is traditionally included in references, *but note* e.g. the *Sunday Times*, the *New York Times* do not follow this rule

time/scale -share (one word)

time/ sheet, — signal (two words)

time-stratigraphic unit (geol.) name given to a specific rock formation formed during a given time in a type area (e.g. Devonian); units of the higher orders (e.g. Cambrian, Ordovician) are given as headwords in this book

time switch (two words)

timetable (one word)

time warp (two words)

time-worn (hyphen, one word in US)

time zone (two words)

Timothy (NT) abbr. **Tim.**

timpan/o (mus.) the orchestral kettledrum, *not* ty-; pl. **-i**; cf. **tympanum**

tin symbol **Sn** (*stannum*)

tinct. tincture

Tindal, Matthew (1656–1733) English theologian, *not* -all; *see also* **Tyn-**

tinfoil (one word)

tingeing *not* -ging

tinhorn (US colloq.) a contemptible person (one word)

tin Lizzie a Model T Ford, hence any old motor car (one cap.)

Tin Pan Alley the world of popular music (three words, caps.), also with reference to the (hist.) district in New York City

tin plate (two words)

tinpot having poor leadership or organization (one word)

tinsel/, -led, -ling

Tintagel Corn., *not* -il

tintinnabulation the ringing sound of bells

tip in (bind.) to insert a plate etc. by pasting its inner margin to the next page

tip-off (noun, hyphen)

Tipperary a town and county, Ireland

tippet a cape, *not* tipet

tipstaff/ a bailiff, pl. **-s**

tip/toe, -toeing (one word)

tip-top (hyphen)

TIR international road transport, esp. with ref. to EU regulations (*transport international routier*)

tirailleur a sharpshooter or skirmisher (not ital.)

Tiranë Albania, *not* -na

tire of a wheel, *use* **ty-** (except in US)

tiré à part (Fr. typ. m.) an offprint

Tir-nan-Og (Ir. myth.) a land of perpetual youth, equivalent to Elysium (two caps., two hyphens)

tiro/ a novice, a new recruit; pl. **-s**; *not* ty- (US)

Tirol(o) *see* **Tyrol**

'tis for *it is* (apos., close up)

tisane an infusion of dried herbs etc.; cf. **ptisan**

Tisiphone (Gr. myth.) one of the Furies

'Tis Pity She's a Whore a play by John Ford, 1633, *not* 'Tis a . . .

Tit. Titus

tit. title

titanic of titanium, colossal (not cap., except with ref. to Titans)

Titanic the White Star liner sunk by an iceberg, 1912

titanium symbol **Ti**

titbit (one word) *not* tid- (US)

Titel/ (Ger. typ. m.) the title, ***-blatt*** (n.) title page, ***-zeile*** (f.) headline (caps.)

titer *use* **titre** (except in US)

tit for tat (three words)

titi a S. American monkey, an American evergreen shrub (one word)

ti-ti the New Zealand mutton-bird (hyphen)

Titian in It. **Tiziano Vecellio** (1477–1576) Venetian painter

Titiens *use* **Tietjens**

titillate excite pleasurably

titivate smarten up, *not* titt-

title deed (two words)

title/ page (typ.) properly the *full-title page*, as distinct from the *half-title page*; — **piece**, — **role** (two words)

titles (**cited**) articles, chapters, shorter poems, songs to be roman, quoted; series of books etc. to be roman, no quotes; books, periodicals, newspapers, epic poems, plays, operas, symphonies, ballets, works of art to be italic

title verso (typ.) the reverse of a title page (two words)

Tito/ pseud. of **Josip Broz** (1892–1980) President of Yugoslavia 1953–80, **-ism, -ist**; **-grad** former name of **Podgorica**

titre (chem.) the strength of a solution determined by titration, *not* -ter (US)

titre (Fr. typ. m.) title

tittivate *use* **titi-**

tittup/ behave or move in a lively way; **-ed, -ing, -py**

Titus/, Epistle to (NT) abbr. **Tit.**; — (Rom. praenomen) abbr. **T.**

T/-joint, -junction (caps., hyphens); *use* a sans serif typeface only where important to represent the actual configuration exactly

TKO technical knockout

Tl thallium (no point)

Tlemcen NW Algeria

TLS *Times Literary Supplement*

TLWM Trinity Low-Water Mark

TM transcendental meditation

Tm thulium (no point)

tmes/is (gram.) the division of a compound word by intervening word(s), pl. **-es**

TN Tennessee (postal abbr.)

tn (US) ton, town

TNT trinitrotoluene

TO Telegraph Office, turn over

toad/fish, -flax (one word)

toad-in-the-hole (hyphens)

toad/stone, -stool (one word)

to and fro (adv., three words)

toast/-master, -mistress (hyphens, one word in US)

toastrack (one word)

Toba Batak *see* **Batak**

Tobago island, part of Trinidad and Tobago; *not* Ta-

Tobermore Co. Londonderry

Tobermory Isle of Mull, Strathclyde

Tobit (Apocr.) not to be abbr.

toboggan/ *not* -ogan; **-er, -ing**

toby/ collar, — jug (two words, not cap.)

Toc H a society, orig. of ex-service personnel founded after the First World War (no point)

Tocharian (of or in) an extinct Indo-European language of a Cent. Asian people in the first millennium AD, or a member of the people speaking this language

Tocqueville, Alexis Charles Henri Maurice Clérel, comte de (1805–59) French statesman and political writer

tocsin an alarm bell or signal

to-do commotion (hyphen)

toe/ (verb), **-d, -ing**

toe/cap, -nail, -rag (one word)

toffee *not* -y

toga/ an ancient Roman mantle, pl. **-s**

together with takes a singular verb if the subject is singular

Togo/ Cent. W. Africa; adj. **-lese**

toile linen cloth

toilet *not* -ette

toilet/ paper, — powder, — roll, — set, — soap, — table (two words)

toilette (Fr. f.) toilet

toilet-train/, -ing (hyphen, two words in US)

toilet water (two words)

toing and froing (three words, no hyphens); (US) to-ing and fro-ing (hyphens)

Toison d'or (Fr. f.) the Golden Fleece

Tokaj Hungary; trad. Eng. **Tokay**, also for the region's **Tokaji** wine

Tokyo Japan, *not* -io; in Jap. **Tōkyō**; in Eng. formerly **Edo**, previously **Yeddo**

Toler in the family name of the Earl of Norbury

Tolkien, J(ohn) R(onald) R(euel) (1892–1973) English writer and scholar, *not* -ein

tollbooth (one word), *not* tol-

toll call (US) a long-distance (non-local) telephone call

Tolstoy, Count Leo (**Lev Nikolaevich**) (1828–1910) Russian novelist, *not* -oi

Toltec (of or related to) (a member of) an American Indian people that flourished in Mexico before the Aztecs, or their language

tomahawk a Native American war-axe, a hatchet

tomato/ pl. **-es**

tombola a kind of lottery using a drum-shaped container

tombolo a spit joining an island to the mainland

Tombouctou Fr. for **Timbuktu**

tom/boy, -cat (one word)

Tom Collins a gin-based iced cocktail

tome a large book or volume, usually thought of as a massive work of obscure learning

tome (Fr. m.) a volume, abbr. **t.**

tomfool/, -ery (one word)

Tommy a British private soldier (cap.)

tommy gun (not cap.; noun, two words; verb, hyphen)

tommyrot (one word)

Tompion, Thomas (?1639–1713) English clock maker

tompion *use* **tam-**

tomtit a small bird (one word)

tom-tom a kind of drum (hyphen)

ton/ (weight), **-s**; abbr. **t**

ton (Fr. m.) style

Tonbridge *but* **Tunbridge Wells** Kent

tond/o (It.) a painting or relief of circular form, pl. **-i** (not ital.)

tone poem (mus.) (two words)

tong a Chinese guild, association, or secret society

tongu/e (verb), **-ed, -ing**

tonic sol-fa (one hyphen)

Tonkin Vietnam; *not* Tongking, Tonquin, Tun-

tonn. tonnage

tonne a metric ton, equal to 1,000 kg, 0.984 long tons, or 1.102 short tons; abbr. **t, te**

tonneau the rear of a motor car

tonneau (Fr. m.) ton, tun, or cask; abbr. **t.**

tonsil/, -lar, -lectomy, -litis

ton/y (US colloq.) having 'tone', stylish or fashionable; *not* -ey; **-ier, -iest**

toolbox (one word)

tooling (bind.) impressing a design or lettering on the (usually leather) binding by hand

toolmaker (one word)

tooth/ache, -brush, -comb, -paste, -pick, -some, -wort (one word)

topcoat (one word)

topgallant (naut.) the mast, sail, yard, or rigging immediately above the topmast and topsail (one word)

top-heavy (hyphen)

Tophet (Scripture) hell, in Heb. *tōpeṯ*

topi (Anglo-Ind.) a hat, *not* -pee

top/knot, -less, -mast (one word)

top-notch first-rate (hyphen)

topog. topograph/y, -ical

top/os a stock theme in literature etc., pl. **-oi**

topsail (one word)

tops and tails (typ.) preliminary matter and index etc.

topside (naut.) the ship's side between waterline and deck, also of beef (one word)

topsoil (one word)

Topsy a character in Stowe's novel *Uncle Tom's Cabin*

topsy-turvy (hyphen)

Torah, the the Jewish term for the Pentateuch, in Heb. *tōrāh*

Tor Bay Devon

Torbay a town, Devon

torc (hist.) a necklace of twisted metal, esp. of the ancient Gauls and Britons; cf. **torque**

torchère a tall stand with a small table for a candlestick etc. (not ital.)

torchlight (one word)

tori pl. of **torus**

torii the gateway of a Shinto shrine; pl. same

Torino It. for **Turin**

tormentor *not* -er

tornado/ pl. **-es**

torniquet *use* **tour-**

torpedo/ pl. **-es**

Torphichen, Baron

torque (mech.) the moment of a system of forces tending to cause rotation; cf. **torc**

Torquemada, Tomás de (1420–98) Spanish Inquisitor

torr (phys.) a unit of pressure, with numbers **Torr** (no point); its use is now discouraged

Torres Vedras a fortified town near Lisbon, Portugal; battle, 1810

torse (her.) a wreath

torso/ (a representation of) the human trunk; something unfinished or mutilated; pl. **-s**

tort/ (law) a breach of duty (other than under contract) leading to liability for damages; **-feasor** a person guilty of tort; **-ious** constituting a tort, wrongful; cf. **tortuous**; **torturous**

torte/ an elaborate sweet cake or tart, pl. **-n**

tortilla (Mexican cook.) a thin flat unleavened maize or wheat cake

tortoiseshell (one word)

tortue/ (Fr. f.) turtle, — *claire* clear turtle soup

tortuous full of twists and turns, devious, circuitous, crooked; cf. **tortious**; **torturous**

torturous concerning torture; cf. **tortious**; **tortuous**

Tory (of or related to) the British Conservative Party; (US hist.) a loyal colonist during the American Revolution

Toscana It. for **Tuscany**

Toscanini, Arturo (1867–1957) Italian conductor

Tosk one of two main dialects of Albanian, the basis for standard Albanian; *see also* **Geg**

total/, -led, -ling (one l in US)

totalizator a betting device, colloq. 'the tote'; *but* **Horserace Totalisator Board**

totalize collect into a total, *not* -ise

t'other (colloq.) the other, *not* tother

totidem verbis (Lat.) in so many words

toties quoties (Lat.) the one as often as the other

toto caelo (Lat.) diametrically opposed, *not* coe-

touchdown (one word) abbr. **TD**

touché acknowledging a hit (not ital.)

touchline (one word)

touch/-tone, -type (hyphen)

touchwood readily inflammable wood (one word)

Toulouse-Lautrec, Henri Marie Raymonde de (1864–1901) French painter

toupee a wig; *not* -ée, -et

tour/ (Fr. m.) a tour; (f.) tower; **— à tour** alternately, in turn (ital.)

touraco *use* tur-

tour de force a feat of strength or skill (not ital.)

tour/ de main (Fr. m.) sleight of hand, **-d'horizon** a broad survey or summary; pl. **-s — —** (ital.)

touring car (two words)

tourmaline a mineral, sometimes cut as a gem; *not* -in

Tournai Belgium; in Fl. **Doornik**, *formerly* in Eng. **Tournay**

Tournay France

tournedos a small round thick cut from a fillet of beef, pl. same

tourney (take part in) a tournament

tourniquet a bandage etc. for stopping flow of blood, *not* torn-

Toussaint L'Ouverture, François (1743–1803) Haitian general and liberator, in Fr. **Louverture** (no apos.)

tout/ à coup (Fr.) suddenly; **— à fait** entirely; **— court** abruptly, or simply; **— de même** all the same; **— de suite** immediately; **— d'un coup** all at once; **le — ensemble** the general effect; **— le monde** all the world, everybody (no hyphens)

tovarishch/ (Russ. m. or f.), comrade, pl. **-i**; in Eng. **tovarish** (not ital.); *see also* **grazhdanin**

towel/, -led, -ling (one *l* in US)

town abbr. **t.**

town councillor *not* -ilor, abbr. **TC** (two words)

town/hall, — house (two words)

townie *not* -ee

Townshend, Marquess

township abbr. **t.**

toxaemia blood poisoning, *not* -xemia (US)

toxicol. toxicolog/y, -ical

toxin a poison, *not* -ine

toxophilite a student or lover of archery

Toys "Я" Us a retail chain (double quotes, reverse *R*)

Tpr. Trooper

Tr. trustee

tr. transitive, translat/ed, -ion, -or; transfer, -red

Trabzon Turkey

tracasserie a fuss or state of annoyance (not ital.)

trace/able, -ability *not* -cable

trache/a the windpipe, pl. **-ae**

track/ record, — shoe (two words)

tracksuit (one word)

Tractarian/, -ism the Oxford or High Church Movement of the mid-19th c. (cap.)

tractor *not* -er

trad (colloq.) traditional (music, no point), also as abbr. (with point)

tradable *not* -eable

trade/ book, — cycle, — edition, — gap (two words)

trademark (one word, *but* two in law)

trade/ name, — secret, — wind (two words)

trades/man, -people, -woman (one word)

trade/ union (*not* trades union) pl. **— unions** (two words), abbr. **TU**; *but* **Trades Union Congress** abbr. **TUC**; **— unionism, — unionist** (two words)

trade wind (two words)

trading post (two words)

traduction (Fr. f.) translation

traffic/, -ked, -ker, -king

traffic circle (US) = **roundabout**

traffic/ jam, — light *or* **— signal, — sign, — warden** (two words)

trag. tragedy, tragic

tragedi/an a writer of tragedies, a tragic actor; **-enne** a tragic actress

tragicomedy a drama of mixed tragic and comic elements (one word)

trahison des clercs (Fr. f.) the betrayal of standards, scholarship, etc. by the intellectuals

trailer an unpowered vehicle towed by another, (US) = **caravan**

train-bearer (hyphen, one word in US)

train/man, -men (one word)

train oil oil obtained from whale blubber (two words)

trainsick (one word)

trainspott/er, -ing (one word)

traipse trudge, *not* -apes

trait a characteristic

trait d'union (Fr. typ. m.) the hyphen

Trajectum ad Rhenum *see* **Utrecht**

tram/, -car, -lines (one word)

trammel/ entangle; **-led, -ling** (one *l* in US)

tramontana a cold north wind in the Adriatic (not ital.)

tramontane (a person) situated or living on the other side of mountains, foreign; *not* trans-; in It. **tramontano**

trampoline a sprung canvas sheet used by acrobats, gymnasts, etc.; *not* -in

tranche a portion of income etc. (not ital.)

tranny (colloq.) a transistor radio, a transparency; *not* -ie

tranquil/, -lity, -lize *not* -ise (one *l* in US), **-ly**

trans. transactions, transitive; translat/ed, -ion, -or

transact/, -or

transalpine beyond the Alps, esp. from the Italian point of view (one word, not cap.); cf. **cisalpine**

transatlantic beyond or crossing the Atlantic, esp. (Brit.) American, and (US) European (one word, not cap.)

transcontinental (one word)

transcript a written or recorded copy (usually of speech)

transexual *use* **transs-**

transf. transferred

transfer/, -able, -ee, -ence, -red, -rer, -ring

transgress/ pass beyond the limit of; **-ible, -or**

tranship/, -ment *use* trans-s-

transition a literary monthly 1927–38 (not cap.)

transitive (gram.) (of verb) taking a direct object; abbr. **trans., transit.**

Transkei S. Africa

translat/ed, -ion, -or abbr. **tr., trans.; -able**

trans/missible (med.), **-mittable** (physics)

transmogrify *not* -morg-

transmontane *use* **tram-**

transonic relating to speeds close to that of sound, *not* trans-sonic

transpacific beyond or crossing the Pacific (one word)

transpontine on the other side of a bridge, esp. on the south side of the Thames; *see also* **cispontine**

transpose/ (typ.) to interchange letters, words, lines of type, etc.; **— mark** ⌊⌐⌐

transsexual *not* transexual

trans-ship/, -ment (hyphens, one word in US), *not* transh-

trans-sonic *use* **transonic**

Transvaal a province of S. Africa, abbr. **Tvl.**

transverse (adj.) situated, arranged, or acting in a crosswise direction; cf. **traverse**

Transylvania a part of Romania, before 1919 part of Hungary; Romanian **Transilvania**, Hung. **Erdély**, Ger. **Siebenbürgen**

trapes *use* **traipse**

trapezi/um a quadrilateral with only one pair of sides parallel; (US) a quadrilateral with no two sides parallel; pl. **-a**

trapezoid/ a quadrilateral with no two sides parallel; (US) a quadrilateral with only one pair of sides parallel; pl. **-s**

trash/ (US) refuse, rubbish; **— can** (US) = **dustbin** (two words)

trattoria an Italian-style restaurant (not ital.)

trauma/ a wound or shock, pl. **-s**

travail/, -ed, -ing

travel/, -led, -ler, -ling (one *l* in US)

travel agent (two words)

Travellers' Club London (*not* 's)

travelogue *not* -og (US)

traverse (verb) travel, lie across, turn horizontally, consider or discuss the whole extent, thwart or oppose, (law) deny; (noun) a sideways movement, a thing that crosses another, an act of traversing; cf. **transverse**

travois a drag sledge used by Native Americans, pl. same

Trawsfynydd Gwynedd

TRC Thames Rowing Club

tread past **trod**, past part. **trodden**

treadmill (one word)

Treas. treasurer, treasury

trecent/o 1300–99, and the Italian art and literature of that century; **-ist** (not ital.)

tre corde (mus.) direction in piano-music to release soft pedal; cf. **una corda**

treen (treated as pl.) small domestic wooden objects, esp. antiques

trefa *or* **tref** not kosher, *not* the many variants; in Heb. **ṱerēpāh**

Treitschke, Heinrich von (1834–96) German historian

trek/ (to make) an arduous journey; *not* -ck; **-ked, -ker, -king**

trellis/ *not* -ice, **-work** (hyphen, one word in US)

trematode (noun or adj.) (of) a flatworm, *not* -oid

tremolo/ (mus.) a tremulous effect or device producing this, pl. **-s**

tremor *not* -our

Trengganu *see* **Malaya, Federation of**

trente-et-quarante (Fr. m.) a game of chance, *rouge-et-noir* (hyphens)

Trento Italy; in hist. contexts the older Eng. form **Trent** is still used, e.g. for the Council of Trent and the Trent Codices; in Fr. **Trente**, Ger. **Trient**

trepan/ (to use) a surgeon's cylindrical saw, a borer; to trap; **-ation, -ned, -ning**

trepang bêche-de-mer, a sea cucumber

Tresco Scilly

Trescowe Corn.

Tresilian Bay S. Glam.

Tresillian Corn.

Tressell, Robert pseud. of **Robert Noonan** (?1870–1911) English novelist

Trèves Fr. for **Trier**

trevet *use* **tri-**

TRH Their Royal Highnesses

Triassic (geol.) (of or relating to) the earliest period of the Mesozoic era

trib. tribal, tribun/e, -al, tributary

tribrach (prosody) a foot of three short or unstressed syllables

tricolour (a flag) having three colours, esp. the French flag; in Fr. m. ***drapeau tricolore***

tricorne (an imaginary animal) with three horns, a cocked hat; *not* -n

Tridentine of or relating to the Council of Trent, held at Trento in Italy 1545–63, esp. as the basis of RC doctrine; a RC adhering to this trad. doctrine and practice (cap.)

trienni/al lasting, or occurring every, three years; **-um** a period of three years, pl. **-ums**

Trier Germany; *not* -rs, Trèves

trig. trigonometry

trigesimo-secundo *use* **thirty-twomo**

trigon. trigonometr/y, -ical

trillion a million million (10^{12}); in France (since 1948), Germany, and formerly in Britain, a million million million (10^{18}); corresponds to the change in use of **billion**; avoid ambiguity

trimeter (prosody) a verse of three measures

Trin. Trinidad, Trinity

Trinidad and Tobago W. Indies

Trinity Sunday the one after Whit Sunday

triphthong a union of three vowels (letters *or* sounds) pron. in one syllable (as in *fire*), or three vowels representing the sound of a single vowel (as in *beau*)

Tripitaka the sacred canon of Theravada Buddhism, written in Pali

Tripoli/ Libya, in Arab. **Ṭarābulus al-Ġarb** ('Tripoli of the West'); Lebanon, in Arab. **Ṭarābulus ash-Shām,** *properly* **Ṭarābulus al-Ša'm** ('Tripoli of Syria'), in local pronunciation **Trâblous**; **-tania** the coastal region surrounding Tripoli in Libya

tripoli rottenstone (not cap.)

tripos the honours examination for the BA degree at Cambridge

triptych a set of three painted or carved panels, hinged together; or a similarly associated set of pictures

triptyque a customs permit serving as a passport for a motor vehicle

triquetr/a a symmetrical ornament of three interlaced arcs, pl. **-ae**; **-al**

trireme an ancient Greek ship with three banks of oars on each side

Tristan da Cunha S. Atlantic, *not* d'Acunha

Tristan und Isolde an opera by Wagner, 1865

Tristram a knight of the Round Table; also spelt Tristran, Tristrand, Trystan, etc.

tritium symbol **T**

triturat/e grind finely, **-or**

triumvir/ one of a committee of three; Eng. pl. **-s**; Lat. pl. **-i** (the earlier and more correct Lat. pl. is **tresviri** (three men)); collective noun **-ate**

trivet an iron tripod or bracket, *not* tre-

trivia trifles, is pl.

trivium (hist.) a medieval university course of grammar, rhetoric, and logic; cf. **quadrivium**

tri-weekly produced or occurring three times a week or every three weeks; to avoid confusion, spell out what is meant

tRNA transfer RNA, *not* sRNA

trocar (med.) an instrument for withdrawing fluid from the body, *not* troch-

troche (med.) a medicated lozenge

troch/ee a foot of two syllables (- ⏑); **-aic**

Troilus and Cressida a play by Shakespeare, *c.*1602; *but* ***Troilus and Criseyde*** a poem by Chaucer, *c.*1387

trolley *not* -lly

trollop a disreputable girl or woman, a prostitute

Trollope,/ Anthony (1815–82) and **— Frances** (1780–1863) his mother, English novelists

trompe l'œil (Fr. m.) an illusion, esp. in still-life painting or plaster ornament

Trondheim Norway; *not* Th-; in Ger. **Dront-**; in Dan. **-hjem**

troop/ an assembly of soldiers etc.; in pl. of armed forces generally; **-er** abbr. **Tpr.**; **-ing the colour** *not* of the colours; cf. **troupe**

tropaeolum/ a trailing plant, pl. **-s**; as a botanical genus, ***Tropaeolum***

trop/e a figurative (e.g. metaphorical or ironical) use of a word or words, **-ology**

trophic of or concerned with nutrition

tropical (not cap.)

tropic/ of Cancer, — of Capricorn; **the -s** region between these two (one cap.)

troposphere the lower atmosphere; cf. **strato-**

troppo/ (mus.) too much, **ma non —** but not too much so

Trotsky/, Leon pseud. of **Lev Davidovich Bronstein** (1879–1940) Russian revolutionary; *not* -tz-, -ki; **-ism, -ist, -ite**

trottoir (Fr. m.) footway, pavement

trouble/maker, -shooter (one word)

troup/e a company of performers; **-er** one of these, or a staunch colleague; cf. **troop**

trousseau/ the clothes collected by a bride for her marriage, pl. **-s** (not ital.)

trouvaille (Fr. f.) a lucky find

trouvère a medieval poet in N. France in the 11th–14th cc., composing in *langue d'oïl*

trowel/, -led, -ling (one *l* in US)

troy weight (not cap.) 1 troy pound (approx. 373 g) = 12 troy ounces or 5,760 grains; 1 troy ounce = 20 pennyweights

TRRL Transport and Road Research Laboratory

trs. (print.) transpose, trustees

Trucial States former name of the United Arab Emirates

Trudeau, Pierre (Elliott) (b. 1919) Canadian Prime Minister 1968–79, 1980–4

Truffaut, François (1932–84) French film director

Truman, Harry S (1884–1972) US politician, President 1945–53 (no point after the *S*, as it stands for nothing: he had no middle name)

trumpet/, -ed, -ing

Truron: the signature of the Bishop of Truro (colon)

Trustee abbr. **Tr.**, pl. **Trs.**

TS (paper) tub-sized, typescript

tsar/ (hist.) the title of the former emperor of Russia; **-evich** his eldest son, *not* cesarevitch; **-evna** his daughter; **-ina** his wife (in Russ. *tsaritsa*) (caps. as titles); *not* cs-, cz- (US), tz-

Tsaritsyn Russia, *now* Volgograd

Tsarskoe Selo the imperial residence near St Petersburg; renamed Detskoe Selo and, later, Pushkin; *not* Tz-, Z-

TSB Trustee Savings Bank

Tschaikowsky, P. I. *use* **Tchaikovsky**

tsetse African fly, *not* tzetze

TSH Their Serene Highnesses, thyroid-stimulating hormone

T-shirt (hyphen) *not* tee shirt

Tsigane (Fr. m. and f.) a Hungarian Gypsy, a tzigane

tsp teaspoon(ful)

T-square (hyphen) *not* tee-

TSS typescripts

tsunami/ a long tidal wave (not ital.); pl. **-s**

t.s.v.p. (Fr.) *tournez s'il vous plaît*, = PTO

Tswana (a member of) a southern African people living in Botswana and neighbouring areas; *see also* **Setswana**

TT teetotal, Tourist Trophy, tuberculin tested

TTS (typ., compositing) teletypesetting

TU trade union, -s

tuba/ the bass saxhorn, pl. **-s**

Tube, the the London Underground system

Tübingen a town and university, Germany

TUC Trades Union Congress

tuck/-box, -net (hyphens)

tuck shop (two words, one word in US)

Tudor (hist.) of, characteristic of, or associated with the royal family of England ruling 1485–1603, or this period

Tuesday abbr. **Tu.**, **Tue.**, **Tues.**

tugrik a monetary unit of Mongolia, pl. same

Tuileries Paris (one *l*)

tularaemia a severe infectious disease of animals transmissible to man, *not* -remia (US)

tulle a fine silk fabric

tumble/down, -weed (one word)

tumbrel a cart, *not* -il

tumour a morbid growth, *not* -or (US)

tumul/us an ancient burial mound, pl. **-i** (not ital.)

tun/ a large beer or wine cask, or a brewer's fermenting vat; a measure of capacity; pl. **-s**; abbr. **t.**

Tunbridge Wells but **Tonbridge** Kent

tuneable *not* tunable

Tungking *use* **Tonkin**

tungsten wolfram, symbol **W**

Tunisia N. Africa; capital Tunis

tunnel/, -led, -ling (one *l* in US)

Tupamaro a Marxist urban guerrilla in Uruguay

Tupi (of or relating to) (a member of) a Native American people living in the Amazon valley, or their language; pl. same

tu quoque! (Lat.) so are you!

turaco/ a large African bird, pl. **-s**; *not* tou-, -cou, -ko

Turanian (of or relating to) the group of Asian languages that are neither Semitic nor Indo-European, esp. the Ural-Altaic family

turbid muddy, thick, unclear; (of a style) confused or disordered

turbo/charger, -fan, -jet, -prop, -shaft (one word)

Turco/ (hist.) an Algerian soldier in the French army, pl. **-s**; *not* -ko

Turco- a prefix meaning *Turkish*, *not* Turko-

Turcoman *use* **Turkoth**

Turcophile one friendly to the Turks

Turgenev, Ivan (Sergeevich) (1818–83) Russian novelist, *not* the many variants

turgid swollen, inflated, enlarged; (of language) pompous, bombastic

Turin Italy, in It. **Torino**

Turk, Young *see* **Young Turk**

Turk. Turk/ey, -ish

Turkey in Turk. **Türkiye**, Fr. **Turquie**, Ger. **Türkei**, It. **Turchia**

Turkey red (one cap.)

Turki (of or relating to) a group of Ural-Altaic languages (including Turkish), and the people speaking them

Turkic a group of languages spoken in Asia Minor

Turkish the language of Turkey

Turkish/ bath, — carpet, — coffee, — delight, — towel (two words, one cap.)

Turkistan a region of Cent. Asia, *not* Turke-

Turkmenistan Cent. Asia, a former Soviet Socialist Republic

Turko- *use* **Turco-**

Turkoman/ an inhabitant or language of Turkmenistan, *not* Turco-; pl. **-s** *not* -men

Turku Finland, in Swed. **Åbo**

turn/coat, -cock (one word)

turned/ comma (typ.) an opening quote produced (as if) by printing a comma upside down ('); **— sort** (typ.) a sort printed upside down or on its side

Turner, Joseph Mallord William *not* Mallad, -ard (1775–1851) English painter

turning/ circle, — point (two words)

turnkey (one word)

turn-line (typ.) a line wider than the measure, which finishes on a following line; the second or subsequent line of a paragraph (hyphen)

turn/-off, -on (nouns, hyphens, one word in US)

Turnour family name of Earl Winterton

turn-out (noun, hyphen, one word in US)

turn over abbr. **TO**

turnover/ (noun and adj., one word); **— line** *see* **turn-line**

turn/pike, -side (one word)

turn signal (US) = **indicator** (vehicle)

turn/spit, -stile, -stone, -table (one word)

turn-up/ an unexpected surprise (hyphen, one word in US), **-s** cuffs on trouser legs (hyphen)

turtle dove (two words, one in US)

turtleneck (one word)

Tuscany Italy; in It. **Toscana**, Fr. **Toscane**, Ger. **Toskana**

Tuskar Rock a lighthouse, Co. Wexford

Tuskegee Institute Ala.

tussock a clump of grass, *not* -ac(k)

tussore an Indian or Chinese silk(worm); *not* -ah (US), -er

Tutankhamun an Egyptian pharaoh, *not* -amen

Tutsi (of or relating to) a people of Rwanda and Burundi, pl. same; *not* Watusi, Watutsi

tutti/ (mus.) (passage performed with) all instruments or voices together, pl. **-s**

tutti-frutti a confection flavoured with mixed fruits (hyphen)

tutu a ballet dancer's skirt, NZ shrub (one word)

tuum (Lat.) thine; *see also* **meum**

Tuvalu/ W. Pacific; **-an**

tu-whit, tu-whoo (make) an owl's cry

tuxedo/ (US) a dinner jacket, black tie; pl. **-s**

tuyère a furnace nozzle, *not* twyer

TV television

TVA (US) Tennessee Valley Authority

Tvl. Transvaal

TVP (propr.) textured vegetable protein

Twain, Mark *see* **Clemens**

'twas for *it was* (apos., close up)

Tweeddale/ a district of Borders; **Marquis of —**

Twelfth/ Day 6 Jan., **— Night** 5–6 Jan.

twelvemo *see* **duodecimo**

twenty-fourmo (typ.) a book based on twenty-four leaves, forty-eight pages, to the sheet; abbr. **24mo**

twentymo (typ.) a book based on twenty leaves, forty pages, to the sheet; abbr. **20mo**

'twere, 'twill for *it were, it will* (apos., close up)

twerp a stupid or objectionable person, *not* -irp

twilit illuminated (as if) by twilight

Twisleton-Wykeham-Fiennes the family name of Baron Saye and Sele (two hyphens); *see also* **Fiennes**

'twixt for *betwixt* (apos.)

two/-bit (US) cheap, petty (hyphen); **— bits** a quarter of a dollar (two words)

two-faced (adj., hyphen)

twofold (one word)

two/pence, -penny (one word)

twosome (one word)

two/-step, -stroke, -time, -timer, -ton, -tone (hyphens)

'twould for *it would* (apos., close up)

two-way (hyphen)

TX Texas (postal abbr.)

TYC Thames Yacht Club

tyke an objectionable fellow, a mongrel, a small child, (sl.) a Yorkshireman; *not* ti-

Tyler,/ John (1790–1862) US President 1841–5; **— Wat** (d. 1381) English rebel

Tylers and Bricklayers livery company

Tylor, Sir Edward Burnett (1832–1917) English anthropologist

tympan (print.) an appliance in a printing press used to equalize pressure between the platen etc. and a printing sheet

tympan/um (med.) the eardrum, (archit.) a vertical triangular space forming the centre of a pediment or arch; pl. **-a**; cf. **timpano**

Tyndale, William (1484–1536) English priest and translator of the Bible, burnt at the stake

Tyndall, John (1820–93) English physicist

Tyne and Wear a metropolitan county

Tynemouth Tyne & Wear; *see also* **Teign-**

Tynwald/ the parliament of the Isle of Man, **— Day** 5 July

typ. typograph/er, -ic, -ical, -ically

type/**cast, -face** (one word)

type/ **founder, — foundry** (two words, one word in US)

type metal an alloy of lead, antimony, and tin (two words)

typescript prefer to *manuscript* for any document typewritten, printed by computer or typesetter, or otherwise not written by hand; abbr. **TS**, pl. **TSS** (no points)

type/**setter, -setting, -writer, -written** (one word)

tyrannize *not* -ise

Tyre Lebanon; in Arab. **Ṣūr**, Fr. **Tyr**, Ger. **Tyrus**

tyre (of a wheel) *not* ti- (US)

Tyrian/ (a native or citizen) of, *or* relating to, ancient Tyre in Phoenicia; **— purple** a crimson dye obtained from some molluscs

tyro *use* **tiro** (except in US)

Tyrol/ a region of Austria and Italy; in Ger. **Tirol**, It. **Tirolo**; adj. **-ean, -ese**; **South —** a region belonging to Italy since 1919; in Ger. **Südtirol**, It. **Alto Adige**

Tyutchev, Fyodor (**Ivanovich**) (1803–73) Russian lyric poet and diplomat

tzar etc., *use* **ts-**

Tzarskoye Selo *use* **Tsarskoe Selo**

tzatziki a Greek side dish of yogurt with cucumber

Tzeltal, Tzotzil the names for two distinct American Indian peoples inhabiting parts of S. Mexico, or the Mayan language of each

tzetze *use* **tsetse**

tzigane a Hungarian Gypsy, or characteristic of the tziganes or (esp.) their music; in Magyar *cigány*, Fr. m. and f. **Tsigane**, Ger. m. **Zigeuner**

tzolkin the cycle of 260 days constituting a year in the Mayan sacred calendar

Tz'u Chou a district in NE China; the pottery made there from the Sui dynasty onwards; in Pinyin **Cizhou**

U upper class (*see also* **non-U**), uranium, a film-censorship classification, the twentieth in a series; Burmese title of respect before a man's name (e.g. U Nu, U Thant), equivalent to 'Mr' (not an abbr.); (Du.) you (polite, sing. and pl.)

U. Unionist

u unified atomic mass unit

u. (meteor.) ugly, threatening weather; (Ger.) *und* (and), *unter* (among)

Ü, ü in German etc., is not to be replaced by *Ue, ue*, except in some proper names and historical spellings, or *U, u*

u. a. (Ger.) *unter anderem* (among other things)

u. ä. (Ger.) *und ähnliche(s)* (and the like) (space in Ger.)

UAE United Arab Emirates

u. a. m. (Ger.) *und andere(s) mehr* (and so on) (spaces in Ger.)

UAR (hist.) United Arab Republic 1958–71

U-bend (cap., hyphen) *use* a sans serif typeface only where it is important to represent the actual configuration exactly

Übersetzung (Ger. f.) translation

ubique (Lat.) everywhere

ubi supra (Lat.) in the place (mentioned) above, abbr. **u.s.**

U-boat a German submarine (hyphen), in Ger. n. (colloq.) **U-Boot**, in full **Unterseeboot**

UC University College

u.c. (typ.) upper case, (It. mus.) una corda

UCATT Union of Construction, Allied Trades, and Technicians

UCC Universal Copyright Convention

UCCA Universities Central Council on Admissions (no apos.)

UCD University College, Dublin

UCH University College Hospital, London

UCL University College London

UCLA University of California at Los Angeles

UCS University College School

UCW Union of Communications Workers, University College of Wales

UDA Ulster Defence Association

Udaipur India; *not* Odeypore, Oodey-, Ude-

udal a freehold right based on uninterrupted possession; *not* od-; **-ler, -man** (one word)

Udall, Nicholas (1505–56) English playwright

UDC Universal Decimal Classification, (hist.) Urban District Council

UDI unilateral declaration of independence

UDR Ulster Defence Regiment

UEA University of East Anglia

UEFA Union of European Football Associations

UFC United Free Church (of Scotland)

Uffizi Gallery *and* **Palace** Florence, *not* -izzi

UFO/ unidentified flying object; pl. **-s**

ufology the study of UFOs (not cap.)

Ugand/a Africa; **-an**

UGC University Grants Committee

Ugley Essex

Ugli/ (propr.) a citrus fruit, pl. **-s** (cap.)

Ugric of or relating to a branch of the Finno-Ugric language family, *also* **Ugrian**

UHF ultra-high frequency

UHT ultra heat treated (esp. of milk, cream, etc. for keeping long)

u.i. *ut infra* (as below)

Uitlander (Afrik.) a foreigner, esp. before the Boer War

UJD *Utriusque Juris Doctor* (Doctor of Laws)

uji/ in feudal and pre-feudal Japan, a name indicating to which ancestral family the bearer belonged; a patriarchal lineage group of all those with the same *uji*; **-gami** the ancestral deity of an *uji*, or (later) a tutelary deity (one word)

UK United Kingdom

UKAEA United Kingdom Atomic Energy Authority

ukase an arbitrary command, (hist.) an edict of the tsarist Russian government; *not* oukaz; in Russ. **ukaz**

ukiyo-e a style and school of Japanese art (hyphen)

Ukrain/e E. Europe; a former republic of the USSR; abbr. **Ukr.**; *not* -ia, Little Russia, the Ukraine (which implies a region rather than a state); **-ian** (of or relating to) (a native or the language of) Ukraine

ukulele a small guitar, *not* uke-

Ulan Bator *properly* **Ulaanbaatar**; **Ulaangom**, **Ulaanhus** Mongolia

Ulan-Burgasy mountains, Russia

ulema (a member of) a body of Muslim doctors of sacred law and theology; in Arab. (pl.) ʿ**ulamā**

Ullswater Cumbria, *not* Ulles-

uln/a lower-arm bone, pl. **-ae** (not ital.)

ulotrich/an (a person) having tightly curled hair, esp. denoting a human type; also **-ous**

Ulster/ Ireland, comprises the present N. Ireland and the counties of Cavan, Donegal, and Monaghan; **-man, -woman** (one word)

ulster a coat (not cap.)

ult. *see* **ultimo**

ultima ratio/ (Lat.) the final sanction, last resource; **— — regum** resort to arms *ultima Thule* a distant unknown region (one cap., ital.)

ultimatum/ a final proposal, pl. **-s**

ultimo in, or of, the last month; better not abbr.

ultimum vale (Lat.) the last farewell

ultimus haeres (Lat., the final heir) the Crown or the State

ultra/ (Lat.) beyond, extreme; — *vires* beyond legal power

ultra-high (of frequency) (hyphen)

ultra/ist, -ism

Ultrajectum *see* **Utrecht**

ultramontane (a person) situated or living on the other side of the Alps from the point of view of the speaker, (a person) advocating supreme papal authority in matters of faith and discipline

ultramundane lying beyond the world or the solar system, *not* extremely dull

ultra/sonic, -violet (one word)

Uluru *see* **Ayers Rock**

Ulyanov *see* **Lenin**

Ulysses *see* **Odysseus**

Um/bala, -balla *use* **Ambala**

umbel/ (bot.) a flower cluster; **-lar, -late**

umble pie *use* **humble**

umbo/ the boss of a shield, pl. **-s**

umbr/a (astr.) a shadow, pl. **-ae**

UMI University Microfilms International

umiak an Inuit skin-and-wood open boat used by women, *not* oom-

UMIST University of Manchester Institute of Science and Technology

umlaut mark (¨) used over a vowel, esp. in Germanic languages to indicate a vowel change

Umritsur *use* **Amritsar**

UN United Nations; *not* UNO, Uno

'un/ colloq. for *one* (as in *good 'un, young 'un*), pl. **-s** (apos.)

UNA United Nations Association

una corda (mus.) direction in piano music to use soft pedal; cf. **tre corde**

unadvisable (of person) not open to advice; cf. **inadvisable**

un-American (hyphen, cap.)

unanim/ous, -ity (**a** *not* an)

unartistic not concerned with or appreciating art; cf. **inartistic**

una voce (Lat.) unanimously

unberufen (Ger.) *absit omen*

unbiblical (one word)

unbusinesslike (one word)

uncared-for (hyphen)

unchristian (one word, not cap.)

uncome-at-able inaccessible (two hyphens)

uncooperative (one word)

uncoordinated (one word)

UNCSTD United Nations Conference on Science and Technology for Development

UNCTAD United Nations Conference on Trade and Development

unctuous greasy (usually of manner), *not* -ious

under- (prefix) when joined to nouns, adjs., advs., and verbs, normally forms one word (*see* entries below), *but note* **under-secretary**.

under/achieve, -act (one word)

under age below an age limit (two words, hyphen when attrib.)

under/brush (US) = **undergrowth, -carriage, -clothes, -coat, -cover** (adj.), **-current, -cut, -developed, -dog, -emphasis, -emphasize** *not* -ise, **-employed, -estimate, -expose, -ground, -growth, -hand** (one word)

underlie *but* **underlying**

underline (typ.) former term for a caption to illustration, diagram, etc. (regardless of position)

under/manned, -mentioned (one word)

Under Milk Wood a radio drama by Dylan Thomas, 1954 (three words)

under/part, -pass, -privileged (one word)

underproof containing less alcohol than proof spirit does (one word); abbr. **u.p.**

underrate (one word)

under-runners (typ.) an excess of marginal notes, which are continued below the body of text, generally at foot of page (hyphen, one word in US), cf. **shoulder note**

undersea (one word)

under-secretary (caps. as title, hyphen, one word in US)

under/sell, -sexed (one word)

under-sheriff a deputy sheriff (hyphen)

undershirt (US) = **vest**

under/shrub, -side, -signed, -sized, -skirt, -staffed, -surface, -tone, -value, -water (adj.) (one word)

under way in motion (two words)

underweight (one word)

underwrite/, -r (one word)

undies (colloq.) (women's) underclothing

undine a female water-spirit

UNDRO United Nations Disaster Relief Organization

un-English (hyphen, cap.)

unequivocal not ambiguous, plain, unmistakable; *not* uni-

UNESCO United Nations Educational, Scientific, and Cultural Organization; also **Unesco**

unexception/able that cannot be faulted, **-al** not unusual

Ungarn Ger. for Hungary

unget-at-able inaccessible (two hyphens)

unguent ointment

ungul/a hoof, talon; pl. **-ae**; **-ate** hoofed, a hoofed mammal

unheard-of (hyphen)

uni/ (colloq.) university, pl. **-s**

Uni/ate (of or relating to) (a member of) any community of Christians in E. Europe or the Near East that acknowledges papal supremacy but retains its own liturgy etc., *also* **-at**; in Russ. *uniyat*; the term is resented by many of those concerned, who would rather be called Greek Catholics

UNICEF United Nations (International) Children's (Emergency) Fund, also **Unicef**

unidea'd having no ideas, *not* -aed

Unido United Nations Industrial Development Organization

uninterested not interested; cf. **disinterested**

Union/ flag the national ensign of the United Kingdom (one cap.), *see also* — **Jack**

Unionist abbr. **U.**

unionize *not* -ise (one word)

un-ionized not ionized; *not* -ised (hyphen)

Union Jack a small Union flag flown from a ship (two caps.)

Union of Soviet Socialist Republics (hist.) abbr. **USSR**

unisex (one word)

Unit. Unitarian, -ism

United Arab Emirates group of seven Emirates on Persian Gulf, namely: Abu Dhabi, Ajman, Dubai, Fujaira, Ras al Khaima, Sharja, Umm al Qaiwain; abbr. **UAE**

United Arab Republic Egypt and Syria 1958–61, Egypt alone 1961–71; abbr. **UAR**

United/ Brethren the Moravians, — **Free Church of Scotland** (caps.) abbr. **UFC**

United Kingdom (caps.) Great Britain and N. Ireland, abbr. **UK**; *see also* **Britain**

United Nations abbr. UN

United Presbyterian/ abbr. **UP**, — — **Church** (caps.) abbr. **UPC**

United Service Club (*not* Services)

United States of America abbr. (noun) **USA**, (adj.) **US**

Univ. University, (in Oxford) University College

Univers (typ.) a sans serif font, *not* a generic term for sans serif face

universal (**a** *not* an) abbr. **univ.**

Universal Copyright Convention adopted 1952, effective in USA from 1955, in UK 1957, and in USSR 1973; each of the more than 90 member states extends benefit of its own

copyright law to works by citizens of other member states; abbr. **UCC**; *see also* **Berne Convention**

universalize *not* -ise

Universal Time = **Greenwich Mean Time**, abbr. **UT**

university (colloq. **uni/**, pl. **-s**), abbr. **univ.**

University College London (no comma) abbr. **UCL**

unjustified setting (typ.) composition with a single invariable word space, giving an uneven (ragged) margin, usually on the right

Unknown Soldier an unidentified soldier representing casualties in war (caps.)

unlicensed *not* -ced

unlisted (US) of a telephone number = **ex-directory**

un/lived-in, -looked-for (hyphens)

unm. unmarried

UNO *or* **Uno** United Nations Organization, *use* **UN**

uno animo (Lat.) unanimously

unperson a person whose identity is denied or ignored (one word); cf. **non-person**

unpractical not suitable for actual conditions, *not* im-; cf. **impracticable**; **impractical**

unpractised *not* -ced (US)

unputdownable (of a book) (one word)

unreadable too dull or too difficult to be worth reading; cf. **illegible**

UNRRA United Nations Relief and Rehabilitation Administration, also **Unrra**

UNRWA United Nations Relief Works Agency, also **Unrwa**

unselfconscious (one word)

unsewn binding (bind.) = **perfect binding**

unshakeable *not* -kable

unwieldy cumbersome, *not* -ldly

UP United Presbyterian, United Press; Uttar Pradesh (*formerly* United Provinces), India

up. upper

u.p. underproof, (colloq.) all up (with someone)

up-and-/coming (colloq.) likely to succeed; **-over** (adj.) of a door; **-under** a type of high kick in League Rugby, in Rugby Union called a **garryowen** (hyphens)

Upanishad each of a series of Sanskrit philosophical compositions concluding the exposition of the Vedas

upbeat (colloq.) optimistic or cheerful (one word)

up-beat (mus.) an unaccented beat (hyphen)

up-country (hyphen)

Updike, John (**Hoyer**) (b. 1932) US author, poet, and critic

up/field, -hill (one word)

up/ish, -ity *use* **upp-**

upmarket (adj., one word)

upper case (typ.) capital letters

upper class the highest social class in society, including the aristocracy (but technically not royalty) (two words, hyphen when attrib.)

upper crust (two words, hyphen when attrib.)

uppercut (strike with) an upwards blow delivered with the arm bent

Upper House the higher house in a legislature, esp. the House of Lords (caps.)

Upper Volta *now* **Burkina Faso**

upper works the part of a ship that is above the water when fully laden

upp/ish self-assertive; **-ity** arrogant, snobbish; *not* upi-

Uppsala Sweden; in Ger. **Upsala**, Fr. **Upsal**

upright (one word)

Upsala Minn.; Ont., Canada

upside down (two words, hyphen when attrib.)

upsilon the twentieth letter of the Gr. alphabet (Y, v)

upskill/, -ed, -ing (econ.) (one word)

up/stage, -stairs (one word)

upstate (US) in, to, of, or relating to part of a state remote from its large cities, esp. the northern part, e.g. 'upstate New York' (one word)

upstream (one word)

upsy-daisy encouragement spoken to child who has fallen over, *also* **ups-a-**

uptight (colloq.) nervously tense, rigidly conventional (one word)

up to date (hyphens when attrib.)

uptown (US) (of or in) the more northerly or residential part of a town or city; (cf. **downtown**)

UPU Universal Postal Union

upwind (one word)

uraemia (med.) *not* ure- (US)

Ural-Altaic of or relating to a family of Finno-Ugric, Turkic, Mongolian, and other agglutinative languages of N. Europe and Asia; of or relating to the Ural and Altaic mountain ranges in E. Europe and Cent. Asia

Urania (Gr. myth) the muse of astronomy

uranium symbol **U**

Uranus (Gr. myth., astr.)

urari (hist.) *now* **curare**

urbanize *not* -ise

urbi et orbi (Lat.) to the city (Rome) and the world

Urdu a language related to Hindi but with many Persian words, an official language of Pakistan also used in India

urethr/a (anat.) pl. **-ae**

URI (med.) upper respiratory infection

urim and thummim in Exod. 28: 30, are plurals

Uruguay/ abbr. **Uru.**, adj. **-an**

urus *use* **aurochs**

US Under-Secretary, United Service, United States (adj.)

u.s. (Lat.) *ubi supra* (in the place (mentioned) above), *ut supra* (as above)

u/s unserviceable

USA United States of America

usable *not* -eable

USAF United States Air Force

USAFA United States Air Force Academy

USCL United Society for Christian Literature

USDAW Union of Shop, Distributive, and Allied Workers

usf. (Ger.) *und so fort* (= etc., and so on)

Ushant an island off Brittany; in Breton **Enez Eusa**, Fr. **l'île d'Ouessant**

Usher Hall Edinburgh

USI United Service Institution (*not* Services)

USIS United States Information Service

Üsküp Turkey

USN United States Navy

USPG United Society for the Propagation of the Gospel

usquebaugh (Gaelic) whisky, in Gaelic *uisge beatha*

USS United States Ship, Universities Superannuation Scheme

Ussher, James (1581–1656) Irish divine, Archbishop of Armagh

US spellings differences from British usage, such as *aluminum, maneuver,* and *pajamas,* are given under headwords in their alphabetical places

USSR (hist.) Union of Soviet Socialist Republics

usu. usual, -ly

usucaption in Roman and Scots law, acquisition of a title or right to property by uninterrupted and undisputed possession for a prescribed term; *not* -capion

usufruct/ in Roman and Scots law, the right of enjoying the use and advantages of another's property short of the destruction or waste of its substance; **-uary**

usurper *not* -or

usw. (Ger.) *und so weiter* (= etc., and so on)

UT Universal Time, Utah (postal abbr.)

Utah off. abbr. **Ut.**, postal **UT**

Utakamand *use* **Ootacamund**

Utd. United

ut dictum (Lat.) as directed, abbr. **ut dict.**

U Thant *see* **Thant, U**

UTI (med.) urinary tract infection

utilize *not* -ise

ut infra (Lat.) as below, abbr. *u.i.*

uti possidetis (Lat.) as you now possess (opposed to *status quo ante*)

utmost *not* utter-

Utopia/ an imagined perfect place or state of things, from the title of a book by Thomas More, 1516; adj. **-n** (caps.); not cap. when referring to a general concept rather than the specific work

Utrecht city and province, the Netherlands; in old imprints sometimes referred to as **Trajectum ad Rhenum** or **Ultrajectum**

UTS ultimate tensile strength

ut supra (Lat.) as above, abbr. *u.s.*

Uttar Pradesh India, *formerly* United Provinces; abbr. **UP**

U/-tube, -turn (caps., hyphens); *use* a sans serif typeface only where it is important to represent the actual configuration exactly

ut videtur (Lat.) as it seems

UU Ulster Unionist

UV ultraviolet

U/W underwriter

UWIST University of Wales Institute of Science and Technology

UWT Union of Women Teachers

uxor (Lat.) wife, abbr. *ux.*

uxor/ial of or relating to a wife; **-icide** the killing of one's wife, or a person who does this; **-ious** greatly or excessively fond of one's wife

Uzbek/ a member (or the language) of a Turkic people living mainly in **Uzbekistan**, *not* Uzbeg-

V v

V five, vanadium, (elec.) volt(s), (Ger.) *Vergeltungswaffe* (reprisal weapon: **V1** flying bomb, **V2** rocket); traditionally (and often still) not used in the numeration of series

V. Vice, Volunteers

V̆ sign for versicle

v velocity, verse, verso, versus, very, (meteor.) unusual visibility, volume (*prefer* **vol.**), (Ger.) *von* (of)

v italic 'v', in some typefaces may appear identical to Greek nu or upsilon; to avoid confusion where both are used, specify an alternative with a pointier or rounder base

v. (Lat.) *vice* (in place of), *vide* (see); (It. mus.) *violino* (violin), *voce* (voice)

VA (US) Veterans' Administration, Vicar Apostolic, vice admiral, (Order of) Victoria and Albert (for women), Virginia (postal abbr.)

Va. Virginia (off. abbr.)

va. (mus.) viola

v.a. verb active, (Lat.) *vixit ... annos* (lived (so many) years)

vaccinat/e inoculate with vaccine; **-ion, -or**

vacillat/e move from side to side, waver; **-ion, -or**; cf. **oscillate**

vacu/um pl. **-ums**, *or* **-a** in scientific and technical use

vacuum/ brake, — cleaner, — flask, — gauge (two words)

vacuum-packed (hyphen)

vacuum pump (two words)

VAD Voluntary Aid Detachment (for nursing)

vade mecum/ a handbook or other article carried on the person, pl. **-s** (two words)

vae victis! (Lat.) woe to the vanquished!

vaille que vaille (Fr.) whatever it may be worth, at all events

vainglor/y, -ious (one word)

Vaishnava (Hinduism) a devotee of Vishnu, in Skt. *vaiṣṇavá*

Vaisya (a member of) the third of the four great Hindu castes, comprising merchants and farmers; in Skt. *vaiśya*

valance a short curtain or drapery; cf. **valence; valency**

vale (arch. or poet. except in place names) a valley, e.g. 'Vale of White Horse'

vale! (Lat.) farewell!, pl. *valete!*; **vale** (noun) a farewell (not ital.)

valence (US) = **valency**, esp. as adj.; cf. **valance**

Valencia Ecuador; island, Ireland; cities, Philippines; autonomous territory, city, and gulf, Spain; N. Mex., Pa.; city and lake, Venezuela

Valenciennes a rich kind of lace (cap.)

valenc/y (chem.) the combining power of an atom, measured by the number of hydrogen atoms it can displace or combine with; pl. **-ies**; *see also* **valence**; cf. **valance**

Valentia, Viscount *not* -cia

valentine a sweetheart, a card or message sent to or received by one (not cap.)

Valentine's Day, St 14 Feb. (apos.)

Valéra, Éamon de *see* de Valéra, Éamon

valet a man's personal attendant etc. (not ital.)

valeta *use* **vel-**

Valetta *use* **Vall-**

valgus a deformity involving the outward displacement of the foot or hand from the midline; cf. **varus**

Valhalla (Norse myth.) the palace in which souls of dead heroes feasted, in Old Norse **Valhǫll**; *not* W-; *see also* **Hel**

valise a kitbag, (US) a small portmanteau

Valkyrie/ (Norse myth.) each of Odin's twelve handmaidens, pl. **-s**; (the opera *The Valkyrie* refers to a single handmaiden); in Norse *Valkyrja*, pl. *Valkyrjur*; in Ger. f. *Walküre*, pl. *Walküren*

Valladolid Spain

Valletta Malta; *not* Vale-, -eta

valley/ pl. **-s**

Vallombrosa N. Italy, *not* Vallam-

valorize artificially raise or fix a price, *not* -ise

valour *not* -or (US), *but* **valorous**

Valparaiso Ind.

Valparaíso Chile

valse waltz (not ital.); *valse/ à deux temps*, **— à trois temps** (Fr.) variations of the waltz (ital., no hyphens)

valuate (esp. US) estimate the worth of a thing, esp. by a professional

value added tax (three words, no hyphen) abbr. **VAT**

valuta (econ.) the value of one currency with respect to another, a currency considered in this way

van, van den, van der in Du. prefixes to proper names, usually not initial cap. except at beginning of a sentence, and alphabetized under the main name; in Fl. may be cap. V, and alphabetized under V; in Afrik. may be either; in UK and US alphabetize under V

vanadium symbol V

Van Allen/ belt *or* **layer** of radiation surrounding the earth, named after **James Alfred — —** (b. 1914), US physicist

Vanbrugh, Sir John (1664–1726) English architect and playwright

Van Buren, Martin (1782–1862) US President 1837–41

Vancouver system a reference system in which each bibliographical source is assigned a number, which is then used to cite that source in text

V&A Victoria and Albert Museum (no points)

Vandal (a member) of, *or* relating to, a Germanic people of 4th–5th cc. (cap.); a wilful destroyer of art or property (not cap.)

vandalize *not* -ise

van de Graaff/, Robert Jemison (1901–67) US physicist; — — — **accelerator,** — — — **generator**

Vanderbilt/, Cornelius (1794–1877) US businessman and philanthropist, founded — **University** Nashville, Tenn.

Van der Hum a South African liqueur

Van der Post, Sir Laurens (**Jan**) (1906–96) South African explorer, writer, and conservationist

van der Rohe *see* **Mies van der Rohe**

van der Waals/, Johannes (1837–1923) Dutch physicist; — — — **forces,** — — — **equation**

van de Velde *see* **Velde, van de**

Van Diemen's Land *not* Dieman's (apos.), *now* **Tasmania**

Van Dijck, Christoffel *see* **Dijck**

V&V verification and validation (to be set close up)

Van Dyck, Sir Anthony (1599–1641) Flemish painter (two words); Anglicized form **Vandyke/** (one word) used to denote a work by him, and in — **beard,** — **brown**; **vandyke** each of a series of points bordering lace etc. (not cap.)

Vane-Tempest-Stewart family name of the Marquess of Londonderry (hyphens)

Van Eyck,/ Hubert (1366–1426) and — — **Jan** (1385–1440) his brother, Flemish painters

Van Gogh, Vincent *see* **Gogh, Vincent Van**

Vanhomrigh, Esther (1692–1723) Swift's 'Vanessa'

Van Nostrand Reinhold publishers

van 't Hoff, Jacobus Hendricus *see* **Hoff**

Vanuatu SW Pacific, *formerly* New Hebrides

Van Vleck/, John Hasbrouck (1899–1980) US physicist (cap. *V*); — — **paramagnetism**

vaporiz/e *not* -ise, **-er** *not* -or

vapour *not* -or (US); *but* **vapor/ific, -iform, -imeter, -ish, -ous**

Var a river and dép. of France

var. (biol.) variety

Varanasi *see* **Benares**

Varèse, Edgar(d) (1883–1965) French-born US composer

Vargas/ (y Chávez), (Joaquín) Alberto (1896–1982) Peruvian-born US surrealist

painter who worked under the name **Varga**; —, **Getúlio Dornelles** (1883–1954) President of Brazil 1930–45, 1951–4; — **Llosa, (Jorge) Mario (Pedro)** (b. 1936) Peruvian novelist, dramatist, and essayist

variables (math.) normally to be set in italics

vari/a lectio (Lat.) a variant reading, abbr. **v.l.**; pl. ***-ae lectiones*** abbr. **vv.ll.**

variety (biol.) abbr. **var.**

variorum (of an edition of a text) having notes by various editors or commentators, (of an edition of an author's works) including variant readings

variorum notae (Lat.) notes by commentators

Varna Bulgaria, *formerly* Stalin

varna each of the four main Hindu castes, in Hind. *varṇa*

varus a deformity involving the inward displacement of the foot or hand from the midline; cf. **valgus**

vas/ (anat.) a duct, pl. **-a**

vascul/um a botanist's specimen case, pl. **-a**

vas deferens the spermatic duct, pl. **vasa deferentia**

vasectomy the excision of vas deferens

Vaseline (propr.) a type of petroleum jelly (cap.)

vassal (hist.) a holder of land by feudal tenure on conditions of homage and allegiance

Vassar College Poughkeepsie, NY

VAT/ value added tax, **-man** a customs and excise officer who administers VAT (one word)

Vatican/ the palace and official residence of the Pope in Rome; — **City** the independent Papal State in Rome, instituted in 1929; — **Council** an ecumenical council of the Roman Catholic Church; abbr. **Vat.**

Vaudois (of or relating to) a native of Vaud in W. Switzerland, or its French dialect; *see also* **Waldenses**

Vaughan Williams, Ralph (1872–1958) English composer

Vauvenargues, Luc de Clapiers, marquis de (1715–47) French writer

v. aux. verb auxiliary

Vaux of Harrowden, Baron

vb. verb

VC vice-chairman, vice-chancellor, vice-consul, Victoria Cross

VCH Victoria County History

v. Chr. (Ger.) *vor Christo* or *vor Christi Geburt*, BC

VCR video cassette recorder, (US) the machine colloq. called **video** in the UK

VD venereal disease, Volunteer (Officers') Decoration

v.d. various dates

v. dep. verb deponent

VDH valvular disease of the heart

VDU (comput.) visual display unit

VE/ victory in Europe; — **Day** 8 May 1945; *not* V-E (US)

v**e** (Fr.) *veuve* (widow), *cinquième*

veau (Fr. m.) calf, (cook.) veal; (bind.) calf, calf-skin

VEB (hist.) *Volkseigener Betrieb* (state-owned company) (GDR)

Veblen, Thorstein (Bunde) (1857–1929) US economist

vectors (math.) to be set in bold

Ved/a (sing. and pl.) the most ancient Hindu scriptures, esp. the four collections called *Rig Veda, Sama Veda, Yajur Veda*, and *Atharva Veda* (caps.; one word, one cap. in specialist contexts); adj. -ic

Vedanta the Upanishads, or the Hindu philosophy based on these, esp. in its monistic form

Vedda (of or relating to) an aboriginal of Sri Lanka

vedette a mounted sentinel, patrol boat; *not* vi-

veg (colloq.) vegetable(s) (no point)

Vega, Garcilaso de la *see* **Garcilaso**

Vega Carpio, Lope Félix de known as **Lope de Vega** (1562–1635) Spanish playwright and poet

Vehmgericht (not ital.), adj. **Vehmic**; *see* **Fehmgericht**

veille (Fr. f.) the day before, eve; cf. *vieille*; **vielle**

Velázquez, Diego Rodríguez de Silva y (1599–1660) Spanish painter, *not* Velas-

Velcro (propr.)

veld (Afrik.) open country, *not* -dt

Velde,/ Willem van de (the Elder) (1611–93) Dutch marine painter; father of — **Willem van de (the Younger)** (1633–1707) Dutch marine painter; brother of — **Adriaen van de** (1636–72) Dutch landscape and portrait painter; — **Henri (Clemens) van de** (1863–1957) Belgian architect, designer, and teacher

veleta a dance in triple time, *not* val-

Velikovsky, Immanuel (1895–1979) Russian-born writer on astronomy

vellum/ fine parchment, — **paper** that imitating vellum

veloce (mus.) quickly

velocity (mech.) symbol **v** (ital.)

velour a plushlike fabric, *not* -ours

velouté (cook.) a sauce of white stock mixed with cooked butter and flour (not ital.)

vel/ simile (Lat.) or the like; pl. — *similia* abbr. **vel sim.**

vel/um a membrane, pl. -a

velveteen a velvet-like cotton fabric

velvety *not* -tty

Ven. Venerable (used for archdeacons only)

ven/a cava (med.) each of the veins carrying blood to heart, pl. -ae cavae

venal/ (of person) bribable, (of conduct) sordid; -ity, -ly; cf. **venial**

venation the arrangement of veins in a leaf

Vendée, La a dép. of France; adj. **Vendean** of the royalist party 1793–5, specifically of a royalist and Catholic rebellion supressed with great brutality

vendee the person to whom one sells

vendetta/ a blood feud, pl. -s (not ital.)

vendeuse (Fr. f.) saleswoman

vendible that may be sold, *not* -able

Vendôme/ dép. Loir-et-Cher, France; **Colonne** —, and **Place** — (l.c. *p* in Fr.), Paris

vendor a seller, *not* -er

vendue (US) a public auction

venepuncture (med.) a puncture of a vein, *not* veni-

venerat/e, -or

venere/al, -ology

venery (arch.) hunting, sexual indulgence; *not* -ary

venesection phlebotomy, *not* veni-

Venet. Venetian

venetian blind (not cap.)

Venetian/ glass, — red, — window (one cap.)

Venezuela abbr. **Venez.**

venial (of sin) pardonable; cf. **venal**

Venice Italy; in It. **Venezia**, Fr. **Venise**, Ger. **Venedig**

Venn diagram a set of circles representing the relation of logical categories (one cap.)

venose having prominent veins

ven/ous of the veins, -osity; *not* vein-

ventilat/e, -or

ventre à terre (Fr.) at full speed, lit. 'belly to the ground'

ventriloquize *not* -ise

Venus de Milo the Melian Aphrodite, in Fr. f. *Vénus de Milo*

Venus flytrap an insect-eating plant (two words); in US, **Venus's-flytrap** (apos., hyphen)

Venus's/ comb shepherd's needle (a plant), — **looking glass** any of various plants of the genus *Legousia*, — **girdle** a ribbon-like jellyfish, — **slipper** lady's slipper (a plant) (one cap.); *not* Venus'

ver (Du. name prefix) combined form of **van der**, usually cap. and run in: as Vermeer; *see also* **van, van den, van der**

veranda *not* -ah

verb abbr. **vb.**

verb. (Ger.) *verbessert* (improved, revised)

verbal of or concerned with words; (gram.) of, or in the nature of, a verb; literal

verbalize put into words, *not* -ise

verbatim (Lat.) word for word (not ital.)

verboten (Ger.) forbidden

verbum satis sapienti (Lat.) a word to the wise suffices, abbr. **verb. sap.**

verd-antique an ornamental marble, *not* verde- (hyphen)

verderer a judicial officer of royal forests, *not* -or

verdigris green rust on copper, *not* verde-

Verein (Ger. m.) Association (cap.)

Vereinigte Staaten/ (Ger. f.) United States (of America), *but* **die Vereinigten Staaten**

Vereshchagin, Vasili (Vasilevich) (1842–1904) Russian painter

Verey/ light, — pistol *use* **Very**

Verfasser/ (Ger. m.) author (of a specific work), f. *-in*; abbr. **Verf.**; cf. *Dichter*, *Schriftsteller*

verger an attendant in a church; *see also* **vir-**

Vergil, Polydore (1470–1555) Italian humanist and historian

Vergilius Maro, Publius (70–19 BC) Roman poet; trad. Anglicized as **Virgil**, in modern classical contexts as **Vergil**; *see also* **Virgilius Maro**

verglas a thin layer of ice or sleet (not ital.)

vergleiche (Ger.) compare, abbr. **vgl.**

verism/ realism in literature or art, pl. **-s**; **-o** realism, esp. in opera (not ital.)

verkrampte (Afrik.) (a person who is) politically or socially conservative or reactionary

Verlag (Ger. m.) publishing house

verligte (Afrik.) (a person who is) progressive or enlightened

vermilion *not* -llion

Vermillion Kan., S. Dak.

Vermont off. abbr. **Vt.**, postal **VT**

vermouth an aperitif wine flavoured with aromatic herbs (not cap.)

vernal of, in, *or* appropriate to, spring

Verner's law (phonetics) relating to voicing of fricatives in Germanic languages (one cap.)

Veronese, Paolo (1528–88) Italian painter, real surname **Cagliari**

Verrazano-Narrows Bridge New York City (hyphen)

Verrocchio, Andrea del (1435–88) Italian painter and sculptor, *not* the many variants

verruc/a a wart or similar growth, pl. **-ae**

Versailles near Paris

vers de société (Fr. m.) society verses

verse abbr. **v., ver.**; pl. **vv.** *but* avoid confusion with lower-case roman numerals

versicle a short verse in liturgy said or sung by minister, followed by the people's (or choir's) response; (typ.) the sign ℣ used in liturgical works; *see also* ℟ (response)

vers libre (Fr. m.) free verse

verso/ (typ.) the left-hand page, opp. of **recto**; abbr. **v**, **v.** (not ital.); pl. **-s**

verst a Russian measure of length, about 1.1 km (0.66 mile); in Russ. **versta**

versus against (not ital.); abbr. **v., vs.** (esp. in sport); in law often in opposite font

vert. vertical

vertebr/a a segment of the backbone, pl. **-ae** (not ital.)

vertebrate an animal with a spinal column, of the subphylum Vertebrata (*or* Craniata)

vert/ex the highest point, angular point of triangle etc.; pl. **-ices**

vertical abbr. **vert.**

vertig/o giddiness, pl. **-os**; **-inous**

vertu *use* **virtu**

Vertue, George (1684–1756) English engraver

verve spirit (not ital.)

vervet a small African monkey

Verwoerd, Hendrik Frensch (1901–66) Dutch-born Prime Minister of the Republic of South Africa 1958–66

Very Large Array astronomic apparatus, New Mex.; abbr. **VLA**

Very/ light a flare fired from a — **pistol**, *not* Verey

Very Revd Very Reverend (for deans, provosts, and former moderators)

vesica piscis (art) a pointed oval used as an aureole in medieval sculpture and painting, *not* mandorla (not ital.)

Vespucci, Amerigo (1454–1512) Italian navigator

vest an undergarment worn on the upper part of the body, (US, Austral.) = **waistcoat**

vestigia (Lat. pl.) traces

vet/ (colloq.) veterinary surgeon (no point); examine carefully; **-ted, -ting**; (US colloq.) a veteran

veterinarian (US) a veterinary surgeon

veto/ a ban, pl. **-es**

veuf (Fr. m.) widower

veuve (Fr. f.) widow; abbr. **v**ᵉ, **Vve**

Veuve Clicquot a champagne

Vevey Switzerland, *not* -ay

vexata quaestio (Lat.) a disputed question

vexillology the study of flags (three ls)

vexill/um an ancient Roman military standard, esp. of a maniple; pl. **-a** (not ital.)

v.f. very fair

VG Vicar General

v.g. very good

vgl. (Ger. for cf.) *vergleiche* (compare)

VHF very high frequency (no points)

VHS video home system (no points)

v.i. verb intransitive

v.i. (Lat.) *vide infra* (see below)

via by way of, *not* -â (not ital.)

vial (Brit. poet. and US) = **phial**

via media (Lat.) a middle course (ital.)

Viaud *see* **Loti**

vibrato/ (mus.) rapid variation of pitch, pl. **-s**

vibrator *not* -er

Vic. vicar, -age; Victoria

vicar/, -ial

Vicar/ Apostolic abbr. **VA**, — **General** abbr. **VG**

Vicar's College a cathedral residence

vice a tool, *not* vise (US)

vice/ abbr. **V.**; — **admiral** abbr. **VA** (two words, caps. as title); **-chairman, -chairperson, -chairwoman** abbr. **VC**; **-chamberlain; -chancellor, -consul** abbr. **VC** (hyphens, caps. as titles)

vice in place of (ital.)

vice-president abbr. **VP** (hyphen, two words in US, caps. as title)

viceregent (cap. as title) (one word, hyphen in US)

vicereine a female viceroy or a viceroy's wife (cap. as title)

viceroy (cap. as title), adj. **viceregal**

vice versa the order being reversed, *not* visa (no hyphen or accent, not ital.); abbr. **v.v.**

vichyssoise a chilled soup of leeks and potatoes

Vichy water (one cap.)

vicomt/e (Fr.) Viscount, f. *-esse* (not cap., not ital. as part of name)

victimize *not* -ise

Victoria/ abbr. **Vic.**; — **and Albert, Order of** for women, abbr. **VA**; — **Cross** abbr. **VC**; — **Nyanza** *use* **Lake Victoria**

victoria a type of carriage, a S. American water lily, a pigeon, a large plum (not cap.)

Victoria County History abbr. **VCH**

victor ludorum the overall champion in a sports competition (not ital.)

victual/, -led, -ler, -ling (one *l* in US)

vicuña a llama-like S. American mammal, the cloth made from its wool or an imitation of it

vide (Fr. mus.) open (of strings)

vide/ (Lat.) see, consult (a reference or passage in a text etc.); abbr. **v.**; — *ante* see above; — *infra* see below, abbr. **v.i.**

videlicet (Lat.) namely (one word), abbr. *viz.*

video/ pl. **-s**; (colloq. for) — **cassette** (two words), — **cassette recorder** abbr. **VCR**

videodisc (one word); *see also* **disc**

video/ game, — nasty (two words)

videophone (one word)

VideoPlus (propr.) (one word, two caps.)

video recorder (two words)

video/tape, -tex (one word)

vide/ post see below; — *supra* see above, abbr. *v.s.*

vidette *use* **ve-**

videtur (Lat.) it seems

vide ut supra (Lat.) see as above

vidimus (Lat. 'we have seen') a certified copy of accounts etc. (not ital.)

vie compete, rival; **vying**

vieille (Fr. f.) an old woman; cf. *veille*

vielle a hurdy-gurdy; cf. *veille*

Vienn/a in Ger. **Wien**, in Fr. **-e**; adj. **-ese**; in classical and scholarly Latin **Vindobona**

Vienne dép. Isère, France; also a river, tributary of River Loire; *see also* **Haute-Vienne**

viennoise, à la (Fr.) in Viennese style (not cap.)

vient de paraître (Fr.) just published

Vientiane Laos

Vierkleur (Afrik.) the flag of the former Transvaal Republic

vi et armis (Lat.) by force and arms

Vietcong a former guerrilla force in S. Vietnam

Vietnam/ SE Asia, divided into N. and S. Vietnam 1954–79; **-ese**

vieux jeu (adj., noun; Fr. m.) (an) outworn, hackneyed (subject)

view/data, -finder, -graph (one word)

view halloo (hunting) a shout on seeing a fox break cover, *not* the many variants

viewpoint (one word)

vif (Fr. mus.) lively, briskly

vigesimo (typ.) *use* **twentymo**

vigesimo-quarto (typ.) *use* **twenty-fourmo**

vigilante/ a member of a vigilance body, pl. **-s** (not ital.)

vignettes (typ.) illustrations with undefined edges

vigoro (Austral.) a team ball game combining elements of cricket and baseball

vigour *not* -or (US), *but* **vigorous**

vihara a Buddhist temple or monastery

Viking (of or relating to) any of the Scandinavian seafaring pirates and traders in the 8th–11th cc.

vilayet a Turkish province, abbr. **vila.**

vilif/y disparage, *not* vill-; **-ied, -ier, -ying**

village abbr. **vil.**

villain/ an evildoer, (colloq.) a rascal; **-ous, -y**; cf. **villein**

Villa-Lobos, Heitor (1887–1959) Brazilian composer

villanell/a a rustic Neapolitan part song, pl. **-e**

villanelle a usually pastoral or lyrical poem of nineteen lines, with only two rhymes throughout, and some lines repeated

Villa-Villa (propr.) a kind of Havana cigar (hyphen)

villeggiatura (It. f.) a country holiday

villégiature (Fr. f.) a country holiday

villein/ a serf, **-age**; cf. **villain**

Villiers/ family name of the Earls of Clarendon and Jersey; **— de l'Isle Adam, Jean Marie Mathias Philippe Auguste, comte de** (1838–89) French writer

Vilnius Lithuania

vinaigrette a salad dressing, an ornamental smelling-bottle; *not* vineg(a)r-

Vinci,/ Leonardo (1690–1730) Italian composer, **— Leonardo da** see **Leonardo**

vin de/ pays (Fr. m.) country wine, **— —** *table* table wine; *not du*

vineg(a)rette *use* **vinaigrette**

vineyard *not* vinyard

vingt-et-un (Fr. m.) a card game, pontoon

vin ordinaire (Fr. m.) cheap (usually red) wine as drunk in France mixed with water, now called *vin de table*

vintager a grape gatherer

vintner a wine merchant, *not* -ter

viola/ **da braccio** a Renaissance term for any member of the violin family played 'on the arm', but now pertaining to an instrument similar to the viola; **— da gamba** any viol held between the player's legs, esp. the bass viol; **— d'amore** a sweet-toned 18th-c. bowed instrument like a modern viola (not ital.)

viol/ate, -able, -ator *not* -er

violencia (Sp.) in Colombia, the decade of violent political conflict 1948–58

violino (It.) violin, abbr. *v.*

Viollet-le-duc, Eugène Emmanuel (1814–79) French architect

violoncell/o *not* violin-; pl. **-os**; usually shortened to **cello** (no apos.); **-ist**

VIP very important person

virago/ a termagant, pl. **-s**

Virchow, Rudolf (1821–1902) German pathologist

virelay a short (esp. Old Fr.) lyric poem

virger the spelling of **verger** traditional at certain cathedrals, such as St Paul's and Winchester

Virgil see **Vergilius**

Virgilius Maro (7th c.) Irish-born grammarian

Virginia/ off. abbr. **Va.**, postal **VA**; **— creeper** (bot.) *not* -ian

virginibus puerisque (Lat.) for girls and boys; (with two caps) book by R. L. Stevenson, 1881

virg/o intacta (a) virgin with hymen intact, pl. **-ines intactae** (not ital.)

virgule (typ.) a solidus, stroke

virgule (Fr. typ. f.) comma

virtu/ the knowledge of or expertise in fine arts, virtuosity; in It. *virtù*; **article of** — an artistic article of interesting workmanship, antiquity, or rarity; *not* ve-, -ue (not ital.)

virtuos/o one skilled in an art, pl. **-i**

virus/ a submicroscopic infective agent, pl. **-es**

Vis. Viscount

vis (Lat. f.) force, pl. *vires*

visa/ a permit or endorsement on a passport (not ital.), pl. **-s**; as verb **-ed** *not* -'d

vis a tergo force from behind

vis-à-vis (Fr.) face to face, as regards, compared to; (US) a social partner (hyphens, not ital.)

visc/era (pl.) interior organs, esp. in the abdomen; sing. **-us**

viscount/, -ess a British nobleman or -woman ranking between an earl and a baron (cap. as title), abbr. **Vis.**

viscount/cy, -ship the rank or jurisdiction of a viscount; **-y** only in hist. use

viscous sticky

vise (US) a tool = **vice**

Vishnu a Hindu god, in Skt. *Viṣṇu*

visier *use* viz-

Visigoth a member of the branch of the Goths who settled in France and Spain in the 5th c., and ruled much of Spain until 711

vis inertiae (Lat.) force of inanimate matter

visit/, -ed, -ing

visiting nurse (US) = **district nurse**

visitor/ *not* -er, **—s' book** *not* -or's

vis/ *major* superior force, **— *medicatrix naturae*** nature's power of healing

visor part of a helmet, the peak of a cap, the sun shield in a car, (hist.) a mask, etc.; *not* viz-

vista/ a view, pl. **-s**

visualize *not* -ise

vis viva (Lat.) living force

vitalize *not* -ise

vitell/us the yolk of an egg, pl. **-i**

vitiat/e impair the quality or efficiency of, make invalid or ineffectual; **-or**

viticulture the culture of vines

Vitoria Spain; battle, 1813

vitriol,/ **oil of** sulphuric acid, **— blue** copper sulphate, **— green** ferrous sulphate, **— white** zinc sulphate

vituperat/e revile, **-or**

viva/ short for **viva voce**, pl. **-s**; as verb **-ed** *not* -'d (not ital.)

viva! (It.) long live!, *also* ***evviva!***

vivace (mus.) lively, quickly

vivandi/er (Fr.) f. **-ère** army sutler

vivant rex et regina! (Lat.) long live the King and Queen!

vivari/um an enclosure for living things, pl. **-a**

vivat/ regina! (Lat.) long live the Queen! — ***rex!*** long live the King!

viva/ voce orally, *not* vivâ; (noun) an oral examination, pl. **— voces**; (with hyphen) verb (not ital.); *see also* **viva**

vive/! (Fr.) long live! — ***la bagatelle!*** long live trifles! — ***la différence!*** long live the difference! (usually between the sexes), — ***la République!*** long live the Republic!

vivisect/, -ion, -or

vixit . . . annos (Lat.) lived (so many) years, abbr. **v.a.**

viz. *videlicet* (namely) (not ital., comma before), *but use* **namely**

vizier (hist.) a high official in some Muslim countries, esp. in Turkey under Ottoman rule; *not* -ir, -sier

vizor *use* **vis-**

VJ/ victory over Japan; **— Day** 15 Aug. 1945; in USA 2 Sept. 1945; *not* V-J (US)

v.l. *varia lectio* (a variant reading)

Vlaanderen Fl. for **Flanders**

Vlach Bulgarian for **Wallachian**

Vlaminck, Maurice de (1876–1958) French painter

vlei (S. Afr.) a hollow in which water collects during the rainy season (not ital.)

VLF very low frequency (no points)

Vlissingen Du. for **Flushing**

Vltava a Czech river, in Ger. **Moldau**

v. M. (Ger.) *vorigen Monats* (last month)

VMH Victoria Medal of Honour

v.n. verb neuter

V-neck (cap., hyphen)

VO Veterinary Officer, Royal Victorian Order

voc. vocative

vocab. vocabulary

vocalize *not* -ise (except when noun as mus. term, *but not* in US)

vocative abbr. **voc.**

voce (It. mus.) voice, abbr. **v.**

Vogüé, Eugène Melchior, vicomte de (1848–1910) French essayist

vogue la galère! (Fr.) happen what may!

voice box (two words)

voicemail (one word, two in US)

voice-over narration without picture of speaker (hyphen)

voiceprint (one word)

***voilà*/** (Fr.) see there! **— tout** that is all

voile a thin semi-transparent dress material (not ital.)

vol. volume

Volapük an artificial international language, invented by J. M. Schleyer, 1879

volatilize *not* -ise

vol-au-vent (Fr. cook. m.) a filled puff pastry case (not ital.)

volcano/ pl. **-es**; **-logy** (US) = **vulcanology**

volet a panel or wing of a triptych

Volgograd Russia, *formerly* **Tsaritsyn**, *later* **Stalingrad**

Völkerwanderung (Ger. f.) the 2nd–11th-c. migration of Germanic and Slavic peoples into Europe

Volksausgabe (Ger. f.) popular edition

***Volkslied*/** (Ger. n.) folk song, pl. **-er** (cap.)

Volkswagen a German make of car, abbr. **VW**

vols. volumes

volt/ (fencing) make a volte; (elec.) abbr. **V**, SI unit of potential difference; **-ampere** (hyphen)

Voltairean *not* -ian

volte (fencing) a quick movement to escape a thrust, (equestrian) a sideways circular movement of a horse; *not* volt

volte-face a turning about (not ital.)

volti subito (It. mus.) turn over quickly, abbr. **v.s.**

voltmeter a device for measuring electric potential in volts, *not* volta-

volume abbr. **vol.**, pl. **vols.**

voluntarism the doctrine of the financial independence of the Church; (philos.) belief in dominance of will; belief in importance of voluntary action; *not* -aryism

Volunteer(s) abbr. **V.**

vom *see* **von**

von/ as Ger. prefix to a proper name, usually not cap. except at the beginning of a sentence, omitted when surname stands alone, and ignored during alphabetization, *but* cap. in some Swiss names; **— dem**, **— den**, **— der**, and **vom** are also not cap. *but* are retained when the surname stands alone, and form the basis for alphabetization

von Neumann, John (b. **Johann**) (1903–57) Hungarian-born US computer scientist and mathematician, usually alphabetized thus

voodoo the use of, or belief in, religious witchcraft as practised esp. in the W. Indies; *not* voudou, vodu, vudu

voortrekker (Afrik.) pioneer

vor/ Christi Geburt, — Christo (Ger.) BC, abbr. **v. Chr.**

vort/ex a whirlpool, whirling mass, engrossing system; pl. **-exes** (*but* **-ices** in scientific and technical use)

vorticist (art) a painter, writer, etc., of a school influenced by Futurism (often cap.); (metaphysics) a person regarding the universe as a plenum in which motion propagates itself in circles

votable *not* -eable

vouch/er a coupon, one who vouches; in law **-or**

voussoir (archit.) a wedge-shaped or tapered stone forming an arch (not ital.)

vowelize *not* -ise

vox/ (Lat. f.) voice, pl. *voces*; — *angelica* an organ stop with a soft, tremulous tone; — *et praeterea nihil* voice and nothing else; — *humana* an organ stop with a voice-like tone; — *populi* public sentiment, colloq. abbr. **vox pop** (no point, not ital.)

voyager one making a voyage

voyageur a Canadian boatman, esp. (hist.) one employed in transporting goods and passengers between trading posts (not ital.)

voyeur one who spies on sexual activity (not ital.)

voyez! (Fr.) see! look!

VP vice-president

VR variant reading, Victoria Regina (Queen Victoria), Volunteer Reserve

vraisemblance the appearance of truth (not ital.)

Vratislavia/ Latin for **Breslau/Wrocław**; locative (used in place-dates) **-e**; *not* to be Anglicized as Bratislava

VRD Royal Air Force Volunteer Reserve Officers' Decoration, Royal Naval Volunteer Reserve Officers' Decoration

v. refl. verb reflexive

VRI Victoria Regina et Imperatrix (Victoria Queen and Empress)

VS Veterinary Surgeon

vs. versus

v.s. (Lat.) *vide supra* (see above), (It. mus.) *volti subito* (turn over quickly)

V-sign (cap., hyphen, two words in US)

VSO Voluntary Service Overseas

VSOP very special old pale (brandy)

VT Vermont (postal abbr.)

Vt. Vermont (off. abbr.)

v.t. verb transitive

VTOL vertical take-off and landing

vudu *use* **voodoo**

Vuillard, Jean Édouard (1868–1940) French painter

Vuillaume, Jean Baptiste (1798–1875) most important of French family of makers of bowed instruments

vulcan/ize treat rubber with sulphur at high temperature, *not* -ise; **-ology** the study of volcanoes, *not* vo- (except in US)

vulg. vulgar, -ly

vulgarize *not* -ise

Vulgate the Latin version of the Bible prepared mainly by St Jerome in the late 4th c., the official RC Latin text as revised in 1592; abbr. **Vulg.**; the accepted text of an author (not cap.)

vulgo (Lat.) commonly

vv. verses, volumes (*prefer* **vols.**), (mus.) first and second violins

v.v. vice versa

Vve (Fr.) Veuve (widow)

vv.ll. (Lat.) *variae lectiones* (variant readings)

VW Very Worshipful, Volkswagen

v.y. (bibliog.) various years

Vyborg Russia

Východočeský a region of the Czech Republic

Východoslovenský a region of Slovakia

vying *see* **vie**

Vyrnwy a lake and river, Powys

W w

W watt, -s; wolfram (tungsten); traditionally (and often still) not used in the numeration of series

W. Wales, warden, Wednesday, Welsh; west, -ern

w week, -s; (cricket) wicket, wide, wife

w. war, (meteor.) wet dew, width, word, work

WA Washington State (postal abbr.), Western Australia

WAAC (hist.) Women's Army Auxiliary Corps; in Britain, 1917–19; in USA, 1942–8

WAAF Women's Auxiliary Air Force, 1939–48; *earlier and later* **WRAF**

wabbl/e, -y *use* **wo-**

WAC (US) Women's Army Corps

waddy an Australian war-club

wad/e, -able *not* -eable

Wade–Giles (en rule, for Sir Thomas Wade and Herbert Giles) a system of transcribing Chinese sounds into Latin alphabet

wadi/ (Arab.) the dry bed of a torrent, *not* -y; pl. **-s**; in Arab. *wādī*

w.a.f. with all faults

waffle (indulge in) verbose but ignorant talk or writing; (esp. US) avoid committing oneself, prevaricate

W. Afr. West Africa

wag/ a joker; **-gery, -gish**

Wagadugu Burkina Faso, *use* **Ouagadougou**

wage earner (two words)

wagon/, -er, -ette *not* wagg-

wagon/ (Fr. m.) a railway carriage; **wagon-lit** a sleeping car, pl. **wagons-lits** (hyphen, not ital. in Eng. usage)

wagtail a bird (one word)

Wahabi a sect of Muslim puritans formed by **Muhammad ibn ʿAbd-al-Wahhab** (1691–1787), following strictly the original words of the Koran; *not* -bees; *properly* **Wahh-**

Wahrheit, Dichtung und (Ger.) ('fiction and truth') by Goethe, 1811–33

wah-wah (mus.) a fluctuating muted effect achieved on brass and electric instruments, *not* wa-wa

Waiapu, Bishop of New Zealand

Wai-hai-wei *use* **Weihaiwei** (one word)

Waikiki Beach Hawaii

Wain, John (**Barrington**) (1925–94) British poet, critic, and novelist

Wainfleet Lincs.

wainscot/ panelled woodwork on an interior wall; **-ed, -ing**

waist/band, -belt, -coat, -line (one word)

waiting/ list, — room (two words)

wake past **woke**, past part. **woken**

Wakefield: the signature of the Bishop of Wakefield (colon)

Wakley, Thomas (1795–1862) English doctor, founded the *Lancet* in 1823; *see also* **Walkley**

Wal. Walloon

Walachia/, -n *use* **Walla-**

Waldenses a much persecuted puritan religious sect, founded *c.*1170; *not* Vaudois

Waldteufel, Émile (1837–1912) French composer

wale *use* **weal**

wale knot (two words) *not* wall-

Waler a horse from New South Wales

Wal/es abbr. **W.**, **-ian** *not* -ean

Wałęsa, Lech (b. 1943) Polish trade union leader, President of Poland 1990–

Walhalla *use* **V-**, in Old Norse *use* **Valhǫll**

walkabout (one word)

walkathon (one word)

walkie-talkie a two-way portable radio, *not* -y -y

walking/ frame, — stick, — tour (two words)

Walkley, Arthur Bingham (1855–1926) English drama critic; *see also* **Wakley**

Walk/man (propr.) a type of compact portable personal stereo equipment, pl. **-mans**

walkover an easy victory (one word), abbr. **w.o.**

Walküre, Die the second part of Wagner's *Ring des Nibelungen*, 1870

walkway (one word)

Walkyrie *use* **V-**

walla *use* **wallah**

wallaby a variety of small kangaroo, *not* the many variants

Wallace,/ Alfred Russel *not* -ell (1823–1913) English naturalist; **— Sir Donald Mackenzie** (1841–1919) English writer; **— George Corley** (b. 1919) US politician; **— Henry Agard** (1888–1965) US politician; **— Lewis ('Lew')** (1827–1905) US general and author; **— Sir Richard** (1818–90) English art collector and philanthropist (Wallace Collection, London); **— Prof. Robert** (1853–1939) Scottish agricultural writer; **— Sir William** (1272–1305) Scottish hero; **— William Vincent** (1812–65) Irish composer; *see also* **Wallas**; **Wallis**

Wallachia/ a former principality, *now* part of Romania; **-n** of or concerning Wallachia or a native of Wallachia, one of a non-Slav people of SE Europe; *not* Wala-

wallah (Anglo-Ind., *now* sl.) a man (usually in some specified connection)

Wallas, Graham (1858–1932) English socialist writer; *see also* **Wallace**; **Wallis**

wall eye(**d**) (two words, one in US)

wallflower (one word)

Wall Game, the a form of football played at Eton (two caps.)

Wallis,/ Sir Barnes (1887–1979) British inventor; — **George Harry** (1847–1936) English art writer; — **John** (1616–1703) English mathematician, a founder of the Royal Society; *see also* **Wallace**; **Wallas**

wall knot *use* wale-

Walloon a member of a French-speaking people inhabiting S. and E. Belgium and neighbouring N. France (cf. **Fleming**); the French dialect spoken by this people; abbr. **Wal.**

Wallop family name of the Earl of Portsmouth

wall painting (two words)

wallpaper (one word)

Wall Street New York City

Walpurgis night the eve of 1 May, when witches are alleged to meet and hold revels with the Devil; in Ger. f. *Walpurgisnacht*

Walton, Izaak *not* Isaac (1593–1683) English author of *The Compleat Angler*

waltz a dance (not ital.), in Fr. f. *valse*, Ger. m. *Walzer* (ital.)

Walvis Bay Namibia

WAN (comput.) wide area network

wanderlust (one word, not ital.)

W. & M./ William and Mary (King and Queen); *also* — **College** Williamsburg, Va.

wangle (colloq.) obtain (a result) by scheming, altering, or faking, or the act of this; cf. **wrangle**

wannabe (sl.) an avid fan or follower who tries to emulate the admired person, *not* -bee

wapiti a N. American deer, *not* wapp-

War. Warwickshire

Warboys Cambs.

war/ bride, — chest, — cloud, — correspondent, — crime, — cry (two words)

Ward,/ Artemas (1727–1800) American Revolutionary general, — **Artemus** pseud. of **Charles Farrar Browne** (1834–67) US humorist, — **Mrs Humphry** *not* -rey (1851–1920) English novelist, b. **Mary Augusta Arnold**

war/ damage, — dance (two words)

warden abbr. **W.**

Wardour Street London

war game (two words)

war-god (hyphen, two words in US)

war grave (two words)

war/head, -horse, -like (one word)

Warlock, Peter pseud. of **Philip Heseltine** (1894–1930) English composer

war/lock, -lord, -monger (one word)

War Office abbr. **WO**, *now* **MOD**

war/paint, -path (one word)

warrant/er one who authorizes or guarantees, **-or** (law) one who gives warranty

warrant officer (two words)

warrigal (Austral.) (noun) a dingo dog, an untamed horse, a wild Aborigine; (adj.) wild, untamed; *not* warra-

Warrnambool Victoria, Australia

Warsaw in Pol. **Warszawa**, Fr. **Varsovie**, Ger. **Warschau**

Warsaw Pact a military and economic alliance between the E. European Communist countries, originally signed in 1955 by Albania, Bulgaria, Czechoslovakia, E. Germany, Hungary, Poland, Romania, and the USSR

warship (one word)

warthog (one word)

wartime (one word)

war-torn (hyphen)

Warwickshire abbr. **War.**

war zone (two words)

Wash. Washington State (off. abbr.)

wash/bag, -basin, -board (one word)

washbowl (US) = **washbasin, washing-up bowl**

washday (one word)

wash drawing one made with a brush and black or grey watercolour (two words)

washerwoman (one word)

wash house (two words, one in US)

Washington a US state; off. abbr. **Wash.**, postal **WA**

Washington, DC the US capital

washing-up (noun) dirty crockery and cutlery ready for cleaning

wash out (noun, one word)

washroom (US) a room with washing and toilet facilities (one word)

wash/stand, -tub (one word)

wash up (Brit.) wash (crockery and cutlery) after use, (US) wash one's (face and) hands

Wasp, WASP (US, usually derog.) white Anglo-Saxon Protestant

Wassermann a blood test for syphilis, from **August von Wassermann** (1866–1925) German bacteriologist

wastable *not* -eable

wastebasket (US) = **waste-paper basket**

wasteland (one word) but *The Waste Land* a poem by T. S. Eliot, 1922

watch case (two words, one in US)

watch chain (two words)

watch/dog, -maker, -man, -tower, -word (one word)

water bailiff an official enforcing fishing laws, (hist.) a customs house official at a port

water/bed, -bird (one word)

water/ biscuit, — bottle, — butt (two words)

water closet abbr. **WC** (two words)

watercolour (one word; -or in US) *but* the Royal Society of Painters in Water Colours

water-cool/ cool with water (hyphen), **-ed**

water cooler (two words)

water/course, -cress, -fall, -fowl, -front, -gate, -hole (one word)

watering/ can, — place (two words)

water/ jump, — level, — lily (two words)

water/line, -log, -logged (one word)

water main (two words)

waterman (one word)

watermark (typ.) a design in the paper itself (one word)

water meadow (two words)

water/melon, -mill (one word)

water/ nymph, — pistol, — polo (two words)

waterproof (one word)

water rates (two words)

watershed a divide or line of separation between waters flowing to different catchments (e.g. basins, rivers, seas); (US) the catchment itself

waterside (one word)

water strider (US) = **pond skater** (insect)

water/ski (one word, two in US), **-skied, -skiing** *not* ski'ing, **-skier** (one word)

waterspout (one word)

water supply (two words)

watertight (one word)

water/ torture, — tower (two words)

water/way, -works (one word)

Watling Street a Roman road between Dover and Shropshire, passing through London

watt (phys.) a unit of power, abbr. **W**

Watteau/, Jean Antoine (1684–1721) French painter, whence **— hat** etc.

Watts-Dunton, Walter Theodore (1832–1914) English man of letters

Watusi, Watutsi *use* **Tutsi**

Waugh,/ Alec (1898–1981); **— Auberon** (b. 1940) son of **— Evelyn (Arthur St John)** (1903–66) English writers

waul a loud cat-cry, *not* -wl

wave/band, -guide (one word)

wavelength (one word) symbol λ (lambda)

wave number (two words)

wavy *not* -ey

wax/cloth, -work (one word)

Waynflete, William of *see* **William of Waynflete**

-ways suffix forming adjs. and advs. of direction or manner (*crossways, sideways*); *see also* **-wise**

wayzgoose/ (orig. **waygoose**) an annual summer dinner or outing held by a printing house for its employees (one word); pl. **-s**, *not* -geese

Waziristan India, *not* **Wazar-**

Wb weber

WBA West Bromwich Albion

WC water closet, West Central (postal district of London), without charge

WCC World Council of Churches

W/Cdr. Wing Commander

WD War Department, Works Department

w/e week ending

WEA Workers' Educational Association

weak abbr. **wk.**

weal a flesh mark, *not* wale

Weald/, the a formerly wooded district including parts of Kent, Surrey, and East Sussex (cap.); (not cap.) **-clay** beds of clay, sandstone, limestone, and ironstone, forming the top of Wealden strata (hyphen)

Wealden (adj.) of the Weald, resembling it geologically; (noun) a series of Lower Cretaceous freshwater deposits above Jurassic strata and below chalk, best exemplified in the Weald

wear a dam, *use* **weir**

weasel/, -lled, -lling (one *l* in US)

weather/ chart *or* **— map** (two words)

weather/cock, -man, -proof (one word)

weather station (two words)

weather/vane, -woman (one word)

weather-worn (hyphen, one word in US)

weazen *use* **wizened**

Web, the (abbr.) the World Wide Web (cap.)

Webb,/ Beatrice (1858–1943) wife of **— Sidney James, Baron Passfield** (1859–1947) English economists and sociologists; **— Mary** (1881–1927) English novelist

Weber,/ Carl Maria (Friedrich Ernst) von (1786–1826) Austrian-born German composer and pianist; **— Ernst Heinrich** (1795–1878) German physiologist and psychologist, **Weber–Fechner law** (en rule) *use* **Weber's law**; **— Max** (1864–1920) German sociologist; **— Max** (1881–1961) Russian-born US painter

weber (phys.) the SI unit of magnetic flux, abbr. **Wb**; named after **Wilhelm Eduard Weber** (1804–91) German physicist, brother of **Ernst Heinrich Weber** (q.v.)

Webern, Anton (Friedrich Ernst) von (1883–1945) Austrian composer

web/-fed (typ.) presses that receive paper from a reel and not as separate sheets (hyphen); **— letterpress, — offset** (two words)

Webster,/ Daniel (1782–1852) US statesman and orator; **— Noah** (1758–1843) US lexicographer

Weddell/, James (1787–1834) British navigator; discovered — **Sea** (two caps.), — **seal** *Leptonychotes weddelli* (one cap.)

wedding/ breakfast, — cake, — day, — march, — night, — ring (two words)

Wedgwood ware a superior kind of pottery, invented by **Josiah Wedgwood** (1730–95); *not* Wedge-

Wednesday abbr. **W.**, **Wed.**

week/, -s abbr. **w.**, **wk.**

week/day, -end (one word)

week-long (hyphen, one word in US)

Weelkes, Thomas (*c*.1575–1623) English composer

weepie (colloq.) a sentimental film, play, etc.

weepy (colloq.) tearful

weever a spiny marine fish, *not* weav-

weevil a destructive beetle

w.e.f. with effect from

Wehrmacht (Ger. hist. f.) the German armed forces, esp. the army, 1921–45 (cap., ital.)

Weidenfeld (**George**) **& Nicolson** publishers

weighbridge (one word)

weight abbr. **wt.**

weightlift/er, -ing (one word)

weights use numerals; abbr. as cwt, g, lb, oz, no *s* added for the plural

Weihaiwei China, *not* **Wai-hai-wei**

Weil,/ Adolf (1848–1916) German physician, — **Simone** (1909–43) French philosopher

Weill, Kurt (1900–50) German-born US composer

Weimar Republic the German republic 1919–33

Weimaraner a breed of dog

Weingartner, Paul Felix (1863–1942) German conductor and composer

Weinstein, Nathan Wallenstein *see* **West, Nathanael**

weir a dam across a river, *not* -ar

weird *not* wie-

Weismann/, August (1834–1914) German zoologist, **-ism** a theory of heredity

Weissnichtwo (Ger. for Know-not-where) in Carlyle's *Sartor Resartus*

Weizmann/, Chaim (1874–1952) Polish-born chemist and Zionist leader, — **Institute** Israel

Weizsäcker,/ Carl Friedrich Freiherr von (b. 1912) German philosopher and physicist, — **Julius** (1828–89) German historian, — **Karl** (1822–99) German theologian

welch *use* -**sh**

Welch Fusiliers, Royal *but* **Welsh Guards**

Welfare State (two words, caps.)

welk *use* whe-

well- prefix joined to participles in -*ed* or -*ing*, takes hyphens when the compound is used attributively, and to preserve the unity of the sense when it is used predicatively, e.g. 'a well-known book', 'the book is well known', 'the action was not well-advised', 'he has not been well advised'

well/-being, -doer (hyphens)

Welles, Orson (1915–85) US actor and director

Wellesley town and college, Mass.

wellington a waterproof rubber or plastic boot (not cap.), colloq. **welly** *not* -ie

well-known *see* **well-**

well-nigh (hyphen)

well-to-do (hyphens)

well-wisher (hyphen)

Welsh abbr. **W.**

welsh/ default in payment, (esp. US) break one's word; *not* -lch; **-er**; *but prefer* another term to avoid offence

Welsh/ corgi, — dresser, — harp, — onion (one cap.)

Welsh rabbit melted cheese on toast; *not* rarebit

Welt/anschauung (Ger.) world-philosophy, **-politik** participation in international politics, **-schmerz** world-sorrow (one word)

Wemyss/ Bay Strathclyde, — **Castle** Fife, **Earl of** —

wen *see* **wyn**

Wend/, -ic, -ish (hist.) (a member of) a Slavonic people of N. Germany, now inhabiting E. Saxony; in modern contexts use **Sorb**; *see also* **Sorbian**

Wensleydale a variety of white or blue cheese, a breed of long-wool sheep (cap.)

werewol/f a mythical being who at times changes from a person to a wolf, pl. **-ves**; *not* werw-

West, Nathanael pseud. of **Nathan Wallenstein Weinstein** (1903–40) US writer

west abbr. **W.**; *see also* **compass points**

West Africa abbr. **W. Afr.**

westbound (one word)

West Bridgford Notts., *not* Bridge-

Westchester NY

West Chester Del., Pa.

West Country the south-western counties of England (two caps.)

West End London (caps.)

westeria *use* wis-

Westermarck, Edward Alexander (1862–1939) Finnish anthropologist

Western a cowboy film (cap.)

western abbr. **W**; *see also* **compass points**

Western Australia abbr. **WA**

Western Isles the formal name for the Hebrides

Westfalen Ger. for **Westphalia**

Westhoughton Gr. Manchester (one word)

Westmeath/ a county of Ireland (one word), **Earl of —**

Westmorland/ a former county of England, **Earl of —** *not* -eland

Westonzoyland Som. (one word)

West Virginia off. abbr. **W. Va.**, postal **WV**

wetlands (one word)

w.f. (typ.) wrong font

WFEO World Federation of Engineering Organizations

WFTU World Federation of Trade Unions

W.G. W. G. Grace (1848–1915) English cricketer

Wg. Comdr., Wg/Cdr. Wing Commander

Wh watt-hour

whalebone (one word)

whallabee *use* **wallaby**

whar/f a landing stage, abbr. **whf.**; pl. **-ves**

Wharfedale Yorks.

Wharncliffe, Earl of

whatchamacallit (US colloq.) (one word)

what-d'you-call-it? (colloq.) (hyphens, apos.)

Whately, Richard (1787–1863) Archbishop of Dublin, *not* -ey

whatever (one word)

Whatman paper a first-quality English handmade drawing paper (cap.)

whatnot an indefinite or trivial thing, a piece of furniture with shelves (one word)

what not many other similar things, e.g. 'pens, pencils, and what not' (two words, one word in US)

what's/-her-name, -his-name, -its-name (hyphens)

whatso (arch.) whatever

whatsoever (one word)

wheal *use* **weal**

wheatear a small migratory bird (one word)

Wheatstone bridge an apparatus for measuring electrical resistances

wheel/barrow, -base, -chair (one word)

wheel clamp (two words)

wheelhouse (one word)

wheel lock (two words)

wheelwright (one word)

whelk a predatory mollusc, a pimple; *not* we-

whence from which (place), and thence; 'from whence' is a tautology

when/ever, -soever (one word)

whereas (law) a word that introduces the recital of a fact (one word)

where/ver, -soever (one word)

whether or not *not* or no

whf. wharf

whidah *use* why-

whiffletree (US) = **whippletree**

Whig/, -gish, -gism (cap.)

whimbrel a small curlew, *not* wim-

whimsy caprice, *not* -ey

whing/e, -er, -ing, -y

whinny (give) a gentle neigh, *not* -ey

whip/cord, -lash (one word)

whipper/-in (hunting) pl. **-s-in**

whippersnapper (one word)

whippletree a swingletree, the crossbar to which the traces of a harness are attached; *not* whiffle- (US)

whippoorwill an American nightjar (one word)

whirligig a child's spinning toy, a merry-go-round

whirl/pool, -wind (one word)

whirlybird (colloq.) a helicopter

whirr (make) a continuous buzzing sound, *not* whir

whisk/ey (Irish and US); **-y** (Scotch and Canadian)

Whistler, James Abbott McNeill, *not* -eil (1834–1903) US painter and etcher

Whitaker & Sons, J. publishers of the Almanack (*not* -ac) etc.

white/ a white person, (typ.) any space of paper not printed upon; **line of —** a line not printed upon (not cap.)

whitebait (one word)

Whitechapel London (one word)

Whitefield, George (1714–70) English preacher, *not* Whitf-; *but* pron. 'Wit-'

Whitehall London (one word)

Whitehorse Yukon (one word)

White Horse, Vale of Oxon. (*formerly* Berks.), *not* of the

White House official residence of the US President, Washington, DC

Whiteing, Richard (1840–1928) English journalist and novelist

white-out a polar blizzard (hyphen, one word in US)

White Paper a Government report giving information or proposals on an issue (caps.) cf. **Blue Book; Green Paper**

White Russian Soviet Socialist Republic a former Soviet Socialist Republic, *properly* **Belorussian Soviet Socialist Republic**, *now* **Belarus**´; avoid 'White Russian' in this sense, since it was the standard term for anti-Bolsheviks

White's Club London

whitewash (one word)

Whitey derog. for a white person, or white people collectively (cap.); cf. **white**; **whity**

whitish *not* -eish

Whitman, Walt (1819–92) US poet

Whit/ Monday, — Sunday seventh after Easter, *but* **Whitsun/, -tide** (one word)

Whittier, John Greenleaf (1807–92) US poet

Whittlesey, Cambs. *not* -sea

whity whitelike, *not* -ey; cf. **Whitey**

whizz/ *not* whiz (US); **-zed, -zing**

whizz-kid (colloq.) (hyphen, **whiz kid** in US)

WHO World Health Organization

whoa/ a command to stop; **-ed, -ing, -s**

whodunit a novel or play of crime detection, *not* -nnit (one word)

whole-bound (bind.) full-bound

whole/food, -grain, -hearted, -meal (one word)

whole note (US) = semibreve

whole/sale, -some (one word)

wholewheat (one word, two words in US)

whoopee/, — cushion *not* -ie

whooping cough *not* hooping

whore/house, -monger, -son (one word)

whose of whom *or* of which

Who's Who*, *Who Was Who reference books

whydah an African weaver-bird, *not* whidah

why ever (two words)

Whymper, Edward (1840–1911) British climber and writer

Whyte-Melville, George John (1821–78) Scottish novelist (hyphen)

WI West Ind/ies, -ian; Windward Islands; Wisconsin (postal abbr.); Women's Institute

wich alder *use* **witch alder**

wich elm *use* **wych elm**

wich hazel *use* **witch hazel**

Wicliffe *use* **Wyclif**

widdershins (Sc.) anticlockwise, opp. to **deasil**; *not* wither-

wide (cricket) abbr. **w.**

wide awake fully awake, (colloq.) alert, knowing (hyphen when attrib.)

wideawake a kind of hat (one word)

widespread (one word)

widgeon a bird, *use* **wigeon**

widow (typ.) the last line of a paragraph at the top of a page or column, *or* word or part of a word at the end of a paragraph on a line by itself; *see also* **orphan**

Wieland, Christoph Martin (1733–1813) German poet and novelist

Wien Ger. for **Vienna**

Wiener, Norbert (1894–1964) US mathematician and writer on cybernetics

Wiener Neustadt Austria (two words)

Wiener schnitzel a veal cutlet dressed with breadcrumbs (two words, one cap.)

Wieniawski,/ Henri (1835–80) Polish violinist and composer; **— Joseph** (1837–1912) his brother, Polish pianist and composer

Wiesbaden Germany

wife abbr. **w.**

wigeon a dabbling duck, *not* widg-

Wiggin, Kate Douglas (1856–1923) US educator and novelist

Wight, Isle of abbr. **IOW, IoW, IW**

Wigorn: the former signature of the Bishop of Worcester (colon)

Wigton Cumbria

Wigtown a district and town, Dumfries & Galloway

wigwam an arched or conical dwelling of the eastern Native American peoples; cf. **tepee**

Wilamowitz(-Mullendorf), Ulrich von (1848–1931) German classical scholar, *not* Moe-

wildcat a hot-tempered person, reckless or sudden, (US) a bobcat (one word)

Wilde,/ Henry (1833–1919) English physicist, **— Oscar** (**Fingal O'Flahertie Wills**) (1854–1900) Irish playwright, author, and poet

wildebeest a gnu, in Afrik. **wildebees/** pl. **-te**

wild/fire, -fowl (one word)

wild-goose chase (one hyphen)

wildlife (one word)

wilful/, -ly, -ness *not* will- (except in US)

Wilhelmj, August Emil Daniel Ferdinand (1845–1908) German violinist

Wilhelmshaven a city, Lower Saxony, and former German naval station (one word)

Wilhelmstrasse Berlin, the diplomatic quarter, named **Otto-Grotewohl-Straße** under Communist rule

William of Waynflete (1395–1486) Bishop of Winchester, Lord Chancellor

Willkie, Wendell (**Lewis**) (1892–1944) US politician

will-o'-the-wisp the ignis fatuus, an elusive person, a delusive hope (apos., hyphens)

willowware (US) willow-pattern pottery (one word)

will-power (hyphen, one word in US)

willy-nilly whether one likes it or not, haphazardly (hyphen)

willy-willy (Austral.) a cyclone or dust storm (hyphen)

Wiltshire abbr. **Wilts.**

Wimborne, Viscount

Wimborne Minster Dorset

wimbrel *use* wh-

Wimpey a British construction company

Wimpy a fast-food hamburger chain

Wimsey, Lord Peter in the novels by Dorothy Sayers

winable *use* **winn-**

wincey/ a cloth, *not* -sey; **-ette** a lightweight flannelette

Winchelsea E. Sussex

Winchilsea,/ Earl of; — Anne Finch, Countess of (1661–1720) English poet

Winckelmann, Johann Joachim (1717–68) German art critic

wind/age, -bag, -bound, -break (one word)

windbreaker (US) = **windcheater** (jacket)

Windermere *not* Lake —

windfall (one word)

Windhoek Namibia

Wind. I. Windward Islands

winding sheet a shroud (two words)

window/ box, — dressing, — ledge (two words)

window pane (two words, one word in US)

window seat (two words)

window-shop/, -per, -ping (hyphens)

window sill (two words)

window tax (hist.) a tax on windows or similar openings (abolished in 1851)

wind/mill, -pipe, -screen (one word)

Windscale *see* **Sellafield**

wind shear (two words)

windshield (US) = **windscreen** (car)

windsurf/, -er, -ing (one word)

windward (the region) on or towards the side from which the wind is blowing; cf. **leeward**

wine bottle (two words)

wine/glass, -glassful, -press (one word)

winery an establishment where wine is made

wineskin (one word)

winey winelike, *not* winy

Winged Victory (Gr. antiquity) (a statue of) Nike (Athena) (caps.)

winnable able to be won, *not* wina-

Winnie-the-Pooh (hyphens)

wino/ (sl.) an alcoholic, pl. **-s**

winsey *use* **-cey**

wint/er, -ry (not cap.)

wintergreen an aromatic plant (one word)

winterize adapt for use in cold weather, *not* -ise

Winton: the signature of the Bishop of Winchester (colon)

winy *use* **winey**

wipe-out (noun, hyphen, one word in US)

WIPO World Intellectual Property Organization

wireless/ (in full — **set**) a radio receiving set; superseded by **radio**

Wis. Wisconsin (off. abbr.)

Wisbech Cambs., *not* -each

Wisconsin off. abbr. **Wis.**, postal **WI**

Wisden Cricketers' Almanak *not* -'s, -ac

Wisdom of Solomon (Apocr.) abbr. **Wisd.**

-wise suffix forming adjs. and advs. of manner (e.g. *crosswise, clockwise, lengthwise*) or respect (*moneywise*); *see also* **-ways**

wiseacre (one word)

wisent the European bison, *Bison bonasus*; *not* aurochs (q.v.)

wishbone (one word)

wishy-washy (hyphen)

Wislicenus, Johannes (1835–1902) German chemist

Wistar/, (*also* **-er), Caspar** (1761–1818) US anatomist; **— rats** (from the Wistar Institute, Philadelphia, founded by Caspar's grand-nephew)

wisteria (bot.) *not* -taria

witch alder *not* wich, wych (except in US)

witch elm *use* **wych elm**

witchetty (Austral.) the larva of beetle or moth, *not* -ety

witch hazel (two words) *not* wich-, wych-

witch-hunt (hyphen)

withal *not* -all

with/e pl. **-es**, *or* **-y** pl. **-ies** a flexible twig, often of willow; *not* wy-

withershins *use* **widder-**

withhold etc. (one word, two *h*s)

without abbr. **w/o**

witness box (two words) *not* -stand (US)

Wittenberg Germany

Witwatersrand University Johannesburg, S. Africa

wivern *use* **wy-**

wizened shrivelled; *not* weaz-, -en

Wk Walk (in place names)

wk. weak; week, -s; work

W. long. west longitude

Wm. William

WMO World Meteorological Organization

WNW west-north-west

WO War Office (*now* **MOD** (q.v.)), Warrant Officer, Wireless Operator

w.o. walkover

w/o without

wobbl/e, -y *not* wa-

Wodehouse/ the family name of the Earl of Kimberley, **—, P. G. (Sir Pelham Grenville)** (1881–1975) English humorous novelist; *see also* **Woodhouse**

woebegone dismal-looking (one word), *but* 'Lake Wobegon' in the novels of Garrison Keillor

Wolcot, Dr John (1738–1819) **'Peter Pindar'**, English writer; *see also* **Wolcott**; **Woollcott**

Wolcott, Oliver (1726–97) and — — (1760–1833) his son, American statesmen; *see also* **Wolcot**; **Woollcott**

Wolf,/ Friedrich August (1759–1824) German classical scholar, — **Hugo** (1860–1903) Austrian composer

Wolfe,/ Charles (1791–1823) Irish poet; — **Humbert** (1885–1940) English poet; — **James** (1727–59) British general, took Quebec; — **Thomas** (**Clayton**) (1900–38) US novelist; — **Tom** (**Thomas Kennerley**) (b. 1931) US journalist and writer

Wolff,/ Sir Henry Drummond Charles (1830–1908) British politician and diplomat; — **Christian von** (1679–1754) German philosopher and mathematician; — **Joseph** (1795–1862) German-born, English-domiciled traveller; — **Kaspar Friedrich** (1733–94) German embryologist; **-ian**

Wolf-Ferrari, Ermanno (1876–1948) Italian composer

wolfhound (one word)

Wollstonecraft/ (**Godwin**), **Mary** (1759–97) English writer, mother of **Mary** — **Godwin, Mrs Shelley** (1797–1851) English writer

wolverine a voracious weasel-like animal, called **glutton** in Europe; *not* -ene

womanize *not* -ise

womankind *not* women- (one word)

Women's Lib (caps., no point)

wonky (Brit. sl.) crooked, loose, unsteady, unreliable; *not* -ey

woo/, -ed, -er, -s

Wood, Anthony à (1632–95) English antiquary

Woodard Foundation of a number of English public schools, named after **Nathaniel Woodard** (1881–91) English Anglican priest; *not* Woodw-

woodbine honeysuckle, *not* -bind

woodchuck a N. American marmot, a groundhog (one word)

woodcock/ (m. and f.) a bird, pl. same

woodcut (typ.) a design cut in the side grain of a type-high block of wood (one word)

wood engraving (typ.) a design cut in the end grain of a type-high block of wood (two words)

Woodhouse the surname of Emma in Jane Austen's *Emma*; *see also* **Wodehouse**

wood/land, -lark, -louse, -man (one word)

wood nymph (two words)

wood/pecker, -pile, -shed, -wind (mus.), **-work, -worm, -yard** (one word)

wool/, -len (one *l* in US), **-ly**

Woolacombe Devon

Wooler Northumb.

Woolf,/ (**Adeline**) **Virginia** née **Stephen** (1882–1941) English novelist and essayist; — **Leonard Sidney** (1880–1969) her husband, English writer

Woollcott, Alexander (**Humphreys**) (1887–1943) US author and drama critic; *see also* **Wolcot**; **Wolcott**

Woolloomooloo Sydney, Australia

woolpack a fleecy cumulus cloud, (hist.) a bale of wool (one word)

Woolsack the official seat of the Lord Chancellor in the House of Lords (one word)

wool-sorters' disease anthrax, *not* -er's

woolverine *use* wolv-

Worcester: the signature of the Bishop of Worcester (colon)

Worcestershire/ a county of England, abbr. **Worcs.**; — **sauce** (US) = (what is in Britain commonly called) **Worcester sauce**

Worde *see* **Wynkyn**

Word of God, the (caps.) *but* in NT a lower-case w

word/play, -smith (one word)

work abbr. **wk.**

workaday (one word)

work and turn (typ.) the printing of two sides of a sheet of paper from one forme

work/bench, -box, -day, -force, -horse (one word)

workhouse (hist.) a public institution in which the destitute of a parish received board and lodging in return for work done, (US) a house of correction for petty offenders (one word)

working class (hyphen when attrib.)

work/load, -man, -manlike, -manship, -mate (one word)

work off (typ.) actually to print the paper

work/out (noun), **-sheet, -shop, -station** (one word)

work study a system of assessing methods of working (two words)

work-study a programme or course combining work with classroom time (hyphen)

worktop (one word)

work-to-rule (noun, hyphens)

World,/ the New America; — **the Old** Europe, Asia, and Africa, known to the ancients (two caps.)

World Bank *formally*, the **International Bank for Reconstruction and Development**, a UN agency administering economic aid between member nations

world/-famous, -shaking (hyphens)

World War I 1914–18, **World War II** 1939–45 are preferred US forms; **First World War** and

Second World War are preferred British forms

worldwide (one word) *but* (comput.) **World Wide Web, World Wide Fund for Nature** (caps.)

worm-eaten (hyphen)

worm's-eye view (apos., one hyphen)

wormwood (bot.) *Artemisia*, (fig.) bitterness

Wormwood Scrubs a prison, London

worry beads (two words)

worry-guts (colloq.) (hyphen)

worrywart (US colloq.) (one word)

worship/, -ped, -per, -ping (one *p* in US)

Wörterbuch (Ger. n.) dictionary

worthwhile (one word, *formerly* two words predicatively, one word attributively)

Wotton, Sir Henry (1568–1639) English diplomat and poet

would-be adj. (hyphen)

Woulfe/, Peter (1727–1803) English chemist, hence **— bottle** for passing gas through liquid

wove paper that which does not show wire marks; cf. **laid paper**

Wozzeck an opera by Berg, 1925, based on **Woyzeck**, a play by Büchner, 1837

WP weather permitting

w.p.b. waste-paper basket

WPC woman police constable

w.p.m. words per minute

WR Western Region, West Riding

WRAC Women's Royal Army Corps

wrack destruction; a seaweed; *see also* **rack**

WRAF (hist.) Women's Royal Air Force, since 1994 integrated into the RAF

Wrangel Island Arctic Ocean

Wrangell Island Alaska

wrangle (engage in) a noisy argument or (US) herd cattle; cf. **wangle**

wrangler one who wrangles, (US) a cowboy, (Cambridge University) one placed in the first class of the mathematical tripos

wraparound (one word)

wrap-round (bind.) a folded section placed outside another section, so that sewing passes through both

wrath (noun) great anger; *see also* **wro-**

Wray *see* **Ray**

wreath/ (noun), **-e** (verb)

Wren a member of the Women's Royal Naval Service

wrick *use* **rick**

wrist/band, -watch (one word)

writable *not* -eable

write/-back, -down, -off, -protect, -up (nouns, hyphens)

writer's cramp *not* -ers' cramp

writing/ desk, — paper, — table (two words)

WRNS Women's Royal Naval Service, a member is a **Wren**

Wrocław Poland; in Ger. **Breslau**, Lat. **Vratislavia**

wrongdo/er, -ing (one word)

wrong font (typ.) said of letter(s) set in wrong size or cut of type, abbr. **w.f.**

wroth (poet. or joc.) angry; *see also* **wra-**

Wrottesley/ a cape, NW Canada; **Baron —**

WRVS Women's Royal Voluntary Service, *formerly* **WVS**

wry/bill, -mouth, -neck (one word)

WS (Sc.) Writer to the Signet (= attorney)

WSW west-south-west

WT *or* **W/T** wireless telegraphy

wt. weight

wunderkind one who achieves success in youth, *not* wo- (not ital.); in Ger. n. **Wunderkind**

Württemberg a German state (two *t*s); *see also* **Baden-Württemberg**

Wuthering Heights a novel by E. Brontë, 1846

WV West Virginia (postal abbr.)

W. Va. West Virginia (off. abbr.)

WVS Women's Voluntary Service, *now* **WRVS**

w/w weight for weight

WWW World Wide Web

WY Wyoming (postal abbr.)

Wyandot (of) (a member of) a Native American subgroup of the Hurons

wyandotte a breed of domestic fowl, *not* -ot

wych alder *use* **witch alder**

wych elm (two words) *not* wich, witch

Wycherley, William (1640–1716) English playwright

wych hazel *use* **witch hazel**

Wyclif/, John (*c.*1324–84) English religious reformer and translator of the Bible, *not* the many variants; **-fite**

Wycliffe/ College Stonehouse; **— Hall** Oxford, a theological college

Wykeham/, William of (1324–1404) English prelate, **-ist** a member of Winchester College (cap.)

Wymondham Leics., Norfolk

wyn the Old English Þ, þ (distinguish from **eth** and **thorn** (qq.v.)); in modern editions *w* is normally substituted

Wyndham/ the family name of Baron Leconfield; **—, Sir Charles** (1837–1919) English actor, **—, George** (1863–1913) English statesman, **—'s Theatre** London

Wyndham Lewis,/ Dominic Bevan (1894–1969) British writer, **— — Percy** (1882–1957) English writer and painter

Wyndham-Quin family name of the Earl of Dunraven

Wynkyn de Worde (1471–1534) early printer in London

Wyoming off. abbr. **Wyo.**, postal **WY**

Wyredrawers, Gold and Silver a livery company

WYSIWYG (comput.) 'what you see is what you get' (caps.), pron. 'wizziwig'

wyth/e, -y *use* **wi-**

Wythenshawe Manchester

wyvern (her.) a winged two-legged dragon with a barbed tail, *not* wi-

X cross; ten; the twenty-first in a series; former film-censorship classification (replaced in the UK in 1983 by **18**, and in 1990 by **NC-17** in the USA)

X (usually **XP** or **Xt.**) the Greek letter chi, for *Christos*, Christ

x (math.) the first unknown quantity

x. (meteor.) hoar frost

Xaime Galician for **James**

Xanthippe the wife of Socrates, used allusively for a shrewish woman

Xavier, St Francis (1506–52) Jesuit missionary

Xᵇʳᵉ (Fr.) December

XC 90

XCIX 99

x.cp. ex (without) coupon

x.d. ex (without) dividend

Xe xenon (no point)

xebec a small Mediterranean boat, *not* z-

Xenocrates (396–314 BC) Greek philosopher

xenon symbol **Xe**

Xenophanes (*c.*570–*c.*500 BC) Greek philosopher and poet

Xenophon (*c.*438–*c.*354 BC) Greek historian, abbr. **Xen.**

Xérès Fr. for **Jerez**

xeric (ecology) having or characterized by dry conditions

xerograph a copy produced by **xerography**, a dry copying process using electrically charged powder after exposure

Xerox (propr.) a xerographic copying machine (cap.); produce (copies) from such a machine (not cap.); *prefer* **photocopy** in general references

Xerxes (519–465 BC) King of Persia

x-height (typ.) the distance between top and bottom of those lower-case letters of a given font that have no ascenders or descenders (e.g. n, x)

Xhosa (of or relating to) (a member of) a Bantu people of Cape Province, S. Africa; or their language (*formerly* called Kaffir)

xi the fourteenth letter of the Gr. alphabet (Ξ, ξ)

x.i. *or* **ex int.** ex (without) next interest

Xianggang Pinyin for **Hong Kong**

Xiaoping, Deng *see* **Deng Xiaoping**

xiphoid (biol.) sword-shaped

Xizang Pinyin for **Tibet**

XL 40

XLIX 49

Xmas Christmas (no point)

XML (comput.) Extended Mark-up Language

Xn. Christian

x.n. (ex new) (without) the right to new shares

Xnty. Christianity

Xoán Galician for **John**

xoan/on (Gr. antiquity) a primitive (usually wooden) image of a deity, supposed to have fallen from heaven; pl. **-a**

Xosa use **Xho-**

XP (as monogram ☧) the Gr. letters *chi rho*, the first two of *Khristos*

X-ray (hyphen)

Xt. Christ

XX 20

XXX 30

XXXX 40 in Roman and early-modern use, though modern writers favour **XL**

xylograph/ a woodcut or wood engraving; **-y** making woodcuts or wood engravings, the use of wood blocks in printing

Xylonite (propr.) a kind of celluloid

xylophon/e, -ist

xyst/us an ancient Greek portico used by athletes, pl. **-i**; in archaeological (rather than literary) contexts *also* **-os**, pl. **-oi**

Y y

Y yen (q.v.), yttrium; the twenty-second in a series

Y, y (**Ŷ, ÿ**) in mod. Dutch *use* **IJ, ij**, as in IJmuiden, Nijmegen

y. year, -s; (meteor.) dry air

y (math.) the second unknown quantity

yacht/, **-sman** (one word)

yager *use* **jaeger**

Yahoo in Swift's *Gulliver's Travels*, an animal with human form but brutish instincts (cap.); a lout or hooligan (not cap.)

Yahweh the probable pronunciation of the Hebrew Tetragrammaton, the consonants YHVW, YHWH, which are traditionally transliterated as **Jehovah**; *not* Jahveh, Yaveh

Yakö (of or relating to) (a member of) a Nigerian people of the Cross River region, *not* Yache

Yakutsk Siberia, *not* J-

yakuza a Japanese gangster or racketeer, pl. same (not ital.)

Yale university, New Haven, Conn.; (propr.) a kind of lock (cap.)

yam any tropical or subtropical climbing plant of the genus *Dioscorea*, or the edible starchy tuber of this; in US also called **sweet potato**

Yamato-e the style or school of art in Japan, culminating in the 12th and 13th cc., that dealt with Japanese subjects in a distinctively Japanese (rather than Chinese) way

Yangtze Kiang a Chinese river (*kiang* = river), in Pinyin **Yangzijiang**

Yank/, **-ee** *not* -i

Yankey in England a comedy by David Humphreys, 1814

Yanomami (of or relating to) (a member of) an Amazonian people, pl. same; *also* **-mö**

yanqui (Sp.) a citizen of the USA

Yaoundé Cameroon, *not* Yasun-

yaourt *use* **yogurt**

yapp a form of bookbinding with a limp leather cover projecting to fold over the edges of the leaves

yarborough a hand in whist or bridge with no card above 9 (not cap.)

yard/, **-s** = 3 feet (0.9144 metre); abbr. **yd**, **yds**

yardarm (naut.) (one word)

yardbird (US sl.) a new military recruit, a convict (one word)

Yarde-Buller family name of Baron Churston

yardstick (one word)

Yarkand Cent. Asia; *not* -end, -und

yarl *use* **j-**

yarmulke/ a Jewish skullcap, pl. **-s**; *not* yarme-, -ka

Yaroslavl'/, — Oblast Russia, *not* J-

Yates/, Dornford pseud. of **Cecil William Mercer** (1885–1960) English novelist; **—, Frank** (1902–94) English statistician, **—'s correction**

YB Year Book

Yb ytterbium (no point)

YC Young Conservative

yclept (arch., joc.) called, named (one word)

Yding Skovhøj a peak, Denmark

yd yard, pl. **yds**

yͤ the; in approximating 15th- to 17th-c. works, the second letter to be superior (no point); *see also* **yͭ**

Yeames, William Frederick (1835–1918) English painter

year/, **-s** abbr. **y.**; **a**; **yr.**, **yrs.**

yearbook (one word), **Year Book** (law reports) (caps., two words) abbr. **YB**

year-long (hyphen, one word in US)

year-round (hyphen)

years when in figures, to be elided except in titles; no apos. except as possessive, e.g. 'the 1940s' *but* '1940's population figure'

Yeats, William Butler (1865-1939) Irish poet

Yeats-Brown, Francis (1886–1944) English author

Yeddo/ a former name (later **Edo**) for Tokyo: **— hawthorn, — spruce**

yellowhammer a bird, *not* -ammer (one word)

Yellowknife NW Territories, Canada

Yellow Pages (caps.)

Yellowplush Papers (two words) by Thackeray, 1841

Yellowstone/ (one word) **National Park, — River**

Yemen/ S. Arabia; **North —** officially **— Arab Republic**; **South —** officially **People's Democratic Republic of —**; adj. **-i**

yen the chief monetary unit of Japan, pl. same; abbr. **Y**, symbol **¥**

Yeniseisk Siberia, on the **River Yenisei**

Yeo. Yeomanry

Yeoman/ Usher, — Warder; pl. **— Ushers, — Warders**; *not* Yeomen

yerba maté = **maté**

Yerevan Armenia; *not* E-, -iv-

yes-man (colloq.) (hyphen)

yesteryear (one word)

yeux *see* **œil**

Yevtushenko, Yevgeni (**Aleksandrovich**) (b. 1933) Russian writer

Y-fronts (propr.) men's or boys' briefs with a Y-shaped seam at the front

Yggdrasil (Scandinavian myth.) the ash tree binding heaven, earth, and hell; Anglicized from Old Norse *yg(g)drasill*; *not* Ygd-

YHA Youth Hostels Association, (US) Youth Hostels of America

YHVH *or* **YHWH** the Tetragrammaton, the Hebrew name of God written in four (usually small-capital) letters, articulated as Yahweh, Jehovah, etc.

Yiddish/ (of or relating to) a vernacular used by Jews in or from Cent. and E. Europe; also called *Judaeo-German* by linguists; **-ist** a scholar of the subject

yield point (two words)

yippee an exclamation of delight

ylang-ylang (the oil from) a Malayan tree (hyphen), in Tagalog *ilang-ilang*

YMCA Young Men's Christian Association

Ymuiden *use* **IJm-**

Ynca *use* **I-**

Ynys Môn Welsh for Anglesey

yob/ (colloq.) a lout, hooligan; *also* **-bo**; pl. **-s**; **-bish**

yod the tenth and smallest letter in the Hebrew alphabet

yodel/ a song, *or* to sing, with inarticulate partly falsetto voice that carries over long distances; **-led, -ling** (one *l* in US); *not* -dle, jodel

yog/a Hindu system of philosophic meditation; **-i** a person proficient in yoga; adj. **-ic**

yogh the ME letter ȝ, ȝ; normally *use* ȝ, ȝ; standing for certain values of g and y

yogurt a semi-solid sour fermented-milk food; *not* -hurt, -ourt; in Fr. **yaourt**

Yoknapatawpha County a fictional setting in Mississippi in the novels and stories of William Faulkner

Yokohama Japan (one word)

Yom Kippur (Jewish relig.) Day of Atonement

Yonge,/ Charles Duke (1812–91) English historian; **— Charlotte Mary** (1823–1901) English novelist; pron. 'Young'; *see also* **Young**

Yorke family name of the Earl of Hardwicke

Yorkshire a former county of England, abbr. **Yorks.**

Yorktown Va. (one word)

Yoruba a Kwa language spoken in SW Nigeria, Benin, and Togo

Yosemite Valley Calif., pron. 'Yo-sem-itty'

Youcon *use* **Yukon**

Youghal Co. Cork

Youl, Sir James Arndell (1809–1904) Tasmanian colonist

Young, Brigham (1801–77) US Mormon leader; *see also* **Yonge**

younger abbr. **yr.**

Young Men's Christian Association abbr. **YMCA**

Young Turk a member of a revolutionary party in Turkey in 1908; a young person eager for radical change to the established order (cap.); (offens.) a violent child or youth (not cap.)

young 'un (colloq.) a youngster

Young Women's Christian Association abbr. **YWCA**

your abbr. **yr.**

yours (no apos.) abbr. **yrs.**

yo-yo/ a kind of toy, pl. **-s** (hyphen, orig. propr. and cap.)

Ypres/ Belgium, in Fl. **Ieper**; **Earl of —**

Yquem/ a vineyard, dép. Gironde; **—, Château-d'** a Sauterne (hyphen)

yr. year, younger, your

YRA Yacht Racing Association, *now* **RYA**

Yriarte, Charles (1832–98) French writer

yrs. years, yours

Ysaye, Eugène (1858–1929) Belgian violinist

Yseult etc., *use* **Is-**

Yssel *use* **IJssel**

YT Yukon Territory, Canada

y^t that; in approximating 15th- to 17th-c. works, the second letter to be superior (no point); *see also* **y^e**

ytterbium symbol **Yb**

yttrium symbol **Y**

Y2K (comput.) year 2000 (caps.)

yuan chief monetary unit of China, pl. same

Yucatán Mexico (accent)

yucca an American white-flowered liliaceous plant, *not* yuca

Yue another name for **Cantonese**

yugen in trad. Japanese court culture and Noh plays, a hidden quality of graceful beauty or mystery; profound aestheticism

Yugoslavia *not* J-; adj. **Yugoslav**, *not* -avian

Yuk a dialect of Yupik

Yukon/ River Alaska, USA; and Canada; **— Territory** Canada; *not* Youcon, -kon

yule log (two words, cap. Y in US)

Yuletide (one word, cap.)

Yupik an Eskimo or Eskimos of NE Siberia, the Aleutian Islands, and Alaska; the language spoken by them; *not* Yuit; *see also* **Eskimo**; **Inuit**; **Inuk**

yupp/ie *also* **-y**

Yvetot dép. Seine-Maritime, France

YWCA Young Women's Christian Association

Z the twenty-third in a series, pron. (UK) 'zed', (US) 'zee'

z. (meteor.) haze

z (math.) the third unknown quantity

zabaglione an Italian sweet of whipped and heated egg yolks, sugar, and (esp. Marsala) wine (not ital.)

Zach. Zachary

Zacynthus the ancient name of **Zante**

Zaehnsdorf, Joseph (1819–86) Austrian-born English-domiciled bookbinder

zaffre an impure cobalt oxide used as a blue pigment, *not* -er (US)

Zagreb Croatia, *not* -ab; in Ger. **Agram**, Hung. **Zágráb**, It. **Zagabria**

Zaharoff, Sir Basil (1849–1936) Greek-born British financier

Zaire name of the Democratic Republic of Congo 1960–97

Zaïre a major river in the Congo, *formerly* the **Congo** (accent, cap.); the monetary unit of the Congo (no accent, not cap.)

Zaïre a tragedy by Voltaire, 1732

zajčyk monetary unit of Belarus'

Zambezi an African river, *not* -si

Zambia Africa

Zamenhof, Ludwig Lazarus (1859–1917) Polish physician, inventor of Esperanto

zamindar *use* **zemin-**

zanana *use* **ze-**

Zangwill, Israel (1864–1926) English novelist and playwright

Zante a Greek island, ancient name **Zacynthus**

ZANU Zimbabwe African National Union

Zanzibar/ island, Tanzania; **-i**

zapateado a flamenco dance with rhythmic stamping of the feet (not ital.)

ZAPU Zimbabwe African People's Union

Zaragoza Sp. for (Catalan and Eng.) **Saragossa**

zarape *use* **ser-**

Zarathustra (Avestan) (6th c. BC) Persian founder of the Magian system of religion; in Gr. **Zoraster**

zariba (Arab.) a fortified enclosure, *not* the many variants

Zarskoe Selo *use* **Tsarskoe Selo**

zarzuela a trad. Spanish form of musical comedy, a fish stew (not cap., not ital.)

zax *use* **s-**

z. B. (Ger.) *zum Beispiel* (for example)

Zealand Denmark, *use* **Sjælland**

Zealand NB, Canada

zealot an uncompromising or extreme partisan, a fanatic (not cap.); (hist.) a member of an ancient Jewish sect aiming at a world Jewish theocracy and resisting the Romans until AD 70 (cap.)

zebec *use* **x-**

Zech. Zechariah (OT)

Zeeland the Netherlands, *not* Zea-; in Fr. **Zélande**, Ger. **Seeland**

Zeitgeist the spirit of the time, the trend of thought of a period (cap., not ital.); in Ger. m. *Zeitgeist*

Zeitschrift (Ger. f.) periodical (cap.)

Zeltinger a Moselle wine

zemindar an official in India under the Mogul empire, an Indian landowner paying tax to Britain; *not* zamin-

Zen a meditative form of Mahayana Buddhism (cap.)

zenana the part of a house for the seclusion of women of high-caste families in India and Iran, *not* za-; in Hind. *zenāna*

Zend/ an interpretation of the Avesta, each Zend being part of the **-Avesta**, the Zoroastrian sacred writings of the Avesta (text) and Zend (commentary)

Zener cards used in ESP research (one cap.)

zenith the highest point, opp. to **nadir**

Zeph. Zephaniah (OT)

Zeppelin/ (hist.) a large German dirigible airship of the early 20th c.; named after **Count Ferdinand von —** (1838–1917) German airman, its first constructor

Zermatt Switzerland

zero/ pl. **-s**

zeroth immediately preceding what is regarded as 'first' in a series, *also* **noughth**

zeta the sixth letter of the Gr. alphabet (Z, ζ)

Zetinje *use* **C-**

Zetland/ former off. name of Shetland county; **Marquess of —**

zeugma/ (gram.) a figure of speech in which a verb or adj. is used with two nouns, to only one of which it is strictly applicable, e.g. 'with weeping eyes and [sc. 'grieving'] hearts'; pl. **-s**, adj. **-tic** cf. **syllepsis**

zho *use* **dzo**

Zhou Enlai (1898–1976) Chinese statesman, Wade–Giles **Chou En-lai**

Zhu De (1886–1976) founder and commander of the Chinese People's Liberation Army 1930–54, *also spelt* **Chu Teh**

Zia/ ul-Haq, Mohammad (1924–88) President of Pakistan 1978–88; *properly* **— al-Haq**

Ziaur Rahman (1935–81) Bengali nationalist, President of Bangladesh 1977–81

zibet an Asian or Indian civet, *not* -eth (US)

Ziegfeld, Florenz (1869–1932) US theatre manager

ziggurat an ancient Mesopotamian tower, *not* zikk-

zigzag/, -ged, -ging (one word)

Zimbabwe/ Africa, **-an**

zinc symbol **Zn**

zinco/ (typ.) a relief block, usually in line, made from zinc; pl. **-s**

zincography the art of engraving and printing from zinc

zingara, à la (Fr. cook.) in the Gypsy style

zingar/o (It.) a Gypsy, pl. **-i**; f. **-a** pl. **-e**

Zinjanthropus an E. African fossil hominid

Zion/, -ism, -ist *not* Si-

zip/, -ped, -per, -ping, -py

zip/-bag (hyphen)

Zip code (US) = **postcode** (one cap., originally **ZIP**)

zip fastener (two words)

zirconium symbol **Zr**

zloty/ monetary unit of Poland, pl. **-s**, abbr. **zl**

Zn zinc (no point)

zo *use* **dzo**

Zoffany, John (1734–1810) German-born English-domiciled painter

Zollverein (Ger. m.) customs union

zombie a revived corpse, a person in a stupor; *not* -i, -y

zoolog/y genera, species, and subspecies to be italic, all other divisions roman, e.g. Carnivora (order), Felidae (family), *Felis* (genus), *Felis catus* (species); specific epithets, even when derived from names of persons, should be lower case: *Myotis daubentoni*; **-ical, -ist**; abbr. **zool.**

zo/on (biol.) an animal, pl. **-a**

zōon politikon (Gr. antiquity) the political animal, man

Zorast/er Gr. form of **Zarathustra**; **-rian** of or relating to Zoroaster, or the religion taught

by him or his followers (*see also* **Zend**); a follower of Zoroaster

Zouave a member of a French light-infantry corps, originally formed of Algerians and retaining their uniform (cap., not ital.)

Zou-Zou (hist.) a Zouave

ZPG zero population growth

Zr zirconium (no point)

ZS Zoological Society

ZST zone standard time

zucchetto/ (RC) a skullcap, pl. **-s**

zucchini (esp. US, Austral.) a courgette, pl. same; in It. ***zucchin/o***, pl. **-i**

zugzwang (chess) a blockade, a position in which any move is undesirable yet some move must be made (not ital.)

Zuider Zee (hist.) the Netherlands, after enclosure **IJsselmeer**

Zuleika/ Potiphar's wife in the Koran, in Arab. *zuleḵhā*; also the heroine of Byron's *The Bride of Abydos*; **— Dobson** a femme fatale, eponymous heroine of a novel by Max Beerbohm, 1911

Zulu (of or relating to) a member of a black S. African people originally inhabiting Zululand and Natal, or the language of this people

Zululand (one word) annexed by S. Africa 1897, *now* **KwaZulu/Natal**

Zuñi (of or relating to) a member of a Pueblo Indian people inhabiting the valley of the River Zuñi

Zurich Switzerland; in Ger. **Zürich**, Romansh **Türich**, Lat. **Turicum**

zwieback a kind of biscuit rusk (not ital.)

Zwingli, Ulrich (*also* **Huldrych**) (1484–1531) Swiss Protestant reformer

zydeco a form of Cajun dance music originating in S. Louisiana (not cap.)

zymurgy originally the art of fermentation in winemaking, brewing, and distilling, *now* the branch of biochemistry dealing with this

Zyryan *use* **Komi**

zythum (hist.) a fermented-malt drink made in ancient times, esp. in Egypt

Appendix 1: Mathematical and logical symbols

π pi
e, **e**, *or* ε base of natural logarithms
∂ partial derivative
i, j   imaginary unit: $i^2 = -1$
∞ infinity
$=$ equal to
$\neq$ not equal to
$\equiv$ identically equal to
$\not\equiv$ not identically equal to
$\triangleq$ corresponds to
$\not\triangleq$ does not correspond to
$\approx$ approximately equal to
$\not\approx$ not approximately equal to
$\simeq$ asymptotically equal to
$\not\simeq$ not asymptotically equal to
$\cong$ isomorphic to, equal or nearly equal to
$\not\cong$ not isomorphic to, not equal or nearly equal to
$\sim$ equivalent to, of the order of
$\not\sim$ not equivalent to, not of the order of
$\propto$ proportional to
$\rightarrow$ approaches, tends to the limit
$\not\rightarrow$ does not approach, does not tend to the limit
$\nearrow$ limit from the left
$\searrow$ limit from the right
$\uparrow$ tends up to
$\downarrow$ tends down to
$\Rightarrow$ implies
$\Leftarrow$ is implied by
$\Leftrightarrow$ double implication
$>$ greater than
$\not>$ not greater than
$<$ less than
$\not<$ not less than
$\gg$ much greater than
$\ll$ much less than
$\geq$ greater than or equal to
$\not\geq$ not greater than or equal to
$\leq$ less than or equal to
$\not\leq$ not less than or equal to

$\succ$ has a higher rank or order
$\not\succ$ has not a higher rank or order
$\prec$ has a lower rank or order
$\not\prec$ has not a lower rank or order
$\succeq$ has a rank or order higher or equal to
$\not\succeq$ has not a rank or order higher or equal to
$\preceq$ has a rank or order lower or equal to
$\not\preceq$ has not a rank or order lower or equal to
( )   parentheses
[ ]   square brackets
{ }   curly brackets, braces
$\langle\,\rangle$ angle brackets
$[\![\,]\!]$ open brackets
$\vee$ sum of two sets
$\wedge$ vector product
$\subset$ strict inclusion
$\not\subset$ not contained in
$\subseteq$ inclusion
$\not\subseteq$ is not contained in
$\supset, \supseteq$ contains
$\not\supset, \not\supseteq$ does not contain
$\cup, \smallfrown$ union
$\cap, \frown$ intersection, concatenation
$\backslash$ difference
$\varnothing$ the empty set
$\textthreequartersemdash$ centre of line
$+$ plus
$\oplus$ direct sum
$-$ minus
$\pm$ plus or minus
$\mp$ minus or plus
$\parallel$ parallel to
$\perp$ perpendicular to
$\Leftrightarrow$ equivalent to
$\not\Leftrightarrow$ not equivalent to
$a, a{\cdot}b, a{\times}b$ a multiplied by b
$\otimes$ direct multiplication
$a/b, a{\div}b, ab^{-1}$ a divided by b
a^n a raised to the power of n
$|a|$ the magnitude of a
$||$ modulus
$\sqrt{a}, a^{1/2}$ square root of a

$\bar{a}$, $\langle a \rangle$	mean value of a	· or & or ∧	conjunction, and
$p!$	factorial p	~ or ¬ or - or N	negation, not
′	minute, prime	∈	belongs to, is a member
″	second, double prime		of (a set or class)
‴	triple prime	∉	does not belong to,
°	degree		negates ∈
∠	angle	∅	null set, empty set
∟	right angle	≡ or ↔	if and only if (material
∠	acute angle		equivalence)
△	triangle	=	is the same as, *or* if and
:	ratio		only if (strict equiva-
::	proportion		lence)
∴	therefore, hence	≠	is not the same as,
∵	because		negates =
exp x, e^x	exponential of x	≡ or ↔ or ⇔	biconditional, 'is identi-
$\log_a x$	logarithm to base a of x		cally equal to'
$\ln x$, $\log_e x$	natural logarithm of x	≢	is not identically equal
$\lg x$, $\log_{10} x$	common logarithm of x		to, negates ≡
$\text{lb } x$, $\log_2 x$	binary logarithm of x	≈	is approximately equal to
$\sin x$	sine of x	∀	universal quantifier, for
$\cos x$	cosine of x		all
$\tan x$, $\text{tg } x$	tangent of x	∃	existential quantifier,
$\cot x$, $\text{ctg } x$	cotangent of x		some, at least one,
$\sec x$	secant of x		there exists
$\text{cosec } x$, $\csc x$	cosecant of x	∄	there does not exist
$\sin^{-1} x$, $\arcsin x$	inverse sine of x	□ or L	necessarily
$\cos^{-1} x$, $\arccos x$	inverse cosine of x	◊ or M	possibly, i.e. not □ not
$\tan^{-1} x$, $\arctan x$	inverse tangent of x	→ or ⇒	implies
∫	integral, antiderivative	← or ⇐	is implied by
∮	contour integral	⊤	constant true sentence
∑	summation	⊥	constant false sentence
Δ	delta	⊃	includes, implies
∇	nabla, del	⊅	does not include, does
∏	product		not imply
Δx	finite increase of x	⊂	is included in
δx	variation of x	⊄	is not included in
dx	total variation of x	∩ or ∧	intersection
$f(x)$	function of x	∪	union
$f{\circ}g$	composite function of f	⊢	syntactic turnstile (prov-
	and g		ability)
f^*g	convolution of f and g	⊨	semantic turnstile
$\lim_{x \to a} f(x)$	limit of $f(x)$		(entailment etc.)
ℵ	aleph	↑,↓	stroke functors
℘	Weierstrass elliptic	$E!$	existence
	function		
□	D'Alembertian operator		
h	Planck constant		
ℏ	Dirac constant		

Appendix 2: Proofreading marks

Proofreading symbols generally in use have been strongly influenced by the British Standard's Institution's BS 5261 Part 2: 1976 and supplements. Traditional or alternative symbols are still found, especially abroad; the most common are included here.

Instruction	Textual mark	Marginal mark
Correction is concluded	None	/
Insert in text the matter indicated in the margin	⅄	New matter followed by ⅄
Insert additional matter identified by a letter in a diamond	⅄ Followed by, e.g. Ⓐ	The relevant section of the copy should be supplied with the corresponding letter marked on it in a diamond, e.g. Ⓐ
Delete	/ through character(s) or ⊢——⊣ through words to be deleted	ᶁ or ℊ
Close up and delete space between characters or words	linking ⌒ characters	⌒/
Delete and close up	ᶁ through character or ⊢⌒⊣ through character, e.g. charac̶ter charac̶ter	ᶁ or ℊ
Substitute character or substitute part of one or more word(s)	/ through character or ⊢——⊣ through words(s)	New character or new word(s) followed by /
Substitute or insert full point or decimal point	/ or ⅄ through character where required	⊙/ or ⊙
Substitute or insert colon	/ or ⅄ through character where required	⊙/ or ⊙
Substitute or insert semicolon	/ or ⅄ through character where required	;/ or ;⅄
Substitute or insert comma	/ or ⅄ through character where required	,/ or ,⅄ or ⌃
Substitute or insert solidus (oblique)	/ or ⅄ through character where required	⟨/⟩
Substitute or insert character in superior (superscript) position	/ or ⅄ through character where required	⌐ or ∨ under character e.g. ⌐ or ⅄
Substitute or insert character in inferior (subscript) position	/ or ⅄ through character where required	⌐ or ∧ over character e.g. ⅄
Substitute or insert opening or closing parenthesis, square bracket, or curly brace	/ or ⅄ through character where required	(/) or {/}, [/], or {/}
Substitute or insert hyphen	/ or ⅄ through character where required	⊢–⊣ / or = or ⊢–⊣⅄
Substitute or insert rule	/ or ⅄ through character, e.g. **2em**	Give the size of rule in marginal mark [1 em] [4 mm]
Set in or change to bold type	‿‿‿ under character(s) to be set or changed	(bold) or (bf) or ‿‿‿
Set in or change to bold italic type	‿‿‿ under character(s) to be set or changed	(bold ital) or (bf ital) or ⨑
Set in or change to italic	—— under character(s) to be set or changed	(ital) or ⨑
Change italic to upright (roman) type	Encircle character(s) to be changed	(rom) or ⨄
Set in or change to capital letters	≣ under character(s) to be set or changed	(cap) or ≣
Change capital letters to lower-case letters	Encircle character(s) to be changed	(lc) or ≢
Spell out number or abbreviation	Encircle matter to be changed (38 pp.)	(sp)
Set in or change to small capital letters	= under character(s) to be set or changed	(sc) or (s. cap) or =
Set in or change to capital letters for initial letters and small capital letters for the rest of the word(s)	≣ under initial letters and = under rest of the word(s)	≣ where space does not permit textual marks, encircle the affected area instead
Change small capital letters to lower-case letters	Encircle character(s) to be changed	(lc) or ≠
Start new paragraph	⌐_	(NP) or ⌐_ or ¶
Run on (no new paragraph)	⌒⌐	(run on) or ⌒

Instruction	Textual mark	Marginal mark
Transpose characters or words	⌐⌐ between characters or words, numbered when necessary	(trs) or (tr) or ⌐⌐
Transpose lines	5	(trs) or (tr) or 5
Invert type	Encircle character to be inverted	◠
Transpose a number of lines	———————————— ③ ———————————— ② ———————————— ①	To be used when the sequence cannot be clearly indicated otherwise. Rules extend from the margin into the text, with each line to be transplanted numbered in the correct sequence
Centre	[ ] or [enclosing matter to be centred]	
Insert space between characters	| between characters affected	Y or #
Insert space between words	Y between words affected	Y or (more #)
Reduce space between characters	| between characters affected	↑ or (less #)
Reduce space between words	↑ between words affected	↑
Equalize space between characters or words	| between characters or words affected	Y or (eq. #)
Close up to normal interlinear spacing	(each side of column linking lines)	
Insert space between lines or paragraphs	—(or)—	The marginal mark extends between the lines of text. Give the size of the space to be inserted if necessary
Reduce space between lines or paragraphs	← or →	The marginal mark extends between the lines of text. Give the amount by which the space is to be reduced if necessary
Take over character(s), word(s), or line to next line, column, or page	⌐———————	The textual mark surrounds the matter to be taken over and extends into the margin
Take back character(s), word(s), or line to previous line, column, or page	———————⌐	The textual mark surrounds the matter to be taken back and extends into the margin
Insert or substitute em space, en space, or thin space	□ (em), ◙ (en), ♯ or ⎸ (thin)	□ (em), ◙ (en), ♯ or ⎸ (thin)
Indent	⊏	⊏
Cancel indent	⊢⊏	⊐
Move matter specified distance to the right	⊏ enclosing matter to be moved to the right ⊐→⎸	⊏
Move matter specified distance to the left	⊢⎸enclosing matter to be the left ⊐	⊐
Correct vertical alignment	‖	‖ or (align)
Correct horizontal alignment	Single line above and below misaligned matter, e.g. m͟i͟s͟a͟l͟i͟g͟n͟e͟d͟	= or (align)
Correction made in error. Leave unchanged	under characters to remain _ _ _ _ _ _ _	⊘ or (stet)
Remove extraneous mark(s) or replace damaged character(s)	Encircle mark(s) to be removed or character(s) to be changed	✗
Wrong font. Replace by character(s) of correct font	Encircle character(s) to be changed	✗ or (wf)
Refer to appropriate authority anything of doubtful accuracy	Encircle word(s) affected	(?)

Note:

All instructions to the typesetter should be circled as shown above, e.g. (align) (stet) Otherwise they can be mistakenly inserted into the text.

Appendix 3: Transliteration tables

Arabic

Alone	Final	Medial	Initial		
ا	ـا			'alif	'
ب	ـب	ـبـ	بـ	bā'	b
ت	ـت	ـتـ	تـ	tā'	t
ث	ـث	ـثـ	ثـ	thā'	th
ج	ـج	ـجـ	جـ	jīm	j
ح	ـح	ـحـ	حـ	ḥā'	ḥ
خ	ـخ	ـخـ	خـ	khā'	kh
د	ـد			dāl	d
ذ	ـذ			dhāl	dh
ر	ـر			rā'	r
ز	ـز			zāy	z
س	ـس	ـسـ	سـ	sīn	s
ش	ـش	ـشـ	شـ	shīn	sh
ص	ـص	ـصـ	صـ	ṣād	ṣ
ض	ـض	ـضـ	ضـ	ḍād	ḍ
ط	ـط	ـطـ	طـ	ṭā'	ṭ
ظ	ـظ	ـظـ	ظـ	ẓā'	ẓ
ع	ـع	ـعـ	عـ	'ayn	'
غ	ـغ	ـغـ	غـ	ghayn	gh
ف	ـف	ـفـ	فـ	fā'	f
ق	ـق	ـقـ	قـ	qāf	q
ك	ـك	ـكـ	كـ	kāf	k
ل	ـل	ـلـ	لـ	lām	l
م	ـم	ـمـ	مـ	mīm	m
ن	ـن	ـنـ	نـ	nūn	n
ه	ـه	ـهـ	هـ	hā'	h
و	ـو			wāw	w
ى	ـى	ـيـ	يـ	yā'	y

Hebrew

א	'aleph	'
ב	beth	b, bh
ג	gimel	g, gh
ד	daleth	d, dh
ה	he	h
ו	waw	w
ז	zayin	z
ח	heth	ḥ
ט	teth	ṭ
י	yodh	y
כ ך	kaph	k, kh
ל	lamedh	l
מ ם	mem	m
נ ן	nun	n
ס	samekh	s
ע	'ayin	'
פ ף	pe	p, ph
צ ץ	sadhe	ṣ
ק	qoph	q
ר	resh	r
שׂ	śin	ś
שׁ	shin	sh
ת	taw	t, th

Greek

A α	alpha	a
B β	beta	b
Γ γ	gamma	g
Δ δ	delta	d
E ε	epsilon	e
Z ζ	zeta	z
H η	eta	ē
Θ θ	theta	th
I ι	iota	i
K κ	kappa	k
Λ λ	lambda	l
M μ	mu	m
N ν	nu	n
Ξ ξ	xi	x
O o	omicron	o
Π π	pi	p
P ρ	rho	r, rh
Σ σ ς	sigma	s
T τ	tau	t
Y υ	upsilon	u
Φ φ	phi	ph
X χ	chi	kh
Ψ ψ	psi	ps
Ω ω	omega	ō

Russian

А а	a
Б б	b
В в	v
Г г	g
Д д	d
Е е	e, ye
Ё ё	yo
Ж ж	zh
З з	z
И и	i
Й й	ĭ
К к	k
Л л	l
М м	m
Н н	n
О о	o
П п	p
Р р	r
С с	s
Т т	t
У у	u
Ф ф	f
Х х	kh
Ц ц	ts
Ч ч	ch
Ш ш	sh
Щ щ	shch
Ъ ъ	" ('hard sign')
Ы ы	y
Ь ь	' ('soft sign')
Э э	e
Ю ю	yu
Я я	ya

Appendix 4: Diacritics, accents, and special sorts

In typography, a *diacritic* is any symbol placed near or through a letter to show how it should be pronounced. Properly, *accent* is used only for a diacritic placed above a letter. Diacritical marks found for example on an ordinary keyboard constitute standard *sorts*; all others are *special sorts*.

Below is a selection of sorts for the expanded Latin alphabet (including transliterations), arranged alphabetically to aid identification by editors, typesetters, and proof-readers. Distinctions in use and context have been ignored, and in some cases a mark may be known by more than one name, depending on the context in which it is found. While all examples are in lower case unless the sort is specific to a capital, this does not suggest that the diacritics apply only to those lower-case forms, or only to those letters used as examples.

acute (high tone): á í ý
acute and macron: ā́ ū́ ŕ̄
acute and superior circule (ring): ǻ
agma: ŋ
'ain, 'ayin, 'ayn: ʿ ʿ
alef (lenis): ʾ
apostrophe: ʼ
asper (rough breathing): ʿ
breve (short-vowel mark): ğ ŏ
breve and acute: ắ ḗ ő́
breve and grave: ằ ḕ ồ
breve and horn (low rising tone): ắ ĕ̛ ờ̆
breve and tilde: ẵ ễ ỗ
candrabindu: m̐
cedilla (hook left): ç ķ ļ ņ
circumflex (falling tone): â ê î ô û ĥ
circumflex and acute: ấ ế ố
circumflex and grave: ầ ề ồ
circumflex and inferior dot: ậ ệ ộ
circumflex and horn (low rising tone): ấ̛ ế̛
circumflex and tilde: ẫ ễ ỗ
crossed (barred) letters: Đ đ Ħ ħ Ŧ ŧ
crossed (Polish) l: Ł ł
diaeresis (umlaut): ï ü ÿ
digraph: æ œ
dotted capital (Turkish) I: İ
dotted l: Ŀ ŀ
double acute: ő ű
double grave: ȅ ȍ
double inferior dot: s̤ t̤ z̤
e sort: ε
Eszett: ß
eth: Đ ð ð
grave (low tone): à è ì ò ù
háček (raising tone): č š ž
hamza: ʾ
hard sign (double prime): ˝

high comma centre: ġ
high comma left: ʼn ʼí ʼy
high comma right: dʼ tʼ
high dot right: ḣ
hooked b: Ɓ ɓ
hooked d: Ɗ ɗ
hooked k: Ƙ ƙ
hook left: ķ ņ
hook right: ą ę
horn (low rising tone): ɑ̛ e̛ r̛ ơ ư
inferior breve: ḫ
inferior circumflex: ḓ ṱ ṋ
inferior dot (underdot): ạ ẹ ḍ ḥ ị ụ y
inverted (turned) c: ɔ
inverted (turned) exclamation mark: ¡
inverted (turned) question mark: ¿
lenis (smooth breathing): ʾ
ligatures: æ œ fi fl ﬀ
long s: ſ (roman) ʃ (italic)
macron (long-vowel mark): ā ē ī
macron and superior circle (ring): å̄ e̊̄
medial dot: ·
ogonek: Ą ą (non-touching)
shwa (inverted e): ə
slash: ø
slash and acute: ǿ
slur beneath: i͜a i͜e i͜u z͜h
soft sign (single prime): ʹ
superior circle (kroužek): å ů
superior dot (dot above): ċ ġ v̇
thorn: Þþ þþ
tilde (til): ã õ ñ
umlaut: ä ö ü
underline (underscore): s̲ d̲ t̲ dh̲ ch̲ sh̲
undotted (Turkish) i: ı
wyn: ƿ ƿ
yogh: ʒ ʒ ẞ ẟ